THE WOMEN'S STUDY NEW

C000259418

Mary Evans is a lecturer at Lond
and is the author of several books including
Woman In The Bible. She is a trustee of the
British and Foreign Bible Society and sits on the
Council of the UK Evangelical Missionary
Alliance.

Catherine Clark Kroeger is founder and president
of Christians for Biblical Equality, and adjunct
associate professor at Gordon-Conwell Theological Seminary, South Hamilton, Massachusetts.
She is the co-author (with her husband, Richard) of
I Suffer Not A Woman.

Elaine Storkey is Director of the London Institute
for Contemporary Christianity and is the author
of numerous books including *What's Right With
Feminism?* and *Mary's Story, Mary's Song.* She is a
member of the General Synod of the Church of
England and sits on the Council of the UK
Evangelical Alliance.

THE
WOMEN'S STUDY
NEW TESTAMENT

BASED ON THE NRSV

EDITED BY

CATHERINE CLARK KROEGER,
MARY EVANS & ELAINE STORKEY

Marshall Pickering
An Imprint of HarperCollins*Publishers*

Marshall Pickering is an Imprint of
HarperCollins*Religious*
Part of HarperCollins*Publishers*
77–85 Fulham Palace Road, London W6 8JB

First published in Great Britain
in 1995 by Marshall Pickering
and in the USA by Baker Book House

1   3   5   7   9   10   8   6   4   2

New Revised Standard Version Bible, Copyright © 1989,
Division of Christian Education of the
National Council of the Churches of Christ
in the United States of America.

Commentary and notes Copyright © 1995
Catherine Clark Kroeger, Mary Evans
and Elaine Storkey

Catherine Clark Kroeger, Mary Evans and Elaine Storkey
assert the moral right to be identified as the authors
and compilers of this work

A catalogue record for this book is
available from the British Library

ISBN 0551 029080

Printed and bound in Great Britain by
Scotprint Limited, Musselburgh, Edinburgh

CONTENTS

LIST OF CONTRIBUTORS

Sally Alsford Greenwich, England
Wilma Ann Bailey Grantham, Pennsylvania, USA
Jill Baker Chicago, Illinois, USA
Priscilla Benham Oakland, California, USA
Pat Burke Windsor Locks, Connecticut, USA
Nancy Calvert Wheaton, Illinois, USA
Deborah Chapman London, England
Rosemary Christmas Leura, New South Wales, Australia
Marlene Cohen Oxford, England
Lynn Cohick Grantham, Pennsylvania, USA
Kaye Cook Collars Wenham, Massachusetts, USA
Trisha Dale Camberley, England
Marva Dawn Vancouver, Washington, USA
Wanda Deifelt Sao Leopoldo, Brazil
Fiona Devlin Greenwich, England
Rosemary Dowsett Glasgow, Scotland
Mary Evans London, England
Ailish Eves London, England
Ruth Ann Foster Waco, Texas, USA
Helen Bray Garretson Sheffield, Massachusetts, USA
Deborah Menken Gill Roseville, Minnesota, USA
Sharon Gritz Fort Worth, Texas, USA
Mimi Haddad Denver, Colorado, USA
Hannah Harrington Oakland, California, USA
Fran Hiebert Highland Park, Illinois, USA
Gay Hubbard Lakewood, Colorado, USA
Gretchen Hull Cold Spring Harbor, New York State, USA
Dorothy Irvin Durham, North Carolina, USA
Diane Johnson Minneapolis, Minnesota, USA
Catherine Clark Kroeger Brewster, Massachusetts, USA
Martha Lady Mechanicsburg, Pennsylvania, USA

Dianne Marshall North York, Ontario, Canada
Faith Martin Pittsburgh, Pennsylvania, USA
Sheila McGinn Cleveland, Ohio, USA
Alvera Mickelsen New Brighton, Minnesota, USA
Keren Morrell London, England
Clelia Thompson Mulally St Paul, Minnesota, USA
Andrea Mysen Denver, Colorado, USA
Ng Peh Cheng Singapore
Daisy Washburn Osborn Tulsa, Oklahoma
T. J. Ostrander Kent, Washington State, USA
Rebecca Patten Oakland, California, USA
Shelley Paul Denver, Colorado, USA
Joyce K. Penniston Rochester, Minnesota, USA
Pancheeta Peterson Wellfleet, Massachusetts, USA
Donna Petter South Hamilton, Massachusetts, USA
Magdalena Pletsch London, England
Claire Powell Ware, England
Mae Alice Reggy Nairobi, Kenya
Vera Sinton Oxford, England
Judy Smith Lakeside, Montana, USA
Aida Besancon Spencer South Hamilton, Massachusetts, USA
K. E. Stegall Pittsburgh, Pennsylvania, USA
Elaine Storkey London, England
Marcia Stroup Irvine, California, USA
Dianne Tidball Marcham, England
Sarah Warren South Hamilton, Massachusetts, USA
Teresa White CSA London, England
Raewynne Whiteley Sydney, Australia
Sylvia Wilkey Adelaide, Australia

INTRODUCTION

The value of a Study New Testament, where notes and articles are provided to give help to the reader in exploring, understanding and applying the teaching of the New Testament has been proved by many people over many years. But why a Women's Study New Testament, and what does that mean anyway? Well, in this instance it means an edition where the notes and articles have all been written by women and where the concerns and interests of women are particularly taken into account. Over the years the vast majority (perhaps 99%) of commentaries, study guides and other helps to understanding the Bible have been written by men. Many of these are excellent and provide tremendous help to both men and women. Most of them in no sense are anti-women or set out to denigrate or exclude women. However, the interests and concerns of men are sometimes different from those of women. It is perhaps inevitable that male commentators will miss certain aspects of the New Testament teaching simply because they have not asked all the questions or even realized sometimes that answers to questions other than their own might exist within the text.

This volume is an attempt to begin redressing the balance. It is not intended to be the final answer to all questions about the New Testament, women's or men's. It is not seeking to be deliberately radical or only dealing with new issues. Much of what is said will be common ground with other studies. There is, of course, far more overlap than distinction between men's interests and women's interests and the primary concern is always to elucidate the text, not to introduce issues or special concerns that do not really exist within the text itself. What we are doing here is beginning to explore the idea that women may have something to say about the New Testament, not that could not be said by men but that perhaps so far has not been said by men. The intention is that the understanding of both men and women of what the New Testament text is saying will be enriched and that the lives of both men and women will be challenged and changed. The reader must be the judge of whether that intention has been fulfilled.

The women who have taken part in this project come from several different parts of the world and have a very wide range of denominational backgrounds. Most are scholars who are involved in higher level theological education but others are involved in different professions or are working in the home. They are all individuals with different interests, different experiences and different perspectives on life and this is reflected in the different approaches to the various books and the different types of issues looked at. All are committed to Scripture as the Word of God and to its value and relevance in the lives of believers. Some have written just one short article, others have made substantial contributions. We list the names without distinction because all share in the desire that attention will be focused not on the writers but on the encouragement and excitement and challenge of the message of the New Testament.

The volume begins with a number of articles discussing issues relating to the inspiration, authority and interpretation of Scripture. The central section includes general comments on the text of the New Testament plus short articles placed in boxes, which expand on points of special interest. The final section consists of longer articles on matters of Christian doctrine in particular as they relate to women. An index of all articles can be found at the end with the authorship of each individual section and article.

INCLUSIVE LANGUAGE
AND THE NRSV

The New Revised Standard Version of the Bible (NRSV) is the first major English translation of the Bible to attempt to redress the inherent bias of the English language toward the masculine gender. The translators recognized many problems for women in the English language and have taken steps in this version to eliminate some of them.

MAN OR PERSON

The first step they took was to eliminate the dual role of the word 'man'. Traditionally, 'man' has had two meanings in English. It could have a relatively narrow meaning of 'a male human being' or it could have a more inclusive meaning of 'a human being of either sex.' When reading or listening to material using the word 'man' in its dual capacity, women are forced to ask and quickly answer a mental question: Does that 'man' include me or exclude me?

English is a fluid and evolving language. Meanings of words change over the generations. We are all participants in this process. It does not require sophisticated linguistic research to observe how the word 'man' is changing within the space of a single generation. Until recently, using 'man' to mean a 'human being or person' was the hallmark of the educated prose style. Students of all disciplines, early in their education, had its dual role pointed out to them and were shown how to select the correct meaning by examining its context.

Granted, there are many – especially those reared in the church – who are familiar with 'man' representing both men and women. But more and more, the usage is confined to theological discourse and translations of the Bible. In conversation, as well as educated prose, people now avoid 'man' except when a male person is specifically intended. Those responsible for the NRSV evidently felt the time had come for English translations of the Bible to conform to current style, especially since using the current style would more accurately reflect the original texts.

We have probably all heard or read, 'Man shall not live by bread alone', and understood that Jesus was talking about both men and women (Matt. 4:4). But gradually, the gender-inclusive nature of the English word 'man' has taken a back seat to what has now become its primary meaning: 'an adult male'. Bowing to this usage, the translators of the NRSV have confined the use of the word 'man' to mean simply an 'adult male'.

Educated readers of lofty English prose who readily recognize the dual role of 'man' might mourn the loss of an historic and beautiful prose style. But the mandate given the NRSV translators was to communicate in 'current English usage'.

Anyone tempted to bemoan this change as a concession to 'the feminists' should consider that while this step is admittedly taken in response to changes in English usage, it also brings the English reader closer to the original texts. Both Greek and Hebrew contain vocabulary which makes a clear distinction between adult males and adult persons. The NRSV, by reserving 'man' for the adult male, is simply reproducing that distinction in a manner consistent with the original text.

The results are interesting. Sometimes passages are just easier to read and understand. For instance, the New International Version (NIV) which retains the old style in John 2:24 says, 'But Jesus would not entrust himself to them, for he knew all men. He did not need man's testimony about man, for he knew what was in a man.' The NRSV eliminates the repetition and says, 'But Jesus on his part would not entrust himself to them, because he knew all people and needed no one to testify about anyone; for he himself knew what was in everyone.'

In other passages the results might change some people's perspective on the role of women. In the NRSV we now read, 'and what you have heard from me through many witnesses entrust to faithful people who will be able to teach others as well' (2 Tim. 2:2). In the former version, the Revised Standard Version (RSV), and the other standard versions – the New International Version (NIV) and the New King James Version (NKJV) – the passage said 'faithful men'. Many a woman has had this verse quoted to her as proof that only men may teach in the church. But the original text will not support that. The Greek says 'people' or 'human beings'.

Consider also 2 Pet. 1:21. The RSV rendered it, 'because no prophecy ever came by the impulse of man, but men moved by the Holy Spirit spoke from God.' (The NKJV and NIV have a similar use of 'man' and 'men' in that verse.) The NRSV, however, gives us what the Greek says: 'because no prophecy ever came by human will, but men and women moved by the Holy Spirit spoke from God.'

The adoption of current English usage with regard to man is particularly welcome to readers who must read the Bible in translation. The modern English reader of the old style translations might easily come away with the impression that God speaks to men first and women only secondarily. That problem is eliminated in this translation.

MATTERS OF STYLE

Traditionally, translators have all too freely inserted the masculine pronouns 'he' and 'him' when there is no justification except literary style. An example is Matt. 7:8. The NIV translated it: 'For everyone who asks receives; he who seeks finds; and to him who knocks, the door will be opened.' Contrast this with the almost word-for-word translation of the Greek as given in the NRSV: 'For everyone who asks receives, and everyone who searches finds, and for everyone who knocks, the door will be opened.'

HE/SHE/IT

In the foregoing, the NRSV translators were not doing anything that required apology. But there is an aspect of their attempt to correct the masculine bias of the English language which required some explanation by the editor in the preface, i.e. their attempt 'to compensate for a deficiency in the English language – the lack of a common gender third person singular pronoun.'

The problem may be illustrated by the sentence, 'Everyone took his seat.' Because the subject of the sentence (everyone) is singular, the pronoun must also be singular. English, however, has no gender inclusive singular pronoun. (We do not call a person 'it'.) So by convention (custom), women are 'understood' to be included in the masculine singular pronouns 'he' and 'his'. But we don't like that very much. No-one really believes that women are included in such sentences anymore. In spoken English one most often hears, 'Everyone took their seat.' This solution, however, is unacceptable in written English and studiously avoided. Writers wishing to be gender inclusive and grammatical are forced to use the awkward phrase 'his or hers' – or to rewrite the sentence in the plural. They say, 'They all took their seats.'

To avoid being gender exclusive with the third person singular pronoun, the NRSV translators chose the latter solution – they put problem sentences in the plural. The best example of this is Ps. 1:1–3. In the NRSV we read, 'Happy are those who do not follow the advice of the wicked, or take the path that sinners tread, or sit in the seat of scoffers; but their delight is in the law of the LORD, and on his law they meditate day and night. They are like trees planted . . .' This replaces, 'Blessed is the man who walks not in the counsel of the wicked, nor stands in the way of sinners, nor sits in the seat of scoffers; but his delight is in the law of the LORD, and on his law he meditates day and night. He is like a tree . . .' There is something of the personal nature of a believer's walk with God that is lost when this passage is rendered in the plural. And that is to be regretted.

In most instances, however, the text is translated in such a way as to eliminate the need for pronouns. The result is more satisfying. 'Everyone therefore who acknowledges me before others, I also will acknowledge before my Father in heaven' (Matt. 10:32).

It is equally pleasing to read, 'Let anyone who is thirsty come to me, and let the one who believes in me drink. As the scripture has said, "Out of the believer's heart shall flow rivers of living water"' (John 7:37–38). The individual, man or woman, is spoken to directly and personally.

BROTHERS AND SISTERS

There is one final way in which the NRSV attempts to be gender inclusive, but it is hardly controversial. It is the decision to translate 'brothers' as 'brothers and sisters' in situations where both men and women are obviously being addressed. Apparently, saying 'brothers', but meaning both sexes, was a convention of Greek. English speakers, however, are generally careful to acknowledge both sexes in direct address – such as 'ladies and gentlemen'. English-speaking women now have the comfort of reading, 'Therefore, my brothers and sisters, whom I love and long for, my joy and crown, stand firm in the Lord in this way, my beloved' (Phil. 4:1).

The NRSV has much to offer readers. Its attempt to address the masculine bias of the English language is particularly welcome. The purpose of the translations of Scripture is to give the Word of God to people in their native tongue. Anything which comes between the original message and the reader should be eliminated. The masculine bias of the English language has been an historic impediment to the spiritual growth of women who must read the Scriptures in translation, and its final removal will be greatly appreciated. The NRSV is an excellent first step.

A HIGH VIEW OF SCRIPTURE: GOOD NEWS FOR WOMEN

Many laypeople are not aware that we have no originals ('autographs') of ancient literary works, but only copies. There is no original of a treatise by Aristotle or a letter by Cicero. But there is no original of any Bible book either. Hence the great excitement over the discovery of the Dead Sea Scrolls: there is always the hope that such an autograph (whole or in fragment) may yet be found.

For ancient literature, therefore, crucial factors in developing a reliable text are (1) determining the earliest copies (those made as close as possible to the accepted date of authorship) and (2) studying and comparing those copies to determine the most accurate rendering of the text as it appeared in the original languages. These investigative tasks can be very complicated when there are only a few known copies of a particular work, or when the only copies are themselves translations from the first language (such as a medieval Latin copy of an ancient Greek work). Many persons who read the Classics in English have little appreciation of the great effort involved in establishing a reliable text for an ancient document.

Notably, in the case of the biblical manuscripts the gap between the accepted time of writing and the earliest extant copies is narrower overall than with other ancient literature, and many of these copies are of ancient-world origin. Equally significant, there are many copies with which to work in establishing the biblical texts (thousands of New Testament Greek fragments, for example). Taken simply as literature, the Bible is the best authenticated of all ancient writings. So the question is: What is found in the content of this remarkable Book of books?

Some critics consider the Bible primarily a collection of myths and folk-lore. These people will feel free to pick and choose which passages to dismiss as fable, and which might have some historical or theological significance in tracing the beginning of the Judeo-Christian religious tradition. However, among even the most hostile critics there is general agreement that certain biblical precepts have enduring social value. Most people agree with 'You shall not kill' and many urge 'Love your neighbor as yourself.'

Other critics say that the Bible writers did attempt to record factual accounts of what they perceived to be God's mighty acts in history, such as the Exodus in the Old Testament or the Incarnation in the New Testament. However, these critics also say that the Bible texts as originally written were then so heavily edited ('redacted') that much of Scripture does still come down to us as narrative or saga whose facts may or may not be true.

Still other critics consider that the question of whether or not the Bible reliably transmits objective fact or propositional truth is not of primary concern. More important should be determining whether or not the Bible becomes God's Word to its readers as they let the text speak to their hearts.

These and similar views pose a severe problem, because only a completely trustworthy medium insures a consistently trustworthy message. It is illogical to base our morality and ethics, much less our belief in God, upon documents whose actual content (however ancient or familiar) only may or may not be trustworthy.

Such low views of Scripture do inestimable disservice to all seekers after truth, because these views send us to other humans for our answers to questions of eternal significance. In the resulting stalemate, 'My word is as good as yours.'

THE INSPIRED WORD

In contrast, a high view of Scripture affirms that the Bible stands independently as God's Word written, regardless of any human assessment of it or reaction to it. God initiated ('inspired') the writing process to the end that Scripture transmits utterly reliable revelation ('unveiling') of the message of the One True Living God who is our Creator, Redeemer and Sustainer. Therefore this Book of books must be humanity's final authority in every matter of individual faith, corporate confession, ecclesiastical polity, and personal practice.

Belief that 'All scripture is inspired by God' (2 Tim. 3:16) does not imply that the biblical authors were mere ciphers taking down some sort of divine dictation. Nor is inspiration in the same category as human intuition or even human genius. The doctrine of full ('plenary') inspiration affirms creative activity by both the Holy Spirit and the many human writers: Scripture's inspired ('God-breathed') words come to us through human voices using understandable language we can study and obey.

Significantly, a most compelling witness to God's activity in the writing process is this very diversity of human authorship. The dozens of Bible writers come from many different historical eras, cultures, and family backgrounds; they reveal widely differing personalities, and they employ various literary styles (such as historical narrative, poetry, prose, or allegory). Yet these authors – many of whom could have had no possible point of contact with each other – nevertheless present a progressively unfolding redemptive and Christological theme that defies human explanation. The resulting supernatural organic unity of the Bible gives evidence that the Scriptures are far more than even an intentional collection of ancient religious documents, but are indeed 'the sacred writings that are able to instruct you for salvation through faith in Jesus Christ' (2 Tim. 3:15).

GOD'S AUTHORITY AND HUMAN FREEDOM

Thus biblical inspiration goes hand in hand with biblical authority. It is just because 'All scripture is inspired by God' that Scripture is therefore 'useful for teaching, for reproof, for correction, and for training in righteousness, so that everyone who belongs to God may be proficient, equipped for every good work' (2 Tim. 3:16–17).

Contrary to what some may think, acknowledging the Bible as our authoritative guide for faith and practice has a liberating effect. We need never fear studying God's Word: God our Creator seeks only good for us (Jer. 29:11); God our Redeemer freely offers salvation to all who come in believing faith (John 1:12; 3:16); God our Sustainer graciously provides for the continuing needs of God's children (Phil. 4:19; 1 Pet. 5:7).

Only accepting God's gift of new life in Christ leads to true freedom and security in an oppressive and insecure world. Yet in the same way that, out of ignorance or misinformation, many persons have wrongly assumed biblical authority will be oppressive rather than life-enhancing, so also many women have assumed that accepting biblical authority must mean accepting subordinate status in church, home, and society. The reality is far different.

Objective study of God's Word reveals that God considers women and men equally created in the image of God (Gen. 1:26–28) and equally morally and spiritually accountable (Rom. 14:12). Women do not need some sort of male oversight as they approach God, but women and men alike are invited to come directly to the Saviour (John 6:37; 1 Tim. 2:5–6). When they trust Christ for their salvation, women and men are equally redeemed, restored, and called to serve their one Lord (2 Cor. 5:16–20).

Nor should women be reluctant to study Scripture because of past hurts or present injustices inflicted on women in the name of Scripture. Once again, the paradox is that the only true liberation for women is found in upholding the authoritative Word of the God who promises 'I will not violate my covenant, or alter the word that went forth from my lips' (Ps. 89:34). It is not some contemporary female wishful thinking, but God's inspired Word which cannot lie that grants both men and women full membership in the priesthood of all believers (1 Pet. 2:9; Rev. 1:5–6).

Scripture also records human case histories as examples for us to heed (1 Cor. 10:11; Rom. 15:4). Some women may avoid the Bible because they have been told only the negative female examples (such as Jezebel or Herodias), when– as with men – Scripture presents an array of positive female role models suitable for all believers to emulate (such as Deborah, Ruth, Huldah, Phoebe, Priscilla). Women familiar with these Bible characters can refute any who would teach a restricted role for women, by pointing out that our common authority – the Bible – shows God using women in a wide variety of roles.

Women will also be greatly encouraged by the inclusive ministry practices of Jesus, Paul, and the New Testament church. In Luke 11:27–28 Jesus made it clear that God's blessing is not gender-restrictive, and Paul's letter to the Galatians urges all believers to stand firm in their new freedom in Christ Jesus (Gal. 5:1). Women who know Scripture will reject any notion that their gender limits that full redemptive freedom.

SEEKING THE WHOLE TRUTH

Sadly, there have been extended periods throughout church history when laypeople in general were thought unfitted to study Scripture on their own, and when women in particular were discouraged or even prevented from opening the Bible for themselves because of their supposedly 'easily deceivable' nature. Yet God's Word commands us to know Scripture. No one is exempt from the biblical injunction: 'Do your best to present yourself to God as one approved by him, a worker who has no need to be ashamed, rightly explaining the word of truth' (2 Tim. 2:15).

In the Old Testament, the priest Ezra called both men and women to hear and obey the law (Neh. 8:2–3). In the New Testament, we find Jesus encouraged women to learn (Luke 10:38–42) and first entrusted some of Christianity's most cherished truths to women (John 11:25–26; 20:17–18).

Jesus also rebuked disciples who failed to take into account the entirety of Scripture (Luke 24:25). Christians are called to engage in careful, thorough study of the whole Bible, including problem passages. When we rise to this challenge we find great rewards. In addition to personal enrichment and spiritual deepening, when we are familiar with the totality of Scripture we are far better equipped to detect and avoid such pitfalls as selective exegesis (failing to consider the entire context), eisegesis (reading into the text what is not there), and extra-biblical arguments (reasoning not supported by Scripture).

Such diligent study of God's Word is hard work, and we must beware of being easily satisfied by superficial answers to difficult questions. Accepting biblical authority over our lives never means blindly accepting even the most familiar human interpretations of God's authority. Rather, we must continually subject our human interpretations to the light of all God's Word. In this discernment process, we have Jesus' own assurance that the Holy Spirit will guide all seeking hearts into more of God's truth (John 16:13–15; see also James 1:5–6).

THE LAST WORD

Most important of all, our Lord and Saviour Jesus Christ affirmed the utter reliability of God's Word by declaring 'scripture cannot be annulled' (John 10:35). Jesus also promised, 'If you continue in my word, you are truly my disciples; and you will know the truth, and the truth will make you free' (John 8:31–32).

In the final analysis, only upholding a high view of Scripture will free us from that stalemate in which 'My word is as good as yours.' Biblical authority must always take precedence over human traditions, entrenched social customs, and even religious dogma. God's Word must have the last word – not only in gender matters, but in everything affecting the faith and practice of God's children.

INTERPRETING THE NEW TESTAMENT

INTRODUCTION

I saw a poster recently which quoted McLuhan saying something like 'I know you believe you understand what you think I said, but I'm not sure you realize that what you heard is not what I meant.' When we read or hear anything, we interpret it; and in most situations of everyday life we interpret correctly. However, sometimes, even when we know the speaker and the situation well, we get things wrong. The New Testament was written 2,000 years ago by people from a society influenced by knowledge of the Old Testament Scriptures, but also permeated by Greek, Roman and Asian cultures. It was written to those in such cultures, many of whom did not have the same knowledge of the Old Testament. It was written in a different language from ours using different thought forms. So although in many cases as we read the New Testament we are likely to get the meaning right, the potential for misunderstanding in some situations is quite high. Hermeneutics, the technical term for the study of the principles and practice of interpretation (it comes from the Greek *hermeneuo*, meaning 'interpret', 'translate', or 'explain') helps us to lessen the possibility of such misunderstanding.

The intention of this article is to explore some of the issues of hermeneutics; the intention of this volume as a whole is to apply principles so that you and I are better enabled to get to grips with what the New Testament is teaching and to apply it in our own lives.

LITERATURE QUESTIONS

Genre. In order to understand a particular passage we need to know its genre, the type or category of literature. Is this passage prose or poetry, is it parable or narrative, is it advice or command, is it a doctrinal statement or is it a personal letter written to a particular group of people in a particular situation? There are subsidiary questions here. Is the narrative simply an account of what happened or is it supposed to stand as a pattern for all behaviour? Priscilla and Aquila, for example, are the only married couple in the New Testament of whom we have any detailed knowledge of their way of life. Does this imply that all couples should travel a lot or that all couples should follow their model of partnership, where each activity seems to have been carried out together? Clearly, narrative is not teaching, but it may be deliberately making a point. Similarly, we must decide whether the teaching in a letter applies only to the specific situation of the original recipients or if it also has a more general application. Do instructions to slaves really have anything to do with employees today?

Imagery. Those who wish to take the Bible seriously and to treat it as authoritative sometimes speak of believing it all 'literally'. But that is not what they really mean. The New Testament is full of metaphors, parables, pictures and all kinds of symbolism; to interpret these 'literally' would be a nonsense. Of course the believers are not sheep in the literal sense. Taking the Bible seriously means looking at this imagery and working out what it would have meant to the original readers.

In passages which refer to the future we have what might be described as a three-dimensional problem with the imagery. Is the picture presented meant to be literal or is it meant to be figurative? Is it a picture of natural events or of supernatural ones? Is it speaking of events within history or at the end of time? Sometimes there are clear indica- tions within the text as to where the picture fits, but sometimes the answers to these ques- tions are not clear. We must be careful not to assume that we have a picture of real events within history involving supernatural intervention when it might be a figurative picture of natural events, and vice versa.

Grammar. Sometimes the grammatical constructions used give us vital clues about the meaning of a passage. In inflected languages like Greek, pronouns which give us infor- mation about, for example, the identity of a speaker, are built into the verbal form. This means that if a pronoun *is* included then that is because the writer wants to put special stress on the fact that it is 'I' who have done this, or it is 'you' who must respond.

The use of the tense can be significant. For example, in 1 Tim. 2:11 the imperative (command tense) is used. This does not always come across in English translations where often the impression is given that a woman ought to be *allowed* to learn rather than that she *must* learn.

There are grammatical ambiguities in every language and we need to be aware of some of these. For example, if the masculine singular or the feminine singular is used, we know the text refers to an individual male or an individual female. If the feminine plural is used then it refers to a group of women. However, if the masculine plural is used it could be referring to a group of men or a mixed group of men and women – it can sometimes only be a matter of judgment as to which of these is meant.

CONTEXT QUESTIONS

External context. In order to understand a passage we may need information about the history, geography or general background of life at the time the passage was written. There could be factors in the surrounding culture which restrict or explain or make more likely the way in which we should understand what is said. And there could be factors in our own culture which mislead us. Apparently in parts of Indonesia the place where women get water is also the place where they go to bathe – one Indonesian graduate quite naturally assumed therefore that in John 4 Jesus was waiting at the well for women to come so that he could watch them bathing. A knowledge of the customs in Samaria and Judea at the time of Jesus shows that this interpretation is impossible. Similarly, if we knew nothing of the Hebrew idiom where exaggeration is used to make a point, Luke 14:26 could give the impression that Jesus was encouraging his disciples to hate their parents.

Internal context (this is sometimes described as the co-text). Is there anything in the surrounding verses or chapters that illuminates the verses we wish to look at? Jesus' state- ment that 'Salt is good' could be taken as advice on diet but the surrounding verses make it very clear that his point is about lifestyle and witness.

Biblical context. It is important to interpret any passage in the light of the teaching of the Bible as a whole. But this assumes that we have an understanding of the overall teaching – and raises the problem of how far things that we assume the Bible teaches really come from the Bible itself or from some kind of tradition. Many are convinced that the Bible clearly states 'wives obey your husbands' and 'the husband is the head of the family', whereas the actual statements are 'wives be subject to your husbands' and 'the husband is the head of the wife'. This may make a difference to our interpretation of a number of other passages. It is essential that we recognize and are open to various hermeneutical circles.

HERMENEUTICAL CIRCLES

This term is used to describe issues of interpretation where it is important to move from one set of questions to another and then back to the first set and so on, being influenced at each stage by the answers that emerge.

The parts and the whole. We come to a passage with a prior understanding of biblical teaching and we quite rightly interpret the passage in the light of that teaching. However, as we look at the passage carefully, we may come to a new insight about its meaning, and that new insight must then be incorporated into our overall understanding of biblical teaching. With this new overall understanding we come back to the passage, and so the circle goes on, with the parts and the whole constantly interacting as our understanding of both improves. Maybe a spiral is a better image here than a circle, which could imply that there is no progress.

Questions raised by the text and by the world. Christians in general accept that the Bible is not only an account of the religious understanding of a group of people who lived many years ago but also has something to say that is relevant to our situation today. But there is sometimes dispute as to whether our starting-point should be the text or the world in which we find ourselves. Should we look at the text and, as we see questions and issues arising from the various sections, then think about the application of those questions and issues in today's world? Or should we consider what questions and issues are at the forefront in our society and then go to the text to seek a biblical perspective on these issues? To see this as another hermeneutical circle recognizes that both approaches by themselves are inadequate but used together may help us to come to a genuine understanding of the Bible as God's Word for today.

TEXTUAL QUESTIONS

Translation. This always involves interpretation. Which, out of several possible translations of a word, should be used in this instance? Sometimes a word has two or more possible meanings in one language and possibly that word has been chosen to create ambiguity and lead the reader in two different directions at once. It is very unlikely that a word can be found in another language which maintains the same ambiguity and the translator has to decide which way to go. Again, is it better to concentrate on translating words or meaning? To speak of dogs, for example, conveys a very different meaning to a society where dogs are seen as vermin than it does to a society where dogs are cosseted pets.

Transmission. The text of the New Testament is very well attested. Although we do not have the autographs of any of the New Testament documents we do have many, many very early copies of almost every verse. One can see slight differences between these copies. Sometimes a letter or a word has been transposed or even a line missed out. In almost all instances it is quite clear where a mistake has been made in copying. However, occasionally there is some doubt as to which of two possible texts most faithfully reflects the original. Most modern translations indicate this kind of problem by a marginal note. It will be noticed that none of these disputed texts in fact have bearing on significant doctrines but it is sometimes a good idea to compare different translations at the points where a problem is noted.

METHODOLOGICAL QUESTIONS

As we seek to discover what a given passage means and how we should apply it in our own lives, certain patterns of interpretation arise.

Primacy of principle or practice? Should we interpret what actually happened in the light of what we see as teaching principles clearly laid down, or should we interpret, or even modify, the teaching in the light of the actions that are described? At first sight, it seems absolutely clear that the principle should always count more than the description of what people actually did. However, it is interesting that Jesus used the example of David's eating the consecrated 'bread of the Presence', which was against the Law, to show that the Law was not the final answer that the Pharisees had assumed it to be. So *do* we interpret Paul's theological statements in the light of his practice – 'He did this, so he can't mean this'? For example, he worked with women teachers, so he cannot be saying that women can never teach. Or do we interpret his practice in the light of his theological statements – 'He said this, so it can't mean that he did that'? For example, he says women must be silent, so when it speaks of them taking part, it cannot be in church. In fact there is a happy medium whereby we take a look at both. The important thing is to be aware of what we are doing.

The use of the Old Testament by the New. This gives us some clues as to the right way for us to use Scripture. There is a certain amount of flexibility. Quotes from the Old Testament are often general rather than exact. Patterns and concepts are sometimes identified which answer contemporary questions but which do not seem to have been present in the mind of the original writer. This leads to dangers and it is possible to follow the extremes of early Jewish rabbis or Christian writers of earlier centuries and make the text say virtually anything without regard to its original context. That danger must be avoided, but where there is a genuine similarity between the situation described in the text and our own situation, then perhaps it is useful for us to look for patterns and parallels.

Standard principles. A number of standard paths to follow in cases of dispute over a text have been identified:

(1) Interpret the difficult and obscure by the straightforward and plain. Of course what seems obvious and plain to one may seem difficult and obscure to others but it is a good principle to follow.

(2) Interpret the isolated by the common.

(3) Look at parallel usage of words or phrases. It used to be taken for granted that all uses of the same words would have the same meaning and that therefore if we knew the sense in one case we would automatically know what it meant everywhere else. This is now known to be nonsense. Words change their meaning over time and even at the same time can be used in all sorts of different ways. The immediate context has to provide the final answer to the meaning of words. But knowing possibilities from other contexts can sometimes help.

Common sense. This is crucial. We can start asking so many questions of the text that it begins to look as if it is impossible for us ever to come to a sensible and accurate understanding of Scripture. However, Luther was convinced that with the application of common sense and the help of the Spirit, Scripture could and should be heard and understood by every Christian, and I see no reason to disagree with him. It is not necessary to have a training in advanced hermeneutics to be able to hear what God is saying through his Word. It is true that we need to acknowledge that, because of our own prejudices and presuppositions, our understanding can be limited. We need to keep looking, listening and learning taking full advantage of all the help that is available to us. It is also true that we can genuinely hear what Scripture is saying to us. Much the bigger problem for most of us is doing something about what we have heard!

ASKING QUESTIONS
OF AN AUTHORITATIVE TEXT

The previous article on 'Interpreting the New Testament' looks at a range of different questions that we have to have in our minds if we are to understand what the New Testament text is all about. However, for some people, that in itself is a problem. Surely if Scripture is the inspired and authoritative Word of God, then isn't it up to the believer to simply accept the text, not to ask questions about it? As Tennyson said of the soldiers at the charge of the light brigade, 'Theirs not to make reply, theirs not to reason why, theirs but to do and die.' In this instance theirs or ours is but to hear and to obey but not to question. It is felt that questioning the text casts doubts on God's sovereignty and stands in the way of obedience. But questions like those dealt with in the article on interpretation are there to help the reader hear so that she or he will know what it is that they ought to obey. They are there to increase, not to lessen, the influence of the text, to assist, not to hinder, obedience.

One can understand the motivation behind reservations of this kind. Many in our generation have seen the Bible scoffed at or ignored, its teaching listened to only when it suits the reader or backs up what their own reason or desire has already convinced them is applicable. There is a feeling that to ask questions of the text is going to lessen its authority and make people even less likely to heed its message. However, I would want to argue that these reservations are misplaced. Asking questions of the text and hearing and obeying the text are very far from being mutually exclusive. The Old Testament is full of occasions where God positively encourages people to raise questions about what he is doing or intends to do. It is almost as if God revels in the interaction and delights in the fact that his people are thinking the issues through for themselves. We see it in Job, with Abraham in Gen. 18 seeking clarification about the issue of an innocent minority suffering because of the wickedness of the majority, with Jacob, and often in the Psalms. Of course the questioner has to be ready to hear God's answer, and it may not be always what is expected or desired. But the questioning process itself is affirmed rather than discouraged. God wants us to be involved with his affairs, and presumably his Word, actively and not just passively.

The responsibility to search and study the Scriptures carefully was taken for granted by the first-century church (Acts 17:2, 11; 18:24, 28; 1 Tim. 4:13; 2 Tim. 3:15–16). They had no problem with the concept that studying the text involved asking questions of it. It has to be said that sometimes they asked so many questions that they never got round to applying what it said, and sometimes they asked the wrong kind of questions (1 Tim. 3:4; Titus 3:9)! However, avoiding the wrong questions most certainly does not mean avoiding all questions. Jesus' own example makes that very clear.

Jesus became very frustrated with the Jewish Bible scholars of the time, the scribes and the rabbis, both Pharisees and Sadducees, because they had not asked enough questions of the text. They had not thought to ask about the implications of saying that God was the God of Abraham, Isaac, and Jacob, when these people were already dead and hence they had not drawn the right conclusions about resurrection (Matt. 22:29–33). They had not delved into what David was talking about when he referred to one of his own descendants as his 'Lord' (Matt. 22:43). They had not considered whether David was right or wrong to break the Law by eating sanctified bread or worked out the relevance of authorized priestly

Sabbath-breaking for a right understanding of what the Sabbath was really all about (Matt. 12:1–8). They had not wrestled enough with Gen. 2:24 to work out that it had implications for the permanence of marriage and the unsuitability of divorce. It is very clear that hearing and obeying the text must involve first coming to a good understanding of its meaning and implications. It is also clear that getting such an understanding involves effort, delving, wrestling and looking at familiar verses with new eyes, recognizing the possibility of new perspectives.

We have already considered questions of literary structure, of context, of starting-point, of text and translation and of interpretative method, but there are also significant questions that relate directly to the content of Scripture. Much of the material in the Old Testament, and quite a bit in the New Testament too, is in the form of narrative, descriptions of events, of what happened to particular people in particular situations. It seems that many of those Christians who have held most passionately to the authoritative nature of the Scriptures have assumed that the only appropriate question to ask of the narrative sections is 'Did this actually happen?' And the only appropriate answer to give is 'Yes it did.' But is it not true that Jesus' 'Haven't you read about what happened and thought about it further?' approach shows this perspective to be at best limited and almost certainly not fulfilling our responsibilities to take the text seriously?

It is important that where particular events are recorded as factual, we accept the integrity of the text and thus the historical nature of what is recorded; but this should be the beginning not the end of our questioning. As John 21:25 indicates, the events that are set down in the Scriptures are a selection from many other things that could have been included. Why was any particular event put down? And why are some incidents described in much more detail than others? We see God at work with various people at various times. What are we supposed to learn from reading about these events and actions?

If Scripture makes it clear that God used a particular person taking particular action to further his purposes, does that mean that the action in itself must be right? Clearly not. Judas' action in betraying Jesus was used, but not approved, by God. But if a person is recognized by God to be in general a righteous person and used as it were on a regular basis, surely that means we can look at their behavior and assume that we ought to behave in the same kind of way in the same kind of circumstances? Well, no again. Joseph, for example, was used and indeed blessed by God in many ways while in slavery in Egypt. But Gen. 47 describes the action he took in selling back grain, which he had collected from the people, at extortionate prices. Firstly he took their livestock in exchange for grain and finally their land so that eventually he 'bought all the land of Egypt for Pharaoh' (Gen. 47:20). This forcing people to sell land to pay debts is something that is heavily frowned upon within the Law which was given to Moses. In other words, the Law causes us to at least ask searching questions about Joseph's action. There is enough information in Scripture telling us about God's attitudes, preferences and commands, which allows us to look critically at all kinds of incidents. We must recognize that the lessons we are intended to learn are not automatically related to following the same example. Questions must be asked.

But the kind of questions that we know how to ask or think about asking are bound to be limited. Certain things simply do not occur to us to ask. If we come to the text simply to answer questions which are raised by the culture and situation in which we find ourselves, then the presuppositions of that culture may never be challenged and we could rightly be accused of 'selling out to the world'. We *may* take it for granted that the values of material prosperity and of individualism are correct and simply read the Bible in the light of such presuppositions. However if we start from the text and never turn our eyes to what is happening in the world, then issues which did not arise in biblical times, such as genetic engineering or chemical pollution, may never be tackled. We could then be rightly accused of a 'head-in-the-sand irrelevance'. Of course the Bible does not directly raise these issues and it would be quite wrong for us to ignore the original context or to abstract verses from the situation in which they were written. But when issues are raised, it is possible to go back to Scripture to discover whether there are any principles which may apply in this new situation. Or whether indeed there are points made by Scripture that have never been noticed before. This is what happened when Christians began to look afresh at the issue of slavery. Many had taken it for granted that this was perfectly acceptable and indeed supported by the Bible. A fresh look from a different perspective convinced them that they had missed much that was there all the time simply because they had asked the wrong questions.

In this context it is important to realize that we are limited by our own background, culture and circumstances. There are some issues that we will simply not notice because our eyes are not open to them. Almost all the interpretative helps available to us – commentaries, Bible dictionaries etc. – are written by Western, white, middle-class males. However excellent their scholarship, it is likely that they miss out on certain areas. This volume is an attempt to introduce the women's perspective, opening up a new range of questions. But white Westerners need to be open too to hearing the voice of Africans and Asians. Educated people need to listen to those who have not had the opportunities or influence of a classical education. Younger folk need to listen to older folk and vice versa.

And all of us, if we have a desire to hear and obey the authoritative voice of Scripture, must search the Scriptures diligently, delving into the text, wrestling with the text, and asking questions of the text.

MATTHEW'S GOSPEL

INTRODUCTION

Matthew's Gospel (ca. AD 85) is the first book in the New Testament. Often this leads people to assume that it was the first Gospel book written, when in fact Mark's Gospel (ca. 70) is probably the earliest of the canonical Gospels. When the canon – the list of biblical books – was compiled, Matthew was placed at the beginning of the New Testament for two primary reasons. First, the author makes very direct connections between the story of Jesus and 'the Law and the Prophets' (the Hebrew Bible or Old Testament); thus, this book forms a conscious bridge between the two parts of the Christian Bible. Second, the author is concerned with principles of organization and behavior of the early Christian community, so this Gospel came to be viewed as 'the book of the church'.

Traditionally, authorship of this Gospel is attributed to one of Jesus' disciples, a tax collector named Matthew (viz. Matt. 9:9–13). This tradition derives from Papias of Hierapolis (fl. 130), who claimed that Matthew provided a Hebrew (or Aramaic) prototype of the sayings of Jesus which are included in this Gospel (quoted in Eusebius, *HE* III.39.16). The earliest extant witnesses to the text of Matthew are papyrus fragments dating from the third century of our era. In the one manuscript which includes the beginning of the Gospel (⨅1), the attribution 'according to Matthew' already is found. The manuscript goes no further in identifying the author of this Gospel.

Through historical research and analysis of the text, scholars have succeeded in extending our knowledge a bit further: (1) the author was a Jewish Christian (2) who is addressing a Christian community that initially was exclusively Jewish but (3) is now beginning to evangelize Gentiles and include them in their membership. Because of the major role played by Peter, and especially the authoritative position accorded him in Matt. 16:9, it often is suggested that the author's community was in Antioch of Syria, where Peter was a significant figure for a time in the AD 40s–50s. Alternatively, the author's familiarity with Palestinian Judaism and its disputes over interpretation of the Jewish Law has been seen as supporting a Palestinian (or, more specifically, a Galilean) origin for the text.

For the broad outline of Jesus' life and ministry, Matthew (as Luke) draws on the Gospel of Mark. The same basic order of events is followed, and in places there are verbatim parallels with the Markan account. Yet the author does not simply repeat the earlier Gospel material.The author uses Mark creatively – sometimes abridging, expanding, summarizing, or explaining elements – reorganizing the Markan material. Prior source materials are incorporated in ways that best suit the purposes of this new Gospel account, written with the needs of a different Christian community in mind. The author probably also had two other sources of information about Jesus, one often called 'Q' (which is shared with Luke) and one called 'M' (which includes material unique to Matthew). Thus, the author/editor of Matthew had three sources for this Gospel (Mark, Q, and M) which are used to tell, in Matthew's own way, the 'good news' of God's saving activity in the words and deeds of Jesus of Nazareth, the long-awaited Messiah of Israel, who now calls the Gentiles as well.

One way this belief is conveyed is through the arrangement of materials within the Gospel. The longest of the four canonical Gospels, Matthew often has been noted for its five great discourses of Jesus: the Sermon on the Mount, the missionary discourse, the parable discourse, the church order discourse, and the eschatological discourse. Each of these is preceded by a narrative section, and together the narrative-discourse units make up five 'books' within the Gospel. The parallel to the Torah, the five books of Moses, is obvious. Especially given the concluding formula to the discourses – 'when Jesus had finished saying these things' (Matt. 7:28; 11:1; 13:53; 19:1; 26:1) – which is so highly reminiscent of the reports of Moses' proclamation of God's covenant with Israel and, especially, of the Ten Commandments (e.g. Exod. 24:3–4; Num. 11:24; Deut. 9:10; 17:19; 27:3, 8; 32:44), it becomes obvious that this is an intentional plan by the author to draw this connection between Moses and Jesus, between God's Word given through Moses and God's Word given through Jesus.

The Genealogy of Jesus the Messiah

1 An account of the genealogy[a] of Jesus the Messiah,[b] the son of David, the son of Abraham.

2 Abraham was the father of Isaac, and Isaac the father of Jacob, and Jacob the father of Judah and his brothers, [3]and Judah the father of Perez and Zerah by Tamar, and Perez the father of Hezron, and Hezron the father of Aram, [4]and Aram the father of Aminadab, and Aminadab the father of Nahshon, and Nahshon the father of Salmon, [5]and Salmon the father of Boaz by Rahab, and Boaz the father of Obed by Ruth, and Obed the father of Jesse, [6]and Jesse the father of King David.

And David was the father of Solomon by the wife of Uriah, [7]and Solomon the father of Rehoboam, and Rehoboam the father of Abijah, and Abijah the father of Asaph,[c] [8]and Asaph[c] the father of Jehoshaphat, and Jehoshaphat the father of Joram, and Joram the father of Uzziah, [9]and Uzziah the father of Jotham, and Jotham the father of Ahaz, and Ahaz the father of Hezekiah, [10]and Hezekiah the father of Manasseh, and Manasseh the father of Amos,[d] and Amos[d] the father of Josiah, [11]and Josiah the father of Jechoniah and his brothers, at the time of the deportation to Babylon.

12 And after the deportation to Babylon: Jechoniah was the father of Salathiel, and Salathiel the father of Zerubbabel, [13]and

[a] Or birth   [b] Or Jesus Christ
[c] Other ancient authorities read Asa
[d] Other ancient authorities read Amon

THE INFANCY NARRATIVE (MATT. 1:1–2:23)

This section in Matthew, and especially Chapter 2, is intended to recall the infancy story of Moses (Exod. 1:8–2:10). Matthew begins with a narrative prologue, delineating the themes that will be developed in the ensuing sections of the book. Rather than using the name 'Gospel', as Mark does, the author calls this 'An account of the genealogy (geneseos) of Jesus the Messiah, the son of David, the son of Abraham' (Matt. 1:1). The pregnant term geneseos would remind readers of the book of Genesis, the book of God's creation, first of the heavens and the earth, and then of the generations leading up to Abraham, the father of Israel. In this way Matthew connects the coming of Jesus with the continuing story of God's creative action in the world of human affairs. That Jesus is son of Abraham makes him an heir to the promises of God to Israel, to the faith and the covenant; that Jesus is son of David asserts that he is heir to the princely reign and unending dynasty promised to David (2 Sam. 7:16). Jesus is named Christ (Messiah), God's anointed one; like the kings, prophets, and priests of old, Jesus is chosen by God and set apart for a special task. Matthew's book is designed to unfold how Jesus comes to be the fulfillment of the blessings of covenant and Kingdom that God had promised to Israel.

The structure of Matthew's genealogy follows the creation theme in its structure of six sets of seven generations leading up to the birth of Jesus the Christ. (Cf. Gen. 1:1–2:3, where the first two days are devoted to the superstructure of the world, the next two days to the infrastructure [the exosphere], and days five and six are devoted to living creatures; the seventh day is the culmination of God's creative work.) Within this framework, the author highlights two turning points in Israelite history which further divide the structure into three sets of 14 generations: the universal reign of David, and the Babylonian Exile. Implied in this outline is Cyrus, King of Persia, who is hailed as God's 'messiah' in Is. 45:1 because he frees the exiles from Babylonian domination.

Counter to the usual practice of listing exclusively fathers and sons, Matthew's genealogy includes five women: Tamar, Rahab, Ruth, 'the wife of Uriah' (Bathsheba), and Mary. This list teaches three ideas which will be keys to the Gospel. (1) Two of these women (Rahab and Ruth) are foreigners, while a third (Bathsheba) is known as 'the wife of Uriah' (the Hittite); this highlights the action of Gentiles in the fulfillment of God's covenant promises to Israel. (2) All five unusual figures mentioned in the genealogy (including Uriah, rather than Bathsheba) are examples of the true righteousness that Jesus will demand, going against social convention when necessary so that God's will may be done. Even a woman's use of her sexuality can serve

Zerubbabel the father of Abiud, and Abiud the father of Eliakim, and Eliakim the father of Azor, [14]and Azor the father of Zadok, and Zadok the father of Achim, and Achim the father of Eliud, [15]and Eliud the father of Eleazar, and Eleazar the father of Matthan, and Matthan the father of Jacob, [16]and Jacob the father of Joseph the husband of Mary, of whom Jesus was born, who is called the Messiah.[e]

17 So all the generations from Abraham to David are fourteen generations; and from David to the deportation to Babylon, fourteen generations; and from the deportation to Babylon to the Messiah,[e] fourteen generations.

The Birth of Jesus the Messiah

18 Now the birth of Jesus the Messiah[f] took place in this way. When his mother Mary had been engaged to Joseph, but before they lived together, she was found to be with child from the Holy Spirit. [19]Her husband Joseph, being a righteous man and unwilling to expose her to public disgrace, planned to dismiss her quietly. [20]But just when he had resolved to do this, an angel of the Lord appeared to him in a dream and said, "Joseph, son of David, do not be afraid to take Mary as your wife, for the child conceived in her is from the Holy Spirit. [21]She will bear a son, and you are to name him Jesus, for he will save his people from their sins." [22]All this took place to fulfill what had been spoken by the Lord through the prophet:

[23] "Look, the virgin shall conceive and
    bear a son,
  and they shall name him
    Emmanuel,"

which means, "God is with us." [24]When Joseph awoke from sleep, he did as the angel of the Lord commanded him; he took her as his wife, [25]but had no marital relations with her until she had borne a son;[g] and he named him Jesus.

---

[e] Or *the Christ*   [f] Or *Jesus Christ*
[g] Other ancient authorities read *her firstborn son*

God's purposes and inspire faithfulness to the Law (e.g. Tamar and Ruth). (3) Tamar and Mary both noted for pregnancies which were questioned, then later revealed to have been legitimate.

Initially, both Tamar and Mary were thought to have committed adultery (Gen. 38:24 and Matt. 1:18–20 respectively). The Law prescribes that an adulteress deserves death, and Judah is quite ready to impose this penalty on Tamar (Gen. 38:24b). We are told that Joseph was 'a righteous man and unwilling to expose [Mary] to public disgrace' (Matt. 1:19); but this clearly assumes that it was his right as her husband to call for the death penalty. Thus, both women faced the risk of death for the sake of their children, but were vindicated and saved from that fate.

One of the key differences between the two stories is precisely how this vindication comes about. In Tamar's story, she is the one who calls Judah publicly to account, and he has to recognize the legitimacy of her child. Matthew preserves the good character of both Mary and Joseph by showing God as actively involved in both Mary's conception of her child and in her vindication (through the dream to Joseph); the 'illegitimate' Jesus is legitimated by God. It is possible that Matthew here is trying to undercut rumors of Jesus' illegitimacy by showing a similar example from Israelite history where such charges were unfounded; Jesus' parentage is important for bolstering Matthew's claim that Jesus is the true Messiah of Israel, the primary burden of the infancy narrative.

One of the key ways Matthew presses his claim that Jesus is the Messiah of Israel is to use supporting quotations from the Hebrew Scriptures, especially excerpts from the prophets and the Psalms. Following rabbinic custom, Matthew believed that these writings – when properly interpreted – could also be used to understand events that would occur long after the death of the prophet. The Jews of Jesus' day recognized that biblical prophecy is not clairvoyance or prediction, but speaking forth 'the word of the Lord' for the people of the prophet's own time and place. Thus, the biblical prophets addressed the audiences of their own times concerning issues that

The Visit of the Wise Men

2 In the time of King Herod, after Jesus was born in Bethlehem of Judea, wise men[h] from the East came to Jerusalem, ²asking, "Where is the child who has been born king of the Jews? For we observed his star at its rising,[i] and have come to pay him homage." ³When King Herod heard this, he was frightened, and all Jerusalem with him; ⁴and calling together all the chief priests and scribes of the people, he inquired of them where the Messiah[j] was to be born. ⁵They told him, "In Bethlehem of Judea; for so it has been written by the prophet:

⁶ 'And you, Bethlehem, in the land of
      Judah,
   are by no means least among the
      rulers of Judah;
for from you shall come a ruler
   who is to shepherd[k] my people
      Israel.' "

7 Then Herod secretly called for the wise men[h] and learned from them the exact time when the star had appeared. ⁸Then he sent them to Bethlehem, saying, "Go and search diligently for the child; and when you have found him, bring me word so that I may also go and pay him homage." ⁹When they had heard the king, they set out; and there, ahead of them, went the star that they had seen at its rising,[i] until it stopped over the place where the child was. ¹⁰When they saw that the star had stopped,[l] they were overwhelmed with joy. ¹¹On entering the house, they saw the child with Mary his mother; and they knelt down and paid him homage. Then, opening their treasure chests, they offered him gifts of gold, frankincense, and myrrh. ¹²And having been warned in a dream not to return to Herod, they left for their own country by another road.

[h] Or *astrologers*; Gk *magi*   [i] Or *in the East*
[j] Or *the Christ*   [k] Or *rule*
[l] Gk *saw the star*

---

were present to them, and referred to events that were current or would take place in the immediate future. However, Jews also understood that God continued to speak to a later time and place through the record of prior 'words' and events – if one knew the proper way of reading the message. During the Second Temple period, a form of exegesis was developed (known as *pesher*) to read biblical texts as also having an eschatological orientation, that is, as referring to ('predicting') an event or situation which would occur in the final age. Such events included, but were not limited to, the coming and activity of God's Messiah. There are several examples of *pesher* among the scrolls found at Kirbet Qumran, which date from ca. 150–50 BC. Matthew's recurrent theme of 'prophecy fulfillment' is undergirded by this tradition of the *pesher* type of exegesis.

Matthew's story of Jesus' birth illustrates several unique features when compared with the more familiar Lukan story of the nativity. The primary character in Matthew's story is Joseph, not Mary. This follows the common assumption of the time that the central representative of a household is the husband/father.

Rather than an angelic 'annunciation', dreams reveal the divine will (e.g. Matt. 1:20–23; 2:12–13, 19–20, 22). It should be noted that, for Matthew, the dreamer is Mary's husband, Joseph son-of Jacob (cf. Luke 3:23: 'Joseph, son of Heli'). No doubt we are to recall a prior Joseph ben Jacob, whose dreams caused strife with his brothers and eventually took him down to Egypt (Gen. 37). Matthew alone mentions that Joseph's initial response to the news of Mary's pregnancy is to divorce her. To a modern reader, there may appear to be a contradiction in the text regarding the relationship between Mary and Joseph. We are told they are 'engaged', but not living together (Matt. 1:18), and then that Joseph is Mary's 'husband' and is determined to 'divorce' her. Confusion arises because of the complexities of first-century Jewish wedding practices. A Jewish wedding was contracted in two stages: (1) 'consent' or 'betrothal', and (2) 'marriage'. (This two-stage pattern is similar to our contemporary 'engagement' and 'wedding'.)

The Escape to Egypt

13 Now after they had left, an angel of the Lord appeared to Joseph in a dream and said, "Get up, take the child and his mother, and flee to Egypt, and remain there until I tell you; for Herod is about to search for the child, to destroy him." [14]Then Joseph[m] got up, took the child and his mother by night, and went to Egypt, [15]and remained there until the death of Herod. This was to fulfill what had been spoken by the Lord through the prophet, "Out of Egypt I have called my son."

The Massacre of the Infants

16 When Herod saw that he had been tricked by the wise men,[n] he was infuriated, and he sent and killed all the children in and around Bethlehem who were two years old or under, according to the time that he had learned from the wise men.[n] [17]Then was fulfilled what had been spoken through the prophet Jeremiah:

[18] "A voice was heard in Ramah,
   wailing and loud lamentation,
   Rachel weeping for her children;
   she refused to be consoled, because
      they are no more."

The Return from Egypt

19 When Herod died, an angel of the Lord suddenly appeared in a dream to Joseph in Egypt and said, [20]"Get up, take the child and his mother, and go to the land of Israel, for those who were seeking the

[m] Gk *he* [n] Or *astrologers*; Gk *magi*

The terms of the marriage contract, including the 'bride price' and dowry, were decided by the father of the bride and the groom (perhaps with his father). Then, when the bride neared the onset of menses (age 12–13), a formal 'betrothal' ceremony was held during which the bride and groom consented (before witnesses) to the marriage. At this point, the husband gained legal rights over the woman and agreed to complete the marriage at some future date (usually about a year later). On her part, the woman incurred the wifely obligation (among other things) of sexual fidelity to her husband. The point at which the bride actually was transferred to the husband's family home constituted the completion of the marriage process; at that time, the husband assumed the financial support of his wife. Matthew says that Mary and Joseph are in between these two stages of marriage, after the betrothal and before the 'transferral' of the bride to the groom's house. Yet, they are indeed married and, if Joseph now chooses to abrogate the marriage, he can do this only by divorce.

The first public witnesses of Jesus' birth recorded by Matthew are not Israelites but Gentiles described as Eastern 'magi' (Matt. 2:1, 9–11). 'Magi' (masculine plural) refers to 'wise persons'. Most often they were versed in mathematics, physics and astronomy; hence 'astrologers' is sometimes the translation. They certainly were wealthy individuals to have traveled so far and to attend Herod's court, but Matthew makes no mention of them being 'kings' (as is conveyed by the traditional carol, 'We Three Kings'). Incidentally, there is no grammatical basis for all the magi being male, since the masculine plural can refer equally to a group of men or to a mixed group. Nor is there any reference to how many magi there were.

The visit of the magi takes place some time after Jesus' birth in Mary and Joseph's house in Bethlehem (Matt. 2:11). King Herod the Great (who is hardly mentioned in Luke) plays the key role in focusing the opposition against Jesus. The flight into Egypt and the slaughter of the innocents are not mentioned by Luke. Matthew reports a move to Nazareth from Egypt, rather than a return to Nazareth.

In spite of the differences in details, Matthew and Luke both agree on five fundamental points regarding Jesus' birth. He was born in Bethlehem. His parents were a Jewish couple, Mary and Joseph. At least one of his parents was descended from the great King David. Jesus' paternity was questioned, but his true 'father' is God. He was raised in Nazareth and, therefore, was known as a 'Nazorean' (Matt. 2:23).

child's life are dead." [o]²¹Then Joseph got up, took the child and his mother, and went to the land of Israel. ²²But when he heard that Archelaus was ruling over Judea in place of his father Herod, he was afraid to go there. And after being warned in a dream, he went away to the district of Galilee. ²³There he made his home in a town called Nazareth, so that what had been spoken through the prophets might be fulfilled, "He will be called a Nazorean."

The Proclamation of John the Baptist

3 In those days John the Baptist appeared in the wilderness of Judea, proclaiming, ²"Repent, for the kingdom of heaven has come near."[p] ³This is the one of whom the prophet Isaiah spoke when he said,

"The voice of one crying out in the
      wilderness:
   'Prepare the way of the Lord,
      make his paths straight.' "

⁴ Now John wore clothing of camel's hair with a leather belt around his waist, and his food was locusts and wild honey. ⁵Then the people of Jerusalem and all Judea were going out to him, and all the region along the Jordan, ⁶and they were baptized by him in the river Jordan, confessing their sins.

7 But when he saw many Pharisees and Sadducees coming for baptism, he said to them, "You brood of vipers! Who warned you to flee from the wrath to come? ⁸Bear fruit worthy of repentance. ⁹Do not presume to say to yourselves, 'We have Abraham as our ancestor'; for I tell you, God is able from these stones to raise up children to Abraham. ¹⁰Even now the ax is lying at the root of the trees; every tree therefore that does not bear good fruit is cut down and thrown into the fire.

11 "I baptize you with[q] water for repentance, but one who is more powerful than I is coming after me; I am not worthy to carry his sandals. He will baptize you with[q] the Holy Spirit and fire. ¹²His winnowing fork is in his hand, and he will clear his threshing floor and will gather his wheat into the granary; but the chaff he will burn with unquenchable fire."

The Baptism of Jesus

13 Then Jesus came from Galilee to John at the Jordan, to be baptized by him. ¹⁴John would have prevented him, saying, "I need to be baptized by you, and do you come to me?" ¹⁵But Jesus answered him, "Let it be so now; for it is proper for us in this way to fulfill all righteousness." Then he consented.¹⁶And when Jesus had been baptized, just as he came up from the water, suddenly the heavens were opened to him and he saw the Spirit of God descending like a dove and alighting on

[o] Gk *he*   [p] Or *is at hand*   [q] Or *in*

THE INAUGURATION OF JESUS' MINISTRY (MATT. 3:1–7:29)

3:1–17 Since Jesus is the focus of Matthew's story, it may seem odd that the account of Jesus' ministry begins with the preaching of John the Baptist. Matthew does this for at least three reasons. First, John was well known among Jews contemporaneous to Jesus, and had many disciples of his own, even after his execution by Herod; thus, John had to be considered as a religious and political force in the Judaism of Jesus' day. Second, Jesus' message was similar to John's (concerning the coming 'kingdom of heaven') and Jesus was known to have been baptized by John; this may have implied that Jesus (at least for a time) was one of John's disciples (viz. 3:11a). Given these first two factors, Matthew is concerned to establish Jesus' distinction from – indeed, superiority to – John, in spite of Jesus' position as a 'follower'. One of the most convincing ways to do this is to note that John himself proclaimed Jesus' superiority (3:11–15). John's affirmation is then confirmed by a heavenly voice, which bestows upon Jesus the messianic titles of 'Son' and 'Beloved' (Matt. 3:17; cf. Is. 42:1; 49:3).

him. [17]And a voice from heaven said, "This is my Son, the Beloved,[r] with whom I am well pleased."

The Temptation of Jesus

4 Then Jesus was led up by the Spirit into the wilderness to be tempted by the devil. [2]He fasted forty days and forty nights, and afterwards he was famished. [3]The tempter came and said to him, "If you are the Son of God, command these stones to become loaves of bread." [4]But he answered, "It is written,

'One does not live by bread alone,
    but by every word that comes from
        the mouth of God.' "

[5] Then the devil took him to the holy city and placed him on the pinnacle of the temple, [6]saying to him, "If you are the Son of God, throw yourself down; for it is written,

'He will command his angels
        concerning you,'
and 'On their hands they will bear
        you up,
so that you will not dash your foot
        against a stone.' "

[7]Jesus said to him, "Again it is written, 'Do not put the Lord your God to the test.' "

◆ The notion of the *theos aner* ('divine man') was widespread at the turn of the era. Such persons were thought to be endowed with superhuman powers, including the ability to work miracles and to fly. The 'Superman' or 'Superwoman' characters are the best parallels in the popular mythology of our own day ◆

[8] Again, the devil took him to a very high mountain and showed him all the kingdoms of the world and their splendor; [9]and he said to him, "All these I will give you, if you will fall down and worship me." [10]Jesus said to him, "Away with you, Satan! for it is written,

'Worship the Lord your God,
    and serve only him.' "

[11]Then the devil left him, and suddenly angels came and waited on him.

Jesus Begins His Ministry in Galilee

[12] Now when Jesus[s] heard that John had been arrested, he withdrew to Galilee. [13]He left Nazareth and made his home in Capernaum by the sea, in the territory of Zebulun and Naphtali, [14]so that what had

[r] Or *my beloved Son*   [s] Gk *he*

4:1–11. The desert, in Israelite history, is a place of sore trial and yet of great intimacy with God. Now marked as God's chosen one, Jesus sojourns in the desert to come to terms with his call. And, like Job before him, his faithfulness is tested; nothing less than total commitment will do. The numerology here, as elsewhere in Matthew, is significant. That three questions are asked is a symbol of totality. Also, the 40 days and nights of fasting is an obvious allusion to the Flood story, where life endures in the Ark until a new creation can be brought forth. It also recalls the 40 years Israel wandered in the wilderness, totally reliant on God's sustenance, before entering the Promised Land.

Jesus must choose whether to use the divine power entrusted to him for his own purposes, or for God's. He could make his own kingdom, gathering popular support by being a miracle worker (4:3) or 'divine man' (4:6), or becoming a political boss through the patronage system. Jesus passes the threefold test and then, as God cared for Israel for 40 years in the wilderness, so now God sustains Jesus.

4:12–23. Jesus returns to Galilee upon hearing of John the Baptist's arrest. After moving from Nazareth to Capernaum, he begins his public preaching. His central message is of repentance to prepare for the imminent final age when God's power will be made manifest: 'Repent, for the kingdom of heaven has come near' (4:17). While the other evangelists write of 'the Kingdom of God', note that Matthew alone of the evangelists uses the phrase 'Kingdom of heaven', reflecting the Jewish avoidance of writing or speaking the divine Name.

been spoken through the prophet Isaiah might be fulfilled:

15 "Land of Zebulun, land of Naphtali,
    on the road by the sea, across the
        Jordan, Galilee of the
        Gentiles –
16 the people who sat in darkness
        have seen a great light,
    and for those who sat in the region
        and shadow of death
        light has dawned."

17From that time Jesus began to proclaim, "Repent, for the kingdom of heaven has come near."[t]

Jesus Calls the First Disciples

18 As he walked by the Sea of Galilee, he saw two brothers, Simon, who is called Peter, and Andrew his brother, casting a net into the sea – for they were fishermen. 19And he said to them, "Follow me, and I will make you fish for people." 20Immediately they left their nets and followed him. 21As he went from there, he saw two other brothers, James son of Zebedee and his brother John, in the boat with their father Zebedee, mending their nets, and he called them. 22Immediately they left the boat and their father, and followed him.

Jesus Ministers to Crowds of People

23 Jesus[u] went throughout Galilee, teaching in their synagogues and proclaiming the good news[v] of the kingdom and curing every disease and every sickness among the people.24So his fame spread throughout all Syria, and they brought to him all the sick, those who were afflicted with various diseases and pains, demoniacs, epileptics, and paralytics, and he cured them.25And great crowds followed him from Galilee, the Decapolis, Jerusalem, Judea, and from beyond the Jordan.

◆ The remark concerning 'their synagogues' is usually understood to reflect the late first-century split between the Jews and the followers of Jesus. 'Their synagogues' is taken to refer to the synagogues of the Jews who do not believe in Jesus as the Messiah, as opposed to the synagogues of Jesus' followers. On the other hand, it may simply reflect a geographical bias, suggesting that the author and intended audience of this Gospel is not Galilean ◆

The Beatitudes

5 When Jesus[w] saw the crowds, he went up the mountain; and after he sat down, his disciples came to him. 2Then he began to speak, and taught them, saying:

3 "Blessed are the poor in spirit, for theirs is the kingdom of heaven.

4 "Blessed are those who mourn, for they will be comforted.

5 "Blessed are the meek, for they will inherit the earth.

[t] Or *is at hand*   [u] Gk *He*   [v] Gk *gospel*
[w] Gk *he*

Unlike other teachers whose disciples choose them, Jesus calls his disciples, who come 'at once' (4:20, 22). He traverses Galilee 'teaching in their synagogues', preaching, working miracles of healing (v. 23) and – consequently – becoming such a sensation that crowds follow from nearly every region of Palestine. Samaria is the one which is notable for its omission.

Having set the stage, Matthew then reports the first of his five discourses, the Sermon on the Mount (chapters 5–7), which outlines the basic elements of Jesus' message about the Kingdom.

5:1–16. As Moses brought the multitude out of Egypt to create a new people under God's Law, which Moses handed down on Mount Sinai, Jesus sees the multitudes following him and goes up to the mountain to hand down a new teaching. The intentional parallels here between Jesus and Moses are unmistakable (as before in the infancy narrative). But one should note that Jesus is more than a 'new Moses' for Matthew. Moses was chosen to deliver God's Word to Israel, but it

6 "Blessed are those who hunger and thirst for righteousness, for they will be filled.

7 "Blessed are the merciful, for they will receive mercy.

8 "Blessed are the pure in heart, for they will see God.

9 "Blessed are the peacemakers, for they will be called children of God.

10 "Blessed are those who are persecuted for righteousness' sake, for theirs is the kingdom of heaven.

11 "Blessed are you when people revile you and persecute you and utter all kinds of evil against you falsely[x] on my account. [12]Rejoice and be glad, for your reward is great in heaven, for in the same way they persecuted the prophets who were before you.

Salt and Light

13 "You are the salt of the earth; but if salt has lost its taste, how can its saltiness be restored? It is no longer good for anything, but is thrown out and trampled under foot.

14 "You are the light of the world. A city built on a hill cannot be hid. [15]No one after lighting a lamp puts it under the bushel basket, but on the lampstand, and it gives light to all in the house. [16]In the same way, let your light shine before others, so that they may see your good works and give glory to your Father in heaven.

The Law and the Prophets

17 "Do not think that I have come to abolish the law or the prophets; I have come not to abolish but to fulfill. [18]For truly I tell you, until heaven and earth pass away, not one letter,[y] not one stroke of a letter, will pass from the law until all is accomplished. [19]Therefore, whoever breaks[z] one of the least of these commandments, and teaches others to do the same, will be called least in the kingdom of heaven; but whoever does them and teaches them will be called great in the kingdom of heaven. [20]For I tell you, unless your righteousness exceeds that of the scribes and Pharisees, you will never enter the kingdom of heaven.

Concerning Anger

21 "You have heard that it was said to those of ancient times, 'You shall not murder'; and 'whoever murders shall be liable to judgment.' [22]But I say to you that if

---

[x] Other ancient authorities lack *falsely*
[y] Gk *one iota*   [z] Or *annuls*

---

was God's Law that Moses handed down. When Jesus delivers a new law, it is one that he gives directly – without mention of any special vision of God or revelation – on his own authority as God's Chosen One.

5:17–48. According to Matthew, Jesus' teaching does not replace but is the fulfillment of God's revelation to Israel ('the law [and] the prophets', 5:17). Jesus demands greater commitment than before, higher righteousness, not lesser. So not only murder makes one liable to judgment, but also hostility, verbal abuse, or contempt of a sister or brother (5:21–22). Thus, Jesus forbids not only physical violence, but also emotional and verbal violence. These two verses offer a scathing condemnation of verbal and physical abuse among Christians.

Not only is adultery forbidden, but even looking at a woman as a sex object (5:27–28). Two points are worth mention here. First, specifying this as a restriction on men's behavior should not be read as giving tacit permission for women to do the same; on the contrary, in a context where women historically had been blamed for men's sexual misconduct, Jesus puts the responsibility where it belongs (i.e. with the one who carries out the behavior). Second, prohibiting 'looking lustfully' at a person refers to things such as open flirtatiousness and sexual harassment; it does not refer to the ability lawfully to enjoy another person (including her or his body) as an expression of the Creator's goodness.

you are angry with a brother or sister,[a] you will be liable to judgment; and if you insult[b] a brother or sister,[c] you will be liable to the council; and if you say, 'You fool,' you will be liable to the hell[d] of fire. [23]So when you are offering your gift at the altar, if you remember that your brother or sister[e] has something against you, [24]leave your gift there before the altar and go; first be reconciled to your brother or sister,[e] and then come and offer your gift. [25]Come to terms quickly with your accuser while you are on the way to court[f] with him, or your accuser may hand you over to the judge, and the judge to the guard, and you will be thrown into prison. [26]Truly I tell you, you will never get out until you have paid the last penny.

Concerning Adultery

[27] "You have heard that it was said, 'You shall not commit adultery.' [28]But I say to you that everyone who looks at a woman with lust has already committed adultery with her in his heart. [29]If your right eye causes you to sin, tear it out and throw it away; it is better for you to lose one of your members than for your whole body to be thrown into hell.[d] [30]And if your right hand causes you to sin, cut it off and throw it away; it is better for you to lose one of your members than for your whole body to go into hell.[d]

Concerning Divorce

[31] "It was also said, 'Whoever divorces his wife, let him give her a certificate of divorce.' [32]But I say to you that anyone who divorces his wife, except on the ground of unchastity, causes her to commit adultery; and whoever marries a divorced woman commits adultery.

Concerning Oaths

[33] "Again, you have heard that it was said to those of ancient times, 'You shall not swear falsely, but carry out the vows you have made to the Lord.' [34]But I say to you, Do not swear at all, either by heaven, for it is the throne of God, [35]or by the earth, for it is his footstool, or by Jerusalem, for it is the city of the great King. [36]And do not swear by your head, for you cannot make one hair white or black. [37]Let your word be 'Yes, Yes' or 'No, No'; anything more than this comes from the evil one.[g]

[a] Gk *a brother*; other ancient authorities add *without cause*   [b] Gk *say Raca to* (an obscure term of abuse)   [c] Gk *a brother*   [d] Gk *Gehenna*   [e] Gk *your brother*   [f] Gk lacks *to court*   [g] Or *evil*

Whereas formerly a man could unilaterally divorce his wife (Deut. 24:1), this is now forbidden, for it causes her to sin (Matt. 5:31–32). Here in Matthew, the one exception is in the case of *porneia* – which could mean adultery, though Matthew uses a different term for that. It could also refer to consanguineous marriage, that is, within close blood or other relationships. Jewish Law (Lev. 18:6–18) entailed more far-reaching provisions for what constituted consanguinity than did Roman law. Matthew's community apparently followed the Levitical provisions; this could pose difficulties for some Gentile converts who, legally married under Roman law, were seen as incestuous by Matthew's church. Thus, this exception allows for the dissolution of such marriages without prohibiting the partners' remarriage under the limits of the Torah.

One must speak the truth always, not only when under oath (5:33–37). Mercy, rather than justice and emphasis on individual rights, is the rule of social relations (5:38–42); this means love of enemies as well as kin (5:43–47). In short, the Commandments are to help one not only follow God's will, but to *become like God* (5:48).

Concerning Retaliation

38 "You have heard that it was said, 'An eye for an eye and a tooth for a tooth.' ³⁹But I say to you, Do not resist an evildoer. But if anyone strikes you on the right cheek, turn the other also; ⁴⁰and if anyone wants to sue you and take your coat, give your cloak as well; ⁴¹and if anyone forces you to go one mile, go also the second mile. ⁴²Give to everyone who begs from you, and do not refuse anyone who wants to borrow from you.

Love for Enemies

43 "You have heard that it was said, 'You shall love your neighbor and hate your enemy.' ⁴⁴But I say to you, Love your enemies and pray for those who persecute you, ⁴⁵so that you may be children of your Father in heaven; for he makes his sun rise on the evil and on the good, and sends rain on the righteous and on the unrighteous. ⁴⁶For if you love those who love you, what reward do you have? Do not even the tax collectors do the same? ⁴⁷And if you greet only your brothers and sisters,ʰ what more are you doing than others? Do not even the Gentiles do the same? ⁴⁸Be perfect, therefore, as your heavenly Father is perfect.

Concerning Almsgiving

6 "Beware of practicing your piety before others in order to be seen by them; for then you have no reward from your Father in heaven.

2 "So whenever you give alms, do not sound a trumpet before you, as the hypocrites do in the synagogues and in the streets, so that they may be praised by others. Truly I tell you, they have received their reward. ³But when you give alms, do not let your left hand know what your right hand is doing, ⁴so that your alms may be done in secret; and your Father who sees in secret will reward you.ⁱ

Concerning Prayer

5 "And whenever you pray, do not be like the hypocrites; for they love to stand and pray in the synagogues and at the street corners, so that they may be seen by others. Truly I tell you, they have received their reward. ⁶But whenever you pray, go into your room and shut the door and pray to your Father who is in secret; and your Father who sees in secret will reward you.ⁱ

7 "When you are praying, do not heap up empty phrases as the Gentiles do; for they think that they will be heard because of their many words. ⁸Do not be like them, for your Father knows what you need before you ask him.

9 "Pray then in this way:
Our Father in heaven,
    hallowed be your name.
10   Your kingdom come.
    Your will be done,
        on earth as it is in heaven.
11   Give us this day our daily bread.ʲ
12   And forgive us our debts,
        as we also have forgiven our
            debtors.

ʰ Gk *your brothers*   ⁱ Other ancient authorities add *openly*   ʲ Or *our bread for tomorrow*

6:1–34. After these remarks on social relations, the discourse shifts to a discussion of religious duties – almsgiving, prayer, and fasting. One can do these things either for love of God or of human praise. Jesus emphasizes the need for single-hearted devotion to God, a point highlighted in the uniquely Matthean portions of the 'Lord's Prayer' (e.g. 6:10b) and then driven home in the section on true riches. If God's reign and God's righteousness are one's central concerns, then all other needs will be met.

[13] And do not bring us to the time of trial,[k]

but rescue us from the evil one.[l] [14]For if you forgive others their trespasses, your heavenly Father will also forgive you; [15]but if you do not forgive others, neither will your Father forgive your trespasses.

Concerning Fasting

[16] "And whenever you fast, do not look dismal, like the hypocrites, for they disfigure their faces so as to show others that they are fasting. Truly I tell you, they have received their reward. [17]But when you fast, put oil on your head and wash your face, [18]so that your fasting may be seen not by others but by your Father who is in secret; and your Father who sees in secret will reward you.[m]

◆ Fasting for the sake of our public appearance is specifically denounced in this passage. As a spiritual discipline, fasting in private is intended to focus our full beings meditatively on the person of Jesus and our longing for spiritual connectedness to God.

Most women diet rather than fast. Dieting in order to develop and maintain a slender, fashionable appearance may well be rooted in the same self-consciousness, the same bondage to appearances as public fasting. Deprivation eating is not evidence of spiritual obedience or self-control. God does not honor thinness more than heaviness, as long as we are eating in a self-nurturant way.

The modern dieting mania has contributed to the upsurge of anorexia, bulimia, and compulsive overeating/undereating patterns, all of which are destructive to our bodies and spirits. The demand for attractiveness of body, as defined by secularized images of beauty, affects girls as they develop a concept of themselves as women, especially in terms of their potential for relationships with men.

The need to be thin, regardless of God-given natural body shapes, push women to diet repetitively and extremely. When deprived of food our bodies push harder for us to eat, and thus lead women into all sorts of chaotic, binge-eating experiences. God calls us to eat in a self-nurturant way, responsive to our own internal cues of physical hunger. We eat to satisfy our hunger, no more, no less. As we move to respond to our hungers, whether physical, social, intellectual, or spiritual, our appearance takes on more of the beauty of Christ which far surpasses the beauty of the fashion model ◆

Concerning Treasures

[19] "Do not store up for yourselves treasures on earth, where moth and rust[n] consume and where thieves break in and steal; [20]but store up for yourselves treasures in heaven, where neither moth nor rust[n] consumes and where thieves do not break in and steal. [21]For where your treasure is, there your heart will be also.

The Sound Eye

[22] "The eye is the lamp of the body. So, if your eye is healthy, your whole body will be full of light; [23]but if your eye is unhealthy, your whole body will be full of darkness. If then the light in you is darkness, how great is the darkness!

Serving Two Masters

[24] "No one can serve two masters; for a slave will either hate the one and love the other, or be devoted to the one and despise the other. You cannot serve God and wealth.[o]

Do Not Worry

[25] "Therefore I tell you, do not worry about your life, what you will eat or what you will drink,[p] or about your body, what you will wear. Is not life more than food,

[k] Or us into temptation   [l] Or from evil. Other ancient authorities add, in some form, For the kingdom and the power and the glory are yours forever. Amen.   [m] Other ancient authorities add openly   [n] Gk eating   [o] Gk mammon
[p] Other ancient authorities lack or what you will drink

and the body more than clothing? [26]Look at the birds of the air; they neither sow nor reap nor gather into barns, and yet your heavenly Father feeds them. Are you not of more value than they? [27]And can any of you by worrying add a single hour to your span of life?[q] [28]And why do you worry about clothing? Consider the lilies of the field, how they grow; they neither toil nor spin,

◆ The immense number of work hours required to spin linen or wool, inch by inch, into thread, set up a loom, and weave the many thousands of yards of thread into cloth made it necessary, on a practical level, for a large part of the population of the ancient world to reach for the spindle any time they were not occupied with other work.

Most spinners and weavers were women. This was true long before the composition of the alphabetic poem in praise of women's work in Prov. 31:10–31. Jesus in this best-loved sermon argues against the social constraints which assigned to housework a higher value for women than the gospel. The women among the crowds that followed him probably had internalized the critical glances and remarks that reminded them they were neglecting their work when they left their houses and set off down the road to hear him. As women still do today in the Middle East, they could spin while listening, even while walking, and the words of Jesus may mirror for us his sight of women spinning while they listened.

The vividness of the wording here suggests a dialogue in which he quotes and answers objections from the audience. As in the Mary and Martha story (Luke 10:38–42), he reminds them that the Kingdom is more important even than their responsibility to provide food and clothing. The firmness of his instruction must have been a great support to the earliest Christian women as they extended their ideas of service beyond the family to teaching, preaching, prophesying, and other recognized ministries ◆

[29]yet I tell you, even Solomon in all his glory was not clothed like one of these. [30]But if God so clothes the grass of the field, which is alive today and tomorrow is thrown into the oven, will he not much more clothe you – you of little faith? [31]Therefore do not worry, saying, 'What will we eat?' or 'What will we drink?' or 'What will we wear?' [32]For it is the Gentiles who strive for all these things; and indeed your heavenly Father knows that you need all these things. [33]But strive first for the kingdom of God[r] and his[s] righteousness, and all these things will be given to you as well.

34 "So do not worry about tomorrow, for tomorrow will bring worries of its own. Today's trouble is enough for today.

Judging Others

7 "Do not judge, so that you may not be judged. [2]For with the judgment you make you will be judged, and the measure you give will be the measure you get. [3]Why do you see the speck in your neighbor's[t] eye, but do not notice the log in your own eye? [4]Or how can you say to your neighbor,[u]

[q] Or *add one cubit to your height*   [r] Other ancient authorities lack *of God*   [s] Or *its*   [t] Gk *brother's*   [u] Gk *brother*

7:1–29. The third portion of this discourse comprises moral exhortation (including the Golden Rule). The primary message here is that doing God's will is required for entrance into 'the kingdom of heaven'; mere lip service will not suffice. The parable of 'the house on the rock' (7:24–27) punctuates this message, with the key point that God's will is made known not only in the Torah but more importantly *in the words of Jesus* (7:24). The persuasive character of Jesus' teaching is attributed to the fact that 'he taught them as one having authority, and not as their scribes' (7:29).

'Let me take the speck out of your eye,' while the log is in your own eye? [5]You hypocrite, first take the log out of your own eye, and then you will see clearly to take the speck out of your neighbor's[v] eye.

Profaning the Holy

6 "Do not give what is holy to dogs; and do not throw your pearls before swine, or they will trample them under foot and turn and maul you.

Ask, Search, Knock

7 "Ask, and it will be given you; search, and you will find; knock, and the door will be opened for you. [8]For everyone who asks receives, and everyone who searches finds, and for everyone who knocks, the door will be opened. [9]Is there anyone among you who, if your child asks for bread, will give a stone? [10]Or if the child asks for a fish, will give a snake? [11]If you then, who are evil, know how to give good gifts to your children, how much more will your Father in heaven give good things to those who ask him!

The Golden Rule

12 "In everything do to others as you would have them do to you; for this is the law and the prophets.

The Narrow Gate

13 "Enter through the narrow gate; for the gate is wide and the road is easy[w] that leads to destruction, and there are many who take it. [14]For the gate is narrow and the road is hard that leads to life, and there are few who find it.

A Tree and Its Fruit

15 "Beware of false prophets, who come to you in sheep's clothing but inwardly are ravenous wolves. [16]You will know them by their fruits. Are grapes gathered from thorns, or figs from thistles? [17]In the same way, every good tree bears good fruit, but the bad tree bears bad fruit. [18]A good tree cannot bear bad fruit, nor can a bad tree bear good fruit. [19]Every tree that does not bear good fruit is cut down and thrown into the fire. [20]Thus you will know them by their fruits.

Concerning Self-Deception

21 "Not everyone who says to me, 'Lord, Lord,' will enter the kingdom of heaven, but only the one who does the will of my Father in heaven. [22]On that day many will say to me, 'Lord, Lord, did we not prophesy in your name, and cast out demons in your name, and do many deeds of power in your name?' [23]Then I will declare to them, 'I never knew you; go away from me, you evil-doers.'

Hearers and Doers

24 "Everyone then who hears these words of mine and acts on them will be like a wise man who built his house on rock. [25]The rain fell, the floods came, and the winds blew and beat on that house, but it did not fall, because it had been founded on rock. [26]And everyone who hears these words of mine and does not act on them will be like a foolish man who built his house on sand. [27]The rain fell, and the floods came, and the winds blew and beat against that house, and it fell – and great was its fall!"

28 Now when Jesus had finished saying these things, the crowds were astounded at his teaching, [29]for he taught them as one having authority, and not as their scribes.

---

[v] Gk *brother's*   [w] Other ancient authorities read *for the road is wide and easy*

Jesus Cleanses a Leper

8 When Jesus[x] had come down from the mountain, great crowds followed him; [2]and there was a leper[y] who came to him and knelt before him, saying, "Lord, if you choose, you can make me clean." [3]He stretched out his hand and touched him, saying, "I do choose. Be made clean!" Immediately his leprosy[y] was cleansed. [4]Then Jesus said to him, "See that you say nothing to anyone; but go, show yourself to the priest, and offer the gift that Moses commanded, as a testimony to them."

Jesus Heals a Centurion's Servant

5 When he entered Capernaum, a centurion came to him, appealing to him [6]and saying, "Lord, my servant is lying at home paralyzed, in terrible distress." [7]And he said to him, "I will come and cure him." [8]The centurion answered, "Lord, I am not worthy to have you come under my roof; but only speak the word, and my servant will be healed. [9]For I also am a man under authority, with soldiers under me; and I say to one, 'Go,' and he goes, and to another, 'Come,' and he comes, and to my slave, 'Do this,' and the slave does it." [10]When Jesus heard him, he was amazed and said to those who followed him, "Truly I tell you, in no one[z] in Israel have I found such faith.

[11]I tell you, many will come from east and west and will eat with Abraham and Isaac and Jacob in the kingdom of heaven, [12]while the heirs of the kingdom will be thrown into the outer darkness, where there will be weeping and gnashing of teeth." [13]And to the centurion Jesus said, "Go; let it be done for you according to your faith." And the servant was healed in that hour.

Jesus Heals Many at Peter's House

14 When Jesus entered Peter's house, he saw his mother-in-law lying in bed with a fever; [15]he touched her hand, and the fever left her, and she got up and began to serve him. [16]That evening they brought to him many who were possessed with demons; and he cast out the spirits with a word, and cured all who were sick. [17]This was to fulfill what had been spoken through the prophet Isaiah, "He took our infirmities and bore our diseases."

Would-Be Followers of Jesus

18 Now when Jesus saw great crowds around him, he gave orders to go over to the other side. [19]A scribe then approached and

[x] Gk *he*　　[y] The terms *leper* and *leprosy* can refer to several diseases　　[z] Other ancient authorities read *Truly I tell you, not even*

ENACTING AND PREACHING THE COMMONWEALTH OF HEAVEN
(MATT. 8:1–11:1)

Jesus' authority is highlighted by Matthew's comment that 'great crowds followed him' when he came down from the mountain, and is illustrated by a series of healing miracles. This set of miracle narratives shows that Jesus not only preaches but also *does* God's work, as he has called others to do.

8:1–9:34. Matthew sees Jesus' message as addressed to all Israel, the marginalized as well as those in power. And Matthew recalls that some well-placed Jews did become disciples of Jesus (e.g. the scribe of 8:18–20). One must not use Matthew's Gospel to support the blatant anti-Judaism that has been part of Christian commentaries in the past.

　　Matthew's selection of miracle stories shows that Jesus' message is not only for those who are privileged under the Law, but for persons on the margins of society as well: the leper (8:1–4); the centurion's servant, a Gentile (8:5–13); Peter's mother-in-law, a woman (8:14–15); the possessed (8:16–17). The Law retains its force, for the leper is to submit to its requirements to return to communal worship (8:4). Yet the scope of Jesus' message goes beyond the Jews, for the Gentile becomes an example of true faith (8:10–12). And it goes beyond male prerogatives: the healthy

said, "Teacher, I will follow you wherever you go." [20]And Jesus said to him, "Foxes have holes, and birds of the air have nests; but the Son of Man has nowhere to lay his head." [21]Another of his disciples said to him, "Lord, first let me go and bury my father." [22]But Jesus said to him, "Follow me, and let the dead bury their own dead."

Jesus Stills the Storm

23 And when he got into the boat, his disciples followed him. [24]A windstorm arose on the sea, so great that the boat was being swamped by the waves; but he was asleep. [25]And they went and woke him up, saying, "Lord, save us! We are perishing!" [26]And he said to them, "Why are you afraid, you of little faith?" Then he got up and rebuked the winds and the sea; and there was a dead calm. [27]They were amazed, saying, "What sort of man is this, that even the winds and the sea obey him?"

Jesus Heals the Gadarene Demoniacs

28 When he came to the other side, to the country of the Gadarenes,[a] two demoniacs coming out of the tombs met him. They were so fierce that no one could pass that way. [29]Suddenly they shouted, "What have you to do with us, Son of God? Have you come here to torment us before the time?" [30]Now a large herd of swine was feeding at some distance from them. [31]The demons begged him, "If you cast us out, send us into the herd of swine." [32]And he said to them, "Go!" So they came out and entered the swine; and suddenly, the whole herd rushed down the steep bank into the sea and perished in the water. [33]The swineherds ran off, and on going into the town, they told the whole story about what had happened to the demoniacs. [34]Then the whole town came out to meet Jesus; and when they saw him, they begged him to leave their neighborhood. [1]And after getting into a boat he crossed the sea and came to his own town.

Jesus Heals a Paralytic

2 And just then some people were carrying a paralyzed man lying on a bed. When Jesus saw their faith, he said to the paralytic, "Take heart, son; your sins are forgiven." [3]Then some of the scribes said to themselves, "This man is blaspheming." [4]But Jesus, perceiving their thoughts, said, "Why do you think evil in your hearts? [5]For

---

[a] Other ancient authorities read *Gergesenes*; others, *Gerasenes*

---

woman becomes a minister for Jesus (8:15), illustrating the model of true discipleship (20:26–28). As Leonard Swidler has pointed out, the tremendous significance of this incident is that, while other Jewish rabbis are said to have performed miraculous cures, Jesus alone is remembered as healing *women*.

The power of Jesus' word is a key point of this set of miracle stories. Jesus does not cure by means of magical incantations; rather, by a single word of command, he heals both body and psyche (8:16). He even has power over nature, rebuking the wind and the sea, the forces of primeval chaos (8:23–27). Matthew's subtle allusion to creation imagery – in the emphasis on the word and the overcoming of chaos – ought not to be missed.

Moses parted the Red Sea, but it was by God's power of command. Clearly, Matthew teaches, we have a greater than Moses here. Even among the Gentiles Jesus' power is made known, although they are not ready to accept him (8:28–34).

Matthew softens the full political significance of Jesus' cure of the Gadarene demoniacs (8:28–34). In the longer version reported in Mark 5:1–17, the demon (who begs not to be driven from the land) is named 'Legion' – an unmistakable reference to the Roman armed forces. Jesus expels the 'Legion' into the swine, favored animals for pagan sacrifice, where the demon thinks it will be safe. But the entire herd throws itself headlong into the lake and drowns, demonstrating the bankruptcy of the pagan cult and of Roman power in comparison to the power of the

which is easier, to say, 'Your sins are forgiven,' or to say, 'Stand up and walk'? [6]But so that you may know that the Son of Man has authority on earth to forgive sins" – he then said to the paralytic – "Stand up, take your bed and go to your home." [7]And he stood up and went to his home. [8]When the crowds saw it, they were filled with awe, and they glorified God, who had given such authority to human beings.

The Call of Matthew

9 As Jesus was walking along, he saw a man called Matthew sitting at the tax booth; and he said to him, "Follow me." And he got up and followed him.

10 And as he sat at dinner[b] in the house, many tax collectors and sinners came and were sitting[c] with him and his disciples. [11]When the Pharisees saw this, they said to his disciples, "Why does your teacher eat with tax collectors and sinners?" [12]But when he heard this, he said, "Those who are well have no need of a physician, but those who are sick. [13]Go and learn what this means, 'I desire mercy, not sacrifice.' For I have come to call not the righteous but sinners."

The Question about Fasting

14 Then the disciples of John came to him, saying, "Why do we and the Pharisees fast often,[d] but your disciples do not fast?" [15]And Jesus said to them, "The wedding guests cannot mourn as long as the bridegroom is with them, can they? The days will come when the bridegroom is taken away from them, and then they will fast. [16]No one sews a piece of unshrunk cloth on an old cloak, for the patch pulls away from the cloak, and a worse tear is made. [17]Neither is new wine put into old wineskins; otherwise, the skins burst, and the wine is spilled, and the skins are destroyed; but new wine is put into fresh wineskins, and so both are preserved."

A Girl Restored to Life and a Woman Healed

18 While he was saying these things to them, suddenly a leader of the synagogue[e] came in and knelt before him, saying, "My daughter has just died; but come and lay your hand on her, and she will live." [19]And Jesus got up and followed him, with his disciples. [20]Then suddenly a woman who had been suffering from hemorrhages for twelve years came up behind him and touched the fringe of his cloak, [21]for she said to herself, "If I only touch his cloak, I will be made well." [22]Jesus turned, and seeing her he said, "Take heart, daughter; your faith has made you well." And instantly the woman was made well. [23]When Jesus came to the leader's house and saw the flute players and the crowd making a commotion, [24]he said, "Go

[b] Gk reclined   [c] Gk were reclining   [d] Other ancient authorities lack often   [e] Gk lacks of the synagogue

---

one, true God. Matthew retains the emphasis on Jesus' power, but without drawing the comparison to Rome. In light of the recent devastation of Palestine due to the Jewish War against Rome (AD 66–73), it is understandable why Matthew would shy from such a politically loaded account as Mark's.

Jesus has power not only to cure the lame (9:2–8), the dumb (9:32–33), and the blind (9:7–31), but even to heal the chronically ill and to raise the dead (9:18–26). And Jesus uses this power for both women and men, the powerful and the disenfranchised. One daughter of Israel was dead; the other may as well have been, since she was excluded from religious and social relations due to her condition. A father speaks for a silent daughter; a silent woman relies on touch. In both cases, Jesus ignores ritual impurity to bring healing. To the dead maiden, he restores life and wholeness with a touch. To the silent woman, he restores speech, proclaiming aloud her saving faith.

away; for the girl is not dead but sleeping." And they laughed at him. ²⁵But when the crowd had been put outside, he went in and took her by the hand, and the girl got up. ²⁶And the report of this spread throughout that district.

> ◆ Matthew mentions the presence of female flute-players whose music could convey either joy or profound sorrow. Mourners were an accepted part of Israelite society (Luke 7:32). The hiring of women to serve in this role is a very alien custom to many modern societies. In antiquity professional mourners were regularly employed to lead family and friends in appropriate expressions of grief. This is sometimes more healthy than the stifling of emotion which can happen at a time of death. The loss needs to be grieved fully and deeply in companionship with others. At such times Christians find support and sympathy in the fellowship of other believers (Rom. 12:15) and in the consolation which is ours through Christ ◆

Jesus Heals Two Blind Men

27 As Jesus went on from there, two blind men followed him, crying loudly, "Have mercy on us, Son of David!" ²⁸When he entered the house, the blind men came to him; and Jesus said to them, "Do you believe that I am able to do this?" They said to him, "Yes, Lord." ²⁹Then he touched their eyes and said, "According to your faith let it be done to you." ³⁰And their eyes were opened. Then Jesus sternly ordered them, "See that no one knows of this." ³¹But they

went away and spread the news about him throughout that district.

Jesus Heals One Who Was Mute

32 After they had gone away, a demoniac who was mute was brought to him. ³³And when the demon had been cast out, the one who had been mute spoke; and the crowds were amazed and said, "Never has anything like this been seen in Israel." ³⁴But the Pharisees said, "By the ruler of the demons he casts out the demons."ᶠ

The Harvest Is Great, the Laborers Few

35 Then Jesus went about all the cities and villages, teaching in their synagogues, and proclaiming the good news of the kingdom, and curing every disease and every sickness. ³⁶When he saw the crowds, he had compassion for them, because they were harassed and helpless, like sheep without a shepherd. ³⁷Then he said to his disciples, "The harvest is plentiful, but the laborers are few; ³⁸therefore ask the Lord of the harvest to send out laborers into his harvest."

The Twelve Apostles

10 Then Jesusᵍ summoned his twelve disciples and gave them authority over unclean spirits, to cast them out, and to cure every disease and every sickness. ²These are the names of the twelve apostles: first, Simon, also known as Peter, and his brother Andrew; James son of Zebedee, and his brother John; ³Philip and

---

ᶠ Other ancient authorities lack this verse   ᵍ Gk *he*

Until this section, Matthew has depicted Jesus as a truly rising star, an irresistible person with an authoritative message. Here we begin to see that not everyone finds Jesus to be good news. The mild reticence of the Gentiles of the Decapolis (8:34) gives way to confrontation with some of the Jews: 'some of the scribes' charge Jesus with blasphemy (9:3); 'the Pharisees' complain of his fraternizing with sinners (9:11) and that he is in league with Satan; the disciples of John the Baptist object to Jesus' laxity (9:14); when Jesus intervenes with the mourners at the ruler's house, they ridicule him (9:24). Through this gradual development of controversy about Jesus, Matthew hints at his ultimate rejection.

10:1–11:1. In the missionary discourse, Jesus makes explicit these hints of rejection, warning that the disciples – like their master – will experience persecution and even death because of the

Bartholomew; Thomas and Matthew the tax collector; James son of Alphaeus, and Thaddaeus;[h] [4]Simon the Cananaean, and Judas Iscariot, the one who betrayed him.

The Mission of the Twelve

5 These twelve Jesus sent out with the following instructions: "Go nowhere among the Gentiles, and enter no town of the Samaritans, [6]but go rather to the lost sheep of the house of Israel. [7]As you go, proclaim the good news, 'The kingdom of heaven has come near.'[i] [8]Cure the sick, raise the dead, cleanse the lepers,[j] cast out demons. You received without payment; give without payment. [9]Take no gold, or silver, or copper in your belts, [10]no bag for your journey, or two tunics, or sandals, or a staff; for laborers deserve their food. [11]Whatever town or village you enter, find out who in it is worthy, and stay there until you leave. [12]As you enter the house, greet it. [13]If the house is worthy, let your peace come upon it; but if it is not worthy, let your peace return to you. [14]If anyone will not welcome you or listen to your words, shake off the dust from your feet as you leave that house or town. [15]Truly I tell you, it will be more tolerable for the land of Sodom and Gomorrah on the day of judgment than for that town.

Coming Persecutions

16 "See, I am sending you out like sheep into the midst of wolves; so be wise as serpents and innocent as doves. [17]Beware of them, for they will hand you over to councils and flog you in their synagogues; [18]and you will be dragged before governors and kings because of me, as a testimony to them and the Gentiles. [19]When they hand you over, do not worry about how you are to speak or what you are to say; for what you

are to say will be given to you at that time; [20]for it is not you who speak, but the Spirit of your Father speaking through you. [21]Brother will betray brother to death, and a father his child, and children will rise against parents and have them put to death; [22]and you will be hated by all because of my name. But the one who endures to the end will be saved. [23]When they persecute you in one town, flee to the next; for truly I tell you, you will not have gone through all the towns of Israel before the Son of Man comes.

24 "A disciple is not above the teacher, nor a slave above the master; [25]it is enough for the disciple to be like the teacher, and the slave like the master. If they have called the master of the house Beelzebul, how much more will they malign those of his household!

Whom to Fear

26 "So have no fear of them; for nothing is covered up that will not be uncovered, and nothing secret that will not become known. [27]What I say to you in the dark, tell in the light; and what you hear whispered, proclaim from the housetops. [28]Do not fear those who kill the body but cannot kill the soul; rather fear him who can destroy both soul and body in hell.[k] [29]Are not two sparrows sold for a penny? Yet not one of them will fall to the ground apart from your Father. [30]And even the hairs of your head are all counted. [31]So do not be afraid; you are of more value than many sparrows.

32 "Everyone therefore who acknowledges me before others, I also will acknowl-

h Other ancient authorities read *Lebbaeus,* or *Lebbaeus called Thaddaeus*   i Or *is at hand*   j The terms *leper* and *leprosy* can refer to several diseases   k Gk *Gehenna*

---

message they preach and the healing works they perform. Even members of the same family will oppose and betray one another (10:21, 35–36). No one is worthy who values parents or children more than Jesus (10:37), but those who endure to the end will be saved (10:22). The end is near (10:23b), and those who receive the 'poor' (those totally dedicated to God) will be rewarded.

edge before my Father in heaven; [33]but whoever denies me before others, I also will deny before my Father in heaven.

Not Peace, but a Sword

34 "Do not think that I have come to bring peace to the earth; I have not come to bring peace, but a sword.

[35] For I have come to set a man against
    his father,
and a daughter against her mother,
and a daughter-in-law against her
    mother-in-law;
[36] and one's foes will be members of
    one's own household.

◆ Note that spouses are not set against one another; there is no idea that one would have to choose between one's spouse and faithfulness to Jesus (cf. Luke 14:26). The predicted strife in the household is purely inter-generational.

Note, however, that Jesus does predict strife in the household where parents or children subordinate faithfulness to Jesus' message to other values (even 'family values'). Seeking to provide security for one's family is an important value for a parent to have, but this must not prevent living up to the demands of covenant justice (e.g. welcoming the child, feeding the hungry, giving drink to the thirsty, clothing the naked, comforting the afflicted). Although children must respect their parents, a child must not deny faith in Jesus simply to please a non-Christian parent. Teens must not violate their relationship with Jesus (e.g. by not participating in prayer and fellowship with other Christians) simply to please their friends.

Finally, 'family values' do not permit Christians to promote a system of family or church authority whereby some Christians exert power over others for any reason whatsoever (sex, age, office, race, etc.). Such a system of domination is what the Gentiles do, according to Jesus (20:25). But the Christian, like Jesus, must be one who serves (20:26–28), using the power that comes from working with and among people, rather than over or against them. This means that husbands must not domineer over wives, and wives must not fall into a slavish subservience; women are responsible directly to God for their own choices and will be held accountable for them (e.g. 24:41; 25:1–13). Parents must guide their children to grow up and make their own mature decisions, as they become able to do this; they must not dominate their children, trying to keep them dependent. And clergy must not act in authoritarian ways, dominating church members, but must recognize the gifts and call of each Christian, the authority which the gospel gives to each one, and responsibility which goes with it. Partnership is the model which Jesus taught his disciples. If nowhere else, this must be the model for Christian family and church life ◆

[37]Whoever loves father or mother more than me is not worthy of me; and whoever loves son or daughter more than me is not worthy of me; [38]and whoever does not take up the cross and follow me is not worthy of me. [39]Those who find their life will lose it, and those who lose their life for my sake will find it.

Rewards

40 "Whoever welcomes you welcomes me, and whoever welcomes me welcomes the one who sent me. [41]Whoever welcomes a prophet in the name of a prophet will receive a prophet's reward; and whoever welcomes a righteous person in the name of a righteous person will receive the reward of the righteous; [42]and whoever gives even a cup of cold water to one of these little ones in the name of a disciple – truly I tell you, none of these will lose their reward."

11 Now when Jesus had finished instructing his twelve disciples, he went on from there to teach and proclaim his message in their cities.

Messengers from John the Baptist

2 When John heard in prison what the Messiah[1] was doing, he sent word by his[m] disciples [3]and said to him, "Are you the one who is to come, or are we to wait for another?" [4]Jesus answered them, "Go and tell John what you hear and see: [5]the blind receive their sight, the lame walk, the lepers[n] are cleansed, the deaf hear, the dead are raised, and the poor have good news brought to them. [6]And blessed is anyone who takes no offense at me."

Jesus Praises John the Baptist

7 As they went away, Jesus began to speak to the crowds about John: "What did you go out into the wilderness to look at? A reed shaken by the wind? [8]What then did you go out to see? Someone[o] dressed in soft robes? Look, those who wear soft robes are in royal palaces. [9]What then did you go out to see? A prophet?[p] Yes, I tell you, and more than a prophet. [10]This is the one about whom it is written,

'See, I am sending my messenger
       ahead of you,
    who will prepare your way before
       you.'

[11]Truly I tell you, among those born of women no one has arisen greater than John the Baptist; yet the least in the kingdom of heaven is greater than he. [12]From the days of John the Baptist until now the kingdom of heaven has suffered violence,[q] and the violent take it by force. [13]For all the

prophets and the law prophesied until John came; [14]and if you are willing to accept it, he is Elijah who is to come. [15]Let anyone with ears[r] listen!

16 "But to what will I compare this generation? It is like children sitting in the marketplaces and calling to one another,

[17]   'We played the flute for you, and you
          did not dance;
       we wailed, and you did not mourn.'

[18]For John came neither eating nor drinking, and they say, 'He has a demon'; [19]the Son of Man came eating and drinking, and they say, 'Look, a glutton and a drunkard, a friend of tax collectors and sinners!' Yet wisdom is vindicated by her deeds."[s]

Woes to Unrepentant Cities

20 Then he began to reproach the cities in which most of his deeds of power had been done, because they did not repent. [21]"Woe to you, Chorazin! Woe to you, Bethsaida! For if the deeds of power done in you had been done in Tyre and Sidon, they would have repented long ago in sackcloth and ashes. [22]But I tell you, on the day of judgment it will be more tolerable for Tyre and Sidon than for you. [23]And you, Capernaum,

---

[1] Or the Christ   [m] Other ancient authorities read two of his   [n] The terms leper and leprosy can refer to several diseases   [o] Or Why then did you go out? To see someone   [p] Other ancient authorities read Why then did you go out? To see a prophet?   [q] Or has been coming violently   [r] Other ancient authorities add to hear   [s] Other ancient authorities read children

---

HE TAUGHT IN PARABLES (MATT. 11:2–13:53)

As the narrative shows an increase in conflict between Jesus and other parties, Matthew begins to emphasize more questions, riddles and parables in Jesus' speech. When the Baptist's disciples ask Jesus if he is the Coming One, Jesus points to his deeds of power rather than giving them a direct answer. He gives thanks to God for the reversal taking place: wisdom is revealed to babes and hidden from the wise. All who are weary are invited to find rest in taking Jesus' yoke (rather than the yoke of the Torah); for burdens in partnership with Jesus are easy to bear.

will you be exalted to heaven?
No, you will be brought down to
Hades.

For if the deeds of power done in you had been done in Sodom, it would have remained until this day. [24]But I tell you that on the day of judgment it will be more tolerable for the land of Sodom than for you."

Jesus Thanks His Father

25 At that time Jesus said, "I thank[t] you, Father, Lord of heaven and earth, because you have hidden these things from the wise and the intelligent and have revealed them to infants; [26]yes, Father, for such was your gracious will.[u] [27]All things have been handed over to me by my Father; and no one knows the Son except the Father, and no one knows the Father except the Son and anyone to whom the Son chooses to reveal him.

28 "Come to me, all you that are weary and are carrying heavy burdens, and I will give you rest. [29]Take my yoke upon you, and learn from me; for I am gentle and humble in heart, and you will find rest for your souls. [30]For my yoke is easy, and my burden is light."

Plucking Grain on the Sabbath

12 At that time Jesus went through the grainfields on the sabbath; his disciples were hungry, and they began to pluck heads of grain and to eat. [2]When the Pharisees saw it, they said to him, "Look, your disciples are doing what is not lawful to do on the sabbath." [3]He said to them, "Have you not read what David did when he and his companions were hungry? [4]He entered the house of God and ate the bread of the Presence, which it was not lawful for him or his companions to eat, but only for the priests. [5]Or have you not read in the law that on the sabbath the priests in the temple break the sabbath and yet are guiltless? [6]I tell you, something greater than the temple is here. [7]But if you had known what this means, 'I desire mercy and not sacrifice,' you would not have condemned the guiltless. [8]For the Son of Man is lord of the sabbath."

The Man with a Withered Hand

9 He left that place and entered their synagogue; [10]a man was there with a withered hand, and they asked him, "Is it lawful to cure on the sabbath?" so that they might accuse him. [11]He said to them, "Suppose one of you has only one sheep and it falls into a pit on the sabbath; will you not lay hold of it and lift it out? [12]How much more valuable is a human being than a sheep! So it is lawful to do good on the sabbath." [13]Then he said to the man, "Stretch out your hand." He stretched it out, and it was restored, as sound as the other. [14]But the Pharisees went out and conspired against him, how to destroy him.

God's Chosen Servant

15 When Jesus became aware of this, he departed. Many crowds[v] followed him, and he cured all of them, [16]and he ordered them not to make him known. [17]This was to fulfill what had been spoken through the prophet Isaiah:

---

[t] Or *praise*   [u] Or *for so it was well-pleasing in your sight*   [v] Other ancient authorities lack *crowds*

Jesus' behavior poses problems for some of his fellow Jews, especially the Pharisees (12:14). In a midrashic argument, Jesus claims that the Sabbath prohibition against work does not apply when one's actions have to do with a person's basic health and well-being (12:1–14). Note that Jesus is not overturning the Sabbath law itself, but arguing for an exception to it where the basic needs of human life are at stake. By the Mishnaic period, this had become a traditional exception in rabbinic circles.

[18] "Here is my servant, whom I have
     chosen,
   my beloved, with whom my soul is
     well pleased.
I will put my Spirit upon him,
   and he will proclaim justice to the
     Gentiles.
[19] He will not wrangle or cry aloud,
   nor will anyone hear his voice in the
     streets.
[20] He will not break a bruised reed
   or quench a smoldering wick
until he brings justice to victory.
[21]   And in his name the Gentiles will
     hope."

Jesus and Beelzebul

[22] Then they brought to him a de-moniac who was blind and mute; and he cured him, so that the one who had been mute could speak and see. [23]All the crowds were amazed and said, "Can this be the Son of David?" [24]But when the Pharisees heard it, they said, "It is only by Beelzebul, the ruler of the demons, that this fellow casts out the demons." [25]He knew what they were thinking and said to them, "Every kingdom divided against itself is laid waste, and no city or house divided against itself will stand. [26]If Satan casts out Satan, he is divided against himself; how then will his kingdom stand? [27]If I cast out demons by Beelzebul, by whom do your own exorcists[w] cast them out? Therefore they will be your judges. [28]But if it is by the Spirit of God that I cast out demons, then the kingdom of God has come to you. [29]Or

how can one enter a strong man's house and plunder his property, without first tying up the strong man? Then indeed the house can be plundered. [30]Whoever is not with me is against me, and whoever does not gather with me scatters. [31]Therefore I tell you, people will be forgiven for every sin and blasphemy, but blasphemy against the Spirit will not be forgiven. [32]Whoever speaks a word against the Son of Man will be forgiven, but whoever speaks against the Holy Spirit will not be forgiven, either in this age or in the age to come.

A Tree and Its Fruit

[33] "Either make the tree good, and its fruit good; or make the tree bad, and its fruit bad; for the tree is known by its fruit. [34]You brood of vipers! How can you speak good things, when you are evil? For out of the abundance of the heart the mouth speaks. [35]The good person brings good things out of a good treasure, and the evil person brings evil things out of an evil treasure. [36]I tell you, on the day of judgment you will have to give an account for every careless word you utter; [37]for by your words you will be justified, and by your words you will be condemned."

The Sign of Jonah

[38] Then some of the scribes and Pharisees said to him, "Teacher, we wish to see a sign from you." [39]But he answered them, "An evil and adulterous generation

[w] Gk sons

Jesus reduces to absurdity the charge that he does exorcisms by the power of Beelzebub. Instead Jesus claims that he works by the power of the divine Spirit, showing that the common-wealth of heaven has already come (12:24–28).

Jesus poses a decision for his hearers: either be with me, or you will be against me; bear good fruit, or it will be bad; accept what you see, or perish in your demand for a sign. The demand of Jesus' message supersedes natural family ties; Jesus' true brother, sister, and mother is the one who hears God's Word and does it (12:46–50). (Notice there are no 'fathers' in Jesus' family, because there is one Father of all to whom alone is obedience due.) For those who give them-selves fully to the message of God's reign, there will be abundance and joy; but those who hold back will lose everything (e.g. 13:22–23, 40–43).

asks for a sign, but no sign will be given to it except the sign of the prophet Jonah. [40]For just as Jonah was three days and three nights in the belly of the sea monster, so for three days and three nights the Son of Man will be in the heart of the earth. [41]The people of Nineveh will rise up at the judgment with this generation and condemn it, because they repented at the proclamation of Jonah, and see, something greater than Jonah is here! [42]The queen of the South will rise up at the judgment with this generation and condemn it, because she came from the ends of the earth to listen to the wisdom of Solomon, and see, something greater than Solomon is here!

The Return of the Unclean Spirit

43 "When the unclean spirit has gone out of a person, it wanders through waterless regions looking for a resting place, but it finds none. [44]Then it says, 'I will return to my house from which I came.' When it comes, it finds it empty, swept, and put in order. [45]Then it goes and brings along seven other spirits more evil than itself, and they enter and live there; and the last state of that person is worse than the first. So will it be also with this evil generation."

The True Kindred of Jesus

46 While he was still speaking to the crowds, his mother and his brothers were standing outside, wanting to speak to him. [47]Someone told him, "Look, your mother and your brothers are standing outside, wanting to speak to you."[x] [48]But to the one who had told him this, Jesus[y] replied, "Who is my mother, and who are my brothers?" [49]And pointing to his disciples, he said, "Here are my mother and my brothers! [50]For whoever does the will of my Father in heaven is my brother and sister and mother."

The Parable of the Sower

13
That same day Jesus went out of the house and sat beside the sea. [2]Such great crowds gathered around him that he got into a boat and sat there, while the whole crowd stood on the beach. [3]And he told them many things in parables, saying: "Listen! A sower went out to sow. [4]And as he sowed, some seeds fell on the path, and the birds came and ate them up. [5]Other seeds fell on rocky ground, where they did not have much soil, and they sprang up quickly, since they had no depth of soil. [6]But when the sun rose, they were scorched; and since they had no root, they withered away. [7]Other seeds fell among thorns, and the thorns grew up and choked them. [8]Other seeds fell on good soil and brought forth grain, some a hundredfold, some sixty, some thirty. [9]Let anyone with ears[z] listen!"

The Purpose of the Parables

10 Then the disciples came and asked him, "Why do you speak to them in parables?" [11]He answered, "To you it has been given to know the secrets[a] of the kingdom of heaven, but to them it has not been given. [12]For to those who have, more will be given, and they will have an abundance; but from those who have nothing, even what they have will be taken away. [13]The reason I speak to them in parables is that 'seeing they do not perceive, and hearing they do not listen, nor do they understand.' [14]With them indeed is fulfilled the prophecy of Isaiah that says:
'You will indeed listen, but never understand,
and you will indeed look, but never perceive.
[15] For this people's heart has grown dull,
and their ears are hard of hearing,
and they have shut their eyes;
so that they might not look with their eyes,
and listen with their ears,
and understand with their heart and turn –
and I would heal them.'

---

[x] Other ancient authorities lack verse 47   [y] Gk *he*
[z] Other ancient authorities add *to hear*   [a] Or *mysteries*

[16]But blessed are your eyes, for they see, and your ears, for they hear. [17]Truly I tell you, many prophets and righteous people longed to see what you see, but did not see it, and to hear what you hear, but did not hear it.

The Parable of the Sower Explained

18 "Hear then the parable of the sower. [19]When anyone hears the word of the kingdom and does not understand it, the evil one comes and snatches away what is sown in the heart; this is what was sown on the path. [20]As for what was sown on rocky ground, this is the one who hears the word and immediately receives it with joy; [21]yet such a person has no root, but endures only for a while, and when trouble or persecution arises on account of the word, that person immediately falls away.[b] [22]As for what was sown among thorns, this is the one who hears the word, but the cares of the world and the lure of wealth choke the word, and it yields nothing. [23]But as for what was sown on good soil, this is the one who hears the word and understands it, who indeed bears fruit and yields, in one case a hundredfold, in another sixty, and in another thirty."

The Parable of Weeds among the Wheat

24 He put before them another parable: "The kingdom of heaven may be compared to someone who sowed good seed in his field; [25]but while everybody was asleep, an enemy came and sowed weeds among the wheat, and then went away. [26]So when the plants came up and bore grain, then the weeds appeared as well. [27]And the slaves of the householder came and said to him, 'Master, did you not sow good seed in your field? Where, then, did these weeds come from?' [28]He answered, 'An enemy has done this.' The slaves said to him, 'Then do you want us to go and gather them?' [29]But he replied, 'No; for in gathering the weeds you would uproot the wheat along with them. [30]Let both of them grow together until the harvest; and at harvest time I will tell the reapers, Collect the weeds first and bind them in bundles to be burned, but gather the wheat into my barn.' "

The Parable of the Mustard Seed

31 He put before them another parable: "The kingdom of heaven is like a mustard seed that someone took and sowed in his field; [32]it is the smallest of all the seeds, but when it has grown it is the greatest of shrubs and becomes a tree, so that the birds of the air come and make nests in its branches."

The Parable of the Yeast

33 He told them another parable: "The kingdom of heaven is like yeast that a woman took and mixed in with[c] three measures of flour until all of it was leavened."

◆ Biblical writers consistently remark on the pervasive power of yeast and often use it as a symbol of evil or corruption (Matt. 16:6–12; Mark 8:15; Luke 12:1; 1 Cor. 5:6–8; Gal. 5:9). In Matt. 13:31–33, however, Jesus tells two parables about the growth of the Kingdom of heaven: the mustard seed and leaven. The mustard seed is sown by a man, but the leaven is introduced into the dough and guided through the bread-making process by a woman. This is a parable of Christian nurture. A very small amount is worked into a much larger amount of dough; but even a little bit of yeast can transform and lift many times its own weight.

Yeast is alive and needs to be carefully guarded and guided in the beginning stages of bread-making. There must be nourishment with a sugar substance, a gently warm temperature, and control of harmful bacteria that would interfere with the action. Once it is off to a good start, the leaven permeates every part of the dough and transforms its very substance.

In order to have a fine texture, dough must be allowed to rise and then punched

[b] Gk stumbles   [c] Gk hid in

down with determined force before the yeast causes it to rise again. Bread rises at its own pace. No exact time schedule can be fixed, nor is a rigidly precise recipe possible. The amount of flour needs to be varied from batch to batch. Since yeast is composed of tiny living organisms, it behaves differently in varying conditions of climate, environment, and freshness. The baker must respond to the consistency and resilience of the dough as she kneads it with her bare hands, adapting to the particular circumstances.

In the same way, the yeast of the gospel works differently in each individual situation. It does not follow a fixed formula or time schedule. Early faith – especially that of a child – must be patiently nourished on the Word of God as well as guarded against harmful influences, set in a conducive environment, and gently but firmly directed. Later this small beginning may transform great masses; but frequently God consigns the early stages to the care and direction of women. At this critical stage there must be personal interaction according to the specific need. Mothers, grandmothers, aunts, child-care givers, Sunday school and vacation church school teachers, youth workers, church librarians etc. all aid in the nurturing process. The beginnings are humble, but the outcome has worldwide consequences ◆

The Use of Parables

34 Jesus told the crowds all these things in parables; without a parable he told them nothing. [35]This was to fulfill what had been spoken through the prophet:[d]

"I will open my mouth to speak in parables;
I will proclaim what has been hidden from the foundation of the world."[e]

Jesus Explains the Parable of the Weeds

36 Then he left the crowds and went into the house. And his disciples approached him, saying, "Explain to us the parable of the weeds of the field." [37]He answered, "The one who sows the good seed is the Son of Man; [38]the field is the world, and the good seed are the children of the kingdom; the weeds are the children of the evil one, [39]and the enemy who sowed them is the devil; the harvest is the end of the age, and the reapers are angels. [40]Just as the weeds are collected and burned up with fire, so will it be at the end of the age. [41]The Son of Man will send his angels, and they will collect out of his kingdom all causes of sin and all evildoers, [42]and they will throw them into the furnace of fire, where there will be weeping and gnashing of teeth. [43]Then the righteous will shine like the sun in the kingdom of their Father. Let anyone with ears[f] listen!

Three Parables

44 "The kingdom of heaven is like treasure hidden in a field, which someone found and hid; then in his joy he goes and sells all that he has and buys that field.

45 "Again, the kingdom of heaven is like a merchant in search of fine pearls; [46]on finding one pearl of great value, he went and sold all that he had and bought it.

47 "Again, the kingdom of heaven is like a net that was thrown into the sea and caught fish of every kind; [48]when it was full, they drew it ashore, sat down, and put the good into baskets but threw out the bad. [49]So it will be at the end of the age. The angels will come out and separate the evil from the righteous [50]and throw them into the furnace of fire, where there will be weeping and gnashing of teeth.

Treasures New and Old

51 "Have you understood all this?" They answered, "Yes." [52]And he said to them, "Therefore every scribe who has been trained for the kingdom of heaven is like the master of a household who brings out of his treasure what is new and what is

---

[d] Other ancient authorities read *the prophet Isaiah*

[e] Other ancient authorities lack *of the world*

[f] Other ancient authorities add *to hear*

old." [53]When Jesus had finished these parables, he left that place.

The Rejection of Jesus at Nazareth

54 He came to his hometown and began to teach the people[g] in their synagogue, so that they were astounded and said, "Where did this man get this wisdom and these deeds of power? [55]Is not this the carpenter's son? Is not his mother called Mary? And are not his brothers James and Joseph and Simon and Judas? [56]And are not all his sisters with us? Where then did this man get all this?" [57]And they took offense at him. But Jesus said to them, "Prophets are not without honor except in their own country and in their own house." [58]And he did not do many deeds of power there, because of their unbelief.

The Death of John the Baptist

14 At that time Herod the ruler[h] heard reports about Jesus; [2]and he said to his servants, "This is John the Baptist; he has been raised from the dead, and for this reason these powers are at work in him." [3]For Herod had arrested John, bound him, and put him in prison on account of Herodias, his brother Philip's wife,[i] [4]because John had been telling him, "It is not lawful for you to have her." [5]Though Herod[j] wanted to put him to death, he feared the crowd, because they regarded him as a prophet. [6]But when Herod's birthday came, the daughter of Herodias danced before the company, and she pleased Herod [7]so much that he promised on oath to grant her whatever she might ask. [8]Prompted by her mother, she said, "Give me the head of John the Baptist here on a platter." [9]The king was grieved, yet out of regard for his oaths and for the guests, he commanded it to be given; [10]he sent and had John beheaded in the prison. [11]The head was brought on a platter and given to the girl, who brought it to her mother. [12]His disciples came and took the body and buried it; then they went and told Jesus.

Feeding the Five Thousand

13 Now when Jesus heard this, he withdrew from there in a boat to a deserted place by himself. But when the crowds heard it, they followed him on foot from the towns. [14]When he went ashore, he saw a great crowd; and he had compassion for them and cured their sick. [15]When it was evening, the disciples came to him and said, "This is a deserted place, and the hour is now late; send the crowds away so that they may go into the villages and buy food for themselves." [16]Jesus said to them, "They need not go away; you give them something to eat." [17]They replied, "We have nothing here but five loaves and two fish." [18]And he said, "Bring them here to me." [19]Then he ordered the crowds to sit down on the grass. Taking the five loaves and the two fish, he looked up to heaven, and blessed and broke the loaves, and gave them to the disciples, and the disciples gave them to the crowds. [20]And all ate and were filled; and they took up what was left over of the broken pieces, twelve baskets full. [21]And those who ate were about five thousand men, besides women and children.

[g] Gk *them*   [h] Gk *tetrarch*   [i] Other ancient authorities read *his brother's wife*   [j] Gk *he*

THE CHURCH DISCOURSE (MATT. 13:54–19:1)

Jesus' rejection in his own hometown (13:54–58) illustrates how Jesus himself fulfills the demand posed earlier. A gruesome aftermath of a birthday celebration (14:6–11) then acts as a foil for Jesus' meal of compassion for God's true family (14:13–21), while the disciples enact their proper role of serving (v. 19). The presence of women and children is noted as an aside, indicating the man-centered perspective of Matthew; yet the mention of the women also shows that Jesus' message appealed to a broad audience.

Jesus Walks on the Water

22 Immediately he made the disciples get into the boat and go on ahead to the other side, while he dismissed the crowds. ²³And after he had dismissed the crowds, he went up the mountain by himself to pray. When evening came, he was there alone, ²⁴but by this time the boat, battered by the waves, was far from the land,ᵏ for the wind was against them. ²⁵And early in the morning he came walking toward them on the sea. ²⁶But when the disciples saw him walking on the sea, they were terrified, saying, "It is a ghost!" And they cried out in fear. ²⁷But immediately Jesus spoke to them and said, "Take heart, it is I; do not be afraid."

28 Peter answered him, "Lord, if it is you, command me to come to you on the water." ²⁹He said, "Come." So Peter got out of the boat, started walking on the water, and came toward Jesus. ³⁰But when he noticed the strong wind,ˡ he became frightened, and beginning to sink, he cried out, "Lord, save me!" ³¹Jesus immediately reached out his hand and caught him, saying to him, "You of little faith, why did you doubt?" ³²When they got into the boat, the wind ceased. ³³And those in the boat worshiped him, saying, "Truly you are the Son of God."

Jesus Heals the Sick in Gennesaret

34 When they had crossed over, they came to land at Gennesaret. ³⁵After the people of that place recognized him, they sent word throughout the region and brought all who were sick to him, ³⁶and begged him that they might touch even the fringe of his cloak; and all who touched it were healed.

The Tradition of the Elders

15 Then Pharisees and scribes came to Jesus from Jerusalem and said,

---

ᵏ Other ancient authorities read *was out on the sea*
ˡ Other ancient authorities read *the wind*

14:22–33. While the disciples, upon Jesus' command, precede him (by boat) to the other side of the sea, Jesus withdraws to the mountain alone to pray. Matthew sets the scene to evoke the audience's memory of the Exodus story – crossing the sea, the mountain, solitary prayer. This point becomes even more clear when the sea becomes turbulent, and Jesus walks on the water to meet the boat (cf. the Israelites walking dryshod through the sea). Jesus calms the fearful disciples with the statement 'It is I' (*ego eimi*); this is God's 'name' given to reassure Moses in Exod. 3:15.

The sequence with Peter in this scene foreshadows Peter's betrayal of Jesus after his arrest (viz. Matt. 26:31–35, 69–75). Peter tests Jesus, and his own faith, asking Jesus to command him to come to him across the water (14:28). Jesus gives the command, and Peter begins to come to Jesus (v. 29). Peter takes fright and falters, floundering in the sea (v. 30); so he is rebuked for his poverty of faith (v. 31). After Peter is fished out of the water, and he and Jesus are in the boat, the wind is calmed and the disciples worship Jesus as God's Son (vv. 32–33). This scene provides an ironic twist to Jesus' call of Peter in 4:19, and demonstrates that the most eager of Jesus' followers is not necessarily the most enduring.

14:34–36. The people in the region of Gennesaret provide a contrast to the 'small faith' rebuked in the sea story. They, like the woman with the hemorrhage (9:20–22), asked only to touch the tassel of Jesus' garment to be healed.

The mention of Jesus' 'tassel' (*kraspedon*) refers to the decoration required on the four corners of an Israelite's outer garment to remind the bearer to keep God's commandments (Num. 15:38–39; Deut. 22:12). This suggests that Matthew remembers Jesus as observant of the Mosaic Law, a point that is both emphasized and clarified in the ensuing exchange with some of the Pharisees and scribes from Jerusalem.

15:1–20. First Jesus demands filial piety and support for elderly parents based on the fourth commandment and related laws (Exod. 20:12; 21:17; Lev. 20:9; Deut. 5:16). He disallows any

2"Why do your disciples break the tradition of the elders? For they do not wash their hands before they eat." [3]He answered them, "And why do you break the commandment of God for the sake of your tradition? [4]For God said,[m] 'Honor your father and your mother,' and, 'Whoever speaks evil of father or mother must surely die.' [5]But you say that whoever tells father or mother, 'Whatever support you might have had from me is given to God,'[n] then that person need not honor the father.[o] [6]So, for the sake of your tradition, you make void the word[p] of God. [7]You hypocrites! Isaiah prophesied rightly about you when he said:

[8] 'This people honors me with their lips,
       but their hearts are far from me;
[9] in vain do they worship me,
       teaching human precepts as
           doctrines.' "

Things That Defile

10 Then he called the crowd to him and said to them, "Listen and understand: [11]it is not what goes into the mouth that defiles a person, but it is what comes out of the mouth that defiles." [12]Then the disciples approached and said to him, "Do you know that the Pharisees took offense when they heard what you said?" [13]He answered, "Every plant that my heavenly Father has not planted will be uprooted. [14]Let them alone; they are blind guides of the blind.[q] And if one blind person guides another, both will fall into a pit." [15]But Peter said to him, "Explain this parable to us." [16]Then he said, "Are you also still without understanding? [17]Do you not see that whatever goes into the mouth enters the stomach, and goes out into the sewer? [18]But what comes out of the mouth proceeds from the heart, and this is what defiles. [19]For out of the heart come evil intentions, murder, adultery, fornication, theft, false witness, slander. [20]These are what defile a person, but to eat with unwashed hands does not defile."

The Canaanite Woman's Faith

21 Jesus left that place and went away to the district of Tyre and Sidon. [22]Just then a Canaanite woman from that region came out and started shouting, "Have mercy on me, Lord, Son of David; my daughter is tormented by a demon." [23]But he did not answer her at all. And his disciples came

---

[m] Other ancient authorities read *commanded, saying* [n] Or *is an offering* [o] Other ancient authorities add *or the mother* [p] Other ancient authorities read *law*; others, *commandment* [q] Other ancient authorities lack *of the blind*

---

legal ruses to avoid such a responsibility. This teaching accords well with what we know of rabbinic teaching contemporaneous with Jesus. However, Jesus then proceeds to turn the laws of ritual purity on their head, declaring that it is not what a person touches or eats that causes impurity, but one's speech and intentions. If this means that moral impurity (i.e. sin) is the root cause of physical impurity, then this accords well with the view of the Hebrew Bible and other traditional Jewish teaching. However, if this were taken to mean that the purity laws are dismissed entirely, then this teaching would scandalize many Jews, specially the Pharisees (as is mentioned in v. 12).

15:21–28. In the scene with the Canaanite woman, Jesus' teaching on ritual purity is put to the test. If the Pharisees go overboard in their emphasis on ritual purity so that they separate Jews from one another, how far will Jesus go in the other direction? At first, he seems not to move at all; he does not even acknowledge the woman's entreaties. When the annoyed disciples ask Jesus to send her away, he finally proclaims his limits: only Israel (15:24). A more clear-cut dismissal could not be found. The audience has had hints, however, that this restriction to Israel is not quite the case (e.g. the adoration of the magi in 2:1–12, the cures of the centurion's servant in 8:5–13 and the Gadarene demoniacs in 8:28–34). For Gentile men, Jesus has gone beyond Israel before, but never for the sake of a woman.

and urged him, saying, "Send her away, for she keeps shouting after us." [24]He answered, "I was sent only to the lost sheep of the house of Israel." [25]But she came and knelt before him, saying, "Lord, help me." [26]He answered, "It is not fair to take the children's food and throw it to the dogs." [27]She said, "Yes, Lord, yet even the dogs eat the crumbs that fall from their masters' table." [28]Then Jesus answered her, "Woman, great is your faith! Let it be done for you as you wish." And her daughter was healed instantly.

Jesus Cures Many People

29 After Jesus had left that place, he passed along the Sea of Galilee, and he went up the mountain, where he sat down. [30]Great crowds came to him, bringing with them the lame, the maimed, the blind, the mute, and many others. They put them at his feet, and he cured them, [31]so that the crowd was amazed when they saw the mute speaking, the maimed whole, the lame walking, and the blind seeing. And they praised the God of Israel.

Feeding the Four Thousand

32 Then Jesus called his disciples to him and said, "I have compassion for the crowd, because they have been with me now for three days and have nothing to eat; and I do not want to send them away hungry, for they might faint on the way." [33]The disciples said to him, "Where are we to get enough bread in the desert to feed so great a crowd?" [34]Jesus asked them, "How many loaves have you?" They said, "Seven, and a few small fish." [35]Then ordering the crowd to sit down on the ground, [36]he took the seven loaves and the fish; and after giving thanks he broke them and gave them to the disciples, and the disciples gave them to the crowds. [37]And all of them ate and were filled; and they took up the broken pieces left over, seven baskets full. [38]Those who had eaten were four thousand men, besides women and children. [39]After sending away the crowds, he got into the boat and went to the region of Magadan.[r]

---

[r] Other ancient authorities read *Magdala* or *Magdalan*

The Gentile woman's audacity and persistence in the face of Jesus' rejection are what finally grant her a hearing – and a cure. The woman breaks social taboos – she speaks publicly to a man, and a Jewish man at that. She does not succumb to Jesus' seeming dismissal, nor submit to his reproof. Even Jesus' second verbal rejection, which insults her ethnic heritage (15:26), does not sway her from her cause. And her rejoinder now earns not rebuke, but affirmation and blessing (v. 28). Jesus affirms the great faith of this woman in terms evocative of 9:22, the story of that other daughter. Of all the conflict stories about Jesus, this alone shows the other party winning. Of this passage Martin Luther wrote, 'Was this not a master stroke? She has worsted the Lord at his own game.'

Jesus now responds very positively to the Gentile woman, and meets her challenge with a cure. In so doing, he not only undermines the laws of ritual purity, but also challenges ancient notions of ethnic purity at their core.

Women who learned that submissiveness in all things is the appropriate response to (male) authority must be challenged by this story, where Jesus affirms the 'assertive' woman. And all of us who live in societies marked by ethnic and racial tensions must learn, like Jesus, to affirm the 'other' – the Gentile, the Jew, the African, the Asian, the white, the black – and to respond to human need where it exists, without branding the 'type' of human beings for whom we will care.

15:29–39. Matthew emphasizes how Jesus' own ministry flourished after this lesson of the Canaanite woman. He cured multitudes from the mountain, and he fed the 4,000 (again 'besides women and children') with a few loaves and fish. We can infer that these crowds were Gentile, since Matthew specifies that 'they praised the God of Israel' (v. 31). If they were Israelites, presumably, to say 'they praised God' would have been enough.

The Demand for a Sign

16 The Pharisees and Sadducees came, and to test Jesus[s] they asked him to show them a sign from heaven. [2]He answered them, "When it is evening, you say, 'It will be fair weather, for the sky is red.' [3]And in the morning, 'It will be stormy today, for the sky is red and threatening.' You know how to interpret the appearance of the sky, but you cannot interpret the signs of the times.[t] [4]An evil and adulterous generation asks for a sign, but no sign will be given to it except the sign of Jonah." Then he left them and went away.

The Yeast of the Pharisees and Sadducees

5 When the disciples reached the other side, they had forgotten to bring any bread. [6]Jesus said to them, "Watch out, and beware of the yeast of the Pharisees and Sadducees." [7]They said to one another, "It is because we have brought no bread." [8]And becoming aware of it, Jesus said, "You of little faith, why are you talking about having no bread? [9]Do you still not perceive? Do you not remember the five loaves for the five thousand, and how many baskets you gathered? [10]Or the seven loaves for the four thousand, and how many baskets you gathered? [11]How could you fail to perceive that I was not speaking about bread? Beware of the yeast of the Pharisees and Sadducees!" [12]Then they understood that he had not told them to beware of the yeast of bread, but of the teaching of the Pharisees and Sadducees.

Peter's Declaration about Jesus

13 Now when Jesus came into the district of Caesarea Philippi, he asked his disciples, "Who do people say that the Son of Man is?" [14]And they said, "Some say John the Baptist, but others Elijah, and still others Jeremiah or one of the prophets." [15]He said to them, "But who do you say that I am?" [16]Simon Peter answered, "You are the Messiah,[u] the Son of the living God." [17]And Jesus answered him, "Blessed are you, Simon son of Jonah! For flesh and blood has not revealed this to you, but my Father in heaven. [18]And I tell you, you are Peter,[v] and on this rock[w] I will build my church, and the gates of Hades will not prevail against it. [19]I will give you the keys of the kingdom of heaven, and whatever you bind on earth will be bound in heaven, and whatever you loose on earth will be loosed in heaven." [20]Then he sternly ordered the disciples not to tell anyone that he was[x] the Messiah.[u]

[s] Gk *him*   [t] Other ancient authorities lack [2]*When it is . . . of the times*   [u] Or *the Christ*   [v] Gk *Petros*   [w] Gk *petra*   [x] Other ancient authorities add *Jesus*

16:1–12. The faithful response of the Gentiles is then contrasted with the doubt of the leaders of Israel: the Pharisees and Sadducees ask Jesus for a sign 'from heaven' (i.e. from God). Jesus points to the one sign they ignore, 'the sign of Jonah' – that the Gentiles repent and turn to the God of Israel (cf. Jonah 3:3–10).

16:13–28. The response Jesus seeks is illustrated by the impulsive Peter, who declares him to be the Messiah, Son of God (16:15–16). In response to this affirmation of faith, Jesus declares Peter to have 'the keys of the kingdom of heaven', with powers that befit a regent of God on earth (16:17–19). But when Jesus begins to outline what it means for him to be the Messiah, Peter shows that his heart again has outrun his understanding and trust, and is soundly rebuked as 'Satan' by Jesus (16:22–23). Peter must learn to hear and risk and understand before he can make use of this power for good; likewise for us, who are regents of God's creation (cf. Gen. 1:28–30; 2:15) and now heirs to the gospel. The gospel of wealth and comfort is not the gospel of Jesus (Matt. 16:24–27).

Jesus Foretells His Death
and Resurrection

21 From that time on, Jesus began to show his disciples that he must go to Jerusalem and undergo great suffering at the hands of the elders and chief priests and scribes, and be killed, and on the third day be raised. ²²And Peter took him aside and began to rebuke him, saying, "God forbid it, Lord! This must never happen to you." ²³But he turned and said to Peter, "Get behind me, Satan! You are a stumbling block to me; for you are setting your mind not on divine things but on human things."

The Cross and Self-Denial

24 Then Jesus told his disciples, "If any want to become my followers, let them deny themselves and take up their cross and follow me. ²⁵For those who want to save their life will lose it, and those who lose their life for my sake will find it. ²⁶For what will it profit them if they gain the whole world but forfeit their life? Or what will they give in return for their life?

27 "For the Son of Man is to come with his angels in the glory of his Father, and then he will repay everyone for what has been done. ²⁸Truly I tell you, there are some standing here who will not taste death before they see the Son of Man coming in his kingdom."

The Transfiguration

17 Six days later, Jesus took with him Peter and James and his brother John and led them up a high mountain, by themselves. ²And he was transfigured before them, and his face shone like the sun, and his clothes became dazzling white. ³Suddenly there appeared to them Moses and Elijah, talking with him. ⁴Then Peter said to Jesus, "Lord, it is good for us to be here; if you wish, Iʸ will make three dwellingsᶻ here, one for you, one for Moses, and one for Elijah." ⁵While he was still speaking, suddenly a bright cloud overshadowed them, and from the cloud a

voice said, "This is my Son, the Beloved;ᵃ with him I am well pleased; listen to him!" ⁶When the disciples heard this, they fell to the ground and were overcome by fear. ⁷But Jesus came and touched them, saying, "Get up and do not be afraid." ⁸And when they looked up, they saw no one except Jesus himself alone.

9 As they were coming down the mountain, Jesus ordered them, "Tell no one about the vision until after the Son of Man has been raised from the dead." ¹⁰And the disciples asked him, "Why, then, do the scribes say that Elijah must come first?" ¹¹He replied, "Elijah is indeed coming and will restore all things; ¹²but I tell you that Elijah has already come, and they did not recognize him, but they did to him whatever they pleased. So also the Son of Man is about to suffer at their hands." ¹³Then the disciples understood that he was speaking to them about John the Baptist.

Jesus Cures a Boy with a Demon

14 When they came to the crowd, a man came to him, knelt before him, ¹⁵and said, "Lord, have mercy on my son, for he is an epileptic and he suffers terribly; he often falls into the fire and often into the water. ¹⁶And I brought him to your disciples, but they could not cure him." ¹⁷Jesus answered, "You faithless and perverse generation, how much longer must I be with you? How much longer must I put up with you? Bring him here to me." ¹⁸And Jesus rebuked the demon,ᵇ and itᶜ came out of him, and the boy was cured instantly. ¹⁹Then the disciples came to Jesus privately and said, "Why could we not cast it out?" ²⁰He said to them, "Because of your little faith. For truly I tell you, if you have faith the size of aᵈ mustard seed, you will say to this mountain, 'Move from here to there,' and it will

---

ʸ Other ancient authorities read *we*   ᶻ Or *tents*
ᵃ Or *my beloved Son*   ᵇ Gk *it* or *him*   ᶜ Gk *the demon*   ᵈ Gk *faith as a grain of*

move; and nothing will be impossible for you."[e]

Jesus Again Foretells His Death and Resurrection

22 As they were gathering[f] in Galilee, Jesus said to them, "The Son of Man is going to be betrayed into human hands, [23]and they will kill him, and on the third day he will be raised." And they were greatly distressed.

Jesus and the Temple Tax

24 When they reached Capernaum, the collectors of the temple tax[g] came to Peter and said, "Does your teacher not pay the temple tax?"[g] [25]He said, "Yes, he does." And when he came home, Jesus spoke of it first, asking, "What do you think, Simon? From whom do kings of the earth take toll or tribute? From their children or from others?" [26]When Peter[h] said, "From others," Jesus said to him, "Then the children are free. [27]However, so that we do not give offense to them, go to the sea and cast a hook; take the first fish that comes up; and when you open its mouth, you will find a coin;[i] take that and give it to them for you and me."

True Greatness

18 At that time the disciples came to Jesus and asked, "Who is the greatest in the kingdom of heaven?" [2]He called a child, whom he put among them, [3]and said, "Truly I tell you, unless you change and become like children, you will never enter the kingdom of heaven.

[4]Whoever becomes humble like this child is the greatest in the kingdom of heaven. [5]Whoever welcomes one such child in my name welcomes me.

Temptations to Sin

6 "If any of you put a stumbling block before one of these little ones who believe in me, it would be better for you if a great millstone were fastened around your neck and you were drowned in the depth of the sea. [7]Woe to the world because of stumbling blocks! Occasions for stumbling are bound to come, but woe to the one by whom the stumbling block comes!

8 "If your hand or your foot causes you to stumble, cut it off and throw it away; it is better for you to enter life maimed or lame than to have two hands or two feet and to be thrown into the eternal fire. [9]And if your eye causes you to stumble, tear it out and throw it away; it is better for you to enter life with one eye than to have two eyes and to be thrown into the hell[j] of fire.

The Parable of the Lost Sheep

10 "Take care that you do not despise one of these little ones; for, I tell you, in heaven their angels continually see the face of my Father in heaven.[k] [12]What do you

---

[e] Other ancient authorities add verse 21, *But this kind does not come out except by prayer and fasting*   [f] Other ancient authorities read *living*   [g] Gk *didrachma*   [h] Gk *he*   [i] Gk *stater*; the stater was worth two didrachmas   [j] Gk *Gehenna*   [k] Other ancient authorities add verse 11, *For the Son of Man came to save the lost*

18:1–19:2. Jesus has declared his followers to be a new entity, a new gathering (*ekklesia*) or political grouping (Matt. 16:18; cf. Deut. 31:30), where membership is marked by humility, hospitality, and forgiveness. Now Jesus fills out the meaning of this new reality. Welcoming the lost and powerless child is identified with welcome of Jesus himself (Matt. 18:1–9). And to embody these traits, the disciples must 'become like children . . .' (Matt. 18:3; cf. John 3:3), the most disenfranchised of all. We must recover the strays (Matt. 18:10–14), correct one another (18:15–18), together ask God to supply our needs (18:19–20), and treat one another with mercy and forgiveness (18:21–35). We must learn anew the way to live, no longer according to the hierarchical structures of lordship and power, but together as equals under God's rule. For it is God alone to whom dominion belongs.

think? If a shepherd has a hundred sheep, and one of them has gone astray, does he not leave the ninety-nine on the mountains and go in search of the one that went astray? ¹³And if he finds it, truly I tell you, he rejoices over it more than over the ninety-nine that never went astray. ¹⁴So it is not the will of your[l] Father in heaven that one of these little ones should be lost.

Reproving Another Who Sins

15 "If another member of the church[m] sins against you,[n] go and point out the fault when the two of you are alone. If the member[o] listens to you, you have regained that one. ¹⁶But if you are not listened to, take one or two others along with you, so that every word may be confirmed by the evidence of two or three witnesses. ¹⁷If the member[o] refuses to listen to them, tell it to the church; and if the offender[o] refuses to listen even to the church, let such a one be to you as a Gentile and a tax collector. ¹⁸Truly I tell you, whatever you bind on earth will be bound in heaven, and whatever you loose on earth will be loosed in heaven. ¹⁹Again, truly I tell you, if two of you agree on earth about anything you ask, it will be done for you by my Father in heaven. ²⁰For where two or three are gathered in my name, I am there among them."

Forgiveness

21 Then Peter came and said to him, "Lord, if another member of the church[p] sins against me, how often should I forgive? As many as seven times?" ²²Jesus said to him, "Not seven times, but, I tell you, seventy-seven[q] times.

The Parable of the Unforgiving Servant

23 "For this reason the kingdom of heaven may be compared to a king who wished to settle accounts with his slaves. ²⁴When he began the reckoning, one who owed him ten thousand talents[r] was brought to him; ²⁵and, as he could not pay, his lord ordered him to be sold, together with his wife and children and all his possessions, and payment to be made. ²⁶So the slave fell on his knees before him, saying, 'Have patience with me, and I will pay you everything.' ²⁷And out of pity for him, the lord of that slave released him and forgave him the debt. ²⁸But that same slave, as he went out, came upon one of his fellow slaves who owed him a hundred denarii;[s] and seizing him by the throat, he said, 'Pay what you owe.' ²⁹Then his fellow slave fell down and pleaded with him, 'Have patience with me, and I will pay you.' ³⁰But he refused; then he went and threw him into prison until he would pay the debt. ³¹When his fellow slaves saw what had happened, they were greatly distressed, and they went and reported to their lord all that had taken place. ³²Then his lord summoned him and said to him, 'You wicked slave! I forgave you all that debt because you pleaded with me. ³³Should you not have had mercy on your fellow slave, as I had mercy on you?' ³⁴And in anger his lord handed him over to be tortured until he would pay his entire debt. ³⁵So my heavenly Father will also do to every one of you, if you do not forgive your brother or sister[t] from your heart."

Teaching about Divorce

19 When Jesus had finished saying these things, he left Galilee and went to the region of Judea beyond the Jordan. ²Large crowds followed him, and he cured them there.

---

[l] Other ancient authorities read *my brother*   [m] Gk *If your brother*   [n] Other ancient authorities lack *against you*   [o] Gk *the brother*   [p] Gk *if my brother*   [q] Or *seventy times seven*   [r] A talent was worth more than fifteen years' wages of a laborer   [s] The denarius was the usual day's wage for a laborer   [t] Gk *brother*

THE ESCHATOLOGICAL DISCOURSE (MATT. 19:2–26:1)

In this section, Matthew reports a series of Jesus' teachings and actions that brought him into conflict with the religious authorities in Jerusalem. Taken together, they serve to answer the

3 Some Pharisees came to him, and to test him they asked, "Is it lawful for a man to divorce his wife for any cause?" [4]He answered, "Have you not read that the one who made them at the beginning 'made them male and female,' [5]and said, 'For this reason a man shall leave his father and mother and be joined to his wife, and the two shall become one flesh'? [6]So they are no longer two, but one flesh. Therefore what God has joined together, let no one separate." [7]They said to him, "Why then did Moses command us to give a certificate of dismissal and to divorce her?" [8]He said to them, "It was because you were so hard-hearted that Moses allowed you to divorce your wives, but from the beginning it was not so. [9]And I say to you, whoever divorces his wife, except for unchastity, and marries another commits adultery."[u]

10 His disciples said to him, "If such is the case of a man with his wife, it is better not to marry." [11]But he said to them, "Not everyone can accept this teaching, but only those to whom it is given. [12]For there are eunuchs who have been so from birth, and

[u] Other ancient authorities read *except on the ground of unchastity, causes her to commit adultery*; others add at the end of the verse *and he who marries a divorced woman commits adultery*

---

readers' question, prompted by the previous section, of how this new way of life under God's rule differs from their customary practices.

19:3–12. For Jesus, relations between women and men are one of the more significant areas in which God's reign differs from the human social conventions that applied in his day. This becomes crystal clear in his disputation with 'the Pharisees' concerning the reasons for which a man can divorce his wife.

Often in commentaries and Bible editions, this section is entitled 'the question of divorce', but such a title obscures the central point of the Pharisees' challenge and the target of Jesus' rejoinder. The Pharisees ask for Jesus' interpretation of a cryptic phrase in Deut. 24:1, where a man who has consummated a marriage later 'is displeased' with his wife because 'he finds in her something indecent'. So, they ask, what qualifies as something 'indecent' enough to legitimate divorce?

It is important to note that Jesus is *not* asked to give his position on what grounds there may be for ending a marriage in which both parties have equal rights, responsibilities, and economic opportunities. Such a marriage did not exist in the Palestine of Jesus' day. The question concerns ending a marriage where one party (the husband) has the preponderance of rights and opportunities, while the other party (the wife) bears most of the responsibilities. In other words, the question asked of Jesus is: 'What are the grounds for which a patriarchal marriage can be *unilaterally* abrogated by a husband (especially one who wishes to marry another woman)?'

There are two main lines of rabbinic interpretation of the law concerning divorce and remarriage in Deut. 24:1. These are represented by the schools of Rabbi Shammai and of Rabbi Hillel, who were early contemporaries of Jesus. R. Shammai taught the more stringent position that the phrase 'something unclean' in Deut. 24:1 refers to adultery, and that a husband may divorce only on these grounds. R. Hillel taught that 'something unclean' can have a much broader meaning, including anything that incites a husband's displeasure. For example, if a husband is displeased because his wife bears only girls, or because she has lost her beauty, or for a variety of other reasons, each of these can be grounds for divorce. Thus, the view of Shammai often has been characterized as 'stringent' and that of Hillel as 'lenient' – although, from the wife's standpoint, one would be hard pressed to characterize the latter as other than capricious. The requirement that the husband return his wife's dowry upon divorce no doubt provided some economic disincentive to prevent Hillel's ruling from being taken to the extreme, but its effectiveness would decline with the size of the dowry, thus providing less of a safeguard for poorer women.

Given these previous answers to how this verse should be interpreted, when 'the Pharisees' ask Jesus to take a position, the audience no doubt expects his teaching to fall somewhere in between. Jesus' retort is all the more remarkable because he not only rejects both these opinions, but repudiates the key assumption which provides the very grounds for the question.

there are eunuchs who have been made eunuchs by others, and there are eunuchs who have made themselves eunuchs for the sake of the kingdom of heaven. Let anyone accept this who can."

◆ It was noted above that, in answering this question, Jesus had in view a particular mode of marriage – i.e. the patriarchal marriage which was customary in first-century Palestine. Among Jews, there was agreement about the rules of consanguinity, since these are explained in the Torah (Lev. 18:6–18). However, Gentiles had different incest taboos, less restrictive than those of the Jews. By the time Matthew is reporting Jesus' teaching, he is addressing a mixed audience of Jewish Christians and Gentile converts. Gentiles who married before they converted to Christianity may have spouses too closely related to be lawful under the Torah regulations. This would cause scandal in the Matthean church, and perhaps also among the wider public.

Jesus' answer to the Pharisees' question also was addressed to quite different conventions of marriage and divorce than are common among Christians today. In applying this teaching to today's situation, then, we do well to follow Matthew's example of following the spirit of Jesus' message rather than the letter. For Matthew, it may have been a question of incestuous marriages. Among us, there are other types of marriage that create scandal; most significant are abusive relationships. If one partner is abusive toward the other, to continue the marriage is to legitimate the abuse as if God approves of such violent behavior. Jesus argued *against* the divorce practices of his day because of the manner in which they allowed one partner to exert power over and victimize the other, but to continue an abusive marriage is to perpetuate precisely what Jesus repudiated in this ruling. In such cases, Christians must not cite Jesus' authority for teaching victims to allow abuse to continue in a marriage. Jesus argued against a husband's abuse of his wife through divorce; *a fortiori*, there is no reason to believe he tolerated spousal abuse in the marriage itself ◆

The questioners – following common patriarchal marriage practices in first-century Palestine – presume that a husband has unilateral power over his wife in marriage, including contracting and divorcing a marriage. The man arranges with the father of the bride; the daughter does her father's bidding. Hence, a wife is simply the object of her husband's choice. The rulings of both Shammai and Hillel, while they differ greatly, agree on this one point: they accept this same assumption of the power of one marriage partner over the other (husband over wife).

Jesus challenges this assumption, charging that it is the result of sin (v. 8). Quoting Gen. 1:27 and 2:24, he argues that the Creator made human beings both male and female, intending that they become one flesh again when a man joins with his wife. A husband is now subject to this new reality that God has ordained; he is not an independent party who happens to have a wife. Since a woman had always been viewed as subject to the marriage, Jesus' new teaching effectively equalizes the situation. No longer is the husband superior to his wife, with unilateral power over her. Now the husband too is subject to the marriage relationship, with permanent obligations toward his wife. She cannot be summarily dismissed, deprived of children, social status and financial support, and left to return to her parental home (if she is welcome) or to eke out what living she can by gleaning, begging, or even prostitution. Once a man accepts a woman as his wife, the husband is obligated by the Creator to honor and keep her.

The male disciples react strongly to Jesus' teaching, arguing that it is better to remain unmarried if a man can never sunder his marriage (v. 10). Jesus admits that it requires God's grace to live up to 'this teaching' – as it does to live a life of celibacy (19:11f.).

Jesus Blesses Little Children

13 Then little children were being brought to him in order that he might lay his hands on them and pray. The disciples spoke sternly to those who brought them; [14]but Jesus said, "Let the little children come to me, and do not stop them; for it is to such as these that the kingdom of heaven belongs." [15]And he laid his hands on them and went on his way.

The Rich Young Man

16 Then someone came to him and said, "Teacher, what good deed must I do to have eternal life?" [17]And he said to him, "Why do you ask me about what is good? There is only one who is good. If you wish to enter into life, keep the commandments." [18]He said to him, "Which ones?" And Jesus said, "You shall not murder; You shall not commit adultery; You shall not steal; You shall not bear false witness; [19]Honor your father and mother; also, You shall love your neighbor as yourself." [20]The young man said to him, "I have kept all these;[v] what do I still lack?" [21]Jesus said to him, "If you wish to be perfect, go, sell your possessions, and give the money[w] to the poor, and you will have treasure in heaven; then come, follow me." [22]When the young man heard this word, he went away grieving, for he had many possessions.

23 Then Jesus said to his disciples, "Truly I tell you, it will be hard for a rich person to enter the kingdom of heaven.

[24]Again I tell you, it is easier for a camel to go through the eye of a needle than for someone who is rich to enter the kingdom of God." [25]When the disciples heard this, they were greatly astounded and said, "Then who can be saved?" [26]But Jesus looked at them and said, "For mortals it is impossible, but for God all things are possible."

27 Then Peter said in reply, "Look, we have left everything and followed you. What then will we have?" [28]Jesus said to them, "Truly I tell you, at the renewal of all things, when the Son of Man is seated on the throne of his glory, you who have followed me will also sit on twelve thrones, judging the twelve tribes of Israel. [29]And everyone who has left houses or brothers or sisters or father or mother or children or fields, for my name's sake, will receive a hundredfold,[x] and will inherit eternal life. [30]But many who are first will be last, and the last will be first.

The Laborers in the Vineyard

20 "For the kingdom of heaven is like a landowner who went out early in the morning to hire laborers for his vineyard. [2]After agreeing with the laborers for the usual daily wage,[y] he sent them into his vineyard. [3]When he went out about nine

---

[v] Other ancient authorities add *from my youth*
[w] Gk lacks *the money*   [x] Other ancient authorities read *manifold*   [y] Gk *a denarius*

19:13–30. The blessing of the children (19:13–15) and the story of the rich youth (19:16–30) emphasize that the commonwealth of heaven belongs to those who are humble, trusting, and marginal – especially the poor. Possessions may be a blessing from God (as many Jews of Jesus' time assumed; cf. v. 25), but they can also pose an obstacle between a person and God. Those with possessions and power must use them to benefit those who have not.

20:1–16. The parable of the workers in the vineyard gives a practical example of how this can be done. The owner pays all the workers the subsistence wage for the day, even if they have not worked a full day. This is not only an act of generosity by the landowner, but an act of divine justice: the landowner's possessions belong to God, and all the workers need their daily bread. The injustice highlighted in the parable is in the response of the earlier workers, whose greed and envy prompt them to protest. Of course, if the owner had simply paid everyone at the same hourly rate, there would have been no argument – and the last of the workers would not have lived 'till the morrow.

o'clock, he saw others standing idle in the marketplace; [4]and he said to them, 'You also go into the vineyard, and I will pay you whatever is right.' So they went. [5]When he went out again about noon and about three o'clock, he did the same. [6]And about five o'clock he went out and found others standing around; and he said to them, 'Why are you standing here idle all day?' [7]They said to him, 'Because no one has hired us.' He said to them, 'You also go into the vineyard.' [8]When evening came, the owner of the vineyard said to his manager, 'Call the laborers and give them their pay, beginning with the last and then going to the first.' [9]When those hired about five o'clock came, each of them received the usual daily wage.[z] [10]Now when the first came, they thought they would receive more; but each of them also received the usual daily wage.[z] [11]And when they received it, they grumbled against the landowner, [12]saying, 'These last worked only one hour, and you have made them equal to us who have borne the burden of the day and the scorching heat.' [13]But he replied to one of them, 'Friend, I am doing you no wrong; did you not agree with me for the usual daily wage?[z] [14]Take what belongs to you and go; I choose to give to this last the same as I give to you. [15]Am I not allowed to do what I choose with what belongs to me? Or are you envious because I am generous?'[a] [16]So the last will be first, and the first will be last."[b]

A Third Time Jesus Foretells His Death and Resurrection

17 While Jesus was going up to Jerusalem, he took the twelve disciples aside by themselves, and said to them on the way, [18]"See, we are going up to Jerusalem, and the Son of Man will be handed over to the chief priests and scribes, and they will condemn him to death; [19]then they will hand him over to the Gentiles to be mocked and flogged and crucified; and on the third day he will be raised."

◆ The mother of James and John comes to Jesus to further her ambitions for her sons. Of course it is laudable that she wishes to equip Christ's Kingdom with capable administrators, but neither she nor her sons have any idea about the true nature of that Kingdom. Her request is not only selfish, but it causes dissension in the fellowship of the disciples. Far from being constructive, this mother has created a major problem.

She is not unique in her inability to see which ambitions for one's children are appropriate and inappropriate. All of us need to beware lest we use our children's successes and achievements as grounds for our own personal pride. Often women have lived vicariously through their children and found meaning for their lives in the attainments of their offspring. Many a son or daughter has been pushed into a career or course of study simply to gratify the mother's satisfaction. Even some in the ministry of the gospel have succumbed to maternal pressure rather than to a genuine call of God.

There are, however, appropriate measures which a mother may take in order to enable her children to fulfill their God-given mission. It is fitting that she do her utmost to make educational opportunities available to them, that she encourage and support them in developing their gifts and talents, that she lead them to a saving knowledge of Jesus Christ and his love. Mothers can give children positive nurturing experiences, introduce them to good books and music, and help them to form constructive attitudes. Above all they can surround them with prayer, laughter, solidarity, and love ◆

---

[z] Gk *a denarius*   [a] Gk *is your eye evil because I am good?*   [b] Other ancient authorities add *for many are called but few are chosen*

The Request of the Mother of James and John

20 Then the mother of the sons of Zebedee came to him with her sons, and kneeling before him, she asked a favor of him. ²¹And he said to her, "What do you want?" She said to him, "Declare that these two sons of mine will sit, one at your right hand and one at your left, in your kingdom." ²²But Jesus answered, "You do not know what you are asking. Are you able to drink the cup that I am about to drink?"ᶜ They said to him, "We are able." ²³He said to them, "You will indeed drink my cup, but to sit at my right hand and at my left, this is not mine to grant, but it is for those for whom it has been prepared by my Father."

24 When the ten heard it, they were angry with the two brothers. ²⁵But Jesus called them to him and said, "You know that the rulers of the Gentiles lord it over them, and their great ones are tyrants over them. ²⁶It will not be so among you; but whoever wishes to be great among you must be your servant, ²⁷and whoever wishes to be first among you must be your slave; ²⁸just as the Son of Man came not to be served but to serve, and to give his life a ransom for many."

Jesus Heals Two Blind Men

29 As they were leaving Jericho, a large crowd followed him. ³⁰There were two blind men sitting by the roadside. When they heard that Jesus was passing by, they shouted, "Lord,ᵈ have mercy on us, Son of David!" ³¹The crowd sternly ordered them to be quiet; but they shouted even more loudly, "Have mercy on us, Lord, Son of David!" ³²Jesus stood still and called them, saying, "What do you want me to do for you?" ³³They said to him, "Lord, let our eyes be opened." ³⁴Moved with compassion, Jesus touched their eyes. Immediately they regained their sight and followed him.

Jesus' Triumphal Entry into Jerusalem

21 When they had come near Jerusalem and had reached Bethphage, at the Mount of Olives, Jesus sent two disciples, ²saying to them, "Go into the village ahead of you, and immediately you will find a donkey tied, and a colt with her; untie them and bring them to me. ³If anyone says anything to you, just say this, 'The Lord needs them.' And he will send them immediately.ᵉ" ⁴This took place to fulfill what had been spoken through the prophet, saying,

⁵ "Tell the daughter of Zion,
    Look, your king is coming to you,
        humble, and mounted on a donkey,
            and on a colt, the foal of a
            donkey."

⁶The disciples went and did as Jesus had directed them; ⁷they brought the donkey

ᶜ Other ancient authorities add *or to be baptized with the baptism that I am baptized with?*
ᵈ Other ancient authorities lack *Lord*   ᵉ Or '*The Lord needs them and will send them back immediately.*'

20:20–28. The dispute about 'first place' demonstrates that the twelve still do not understand Jesus' teaching about power relationships in the reign of God. They seek honor, but are promised the cup of suffering instead. They seek glory, but are called to servitude.

20:29–21:17. Jesus follows this with a living demonstration of his teaching. When the two blind people cry out, the crowd tries to silence and marginalize them. Jesus responds to their need; and 'Immediately they regained their sight and followed him' (20:34b). When Jesus enters Jerusalem, acclaimed as King and Messiah ('Son of David'), he rides not on a war horse but a she-ass; he comes not to a fortress but to 'daughter Zion'. Familial language predominates over political images, so that Jesus' most political act (cleansing the Temple) is interpreted in light of the praise of infants and children. And just when Jesus would have been expected to establish his new order as king in Jerusalem, he leaves the city to spend the night in Bethany. It is suggestive that one of the possible derivations for this place name is 'house of the poor'.

and the colt, and put their cloaks on them, and he sat on them. [8]A very large crowd[f] spread their cloaks on the road, and others cut branches from the trees and spread them on the road. [9]The crowds that went ahead of him and that followed were shouting,

"Hosanna to the Son of David!
　Blessed is the one who comes in the
　　name of the Lord!
　Hosanna in the highest heaven!"

[10]When he entered Jerusalem, the whole city was in turmoil, asking, "Who is this?" [11]The crowds were saying, "This is the prophet Jesus from Nazareth in Galilee."

Jesus Cleanses the Temple

12 Then Jesus entered the temple[g] and drove out all who were selling and buying in the temple, and he overturned the tables of the money changers and the seats of those who sold doves. [13]He said to them, "It is written,

'My house shall be called a house of
　prayer';

but you are making it a den of
　robbers."

14 The blind and the lame came to him in the temple, and he cured them. [15]But when the chief priests and the scribes saw the amazing things that he did, and heard[h] the children crying out in the temple, "Hosanna to the Son of David," they became angry [16]and said to him, "Do you hear what these are saying?" Jesus said to them, "Yes; have you never read,

'Out of the mouths of infants and
　nursing babies
you have prepared praise for
　yourself'?"

[17]He left them, went out of the city to Bethany, and spent the night there.

Jesus Curses the Fig Tree

18 In the morning, when he returned to the city, he was hungry. [19]And seeing a fig tree by the side of the road, he went to it and found nothing at all on it but leaves. Then he said to it, "May no fruit ever come from you again!" And the fig tree withered at once. [20]When the disciples saw it, they were amazed, saying, "How did the fig tree wither at once?" [21]Jesus answered them, "Truly I tell you, if you have faith and do not doubt, not only will you do what has been done to the fig tree, but even if you say to this mountain, 'Be lifted up and thrown into the sea,' it will be done. [22]Whatever you ask for in prayer with faith, you will receive."

The Authority of Jesus Questioned

23 When he entered the temple, the chief priests and the elders of the people came to him as he was teaching, and said, "By what authority are you doing these things, and who gave you this authority?" [24]Jesus said to them, "I will also ask you one question; if you tell me the answer, then I will also tell you by what authority I do these things. [25]Did the baptism of John come from heaven, or was it of human origin?" And they argued with one another, "If we say, 'From heaven,' he will say to us, 'Why then did you not believe him?' [26]But if we say, 'Of human origin,' we are afraid of the crowd; for all regard John as a prophet."

---

[f] Or *Most of the crowd*　[g] Other ancient authorities add *of God*　[h] Gk lacks *heard*

21:18–22:14. Matthew then reports a series of four parables, all of which are thematically connected with the question of response to Jesus and the 'new order' of the commonwealth of heaven that is coming about through him. The set begins with the 'parable-in-action' of the cursing of the fig tree (21:18–22), continues with the parables of the two sons (21:28–32) and the wicked tenants (21:33–41), and concludes with the parable of the wedding banquet (22:1–14). It is punctuated with interchanges between 'the chief priests and the elders' (21:23–27) and 'the chief priests and the Pharisees' (21:42–46), where the choice set forth in the parables (for or against *God and God's rule*) is interpreted as equivalent to a choice for or against *Jesus*.

[27]So they answered Jesus, "We do not know." And he said to them, "Neither will I tell you by what authority I am doing these things.

The Parable of the Two Sons

28 "What do you think? A man had two sons; he went to the first and said, 'Son, go and work in the vineyard today.' [29]He answered, 'I will not'; but later he changed his mind and went. [30]The father[i] went to the second and said the same; and he answered, 'I go, sir'; but he did not go. [31]Which of the two did the will of his father?" They said, "The first." Jesus said to them, "Truly I tell you, the tax collectors and the prostitutes are going into the kingdom of God ahead of you. [32]For John came to you in the way of righteousness and you did not believe him, but the tax collectors and the prostitutes believed him; and even after you saw it, you did not change your minds and believe him.

◆ In reflecting upon the parable of the two sons, Jesus tells some Jewish leaders that 'the tax collectors and the prostitutes are going into the kingdom of God ahead of you' (21:31–32). Because these two groups were among the most despised in his time, Jesus' audience would likely have found this atrocious. Tax collectors were in league with Rome, extorting money from their fellow Jews for the benefit of a regime many Jews saw as directly opposed to God. Prostitutes, for somewhat more complicated reasons, were seen as threatening Jewish faithfulness to the Law (and, therefore, to God). Neither were viewed by fellow Jews as model citizens of God's Kingdom, and Jesus' bracing remark that they would enter first could only have been heard as offensive.

Prostitution, in the biblical tradition, frequently is linked with apostasy (cf. Lev. 19:29). For example, Hosea's wife, Gomer, is compared with Israel; both are accused of 'harlotry', she for being faithless to her husband, and Israel for being faithless to Yahweh by worshipping other gods (Hos. 1:2 and *passim*). This link arose from the actual connection which existed in Canaanite religion and other fertility cults, where the most important form of worship involved what has been called 'sacred prostitution' (i.e. sexual intercourse with a priest or priestess who represented the deity). By the time of Jesus, the comparison between prostitution and idolatry is so ingrained that it need no longer be made explicit; the revulsion is the same.

Jesus proclaims that 'the tax collectors and the prostitutes' – who are judged by their neighbors as living in radical opposition to God – are the ones who first responded to God's call to repentance. Because they do repent, they will enter God's commonwealth before those who judge them; it is better to be the daughter or son who says 'no' to God, and then repents and acts in obedience, than the one who says 'yes' but does not act. Jesus does not approve of either extortion or prostitution as a profession. But Jesus takes a severe stance against those who will judge other persons, rather than recognizing that all are sinners before God (Matt. 7:1–5) ◆

The Parable of the Wicked Tenants

33 "Listen to another parable. There was a landowner who planted a vineyard, put a fence around it, dug a wine press in it, and built a watchtower. Then he leased it to tenants and went to another country. [34]When the harvest time had come, he sent his slaves to the tenants to collect his produce. [35]But the tenants seized his slaves and beat one, killed another, and stoned another. [36]Again he sent other slaves, more than the first; and they treated them in the same way. [37]Finally he sent his son to them, saying, 'They will respect my son.' [38]But when the tenants saw the son, they said to themselves, 'This is the heir; come, let us kill him and get his inheritance.' [39]So they

[i] Gk *He*

seized him, threw him out of the vineyard, and killed him. ⁴⁰Now when the owner of the vineyard comes, what will he do to those tenants?" ⁴¹They said to him, "He will put those wretches to a miserable death, and lease the vineyard to other tenants who will give him the produce at the harvest time."

42 Jesus said to them, "Have you never read in the scriptures:

'The stone that the builders rejected
    has become the cornerstone;ʲ
this was the Lord's doing,
    and it is amazing in our eyes'?

⁴³Therefore I tell you, the kingdom of God will be taken away from you and given to a people that produces the fruits of the kingdom.ᵏ ⁴⁴The one who falls on this stone will be broken to pieces; and it will crush anyone on whom it falls."ˡ

45 When the chief priests and the Pharisees heard his parables, they realized that he was speaking about them. ⁴⁶They wanted to arrest him, but they feared the crowds, because they regarded him as a prophet.

The Parable of the Wedding Banquet

22 Once more Jesus spoke to them in parables, saying: ²"The kingdom of heaven may be compared to a king who gave a wedding banquet for his son. ³He sent his slaves to call those who had been invited to the wedding banquet, but they would not come. ⁴Again he sent other slaves, saying, 'Tell those who have been invited: Look, I have prepared my dinner, my oxen and my fat calves have been slaughtered, and everything is ready; come to the wedding banquet.' ⁵But they made light of it and went away, one to his farm, another to his business, ⁶while the rest seized his slaves, mistreated them, and killed them. ⁷The king was enraged. He sent his troops, destroyed those murderers, and burned their city. ⁸Then he said to his slaves, 'The wedding is ready, but those invited were not worthy. ⁹Go therefore into the main streets, and invite everyone you find to the wedding banquet.' ¹⁰Those slaves went out into the streets and gathered all whom they found, both good and bad; so the wedding hall was filled with guests.

11 "But when the king came in to see the guests, he noticed a man there who was not wearing a wedding robe, ¹²and he said to him, 'Friend, how did you get in here without a wedding robe?' And he was speechless. ¹³Then the king said to the attendants, 'Bind him hand and foot, and throw him into the outer darkness, where there will be weeping and gnashing of teeth.' ¹⁴For many are called, but few are chosen."

The Question about Paying Taxes

15 Then the Pharisees went and plotted to entrap him in what he said. ¹⁶So they sent their disciples to him, along with the Herodians, saying, "Teacher, we know that you are sincere, and teach the way of God

---

ʲ Or keystone ᵏ Gk the fruits of it ˡ Other ancient authorities lack verse 44

22:15–23:36. Immediately following is a series of challenges to Jesus' authority, depicted in the form of question and answer. Both 'the Pharisees' and 'the Sadducees' are portrayed as Jesus' opponents in debate, first over *halakah*, i.e. interpretation of the Law (22:15–22, 23–33, 34–40), and then over interpretation of the messianic predictions in the Scriptures (22:41–46). Both groups mentioned here serve to illustrate a negative response to Jesus and his message. In contrast, the disciples are invited to make a positive response to Jesus by living lives of humility and service, free from the domination or mastery of others (23:1–12). The 'scribes and Pharisees' are accused of hypocrisy and elitism – thereby becoming the objects of seven 'woes' (23:13–36) – because they are more scrupulous for ritual laws than for the matters of social justice inherent to the Covenant.

in accordance with truth, and show deference to no one; for you do not regard people with partiality. [17]Tell us, then, what you think. Is it lawful to pay taxes to the emperor, or not?" [18]But Jesus, aware of their malice, said, "Why are you putting me to the test, you hypocrites? [19]Show me the coin used for the tax." And they brought him a denarius. [20]Then he said to them, "Whose head is this, and whose title?" [21]They answered, "The emperor's." Then he said to them, "Give therefore to the emperor the things that are the emperor's, and to God the things that are God's." [22]When they heard this, they were amazed; and they left him and went away.

The Question about the Resurrection

23 The same day some Sadducees came to him, saying there is no resurrection;[m] and they asked him a question, saying, [24]"Teacher, Moses said, 'If a man dies childless, his brother shall marry the widow, and raise up children for his brother.' [25]Now there were seven brothers among us; the first married, and died childless, leaving the widow to his brother. [26]The second did the same, so also the third, down to the seventh. [27]Last of all, the woman herself died. [28]In the resurrection, then, whose wife of the seven will she be? For all of them had married her."

29 Jesus answered them, "You are wrong, because you know neither the scriptures nor the power of God. [30]For in the resurrection they neither marry nor are given in marriage, but are like angels[n] in heaven. [31]And as for the resurrection of the dead, have you not read what was said to you by God, [32]'I am the God of Abraham, the God of Isaac, and the God of Jacob'? He is God not of the dead, but of the living." [33]And when the crowd heard it, they were astounded at his teaching.

The Greatest Commandment

34 When the Pharisees heard that he had silenced the Sadducees, they gathered together, [35]and one of them, a lawyer, asked him a question to test him. [36]"Teacher, which commandment in the law is the greatest?" [37]He said to him, " 'You shall love the Lord your God with all your heart, and with all your soul, and with all your mind.' [38]This is the greatest and first commandment. [39]And a second is like it: 'You shall love your neighbor as yourself.' [40]On these two commandments hang all the law and the prophets."

The Question about David's Son

41 Now while the Pharisees were gathered together, Jesus asked them this question: [42]"What do you think of the Messiah?[o] Whose son is he?" They said to him, "The son of David." [43]He said to them, "How is it then that David by the Spirit[p] calls him Lord, saying,

[44] 'The Lord said to my Lord,
   "Sit at my right hand,
      until I put your enemies under your
         feet" '?

[45]If David thus calls him Lord, how can he be his son?" [46]No one was able to give him an answer, nor from that day did anyone dare to ask him any more questions.

Jesus Denounces Scribes and Pharisees

23 Then Jesus said to the crowds and to his disciples, [2]"The scribes and the Pharisees sit on Moses' seat; [3]therefore, do whatever they teach you and follow it; but do not do as they do, for they do not practice what they teach. [4]They tie up heavy burdens, hard to bear,[q] and lay them on the shoulders of others; but they themselves are unwilling to lift a finger to move them. [5]They do all their deeds to be seen by others; for they make their phylacteries broad and their fringes long. [6]They love to have the place of honor at banquets and the best seats in the synagogues, [7]and to be greeted with respect in the marketplaces, and to

---

[m] Other ancient authorities read *who say that there is no resurrection*   [n] Other ancient authorities add *of God*   [o] Or *Christ*   [p] Gk *in spirit*   [q] Other ancient authorities lack *hard to bear*

have people call them rabbi. [8]But you are not to be called rabbi, for you have one teacher, and you are all students.[r] [9]And call no one your father on earth, for you have one Father – the one in heaven. [10]Nor are you to be called instructors, for you have one instructor, the Messiah.[s] [11]The greatest among you will be your servant. [12]All who exalt themselves will be humbled, and all who humble themselves will be exalted.

[13] "But woe to you, scribes and Pharisees, hypocrites! For you lock people out of the kingdom of heaven. For you do not go in yourselves, and when others are going in, you stop them.[t] [15]Woe to you, scribes and Pharisees, hypocrites! For you cross sea and land to make a single convert, and you make the new convert twice as much a child of hell[u] as yourselves.

◆ Compare the eight Beatitudes of Matt. 6 with the seven woes of Matt. 23:13–16. Some manuscripts of Matthew include an extra 'woe' after 23:12 or 13. In the RSV translation, the verse reads: 'woe to you, scribes and Pharisees, hypocrites! for you devour widows' houses and for a pretense you make long prayers; therefore you will receive the greater condemnation' (Matt. 23:14; parallels in Mark 12:40; Luke 20:47). The treatment of widows and orphans is the 'litmus test' of justice in the Hebrew Bible, for these are the people who are most marginalized in the political system, and who are financially destitute (e.g. Exod. 22:22; Deut. 10:18). This saying of Jesus adopts the prophetic critique of unjust leaders in Israel (e.g. Is. 10:1–4), applying it here to the 'scribes and Pharisees'. Obedience to God's covenant requires justice among human beings. And justice is to be measured not by the nation's care for those who have power and are comfortable, but by its care for the poor, the single mother, the unprotected child, the marginalized homeless person, the truly destitute. If 'the poor are always with [us]' (Matt. 26:11), it is not because this is God's desire; it is because we are not faithful to God's covenant of justice. ◆

[16] "Woe to you, blind guides, who say, 'Whoever swears by the sanctuary is bound by nothing, but whoever swears by the gold of the sanctuary is bound by the oath.' [17]You blind fools! For which is greater, the gold or the sanctuary that has made the gold sacred? [18]And you say, 'Whoever swears by the altar is bound by nothing, but whoever swears by the gift that is on the altar is bound by the oath.' [19]How blind you are! For which is greater, the gift or the altar that makes the gift sacred? [20]So whoever swears by the altar, swears by it and by everything on it; [21]and whoever swears by the sanctuary, swears by it and by the one who dwells in it; [22]and whoever swears by heaven, swears by the throne of God and by the one who is seated upon it.

[23] "Woe to you, scribes and Pharisees, hypocrites! For you tithe mint, dill, and cummin, and have neglected the weightier matters of the law: justice and mercy and faith. It is these you ought to have practiced without neglecting the others. [24]You blind guides! You strain out a gnat but swallow a camel!

[25] "Woe to you, scribes and Pharisees, hypocrites! For you clean the outside of the cup and of the plate, but inside they are full of greed and self-indulgence. [26]You blind Pharisee! First clean the inside of the cup,[v] so that the outside also may become clean.

[27] "Woe to you, scribes and Pharisees, hypocrites! For you are like whitewashed tombs, which on the outside look beautiful, but inside they are full of the bones of the dead and of all kinds of filth. [28]So you also on the outside look righteous to others, but inside you are full of hypocrisy and lawlessness.

[29] "Woe to you, scribes and Pharisees,

[r] Gk brothers   [s] Or the Christ   [t] Other authorities add here (or after verse 12) verse 14, Woe to you, scribes and Pharisees, hypocrites! For you devour widows' houses and for the sake of appearance you make long prayers; therefore you will receive the greater condemnation   [u] Gk Gehenna   [v] Other ancient authorities add and of the plate

hypocrites! For you build the tombs of the prophets and decorate the graves of the righteous, [30]and you say, 'If we had lived in the days of our ancestors, we would not have taken part with them in shedding the blood of the prophets.' [31]Thus you testify against yourselves that you are descendants of those who murdered the prophets. [32]Fill up, then, the measure of your ancestors. [33]You snakes, you brood of vipers! How can you escape being sentenced to hell?[w] [34]Therefore I send you prophets, sages, and scribes, some of whom you will kill and crucify, and some you will flog in your synagogues and pursue from town to town, [35]so that upon you may come all the righteous blood shed on earth, from the blood of righteous Abel to the blood of Zechariah son of Barachiah, whom you murdered between the sanctuary and the altar. [36]Truly I tell you, all this will come upon this generation.

The Lament over Jerusalem

[37] "Jerusalem, Jerusalem, the city that kills the prophets and stones those who are sent to it! How often have I desired to gather your children together as a hen gathers her brood under her wings, and you were not willing! [38]See, your house is left to you, desolate.[x] [39]For I tell you, you will not see me again until you say, 'Blessed is the one who comes in the name of the Lord.'"

The Destruction of the Temple Foretold

24 As Jesus came out of the temple and was going away, his disciples came to point out to him the buildings of the temple. [2]Then he asked them, "You see all these, do you not? Truly I tell you, not one stone will be left here upon another; all will be thrown down."

Signs of the End of the Age

[3] When he was sitting on the Mount of Olives, the disciples came to him privately, saying, "Tell us, when will this be, and what will be the sign of your coming and of the end of the age?" [4]Jesus answered them, "Beware that no one leads you astray. [5]For many will come in my name, saying, 'I am the Messiah!'[y] and they will lead many astray. [6]And you will hear of wars and rumors of wars; see that you are not alarmed; for this must take place, but the end is not yet. [7]For nation will rise against nation, and kingdom against kingdom, and there will be famines[z] and earthquakes in various places: [8]all this is but the beginning of the birth pangs.

[w] Gk *Gehenna*   [x] Other ancient authorities lack *desolate*   [y] Or *the Christ*   [z] Other ancient authorities add *and pestilences*

23:37–39. Jesus himself then portrays the model of what is expected of the disciples, using a surprisingly feminine metaphor. Publicly mourning over Jerusalem (traditionally the role of women), Jesus longs to 'gather [her] children' as a mother hen gathers and protects her brood. Though indeed he comes 'in the name of the Lord', Jesus does not command or domineer; he neither chastises nor returns blows. Like Lady Wisdom (Prov. 1:20–33), Jesus calls, cajoles, and warns all those who will hear – and mourns those who will not. (Cf. Rachel in Matt. 2:18.)

24:1–25:30. Jesus' warnings in these two chapters are not only for those who refuse to hear, but also – even primarily – for those who have begun to be disciples (cf. 24:24), to ensure that they continue on their chosen path. The few additions Matthew has made to Mark's version of the eschatological warnings (in Mark 13) fall into a pattern; they reflect a delay in the expected time of the *parousia* (e.g. Matt. 24:14), and the idea that false prophets will test the commitment of 'the elect', leading many astray and causing the love of many to 'grow cold' (24:11–12). That the audience will not succumb to such a temptation, Matthew follows Jesus' warnings with a set of his parables depicting the suddenness of the *parousia* and the choice that each person must make to be ready for that Day (24:36–44, 45–51; 25:1–13, 14–30).

Persecutions Foretold

9 "Then they will hand you over to be tortured and will put you to death, and you will be hated by all nations because of my name. [10]Then many will fall away,[a] and they will betray one another and hate one another. [11]And many false prophets will arise and lead many astray. [12]And because of the increase of lawlessness, the love of many will grow cold. [13]But the one who endures to the end will be saved. [14]And this good news[b] of the kingdom will be proclaimed throughout the world, as a testimony to all the nations; and then the end will come.

The Desolating Sacrilege

15 "So when you see the desolating sacrilege standing in the holy place, as was spoken of by the prophet Daniel (let the reader understand), [16]then those in Judea must flee to the mountains; [17]the one on the housetop must not go down to take what is in the house; [18]the one in the field must not turn back to get a coat. [19]Woe to those who are pregnant and to those who are nursing infants in those days! [20]Pray that your flight may not be in winter or on a sabbath. [21]For at that time there will be great suffering, such as has not been from the beginning of the world until now, no,

and never will be. [22]And if those days had not been cut short, no one would be saved; but for the sake of the elect those days will be cut short. [23]Then if anyone says to you, 'Look! Here is the Messiah!'[c] or 'There he is!' – do not believe it. [24]For false messiahs[d] and false prophets will appear and produce great signs and omens, to lead astray, if possible, even the elect. [25]Take note, I have told you beforehand. [26]So, if they say to you, 'Look! He is in the wilderness,' do not go out. If they say, 'Look! He is in the inner rooms,' do not believe it. [27]For as the lightning comes from the east and flashes as far as the west, so will be the coming of the Son of Man. [28]Wherever the corpse is, there the vultures will gather.

The Coming of the Son of Man

29 "Immediately after the suffering of those days
　the sun will be darkened,
　　and the moon will not give its light;
　the stars will fall from heaven,
　　and the powers of heaven will be
　　　shaken.
[30]Then the sign of the Son of Man will appear in heaven, and then all the tribes of

[a] Or *stumble*　[b] Or *gospel*　[c] Or *the Christ*
[d] Or *christs*

As elsewhere, Matthew parallels images of men and women responding to this challenge. The judgment comes upon both women and men – e.g. two men in the field, two women grinding meal (24:40–41) – and both must be ready. The parable of the faithful slave (24:45–51) is paired with the one about the ten maids (25:1–13). Whereas the former is also told by Luke (Luke 12:42–46), the latter is unique to Matthew. Thus, it is distinctive that Matthew chooses to use five young women as examples of faithful anticipation of the coming of the Lord. While five of the virgins are not prepared for the coming of the bridegroom, the other five are; and it is these last who provide the light *for the entire wedding party* (cf. Matt. 5:16). I find it puzzling that commentators, both in texts and in the pulpit, so frequently focus on the five maids who are *not* prepared, rather than the five who *are*.

These unmarried women each are responsible directly to their Lord (just as are the male slaves in the previous parable). Their decisions and their own preparatory actions (or lack thereof) have a direct impact not only on their own destiny, but on the 'light' (salvation) of the entire wedding party. These young women provide the advance welcome to the bridegroom, and make the party possible because of the light they bear. This parable provides a powerful challenge to us as women when we want to sit back, denying the God-given leadership and responsibility that are our own.

the earth will mourn, and they will see 'the Son of Man coming on the clouds of heaven' with power and great glory. [31]And he will send out his angels with a loud trumpet call, and they will gather his elect from the four winds, from one end of heaven to the other.

The Lesson of the Fig Tree

32 "From the fig tree learn its lesson: as soon as its branch becomes tender and puts forth its leaves, you know that summer is near. [33]So also, when you see all these things, you know that he[e] is near, at the very gates. [34]Truly I tell you, this generation will not pass away until all these things have taken place. [35]Heaven and earth will pass away, but my words will not pass away.

The Necessity for Watchfulness

36 "But about that day and hour no one knows, neither the angels of heaven, nor the Son,[f] but only the Father. [37]For as the days of Noah were, so will be the coming of the Son of Man. [38]For as in those days before the flood they were eating and drinking, marrying and giving in marriage, until the day Noah entered the ark, [39]and they knew nothing until the flood came and swept them all away, so too will be the coming of the Son of Man. [40]Then two will be in the field; one will be taken and one will be left. [41]Two women will be grinding meal together; one will be taken and one will be left. [42]Keep awake therefore, for you do not know on what day[g] your Lord is coming. [43]But understand this: if the owner of the house had known in what part of the night the thief was coming, he would have stayed awake and would not have let his house be broken into. [44]Therefore you also must be ready, for the Son of Man is coming at an unexpected hour.

The Faithful or the Unfaithful Slave

45 "Who then is the faithful and wise slave, whom his master has put in charge of his household, to give the other slaves[h] their allowance of food at the proper time? [46]Blessed is that slave whom his master will find at work when he arrives. [47]Truly I tell you, he will put that one in charge of all his possessions. [48]But if that wicked slave says to himself, 'My master is delayed,' [49]and he begins to beat his fellow slaves, and eats and drinks with drunkards, [50]the master of that slave will come on a day when he does not expect him and at an hour that he does not know. [51]He will cut him in pieces[i] and put him with the hypocrites, where there will be weeping and gnashing of teeth.

The Parable of the Ten Bridesmaids

25 "Then the kingdom of heaven will be like this. Ten bridesmaids[j] took their lamps and went to meet the bridegroom.[k] [2]Five of them were foolish, and five were wise. [3]When the foolish took their lamps, they took no oil with them; [4]but the wise took flasks of oil with their lamps. [5]As the bridegroom was delayed, all of them became drowsy and slept. [6]But at midnight there was a shout, 'Look! Here is the bridegroom! Come out to meet him.' [7]Then all those bridesmaids[j] got up and trimmed their lamps. [8]The foolish said to the wise, 'Give us some of your oil, for our lamps are going out.' [9]But the wise replied, 'No! there will not be enough for you and for us; you had better go to the dealers and buy some for yourselves.' [10]And while they went to buy it, the bridegroom came, and those who were ready went with him into the wedding banquet; and the door was shut. [11]Later the other bridesmaids[j] came also, saying, 'Lord, lord, open to us.' [12]But he replied, 'Truly I tell you, I do not know you.' [13]Keep awake therefore, for you know neither the day nor the hour.[l]

[e] Or *it*   [f] Other ancient authorities lack *nor the Son*   [g] Other ancient authorities read *at what hour*
[h] Gk *to give them*   [i] Or *cut him off*   [j] Gk *virgins*
[k] Other ancient authorities add *and the bride*
[l] Other ancient authorities add *in which the Son of Man is coming*

The Parable of the Talents

14 "For it is as if a man, going on a journey, summoned his slaves and entrusted his property to them; ¹⁵to one he gave five talents,ᵐ to another two, to another one, to each according to his ability. Then he went away. ¹⁶The one who had received the five talents went off at once and traded with them, and made five more talents. ¹⁷In the same way, the one who had the two talents made two more talents. ¹⁸But the one who had received the one talent went off and dug a hole in the ground and hid his master's money. ¹⁹After a long time the master of those slaves came and settled accounts with them. ²⁰Then the one who had received the five talents came forward, bringing five more talents, saying, 'Master, you handed over to me five talents; see, I have made five more talents.' ²¹His master said to him, 'Well done, good and trustworthy slave; you have been trustworthy in a few things, I will put you in charge of many things; enter into the joy of your master.' ²²And the one with the two talents also came forward, saying, 'Master, you handed over to me two talents; see, I have made two more talents.' ²³His master said to him, 'Well done, good and trustworthy slave; you have been trustworthy in a few things, I will put you in charge of many things; enter into the joy of your master.' ²⁴Then the one who had received the one talent also came forward, saying, 'Master, I knew that you were a harsh man, reaping where you did not sow, and gathering where you did not scatter seed; ²⁵so I was afraid, and I went and hid your talent in the ground. Here you have what is yours.' ²⁶But his master replied, 'You wicked and lazy slave! You knew, did you, that I reap where I did not sow, and gather where I did not scatter? ²⁷Then you ought to have invested my money with the bankers, and on my return I would have received what was my own with interest. ²⁸So take the talent from him, and give it to the one with the ten talents. ²⁹For to all those who have, more will be given, and they will have an abundance; but from those who have nothing, even what they have will be taken away. ³⁰As for this worthless slave, throw him into the outer darkness, where there will be weeping and gnashing of teeth.'

The Judgment of the Nations

31 "When the Son of Man comes in his glory, and all the angels with him, then he will sit on the throne of his glory. ³²All the nations will be gathered before him, and he will separate people one from another as a shepherd separates the sheep from the goats, ³³and he will put the sheep at his right hand and the goats at the left. ³⁴Then the king will say to those at his right hand, 'Come, you that are blessed by my Father, inherit the kingdom prepared for you from the foundation of the world; ³⁵for I was hungry and you gave me food, I was thirsty and you gave me something to drink, I was a stranger and you welcomed me, ³⁶I was naked and you gave me clothing, I was sick and you took care of me, I was in prison and you visited me.' ³⁷Then the righteous will answer him, 'Lord, when was it that we saw you hungry and gave you food, or thirsty and gave you something to drink? ³⁸And when was it that we saw you a

---

ᵐ A talent was worth more than fifteen years' wages of a laborer

---

25:31–46. The image of the final judgment provides the final exclamation point to Matthew's discourse about the end times, confirming that the Lord will render judgment to each based upon her or his response to those who are most marginalized. True discipleship is equated, once again, with service to those in need. And it is of more than passing interest that the deeds which provide the basis for divine judgment are precisely tasks which traditionally have been viewed as 'women's work' (providing food, drink, clothing, comfort, and personal connection).

stranger and welcomed you, or naked and gave you clothing? ³⁹And when was it that we saw you sick or in prison and visited you?' ⁴⁰And the king will answer them, 'Truly I tell you, just as you did it to one of the least of these who are members of my family,ⁿ you did it to me.' ⁴¹Then he will say to those at his left hand, 'You that are accursed, depart from me into the eternal fire prepared for the devil and his angels; ⁴²for I was hungry and you gave me no food, I was thirsty and you gave me nothing to drink, ⁴³I was a stranger and you did not welcome me, naked and you did not give me clothing, sick and in prison and you did not visit me.' ⁴⁴Then they also will answer, 'Lord, when was it that we saw you hungry or thirsty or a stranger or naked or sick or in prison, and did not take care of you?' ⁴⁵Then he will answer them, 'Truly I tell you, just as you did not do it to one of the least of these, you did not do it to me.' ⁴⁶And these will go away into eternal punishment, but the righteous into eternal life."

The Plot to Kill Jesus

26 When Jesus had finished saying all these things, he said to his disciples, ²"You know that after two days the Passover is coming, and the Son of Man will be handed over to be crucified."

³Then the chief priests and the elders of the people gathered in the palace of the high priest, who was called Caiaphas, ⁴and they conspired to arrest Jesus by stealth and kill him. ⁵But they said, "Not during the festival, or there may be a riot among the people."

The Anointing at Bethany

⁶Now while Jesus was at Bethany in the house of Simon the leper,° ⁷a woman came to him with an alabaster jar of very costly ointment, and she poured it on his head as he sat at the table. ⁸But when the disciples saw it, they were angry and said, "Why this waste? ⁹For this ointment could have been sold for a large sum, and the money given to the poor." ¹⁰But Jesus, aware of this, said to them, "Why do you trouble the woman? She has performed a good service for me. ¹¹For you always have the poor with you, but you will not always have me. ¹²By pouring this ointment on my body she has prepared me for burial. ¹³Truly I tell you, wherever this good newsᵖ is proclaimed in the whole world, what she has done will be told in remembrance of her."

ⁿ Gk *these my brothers* ° The terms *leper* and *leprosy* can refer to several diseases ᵖ Or *gospel*

THE PASSION AND RESURRECTION (MATT. 26:2–28:20)

Jesus' prediction of the passion and the report of the plot against him (26:1–5) provide the literary transition between the final judgment scene and the final section of Matthew's Gospel, the passion-resurrection account. Several episodes with women in key roles punctuate these last three chapters (26:6–13, 69–75; 27:15–23, 45–56, 57–61; 28:1–10). In these scenes, the author applies and further illustrates the message of the responsible discipleship of women.

26:6–13. The first of these episodes is the story of the anointing of Jesus. Matthew follows Mark's account verbatim, except for the one significant change of identifying the protesters as 'the disciples' (v. 8; cf. Mark 14:3–9). Through her prophetic action of anointing Jesus, the woman proclaims him the Messiah-King of Israel. 'Messiah' means 'anointed one', and Samuel had anointed Saul (1 Sam. 10:1) and David (1 Sam. 16:1–13) as king and 'messiah' (1 Sam. 16:6).

The disciples' reproach of the woman centers on the charge that she was wasteful – 'this ointment could have been sold for a large sum, and the money given to the poor' (v. 9). Matthew omits Mark's detail that it was worth 'more than three hundred denarii', that is, 300 days' wages. For purposes of comparison, if one assumes a minimum wage of $5.00 an hour, the value in current funds would be over $12,000 US.

Judas Agrees to Betray Jesus

14 Then one of the twelve, who was called Judas Iscariot, went to the chief priests [15]and said, "What will you give me if I betray him to you?" They paid him thirty pieces of silver. [16]And from that moment he began to look for an opportunity to betray him.

The Passover with the Disciples

17 On the first day of Unleavened Bread the disciples came to Jesus, saying, "Where do you want us to make the preparations for you to eat the Passover?" [18]He said, "Go into the city to a certain man, and say to him, 'The Teacher says, My time is near; I will keep the Passover at your house with my disciples.'" [19]So the disciples did as Jesus had directed them, and they prepared the Passover meal.

20 When it was evening, he took his place with the twelve;[q] [21]and while they were eating, he said, "Truly I tell you, one of you will betray me." [22]And they became greatly distressed and began to say to him one after another, "Surely not I, Lord?" [23]He answered, "The one who has dipped his hand into the bowl with me will betray me. [24]The Son of Man goes as it is written of him, but woe to that one by whom the Son of Man is betrayed! It would have been better for that one not to have been born." [25]Judas, who betrayed him, said, "Surely not I, Rabbi?" He replied, "You have said so."

The Institution of the Lord's Supper

26 While they were eating, Jesus took a loaf of bread, and after blessing it he broke it, gave it to the disciples, and said, "Take, eat; this is my body." [27]Then he took a cup, and after giving thanks he gave it to them, saying, "Drink from it, all of you; [28]for this is my blood of the[r] covenant, which is poured out for many for the forgiveness of sins. [29]I tell you, I will never again drink of this fruit of the vine until that day when I drink it new with you in my Father's kingdom."

30 When they had sung the hymn, they went out to the Mount of Olives.

Peter's Denial Foretold

31 Then Jesus said to them, "You will all become deserters because of me this night; for it is written,

'I will strike the shepherd,
and the sheep of the flock will be scattered.'

[32]But after I am raised up, I will go ahead of you to Galilee." [33]Peter said to him, "Though all become deserters because of you, I will never desert you." [34]Jesus said to him, "Truly I tell you, this very night, before the cock crows, you will deny me three times." [35]Peter said to him, "Even though I must die with you, I will not deny you." And so said all the disciples.

Jesus Prays in Gethsemane

36 Then Jesus went with them to a place called Gethsemane; and he said to his disciples, "Sit here while I go over there and pray." [37]He took with him Peter and the two sons of Zebedee, and began to be grieved and agitated. [38]Then he said to them, "I am

[q] Other ancient authorities add *disciples*   [r] Other ancient authorities add *new*

Yet, after centuries of waiting, would not the Messiah be worth such a price? She would be 'wasting' the ointment only if her prophetic action were false – either because a woman by definition can have no prophetic authority, or because she is mistaken about Jesus' identity. She and 'the disciples' cannot both be right.

Matthew follows Mark in reporting Jesus' defense of the woman, interpreting her action as both prophetic and caring (vv. 10, 12). The unnamed woman is the first and only one so far who recognizes Jesus as the Messiah-King who will reign because of his suffering and death. Judas' betrayal, which immediately follows this story, provides a sharp contrast with the faithfulness of this prophetess.

deeply grieved, even to death; remain here, and stay awake with me." [39]And going a little farther, he threw himself on the ground and prayed, "My Father, if it is possible, let this cup pass from me; yet not what I want but what you want." [40]Then he came to the disciples and found them sleeping; and he said to Peter, "So, could you not stay awake with me one hour? [41]Stay awake and pray that you may not come into the time of trial;[s] the spirit indeed is willing, but the flesh is weak." [42]Again he went away for the second time and prayed, "My Father, if this cannot pass unless I drink it, your will be done." [43]Again he came and found them sleeping, for their eyes were heavy. [44]So leaving them again, he went away and prayed for the third time, saying the same words. [45]Then he came to the disciples and said to them, "Are you still sleeping and taking your rest? See, the hour is at hand, and the Son of Man is betrayed into the hands of sinners. [46]Get up, let us be going. See, my betrayer is at hand."

The Betrayal and Arrest of Jesus

47 While he was still speaking, Judas, one of the twelve, arrived; with him was a large crowd with swords and clubs, from the chief priests and the elders of the people. [48]Now the betrayer had given them a sign, saying, "The one I will kiss is the man; arrest him." [49]At once he came up to Jesus and said, "Greetings, Rabbi!" and kissed him. [50]Jesus said to him, "Friend, do what you are here to do." Then they came and laid hands on Jesus and arrested him. [51]Suddenly, one of those with Jesus put his hand on his sword, drew it, and struck the slave of the high priest, cutting off his ear. [52]Then Jesus said to him, "Put your sword back into its place; for all who take the sword will perish by the sword. Do you think that I cannot appeal to my Father, and he will at once send me more than twelve legions of angels? [54]But how then would the scriptures be fulfilled, which say it must happen in this way?" [55]At that hour Jesus said to the crowds, "Have you come

out with swords and clubs to arrest me as though I were a bandit? Day after day I sat in the temple teaching, and you did not arrest me. [56]But all this has taken place, so that the scriptures of the prophets may be fulfilled." Then all the disciples deserted him and fled.

Jesus before the High Priest

57 Those who had arrested Jesus took him to Caiaphas the high priest, in whose house the scribes and the elders had gathered. [58]But Peter was following him at a distance, as far as the courtyard of the high priest; and going inside, he sat with the guards in order to see how this would end. [59]Now the chief priests and the whole council were looking for false testimony against Jesus so that they might put him to death, [60]but they found none, though many false witnesses came forward. At last two came forward [61]and said, "This fellow said, 'I am able to destroy the temple of God and to build it in three days.' " [62]The high priest stood up and said, "Have you no answer? What is it that they testify against you?" [63]But Jesus was silent. Then the high priest said to him, "I put you under oath before the living God, tell us if you are the Messiah,[t] the Son of God." [64]Jesus said to him, "You have said so. But I tell you,

> From now on you will see the Son of
>   Man
>   seated at the right hand of Power
>   and coming on the clouds of
>   heaven."

[65]Then the high priest tore his clothes and said, "He has blasphemed! Why do we still need witnesses? You have now heard his blasphemy. [66]What is your verdict?" They answered, "He deserves death." [67]Then they spat in his face and struck him; and some slapped him, [68]saying, "Prophesy to us, you Messiah![t] Who is it that struck you?"

---

[s] Or *into temptation*   [t] Or *Christ*

Peter's Denial of Jesus

69 Now Peter was sitting outside in the courtyard. A servant-girl came to him and said, "You also were with Jesus the Galilean." [70]But he denied it before all of them, saying, "I do not know what you are talking about." [71]When he went out to the porch, another servant-girl saw him, and she said to the bystanders, "This man was with Jesus of Nazareth."[u] [72]Again he denied it with an oath, "I do not know the man." [73]After a little while the bystanders came up and said to Peter, "Certainly you are also one of them, for your accent betrays you." [74]Then he began to curse, and he swore an oath, "I do not know the man!" At that moment the cock crowed. [75]Then Peter remembered what Jesus had said: "Before the cock crows, you will deny me three times." And he went out and wept bitterly.

Jesus Brought before Pilate

27 When morning came, all the chief priests and the elders of the people conferred together against Jesus in order to bring about his death. [2]They bound him, led him away, and handed him over to Pilate the governor.

The Suicide of Judas

3 When Judas, his betrayer, saw that Jesus[v] was condemned, he repented and brought back the thirty pieces of silver to the chief priests and the elders. [4]He said, "I have sinned by betraying innocent[w] blood." But they said, "What is that to us? See to it yourself." [5]Throwing down the pieces of silver in the temple, he departed; and he went and hanged himself. [6]But the chief priests, taking the pieces of silver, said, "It is not lawful to put them into the treasury, since they are blood money." [7]After conferring together, they used them to buy the potter's field as a place to bury foreigners. [8]For this reason that field has been called the Field of Blood to this day. [9]Then was fulfilled what had been spoken through the prophet Jeremiah,[x] "And they took[y] the thirty pieces of silver, the price of the one on whom a price had been set,[z] on whom some of the people of Israel had set a price, [10]and they gave[a] them for the potter's field, as the Lord commanded me."

Pilate Questions Jesus

11 Now Jesus stood before the governor; and the governor asked him, "Are you the King of the Jews?" Jesus said, "You say so." [12]But when he was accused by the chief priests and elders, he did not answer. [13]Then Pilate said to him, "Do you not hear how many accusations they make against you?" [14]But he gave him no answer, not even to a single charge, so that the governor was greatly amazed.

Barabbas or Jesus?

15 Now at the festival the governor was accustomed to release a prisoner for the crowd, anyone whom they wanted. [16]At that time they had a notorious prisoner, called Jesus[b] Barabbas. [17]So after they had gathered, Pilate said to them, "Whom do you want me to release for you,

[u] Gk *the Nazorean*   [v] Gk *he*   [w] Other ancient authorities read *righteous*   [x] Other ancient authorities read *Zechariah* or *Isaiah*   [y] Or *I took*   [z] Or *the price of the precious One*   [a] Other ancient authorities read *I gave*   [b] Other ancient authorities lack *Jesus*

26:69–75. The second episode in which women figure is the account of Peter's threefold denial of Jesus. Two servant-girls see Peter in the courtyard, during Jesus' hearing before the high priest. The women know Jesus well enough to recognize his disciple. They speak to Peter and to the bystanders: 'You also were with Jesus the Galilean' (v. 69); 'This man was with Jesus of Nazareth' (v. 71). The women offer Peter his chance to show his faithfulness, to proclaim that he indeed is a disciple of Jesus. But the disciple 'do[es] not know' Jesus; he turns faithless, and denies Jesus instead.

27:15–61. In the next three scenes where women figure, they are less central characters, but their behavior is unusual enough that they are mentioned explicitly, and sometimes even

Jesus[c] Barabbas or Jesus who is called the Messiah?"[d] [18]For he realized that it was out of jealousy that they had handed him over. [19]While he was sitting on the judgment seat, his wife sent word to him, "Have nothing to do with that innocent man, for today I have suffered a great deal because of a dream about him." [20]Now the chief priests and the elders persuaded the crowds to ask for Barabbas and to have Jesus killed. [21]The governor again said to them, "Which of the two do you want me to release for you?" And they said, "Barabbas." [22]Pilate said to them, "Then what should I do with Jesus who is called the Messiah?"[d] All of them said, "Let him be crucified!" [23]Then he asked, "Why, what evil has he done?" But they shouted all the more, "Let him be crucified!"

Pilate Hands Jesus over to Be Crucified

24 So when Pilate saw that he could do nothing, but rather that a riot was beginning, he took some water and washed his hands before the crowd, saying, "I am innocent of this man's blood;[e] see to it yourselves." [25]Then the people as a whole answered, "His blood be on us and on our children!" [26]So he released Barabbas for them; and after flogging Jesus, he handed him over to be crucified.

The Soldiers Mock Jesus

27 Then the soldiers of the governor took Jesus into the governor's headquarters,[f] and they gathered the whole cohort around him. [28]They stripped him and put a scarlet robe on him, [29]and after twisting some thorns into a crown, they put it on his head. They put a reed in his right hand and knelt before him and mocked him, saying, "Hail, King of the Jews!" [30]They spat on him, and took the reed and struck him on the head. [31]After mocking him, they stripped him of the robe and put his own clothes on him. Then they led him away to crucify him.

The Crucifixion of Jesus

32 As they went out, they came upon a man from Cyrene named Simon; they compelled this man to carry his cross.

[c] Other ancient authorities lack *Jesus*   [d] Or *the Christ*   [e] Other ancient authorities read *this righteous blood,* or *this righteous man's blood*   [f] Gk *the praetorium*

---

named. We probably can assume 'the crowd' (e.g. 27:15) included some women, although they are not mentioned explicitly.

In the first of these scenes (27:15–23), Pilate's wife intercedes for Jesus with her husband, claiming Jesus' innocence on the basis of a dream. (This detail is mentioned only in Matthew.) In the infancy narrative (Matt. 1–2), we found that dreams are means of divine revelation. No doubt we are also to assess this message as divine revelation. So, the wife of Pilate recognizes God's Word concerning Jesus, and 'sends' it to her husband.(The verb here is *apesteilen,* a form of *apostello,* from which we get the noun, 'apostle'.) Whether or not he obeys this divine message is left open to debate (27:24).

The crucifixion and burial scenes (27:45–56, 57–61) also include vignettes of women (vv. 55–56, 61). In both cases, the women are mentioned only at the end of the scene, after the men's actions have been described.

The women were 'looking on' at the crucifixion, after having 'followed Jesus from Galilee' and having provided for him (v. 55); and they 'remained sitting' opposite the tomb (v. 61). The term for their 'watching' is *theorousai,* from *theoreo.* The term implies true perception, rather than simply looking. In John (14:17, 19b; 17:24), we find this verb used to express 'the spiritual perception of the one sent by God, which is possible only to the believer' (Bauer, Arndt, Gingrich, and Danker, eds., *A Greek-English Lexicon of the New Testament and Other Early Christian Literature,* 2nd edn. [Chicago and London: University of Chicago Press, 1957, 1979] p. 360). The author could have used *orao* to report the women's 'seeing', and yet chose *theoreo* instead. This suggests a meaning akin to John's.

³³And when they came to a place called Golgotha (which means Place of a Skull), ³⁴they offered him wine to drink, mixed with gall; but when he tasted it, he would not drink it. ³⁵And when they had crucified him, they divided his clothes among themselves by casting lots;^g ³⁶then they sat down there and kept watch over him. ³⁷Over his head they put the charge against him, which read, "This is Jesus, the King of the Jews."

38 Then two bandits were crucified with him, one on his right and one on his left. ³⁹Those who passed by derided^h him, shaking their heads ⁴⁰and saying, "You who would destroy the temple and build it in three days, save yourself! If you are the Son of God, come down from the cross." ⁴¹In the same way the chief priests also, along with the scribes and elders, were mocking him, saying, ⁴²"He saved others; he cannot save himself.ⁱ He is the King of Israel; let him come down from the cross now, and we will believe in him. ⁴³He trusts in God; let God deliver him now, if he wants to; for he said, 'I am God's Son.'" ⁴⁴The bandits who were crucified with him also taunted him in the same way.

The Death of Jesus

45 From noon on, darkness came over the whole land^j until three in the afternoon. ⁴⁶And about three o'clock Jesus cried with a loud voice, "Eli, Eli, lema sabachthani?" that is, "My God, my God, why have you forsaken me?" ⁴⁷When some of the bystanders heard it, they said, "This man is calling for Elijah." ⁴⁸At once one of them ran and got a sponge, filled it with sour wine, put it on a stick, and gave it to him to drink. ⁴⁹But the others said, "Wait, let us see whether Elijah will come to save him."^k ⁵⁰Then Jesus cried again with a loud voice and breathed his last.^l ⁵¹At that moment the curtain of the temple was torn in two, from top to bottom. The earth shook, and the rocks were split. ⁵²The tombs also were opened, and many bodies

---

^g Other ancient authorities add *in order that what had been spoken through the prophet might be fulfilled, "They divided my clothes among themselves, and for my clothing they cast lots."* ^h Or *blasphemed* ⁱ Or *is he unable to save himself?* ^j Or *earth* ^k Other ancient authorities add *And another took a spear and pierced his side, and out came water and blood* ^l Or *gave up his spirit*

We now discover that these faithful women – who, like the children, were 'not count[ed]' – indeed have followed Jesus from the beginning of his ministry in Galilee. They have been true disciples, for they 'ministered' to him, offering service in the way all disciples are called to do. The verb is *diakonousai*, from *diakoneo*, meaning 'to minister' or 'to serve'. The English term 'deacon' derives from the noun form, *diakonos*. Now these 'many women' have perceived, at Jesus' crucifixion, God's truth about him. As Peter was singled out to represent the male disciples who fled, three female disciples are singled out to represent the faithful group: Mary Magdalene, Mary 'the mother of James and Joseph', and 'the [unnamed] mother of the sons of Zebedee' (v. 56). There is a poignant irony in the mention of these sons' names, since they are the ones *named* as disciples throughout the Gospel, yet now the sons are nowhere to be found. These women, faithful all along, come to the fore only now that the men have left the stage. This is particularly true of 'the mother of the sons of Zebedee'. She was last seen kneeling before Jesus and asking him for glory for her sons, both of whom vowed they would follow Jesus to the end (20:20–23). Now they have fled. 'The mother' made no vow, yet she is present.

At the burial, another unknown disciple – this time a man, Joseph of Arimathea – rises to the occasion. The scene depicts Joseph as a law-abiding Jew, who risks the wrath of the Roman authorities to ensure Jesus a proper burial. The action also demonstrates Joseph's faith for, if Jesus truly had been guilty of blasphemy, those who do not shun him risk the wrath of God. Sealing the tomb with a great stone, Joseph retires.

of the saints who had fallen asleep were raised. [53]After his resurrection they came out of the tombs and entered the holy city and appeared to many. [54]Now when the centurion and those with him, who were keeping watch over Jesus, saw the earthquake and what took place, they were terrified and said, "Truly this man was God's Son!"[m]

55 Many women were also there, looking on from a distance; they had followed Jesus from Galilee and had provided for him. [56]Among them were Mary Magdalene, and Mary the mother of James and Joseph, and the mother of the sons of Zebedee.

The Burial of Jesus

57 When it was evening, there came a rich man from Arimathea, named Joseph, who was also a disciple of Jesus. [58]He went to Pilate and asked for the body of Jesus; then Pilate ordered it to be given to him. [59]So Joseph took the body and wrapped it in a clean linen cloth [60]and laid it in his own new tomb, which he had hewn in the rock. He then rolled a great stone to the door of the tomb and went away. [61]Mary Magdalene and the other Mary were there, sitting opposite the tomb.

The Guard at the Tomb

62 The next day, that is, after the day of Preparation, the chief priests and the Pharisees gathered before Pilate [63]and said, "Sir, we remember what that impostor said while he was still alive, 'After three days I will rise again.' [64]Therefore command the tomb to be made secure until the third day; otherwise his disciples may go and steal him away, and tell the people, 'He has been raised from the dead,' and the last deception would be worse than the first." [65]Pilate said to them, "You have a guard[n] of soldiers; go, make it as secure as you can."[o] [66]So they went with the guard and made the tomb secure by sealing the stone.

The Resurrection of Jesus

28 After the sabbath, as the first day of the week was dawning, Mary Magdalene and the other Mary went to see the tomb. [2]And suddenly there was a great earthquake; for an angel of the Lord, descending from heaven, came and rolled back the stone and sat on it. [3]His appearance was like lightning, and his clothing white as snow. [4]For fear of him the guards

[m] Or *a son of God*   [n] Or *Take a guard*   [o] Gk *you know how*

Only then do we find 'Mary Magdalene and the other Mary', yet they had been there all along, 'sitting opposite the tomb' and watching Joseph's service to Jesus (v. 61). A second time, the author catches us forgetting them because the narrator omits to mention them. These two women contrast with another pair of disciples, James and John. Unlike 'the sons of Zebedee', who desired to sit in Jesus' glory (20:20–23), the women know the disciple's place is 'sitting opposite the tomb'. Faithful to the end, they keep vigil and share in Jesus' humiliation.

27:62–28:10. Others are there keeping watch, too. A guard of soldiers is sent to ensure that Jesus remains in the tomb (27:62–66). But they are impotent in the face of God's power, which the faithful women are there to witness (28:1–10). In their fear of the divine messenger, the guards become like zombies, incoherent and trembling. By contrast, the women receive the angel's message with 'fear and great joy' (28:8). Seeking Jesus with their whole hearts (28:5), they had been satisfied to remain with him in his humiliation. But God is gracious, and neither Jesus nor the women are left humiliated. All are rewarded by entering into glory, Jesus by being raised from death (28:7), and the women by entering into the presence of Jesus himself (28:9).

The reward is not for the women alone. Discipleship does not permit possessiveness, even of good news and great joy. The angelic message that Jesus has conquered death is joined with the divine command: 'go' and 'tell' the other disciples (28:7).

shook and became like dead men. [5]But the angel said to the women, "Do not be afraid; I know that you are looking for Jesus who was crucified. [6]He is not here; for he has been raised, as he said. Come, see the place where he[p] lay. [7]Then go quickly and tell his disciples, 'He has been raised from the dead,[q] and indeed he is going ahead of you to Galilee; there you will see him.' This is my message for you." [8]So they left the tomb quickly with fear and great joy, and ran to tell his disciples. [9]Suddenly Jesus met them and said, "Greetings!" And they came to him, took hold of his feet, and worshiped him. [10]Then Jesus said to them, "Do not be afraid; go and tell my brothers to go to Galilee; there they will see me."

◆ Frequently commentators exclude the women from the references to 'the disciples' in Matt. 27:7. But the author has caught us making this assumption twice before, in the two immediately preceding scenes where women figure (27:45–56; 57–61). Only at the end of the scenes do we find out our mistake.

Since we now know that there have been unmentioned Galilean women disciples *all along* (27:55), I would argue that we should read this reference as including them – perhaps even primarily them. If this is the case, then Jesus' command to the women is not simply a repetition of the angelic message. Having obeyed the first divine command, which they received from the angel, the women are now given a second command to tell Jesus' 'brothers' – that is, specifically, the Eleven. This would further imply that the Eleven were not present with the other 'disciples' (v. 7), but were still scattered after they had fled before Jesus crucifixion. This allows a perfect transition to the commissioning scene (28:16–20), which begins with the Eleven, and which proves that the women were obedient to this second command as well ◆

The Report of the Guard

11 While they were going, some of the guard went into the city and told the chief priests everything that had happened. [12]After the priests[r] had assembled with the elders, they devised a plan to give a large sum of money to the soldiers, [13]telling them, "You must say, 'His disciples came by night and stole him away while we were asleep.' [14]If this comes to the governor's ears, we will satisfy him and keep you out of trouble." [15]So they took the money and did as they were directed. And this story is still told among the Jews to this day.

The Commissioning of the Disciples

16 Now the eleven disciples went to Galilee, to the mountain to which Jesus had directed them. [17]When they saw him, they worshiped him; but some doubted. [18]And Jesus came and said to them, "All authority in heaven and on earth has been given to me. [19]Go therefore and make

[p] Other ancient authorities read *the Lord* [q] Other ancient authorities lack *from the dead* [r] Gk *they*

Joyfully the women run to obey, and they find themselves running from glory to glory: they meet Jesus himself and worship at his feet. The command of the apostleship is repeated; now Jesus directly commissions the women to 'go and tell my brothers' (28:10). Women are validated as apostles to men, out of Jesus' own mouth.

28:16–20. Much has been made of the absence of women in the final scene of Matthew's Gospel, 'the Great Commission'. This is easy to do when the episode is taken out of its context. To read it in context, three points must be kept in mind. First, the eleven would not have been present to be commissioned by Jesus had not *the apostolic women* brought to them the twofold message of Jesus' resurrection and his coming to Galilee. Second, the reaction of the eleven to Jesus' appearance there is not univocal: 'they worshiped him; but some doubted' (v. 17). In contrast, there was

disciples of all nations, baptizing them in the name of the Father and of the Son and of the Holy Spirit, ²⁰and teaching them to obey everything that I have commanded you. And remember, I am with you always, to the end of the age."ˢ

ˢ Other ancient authorities add *Amen*

---

no mention of doubt when Jesus appeared to the apostolic women (v. 9); and their faith has been proven by their obedience to Jesus' command. Finally, the 'commissioning' of the eleven differs from the two 'commissionings' of the women (by the angel and then Jesus) in audience rather than in kind. The eleven are sent to 'all the nations' to teach them to obey all Jesus' commands; the women are sent to other Jews: the disciples, and then the eleven.

This distinction of audiences for the evangelistic activity of the female and male apostles allows the author both to recognize Jesus' affirmation of the women and to retain the traditional (Jewish and Graeco-Roman) 'separation of spheres' of male and female influence. Men traditionally took the role of leadership in the public arena, and women had the role of household management (leadership in the private sphere). Matthew stretches the 'private sphere' for the apostolic women, in conformity to Jesus' commission to them: the 'household' becomes the whole people of Israel. The 'public sphere' for apostolic men must then be shifted; it becomes the world beyond Israel, the Gentile nations.

Explicitly, they bring the message of the resurrection and of Jesus' return. Although they are not explicitly told to do so, the women also teach the other disciples (even the eleven!) to obey Jesus' commands, for they are the few unfaltering models of such behavior in the entire Gospel.

These faithful and apostolic women lived through the end of their world at the crucifixion, death, and burial of Jesus. They waited in vigil, and then saw it reborn and transformed at Jesus' resurrection and meeting with them. Who has more authority to proclaim Jesus' final words to us? 'And remember, I am with you always, to the end of the age.'

MARK'S GOSPEL

INTRODUCTION

Characteristics

Whether one reads the Gospel of Mark in Greek or in translations, one is struck by the motion, the urgency. Jesus literally rushes from event to event, never staying very long in any one place. This effect is heightened by Mark's frequent use of 'immediately' (*euthus*). Mark also begins almost every sentence with the word 'and', again giving the feeling of forward motion.

Besides these grammatical aspects, the first eight chapters comprise an album of candid snapshots – miracles, exorcisms, healings, interactions; all short, sharply drawn pictures of the active Jesus.

Mark further adds vivid strokes by specific details: the men break up the roof to let the palsied man down (Mark 2), Jesus sleeps with his head on a pillow during a violent storm (4:37–38), he arranges the crowds in orderly groups like a vegetable patch on the green grass (6:39), he heals the deaf and dumb man by putting his fingers into the ears and touching the tongue (7:33), the blind man sees men like trees before his sight is fully restored (8:23ff.), Jesus' clothes become radiant and exceedingly white as no launderer on earth can whiten them (9:3), Peter sits by the fire warming himself in the palace of the high priest (14:54).

Although much of Marcan material can also be found in Matthew and Luke, the tone and style are remarkably different, especially with regard to the feeling of action.

Mark's portrait of Jesus

Mark presents a clear picture of Jesus but he also presents alternative perspectives and Jesus' correctives of these viewpoints. These alternatives are interwoven in the first seven chapters and are articulated in Mark 8, where Jesus asks who the crowd sees him as. The disciples respond 'John the Baptist; and others, Elijah; and still others, one of the prophets', all prophetic figures. A consideration of the crowd's responses to Jesus' miracles and teaching supports this – they respond to him as 'one having authority', 'we have never seen anything like this', etc. The miracles of the multiplication of food and the healing of the blind indicate a prophet figure as well. In contrast, the disciples (Peter as spokesperson) acclaim Jesus as Christ (literally Messiah) probably indicating the political Messiah figure denoted by this title in the Old Testament. Jesus clarifies this position by explaining what kind of Messiah he is – a suffering Son of Man who will suffer and die in Jerusalem.

These three views continue to interweave through the remainder of the book with Jesus' view – the Suffering Son of Man – being fulfilled in the passion.

Purpose

Mark's opening statement, as Guthrie points out, sets the gospel message in a theological rather than a biographical context: 'The beginning of the good news of Jesus Christ, the Son of God . . .' (1:1).

In this setting, neither rigid chronology nor comprehensive data are of primary importance. For example, it is the good news that must be announced and Jesus himself states it in his first appearance in the text: 'The time is fulfilled, and the kingdom of God has come near; repent, and believe in the good news' (1:15). Mark proceeds to unfold what that means – sins are forgiven, demons are exorcized, diseased people are healed, people are taught and fed. All of this presses forward to the main event from which the Kingdom itself is born – the salvific death and resurrection of Jesus.

Authorship

The author of the Gospel is most likely John Mark, for which we have a number of references in the Gospels, in Acts and in the Epistles. If this is the case, the author probably was in Palestine as a child during Jesus' ministry and was an active member of the early church. Paul himself states that he was 'profitable for the Gospel' (2 Tim. 4:11).

The authorship of Mark is attested to at an early date by Papias who states that Mark wrote down the reports of Peter. Irenaeus, Clement, Origen, Hieronymus, Jerome and others follow Papias in this. However, there is no reliable evidence for the relationship of the author (Mark) and Peter. The difficult question seems to be who Mark is and whether he knew Peter. Again, this question can be dealt with at length, but the important aspect is, if the Mark of the Gospel is not John Mark (Marcus was a common Roman name) then there is no biblical nor traditional reference to this author at all.

Date

The dating of the Gospel of Mark is another problem which is to some extent dependent on the position one takes on the issues of authorship and Mark's relationship to Peter. Irenaeus and Clement disagree as to whether Mark wrote before Peter's death (Clement) or after (Irenaeus).

The key to the dating is the relationship of the fall of Jerusalem to the Gospel. In the text there is no direct mention of the fall but it is thought by some scholars that the reference to the 'abomination of desolation' (Mark 13) and the urgency of Mark 13 refer to the coming invasion by Rome (AD 70). Other scholars maintain that this refers to Caligula's attempt to set up his image in the Temple around AD 40 but other aspects of the Gospel as well as the apocalyptic nature of Mark 13 would indicate a later date.

In any case, although a majority of scholars hold to a date around AD 65–70, there are some who suggest an earlier date (before AD 50) and still others who hold to a later date (AD 75). For our purposes in this study, we will assume a date around AD 70.

Audience: the location of Mark's community (or church)

Although the traditional view that Mark's Gospel is written to a church at Rome is based on some evidence, Howard Clark Kee points out that this view is opposed by cultural and linguistic features of the Eastern Mediterranean rural or village culture preserved by Mark. Others suggest Galilee. According to Kee, the reflection of practices involving agriculture, housing, employment, land-ownership, and taxation seem to indicate the larger area of Syria-Palestine. He also addresses other Palestinian location alternatives such as Antioch and gives textual evidence against Mark being addressed to a city. Although the issue is not conclusively resolved, for the purposes of this study, we will hold that the Gospel of Mark was written to a community located somewhere in Syria-Palestine.

The Proclamation of John the Baptist

1 The beginning of the good news[a] of Jesus Christ, the Son of God.[b] 2 As it is written in the prophet Isaiah,[c]

"See, I am sending my messenger
    ahead of you,[d]
who will prepare your way;
3 the voice of one crying out in the
    wilderness:
    'Prepare the way of the Lord,
    make his paths straight,' "

4John the baptizer appeared[e] in the wilderness, proclaiming a baptism of repentance for the forgiveness of sins. 5And people from the whole Judean countryside and all the people of Jerusalem were going out to him, and were baptized by him in the river Jordan, confessing their sins. 6Now John was clothed with camel's hair, with a leather belt around his waist, and he ate locusts and wild honey. 7He proclaimed, "The one who is more powerful than I is coming after me; I am not worthy to stoop down and untie the thong of his sandals. 8I have baptized you with[f] water; but he will baptize you with[f] the Holy Spirit."

The Baptism of Jesus

9 In those days Jesus came from Nazareth of Galilee and was baptized by John in the Jordan. 10And just as he was coming up out of the water, he saw the heavens torn apart and the Spirit descending like a dove on him. 11And a voice came from heaven, "You are my Son, the Beloved;[g] with you I am well pleased."

The Temptation of Jesus

12 And the Spirit immediately drove him out into the wilderness. 13He was in the wilderness forty days, tempted by Satan; and he was with the wild beasts; and the angels waited on him.

The Beginning of the Galilean Ministry

14 Now after John was arrested, Jesus came to Galilee, proclaiming the good news[h]

[a] Or gospel   [b] Other ancient authorities lack the Son of God   [c] Other ancient authorities read in the prophets   [d] Gk before your face   [e] Other ancient authorities read John was baptizing   [f] Or in   [g] Or my beloved Son   [h] Or gospel

---

THE BEGINNING OF THE GOSPEL (MARK 1:1–13)

1. In keeping with the vivid urgency of Mark's Gospel the author goes straight into the action with only a brief sentence of introduction. He leaves out the birth narratives, found in Matthew's and Luke's Gospels, and begins with the appearance of John in the wilderness preaching and baptizing. In verse 9 Jesus is introduced to the readers at the point of his baptism in the Jordan by John.

10–11. The Spirit descending on Jesus and the voice from heaven confirm Jesus as God's Son.

12–13. Jesus is compelled by the Spirit to go into the desert where he is tempted by Satan. Unlike Matthew and Luke – whose versions of the temptation are quite detailed – Mark does not give any details of the temptations directed at Jesus; he merely states that it happened.

13. 'with the wild beasts (*meta* = 'among') indicates close and intimate communion (cf. 3:14; 5:18; 14:67). The reference to animals probably aligns this event with the restoration of paradise introduced by Jesus himself (Is. 11:6–8; 65:25; Hos. 2:18). These beasts could possibly have included the jungle cat, foxes and jackals.

JESUS CALLS HIS FIRST DISCIPLES (MARK 1:14–20)

Jesus' public ministry commences with him calling his first disciples. Mark then goes on to narrate a series of healings, exorcisms, conflicts with the religious authorities, the teaching of parables and preaching which make up the largest part of this Gospel.

of God,[i] [15]and saying, "The time is fulfilled, and the kingdom of God has come near;[j] repent, and believe in the good news."[k]

Jesus Calls the First Disciples

16 As Jesus passed along the Sea of Galilee, he saw Simon and his brother Andrew casting a net into the sea – for they were fishermen. [17]And Jesus said to them, "Follow me and I will make you fish for people." [18]And immediately they left their nets and followed him. [19]As he went a little farther, he saw James son of Zebedee and his brother John, who were in their boat mending the nets. [20]Immediately he called them; and they left their father Zebedee in the boat with the hired men, and followed him.

The Man with an Unclean Spirit

21 They went to Capernaum; and when the sabbath came, he entered the synagogue and taught. [22]They were astounded at his teaching, for he taught them as one having authority, and not as the scribes. [23]Just then there was in their synagogue a man with an unclean spirit, [24]and he cried out, "What have you to do with us, Jesus of Nazareth? Have you come to destroy us? I know who you are, the Holy One of God." [25]But Jesus rebuked him, saying, "Be silent, and come out of him!" [26]And the unclean spirit, convulsing him and crying with a loud voice, came out of him. [27]They were all amazed, and they kept on asking one another, "What is this? A new teaching – with authority! He[l] commands even the unclean spirits, and they obey him." [28]At once his fame began to spread throughout the surrounding region of Galilee.

Jesus Heals Many at Simon's House

29 As soon as they[m] left the synagogue, they entered the house of Simon and Andrew, with James and John. [30]Now Simon's mother-in-law was in bed with a fever, and they told him about her at once. [31]He came and took her by the hand and lifted her up. Then the fever left her, and she began to serve them.

32 That evening, at sundown, they brought to him all who were sick or possessed with demons. [33]And the whole city was gathered around the door. [34]And he cured many who were sick with various diseases, and cast out many demons; and he would not permit the demons to speak, because they knew him.

◆ The term 'crowd' appears 37 times throughout the Gospel. Other terms which imply the crowd are also used: the undefined 'they' (e.g. 1:22, 32, 45); the 'many' (2:2, 13; 6:2, 31, 33; 10:48; 11:8); the 'all' (1:27; 2:12; 5:20); the 'multitude' (3:7, 8); and the 'people' (14:2). Because the crowd appears so frequently in the Gospel, the crowd must have played a special role in the intention of Mark.

There are several views on the role of the crowd in the Gospel of Mark. Robinson sees them in a derogatory sense,

---

[i] Other ancient authorities read *of the kingdom* [j] Or *is at hand*   [k] Or *gospel*   [l] Or *A new teaching! With authority he*   [m] Other ancient authorities read *he*

THE MINISTERING WOMAN (MARK 1:29–34)

The first woman who appears in the Gospel of Mark is healed by Jesus. According to custom, she is identified by her husband or male relative, in this case, probably Simon Peter. Remarkably, however, Jesus, a male outsider to the family, goes to her and touching her, heals her. Her response is to serve or minister to Jesus. It is worthy of note that the same word is used of the angels ministering to Jesus (1:13). Mary Ann Tolbert suggests that this could indicate for Mark that the same way angels ministered to Jesus in the wilderness this woman ministered to him in her home. Indeed, her home becomes the location for the healing of many in the city (1:32–34).

as an obstacle to Jesus' ministry. Weeden disagrees, suggesting that although they appear as an obstacle (2:4; 3:20; 5:30), they are a literary device 'to dramatize, by contrast with the religious leaders, the positive response to Jesus' (T. J. Weeden, *Mark: Traditions in Conflict*, Fortress Press, Philadelphia, 1971, 1979, p. 22). I suggest that the crowd is a literary device playing the role of one of the incorrect Christologies.

Mark presents the crowd in Mark 1–8 as responding with enthusiasm to Jesus' teaching and miracles. The miracles, however, are subordinate to the teaching. In 6:14f. and 8:27f., he describes the crowd's opinion of Jesus as Elijah, the prophet, or John the Baptist – Jewish prophet figures. In 8:34a Jesus calls the crowd and tells them about the Son of Man, discipleship, and the imminent coming of the Kingdom. They continue to respond with amazement to Jesus' miracles (e.g. the epileptic boy, Mark 9); they listen to Jesus' teaching with enthusiasm (11:18b; 12:37b) and follow Jesus on the road (10:46). At the Triumphal Entry (11:1–12) they hail him as the one who comes in the name of the Lord announcing the imminence of the Kingdom of God. They expect the Kingdom itself to follow shortly.

The pericope of the Triumphal Entry (11:1–11) precedes Mark's account of Jesus throwing the money-changers out of the Temple, which is a dramatic representation of his prophetic function as restorer of Israel. In the next reference to the crowd they ask Pilate to follow the custom of releasing a prisoner (possibly they were asking for Jesus). It is then that the religious leaders influence the crowd to reject Jesus. Mark holds these leaders responsible in this rejection (15:11–15). Evidently, when the crowd's expectation of the imminent coming of the Kingdom is not fulfilled, they turn to a political figure. At the cross, the bystanders (possibly connected with the religious leaders) ridicule Jesus on the basis of the expected but unfulfilled rebuilding of the Temple. Thus, throughout the Gospel the crowd sees Jesus as the Prophet who will announce the Kingdom of God, but when the Kingdom does not come, they turn to a political type of messiah, Barabbas.

What is the role of the crowd for Mark? We have seen that the crowd reflects the popular opinion of Jesus as the eschatological Prophet. They have listened to Jesus' teaching and seen his miracles, but have come to the wrong conclusion. Mark 1–8 shows the crowd gathering and flocking to Jesus in the belief that he is the prophet (8:27–33). From this point on, however, their identification is seen as incorrect: Jesus ignores their opinion (8:27) and explains to the disciples the Son-of-Man Christology. He also explains to them, but not to the crowd, the relation of Elijah to the Messiah (9:11–13). Then, in Mark 11, the crowd identification reaches its peak with the Triumphal Entry: they publicly proclaim him as the Prophet 'who comes in the name of the Lord' and proclaims 'the coming kingdom of our ancestor David' (11:9–10).

From this time on, the crowd is recorded as merely enjoying the teaching of Jesus (11:18; 12:37). But they are easily swayed. When the Kingdom does not automatically follow Jesus' ministry, as the crowd had expected, their rejection of Jesus and espousal of the political Barabbas demonstrates how greatly the popular opinion of Jesus is misguided.

Whether or not the crowd is a literary device, there is no doubt that Jesus is incorrectly identified by them. Perhaps we can infer that the crowd reflects a minor group outside of Mark's community that sees Jesus as the fulfillment of the popular Jewish expectation of the eschatological Prophet ◆

A Preaching Tour in Galilee

35 In the morning, while it was still very dark, he got up and went out to a deserted place, and there he prayed. [36]And Simon and his companions hunted for him. [37]When they found him, they said to him, "Everyone is searching for you." [38]He answered, "Let us go on to the neighboring towns, so that I may proclaim the message there also; for that is what I came out to do." [39]And he went throughout Galilee, proclaiming the message in their synagogues and casting out demons.

Jesus Cleanses a Leper

[40] A leper[n] came to him begging him, and kneeling[o] he said to him, "If you choose, you can make me clean." [41]Moved with pity,[p] Jesus[q] stretched out his hand and touched him, and said to him, "I do choose. Be made clean!" [42]Immediately the leprosy[n] left him, and he was made clean. [43]After sternly warning him he sent him away at once, [44]saying to him, "See that you say nothing to anyone; but go, show yourself to the priest, and offer for your cleansing what Moses commanded, as a testimony to them." [45]But he went out and began to proclaim it freely, and to spread the word, so that Jesus[q] could no longer go into a town openly, but stayed out in the country; and people came to him from every quarter.

Jesus Heals a Paralytic

2 When he returned to Capernaum after some days, it was reported that he was at home. [2]So many gathered around that there was no longer room for them, not even in front of the door; and he was speaking the word to them. [3]Then some people[r] came, bringing to him a paralyzed man, carried by four of them. [4]And when they could not bring him to Jesus because of the crowd, they removed the roof above him; and after having dug through it, they let down the mat on which the paralytic lay. [5]When Jesus saw their faith, he said to the paralytic, "Son, your sins are forgiven." [6]Now some of the scribes were sitting there, questioning in their hearts, [7]"Why does this fellow speak in this way? It is blasphemy! Who can forgive sins but God alone?" [8]At once Jesus perceived in his spirit that they were discussing these questions among themselves; and he said

[n] The terms *leper* and *leprosy* can refer to several diseases   [o] Other ancient authorities lack *kneeling*   [p] Other ancient authorities read *anger*   [q] Gk *he*   [r] Gk *they*

CONFLICT WITH THE RELIGIOUS AUTHORITIES (MARK 2FF.)

Mark includes a number of incidents in which Jesus is found to be in conflict with the religious authorities. Jesus has shown himself to be very popular with the ordinary people and has demonstrated an authority which the scribes and Pharisees did not have. In Mark 2 the scribes accuse him of blasphemy when he forgives the sins of the paralytic he is healing. Jesus eats with those who are considered to be unclean sinners and socially unacceptable (2:15–17) and does not impose fasting on his followers (2:18ff.). He angers the Pharisees further when he shows little regard for the Sabbath laws instead taking the view that people – helping and healing them – are more important than regulations (2:23–3:12). The opposition to Jesus grows throughout his ministry and he is confronted by opponents over issues of tradition (7:1–23) and the Law (10:1–12). Finally their opposition to Jesus results in his arrest, trial and execution.

THE MAN LET DOWN THROUGH THE ROOF (MARK 2:1–12)

This miracle is set in Capernaum 'at home'. It is not clear however, exactly whose home it is. It is clear that there is a vast crowd, probably spilling out of the modest house into the street.

The word describing the man's illness is found neither in classical literature nor the LXX and Mark alone includes the detail of four men carrying the stretcher. These men literally 'unroof' the house to reach Jesus, inferring a flat roof, probably with an earth covering, although Luke implies tiles (5:19).

to them, "Why do you raise such questions in your hearts? ⁹Which is easier, to say to the paralytic, 'Your sins are forgiven,' or to say, 'Stand up and take your mat and walk'? ¹⁰But so that you may know that the Son of Man has authority on earth to forgive sins" – he said to the paralytic – ¹¹"I say to you, stand up, take your mat and go to your home." ¹²And he stood up, and immediately took the mat and went out before all of them; so that they were all amazed and glorified God, saying, "We have never seen anything like this!"

Jesus Calls Levi

13 Jesus[s] went out again beside the sea; the whole crowd gathered around him, and he taught them. ¹⁴As he was walking along, he saw Levi son of Alphaeus sitting at the tax booth, and he said to him, "Follow me." And he got up and followed him.

15 And as he sat at dinner[t] in Levi's[u] house, many tax collectors and sinners were also sitting[v] with Jesus and his disciples – for there were many who followed him. ¹⁶When the scribes of[w] the Pharisees saw that he was eating with sinners and tax collectors, they said to his disciples, "Why does he eat[x] with tax collectors and sinners?" ¹⁷When Jesus heard this, he said to them, "Those who are well have no need of a physician, but those who are sick; I have come to call not the righteous but sinners."

The Question about Fasting

18 Now John's disciples and the Pharisees were fasting; and people[y] came and said to him, "Why do John's disciples and the disciples of the Pharisees fast, but your disciples do not fast?" ¹⁹Jesus said to them, "The wedding guests cannot fast while the bridegroom is with them, can they? As long as they have the bridegroom with them, they cannot fast. ²⁰The days will come when the bridegroom is taken away from them, and then they will fast on that day.

21 "No one sews a piece of unshrunk cloth on an old cloak; otherwise, the patch pulls away from it, the new from the old, and a worse tear is made. ²²And no one puts new wine into old wineskins; otherwise, the wine will burst the skins, and the wine is lost, and so are the skins; but one puts new wine into fresh wineskins."[z]

Pronouncement about the Sabbath

23 One sabbath he was going through the grainfields; and as they made their way his disciples began to pluck heads of grain. ²⁴The Pharisees said to him, "Look, why are they doing what is not lawful on the sabbath?" ²⁵And he said to them, "Have you

---

[s] Gk He   [t] Gk reclined   [u] Gk his   [v] Gk reclining   [w] Other ancient authorities read and   [x] Other ancient authorities add and drink   [y] Gk they   [z] Other ancient authorities lack but one puts new wine into fresh wineskins

---

It is noteworthy that when the man is placed before Jesus, Jesus responds with 'your sins are forgiven' (v. 5). The present tense of 'forgiven' probably indicates the immediate act of the sin's being forgiven, 'your sins are at this moment forgiven'. The scribes 'get' the significance of the act and begin debating and reasoning 'in their hearts'. Jesus responds to this non-verbal response by explaining that indeed the act of forgiveness of sins has significance. Furthermore, that it might be known that the 'Son of Man has authority on earth to forgive sins' Jesus heals the physical illness of the man who takes up his pallet or mat and goes out (v. 12).

This miracle, perhaps more clearly than most of the other miracles, shows the role of miracle for Mark – to show that Jesus is not merely a miracle-worker for miracles' sake alone, but that he does miracles for a deeper significance – to show his authority and divine power on earth.

never read what David did when he and his companions were hungry and in need of food? [26]He entered the house of God, when Abiathar was high priest, and ate the bread of the Presence, which it is not lawful for any but the priests to eat, and he gave some to his companions." [27]Then he said to them, "The sabbath was made for humankind, and not humankind for the sabbath; [28]so the Son of Man is lord even of the sabbath."

The Man with a Withered Hand

3 Again he entered the synagogue, and a man was there who had a withered hand. [2]They watched him to see whether he would cure him on the sabbath, so that they might accuse him. [3]And he said to the man who had the withered hand, "Come forward." [4]Then he said to them, "Is it lawful to do good or to do harm on the sabbath, to save life or to kill?" But they were silent. [5]He looked around at them with anger; he was grieved at their hardness of heart and said to the man, "Stretch out your hand." He stretched it out, and his hand was restored. [6]The Pharisees went out and immediately conspired with the Herodians against him, how to destroy him.

A Multitude at the Seaside

7 Jesus departed with his disciples to the sea, and a great multitude from Galilee followed him; [8]hearing all that he was doing, they came to him in great numbers from Judea, Jerusalem, Idumea, beyond the Jordan, and the region around Tyre and Sidon. [9]He told his disciples to have a boat ready for him because of the crowd, so that they would not crush him; [10]for he had cured many, so that all who had diseases pressed upon him to touch him. [11]Whenever the unclean spirits saw him, they fell down before him and shouted, "You are the Son of God!" [12]But he sternly ordered them not to make him known.

Jesus Appoints the Twelve

13 He went up the mountain and called to him those whom he wanted, and they came to him. [14]And he appointed twelve, whom he also named apostles,[a] to be with him, and to be sent out to proclaim the message, [15]and to have authority to cast out demons. [16]So he appointed the twelve:[b] Simon (to whom he gave the name Peter); [17]James son of Zebedee and John the brother of James (to whom he gave the name Boanerges, that is, Sons of Thunder); [18]and Andrew, and Philip, and Bartholomew, and Matthew, and Thomas, and James son of Alphaeus, and Thaddaeus, and Simon the Cananaean, [19]and Judas Iscariot, who betrayed him.

Jesus and Beelzebul

Then he went home; [20]and the crowd came together again, so that they could not even eat. [21]When his family heard it, they went out to restrain him, for people were saying, "He has gone out of his mind." [22]And the scribes who came down from Jerusalem said, "He has Beelzebul, and by the ruler of the demons he casts out demons." [23]And he called them to him, and spoke to them in parables, "How can Satan cast out Satan? [24]If a kingdom is divided against itself, that kingdom cannot stand.

[a] Other ancient authorities lack *whom he also named apostles*   [b] Other ancient authorities lack *So he appointed the twelve*

THE HUMAN FAMILY OF JESUS AND HUMAN RELATIONSHIPS
(MARK 3:21, 31–32; 6:3–4)

The only references to members of Jesus' family in the Gospel of Mark are negative: they think he has 'gone out of his mind' (3:21), they are not acknowledged by Jesus as his 'real' family (3:31–2), and they do not accept Jesus as divine miracle-worker (6:3–4).

²⁵And if a house is divided against itself, that house will not be able to stand. ²⁶And if Satan has risen up against himself and is divided, he cannot stand, but his end has come. ²⁷But no one can enter a strong man's house and plunder his property without first tying up the strong man; then indeed the house can be plundered.

28 "Truly I tell you, people will be forgiven for their sins and whatever blasphemies they utter; ²⁹but whoever blasphemes against the Holy Spirit can never have forgiveness, but is guilty of an eternal sin" – ³⁰for they had said, "He has an unclean spirit."

The True Kindred of Jesus

31 Then his mother and his brothers came; and standing outside, they sent to him and called him. ³²A crowd was sitting around him; and they said to him, "Your mother and your brothers and sistersᶜ are outside, asking for you." ³³And he replied, "Who are my mother and my brothers?"

³⁴And looking at those who sat around him, he said, "Here are my mother and my brothers! ³⁵Whoever does the will of God is my brother and sister and mother."

The Parable of the Sower

4 Again he began to teach beside the sea. Such a very large crowd gathered around him that he got into a boat on the sea and sat there, while the whole crowd was beside the sea on the land. ²He began to teach them many things in parables, and in his teaching he said to them: ³"Listen! A sower went out to sow. ⁴And as he sowed, some seed fell on the path, and the birds came and ate it up. ⁵Other seed fell on rocky ground, where it did not have much soil, and it sprang up quickly, since it had no depth of soil. ⁶And when the sun rose, it was scorched; and since it had no root, it withered away. ⁷Other seed fell among thorns, and

ᶜ Other ancient authorities lack *and sisters*

Several New Testament scholars explain that the main idea in these passages, particularly in 3:31–2 is to define the eschatological family of Jesus in light of his proclamation of the Kingdom. The clearer his announcement of the Kingdom becomes, the less his relatives understand about his mission and person. Hence, when he is teaching such a crowd that 'he could not even eat a meal' (3:21), his relatives attempt to take custody of him, assuming he is 'beside himself'. Again, in 3:21–2, he is teaching and they send word to him that they are present. Here he clearly articulates the replacement of his natural family by the eschatological one – he looks at those around him (Matthew specifies even further that these are the disciples) and says that 'Whoever does the will of God is my brother and sister and mother' (3:35).

Mark 6 takes the issue even further and indicates that his human family is actually a hindrance to the working of the Kingdom: 'Prophets are not without honor, except in their home-town and among their own kin [Matthew leaves out this explicit phrase], and in their own house' (6:3–4).

Nevertheless, Jesus acknowledges the value of the family: marriage is instituted by God (10:6–9); and only those who become like children will enter the Kingdom (10:15). The key is that human relationships are replaced by eschatological ones, so that whoever gives up natural relatives will regain eschatological ones a hundred times more numerous (10:29–30).

PARABLES OF THE KINGDOM (MARK 4)

Interspersed throughout the accounts of Jesus' miracles and opposition to him Mark includes some of Jesus' teaching. Here in Mark 4 it takes the form of parables. By using everyday objects and situations Jesus taught the truths of the Kingdom of God in such a way as to make his listeners think about what they had heard.

the thorns grew up and choked it, and it yielded no grain. ⁸Other seed fell into good soil and brought forth grain, growing up and increasing and yielding thirty and sixty and a hundredfold." ⁹And he said, "Let anyone with ears to hear listen!"

The Purpose of the Parables

10 When he was alone, those who were around him along with the twelve asked him about the parables. ¹¹And he said to them, "To you has been given the secret^d of the kingdom of God, but for those outside, everything comes in parables; ¹²in order that

'they may indeed look, but not
    perceive,
and may indeed listen, but not
    understand;
so that they may not turn again and be
    forgiven.' "

13 And he said to them, "Do you not understand this parable? Then how will you understand all the parables? ¹⁴The sower sows the word. ¹⁵These are the ones on the path where the word is sown: when they hear, Satan immediately comes and takes away the word that is sown in them. ¹⁶And these are the ones sown on rocky ground: when they hear the word, they immediately receive it with joy. ¹⁷But they have no root, and endure only for a while; then, when trouble or persecution arises on account of the word, immediately they fall away.^e ¹⁸And others are those sown among the thorns: these are the ones who hear the word, ¹⁹but the cares of the world, and the lure of wealth, and the desire for other things come in and choke the word, and it yields nothing. ²⁰And these are the ones sown on the good soil: they hear the word and accept it and bear fruit, thirty and sixty and a hundredfold."

A Lamp under a Bushel Basket

21 He said to them, "Is a lamp brought in to be put under the bushel basket, or under the bed, and not on the lampstand? ²²For there is nothing hidden, except to be disclosed; nor is anything secret, except to come to light. ²³Let anyone with ears to hear listen!" ²⁴And he said to them, "Pay attention to what you hear; the measure you give will be the measure you get, and still more will be given you. ²⁵For to those who have, more will be given; and from those who have nothing, even what they have will be taken away."

The Parable of the Growing Seed

26 He also said, "The kingdom of God is as if someone would scatter seed on the ground, ²⁷and would sleep and rise night and day, and the seed would sprout and grow, he does not know how. ²⁸The earth produces of itself, first the stalk, then the head, then the full grain in the head. ²⁹But when the grain is ripe, at once he goes in with his sickle, because the harvest has come."

The Parable of the Mustard Seed

30 He also said, "With what can we compare the kingdom of God, or what parable will we use for it? ³¹It is like a mustard seed, which, when sown upon the ground, is the smallest of all the seeds on earth; ³²yet when it is sown it grows up and becomes the greatest of all shrubs, and puts forth large branches, so that the birds of the air can make nests in its shade."

The Use of Parables

33 With many such parables he spoke the word to them, as they were able to hear it; ³⁴he did not speak to them except in parables, but he explained everything in private to his disciples.

^d Or *mystery* ^e Or *stumble*

Jesus Stills a Storm

35 On that day, when evening had come, he said to them, "Let us go across to the other side." ³⁶And leaving the crowd behind, they took him with them in the boat, just as he was. Other boats were with him. ³⁷A great windstorm arose, and the waves beat into the boat, so that the boat was already being swamped. ³⁸But he was in the stern, asleep on the cushion; and they woke him up and said to him, "Teacher, do you not care that we are perishing?" ³⁹He woke up and rebuked the wind, and said to the sea, "Peace! Be still!" Then the wind ceased, and there was a dead calm. ⁴⁰He said to them, "Why are you afraid? Have you still no faith?" ⁴¹And they were filled with great awe and said to one another, "Who then is this, that even the wind and the sea obey him?"

Jesus Heals the Gerasene Demoniac

5 They came to the other side of the sea, to the country of the Gerasenes.ᶠ ²And when he had stepped out of the boat, immediately a man out of the tombs with an unclean spirit met him. ³He lived among the tombs; and no one could restrain him any more, even with a chain; ⁴for he had often been restrained with shackles and chains, but the chains he wrenched apart, and the shackles he broke in pieces; and no one had the strength to subdue him. ⁵Night and day among the tombs and on the mountains he was always howling and bruising himself with stones. ⁶When he saw Jesus from a distance, he ran and bowed down before him; ⁷and he shouted at the top of his voice, "What have you to do with me, Jesus, Son of the Most High God? I adjure you by God, do not torment me." ⁸For he had said to him, "Come out of the man, you unclean spirit!" ⁹Then Jesusᵍ asked him, "What is your name?" He replied, "My name is Legion; for we are many." ¹⁰He begged him earnestly not to send them out of the country. ¹¹Now there on the hillside a great herd of swine was feeding; ¹²and the unclean spiritsʰ begged him, "Send us into the swine; let us enter them." ¹³So he gave them permission. And the unclean spirits came out and entered the swine; and the herd, numbering about two thousand, rushed down the steep bank into the sea, and were drowned in the sea.

14 The swineherds ran off and told it in the city and in the country. Then people came to see what it was that had happened. ¹⁵They came to Jesus and saw the demoniac sitting there, clothed and in his right mind, the very man who had had the legion; and they were afraid. ¹⁶Those who had seen what had happened to the demoniac and to the swine reported it. ¹⁷Then they began to beg

---

ᶠ Other ancient authorities read *Gergesenes*; others, *Gadarenes*   ᵍ Gk *he*   ʰ Gk *they*

4:35–41. Mark, as usual, uses vivid language to describe the calming of the storm. For example, he describes the waves as 'breaking over' the boat, literally meaning they were 'hurled upon' the boat. Also, Mark's use of the present tenses for 'they rouse him' and 'they say to him' (v. 38) offers a dynamic sense of the scene (Matthew and Luke use participles and past tenses which give a sense of a completed action).

The command of Jesus to the sea 'be still' is intriguing in that it is the same word used by Jesus to cast out the demons (1:25). Scholars have suggested various significances for this, but most likely it indicates that Jesus had power over nature just as he had over demons.

The fear of the disciples because of the intensity of the storm (these sudden storms are frequent on inland lakes such as Galilee) is understandable to us but for Jesus their desperate cry was evidently a sign of 'little faith' (v. 40). It is worthy of note that although Jesus rebukes them for their timidity (little faith) he nevertheless calms the sea and rescues them. The response of the disciples is again understandable – awe and wonder about who Jesus is (v. 41).

Jesus[i] to leave their neighborhood. [18]As he was getting into the boat, the man who had been possessed by demons begged him that he might be with him. [19]But Jesus[j] refused, and said to him, "Go home to your friends, and tell them how much the Lord has done for you, and what mercy he has shown you." [20]And he went away and began to proclaim in the Decapolis how much Jesus had done for him; and everyone was amazed.

A Girl Restored to Life and a Woman Healed

21 When Jesus had crossed again in the boat[k] to the other side, a great crowd gathered around him; and he was by the sea. [22]Then one of the leaders of the synagogue named Jairus came and, when he saw him, fell at his feet [23]and begged him repeatedly, "My little daughter is at the point of death. Come and lay your hands on her, so that she may be made well, and live." [24]So he went with him.

And a large crowd followed him and pressed in on him. [25]Now there was a woman who had been suffering from

◆ The story in Mark 5:21–43 of a woman with a twelve-year hemorrhage who approached Jesus for healing reflects the tip of a larger issue: the status of the menstruant in Jewish Palestine. In healing this desperate woman, Jesus challenges socio-cultural boundaries and early Jewish traditions.

In the Ancient Near East, persons with flows were considered contagiously impure and thus isolated from society. In Babylon and Southern Arabia anyone who touched a menstruant became impure. Zoroastrian and ancient Greek culture regarded even the glance of a menstruant as defiling.

In Israel too the condition and restriction of the menstruant was severe. The Hebrew term *nidda* literally means, 'expulsion' or 'elimination' and may have originally referred to the vaginal blood flow. In any case, the term was certainly used to refer to the menstruant herself who was not only discharging blood but was herself 'discharged' or excluded from society during this time (*Ant.* 3:261; *m.Nid.* 7:4).

Not only was the menstruant considered impure, but she could contaminate other persons and objects merely by touching, shifting, spitting on or carrying them. Even those who touched her bed or chair would become impure (Lev. 15:21). Sexual intercourse with a menstruant was not only contaminating but forbidden (Lev. 18:19).

The woman with a flow of blood in Mark 5 is in a more desperate situation than routine menstruation. She has been abnormally hemorrhaging for twelve years. Only a miracle will change her status. The fact that the woman touches Jesus' garment (Matthew says 'hem' or 'tassels') rather than Jesus himself may be due to her fear of contaminating as well as generally irritating him.

The woman's touch on Jesus' garment should have rendered it impure. Furthermore, she did not merely touch Jesus' garment; she made contact with him because he says power went out of him. Under these circumstances, Jesus' touch on certain other items (e.g. persons, food, cooking vessels and clothing) would contaminate them, and he would have been obligated to immerse his whole body in water for purification.

To the contrary, Jesus not only appears immune to impurity, he transforms an impure situation into a pure one. As a religious Jew, Jesus should have become impure, but instead he makes the impure woman pure. His clothes do not contract impurity; they serve as a vehicle of purification.

It is significant that Jesus attends to this unfortunate woman at the expense of the religious ruler, Jairus, who is anxious for Jesus to heal his dying daughter. Jairus has asked Jesus to lay

[i] Gk *him*　[j] Gk *he*　[k] Other ancient authorities lack *in the boat*

hands on his daughter, but Jesus allows the defiling touch of an impure woman to detain him.

To the reader's surprise, the woman is the one who receives the title of 'daughter' from Jesus' lips. Her faith is acclaimed, whereas the disciples have been strongly rebuked for their lack of faith (Mark 4:40) and Jairus is exhorted to hold on to what faith he has (5:36). Jesus is not repulsed by the ostracized woman's contagious, impure condition. He is willing to cross social and religious boundaries in order to bring her healing and self-esteem ◆

hemorrhages for twelve years. [26]She had endured much under many physicians, and had spent all that she had; and she was no better, but rather grew worse. [27]She had heard about Jesus, and came up behind him in the crowd and touched his cloak, [28]for she said, "If I but touch his clothes, I will be made well." [29]Immediately her hemorrhage stopped; and she felt in her body that she was healed of her disease. [30]Immediately aware that power had gone forth from him, Jesus turned about in the crowd and said, "Who touched my clothes?" [31]And his disciples said to him, "You see the crowd pressing in on you; how can you say, 'Who touched me?' " [32]He looked all around to see who had done it. [33]But the woman, knowing what had happened to her, came in fear and trembling, fell down before him, and told him the whole truth. [34]He said to her, "Daughter, your faith has made you well; go in peace, and be healed of your disease."

[35] While he was still speaking, some people came from the leader's house to say, "Your daughter is dead. Why trouble the teacher any further?" [36]But overhearing[l] what they said, Jesus said to the leader of the synagogue, "Do not fear, only believe." [37]He allowed no one to follow him except Peter, James, and John, the brother of James. [38]When they came to the house of the leader of the synagogue, he saw a commotion, people weeping and wailing loudly. [39]When he had entered, he said to them, "Why do you make a commotion and weep? The child is not dead but sleeping." [40]And they laughed at him. Then he put them all outside, and took the child's father and mother and those who were with him, and went in where the child was. [41]He took her by the hand and said to her, "Talitha cum," which means, "Little girl, get up!" [42]And immediately the girl got up and began to walk about (she was twelve years of age). At this they were overcome with amazement. [43]He strictly ordered them that no one should know this, and told them to give her something to eat.

The Rejection of Jesus at Nazareth

6 He left that place and came to his hometown, and his disciples followed him. [2]On the sabbath he began to teach in the synagogue, and many who heard him were astounded. They said, "Where did this man get all this? What is this wisdom that has been given to him? What deeds of power are being done by his hands! [3]Is not this the carpenter, the son of Mary[m] and brother of James and Joses and Judas and Simon, and are not his sisters here with us?" And they took offense[n] at him. [4]Then Jesus said to them, "Prophets are not without honor, except in their hometown, and among their own kin, and in their own house." [5]And he could do no deed of power there, except that he laid his hands on a few sick people and cured them. [6]And he was amazed at their unbelief.

The Mission of the Twelve

Then he went about among the villages teaching. [7]He called the twelve and began to send them out two by two, and gave them authority over the unclean spirits. [8]He ordered them to take nothing for their journey except a staff; no bread, no bag, no

[l] Or *ignoring*; other ancient authorities read *hearing*
[m] Other ancient authorities read *son of the carpenter and of Mary*   [n] Or *stumbled*

money in their belts; [9]but to wear sandals
and not to put on two tunics. [10]He said to
them, "Wherever you enter a house, stay
there until you leave the place. [11]If any
place will not welcome you and they refuse
to hear you, as you leave, shake off the dust
that is on your feet as a testimony against
them." [12]So they went out and proclaimed
that all should repent. [13]They cast out
many demons, and anointed with oil many
who were sick and cured them.

The Death of John the Baptist

14 King Herod heard of it, for Jesus'[o]
name had become known. Some were[p]
saying, "John the baptizer has been raised
from the dead; and for this reason these
powers are at work in him." [15]But others
said, "It is Elijah." And others said, "It is a
prophet, like one of the prophets of old."
[16]But when Herod heard of it, he said,
"John, whom I beheaded, has been raised."

◆ Herodias (6:14–24) was the daughter of Aristobulus, son of Herod the Great and Mariamne, daughter of Hyrcanus. She married Philip I, son of Herod the Great and Mariamne. This produced a daughter, Salome. When Herod Antipas, Philip's brother, visited Rome, he became involved with her and brought her back to Israel to reign as Queen. It was this illicit union that John the Baptist condemned. Herodias avenged this rebuke by asking for John's head. In this role, Herodias occupies an extremely negative place in the Gospel of Mark. It is worthy of note that although her political power does not extend to ensuring John's death by legal means, she used subterfuge and trickery to accomplish her ends. Perhaps it is worthy of note that whereas men (the religious leaders) are the ones who plot and accomplish Jesus' death, a woman (a minor but important character) masterminds the death of John the Baptist.

Drusilla was the great granddaughter of Herod the Great and the youngest daughter of Herod Agrippa I. At 15 years of age, she married King Aziz of Emesa after he became a Jew. She illegitimately married Felix, the Roman governor. Agrippa was her only child and Josephus relates that Drusilla was killed attempting to rescue her child in the eruption of Vesuvius.

Bernice was the eldest daughter of Herod Agrippa I (AD 38–45). Josephus says that she first married Marcus, then married her uncle Herod, king of Chaldis. After his death, it was rumored that she had incestuous relations with her brother Agrippa. She then married Ptolemy, king of Cilicia, and then returned to her brother Agrippa. Later, she became mistress of Vespasian, and then of Titus, son of Vespasian until he became Emperor. Along with her sister Drusilla, Bernice is outstanding for her wicked life. She, along with Agrippa heard Paul's message when Agrippa proclaimed, 'Are you so quickly persuading me to become a Christian?' (Acts 25:23; 26:28).

By considering, even briefly, the lives of these women in Herod's life, we can conclude that although they led lives of wealth, prestige, and luxury, basically, they stand as indications of the debauchery and licentiousness of the Roman era. As women, they were respected to some degree, having some say in matters such as the welfare of John the Baptist and Paul. However, Mark shows them using intrigue and trickery rather than actual political power to accomplish their ends ◆

17 For Herod himself had sent men who
arrested John, bound him, and put him in
prison on account of Herodias, his brother
Philip's wife, because Herod[q] had married
her. [18]For John had been telling Herod, "It is
not lawful for you to have your brother's
wife." [19]And Herodias had a grudge against
him, and wanted to kill him. But she could
not, [20]for Herod feared John, knowing that
he was a righteous and holy man, and he

[o] Gk *his* [p] Other ancient authorities read *He was*
[q] Gk *he*

protected him. When he heard him, he was greatly perplexed;[r] and yet he liked to listen to him. [21]But an opportunity came when Herod on his birthday gave a banquet for his courtiers and officers and for the leaders of Galilee. [22]When his daughter Herodias[s] came in and danced, she pleased Herod and his guests; and the king said to the girl, "Ask me for whatever you wish, and I will give it." [23]And he solemnly swore to her, "Whatever you ask me, I will give you, even half of my kingdom." [24]She went out and said to her mother, "What should I ask for?" She replied, "The head of John the baptizer." [25]Immediately she rushed back to the king and requested, "I want you to give me at once the head of John the Baptist on a platter." [26]The king was deeply grieved; yet out of regard for his oaths and for the guests, he did not want to refuse her. [27]Immediately the king sent a soldier of the guard with orders to bring John's[t] head. He went and beheaded him in the prison, [28]brought his head on a platter, and gave it to the girl. Then the girl gave it to her mother. [29]When his disciples heard about it, they came and took his body, and laid it in a tomb.

Feeding the Five Thousand

30 The apostles gathered around Jesus, and told him all that they had done and taught. [31]He said to them, "Come away to a deserted place all by yourselves and rest a while." For many were coming and going, and they had no leisure even to eat. [32]And they went away in the boat to a deserted place by themselves. [33]Now many saw them going and recognized them, and they hurried there on foot from all the towns and arrived ahead of them. [34]As he went ashore, he saw a great crowd; and he had compassion for them, because they were like sheep without a shepherd; and he began to teach them many things. [35]When it grew late, his disciples came to him and said, "This is a deserted place, and the hour is now very late; [36]send them away so that they may go into the surrounding country and villages and

buy something for themselves to eat." [37]But he answered them, "You give them something to eat." They said to him, "Are we to go and buy two hundred denarii[u] worth of bread, and give it to them to eat?" [38]And he said to them, "How many loaves have you? Go and see." When they had found out, they said, "Five, and two fish." [39]Then he ordered them to get all the people to sit down in groups on the green grass. [40]So they sat down in groups of hundreds and of fifties. [41]Taking the five loaves and the two fish, he looked up to heaven, and blessed and broke the loaves, and gave them to his disciples to set before the people; and he divided the two fish among them all. [42]And all ate and were filled; [43]and they took up twelve baskets full of broken pieces and of the fish. [44]Those who had eaten the loaves numbered five thousand men.

Jesus Walks on the Water

45 Immediately he made his disciples get into the boat and go on ahead to the other side, to Bethsaida, while he dismissed the crowd. [46]After saying farewell to them, he went up on the mountain to pray.

47 When evening came, the boat was out on the sea, and he was alone on the land. [48]When he saw that they were straining at the oars against an adverse wind, he came towards them early in the morning, walking on the sea. He intended to pass them by. [49]But when they saw him walking on the sea, they thought it was a ghost and cried out; [50]for they all saw him and were terrified. But immediately he spoke to them and said, "Take heart, it is I; do not be afraid." [51]Then he got into the boat with them and the wind ceased. And they were utterly astounded, [52]for they did not understand about the loaves, but their hearts were hardened.

---

[r] Other ancient authorities read *he did many things*
[s] Other ancient authorities read *the daughter of Herodias herself*   [t] Gk *his*   [u] The denarius was the usual day's wage for a laborer

Healing the Sick in Gennesaret

53 When they had crossed over, they came to land at Gennesaret and moored the boat. [54]When they got out of the boat, people at once recognized him, [55]and rushed about that whole region and began to bring the sick on mats to wherever they heard he was. [56]And wherever he went, into villages or cities or farms, they laid the sick in the marketplaces, and begged him that they might touch even the fringe of his cloak; and all who touched it were healed.

The Tradition of the Elders

7 Now when the Pharisees and some of the scribes who had come from Jerusalem gathered around him, [2]they noticed that some of his disciples were eating with defiled hands, that is, without

---

◆ Ritual purity among ancient cultures was a state of physical cleanness required for participation in the worship of the gods. Purification rites, including immersion in water, had to be observed after certain physical impurities, e.g. menstruation, and especially before entering a sacred area.

In first-century Jewish Palestine, purity was a serious concern. The Tosefta, an early rabbinic text, claims, 'Purity was a stronger concern than incest' (t. Shab. 1:14), and 'Impurity of knife was of greater concern to Israel than the shedding of blood' (t. Yoma 1:12).

Impurity concerns among Jews of the Second Temple period can be categorized in three areas: (1) death, (2) leprosy, and (3) sexual flows. A corpse was the most impure of all impurities and had to be buried outside city walls. Likewise, animals associated with death: carnivores, preying birds, and scavenging fish, were excluded from Israel's diet. Animal carcasses and human corpses conveyed impurity to anyone who touched them. Blood, because it represented life, had to be revered and never ingested (Lev. 17:10).

Lepers were considered cursed by God for wrongdoing (cf. Num. 12:10; 2 Sam. 3:29; 2 Kings 5:27; 2 Chron. 26:19). No cure was available; healing could come only from God. The nature of leprosy in biblical times, unlike the modern definition, encompassed a broad variety of skin diseases (Lev. 13). A significant feature was the extreme flaking of the skin. On more than one occasion the ancient Hebrew associated this with the appearance of death (Num. 12:12; Job 18:13). Lepers, like corpses, were banned from the cities of human habitation.

The final category of impurity concerns sexual flows. Sexual intercourse and menstruation, although part of the normal life-cycle, caused ritual impurity. After intercourse, persons had to bathe and wait until sundown before they could enter sacred precincts (Lev. 15:19). Abnormal sexual impurities, such as gonorrhea or excessive menstrual bleeding outside of the normal period were considered serious diseases which only God could heal. A woman who had just given birth was especially impure because of the amount of bleeding which ensues (Lev. 12:2–4).

According to Jewish Law, certain items which came into contact with persons in any of these three categories also became impure. Susceptible items included other persons, cooking utensils, clothes, food, and liquids. The major concern was that the impurity would come into contact with persons or foods which were going to the Temple.

Scholars have long struggled to determine a rationale for these laws. The Bible explains that these constraints will distinguish the holy people of Israel from pagan nations (Lev. 20:22–26). Perhaps there is also an underlying symbolism illustrating this polarity in terms of life and death. Israel's diet and purity traditions reflect her position as the people who have chosen life (Deut. 31:15–20). The corpse and carcass obviously represent death. The leper too, although alive, reminds one of death since he is visibly deteriorating.

In the third category, the body is losing fluids, semen or blood, which combine to give life. Instead of producing life, they are wasting from the body ◆

washing them. [3](For the Pharisees, and all the Jews, do not eat unless they thoroughly wash their hands,[v] thus observing the tradition of the elders; [4]and they do not eat anything from the market unless they wash it;[w] and there are also many other traditions that they observe, the washing of cups, pots, and bronze kettles.[x]) [5]So the Pharisees and the scribes asked him, "Why do your disciples not live[y] according to the tradition of the elders, but eat with defiled hands?" [6]He said to them, "Isaiah prophesied rightly about you hypocrites, as it is written,

'This people honors me with their
     lips,
   but their hearts are far from me;
[7] in vain do they worship me,
     teaching human precepts as
        doctrines.'

[8]You abandon the commandment of God and hold to human tradition."

9 Then he said to them, "You have a fine way of rejecting the commandment of God in order to keep your tradition! [10]For Moses said, 'Honor your father and your mother'; and, 'Whoever speaks evil of father or mother must surely die.' [11]But you say that if anyone tells father or mother, 'Whatever support you might have had from me is Corban' (that is, an offering to God[z])— [12]then you no longer permit doing anything for a father or mother, [13]thus making void the word of God through your tradition that you have handed on. And you do many things like this."

14 Then he called the crowd again and said to them, "Listen to me, all of you, and understand: [15]there is nothing outside a person that by going in can defile, but the things that come out are what defile."[a]

[17] When he had left the crowd and entered the house, his disciples asked him about the parable. [18]He said to them, "Then do you also fail to understand? Do you not see that whatever goes into a person from outside cannot defile, [19]since it enters, not the heart but the stomach, and goes out into the sewer?" (Thus he declared all foods clean.) [20]And he said, "It is what comes out of a person that defiles. [21]For it is from within, from the human heart, that evil intentions come: fornication, theft, murder, [22]adultery, avarice, wickedness, deceit, licentiousness, envy, slander, pride, folly. [23]All these evil things come from within, and they defile a person."

◆ The Jewish woman in the first century AD spent a considerable portion of each day preparing food. She was required to grind flour, bake bread, prepare meals and feed her family (m. Ket. 5:5). From known archaeological findings and early Jewish sources, the agricultural economy of Roman Palestine and the diet of a typical Jewish family can be established with reasonable certainty.

In the time of Jesus, strict food laws were observed among Jews. These rules governed the type of animal eaten and the manner in which it was slaughtered and cooked (Lev. 11; Deut. 14). Only animals which have a split hoof and chew a cud could be eaten. This rule, in effect, limited the acceptable animals to a few mostly domesticated types: cattle, goats and sheep. Deer too could be eaten. Among birds those which eat carrion and prey on other creatures were excluded. Fish had to have both scales and fins to be acceptable for the table.

The Jewish cook was guided by explicit rules in the preparation of meat dishes.

[v] Meaning of Gk uncertain   [w] Other ancient authorities read *and when they come from the marketplace, they do not eat unless they purify themselves*   [x] Other ancient authorities add *and beds*   [y] Gk *walk*   [z] Gk lacks *to God*   [a] Other ancient authorities add verse 16, *"Let anyone with ears to hear listen"*

The ingestion of blood was strictly forbidden under Jewish Law (Lev. 17:10). Thus, all meat, whether poultry or cattle, had to be slaughtered cleanly with a sharp knife, so that all of its blood could then be drained. Animals which died of old age or had been the prey of other animals could not be eaten (Lev. 17:15).

It is also possible that the rabbinic law separating the consumption of dairy and meat products extends back to the first century AD. If this is the case, no butter, milk, cream, or cheese could have been cooked or eaten with animal meat. According to the rule, some foods are considered *parve*, natural, and can be eaten with either dairy or meat dishes.

That these regulations were carefully observed by the general Jewish populace of Second Temple times is attested in many places. The books of Maccabees describe the courage of many Jews who chose torture and death rather than to eat pork (2 Macc. 6:18; 7:1; 4 Macc.; cf. also Dan. 1:12–16; Ezek. 4:14; Judith 12:2). Peter is revolted by the unclean animals which he is told to kill and eat, claiming that all of his life he has been faithful to the Jewish food code (Acts 10:14).

According to a second-century Jewish document known as Mishna, the daily diet of a day laborer consisted of bread, pulse, oil and fresh or dried fruit (m. Baba Metzia 7:1). Honey, too, was a major agricultural product. Vinegar was used for sauces into which bread was dipped.

On the Sabbath, this meager diet would have been supplemented with fish and green vegetables. The availability of fish, especially in the Sea of Galilee and Mediterranean Sea, provided a fine economic and nutritional source. Wine too was limited to the Sabbath and other occasions, but it was usually diluted with a fair amount of water.

The Mishna records specific provisions to be given a woman living alone, apparently divorced from her husband. She was to be given a weekly allotment of 4.4 liters of wheat, 1.1 liters of pulse, 0.25 liters of oil and 2.2 liters of figs and other fruits ◆

The Syrophoenician Woman's Faith

24 From there he set out and went away to the region of Tyre.[b] He entered a house and did not want anyone to know he was there. Yet he could not escape notice, [25]but a woman whose little daughter had an unclean spirit immediately heard about him, and she came and bowed down at his feet. [26]Now the woman was a Gentile, of

[b] Other ancient authorities add *and Sidon*

THE SYROPHOENICIAN WOMAN (MARK 7:25–30)

This interplay between a Gentile woman (a Canaanite, according to Matthew) and Jesus must be addressed since it is one of the harshest responses of Jesus to anyone. Mary Ann Tolbert suggests an interesting interpretation of this event. She notes that the woman breaks many conventional social rules by her approaching Jesus and asking him to heal her daughter. Jesus' abrupt response acknowledges this unconventional behavior. Her bold, clever response to his rebuke, however, shows her desperation. Tolbert suggests that Jesus' response – calling her a 'little dog' (the diminutive of *Kyon*, 'dog') – could be associated with the name of one of the philosophical movements of the day. Around the fourth century BC, Diogenes of Sinope developed a group with anti-establishment views; his followers not only mocked the customs and social mores of the day, but because of their aggressive, rude and obnoxious behavior, they adopted the name 'dogs' (Cynics) to describe their group. If Jesus by calling the Syrophoenician woman 'little dog' was actually aligning her with this philosophical group because of her behavior, it could be seen as considerably less harsh and condescending than if he were using the term by which the Jews usually referred to the Gentiles.

In any case, her witty and courageous response to Jesus' harsh words wins her a commendation from Jesus, (one of the *few* commendations in the Gospel), healing for her daughter, and admiration from the thousands who have read about her through the centuries. Her behavior and Jesus' response clearly indicate to us that Christ calls us to a perseverance that overcomes obstacles.

Syrophoenician origin. She begged him to cast the demon out of her daughter. [27]He said to her, "Let the children be fed first, for it is not fair to take the children's food and throw it to the dogs." [28]But she answered him, "Sir,[c] even the dogs under the table eat the children's crumbs." [29]Then he said to her, "For saying that, you may go – the demon has left your daughter." [30]So she went home, found the child lying on the bed, and the demon gone.

Jesus Cures a Deaf Man

31 Then he returned from the region of Tyre, and went by way of Sidon towards the Sea of Galilee, in the region of the Decapolis. [32]They brought to him a deaf man who had an impediment in his speech; and they begged him to lay his hand on him. [33]He took him aside in private, away from the crowd, and put his fingers into his ears, and he spat and touched his tongue. [34]Then looking up to heaven, he sighed and said to him, "Ephphatha," that is, "Be opened." [35]And immediately his ears were opened, his tongue was released, and he spoke plainly. [36]Then Jesus[d] ordered them to tell no one; but the more he ordered them, the more zealously they proclaimed it. [37]They were astounded beyond measure, saying, "He has done everything well; he even makes the deaf to hear and the mute to speak."

Feeding the Four Thousand

8 In those days when there was again a great crowd without anything to eat, he called his disciples and said to them, [2]"I have compassion for the crowd, because they have been with me now for three days and have nothing to eat. [3]If I send them away hungry to their homes, they will faint on the way – and some of them have come from a great distance." [4]His disciples replied, "How can one feed these people with bread here in the desert?" [5]He asked them, "How many loaves do you have?" They said, "Seven." [6]Then he ordered the crowd to sit down on the ground; and he

took the seven loaves, and after giving thanks he broke them and gave them to his disciples to distribute; and they distributed them to the crowd. [7]They had also a few small fish; and after blessing them, he ordered that these too should be distributed. [8]They ate and were filled; and they took up the broken pieces left over, seven baskets full. [9]Now there were about four thousand people. And he sent them away. [10]And immediately he got into the boat with his disciples and went to the district of Dalmanutha.[e]

> ◆ There were different kinds of baskets used in each of the miracles of the feedings – the 5,000 (Mark 6) and the 4,000 (Mark 8). In the former, the basket is a small coffin shaped basket used to carry Levitically clean food whereas in the feeding of the 4,000 the word indicates a large provision basket, the kind used to lower Paul over the wall (Acts 9:25). In both cases, there was plenty of food left over, perhaps implying that God's blessings are always bountiful ◆

The Demand for a Sign

11 The Pharisees came and began to argue with him, asking him for a sign from heaven, to test him. [12]And he sighed deeply in his spirit and said, "Why does this generation ask for a sign? Truly I tell you, no sign will be given to this generation." [13]And he left them, and getting into the boat again, he went across to the other side.

The Yeast of the Pharisees and of Herod

14 Now the disciples[f] had forgotten to bring any bread; and they had only one loaf with them in the boat. [15]And he cautioned them, saying, "Watch out – beware of the yeast of the Pharisees and the yeast of Herod."[g] [16]They said to one another, "It is

[c] Or *Lord*; other ancient authorities prefix *Yes*
[d] Gk *he*   [e] Other ancient authorities read *Mageda* or *Magdala*   [f] Gk *they*   [g] Other ancient authorities read *the Herodians*

because we have no bread." [17]And becoming aware of it, Jesus said to them, "Why are you talking about having no bread? Do you still not perceive or understand? Are your hearts hardened? [18]Do you have eyes, and fail to see? Do you have ears, and fail to hear? And do you not remember? [19]When I broke the five loaves for the five thousand, how many baskets full of broken pieces did you collect?" They said to him, "Twelve." [20]"And the seven for the four thousand, how many baskets full of broken pieces did you collect?" And they said to him, "Seven." [21]Then he said to them, "Do you not yet understand?"

Jesus Cures a Blind Man at Bethsaida

22 They came to Bethsaida. Some people[h] brought a blind man to him and begged him to touch him. [23]He took the blind man by the hand and led him out of the village; and when he had put saliva on his eyes and laid his hands on him, he asked him, "Can you see anything?" [24]And the man[i] looked up and said, "I can see people, but they look like trees, walking." [25]Then Jesus[i] laid his hands on his eyes again; and he looked intently and his sight was restored, and he saw everything clearly. [26]Then he sent him away to his home, saying, "Do not even go into the village."[j]

Peter's Declaration about Jesus

27 Jesus went on with his disciples to the villages of Caesarea Philippi; and on the way he asked his disciples, "Who do people say that I am?" [28]And they answered him, "John the Baptist; and others, Elijah; and still others, one of the prophets." [29]He asked them, "But who do you say that I am?" Peter answered him, "You are the Messiah."[k] [30]And he sternly ordered them not to tell anyone about him.

Jesus Foretells His Death and Resurrection

31 Then he began to teach them that the Son of Man must undergo great suffering, and be rejected by the elders, the chief priests, and the scribes, and be killed, and

◆ This passage includes the various perceptions of Jesus reflected in the Gospel of Mark: Prophet (by the crowd), Messiah (by the disciples), and Son of Man (by Jesus himself). Each of these represent the expectation of someone who was to come at the end of the age to redeem Israel from foreign rule. Each figure, however, differs as to its function and role in the eschatological events. Each perception, as recorded by Mark reflects the response to Jesus by various groups who heard him.

The Prophet. The belief that one of the Old Testament prophets would return in the last days was widespread in the time of Jesus. Although some hold that this Prophet could be any one of the Old Testament prophets, Elijah and Moses were the most commonly held, probably because of their unusual departures from the earth. Also, the prophecies were another major reason for the belief in the return (see Mal. 4:5–6 [Elijah] and Deut. 18:18 [Moses]).

The tradition about the return of Elijah developed through the centuries by various interpretations and legends and generally includes four aspects of expected activity: repentance, reconciliation, restoration, and resurrection. These activities are to prepare Israel for the imminent coming of the Kingdom of God. In all of the traditions, however – Old Testament, Qumran, and apocalyptic circles – the Prophet is seen against an eschatological expectation: he is expected to announce and to prepare for the imminent coming of the Kingdom of God.

Moses. Moses was another of the ancient prophets whom the Jews expected to arise again at the end-time. This belief, although not so prevalent as that in the return of Elijah, arose through the general opinion that Mosaic times would return to Israel.

Moses is known as the great prophet of Israel, the Savior of the exodus from Egypt, the prophet mediator, the author of the Torah. His miracles were seen in connection with God's redemptive plan for Israel. The nature of miracles as authentication

---

[h] Gk *They*   [i] Gk *he*   [j] Other ancient authorities add *or tell anyone in the village*   [k] Or *the Christ*

of a prophet's status is viewed differently by different traditions. In literary circles, such as those which Josephus and Philo represent, Moses is presented as sage, lawgiver, and possessor of virtue. In other spheres, miracles play a greater role and Moses is presented as the great miracleworker, prophet and magician. The writers emphasized the elements which would be most appealing to their audiences. In whatever context Moses appears, it is noteworthy that he appears in connection with the Exodus, the redemption of Israel. Even in the magical traditions, his magic is performed in order to redeem Israel. Thus, even when Moses appears as a magician, the Exodus can be perceived in the background. The miracles are set in an eschatological setting; they have a far broader purpose than the exaltation of their performer. Rather, they are seen in the context of God's redemptive history: the prophet appears as God's agent on earth.

These prophet figures are reflected in the response of the crowd to Jesus – they respond to Jesus' teaching and miracles (Mark 1–8), and Mark records their identification of Jesus as Elijah or John the Baptist or one of the prophets (8:27).

In contrast, the disciples represented by Peter identify Jesus as the Messiah. Like the expected prophet, this was also an eschatological figure expected in the endtime. This figure, however, has more political overtones than the Prophet figure.

The Greek word means 'anointed' and refers to the anointing of priests and kings in the Old Testament. In the eschatological time the Messiah was expected to restore Israel politically, to conquer other nations and to rule over Israel as king.

Like the expectations of the Prophet figure, there were variations in the expectations of the Messiah figure, but there were basically two aspects of the Messiah which were widely held at the time of Jesus: 'One was the national, political, this-worldly [concept], with particularistic tendencies, though universalistic at its best. The other was a super-terrestrial, other-worldly [concept] rich in religious content and mythological concepts, universalistic,

numinous, at home in the sphere of "Holy" and the "wholly other"' (S. O. Mowinckel, *He That Cometh*, trans. G. W. Anderson, Abingdon Press, New York, 1954, p. 194).

The expectation of an earthly kingship developed more fully during the Babylonian Exile when the throne of David no longer existed, and the Jews were forced to accept that the fulfillment of the promise was postponed to a distant future. It became more active under the rule of Greece as Jewish nationalism developed, and the expectation of a political warrior emerged. This concept of Messiah (political, national warrior) prevailed at the time of Jesus.

The older, nationalistic future hope prevailed among the masses because it appealed to the economic, social and political pressures, whereas the other-worldly concept was current in certain literary circles, among the learned, religious sects. That the Messiah was regarded as an earthly figure is evident by the accounts of several people being proclaimed as such. For example, Zerubbabel was proclaimed king of the restoration by Zechariah and Haggai; Simon, during the Hasmonean rule, was considered the Messiah (1 Macc. 14:4ff.); the false messiahs, mentioned by Josephus, were called brigands, rioters, and saboteurs. Hezekiah, the 'robber-chief', so called by Josephus, was called 'messiah' by R. Hillel. At the time of Jesus, the mission of the Messiah was the salvation of Israel, i.e. to restore Israel as a people to her former glory, to a leading position among all nations; to free her from enemies and destroy the world powers. This concept was influenced by the growing intolerance of everything foreign as a result of the Maccabean revolt and Roman rule. The future hope concentrated more and more on deliverance. The Messiah would be primarily a royal deliverer, the enemy of Rome, a zealot. His qualities and deeds would surpass ordinary standards, but had also been done by others (e.g. miracles had been done by Elijah). 'Only as a mighty ruler and an exalted and unequaled moral personality would the Messiah be superior to all the rest of the saints and prophets of

Israel. His Kingdom was still *of this world'* (S. O. Mowinckel, *He That Cometh*, trans. G. W. Anderson, Abingdon Press, New York, 1954, p. 314).

The Son of Man. Finally, Jesus' identification of himself (most likely reflecting Mark's own view) is that he is the suffering Son of Man. Mowinckel, in his study on messiah figures, says that there was not a strongly existing expectation of a suffering or dying Messiah in Judaism, though this theme was sounded by Isaiah (Is. 53). The concept of the eternal Messiah is associated with the Son of Man figure (Daniel). Jesus revealed himself as the bearer of salvation, the uniquely pre-existing Son of God. He merges the two concepts of sacrificial death and eternal reign of glory. Although he ignores the identification of the crowd, he responds to the opinion of the disciples by clarifying that he is a Messiah (the Son of Man) who will suffer and die. Peter rejects this idea and is sharply rebuked by Jesus ('you are setting your mind not on divine things but on human things' Mark 8:33).

There is much debate about the origin of the Son of Man figure but most likely Jesus is referring to the figure described by Daniel – the Son of Man coming in the clouds with his angels (e.g. Dan. 7:13–14). This title, then, is not a title indicating the humanity of Jesus, rather it represents his glorious eschatological nature when he returns with the Kingdom in the end time ◆

began to rebuke him. [33]But turning and looking at his disciples, he rebuked Peter and said, "Get behind me, Satan! For you are setting your mind not on divine things but on human things."

34 He called the crowd with his disciples, and said to them, "If any want to become my followers, let them deny themselves and take up their cross and follow me.[35]For those who want to save their life will lose it, and those who lose their life for my sake, and for the sake of the gospel,[1] will save it. [36]For what will it profit them to gain the whole world and forfeit their life? [37]Indeed, what can they give in return for their life? [38]Those who are ashamed of me and of my words[m] in this adulterous and sinful generation, of them the Son of Man will also be ashamed when he comes in the glory of his Father with the **9** holy angels." [1]And he said to them, "Truly I tell you, there are some standing here who will not taste death until they see that the kingdom of God has come with[n] power."

The Transfiguration

2 Six days later, Jesus took with him Peter and James and John, and led them up a high mountain apart, by themselves. And he was transfigured before them, [3]and his

after three days rise again. [32]He said all this quite openly. And Peter took him aside and

[1] Other ancient authorities read *lose their life for the sake of the gospel* [m] Other ancient authorities read *and of mine* [n] Or *in*

THE PRICE OF DISCIPLESHIP (MARK 8:34–35)

It is worthy of note that the 'price' of discipleship mentioned by Jesus here is not the denial *to* oneself of riches, fame, fortune, etc. Rather, it is the denial *of* oneself. Most likely, this indicates the relinquishing of the role of master of one's life to Jesus rather than oneself. Crucifixion (taking up the cross), after all, implies death. When one has relinquished the role of master, one 'loses' one's life, only to find it, according to Jesus in the Gospel of Mark.

THE TRANSFIGURATION (MARK 9:1FF.)

Mark describes the transfiguration using vivid language. The word 'transfigures' translates the Greek word *metamorphe*, from which our English word 'metamorphosis' comes. It indicates a

clothes became dazzling white, such as
no one[o] on earth could bleach them. [4]And
there appeared to them Elijah with Moses,
who were talking with Jesus. [5]Then Peter
said to Jesus, "Rabbi, it is good for us to be
here; let us make three dwellings,[p] one for
you, one for Moses, and one for Elijah." [6]He
did not know what to say, for they were
terrified. [7]Then a cloud overshadowed
them, and from the cloud there came a
voice, "This is my Son, the Beloved;[q] listen
to him!" [8]Suddenly when they looked
around, they saw no one with them any
more, but only Jesus.

The Coming of Elijah

9 As they were coming down the mountain, he ordered them to tell no one about
what they had seen, until after the Son of
Man had risen from the dead. [10]So they kept
the matter to themselves, questioning
what this rising from the dead could mean.
[11]Then they asked him, "Why do the scribes
say that Elijah must come first?" [12]He said
to them, "Elijah is indeed coming first to
restore all things. How then is it written
about the Son of Man, that he is to go
through many sufferings and be treated
with contempt? [13]But I tell you that Elijah
has come, and they did to him whatever
they pleased, as it is written about him."

The Healing of a Boy with a Spirit

14 When they came to the disciples,
they saw a great crowd around them, and
some scribes arguing with them. [15]When
the whole crowd saw him, they were immediately overcome with awe, and they
ran forward to greet him. [16]He asked them,
"What are you arguing about with them?"
[17]Someone from the crowd answered him,
"Teacher, I brought you my son; he has a
spirit that makes him unable to speak;
[18]and whenever it seizes him, it dashes him
down; and he foams and grinds his teeth
and becomes rigid; and I asked your disciples to cast it out, but they could not
do so." [19]He answered them, "You faithless
generation, how much longer must I be
among you? How much longer must I put
up with you? Bring him to me." [20]And they
brought the boy[r] to him. When the spirit
saw him, immediately it convulsed the
boy,[r] and he fell on the ground and rolled
about, foaming at the mouth. [21]Jesus[s] asked
the father, "How long has this been
happening to him?" And he said, "From
childhood. [22]It has often cast him into the
fire and into the water, to destroy him; but
if you are able to do anything, have pity on

[o] Gk *no fuller* [p] Or *tents* [q] Or *my beloved Son*
[r] Gk *him* [s] Gk *He*

---

notable change. Dr Merrill Tenney suggests that this change which takes place is probably a change similar to when a light is turned on – the object becomes bright and almost translucent in quality. This would explain Mark's description, 'and his clothes became dazzling white, such as no one on earth could bleach them' (v. 3).

Scholars have suggested many explanations for the appearance of Elijah and Moses with Jesus. The crowd had identified Jesus as a prophet, or Elijah, or John the Baptist, and this appearance dynamically clarifies the relation of Jesus to the eschatological prophets. Of course, Moses and Elijah can be seen in symbolic terms as representing the Law and the prophets and Jesus' relation to them. The eschatological idea is significant here, though, as can be seen by the discussion of Jesus and the disciples as they leave the mountain – they discuss the relation of Elijah to the Son of Man (vv. 11–13).

BELIEF AND UNBELIEF (MARK 9:22–23)

There is a notable word-play in these verses. The epileptic boy's father, discouraged by the inability of the disciples to heal, asks Jesus, 'if you are able to do anything, have pity on us and us and help us." [23]Jesus said to him, "If you are able! – All things can be done for the one who believes." [24]Immediately the father of the child cried out,[t] "I believe; help my unbelief!" [25]When Jesus saw that a crowd came running together, he rebuked the unclean spirit, saying to it, "You spirit that keeps this boy from speaking and hearing, I command you, come out of him, and never enter him again!" [26]After crying out and convulsing him terribly, it came out, and the boy was like a corpse, so that most of them said, "He is dead." [27]But Jesus took him by the hand and lifted him up, and he was able to stand. [28]When he had entered the house, his disciples asked him privately, "Why could we not cast it out?" [29]He said to them, "This kind can come out only through prayer."[u]

Jesus Again Foretells His Death and Resurrection

30 They went on from there and passed through Galilee. He did not want anyone to know it; [31]for he was teaching his disciples, saying to them, "The Son of Man is to be betrayed into human hands, and they will kill him, and three days after being killed, he will rise again." [32]But they did not understand what he was saying and were afraid to ask him.

Who Is the Greatest?

33 Then they came to Capernaum; and when he was in the house he asked them, "What were you arguing about on the way?" [34]But they were silent, for on the way they had argued with one another who was the greatest. [35]He sat down, called the twelve, and said to them, "Whoever wants to be first must be last of all and servant of all." [36]Then he took a little child and put it among them; and taking it in his arms, he

said to them, [37]"Whoever welcomes one such child in my name welcomes me, and whoever welcomes me welcomes not me but the one who sent me."

Another Exorcist

38 John said to him, "Teacher, we saw someone[v] casting out demons in your name, and we tried to stop him, because he was not following us." [39]But Jesus said, "Do not stop him; for no one who does a deed of power in my name will be able soon afterward to speak evil of me. [40]Whoever is not against us is for us. [41]For truly I tell you, whoever gives you a cup of water to drink because you bear the name of Christ will by no means lose the reward.

Temptations to Sin

42 "If any of you put a stumbling block before one of these little ones who believe in me,[w] it would be better for you if a great millstone were hung around your neck and you were thrown into the sea. [43]If your hand causes you to stumble, cut it off; it is better for you to enter life maimed than to have two hands and to go to hell,[x] to the unquenchable fire.[y] [45]And if your foot causes you to stumble, cut it off; it is better for you to enter life lame than to have two feet and to be thrown into hell.[x,y] [47]And if your eye causes you to stumble, tear it out; it is better for you to enter the kingdom of God with one eye than to have two eyes and

[t] Other ancient authorities add *with tears*   [u] Other ancient authorities add *and fasting*   [v] Other ancient authorities add *who does not follow us*   [w] Other ancient authorities lack *in me*   [x] Gk *Gehenna*   [y] Verses 44 and 46 (which are identical with verse 48) are lacking in the best ancient authorities

---

help us.' Jesus answers by putting the emphasis back on the father – 'If *you* [emphatic] are able! – All things can be done for the one who believes.' The father responds with a phrase we can all relate to 'I do believe; help my unbelief!'

to be thrown into hell,[z] [48]where their worm never dies, and the fire is never quenched.

49 "For everyone will be salted with fire.[a] [50]Salt is good; but if salt has lost its saltiness, how can you season it?[b] Have salt in yourselves, and be at peace with one another."

Teaching about Divorce

10 He left that place and went to the region of Judea and[c] beyond the Jordan. And crowds again gathered around him; and, as was his custom, he again taught them.

2 Some Pharisees came, and to test him they asked, "Is it lawful for a man to divorce his wife?" [3]He answered them, "What did Moses command you?" [4]They said, "Moses allowed a man to write a certificate of dismissal and to divorce her." [5]But Jesus said to them, "Because of your hardness of heart he wrote this commandment for you. [6]But from the beginning of creation, 'God made them male and female.' [7]For this reason a man shall leave his father and mother and be joined to his wife,[d] [8]and the two shall become one flesh.' So they are no longer two, but one flesh. [9]Therefore what God has joined together, let no one separate."

◆ The passage where Jesus comments on divorce is interesting when set in its Jewish context. According to the Talmud, divorce was not difficult; but there were rules concerning the grounds for the dissolution of marriage. The entire issue must be considered within the context of the high ideal placed on marriage. Although there were carefully circumscribed grounds for the dissolution, it was never taken lightly (this was emphasized by the high price to attain a divorce).

In first-century Judaism, opposing views of Deut. 24:1 were represented by the schools of Hillel and Shammai. Shammai interpreted it as meaning that a man could obtain a divorce only in the case of unfaithfulness, whereas Hillel took a more lenient view that a divorce could be obtained if a woman did 'anything unseemly', e.g. spoil his dinner. Rabbi Akiva went even further to state that divorce was possible if a man 'found a woman more beautiful than she' (Git. IX.10).

The Rabbis agreed on the authority of the husband in respect to divorce, so the man could divorce a woman without her consent, whereas a woman could only divorce with the man's consent (Jeb. XIV.1; Cohen, 1975, p. 167).

The strongest ground for divorce was adultery, for which divorce was obligatory. Other grounds were possible, but with contingencies. Sterility was recognized

[z] Gk *Gehenna*   [a] Other ancient authorities either add or substitute *and every sacrifice will be salted with salt*   [b] Or *how can you restore its saltiness?*   [c] Other ancient authorities lack *and*   [d] Other ancient authorities lack *and be joined to his wife*

THE SALT OF THE EARTH (MARK 9:50)

In the ancient world, salt was a valuable commodity – it was even used to pay people. In fact our English word 'salary' comes from the word 'salt'. It was also used to preserve food before refrigeration and as an antiseptic to disinfect wounds. In the valley in Judea from which salt comes, the veins of salt are visible. If you break off a piece of salt which has been exposed to the elements, although it still retains its parts and particles of salt, it has lost its taste. Only the inner part which is still connected to the rock retains its savor. When salt had lost its taste, it was used on the Temple floor so that people would not slip. Without its taste, it was only good to be trampled on. This has a very special lesson for us – as long as we remain 'connected' to the 'Rock', we retain our 'savor' as Christians, whereas, alone, we lose our flavor and viability for witness and as Jesus said, we become worthless. From this point on Jesus begins his journey towards Jerusalem.

only after waiting ten years; insanity was actually strong grounds for *not* obtaining a divorce, since the insane person needed protection. Failure to consummate the marriage or to have intercourse were grounds for both men or women; impotence and the inability or unwillingness to support a woman properly were also recognized as acceptable grounds for a woman. Desertion was only recognized if testified to by one or two reliable witnesses.

Jesus' brief comment in Mark 10:1–10 seems to reflect Jewish high views of marriage as sanctioned by God and dissolved only by a concession by Moses. It is interesting that only Matthew adds the phrase that divorce is acceptable in the case of unfaithfulness, thus echoing the position of Shammai. Jesus in Mark takes an even stronger view ◆

10 Then in the house the disciples asked him again about this matter. ¹¹He said to them, "Whoever divorces his wife and marries another commits adultery against her; ¹²and if she divorces her husband and marries another, she commits adultery."

Jesus Blesses Little Children
13 People were bringing little children to him in order that he might touch them; and the disciples spoke sternly to them. ¹⁴But when Jesus saw this, he was indignant and said to them, "Let the little children come to me; do not stop them; for it is to such as these that the kingdom of God belongs. ¹⁵Truly I tell you, whoever does not receive the kingdom of God as a little child will never enter it." ¹⁶And he took them up in his arms, laid his hands on them, and blessed them.

The Rich Man
17 As he was setting out on a journey, a man ran up and knelt before him, and asked him, "Good Teacher, what must I do to inherit eternal life?" ¹⁸Jesus said to him, "Why do you call me good? No one is good but God alone. ¹⁹You know the commandments: 'You shall not murder; You shall not commit adultery; You shall not steal; You shall not bear false witness; You shall not defraud; Honor your father and mother.' " ²⁰He said to him, "Teacher, I have kept all these since my youth." ²¹Jesus, looking at him, loved him and said, "You lack one thing; go, sell what you own, and give the

---

JESUS' ATTITUDE TO CHILDREN (MARK 10:13–16)
This passage indicates Jesus' feeling about children – that he sees them as symbolic of those who are acceptable to enter the Kingdom of heaven.

There are two components to this passage. First, the coming of the children to Jesus; secondly, Jesus' comment on the relation of children to the Kingdom.

It is not clear who brought the children or why the disciples felt they should not approach Jesus. In v. 13 the purpose is stated: 'in order that he might touch them'. Elsewhere in Mark 'touch' usually refers to his healing touch, but probably refers here to blessing (as in the Old Testament, cf. Gen. 48:14). Jesus responds in anger (one of the few instances that his anger is noted). His remarks are very strong: 'Let the little children come to me; do not stop them.' He continues to explain the relation of children to the Kingdom of God – that the Kingdom indeed 'belongs' to them. Many interpretations can be given as to what this means, but most likely the implication is in terms of how the Kingdom is received. Jesus says it is important to *receive* the Kingdom like a child, perhaps referring to the enthusiasm of a child when receiving a gift. Further, a child does not expect to have *earned* a gift; a child simply joyfully receives it.

In any case, Jesus takes the children in his arms and blesses them – perhaps symbolizing the manner of acceptance into the Kingdom. This notable blessing of Jesus heralded the Kingdom, and is a symbol of the Kingdom itself.

money[e] to the poor, and you will have treasure in heaven; then come, follow me." [22]When he heard this, he was shocked and went away grieving, for he had many possessions.

[23] Then Jesus looked around and said to his disciples, "How hard it will be for those who have wealth to enter the kingdom of God!" [24]And the disciples were perplexed at these words. But Jesus said to them again, "Children, how hard it is[f] to enter the kingdom of God! [25]It is easier for a camel to go through the eye of a needle than for someone who is rich to enter the kingdom of God."[26]They were greatly astounded and said to one another,[g] "Then who can be saved?" [27]Jesus looked at them and said, "For mortals it is impossible, but not for God; for God all things are possible."

[28] Peter began to say to him, "Look, we have left everything and followed you." [29]Jesus said, "Truly I tell you, there is no one who has left house or brothers or sisters or mother or father or children or fields, for my sake and for the sake of the good news,[h] [30]who will not receive a hundredfold now in this age – houses, brothers and sisters, mothers and children, and fields with persecutions – and in the age to come eternal life. [31]But many who are first will be last, and the last will be first."

A Third Time Jesus Foretells His Death and Resurrection

[32] They were on the road, going up to Jerusalem, and Jesus was walking ahead of them; they were amazed, and those who followed were afraid. He took the twelve aside again and began to tell them what was to happen to him, [33]saying, "See, we are going up to Jerusalem, and the Son of Man will be handed over to the chief priests and the scribes, and they will condemn him to death; then they will hand him over to the Gentiles; [34]they will mock him, and spit upon him, and flog him, and kill him; and after three days he will rise again."

The Request of James and John

[35] James and John, the sons of Zebedee, came forward to him and said to him, "Teacher, we want you to do for us whatever we ask of you." [36]And he said to them, "What is it you want me to do for you?" [37]And they said to him, "Grant us to sit, one at your right hand and one at your left, in your glory." [38]But Jesus said to them, "You do not know what you are asking. Are you able to drink the cup that I drink, or be baptized with the baptism that I am baptized with?" [39]They replied, "We are able." Then Jesus said to them, "The cup that I drink you will drink; and with the baptism with which I am baptized, you will be baptized; [40]but to sit at my right hand or at my left is not mine to grant, but it is for those for whom it has been prepared."

[41] When the ten heard this, they began to be angry with James and John. [42]So Jesus called them and said to them, "You know that among the Gentiles those whom they recognize as their rulers lord it over them, and their great ones are tyrants over them. [43]But it is not so among you; but whoever wishes to become great among you must be

[e] Gk lacks *the money*   [f] Other ancient authorities add *for those who trust in riches*   [g] Other ancient authorities read *to him*   [h] Or *gospel*

THE NEEDLE'S EYE (MARK 10:25)

In the past, commentators interpreted the needle's eye to refer to a small gate alongside a main city gate through which it was difficult for a camel to pass. It is perhaps simply a hyperbole to show the nearly impossible difficulty of a rich person to enter the Kingdom. In any case, Jesus is stressing the *difficulty* rather than the *impossibility* of entrance, so that whether it should be understood as a literal gate or in a figurative sense, its meaning is clear.

your servant, [44]and whoever wishes to be first among you must be slave of all. [45]For the Son of Man came not to be served but to serve, and to give his life a ransom for many."

The Healing of Blind Bartimaeus

46 They came to Jericho. As he and his disciples and a large crowd were leaving Jericho, Bartimaeus son of Timaeus, a blind beggar, was sitting by the roadside. [47]When he heard that it was Jesus of Nazareth, he began to shout out and say, "Jesus, Son of David, have mercy on me!" [48]Many sternly ordered him to be quiet, but he cried out even more loudly, "Son of David, have mercy on me!" [49]Jesus stood still and said, "Call him here." And they called the blind man, saying to him, "Take heart; get up, he is calling you." [50]So throwing off his cloak, he sprang up and came to Jesus. [51]Then Jesus said to him, "What do you want me to do for you?" The blind man said to him, "My teacher,[i] let me see again." [52]Jesus said to him, "Go; your faith has made you well." Immediately he regained his sight and followed him on the way.

Jesus' Triumphal Entry into Jerusalem

11 When they were approaching Jerusalem, at Bethphage and Bethany, near the Mount of Olives, he sent two of his disciples [2]and said to them, "Go into the village ahead of you, and immediately as you enter it, you will find tied there a colt that has never been ridden; untie it and bring it. [3]If anyone says to you, 'Why are you doing this?' just say this, 'The Lord needs it and will send it back here immediately.'" [4]They went away and found a colt tied near a door, outside in the street. As they were untying it, [5]some of the bystanders said to them, "What are you doing, untying the colt?" [6]They told them what Jesus had said; and they allowed them to take it. [7]Then they brought the colt to Jesus and threw their cloaks on it; and he sat on it. [8]Many people spread their cloaks on the road, and others spread leafy branches that they had cut in the fields. [9]Then those who went ahead and those who followed were shouting,

"Hosanna!
> Blessed is the one who comes in the
> > name of the Lord!
[10] > Blessed is the coming kingdom of
> > our ancestor David!
> Hosanna in the highest heaven!"

11 Then he entered Jerusalem and went into the temple; and when he had looked around at everything, as it was already late, he went out to Bethany with the twelve.

Jesus Curses the Fig Tree

12 On the following day, when they came from Bethany, he was hungry. [13]Seeing in the

---

[i] Aramaic *Rabbouni*

'HOSANNA!' (MARK 11:9–10)

The last week of Jesus' ministry (11:1–15:47) begins with great excitement and anticipation, rejoicing and welcoming Jesus with great shouts of praise and blessings but it ends with sadness and sorrow, rejection and injustice as Jesus spends his last days with his disciples, is unfairly tried and crucified.

The cry of 'Hosanna!', associated with Passover, Booths and Dedication, means literally 'save now'. It was part of the usual liturgy when branches were carried around the altar. The Psalm verse (118:25–26) also was apparently added and the Gospel writers included the record of the cry to emphasize the importance of a shout that had Messianic overtones and had been used at political celebrations such as the inauguration of Judas Maccabeus.

THE FIG TREE (MARK 11:12–14, 22)

This is the only 'negative' miracle Jesus does in the Gospels. It is curious that Mark states that there were no figs, 'for it was not the season for figs' (v. 13). Professor Edersheim, being bothered

distance a fig tree in leaf, he went to see whether perhaps he would find anything on it. When he came to it, he found nothing but leaves, for it was not the season for figs. ¹⁴He said to it, "May no one ever eat fruit from you again." And his disciples heard it.

Jesus Cleanses the Temple

15 Then they came to Jerusalem. And he entered the temple and began to drive out those who were selling and those who were buying in the temple, and he overturned the tables of the money changers and the seats of those who sold doves; ¹⁶and he would not allow anyone to carry anything through the temple. ¹⁷He was teaching and saying, "Is it not written,

'My house shall be called a house of
     prayer for all the nations'?
But you have made it a den of
     robbers."

¹⁸And when the chief priests and the scribes heard it, they kept looking for a way to kill him; for they were afraid of him, because the whole crowd was spellbound by his teaching. ¹⁹And when evening came, Jesus and his disciples[j] went out of the city.

The Lesson from the Withered Fig Tree

20 In the morning as they passed by, they saw the fig tree withered away to its roots. ²¹Then Peter remembered and said to him, "Rabbi, look! The fig tree that you cursed has withered." ²²Jesus answered them, "Have[k] faith in God. ²³Truly I tell you, if you say to this mountain, 'Be taken up and thrown into the sea,' and if you do not doubt in your heart, but believe that what you say will come to pass, it will be done for you. ²⁴So I tell you, whatever you ask for in prayer, believe that you have received[l] it, and it will be yours.

♦ Jesus prayed often. Mark indicates that Jesus prayed alone in the morning during his busy ministry (1:35); before important turning-points (e.g. after the feeding of the 5,000 he prays instead of accepting the crowd's desire to make him king, 6:46). Of course, in Gethsemane Jesus prayed the most difficult prayer of his life, as he submitted himself to God's will.

Another purpose for prayer emerges: Jesus says, 'Whenever you stand praying, *forgive*, if you have anything against anyone' (11:25). He also says, 'whatever you ask for in prayer, believe that you have received it, and it will be yours' (11:24). This follows the remarkable passage about faith being able to move mountains, implying perhaps that it is in the relation of prayer and faith that strength and power with God reside. We see in this passage echoes of the Sermon on the Mount in Matt. 7:7–8 and 18:19, 'search and you will find . . .' Mark, however, links faith, prayer and forgiveness (see also Matt. 5:23–24) ♦

25 "Whenever you stand praying, forgive, if you have anything against anyone; so that your Father in heaven may also forgive you your trespasses."[m]

Jesus' Authority Is Questioned

27 Again they came to Jerusalem. As he was walking in the temple, the chief priests, the scribes, and the elders came to him ²⁸and said, "By what authority are you

---

[j] Gk *they*: other ancient authorities read *he*
[k] Other ancient authorities read *"If you have*
[l] Other ancient authorities read *are receiving*
[m] Other ancient authorities add verse 26, *"But if you do not forgive, neither will your Father in heaven forgive your trespasses."*

---

by this, researched this by visiting this geographical area at the stated time of year and exploring the nature of fig trees. He found out that fig trees, if they will bear fruit in the season, have small raisin-like fruit on them. These are tasty and tend to curb hunger pains. If a tree is barren these pods or seeds are not present. Hence Jesus was appropriately justified for cursing the fig tree for its barren state.

doing these things? Who gave you this authority to do them?" ²⁹Jesus said to them, "I will ask you one question; answer me, and I will tell you by what authority I do these things. ³⁰Did the baptism of John come from heaven, or was it of human origin? Answer me." ³¹They argued with one another, "If we say, 'From heaven,' he will say, 'Why then did you not believe him?' ³²But shall we say, 'Of human origin'?" – they were afraid of the crowd, for all regarded John as truly a prophet. ³³So they answered Jesus, "We do not know." And Jesus said to them, "Neither will I tell you by what authority I am doing these things."

The Parable of the Wicked Tenants

12 Then he began to speak to them in parables. "A man planted a vineyard, put a fence around it, dug a pit for the wine press, and built a watchtower; then he leased it to tenants and went to another country. ²When the season came, he sent a slave to the tenants to collect from them his share of the produce of the vineyard. ³But they seized him, and beat him, and sent him away empty-handed. ⁴And again he sent another slave to them; this one they beat over the head and insulted. ⁵Then he sent another, and that one they killed. And so it was with many others; some they beat, and others they killed. ⁶He had still one other, a beloved son. Finally he sent him to them, saying, 'They will respect my son.' ⁷But those tenants said to one

another, 'This is the heir; come, let us kill him, and the inheritance will be ours.' ⁸So they seized him, killed him, and threw him out of the vineyard. ⁹What then will the owner of the vineyard do? He will come and destroy the tenants and give the vineyard to others. ¹⁰Have you not read this scripture:

'The stone that the builders rejected
    has become the cornerstone;ⁿ
¹¹ this was the Lord's doing,
    and it is amazing in our eyes'?"

12 When they realized that he had told this parable against them, they wanted to arrest him, but they feared the crowd. So they left him and went away.

The Question about Paying Taxes

13 Then they sent to him some Pharisees and some Herodians to trap him in what he said. ¹⁴And they came and said to him, "Teacher, we know that you are sincere, and show deference to no one; for you do not regard people with partiality, but teach the way of God in accordance with truth. Is it lawful to pay taxes to the emperor, or not? ¹⁵Should we pay them, or should we not?" But knowing their hypocrisy, he said to them, "Why are you putting me to the test? Bring me a denarius and let me see it." ¹⁶And they brought one. Then he said to them, "Whose head is this, and whose title?" They answered, "The emperor's." ¹⁷Jesus said to them, "Give to

ⁿ Or *keystone*

GOD AND THE EMPEROR (MARK 12:13–17)

In this passage, Jesus is confronted by the Herodians. Scholars are uncertain who the Herodians actually were. Only Matthew and Mark allude to them and these allusions tend to be vague and indecisive. Although various opinions abound, most likely the term refers to the supporters and followers of Herod Antipas. If this is the case, they were a political group and it follows that they would use the issue of taxes to trap Jesus. The term 'trap' is the classical word used of hunting or fishing. The question posed by the Herodians was indeed a 'trap' – either a yes or no answer was politically risky: a 'yes' would incur disfavor and a 'no' would imply political disloyalty to Rome.

The tax being referred to here is the poll tax, paid, however resentfully, by the Jews to the Roman treasury. The silver coin bore the image of the Roman Caesar, in this case Tiberius. It was worth a day's wages for an unskilled worker.

the emperor the things that are the emperor's, and to God the things that are God's." And they were utterly amazed at him.

The Question about the Resurrection

18 Some Sadducees, who say there is no resurrection, came to him and asked him a question, saying, [19]"Teacher, Moses wrote for us that if a man's brother dies, leaving a wife but no child, the man° shall marry the widow and raise up children for his brother. [20]There were seven brothers; the first married and, when he died, left no children; [21]and the second married her and died, leaving no children; and the third likewise; [22]none of the seven left children. Last of all the woman herself died. [23]In the resurrection[p] whose wife will she be? For the seven had married her."

◆ Women in the ancient world could in some cases buy, own and inherit property, but much more frequently they did not, and if not closely related to a land-owning male, were at great risk for poverty, slavery and prostitution. Recognizing this, the legal/religious system somewhat clumsily acknowledged every woman's right, in the patrilinear inheritance system, to survive financially by getting married and bearing a son. If a husband died without having begotten a son, other males in his family were obligated to give his widow a chance to conceive a son. This was usually a brother, but if there was no brother, the obligation could pass to the father-in-law as in the story of

---

Tamar (Gen. 38) or to a more remote kinsman, as in Ruth 3:1ff.

In Gen. 38, Onan plans to steal his older brother's inheritance by going through the form of his obligation to Tamar while making sure that she will not conceive. God kills him for this dishonesty, supporting the woman's rights as understood at that time. It is now recognized that the Tamar story is about a long-dead custom foreign to our society and to our religious beliefs, and cannot be used to argue against family planning.

In Mark, the Sadducees refer to this custom in an attempt to make Jesus' teaching about the resurrection look ridiculous. But he counters with the teaching that marriage is an earthly arrangement and that women's salvation is a matter of their own spirituality, quite apart from their marital status and from their relationship to a husband. This passage echoes others in which Jesus places faithfulness to the gospel above everything else, even so important an obligation as family relationships ◆

---

24 Jesus said to them, "Is not this the reason you are wrong, that you know neither the scriptures nor the power of God? [25]For when they rise from the dead, they neither marry nor are given in marriage, but are like angels in heaven.

° Gk *his brother*   [p] Other ancient authorities add *when they rise*

Jesus' response, as usual, is masterful – Jesus acknowledges that since the coin bears the Emperor's image, it therefore belongs to him and should be returned to him. The verb 'pay back' (*apodote*) is not the word usually used for payment (*dounai*): whereas the latter word has the sense of pay as a gift, the former has the sense of 'giving back what is due' or 'what belongs'.

In this passage, Jesus recognizes that although one may have acknowledged God as Lord of life, one remains in the natural environment and hence should be responsible to its rulers whenever possible.

26And as for the dead being raised, have you
not read in the book of Moses, in the story
about the bush, how God said to him, 'I am
the God of Abraham, the God of Isaac, and
the God of Jacob'? 27He is God not of the
dead, but of the living; you are quite
wrong."

The First Commandment

28 One of the scribes came near and
heard them disputing with one another,
and seeing that he answered them well,
he asked him, "Which commandment is
the first of all?" 29Jesus answered, "The first
is, 'Hear, O Israel: the Lord our God, the
Lord is one; 30you shall love the Lord your
God with all your heart, and with all your
soul, and with all your mind, and with all
your strength.' 31The second is this, 'You
shall love your neighbor as yourself.' There
is no other commandment greater than
these." 32Then the scribe said to him, "You
are right, Teacher; you have truly said
that 'he is one, and besides him there is
no other'; 33and 'to love him with all the
heart, and with all the understanding, and
with all the strength,' and 'to love one's
neighbor as oneself,' – this is much more
important than all whole burnt offerings
and sacrifices." 34When Jesus saw that
he answered wisely, he said to him, "You
are not far from the kingdom of God."
After that no one dared to ask him any
question.

The Question about David's Son

35 While Jesus was teaching in the
temple, he said, "How can the scribes say
that the Messiah[q] is the son of David?
36David himself, by the Holy Spirit,
declared,

'The Lord said to my Lord,
"Sit at my right hand,
until I put your enemies under your
feet." '

37David himself calls him Lord; so how can
he be his son?" And the large crowd was
listening to him with delight.

Jesus Denounces the Scribes

38 As he taught, he said, "Beware of the
scribes, who like to walk around in long
robes, and to be greeted with respect in the
marketplaces, 39and to have the best seats
in the synagogues and places of honor at
banquets! 40They devour widows' houses
and for the sake of appearance say long
prayers. They will receive the greater
condemnation."

The Widow's Offering

41 He sat down opposite the treasury,
and watched the crowd putting money into
the treasury. Many rich people put in large
sums. 42A poor widow came and put in
two small copper coins, which are worth a
penny. 43Then he called his disciples and
said to them, "Truly I tell you, this poor
widow has put in more than all those who
are contributing to the treasury. 44For all of
them have contributed out of their abundance; but she out of her poverty has put in
everything she had, all she had to live on."

The Destruction of the Temple Foretold

13 As he came out of the temple, one
of his disciples said to him, "Look,
Teacher, what large stones and what large
buildings!" 2Then Jesus asked him, "Do you
see these great buildings? Not one stone
will be left here upon another; all will be
thrown down."

3 When he was sitting on the Mount of
Olives opposite the temple, Peter, James,
John, and Andrew asked him privately,
4"Tell us, when will this be, and what will
be the sign that all these things are about
to be accomplished?" 5Then Jesus began to
say to them, "Beware that no one leads you
astray. 6Many will come in my name and
say, 'I am he!'[r] and they will lead many
astray. 7When you hear of wars and rumors
of wars, do not be alarmed; this must take
place, but the end is still to come. 8For

[q] Or *the Christ* [r] Gk *I am*

nation will rise against nation, and kingdom against kingdom; there will be earthquakes in various places; there will be famines. This is but the beginning of the birth pangs.

Persecution Foretold

9 "As for yourselves, beware; for they will hand you over to councils; and you will be beaten in synagogues; and you will stand before governors and kings because of me, as a testimony to them. [10]And the good news[s] must first be proclaimed to all nations. [11]When they bring you to trial and hand you over, do not worry beforehand about what you are to say; but say whatever is given you at that time, for it is not you who speak, but the Holy Spirit. [12]Brother will betray brother to death, and a father his child, and children will rise against parents and have them put to death; [13]and you will be hated by all because of my name. But the one who endures to the end will be saved.

The Desolating Sacrilege

14 "But when you see the desolating sacrilege set up where it ought not to be (let the reader understand), then those in Judea must flee to the mountains; [15]the one on the housetop must not go down or enter the house to take anything away; [16]the one in the field must not turn back to get a coat. [17]Woe to those who are pregnant and to those who are nursing infants in those days! [18]Pray that it may not be in winter. [19]For in those days there will be suffering, such as has not been from the beginning of the creation that God created until now, no, and never will be. [20]And if the Lord had not cut short those days, no one would be saved; but for the sake of the elect, whom he chose, he has cut short those days. [21]And if anyone says to you at that time, 'Look! Here is the Messiah!'[t] or 'Look! There he is!' – do not believe it. [22]False messiahs[u] and false prophets will appear and produce signs and omens, to lead astray, if possible, the elect. [23]But be alert; I have already told you everything.

The Coming of the Son of Man

24 "But in those days, after that suffering,

the sun will be darkened,
　and the moon will not give its light,
[25] and the stars will be falling from heaven,
　and the powers in the heavens will
　　be shaken.

[26]Then they will see 'the Son of Man coming in clouds' with great power and glory. [27]Then he will send out the angels, and gather his elect from the four winds, from the ends of the earth to the ends of heaven.

The Lesson of the Fig Tree

28 "From the fig tree learn its lesson: as soon as its branch becomes tender and puts forth its leaves, you know that summer is near. [29]So also, when you see these things taking place, you know that he[v] is near, at the very gates. [30]Truly I tell you, this generation will not pass away until all these things have taken place. [31]Heaven and earth will pass away, but my words will not pass away.

The Necessity for Watchfulness

32 "But about that day or hour no one knows, neither the angels in heaven, nor the Son, but only the Father. [33]Beware, keep alert;[w] for you do not know when the time will come. [34]It is like a man going on a journey, when he leaves home and puts his slaves in charge, each with his work, and commands the doorkeeper to be on the watch. [35]Therefore, keep awake – for you do not know when the master of the house will come, in the evening, or at midnight, or at cockcrow, or at dawn, [36]or else he may find you asleep when he comes suddenly. [37]And what I say to you I say to all: Keep awake."

[s] Gk gospel　[t] Or the Christ　[u] Or christs　[v] Or it
[w] Other ancient authorities add and pray

The Plot to Kill Jesus

14 It was two days before the Passover and the festival of Unleavened Bread. The chief priests and the scribes were looking for a way to arrest Jesus[x] by stealth and kill him; [2]for they said, "Not during the festival, or there may be a riot among the people."

The Anointing at Bethany

[3] While he was at Bethany in the house of Simon the leper,[y] as he sat at the table, a woman came with an alabaster jar of very costly ointment of nard, and she broke open the jar and poured the ointment on his head. [4]But some were there who said to one another in anger, "Why was the ointment wasted in this way? [5]For this ointment could have been sold for more than three hundred denarii,[z] and the money given to the poor." And they scolded her. [6]But Jesus said, "Let her alone; why do you trouble her? She has performed a good service for me. [7]For you always have the poor with you, and you can show kindness to them whenever you wish; but you will not always have me. [8]She has done what she could; she has anointed my body beforehand for its burial. [9]Truly I tell you, wherever the good news[a] is proclaimed in the whole world, what she has done will be told in remembrance of her."

Judas Agrees to Betray Jesus

[10] Then Judas Iscariot, who was one of the twelve, went to the chief priests in order to betray him to them. [11]When they heard it, they were greatly pleased, and promised to give him money. So he began to look for an opportunity to betray him.

The Passover with the Disciples

[12] On the first day of Unleavened Bread, when the Passover lamb is sacrificed, his disciples said to him, "Where do you want us to go and make the preparations for you to eat the Passover?" [13]So he sent two of his disciples, saying to them, "Go into the city, and a man carrying a jar of water will meet you; follow him, [14]and wherever he enters, say to the owner of the house, 'The Teacher asks, Where is my guest room where I may eat the Passover with my disciples?' [15]He will show you a large room upstairs, furnished and ready. Make preparations for us there." [16]So the disciples set out and went to the city, and found everything as he had told them; and they prepared the Passover meal.

[17] When it was evening, he came with the twelve. [18]And when they had taken their places and were eating, Jesus said, "Truly I tell you, one of you will betray me, one who is eating with me." [19]They began to be distressed and to say to him one after another, "Surely, not I?" [20]He said to them, "It is one of the twelve, one who is dipping bread[b] into the bowl[c] with me. [21]For the Son of Man goes as it is written of him, but woe

---

[x] Gk *him*   [y] The terms *leper* and *leprosy* can refer to several diseases   [z] The denarius was the usual day's wage for a laborer   [a] Or *gospel*   [b] Gk lacks *bread*   [c] Other ancient authorities read *same bowl*

A WOMAN'S GIFT (MARK 14:1-9)

Although it is uncertain what exact kind of perfume the alabaster vial contained, it is clear that it was expensive: the woman had most likely been keeping this for a special occasion. The act of pouring it over Jesus' head connotes the anointing of kings and priests in the Old Testament and can be particularly related to the Messiah. Hence, an unknown, possibly a servant or a visiting prostitute – most likely the former – performs a special prophetic service for Jesus at a time when his death was near. Jesus' acceptance and commendation of this act says much about his view of women – he recognized her anointing for his burial, which was part of his most important mission – his death and resurrection for our salvation.

to that one by whom the Son of Man is betrayed! It would have been better for that one not to have been born."

The Institution of the Lord's Supper

22 While they were eating, he took a loaf of bread, and after blessing it he broke it, gave it to them, and said, "Take; this is my body." [23]Then he took a cup, and after giving thanks he gave it to them, and all of them drank from it. [24]He said to them, "This is my blood of the[d] covenant, which is poured out for many. [25]Truly I tell you, I will never again drink of the fruit of the vine until that day when I drink it new in the kingdom of God."

Peter's Denial Foretold

26 When they had sung the hymn, they went out to the Mount of Olives. [27]And Jesus said to them, "You will all become deserters; for it is written,

'I will strike the shepherd,
    and the sheep will be scattered.'

[28]But after I am raised up, I will go before you to Galilee." [29]Peter said to him, "Even though all become deserters, I will not." [30]Jesus said to him, "Truly I tell you, this day, this very night, before the cock crows twice, you will deny me three times." [31]But he said vehemently, "Even though I must die with you, I will not deny you." And all of them said the same.

Jesus Prays in Gethsemane

32 They went to a place called Gethsemane; and he said to his disciples, "Sit here while I pray." [33]He took with him Peter and James and John, and began to be distressed and agitated. [34]And he said to them, "I am deeply grieved, even to death; remain here, and keep awake." [35]And going a little farther, he threw himself on the ground and prayed that, if it were possible, the hour might pass from him. [36]He said, "Abba,[e] Father, for you all things are possible; remove this cup from me; yet, not what I want, but what you want." [37]He came and found them sleeping; and he said to Peter, "Simon, are you asleep? Could you not keep awake one hour? [38]Keep awake and pray that you may not come into the time of trial;[f] the spirit indeed is willing, but the flesh is weak." [39]And again he went away and prayed, saying the same words. [40]And once more he came and found them sleeping, for their eyes were very heavy; and they did not know what to say to him. [41]He came a third time and said to them, "Are you still sleeping and taking your rest? Enough! The hour has come; the Son of Man is betrayed into the hands of sinners. [42]Get up, let us be going. See, my betrayer is at hand."

The Betrayal and Arrest of Jesus

43 Immediately, while he was still speaking, Judas, one of the twelve, arrived; and with him there was a crowd with swords and clubs, from the chief priests, the scribes, and the elders. [44]Now the betrayer had given them a sign, saying, "The one I will kiss is the man; arrest him and lead him away under guard." [45]So when he came, he went up to him at once and said, "Rabbi!" and kissed him. [46]Then they laid hands on him and arrested him. [47]But one of those who stood near drew his sword and struck the slave of the high priest, cutting off his ear. [48]Then Jesus said to them, "Have you come out with swords and clubs to arrest me as though I were a bandit? [49]Day after day I was with you in the temple teaching, and you did not arrest

[d] Other ancient authorities add *new*   [e]Aramaic for *Father*   [f] Or *into temptation*

SINGING A HYMN (MARK 14:25)

Since this occasion was apparently the celebration of Passover, the hymn would be the Hallel (Pss. 113–18). This particular hymn is still used today in the Jewish celebration of Passover.

me. But let the scriptures be fulfilled." [50]All of them deserted him and fled.

51 A certain young man was following him, wearing nothing but a linen cloth. They caught hold of him, [52]but he left the linen cloth and ran off naked.

Jesus before the Council

53 They took Jesus to the high priest; and all the chief priests, the elders, and the scribes were assembled. [54]Peter had followed him at a distance, right into the courtyard of the high priest; and he was sitting with the guards, warming himself at the fire. [55]Now the chief priests and the whole council were looking for testimony against Jesus to put him to death; but they found none. [56]For many gave false testimony against him, and their testimony did not agree. [57]Some stood up and gave false testimony against him, saying, [58]"We heard him say, 'I will destroy this temple that is made with hands, and in three days I will build another, not made with hands.'" [59]But even on this point their testimony did not agree. [60]Then the high priest stood up before them and asked Jesus, "Have you no answer? What is it that they testify against you?" [61]But he was silent and did not answer. Again the high priest asked him, "Are you the Messiah,[g] the Son of the Blessed One?" [62]Jesus said, "I am; and

'you will see the Son of Man
  seated at the right hand of the Power,'
and 'coming with the clouds of
    heaven.'"

[63]Then the high priest tore his clothes and said, "Why do we still need witnesses? [64]You have heard his blasphemy! What is your decision?" All of them condemned him as deserving death. [65]Some began to spit on him, to blindfold him, and to strike him, saying to him, "Prophesy!" The guards also took him over and beat him.

Peter Denies Jesus

66 While Peter was below in the courtyard, one of the servant-girls of the high priest came by. [67]When she saw Peter warming himself, she stared at him and said, "You also were with Jesus, the man from Nazareth." [68]But he denied it, saying, "I do not know or understand what you are talking about." And he went out into the forecourt.[h] Then the cock crowed.[i] [69]And the servant-girl, on seeing him, began again to say to the bystanders, "This man is one of them." [70]But again he denied it. Then after a little while the bystanders again said to Peter, "Certainly you are one of them; for you are a Galilean." [71]But he began to curse, and he swore an oath, "I do not know this man you are talking about." [72]At that moment the cock crowed for the second time. Then Peter remembered that Jesus had said to him, "Before the cock crows twice, you will deny me three times." And he broke down and wept.

Jesus before Pilate

15 As soon as it was morning, the chief priests held a consultation with the elders and scribes and the whole council. They bound Jesus, led him away, and handed him over to Pilate. [2]Pilate asked him, "Are you the King of the Jews?" He answered him, "You say so." [3]Then the chief priests accused him of many things. [4]Pilate asked him again, "Have you no answer? See how many charges they bring against you." [5]But Jesus made no further reply, so that Pilate was amazed.

Pilate Hands Jesus over to Be Crucified

6 Now at the festival he used to release a prisoner for them, anyone for whom they asked. [7]Now a man called Barabbas was in prison with the rebels who had committed murder during the insurrection. [8]So the crowd came and began to ask Pilate to do for them according to his custom. [9]Then he answered them, "Do you want me to release for you the King of the Jews?" [10]For he realized that it was out of jealousy that

---

[g] Or *the Christ*   [h] Or *gateway*   [i] Other ancient authorities lack *Then the cock crowed*

the chief priests had handed him over. [11]But the chief priests stirred up the crowd to have him release Barabbas for them instead. [12]Pilate spoke to them again, "Then what do you wish me to do[j] with the man you call[k] the King of the Jews?" [13]They shouted back, "Crucify him!" [14]Pilate asked them, "Why, what evil has he done?" But they shouted all the more, "Crucify him!" [15]So Pilate, wishing to satisfy the crowd, released Barabbas for them; and after flogging Jesus, he handed him over to be crucified.

The Soldiers Mock Jesus

16 Then the soldiers led him into the courtyard of the palace (that is, the governor's headquarters[l]); and they called together the whole cohort. [17]And they clothed him in a purple cloak; and after twisting some thorns into a crown, they put it on him. [18]And they began saluting him, "Hail, King of the Jews!" [19]They struck his head with a reed, spat upon him, and knelt down in homage to him. [20]After mocking him, they stripped him of the purple cloak and put his own clothes on him. Then they led him out to crucify him.

The Crucifixion of Jesus

21 They compelled a passer-by, who was coming in from the country, to carry his cross; it was Simon of Cyrene, the father of Alexander and Rufus. [22]Then they brought Jesus[m] to the place called Golgotha (which means the place of a skull). [23]And they offered him wine mixed with myrrh; but he did not take it. [24]And they crucified him, and divided his clothes among them, casting lots to decide what each should take.

25 It was nine o'clock in the morning when they crucified him. [26]The inscription of the charge against him read, "The King of the Jews." [27]And with him they crucified two bandits, one on his right and one on his left.[n] [29]Those who passed by derided[o] him, shaking their heads and saying, "Aha! You who would destroy the temple and build it in three days, [30]save yourself, and come

down from the cross!" [31]In the same way the chief priests, along with the scribes, were also mocking him among themselves and saying, "He saved others; he cannot save himself. [32]Let the Messiah,[p] the King of Israel, come down from the cross now, so that we may see and believe." Those who were crucified with him also taunted him.

The Death of Jesus

33 When it was noon, darkness came over the whole land[q] until three in the afternoon. [34]At three o'clock Jesus cried out with a loud voice, "Eloi, Eloi, lema sabachthani?" which means, "My God, my God, why have you forsaken me?"[r] [35]When some of the bystanders heard it, they said, "Listen, he is calling for Elijah." [36]And someone ran, filled a sponge with sour wine, put it on a stick, and gave it to him to drink, saying, "Wait, let us see whether Elijah will come to take him down." [37]Then Jesus gave a loud cry and breathed his last. [38]And the curtain of the temple was torn in two, from top to bottom. [39]Now when the centurion, who stood facing him, saw that in this way he[s] breathed his last, he said, "Truly this man was God's Son!"[t]

40 There were also women looking on from a distance; among them were Mary Magdalene, and Mary the mother of James the younger and of Joses, and Salome. [41]These used to follow him and provided for him when he was in Galilee; and there were many other women who had come up with him to Jerusalem.

The Burial of Jesus

42 When evening had come, and since it was the day of Preparation, that is, the day

---

[j] Other ancient authorities read *what should I do*
[k] Other ancient authorities lack *the man you call*
[l] Gk *the praetorium*   [m] Gk *him*   [n] Other ancient authorities add verse 28, *And the scripture was fulfilled that says, "And he was counted among the lawless."*   [o] Or *blasphemed*   [p] Or *the Christ*
[q] Or *earth*   [r] Other ancient authorities read *made me a reproach*   [s] Other ancient authorities add *cried out and*   [t] Or *a son of God*

before the sabbath, ⁴³Joseph of Arimathea, a respected member of the council, who was also himself waiting expectantly for the kingdom of God, went boldly to Pilate and asked for the body of Jesus. ⁴⁴Then Pilate wondered if he were already dead; and summoning the centurion, he asked him whether he had been dead for some time. ⁴⁵When he learned from the centurion that he was dead, he granted the body to Joseph. ⁴⁶Then Joseph^u bought a linen cloth, and taking down the body,^v wrapped it in the linen cloth, and laid it in a tomb that had been hewn out of the rock. He then rolled a stone against the door of the tomb. ⁴⁷Mary Magdalene and Mary the mother of Joses saw where the body^v was laid.

The Resurrection of Jesus

16 When the sabbath was over, Mary Magdalene, and Mary the mother of James, and Salome bought spices, so that they might go and anoint him. ²And very early on the first day of the week, when the sun had risen, they went to the tomb. ³They had been saying to one another, "Who will roll away the stone for us from the entrance to the tomb?" ⁴When they looked up, they saw that the stone, which was very large, had already been rolled back. ⁵As they entered the tomb, they saw a young man, dressed in a white robe, sitting

◆ Life is like a journey. Its various stages are often marked by rites of passage, symbolic events which proclaim the transitory, pilgrim nature of the Christian life.

Such rites perform particularly crucial roles in the major transitions of life, helping to order experience when uncertainty is at its greatest, and addressing the meaning and significance of life itself. The major purpose of these rites is to name God as present – clearly, unambiguously and personally. Only God's grace is sufficient for the journey of life. Thus these rites are particularly important, for example, at the time of birth and the time of death. However, they also mark other significant events in life, such as marriage or the transition from childhood to adulthood.

Women have traditionally been at the forefront of care in such times of transition, and have had a strong role in rites of passage. Women's care of the newly born and the dying has extended to the rites accompanying these events. In some traditions, midwives have been authorized to baptize at the time of birth when necessary; women in many traditional societies are the key participants in such funeral preparations as laying out the body, as well as caring for those who mourn. At such times, when the basics of life are involved, women have great gifts for the community. Their spiritual resources of faith and hope, expressing the love and care of God in practical action, bring the presence of God near to those undergoing the most basic experiences of life itself. Thus they offer a hope and a care rooted in the present love of God and the promise of future re-creation ◆

^u Gk *he* ^v Gk *it*

THE RESURRECTION OF JESUS (MARK 16:1–8)

After the cruel treatment of Jesus, his humiliation and the injustice of all the events surrounding his death, Jesus' followers are left in total despair and bewilderment. The man they loved, the man who they thought was their Messiah, 'the Christ' (8:29), was gone. Their emptiness and hopelessness, their loneliness could never be repaired – everything was over, all their hopes and dreams gone. Even so, Mary Magdalene and Mary the mother of James wanted to do the little they could and went to the tomb with spices to anoint his body. On their arrival they are greeted by a young man in white who tells them that Jesus is not there, he is risen and will meet the disciples in Galilee. Out of sheer terror the women flee from the empty tomb.

on the right side; and they were alarmed. [6]But he said to them, "Do not be alarmed; you are looking for Jesus of Nazareth, who was crucified. He has been raised; he is not here. Look, there is the place they laid him. [7]But go, tell his disciples and Peter that he is going ahead of you to Galilee; there you will see him, just as he told you." [8]So they went out and fled from the tomb, for terror and amazement had seized them; and they said nothing to anyone, for they were afraid.[w]

THE SHORTER ENDING OF MARK

[[And all that had been commanded them they told briefly to those around Peter. And afterward Jesus himself sent out through them, from east to west, the sacred and imperishable proclamation of eternal salvation.[x]]]

THE LONGER ENDING OF MARK
Jesus Appears to Mary Magdalene

9 [[Now after he rose early on the first day of the week, he appeared first to Mary Magdalene, from whom he had cast out seven demons. [10]She went out and told those who had been with him, while they were mourning and weeping. [11]But when they heard that he was alive and had been seen by her, they would not believe it.

Jesus Appears to Two Disciples

12 After this he appeared in another form to two of them, as they were walking into the country. [13]And they went back and told the rest, but they did not believe them.

Jesus Commissions the Disciples

14 Later he appeared to the eleven themselves as they were sitting at the table; and he upbraided them for their lack of faith and stubbornness, because they had not

believed those who saw him after he had risen.[y] [15]And he said to them, "Go into all the world and proclaim the good news[z] to the whole creation. [16]The one who believes and is baptized will be saved; but the one who does not believe will be condemned. [17]And these signs will accompany those who believe: by using my name they will cast out demons; they will speak in new tongues; [18]they will pick up snakes in their hands,[a] and if they drink any deadly thing, it will not hurt them; they will lay their hands on the sick, and they will recover."

The Ascension of Jesus

19 So then the Lord Jesus, after he had spoken to them, was taken up into heaven and sat down at the right hand of God. [20]And they went out and proclaimed the good news everywhere, while the Lord worked with them and confirmed the message by the signs that accompanied it.[x]]]

[w] Some of the most ancient authorities bring the book to a close at the end of verse 8. One authority concludes the book with the shorter ending; others include the shorter ending and then continue with verses 9-20. In most authorities verses 9-20 follow immediately after verse 8, though in some of these authorities the passage is marked as being doubtful.   [x] Other ancient authorities add *Amen*
[y] Other ancient authorities add, in whole or in part, *And they excused themselves, saying, "This age of lawlessness and unbelief is under Satan, who does not allow the truth and power of God to prevail over the unclean things of the spirits. Therefore reveal your righteousness now" – thus they spoke to Christ. And Christ replied to them, "The term of years of Satan's power has been fulfilled, but other terrible things draw near. And for those who have sinned I was handed over to death, that they may return to the truth and sin no more, that they may inherit the spiritual and imperishable glory of righteousness that is in heaven."*   [z] Or *gospel*
[a] Other ancient authorities lack *in their hands*

16:9–20. (Some older manuscripts do not include these verses.) Jesus appears a number of times to his disciples before ascending to heaven, leaving them with a commission to 'Go into all the world and proclaim the good news.'

LUKE'S GOSPEL

INTRODUCTION

'The Spirit of the Lord is upon me, because he has anointed me to bring good news to the poor. He has sent me to proclaim release to the captives and recovery of sight to the blind, to let the oppressed go free, to proclaim the year of the Lord's favor' (Luke 4:18–19, from Is. 61:1–2).

Only in the Gospel of Luke is Jesus' ministry introduced with this prophecy from Isaiah which particularly emphasizes God's redeeming works: good news, concern for the disadvantaged, release from constraints and oppression, healing and restoration, and fulfillment of God's purposes in the Anointed One. Both the Gospel of Luke and its sequel, the Acts of the Apostles, weave these themes throughout their depiction of Jesus' ministry, his death, resurrection, and ascension, and the working of the Holy Spirit in the lives of early believers.

Who is Luke?

Nowhere in the text of his Gospel or Acts is Luke mentioned as the author. But by the end of the second century, Christian tradition identified the author of this Gospel with Luke, the 'beloved physician' (Col. 4:14), Paul's fellow worker (Philem. 25) and companion (2 Tim. 4:11). In Acts, there are three passages (the 'we' sections: 16:10–17; 20:5–21:18; 27:1–28:16) in which the author gives an eyewitness account of his journeys with Paul. Luke could have been this companion. The author indicates in his prologue to the Gospel that he is among the second generation of believers: he received accounts of events from 'eyewitnesses and servants of the word' (Luke 1:2). One tradition states that Luke was from Antioch in Syria, was unmarried, journeyed with Paul and stayed with him until Paul's martyrdom (about AD 65), and wrote the Gospel sometime afterwards in Greece.

Some modern scholars are sceptical about the traditional identification of Luke with the author of this Gospel, but no other candidates for authorship have been successfully presented. Contemporary scholars offer a wide range of dating for the Gospel, ranging from immediately after Paul's death until near the end of the first century. A date between AD 65–80 seems most likely.

Who is Theophilus?

Both the Gospel of Luke and Acts are dedicated to a man named Theophilus. In Luke 1:3 Theophilus is addressed as 'most excellent' (Greek *kratiste*), a term often used for public officials or men of some social and economic standing (see, e.g., Acts 23:26; 26:25). Nothing else is known about Theophilus. Was he a Christian? An interested pagan? An official charged with getting information about Paul and his beliefs prior to his trial at Rome? It seems likely that he was a new believer who wanted assurance about the events of Jesus' life and the subsequent spread of the new faith. But Luke was not writing for one person only. Ancient works of this sort were dedicated to one person, but the author expected a wider audience.

What are Luke's sources?

In his prologue to the Gospel, Luke tells Theophilus that many people 'have undertaken to set down an orderly account of the events that have been fulfilled among us' (1:1). These accounts, says Luke, are based on eyewitnesses of the actual events (1:2). Since Luke knows of other accounts of the events surrounding Jesus' life, presumably he has used some of them in creating his own Gospel. Comparative studies with Mark and Matthew, the other 'Synoptic' Gospels, suggest that Luke knew the Gospel of Mark as well as collections of Jesus' sayings.

Luke is the evangelist most interested in female imagery and in the activities involving women. He includes accounts of women not present in the other Gospels. It seems likely that during his life he met women who knew Jesus, for he emphasizes the role of Jesus' female followers (8:1-3; 23:27-29, 48-49, 55-56; 24:1-11, 22-25), and clearly uses them as sources for his information (1:4-2:52; 8:1-3, 18-21; 23:48-56; 24:1-11, 22-24).

Luke's special concerns

He notes that Jesus uses women as spiritual examples, both those whom he encountered in his own ministry (7:36; 10:38-42; 21:1-4) and those whose stories were part of the history of Israel (4:26; 11:31; 17:32). Luke records six of Jesus' healing miracles in which women were involved (4:38-39; 7:11-17; 8:2-33, 41-56; 13:10-17) and three parables (13:20-21; 15:8-10; 18:1-9). Frequently he displays a rejection of traditional, legalistic standards in his presentation of Jesus' encounters with women (7:36-50; 8:43-48; 10:38-42; 13:10-17; 11:27-28; 16:18; 20:27-38; 24:66-68). Luke is aware of Jesus' concern for the safety and salvation of women (17:35; 21:23; 23:28-31). The only description of a woman unsympathetic to Jesus' mission is of the serving girl (22:56-57).

Both Luke's Gospel and Acts share two further distinctive motifs: emphasis on journeys and pairings of stories, one which deals with a man and another which deals with a woman. More than the other three Gospels, Luke's Gospel is structured on the concept of a journey to fulfill God's purposes. Jesus' ministry begins in Galilee (Luke 4), and after he journeys around that region, he moves deliberately towards his ministry's fulfillment in Jerusalem (19:11ff.). There are numerous journeys found only in Luke's Gospel. Mary travels to see Elizabeth and receives confirmation that her unborn child is blessed (1:39-45). Mary and Joseph travel from Nazareth to Bethelehem where Jesus is born (2:3-7). Two parables found only in Luke's Gospel involve significant journeys: the Good Samaritan (10:29-45), and the Prodigal Son (15:11-32). Only this Gospel depicts the walk to Emmaus during which the risen Lord appears to two followers and breaks bread with them (24:13-35). Jesus' final acts with the disciples involve a journey to Bethany, outside Jerusalem, just before his ascension (24:50-53). The Acts of the Apostles, likewise, includes the journeys of the early believers from Jerusalem and surrounding areas into the Gentile territory of Asia Minor, Greece, and finally to Rome, the capital of the Roman Empire. Perhaps Luke's own experiences travelling with Paul impressed him that life itself is a journey toward fulfillment of God's purposes.

Luke pairs stories about men and women in both his Gospel and Acts. Mary's song (Luke 1:46-55) is paired with Zecharias' prophecy (1:67-79). Two elderly people, the devout Simeon and the prophet Anna, both recognize the infant Jesus as the Lord's Messiah (2:25-38). The healing of the man with an unclean spirit and that of Peter's mother-in-law are paired in 4:31-39. Another pair of healings – the centurion with a sick slave and the widow with a sick son – occur in 7:2-17. In his parables, the man who finds his lost sheep is paired with the woman who finds her lost coin (15:3-10). Both women and men experience the empty tomb and the risen Lord (24:1-12, 22-24). Only the healings in Luke 4 and the resurrection experiences in Luke 24 are paired in any of the other Gospels. (See the introduction to Acts for similar pairs there.) Why does Luke pair such events? Perhaps by these pairings he is emphasizing to his readers that God equally cares for and works through both men and women.

Questions on Luke's Gospel

(1) If Luke suggests that the experiences of men and women are equally important to God, do I believe that *my* experiences are as important to God as those of others are?

(2) How is my own life a journey whether I stay at home or travel widely? Where am I going on my journey? What are my experiences? How could I describe my journey as a Christian to someone else?

(3) How can I incorporate some of Luke's themes – compassion, release, healing, restoration, acceptance and fulfillment of God's purposes – more fully into my own life?

Dedication to Theophilus

1 Since many have undertaken to set down an orderly account of the events that have been fulfilled among us, ²just as they were handed on to us by those who from the beginning were eyewitnesses and servants of the word, ³I too decided, after investigating everything carefully from the very first,ᵃ to write an orderly account for you, most excellent Theophilus, ⁴so that you may know the truth concerning the things about which you have been instructed.

The Birth of John the Baptist Foretold

5 In the days of King Herod of Judea, there was a priest named Zechariah, who belonged to the priestly order of Abijah. His wife was a descendant of Aaron, and her name was Elizabeth. ⁶Both of them were righteous before God, living blamelessly according to all the commandments and regulations of the Lord. ⁷But they had no children, because Elizabeth was barren, and both were getting on in years.

ᵃOr *for a long time*

LUKE 1

1. Luke here tells us that he has examined the accounts of Christ's life which were already in circulation. None of them met the need which he perceived, and so he was prompted to produce a more 'orderly' narrative. This does not necessarily mean that the events occurred in precisely the order in which they are now arranged. Rather, Luke sensed certain basic themes which caused him to construct his outline to emphasize certain features.

St John observed that he did not think the world itself could contain the books which might be written concerning the events relative to the life of Christ (John 20:30–31). He too was selective with a different set of objectives (John 21:25). Luke's purpose is to present the material in a sequence which might appeal to a mind trained in the logical and legal systems of the Roman world. He stresses the accuracy and thoroughness of his inquiry.

Although Luke's account contains considerable material which is essentially the same as that found in Matthew and Mark, he includes those features necessary to give credibility in the investigative world of antiquity: geographic location, names of rulers which are essential for dating, medical descriptions, and even formal information about legal charges.

He is careful to tell us that he has used eyewitnesses (Luke 1:2); and many of these appear to have been women. The birth narrative, the crucifixion and the resurrection account must of necessity have come from female witnesses. It is possible that he also consulted the prophesying daughters of Philip, who were said by the apostolic father Papias to have preserved certain of the traditions about Christ. The reliability of the women witnesses becomes a theme in Luke. Their testimony is a significant part of the framework which Luke has constructed to give the reader a more adequate comprehension of the Gospel narrative.

5. Although much of the activity of this Gospel will take place in Galilee, the cycle of events will begin and end in Jerusalem. The Temple is a focal point to which the action will return again and again. Luke alone of the four evangelists stresses the place of Mary and Anna in the Temple (Luke 2:37, 42).

6. Though admirably suited for parenthood, Elizabeth and Zechariah know the frustration and heartbreak of childlessness. Like Sarah and Abraham, Hannah and the Shunammite woman (Gen. 11:30, 1 Sam. 1:5; 2 Kings 4:14), these childless saints appear to have possessed a spirituality deeply attuned to the mind and purposes of God (Gal. 4:27).

Often the woman with no children of her own develops a mothering ministry to others. Despite her own childlessness, Elizabeth was well able to nurture young people. Thus she could render the support and guidance which her young cousin Mary would need in preparation for the Messiah's birth.

8 Once when he was serving as priest before God and his section was on duty, [9]he was chosen by lot, according to the custom of the priesthood, to enter the sanctuary of the Lord and offer incense. [10]Now at the time of the incense offering, the whole assembly of the people was praying outside. [11]Then there appeared to him an angel of the Lord, standing at the right side of the altar of incense. [12]When Zechariah saw him, he was terrified; and fear overwhelmed him. [13]But the angel said to him, "Do not be afraid, Zechariah, for your prayer has been heard. Your wife Elizabeth will bear you a son, and you will name him John. [14]You will have joy and gladness, and many will rejoice at his birth, [15]for he will be great in the sight of the Lord. He must never drink wine or strong drink; even before his birth he will be filled with the Holy Spirit. [16]He will turn many of the people of Israel to the Lord their God. [17]With the spirit and power of Elijah he will go before him, to turn the hearts of parents to their children, and the disobedient to the wisdom of the righteous, to make ready a people prepared for the Lord." [18]Zechariah said to the angel, "How will I know that this is so? For I am an old man, and my wife is getting on in years." [19]The angel replied, "I am Gabriel. I stand in the presence of God, and I have been sent to speak to you and to bring you this good news. [20]But now, because you did not believe my words, which will be fulfilled in their time, you will become mute, unable to speak, until the day these things occur."

21 Meanwhile the people were waiting for Zechariah, and wondered at his delay in the sanctuary. [22]When he did come out, he could not speak to them, and they realized that he had seen a vision in the sanctuary. He kept motioning to them and remained unable to speak. [23]When his time of service was ended, he went to his home.

24 After those days his wife Elizabeth conceived, and for five months she remained in seclusion. She said, [25]"This is

---

8–9. The ranks of the priesthood were so large that priests ordinarily gave only two months of service a year. Their duties were assigned by lot, and it may have been a very rare experience for Zechariah to make the incense offering.

While Matthew stresses the role of the prophets in foretelling the coming of the Messiah, Luke begins with the official priesthood. This gives a different sort of legitimacy to the story. Although much of the rest of the story will take place in impromptu and unofficial circumstances (a stable, the wilderness, the carpenter shop, the dusty roads and lake of Galilee), it is in the Holy Place, during the performance of a sacred act by a duly appointed functionary, that the birth of Messiah's forerunner is announced.

17. Malachi records God's promise to send the prophet Elijah before the day of the LORD (Mal. 4:5–6). It would be his mission to 'turn the hearts of parents to their children'. That promise is here repeated for the ministry of John the Baptist, who was to come in the spirit and power of Elijah.

20. The enforced silence of Zechariah could not have been an easy circumstance for his elderly wife experiencing the discomforts and anxieties of her first pregnancy. He was unable to offer her the verbal support, sympathy and encouragement which she might have welcomed; but neither could he offer advice or observations which might have been less than helpful.

Zechariah, though righteous and blameless, had failed to respond with faith to the angel's message. As the two women, Mary and Elizabeth, prepared themselves to raise children ordained to be instruments of God, they were spared his possibly sceptical comments. If he had doubted the working of God's power to cause conception in his aged wife, how much less could he have accepted the circumstances attending the pregnancy of Mary? As a mute, he could question neither the possible paternity of her child nor her ability to raise him. She was mercifully spared a voice that might have filled her with alarm, uncertainty and anxiety.

what the Lord has done for me when he looked favorably on me and took away the disgrace I have endured among my people."

◆ Three women stand out because of their wisdom in dealing with the astonishing events surrounding the birth of Christ: Mary, Elizabeth, and Anna. Elizabeth not only accepts her own pregnancy at an advanced age, but also provides support to the young virgin who has been told to expect the birth of Messiah. Elizabeth demonstrates remarkable spiritual perception not only of the upcoming divine event but also of Mary's attitude. The older woman welcomes Messiah's mother without causing Mary to make any painful explanations, and she directs praise toward the God who is bringing to pass his redemptive purposes. It is only after Elizabeth's joyful affirmation of Mary's condition and approbation of her faith that the virgin herself bursts into song.

The second wise woman, Mary, has displayed remarkable maturity in seeking out godly counsel as she faces an unplanned pregnancy without a husband. She regarded Elizabeth as one having the wisdom and love to guide her in her perplexity. She must have already felt a confidence born of other associations with her saintly cousin. Still, she could not know what sort of reception she might expect from Zechariah and Elizabeth. Instead of being met with doubts or even condemnation, she finds an exuberant welcome. The weariness and uncertainties of Mary's journey are dissolved into a paean of praise. She has entered into a house of faith and love where she may share her thoughts, her prayers, and her needs.

Fortified by her three months' stay with Elizabeth, Mary can accept the distressing and perplexing circumstances attendant upon her son's birth and maintain a poised equilibrium. If she cannot understand all that is taking place, she can 'keep all these things and ponder them in her heart'. If she must give birth in a stable after rejection at the inn, she does not question God's provision or purpose. She believes despite adversity and is faithful in her calling.

The third wise woman is Anna, the prophet who recognizes the divine child despite the humble appearance of the couple who present him at the Temple (2:36–38). Thereupon she assumes a prophetic ministry of proclamation. She had a consuming passion to serve God, having given some 50 years to the ministry of prayer. Although she remained in the Temple, her perspective was not that of the Temple authorities, who had made a political alliance with their Roman conquerors. Her influence lay with those who awaited the coming of God's Anointed One as a spiritual rather than a political event. To those who had faithfully watched and prayed, she communicated the fulfillment of their desire.

These three wise women demonstrate the qualities of patience, prayer, praise, and faith ◆

The Birth of Jesus Foretold

26 In the sixth month the angel Gabriel was sent by God to a town in Galilee called Nazareth, [27]to a virgin engaged to a man whose name was Joseph, of the house of David. The virgin's name was Mary. [28]And he came to her and said, "Greetings, favored one! The Lord is with you."[b] [29]But

[b] Other ancient authorities add *Blessed are you among women*

---

26. The angel Gabriel goes first to the Temple, then to the hill country of Galilee, first to one engaged in an official act of worship on behalf of all Israel, the second time to a humble young woman in a very obscure village.
27. Hebrew betrothal ceremonies were formal and binding, but the actual union did not take place until later. It is during this period of waiting that Mary is visited by the angel.

she was much perplexed by his words and pondered what sort of greeting this might be. ³⁰The angel said to her, "Do not be afraid, Mary, for you have found favor with God. ³¹And now, you will conceive in your womb and bear a son, and you will name him Jesus. ³²He will be great, and will be called the Son of the Most High, and the Lord God will give to him the throne of his ancestor David. ³³He will reign over the house of Jacob forever, and of his kingdom there will be no end." ³⁴Mary said to the angel, "How can this be, since I am a virgin?"ᶜ ³⁵The angel said to her, "The Holy Spirit will come upon you, and the power of the Most High will overshadow you; therefore the child to be bornᵈ will be holy; he will be called Son of God. ³⁶And now, your relative Elizabeth in her old age has also conceived a son; and this is the sixth month for her who was said to be barren. ³⁷For nothing will be impossible with God." ³⁸Then Mary said, "Here am I, the servant of the Lord; let it be with me according to your word." Then the angel departed from her.

Mary Visits Elizabeth

39 In those days Mary set out and went with haste to a Judean town in the hill country, ⁴⁰where she entered the house of Zechariah and greeted Elizabeth. ⁴¹When Elizabeth heard Mary's greeting, the child leaped in her womb. And Elizabeth was filled with the Holy Spirit ⁴²and exclaimed with a loud cry, "Blessed are you among women, and blessed is the fruit of your womb. ⁴³And why has this happened to me, that the mother of my Lord comes to me? ⁴⁴For as soon as I heard the sound of your greeting, the child in my womb leaped for

ᶜ Gk *I do not know a man*   ᵈ Other ancient authorities add *of you*

---

30. God's redemptive plan depends upon the faith and collaboration of a woman. Her body will bring the Messiah into the world, but her mind and spirit must also be engaged. Hers will be the task of nurturing and guiding the young child who will be called the Son of the Most High (v. 32). The task of motherhood is always taxing, but it is also rewarding.

34. Her question does not imply lack of faith, as did that of Zechariah, but rather a request for an explanation as to how such a circumstance might be possible.

35. The angel's response makes it clear that the process will be spiritual rather than sexual, that it will be full of God's power, and that the child shall be called the Son of God.

38. Mary of her own free will chooses her role of motherhood. It has not been forced upon her. Myths abounded in the ancient world about the impregnation of women by the gods. The stories are full of violence, seduction, and deceit. By contrast, Mary has been given a straightforward explanation and then willingly becomes the instrument of God's plan in the incarnation of Jesus Christ. God never forces himself upon us but waits to be invited into our hearts and lives.

39. The Gospel of Luke is a book of journeys, and the first is that of Mary to the home of Elizabeth. She goes in search of both practical and spiritual counsel. Nevertheless she must have wondered along the way how she could explain her condition to the elderly couple whom she hoped would receive her.

40. Her anxiety is dispelled by Elizabeth, whose joyous burst of praise, guided by the Holy Spirit, must indeed have fortified Mary's own spirit.

41. Not only is Elizabeth filled with the Spirit, but also the unborn babe within her, as had been prophesied by the angel (v. 15). The mother maintains that the child himself has led her to the conviction that Mary is actually the mother of the Messiah. She is indeed open to God's direction.

44. The stirring of an infant within the womb can be a spiritual experience, one that leads us closer to Christ. Certain Scripture passages raise the possibility of spiritual guidance and awareness before birth (Gen. 25:22–26; Judg. 13:4–5; Job 10:8–12; Ps. 139:13–16; Is. 44:2, 24; 46:3; 49:1, 5; Jer. 1:5; Gal. 1:15). Prenatal influence can in some instances shape children and their spiritual

joy. ⁴⁵And blessed is she who believed that there would be^e a fulfillment of what was spoken to her by the Lord."

◆ Luke introduces significant ministries with the use of songs, often deeply reminiscent of songs in the Old testament. Elizabeth is the first to break into prophetic song (1:42–45), and Mary is next to express her joy and her sense of mission in a hymn of praise (1:46–55). This is followed by the song of Zechariah (1:68–79), who also extols God for what he is performing in the redemption of Israel and for the part to be played by his son. The angels' song (2:14) extends the promise of blessing beyond Israel to all who open their hearts to God. Simeon's hymn (2:29–32) describes the joy of the elderly at seeing at last the fulfillment of their dearest hopes and prayers. He emphasizes the universality of the Savior's outreach 'to all people'. At the outset of the ministries of John the Baptist and Jesus, each again defines his mission by applying a song from Isaiah to his own activities (3:4; 4:18–19).

These songs, rooted in the Old Testament, are skillfully placed to provide the reader with an interpretation of what is to follow. They build a sense of continuity and divine proclamation for the beginning of Christ's earthly mission ◆

Mary's Song of Praise

46 And Mary^f said,
"My soul magnifies the Lord,
⁴⁷ and my spirit rejoices in God my Savior,
⁴⁸ for he has looked with favor on the lowliness of his servant.
Surely, from now on all generations will call me blessed;
⁴⁹ for the Mighty One has done great things for me,
and holy is his name.
⁵⁰ His mercy is for those who fear him from generation to generation.
⁵¹ He has shown strength with his arm;
he has scattered the proud in the thoughts of their hearts.
⁵² He has brought down the powerful from their thrones,
and lifted up the lowly;
⁵³ he has filled the hungry with good things,
and sent the rich away empty.
⁵⁴ He has helped his servant Israel, in remembrance of his mercy,
⁵⁵ according to the promise he made to our ancestors,
to Abraham and to his descendants forever."

^e Or *believed, for there will be* ^f Other ancient authorities read *Elizabeth*

attitudes. Pregnant women might find the months of waiting less wearisome if they realized that God was doing his work not only upon the bodies but in the souls of their unborn children and of themselves as well.

45. Elizabeth singles out Mary's faith in believing what has been spoken, in contrast to Zechariah who disbelieved the words of the angel.

46. Mary's song of praise resembles that of Hannah, who rejoiced in God's mercy after the birth of her long-desired son (1 Sam. 2:1–10). This indicates Mary's familiarity with the Scriptures which well up from deep within her.

48. Mary is filled with wonder that God has chosen one of a low social and economic condition to bring to the world the Son of God. She calls herself God's slavewoman, aware that her gender has not deflected the design of God but rather fulfilled it (Gal. 4:4, 'born of a woman'). Her use of the word 'slave' expresses again her identity with the marginalized and disenfranchised of human society. (See note on 'Slavery', p. 336.)

Mary is overwhelmed by God's goodness to the lowly and by the honor which he can bring to the despised of earth. Her focus is on the liberating and levelling work of God in human hearts and lives. This song will be echoed in Jesus' manifestation of himself as anointed to preach to the poor, the downtrodden, and the afflicted (Luke 4:18–19).

56 And Mary remained with her about three months and then returned to her home.

The Birth of John the Baptist

57 Now the time came for Elizabeth to give birth, and she bore a son. ⁵⁸Her neighbors and relatives heard that the Lord had shown his great mercy to her, and they rejoiced with her.

59 On the eighth day they came to circumcise the child, and they were going to name him Zechariah after his father. ⁶⁰But his mother said, "No; he is to be called John." ⁶¹They said to her, "None of your relatives has this name." ⁶²Then they began motioning to his father to find out what name he wanted to give him. ⁶³He asked for a writing tablet and wrote, "His name is John." And all of them were amazed. ⁶⁴Immediately his mouth was opened and his tongue freed, and he began to speak, praising God. ⁶⁵Fear came over all their neighbors, and all these things were talked about throughout the entire hill country of Judea. ⁶⁶All who heard them pondered them and said, "What then will this child become?" For, indeed, the hand of the Lord was with him.

Zechariah's Prophecy

67 Then his father Zechariah was filled with the Holy Spirit and spoke this prophecy:

⁶⁸ "Blessed be the Lord God of Israel,
　　for he has looked favorably on his
　　　　people and redeemed them.
⁶⁹ He has raised up a mighty savior[g] for
　　us
　　in the house of his servant David,
⁷⁰ as he spoke through the mouth of his
　　　　holy prophets from of old,
⁷¹ 　that we would be saved from our
　　　　enemies and from the hand of
　　　　all who hate us.
⁷² Thus he has shown the mercy
　　　　promised to our ancestors,

[g] Gk *a horn of salvation*

---

56. Mary leaves before the actual birth of John the Baptist, but she has observed all the preparations necessary before a birth, and she has discussed freely with a mature woman the significance of the miraculous process in which they are both involved.

58. The neighbors and relatives are not simply meddlers. Their role is far more than this, as they give support to a first-time mother who must have known the uncertainties and insecurities that almost all women feel at the birth or adoption of their first child. The care of a newborn, so different from that required by older human beings, is not assimilated from books or lectures. Rather it is taught one-on-one within a home that has been blessed with a new arrival. This precious lore, preserved from time immemorial by women, is usually passed on from an older mother to a younger one. Even a mother who is quite experienced in taking care of other people's babies sometimes feels a need for reinforcement when the infant is her very own.

Elizabeth's neighbors and kinfolk are there to support her, to help as they can, to care for her and the newborn infant. Their joy and praise for God's goodness must have nurtured the elderly woman whose own husband could not voice the words at this, the happiest and most astounding event in their lives. Theirs is an effort to stress the spiritual importance of the occasion.

The insistence of the neighbors and relatives upon the naming of the child is unwarranted: like many other well-intentioned people, they have overstepped their role. Here the officious behavior of neighbors and kinsfolk results in the freeing of Zechariah's speech to proclaim the praises and purposes of God.

68. Zechariah's song centers upon the fulfillment of the words of the prophets and the anticipation that John himself will be a prophet. In terms of literary influence, the old priest draws his inspiration and language largely from the prophetic writings, while Mary's song looks to the Psalms and the canticle of Hannah (1 Sam. 2:1–10).

and has remembered his holy
    covenant,
73 the oath that he swore to our ancestor
    Abraham,
    to grant us 74that we, being rescued
      from the hands of our enemies,
might serve him without fear, 75in
    holiness and righteousness
    before him all our days.
76 And you, child, will be called the
    prophet of the Most High;
    for you will go before the Lord to
    prepare his ways,
77 to give knowledge of salvation to his
    people
    by the forgiveness of their sins.
78 By the tender mercy of our God,
    the dawn from on high will break
    upon[h] us,
79 to give light to those who sit in
    darkness and in the shadow of
    death,
    to guide our feet into the way of
    peace."

80 The child grew and became strong in spirit, and he was in the wilderness until the day he appeared publicly to Israel.

The Birth of Jesus

2 In those days a decree went out from Emperor Augustus that all the world should be registered. 2This was the first registration and was taken while Quirinius was governor of Syria. 3All went to their own towns to be registered. 4Joseph also went from the town of Nazareth in Galilee to Judea, to the city of David called Bethlehem, because he was descended from the house and family of David. 5He went to be registered with Mary, to whom he was engaged and who was expecting a child. 6While they were there, the time

◆ Mary the mother of Jesus was pregnant outside of wedlock, as many another woman has found herself to be. Those who lament the inhospitality of the inn should examine their own hearts as they encounter women in such circumstances. The condition of these women may have been caused by their own indiscretion; but they may have been the victims of rape, incest, manipulation, trickery, seduction, or outright ignorance. Let us remember that Mary willingly accepted her pregnancy despite the obvious complications.

There is no indication in the biblical text that Mary's parents offered her support, understanding, or even a place to stay in their home. These are afforded first by Elizabeth and then by Joseph. The carpenter, upon discovering that his betrothed is already impregnated, at first assumes that she has been guilty of sexual impropriety. While he is seeking to deal with this situation as wisely and kindly as he can, God's enlightenment leads him to take Mary into his home as his wedded wife. Righteous Joseph stands as a precursor of other men who have assumed the protection and support of a woman

[h] Other ancient authorities read *has broken upon*

---

80. It is often speculated that John's elderly parents passed away while he was quite young, and he may well have been raised in a desert community of holy men. The Qumran community in the Dead Sea area is known to have adopted a number of children.

LUKE 2

1–2. The order for this census is known from non-biblical accounts and probably was executed in Palestine about 4 BC. It required that families be registered at the residence of the oldest living ancestor, who was recognized as holding jurisdiction over all the others. If Joseph's father or grandfather were still living, this would necessitate the trip. Probably Mary's presence would not have been required for the census, but the circumstances of her condition would have rendered it expedient.

and her unborn child, even if he was not the biological father. Concerned for all her needs, he seeks out a stable after the rejection at the inn.

Women in crisis pregnancy are often overwhelmed by a swirl of emotions: fear, bitterness, despair, a sense of guilt and betrayal, shame, uncertainty, and bewilderment. One of the greatest needs is for wise and kindly counsel, provided in the case of Mary by Elizabeth. Frequently they do not know where they may turn for an understanding reception. How slow other Christian women have been to lend their hearts and ears and helping hands!

The Gospel stories explain how Mary was given a confidante, strength for what lay before her, instruction on the care of the newborn, and provision for her material needs. Joseph, Elizabeth, Zaccharias, Anna, Simeon, the shepherds and the Magi are all God's endowment for a network of support during the pregnancy, birth, and early days after the delivery.

Women pregnant out of wedlock experience rejection, as Mary did; but their hearts are frequently open to God as was that of Mary. Often they develop an increased spiritual awareness. As new life grows inside them, Christ may be born in their hearts to be their Savior and guide. Many a woman in such circumstances has turned to God in a new way, thereby finding strength and sustaining grace for the future ◆

---

came for her to deliver her child. [7]And she gave birth to her firstborn son and wrapped him in bands of cloth, and laid him in a manger, because there was no place for them in the inn.

The Shepherds and the Angels

8 In that region there were shepherds living in the fields, keeping watch over their flock by night. [9]Then an angel of the Lord stood before them, and the glory of the Lord shone around them, and they were terrified. [10]But the angel said to them, "Do not be afraid; for see – I am bringing you good news of great joy for all the people: [11]to you is born this day in the city of David a Savior, who is the Messiah,[i] the Lord. [12]This will be a sign for you: you

[i] Or *the Christ*

---

7. The stopping place for travellers was not a hotel as we know it, but rather a rectangular building with apartments ranged along the outside porches for the accommodation of travellers. The central part of the courtyard was reserved for the enclosure of the animals accompanying them. The overcrowded conditions would have given no privacy in which a birth might take place.

Swaddling clothes were woven of linen and were very absorbent. This was especially useful in cold weather as the bands were so thick that the baby needed to be unwrapped for change only a few times during a day. The custom of swaddling infants continued in Europe into this century. We may suppose that the swaddling bands had been prepared – or at least planned – during Mary's visit to Elizabeth. Although God was working a mighty miracle, Mary was not negligent in her part of making ready all that the child would need.

After the tight constriction of the womb, babies often rest more comfortably in a small enclosed space. On many occasions women have had to improvise a safe bed for a baby so that it would not squirm its way into danger. Even a bureau drawer or a suitcase has served. A stone manger was sometimes used in the Near East as a crib for the newborn. Cushioned with hay, it provided a safe and snug place for an infant, protected from cold drafts, falls, and intrusions.

8. Ordinarily no flocks were permitted to graze in the fields around the town except those intended for sacrifice in the Temple. The presence of shepherds watching all night in the fields close to Bethlehem may suggest that the event took place in the lambing season.

12. The signs given to the shepherds indicate that Mary has conscientiously prepared and cared for the newborn child.

will find a child wrapped in bands of cloth and lying in a manger." [13]And suddenly there was with the angel a multitude of the heavenly host,[j] praising God and saying,

[14] "Glory to God in the highest heaven,
and on earth peace among those
whom he favors!"[k]

15 When the angels had left them and gone into heaven, the shepherds said to one another, "Let us go now to Bethlehem and see this thing that has taken place, which the Lord has made known to us." [16]So they went with haste and found Mary and Joseph, and the child lying in the manger. [17]When they saw this, they made known what had been told them about this child; [18]and all who heard it were amazed at what the shepherds told them. [19]But Mary treasured all these words and pondered them in her heart. [20]The shepherds returned, glorifying and praising God for all they had heard and seen, as it had been told them.

Jesus Is Named

21 After eight days had passed, it was time to circumcise the child; and he was called Jesus, the name given by the angel before he was conceived in the womb.

Jesus Is Presented in the Temple

22 When the time came for their purification according to the law of Moses, they brought him up to Jerusalem to present him to the Lord [23](as it is written in the law of the Lord, "Every firstborn male shall be designated as holy to the Lord"), [24]and they offered a sacrifice according to what is stated in the law of the Lord, "a pair of turtledoves or two young pigeons."

25 Now there was a man in Jerusalem whose name was Simeon;[l] this man was righteous and devout, looking forward to the consolation of Israel, and the Holy Spirit rested on him. [26]It had been revealed to him by the Holy Spirit that he would not see death before he had seen the Lord's Messiah.[m] [27]Guided by the Spirit, Simeon[n] came into the temple; and when the parents brought in the child Jesus, to do for him what was customary under the law, [28]Simeon[o] took him in his arms and praised God, saying,

[29] "Master, now you are dismissing your
servant[p] in peace,
according to your word;

[j] Gk *army*   [k] Other ancient authorities read *peace, goodwill among people*   [l] Gk *Symeon*   [m] Or *the Lord's Christ*   [n] Gk *In the Spirit, he*   [o] Gk *he*   [p] Gk *slave*

---

14. The song of the angels declares peace to human beings of good will. There is God's part and our part in this blessing. Peace comes to those who are open and receptive to God's prompting and provision.

17. The shepherds share the angel's news and add their own experience of finding the babe. Like all who bear witness to finding Christ, their testimony is a source of wonder to those who hear the news.

19. Mary's attitude is one of reflective patience and trust as she treasures in her heart all the incomprehensible promises and seemingly contradictory events. She is willing to wait for God to clarify the puzzle for her.

21–22. Both the circumcision and the presentation in the Temple are a fulfillment of the Law of Israel. An observance is made at the end of Mary's ritual purification from childbirth (Lev. 12:1–8). A strict sanitary code prohibiting sexual contact for six weeks following a birth gave Israel a far higher standard of health than that of the surrounding nations. The first-born male of an Israelite woman was considered the property of God and must be ransomed back (Exod. 13:2, 12–13; Num. 3:12–13, 40–51; 8:16–18; 18:15–16). Later Jesus will again be reclaimed by Mary in the Temple (Luke 2:49–51).

30 for my eyes have seen your salvation,
31 which you have prepared in the
presence of all peoples,
32 a light for revelation to the Gentiles
and for glory to your people Israel."

33 And the child's father and mother
were amazed at what was being said
about him. 34Then Simeon[q] blessed
them and said to his mother Mary, "This
child is destined for the falling and
the rising of many in Israel, and to be
a sign that will be opposed 35so that
the inner thoughts of many will be revealed
– and a sword will pierce your own soul
too."

36 There was also a prophet, Anna[r] the
daughter of Phanuel, of the tribe of Asher.
She was of a great age, having lived with
her husband seven years after her marriage,
37then as a widow to the age of eighty-four.
She never left the temple but worshiped
there with fasting and prayer night and day.
38At that moment she came, and began to
praise God and to speak about the child[s] to
all who were looking for the redemption of
Jerusalem.

◆ The female prophets are proof that God calls and equips women for religious leadership. Two of the five pre-monarchical personalities identified by title as prophets were women. Miriam and Deborah are included along with Abraham (Gen. 20:7), Aaron (Exod. 7:1), and Moses (Deut. 18:15; 34:10; Num. 12:5–8; Hos. 12:13). Miriam celebrated at the Exodus (Exod. 15:20–21), opposed Moses (Num. 12:1–15; Deut. 24:9), yet was lauded in later prophetical tradition (Mic. 6:4). Two full chapters, Judg. 4–5, are devoted to the leadership of Deborah as prophet, judge, and military leader.

In the period of the kings, though both prophets Jeremiah and Zephaniah were active at the time, when the scroll of the Law was found in the Temple, the royal officials went to prophet Huldah for its authentication (2 Kings 22:8–20; 2 Chron. 34:14–28). The word of this woman was the basis of the most extensive reform in Israel's history.

[q] Gk *Symeon* [r] Gk *Hanna* [s] Gk *him*

---

34. Here we find a sense of completion, one of the ultimate satisfactions of old age. Simeon's waiting has not been in vain, nor his life wasted. He will leave this world knowing that his life has been full of meaning, in tune with the purposes of God. The four old people who frame the nativity story (Zechariah, Elizabeth, Simeon and Anna) all tell of continuity with the old covenant and the promise of the new. All find in Christ the consummation of their dearest hopes.

35. The prophecy of Simeon, directed particularly at Mary, must have brought great shock to her. Yet it also provided a preparation for what she must later experience, as had the earlier annunciation by the angel. Under the guidance of the Holy Spirit, Simeon empathizes with her and understands the emotion of a mother at the death of a child. This Gospel story is permeated with remarkable understandings of women's emotions and perceptions.

36–38. The prophet appointed by God to announce the birth of the Messiah is a woman named Anna. Just as the proclamation of the resurrection is entrusted to angels and to women, so too the proclamation of Christ's arrival on earth is entrusted to angels and a woman. She is specifically called a prophet (v. 36), as are nine other women of the Bible (Exod. 15:20; Judg. 4:4; Is. 8:3; 2 Kings 22:14; Neh. 6:14; Acts 21:9). Prophecy is defined as communication which strengthens, encourages and builds up God's people (1 Cor. 14:3–4).

38. She communicated the news of Jesus' birth only after first giving thanks to God. The word that is used here for her praise also means 'to confess freely and openly'. Let us not forget that praise is an integral part of prophecy. To those faithful ones who wait for the redemption of Israel she makes her confession, fearlessly and freely. The long years of their waiting were over, for God had fulfilled the promise.

Comparing the description of the office of musician-prophets in 1 Chron. 25 with Ps. 68 (vv. 11–14, 24–26) it seems evident that women were included among those whose music ministry was identified by the Chronicler as prophecy. (The Hebrew text makes it clear that the host of those who bear the tidings in Ps. 68:11 are female.)

In the prophetical books, the wife of Isaiah is called a prophet (Is. 8:3), and Joel promises a day when the Holy Spirit and the gift of prophecy will be dispensed regardless of gender (Joel 2:28–29). In fact, the appearance of female prophets is to be validation of the day of the LORD.

In light of Joel's prophecy, Luke demonstrates the Messianic age has come when this promise is fulfilled in Acts – women are pictured among the 120 who are filled with the Spirit and prophesy (Acts 1:14–15; cf. 2:14–21). There are even flurries of Pentecost in the birth narratives of Christ when prophecy is revived – and women are included among those who prophesy (Elizabeth, Luke 1:41–45; Mary, Luke 1:46–55; and Anna, Luke 2:36–38). As the church expands, the ripples of Pentecost extend, and women, such as Philip's four daughters, continue to be identified among New Testament prophets (Acts 21:8–9).

Paul, in describing church decorum appropriate to his day and age allows for, and thus affirms, women's prophesying in the public worship service (1 Cor. 11:5).

Scripture recognizes the divine appointment of these women. The God of the Bible is an *equal opportunity employer* ◆

The Return to Nazareth

39 When they had finished everything required by the law of the Lord, they returned to Galilee, to their own town of Nazareth. ⁴⁰The child grew and became strong, filled with wisdom; and the favor of God was upon him.

The Boy Jesus in the Temple

41 Now every year his parents went to Jerusalem for the festival of the Passover. ⁴²And when he was twelve years old, they went up as usual for the festival. ⁴³When the festival was ended and they started to return, the boy Jesus stayed behind in Jerusalem, but his parents did not know it. ⁴⁴Assuming that he was in the group of travelers, they went a day's journey. Then they started to look for him among their relatives and friends. ⁴⁵When they did not find him, they returned to Jerusalem to search for him. ⁴⁶After three days they found him in the temple, sitting among the teachers, listening to them and asking them questions. ⁴⁷And all who heard him were amazed at his understanding and his

---

42. Although women might be excused from the Passover pilgrimage required of men, devoted women, such as Hannah (1 Sam. 1:3–7), made the trip yearly to bring their own devotion to God. Mary does not simply depend upon her husband to discharge the call for God's people to assemble before the Lord (Exod. 23:14, 17; 34:23; Deut. 16:5–8, 16).

43. It was probably at this time that Jesus made his Bar Mitzveh, by which a boy is considered a man under the Law. A Jewish lad without a living father took this step at the age of 12 rather than 13. This may have constituted tacit recognition that Joseph was not his biological father.

Apparently well prepared by his parents for the spiritual responsibility, Jesus assumes that his proper place is now in the Temple. Within its precincts, several schools of thought under the leadership of some of Israel's most brilliant thinkers (especially rabbis Shammai and Hillel) were involved daily in formulative discourse.

46. Jesus rapidly becomes part of the intellectual excitement and finds a place in its midst as the intelligence and spiritual perceptions of the adolescent boy are readily recognized.

answers. [48]When his parents[t] saw him they were astonished; and his mother said to him, "Child, why have you treated us like this? Look, your father and I have been searching for you in great anxiety." [49]He said to them, "Why were you searching for me? Did you not know that I must be in my Father's house?"[u] [50]But they did not understand what he said to them. [51]Then he went down with them and came to Nazareth, and was obedient to them. His mother treasured all these things in her heart.

◆ For many centuries throughout Christendom, Mary the mother of Jesus has been the subject of much theological, mythological and artistic speculation, and the object of great devotion. The most extensive biblical treatment of Mary is to be found in the infancy narratives in Luke's Gospel, including the annunciation of Jesus' conception and birth by the angel, Mary's response, and her encounter with Elizabeth and the recitation of the Magnificat. It is primarily these events which provide the scriptural foundation from which mariology has evolved.

Luke's purpose in appending the infancy narrative to his Gospel was Christological: to establish the identity of Jesus from his conception; and within salvation history, to provide a transition from the era of Israel to the era of Jesus. Characters such as Zechariah and Elizabeth, Simeon and Anna, represent the old Israel: Mary is representative of both Israel and the new era in that she bears Jesus and is identified by Luke as the first disciple. In Luke's narrative, Mary's significance is subordinate to his Christological concern: her special status is constituted solely by her role in God's salvific plan, because of the divine favor bestowed on her in the conception of the Messiah.

Yet Luke emphasizes Mary as the recipient of the angel's message, and as the dominant character in the infancy

[t] Gk *they*   [u] Or *be about my Father's interests?*

---

48. Any mother who has ever lost a child, even for a few minutes, understands the agonizing distress which Mary has suffered. Also disconcerting to her must have been the ease with which Jesus has accommodated himself to the surroundings of the Temple.

49. His response shows that he is already starting to develop a thought life quite independent of his mother. Jesus, now a man in the eyes of the Law and probably aware of the angel's promise, had considered the world of the Temple to be his appropriate habitat. It was there that his parents had brought him, and he may well have viewed it as the place where he might grow to full spiritual maturity.

50. Mark 3:21 shows that the family continued to misunderstand Jesus and his mission. Often we grieve because we as parents fail to understand our adolescent children and their motivation. Mary knew the same frustration and kept the saying in her heart. She was not immune from family tension but was slow to speak and swift to pray.

51. Though his parents do not understand him, he consents to accompany them back to Galilee, exchanging the rarefied and intellectually stimulating life of the Temple and its cult for the everyday existence of Nazareth. Rather than the hair-splitting debates of contemporary Judaism, his teaching will reflect the common experiences of housewives and shepherds, children and fishermen, farmers and tenants.

He becomes assimilated to the world of his family. The word here translated 'was obedient' is *hupotasso*, usually rendered 'submit' when it is applied to women (see note on 1 Cor. 14:32–35). The word can imply being joined, associated with or identified with another. One Greek writer of about the same period used the term to mean attaching one person or thing to another in order to make a meaningful relationship. Jesus' relationship to his family was one of responsibility, commitment and loving association rather than of absolute obedience (Matt. 12:46–50; 13:55–56; Mark 3:21, 31–35; 6:3; Luke 2:49; 8:19–21; John 2:4; 19:25–27).

narrative, in contrast with the Matthean emphasis on Joseph. Moreover, there are strong parallels between Mary and Elizabeth, and women in the Old Testament who play a prominent part in salvation history, particularly Sarah, Abraham's wife, and Hannah, the mother of Samuel. These suggest a recognition of the contribution of women in God's plan (albeit centered on their biological function as mothers) unequaled elsewhere in the New Testament. When Mary gives voice to the Magnificat she echoes Hannah's canticle in 1 Sam. 2. In recording the words of Mary in the Magnificat, Luke shows her as a symbol of the poor remnant of Israel, the oppressed of the community whom God would save: as the handmaid of the Lord, obedient to God's word, Mary typifies the piety of these faithful of Israel, expressing their hopes and expectations.

Some feminist theologians have attempted to provide a more holistic understanding of women and men, transcending a purely biological focus. They see Luke's account of Mary as placing her in a significant position as a model of discipleship for female and male alike. Mary's faith and obedience enable her to be the means through which God is incarnate: thus she is able to participate in the liberating activity of God in history. Mary's faithfulness did not end at Jesus' birth. Although references to her are not frequent in the rest of the Gospel, Luke mentions the women who wait alongside Jesus' disciples at the crucifixion (Luke 23:49); John's Gospel names Mary the

mother of Jesus as being among them (John 19:25). So we see that Mary continues to live a life of obedience and faith in God. Thus the portrayal of Mary in Luke's Gospel may provide the basis for a positive and realistic model for women of faith today ◆

52 And Jesus increased in wisdom and in years,ᵛ and in divine and human favor.

The Proclamation of John the Baptist

3 In the fifteenth year of the reign of Emperor Tiberius, when Pontius Pilate was governor of Judea, and Herod was rulerʷ of Galilee, and his brother Philip rulerʷ of the region of Ituraea and Trachonitis, and Lysanias rulerʷ of Abilene, ²during the high priesthood of Annas and Caiaphas, the word of God came to John son of Zechariah in the wilderness. ³He went into all the region around the Jordan, proclaiming a baptism of repentance for the forgiveness of sins, ⁴as it is written in the book of the words of the prophet Isaiah,
"The voice of one crying out in the
    wilderness:
'Prepare the way of the Lord,
    make his paths straight.
⁵ Every valley shall be filled,
    and every mountain and hill shall be
        made low,
and the crooked shall be made
        straight,

ᵛ Or *in stature*   ʷ Gk *tetrarch*

LUKE 3

1. In antiquity, dates were identified by the names of individuals who held office at that point in time; and Luke takes exact pains to pinpoint as precisely as possible the dating of the divine event. He wishes to show that this is not myth but historic fact. The date that appears best to fit the information is AD 25–26.

4. John the Baptist is now ready to begin his ministry, and Luke appropriately introduces it with a quotation from the prophet Isaiah. It is a text speaking of spiritual preparation. John wears the clothing of Elijah (2 Kings 1:8; Matt. 3:4) and gives a stern message of repentance. He fulfills the promise that Elijah would come before the Lord (Mal. 4:5) as he calls soldiers and tax-gatherers to paths of personal repentance and righteousness.

and the rough ways made smooth;
6 and all flesh shall see the salvation of
God.' "

7 John said to the crowds that came out to be baptized by him, "You brood of vipers! Who warned you to flee from the wrath to come? 8Bear fruits worthy of repentance. Do not begin to say to yourselves, 'We have Abraham as our ancestor'; for I tell you, God is able from these stones to raise up children to Abraham. 9Even now the ax is lying at the root of the trees; every tree therefore that does not bear good fruit is cut down and thrown into the fire."

10 And the crowds asked him, "What then should we do?" 11In reply he said to them, "Whoever has two coats must share with anyone who has none; and whoever has food must do likewise." 12Even tax collectors came to be baptized, and they asked him, "Teacher, what should we do?" 13He said to them, "Collect no more than the amount prescribed for you." 14Soldiers also asked him, "And we, what should we do?" He said to them, "Do not extort money from anyone by threats or false accusation, and be satisfied with your wages."

15 As the people were filled with expectation, and all were questioning in their hearts concerning John, whether he might be the Messiah,[x] 16John answered all of them by saying, "I baptize you with water; but one who is more powerful than I is coming; I am not worthy to untie the thong of his sandals. He will baptize you with[y] the Holy Spirit and fire. 17His winnowing fork is in his hand, to clear his threshing floor and to gather the wheat into his granary; but the chaff he will burn with unquenchable fire."

18 So, with many other exhortations, he proclaimed the good news to the people. 19But Herod the ruler,[z] who had been rebuked by him because of Herodias, his brother's wife, and because of all the evil things that Herod had done, 20added to them all by shutting up John in prison.

The Baptism of Jesus

21 Now when all the people were baptized, and when Jesus also had been baptized and was praying, the heaven was opened, 22and the Holy Spirit descended upon him in bodily form like a dove. And a voice came from heaven, "You are my Son, the Beloved;[a] with you I am well pleased."[b]

[x] Or the Christ [y] Or in [z] Gk tetrarch [a] Or my beloved Son [b] Other ancient authorities read You are my Son, today I have begotten you

---

8. Sometimes we are told that women were given significant roles in the Bible only because males were not available. Here we are reassured that God can raise up at the proper time those whom he wills to do his appointed task (cf. Est. 4:4).

11. John's message is distinguished by a strong sense of social justice, a theme to which Luke returns again and again.

19. Jewish Law did not permit marrying the wife of one's brother; and John the Baptist proclaimed a strict standard of sexual morality that was to cost him his life.

Clearly John must have baptized Jesus before Herod seized him, although Luke describes the imprisonment and execution first. Here we see evidence that Luke arranges his material according to certain themes rather than in strict time sequence.

21. As the sinless Son of God, Jesus does not need 'a baptism of repentance for the forgiveness of sins' (v. 3). Here, as at his death, he wholly identifies with sinners and shares in the experience of the righteous who seek to do God's will.

22. Here for the first time we find the combined activity of Father, Son and Holy Spirit recorded at the same event.

The Ancestors of Jesus

23 Jesus was about thirty years old when he began his work. He was the son (as was thought) of Joseph son of Heli, ²⁴son of Matthat, son of Levi, son of Melchi, son of Jannai, son of Joseph, ²⁵son of Mattathias, son of Amos, son of Nahum, son of Esli, son of Naggai, ²⁶son of Maath, son of Mattathias, son of Semein, son of Josech, son of Joda, ²⁷son of Joanan, son of Rhesa, son of Zerubbabel, son of Shealtiel,ᶜ son of Neri, ²⁸son of Melchi, son of Addi, son of Cosam, son of Elmadam, son of Er, ²⁹son of Joshua, son of Eliezer, son of Jorim, son of Matthat, son of Levi, ³⁰son of Simeon, son of Judah, son of Joseph, son of Jonam, son of Eliakim, ³¹son of Melea, son of Menna, son of Mattatha, son of Nathan, son of David, ³²son of Jesse, son of Obed, son of Boaz, son of Sala,ᵈ son of Nahshon, ³³son of Amminadab, son of Admin, son of Arni,ᵉ son of Hezron, son of Perez, son of Judah, ³⁴son of Jacob, son of Isaac, son of Abraham, son of Terah, son of Nahor, ³⁵son of Serug, son of Reu, son of Peleg, son of Eber, son of Shelah, ³⁶son of Cainan, son of Arphaxad, son of Shem, son of Noah, son of Lamech, ³⁷son of Methuselah, son of Enoch, son of Jared, son of Mahalaleel, son of Cainan, ³⁸son of Enos, son of Seth, son of Adam, son of God.

The Temptation of Jesus

4 Jesus, full of the Holy Spirit, returned from the Jordan and was led by the Spirit in the wilderness, ²where for forty days he was tempted by the devil. He ate nothing at all during those days, and when they were over, he was famished. ³The devil said to him, "If you are the Son of God, command this stone to become a loaf of bread." ⁴Jesus answered him, "It is written, 'One does not live by bread alone.' "

5 Then the devilᶠ led him up and showed him in an instant all the kingdoms of the world. ⁶And the devilᶠ said to him, "To you I will give their glory and all this authority; for it has been given over to me, and I give it to anyone I please. ⁷If you, then, will worship me, it will all be yours." ⁸Jesus answered him, "It is written,

'Worship the Lord your God,
and serve only him.' "

ᶜ Gk *Salathiel*   ᵈ Other ancient authorities read *Salmon*   ᵉ Other ancient authorities read *Amminadab, son of Aram*; others vary widely   ᶠ Gk *he*

---

23. In keeping with the previous emphasis upon Mary, we are now apparently given her genealogy rather than that of Joseph. This accounts for the difference in the names listed by Matthew, who enables us to glimpse the heritage and influences that the earthly father of Jesus brought to the home. Matthew includes the names of some ancestresses but Luke's approach is different. In keeping with the initiatory role of women in the Exodus, the great saving event of the Old Testament (Exod. 1:15–21; 2:1–10; 3:22), he emphasizes the importance of women at the beginning of the great salvation story contained in his Gospel.

LUKE 4

3. Jesus, newly baptized, must now reach some difficult decisions as to how he will approach his public ministry and the mission to which he knows he is called. Many scholars feel that he grew in his awareness of being the Messiah. With this recognition, he rejects the temptation to deal with his legitimate personal needs first, renouncing the demands of his own body to bring spiritual food to others.

5–8. Political power was also a temptation. Precisely because Jesus could have assumed control over the entire world, he can identify with the powerless. He deliberately rejects the use of power in order to be the Savior of the disempowered, including women.

9 Then the devil[g] took him to Jerusalem, and placed him on the pinnacle of the temple, saying to him, "If you are the Son of God, throw yourself down from here, [10]for it is written,

'He will command his angels
    concerning you,
  to protect you,'

[11]and

'On their hands they will bear you up,
  so that you will not dash your foot
      against a stone.' "

[12]Jesus answered him, "It is said, 'Do not put the Lord your God to the test.' " [13]When the devil had finished every test, he departed from him until an opportune time.

The Beginning of the Galilean Ministry

14 Then Jesus, filled with the power of the Spirit, returned to Galilee, and a report about him spread through all the surrounding country. [15]He began to teach in their synagogues and was praised by everyone.

The Rejection of Jesus at Nazareth

16 When he came to Nazareth, where he had been brought up, he went to the synagogue on the sabbath day, as was his custom. He stood up to read, [17]and the scroll of the prophet Isaiah was given to him. He unrolled the scroll and found the place where it was written:

[18] "The Spirit of the Lord is upon me,
    because he has anointed me
      to bring good news to the poor.
  He has sent me to proclaim release to
      the captives
    and recovery of sight to the blind,
      to let the oppressed go free,
[19] to proclaim the year of the Lord's
      favor."

[20]And he rolled up the scroll, gave it back to the attendant, and sat down. The eyes of all in the synagogue were fixed on him. [21]Then he began to say to them, "Today this scripture has been fulfilled in your hearing." [22]All spoke well of him and were amazed at the gracious words that came from his mouth. They said, "Is not this Joseph's son?" [23]He said to them, "Doubtless you will quote to me this proverb, 'Doctor, cure yourself!' And you will say, 'Do here also in your hometown the things that we have heard you did at Capernaum.' " [24]And he said, "Truly I tell you, no prophet is accepted in the prophet's hometown. [25]But the truth is, there were many widows in Israel in the time of Elijah, when the heaven was shut up three years and six months, and there was a severe famine over all the land; [26]yet Elijah was sent to none of them except to a widow at Zarephath in Sidon. [27]There were also many lepers[h] in

[g] Gk he   [h] The terms *leper* and *leprosy* can refer to several diseases

---

9–12. The desire to be the center of attention is all too human, as is the need for acclamation, and legitimation, even if by rather dubious means. Jesus will gain adherents through reaching out to those in need rather than through resorting to tawdry showmanship.

17. As he embarks upon his calling, Jesus presents himself not to an electrified crowd at the Temple but in humble fashion to his fellow townsfolk in the synagogue. Just as his repudiation of Satan's lures was based upon quotations of Israel's sacred Scriptures (Deut. 6:13; 8:3), so too is the proclamation of his own ministry. His great manifesto of mission is epitomized in the writings of Isaiah (Is. 61:1–2; 58:6). It emphasizes his calling to the poor, the captives, the blind and the oppressed. Jesus understands himself in this context rather than in that of world power or of dazzling spectacle.

25. Here as so often, Jesus points to a woman as a spiritual example, in this case one from prophetic tradition: a Sidonian woman who demonstrated great faith and courage (1 Kings 17:9–24). The area is ruled by the father of the vicious and vindictive Queen Jezebel, but this

Israel in the time of the prophet Elisha, and none of them was cleansed except Naaman the Syrian." [28]When they heard this, all in the synagogue were filled with rage. [29]They got up, drove him out of the town, and led him to the brow of the hill on which their town was built, so that they might hurl him off the cliff. [30]But he passed through the midst of them and went on his way.

The Man with an Unclean Spirit

[31] He went down to Capernaum, a city in Galilee, and was teaching them on the sabbath. [32]They were astounded at his teaching, because he spoke with authority. [33]In the synagogue there was a man who had the spirit of an unclean demon, and he cried out with a loud voice, [34]"Let us alone! What have you to do with us, Jesus of Nazareth? Have you come to destroy us? I know who you are, the Holy One of God." [35]But Jesus rebuked him, saying, "Be silent, and come out of him!" When the demon had thrown him down before them, he came out of him without having done him any harm. [36]They were all amazed and kept saying to one another, "What kind of utterance is this? For with authority and power he commands the unclean spirits, and out they come!" [37]And a report about him began to reach every place in the region.

Healings at Simon's House

[38] After leaving the synagogue he entered Simon's house. Now Simon's mother-in-law was suffering from a high fever, and they asked him about her. [39]Then he stood over her and rebuked the fever, and it left her. Immediately she got up and began to serve them.

[40] As the sun was setting, all those who had any who were sick with various kinds of diseases brought them to him; and he laid his hands on each of them and cured them. [41]Demons also came out of many, shouting, "You are the Son of God!" But he rebuked them and would not allow them to speak, because they knew that he was the Messiah.[i]

Jesus Preaches in the Synagogues

[42] At daybreak he departed and went into a deserted place. And the crowds were looking for him; and when they reached him, they wanted to prevent him from leaving them. [43]But he said to them, "I must proclaim the good news of the kingdom of God to the other cities also; for I was sent for this purpose." [44]So he continued proclaiming the message in the synagogues of Judea.[j]

---

[i] Or the Christ   [j] Other ancient authorities read Galilee

---

widow at personal risk receives Elijah into her home and sustains him throughout three years of terrible drought. Reduced to destitution, she gives her last loaf of bread to the prophet and finds that God continues to supply her needs and that of her child. When the young boy sickens and dies, God's power restores him in answer to Elijah's prayer, and the woman is convinced that he is truly God's messenger: 'Now I know that you are a man of God, and that the word of the LORD in your mouth is truth' (1 Kings 17:24). Jesus calls his hearers to the same kind of receptive faith. **28–31.** With his life endangered at Nazareth, Jesus moves his base of operation to Capernaum (Matt. 4:13) beside the Sea of Galilee. When the early and later rainy seasons rendered travel and outdoor preaching impossible, he was to be found there.
38–39. All of the Synoptic Gospels tell of the healing of Peter's mother-in-law. Luke as physician mentions that she has 'a high fever' which is broken at the command of Jesus. Like many other women in the Gospel story, she 'ministers' to Jesus; for the theme of ministering women catches the attention of Luke (Luke 8:3; 10:40–41; see also John 12:2).

Jesus Calls the First Disciples

5 Once while Jesus[k] was standing beside the lake of Gennesaret, and the crowd was pressing in on him to hear the word of God, [2]he saw two boats there at the shore of the lake; the fishermen had gone out of them and were washing their nets. [3]He got into one of the boats, the one belonging to Simon, and asked him to put out a little way from the shore. Then he sat down and taught the crowds from the boat. [4]When he had finished speaking, he said to Simon, "Put out into the deep water and let down your nets for a catch." [5]Simon answered, "Master, we have worked all night long but have caught nothing. Yet if you say so, I will let down the nets." [6]When they had done this, they caught so many fish that their nets were beginning to break. [7]So they signaled their partners in the other boat to come and help them. And they came and filled both boats, so that they began to sink. [8]But when Simon Peter saw it, he fell down at Jesus' knees, saying, "Go away from me, Lord, for I am a sinful man!" [9]For he and all who were with him were amazed at the catch of fish that they had taken; [10]and so also were James and John, sons of Zebedee, who were partners with Simon. Then Jesus said to Simon, "Do not be afraid; from now on you will be catching people." [11]When they had brought their boats to shore, they left everything and followed him.

Jesus Cleanses a Leper

[12] Once, when he was in one of the cities, there was a man covered with leprosy.[l] When he saw Jesus, he bowed with his face to the ground and begged him, "Lord, if you choose, you can make me clean." [13]Then Jesus[k] stretched out his hand, touched him, and said, "I do choose. Be made clean." Immediately the leprosy[l] left him. [14]And he ordered him to tell no one. "Go," he said, "and show yourself to the priest, and, as Moses commanded, make an offering for your cleansing, for a testimony to them." [15]But now more than ever the word about Jesus[m] spread abroad; many crowds would gather to hear him and to be cured of their diseases. [16]But he would withdraw to deserted places and pray.

Jesus Heals a Paralytic

[17] One day, while he was teaching, Pharisees and teachers of the law were sitting near by (they had come from every village of Galilee and Judea and from Jerusalem); and the power of the Lord was with him to heal.[n] [18]Just then some men came, carrying a paralyzed man on a bed. They were trying to bring him in and lay him before Jesus;[m] [19]but finding no way to bring him in because of the crowd, they went up on the roof and let him down with his bed through the tiles into the middle of the crowd[o] in front of Jesus. [20]When he saw their faith, he said, "Friend,[p] your sins are forgiven you." [21]Then the scribes and the Pharisees began to question, "Who is this who is speaking blasphemies? Who can forgive sins but God alone?" [22]When Jesus perceived their questionings, he answered them, "Why do you raise such questions in

---

[k] Gk *he*   [l] The terms *leper* and *leprosy* can refer to several diseases   [m] Gk *him*   [n] Other ancient authorities read *was present to heal them*   [o] Gk *into the midst*   [p] Gk *Man*

LUKE 5

13. Jesus loved to touch the untouchables, whether a leper, a sinful woman, or a woman with an issue of blood. The laws against contact with lepers and women having a discharge had both been formulated in a primitive society for reasons of hygiene; but in Jesus' day these laws had been carried to excessive and cruel lengths.

your hearts? [23]Which is easier, to say 'Your sins are forgiven you,' or to say, 'Stand up and walk'? [24]But so that you may know that the Son of Man has authority on earth to forgive sins" – he said to the one who was paralyzed – "I say to you, stand up and take your bed and go to your home." [25]Immediately he stood up before them, took what he had been lying on, and went to his home, glorifying God. [26]Amazement seized all of them, and they glorified God and were filled with awe, saying, "We have seen strange things today."

◆ The Gospels place a special emphasis upon the testimony of persons with disabilities. I first realized this when I was a volunteer-in-mission in an area that provided no services for disabled persons. Disappointed personally because the ministry to which I had been assigned was closed to me by reason of my gender, I felt led to use my skills and training as a swimming instructor of handicapped persons. Soon I had 42 students a week and found myself filled with an enormous sense of blessing. I did not understand how this could be when I had been so roundly rejected in my anticipated field of service. Certainly I was humbled as these people entered the water and put their very lives in my hands, but I felt that there must be a deeper answer within the Scriptures. As I searched, I began to see that many of the movements of God's Spirit among people began with the testimony of a person who had known some sort of disability (Matt. 9:7, 33; 15:31–32; Mark 2:12; 7:35–7; Luke 5:25–26; 13:13, 17; 18:43; John 9:25–39; Acts 3:6–10). How we need such sharing of contagious faith in today's world! Just as blind persons sometimes develop an unusually keen sense of hearing, so God sometimes gifts disabled persons with exceptionally profound spiritual perceptions. May God enable us to listen and affirm with humble, receptive hearts ◆

Jesus Calls Levi

27 After this he went out and saw a tax collector named Levi, sitting at the tax booth; and he said to him, "Follow me." [28]And he got up, left everything, and followed him.

29 Then Levi gave a great banquet for him in his house; and there was a large crowd of tax collectors and others sitting at the table[q] with them. [30]The Pharisees and their scribes were complaining to his disciples, saying, "Why do you eat and drink with tax collectors and sinners?" [31]Jesus answered, "Those who are well have no need of a physician, but those who are sick; [32]I have come to call not the righteous but sinners to repentance."

The Question about Fasting

33 Then they said to him, "John's disciples, like the disciples of the Pharisees, frequently fast and pray, but your disciples eat and drink. [34]Jesus said to them, "You cannot make wedding guests fast while the bridegroom is with them, can you? [35]The days will come when the bridegroom will be taken away from them, and then they will fast in those days." [36]He also told them a parable: "No one tears a piece from a new garment and sews it on an old garment; otherwise the new will be torn, and the piece from the new will not match the old. [37]And no one puts new wine into old wineskins; otherwise the new wine will burst the skins and will be spilled, and the skins will be destroyed. [38]But new wine must be put into fresh wineskins. [39]And no one after drinking old wine desires new wine, but says, 'The old is good.' "[r]

---

[q] Gk reclining   [r] Other ancient authorities read better; others lack verse 39

The Question about the Sabbath

6 One sabbath[s] while Jesus[t] was going through the grainfields, his disciples plucked some heads of grain, rubbed them in their hands, and ate them. [2]But some of the Pharisees said, "Why are you doing what is not lawful[u] on the sabbath?" [3]Jesus answered, "Have you not read what David did when he and his companions were hungry? [4]He entered the house of God and took and ate the bread of the Presence, which it is not lawful for any but the priests to eat, and gave some to his companions?" [5]Then he said to them, "The Son of Man is lord of the sabbath."

The Man with a Withered Hand

6 On another sabbath he entered the synagogue and taught, and there was a man there whose right hand was withered. [7]The scribes and the Pharisees watched him to see whether he would cure on the sabbath, so that they might find an accusation against him. [8]Even though he knew what they were thinking, he said to the man who had the withered hand, "Come and stand here." He got up and stood there. [9]Then Jesus said to them, "I ask you, is it lawful to do good or to do harm on the sabbath, to save life or to destroy it?" [10]After looking around at all of them, he said to him, "Stretch out your hand." He did so, and his hand was restored. [11]But they were filled with fury and discussed with one another what they might do to Jesus.

Jesus Chooses the Twelve Apostles

12 Now during those days he went out to the mountain to pray; and he spent the night in prayer to God. [13]And when day came, he called his disciples and chose twelve of them, whom he also named apostles: [14]Simon, whom he named Peter, and his brother Andrew, and James, and John, and Philip, and Bartholomew, [15]and Matthew, and Thomas, and James son of Alphaeus, and Simon, who was called the Zealot, [16]and Judas son of James, and Judas Iscariot, who became a traitor.

Jesus Teaches and Heals

17 He came down with them and stood on a level place, with a great crowd of his disciples and a great multitude of people from all Judea, Jerusalem, and the coast of Tyre and Sidon. [18]They had come to hear him and to be healed of their diseases; and those who were troubled with unclean spirits were cured. [19]And all in the crowd were trying to touch him, for power came out from him and healed all of them.

Blessings and Woes

20 Then he looked up at his disciples and said:
"Blessed are you who are poor,
　for yours is the kingdom of God.
[21] "Blessed are you who are hungry now,
　for you will be filled.
"Blessed are you who weep now,
　for you will laugh.
22 "Blessed are you when people hate you, and when they exclude you, revile you, and defame you[v] on account of the Son of Man. [23]Rejoice in that day and leap for joy, for surely your reward is great in heaven; for that is what their ancestors did to the prophets.
[24] "But woe to you who are rich,
　for you have received your
　　consolation.
[25] "Woe to you who are full now,
　for you will be hungry.

[s] Other ancient authorities read *On the second first sabbath* [t] Gk *he* [u] Other ancient authorities add *to do* [v] Gk *cast out your name as evil*

LUKE 6

12. The commissioning of male disciples will be balanced by the inclusion of women in Luke 8:1–3.

"Woe to you who are laughing now,
    for you will mourn and weep.

26 "Woe to you when all speak well of you, for that is what their ancestors did to the false prophets.

Love for Enemies

27 "But I say to you that listen, Love your enemies, do good to those who hate you, [28]bless those who curse you, pray for those who abuse you. [29]If anyone strikes you on the cheek, offer the other also; and from anyone who takes away your coat do not withhold even your shirt. [30]Give to everyone who begs from you; and if anyone takes away your goods, do not ask for them again. [31]Do to others as you would have them do to you.

32 "If you love those who love you, what credit is that to you? For even sinners love those who love them. [33]If you do good to those who do good to you, what credit is that to you? For even sinners do the same. [34]If you lend to those from whom you hope to receive, what credit is that to you? Even sinners lend to sinners, to receive as much again. [35]But love your enemies, do good, and lend, expecting nothing in return.[w] Your reward will be great, and you will be children of the Most High; for he is kind to the ungrateful and the wicked. [36]Be merciful, just as your Father is merciful.

Judging Others

37 "Do not judge, and you will not be judged; do not condemn, and you will not be condemned. Forgive, and you will be forgiven; [38]give, and it will be given to you. A good measure, pressed down, shaken together, running over, will be put into your lap; for the measure you give will be the measure you get back."

39 He also told them a parable: "Can a blind person guide a blind person? Will not both fall into a pit? [40]A disciple is not above the teacher, but everyone who is fully qualified will be like the teacher. [41]Why do you see the speck in your neighbor's[x] eye, but do not notice the log in your own eye? [42]Or how can you say to your neighbor,[y] 'Friend,[y] let me take out the speck in your eye,' when you yourself do not see the log in your own eye? You hypocrite, first take the log out of your own eye, and then you will see clearly to take the speck out of your neighbor's[x] eye.

A Tree and Its Fruit

43 "No good tree bears bad fruit, nor again does a bad tree bear good fruit; [44]for each tree is known by its own fruit. Figs are not gathered from thorns, nor are grapes picked from a bramble bush. [45]The good person out of the good treasure of the heart produces good, and the evil person out of evil treasure produces evil; for it is out of the abundance of the heart that the mouth speaks.

The Two Foundations

46 "Why do you call me 'Lord, Lord,' and do not do what I tell you? [47]I will show you what someone is like who comes to me, hears my words, and acts on them. [48]That one is like a man building a house, who dug deeply and laid the foundation on rock; when a flood arose, the river burst against that house but could not shake it, because it had been well built.[z] [49]But the one who hears and does not act is like a man who built a house on the ground without a foundation. When the river burst against it,

---

[w] Other ancient authorities read *despairing of no one*   [x] Gk *brother's*   [y] Gk *brother*   [z] Other ancient authorities read *founded upon the rock*

27–31. This saying of Jesus is not intended to turn us into doormats, for Jesus was not a doormat (Matt. 21:12–13; Mark 11:15–17; Luke 12:14; 19:45–46). Like Jesus, we need to set limits; for this is an application of the Golden Rule (Luke 6:31). To permit persons to mistreat others does great harm to both the abuser and the abused.

immediately it fell, and great was the ruin of that house."

Jesus Heals a Centurion's Servant

7 After Jesus[a] had finished all his sayings in the hearing of the people, he entered Capernaum. [2]A centurion there had a slave whom he valued highly, and who was ill and close to death. [3]When he heard about Jesus, he sent some Jewish elders to him, asking him to come and heal his slave. [4]When they came to Jesus, they appealed to him earnestly, saying, "He is worthy of having you do this for him, [5]for he loves our people, and it is he who built our synagogue for us." [6]And Jesus went with them, but when he was not far from the house, the centurion sent friends to say to him, "Lord, do not trouble yourself, for I am not worthy to have you come under my roof; [7]therefore I did not presume to come to you. But only speak the word, and let my servant be healed. [8]For I also am a man set under authority, with soldiers under me; and I say to one, 'Go,' and he goes, and to another, 'Come,' and he comes, and to my slave, 'Do this,' and the slave does it." [9]When Jesus heard this he was amazed at him, and turning to the crowd that followed him, he said, "I tell you, not even in Israel have I found such faith." [10]When those who had been sent returned to the house, they found the slave in good health.

Jesus Raises the Widow's Son at Nain

[11] Soon afterwards[b] he went to a town called Nain, and his disciples and a large crowd went with him. [12]As he approached the gate of the town, a man who had died was being carried out. He was his mother's only son, and she was a widow; and with her was a large crowd from the town.

◆ In this story of the widow of Nain, it is of significance that this widow lost her only son. In ancient times the primary issues of a desolate widow were that she would not have a son to carry on the family name, a protector to care for and comfort her in old age. Such a widow would be dependent on her son for economic support, as there were few opportunities for women to earn their own living in the first century. Nain was not far from Shunem, where Elisha had raised the son of the Shunamite back to life (2 Kings 4:18). Another prophet (Elijah) had been empowered by God to restore life to a widow's son at Zarephath (1 Kings 17:17). Jesus was acknowledged as a great prophet by the people, as a result of this miracle. Jesus' unfathomable compassion for the heavy-hearted widow moved him to reach out and heal her son with his powerful touch. The prophet Isaiah prophesied of the Messiah's healing ministry in which he would bind up the broken-hearted, comfort all who mourn and 'give them a garland instead of ashes, the oil of gladness instead of mourning, the mantle of praise instead of a faint spirit' (Is. 61:1–3). Truly, after the miracle, we picture the widow of Nain with a changed countenance of surprise, relief, and exuberant joy. What amazing grace!

The death of a child is one of the most heart-rending losses a parent can experience. While Jesus resurrected the child in this Luke incident, what about the Christian parents who lost a daughter suddenly in a car accident while three of her friends walked away without a scratch? What about the parents of a 24-year-old eldest daughter struck down in the prime of life by Hodgkin's disease

[a] Gk *he*   [b] Other ancient authorities read *Next day*

LUKE 7

11. This story is told in terms of sympathy for the widowed mother who has lost her only child. As Jesus gives the son back to the grief-stricken mother, the emphasis is on her rather than the son whom she receives back from the dead. Women are intimately involved in all of the Gospel stories about Jesus restoring people to life.

when she had so much to offer the world? God does not always intervene in these tragic circumstances. Oh, the loud, loud silence and painful separation of parents who survive the loss of a child, the restless nights of dreams of happy reunions, only to awaken to the reality of loss and the accompanying feelings of excruciating pain, the dreams in which pent-up, unfinished emotions are surfaced and released, and even the dreams that God uses to bring gradual healing and wholeness through his grace. It is this author's experience that God comforts us in adversity, that even when he does not intervene and remove us from the fiery furnace, his presence is with us through the fire. The Jesus who showed compassion for the widow of Nain weeps with us in our brokenness, grieves for the groanings of his loved ones in this unnatural state of death, and finally, will come to conquer death and ransom us from the effects of the Fall (1 Cor. 15:54–57; John 14:19) ◆

[13]When the Lord saw her, he had compassion for her and said to her, "Do not weep." [14]Then he came forward and touched the bier, and the bearers stood still. And he said, "Young man, I say to you, rise!" [15]The dead man sat up and began to speak, and Jesus[c] gave him to his mother. [16]Fear seized all of them; and they glorified God, saying, "A great prophet has risen among us!" and "God has looked favorably on his people!" [17]This word about him spread throughout Judea and all the surrounding country.

Messengers from John the Baptist

18 The disciples of John reported all these things to him. So John summoned two of his disciples [19]and sent them to the Lord to ask, "Are you the one who is to come, or are we to wait for another?" [20]When the men had come to him, they said, "John the Baptist has sent us to you to ask, 'Are you the one who is to come, or are we to wait for another?' " [21]Jesus[c] had just then cured many people of diseases, plagues, and evil spirits, and had given sight to many who were blind. [22]And he answered them, "Go and tell John what you have seen and heard: the blind receive their sight, the lame walk, the lepers[d] are cleansed, the deaf hear, the dead are raised, the poor have good news brought to them. [23]And blessed is anyone who takes no offense at me."

24 When John's messengers had gone, Jesus[e] began to speak to the crowds about John:[e] "What did you go out into the wilderness to look at? A reed shaken by the wind? [25]What then did you go out to see? Someone[f] dressed in soft robes? Look, those who put on fine clothing and live in luxury are in royal palaces. [26]What then did you go out to see? A prophet? Yes, I tell you, and more than a prophet. [27]This is the one about whom it is written,

'See, I am sending my messenger
    ahead of you,
  who will prepare your way before
      you.'
[28]I tell you, among those born of women no one is greater than John; yet the least in the kingdom of God is greater than he." [29](And all the people who heard this, including the tax collectors, acknowledged the justice of God,[g] because they had been baptized with John's baptism. [30]But by refusing to be baptized by him, the Pharisees and the lawyers rejected God's purpose for themselves.)

31 "To what then will I compare the people of this generation, and what are they like? [32]They are like children sitting in

[c] Gk *he*   [d] The terms *leper* and *leprosy* can refer to several diseases   [e] Gk *him*   [f] Or *Why then did you go out? To see someone*   [g] Or *praised God*

---

32. Jesus not only loves to have children around him, but he has been an astute observer of their play. His amusement shines through the remark, while the sarcasm is directed at supposedly mature individuals.

the marketplace and calling to one another,

'We played the flute for you, and you
did not dance;

we wailed, and you did not weep.'

³³For John the Baptist has come eating no bread and drinking no wine, and you say, 'He has a demon'; ³⁴the Son of Man has come eating and drinking, and you say, 'Look, a glutton and a drunkard, a friend of tax collectors and sinners!' ³⁵Nevertheless, wisdom is vindicated by all her children."

A Sinful Woman Forgiven

36 One of the Pharisees asked Jesusʰ to eat with him, and he went into the Pharisee's house and took his place at the table. ³⁷And a woman in the city, who was a sinner, having learned that he was eating in the Pharisee's house, brought an alabaster jar of ointment. ³⁸She stood behind him at his feet, weeping, and began to bathe his feet with her tears and to dry them with her hair. Then she continued kissing his feet and anointing them with the ointment. ³⁹Now when the Pharisee who had invited him saw it, he said to himself, "If this man were a prophet, he would have known who and what kind of woman this is who is touching him – that she is a sinner." ⁴⁰Jesus spoke up and said to him, "Simon, I have something to say to you." "Teacher," he replied, "Speak." ⁴¹"A certain creditor had two debtors; one owed five hundred denarii,ⁱ and the other fifty. ⁴²When they could not pay, he canceled the debts for both of them. Now which of them will love him more?" ⁴³Simon answered, "I suppose the one for whom he canceled the greater debt." And Jesusʲ said to him, "You have judged rightly." ⁴⁴Then turning toward the woman, he said to Simon, "Do you see this woman? I entered your house; you gave me no water for my feet, but she has bathed my feet with her tears and dried them with her hair. ⁴⁵You gave me no kiss, but from the time I came in she has not stopped kissing my feet. ⁴⁶You did not anoint my head with oil, but she has anointed my feet with ointment.

ʰ Gk *him*   ⁱ The denarius was the usual day's wage for a laborer   ʲ Gk *he*

---

35. Here, as at 11:49, wisdom is discussed as though it were a real person. The literary term for such a device is 'personification'. Jesus also addresses Jerusalem as though it were a person (13:34–35).

36. Jesus has just declared himself a friend of tax-gatherers and sinners (v. 34). Now we are afforded a glimpse of an actual interaction with a sinner, in this case a woman. As Jesus reclines at dinner in the house of a Pharisee, a sinful woman approaches the back of his couch, where his feet are extended.

Tears, sometimes the contrived tool of a manipulative mistress, burst forth in a flood of genuine repentance, washing off the dust of the road. Hair, considered the glory of women, was customarily covered outside the home, but the weeping sinner readily employs her tresses not for allurement but to perform the homely function of wiping the grime from his feet. Her kisses are not for a paramour but for one who could transform sinners. Her alabaster jar (*alabastron*, as it is called in the text) was ordinarily a vessel containing perfumed oil to be used in sexual encounters, especially on the wedding night. Here the woman transforms the normal use of the ointment into a service of repentence, love and worship.

Jesus accepts both the woman and the past which she has left behind as he commends her for her great love. She has found a new meaning for life that lies above and beyond her sexuality. Thus she becomes one of the many women whom Luke uses as a spiritual example. The phrase 'Your faith has saved you' often recurs in Luke (8:28; 17:19; 18:42).

The Pharisee too has been called to repentance but fails to respond to the challenge. He is well acquainted with the woman's previous misuse of her sexuality, but is unable to comprehend the rechanneling of her soul's affection. He is blind to the true import of her acts of penitent devotion, not knowing the sanctifying power of human touch and divine forgiveness.

⁴⁷Therefore, I tell you, her sins, which were many, have been forgiven; hence she has shown great love. But the one to whom little is forgiven, loves little." ⁴⁸Then he said to her, "Your sins are forgiven." ⁴⁹But those who were at the table with him began to say among themselves, "Who is this who even forgives sins?" ⁵⁰And he said to the woman, "Your faith has saved you; go in peace."

Some Women Accompany Jesus

8 Soon afterwards he went on through cities and villages, proclaiming and bringing the good news of the kingdom of God. The twelve were with him, ²as well as some women who had been cured of evil spirits and infirmities: Mary, called Magdalene, from whom seven demons had gone out, ³and Joanna, the wife of Herod's steward Chuza, and Susanna, and many others, who provided for them^k out of their resources.

The Parable of the Sower

4 When a great crowd gathered and people from town after town came to him, he said in a parable: ⁵"A sower went out to sow his seed; and as he sowed, some fell on the path and was trampled on, and the birds of the air ate it up. ⁶Some fell on the rock; and as it grew up, it withered for lack of moisture. ⁷Some fell among thorns, and the thorns grew with it and choked it. ⁸Some fell into good soil, and when it grew, it produced a hundredfold." As he said this, he called out, "Let anyone with ears to hear listen!"

The Purpose of the Parables

9 Then his disciples asked him what this parable meant. ¹⁰He said, "To you it has been given to know the secrets^l of the kingdom of God; but to others I speak^m in parables, so that

^k Other ancient authorities read *him*   ^l Or *mysteries*   ^m Gk lacks *I speak*

LUKE 8

1–3. Women as well as men are identified as disciples who composed part of the travelling band who accompany Jesus. The names of the male disciples have already been given, and to these are now added a significant group of women, some of them specifically named.

Despite the common misapprehension, the New Testament nowhere describes Mary Magdalen as a prostitute. Rather she has experienced the freeing power of Jesus from a serious mental affliction. The other women too appear to have been socially and religiously marginalized by the severity of their infirmities. Their subsequent healing may have left them with fewer family constraints so that they were free to travel with Jesus. Like Peter's mother-in-law (Luke 4:38–39), the women made well by Jesus become his ministers.

Joanna, Mary Magdalen, and Mary the mother of James are specifically mentioned as having borne witness to the resurrection of their Lord (Luke 24:10). It was during the Galilean ministry that they were prepared for this important task and given specific instruction by Jesus (Luke 24:6–8). They were later to serve as the major witnesses to the death and resurrection of Christ.

There is no record of women have been sent out two by two into the dangers of the countryside, but all of the Synoptic Gospels speak of women accompanying Jesus in his travelling ministry (Matt. 27:55–56; Mark 15:40–41; Luke 23:49). Like the women who were financiers of the Exodus (Exod. 3:22; 11:2–3; 12:35–36), these women promoted the ministry of Jesus with their gifts, prayers and concern.

The Greek word used for their service is *diakoneo* – to minister or serve as deacon. The same term is used for women's ministry at Matt 27:55; Mark 1:31; 15:41; Luke 4:39; 8:3; 10:40; John 12:2. It is used of men at Acts 19:22; Rom. 15:25; 2 Tim. 1:18; Philem. 13, of prophets at 1 Pet. 1:12, of angels at Matt. 4:11; Mark 1:13, and of Jesus at Matt. 20:28; Mark 10:45; Luke 22:27.

'looking they may not perceive,
and listening they may not
understand.'

The Parable of the Sower Explained

11 "Now the parable is this: The seed is the word of God. [12]The ones on the path are those who have heard; then the devil comes and takes away the word from their hearts, so that they may not believe and be saved. [13]The ones on the rock are those who, when they hear the word, receive it with joy. But these have no root; they believe only for a while and in a time of testing fall away. [14]As for what fell among the thorns, these are the ones who hear; but as they go on their way, they are choked by the cares and riches and pleasures of life, and their fruit does not mature. [15]But as for that in the good soil, these are the ones who, when they hear the word, hold it fast in an honest and good heart, and bear fruit with patient endurance.

A Lamp under a Jar

16 "No one after lighting a lamp hides it under a jar, or puts it under a bed, but puts it on a lampstand, so that those who enter may see the light. [17]For nothing is hidden that will not be disclosed, nor is anything secret that will not become known and come to light. [18]Then pay attention to how you listen; for to those who have, more will be given; and from those who do not have, even what they seem to have will be taken away."

The True Kindred of Jesus

19 Then his mother and his brothers came to him, but they could not reach him because of the crowd. [20]And he was told, "Your mother and your brothers are standing outside, wanting to see you." [21]But he said to them, "My mother and my brothers are those who hear the word of God and do it."

Jesus Calms a Storm

22 One day he got into a boat with his disciples, and he said to them, "Let us go across to the other side of the lake." So they put out, [23]and while they were sailing he fell asleep. A windstorm swept down on the lake, and the boat was filling with water, and they were in danger. [24]They went to him and woke him up, shouting, "Master, Master, we are perishing!" And he woke up and rebuked the wind and the raging waves; they ceased, and there was a calm. [25]He said to them, "Where is your faith?" They were afraid and amazed, and said to one another, "Who then is this, that he commands even the winds and the water, and they obey him?"

Jesus Heals the Gerasene Demoniac

26 Then they arrived at the country of the Gerasenes,[n] which is opposite Galilee. [27]As he stepped out on land, a man of the city who had demons met him. For a long time he had worn[o] no clothes, and he did not live in a house but in the tombs. [28]When he saw Jesus, he fell down before him and shouted at the top of his voice, "What have you to do with me, Jesus, Son

---

[n] Other ancient authorities read *Gadarenes*; others, *Gergesenes*   [o] Other ancient authorities read *a man of the city who had had demons for a long time met him. He wore*

19–21. Here Jesus recognizes family values that lie beyond the claims of blood relationship. True kinship is with those who hear the Word of God and do it. Rather than acceding to the claims of his family and dismissing the crowd, Jesus has emphasized the claims of God upon the lives of each person. Perhaps Jesus intended his words as a provocative challenge. John records the unbelief of his brothers (John 7:5), though later on as members of the family understand his message, they become strong adherents (Acts 1:14; 12:17; 15:13; 1 Cor. 9:5; Gal. 1:19; 2:9; James 1:1; Jude 1).

of the Most High God? I beg you, do not torment me" – [29]for Jesus[p] had commanded the unclean spirit to come out of the man. (For many times it had seized him; he was kept under guard and bound with chains and shackles, but he would break the bonds and be driven by the demon into the wilds.) [30]Jesus then asked him, "What is your name?" He said, "Legion"; for many demons had entered him. [31]They begged him not to order them to go back into the abyss.

32 Now there on the hillside a large herd of swine was feeding; and the demons[q] begged Jesus[r] to let them enter these. So he gave them permission. [33]Then the demons came out of the man and entered the swine, and the herd rushed down the steep bank into the lake and was drowned.

34 When the swineherds saw what had happened, they ran off and told it in the city and in the country. [35]Then people came out to see what had happened, and when they came to Jesus, they found the man from whom the demons had gone sitting at the feet of Jesus, clothed and in his right mind. And they were afraid. [36]Those who had seen it told them how the one who had been possessed by demons had been healed. [37]Then all the people of the surrounding country of the Gerasenes[s] asked Jesus[r] to leave them; for they were seized with great fear. So he got into the boat and returned. [38]The man from whom

the demons had gone begged that he might be with him; but Jesus[p] sent him away, saying, [39]"Return to your home, and declare how much God has done for you." So he went away, proclaiming throughout the city how much Jesus had done for him.

A Girl Restored to Life and a Woman Healed

40 Now when Jesus returned, the crowd welcomed him, for they were all waiting for him. [41]Just then there came a man named Jairus, a leader of the synagogue. He fell at Jesus' feet and begged him to come to his house, [42]for he had an only daughter, about twelve years old, who was dying.

As he went, the crowds pressed in on him. [43]Now there was a woman who had been suffering from hemorrhages for twelve years; and though she had spent all she had on physicians,[t] no one could cure her. [44]She came up behind him and touched the fringe of his clothes, and immediately her hemorrhage stopped. [45]Then Jesus asked, "Who touched me?" When all denied it, Peter[u] said, "Master, the crowds surround you and press in on you." [46]But Jesus said, "Someone touched me; for I noticed that power had gone out from me."

[p] Gk *he*   [q] Gk *they*   [r] Gk *him*   [s] Other ancient authorities read *Gadarenes*; others, *Gergesenes*   [t] Other ancient authorities lack *and had spent all she had on physicians*   [u] Other ancient authorities add *and those who were with him*

---

40. We see Jesus caught between the claims of two women. The young girl is at the point of death, while the older woman is at the brink of despair because of the hopelessness of her condition. Each situation is equally desperate, and Jesus responds to both needs.

42. The young girl, just at the age of puberty and the onset of menstruation, lies dying; and Jesus comes at the urgent appeal of the father.

43. Luke the Greek physician matter-of-factly explains the woman's hemorrhaging, a condition viewed as unclean by Jewish Law. Despite the prohibition against contact with women experiencing a discharge (Lev. 15:19–30), she pushed forward through the crowd to touch the hem of Christ's cloak.

46. One might suppose that delicacy would keep Jesus from asking such a question, but secrecy at this point would only reinforce the concept of vaginal discharge as shameful rather than as a basic feminine function.

⁴⁷When the woman saw that she could not remain hidden, she came trembling; and falling down before him, she declared in the presence of all the people why she had touched him, and how she had been immediately healed. ⁴⁸He said to her, "Daughter, your faith has made you well; go in peace."

49 While he was still speaking, someone came from the leader's house to say, "Your daughter is dead; do not trouble the teacher any longer." ⁵⁰When Jesus heard this, he replied, "Do not fear. Only believe, and she will be saved." ⁵¹When he came to the house, he did not allow anyone to enter with him, except Peter, John, and James, and the child's father and mother. ⁵²They were all weeping and wailing for her; but he said, "Do not weep; for she is not dead but sleeping." ⁵³And they laughed at him, knowing that she was dead. ⁵⁴But he took her by the hand and called out, "Child, get up!" ⁵⁵Her spirit returned, and she got up at once. Then he directed them to give her something to eat. ⁵⁶Her parents were astounded; but he ordered them to tell no one what had happened.

The Mission of the Twelve

9 Then Jesusᵛ called the twelve together and gave them power and authority over all demons and to cure diseases, ²and he sent them out to proclaim the kingdom of God and to heal. ³He said to them, "Take nothing for your journey, no staff, nor bag, nor bread, nor money – not even an extra tunic. ⁴Whatever house you enter, stay there, and leave from there. ⁵Wherever they do not welcome you, as you are leaving that town shake the dust off your feet as a testimony against them." ⁶They departed and went through the villages, bringing the good news and curing diseases everywhere.

Herod's Perplexity

7 Now Herod the rulerʷ heard about all that had taken place, and he was perplexed, because it was said by some that John had been raised from the dead, ⁸by some that Elijah had appeared, and by others that one of the ancient prophets had arisen. ⁹Herod said, "John I beheaded; but who is this about whom I hear such things?" And he tried to see him.

Feeding the Five Thousand

10 On their return the apostles told Jesusˣ all they had done. He took them with him and withdrew privately to a city called Bethsaida. ¹¹When the crowds found out about it, they followed him; and he welcomed them, and spoke to them about the kingdom of God, and healed those who needed to be cured.

12 The day was drawing to a close, and the twelve came to him and said, "Send the crowd away, so that they may go into the surrounding villages and countryside, to lodge and get provisions; for we are here in a deserted place." ¹³But he said to them, "You give them something to eat." They said, "We have no more than five loaves and two fish – unless we are to go and buy food for all these people." ¹⁴For there were about five thousand men. And he said to his disciples, "Make them sit down in groups of about fifty each." ¹⁵They did so and made them all sit down. ¹⁶And taking the five loaves and the two fish, he looked up to

ᵛ Gk *he*   ʷ Gk *tetrarch*   ˣ Gk *him*

---

47. Jesus insists that the woman share her testimony before the crowd – she is not allowed the luxury of silence, although one might suppose that she would experience embarrassment as well as fear.
48. His affirmation of her faith includes the repudiation of the traditional taboo regarding menstruation and other feminine discharge. Jesus has accepted both her touch and her testimony.

heaven, and blessed and broke them, and gave them to the disciples to set before the crowd. [17]And all ate and were filled. What was left over was gathered up, twelve baskets of broken pieces.

Peter's Declaration about Jesus

18 Once when Jesus[y] was praying alone, with only the disciples near him, he asked them, "Who do the crowds say that I am?" [19]They answered, "John the Baptist; but others, Elijah; and still others, that one of the ancient prophets has arisen." [20]He said to them, "But who do you say that I am?" Peter answered, "The Messiah[z] of God."

Jesus Foretells His Death and Resurrection

21 He sternly ordered and commanded them not to tell anyone, [22]saying, "The Son of Man must undergo great suffering, and be rejected by the elders, chief priests, and scribes, and be killed, and on the third day be raised."

23 Then he said to them all, "If any want to become my followers, let them deny themselves and take up their cross daily and follow me. [24]For those who want to save their life will lose it, and those who lose their life for my sake will save it. [25]What does it profit them if they gain the whole world, but lose or forfeit themselves? [26]Those who are ashamed of me and of my words, of them the Son of Man will be ashamed when he comes in his glory and the glory of the Father and of the holy angels. [27]But truly I tell you, there are some standing here who will not taste death before they see the kingdom of God."

The Transfiguration

28 Now about eight days after these sayings Jesus[y] took with him Peter and John and James, and went up on the mountain to pray. [29]And while he was praying, the appearance of his face changed, and his clothes became dazzling white. [30]Suddenly they saw two men, Moses and Elijah, talking to him. [31]They appeared in glory and were speaking of his departure, which he was about to accomplish at Jerusalem. [32]Now Peter and his companions were weighed down with sleep; but since they had stayed awake,[a] they saw his glory and the two men who stood with him. [33]Just as they were leaving him, Peter said to Jesus, "Master, it is good for us to be here; let us make three dwellings,[b] one for you, one for Moses, and one for Elijah" – not knowing what he said. [34]While he was saying this, a cloud came and overshadowed them; and they were terrified as they entered the cloud. [35]Then from the cloud came a voice that said, "This is my Son, my Chosen;[c] listen to him!" [36]When the voice had spoken, Jesus was found alone. And they kept silent and in those days told no one any of the things they had seen.

Jesus Heals a Boy with a Demon

37 On the next day, when they had come down from the mountain, a great crowd met him. [38]Just then a man from the crowd shouted, "Teacher, I beg you to look at my son; he is my only child. [39]Suddenly a spirit

[y] Gk *he*   [z] Or *The Christ*   [a] Or *but when they were fully awake*   [b] Or *tents*   [c] Other ancient authorities read *my Beloved*

LUKE 9

22. The theme of Jesus' impending death appears repeatedly in Luke from the time of his presentation in the Temple (2:35; 9:44–45; 18:31–34). He speaks of the cross as a matter of his own choosing and specifically challenges his followers to a similar self-renunciation. The cross makes him not victim but victor. It is a stepping stone from which the Son of Man shall come with the holy angels.

seizes him, and all at once he[d] shrieks. It convulses him until he foams at the mouth; it mauls him and will scarcely leave him. ⁴⁰I begged your disciples to cast it out, but they could not." ⁴¹Jesus answered, "You faithless and perverse generation, how much longer must I be with you and bear with you? Bring your son here." ⁴²While he was coming, the demon dashed him to the ground in convulsions. But Jesus rebuked the unclean spirit, healed the boy, and gave him back to his father. ⁴³And all were astounded at the greatness of God.

Jesus Again Foretells His Death

While everyone was amazed at all that he was doing, he said to his disciples, ⁴⁴"Let these words sink into your ears: The Son of Man is going to be betrayed into human hands." ⁴⁵But they did not understand this saying; its meaning was concealed from them, so that they could not perceive it. And they were afraid to ask him about this saying.

True Greatness

46 An argument arose among them as to which one of them was the greatest. ⁴⁷But Jesus, aware of their inner thoughts, took a little child and put it by his side, ⁴⁸and said to them, "Whoever welcomes this child in my name welcomes me, and whoever welcomes me welcomes the one who sent me; for the least among all of you is the greatest."

◆ The care of children has traditionally been the prerogative of Christian women. Women were the leaders in taking ragged hungry children into Sabbath schools to feed them, to teach them reading and writing and to tell them of Jesus. The daughter of Count Zinzendorf started the first public school for children in America, while Pandita Ramabai rescued hundreds of children from a terrible fate in India. Mary Slessor opened her heart and home to many unwanted African babies, and Christian women have established orphanages and schools all over the world.

To receive a needy or troubled child into our own homes can represent a considerable challenge. Such an action is unlikely at first to produce domestic peace or tranquillity. We can, however, move forward with the conviction that this is what Christ asked us to do. Our kindness and firmness and patience will indubitably be strained, but we may in the end build a loving and stable relationship. Adoption may be less complicated than providing shelter and nurturance for a child with shorter-term needs, and fewer people are willing to accept the challenge. Sometimes illness or death or other circumstances necessitate children staying outside their own homes for a temporary period, but they may return when the time is suitable with a knowledge of Christ and an experience of Christian love ◆

Another Exorcist

49 John answered, "Master, we saw someone casting out demons in your name, and we tried to stop him, because he does not follow with us." ⁵⁰But Jesus said to him, "Do not stop him; for whoever is not against you is for you."

A Samaritan Village Refuses to Receive Jesus

51 When the days drew near for him to be taken up, he set his face to go to

[d] Or it

44–45. Jesus again attempts to prepare the disciples for his execution, and again they do not wish to know what he is telling them. He is also preparing the women (24:6–8), although they 'forget' the painful information.

Jerusalem. [52]And he sent messengers ahead of him. On their way they entered a village of the Samaritans to make ready for him; [53]but they did not receive him, because his face was set toward Jerusalem. [54]When his disciples James and John saw it, they said, "Lord, do you want us to command fire to come down from heaven and consume them?"[e] [55]But he turned and rebuked them. [56]Then[f] they went on to another village.

Would-Be Followers of Jesus

[57] As they were going along the road, someone said to him, "I will follow you wherever you go." [58]And Jesus said to him, "Foxes have holes, and birds of the air have nests; but the Son of Man has nowhere to lay his head." [59]To another he said, "Follow me." But he said, "Lord, first let me go and bury my father." [60]But Jesus[g] said to him, "Let the dead bury their own dead; but as for you, go and proclaim the kingdom of God." [61]Another said, "I will follow you, Lord; but let me first say farewell to those at my home." [62]Jesus said to him, "No one who puts a hand to the plow and looks back is fit for the kingdom of God."

The Mission of the Seventy

10 After this the Lord appointed seventy[h] others and sent them on ahead of him in pairs to every town and place where he himself intended to go. [2]He said to them, "The harvest is plentiful, but the laborers are few; therefore ask the Lord of the harvest to send out laborers into his harvest. [3]Go on your way. See, I am sending you out like lambs into the midst of wolves. [4]Carry no purse, no bag, no sandals; and greet no one on the road. [5]Whatever house you enter, first say, 'Peace to this house!' [6]And if anyone is there who shares

in peace, your peace will rest on that person; but if not, it will return to you. [7]Remain in the same house, eating and drinking whatever they provide, for the laborer deserves to be paid. Do not move about from house to house. [8]Whenever you enter a town and its people welcome you, eat what is set before you; [9]cure the sick who are there, and say to them, 'The kingdom of God has come near to you.'[i] [10]But whenever you enter a town and they do not welcome you, go out into its streets and say, [11]'Even the dust of your town that clings to our feet, we wipe off in protest against you. Yet know this: the kingdom of God has come near.'[j] [12]I tell you, on that day it will be more tolerable for Sodom than for that town.

Woes to Unrepentant Cities

[13] "Woe to you, Chorazin! Woe to you, Bethsaida! For if the deeds of power done in you had been done in Tyre and Sidon, they would have repented long ago, sitting in sackcloth and ashes. [14]But at the judgment it will be more tolerable for Tyre and Sidon than for you. [15]And you, Capernaum,
will you be exalted to heaven?
No, you will be brought down to
Hades.
[16] "Whoever listens to you listens to me, and whoever rejects you rejects me, and whoever rejects me rejects the one who sent me."

[e] Other ancient authorities add *as Elijah did*
[f] Other ancient authorities read *rebuked them, and said, "You do not know what spirit you are of,*[56] *for the Son of Man has not come to destroy the lives of human beings but to save them." Then* [g] Gk *he*
[h] Other ancient authorities read *seventy-two*
[i] Or *is at hand for you* [j] Or *is at hand*

---

58. Like many people in today's world, Jesus knew homelessness. He who might have ruled the world had not even a bed on which to lay his head. He becomes one with those who have no fixed abode, that he might give to their hearts a secure resting place. Scripture calls us to receive those in need of shelter (Is. 16:4; 58:7; Rom. 12:13), for thereby we provide for heavenly guests (Matt. 25:35; Heb. 13:2).

The Return of the Seventy

17 The seventy[k] returned with joy, saying, "Lord, in your name even the demons submit to us!" [18]He said to them, "I watched Satan fall from heaven like a flash of lightning. [19]See, I have given you authority to tread on snakes and scorpions, and over all the power of the enemy; and nothing will hurt you. [20]Nevertheless, do not rejoice at this, that the spirits submit to you, but rejoice that your names are written in heaven."

Jesus Rejoices

21 At that same hour Jesus[l] rejoiced in the Holy Spirit[m] and said, "I thank[n] you, Father, Lord of heaven and earth, because you have hidden these things from the wise and the intelligent and have revealed them to infants; yes, Father, for such was your gracious will.[o] [22]All things have been handed over to me by my Father; and no one knows who the Son is except the Father, or who the Father is except the Son and anyone to whom the Son chooses to reveal him."

23 Then turning to the disciples, Jesus[l] said to them privately, "Blessed are the eyes that see what you see! [24]For I tell you that many prophets and kings desired to see what you see, but did not see it, and to hear what you hear, but did not hear it."

The Parable of the Good Samaritan

25 Just then a lawyer stood up to test Jesus.[p] "Teacher," he said, "what must I do to inherit eternal life?" [26]He said to him,

---

◆ The words Samaritan and neighbor become the two most important words for me in this passage. In many ways they carry the weight of extremes.

Samaritans were hated by Jews. The Jews avoided them and called them 'dogs'. The separation was nearly total, the walls of resentment and distrust were solidly in place and though there is some evidence that they were related somewhat by 'blood', there was no danger of their engagement in a family gathering. Their estrangement was now cultural, religious and racial, with no expectation of change for the better.

'Neighbor', on the other hand suggests nearness, cooperation and the possibility of friendship. Neighborliness is a positive quality suggesting a place of acceptance, a place where one feels safe and certainly a place where one's family can grow and flourish.

Who is my neighbor indeed, when the modern era still finds us separated racially, culturally and ethnically? Is Jesus suggesting, by presenting a Samaritan who acts in a kind and neighborly way, that a history of differences and separation are insufficient reasons to withhold love? Must I, a woman who is black, continue to love and care even when the object of that love has humiliated and abased me as long as I can remember? How can I do that? Will I not seem to be weak and foolish? Won't I leave myself vulnerable to further attacks and other degradations?

Even as the words of protestation form in my mind I am reminded of the example of Jesus as he is persecuted and crucified. His proactive stance on my behalf is forgiveness based on my lack of awareness. The fact of our separation does not prevent him from coming to my aid. Being reconciled with God, through forgiveness of my sins, I in turn am called to forgive. This is quite a challenge for me as a woman of color who must live in a world where I am devalued and my talents often ignored. Can God really turn my pain and humiliation into the perfumed balm of reconciliation? No wonder then that the gift of forgiveness offered by the insulted or demeaned has such a powerful impact on the community. Certainly, this can only be accomplished through God's grace. Freely have I received, freely can I offer myself and my talent to be used for

---

[k] Other ancient authorities read *seventy-two*
[l] Gk *he*   [m] Other authorities read *in the spirit*
[n] Or *praise*   [o] Or *for so it was well-pleasing in your sight*   [p] Gk *him*

my Lord's purpose. We, women and persons of color, have many opportunities to use those gifts and talents which we developed through pain and oppression. We can answer God's call for workers in the field of reconciliation. All around us are persons who lack understanding in this area.

I well understand the Samaritan and his choices. It would have been so easy to recount his painful history with the Jews or to itemize his busy itinerary. Like the priest and Levite, he could have chosen piety over community involvement and so maintained his security of self-protection. This Samaritan is a risk-taker. In 2 Cor. 1:3–4 we are encouraged to give away what we have been given. He had learned one of life's precious secrets: learning to forgive frees us to love.

History records that Sojourner Truth, Eleanor Roosevelt and Maya Angelou were able to transform the pain of rejection, prejudice and discrimination into launchpads of love and reconciliation. This Samaritan model of a loving, caring neighbor challenges me. I *can* do all things through Christ who strengthens me ◆

"What is written in the law? What do you read there?" 27He answered, "You shall love the Lord your God with all your heart, and with all your soul, and with all your strength, and with all your mind; and your neighbor as yourself." 28And he said to him, "You have given the right answer; do this, and you will live."

29 But wanting to justify himself, he asked Jesus, "And who is my neighbor?" 30Jesus replied, "A man was going down from Jerusalem to Jericho, and fell into the hands of robbers, who stripped him, beat him, and went away, leaving him half dead. 31Now by chance a priest was going down that road; and when he saw him, he passed by on the other side. 32So likewise a Levite, when he came to the place and saw him, passed by on the other side. 33But a Samaritan while traveling came near him; and when he saw him, he was moved with pity. 34He went to him and bandaged his wounds, having poured oil and wine on them. Then he put him on his own animal, brought him to an inn, and took care of him. 35The next day he took out two denarii,q gave them to the innkeeper, and said, 'Take care of him; and when I come back, I will repay you whatever more you spend.' 36Which of these three, do you think, was a neighbor to the man who fell into the hands of the robbers?" 37He said, "The one who showed him mercy." Jesus said to him, "Go and do likewise."

Jesus Visits Martha and Mary

38 Now as they went on their way, he entered a certain village, where a woman named Martha welcomed him into her home. 39She had a sister named Mary, who sat at the Lord's feet and listened to what he was saying. 40But Martha was distracted

q The denarius was the usual day's wage for a laborer

39. Mary sits at the feet of Jesus in the traditional position of a learner (Acts 22:3). Indeed, every time we meet Mary in the Gospel stories, she is at the feet of Jesus (John 11:32; 12:3).
40. Martha typifies many of our own efforts at entertaining. She is so flustered with the preparation of an elaborate meal that she cannot give her attention to her guest. Her preoccupation is with a myriad of details. Like many another woman, she may find it necessary to prove her worth by the spread which she sets forth upon the table. Instead, her true definition must lie in her relationship with Jesus. The Greek text says that she was distracted by 'much ministry' (*diakonia*) – a term frequently used in the New Testament for ministry (see in particular Acts 1:17, 25; 20:24; Rom. 12:7). Jesus' first purpose in calling the disciples was that they should 'be with him' (Mark 3:14). Martha has yet to learn this.

by her many tasks; so she came to him and asked, "Lord, do you not care that my sister has left me to do all the work by myself? Tell her then to help me." [41]But the Lord answered her, "Martha, Martha, you are worried and distracted by many things; [42]there is need of only one thing.[r] Mary has chosen the better part, which will not be taken away from her."

The Lord's Prayer

11 He was praying in a certain place, and after he had finished, one of his disciples said to him, "Lord, teach us to pray, as John taught his disciples." [2]He said to them, "When you pray, say:

Father,[s] hallowed be your name.
Your kingdom come.[t]
[3]   Give us each day our daily bread.[u]
[4]   And forgive us our sins,
        for we ourselves forgive everyone
            indebted to us.
        And do not bring us to the time of
            trial."[v]

Perseverance in Prayer

[5] And he said to them, "Suppose one of you has a friend, and you go to him at midnight and say to him, 'Friend, lend me three loaves of bread; [6]for a friend of mine has arrived, and I have nothing to set before him.' [7]And he answers from within, 'Do not bother me; the door has already been locked, and my children are with me in bed; I cannot get up and give you anything.' [8]I tell you, even though he will not get up and give him anything because he is his friend, at least because of his persistence he will get up and give him whatever he needs.

[9] "So I say to you, Ask, and it will be given you; search, and you will find; knock,

and the door will be opened for you. [10]For everyone who asks receives, and everyone who searches finds, and for everyone who knocks, the door will be opened. [11]Is there anyone among you who, if your child asks for[w] a fish, will give a snake instead of a fish? [12]Or if the child asks for an egg, will give a scorpion? [13]If you then, who are evil, know how to give good gifts to your children, how much more will the heavenly Father give the Holy Spirit[x] to those who ask him!"

Jesus and Beelzebul

[14] Now he was casting out a demon that was mute; when the demon had gone out, the one who had been mute spoke, and the crowds were amazed. [15]But some of them said, "He casts out demons by Beelzebul, the ruler of the demons." [16]Others, to test him, kept demanding from him a sign from heaven. [17]But he knew what they were thinking and said to them, "Every kingdom divided against itself becomes a desert, and house falls on house. [18]If Satan also is divided against himself, how will his kingdom stand? – for you say that I cast out the demons by Beelzebul. [19]Now if I cast out the demons by Beelzebul, by whom do your exorcists[y] cast them out? Therefore they will be your judges. [20]But if

[r] Other ancient authorities read *few things are necessary, or only one*   [s] Other ancient authorities read *Our Father in heaven*   [t] A few ancient authorities read *Your Holy Spirit come upon us and cleanse us*. Other ancient authorities add *Your will be done, on earth as in heaven*   [u] Or *our bread for tomorrow*   [v] Or *us into temptation*. Other ancient authorities add *but rescue us from the evil one* (or *from evil*)   [w] Other ancient authorities add *bread, will give a stone; or if your child asks for*   [x] Other ancient authorities read *the Father give the Holy Spirit from heaven*   [y] Gk *sons*

---

41. She complains that Mary is not ministering (*diakoneo*) with her, but Jesus shows that learning the Word of God is also part of ministry, and indeed the better part. Ministry may involve serving tables, but it also involves hearing and sharing the Word of God.

42. In the face of rabbinic sayings that it was better for the Torah to be given to swine or to be burned than taught to a woman, Jesus maintains women's right to learn and to respond appropriately.

it is by the finger of God that I cast out the demons, then the kingdom of God has come to you. ²¹When a strong man, fully armed, guards his castle, his property is safe. ²²But when one stronger than he attacks him and overpowers him, he takes away his armor in which he trusted and divides his plunder. ²³Whoever is not with me is against me, and whoever does not gather with me scatters.

The Return of the Unclean Spirit

24 "When the unclean spirit has gone out of a person, it wanders through waterless regions looking for a resting place, but not finding any, it says, 'I will return to my house from which I came.' ²⁵When it comes, it finds it swept and put in order. ²⁶Then it goes and brings seven other spirits more evil than itself, and they enter and live there; and the last state of that person is worse than the first."

True Blessedness

27 While he was saying this, a woman in the crowd raised her voice and said to him, "Blessed is the womb that bore you and the breasts that nursed you!" ²⁸But he said, "Blessed rather are those who hear the word of God and obey it!"

◆ Although we know almost nothing about this woman, we can guess that she is a mother. She praises Jesus as the Son of God (as he calls her to in the preceding verses) by honoring his mother. Any woman who has given birth recognizes this urge: to know the mother behind the child, even if the child is an adult. Perhaps she identified with his mother. Perhaps she thought of her own son. Truly, an outstanding son does honor his mother . . . especially when he is the Son of God!

Jesus challenges this mother *not* to

honor his mother. How could he? Surely his mother was worthy of honor and care – as he affirmed at the cross (John 19:26–27). Jesus wanted this woman to know that the response made to God's Word is more important than any identity as a mother. How we respond to the biblical message is more important than who we are.

Many women today need to hear these words. Too often, women identify themselves by their children and feel their primary worth is through child-rearing. To glory in one's children is praiseworthy and the mark of a good parent (see, e.g., Pss. 147:13; 128:3–4). But a maternal (or paternal) identity is not enough. Some agonize that their children are not believers, or that their children struggle. Yet others feel a lack of identity if they are childless (a struggle to which the Bible speaks, e.g., in Gal. 4:27). In their pain, and their pain is great, mothers and those who wish to be mothers may forget or devalue their identity in Christ. Yet Jesus reminds us that our identity as mothers is not our primary identity.

Luke 11:27 describes the biological qualities of femaleness (i.e. womb and breasts), but the media bombards us daily with other qualities of femaleness: attractiveness, thinness, relationship. Many women believe these qualities are necessary to their femaleness, and define themselves as attractive . . . or not; as thin . . . or not; as having a perfect relationship . . . or a poor relationship . . . or no relationship at all. These women may find it difficult to worship on Sunday morning or to believe that God loves them and provides for them because of their struggles. These struggles are not minor, and God is concerned about them. But our worth in the Kingdom does not hinge on these criteria.

In Luke 11:27, as in 8:11, Jesus reminds us that our spiritual identity transcends

---

LUKE 11

27–28. Women who find their worth only in child-bearing or breast-feeding should examine Jesus' priorities. Do we define ourselves in terms of our sexuality or of our spirituality?

gender identity. We are called first to define ourselves by our membership in the Kingdom. We are God's children; no identity is more important than that.

Luke 11:28 calls us further to be doers of the Word and not hearers only. We are to serve God, making each day count. We are not just to know God but to act on our knowledge. Women in particular, who often feel themselves branded as women and limited by their femaleness, can feel free to respond to God's calling to develop and use their gifts, whatever those may be. Women can glory in their relationships and their children, if they have them, because they have first trusted themselves to God and responded to God's call to action.

Being a woman and a mother is a high calling, but serving God is a higher calling yet. There is no higher calling ◆

The Sign of Jonah

29 When the crowds were increasing, he began to say, "This generation is an evil generation; it asks for a sign, but no sign will be given to it except the sign of Jonah. [30]For just as Jonah became a sign to the people of Nineveh, so the Son of Man will be to this generation. [31]The queen of the South will rise at the judgment with the people of this generation and condemn them, because she came from the ends of the earth to listen to the wisdom of Solomon, and see, something greater than Solomon is here! [32]The people of Nineveh will rise up at the judgment with this generation and condemn it, because they repented at the proclamation of Jonah, and see, something greater than Jonah is here!

The Light of the Body

33 "No one after lighting a lamp puts it in a cellar,[z] but on the lampstand so that those who enter may see the light. [34]Your eye is the lamp of your body. If your eye is healthy, your whole body is full of light; but if it is not healthy, your body is full of darkness. [35]Therefore consider whether the light in you is not darkness. [36]If then your whole body is full of light, with no part of it in darkness, it will be as full of light as when a lamp gives you light with its rays."

Jesus Denounces Pharisees and Lawyers

37 While he was speaking, a Pharisee invited him to dine with him; so he went in and took his place at the table. [38]The Pharisee was amazed to see that he did not first wash before dinner. [39]Then the Lord said to him, "Now you Pharisees clean the outside of the cup and of the dish, but

[z] Other ancient authorities add *or under the bushel basket*

---

31. To those who ask for a sign, Jesus points to characters from the Old Testament. The Queen of Sheba, like the hearers of Jonah, experienced a radical transformation in attitude (1 Kings 10:1–13; 2 Chron. 9:1–12). There is scholarly debate as to whether Sheba lay on the coast of Africa or of Arabia. The queen may have come originally to negotiate a trade agreement for maritime commerce in the Red Sea, and the 'hard questions' with which she came to test Solomon may have concerned economic considerations. Like the inhabitants of Nineveh to whom Jonah preached, her mind is turned to her own spiritual condition; and she returns with a new understanding of the God of Israel. St Ephraem the Syrian (died 373) wrote, 'The lamp of truth did Solomon give her . . . she was enlightened and went away . . . The bright spark which went down home with that blessed Queen, held on its shining amid the darkness, till the new Day-spring came.'

The Queen of Sheba is one of three Old Testament women used as spiritual examples in Luke (4:26; 11:31; 17:32). Like other black and African women of the Bible, she demonstrates an unusual readiness to hear and do God's will (Gen. 16:7–14; 21:15–19; Exod. 1:15–21; 2:5–10, 21; 3:22; 4:24–26; Num. 12:1; Song of Sol. 1:5).

inside you are full of greed and wickedness. [40]You fools! Did not the one who made the outside make the inside also? [41]So give for alms those things that are within; and see, everything will be clean for you.

42 "But woe to you Pharisees! For you tithe mint and rue and herbs of all kinds, and neglect justice and the love of God; it is these you ought to have practiced, without neglecting the others. [43]Woe to you Pharisees! For you love to have the seat of honor in the synagogues and to be greeted with respect in the marketplaces. [44]Woe to you! For you are like unmarked graves, and people walk over them without realizing it."

45 One of the lawyers answered him, "Teacher, when you say these things, you insult us too." [46]And he said, "Woe also to you lawyers! For you load people with burdens hard to bear, and you yourselves do not lift a finger to ease them. [47]Woe to you! For you build the tombs of the prophets whom your ancestors killed. [48]So you are witnesses and approve of the deeds of your ancestors; for they killed them, and you build their tombs. [49]Therefore also the Wisdom of God said, 'I will send them prophets and apostles, some of whom they will kill and persecute,' [50]so that this generation may be charged with the blood of all the prophets shed since the foundation of the world, [51]from the blood of Abel to the blood of Zechariah, who perished between the altar and the sanctuary. Yes, I tell you, it will be charged against this generation. [52]Woe to you lawyers! For you have taken away the key of knowledge; you did not enter yourselves, and you hindered those who were entering."

53 When he went outside, the scribes and the Pharisees began to be very hostile toward him and to cross-examine him about many things, [54]lying in wait for him, to catch him in something he might say.

A Warning against Hypocrisy

12 Meanwhile, when the crowd gathered by the thousands, so that they trampled on one another, he began to speak first to his disciples, "Beware of the yeast of the Pharisees, that is, their hypocrisy. [2]Nothing is covered up that will not be uncovered, and nothing secret that will not become known. [3]Therefore whatever you

---

49–51. Here Jesus uses a figure of speech to depict wisdom (*Sophia*) as a person giving expression to the purposes of God. This is the only New Testament representation of wisdom as speaking with its own voice, though there is another personification at Luke 7:35. The writer of Proverbs pictures both Wisdom and Folly as women calling advice to their adherents (Prov. 1:20–33; 3:15–18; 8:1–9:12–17). Many other abstract qualities are also personified in the Bible. (See Pss. 23:6; 25:21; 43:3; 79:8; 85:10–13; 89:14; 96:6; Prov. 20:28; Is. 59:14–16.) In the New Testament wisdom is viewed as an attribute or characteristic of God, along with many other virtues such as mercy, justice, truth and holiness. These individual characteristics are not divine personages to be worshipped in their own right but rather give us a deeper understanding of God's perfection. For instance, when Jesus declares that the truth shall make us free, he does not mean that truth is a religious entity capable of action in its own right. The empowerment comes from God who sends both message and messenger. Under no circumstances should we worship an individual attribute rather than the God who encompasses every perfection. In Christ are hidden all the treasures of wisdom and knowledge (Col. 2:30) and in Christ all things are summed up (Eph. 1:10).

Interestingly enough, wisdom (*Sophia*) is here shown as planning the sending of emissaries whose message may not be heeded, and some of whom will even be killed. Jesus declares that the religious leaders of his own time would be involved in the culmination of this long process. The saying must be understood in connection with his three-fold prediction of his death, his lament over Jerusalem (Luke 13:34–35) and with the parable of Luke 20:9–16. Luke persistently represents Jesus as aware of his coming death and as being involved in the decision-making.

have said in the dark will be heard in the light, and what you have whispered behind closed doors will be proclaimed from the housetops.

Exhortation to Fearless Confession

4 "I tell you, my friends, do not fear those who kill the body, and after that can do nothing more. ⁵But I will warn you whom to fear: fear him who, after he has killed, has authority[a] to cast into hell.[b] Yes, I tell you, fear him! ⁶Are not five sparrows sold for two pennies? Yet not one of them is forgotten in God's sight. ⁷But even the hairs of your head are all counted. Do not be afraid; you are of more value than many sparrows.

8 "And I tell you, everyone who acknowledges me before others, the Son of Man also will acknowledge before the angels of God; ⁹but whoever denies me before others will be denied before the angels of God. ¹⁰And everyone who speaks a word against the Son of Man will be forgiven; but whoever blasphemes against the Holy Spirit will not be forgiven. ¹¹When they bring you before the synagogues, the rulers, and the authorities, do not worry about how[c] you are to defend yourselves or what you are to say; ¹²for the Holy Spirit will teach you at that very hour what you ought to say."

The Parable of the Rich Fool

13 Someone in the crowd said to him, "Teacher, tell my brother to divide the family inheritance with me." ¹⁴But he said to him, "Friend, who set me to be a judge or arbitrator over you?" ¹⁵And he said to them, "Take care! Be on your guard against all kinds of greed; for one's life does not consist in the abundance of possessions." ¹⁶Then he told them a parable: "The land of a rich man produced abundantly. ¹⁷And he thought to himself, 'What should I do, for I have no place to store my crops?' ¹⁸Then he said, 'I will do this: I will pull down my barns and build larger ones, and there I will store all my grain and my goods. ¹⁹And I will say to my soul, 'Soul, you have ample goods laid up for many years; relax, eat, drink, be merry.' ²⁰But God said to him, 'You fool! This very night your life is being demanded of you. And the things you have prepared, whose will they be?' ²¹So it is with those who store up treasures for themselves but are not rich toward God."

Do Not Worry

22 He said to his disciples, "Therefore I tell you, do not worry about your life, what you will eat, or about your body, what you will wear. ²³For life is more than food, and the body more than clothing. ²⁴Consider the ravens: they neither sow nor reap, they have neither storehouse nor barn, and yet God feeds them. Of how much more value are you than the birds! ²⁵And can any of you by worrying add a single hour to your span of life?[d] ²⁶If then you are not able to do so small a thing as that, why do you worry about the rest? ²⁷Consider the lilies, how they grow: they neither toil nor spin;[e] yet I tell you, even Solomon in all his glory was not clothed like one of these. ²⁸But if God so clothes the grass of the field, which is alive today and tomorrow is thrown into the oven, how much more will he clothe you – you of little faith! ²⁹And do not keep striving for what you are to eat and what you are to drink, and do not keep worrying.

---

[a] Or *power*   [b] Gk *Gehenna*   [c] Other ancient authorities add *or what*   [d] Or *add a cubit to your stature*   [e] Other ancient authorities read *Consider the lilies; they neither spin nor weave*

LUKE 12

14. On more than one occasion, Jesus refuses to accede to demands that are inappropriate. See Matt. 15:24; 20:20–23; John 2:4; 12:13.

[30]For it is the nations of the world that strive after all these things, and your Father knows that you need them. [31]Instead, strive for his[f] kingdom, and these things will be given to you as well.

32 "Do not be afraid, little flock, for it is your Father's good pleasure to give you the kingdom. [33]Sell your possessions, and give alms. Make purses for yourselves that do not wear out, an unfailing treasure in heaven, where no thief comes near and no moth destroys. [34]For where your treasure is, there your heart will be also.

Watchful Slaves

35 "Be dressed for action and have your lamps lit; [36]be like those who are waiting for their master to return from the wedding banquet, so that they may open the door for him as soon as he comes and knocks. [37]Blessed are those slaves whom the master finds alert when he comes; truly I tell you, he will fasten his belt and have them sit down to eat, and he will come and serve them. [38]If he comes during the middle of the night, or near dawn, and finds them so, blessed are those slaves.

39 "But know this: if the owner of the house had known at what hour the thief was coming, he[g] would not have let his house be broken into. [40]You also must be ready, for the Son of Man is coming at an unexpected hour."

The Faithful or the Unfaithful Slave

41 Peter said, "Lord, are you telling this parable for us or for everyone?" [42]And the Lord said, "Who then is the faithful and prudent manager whom his master will put in charge of his slaves, to give them their allowance of food at the proper time? [43]Blessed is that slave whom his master will find at work when he arrives. [44]Truly I tell you, he will put that one in charge of all his possessions. [45]But if that slave says to himself, 'My master is delayed in coming,' and if he begins to beat the other slaves, men and women, and to eat and drink and get drunk, [46]the master of that slave will come on a day when he does not expect him and at an hour that he does not know, and will cut him in pieces,[h] and put him with the unfaithful. [47]That slave who knew what his master wanted, but did not prepare himself or do what was wanted, will receive a severe beating. [48]But the one who did not know and did what deserved a beating will receive a light beating. From everyone to whom much has been given, much will be required; and from the one to whom much has been entrusted, even more will be demanded.

Jesus the Cause of Division

49 "I came to bring fire to the earth, and how I wish it were already kindled! [50]I have a baptism with which to be baptized, and what stress I am under until it is completed! [51]Do you think that I have come to bring peace to the earth? No, I tell you, but rather division! [52]From now on five in one household will be divided, three

[f] Other ancient authorities read *God's*   [g] Other ancient authorities add *would have watched and*   [h] Or *cut him off*

---

50. Jesus is able both to accept the ordeal which lies before him and to express the dread honestly. Though there is no shirking the challenge, there is anxiety until the task could be finished (Mark 10:38; Luke 22:42; John 19:28, 30).

52–53. Christ is quite honest that commitment to him does not always bring peace within a household. Mother may be pitted against daughter and mother-in-law against daughter-in-law. This is a difficult concept for women who desire to create domestic harmony at any price. Spiritual priorities may complicate relationships and bring severe alienation from family members who hold a different set of values. It is easier to accept this if we understand that we have been forewarned by Jesus.

against two and two against three; [53]they will be divided:

father against son
and son against father,
mother against daughter
and daughter against mother,
mother-in-law against her daughter-in-law
and daughter-in-law against mother-in-law."

Interpreting the Time

54 He also said to the crowds, "When you see a cloud rising in the west, you immediately say, 'It is going to rain'; and so it happens. [55]And when you see the south wind blowing, you say, 'There will be scorching heat'; and it happens. [56]You hypocrites! You know how to interpret the appearance of earth and sky, but why do you not know how to interpret the present time?

Settling with Your Opponent

57 "And why do you not judge for yourselves what is right? [58]Thus, when you go with your accuser before a magistrate, on the way make an effort to settle the case,[1] or you may be dragged before the judge, and the judge hand you over to the officer, and the officer throw you in prison. [59]I tell you, you will never get out until you have paid the very last penny."

Repent or Perish

13 At that very time there were some present who told him about the

Galileans whose blood Pilate had mingled with their sacrifices. [2]He asked them, "Do you think that because these Galileans suffered in this way they were worse sinners than all other Galileans? [3]No, I tell you; but unless you repent, you will all perish as they did. [4]Or those eighteen who were killed when the tower of Siloam fell on them – do you think that they were worse offenders than all the others living in Jerusalem? [5]No, I tell you; but unless you repent, you will all perish just as they did."

The Parable of the Barren Fig Tree

6 Then he told this parable: "A man had a fig tree planted in his vineyard; and he came looking for fruit on it and found none. [7]So he said to the gardener, 'See here! For three years I have come looking for fruit on this fig tree, and still I find none. Cut it down! Why should it be wasting the soil?' [8]He replied, 'Sir, let it alone for one more year, until I dig around it and put manure on it. [9]If it bears fruit next year, well and good; but if not, you can cut it down.' "

Jesus Heals a Crippled Woman

10 Now he was teaching in one of the synagogues on the sabbath. [11]And just then there appeared a woman with a spirit that had crippled her for eighteen years. She was bent over and was quite unable to stand up straight. [12]When Jesus saw her, he called her over and said, "Woman, you are set free from your ailment." [13]When he laid his

---

[1] Gk *settle with him*

LUKE 13

10–16. The crippled woman has endured her affliction for 18 years, but she is still faithful in coming to the house of God on the Sabbath. Here she meets the Great Physician who perceives that her first need is spiritual rather than physical. The weight of her sins is first removed before her back is straightened, and she stands erect to praise God. The synagogue officials appear more jealous of Jesus' power than concerned over Sabbath proprieties, but Jesus points to the true priorities of the Sabbath. To the religious functionaries the handicapped woman had less value than an animal, but to Jesus she is a covenant member of believing Israel. If livestock may be loosed in order to have water on the Sabbath, how much more should the daughter of Abraham be loosed from the painful constriction of her body? Contrary to the common assumption that

hands on her, immediately she stood up straight and began praising God. ¹⁴But the leader of the synagogue, indignant because Jesus had cured on the sabbath, kept saying to the crowd, "There are six days on which work ought to be done; come on those days and be cured, and not on the sabbath day." ¹⁵But the Lord answered him and said, "You hypocrites! Does not each of you on the sabbath untie his ox or his donkey from the manger, and lead it away to give it water? ¹⁶And ought not this woman, a daughter of Abraham whom Satan bound for eighteen long years, be set free from this bondage on the sabbath day?" ¹⁷When he said this, all his opponents were put to shame; and the entire crowd was rejoicing at all the wonderful things that he was doing.

The Parable of the Mustard Seed

18 He said therefore, "What is the kingdom of God like? And to what should I compare it? ¹⁹It is like a mustard seed that someone took and sowed in the garden; it grew and became a tree, and the birds of the air made nests in its branches."

The Parable of the Yeast

20 And again he said, "To what should I compare the kingdom of God? ²¹It is like yeast that a woman took and mixed in with[j] three measures of flour until all of it was leavened."

The Narrow Door

22 Jesus[k] went through one town and village after another, teaching as he made his way to Jerusalem. ²³Someone asked him, "Lord, will only a few be saved?" He said to them, ²⁴"Strive to enter through the narrow door; for many, I tell you, will try to enter and will not be able. ²⁵When once the owner of the house has got up and shut the door, and you begin to stand outside and to knock at the door, saying, 'Lord, open to us,' then in reply he will say to you, 'I do not know where you come from.' ²⁶Then you will begin to say, 'We ate and drank with you, and you taught in our streets.' ²⁷But he will say, 'I do not know where you come from; go away from me, all you evildoers!' ²⁸There will be weeping and gnashing of teeth when you see Abraham and Isaac and Jacob and all the prophets in the kingdom of God, and you yourselves thrown out. ²⁹Then people will come from east and west, from north and south, and will eat in the kingdom of God. ³⁰Indeed, some are last who will be first, and some are first who will be last."

The Lament over Jerusalem

31 At that very hour some Pharisees came and said to him, "Get away from here, for Herod wants to kill you." ³²He said to them, "Go and tell that fox for me,[l] 'Listen, I am casting out demons and performing cures today and tomorrow, and on the third day I finish my work. ³³Yet today, tomorrow, and the next day I must be on my way, because it is impossible for a prophet to be killed outside of Jerusalem.' ³⁴Jerusalem,

[j] Gk hid in   [k] Gk He   [l] Gk lacks for me

---

handicapped persons were suffering on account of their own wrongdoing, Jesus insists that the woman has been afflicted not by her own misdeeds but by the binding of Satan. Both soul and body are now free to glorify God.

How often have we come to the house of God, bent over with the weight of our anger, resentment, jealousy, pride and guilt, there to be delivered by the Great Physician!

20–21. See note on yeast at Matt. 13:33. For Luke's other parables involving women, see Luke 15:8–10; 18:1–9.

34. Here Jesus likens his love and compassion for Jerusalem to the proverbial concern of a mother hen for her chicks. This maternal image is close to that of God as a mother eagle hovering over her young and bearing them on her wings (Exod. 19:4; Deut. 32:11). For other similes of God as mother, see Deut. 32:18; Ps. 131:2–3; Is. 42:13–14; 49:15; 66:13; Hos. 13:8.

Jerusalem, the city that kills the prophets and stones those who are sent to it! How often have I desired to gather your children together as a hen gathers her brood under her wings, and you were not willing! [35]See, your house is left to you. And I tell you, you will not see me until the time comes when[m] you say, 'Blessed is the one who comes in the name of the Lord.' "

Jesus Heals the Man with Dropsy

14 On one occasion when Jesus[n] was going to the house of a leader of the Pharisees to eat a meal on the sabbath, they were watching him closely. [2]Just then, in front of him, there was a man who had dropsy. [3]And Jesus asked the lawyers and Pharisees, "Is it lawful to cure people on the sabbath, or not?" [4]But they were silent. So Jesus[n] took him and healed him, and sent him away. [5]Then he said to them, "If one of you has a child[o] or an ox that has fallen into a well, will you not immediately pull it out on a sabbath day?" [6]And they could not reply to this.

Humility and Hospitality

7 When he noticed how the guests chose the places of honor, he told them a parable. [8]"When you are invited by someone to a wedding banquet, do not sit down at the place of honor, in case someone more distinguished than you has been invited by your host; [9]and the host who invited both of you may come and say to you, 'Give this person your place,' and then in disgrace you would start to take the lowest place. [10]But when you are invited, go and sit down at the lowest place, so that when your host comes, he may say to you, 'Friend, move up

higher'; then you will be honored in the presence of all who sit at the table with you. [11]For all who exalt themselves will be humbled, and those who humble themselves will be exalted."

12 He said also to the one who had invited him, "When you give a luncheon or a dinner, do not invite your friends or your brothers or your relatives or rich neighbors, in case they may invite you in return, and you would be repaid. [13]But when you give a banquet, invite the poor, the crippled, the lame, and the blind. [14]And you will be blessed, because they cannot repay you, for you will be repaid at the resurrection of the righteous."

The Parable of the Great Dinner

15 One of the dinner guests, on hearing this, said to him, "Blessed is anyone who will eat bread in the kingdom of God!" [16]Then Jesus[n] said to him, "Someone gave a great dinner and invited many. [17]At the time for the dinner he sent his slave to say to those who had been invited, 'Come; for everything is ready now.' [18]But they all alike began to make excuses. The first said to him, 'I have bought a piece of land, and I must go out and see it; please accept my regrets.' [19]Another said, 'I have bought five yoke of oxen, and I am going to try them out; please accept my regrets.' [20]Another said, 'I have just been married, and therefore I cannot come.' [21]So the slave returned and reported this to his master. Then the owner of the house became angry and said

---

[m] Other ancient authorities lack *the time comes when*   [n] Gk *he*   [o] Other ancient authorities read *a donkey*

LUKE 14

4. The word describing the reaction of Jesus' opponents is *hesuchazo*, containing a root stem that is also applied to women (1 Tim. 2:11–12). Sometimes, as here, it may indeed mean to hold one's tongue but sometimes it means to cease one's objections. Twice in the book of Acts, the term is used of people who continued to speak and even made theological statements (Acts 11:18; 21:14). Women would do well to bear in mind that 'to be silent' may imply refraining from further resistance rather than saying nothing at all.

to his slave, 'Go out at once into the streets and lanes of the town and bring in the poor, the crippled, the blind, and the lame.' [22]And the slave said, 'Sir, what you ordered has been done, and there is still room.' [23]Then the master said to the slave, 'Go out into the roads and lanes, and compel people to come in, so that my house may be filled. [24]For I tell you,[p] none of those who were invited will taste my dinner.' "

The Cost of Discipleship

25 Now large crowds were traveling with him; and he turned and said to them, [26]"Whoever comes to me and does not hate father and mother, wife and children, brothers and sisters, yes, and even life itself, cannot be my disciple. [27]Whoever does not carry the cross and follow me cannot be my disciple. [28]For which of you, intending to build a tower, does not first sit down and estimate the cost, to see whether he has enough to complete it? [29]Otherwise, when he has laid a foundation and is not able to finish, all who see it will begin to ridicule him, [30]saying, 'This fellow began to build and was not able to finish.' [31]Or what king, going out to wage war against another king, will not sit down first and consider whether he is able with ten thousand to oppose the one who comes against him with twenty thousand? [32]If he cannot, then, while the other is still far away, he sends a delegation and asks for the terms of peace. [33]So therefore, none of you can become my disciple if you do not give up all your possessions.

About Salt

34 "Salt is good; but if salt has lost its taste, how can its saltiness be restored?[q] [35]It is fit neither for the soil nor for the manure pile; they throw it away. Let anyone with ears to hear listen!"

The Parable of the Lost Sheep

15 Now all the tax collectors and sinners were coming near to listen to him. [2]And the Pharisees and the scribes were grumbling and saying, "This fellow welcomes sinners and eats with them."

3 So he told them this parable: [4]"Which one of you, having a hundred sheep and losing one of them, does not leave the ninety-nine in the wilderness and go after the one that is lost until he finds it? [5]When he has found it, he lays it on his shoulders and rejoices. [6]And when he comes home, he calls together his friends and neighbors, saying to them, 'Rejoice with me, for I have found my sheep that was lost.' [7]Just so, I tell you, there will be more joy in heaven over one sinner who repents than over ninety-nine righteous persons who need no repentance.

The Parable of the Lost Coin

8 "Or what woman having ten silver coins,[r] if she loses one of them, does not light a lamp, sweep the house, and search carefully until she finds it? [9]When she has

[p] The Greek word for *you* here is plural   [q] Or *how can it be used for seasoning?*   [r] Gk *drachmas*, each worth about a day's wage for a laborer

---

26. The paramount call is to follow Christ. Many Christian women have been told that the greatest good in their lives is to live harmoniously with their husbands; and some will sacrifice their own spiritual integrity to keep peace within the home. Jesus insists that marriage and family must not be placed ahead of God's will.

LUKE 15

8–10. These three parables tell about something that is lost. In the parable of the lost sheep, God is represented as the Good Shepherd. In the story of the lost son, God is shown as a loving and forgiving Father. In the parable of the lost coin, God is represented by the woman seeking that which was hers.

found it, she calls together her friends and neighbors, saying, 'Rejoice with me, for I have found the coin that I had lost.' [10]Just so, I tell you, there is joy in the presence of the angels of God over one sinner who repents."

The Parable of the Prodigal and His Brother

11 Then Jesus[s] said, "There was a man who had two sons. [12]The younger of them said to his father, 'Father, give me the share of the property that will belong to me.' So he divided his property between them. [13]A

◆ Jesus' story of the Prodigal Son brings important insights to godly parents who grieve over the misbehavior and/or lack of faith displayed by their sons or daughters. In this parable, the father personifies God as a faithful parent, always waiting to receive back the wayward child. The first point to note is that *the father is not to blame for the son's misconduct.* How often we have channeled our spiritual energies into blaming ourselves rather than into prayer! A mother's self-definition or worth is not tied to the performance of her child but rather to her relationship with Christ.

The Scriptures are very clear that grown children make their own decisions and are responsible for them. They cannot become fully mature human beings unless they are allowed to make choices. The father in this story not only permits the son to make his ill-advised choice, but even enables him to put it into action. At

great personal cost, the father turns over to the younger son his portion of all that the father has labored so hard to conserve. It is precisely when the son has to face the consequences of his choices that his heart turns back to his father. His decision to return takes place 'in the far country' where he has had opportunity to reflect upon his condition away from the influences of home.

Psychologists tell us that human beings may pass through stages of dependence, independence, counterdependence and interdependence as they struggle toward full maturity. The loving father in this story gave the son the space that he needed and did not crowd him. Young people need to have the freedom to make a decision that is their own and to know that it has not been forced upon them by parental pressure.

The process goes much better and faster if parents respect their children's need for distancing themselves while they are thinking through their own relationship to God. The Holy Spirit may be most at work when our sons or daughters appear most deeply alienated. For the promise of the Spirit to the children of believers, see Acts 2:39; 16:31; 1 Cor. 7:14. Some of the world's most powerful Christians are those who have returned to serve Christ with the passion and repentance of the Prodigal. One might mention St Augustine, Francis of Assisi, John Bunyan and many more as trophies of this grace.

[s] Gk *he*

In the Near East, women often wear their dowry coins sewn to a headband or on chains about their necks. These coins are very valuable and represent an investment against any kind of financial need. When the woman in the story loses one, one tenth of her capital is gone; and at last her diligent search is rewarded by the recovery of the precious silver piece. The neighbor women join her in rejoicing at the restoration, just as the angels rejoice over a sinner who repents.

Many women find it difficult to see the seeking love of God in the representation of the woman. More than once the Bible depicts God with feminine imagery, and women need to perceive themselves as made in the image of God (Gen. 1:26–27; 5:2–3). This biblical understanding could greatly enhance women's self respect and give them the assurance to reach out to others in ministry.

We note that the father was not only waiting but also watching, as we must watch in prayer. Sometimes we ask about the role of the mother in this parable. Whatever the reason, she is keeping hands off. We must assume that she was busy with prayer and with preparing a comfortable and welcoming environment for the return of the Prodigal. Even when a beloved son or daughter is far from Christ, we may proceed about our tasks with a cheerful confidence that the restoration depends upon God rather than upon ourselves ◆

few days later the younger son gathered all he had and traveled to a distant country, and there he squandered his property in dissolute living. ¹⁴When he had spent everything, a severe famine took place throughout that country, and he began to be in need. ¹⁵So he went and hired himself out to one of the citizens of that country, who sent him to his fields to feed the pigs. ¹⁶He would gladly have filled himself with ᵗ the pods that the pigs were eating; and no one gave him anything. ¹⁷But when he came to himself he said, 'How many of my father's hired hands have bread enough and to spare, but here I am dying of hunger! ¹⁸I will get up and go to my father, and I will say to him, "Father, I have sinned against heaven and before you; ¹⁹I am no longer worthy to be called your son; treat me like one of your hired hands." ' ²⁰So he set off and went to his father. But while he was still far off, his father saw him and was filled with compassion; he ran and put his arms around him and kissed him. ²¹Then the son said to him, 'Father, I have sinned against heaven and before you; I am no longer worthy to be called your son.'ᵘ ²²But the father said to his slaves, 'Quickly, bring out a robe – the best one – and put it on him; put a ring on his finger and sandals on his feet. ²³And get the fatted calf and kill it, and let us eat and celebrate; ²⁴for this son of mine was dead and is alive again; he was

lost and is found!' And they began to celebrate.

25 "Now his elder son was in the field; and when he came and approached the house, he heard music and dancing. ²⁶He called one of the slaves and asked what was going on. ²⁷He replied, 'Your brother has come, and your father has killed the fatted calf, because he has got him back safe and sound.' ²⁸Then he became angry and refused to go in. His father came out and began to plead with him. ²⁹But he answered his father, 'Listen! For all these years I have been working like a slave for you, and I have never disobeyed your command; yet you have never given me even a young goat so that I might celebrate with my friends. ³⁰But when this son of yours came back, who has devoured your property with prostitutes, you killed the fatted calf for him!' ³¹Then the fatherᵛ said to him, 'Son, you are always with me, and all that is mine is yours. ³²But we had to celebrate and rejoice, because this brother of yours was dead and has come to life; he was lost and has been found.' "

The Parable of the Dishonest Manager

16 Then Jesusᵛ said to the disciples, "There was a rich man who had a manager, and charges were brought to him that this man was squandering his property. ²So he summoned him and said to him, 'What is this that I hear about you? Give me an accounting of your management, because you cannot be my manager any longer.' ³Then the manager said to himself, 'What will I do, now that my master is taking the position away from me? I am not strong enough to dig, and I am ashamed to beg. ⁴I have decided what to do so that, when I am dismissed as manager, people may welcome me into their homes.' ⁵So, summoning his master's debtors one by

ᵗ Other ancient authorities read *filled his stomach with*   ᵘ Other ancient authorities add *treat me as one of your hired servants*   ᵛ Gk *he*

one, he asked the first, 'How much do you owe my master?' [6]He answered, 'A hundred jugs of olive oil.' He said to him, 'Take your bill, sit down quickly, and make it fifty.' [7]Then he asked another, 'And how much do you owe?' He replied, 'A hundred containers of wheat.' He said to him, 'Take your bill and make it eighty.' [8]And his master commended the dishonest manager because he had acted shrewdly; for the children of this age are more shrewd in dealing with their own generation than are the children of light. [9]And I tell you, make friends for yourselves by means of dishonest wealth[w] so that when it is gone, they may welcome you into the eternal homes.[x]

[10] "Whoever is faithful in a very little is faithful also in much; and whoever is dishonest in a very little is dishonest also in much. [11]If then you have not been faithful with the dishonest wealth,[w] who will entrust to you the true riches? [12]And if you have not been faithful with what belongs to another, who will give you what is your own? [13]No slave can serve two masters; for a slave will either hate the one and love the other, or be devoted to the one and despise the other. You cannot serve God and wealth."[w]

The Law and the Kingdom of God

[14] The Pharisees, who were lovers of money, heard all this, and they ridiculed him. [15]So he said to them, "You are those who justify yourselves in the sight of others; but God knows your hearts; for what is prized by human beings is an abomination in the sight of God.

[16] "The law and the prophets were in effect until John came; since then the good news of the kingdom of God is proclaimed, and everyone tries to enter it by force.[y] [17]But it is easier for heaven and earth to pass away, than for one stroke of a letter in the law to be dropped.

[18] "Anyone who divorces his wife and marries another commits adultery, and whoever marries a woman divorced from her husband commits adultery.

The Rich Man and Lazarus

[19] "There was a rich man who was dressed in purple and fine linen and who feasted sumptuously every day. [20]And at his gate lay a poor man named Lazarus, covered with sores, [21]who longed to satisfy his hunger with what fell from the rich man's table; even the dogs would come and lick his sores. [22]The poor man died and was carried away by the angels to be with Abraham.[z] The rich man also died and was buried. [23]In Hades, where he was being tormented, he looked up and saw Abraham far away with Lazarus by his side.[a] [24]He called out, 'Father Abraham, have mercy on me, and send Lazarus to dip the tip of his finger in water and cool my tongue; for I am in agony in these flames.' [25]But Abraham said, 'Child, remember that during your lifetime you received your good things, and Lazarus in like manner evil things; but now he is comforted here,

[w] Gk mammon [x] Gk tents [y] Or everyone is strongly urged to enter it [z] Gk to Abraham's bosom [a] Gk in his bosom

---

LUKE 16

18. This is often viewed as a very legalistic text. In point of fact, Jesus makes the declaration to safeguard the rights and needs of woman in a system that allowed men to discard their wives with impunity. (See the note on 'Divorce', p. 97.) Even today many systems of divorce leave women impoverished and disadvantaged, without adequate means to support themselves and their children. The former husband who marries again frequently fails to provide for the family to which he originally committed himself, and there is, as well, great emotional, social and psychological deprivation.

and you are in agony. ²⁶Besides all this, between you and us a great chasm has been fixed, so that those who might want to pass from here to you cannot do so, and no one can cross from there to us.' ²⁷He said, 'Then, father, I beg you to send him to my father's house – ²⁸for I have five brothers – that he may warn them, so that they will not also come into this place of torment.' ²⁹Abraham replied, 'They have Moses and the prophets; they should listen to them.' ³⁰He said, 'No, father Abraham; but if someone goes to them from the dead, they will repent.' ³¹He said to him, 'If they do not listen to Moses and the prophets, neither will they be convinced even if someone rises from the dead.' "

Some Sayings of Jesus

17 Jesus[b] said to his disciples, "Occasions for stumbling are bound to come, but woe to anyone by whom they come! ²It would be better for you if a millstone were hung around your neck and you were thrown into the sea than for you to cause one of these little ones to stumble. ³Be on your guard! If another disciple[c] sins, you must rebuke the offender, and if there is repentance, you must forgive. ⁴And if the same person sins against you seven times a day, and turns back to you seven times and says, 'I repent,' you must forgive."

5 The apostles said to the Lord, "Increase our faith!" ⁶The Lord replied, "If you had faith the size of a[d] mustard seed, you could say to this mulberry tree, 'Be uprooted and planted in the sea,' and it would obey you.

7 "Who among you would say to your slave who has just come in from plowing or tending sheep in the field, 'Come here at once and take your place at the table'? ⁸Would you not rather say to him, 'Prepare supper for me, put on your apron and serve me while I eat and drink; later you may eat and drink'? ⁹Do you thank the slave for doing what was commanded? ¹⁰So you also, when you have done all that you were

ordered to do, say, 'We are worthless slaves; we have done only what we ought to have done!' "

Jesus Cleanses Ten Lepers

11 On the way to Jerusalem Jesus[b] was going through the region between Samaria and Galilee. ¹²As he entered a village, ten lepers[e] approached him. Keeping their distance, ¹³they called out, saying, "Jesus, Master, have mercy on us!" ¹⁴When he saw them, he said to them, "Go and show yourselves to the priests." And as they went, they were made clean. ¹⁵Then one of them, when he saw that he was healed, turned back, praising God with a loud voice. ¹⁶He prostrated himself at Jesus'[f] feet and thanked him. And he was a Samaritan. ¹⁷Then Jesus asked, "Were not ten made clean? But the other nine, where are they? ¹⁸Was none of them found to return and give praise to God except this foreigner?" ¹⁹Then he said to him, "Get up and go on your way; your faith has made you well."

The Coming of the Kingdom

20 Once Jesus[b] was asked by the Pharisees when the kingdom of God was coming, and he answered, "The kingdom of God is not coming with things that can be observed; ²¹nor will they say, 'Look, here it is!' or 'There it is!' For, in fact, the kingdom of God is among[g] you."

22 Then he said to the disciples, "The days are coming when you will long to see one of the days of the Son of Man, and you will not see it. ²³They will say to you, 'Look there!' or 'Look here!' Do not go, do not set off in pursuit. ²⁴For as the lightning flashes and lights up the sky from one side to the other, so will the Son of Man be in his day.[h] ²⁵But first he must endure much suffering and be rejected by this generation. ²⁶Just as it was in the days of Noah, so too it will be

[b] Gk *He*　[c] Gk *your brother*　[d] Gk *faith as a grain of*　[e] The terms *leper* and *leprosy* can refer to several diseases　[f] Gk *his*　[g] Or *within*　[h] Other ancient authorities lack *in his day*

in the days of the Son of Man. ²⁷They were eating and drinking, and marrying and being given in marriage, until the day Noah entered the ark, and the flood came and destroyed all of them. ²⁸Likewise, just as it was in the days of Lot: they were eating and drinking, buying and selling, planting and building, ²⁹but on the day that Lot left Sodom, it rained fire and sulfur from heaven and destroyed all of them ³⁰ – it will be like that on the day that the Son of Man is revealed. ³¹On that day, anyone on the housetop who has belongings in the house must not come down to take them away; and likewise anyone in the field must not turn back. ³²Remember Lot's wife. ³³Those who try to make their life secure will lose it, but those who lose their life will keep it. ³⁴I tell you, on that night there will be two in one bed; one will be taken and the other left. ³⁵There will be two women grinding meal together; one will be taken and the other left."ⁱ ³⁷Then they asked him, "Where, Lord?" He said to them, "Where the corpse is, there the vultures will gather."

The Parable of the Widow and the Unjust Judge

18 Then Jesusʲ told them a parable about their need to pray always and not to lose heart. ²He said, "In a certain city there was a judge who neither feared God nor had respect for people. ³In that city there was a widow who kept coming to him and saying, 'Grant me justice against my opponent.' ⁴For a while he refused; but later he said to himself, 'Though I have no fear of God and no respect for anyone, ⁵yet because this widow keeps bothering me, I will grant her justice, so that she may not wear me out by continually coming.' "ᵏ ⁶And the Lord said, "Listen to what the unjust judge says. ⁷And will not God grant justice to his chosen ones who cry to him day and night? Will he delay long in helping them? ⁸I tell you, he will quickly grant justice to them. And yet, when the Son of Man comes, will he find faith on earth?"

The Parable of the Pharisee and the Tax Collector

9 He also told this parable to some who trusted in themselves that they were righteous and regarded others with contempt: ¹⁰"Two men went up to the temple to pray, one a Pharisee and the other a tax collector. ¹¹The Pharisee, standing by himself, was praying thus, 'God, I thank you that I am not like other people: thieves, rogues, adulterers, or even like this tax collector. ¹²I fast twice a week; I give a tenth of all my income.' ¹³But the tax collector, standing

ⁱ Other ancient authorities add verse 36, *"Two will be in the field; one will be taken and the other left."* ʲ Gk *he* ᵏ Or *so that she may not finally come and slap me in the face*

LUKE 17

28–33. As Jesus speaks of a time of future judgment, he likens it to the destruction of Sodom and Gomorrah, when Lot's family was led to safety by angels (Gen. 19:15–28). Lot's wife, still attached to the life and society she was leaving, turned back and was destroyed. This is the one instance of Jesus' use of a woman as a negative spiritual example. He considered her an individual in her own right who made a wrong moral choice and suffered the consequences. Cf. Acts 5:1–11.

LUKE 18

1–9. Here as at Matt. 15:21–28 and Mark 7:24–30, Jesus applauds the assertiveness of a woman. Denied justice by an indifferent judge, she persists until he accedes to her demands. This parable was told to encourage those who do not immediately receive an answer to their prayers. God is by no means indifferent, but there are often obstacles that must be overcome by persistent believing prayer.

far off, would not even look up to heaven, but was beating his breast and saying, 'God, be merciful to me, a sinner!' [14]I tell you, this man went down to his home justified rather than the other; for all who exalt themselves will be humbled, but all who humble themselves will be exalted."

Jesus Blesses Little Children

15 People were bringing even infants to him that he might touch them; and when the disciples saw it, they sternly ordered them not to do it. [16]But Jesus called for them and said, "Let the little children come to me, and do not stop them; for it is to such as these that the kingdom of God belongs. [17]Truly I tell you, whoever does not receive the kingdom of God as a little child will never enter it."

The Rich Ruler

18 A certain ruler asked him, "Good Teacher, what must I do to inherit eternal life?" [19]Jesus said to him, "Why do you call me good? No one is good but God alone. [20]You know the commandments: 'You shall not commit adultery; You shall not murder; You shall not steal; You shall not bear false witness; Honor your father and mother.' " [21]He replied, "I have kept all these since my youth." [22]When Jesus heard this, he said to him, "There is still one thing lacking. Sell all that you own and distribute the money[1] to the poor, and you

will have treasure in heaven; then come, follow me." [23]But when he heard this, he became sad; for he was very rich. [24]Jesus looked at him and said, "How hard it is for those who have wealth to enter the kingdom of God! [25]Indeed, it is easier for a camel to go through the eye of a needle than for someone who is rich to enter the kingdom of God."

26 Those who heard it said, "Then who can be saved?" [27]He replied, "What is impossible for mortals is possible for God."

28 Then Peter said, "Look, we have left our homes and followed you." [29]And he said to them, "Truly I tell you, there is no one who has left house or wife or brothers or parents or children, for the sake of the kingdom of God, [30]who will not get back very much more in this age, and in the age to come eternal life."

A Third Time Jesus Foretells His Death and Resurrection

31 Then he took the twelve aside and said to them, "See, we are going up to Jerusalem, and everything that is written about the Son of Man by the prophets will be accomplished. [32]For he will be handed over to the Gentiles; and he will be mocked and insulted and spat upon. [33]After they have flogged him, they will kill him, and

[1] Gk lacks *the money*

15–17. The mothers with their children are rebuffed by the disciples but welcomed by Christ. Those who care for children lovingly do Christ's work in a hostile world (Matt. 18:5) and prepare new citizens for the Kingdom of Heaven.

31–34. This third declaration of his death shows Jesus willingly going up to Jerusalem, where the gathering opposition will surely seek to exterminate him. Remaining in Galilee would have been far safer. Jesus makes the choice freely, with full knowledge of the consequences. He is also aware that others will make their own choices. Once he is handed over to the Gentiles, he will be ridiculed, abused, spit upon, beaten and ultimately slain. Here we see one of the paradoxes of evil: God gives free will, and human beings exploit that freedom to harm others in defiance of the laws of God.

Jesus foretells that he will endure verbal, emotional and physical abuse. As Son of God, he could escape; but as Son of Man, he chooses to become identified with all those who have known mistreatment at the hands of another. It is important to understand that the abuse will come from human beings and not from the Father.

on the third day he will rise again." ³⁴But they understood nothing about all these things; in fact, what he said was hidden from them, and they did not grasp what was said.

Jesus Heals a Blind Beggar Near Jericho

35 As he approached Jericho, a blind man was sitting by the roadside begging. ³⁶When he heard a crowd going by, he asked what was happening. ³⁷They told him, "Jesus of Nazarethᵐ is passing by." ³⁸Then he shouted, "Jesus, Son of David, have mercy on me!" ³⁹Those who were in front sternly ordered him to be quiet; but he shouted even more loudly, "Son of David, have mercy on me!" ⁴⁰Jesus stood still and ordered the man to be brought to him; and when he came near, he asked him, ⁴¹"What do you want me to do for you?" He said, "Lord, let me see again." ⁴²Jesus said to him, "Receive your sight; your faith has saved you." ⁴³Immediately he regained his sight and followed him, glorifying God; and all the people, when they saw it, praised God.

Jesus and Zacchaeus

19 He entered Jericho and was passing through it. ²A man was there named Zacchaeus; he was a chief tax collector and was rich. ³He was trying to see who Jesus was, but on account of the crowd he could not, because he was short in stature. ⁴So he ran ahead and climbed a sycamore tree to see him, because he was going to pass that way. ⁵When Jesus came to the place, he looked up and said to him, "Zacchaeus, hurry and come down; for I must stay at your house today." ⁶So he hurried down and was happy to welcome him. ⁷All who saw it began to grumble and said, "He has gone to be the guest of one who is a sinner." ⁸Zacchaeus stood there and said to the Lord, "Look, half of my possessions, Lord, I will give to the poor; and if I have defrauded anyone of anything, I will pay back four times as much." ⁹Then Jesus said

to him, "Today salvation has come to this house, because he too is a son of Abraham. ¹⁰For the Son of Man came to seek out and to save the lost."

The Parable of the Ten Pounds

11 As they were listening to this, he went on to tell a parable, because he was near Jerusalem, and because they supposed that the kingdom of God was to appear immediately. ¹²So he said, "A nobleman went to a distant country to get royal power for himself and then return. ¹³He summoned ten of his slaves, and gave them ten pounds,ⁿ and said to them, 'Do business with these until I come back.' ¹⁴But the citizens of his country hated him and sent a delegation after him, saying, 'We do not want this man to rule over us.' ¹⁵When he returned, having received royal power, he ordered these slaves, to whom he had given the money, to be summoned so that he might find out what they had gained by trading. ¹⁶The first came forward and said, 'Lord, your pound has made ten more pounds.' ¹⁷He said to him, 'Well done, good slave! Because you have been trustworthy in a very small thing, take charge of ten cities.' ¹⁸Then the second came, saying, 'Lord, your pound has made five pounds.' ¹⁹He said to him, 'And you, rule over five cities.' ²⁰Then the other came, saying, 'Lord, here is your pound. I wrapped it up in a piece of cloth, ²¹for I was afraid of you, because you are a harsh man; you take what you did not deposit, and reap what you did not sow.' ²²He said to him, 'I will judge you by your own words, you wicked slave! You knew, did you, that I was a harsh man, taking what I did not deposit and reaping what I did not sow? ²³Why then did you not put my money into the bank? Then when I returned, I could have collected it with interest.' ²⁴He said to the bystanders, 'Take the pound from him and give it to the one who has ten pounds.' ²⁵(And they said

ᵐ Gk *the Nazorean*　ⁿ The mina, rendered here by *pound*, was about three months' wages for a laborer

to him, 'Lord, he has ten pounds!') ²⁶'I tell you, to all those who have, more will be given; but from those who have nothing, even what they have will be taken away. ²⁷But as for these enemies of mine who did not want me to be king over them – bring them here and slaughter them in my presence.' "

Jesus' Triumphal Entry into Jerusalem

28 After he had said this, he went on ahead, going up to Jerusalem.

29 When he had come near Bethphage and Bethany, at the place called the Mount of Olives, he sent two of the disciples, ³⁰saying, "Go into the village ahead of you, and as you enter it you will find tied there a colt that has never been ridden. Untie it and bring it here. ³¹If anyone asks you, 'Why are you untying it?' just say this, 'The Lord needs it.' " ³²So those who were sent departed and found it as he had told them. ³³As they were untying the colt, its owners asked them, "Why are you untying the colt?" ³⁴They said, "The Lord needs it." ³⁵Then they brought it to Jesus; and after throwing their cloaks on the colt, they set Jesus on it. ³⁶As he rode along, people kept spreading their cloaks on the road. ³⁷As he was now approaching the path down from the Mount of Olives, the whole multitude of the disciples began to praise God joyfully with a loud voice for all the deeds of power that they had seen, ³⁸saying,

"Blessed is the king
    who comes in the name of the Lord!
Peace in heaven,
    and glory in the highest heaven!"

³⁹Some of the Pharisees in the crowd said to him, "Teacher, order your disciples to stop." ⁴⁰He answered, "I tell you, if these were silent, the stones would shout out."

Jesus Weeps over Jerusalem

41 As he came near and saw the city, he wept over it, ⁴²saying, "If you, even you, had only recognized on this day the things that make for peace! But now they are hidden from your eyes. ⁴³Indeed, the days will come upon you, when your enemies will set up ramparts around you and surround you, and hem you in on every side. ⁴⁴They will crush you to the ground, you and your children within you, and they will not leave within you one stone upon another; because you did not recognize the time of your visitation from God."°

Jesus Cleanses the Temple

45 Then he entered the temple and began to drive out those who were selling things there; ⁴⁶and he said, "It is written,

'My house shall be a house of
        prayer';
but you have made it a den of robbers."

47 Every day he was teaching in the temple. The chief priests, the scribes, and the leaders of the people kept looking for a way to kill him; ⁴⁸but they did not find anything they could do, for all the people were spellbound by what they heard.

The Authority of Jesus Questioned

20 One day, as he was teaching the people in the temple and telling the good news, the chief priests and the scribes came with the elders ²and said to him, "Tell us, by what authority are you doing these things? Who is it who gave you this authority?" ³He answered them, "I will also ask you a question, and you tell me: ⁴Did the baptism of John come from heaven, or was it of human origin?" ⁵They discussed it with one another, saying, "If we say, 'From heaven,' he will say, 'Why did you not believe him?' ⁶But if we say, 'Of human origin,' all the people will stone us; for they are convinced that John was a prophet." ⁷So they answered that they did not know where it came from. ⁸Then Jesus said to them, "Neither will I tell you by what authority I am doing these things."

° Gk lacks *from God*

The Parable of the Wicked Tenants

9 He began to tell the people this
parable: "A man planted a vineyard, and
leased it to tenants, and went to another
country for a long time. 10 When the season
came, he sent a slave to the tenants in order
that they might give him his share of the
produce of the vineyard; but the tenants
beat him and sent him away empty-
handed. 11 Next he sent another slave; that
one also they beat and insulted and sent
away empty-handed. 12 And he sent still a
third; this one also they wounded and
threw out. 13 Then the owner of the vineyard
said, 'What shall I do? I will send my
beloved son; perhaps they will respect
him.' 14 But when the tenants saw him, they
discussed it among themselves and said,
'This is the heir; let us kill him so that the
inheritance may be ours.' 15 So they threw
him out of the vineyard and killed him.
What then will the owner of the vineyard
do to them? 16 He will come and destroy
those tenants and give the vineyard to
others." When they heard this, they said,
"Heaven forbid!" 17 But he looked at them
and said, "What then does this text mean:

'The stone that the builders rejected
has become the cornerstone'?[p]

18 Everyone who falls on that stone will be
broken to pieces; and it will crush anyone
on whom it falls." 19 When the scribes and
chief priests realized that he had told this
parable against them, they wanted to lay
hands on him at that very hour, but they
feared the people.

The Question about Paying Taxes

20 So they watched him and sent spies
who pretended to be honest, in order to trap
him by what he said, so as to hand him
over to the jurisdiction and authority of the
governor. 21 So they asked him, "Teacher, we
know that you are right in what you say
and teach, and you show deference to no
one, but teach the way of God in accordance with truth. 22 Is it lawful for us to pay
taxes to the emperor, or not?" 23 But he
perceived their craftiness and said to them,
24 "Show me a denarius. Whose head and
whose title does it bear?" They said, "The
emperor's." 25 He said to them, "Then give
to the emperor the things that are the
emperor's, and to God the things that are
God's." 26 And they were not able in the
presence of the people to trap him by what
he said; and being amazed by his answer,
they became silent.

The Question about the Resurrection

27 Some Sadducees, those who say
there is no resurrection, came to him 28 and
asked him a question, "Teacher, Moses
wrote for us that if a man's brother dies,
leaving a wife but no children, the man[q]
shall marry the widow and raise up

[p] Or *keystone* [q] Gk *his brother*

LUKE 20

9–16. The father sends the son not to be killed but to communicate his concerns to the wicked tenants. The son is admittedly exposed to risk, but the tenants are afforded free choice as to how they will receive him. Some critics have spoken of God as an abusive father and the son as divine victim. This parable tells of a father and son who devise a plan in which they are willing to be vulnerable as they afford one last opportunity to those who have already repudiated and slain the earlier prophets. Luke 11:49 speaks of this plan as being propounded by the Wisdom (*Sophia*) of God.
27. The Sadducees do not appear to have any concern about what emotional significance this hypothetical situation might have for a woman. They are simply setting a trap for Jesus, intended to ridicule the doctrine of the resurrection. Christ stresses the new relationships which shall be ours in the life everlasting. Marriage, physical sexuality and death no longer have any part in the lives of the redeemed. Instead there is a spiritual and eternal bonding to God and to one another that far supercedes the bonding of the flesh. Cf. John 3:6; 1 Cor. 15:35–54; 2 Cor. 5:1–4.

children for his brother. ²⁹Now there were seven brothers; the first married, and died childless; ³⁰then the second ³¹and the third married her, and so in the same way all seven died childless. ³²Finally the woman also died. ³³In the resurrection, therefore, whose wife will the woman be? For the seven had married her."

34 Jesus said to them, "Those who belong to this age marry and are given in marriage; ³⁵but those who are considered worthy of a place in that age and in the resurrection from the dead neither marry nor are given in marriage. ³⁶Indeed they cannot die anymore, because they are like angels and are children of God, being children of the resurrection. ³⁷And the fact that the dead are raised Moses himself showed, in the story about the bush, where he speaks of the Lord as the God of Abraham, the God of Isaac, and the God of Jacob. ³⁸Now he is God not of the dead, but of the living; for to him all of them are alive." ³⁹Then some of the scribes answered, "Teacher, you have spoken well." ⁴⁰For they no longer dared to ask him another question.

The Question about David's Son

41 Then he said to them, "How can they say that the Messiahʳ is David's son? ⁴²For David himself says in the book of Psalms,

'The Lord said to my Lord,
"Sit at my right hand,
⁴³   until I make your enemies your
       footstool." '

⁴⁴David thus calls him Lord; so how can he be his son?"

Jesus Denounces the Scribes

45 In the hearing of all the people he said to theˢ disciples, ⁴⁶"Beware of the scribes, who like to walk around in long robes, and love to be greeted with respect in the marketplaces, and to have the best seats in the synagogues and places of honor at banquets. ⁴⁷They devour widows' houses and for the sake of appearance say long prayers. They will receive the greater condemnation."

The Widow's Offering

21 He looked up and saw rich people putting their gifts into the treasury; ²he also saw a poor widow put in two small copper coins. ³He said, "Truly I tell you, this poor widow has put in more than all of them; ⁴for all of them have contributed out of their abundance, but she out of her poverty has put in all she had to live on."

ʳ Or the Christ   ˢ Other ancient authorities read his

---

47. Jesus' concern for widows is often overlooked. The Greek word *cheira* meant a destitute or deprived woman, usually one who had lost her husband. Our present society often fails to anticipate the needs of women while their husbands are still living.

LUKE 21

1. The poor widow is one of several women whom Jesus uses as spiritual examples (Matt. 15:21–18; Mark 7:24–30; 12:41–44; 14:3–9; Luke 7:36–50). Though she possesses very little and no longer has a husband to supply a fixed source of income, she honors God with her gift at great personal sacrifice. She is not afraid to part with her last bit of money.

Jesus notes that her management of money is based upon a different set of priorities from those of the affluent who give from their excess of property. Others give in ostentation, she in humility and the utmost simplicity. She gives her all while others give trifles. She gives that God might be glorified and that the people of God might have a place of prayer and worship. She gives to maintain the spiritual focus of believing Israel, and to be an obedient daughter of God's Law.

The Destruction of the Temple Foretold

5 When some were speaking about the temple, how it was adorned with beautiful stones and gifts dedicated to God, he said, ⁶"As for these things that you see, the days will come when not one stone will be left upon another; all will be thrown down."

Signs and Persecutions

7 They asked him, "Teacher, when will this be, and what will be the sign that this is about to take place?" ⁸And he said, "Beware that you are not led astray; for many will come in my name and say, 'I am he!'ᵗ and, 'The time is near!'ᵘ Do not go after them.

9 "When you hear of wars and insurrections, do not be terrified; for these things must take place first, but the end will not follow immediately." ¹⁰Then he said to them, "Nation will rise against nation, and kingdom against kingdom; ¹¹there will be great earthquakes, and in various places famines and plagues; and there will be dreadful portents and great signs from heaven.

12 "But before all this occurs, they will arrest you and persecute you; they will hand you over to synagogues and prisons, and you will be brought before kings and governors because of my name. ¹³This will give you an opportunity to testify. ¹⁴So make up your minds not to prepare your defense in advance; ¹⁵for I will give you wordsᵛ and a wisdom that none of your opponents will be able to withstand or contradict. ¹⁶You will be betrayed even by parents and brothers, by relatives and friends; and they will put some of you to death. ¹⁷You will be hated by all because of my name. ¹⁸But not a hair of your head will perish. ¹⁹By your endurance you will gain your souls.

The Destruction of Jerusalem Foretold

20 "When you see Jerusalem surrounded by armies, then know that its desolation has come near.ʷ ²¹Then those in Judea must flee to the mountains, and those inside the city must leave it, and those out in the country must not enter it; ²²for these are days of vengeance, as a fulfillment of all that is written. ²³Woe to those who are pregnant and to those who are nursing infants in those days! For there will be great distress on the earth and wrath against this people; ²⁴they will fall by the edge of the sword and be taken away as captives among all nations; and Jerusalem will be trampled on by the Gentiles, until the times of the Gentiles are fulfilled.

The Coming of the Son of Man

25 "There will be signs in the sun, the moon, and the stars, and on the earth distress among nations confused by the roaring of the sea and the waves. ²⁶People will faint from fear and foreboding of what is coming upon the world, for the powers of the heavens will be shaken. ²⁷Then they will see 'the Son of Man coming in a cloud' with power and great glory. ²⁸Now when these things begin to take place, stand up

ᵗ Gk *I am*   ᵘ Or *at hand*   ᵛ Gk *a mouth*   ʷ Or *is at hand*

---

23. Just as the prophets of old foresaw the impending overthrow of Jerusalem, so Jesus can perceive the coming destruction. Rebellion against an enormously superior force is full of risks, especially for those who are the most vulnerable. Here Jesus displays a deep concern for the particular needs of women. Those who are pregnant or nursing will be placed at special risk. We shall see this same sympathy for the bodily experiences of women displayed again at Luke 23. In the Gospel accounts, we find that Jesus particularly addresses the emotions and conditions of women in childlessness, pregnancy (Luke 21:23; 23:28–29), birthing (John 16:21) and menstruation (Luke 8:43–47), though he refused to prize reproductive activity above spiritual attitude (Luke 11:27–28).

and raise your heads, because your redemption is drawing near."

The Lesson of the Fig Tree

29 Then he told them a parable: "Look at the fig tree and all the trees; ³⁰as soon as they sprout leaves you can see for yourselves and know that summer is already near. ³¹So also, when you see these things taking place, you know that the kingdom of God is near. ³²Truly I tell you, this generation will not pass away until all things have taken place. ³³Heaven and earth will pass away, but my words will not pass away.

Exhortation to Watch

34 "Be on guard so that your hearts are not weighed down with dissipation and drunkenness and the worries of this life, and that day catch you unexpectedly, ³⁵like a trap. For it will come upon all who live on the face of the whole earth. ³⁶Be alert at all times, praying that you may have the strength to escape all these things that will take place, and to stand before the Son of Man."

37 Every day he was teaching in the temple, and at night he would go out and spend the night on the Mount of Olives, as it was called. ³⁸And all the people would get up early in the morning to listen to him in the temple.

The Plot to Kill Jesus

22 Now the festival of Unleavened Bread, which is called the Passover, was near. ²The chief priests and the scribes were looking for a way to put Jesusˣ to death, for they were afraid of the people.

3 Then Satan entered into Judas called Iscariot, who was one of the twelve; ⁴he went away and conferred with the chief priests and officers of the temple police about how he might betray him to them. ⁵They were greatly pleased and agreed to give him money. ⁶So he consented and began to look for an opportunity to betray him to them when no crowd was present.

The Preparation of the Passover

7 Then came the day of Unleavened Bread, on which the Passover lamb had to be sacrificed. ⁸So Jesusʸ sent Peter and John, saying, "Go and prepare the Passover meal for us that we may eat it." ⁹They asked him, "Where do you want us to make preparations for it?" ¹⁰"Listen," he said to them, "when you have entered the city, a man carrying a jar of water will meet you; follow him into the house he enters ¹¹and say to the owner of the house, 'The teacher asks you, "Where is the guest room, where I may eat the Passover with my disciples?" ' ¹²He will show you a large room upstairs, already furnished. Make preparations for us there." ¹³So they went and found everything as he had told them; and they prepared the Passover meal.

ˣ Gk *him*   ʸ Gk *he*

LUKE 22

7–22. The Passover meal was celebrated on two succeeding nights, and women were very much in evidence at the supper the previous night in Bethany (Matt. 26:6–13; Mark 14:3–9; John 12:1–8). Of particular importance at that time was the anointing of Christ's head. As the Anointed One of Israel, Jesus receives this ministry from the hands of a woman and recognizes the unction as preparatory to his burial as Messiah.

There is no mention of the presence of women at this Passover meal. They will become the major witnesses of the crucifixion and resurrection, but only males are recorded to have participated with Christ at the Last Supper. Jesus has a clear premonition of the approaching danger and may have chosen not to expose the women to the possibility of violence. The men were included in a foreshadowing of his death for our sin, while the women were present at the actual event.

The Institution of the Lord's Supper

14 When the hour came, he took his place at the table, and the apostles with him. [15]He said to them, "I have eagerly desired to eat this Passover with you before I suffer; [16]for I tell you, I will not eat it[z] until it is fulfilled in the kingdom of God." [17]Then he took a cup, and after giving thanks he said, "Take this and divide it among yourselves; [18]for I tell you that from now on I will not drink of the fruit of the vine until the kingdom of God comes." [19]Then he took a loaf of bread, and when he had given thanks, he broke it and gave it to them, saying, "This is my body, which is given for you. Do this in remembrance of me." [20]And he did the same with the cup after supper, saying, "This cup that is poured out for you is the new covenant in my blood.[a] [21]But see, the one who betrays me is with me, and his hand is on the table. [22]For the Son of Man is going as it has been determined, but woe to that one by whom he is betrayed!" [23]Then they began to ask one another, which one of them it could be who would do this.

The Dispute about Greatness

24 A dispute also arose among them as to which one of them was to be regarded as the greatest. [25]But he said to them, "The kings of the Gentiles lord it over them; and those in authority over them are called benefactors. [26]But not so with you; rather the greatest among you must become like the youngest, and the leader like one who serves. [27]For who is greater, the one who is at the table or the one who serves? Is it not the one at the table? But I am among you as one who serves.

28 "You are those who have stood by me in my trials; [29]and I confer on you, just as my Father has conferred on me, a kingdom, [30]so that you may eat and drink at my table in my kingdom, and you will sit on thrones judging the twelve tribes of Israel.

Jesus Predicts Peter's Denial

31 "Simon, Simon, listen! Satan has demanded[b] to sift all of you like wheat, [32]but I have prayed for you that your own faith may not fail; and you, when once you have turned back, strengthen your brothers." [33]And he said to him, "Lord, I am ready to go with you to prison and to death!" [34]Jesus[c] said, "I tell you, Peter, the cock will not crow this day, until you have denied three times that you know me."

Purse, Bag, and Sword

35 He said to them, "When I sent you out without a purse, bag, or sandals, did you lack anything?" They said, "No, not a thing." [36]He said to them, "But now, the one who has a purse must take it, and

[z] Other ancient authorities read *never eat it again*
[a] Other ancient authorities lack, in whole or in part, verses 19b-20 (*which is given . . . in my blood*)
[b] Or *has obtained permission*   [c] Gk *He*

---

24. How often Christians squabble over who is to be 'the boss'! The emphasis of Jesus was upon ministry to others rather than upon holding authority over others. Indeed, he specifically declares that the desire to rule over others is a heathen attitude (v. 25). Just as it was not God's original purpose that one individual should be king over Israel (Num. 23:21; Deut. 33:5; 1 Sam. 8:4-22; 10:19; 12:12, 17, 19), so Jesus left a committed band of followers rather than a commander-in-chief.

The true benefactor is not the one in command but the one dedicated to serving others (cf. Matt. 18:1; Mark 9:34; Luke 9:46). Whether in home or church our concern should be for servanthood rather than for supremacy. It is sometimes the failing of women that they empower the dominance of another, to the detriment of all concerned.

27. Jesus points to himself as an example only when he speaks of servanthood and humility (see John 13:13-17).

likewise a bag. And the one who has no sword must sell his cloak and buy one. ³⁷For I tell you, this scripture must be fulfilled in me, 'And he was counted among the lawless'; and indeed what is written about me is being fulfilled." ³⁸They said, "Lord, look, here are two swords." He replied, "It is enough."

Jesus Prays on the Mount of Olives

39 He came out and went, as was his custom, to the Mount of Olives; and the disciples followed him. ⁴⁰When he reached the place, he said to them, "Pray that you may not come into the time of trial."ᵈ ⁴¹Then he withdrew from them about a stone's throw, knelt down, and prayed, ⁴²"Father, if you are willing, remove this cup from me; yet, not my will but yours be done." [[⁴³Then an angel from heaven appeared to him and gave him strength. ⁴⁴In his anguish he prayed more earnestly, and his sweat became like great drops of blood falling down on the ground.]]ᵉ ⁴⁵When he got up from prayer, he came to the disciples and found them sleeping because of grief, ⁴⁶and he said to them, "Why are you sleeping? Get up and pray that you may not come into the time of trial."ᵈ

The Betrayal and Arrest of Jesus

47 While he was still speaking, suddenly a crowd came, and the one called Judas, one of the twelve, was leading them. He approached Jesus to kiss him; ⁴⁸but Jesus said to him, "Judas, is it with a kiss that you are betraying the Son of Man?" ⁴⁹When those who were around him saw what was coming, they asked, "Lord, should we strike with the sword?" ⁵⁰Then one of them struck the slave of the high priest and cut off his right ear. ⁵¹But Jesus said, "No more of this!" And he touched his ear and healed him. ⁵²Then Jesus said to the chief priests, the officers of the temple police, and the elders who had come for him, "Have you come out with swords and clubs as if I were a bandit? ⁵³When I was with you day after day in the temple, you did not lay hands on me. But this is your hour, and the power of darkness!"

Peter Denies Jesus

54 Then they seized him and led him away, bringing him into the high priest's house. But Peter was following at a distance. ⁵⁵When they had kindled a fire in the middle of the courtyard and sat down together, Peter sat among them. ⁵⁶Then a servant-girl, seeing him in the firelight, stared at him and said, "This man also was with him." ⁵⁷But he denied it, saying, "Woman, I do not know him." ⁵⁸A little

ᵈ Or *into temptation*   ᵉ Other ancient authorities lack verses 43 and 44

---

39. In the Garden of Gethsemane we are afforded a wonderful glimpse of the humanity of Jesus. Here he knew fear, dread, and anguish. He could be torn between a desire to fulfill the purposes of God and a knowledge of the personal cost to himself. He begs the Father to stop the work of the evil-doers if this can be done without obstructing the divine plan.

Even to save the life of his Son, God would not intervene. This remains a mystery which we cannot explain: why does God allow the wicked to destroy the innocent? Why does their will triumph over that which is right?

Many times women find themselves in situations in which they beg God to stop the evil of the abuser. In this Christ is one with them. Not only did he experience the atrocities of human hatred, power, lust and perversity, but he became the sin-bearer.

Gethsemane is not the end of the passion story, and Christ's death has wrought our redemption. The redeemed are called to deliver the innocent from the hands of the violent and the oppressor (Ps. 72:1–4, 14; Eccl. 4:1; Is. 58:6–10; Jer. 21:12; 22:3, 15–16).

55–57. The vignette of the saucy servant girl is a pert touch in an otherwise grim story. She is characterized with deft strokes. Like Rhoda who was entrusted with guarding the door in the

◆ Immediately after his arrest in the middle of the night, Jesus was taken to the house of Annas, the son-in-law of the high priest Caiaphas (Luke 22:54). At dawn he was taken before the Council, known as the Sanhedrin, within the Temple precinct (22:66). Next he was brought to the provincial governor Pontius Pilate, with the allegation that he was a danger to the peace and stability of Roman rule (23:1–5). Pilate, unable to find any legitimate accusation, sent him to Herod since he was tetrarch of Galilee and might properly be asked to adjudicate the case (23:6–12). This was a clever diplomatic move to rid Pilate of the problem, and to create good will with Herod; but the tetrarch could discover no basis for an execution and returned the prisoner to Pilate. The governor, unable to reason with the priests and the raging mob and incapable of administering justice, accedes to their wishes and gives the order for the crucifixion ◆

later someone else, on seeing him, said, "You also are one of them." But Peter said, "Man, I am not!" 59Then about an hour later still another kept insisting, "Surely this man also was with him; for he is a Galilean." 60But Peter said, "Man, I do not know what you are talking about!" At that moment, while he was still speaking, the cock crowed. 61The Lord turned and looked at Peter. Then Peter remembered the word of the Lord, how he had said to him, "Before the cock crows today, you will deny me three times." 62And he went out and wept bitterly.

The Mocking and Beating of Jesus

63 Now the men who were holding Jesus began to mock him and beat him;

64they also blindfolded him and kept asking him, "Prophesy! Who is it that struck you?" 65They kept heaping many other insults on him.

Jesus before the Council

66 When day came, the assembly of the elders of the people, both chief priests and scribes, gathered together, and they brought him to their council. 67They said, "If you are the Messiah,ᶠ tell us." He replied, "If I tell you, you will not believe; 68and if I question you, you will not answer. 69But from now on the Son of Man will be seated at the right hand of the power of God." 70All of them asked, "Are you, then, the Son of God?" He said to them, "You say that I am." 71Then they said, "What further testimony do we need? We have heard it ourselves from his own lips!"

Jesus before Pilate

23 Then the assembly rose as a body and brought Jesusᵍ before Pilate. 2They began to accuse him, saying, "We found this man perverting our nation, forbidding us to pay taxes to the emperor, and saying that he himself is the Messiah, a king."ʰ 3Then Pilate asked him, "Are you the king of the Jews?" He answered, "You say so." 4Then Pilate said to the chief priests and the crowds, "I find no basis for an accusation against this man." 5But they were insistent and said, "He stirs up the people by teaching throughout all Judea, from Galilee where he began even to this place."

ᶠ Or the Christ   ᵍ Gk him   ʰ Or is an anointed king

---

story of Acts 12:1–17, she is called *paidiske*, a slave woman. This woman is alert and articulate, capable of speaking the truth as she knows it. It is she who first calls upon Peter to own his Lord, as it is the wife of Pilate who calls upon the Roman governor to deal honestly and justly with Jesus (Matt. 27:19).

Jesus before Herod

6 When Pilate heard this, he asked whether the man was a Galilean. ⁷And when he learned that he was under Herod's jurisdiction, he sent him off to Herod, who was himself in Jerusalem at that time. ⁸When Herod saw Jesus, he was very glad, for he had been wanting to see him for a long time, because he had heard about him and was hoping to see him perform some sign. ⁹He questioned him at some length, but Jesusⁱ gave him no answer. ¹⁰The chief priests and the scribes stood by, vehemently accusing him. ¹¹Even Herod with his soldiers treated him with contempt and mocked him; then he put an elegant robe on him, and sent him back to Pilate. ¹²That same day Herod and Pilate became friends with each other; before this they had been enemies.

Jesus Sentenced to Death

13 Pilate then called together the chief priests, the leaders, and the people, ¹⁴and said to them, "You brought me this man as one who was perverting the people; and here I have examined him in your presence and have not found this man guilty of any of your charges against him. ¹⁵Neither has Herod, for he sent him back to us. Indeed, he has done nothing to deserve death. ¹⁶I will therefore have him flogged and release him."ʲ

18 Then they all shouted out together, "Away with this fellow! Release Barabbas for us!" ¹⁹(This was a man who had been put in prison for an insurrection that had taken place in the city, and for murder.) ²⁰Pilate, wanting to release Jesus, addressed them again; ²¹but they kept shouting, "Crucify, crucify him!" ²²A third time he said to them, "Why, what evil has he done? I have found in him no ground for the sentence of death; I will therefore have him flogged and then release him." ²³But they kept urgently demanding with loud shouts that he should be crucified; and their voices prevailed. ²⁴So Pilate gave his verdict that their demand should be granted. ²⁵He released the man they asked for, the one who had been put in prison for insurrection and murder, and he handed Jesus over as they wished.

The Crucifixion of Jesus

26 As they led him away, they seized a man, Simon of Cyrene, who was coming from the country, and they laid the cross on him, and made him carry it behind Jesus. ²⁷A great number of the people followed him, and among them were women who were beating their breasts and wailing for

ⁱ Gk *he*   ʲ Here, or after verse 19, other ancient authorities add verse 17, *Now he was obliged to release someone for them at the festival*

LUKE 23

26. Cyrene was the capital city of Cyrenaica on the northern coast of Africa. Its citizens travelled and traded throughout the Mediterannean world in medicines, corn, wheat, wool, and oil. Other trade routes led deep into the heart of Africa so that there was an intermingling of merchandise, cultures and races. The city was famed for its philosophers, mathematicians, poets, physicians and athletes. One astronomer computed the circumference of the world with remarkable accuracy some 1,700 years before Columbus. Cyrene's famous school of philosphy attracted students and scholars from many parts of the world. Originally settled by Greek colonists, the city soon attracted such diverse ethnic elements that it was said of one philosopher, 'All colors and all conditions become him.'

There was a significant Jewish element in the population, and Christian burials were found in Jewish cemeteries by the end of the first century. Presumably Simon had affinities with the Jewish community and had come to Jerusalem for the Passover celebration. He may appear as 'Simon the Black', a Christian leader in Acts 13:1. His sons were known to the Christian community (Mark 15:21; Rom. 16:13).

◆ In the passion narrative, we are told repeatedly of women who 'followed' Jesus. The Greek word *akoloutheo* (meaning both 'to follow' and 'to be a disciple') is used here of women who follow along on the way to Calvary. Jesus specifically stops to address his paramount concern for their safety even as he goes to his own death. He has a remarkable sensitivity and sympathy for the vulnerability of women who are pregnant or nursing, and his own calmness stands in marked contrast to the terror and panic which would overwhelm them.

The women who followed are mentioned again at Luke 23:49 as they stand at a distance from the cross, watching their Lord's cruel death. They had been with their Master throughout his earthly ministry (cf. Luke 8:2–3), and they are there at the end. Luke tells us that they had 'followed along with Jesus' from Galilee. They stand in the company of others who are called only 'acquaintances', for the male disciples are not present. Thus the presence and testimony of these women followers becomes essential for the Gospel record.

As the body was removed from the cross and carried to the grave, Luke tells us that the women 'followed along' so that they might see the grave and how the body was laid (23:55). They can attest as first-hand witnesses to every part of the proceedings on Calvary as they will be able to attest to the events on Easter morning ◆

him. ²⁸But Jesus turned to them and said, "Daughters of Jerusalem, do not weep for me, but weep for yourselves and for your children. ²⁹For the days are surely coming when they will say, 'Blessed are the barren, and the wombs that never bore, and the breasts that never nursed.' ³⁰Then they will begin to say to the mountains, 'Fall on us'; and to the hills, 'Cover us.' ³¹For if they do this when the wood is green, what will happen when it is dry?"

32 Two others also, who were criminals, were led away to be put to death with him. ³³When they came to the place that is called The Skull, they crucified Jesus^k there with the criminals, one on his right and one on his left. [[³⁴Then Jesus said, "Father, forgive them; for they do not know what they are

^k Gk *him*

32. In life, Jesus identified himself with those in prison (Matt. 25:36) and in death, he shared a common experience with those who are executed by the law.

33. On the cross, Jesus endures all that inhumanity can wreak upon a mortal being. As a citizen of a subject nation, he is falsely accused in the courts and sentenced to die by a foreign official who follows the demands of political expediency rather than those of justice. He is mocked, trivialized, demeaned, scourged and given an excruciating execution by those who denied him a fair trial. But the instigators of the outrage are the religious leaders of his own nation. Betrayed by one of his own followers, deserted by his friends and derided by his enemies, he is ignominiously executed between two common criminals. In many cases of abuse, people ask, 'What did the victim do to provoke this?' Jesus, the only human being without sin, had called forth the treatment he received by going about doing good.

Although his own Son endured the ultimate in abuse, God did nothing to halt the outrage. Instead, he transformed the suffering and death so that it became an expiation for all of human sin. Evil inflicted by wicked men was rendered an instrument for salvation in the hands of God (cf. Gen. 45:5–8; 50:19; 2 Sam. 7:14). Human imagination and intellect cannot fully comprehend this transposition whereby the victim became the victor. Women sometimes have the notion that they too can have a redemptive effect when they suffer at the hands of their abusers, but the Bible is clear that Jesus suffered once for all at a specific time in human history (Heb. 9:12, 25–28; cf. 6:6). God's purpose is to free human beings from all types of bondage and to make them liberators of the oppressed.

doing."]][And they cast lots to divide his clothing. [35]And the people stood by, watching; but the leaders scoffed at him, saying, "He saved others; let him save himself if he is the Messiah[m] of God, his chosen one!" [36]The soldiers also mocked him, coming up and offering him sour wine, [37]and saying, "If you are the King of the Jews, save yourself!" [38]There was also an inscription over him,[n] "This is the King of the Jews."

[39] One of the criminals who were hanged there kept deriding[o] him and saying, "Are you not the Messiah?[m] Save yourself and us!" [40]But the other rebuked him, saying, "Do you not fear God, since you are under the same sentence of condemnation? [41]And we indeed have been condemned justly, for we are getting what we deserve for our deeds, but this man has done nothing wrong." [42]Then he said, "Jesus, remember me when you come into[p] your kingdom." [43]He replied, "Truly I tell you, today you will be with me in Paradise."

The Death of Jesus

[44] It was now about noon, and darkness came over the whole land[q] until three in the afternoon, [45]while the sun's light failed;[r] and the curtain of the temple was torn in two. [46]Then Jesus, crying with a loud voice, said, "Father, into your hands I commend my spirit." Having said this, he breathed his last. [47]When the centurion saw what had taken place, he praised God and said, "Certainly this man was innocent."[s] [48]And when all the crowds who had gathered there for this spectacle saw what had taken place, they returned home, beating their breasts. [49]But all his acquaintances, including the women who had followed him from Galilee, stood at a distance, watching these things.

The Burial of Jesus

[50] Now there was a good and righteous man named Joseph, who, though a member of the council, [51]had not agreed to their plan and action. He came from the Jewish town of Arimathea, and he was waiting expectantly for the kingdom of God. [52]This man went to Pilate and asked for the body of Jesus. [53]Then he took it down, wrapped it in a linen cloth, and laid it in a rock-hewn tomb where no one had ever been laid. [54]It was the day of Preparation, and the sabbath was beginning.[t] [55]The women who had come with him from Galilee followed, and they saw the tomb and how his body was

[l] Other ancient authorities lack the sentence *Then Jesus . . . what they are doing*   [m] Or *the Christ*
[n] Other ancient authorities add *written in Greek and Latin and Hebrew* (that is, *Aramaic*)   [o] Or *blaspheming*   [p] Other ancient authorities read *in*
[q] Or *earth*   [r] Or *the sun was eclipsed.* Other ancient authorities read *the sun was darkened*
[s] Or *righteous*   [t] Gk *was dawning*

---

35. This Gospel alone records Jesus' prayer for forgiveness for his tormentors, and his words of forgiveness for the penitent thief (v. 43). Throughout his account Luke emphasizes remission of sin through Christ.

49. The presence of Jesus' female followers is also mentioned in Matt. 27:55–56; Mark 15:40–41. They stand afar, while John tells of a group standing at the foot of the cross (John 19:25). Here John, the only male disciple present, has his place. As Mary Magdalene comprises part of both groups, one might presume that she paces back and forth during the long, excruciating agony. All of the Gospel writers attest to the presence of dedicated women as witnesses to the atoning death of Christ.

55. The observation of the women will be critical in establishing the circumstances of the burial and resurrection. Some critics have maintained that the women on Easter morning became confused and went to the wrong tomb. Finding it empty, they supposed that Jesus had risen from the dead.

laid. ⁵⁶Then they returned, and prepared spices and ointments.

On the sabbath they rested according to the commandment.

The Resurrection of Jesus

24 But on the first day of the week, at early dawn, they came to the tomb, taking the spices that they had prepared.

◆ The records given by the four Gospels are not entirely consistent. That stupefied witnesses, their senses reeling, should have different aspects emblazoned upon their memories is not surprising. No one account appears to tell the story in its entirety, but it is possible to reconstruct the various occurrences as follows:

(1) The women arrive at the sealed tomb by the first light of dawn, with Mary Magdalene perhaps coming separately from the others (Matt. 28:1; Mark 16:1–3; Luke 24:1; John 20:1).

(2) The stone covering the entrance to the tomb is rolled back during an earthquake and angelic visitation (Matt. 28:2–3; Mark 16:4–6; Luke 24:2).

(3) The women discover that the grave is empty. As they are instructed by angels, they go to tell the male disciples that the Lord is risen (Matt. 28:5–8; Mark 16:7–8; Luke 24:3–11; John 20:2).

(4) The guards report the disappearance of the body to the authorities (Matt. 28:11–15).

(5) When Peter and John hear the news, they run to the tomb and find it empty (Luke 24:12; John 20:3–9).

(6) Mary Magdalene returns and meets the risen Christ. She obeys his commission to tell the others (Mark 16:9–10; John 20:11–18).

(7) The other women return and also see Christ, who instructs them to proclaim the news of his resurrection (Matt. 28:9–10).

(8) Peter encounters Christ (Luke 24:34; 1 Cor. 15:5).

(9) Jesus walks with two disciples on the way to Emmaus (Mark 16:12–13; Luke 24:13–32).

(10) He visits the Upper Room (Mark 16:14; Luke 24:36–44; John 20:19–23). The involvement and witness of the women is critical in all four of the accounts ◆

²They found the stone rolled away from the tomb, ³but when they went in, they did not find the body.ᵘ ⁴While they were perplexed about this, suddenly two men in dazzling clothes stood beside them. ⁵The womenᵛ were terrified and bowed their faces to the ground, but the menʷ said to them, "Why

ᵘ Other ancient authorities add *of the Lord Jesus*
ᵛ Gk *They*   ʷ Gk *but they*

Luke, the careful historian, notes that the women were particularly concerned to observe the location of their Lord's grave. Mark (15:47) gives the names of Mary Magdalene and Mary the mother of Joses as those who marked the place, while Matthew (27:61) tells us that Mary Magdalene and 'the other Mary' sat in full view of the tomb after Nicodemus and Joseph of Arimathea had left.

56. The word used here for the Sabbath rest of the women (*hesuchazo*) has the same root as that used elsewhere for the silence of women (1 Tim. 2:11–12). The term could indicate remaining in peace, calm, tranquillity or rest.

LUKE 24

1. Preparation of the dead for burial is usually the task of women. In John's Gospel, Jesus himself maintained that the anointing by Mary was in anticipation of his burial (John 12:7). Ordinarily women did not participate in the burial of an executed criminal, but the hasty pre-Sabbath ministrations of Joseph of Arimathea and Nicodemus (Matt. 27:59; Mark 15:46; John 19:39–40) were evidently considered inadequate by the women. Hence they prepared their own embalming spices and came to finish the task at the close of the Sabbath during which no such activities could be undertaken.

do you look for the living among the dead? He is not here, but has risen.[x] 6Remember how he told you, while he was still in Galilee, 7'that the Son of Man must be handed over to sinners, and be crucified, and on the third day rise again." 8Then they remembered his words, 9and returning from the tomb, they told all this to the eleven and to all the rest. 10Now it was Mary Magdalene, Joanna, Mary the mother of James, and the other women with them who told this to the apostles. 11But these words seemed to them an idle tale, and they did not believe them. 12But Peter got up and ran to the tomb; stooping and looking in, he saw the linen cloths by themselves; then he went home, amazed at what had happened.[y]

◆ At least seven individuals in the New Testament have the name Mary. These are Mary the mother of Jesus, Mary Magdalene, Mary of Bethany, Mary the mother of James and Joses (Matt. 27:56; Luke 24:10), Mary the wife of Clopas (John 19:25), Mary the mother of Mark (Acts 12:12), Mary, an active member of the church at Rome (Rom. 16:6). The name was a favorite for Jewish women because of the powerful leadership which Miriam, the sister of Aaron and Moses, had given to Israel at the time of the Exodus (Exod. 2:1-10; 15:20-21; Num. 12:1-15; 20:1; 26:59; 1 Chron. 6:3; Mic. 6:4) ◆

The Walk to Emmaus

13 Now on that same day two of them were going to a village called Emmaus, about seven miles[z] from Jerusalem, 14and talking with each other about all these things that had happened. 15While they were talking and discussing, Jesus himself came near and went with them, 16but their eyes were kept from recognizing him. 17And he said to them, "What are you discussing with each other while you walk along?" They stood still, looking sad.[a] 18Then one of them, whose name was Cleopas, answered him, "Are you the only stranger in Jerusalem who does not know the things that have taken place there in these days?" 19He asked them, "What things?" They

[x] Other ancient authorities lack *He is not here, but has risen* [y] Other ancient authorities lack verse 12 [z] Gk *sixty stadia;* other ancient authorities read *a hundred sixty stadia* [a] Other ancient authorities read *walk along, looking sad?"*

6-7. Here we discover that Jesus had given special preparatory instruction to the women so that they might better convey the important news which they must bring to the rest of his followers. While he had been training the male disciples to go out preaching, he had been preparing his female disciples to be the major witnesses of the death, burial, and resurrection. Although the women had put the painful prediction out of their minds, they now recollected it and set about their task of proclamation. The men who had refused to accept Jesus' announcements of his impending death, also refused to accept the witness of the women to the resurrection (v. 11).

7. Jesus' executioners are here called 'sinners'. This would have special significance to women who have known abuse at the hands of sinful people. Our great high priest has been tested in all points as has suffering humanity. He did not exempt himself from experiencing the evil that sinful human beings may wreak upon the innocent.

9-11. Christ arranges the situation so that the disciples shall hear from his female followers the news that he is alive again from the dead. His birth had been announced by angels, and it was angels who brought the news to the women; but their task was to tell the others. Although Peter and John came to the tomb, it was only after their departure that Jesus revealed himself to Mary and the others. As emissaries the women are disbelieved and trivialized; but the truth of their message is soon incontrovertibly authenticated.

13-17. The Greek indicates that a vigorous argument had been under way as Jesus joins the two disciples. One is surely a man (v. 18), but we do not know the gender of the other.

replied, "The things about Jesus of Nazareth,[b] who was a prophet mighty in deed and word before God and all the people, [20]and how our chief priests and leaders handed him over to be condemned to death and crucified him. [21]But we had hoped that he was the one to redeem Israel.[c] Yes, and besides all this, it is now the third day since these things took place. [22]Moreover, some women of our group astounded us. They were at the tomb early this morning, [23]and when they did not find his body there, they came back and told us that they had indeed seen a vision of angels who said that he was alive. [24]Some of those who were with us went to the tomb and found it just as the women had said; but they did not see him." [25]Then he said to them, "Oh, how foolish you are, and how slow of heart to believe all that the prophets have declared! [26]Was it not necessary that the Messiah[d] should suffer these things and then enter into his glory?" [27]Then beginning with Moses and all the prophets, he interpreted to them the things about himself in all the scriptures.

28 As they came near the village to which they were going, he walked ahead as if he were going on. [29]But they urged him strongly, saying, "Stay with us, because it is almost evening and the day is now nearly over." So he went in to stay with them. [30]When he was at the table with them, he took bread, blessed and broke it, and gave it to them. [31]Then their eyes were opened, and they recognized him; and he vanished from their sight. [32]They said to each other, "Were not our hearts burning within us[e] while he was talking to us on the road, while he was opening the scriptures to us?" [33]That same hour they got up and returned to Jerusalem; and they found the eleven and their companions gathered together. [34]They were saying, "The Lord has risen indeed, and he has appeared to Simon!" [35]Then they told what had happened on the road, and how he had been made known to them in the breaking of the bread.

Jesus Appears to His Disciples

36 While they were talking about this, Jesus himself stood among them and said to them, "Peace be with you."[f] [37]They were startled and terrified, and thought that they were seeing a ghost. [38]He said to them, "Why are you frightened, and why do doubts arise in your hearts? [39]Look at my

[b] Other ancient authorities read *Jesus the Nazorean*
[c] Or *to set Israel free*   [d] Or *the Christ*   [e]Other ancient authorities lack *within us*   [f] Other ancient authorities lack *and said to them, "Peace be with you."*

25–27. The Emmaus disciples, like the others, failed to believe the women (Mark 16:11; Luke 24:11). After Jesus gently chides them for their disbelief, he returns to a theme raised by others in the passion narrative: is he the Messiah (Luke 23:2, 35, 39)? Here, although they do not yet recognize him as the risen Christ, he clearly identifies the risen Christ with the suffering and glorified Messiah and interprets for them all the Scriptures concerning the Messiah.

28–35. As the two disciples reach Emmaus, they invite their unknown companion to stay with them, since the hour is late. As they eat, the Lord reveals himself to them when he takes bread, blesses it, breaks it, and gives it to them – a sequence similar to Luke 22:19 and 1 Cor. 10:23–24 – thus suggesting a connection with the Lord's Supper. When they return to Jerusalem, they share in the excitement over Jesus' resurrection by relating their own experiences with the risen Lord. Their experiences suggest many Christians' experience with Christ: we are led from ignorance to faith as we meet the Lord and ask him to stay with us, and we are fed at his table.

36–43. As they discuss these stunning events, Jesus stands among them. Because he realizes the turmoil and terror his presence will cause, he bids them peace. He urges them to test the physical nature of his resurrected body by touching him, seeing his (wounded) hands and feet, and watching him eat. Behind this incident lies the obvious need to ascertain that he is neither a ghost nor a hoax.

hands and my feet; see that it is I myself. Touch me and see; for a ghost does not have flesh and bones as you see that I have." [40]And when he had said this, he showed them his hands and his feet.[g] [41]While in their joy they were disbelieving and still wondering, he said to them, "Have you anything here to eat?" [42]They gave him a piece of broiled fish, [43]and he took it and ate in their presence.

44 Then he said to them, "These are my words that I spoke to you while I was still with you – that everything written about me in the law of Moses, the prophets, and the psalms must be fulfilled." [45]Then he opened their minds to understand the scriptures, [46]and he said to them, "Thus it is written, that the Messiah[h] is to suffer and to rise from the dead on the third day, [47]and that repentance and forgiveness of sins is to be proclaimed in his name to all nations,[i] beginning from Jerusalem. [48]You are witnesses of these things. [49]And see, I am sending upon you what my Father promised; so stay here in the city until you have been clothed with power from on high."

The Ascension of Jesus

50 Then he led them out as far as Bethany, and, lifting up his hands, he blessed them. [51]While he was blessing them, he withdrew from them and was carried up into heaven.[j] [52]And they worshiped him, and[k] returned to Jerusalem with great joy; [53]and they were continually in the temple blessing God.[l]

---

[g] Other ancient authorities lack verse 40   [h] Or *the Christ*   [i] Or *nations. Beginning from Jerusalem you are witnesses*   [j] Other ancient authorities lack *and was carried up into heaven*   [k] Other ancient authorities lack *worshiped him, and*   [l] Other ancient authorities add *Amen*

44–49. As Luke ends his Gospel, he is thinking about integrating it with his sequel, Acts. Instead of enumerating the passages from 'the law of Moses, the prophets, and the psalms' which are fulfilled in the Messiah, Luke will leave many of these for the speeches in Acts. V. 46 interprets the events of Luke 22–24 in light of the resurrection, and vv. 47–49 suggest the upcoming themes and events of Acts: the gospel will be proclaimed starting in Jerusalem and will then spread 'to all nations'; and they will receive what the 'Father [has] promised' – 'power from on high' (the Holy Spirit in Acts 2) – as they wait in Jerusalem.

50–53. Luke concludes his Gospel with the picture of Jesus ascending into heaven and blessing them. This scene is repeated, with amplification at the beginning of Acts (1:6–11). Luke leaves readers of his Gospel at a point of temporary satisfaction and contentment: the disciples return joyfully to Jerusalem and spend their time in the Temple blessing God. The last words of the Gospel, 'blessing God', suggest an appropriate response for us as we constantly await God's new directions for our lives.

JOHN'S GOSPEL

INTRODUCTION

At first glance, John's Gospel is amazingly, perhaps even bewilderingly, different from Matthew, Mark and Luke. Where are the lovely birth narratives of Matthew and Luke, the brain-teasing parables, the down-to-earthness of the Sermon on the Mount?

Well, in the generosity of God, we can find those things where they are, in the first three Gospels, and then turn to John for a totally different kind of biography of the Lord Jesus. Here is divine complementarity at work! For John's portrait of Christ, so distinct, so different, is not one of the great gaps but rather one that adds immeasurably to our knowledge and to our faith.

It is John who sets the Lord's brief lifespan on earth most clearly against the backdrop of eternity and the breadth of the heavens. It is John who takes us into the heart of a remarkable series of conversations between the Lord Jesus and a range of individuals, explicating the universals that lie behind the specifics. It is John who gives us the beautiful series of 'I ams', through which the Lord vividly illustrates his relationship with his followers by means of symbols. It is John who gives us in great detail the Lord's teaching immediately before his arrest and death, and who gives us many facts about his death and resurrection not recorded elsewhere.

John's Gospel also includes special insights into the Savior's attitude towards women. For example, the first miracle or 'sign' of Jesus' unique identity as the Son of God, recorded by John is that at the wedding feast at Cana: the Lord responds to his mother's faith and creates wine from water (John 2). The encounter with a Samaritan woman beside a village well (John 4) and Jesus' tender dealings with Mary and Martha following the death of their brother, Lazarus (John 11), show the Lord in deep theological discussion with those who by their gender would be regarded by the religious establishment as being barred from such respect. John's record of the woman taken in adultery (John 8) shows the Lord challenging another male perversion of God's Law. And it is John's Gospel that scrupulously underlines the way in which it was to women that God entrusted the primary witness to both Calvary and the resurrection, those pivotal events that lie at the very heart of the Good News.

Who exactly was the author of the Fourth Gospel? Although we are not told in so many words, there is good internal and external evidence for believing him to be John, son of Zebedee and brother of James. This John was one of the disciples closest to Jesus, his companion throughout this ministry, and an apostle of the infant church. In the second century, Bishop Irenaeus of Lyons tells us that the saintly elderly Polycarp had known John at the end of the latter's life and that it was indeed he who was the author of the Gospel. It seems that John may have been a very young man when he first followed the Lord, and a very old one when he died at the end of the century.

If it was indeed he who wrote the Gospel, and if he wrote some years after the other Gospels were already in circulation, perhaps even as late as around AD 80, as many scholars believe, we may have an important key as to why John's is so very different a biography of Jesus from the others. John would have been writing reflectively, in the light of both the growth and the struggle of the young church. He wrote as a Jew, yet aware of the strength of the church already passing over into the Gentile world. Many of his fellow apostles would have already died. He who had precious extra information about the Master's life and teaching, and who understood their deep Jewish cultural roots, must preserve it for the church, and build bridges of understanding into the Greek and Roman worlds.

He tells us himself that his purpose in writing is 'so that you may come to believe that Jesus is the Messiah, the Son of God, and that through believing you may have life in his name' (John 20:31). That purpose shapes the way in which he records his material. In Jewish thinking, significance was always even more important than exact chronology, important though that was, too. So John moves from one 'sign', symbol or event to the next, each adding yet more weight to his evidence that the Jesus he knew and watched and loved and now describes is truly none other than the Son of God.

When, then, he moves on to the climax of Jesus' death and resurrection, the reader is faced with the crucial question: 'What does this mean for me today?' No wonder that down through the years countless men and women have come to faith as they have encountered Christ compellingly introduced by John.

The Word Became Flesh

1 In the beginning was the Word, and the Word was with God, and the Word was God. ²He was in the beginning with God. ³All things came into being through him, and without him not one thing came into being. What has come into being ⁴in him was life,ᵃ and the life was the light of all people. ⁵The light shines in the darkness, and the darkness did not overcome it.

6 There was a man sent from God, whose name was John. ⁷He came as a witness to testify to the light, so that all might believe through him. ⁸He himself was not the light, but he came to testify to the light. ⁹The true light, which enlightens everyone, was coming into the world.ᵇ

10 He was in the world, and the world came into being through him; yet the world did not know him. ¹¹He came to what was his own,ᶜ and his own people did not accept him. ¹²But to all who received him, who believed in his name, he gave power to become children of God, ¹³who were born, not of blood or of the will of the flesh or of the will of man, but of God.

14 And the Word became flesh and lived among us, and we have seen his glory, the glory as of a father's only son,ᵈ full of grace and truth. ¹⁵(John testified to him and cried out, "This was he of whom I said, 'He who comes after me ranks ahead of me because he was before me.' ") ¹⁶From his fullness we have all received, grace upon grace. ¹⁷The law indeed was given through Moses; grace and truth came through Jesus Christ. ¹⁸No one has ever seen God. It is God the only Son,ᵉ who is close to the Father's heart,ᶠ who has made him known.

The Testimony of John the Baptist

19 This is the testimony given by John when the Jews sent priests and Levites from Jerusalem to ask him, "Who are you?"

ᵃ Or ³through him. And without him not one thing came into being that has come into being. ⁴In him was life ᵇ Or He was the true light that enlightens everyone coming into the world ᶜ Or to his own home ᵈ Or the Father's only Son ᵉ Other ancient authorities read It is an only Son, God, or It is the only Son ᶠ Gk bosom

---

THE PROLOGUE (JOHN 1:1–18)

The Gospels are essentially narrative biographies. But John begins his Gospel with a declaration about the true identity of Jesus Christ, because it is only because this man was also truly God that all that follows makes sense.

First, John deliberately echoes Gen. 1:1 (John 1:1); then he establishes that the Word was and is eternally Creator: personal, all-powerful, ultimate source of all life, God himself, in sheer contrast to the world and its rejecting darkness (vv. 1–5). Then, eternity and time meet as the Word enters time and space and makes the invisible visible (vv. 9, 14). Why? To make God known in a way that would otherwise have been impossible; the Son comes from God's heart (v. 18).

John the Baptist's ministry marks the beginning of this extraordinary public disclosure of God in the person of Jesus Christ. It is response to Jesus – recognition or denial – that becomes the gateway into the family of God (v. 12), or exclusion from it. In receiving him, we are ushered into life and light, grace and truth, in a categorically new dimension: the dimension of eternity.

A PRELUDE (JOHN 1:19–2:12)

Baptism was not invented by John the Baptist. But the combination of practice and message as he preached implied that he knew he had special authority from God – and that being born a Jew was no guarantee of being acceptable to God (cf. Matt. 3). People were right to wonder whether this was the start of the new era prophesied often in the past (e.g. Mal. 4:5; Deut. 18:15–18), but John points firmly past himself to Jesus (John 1: 23, 27, 30, 36). It is Jesus who will deal with sin (v. 29). While water baptism is a dramatic symbol, it remains external; Jesus, by contrast, will create the very life of God within a person (v. 34).

[20]He confessed and did not deny it, but confessed, "I am not the Messiah."[g] [21]And they asked him, "What then? Are you Elijah?" He said, "I am not." "Are you the prophet?" He answered, "No." [22]Then they said to him, "Who are you? Let us have an answer for those who sent us. What do you say about yourself?" [23]He said,

"I am the voice of one crying out in
        the wilderness,
'Make straight the way of the Lord,' "

as the prophet Isaiah said.

[24] Now they had been sent from the Pharisees. [25]They asked him, "Why then are you baptizing if you are neither the Messiah,[g] nor Elijah, nor the prophet?" [26]John answered them, "I baptize with water. Among you stands one whom you do not know, [27]the one who is coming after me; I am not worthy to untie the thong of his sandal." [28]This took place in Bethany across the Jordan where John was baptizing.

The Lamb of God

[29] The next day he saw Jesus coming toward him and declared, "Here is the Lamb of God who takes away the sin of the world! [30]This is he of whom I said, 'After me comes a man who ranks ahead of me because he was before me.' [31]I myself did not know him; but I came baptizing with water for this reason, that he might be revealed to Israel." [32]And John testified, "I saw the Spirit descending from heaven like a dove, and it remained on him. [33]I myself did not know him, but the one who sent me to baptize with water said to me, 'He on whom you see the Spirit descend and remain is the one who baptizes with the Holy Spirit.' [34]And I myself have seen and have testified that this is the Son of God."[h]

The First Disciples of Jesus

[35] The next day John again was standing with two of his disciples, [36]and as he watched Jesus walk by, he exclaimed, "Look, here is the Lamb of God!" [37]The two disciples heard him say this, and they followed Jesus. [38]When Jesus turned and saw them following, he said to them, "What are you looking for?" They said to him, "Rabbi" (which translated means Teacher), "where are you staying?" [39]He said to them, "Come and see." They came and saw where he was staying, and they remained with him that day. It was about four o'clock in the afternoon. [40]One of the two who heard John speak and followed him was Andrew, Simon Peter's brother. [41]He first found his brother Simon and said to him, "We have found the Messiah" (which is translated Anointed[i]). [42]He

[g] Or the Christ   [h] Other ancient authorities read is God's chosen one   [i] Or Christ

---

John twice (vv. 31, 33) says that he 'did not know' Jesus before baptizing him. John's mother, Elizabeth, and Jesus' mother, Mary, were cousins and it's hard to believe that each had not talked with her son about the amazing events that accompanied his birth, and the way those births were interlocked (see Luke 1). But the dramatic symbol of the dove that came upon Jesus, and more importantly remained, at his baptism is clear evidence to John that his cousin is no temporary instrument of God but unique in human history: the Son of God.

John's mission is now complete. Like a mother raising children, the point has come to 'let go' of his disciples in order that they may follow Jesus (1:35–37). The Lord Jesus gathers those who are to be his close disciples for the next three years. There is a strong strand of relationship and friendship as one person brings another to meet Jesus (1:40, 41, 45). Three times there is testimony to Jesus' true identity (1: 41, 45, 49): Messiah ('God's Anointed'), the one foretold by the law and the prophets, Son of God and King of Israel. Nathanael initially is puzzled, not knowing that Jesus was born in Bethlehem (1:46), but is quickly convinced by Jesus' insight without former instruction. Nathanael, says Jesus, is transparently honest, unlike Jacob who is alluded to in 1:51 (see Gen. 27:36; 28:12).

brought Simon[j] to Jesus, who looked at him and said, "You are Simon son of John. You are to be called Cephas" (which is translated Peter[k]).

Jesus Calls Philip and Nathanael

43 The next day Jesus decided to go to Galilee. He found Philip and said to him, "Follow me." [44]Now Philip was from Bethsaida, the city of Andrew and Peter. [45]Philip found Nathanael and said to him, "We have found him about whom Moses in the law and also the prophets wrote, Jesus son of Joseph from Nazareth." [46]Nathanael said to him, "Can anything good come out of Nazareth?" Philip said to him, "Come and see." [47]When Jesus saw Nathanael coming toward him, he said of him, "Here is truly an Israelite in whom there is no deceit!" [48]Nathanael asked him, "Where did you get to know me?" Jesus answered, "I saw you under the fig tree before Philip called you." [49]Nathanael replied, "Rabbi, you are the Son of God! You are the King of Israel!" [50]Jesus answered, "Do you believe because I told you that I saw you under the fig tree? You will see greater things than these." [51]And he said to him, "Very truly I tell you,[l] you will see heaven opened and the angels of God ascending and descending upon the Son of Man."

The Wedding at Cana

2 On the third day there was a wedding in Cana of Galilee, and the mother of Jesus was there. [2]Jesus and his disciples had also been invited to the wedding. [3]When the wine gave out, the mother of Jesus said to him, "They have no wine." [4]And Jesus said to her, "Woman, what concern is that to you and to me? My hour has not yet come." [5]His mother said to the servants, "Do whatever he tells you." [6]Now standing there were six stone water jars for the Jewish rites of purification, each holding twenty or thirty gallons. [7]Jesus said to them, "Fill the jars with water." And they filled them up to the brim. [8]He said to them, "Now draw some out, and take it to the chief steward." So they took it. [9]When the steward tasted the water that had become wine, and did not know where it came from (though the servants who had drawn the water knew), the steward called the bridegroom [10]and said to him, "Everyone serves the good wine first, and then the inferior wine after the guests have become drunk. But you have kept the good wine until now." [11]Jesus did this, the first of his signs, in Cana of Galilee, and revealed his glory; and his disciples believed in him.

12 After this he went down to Capernaum with his mother, his brothers, and his disciples; and they remained there a few days.

---

[j] Gk *him*   [k] From the word for *rock* in Aramaic (*kepha*) and Greek (*petra*), respectively   [l] Both instances of the Greek word for *you* in this verse are plural

---

After three days' journey between Bethany and Cana, Jesus and his friends join a wedding celebration. Such an event would have been a whole community affair. Perhaps Mary was closely involved; certainly she feels keenly responsible to avert a hospitality crisis which would reflect badly on the host family. Perhaps she sensed that the moment had come for all those extraordinary promises of God that she had pondered (e.g. Luke 2:19) now to be fulfilled. Jesus' gentle rebuke (John 2:4) sets Mary at a little distance; the fact is that though she is his mother, she needs him as her Savior. The humble handmaid of Luke 1:38 must relinquish any hint of maternal privilege. It is his Father's will alone that must prevail.

Nonetheless, Jesus miraculously changes water set aside for ritual purification into the very best wine imaginable. He shows in symbol form that the water that can only wash away external dirt must be replaced by the new wine of the gospel, the blood of the man-who-is-God, the Lamb who really takes away the sin of the world. Jesus' glory (John 2:11) lies not just in a physical miracle, but more in what that miracle points to.

Jesus Cleanses the Temple

13 The Passover of the Jews was near, and Jesus went up to Jerusalem. ¹⁴In the temple he found people selling cattle, sheep, and doves, and the money changers seated at their tables. ¹⁵Making a whip of cords, he drove all of them out of the temple, both the sheep and the cattle. He also poured out the coins of the money changers and overturned their tables. ¹⁶He told those who were selling the doves, "Take these things out of here! Stop making my Father's house a marketplace!" ¹⁷His disciples remembered that it was written, "Zeal for your house will consume me." ¹⁸The Jews then said to him, "What sign can you show us for doing this?" ¹⁹Jesus answered them, "Destroy this temple, and in three days I will raise it up." ²⁰The Jews then said, "This temple has been under construction for forty-six years, and will you raise it up in three days?" ²¹But he was speaking of the temple of his body. ²²After he was raised from the dead, his disciples remembered that he had said this; and they believed the scripture and the word that Jesus had spoken.

23 When he was in Jerusalem during the Passover festival, many believed in his name because they saw the signs that he was doing. ²⁴But Jesus on his part would not entrust himself to them, because he knew all people ²⁵and needed no one to testify about anyone; for he himself knew what was in everyone.

Nicodemus Visits Jesus

3 Now there was a Pharisee named Nicodemus, a leader of the Jews. ²He came to Jesus^m by night and said to him, "Rabbi, we know that you are a teacher who has come from God; for no one can do these signs that you do apart from the presence of God." ³Jesus answered him, "Very truly, I tell you, no one can see the kingdom of God without being born from above."^n ⁴Nicodemus said to him, "How can anyone be born after having grown old? Can one enter a second time into the mother's womb and be born?" ⁵Jesus answered, "Very truly, I tell you, no one can enter the kingdom of God without being born of water and Spirit. ⁶What is born of the flesh is flesh, and what is born of the Spirit is spirit.^o ⁷Do not be astonished that I said to you, 'You^p must be born from above.'^q ⁸The wind^o blows where it chooses, and you hear the sound of it, but you do not know where it comes from or where it goes. So it is with everyone who is born of the Spirit." ⁹Nicodemus said to him, "How can these things be?" ¹⁰Jesus answered him,

---

^m Gk *him*   ^n Or *born anew*   ^o The same Greek word means both *wind* and *spirit*   ^p The Greek word for *you* here is plural   ^q Or *anew*

SEEING AND BELIEVING (JOHN 2:13–4:54)

Jesus and his disciples travel from Cana to Capernaum to Jerusalem; then, on into the Judean countryside, round through Samaria, and back up to Cana. Life on foot may be exhausting, but it allows for personal encounters. In today's hectic world, it is often women who most closely identify with Jesus' focus on people and relationships.

John locates the confrontation with traders and money-lenders in the Temple at the start of Jesus' public ministry, where the other Gospels place it towards the end. Maybe the same incident happened twice, or maybe John puts it here to highlight why it was inevitable that Jesus must clash with the religious authorities. Religious observance had been twisted into an occasion for exploitation; the place that was supposed to be 'a house of prayer for all nations' (Is. 56:7) was reduced to a thieves' market. Moreover, it is the person of Christ, not the Temple, that is the literal dwelling place of God; in his coming resurrection Jesus will demonstrate that though the Temple can be destroyed (as it soon was to be, yet again), he cannot be (John 2: 18–22).

"Are you a teacher of Israel, and yet you do not understand these things?

11 "Very truly, I tell you, we speak of what we know and testify to what we have seen; yet you[r] do not receive our testimony. [12]If I have told you about earthly things and you do not believe, how can you believe if I tell you about heavenly things? [13]No one has ascended into heaven except the one who descended from heaven, the Son of Man.[s] [14]And just as Moses lifted up the serpent in the wilderness, so must the Son of Man be lifted up, [15]that whoever believes in him may have eternal life.[t]

16 "For God so loved the world that he gave his only Son, so that everyone who believes in him may not perish but may have eternal life.

17 "Indeed, God did not send the Son into the world to condemn the world, but in order that the world might be saved through him. [18]Those who believe in him are not condemned; but those who do not believe are condemned already, because they have not believed in the name of the only Son of God. [19]And this is the judgment, that the light has come into the world, and people loved darkness rather than light because their deeds were evil. [20]For all who do evil hate the light and do not come to the light, so that their deeds may not be exposed. [21]But those who do what is true come to the light, so that it may be clearly seen that their deeds have been done in God."[t]

Jesus and John the Baptist

22 After this Jesus and his disciples went into the Judean countryside, and he spent some time there with them and baptized. [23]John also was baptizing at Aenon near Salim because water was abundant there; and people kept coming and were being baptized [24] – John, of course, had not yet been thrown into prison.

25 Now a discussion about purification arose between John's disciples and a Jew.[u] [26]They came to John and said to him, "Rabbi, the one who was with you across the Jordan, to whom you testified, here he is baptizing, and all are going to him." [27]John answered, "No one can receive anything except what has been given from heaven. [28]You yourselves are my witnesses that I said, 'I am not the Messiah,[v] but I have been sent ahead of him.' [29]He who has the bride is the bridegroom. The friend of the bridegroom, who stands and hears him, rejoices greatly at the bridegroom's voice. For this reason my joy has been fulfilled.

[r] The Greek word for *you* here and in verse 12 is plural   [s] Other ancient authorities add *who is in heaven*   [t] Some interpreters hold that the quotation concludes with verse 15   [u] Other ancient authorities read *the Jews*   [v] Or *the Christ*

As the narrative unfolds, John frequently underlines that as people encounter Jesus, see what he does and hear what he says, they believe (e.g. John 2:11, 23; 4:42, 53). Some, like Nicodemus (3:1-21), are confused; on the one hand, there is no explanation for the 'signs' unless God is with Jesus; on the other, Jesus is radically challenging the adequacy of the external observances around which the Pharisees' lives revolved. Just as John the Baptist had to point to the really important baptism being not that of water but that of the Spirit, so Jesus has to point to a spiritual birth that has nothing to do with mere physical birth, even as a Jew. Surely, says Jesus, Nicodemus should have understood that from the Old Testament.

It is in response to Jesus that people put themselves among the condemned or among those who have already received eternal life. The contrast is sharp, as sharp as the contrast between light and darkness or between life and death. There is a profoundly moral element; this is not just about knowledge or ignorance, but above loving to live the truth so that one draws close to the light. Love, life, light and truth: all are found supremely in Jesus. He offers them to the whole wide world. Each person must respond (3:16).

³⁰He must increase, but I must decrease."ʷ

The One Who Comes from Heaven

31 The one who comes from above is above all; the one who is of the earth belongs to the earth and speaks about earthly things. The one who comes from heaven is above all. ³²He testifies to what he has seen and heard, yet no one accepts his testimony. ³³Whoever has accepted his testimony has certifiedˣ this, that God is true. ³⁴He whom God has sent speaks the words of God, for he gives the Spirit without measure. ³⁵The Father loves the Son and has placed all things in his hands. ³⁶Whoever believes in the Son has eternal life; whoever disobeys the Son will not see life, but must endure God's wrath.

Jesus and the Woman of Samaria

4 Now when Jesusʸ learned that the Pharisees had heard, "Jesus is making and baptizing more disciples than John" ² – although it was not Jesus himself but his disciples who baptized – ³he left Judea and started back to Galilee. ⁴But he had to go through Samaria. ⁵So he came to a Samaritan city called Sychar, near the plot of ground that Jacob had given to his son Joseph. ⁶Jacob's well was there, and Jesus, tired out by his journey, was sitting by the well. It was about noon.

7 A Samaritan woman came to draw water, and Jesus said to her, "Give me a drink." ⁸(His disciples had gone to the city to buy food.) ⁹The Samaritan woman said to him, "How is it that you, a Jew, ask a drink of me, a woman of Samaria?" (Jews do not share things in common with Samaritans.)ᶻ ¹⁰Jesus answered her, "If you knew the gift of God, and who it is that is saying to you, 'Give me a drink,' you would have asked him, and he would have given you living water." ¹¹The woman said to him, "Sir, you have no bucket, and the well is deep. Where do you get that living water? ¹²Are you greater than our ancestor Jacob, who gave us the well, and with his sons and his flocks drank from it?" ¹³Jesus said to her, "Everyone who drinks of this water will be thirsty again, ¹⁴but those who drink of the water that I will give them will never be thirsty. The water that I will give will become in them a spring of water gushing up to eternal life." ¹⁵The woman said to him, "Sir, give me this water, so that I may never be thirsty or have to keep coming here to draw water."

16 Jesus said to her, "Go, call your husband, and come back." ¹⁷The woman answered him, "I have no husband." Jesus said to her, "You are right in saying, 'I have no husband'; ¹⁸for you have had five

---

ʷ Some interpreters hold that the quotation continues through verse 36   ˣ Gk *set a seal to*   ʸ Other ancient authorities read *the Lord*   ᶻ Other ancient authorities lack this sentence

---

Once more (3:25–30) John the Baptist affirms that it is Jesus who brings purification that is more than skin-deep. He likens himself to a best man at a wedding: he has a real role, but does not compete with the bridegroom for the bride. After the wedding, the best man's task is done. 3:31–36 appear to be a comment from John the Evangelist rather than a continuation of John the Baptist's teaching, and build on Jesus' discussion with Nicodemus. Now John introduces the connection between belief and obedience; what is at stake is response to the one who carries the very authority of God.

If Nicodemus represents the privileged, educated, male religious leader, who externally at least seemed to do everything right, the Samaritan woman (4:4–42) could not be more different. She was of a despised group whom the Jews regarded as apostate beyond recall, she was personally outrageously immoral, and she was a woman. The more orthodox a Jewish male was, the more passionately he believed that to communicate with a female outside his own immediate family circle was to be contaminated; and to discuss religion with a woman was to trample God's Word in the dirt.

husbands, and the one you have now is not your husband. What you have said is true!" ¹⁹The woman said to him, "Sir, I see that you are a prophet. ²⁰Our ancestors worshiped on this mountain, but you[a] say that the place where people must worship is in Jerusalem." ²¹Jesus said to her, "Woman, believe me, the hour is coming when you will worship the Father neither on this mountain nor in Jerusalem. ²²You worship what you do not know; we worship what we know, for salvation is from the Jews. ²³But the hour is coming, and is now here, when the true worshipers will worship the Father in spirit and truth, for the Father seeks such as these to worship him. ²⁴God is spirit, and those who worship him must worship in spirit and truth." ²⁵The woman said to him, "I know that Messiah is coming" (who is called Christ). "When he comes, he will proclaim all things to us." ²⁶Jesus said to her, "I am he,[b] the one who is speaking to you."

27 Just then his disciples came. They were astonished that he was speaking with a woman, but no one said, "What do you want?" or, "Why are you speaking with her?" ²⁸Then the woman left her water jar and went back to the city. She said to the people, ²⁹"Come and see a man who told me everything I have ever done!

He cannot be the Messiah,[c] can he?" ³⁰They left the city and were on their way to him.

31 Meanwhile the disciples were urging him, "Rabbi, eat something." ³²But he said to them, "I have food to eat that you do not know about." ³³So the disciples said to one another, "Surely no one has brought him something to eat?" ³⁴Jesus said to them, "My food is to do the will of him who sent me and to complete his work. ³⁵Do you not say, 'Four months more, then comes the harvest'? But I tell you, look around you, and see how the fields are ripe for harvesting. ³⁶The reaper is already receiving[d] wages and is gathering fruit for eternal life, so that sower and reaper may rejoice together. ³⁷For here the saying holds true, 'One sows and another reaps.' ³⁸I sent you to reap that for which you did not labor. Others have labored, and you have entered into their labor."

39 Many Samaritans from that city believed in him because of the woman's testimony, "He told me everything I have ever done." ⁴⁰So when the Samaritans came to him, they asked him to stay with them;

[a] The Greek word for *you* here and in verses 21 and 22 is plural [b] Gk *I am* [c] Or *the Christ* [d] Or ³⁵. . . *the fields are already ripe for harvesting.* ³⁶*The reaper is receiving*

The Lord turns it all on its head, shocking the woman (4:9) and shaking the disciples (4:27) in the process. He discusses religious questions with her. He puts himself in her debt by asking her for water, ignoring laws of ritual cleanness. The fact that she comes to draw water in the heat of the day, and alone, probably means that even the local women regarded her as too immoral to have anything to do with; but Jesus does not condemn her, just gently but persistently presses her to face the fact that her real needs are much deeper than the hassle of daily chores. In a culture where a woman without a male protector was destitute indeed, who knows what may have lain behind her apparent promiscuity? It is to this most unlikely of people that Jesus confirms explicitly that he is the Messiah (4:26).

Moreover, it is this woman's testimony that brings a crowd of other people to meet Jesus, a crowd who then come to recognize Jesus as 'the Savior of the world' (4:42) (as he truly is, and in a way few Jews could see). Jesus clearly does not underwrite the prevailing marginalization of women. He treats her with dignity and compassion, and as one who as much as any man has the right and the responsibility to face God personally, and then to serve him.

The incident of the royal official who begs Jesus to heal his son (4:46–54) is not only the occasion for another 'sign', but also leads to a whole household believing because they have seen.

and he stayed there two days. [41]And many more believed because of his word. [42]They said to the woman, "It is no longer because of what you said that we believe, for we have heard for ourselves, and we know that this is truly the Savior of the world."

Jesus Returns to Galilee

43 When the two days were over, he went from that place to Galilee [44](for Jesus himself had testified that a prophet has no honor in the prophet's own country). [45]When he came to Galilee, the Galileans welcomed him, since they had seen all that he had done in Jerusalem at the festival; for they too had gone to the festival.

Jesus Heals an Official's Son

46 Then he came again to Cana in Galilee where he had changed the water into wine. Now there was a royal official whose son lay ill in Capernaum. [47]When he heard that Jesus had come from Judea to Galilee, he went and begged him to come down and heal his son, for he was at the point of death. [48]Then Jesus said to him, "Unless you[e] see signs and wonders you will not believe." [49]The official said to him, "Sir, come down before my little boy dies." [50]Jesus said to him, "Go; your son will live." The man believed the word that Jesus spoke to him and started on his way. [51]As he was going down, his slaves met him and told him that his child was alive. [52]So he asked them the hour when he began to recover, and they said to

him, "Yesterday at one in the afternoon the fever left him." [53]The father realized that this was the hour when Jesus had said to him, "Your son will live." So he himself believed, along with his whole household. [54]Now this was the second sign that Jesus did after coming from Judea to Galilee.

Jesus Heals on the Sabbath

5 After this there was a festival of the Jews, and Jesus went up to Jerusalem.

2 Now in Jerusalem by the Sheep Gate there is a pool, called in Hebrew[f] Bethzatha,[g] which has five porticoes. [3]In these lay many invalids – blind, lame, and paralyzed.[h] [5]One man was there who had been ill for thirty-eight years. [6]When Jesus saw him lying there and knew that he had been there a long time, he said to him, "Do you want to be made well?" [7]The sick man answered him, "Sir, I have no one to put me into the pool when the water is stirred up; and while I am making my way, someone else steps down ahead of me." [8]Jesus said to him, "Stand up, take your mat and walk."

[e] Both instances of the Greek word for *you* in this verse are plural   [f] That is, *Aramaic*   [g] Other ancient authorities read *Bethesda*, others *Bethsaida*   [h] Other ancient authorities add, wholly or in part, *waiting for the stirring of the water;* [4]*for an angel of the Lord went down at certain seasons into the pool, and stirred up the water; whoever stepped in first after the stirring of the water was made well from whatever disease that person had.*

BY WHOSE AUTHORITY? (JOHN 5:1–47)

Jesus repeatedly challenged the endless rules developed by the religious establishment. It was inevitable that this would bring him into conflict with the Temple authorities. Who did he think he was!

At first glance, Jesus' question (5:6) to the invalid beside the pool seems silly: of course he would want to be healed. Yet the fact is that in the complexity of the human personality there are some for whom chronic illness may be a refuge from reality, an evasion. For this man there were certain advantages, including a source of income. The test of his genuineness is what he does when offered healing. The test of our sincerity may be what we do when God offers the opportunity for real change, because change carries its own pricetag, including responsibility (5:14).

⁹At once the man was made well, and he took up his mat and began to walk.

Now that day was a sabbath. ¹⁰So the Jews said to the man who had been cured, "It is the sabbath; it is not lawful for you to carry your mat." ¹¹But he answered them, "The man who made me well said to me, 'Take up your mat and walk.' " ¹²They asked him, "Who is the man who said to you, 'Take it up and walk'?" ¹³Now the man who had been healed did not know who it was, for Jesus had disappeared in¹ the crowd that was there. ¹⁴Later Jesus found him in the temple and said to him, "See, you have been made well! Do not sin any more, so that nothing worse happens to you." ¹⁵The man went away and told the Jews that it was Jesus who had made him well. ¹⁶Therefore the Jews started persecuting Jesus, because he was doing such things on the sabbath. ¹⁷But Jesus answered them, "My Father is still working, and I also am working." ¹⁸For this reason the Jews were seeking all the more to kill him, because he was not only breaking the sabbath, but was also calling God his own Father, thereby making himself equal to God.

◆ God rested after completing the task of creation (Gen. 2:2–3). Human beings, made in God's image, also need a rhythm of rest after labor. In his wisdom, God enshrined this in the Fourth Commandment (Exod. 20:8–11). The purpose was to devote a day in a special way to the worship of the Lord, to take stock and to tie one's life's moorings firmly back into God, and to be renewed for another cycle of work. The early church soon came to celebrate Sabbath on Sunday, the day of the Lord's resurrection.

By the time of Jesus, the Pharisees had taken a beautiful principle and weighed it down with thousands of detailed rules, mostly negative, guaranteeing condemnation rather than recommissioning. Jesus condemns the legalism, and refocuses the principle. The pastor or nurse, for whom Sunday may be a busy workday, is not to feel guilty – but needs to set aside other rest time instead. A rural Tanzanian woman must still milk her goats and fetch water on a Sunday, but in other ways she may be able to make the day different from the rest of her week. A Christian believer within a Muslim community may celebrate Sunday on Friday! Public worship, quiet reflection, family time, healing care for the lonely: all these can positively express Sabbath. Children in Christian families should be helped to celebrate Sunday as the joyful 'best day of the week' rather than being circumscribed only by negative restrictions ◆

The Authority of the Son

19 Jesus said to them, "Very truly, I tell you, the Son can do nothing on his own, but only what he sees the Father doing; for whatever the Father¹ does, the Son does likewise. ²⁰The Father loves the Son and

¹ Or *had left because of*   ¹ Gk *that one*

Jesus' action angers those Jews whose orthodoxy is tightly tied to detailed rules: work on the Sabbath is forbidden, and that includes healing and carrying anything. They are angered, too, by his claim to special relationship with God (5:18). From this point on, they seek to kill him.

Jesus makes it very clear that he does indeed have a unique relationship with God. As Son, he has full authority from his Father (5:19, 22, 23, 27 etc.). There is complete harmony between what the Father does and what the Son does. This embraces authority over life and death, over judgment and revelation. Further, the Jews' confidence that they are defending the Law of Moses is misplaced (5:46). In their preoccupation with keeping their many rules, they have lost touch with the ultimate Lawgiver, God. They scour the Scriptures for rules, and miss their throbbing testimony to Jesus (5:39). The Old Testament, Jesus' own demonstrated power in miracles, the testimony of John, and of the Father himself at Jesus' baptism, all bear witness to his authority.

shows him all that he himself is doing; and he will show him greater works than these, so that you will be astonished. ²¹Indeed, just as the Father raises the dead and gives them life, so also the Son gives life to whomever he wishes. ²²The Father judges no one but has given all judgment to the Son, ²³so that all may honor the Son just as they honor the Father. Anyone who does not honor the Son does not honor the Father who sent him. ²⁴Very truly, I tell you, anyone who hears my word and believes him who sent me has eternal life, and does not come under judgment, but has passed from death to life.

25 "Very truly, I tell you, the hour is coming, and is now here, when the dead will hear the voice of the Son of God, and those who hear will live. ²⁶For just as the Father has life in himself, so he has granted the Son also to have life in himself; ²⁷and he has given him authority to execute judgment, because he is the Son of Man. ²⁸Do not be astonished at this; for the hour is coming when all who are in their graves will hear his voice ²⁹and will come out – those who have done good, to the resurrection of life, and those who have done evil, to the resurrection of condemnation.

Witnesses to Jesus

30 "I can do nothing on my own. As I hear, I judge; and my judgment is just, because I seek to do not my own will but the will of him who sent me.

31 "If I testify about myself, my testimony is not true. ³²There is another who testifies on my behalf, and I know that his testimony to me is true. ³³You sent messengers to John, and he testified to the truth.

³⁴Not that I accept such human testimony, but I say these things so that you may be saved. ³⁵He was a burning and shining lamp, and you were willing to rejoice for a while in his light. ³⁶But I have a testimony greater than John's. The works that the Father has given me to complete, the very works that I am doing, testify on my behalf that the Father has sent me. ³⁷And the Father who sent me has himself testified on my behalf. You have never heard his voice or seen his form, ³⁸and you do not have his word abiding in you, because you do not believe him whom he has sent.

39 "You search the scriptures because you think that in them you have eternal life; and it is they that testify on my behalf. ⁴⁰Yet you refuse to come to me to have life. ⁴¹I do not accept glory from human beings. ⁴²But I know that you do not have the love of God in^k you. ⁴³I have come in my Father's name, and you do not accept me; if another comes in his own name, you will accept him. ⁴⁴How can you believe when you accept glory from one another and do not seek the glory that comes from the one who alone is God? ⁴⁵Do not think that I will accuse you before the Father; your accuser is Moses, on whom you have set your hope. ⁴⁶If you believed Moses, you would believe me, for he wrote about me. ⁴⁷But if you do not believe what he wrote, how will you believe what I say?"

Feeding the Five Thousand

6 After this Jesus went to the other side of the Sea of Galilee, also called the Sea of Tiberias.¹ ²A large crowd kept

---

^{k} Or *among*   ¹ Gk *of Galilee of Tiberias*

JESUS THE BREAD OF LIFE (JOHN 6:1–71)

By now a large crowd was following Jesus, fascinated by his miraculous healing power. There is an almost ludicrous disparity between the small boy's picnic (6:9) and the size of the crowd (perhaps 10,000 or more, since the women and children were not included in the 5,000 of Matthew and Mark's accounts: see Matt. 14:21; Mark 6:44; official numbering usually referred to adult males only). Yet, for the Creator of the universe, who created everything out of nothing, the provision of food on this scale is no problem. This is not magic, but creatorhood being exercised.

following him, because they saw the signs that he was doing for the sick. ³Jesus went up the mountain and sat down there with his disciples. ⁴Now the Passover, the festival of the Jews, was near. ⁵When he looked up and saw a large crowd coming toward him, Jesus said to Philip, "Where are we to buy bread for these people to eat?" ⁶He said this to test him, for he himself knew what he was going to do. ⁷Philip answered him, "Six months' wages[m] would not buy enough bread for each of them to get a little." ⁸One of his disciples, Andrew, Simon Peter's brother, said to him, ⁹"There is a boy here who has five barley loaves and two fish. But what are they among so many people?" ¹⁰Jesus said, "Make the people sit down." Now there was a great deal of grass in the place; so they[n] sat down, about five thousand in all. ¹¹Then Jesus took the loaves, and when he had given thanks, he distributed them to those who were seated; so also the fish, as much as they wanted. ¹²When they were satisfied, he told his disciples, "Gather up the fragments left over, so that nothing may be lost." ¹³So they gathered them up, and from the fragments of the five barley loaves, left by those who had eaten, they filled twelve baskets. ¹⁴When the people saw the sign that he had done, they began to say, "This is indeed the prophet who is to come into the world."

15 When Jesus realized that they were about to come and take him by force to make him king, he withdrew again to the mountain by himself.

Jesus Walks on the Water

16 When evening came, his disciples went down to the sea, ¹⁷got into a boat, and started across the sea to Capernaum. It was now dark, and Jesus had not yet come to them. ¹⁸The sea became rough because a strong wind was blowing. ¹⁹When they had rowed about three or four miles,[o] they saw Jesus walking on the sea and coming near the boat, and they were terrified. ²⁰But he said to them, "It is I;[p] do not be afraid." ²¹Then they wanted to take him into the boat, and immediately the boat reached the land toward which they were going.

The Bread from Heaven

22 The next day the crowd that had stayed on the other side of the sea saw that there had been only one boat there. They also saw that Jesus had not got into the boat with his disciples, but that his disciples had gone away alone. ²³Then some boats from Tiberias came near the place where they had eaten the bread after the Lord had given thanks.[q] ²⁴So when the crowd saw that neither Jesus nor his disciples were there, they themselves got into the boats and went to Capernaum looking for Jesus.

25 When they found him on the other side of the sea, they said to him, "Rabbi,

[m] Gk *Two hundred denarii*; the denarius was the usual day's wage for a laborer   [n] Gk *the men*
[o] Gk *about twenty-five or thirty stadia*   [p] Gk *I am*
[q] Other ancient authorities lack *after the Lord had given thanks*

The time was not yet right for Jesus to be declared king, and in any case his kingship would never be expressed in the terms expected by the crowd. Chafing under the rule of the Romans, they expected a Messiah who would bring political deliverance. By contrast, Jesus shows his kingly authority over creation to his disciples as he walks on the sea (6:19).

When the crowd catch up with him again (6:25), Jesus reinterprets for them the familiar story of that great deliverance of the past, the Exodus, and especially God's provision for his people in the wilderness (Exod. 16). The manna by which the children of Israel survived in the wilderness lasted only a day at a time. Still in the present much of each day's activity would have revolved around the need to provide food for survival. All the same, says Jesus, there is an even deeper need, an even more important food, that which makes possible and then sustains eternal life (John 6:27, 48–51). He himself is that food.

when did you come here?" ²⁶Jesus answered them, "Very truly, I tell you, you are looking for me, not because you saw signs, but because you ate your fill of the loaves. ²⁷Do not work for the food that perishes, but for the food that endures for eternal life, which the Son of Man will give you. For it is on him that God the Father has set his seal." ²⁸Then they said to him, "What must we do to perform the works of God?" ²⁹Jesus answered them, "This is the work of God, that you believe in him whom he has sent." ³⁰So they said to him, "What sign are you going to give us then, so that we may see it and believe you? What work are you performing? ³¹Our ancestors ate the manna in the wilderness; as it is written, 'He gave them bread from heaven to eat.' " ³²Then Jesus said to them, "Very truly, I tell you, it was not Moses who gave you the bread from heaven, but it is my Father who gives you the true bread from heaven. ³³For the bread of God is that which[r] comes down from heaven and gives life to the world." ³⁴They said to him, "Sir, give us this bread always."

35 Jesus said to them, "I am the bread of life. Whoever comes to me will never be hungry, and whoever believes in me will never be thirsty. ³⁶But I said to you that you have seen me and yet do not believe. ³⁷Everything that the Father gives me will come to me, and anyone who comes to me I will never drive away; ³⁸for I have come down from heaven, not to do my own will, but the will of him who sent me. ³⁹And this is the will of him who sent me, that I should lose nothing of all that he has given me, but raise it up on the last day. ⁴⁰This is indeed the will of my Father, that all who see the

Son and believe in him may have eternal life; and I will raise them up on the last day."

41 Then the Jews began to complain about him because he said, "I am the bread that came down from heaven." ⁴²They were saying, "Is not this Jesus, the son of Joseph, whose father and mother we know? How can he now say, 'I have come down from heaven'?" ⁴³Jesus answered them, "Do not complain among yourselves. ⁴⁴No one can come to me unless drawn by the Father who sent me; and I will raise that person up on the last day. ⁴⁵It is written in the prophets, 'And they shall all be taught by God.' Everyone who has heard and learned from the Father comes to me. ⁴⁶Not that anyone has seen the Father except the one who is from God; he has seen the Father. ⁴⁷Very truly, I tell you, whoever believes has eternal life. ⁴⁸I am the bread of life. ⁴⁹Your ancestors ate the manna in the wilderness, and they died. ⁵⁰This is the bread that comes down from heaven, so that one may eat of it and not die. ⁵¹I am the living bread that came down from heaven. Whoever eats of this bread will live forever; and the bread that I will give for the life of the world is my flesh."

52 The Jews then disputed among themselves, saying, "How can this man give us his flesh to eat?" ⁵³So Jesus said to them, "Very truly, I tell you, unless you eat the flesh of the Son of Man and drink his blood, you have no life in you. ⁵⁴Those who eat my flesh and drink my blood have eternal life, and I will raise them up on the last day; ⁵⁵for my flesh is true food and my blood is true drink. ⁵⁶Those who eat my flesh and drink

[r] Or *he who*

Once again, the crowd are unable to see beyond the symbol and the literal meaning of what Jesus says. How could he have come down from heaven when they knew his parents perfectly well? Was he advocating some gruesome form of cannibalism?

Jesus looks back to the Passover and forward to Calvary (6:53ff.), but it is beyond most people's comprehension. Many left him, perhaps thinking him to be insane, perhaps disappointed that he wasn't fulfilling their agenda. The Twelve remain: despite the things they don't understand, they know enough to know they need to stay (6:68–69).

my blood abide in me, and I in them. [57]Just as the living Father sent me, and I live because of the Father, so whoever eats me will live because of me. [58]This is the bread that came down from heaven, not like that which your ancestors ate, and they died. But the one who eats this bread will live forever." [59]He said these things while he was teaching in the synagogue at Capernaum.

The Words of Eternal Life

60 When many of his disciples heard it, they said, "This teaching is difficult; who can accept it?" [61]But Jesus, being aware that his disciples were complaining about it, said to them, "Does this offend you? [62]Then what if you were to see the Son of Man ascending to where he was before? [63]It is the spirit that gives life; the flesh is useless. The words that I have spoken to you are spirit and life. [64]But among you there are some who do not believe." For Jesus knew from the first who were the ones that did not believe, and who was the one that would betray him. [65]And he said, "For this reason I have told you that no one can come to me unless it is granted by the Father."

66 Because of this many of his disciples turned back and no longer went about with him. [67]So Jesus asked the twelve, "Do you also wish to go away?" [68]Simon Peter answered him, "Lord, to whom can we go? You have the words of eternal life. [69]We have

come to believe and know that you are the Holy One of God."[s] [70]Jesus answered them, "Did I not choose you, the twelve? Yet one of you is a devil." [71]He was speaking of Judas son of Simon Iscariot,[t] for he, though one of the twelve, was going to betray him.

The Unbelief of Jesus' Brothers

7 After this Jesus went about in Galilee. He did not wish[u] to go about in Judea because the Jews were looking for an opportunity to kill him. [2]Now the Jewish festival of Booths[v] was near. [3]So his brothers said to him, "Leave here and go to Judea so that your disciples also may see the works you are doing; [4]for no one who wants[w] to be widely known acts in secret. If you do these things, show yourself to the world." [5](For not even his brothers believed in him.) [6]Jesus said to them, "My time has not yet come, but your time is always here. [7]The world cannot hate you, but it hates me because I testify against it that its works are evil. [8]Go to the festival yourselves. I am not[x] going to this festival, for my time has not yet fully come." [9]After saying this, he remained in Galilee.

[s] Other ancient authorities read *the Christ, the Son of the living God* [t] Other ancient authorities read *Judas Iscariot son of Simon*; others, *Judas son of Simon from Karyot* (Kerioth) [u] Other ancient authorities read *was not at liberty* [v] Or *Tabernacles* [w] Other ancient authorities read *wants it* [x] Other ancient authorities add *yet*

JESUS AND THE LAW (JOHN 7:1–8:59)

The Festival of Booths (7:2) or Tabernacles was a week-long celebration at the end of the fruit harvest. Jesus' brothers think he should exploit the situation when people have time on their hands to raise his public profile. Jesus refuses; it is neither the time nor the method.

Nonetheless, he is already the subject of debate (7:12) and, when he slips up to Jerusalem and begins teaching in the Temple, that debate intensifies. How can someone who has never been properly trained in the authorized schools know so much? Jesus claims that his teaching comes directly from God. At the very least he is setting himself up on a level with Moses, whose Law is their pride. Yet they've even missed the point of that, says Jesus (7:19–24). Once again he is challenging them as to the difference between the external and the internal, between the form and the reality. 'Go to the inner meaning!' he says (7:24).

Because the religious authorities do not arrest him, the people are confused (7:25–27). Jesus seems to speak in riddles (7:33, 36, 38) and he doesn't fit their identikit for the Messiah (7:27, 41–43, 52); what should they make of him? Some can't believe that he isn't the Messiah (7:31), some are sure he's a dangerous imposter (7:44, 48), and some want to wait and see (7:46, 50–51).

Jesus at the Festival of Booths

10 But after his brothers had gone to the festival, then he also went, not publicly but as it were[y] in secret. [11]The Jews were looking for him at the festival and saying, "Where is he?" [12]And there was considerable complaining about him among the crowds. While some were saying, "He is a good man," others were saying, "No, he is deceiving the crowd." [13]Yet no one would speak openly about him for fear of the Jews.

14 About the middle of the festival Jesus went up into the temple and began to teach. [15]The Jews were astonished at it, saying, "How does this man have such learning,[z] when he has never been taught?" [16]Then Jesus answered them, "My teaching is not mine but his who sent me. [17]Anyone who resolves to do the will of God will know whether the teaching is from God or whether I am speaking on my own. [18]Those who speak on their own seek their own glory; but the one who seeks the glory of him who sent him is true, and there is nothing false in him.

19 "Did not Moses give you the law? Yet none of you keeps the law. Why are you looking for an opportunity to kill me?" [20]The crowd answered, "You have a demon! Who is trying to kill you?" [21]Jesus answered them, "I performed one work, and all of you are astonished. [22]Moses gave you circumcision (it is, of course, not from Moses, but from the patriarchs), and you circumcise a man on the sabbath. [23]If a man receives circumcision on the sabbath in order that the law of Moses may not be broken, are you angry with me because I healed a man's whole body on the sabbath? [24]Do not judge by appearances, but judge with right judgment."

Is This the Christ?

25 Now some of the people of Jerusalem were saying, "Is not this the man whom they are trying to kill? [26]And here he is, speaking openly, but they say nothing to him! Can it be that the authorities really know that this is the Messiah?[a] [27]Yet we know where this man is from; but when the Messiah[a] comes, no one will know where he is from." [28]Then Jesus cried out as he was teaching in the temple, "You know me, and you know where I am from. I have not come on my own. But the one who sent me is true, and you do not know him. [29]I know him, because I am from him, and he sent me." [30]Then they tried to arrest him, but no one laid hands on him, because his hour had not yet come. [31]Yet many in the crowd believed in him and were saying, "When the Messiah[a] comes, will he do more signs than this man has done?"[b]

---

[y] Other ancient authorities lack *as it were*   [z] Or *this man know his letters*   [a] Or *the Christ*   [b] Other ancient authorities read *is doing*

Jesus makes stunning claims: his teaching comes straight from God; his interpretation of the Old Testament is right, and theirs is often wrong; he is the giver of the Spirit (7:37–39). Angry and eager to trap him, the scribes and the Pharisees next day bring a woman caught in adultery and ask Jesus what should be done. Their blatant using of the woman as a tool for their own ends, and their concern to catch Jesus out under the guise of upholding the Law, show painfully how worldly these men are. Their double standards are sickening: if they really had caught the woman in the act of adultery, where is the man? Under the Law, he too must be punished (see further the note on 'Sexual ethics', p. 197).

Jesus' response is masterly. He neither denies the Law of Moses nor affirms it. Instead, he puts the spotlight on the men (8:7). If they 'throw the first stone', and thereby claim freedom from sin, they are clearly denying the Scripture. The would-be trappers are themselves trapped, and melt away. The Lord, with great compassion, releases the woman from the sentence of a cruel death while still insisting that sin is sin and must be abandoned.

Officers Are Sent to Arrest Jesus

32 The Pharisees heard the crowd muttering such things about him, and the chief priests and Pharisees sent temple police to arrest him. [33]Jesus then said, "I will be with you a little while longer, and then I am going to him who sent me. [34]You will search for me, but you will not find me; and where I am, you cannot come." [35]The Jews said to one another, "Where does this man intend to go that we will not find him? Does he intend to go to the Dispersion among the Greeks and teach the Greeks? [36]What does he mean by saying, 'You will search for me and you will not find me' and 'Where I am, you cannot come'?"

Rivers of Living Water

37 On the last day of the festival, the great day, while Jesus was standing there, he cried out, "Let anyone who is thirsty come to me, [38]and let the one who believes in me drink. As[c] the scripture has said, 'Out of the believer's heart[d] shall flow rivers of living water.' " [39]Now he said this about the Spirit, which believers in him were to receive; for as yet there was no Spirit,[e] because Jesus was not yet glorified.

Division among the People

40 When they heard these words, some in the crowd said, "This is really the prophet." [41]Others said, "This is the Messiah."[f] But some asked, "Surely the Messiah[f] does not come from Galilee,

does he? [42]Has not the scripture said that the Messiah[f] is descended from David and comes from Bethlehem, the village where David lived?" [43]So there was a division in the crowd because of him. [44]Some of them wanted to arrest him, but no one laid hands on him.

The Unbelief of Those in Authority

45 Then the temple police went back to the chief priests and Pharisees, who asked them, "Why did you not arrest him?" [46]The police answered, "Never has anyone spoken like this!" [47]Then the Pharisees replied, "Surely you have not been deceived too, have you? [48]Has any one of the authorities or of the Pharisees believed in him? [49]But this crowd, which does not know the law – they are accursed." [50]Nicodemus, who had gone to Jesus[g] before, and who was one of them, asked, [51]"Our law does not judge people without first giving them a hearing to find out what they are doing, does it?" [52]They replied, "Surely you are not also from Galilee, are you? Search and you will see that no prophet is to arise from Galilee."

The Woman Caught in Adultery

8 [[[53]Then each of them went home, [1]while Jesus went to the Mount of

[c] Or *come to me and drink.* [38]*The one who believes in me, as*   [d] Gk *out of his belly*   [e] Other ancient authorities read *for as yet the Spirit* (others, [Holy Spirit]) *had not been given*   [f] Or *the Christ*   [g] Gk *him*

Each evening of the Feast of Booths, there was a joyful celebration in the Temple courtyard, lighted by four huge lamps. It is probably these that prompt Jesus, ever one to use visual aids to hand, to call himself the 'light of the world' (8:12). For the Jew, light symbolizes life, purity and guidance, and Jesus is claiming to be the true source of all three. Again he insists on his special relationship with his Father (8:16, 18, 26, 42, 54).

By contrast, he says that the Pharisees, who pride themselves on being the most acceptable of all to God, are actually earth-bound in their judgments (8:15), ignorant of God (8:19), slaves to sin (8:34), the children of the devil (8:44), and liars (8:55). Neither physical descent from Abraham (i.e. privileges of race), nor adherence to the externals of the Law while ignoring the inner demands of it, can save. No wonder the Jews are furious! From their point of view, Jesus is now clearly seen as a dangerous heretic attacking the Law: he must be destroyed (8:59).

Olives. [2]Early in the morning he came again to the temple. All the people came to him and he sat down and began to teach them. [3]The scribes and the Pharisees brought a woman who had been caught in adultery; and making her stand before all of them, [4]they said to him, "Teacher, this woman was caught in the very act of committing adultery. [5]Now in the law

♦ In the incident recorded by John, it is quite clear that the scribes and Pharisees were not really interested in upholding the Law but rather wanted to trap Jesus (John 8:6). In Deut. 22:23–4, stoning is the punishment decreed for both the man and the woman where the woman is engaged to be married to another man. The death penalty is prescribed in a number of other instances of sexual unfaithfulness (see, e.g. Lev 20:10ff.) but generally the exact mode of death is not specified. Had the Jewish leaders genuinely been indignant at the breaking of the law, they must have brought the guilty man also to Jesus. In fact, though the Law was indeed there in the Scriptures, it was probably only very rarely implemented in Jesus' day.

Why should there have been such strict laws in the first place? The reason is not primarily negative at all, but very positive. Marriage, the faithful permanent committedness to one another of a man and a woman, was God's good plan from before the Fall (Gen. 2:18–24). This relationship, and this alone, was to be the context within which man and woman expressed their sexuality. Any other sexual relationship, heterosexual or homosexual, temporary or long-term, was (and is) outside the will of God. In order to protect the divine blueprint of marriage, all other sexual relationships must be severely punished. In fact, so important is God's concept of marriage that it is used as a symbolic description of the relationship between Christ and the church (e.g. Eph. 5:25ff.).

The fact that the Bible has so much to say about sexual sin probably reflects the fact that our sexuality is a very powerful part of our personality and that it is all too easy to misuse what God designed to be a most beautiful and creative gift. There are many biblical examples of the suffering that follows from abusing the gift: David and Bathsheba (2 Sam. 11), Amnon and Tamar (2 Sam. 13), the story of Hosea, etc. The Scriptures realistically recount examples of adultery (sex outside marriage), fornication (usually but not exclusively sex before marriage), rape, and homosexuality, among others.

Modern Western culture strongly advocates the individual's right to total sexual freedom, though some activities (e.g. sexual abuse of children) are still theoretically repugnant; the frequency of their occurrence suggests that sanctions against them are not as strong as we might suppose. The fact is that any deviation from the Creator's design is not only sinful, but is also destructive. While women are, sadly, perfectly capable of being responsible for sexual sin, it is also true that women and children may suffer greatly at the hands of men in their lives. Further, sexual sin in one generation often bitterly damages the next. The church has a critical responsibility today to demonstrate faithful, winsome marriages.

Some women have been troubled by the apparent unfairness of the Old Testament rules that described a woman as being 'unclean' during menstruation (e.g. Lev. 15:25–30) or while still bleeding following the birth of a baby. Whatever the reasons behind those laws, clearly the Lord Jesus shows that they are no longer applicable when he deals with the woman with a longstanding gynaecological problem in Luke 8:43ff.

The story of John 8:3ff. does not by any means suggest that Jesus says sexual sin does not matter; he calls it sin, and tells the woman to turn from it. The story almost certainly expresses his indignation at the exploitation of a woman by men. It also shows us that for sexual sin as well as any other sin, there is the possibility of forgiveness and a new start. Jesus is the Savior of sinners. That is a crucial message for our generation ♦

Moses commanded us to stone such women. Now what do you say?" [6]They said this to test him, so that they might have some charge to bring against him. Jesus bent down and wrote with his finger on the ground. [7]When they kept on questioning him, he straightened up and said to them, "Let anyone among you who is without sin be the first to throw a stone at her." [8]And once again he bent down and wrote on the ground.[h] [9]When they heard it, they went away, one by one, beginning with the elders; and Jesus was left alone with the woman standing before him. [10]Jesus straightened up and said to her, "Woman, where are they? Has no one condemned you?" [11]She said, "No one, sir."[i] And Jesus said, "Neither do I condemn you. Go your way, and from now on do not sin again."]][j]

Jesus the Light of the World

[12] Again Jesus spoke to them, saying, "I am the light of the world. Whoever follows me will never walk in darkness but will have the light of life." [13]Then the Pharisees said to him, "You are testifying on your own behalf; your testimony is not valid." [14]Jesus answered, "Even if I testify on my own behalf, my testimony is valid because I know where I have come from and where I am going, but you do not know where I come from or where I am going. [15]You judge by human standards;[k] I judge no one. [16]Yet even if I do judge, my judgment is valid; for it is not I alone who judge, but I and the Father[l] who sent me. [17]In your law it is written that the testimony of two witnesses is valid. [18]I testify on my own behalf, and the Father who sent me testifies on my behalf." [19]Then they said to him, "Where is your Father?" Jesus answered, "You know neither me nor my Father. If you knew me, you would know my Father also." [20]He spoke these words while he was teaching in the treasury of the temple, but no one arrested him, because his hour had not yet come.

Jesus Foretells His Death

[21] Again he said to them, "I am going away, and you will search for me, but you will die in your sin. Where I am going, you cannot come." [22]Then the Jews said, "Is he going to kill himself? Is that what he means by saying, 'Where I am going, you cannot come'?" [23]He said to them, "You are from below, I am from above; you are of this world, I am not of this world. [24]I told you that you would die in your sins, for you will die in your sins unless you believe that I am he."[m] [25]They said to him, "Who are you?" Jesus said to them, "Why do I speak to you at all? [26]I have much to say about you and much to condemn; but the one who sent me is true, and I declare to the world what I have heard from him." [27]They did not understand that he was speaking to them about the Father. [28]So Jesus said, "When you have lifted up the Son of Man, then you will realize that I am he,[m] and that I do nothing on my own, but I speak these things as the Father instructed me. [29]And the one who sent me is with me; he has not left me alone, for I always do what is pleasing to him." [30]As he was saying these things, many believed in him.

True Disciples

[31] Then Jesus said to the Jews who had believed in him, "If you continue in my word, you are truly my disciples; [32]and you will know the truth, and the truth will make you free." [33]They answered him, "We are descendants of Abraham and have never been slaves to anyone. What do you mean by saying, 'You will be made free'?"

[34] Jesus answered them, "Very truly, I tell you, everyone who commits sin is a

[h] Other ancient authorities add *the sins of each of them*   [i] Or *Lord*   [j] The most ancient authorities lack 7.53–8.11; other authorities add the passage here or after 7.36 or after 21.25 or after Luke 21.38, with variations of text; some mark the passage as doubtful.   [k] Gk *according to the flesh*   [l] Other ancient authorities read *he*   [m] Gk *I am*   [n] Or *What I have told you from the beginning*

slave to sin. ³⁵The slave does not have a permanent place in the household; the son has a place there forever. ³⁶So if the Son makes you free, you will be free indeed. ³⁷I know that you are descendants of Abraham; yet you look for an opportunity to kill me, because there is no place in you for my word. ³⁸I declare what I have seen in the Father's presence; as for you, you should do what you have heard from the Father."^o

Jesus and Abraham

³⁹ They answered him, "Abraham is our father." Jesus said to them, "If you were Abraham's children, you would be doing^p what Abraham did, ⁴⁰but now you are trying to kill me, a man who has told you the truth that I heard from God. This is not what Abraham did. ⁴¹You are indeed doing what your father does." They said to him, "We are not illegitimate children; we have one father, God himself." ⁴²Jesus said to them, "If God were your Father, you would love me, for I came from God and now I am here. I did not come on my own, but he sent me. ⁴³Why do you not understand what I say? It is because you cannot accept my word. ⁴⁴You are from your father the devil, and you choose to do your father's desires. He was a murderer from the beginning and does not stand in the truth, because there is no truth in him. When he lies, he speaks according to his own nature, for he is a liar and the father of lies. ⁴⁵But because I tell the truth, you do not believe me. ⁴⁶Which of you convicts me of sin? If I tell the truth, why do you not believe me? ⁴⁷Whoever is from God hears the words of God. The reason you do not hear them is that you are not from God."

⁴⁸ The Jews answered him, "Are we not right in saying that you are a Samaritan and have a demon?" ⁴⁹Jesus answered, "I do not have a demon; but I honor my Father, and you dishonor me. ⁵⁰Yet I do not seek my own glory; there is one who seeks it and he is the judge. ⁵¹Very truly, I tell you, whoever keeps my word will never see death." ⁵²The Jews said to him, "Now we know that you have a demon. Abraham died, and so did the prophets; yet you say, 'Whoever keeps my word will never taste death.' ⁵³Are you greater than our father Abraham, who died? The prophets also died. Who do you claim to be?" ⁵⁴Jesus answered, "If I glorify myself, my glory is nothing. It is my Father who glorifies me, he of whom you say, 'He is our God,' ⁵⁵though you do not know him. But I know him; if I would say that I do not know him, I would be a liar like you. But I do know him and I keep his word. ⁵⁶Your ancestor Abraham rejoiced that he would see my day; he saw it and was glad." ⁵⁷Then the Jews said to him, "You are not yet fifty years old, and have you seen Abraham?"^q ⁵⁸Jesus said to them, "Very truly, I tell you, before Abraham was, I am." ⁵⁹So they picked up stones to throw at him, but Jesus hid himself and went out of the temple.

A Man Born Blind Receives Sight

9 As he walked along, he saw a man blind from birth. ²His disciples asked him, "Rabbi, who sinned, this man or his parents, that he was born blind?" ³Jesus answered, "Neither this man nor his

---

^o Other ancient authorities read *you do what you have heard from your father*   ^p Other ancient authorities read *If you are Abraham's children, then do*   ^q Other ancient authorities read *has Abraham seen you?*

THE MAN BORN BLIND (JOHN 9:1–41)

The disciples display a common assumption of their day, that to bear a handicapped child must be judgment for sin (see further the note on 'Children born with a handicap', p. 200). While indeed sin may lead to suffering, Jesus demolishes the disciples' simplistic equation. In this case, he says, God has a special purpose: to reveal through the blind man his powerful activity.

◆ In many cultures, parental grief (mourning for the loss of the perfect, anxiety over caring for the child in the future, heartache for what the child may face), especially for the mother, may be complicated by a sense of shame ('How can I face the world with this damaged child? I have failed') and a sense of guilt ('I must have done something wrong'). In some societies, there may be a belief that some spirit is taking revenge. Later, the child may also come to experience (false) guilt and shame. His or her anger may then be directed both at God and at the parents ('It's your fault that I'm suffering like this').

If the handicap is severe, there may be rejection. Some modern societies are obsessed with physical perfection. Women in particular can be burdened by failure to match up to what is perceived as a beautiful body. A mother who has come to a healthy acceptance of her own body may be best able to accept a handicapped child.

While it is true that sometimes parental sin can lead to a child's handicap (for example, parental sexual promiscuity may lead to disease which can blind the child before or at birth), Jesus makes it clear that there may be no direct connection in any individual between handicap and sin, except in so far as all imperfection is a result of the Fall.

Where handicap is detected before birth, a mother may be under great pressure to have an abortion. Most Christians believe abortion to be wrong because it destroys God-given life; if we oppose abortion, we must follow through with realistic support for families who carry the heavy burden of care for a handicapped person.

How can a handicap glorify God? Sometimes the Lord may intervene with direct healing. More often, it may be the compassionate love of the carers, or the grace to live positively with the handicap,

or demonstrating that all human life is precious, that honors God. Caring for the handicapped is an object lesson in God's love for us all: unconditional love for the helpless ◆

parents sinned; he was born blind so that God's works might be revealed in him. 4We[r] must work the works of him who sent me[s] while it is day; night is coming when no one can work. 5As long as I am in the world, I am the light of the world." 6When he had said this, he spat on the ground and made mud with the saliva and spread the mud on the man's eyes, 7saying to him, "Go, wash in the pool of Siloam" (which means Sent). Then he went and washed and came back able to see. 8The neighbors and those who had seen him before as a beggar began to ask, "Is this not the man who used to sit and beg?" 9Some were saying, "It is he." Others were saying, "No, but it is someone like him." He kept saying, "I am the man." 10But they kept asking him, "Then how were your eyes opened?" 11He answered, "The man called Jesus made mud, spread it on my eyes, and said to me, 'Go to Siloam and wash.' Then I went and washed and received my sight." 12They said to him, "Where is he?" He said, "I do not know."

The Pharisees Investigate the Healing

13 They brought to the Pharisees the man who had formerly been blind. 14Now it was a sabbath day when Jesus made the mud and opened his eyes. 15Then the Pharisees also began to ask him how he had received his sight. He said to them, "He put mud on my eyes. Then I washed, and now I see." 16Some of the Pharisees said, "This

[r] Other ancient authorities read *I*   [s] Other ancient authorities read *us*

John makes no suggestion that the blind man took any initiative, but when Jesus gives him orders he obeys without question. With his sight restored, all he can say to his neighbors is that 'I did what he said and now I can see' (9:11). To the Pharisees, consulted by the neighbors, he can only say the same again.

man is not from God, for he does not observe the sabbath." But others said, "How can a man who is a sinner perform such signs?" And they were divided. [17]So they said again to the blind man, "What do you say about him? It was your eyes he opened." He said, "He is a prophet."

[18] The Jews did not believe that he had been blind and had received his sight until they called the parents of the man who had received his sight [19]and asked them, "Is this your son, who you say was born blind? How then does he now see?" [20]His parents answered, "We know that this is our son, and that he was born blind; [21]but we do not know how it is that now he sees, nor do we know who opened his eyes. Ask him; he is of age. He will speak for himself." [22]His parents said this because they were afraid of the Jews; for the Jews had already agreed that anyone who confessed Jesus[t] to be the Messiah[u] would be put out of the synagogue. [23]Therefore his parents said, "He is of age; ask him."

[24] So for the second time they called the man who had been blind, and they said to him, "Give glory to God! We know that this man is a sinner." [25]He answered, "I do not know whether he is a sinner. One thing I do know, that though I was blind, now I see." [26]They said to him, "What did he do to you? How did he open your eyes?" [27]He answered them, "I have told you already, and you would not listen. Why do you want to hear it again? Do you also want to become his disciples?" [28]Then they reviled him, saying, "You are his disciple, but we are disciples of Moses. [29]We know that God has spoken to Moses, but as for this man, we do not know where he comes from." [30]The man answered, "Here is an astonishing thing! You do not know where he comes from, and yet he opened my eyes. [31]We know that God does not listen to sinners, but he does listen to one who worships him and obeys his will. [32]Never since the world began has it been heard that anyone opened the eyes of a person born blind. [33]If this man were not from God, he could do nothing." [34]They answered him, "You were born entirely in sins, and are you trying to teach us?" And they drove him out.

Spiritual Blindness

[35] Jesus heard that they had driven him out, and when he found him, he said, "Do you believe in the Son of Man?"[v] [36]He answered, "And who is he, sir?[w] Tell me, so that I may believe in him." [37]Jesus said to him, "You have seen him, and the one speaking with you is he." [38]He said, "Lord,[w] I believe." And he worshiped him. [39]Jesus said, "I came into this world for judgment so that those who do not see may see, and those who do see may become blind." [40]Some of the Pharisees near him heard this and said to him, "Surely we are not blind, are we?" [41]Jesus said to them, "If you were blind, you would not have sin. But now that you say, 'We see,' your sin remains.

[t] Gk *him*   [u] Or *the Christ*   [v] Other ancient authorities read *the Son of God*   [w] *Sir* and *Lord* translate the same Greek word

---

Their response is mixed. To some, it is inconceivable that a wicked man should be able to perform miracles (9:16). To others, the fact that yet again Jesus has ignored the traditions of Sabbath-keeping is proof positive that he can't have God's approval. Some want to discount the miracle: the man couldn't have been blind in the first place. His parents when summoned, fearful of social ostracism (9:22), do not wish to get involved. The healed man, questioned again, has no more information to give but has clearly decided that Jesus must be from God – and says so in no uncertain terms (9:30–33). Even punishment for daring to say such a thing does not deter his budding faith. When Jesus seeks him out again, and reveals his identity, the man responds in faith and worship. Physical sight is beautifully matched by spiritual sight.

Jesus the Good Shepherd

10 "Very truly, I tell you, anyone who does not enter the sheepfold by the gate but climbs in by another way is a thief and a bandit. ²The one who enters by the gate is the shepherd of the sheep. ³The gatekeeper opens the gate for him, and the sheep hear his voice. He calls his own sheep by name and leads them out. ⁴When he has brought out all his own, he goes ahead of them, and the sheep follow him because they know his voice. ⁵They will not follow a stranger, but they will run from him because they do not know the voice of strangers." ⁶Jesus used this figure of speech with them, but they did not understand what he was saying to them.

7 So again Jesus said to them, "Very truly, I tell you, I am the gate for the sheep. ⁸All who came before me are thieves and bandits; but the sheep did not listen to them. ⁹I am the gate. Whoever enters by me will be saved, and will come in and go out and find pasture. ¹⁰The thief comes only to steal and kill and destroy. I came that they may have life, and have it abundantly.

◆ What does Jesus mean when he speaks of 'life more abundantly'? To be sure, he includes the idea of eternal life: life that has no end, outside the realm of time, and the Christian's inheritance in the new birth. But Jesus also means us to understand that he came to bring qualitatively different life from that which we experience by being born physically.

This is the life of restored relationship with God, through which we become truly human. This is the life that comes when he who is the very origin of life itself makes his permanent home within us, and his life bubbles up through us. It is the life that is fully realized in the Kingdom, but which is already being formed within us. It is the life that nourishes us at the deepest possible level of our beings, and that gradually transforms our personalities so that we may more clearly reflect the life of Christ. It is the life that makes sin look tawdry to us, and holiness beautiful.

In John 10:10, while the thief comes only to diminish and destroy, Jesus is the one who protects and nurtures and provides for his people.

Some people have concluded that the promise of 'abundant life' guarantees them health, wealth and prosperity in the material and physical sphere. This cannot be what Jesus means, because on numerous occasions he makes it clear that suffering is part of Christian discipleship. He heals some, but not all, of those he meets. On no occasion is he recorded as making anyone wealthy. Rather, abundant life is God's gift to us in our circumstances, not as an escape from them ◆

11 "I am the good shepherd. The good shepherd lays down his life for the sheep. ¹²The hired hand, who is not the shepherd and does not own the sheep, sees the wolf coming and leaves the sheep and runs

JESUS THE GOOD SHEPHERD (JOHN 10:1–42)

The image of God as shepherd and of his people as sheep is a familiar one from the Old Testament. Jesus' application of the same metaphor to himself is another clear example of his persistent claim to be the Messiah, and John's Jewish readers would have been left in no doubt at all about what it meant.

The Jewish shepherd led, not drove, his sheep. He knew each beast individually and by name, and the sheep would respond to his voice and to no other. His life was bound up in his sheep; where a hired hand might run away in the event of attack, the genuine owner would defend them with his life. At night, he would lie across the doorway of the sheepfold to prevent either thieves or wild animals harming his flock. If necessary, he would die to defend them. Sometimes a large flock might be temporarily divided between different places for better feeding, but the shepherd's aim was to bring them all together as soon as possible.

away – and the wolf snatches them and scatters them. [13]The hired hand runs away because a hired hand does not care for the sheep. [14]I am the good shepherd. I know my own and my own know me, [15]just as the Father knows me and I know the Father. And I lay down my life for the sheep. [16]I have other sheep that do not belong to this fold. I must bring them also, and they will listen to my voice. So there will be one flock, one shepherd. [17]For this reason the Father loves me, because I lay down my life in order to take it up again. [18]No one takes[x] it from me, but I lay it down of my own accord. I have power to lay it down, and I have power to take it up again. I have received this command from my Father."

19 Again the Jews were divided because of these words. [20]Many of them were saying, "He has a demon and is out of his mind. Why listen to him?" [21]Others were saying, "These are not the words of one who has a demon. Can a demon open the eyes of the blind?"

Jesus Is Rejected by the Jews

22 At that time the festival of the Dedication took place in Jerusalem. It was winter, [23]and Jesus was walking in the temple, in the portico of Solomon. [24]So the Jews gathered around him and said to him, "How long will you keep us in suspense? If you are the Messiah,[y] tell us plainly." [25]Jesus answered, "I have told you, and you do not believe. The works that I do in my Father's name testify to me; [26]but you do not believe, because you do not belong to my sheep. [27]My sheep hear my voice. I know them, and they follow me. [28]I give them eternal life, and they will never perish. No one will snatch them out of my hand. [29]What my Father has given me is greater than all else, and no one can snatch it out of the Father's hand.[z] [30]The Father and I are one."

31 The Jews took up stones again to stone him. [32]Jesus replied, "I have shown you many good works from the Father. For which of these are you going to stone me?" [33]The Jews answered, "It is not for a good work that we are going to stone you, but for blasphemy, because you, though only a human being, are making yourself God." [34]Jesus answered, "Is it not written in your law,[a] 'I said, you are gods'? [35]If those to whom the word of God came were called 'gods' – and the scripture cannot be annulled – [36]can you say that the one whom the Father has sanctified and sent into the world is blaspheming because I said, 'I am God's Son'? [37]If I am not doing the works of my Father, then do not believe me. [38]But if I do them, even though you do not believe me, believe the works, so that you may know and understand[b] that the Father is in me and I am in the Father." [39]Then they tried to arrest him again, but he escaped from their hands.

40 He went away again across the Jordan to the place where John had been baptizing earlier, and he remained there. [41]Many came to him, and they were saying, "John performed no sign, but everything that John said about this man was true." [42]And many believed in him there.

[x] Other ancient authorities read *has taken*   [y] Or *the Christ*   [z] Other ancient authorities read *My Father who has given them to me is greater than all, and no one can snatch them out of the Father's hand*   [a] Other ancient authorities read *in the law*   [b] Other ancient authorities lack *and understand;* others read *and believe*

All these characteristics of the good shepherd Jesus picks up and applies to himself in relation to his 'people-sheep'. Once more, the response from the Jews is divided: is he demon possessed? Is he sane but a blasphemer? Is he who he says he is? Jesus says that if they do not recognize his divine authority, that is in itself proof that they are not numbered among the Father's flock (10:26). Beside themselves in their anger, the Jews try first to stone him and then to arrest him, but Jesus escapes to the countryside.

The Death of Lazarus

11 Now a certain man was ill, Lazarus of Bethany, the village of Mary and her sister Martha. ²Mary was the one who anointed the Lord with perfume and wiped his feet with her hair; her brother Lazarus was ill. ³So the sisters sent a message to Jesus,ᶜ "Lord, he whom you love is ill." ⁴But when Jesus heard it, he said, "This illness does not lead to death; rather it is for God's glory, so that the Son of God may be glorified through it." ⁵Accordingly, though Jesus loved Martha and her sister and Lazarus, ⁶after having heard that Lazarusᵈ was ill, he stayed two days longer in the place where he was.

7 Then after this he said to the disciples, "Let us go to Judea again." ⁸The disciples said to him, "Rabbi, the Jews were just now trying to stone you, and are you going there again?" ⁹Jesus answered, "Are there not twelve hours of daylight? Those who walk during the day do not stumble, because they see the light of this world. ¹⁰But those who walk at night stumble, because the light is not in them." ¹¹After saying this, he told them, "Our friend Lazarus has fallen asleep, but I am going there to awaken him." ¹²The disciples said to him, "Lord, if he has fallen asleep, he will be all right." ¹³Jesus, however, had been speaking about his death, but they thought that he was referring merely to sleep. ¹⁴Then Jesus told them plainly, "Lazarus is dead. ¹⁵For your sake I am glad I was not there, so that you may believe. But let us go to him." ¹⁶Thomas, who was called the Twin,ᵉ said to his fellow disciples, "Let us also go, that we may die with him."

Jesus the Resurrection and the Life

17 When Jesus arrived, he found that Lazarusᵈ had already been in the tomb four days. ¹⁸Now Bethany was near Jerusalem, some two milesᶠ away, ¹⁹and many of the Jews had come to Martha and Mary to console them about their brother. ²⁰When Martha heard that Jesus was coming, she went and met him, while Mary stayed at home. ²¹Martha said to Jesus, "Lord, if you had been here, my brother would not have died. ²²But even now I know that God will give you whatever you ask of him." ²³Jesus said to her, "Your brother will rise again." ²⁴Martha said to him, "I know that he will rise again in the resurrection on the last day." ²⁵Jesus said to her, "I am the resurrection and the life.ᵍ Those who believe in me,

ᶜ Gk *him* ᵈ Gk *he* ᵉ Gk *Didymus* ᶠ Gk *fifteen stadia* ᵍ Other ancient authorities lack *and the life*

JESUS, THE RESURRECTION AND THE LIFE (JOHN 11:1-57)

Repeatedly, Jesus demonstrates his descriptive titles: as the bread of life, he feeds a hungry crowd; as the light of the world, he restores sight to a blind man; as the good shepherd, he will die for his sheep. Now, as the resurrection and the life, he brings a dead man back to life. In each case, the visible symbol points to a greater invisible reality.

Lazarus, Martha and Mary are clearly dear friends of Jesus (11:5). We, like the sisters, might have expected Jesus to hurry to their aid as soon as he learnt of Lazarus' illness. But Jesus does not always do what we expect; he sees beyond the immediate circumstances to what may be far better. In this case, his delay brings great glory to God. His going at all, against the advice of his disciples who fear for his life, is secure because he knows the moment has not yet come for him to die.

For Martha and Mary, genuine grief at losing a loved brother is probably compounded by their vulnerability in losing their male protector. What will the future hold? Martha's 'If only . . .!' (11:21) is echoed by Mary (11:32). Yet each sister also clearly expresses deep trust in Jesus as Lord, and, in Martha's case, a profound recognition of his true identity (11:27). Jesus enters into their grief (11:35; see further the note on 'Mourning', p. 205).

even though they die, will live, ²⁶and everyone who lives and believes in me will never die. Do you believe this?" ²⁷She said to him, "Yes, Lord, I believe that you are the Messiah,ʰ the Son of God, the one coming into the world."

Jesus Weeps

28 When she had said this, she went back and called her sister Mary, and told her privately, "The Teacher is here and is calling for you." ²⁹And when she heard it, she got up quickly and went to him. ³⁰Now Jesus had not yet come to the village, but was still at the place where Martha had met him. ³¹The Jews who were with her in the house, consoling her, saw Mary get up quickly and go out. They followed her because they thought that she was going to the tomb to weep there. ³²When Mary came where Jesus was and saw him, she knelt at his feet and said to him, "Lord, if you had been here, my brother would not have died." ³³When Jesus saw her weeping, and the Jews who came with her also weeping, he was greatly disturbed in spirit and deeply moved. ³⁴He said, "Where have you laid him?" They said to him, "Lord, come and see." ³⁵Jesus began to weep. ³⁶So the Jews said, "See how he loved him!" ³⁷But some of them said, "Could not he who opened the eyes of the blind man have kept this man from dying?"

Jesus Raises Lazarus to Life

38 Then Jesus, again greatly disturbed, came to the tomb. It was a cave, and a stone was lying against it. ³⁹Jesus said, "Take away the stone." Martha, the sister of the dead

◆ John carefully records for us that Jesus wept in the face of the death of his friend, Lazarus. This should encourage us to accept that while we are not to grieve 'as those who have no hope' (1 Thess. 4:13), it is nonetheless perfectly natural to feel grief at the death of a loved one. Weeping is an expression of the pain at being torn apart, even though between believers the parting is only temporary. To weep can be profoundly therapeutic, though when it continues over a long period, or when it is accompanied by heavy despair, the bereaved person almost certainly needs professional help.

In Jesus' day, although burial had to take place as rapidly as possible, formal mourning usually lasted for seven days, during which family and friends would stay as much as possible with the bereaved. Such a pattern helps the bereaved person to pass from denial to acceptance that the one who has died really has gone, and provides a framework within which grief can be expressed very openly. This is much healthier than smothering it and 'putting on a brave face'. The latter usually leads to serious problems later. In some cultures, a bereaved person hides away in private. This may make it harder to face other people again afterwards, and intensify loneliness and dislocation.

Jewish custom expected that those who could afford to do so would hire professional mourners, including musicians. Perhaps it was the contrast between their (almost certainly) rather insincere mourning, and the deep grief of Martha

ʰ Or *the Christ*

Jesus' very public prayer (11:41–42), and direct command to the dead man, leads to Lazarus' resurrection. John includes details that highlight Lazarus' complete helplessness (11:44) but does not dwell on what must have been a totally extraordinary experience as the crowd watched him emerge. What does matter is that God is glorified as observers become believers.

The Pharisees' reaction is predictable. Jesus' activities may cause such social upheaval that the fragile truce with the Romans will be endangered, risking the annihilation of Temple and nation. Thus they rationalize (very plausibly) their rejection of their Messiah. Under Caiaphas' leadership, they actively plan Jesus' death.

and Mary, that made Jesus 'greatly disturbed in spirit' (John 11:33). Probably 'disturbed' means 'angry' or 'outraged'. More likely, Jesus is angered by death itself, the temporary victory of Satan. He would also be distressed that these dear friends could not yet comprehend what it meant that he was 'the resurrection and the life' (11:25) ◆

man, said to him, "Lord, already there is a stench because he has been dead four days." [40]Jesus said to her, "Did I not tell you that if you believed, you would see the glory of God?" [41]So they took away the stone. And Jesus looked upward and said, "Father, I thank you for having heard me. [42]I knew that you always hear me, but I have said this for the sake of the crowd standing here, so that they may believe that you sent me." [43]When he had said this, he cried with a loud voice, "Lazarus, come out!" [44]The dead man came out, his hands and feet bound with strips of cloth, and his face wrapped in a cloth. Jesus said to them, "Unbind him, and let him go."

The Plot to Kill Jesus

45 Many of the Jews therefore, who had come with Mary and had seen what Jesus did, believed in him. [46]But some of them went to the Pharisees and told them what he had done. [47]So the chief priests and the Pharisees called a meeting of the council, and said, "What are we to do? This man is performing many signs. [48]If we let him go on like this, everyone will believe in him, and the Romans will come and destroy both our holy place[i] and our nation." [49]But one of them, Caiaphas, who was high priest that year, said to them, "You know nothing at all! [50]You do not understand that it is better for you to have one man die for the people than to have the whole nation destroyed." [51]He did not say this on his own, but being high priest that year he prophesied that Jesus was about to die for the nation, [52]and not for the nation only, but to gather into one the dispersed children of God. [53]So from that day on they planned to put him to death.

54 Jesus therefore no longer walked about openly among the Jews, but went from there to a town called Ephraim in the region near the wilderness; and he remained there with the disciples.

55 Now the Passover of the Jews was near, and many went up from the country to Jerusalem before the Passover to purify themselves. [56]They were looking for Jesus and were asking one another as they stood in the temple, "What do you think? Surely he will not come to the festival, will he?" [57]Now the chief priests and the Pharisees had given orders that anyone who knew where Jesus[j] was should let them know, so that they might arrest him.

Mary Anoints Jesus

12 Six days before the Passover Jesus came to Bethany, the home of Lazarus, whom he had raised from the dead. [2]There they gave a dinner for him. Martha served, and Lazarus was one of those at the table with him. [3]Mary took a pound of

---

[i] Or *our temple*; Greek *our place*　[j] Gk *he*

THE HOUR HAS COME (JOHN 12:1-50)

Mary's true love for Jesus (12:3 – extravagant, costly, intuitive of what lay ahead – contrasts starkly with the fickle acclaim of the crowds (12:13, 18, 37). Only a slave was required to wash other people's dirty, sweaty feet. Mary declares herself the Lord's glad servant as she replaces water with perfume, a towel with her hair. Judas, perhaps finding Mary's open expression of love distasteful, certainly coveting wealth for himself, objects; Jesus gently affirms a woman's love expressed in a transparent woman's way, and commends her priorities (12:7-8; see further the note on 'Poverty, hunger and human need', p. 207).

costly perfume made of pure nard, anointed Jesus' feet, and wiped them[k] with her hair. The house was filled with the fragrance of the perfume. ⁴But Judas Iscariot, one of his disciples (the one who was about to betray him), said, ⁵"Why was this perfume not sold for three hundred denarii[l] and the money given to the poor?" ⁶(He said this not because he cared about the poor, but because he was a thief; he kept the common purse and used to steal what was put into it.) ⁷Jesus said, "Leave her alone. She bought it[m] so that she might keep it for the day of my burial. ⁸You always have the poor with you, but you do not always have me."

◆ Jesus is not justifying the existence of poverty; he is simply stating a fact. There is no biblical evidence that poverty will be eliminated on earth.

While sin or laziness may lead to poverty, more often in the Bible it is associated with exploitation or factors beyond the control of those who are poor. Consequently there are frequent injunctions addressed to those who are either wealthy or at least have material resources to care for the poor and needy (e.g. Deut. 15:1–11). On the one hand, personal possession is not wrong (otherwise, e.g., the Tenth Commandment becomes nonsense). On the other, ownership of material possessions carries with it responsibility to care compassionately for those who are in need rather than to be personally greedy and self-indulgent. This applies on an individual level and also for societies as a whole. Wealth is not wicked in and of itself (though it may have been acquired wickedly); but it is fraught with dangerous temptations.

Poverty does not make a person automatically acceptable to God, as some Liberation Theology implies. Whether we are rich or poor, we are sinners who need salvation through Jesus Christ. However, while the rich may be tempted to rely on their wealth, the poor may more readily know their dependence on God and their powerlessness to work out their own salvation. This may be why Jesus stated that he came to bring good news to the poor (Luke 4:18) and said, 'Blessed are you who are poor, for yours is the kingdom of God' (Luke 6:20). Self-reliance is a powerful obstacle to faith. Generosity from the poor is especially precious to God (see, e.g., the account in Mark 12:41–44 of the poor widow who gave all she had to God). This is because generosity reflects the very nature of God himself.

Christians today in the wealthy First World need to search our hearts. Much world poverty is exacerbated by greedy exploitation by our powerful governments and multi-national corporations. Our high lifestyle is at least in part at the expense of the world's poor. God holds us morally answerable for the way we obtain our wealth and for the way in which we spend it. Christians need to influence politics at every level to seek a more just society. At the same time, we need to support sacrificially those agencies that minister to the poor.

In the incident John records, the contrast is between ongoing care for the poor and an extraordinary pouring out of

---

[k] Gk *his feet*   [l] Three hundred denarii would be nearly a year's wages for a laborer   [m] Gk lacks *She bought it*

Already Jews from all over the world had gathered for Passover in Jerusalem. Excitedly, they greet him as victorious king, caught up in the testimony of those who have seen Lazarus alive and well again. The worst fears of the Pharisees are being realized, and they plot to kill Lazarus as well as Jesus (12:10) in order to destroy the evidence.

Now, says Jesus, the moment has come (12:23, 27). John's account does not draw much attention to the fact that years have passed since Jesus' ministry began. But he does now underline that 'not yet' has become 'now'.

an expensive love-gift for Jesus. Some would see that as justification for spending a large sum on a church building, for example. We need to be careful that that is not self-indulgence. The context of Mary's gift was unique. Perhaps today the Lord would rather we gave extravagantly to help the needy ◆

The Plot to Kill Lazarus

9 When the great crowd of the Jews learned that he was there, they came not only because of Jesus but also to see Lazarus, whom he had raised from the dead. [10]So the chief priests planned to put Lazarus to death as well, [11]since it was on account of him that many of the Jews were deserting and were believing in Jesus.

Jesus' Triumphal Entry into Jerusalem

12 The next day the great crowd that had come to the festival heard that Jesus was coming to Jerusalem. [13]So they took branches of palm trees and went out to meet him, shouting,

"Hosanna!
Blessed is the one who comes in the
    name of the Lord –
the King of Israel!"

[14]Jesus found a young donkey and sat on it; as it is written:
[15] "Do not be afraid, daughter of Zion.
    Look, your king is coming,
        sitting on a donkey's colt!"

[16]His disciples did not understand these things at first; but when Jesus was glorified, then they remembered that these things had been written of him and had been done to him. [17]So the crowd that had been with him when he called Lazarus out of the tomb and raised him from the dead continued to testify.[n] [18]It was also because they heard that he had performed this sign that the crowd went to meet him. [19]The Pharisees then said to one another, "You see, you can do nothing. Look, the world has gone after him!"

Some Greeks Wish to See Jesus

20 Now among those who went up to worship at the festival were some Greeks. [21]They came to Philip, who was from Bethsaida in Galilee, and said to him, "Sir, we wish to see Jesus." [22]Philip went and told Andrew; then Andrew and Philip went and told Jesus. [23]Jesus answered them, "The hour has come for the Son of Man to be glorified. [24]Very truly, I tell you, unless a grain of wheat falls into the earth and dies, it remains just a single grain; but if it dies, it bears much fruit. [25]Those who love their life lose it, and those who hate their life in this world will keep it for eternal life. [26]Whoever serves me must follow me, and where I am, there will my servant be also. Whoever serves me, the Father will honor.

Jesus Speaks about His Death

27 "Now my soul is troubled. And what should I say – 'Father, save me from this hour'? No, it is for this reason that I have come to this hour. [28]Father, glorify your name." Then a voice came from heaven, "I have glorified it, and I will glorify it again." [29]The crowd standing there heard it and said that it was thunder. Others said, "An angel has spoken to him." [30]Jesus answered, "This

[n] Other ancient authorities read *with him began to testify that he had called . . . from the dead*

It is in his death that he will be supremely glorified; it is through his death that he will draw people to himself (12:32). For all the signs of his life, few have truly believed (12:37ff.), and some of those who have are unwilling to pay the price of open allegiance (12:42). The paradoxical turning point will be his death. As at Jesus' baptism, the Father's confirming voice is heard from heaven (12:28). The Old Testament Scriptures bear witness to what is happening. Once more, Jesus claims without apology that he has the full authority of his Father, and that it is response to himself that is crucial.

voice has come for your sake, not for mine.
31 Now is the judgment of this world; now the
ruler of this world will be driven out. 32 And I,
when I am lifted up from the earth, will draw
all people[o] to myself." 33 He said this to indicate the kind of death he was to die. 34 The
crowd answered him, "We have heard from
the law that the Messiah[p] remains forever.
How can you say that the Son of Man must
be lifted up? Who is this Son of Man?" 35 Jesus
said to them, "The light is with you for a
little longer. Walk while you have the light,
so that the darkness may not overtake you. If
you walk in the darkness, you do not know
where you are going. 36 While you have the
light, believe in the light, so that you may
become children of light."

The Unbelief of the People

After Jesus had said this, he departed
and hid from them. 37 Although he had performed so many signs in their presence,
they did not believe in him. 38 This was to
fulfill the word spoken by the prophet
Isaiah:

"Lord, who has believed our message,
and to whom has the arm of the
Lord been revealed?"

39 And so they could not believe, because
Isaiah also said,

40 "He has blinded their eyes
and hardened their heart,
so that they might not look with their
eyes,
and understand with their heart and
turn –
and I would heal them."

41 Isaiah said this because[q] he saw his glory
and spoke about him. 42 Nevertheless many,
even of the authorities, believed in him.
But because of the Pharisees they did not
confess it, for fear that they would be
put out of the synagogue; 43 for they loved
human glory more than the glory that
comes from God.

Summary of Jesus' Teaching

44 Then Jesus cried aloud: "Whoever
believes in me believes not in me but in
him who sent me. 45 And whoever sees me
sees him who sent me. 46 I have come as
light into the world, so that everyone who
believes in me should not remain in the
darkness. 47 I do not judge anyone who hears
my words and does not keep them, for I
came not to judge the world, but to save the
world. 48 The one who rejects me and does
not receive my word has a judge; on the last
day the word that I have spoken will serve
as judge, 49 for I have not spoken on my own,
but the Father who sent me has himself
given me a commandment about what to
say and what to speak. 50 And I know that
his commandment is eternal life. What I
speak, therefore, I speak just as the Father
has told me."

Jesus Washes the Disciples' Feet

13 Now before the festival of the
Passover, Jesus knew that his hour
had come to depart from this world and go

[o] Other ancient authorities read *all things* [p] Or *the Christ* [q] Other ancient witnesses read *when*

THE LAST SUPPER (JOHN 13:1–30)

Luke tells us (Luke 22:24) the disciples had been arguing about rank and power. Jesus, secure in the knowledge that he truly is the one above all (John 13:3), vividly displays that true leadership lies in serving, not in self-aggrandizement. The King of Glory fulfills the role of a slave (cf. Phil. 2:5ff.). Behind this lesson lies another: Jesus alone can wash away the dirt of our lives that we call sin. At one moment, impetuous Peter wants less than Jesus offers; at the next, he wants more. But Jesus makes it clear that nothing must be taken away, and nothing can be added: his cleansing is perfect. The symbol of 'bathing' (John 13:10) is not a reference to baptism so much as to the spiritual truth to which baptism points: the need to be made clean by the atoning blood of the Lamb of God.

to the Father. Having loved his own who were in the world, he loved them to the end. ²The devil had already put it into the heart of Judas son of Simon Iscariot to betray him. And during supper ³Jesus, knowing that the Father had given all things into his hands, and that he had come from God and was going to God, ⁴got up from the table,ʳ took off his outer robe, and tied a towel around himself. ⁵Then he poured water into a basin and began to wash the disciples' feet and to wipe them with the towel that was tied around him. ⁶He came to Simon Peter, who said to him, "Lord, are you going to wash my feet?" ⁷Jesus answered, "You do not know now what I am doing, but later you will understand." ⁸Peter said to him, "You will never wash my feet." Jesus answered, "Unless I wash you, you have no share with me." ⁹Simon Peter said to him, "Lord, not my feet only but also my hands and my head!" ¹⁰Jesus said to him, "One who has bathed does not need to wash, except for the feet,ˢ but is entirely clean. And youᵗ are clean, though not all of you." ¹¹For he knew who was to betray him; for this reason he said, "Not all of you are clean."

12 After he had washed their feet, had put on his robe, and had returned to the table, he said to them, "Do you know what I have done to you? ¹³You call me Teacher and Lord – and you are right, for that is what I am. ¹⁴So if I, your Lord and Teacher, have washed your feet, you also ought to wash one another's feet. ¹⁵For I have set you an example, that you also should do as I have done to you. ¹⁶Very truly, I tell you, servantsᵘ are not greater than their master, nor are messengers greater than the one who sent them. ¹⁷If you know these things,

you are blessed if you do them. ¹⁸I am not speaking of all of you; I know whom I have chosen. But it is to fulfill the scripture, 'The one who ate my breadᵛ has lifted his heel against me.' ¹⁹I tell you this now, before it occurs, so that when it does occur, you may believe that I am he.ʷ ²⁰Very truly, I tell you, whoever receives one whom I send receives me; and whoever receives me receives him who sent me."

Jesus Foretells His Betrayal

21 After saying this Jesus was troubled in spirit, and declared, "Very truly, I tell you, one of you will betray me." ²²The disciples looked at one another, uncertain of whom he was speaking. ²³One of his disciples – the one whom Jesus loved – was reclining next to him; ²⁴Simon Peter therefore motioned to him to ask Jesus of whom he was speaking. ²⁵So while reclining next to Jesus, he asked him, "Lord, who is it?" ²⁶Jesus answered, "It is the one to whom I give this piece of bread when I have dipped it in the dish."ˣ So when he had dipped the piece of bread, he gave it to Judas son of Simon Iscariot.ʸ ²⁷After he received the piece of bread,ᶻ Satan entered into him. Jesus said to him, "Do quickly what you are going to do." ²⁸Now no one at the table knew why he said this to him. ²⁹Some thought that, because Judas had the common purse, Jesus was telling him, "Buy what we need for the festival"; or, that he

---

ʳ Gk *from supper*   ˢ Other ancient authorities lack *except for the feet*   ᵗ The Greek word for *you* here is plural   ᵘ Gk *slaves*   ᵛ Other ancient authorities read *ate bread with me*   ʷ Gk *I am*   ˣ Gk *dipped it*   ʸ Other ancient authorities read *Judas Iscariot son of Simon*; others, *Judas son of Simon from Karyot* (Kerioth)   ᶻ Gk *After the piece of bread*

The disciples are all too well aware of the danger posed by the religious leaders. Now Jesus stuns them by declaring that it is from among themselves that he will be betrayed. In their confusion, they do not understand the pointer Jesus has given them; when Judas leaves, they assume he has an errand to run for the Master. Poignantly, so he has: to fulfill the Scripture (13:18). Rejecting Jesus' proffered love and light, Judas by choice becomes the instrument of Satan, symbolized by darkness (13:30). The greatest battle of all is joined.

should give something to the poor. ³⁰So, after receiving the piece of bread, he immediately went out. And it was night.

The New Commandment

31 When he had gone out, Jesus said, "Now the Son of Man has been glorified, and God has been glorified in him. ³²If God has been glorified in him,ᵃ God will also glorify him in himself and will glorify him at once. ³³Little children, I am with you only a little longer. You will look for me; and as I said to the Jews so now I say to you, 'Where I am going, you cannot come.' ³⁴I give you a new commandment, that you love one another. Just as I have loved you, you also should love one another. ³⁵By this everyone will know that you are my disciples, if you have love for one another."

Jesus Foretells Peter's Denial

36 Simon Peter said to him, "Lord, where are you going?" Jesus answered, "Where I am going, you cannot follow me now; but you will follow afterward." ³⁷Peter said to him, "Lord, why can I not follow you now? I will lay down my life for you." ³⁸Jesus answered, "Will you lay down your life for me? Very truly, I tell you, before the cock crows, you will have denied me three times.

Jesus the Way to the Father

14 "Do not let your hearts be troubled. Believeᵇ in God, believe also in me.

²In my Father's house there are many dwelling places. If it were not so, would I have told you that I go to prepare a place for you?ᶜ ³And if I go and prepare a place for you, I will come again and will take you to myself, so that where I am, there you may be also. ⁴And you know the way to the place where I am going."ᵈ ⁵Thomas said to him, "Lord, we do not know where you are going. How can we know the way?" ⁶Jesus said to him, "I am the way, and the truth, and the life. No one comes to the Father except through me. ⁷If you know me, you will knowᵉ my Father also. From now on you do know him and have seen him."

8 Philip said to him, "Lord, show us the Father, and we will be satisfied." ⁹Jesus said to him, "Have I been with you all this time, Philip, and you still do not know me? Whoever has seen me has seen the Father. How can you say, 'Show us the Father'? ¹⁰Do you not believe that I am in the Father and the Father is in me? The words that I say to you I do not speak on my own; but the Father who dwells in me does his works. ¹¹Believe me that I am in the Father and the Father is in me; but if you do not, then believe me because of the works themselves. ¹²Very

ᵃ Other ancient authorities lack *If God has been glorified in him*   ᵇ Or *You believe*   ᶜ Or *If it were not so, I would have told you; for I go to prepare a place for you*   ᵈ Other ancient authorities read *Where I am going you know, and the way you know*   ᵉ Other ancient authorities read *If you had known me, you would have known*

JESUS' FINAL TEACHING: PART 1 (JOHN 13:31–14:31)

Judas' leaving to set in motion Jesus' arrest, trial and death, is a decisive moment (13:31): the Father affirms that the glory of his son is seen above all in his crucifixion.

Jesus builds on the lessons he has just taught and calls the disciples to sacrificial love for one another, not competition with each other, nor the seeking to dominate which is the hallmark of fallen relationships. There is a compelling testimony to Jesus in such love (13:35). Peter promises the dramatic gesture of dying for his Lord; Jesus knows such a promise is soon to be broken. The proof of love is deed, not word.

Even at this late juncture, John shows how limited is the disciples' grasp of Jesus' mission (14:5, 9). Jesus asserts that he exclusively is 'the way, and the truth, and the life' (14:6), and that in seeing him the disciples are seeing God (14:9). Because he is returning to his Father, he will do greater things than they have already seen (14:12). His death is a gateway, not a shut door.

truly, I tell you, the one who believes in me will also do the works that I do and, in fact, will do greater works than these, because I am going to the Father. [13]I will do whatever you ask in my name, so that the Father may be glorified in the Son. [14]If in my name you ask me[f] for anything, I will do it.

The Promise of the Holy Spirit

15 "If you love me, you will keep[g] my commandments. [16]And I will ask the Father, and he will give you another Advocate,[h] to be with you forever. [17]This is the Spirit of truth, whom the world cannot receive, because it neither sees him nor knows him. You know him, because he abides with you, and he will be in[i] you.

18 "I will not leave you orphaned; I am coming to you. [19]In a little while the world will no longer see me, but you will see me; because I live, you also will live. [20]On that day you will know that I am in my Father, and you in me, and I in you. [21]They who have my commandments and keep them are those who love me; and those who love me will be loved by my Father, and I will love them and reveal myself to them." [22]Judas (not Iscariot) said to him, "Lord, how is it that you will reveal yourself to us, and not to the world?" [23]Jesus answered him, "Those who love me will keep my word, and my Father will love them, and we will come to

them and make our home with them. [24]Whoever does not love me does not keep my words; and the word that you hear is not mine, but is from the Father who sent me.

25 "I have said these things to you while I am still with you. [26]But the Advocate,[h] the Holy Spirit, whom the Father will send in my name, will teach you everything, and remind you of all that I have said to you. [27]Peace I leave with you; my peace I give to you. I do not give to you as the world gives. Do not let your hearts be troubled, and do not let them be afraid. [28]You heard me say to you, 'I am going away, and I am coming to you.' If you loved me, you would rejoice that I am going to the Father, because the Father is greater than I. [29]And now I have told you this before it occurs, so that when it does occur, you may believe. [30]I will no longer talk much with you, for the ruler of this world is coming. He has no power over me; [31]but I do as the Father has commanded me, so that the world may know that I love the Father. Rise, let us be on our way.

Jesus the True Vine

15 "I am the true vine, and my Father is the vinegrower. [2]He removes

[f] Other ancient authorities lack *me*   [g] Other ancient authorities read *me, keep*   [h] Or *Helper*   [i] Or *among*

Because he has authority to ask the Father for anything, and be granted it (14:14), he promises that the Spirit of truth, whom they have already begun to know, will make his permanent home within them (14:16–17). The Spirit will recall to them all that Jesus has taught them, the significance of much of which they only very dimly discern as yet. It will become clear in the light of Jesus' death and resurrection, and the events of Pentecost. As they remember and understand what Jesus has taught, obeying that word will be the evidence of love (14:21). Father, Son and Spirit will delight to 'make their home' (14:23) with such disciples.

Aware of their deep fear and distress, Jesus repeatedly comforts them with the promise that his death is not the end. Rather it is the beginning of something far more glorious: provision for the sin of the past, the ministry of the Spirit in the present, and a place face to face with God in the future. No wonder their hearts, and ours, are to be at peace!

JESUS' FINAL TEACHING: PART 2 (JOHN 15:1–16:33)

Perhaps at this point (14:31) Jesus and the disciples start on their walk to Gethsemane. Time to teach them is running out. Every word is etched on their memories, recalled by the Spirit.

every branch in me that bears no fruit. Every branch that bears fruit he prunes[j] to make it bear more fruit. [3]You have already been cleansed[j] by the word that I have spoken to you. [4]Abide in me as I abide in you. Just as the branch cannot bear fruit by itself unless it abides in the vine, neither can you unless you abide in me. [5]I am the vine, you are the branches. Those who abide in me and I in them bear much fruit, because apart from me you can do nothing. [6]Whoever does not abide in me is thrown away like a branch and withers; such branches are gathered, thrown into the fire, and burned. [7]If you abide in me, and my words abide in you, ask for whatever you wish, and it will be done for you. [8]My Father is glorified by this, that you bear much fruit and become[k] my disciples. [9]As the Father has loved me, so I have loved you; abide in my love. [10]If you keep my commandments, you will abide in my love, just as I have kept my Father's commandments and abide in his love. [11]I have said these things to you so that my joy may be in you, and that your joy may be complete.

12 "This is my commandment, that you love one another as I have loved you. [13]No one has greater love than this, to lay down one's life for one's friends. [14]You are my friends if you do what I command you. [15]I do not call you servants[l] any longer, because the servant[m] does not know what the master is doing; but I have called you friends, because I have made known to you everything that I have heard from my Father. [16]You did not choose me but I chose you. And I appointed you to go and bear fruit, fruit that will last, so that the Father will give you whatever you ask him in my name. [17]I am giving you these commands so that you may love one another.

The World's Hatred
18 "If the world hates you, be aware that it hated me before it hated you. [19]If you belonged to the world,[n] the world would love you as its own. Because you do not belong to the world, but I have chosen you out of the world – therefore the world hates you. [20]Remember the word that I said to you, 'Servants[l] are not greater than their master.' If they persecuted me, they will

---

[i] The same Greek root refers to pruning and cleansing   [k] Or *be*   [l] Gk *slaves*   [m] Gk *slave*   [n] Gk *were of the world*

Jesus develops the metaphor of the vine (15:1–8) and then comments on it (15:9–17). Both sections revolve around 'abiding' (15:4–7, 9–10) and fruitfulness (15:5, 16). Each draws attention to a new beginning: the vine is no longer faithless Israel but Jesus the perfect one (15:1); and a new intimate and privileged relationship is established as servants become friends (15:15). It is incorporation into Jesus rather than into Israel that matters. It is intimacy with Jesus that produces fruit. The Father will strip away the unfruitful, by definition those who are not embracing the Son, and destroy them (15:6). Love for Jesus, evidenced by keeping his commandments, must also produce love for one another that is willing to lay down one's life. Love, abiding (ongoing relationship), fruitfulness and prayer are inextricably linked (15:7, 16) and bring glory to God (15:8).

John has earlier told us that it was because of his love for the world that God gave his only son (3:16). Now Jesus sadly shows how that love is met with hatred: hatred for himself, and, by extension, hatred for his disciples. The reason is given in 7:7: 'it hates me because I testify against it that its works are evil'. Those who abide in Christ will surely produce fruits of godliness, and it is this that angers the world and leads to persecution. Persecution of Christian disciples, says Jesus, is not some aberration but the inevitable consequence of the world's rejection of himself. The world no longer has any excuse for its sin (15:22). Even those who are religious leaders, thinking they are serving God, will persecute them (16:2); the awesome truth is that in rejecting Jesus they show that they do not know God at all.

persecute you; if they kept my word, they will keep yours also. [21]But they will do all these things to you on account of my name, because they do not know him who sent me. [22]If I had not come and spoken to them, they would not have sin; but now they have no excuse for their sin. [23]Whoever hates me hates my Father also. [24]If I had not done among them the works that no one else did, they would not have sin. But now they have seen and hated both me and my Father. [25]It was to fulfill the word that is written in their law, 'They hated me without a cause.'

[26] "When the Advocate° comes, whom I will send to you from the Father, the Spirit of truth who comes from the Father, he will testify on my behalf. [27]You also are to testify because you have been with me from the beginning.

16 "I have said these things to you to keep you from stumbling. [2]They will put you out of the synagogues. Indeed, an hour is coming when those who kill you will think that by doing so they are offering worship to God. [3]And they will do this because they have not known the Father or me. [4]But I have said these things to you so that when their hour comes you may remember that I told you about them.

The Work of the Spirit

"I did not say these things to you from the beginning, because I was with you. [5]But now I am going to him who sent me; yet none of you asks me, 'Where are you going?' [6]But because I have said these things to you, sorrow has filled your hearts. [7]Nevertheless I tell you the truth: it is to your advantage that I go away, for if I do not go away, the Advocate° will not come to you; but if I go, I will send him to you. [8]And when he comes, he will prove the world wrong about[p] sin and righteousness and judgment: [9]about sin, because they do not believe in me; [10]about righteousness, because I am going to the Father and you will see me no longer; [11]about judgment, because the ruler of this world has been condemned.

[12] "I still have many things to say to you, but you cannot bear them now. [13]When the Spirit of truth comes, he will guide you into all the truth; for he will not speak on his own, but will speak whatever he hears, and he will declare to you the things that are to come. [14]He will glorify me, because he will take what is mine and declare it to you. [15]All that the Father has is mine. For this reason I said that he will take what is mine and declare it to you.

Sorrow Will Turn into Joy

[16] "A little while, and you will no longer see me, and again a little while, and

° Or *Helper*   [p] Or *convict the world of*

Jesus returns to his earlier theme of the advantage that comes from his leaving the disciples (16:7). In particular, the Spirit will powerfully bear witness to Jesus (15:26) and force the world to face sin, righteousness and judgment on Jesus' terms. As a result, some will turn in repentance and faith, acknowledging Jesus for who he is, the Son of God. Others will reject the Spirit's witness as the world did Jesus in the flesh, and be confirmed in their route to destruction.

There is no way in which the disciples can be spared the coming trauma of their Master's death, any more than a woman can be spared the realities of childbirth when she comes to term (16:20ff.; see further the note on 'Labor and childbirth', p. 215). But, just as the suffering for the woman is swallowed up in delight when she holds her baby in her arms, so the disciples' grief will give way to joy when the Lord returns from the dead. After that, they will know that 'nothing can separate us from the love of God that is in Christ Jesus our Lord' (Rom. 8:39). There will be joy that cannot be taken away (John 16:22) and prayerful confidence (16:23–24). Moreover, then all that now seems puzzling will be radiantly clear (16:25).

Indeed, already the disciples begin to see (16:29): now they know and believe (16:30). Yet, says Jesus, they are all about to desert him (16:32). Only his Father will stand by him now.

you will see me." [17]Then some of his disciples said to one another, "What does he mean by saying to us, 'A little while, and you will no longer see me, and again a little while, and you will see me'; and 'Because I am going to the Father'?" [18]They said, "What does he mean by this 'a little while'? We do not know what he is talking about." [19]Jesus knew that they wanted to ask him, so he said to them, "Are you discussing among yourselves what I meant when I said, 'A little while, and you will no longer see me, and again a little while, and you will see me'? [20]Very truly, I tell you, you will weep and mourn, but the world will rejoice; you will have pain, but your pain will turn into joy. [21]When a woman is in labor, she has pain, because her hour has come. But when her child is born, she no longer remembers the anguish because of the joy of having brought a human being into the world. [22]So you have pain now; but I will see you again, and your hearts will rejoice, and no one will take your joy from you. [23]On that day you will ask nothing of me.[q] Very truly, I tell you, if you ask anything of the Father in my name, he will give it to you.[r] [24]Until now you have not asked for anything in my name. Ask and you will receive, so that your joy may be complete.

◆ In some Western societies, pain associated with childbirth may be greatly reduced by medical intervention. While not condoning the attitude of former generations (especially the men!) that women deserved to suffer as much pain as possible in childbirth (deriving from a faulty interpretation of Gen. 3:16 as prescriptive; cf. the widespread hostility towards the introduction of anaesthetics in childbirth in the mid-nineteenth century), nor believing in suffering for suffering's sake, nonetheless Christians would do well to ponder the biblical truth that suffering can be very fruitful. Our hedonistic society believes suffering should be avoided at all costs. God says

there are good things to be learned and achieved through suffering (cf. 1 Pet. 1:3–7; 4:12–13). Above all, our model is the Lord Jesus, whose name is 'Suffering Servant'.

Jesus uses the illustration of childbirth here precisely because there has to be a time of pain, grief and suffering before joy can come. While it lasts, the suffering may fill our consciousness. But, so great will be the quality of the joy, the memory of the suffering will fade away. This is not denial of real pain; it is recognition that its productive end is such as to make it all worthwhile.

The picture Jesus uses is a common Old Testament motif. Isaiah, for example (e.g. Is. 21:2–3; 26:16–21; 66:7–14) uses the metaphor of childbirth to describe the great suffering God's people must endure before the promised Messiah comes; then their pain will be swallowed up in joy unspeakable. In Jesus' day, there was a widespread expectation that current suffering as a subject nation might soon be ushering in the Messiah. Sadly, they didn't recognize him when he came ◆

Peace for the Disciples

25 "I have said these things to you in figures of speech. The hour is coming when I will no longer speak to you in figures, but will tell you plainly of the Father. [26]On that day you will ask in my name. I do not say to you that I will ask the Father on your behalf; [27]for the Father himself loves you, because you have loved me and have believed that I came from God.[s] [28]I came from the Father and have come into the world; again, I am leaving the world and am going to the Father."

29 His disciples said, "Yes, now you are speaking plainly, not in any figure of speech! [30]Now we know that you know all things, and do not need to have anyone question you; by this we believe that you

[q] Or *will ask me no question*   [r] Other ancient authorities read *Father, he will give it to you in my name*   [s] Other ancient authorities read *the Father*

came from God." [31]Jesus answered them, "Do you now believe? [32]The hour is coming, indeed it has come, when you will be scattered, each one to his home, and you will leave me alone. Yet I am not alone because the Father is with me. [33]I have said this to you, so that in me you may have peace. In the world you face persecution. But take courage; I have conquered the world!"

Jesus Prays for His Disciples

17 After Jesus had spoken these words, he looked up to heaven and said, "Father, the hour has come; glorify your Son so that the Son may glorify you, [2]since you have given him authority over all people,[t] to give eternal life to all whom you have given him. [3]And this is eternal life, that they may know you, the only true God, and Jesus Christ whom you have sent. [4]I glorified you on earth by finishing the work that you gave me to do. [5]So now, Father, glorify me in your own presence with the glory that I had in your presence before the world existed.

[6] "I have made your name known to those whom you gave me from the world. They were yours, and you gave them to me, and they have kept your word. [7]Now they know that everything you have given me is from you; [8]for the words that you gave to me I have given to them, and they have received them and know in truth that I came from you; and they have believed that you sent me. [9]I am asking on their behalf; I am not asking on behalf of the world, but on behalf of those whom you gave me, because they are yours. [10]All mine are yours, and yours are mine; and I have been glorified in them. [11]And now I am no longer in the world, but they are in the world, and I am coming to you. Holy Father, protect them in your name that[u] you have given me, so that they may be one, as we are one. [12]While I was with them, I protected them in your name that[u] you have given me. I guarded them, and not one of them was lost except the one destined to be lost,[v] so that the scripture might be fulfilled. [13]But now I am coming to you, and I speak these things in the world so that they may have my joy made complete in themselves.[w] [14]I have given them your word, and the world has hated them because they do not belong to the world, just as I do not belong to the world. [15]I am not asking you to take them out of the world, but I ask you to protect them from the evil one.[x] [16]They do not belong to the world, just as I do not belong to the world. [17]Sanctify them in the truth;

[t] Gk *flesh*　[u] Other ancient authorities read *protected in your name those whom*　[v] Gk *except the son of destruction*　[w] Or *among themselves*　[x] Or *from evil*

JESUS PRAYS (JOHN 17:1–26)

We do not know whether John, memory jogged by the Spirit, is quoting Jesus exactly, or whether he is reconstructing this great prayer. Nor do we know whether, as in 11:41–42, Jesus prays out loud primarily for the benefit of the people around him, in this case the disciples. In neither case does it matter very much. Whether literal transcription or literary device, whether eavesdropping or not, the prayer gathers up the themes of the Gospel so far and then ushers us towards the climax of death and resurrection.

The prayer has three main sections. First, Jesus prays for himself (17:1–5); then he prays for his disciples (17:6–19); lastly he prays for the church that is to come (17:20–26). Each section is both recapitulation and development.

For himself, the key lies in his prayer for reciprocal glory. Indeed, it had already been there before creation (17:5). Now it needs to be established again; the very purpose for which he came, to give eternal life, rests upon it. The glory of the Creator, and the glory of the Re-creator, are one and the same. Although the terrible cross still lies ahead, it is totally inevitable, and so Jesus may rightly say that he has finished the work he had been given to do (17:4).

your word is truth. [18]As you have sent me into the world, so I have sent them into the world. [19]And for their sakes I sanctify myself, so that they also may be sanctified in truth.

20 "I ask not only on behalf of these, but also on behalf of those who will believe in me through their word, [21]that they may all be one. As you, Father, are in me and I am in you, may they also be in us,[y] so that the world may believe that you have sent me. [22]The glory that you have given me I have given them, so that they may be one, as we are one, [23]I in them and you in me, that they may become completely one, so that the world may know that you have sent me and have loved them even as you have loved me. [24]Father, I desire that those also, whom you have given me, may be with me where I am, to see my glory, which you have given me because you loved me before the foundation of the world.

25 "Righteous Father, the world does not know you, but I know you; and these know that you have sent me. [26]I made your name known to them, and I will make it known, so that the love with which you have loved me may be in them, and I in them."

The Betrayal and Arrest of Jesus

18 After Jesus had spoken these words, he went out with his disciples across the Kidron valley to a place where there was a garden, which he and his disciples entered. [2]Now Judas, who betrayed him, also knew the place, because Jesus often met there with his disciples. [3]So Judas brought a detachment of soldiers together with police from the chief priests and the Pharisees, and they came there with lanterns and torches and weapons. [4]Then Jesus, knowing all that was to happen to him, came forward and asked them, "Whom are you looking for?" [5]They answered, "Jesus of Nazareth."[z] Jesus replied, "I am he."[a] Judas, who betrayed him, was standing with them. [6]When Jesus[b] said to them, "I am he,"[a] they stepped back and fell to the ground. [7]Again he asked them, "Whom are you looking for?" And they said, "Jesus of Nazareth."[z] [8]Jesus answered, "I told you that I am he.[a] So if you are looking for me, let these men go." [9]This was to fulfill the word that he had

[y] Other ancient authorities read *be one in us*
[z] Gk *the Nazorean*   [a] Gk *I am*   [b] Gk *he*

The disciples were the Father's gift to the Son out of the world (17:6), and they have come to acknowledge Christ's origin in God. Now, as he must leave them, and as the hatred of the world intensifies, Jesus prays for their protection from all the onslaughts of the devil (17:15). The solution is not that they should be withdrawn from the world, but that they should have the resources of God to remain faithful to him in it. Let God's Word – alive, conveying his creative power and authority (John 1:1–3; cf. Gen. 1:3, 9, 11 etc.) – set the disciples apart to reflect God's holiness, even within the context of an opposing world. Harmony and oneness is one way in which that reflection will be displayed (John 17:11).

That unity is clear evidence of the supernatural activity of God; it is humanly impossible. But, not only do the disciples need it; so too do all those who are yet to come who will belong to Jesus as the rest of time unrolls. These are already gifted to him by the Father, and their destiny is to 'be with me where I am, to see my glory' (17:24). John has brought us back full circle to where he began in his great Prologue: in Christ, time and eternity meet.

THE TRIAL AND CRUCIFIXION (JOHN 18:1–19:42)

Both Roman and Jewish authorities were sensitive to the possibility of an uprising when crowds gathered to celebrate a religious festival, above all at Passover with its strong reminiscence of past deliverance. Probably unsure as to how much popular support there might be for Jesus, a large group of Roman soldiers and Jewish Temple police arrive to arrest him. Judas knows exactly where to find him.

spoken, "I did not lose a single one of those whom you gave me." [10]Then Simon Peter, who had a sword, drew it, struck the high priest's slave, and cut off his right ear. The slave's name was Malchus. [11]Jesus said to Peter, "Put your sword back into its sheath. Am I not to drink the cup that the Father has given me?"

Jesus before the High Priest

12 So the soldiers, their officer, and the Jewish police arrested Jesus and bound him. [13]First they took him to Annas, who was the father-in-law of Caiaphas, the high priest that year. [14]Caiaphas was the one who had advised the Jews that it was better to have one person die for the people.

Peter Denies Jesus

15 Simon Peter and another disciple followed Jesus. Since that disciple was known to the high priest, he went with Jesus into the courtyard of the high priest, [16]but Peter was standing outside at the gate. So the other disciple, who was known to the high priest, went out, spoke to the woman who guarded the gate, and brought Peter in. [17]The woman said to Peter, "You are not also one of this man's disciples, are you?" He said, "I am not." [18]Now the slaves and the police had made a charcoal fire because it was cold, and they were standing around it and warming themselves. Peter also was standing with them and warming himself.

The High Priest Questions Jesus

19 Then the high priest questioned Jesus about his disciples and about his teaching. [20]Jesus answered, "I have spoken openly to the world; I have always taught in synagogues and in the temple, where all the Jews come together. I have said nothing in secret. [21]Why do you ask me? Ask those who heard what I said to them; they know what I said." [22]When he had said this, one of the police standing nearby struck Jesus on the face, saying, "Is that how you answer the high priest?" [23]Jesus answered, "If I have spoken wrongly, testify to the wrong. But if I have spoken rightly, why do you strike me?" [24]Then Annas sent him bound to Caiaphas the high priest.

Peter Denies Jesus Again

25 Now Simon Peter was standing and warming himself. They asked him, "You

---

Jesus gives himself up. No force is required. He deliberately and steadfastly walks into the will of God (18:11). Only Peter makes a gesture of defiance.

Desperate not to have Jesus give them the slip, the soldiers and police bind Jesus and take him first to Annas, then to Caiaphas, the senior leaders of the religious establishment. Both in turn interrogate him. Clearly, if they can get him to incriminate himself by claiming to be the Son of God in their hearing, they can charge him with blasphemy of the gravest order and make themselves look innocent. Jesus throws the onus back on them by countering question with question (18:21, 23).

Peter, too, is faced with questions. Torn between wanting to know what was happening to his Master, and fear for his own life, he three times denies having any association with Jesus. As the cock crows, how heartbreakingly hollow now must sound his passionate promise of only a few hours before (13:37–38). He too, like Judas, has betrayed the Lord. Unlike Judas, Peter will have a way back.

Determined to do away with Jesus, yet frustrated in not being able to pin an exact charge upon him (18:30), the Jews take Jesus to Pilate, the Roman Governor and the one responsible to the Roman Emperor for keeping the peace in Palestine. If there were to be an uprising, Pilate would be likely to lose his head as punishment. He would prefer not to take responsibility for condemning a man whose guilt eluded him (18:31, 38), yet he dare not precipitate a riot either. The Jews are clearly bent on having Jesus' blood, but may not themselves put anyone to death, so they need Pilate. At the same time, they can manipulate him by threatening to report that he did nothing about a man who claimed to be the King of the Jews, a threat to Rome.

are not also one of his disciples, are you?" He denied it and said, "I am not." ²⁶One of the slaves of the high priest, a relative of the man whose ear Peter had cut off, asked, "Did I not see you in the garden with him?" ²⁷Again Peter denied it, and at that moment the cock crowed.

Jesus before Pilate

28 Then they took Jesus from Caiaphas to Pilate's headquarters.ᶜ It was early in the morning. They themselves did not enter the headquarters,ᶜ so as to avoid ritual defilement and to be able to eat the Passover. ²⁹So Pilate went out to them and said, "What accusation do you bring against this man?" ³⁰They answered, "If this man were not a criminal, we would not have handed him over to you." ³¹Pilate said to them, "Take him yourselves and judge him according to your law." The Jews replied, "We are not permitted to put anyone to death." ³²(This was to fulfill what Jesus had said when he indicated the kind of death he was to die.)

33 Then Pilate entered the headquartersᶜ again, summoned Jesus, and asked him, "Are you the King of the Jews?" ³⁴Jesus answered, "Do you ask this on your own, or did others tell you about me?" ³⁵Pilate replied, "I am not a Jew, am I? Your own nation and the chief priests have handed you over to me. What have you done?" ³⁶Jesus answered, "My kingdom is not from this world. If my kingdom were from this world, my followers would be fighting to keep me from being handed over to the Jews. But as it is, my kingdom is not from here." ³⁷Pilate asked him, "So you are a king?" Jesus answered, "You say that I am a king. For this I was born, and for this I came into the world, to testify to the truth. Everyone who belongs to the truth listens to my voice." ³⁸Pilate asked him, "What is truth?"

Jesus Sentenced to Death

After he had said this, he went out to the Jews again and told them, "I find no case against him. ³⁹But you have a custom that I release someone for you at the Passover. Do you want me to release for you the King of the Jews?" ⁴⁰They shouted in reply, "Not this man, but Barabbas!" Now Barabbas was a bandit.

19 Then Pilate took Jesus and had him flogged. ²And the soldiers wove a crown of thorns and put it on his head, and they dressed him in a purple robe. ³They kept coming up to him, saying, "Hail, King of the Jews!" and striking him on the face. ⁴Pilate went out again and said to them, "Look, I am bringing him out to you to let you know that I find no case against him."

ᶜ Gk *the praetorium*

Pilate knows full well that Jesus poses no threat to Rome, but wriggles out of the dilemma by appeal to custom (18:39). Jesus, the innocent, becomes a substitute for a guilty man, Barabbas. So the symbolism of Passover, and the shedding of the blood of a spotless lamb so that death and judgment might be averted, is consummated as Jesus, the Lamb of God, goes out to die in the sinner's place.

John does not dwell on the details of Jesus' flogging, brutal though that must have been, though he tells us more about the taunting that followed. Did Pilate think that if he flogged an innocent man, the Jews would be ashamed and let him go with his life? Twice more Pilate disclaims responsibility (19:4, 6), but the crowd, urged on by the priests and police, is becoming frenzied. Now frightened, Pilate nonetheless tries once more to find a legitimate reason to release Jesus (19:10, 12), but is trapped by the Jews (19:12). In the face of the united cry of the crowd outside (19:15) he capitulates. Jesus is led away and crucified.

It is Pilate who has the caption 'Jesus of Nazareth, the King of the Jews' (19:19) put on the cross. The Jews object, but Pilate writes more wisely than he knows, for truly Jesus is their supreme King.

[5]So Jesus came out, wearing the crown of thorns and the purple robe. Pilate said to them, "Here is the man!" [6]When the chief priests and the police saw him, they shouted, "Crucify him! Crucify him!" Pilate said to them, "Take him yourselves and crucify him; I find no case against him." [7]The Jews answered him, "We have a law, and according to that law he ought to die because he has claimed to be the Son of God."

[8] Now when Pilate heard this, he was more afraid than ever. [9]He entered his head-quarters[d] again and asked Jesus, "Where are you from?" But Jesus gave him no answer. [10]Pilate therefore said to him, "Do you refuse to speak to me? Do you not know that I have power to release you, and power to crucify you?" [11]Jesus answered him, "You would have no power over me unless it had been given you from above; therefore the one who handed me over to you is guilty of a greater sin." [12]From then on Pilate tried to release him, but the Jews cried out, "If you release this man, you are no friend of the emperor. Everyone who claims to be a king sets himself against the emperor."

[13] When Pilate heard these words, he brought Jesus outside and sat[e] on the judge's bench at a place called The Stone Pavement, or in Hebrew[f] Gabbatha. [14]Now it was the day of Preparation for the Passover; and it was about noon. He said to the Jews, "Here is your King!" [15]They cried out, "Away with him! Away with him! Crucify him!" Pilate asked them, "Shall I crucify your King?" The chief priests answered, "We have no king but the emperor." [16]Then he handed him over to them to be crucified.

The Crucifixion of Jesus

So they took Jesus; [17]and carrying the cross by himself, he went out to what is called The Place of the Skull, which in Hebrew[f] is called Golgotha. [18]There they crucified him, and with him two others, one on either side, with Jesus between them. [19]Pilate also had an inscription written and put on the cross. It read, "Jesus of Nazareth,[g] the King of the Jews." [20]Many of the Jews read this inscription, because the place where Jesus was crucified was near the city; and it was written in Hebrew,[f] in Latin, and in Greek. [21]Then the chief priests of the Jews said to Pilate, "Do not write, 'The King of the Jews,' but, 'This

[d] Gk *the praetorium*   [e] Or *seated him*   [f] That is, *Aramaic*   [g] Gk *the Nazorean*

John records again and again how each detail of prophecy is fulfilled (19:24, 28, 36, 37 etc.). As the disciples reflected later on all that happened, how important the fulfilling of Scripture must have been. And, as John writes for Jewish readers years later, every tiny point that links Jesus with the Old Testament is important. Did the Psalmist, or Zechariah, have any idea of the significance of what they were writing so many years before?

Wherever most of the disciples may have been, it is the three Marys (19:25) and 'the disciple whom he loved' (19:26, a reference to John himself) who watch him die. What passed through their minds? In the midst of his own agony, Jesus is aware of their anguish and tenderly entrusts his mother to John's care (see further the note on 'Mother-child relationships', p. 221).

It is noteworthy that John draws special attention to the women. Were they less fearful than the men of reprisals? Were they just much more direct than the men about admitting and expressing their love for Jesus? Did they hope that their presence might in some tiny way alleviate the terrible loneliness of a terrible death, that just being there might be precious to their loved one? Mary, his mother, had given him birth. How did she make sense of all that had happened? Mary Magdalene owed him her sanity and deliverance (Luke 8:2). They could not keep away.

At last, Jesus died. John deliberately tells us that Jesus 'gave up his spirit' (John 19:30); no-one could take his life from him (see further the note on 'Death', p. 222).

man said, I am King of the Jews.' " [22]Pilate answered, "What I have written I have written." [23]When the soldiers had crucified Jesus, they took his clothes and divided them into four parts, one for each soldier. They also took his tunic; now the tunic was seamless, woven in one piece from the top. [24]So they said to one another, "Let us not tear it, but cast lots for it to see who will get it." This was to fulfill what the scripture says,

"They divided my clothes among
themselves,

and for my clothing they cast lots."
[25]And that is what the soldiers did.

Meanwhile, standing near the cross of Jesus were his mother, and his mother's sister, Mary the wife of Clopas, and Mary Magdalene. [26]When Jesus saw his mother and the disciple whom he loved standing beside her, he said to his mother, "Woman, here is your son." [27]Then he said to the disciple, "Here is your mother." And from that hour the disciple took her into his own home.

◆ Jesus' loving provision for Mary is not simply that John should keep an eye on her, nor even bring her into his home. He declares to Mary that John is now her son; he declares to John that Mary is now his mother.

Some Christians have seen this as the basis for regarding Mary as the mother of the church; in other words, provision for John who then symbolizes all believers. This is an unlikely interpretation because we are told that 'from that hour the disciple took her into his own home'; that is, John is providing for Mary. A widow was vulnerable; without a son, she was destitute. Why didn't Mary's other sons, Jesus' brothers, take care of her? Perhaps the bond of love was closer with John because they had shared all the events of the past three years. Certainly, earlier (John 7:5) Jesus' brothers had been unsympathetic and unbelieving, and there is no mention of them being at hand during the closing days of the Lord's life, though they appear in Acts 1:14.

Perhaps Jesus was underwriting what he had already taught, that 'whoever does the will of my Father in heaven is my brother and sister and mother' (Matt. 12:50) and that his disciples were thus his true family. When we are born into the family of God, we have a new set of relationships alongside our biological ones. This means that no believer should be 'alone in the world'; our churches should live out the family-ness of God's people with special care of those whose biological family is missing or dysfunctional. This is a powerful sign of the Kingdom of

---

Roman custom was to leave those crucified to a long, slow death, which could take days, and then let their bodies be picked by vultures. The Jews, however, removed a body before sunset to avoid defiling the land. On this occasion, there was even greater urgency: the Sabbath, and even more the Passover, must not be defiled. Breaking the victim's legs hastened death as his body sagged and he choked. To the soldiers' amazement, Jesus was already dead; they left his legs unbroken (19:36). But they plunged a spear into his side, and John records carefully that both blood and water flowed from the wound. It is difficult to be absolutely sure why John draws attention to this. Is it evidence that he was truly dead, and not just in a swoon as some were to claim after the resurrection? Or does it bring together the two great symbols of cleansing?

Pilate releases Jesus' body for burial to two secret believers: Joseph of Arimathea and Nicodemus. Both were wealthy and influential. But for their intervention, Jesus would have been taken to a common grave for criminals outside the city. The body is wrapped in a great quantity of sweet-smelling spices (reminiscent both of Mary's recent homage, and of the gift of the Magi long ago: Matt. 2:11) and laid in an unused tomb in a nearby garden. To the Jews, to have put the body of a criminal in a family tomb would have been to have defiled the bodies already there.

God to the world. So, in Christ, even a single childless woman may have many sons and daughters on whom to pour out motherly care; an orphan, in Christ, has grandparents, parents, brothers and sisters to cherish him. May our churches be such families! ◆

28 After this, when Jesus knew that all was now finished, he said (in order to fulfill the scripture), "I am thirsty." ²⁹A jar full of sour wine was standing there. So they put a sponge full of the wine on a branch of hyssop and held it to his mouth. ³⁰When Jesus had received the wine, he said, "It is finished." Then he bowed his head and gave up his spirit.

◆ Death entered the world that God had created perfect as a direct result of Adam and Eve's disobedience (Gen. 2:17; Rom. 5:12). Its significance is first described in Gen. 3:14–19, where we are given a horrifying picture of alienation from God, from one another and from our environment; of life disjointed; and of ultimate decay. The total human personality is given over to death. It is neither simply an event nor a process, but a state of being. Body and spirit are engulfed.

Jesus' death, and the voluntary relinquishing of his life, is the substitution by which I may be delivered from death and enabled to enter into the state of eternal life. Whilst I must still go through the process of physical death, the guarantee of the resurrection is that I may look forward with quiet confidence not only to the immortality of the soul but also to the resurrection of the body. Just as sin destroys the total personality, so Christ's death restores the total personality. Beyond physical death, I will be raised to perfection and restored joyfully to God's visible presence.

While our Lord Jesus deliberately gave himself up to death, it was a terrible thing for him. Paul describes it like this: 'For our sake he [God] made him [Jesus] to be sin who knew no sin, so that in him we might become the righteousness of God' (2 Cor. 5:21). In some mysterious way that we can never fully understand, but which is pictured in the Bible in the language of sacrifice and of the lamb, Jesus' sacrifice of himself and the shedding of his blood becomes the gateway to life for those who trust in him.

For the Christian, physical death may still be a great barrier, and the dying process may be sometimes dreadful and dreaded. Nonetheless, because of Christ's death, the 'sting' has been taken out of death, and it no longer has the last triumphant word (1 Cor. 15:54ff.). We are to focus not on death but on Glory. In the face of death, we are not to 'grieve as others do who have no hope' (1 Thess. 4:13) but rather to look forward with joyful confidence to entering into the fullness of Christ's victory, and resurrection life with him in heaven.

In today's Western world, where the prospect of death faces people with the sheer hopelessness and ultimate meaninglessness of their existence, causing great fear, the Christian's testimony to life in Christ that is stronger than death is immensely powerful ◆

Jesus' Side Is Pierced

31 Since it was the day of Preparation, the Jews did not want the bodies left on the cross during the sabbath, especially because that sabbath was a day of great solemnity. So they asked Pilate to have the legs of the crucified men broken and the bodies removed. ³²Then the soldiers came and broke the legs of the first and of the other who had been crucified with him. ³³But when they came to Jesus and saw that he was already dead, they did not break his legs. ³⁴Instead, one of the soldiers pierced his side with a spear, and at once blood and water came out. ³⁵(He who saw this has testified so that you also may believe. His testimony is true, and he knowsʰ that he tells the truth.) ³⁶These things occurred so

ʰ Or *there is one who knows*

that the scripture might be fulfilled, "None of his bones shall be broken." [37]And again another passage of scripture says, "They will look on the one whom they have pierced."

The Burial of Jesus

38 After these things, Joseph of Arimathea, who was a disciple of Jesus, though a secret one because of his fear of the Jews, asked Pilate to let him take away the body of Jesus. Pilate gave him permission; so he came and removed his body. [39]Nicodemus, who had at first come to Jesus by night, also came, bringing a mixture of myrrh and aloes, weighing about a hundred pounds. [40]They took the body of Jesus and wrapped it with the spices in linen cloths, according to the burial custom of the Jews. [41]Now there was a garden in the place where he was crucified, and in the garden there was a new tomb in which no one had ever been laid. [42]And so, because it was the Jewish day of Preparation, and the tomb was nearby, they laid Jesus there.

The Resurrection of Jesus

20 Early on the first day of the week, while it was still dark, Mary Magdalene came to the tomb and saw that the stone had been removed from the tomb. [2]So she ran and went to Simon Peter and

◆ Mary Magdalene, probably so called because she came from Magdala, a town in Galilee, is described by Luke as having been delivered by Jesus of seven demons (Luke 8:2). She then became one of the group who travelled with Jesus. While we are given no details about her demon possession and deliverance, the depth of her gratitude may be deduced from her wanting to stay near her Master.

Clearly, she became one of the inner circle of companions, alongside the Twelve, because she stands with Mary, Jesus' mother, through the awfulness of the crucifixion, and then shares in the anointing of his body with spices for burial. It is Mary Magdalene whom John especially notes as going ahead to the tomb at the earliest permitted moment (it would have been unthinkable during the Sabbath), discovering the empty cave, and telling the others. It is to her that the Lord first reveals himself in risen form. It is safe to assume that she was with the disciples, waiting as instructed, between the ascension and Pentecost (Acts 1:14).

After that, we are given no reference to Mary Magdalene by name. She is not subsequently named as first witness to the resurrection, perhaps because in contemporary society the witness of a woman was judged to be worthless. Yet, it is clear that Jesus greatly loved and honored her, and entrusted her, woman

---

JESUS' RESURRECTION (JOHN 20:1–31)

Early in the morning after Sabbath has been completed, Mary Magdalene (see further the note on 'Sabbath', p. 190) returns to the tomb. Perhaps after the haste of the burial she needs to come back to continue her grieving; in many cultures, there is a deep pull inside ourselves to go back to the place where a loved one is buried.

Shocked to find the stone placed across the entrance of the tomb rolled back, she knows it was far too heavy to have shifted by accident. Not unreasonably, she assumes that the Jews have taken the body for reasons of their own, perhaps to place it ignominiously in the despicable common grave for criminals. Without stopping to look closely, she runs to Peter and John and pours out her story. They in turn run to see for themselves, but go right in. The linen cloths in which the body had been buried are all there in order. No robbers would have removed them from the body and left them. It would have been a time-consuming and an unpleasant task. In any case, the spices were very valuable, and, had they removed the cloths, they wouldn't have left them. Although 'as yet they did not understand the scripture' (20:9), John at least is convinced that the Lord has come back from the dead, just as he promised.

notwithstanding, with witnessing both his death and his resurrection. Looking back, the men would have realized that they were told about this key event in history by a woman, and John records the point carefully.

Mary Magdalene has sometimes been assumed to be the 'sinful woman' in Luke 7:36ff., but this is unlikely ◆

the other disciple, the one whom Jesus loved, and said to them, "They have taken the Lord out of the tomb, and we do not know where they have laid him." ³Then Peter and the other disciple set out and went toward the tomb. ⁴The two were running together, but the other disciple outran Peter and reached the tomb first. ⁵He bent down to look in and saw the linen wrappings lying there, but he did not go in. ⁶Then Simon Peter came, following him, and went into the tomb. He saw the linen wrappings lying there, ⁷and the cloth that had been on Jesus' head, not lying with the linen wrappings but rolled up in a place by itself. ⁸Then the other disciple, who reached the tomb first, also went in, and he saw and believed; ⁹for as yet they did not understand the scripture, that he must rise from the dead. ¹⁰Then the disciples returned to their homes.

Jesus Appears to Mary Magdalene

11 But Mary stood weeping outside the tomb. As she wept, she bent over to look[i] into the tomb; ¹²and she saw two angels in white, sitting where the body of Jesus had been lying, one at the head and the other at the feet. ¹³They said to her, "Woman, why are you weeping?" She said to them, "They have taken away my Lord, and I do not know where they have laid him." ¹⁴When she had said this, she turned around and saw Jesus standing there, but she did not know that it was Jesus. ¹⁵Jesus said to her, "Woman, why are you weeping? Whom are you looking for?" Supposing him to be the gardener, she said to him, "Sir, if you have carried him away, tell me where you have laid him, and I will take him away." ¹⁶Jesus said to her, "Mary!" She turned and said to him in Hebrew,[j] "Rabbouni!" (which means Teacher). ¹⁷Jesus said to her, "Do not hold on to me, because I have not yet ascended to the Father. But go to my brothers and say to them, 'I am ascending to my Father and your Father, to my God and your God.' " ¹⁸Mary Magdalene went and announced to the disciples, "I have seen the Lord"; and she told them that he had said these things to her.

---

[i] Gk lacks *to look*   [j] That is, *Aramaic*

Mary stays to mourn, and it is to her that first the angels appear (20:12), and then the risen Jesus himself. Because of her conviction that he is dead, or maybe because he is already gloriously transfigured, Mary does not recognize Jesus until he gently says her name (20:16). Probably Mary turns to clasp him as though, having found him again, she is determined not to lose him again. Jesus' gentle rebuke (20:17) then makes sense: it is not that she may not clutch at a ghost, but, rather, that it will be awhile until the ascension and Jesus' permanent departure.

It is Mary who is charged with the message to the disciples. Woman though she is, it has been she who has witnessed her Master's death and now is the first to see him risen again. God gladly includes women as witnesses to the central events of history, ushering them into the heart of the new era. Jewish custom may have sadly marginalized women; God demonstrates that such custom is man-made and sinful.

Jesus appears to the gathered disciples (20:19). His resurrection body can pass through locked doors (20: 19, 26), is recognizable as the one they have known and loved, can be touched (20:27), and clearly bears the marks of his crucifixion (20:20, 27). Thomas, skeptical in the face of hearsay (20:24–25), sees for himself and declares, 'My Lord and my God!' (20:28). For John, such a response of faith is the very reason for the writing of his book (20:31). It is faith such as this that opens the way to eternal life.

Jesus Appears to the Disciples

19 When it was evening on that day, the first day of the week, and the doors of the house where the disciples had met were locked for fear of the Jews, Jesus came and stood among them and said, "Peace be with you." [20]After he said this, he showed them his hands and his side. Then the disciples rejoiced when they saw the Lord. [21]Jesus said to them again, "Peace be with you. As the Father has sent me, so I send you." [22]When he had said this, he breathed on them and said to them, "Receive the Holy Spirit. [23]If you forgive the sins of any, they are forgiven them; if you retain the sins of any, they are retained."

Jesus and Thomas

24 But Thomas (who was called the Twin[k]), one of the twelve, was not with them when Jesus came. [25]So the other disciples told him, "We have seen the Lord." But he said to them, "Unless I see the mark of the nails in his hands, and put my finger in the mark of the nails and my hand in his side, I will not believe."

26 A week later his disciples were again in the house, and Thomas was with them. Although the doors were shut, Jesus came and stood among them and said, "Peace be with you." [27]Then he said to Thomas, "Put your finger here and see my hands. Reach out your hand and put it in my side. Do not doubt but believe." [28]Thomas answered him, "My Lord and my God!" [29]Jesus said to him, "Have you believed because you have seen me? Blessed are those who have not seen and yet have come to believe."

The Purpose of This Book

30 Now Jesus did many other signs in the presence of his disciples, which are not written in this book. [31]But these are written so that you may come to believe[l] that Jesus is the Messiah,[m] the Son of God, and that through believing you may have life in his name.

◆ Some commentators have argued that John was writing for believers. But John here quite clearly states that his purpose is to convince his readers as to the identity of Jesus so that they might come to believe and thus enter into eternal life. That sounds like evangelism!

Whatever John's original purpose, this Gospel, like the other three, has a dual ministry: to describe clearly to the unbeliever who Jesus is and what he has done; and to enable Christians to know their Lord better.

Each Gospel preserves precious eyewitness accounts. It is normally through the record of the Scriptures, brought to life by the Spirit, and declared by the Lord's people, that others are brought to faith. In the same way, the Scriptures, or at least the contents of them, however communicated, illuminated by the Spirit, are God's normal instrument to instruct his people.

It may well be that John's original audience was Jewish (including those who were not Jews by birth but who had identified with the Jewish faith). It would be they who would be aware of the significance of proving that Jesus was the Messiah (John 20:31), the anointed and promised one who was to come from God. By the time of John's writing, almost certainly after the destruction of Jerusalem in AD 70, the church had become overwhelmingly Gentile. John, like Paul (Rom. 10:1), would have longed for his own people to yet recognize their Messiah ◆

[k] Gk *Didymus*   [l] Other ancient authorities read *may continue to believe*   [m] Or *the Christ*

The risen Jesus not only blesses them with his peace (20:19, 21) but sends them into the world in just the same manner as his Father had sent him. His mission is to be continued through them, empowered by the Spirit (20:22). John the Baptist had promised that Jesus would baptize not with water but with the Spirit. With Calvary and resurrection completed, the way is open for the Spirit to make his permanent home within believers.

Jesus Appears to Seven Disciples

21 After these things Jesus showed himself again to the disciples by the Sea of Tiberias; and he showed himself in this way. ²Gathered there together were Simon Peter, Thomas called the Twin,ⁿ Nathanael of Cana in Galilee, the sons of Zebedee, and two others of his disciples. ³Simon Peter said to them, "I am going fishing." They said to him, "We will go with you." They went out and got into the boat, but that night they caught nothing.

4 Just after daybreak, Jesus stood on the beach; but the disciples did not know that it was Jesus. ⁵Jesus said to them, "Children, you have no fish, have you?" They answered him, "No." ⁶He said to them, "Cast the net to the right side of the boat, and you will find some." So they cast it, and now they were not able to haul it in because there were so many fish. ⁷That disciple whom Jesus loved said to Peter, "It is the Lord!" When Simon Peter heard that it was the Lord, he put on some clothes, for he was naked, and jumped into the sea. ⁸But the other disciples came in the boat, dragging the net full of fish, for they were not far from the land, only about a hundred yardsᵒ off.

9 When they had gone ashore, they saw a charcoal fire there, with fish on it, and bread. ¹⁰Jesus said to them, "Bring some of the fish that you have just caught." ¹¹So Simon Peter went aboard and hauled the net ashore, full of large fish, a hundred fifty-three of them; and though there were so many, the net was not torn. ¹²Jesus said to them, "Come and have breakfast." Now none of the disciples dared to ask him, "Who are you?" because they knew it was the Lord. ¹³Jesus came and took the bread and gave it to them, and did the same with the fish. ¹⁴This was now the third time that Jesus appeared to the disciples after he was raised from the dead.

Jesus and Peter

15 When they had finished breakfast, Jesus said to Simon Peter, "Simon son of John, do you love me more than these?" He said to him, "Yes, Lord; you know that I love you." Jesus said to him, "Feed my lambs." ¹⁶A second time he said to him, "Simon son of John, do you love me?" He said to him, "Yes, Lord; you know that I love you." Jesus said to him, "Tend my

ⁿ Gk *Didymus*   ᵒ Gk *two hundred cubits*

CODA AND EPILOGUE (JOHN 21:1–25)

At first glance, 20:31 appears to be a final statement so that another chapter is unexpected. But, on closer reading, there is a beautiful rightness about John's final section, a satisfying tying up of the threads, and a balance to the calling of the disciples in the Prelude of 1:19ff.

Jesus had called several of his disciples out of their lives as fishermen. The Gospels seem to imply that they continued to fish from time to time, but it was no longer their primary absorption. Now, seven of them are fishing again, but 'they caught nothing' (21:3). Even though they didn't yet know quite how to go forward, God was saying they couldn't go backwards.

From the shore, the risen Lord Jesus, unrecognized by them, tells them to do their job differently. After a whole night of fruitless toil, suddenly their catch is phenomenal. Even the exact number – 153 large fish (21:11) – is engraved on their memory. It must be the Lord, realizes John!

With haunting echoes of the Last Supper, Jesus gives them breakfast: another shared meal at which he is host to honored friends. To accept hospitality was to commit oneself to loyalty. Then, lovingly but persistently, the Lord confronts Peter with his broken promise; for each of his three denials there is opportunity to testify to his love for Jesus. The brash extravagance of the dramatic gesture is to give way to faithful, steady servanthood (21:15–17). Peter's personal agenda must give way to God's, even though it might not be what he could possibly have chosen for himself. It is a chastened but gloriously welcomed Peter who is recommissioned by Jesus for a future that will glorify God (21:19). The servant will be like his Master!

sheep." [17]He said to him the third time, "Simon son of John, do you love me?" Peter felt hurt because he said to him the third time, "Do you love me?" And he said to him, "Lord, you know everything; you know that I love you." Jesus said to him, "Feed my sheep. [18]Very truly, I tell you, when you were younger, you used to fasten your own belt and to go wherever you wished. But when you grow old, you will stretch out your hands, and someone else will fasten a belt around you and take you where you do not wish to go." [19](He said this to indicate the kind of death by which he would glorify God.) After this he said to him, "Follow me."

Jesus and the Beloved Disciple

20 Peter turned and saw the disciple whom Jesus loved following them; he was the one who had reclined next to Jesus at the supper and had said, "Lord, who is it that is going to betray you?" [21]When Peter saw him, he said to Jesus, "Lord, what about him?" [22]Jesus said to him, "If it is my will that he remain until I come, what is that to you? Follow me!" [23]So the rumor spread in the community[p] that this disciple would not die. Yet Jesus did not say to him that he would not die, but, "If it is my will that he remain until I come, what is that to you?"[q]

24 This is the disciple who is testifying to these things and has written them, and we know that his testimony is true. [25]But there are also many other things that Jesus did; if every one of them were written down, I suppose that the world itself could not contain the books that would be written.

[p] Gk *among the brothers*   [q] Other ancient authorities lack *what is that to you*

Now John brings his lovely record to a close, humbly urging his truthfulness in writing. Selective he has been; there is so much more that could have been told. Not even the whole world is big enough to contain all the glory of Christ. That waits for heaven and eternity.

THE ACTS OF THE APOSTLES

INTRODUCTION

'The LORD sets the prisoners free; the LORD opens the eyes of the blind. The LORD lifts up those who are bowed down; the LORD loves the righteous. The LORD watches over the strangers; he upholds the orphan and the widow, but the way of the wicked he brings to ruin' (Ps. 146:7b–9).

In the late second century the church theologian Irenaeus referred to Luke's second book, written to the unknown Roman official Theophilus, as the 'Acts of the Apostles'. A careful reading of Acts, however, reveals that Luke, writing probably about AD 70–80, sees the events of the early church as the 'Acts of God'. God's power, described in Ps. 146, shows itself throughout Acts: through the generous outpouring of the Holy Spirit, God frees prisoners, heals, vindicates the persecuted, and triumphs over wickedness. Luke himself uses the term 'apostles' for Jesus' chosen Twelve, and rarely for Paul, whose missionary efforts comprise about half of Acts.

From the opening scene of Jesus' ascension to the final description of the prisoner Paul preaching the gospel unhindered in Rome, the great themes of Acts are the powerful acts of God and the spread of the gospel after Pentecost. From Jerusalem and Judea to Asia Minor, Greece, and finally the capital of the Roman Empire itself, God's faithful witnesses, led powerfully by the Holy Spirit, proclaim that Jesus has been raised from the dead, the prophetic scriptures are fulfilled, and salvation is offered to both Jew and Gentile. Writing before the final separation of Judaism and Christianity, Luke portrays difficulties and joys as the Holy Spirit leads Jewish believers to reach out to Gentiles as well as other Jews.

To study Acts is to meet people of differing languages and cultures, religious experience, economic and social status and to observe their responses to the good news. Luke envisions each person, each city, each culture as important in God's sight. Luke portrays women of varying occupations and social positions: slaves, businesswomen, prominent women, widows. Active in the worship and work of the believers' fellowship, they pray, receive the Holy Spirit, prophesy, teach, and take the initiative in various ways.

The Introduction to the Gospel of Luke (pp. 112–113) has details on the identities of Luke and Theophilus and the dating of Luke–Acts.

The beginning of Luke's Gospel (1:1–4) indicates that Luke knows of many accounts of the 'events that have been fulfilled among us'. These accounts are the sources for both Luke's Gospel and Acts. In Acts, Luke skillfully weaves together the various threads of these sources into a nearly seamless whole. Scholars have detected several types of sources: accounts which center on the deeds of important figures – Peter, Stephen, Philip, and Paul – as well as travel documents and itineraries for Paul's travels. One distinctive source of information on Paul's journeys is Luke's eyewitness account of three of Paul's sea journeys, found in the 'we' sections (Acts 16:10–17; 20:5–21:18; 27:1–28:16).

To depict the progress of the gospel from Jerusalem to Rome, Luke focuses his source material in several ways. First, he concentrates on the words and deeds of a few major figures – Peter, Stephen, Philip, and Paul – as the Holy Spirit leads them through unanticipated conflict and growth.

Second, since Luke cannot use all the known experiences of the emerging community of faith, he carefully chooses vivid events and skillfully condenses them to make his points. Every episode and character has specific purposes. The numerous speeches – briefer than actual speeches would be – address issues crucial to the emerging Christian community. Speeches to Jewish audiences usually follow a pattern: interpretation of aspects of Hebrew history and prophetic scriptures which point to the Messiah, their fulfillment in the death and resurrection of Jesus, and an appeal for listeners' belief. Speeches to Gentiles begin by urging them to forego idol worship, and turn to the Creator God who cares for them by sending Jesus who has been raised from the dead.

Third, Luke often arranges events so that careful readers may find additional underlying meanings. One such example, familiar from Luke's Gospel, is the pairing of stories about men and women: Aeneas and Tabitha healed and restored (Acts 9:32–42), Lydia and the jailer converted (16:11–40), and Philip's four unmarried daughters and Agabus as prophets (21:7–14). He also emphasizes that both men and women respond to the gospel (e.g. 5:14; 8:3; 9:2;17:4, 34). By such pairings, Luke suggests that God cares equally for men and women and that they have equal responsibilities under Christ's authority.

The Promise of the Holy Spirit

1 In the first book, Theophilus, I wrote about all that Jesus did and taught from the beginning ²until the day when he was taken up to heaven, after giving instructions through the Holy Spirit to the apostles whom he had chosen. ³After his suffering he presented himself alive to them by many convincing proofs, appearing to them during forty days and speaking about the kingdom of God. ⁴While staying[a] with them, he ordered them not to leave Jerusalem, but to wait there for the promise of the Father. "This," he said, "is what you have heard from me; ⁵for John baptized with water, but you will be baptized with[b] the Holy Spirit not many days from now."

The Ascension of Jesus

6 So when they had come together, they asked him, "Lord, is this the time when you will restore the kingdom to Israel?" ⁷He replied, "It is not for you to know the times or periods that the Father has set by his own authority. ⁸But you will receive power when the Holy Spirit has come upon you; and you will be my witnesses in Jerusalem, in all Judea and Samaria, and to the ends of the earth." ⁹When he had said this, as they were watching, he was lifted up, and a cloud took him out of their sight. ¹⁰While he was going and they were gazing up toward heaven, suddenly two men in white robes stood by them. ¹¹They said, "Men of Galilee, why do you stand looking up toward heaven? This Jesus, who has been taken up from you into heaven, will come in the same way as you saw him go into heaven."

Matthias Chosen to Replace Judas

12 Then they returned to Jerusalem from the mount called Olivet, which is near Jerusalem, a sabbath day's journey away. ¹³When they had entered the city, they went to the room upstairs where they were staying, Peter, and John, and James, and Andrew, Philip and Thomas, Bartholomew and Matthew, James son of Alphaeus, and Simon the Zealot, and Judas son of[c] James. ¹⁴All these were constantly devoting themselves to prayer, together with certain women, including Mary the mother of Jesus, as well as his brothers.

[a] Or eating [b] Or by [c] Or the brother of

ACTS 1

1–26. Luke briefly summarizes his first book – the Gospel of Luke – and lays the groundwork for the themes and events of Acts (see Luke 1:1–4).

2. Luke often anticipates events or people. Here he mentions Jesus' chosen apostles. In 1:12–26, he will describe the selection of an apostle to take Judas' place.

4. Again Luke anticipates: believers will receive the promised Holy Spirit (Acts 2).

6–7. Luke asserts that humans cannot know beforehand when God will act decisively in history. The apostles must not waste energy speculating about God's next move, but they are assured (v. 11) that Jesus will come again.

8. Just before his ascension, Jesus tells the apostles where the Holy Spirit will lead them: they will be Jesus' witnesses at home, among people like them (Jerusalem and Judea), among people with different religious beliefs (Samaria), and far away from everything familiar (the ends of the earth). The important theme of Acts will indeed be the unhindered spread of the gospel.

12–14. Upper rooms could be rented as lodgings or gathering places. This one is large, holding about 120 people (v. 15). The Gospels do not record that Jesus' followers prayed this fervently before Jesus' death. They have learned from his example and from intense experiences with the risen Lord.

The 'certain women' are likely those mentioned in Luke's Gospel (see Luke 8:1–3; 23:49, 55; 24:10). After the resurrection, Jesus' mother Mary joins them.

In first-century Judaism, women usually did not participate in ritual prayers and blessings. These women's participation in constant prayer would be a new experience for them.

15 In those days Peter stood up among the believers[d] (together the crowd numbered about one hundred twenty persons) and said, [16]"Friends,[e] the scripture had to be fulfilled, which the Holy Spirit through David foretold concerning Judas, who became a guide for those who arrested Jesus – [17]for he was numbered among us and was allotted his share in this ministry." [18](Now this man acquired a field with the reward of his wickedness; and falling head-long,[f] he burst open in the middle and all his bowels gushed out. [19]This became known to all the residents of Jerusalem, so that the field was called in their language Hakeldama, that is, Field of Blood.) [20]"For it is written in the book of Psalms,

'Let his homestead become desolate,
    and let there be no one to live in it';
and
'Let another take his position of
        overseer.'

[21]So one of the men who have accompanied us during all the time that the Lord Jesus went in and out among us, [22]beginning from the baptism of John until the day when he was taken up from us – one of these must become a witness with us to his resurrection." [23]So they proposed two, Joseph called Barsabbas, who was also known as Justus, and Matthias. [24]Then they prayed and said, "Lord, you know everyone's heart. Show us which one of these two you have chosen [25]to take the place[g] in this ministry and apostleship from which Judas turned aside to go to his own place." [26]And they cast lots for them, and the lot fell on Matthias; and he was added to the eleven apostles.

The Coming of the Holy Spirit

2 When the day of Pentecost had come, they were all together in one place. [2]And suddenly from heaven there came a sound like the rush of a violent wind, and it filled the entire house where they were sitting. [3]Divided tongues, as of fire, appeared among them, and a tongue rested on each of them. [4]All of them were filled with the Holy Spirit and began to speak in other languages, as the Spirit gave them ability.

[d] Gk *brothers* [e] Gk *Men, brothers* [f] Or *swelling up* [g] Other ancient authorities read *the share*

---

15. The Greek text has 'brothers' (NRSV footnote d) instead of 'believers'. The Greek words for 'brother' (*adelphos*) and 'sister' (*adelphe*) have the same root, and the plural of *adelphos* can be used collectively for both brothers and sisters. NRSV 'believers' captures the potential of the Greek to refer to both men and women and occurs throughout Acts (e.g. 9:30; 11:1; 12:17; 16:2; 17:14; 18:27; 21:7).

16. As the NRSV footnote e states, the Greek text refers specifically to men. In Acts, in deliber-ative or persuasive speeches, speakers often address men only, since men of that era were customarily decision-makers in political and religious matters in Jewish and most Gentile cultures (see 2:14; 5:35; 7:2; 13:16; 15:6; 23:1). Women are, however, present (1:14).

21–26. In Acts, Luke normally reserves the term 'apostle' for one of the Twelve. Judas' successor as apostle will have been a companion of Jesus throughout his ministry, including his ascension. After prayer, lots are cast so that God's choice for the twelfth apostle may emerge. The believers are still unsure of themselves, groping for God's will.

ACTS 2

1–4. Fifty days after the Passover festival is the Jewish harvest festival of Shavuot (Hebrew = 'weeks') or Pentecost (Greek *pentecoste* = 'fiftieth day') at which the first-fruits of new wheat would be offered to the LORD (Lev. 23:15–22). Pentecost also commemorates God's giving the Law at Mt Sinai. The dual nature of this festival and the early believers' experience of the Holy Spirit on Pentecost have led Christians to celebrate God's gift of the Holy Spirit as the first-fruits of the fulfillment of God's new covenant in Christ.

5 Now there were devout Jews from every nation under heaven living in Jerusalem. ⁶And at this sound the crowd gathered and was bewildered, because each one heard them speaking in the native language of each. ⁷Amazed and astonished, they asked, "Are not all these who are speaking Galileans? ⁸And how is it that we hear, each of us, in our own native language? ⁹Parthians, Medes, Elamites, and residents of Mesopotamia, Judea and Cappadocia, Pontus and Asia, ¹⁰Phrygia and Pamphylia, Egypt and the parts of Libya belonging to Cyrene, and visitors from Rome, both Jews and proselytes, ¹¹Cretans and Arabs – in our own languages we hear them speaking about God's deeds of power." ¹²All were amazed and perplexed, saying to one another, "What does this mean?" ¹³But others sneered and said, "They are filled with new wine."

Peter Addresses the Crowd

14 But Peter, standing with the eleven, raised his voice and addressed them, "Men of Judea and all who live in Jerusalem, let this be known to you, and listen to what I say. ¹⁵Indeed, these are not drunk, as you suppose, for it is only nine o'clock in the morning. ¹⁶No, this is what was spoken through the prophet Joel:

¹⁷ 'In the last days it will be, God
        declares,
    that I will pour out my Spirit upon all
        flesh,
    and your sons and your daughters
        shall prophesy,
    and your young men shall see visions,
    and your old men shall dream
        dreams.
¹⁸ Even upon my slaves, both men and
        women,
    in those days I will pour out my
        Spirit;
    and they shall prophesy.
¹⁹ And I will show portents in the
        heaven above
    and signs on the earth below,
        blood, and fire, and smoky mist.
²⁰ The sun shall be turned to darkness
    and the moon to blood,
        before the coming of the Lord's
        great and glorious day.
²¹ Then everyone who calls on the name
        of the Lord shall be saved.'
22 "You that are Israelites,ʰ listen to

ʰ Gk *Men, Israelites*

1–2. Luke does not limit the 'all' who are gathered to any particular group. Thus, the women (1:14) participate in the events of Pentecost. Since the event takes place inside a house, women are easily included. The 'sound like the rush of a violent wind (Greek *pnoe*)' fills the whole house, not just the upper room (1:13). *Pnoe* ('wind, breath') shares the same root with *pneuma* ('wind, breath, spirit', particularly the Holy Spirit). John 3:3–10 plays on these meanings of *pneuma*. For similar Hebrew word-play, see Ezek. 37:1–14, the valley of Dry Bones.

3–4. In another supernatural event tongues like fire rest on everyone. Before Moses received the Law, the Lᴏʀᴅ descended upon Mt Sinai in fire (Exod. 19:18). For the new covenant a gentler, more personal flame announces God's presence. In Luke 3:16, John the Baptist proclaims that Jesus will baptize with Holy Spirit and fire, a prophecy fulfilled here. Luke emphasizes that the Holy Spirit fills all present and they speak in other languages.

5–36. The scene shifts from inside to outside, where Jews from throughout the known world hear and understand the believers as they speak about God's 'deeds of power'. Peter interprets scriptures fulfilled by Jesus' death and resurrection and by the dramatic coming of the Holy Spirit to show to the Jewish community that Jesus is 'Lord and Messiah'. Luke describes Peter's audience as primarily male (2:14, 22, 29) because normally men decided religious matters, but local women may have been attracted to the event by the unusual activity.

17–18. Peter emphasizes from Joel 2:28–32 that the Spirit is being poured upon all flesh: both sons and daughters will prophesy as will male and female slaves. Both sexes, all social classes will receive the Spirit and proclaim the Word of God.

what I have to say: Jesus of Nazareth,[i] a man attested to you by God with deeds of power, wonders, and signs that God did through him among you, as you yourselves know – [23]this man, handed over to you according to the definite plan and foreknowledge of God, you crucified and killed by the hands of those outside the law. [24]But God raised him up, having freed him from death,[j] because it was impossible for him to be held in its power. [25]For David says concerning him,

'I saw the Lord always before me,
    for he is at my right hand so that I
        will not be shaken;
[26] therefore my heart was glad, and my
        tongue rejoiced;
    moreover my flesh will live in hope.
[27] For you will not abandon my soul to
        Hades,
    or let your Holy One experience
        corruption.
[28] You have made known to me the ways
        of life;
    you will make me full of gladness
        with your presence.'

[29] "Fellow Israelites,[k] I may say to you confidently of our ancestor David that he both died and was buried, and his tomb is with us to this day. [30]Since he was a prophet, he knew that God had sworn with

an oath to him that he would put one of his descendants on his throne. [31]Foreseeing this, David[l] spoke of the resurrection of the Messiah,[m] saying,

'He was not abandoned to Hades,
    nor did his flesh experience
        corruption.'

[32]This Jesus God raised up, and of that all of us are witnesses. [33]Being therefore exalted at[n] the right hand of God, and having received from the Father the promise of the Holy Spirit, he has poured out this that you both see and hear. [34]For David did not ascend into the heavens, but he himself says,

'The Lord said to my Lord,
    "Sit at my right hand,
[35]   until I make your enemies your
        footstool." '

[36]Therefore let the entire house of Israel know with certainty that God has made him both Lord and Messiah,[o] this Jesus whom you crucified."

The First Converts

37 Now when they heard this, they were cut to the heart and said to Peter and to the

[i] Gk *the Nazorean*   [j] Gk *the pains of death*   [k] Gk *Men, brothers*   [l] Gk *he*   [m] Or *the Christ*   [n] Or *by*   [o] Or *Christ*

---

24. NRSV footnote j gives an alternate translation, 'pains of death'. The Greek word *odines* refers primarily to labor pains in childbirth. Jesus' release from death is compared with the mother's release from labor pain at the birth of an infant. Some scholars see the words as a mistranslation of the Hebrew phrase 'cords' of death (Ps. 18:4; 2 Sam. 22:6) in the Septuagint, the Greek translation of the Hebrew Scriptures which Luke knew well. In any case, the image of new life emerging from suffering and death is powerful.

32–33. The 'we' who are witnesses to the risen Jesus are the twelve apostles, certainly, since they are standing there (2:14). But those inside who are witnesses also include the women who were the first to experience the empty tomb. The Spirit continues to be poured out on those inside while Peter speaks outside: the Greek verbs 'you see and hear' are in the present tense, indicating an event in progress.

37–47. Luke's first description of becoming a believer includes repentance, baptism in Jesus' name, forgiveness of sins, and receiving the Holy Spirit. About 3,000 people – the Greek *psychai* ('souls') includes men and women – join the 120. After their conversion, they all participate in activities inside houses: study, breaking bread, prayer. Although women could not enter parts of the Temple that men could, they could participate in house fellowships (v. 46). Positive inclusion of women in the believers' fellowship contrasts with women's very limited role in first-century Jewish rituals.

other apostles, "Brothers,[p] what should we do?" [38]Peter said to them, "Repent, and be baptized every one of you in the name of Jesus Christ so that your sins may be forgiven; and you will receive the gift of the Holy Spirit. [39]For the promise is for you, for your children, and for all who are far away, everyone whom the Lord our God calls to him." [40]And he testified with many other arguments and exhorted them, saying, "Save yourselves from this corrupt generation." [41]So those who welcomed his message were baptized, and that day about three thousand persons were added. [42]They devoted themselves to the apostles' teaching and fellowship, to the breaking of bread and the prayers.

Life among the Believers

43 Awe came upon everyone, because many wonders and signs were being done by the apostles. [44]All who believed were together and had all things in common; [45]they would sell their possessions and goods and distribute the proceeds[q] to all, as any had need. [46]Day by day, as they spent much time together in the temple, they broke bread at home[r] and ate their food with glad and generous[s] hearts, [47]praising God and having the goodwill of all the people. And day by day the Lord added to their number those who were being saved.

Peter Heals a Crippled Beggar

3 One day Peter and John were going up to the temple at the hour of prayer, at three o'clock in the afternoon. [2]And a man lame from birth was being carried in. People would lay him daily at the gate of the temple called the Beautiful Gate so that he could ask for alms from those entering the temple. [3]When he saw Peter and John about to go into the temple, he asked them for alms. [4]Peter looked intently at him, as did John, and said, "Look at us." [5]And he fixed his attention on them, expecting to receive something from them. [6]But Peter said, "I have no silver or gold, but what I have I give you; in the name of Jesus Christ of Nazareth,[t] stand up and walk." [7]And he took him by the right hand and

[p] Gk *Men, brothers* [q] Gk *them* [r] Or *from house to house* [s] Or *sincere* [t] Gk *the Nazorean*

ACTS 3:1–4:37

Healing the lame beggar at the Temple's Beautiful Gate results in unexpected opportunities to witness to God's power: Peter and John address amazed onlookers, are arrested for disturbing the peace, defend themselves before the Council (NRSV translation of the Sanhedrin), are freed with only a warning, return to the believers, and pray for boldness.

3:1. In first-century Jewish custom, men normally prayed three times a day: around 9 a.m. (the time of the morning sacrifice in the Temple); 3 p.m. (the time of the burnt offering in the Temple); and at sunset. The apostles go to the Temple for customary afternoon rituals. The location of the Beautiful Gate is conjectural, but probably it led from outside into the Court of the Women. In Herod's temple women could not go beyond this Court into the Court of Israel and were not encouraged to participate in some of the yearly festivals and daily rituals connected with the Temple.

3:2. 'Lame from birth' is 'lame from his mother's womb' in Greek, emphasizing the length of time the man has been crippled (40 years, 4:22; also 14:8). John 9:1–41 relates another instance of a man disabled from birth: Jesus strongly refutes traditional notions that such disabilities are caused by someone's sin (see note on 'Children born with a handicap', p. 200).

3:3–10. This, the first of the apostles' healings after Jesus' ascension, is done in the power of Jesus' name (see Luke 10:1–20 for Jesus' instructions to heal in his name). In ancient cultures, a person's name was inextricably related to that individual's essential character. The name Jesus (Hebrew Joshua) means 'The Lord is salvation'. 'All the people' (Acts 3:9) – presumably men and women, since the Beautiful Gate was probably outside the Court of Israel – are amazed.

raised him up; and immediately his feet and ankles were made strong. ⁸Jumping up, he stood and began to walk, and he entered the temple with them, walking and leaping and praising God. ⁹All the people saw him walking and praising God, ¹⁰and they recognized him as the one who used to sit and ask for alms at the Beautiful Gate of the temple; and they were filled with wonder and amazement at what had happened to him.

Peter Speaks in Solomon's Portico

11 While he clung to Peter and John, all the people ran together to them in the portico called Solomon's Portico, utterly astonished. ¹²When Peter saw it, he addressed the people, "You Israelites,ᵘ why do you wonder at this, or why do you stare at us, as though by our own power or piety we had made him walk? ¹³The God of Abraham, the God of Isaac, and the God of Jacob, the God of our ancestors has glorified his servantᵛ Jesus, whom you handed over and rejected in the presence of Pilate, though he had decided to release him. ¹⁴But you rejected the Holy and Righteous One and asked to have a murderer given to you, ¹⁵and you killed the Author of life, whom God raised from the dead. To this we are witnesses. ¹⁶And by faith in his name, his name itself has made this man strong, whom you see and know; and the faith that is through Jesusʷ has given him this perfect health in the presence of all of you.

17 "And now, friends,ˣ I know that you acted in ignorance, as did also your rulers.

¹⁸In this way God fulfilled what he had foretold through all the prophets, that his Messiahʸ would suffer. ¹⁹Repent therefore, and turn to God so that your sins may be wiped out, ²⁰so that times of refreshing may come from the presence of the Lord, and that he may send the Messiahᶻ appointed for you, that is, Jesus, ²¹who must remain in heaven until the time of universal restoration that God announced long ago through his holy prophets. ²²Moses said, 'The Lord your God will raise up for you from your own peopleˣ a prophet like me. You must listen to whatever he tells you. ²³And it will be that everyone who does not listen to that prophet will be utterly rooted out of the people.' ²⁴And all the prophets, as many as have spoken, from Samuel and those after him, also predicted these days. ²⁵You are the descendants of the prophets and of the covenant that God gave to your ancestors, saying to Abraham, 'And in your descendants all the families of the earth shall be blessed.' ²⁶When God raised up his servant,ᵛ he sent him first to you, to bless you by turning each of you from your wicked ways."

Peter and John before the Council

4 While Peter and Johnᵃ were speaking to the people, the priests, the captain of the temple, and the Sadducees came to them, ²much annoyed because they

ᵘ Gk *Men, Israelites*   ᵛ Or *child*   ʷ Gk *him*
ˣ Gk *brothers*   ʸ Or *his Christ*   ᶻ Or *the Christ*
ᵃ Gk *While they*

3:11–16. Luke highlights the healing's ongoing consequences. Peter, now in Solomon's Portico, seizes the opportunity to proclaim that God, not the apostles' power or piety, has healed the man to glorify the risen Jesus whom Peter's audience has crucified. Peter also emphasizes that the lame man's faith in Jesus' name has restored him.

3:17–26. Peter insists that his listeners acted from ignorance in crucifying Jesus, but as a result God has fulfilled prophecy. He urges them into twofold action: repent *and* turn to God (3:19). 'Times of refreshing' as well as blessing will result from the restoration of the Messiah as foretold by Moses (Deut. 18:15–19) and the prophets.

4:1–4. Religious authorities, disturbed by large gatherings and preaching of the resurrection, arrest Peter and John. The Greek text indicates that these 5,000 believers were specifically men (*andres*). The population of Jerusalem was then about 30,000 people.

were teaching the people and proclaiming that in Jesus there is the resurrection of the dead. ³So they arrested them and put them in custody until the next day, for it was already evening. ⁴But many of those who heard the word believed; and they numbered about five thousand.

5 The next day their rulers, elders, and scribes assembled in Jerusalem, ⁶with Annas the high priest, Caiaphas, John,ᵇ and Alexander, and all who were of the high-priestly family. ⁷When they had made the prisonersᶜ stand in their midst, they inquired, "By what power or by what name did you do this?" ⁸Then Peter, filled with the Holy Spirit, said to them, "Rulers of the people and elders, ⁹if we are questioned today because of a good deed done to someone who was sick and are asked how this man has been healed, ¹⁰let it be known to all of you, and to all the people of Israel, that this man is standing before you in good health by the name of Jesus Christ of Nazareth,ᵈ whom you crucified, whom God raised from the dead. ¹¹This Jesusᵉ is

'the stone that was rejected by you,
     the builders;

   it has become the cornerstone.'ᶠ

¹²There is salvation in no one else, for there is no other name under heaven given among mortals by which we must be saved."

13 Now when they saw the boldness of Peter and John and realized that they were uneducated and ordinary men, they were amazed and recognized them as companions of Jesus. ¹⁴When they saw the man who had been cured standing beside them, they had nothing to say in opposition. ¹⁵So they ordered them to leave the council while they discussed the matter with one another. ¹⁶They said, "What will we do with them? For it is obvious to all who live in Jerusalem that a notable sign has been done through them; we cannot deny it. ¹⁷But to keep it from spreading further among the people, let us warn them to speak no more to anyone in this name." ¹⁸So they called them and ordered them not to speak or teach at all in the name of Jesus. ¹⁹But Peter and John answered them, "Whether it is right in God's sight to listen to you rather than to God, you must judge; ²⁰for we cannot keep from speaking about what we have seen and heard." ²¹After threatening them again, they let them go, finding no way to punish them because of the people, for all of them praised God for what had happened. ²²For the man on whom this sign of healing had been performed was more than forty years old.

ᵇ Other ancient authorities read *Jonathan*
ᶜ Gk *them*   ᵈ Gk *the Nazorean*   ᵉ Gk *This*
ᶠ Or *keystone*

4:5–6. The next day, the leading religious officials conduct the hearing. Throughout Acts, Luke mentions two major Jewish theological factions: the Sadducees and the Pharisees. The Sadducees did not believe in resurrection from the dead. The Pharisees (many scribes were Pharisees) believed in resurrection at the end of the age, and Luke portrays them as potentially more sympathetic to news of Jesus' resurrection.

4:7–11. The authorities do not dispute the healing but ask 'By what power or by what name' the healing was done. Peter asserts that the man has been healed by the name of Jesus whom they crucified and God has raised from the dead.

4:13–21. The authorities debate options. They cannot deny the 'notable sign', but they want to keep control of the situation. They know that the Romans, in control of Palestine, do not tolerate uprisings, and they fear threats to their traditional beliefs and power. Their solution is to forbid Peter and John to speak in Jesus' name. The apostles insist upon testifying to what they have 'seen and heard'. At this impasse the authorities, concerned for their own public image, threaten them but release them.

The Believers Pray for Boldness

23 After they were released, they went to their friends[g] and reported what the chief priests and the elders had said to them. [24]When they heard it, they raised their voices together to God and said, "Sovereign Lord, who made the heaven and the earth, the sea, and everything in them, [25]it is you who said by the Holy Spirit through our ancestor David, your servant:[h]

'Why did the Gentiles rage,
and the peoples imagine vain
things?
[26] The kings of the earth took their
stand,
and the rulers have gathered
together
against the Lord and against his
Messiah.'[i]

[27]For in this city, in fact, both Herod and Pontius Pilate, with the Gentiles and the peoples of Israel, gathered together against your holy servant[h] Jesus, whom you anointed, [28]to do whatever your hand and your plan had predestined to take place. [29]And now, Lord, look at their threats, and grant to your servants[j] to speak your word with all boldness, [30]while you stretch out your hand to heal, and signs and wonders are performed through the name of your holy servant[h] Jesus." [31]When they had prayed, the place in which they were gathered together was shaken; and they were all filled with the Holy Spirit and spoke the word of God with boldness.

The Believers Share Their Possessions

32 Now the whole group of those who believed were of one heart and soul, and no one claimed private ownership of any possessions, but everything they owned was held in common. [33]With great power the apostles gave their testimony to the resurrection of the Lord Jesus, and great grace was upon them all. [34]There was not a needy person among them, for as many as owned lands or houses sold them and brought the proceeds of what was sold. [35]They laid it at the apostles' feet, and it was distributed to each as any had need. [36]There was a Levite, a native of Cyprus, Joseph, to whom the apostles gave the name Barnabas (which means "son of encouragement"). [37]He sold a field that belonged to him, then brought the money, and laid it at the apostles' feet.

Ananias and Sapphira

5 But a man named Ananias, with the consent of his wife Sapphira, sold a piece of property; [2]with his wife's knowledge, he kept back some of the proceeds, and brought only a part and laid it at the

[g] Gk their own   [h] Or child   [i] Or his Christ
[j] Gk slaves

4:23–31. After this first confrontation after Pentecost, Peter and John seek out close friends (NRSV footnote f: 'Their own', Greek *idioi*, implies closeness). After experiencing the authorities' hostility, they pray for boldness in speaking God's Word.

4:32–5:11. The next two episodes contrast attitudes toward personal possessions.

4:32–35. Luke repeats that these believers hold their possessions in common (2:44–47). Those with property choose to sell it when needed and give the money to the apostles to distribute.

4:36–37. Luke cites the generosity of Barnabas, from Cyprus, who sells a field and gives the apostles the money. Barnabas later mediates potential conflict (9:27; 11:22–26) and is one of Paul's travelling companions (Acts 13–15).

ACTS 5

1–11. The story of Ananias and Sapphira with their harsh punishment for deceit is Luke's first report of sin and discord within the believers' community. They voluntarily sell their property – perhaps to try to gain status in the community – and deliberately withhold some of the proceeds while claiming to have given all. The results of their deceit, death for both, is hard to understand.

apostles' feet. [3]"Ananias," Peter asked, "why has Satan filled your heart to lie to the Holy Spirit and to keep back part of the proceeds of the land? [4]While it remained unsold, did it not remain your own? And after it was sold, were not the proceeds at your disposal? How is it that you have contrived this deed in your heart? You did not lie to us[k] but to God!" [5]Now when Ananias heard these words, he fell down and died. And great fear seized all who heard of it. [6]The young men came and wrapped up his body,[l] then carried him out and buried him.

[7] After an interval of about three hours his wife came in, not knowing what had happened. [8]Peter said to her, "Tell me whether you and your husband sold the land for such and such a price." And she said, "Yes, that was the price." [9]Then Peter said to her, "How is it that you have agreed together to put the Spirit of the Lord to the test? Look, the feet of those who have buried your husband are at the door, and they will carry you out." [10]Immediately she fell down at his feet and died. When the young men came in they found her dead, so they carried her out and buried her beside her husband. [11]And great fear seized the whole church and all who heard of these things.

The Apostles Heal Many

[12] Now many signs and wonders were done among the people through the apostles. And they were all together in Solomon's Portico. [13]None of the rest dared to join them, but the people held them in high esteem. [14]Yet more than ever believers were added to the Lord, great numbers of both men and women, [15]so that they even carried out the sick into the streets, and laid them on cots and mats, in order that Peter's shadow might fall on some of them as he came by. [16]A great number of people would also gather from the towns around Jerusalem, bringing the sick and those tormented by unclean spirits, and they were all cured.

[k] Gk *to men*   [l] Meaning of Gk uncertain

Luke strongly suggests that sin is a life-and-death matter. He underscores that the entrance of sin into the 'Garden of Eden' of the believers' community is the shared responsibility of both a man and a woman.

This passage raises two issues about women's roles in first-century Judaism: property ownership and participation in funerals.

Although the property described here probably belongs to Ananias, a first-century Jewish woman could own property, particularly through her dowry. Managed by her husband, the dowry remained the wife's possession and returned to her when she was widowed or divorced. Here, Sapphira fully participates with Ananias in decisions to sell and deceive.

Death and burial practices in this story are unusual for first-century Jewish custom. Normally after a death, women cared for the body by washing it and preparing it for burial. They raised loud lamentations and followed the body to its burial place, usually in a rock-cut tomb. With criminals' deaths or cases of vengeance or unrighteousness traditional funeral procedures were changed (as in Jesus' burial). Here, normal female participation is omitted. Men simply wrap up the bodies and carry them out for burial. This suggests that the believers view Ananias' and Sapphira's sin as virtually criminal, and they deny them customary rites due family members. For traditional funeral practices see 9:36–42.

12–42. Luke further portrays God's power in the early believers' lives: people are healed, and the apostles, arrested and imprisoned, are delivered. Gamaliel, a Pharisee, advises the council to leave the apostles alone to determine whether the movement is of divine or human origin. Flogged and again forbidden to speak in Jesus' name, the apostles rejoice that they have 'suffered dishonor' for Jesus' sake. They continue their ministry. Luke again emphasizes that both men and women become believers.

The Apostles Are Persecuted

17 Then the high priest took action; he and all who were with him (that is, the sect of the Sadducees), being filled with jealousy, [18]arrested the apostles and put them in the public prison. [19]But during the night an angel of the Lord opened the prison doors, brought them out, and said, [20]"Go, stand in the temple and tell the people the whole message about this life." [21]When they heard this, they entered the temple at daybreak and went on with their teaching.

When the high priest and those with him arrived, they called together the council and the whole body of the elders of Israel, and sent to the prison to have them brought. [22]But when the temple police went there, they did not find them in the prison; so they returned and reported, [23]"We found the prison securely locked and the guards standing at the doors, but when we opened them, we found no one inside." [24]Now when the captain of the temple and the chief priests heard these words, they were perplexed about them, wondering what might be going on. [25]Then someone arrived and announced, "Look, the men whom you put in prison are standing in the temple and teaching the people!" [26]Then the captain went with the temple police and brought them, but without violence, for they were afraid of being stoned by the people.

27 When they had brought them, they had them stand before the council. The high priest questioned them, [28]saying, "We gave you strict orders not to teach in this name,[m] yet here you have filled Jerusalem with your teaching and you are determined to bring this man's blood on us." [29]But Peter and the apostles answered, "We must obey God rather than any human authority.[n] [30]The God of our ancestors raised up Jesus, whom you had killed by hanging him on a tree. [31]God exalted him at his right hand as Leader and Savior that he might give repentance to Israel and forgiveness of sins. [32]And we are witnesses to these things, and so is the Holy Spirit whom God has given to those who obey him."

33 When they heard this, they were enraged and wanted to kill them. [34]But a Pharisee in the council named Gamaliel, a teacher of the law, respected by all the people, stood up and ordered the men to be put outside for a short time. [35]Then he said to them, "Fellow Israelites,[o] consider carefully what you propose to do to these men. [36]For some time ago Theudas rose up, claiming to be somebody, and a number of men, about four hundred, joined him; but he was killed, and all who followed him were dispersed and disappeared. [37]After him Judas the Galilean rose up at the time of the census and got people to follow him; he also perished, and all who followed him were scattered. [38]So in the present case, I tell you, keep away from these men and let them alone; because if this plan or this undertaking is of human origin, it will fail; [39]but if it is of God, you will not be able to overthrow them – in that case you may even be found fighting against God!"

They were convinced by him, [40]and when

m Other ancient authorities read *Did we not give you strict orders not to teach in this name?*
n Gk *than men*   o Gk *Men, Israelites*

---

29. NRSV footnote m gives 'men' as an alternate translation for 'human authority'. The Greek word used here is *anthropoi* (plural of *anthropos*) and is the generic term for human beings, male and female. *Anthropos* is often translated as 'man' generically but should usually be understood as referring to a human being, person, or individual. Here, Luke uses *anthropos*, 'human being', to contrast with *theos*, 'God'. For Judaism, equating a human being with God is blasphemy (see 5:38–39; 10:26; 12:22; 14:11, 15; 17:29; 24:16).

35–39. Gamaliel's speech urges caution. He concludes (vv. 38–39) with another human-divine contrast (see 5:29).

they had called in the apostles, they had them flogged. Then they ordered them not to speak in the name of Jesus, and let them go. ⁴¹As they left the council, they rejoiced that they were considered worthy to suffer dishonor for the sake of the name. ⁴²And every day in the temple and at home^p they did not cease to teach and proclaim Jesus as the Messiah.^q

Seven Chosen to Serve

6 Now during those days, when the disciples were increasing in number, the Hellenists complained against the Hebrews because their widows were being neglected in the daily distribution of food.

◆ A recurring theme in both Old and New Testament is the care of widows (Deut. 10:18; Job 22:9; 24:3; 31:16; Ps. 94:6; Is. 1:23; 10:2; Mark 12:40; James 1:18). God pronounces a curse against those who withhold justice from widows (Deut. 27:19) while those who care for them are promised God's blessing (Jere. 7:5–7) "Do not take advantage of a widow," warms Exod. 22:22, for God is the defender of widows (Deut. 10:17; Ps. 68:5;146:9). Malachi 3:5 declares that those who defraud laborers of their wages and oppress widows do not fear the Lord Almighty. God repeatedly commanded that His people should relieve the affliction of widows.

There is also an emphasis on letting widows help themselves. The tithe of the produce every third year was designated for the widow, the fatherless, the stranger and the Levite (Deut. 26:12; 27:19). Widows and other economically disadvantaged persons were given special rights to glean at harvest time (Deut. 24:19–21). Ruth, a foreign widow who is further burdened by having taken on the care of the widowed Naomi, is given an opportunity by Boaz to provide for both her mother-in-law and herself. His generosity ensures that her many hours of hot, hard labor bring adequate compensation. Often we see Ruth as a love story. It is also the story of a man righteous enough to support the legitimate claims of a widow. (See Is. 1:17 for the command to defend the rights of widows.) Her rights are to glean and to contract a levirate marriage.

Behind the story of Ruth lies the ancient law whereby a widow was given in marriage to her dead husband's brother, so that she might have a man to provide for her old age (Deut. 25:5–10). A story of another widow's rights is told in Gen. 38, where the father-in-law declares that Tamar acted more righteously than he in her efforts to gain the protection afforded her by law.

The Bible mentions other ways in which widows were enabled to improve their own

^p Or *from house to house*   ^q Or *the Christ*

---

42. By teaching and preaching in homes as well as the Temple, the apostles reach women who may not enter the central parts of the Temple.

ACTS 6

1–7. Luke describes the community's successful solution of a problem: some widows, a socially vulnerable group (see Acts 9:39; James 1:29) are overlooked as food is distributed. Luke introduces Stephen's role in the community.

1. Luke uses several terms to describe the early believers. Here he chooses 'disciples' (e.g. 9:1, 10, 26, 36; 10:36; 14:20–21 etc.). Elsewhere he calls them those 'who belonged to the Way' (9:2), 'saints' (9:13), 'brother (or sister)' (9:17, 30), 'believers (or faithful ones)' (10:45). They are not called 'Christians' until 11:26, in Antioch.

Enough time has passed, maybe three years, since Pentecost, that the believers have formed distinct groups. The Hellenists are native Greek-speaking Jews who have come to Jerusalem from elsewhere in the Roman Empire. They would attend synagogue services in Greek; the Hebrews are native Hebrew (Aramaic) speakers. Both groups probably have numerous bilingual members.

condition. Elijah asked an impoverished widow to supply what she had – enough flour and oil to make a little cake for him. As she ministered to his needs, her own were miraculously supplied during the three and a half years of the drought. She was helped to help herself (1 Kings 17:7–16). Elisha was once approached by a destitute widow who was threatened with the sale of her two sons into slavery. His first command was that she go out and borrow jars from the neighbors. Next she must utilize what she had: the little oil she still possessed. By God's grace it is multiplied until she has enough to provide for herself and her sons (2 Kings 4:17).

Jesus expressed concern for the legal rights of widows and told a parable affirming a widow who persisted in her struggles to obtain justice (Luke 18:2–5). He restored to life a widow's only son, so that he might continue to support her in her old age (Luke 7:11–17). The early church appointed deacons to see that the needs of widows were being met equitably and adequately. (Acts 6:1ff) Peter's prayers returned to life a disciple named Dorcas because of her ministry to widows (Acts 9:36–41).

An individual who leaves a widow in destitution has denied the faith and is worse than an infidel (1 Tim. 5:4, 8). The First Epistle to Timothy arranged for widows in financial need to be compensated in return for their labors in the church (1 Tim. 5:3–16); and Paul was of the opinion that a laborer was worthy of her hire (1 Tim. 5:18).

Widows were regarded as persons having special opportunities for Christian service. They were widely used in the ministry of the early church and given special seats of honor in front of the congregation. A large church, such as Hagia Sophia in Constantinople, might have hundreds of widows on its staff. They visited homes, brought food for the hungry, cared for the sick, comforted the bereaved, prayed for all who made their requests known, assisted in Christian instruction and baptism, and counselled those in need. So powerful were they in prayer that early Christian literature sometimes calls widows "the altar of God" ◆

²And the twelve called together the whole community of the disciples and said, "It is not right that we should neglect the word of God in order to wait on tables.ᵗ ³Therefore, friends,ˢ select from among yourselves seven men of good standing, full of the Spirit and of wisdom, whom we may appoint to this task, ⁴while we, for our part, will devote ourselves to prayer and to serving the word." ⁵What they said pleased the whole community, and they chose Stephen, a man full of faith and the Holy Spirit, together with Philip, Prochorus, Nicanor, Timon, Parmenas, and Nicolaus, a proselyte of Antioch. ⁶They had these men stand before the apostles, who prayed and laid their hands on them.

7 The word of God continued to spread; the number of the disciples increased greatly in Jerusalem, and a great many of the priests became obedient to the faith.

ᵗ Or *keep accounts*   ˢ Gk *brothers*

2–6. The apostles, their schedules already full, urge selection of seven men to take care of the situation. Stephen and six other men (they were presumably Hellenists, since they had Greek names) are chosen. Although it is unclear whether they are to supervise the food distribution or do it themselves (a task normally reserved for servants, slaves, or women), their service is sufficiently important to receive laying on of hands (v. 6), normally a sign of consecration or healing (see Num. 27:15–23; Acts 8:17; 9:17; 13:3; 19:6; 28:8; 1 Tim. 4:14; 2 Tim. 1:6). Over the centuries, this position of service has evolved in many churches into the role of 'deacon', from the Greek *diakoneo*, 'I serve', found in Acts 6:2 ('wait on', NRSV).

The Arrest of Stephen

8 Stephen, full of grace and power, did great wonders and signs among the people. ⁹Then some of those who belonged to the synagogue of the Freedmen (as it was called), Cyrenians, Alexandrians, and others of those from Cilicia and Asia, stood up and argued with Stephen. ¹⁰But they could not withstand the wisdom and the Spirit' with which he spoke. ¹¹Then they secretly instigated some men to say, "We have heard him speak blasphemous words against Moses and God." ¹²They stirred up the people as well as the elders and the scribes; then they suddenly confronted him, seized him, and brought him before the council. ¹³They set up false witnesses who said, "This man never stops saying things against this holy place and the law; ¹⁴for we have heard him say that this Jesus of Nazareth" will destroy this place and will change the customs that Moses handed on to us." ¹⁵And all who sat in the council looked intently at him, and they saw that his face was like the face of an angel.

Stephen's Speech to the Council

7 Then the high priest asked him, "Are these things so?" ²And Stephen replied:

"Brothers' and fathers, listen to me. The God of glory appeared to our ancestor Abraham when he was in Mesopotamia, before he lived in Haran, ³and said to him, 'Leave your country and your relatives and go to the land that I will show you.' ⁴Then he left the country of the Chaldeans and settled in Haran. After his father died, God had him move from there to this country in which you are now living. ⁵He did not give him any of it as a heritage, not even a foot's length, but promised to give it to him as his possession and to his descendants after him, even though he had no child. ⁶And God spoke in these terms, that his descendants would be resident aliens in a country belonging to others, who would enslave them and mistreat them during four hundred years. ⁷'But I will judge the nation that they serve,' said God, 'and after that they shall come out and worship me in this place.' ⁸Then he gave him the covenant of circumcision. And so Abraham" became the father of Isaac and circumcised him on the eighth day; and Isaac became the father of Jacob, and Jacob of the twelve patriarchs.

9 "The patriarchs, jealous of Joseph, sold him into Egypt; but God was with him, ¹⁰and rescued him from all his afflictions, and enabled him to win favor and to show wisdom when he stood before Pharaoh,

---

' Or *spirit*   " Gk *the Nazorean*
' Gk *Men, brothers*   " Gk *he*

6:8–8:1. Stephen, a powerful, radical speaker with unorthodox attitudes toward Judaism as practised in the first century, first confronts other Hellenist Jews at the Synagogue of the Freedmen, then faces the Council, and is stoned to death.

6:13–15. Charges against Stephen – he speaks 'against this holy place [i.e. the Temple] and the law' – suggest that he considers some aspects of Temple worship unnecessary and believes that Jesus, upon his return, will destroy the Temple and change the laws given by Moses.

ACTS 7

1–53. Stephen's speech indirectly addresses these charges. Not seeking acquittal, he interprets Hebrew history. He concentrates on Abraham (vv. 2–8), Joseph (vv. 9–16), and Moses (vv. 20–44), patriarchs whom God led from their homes into uncertain futures. Stephen stresses that when the Hebrew people felt secure as a nation, they built a Temple (under Solomon, vv. 47–50) rather than keep the portable Tent of Testimony as God directed under Moses. Throughout his speech, Stephen emphasizes that the Patriarchs who obeyed God lived uprooted lives (tent-like), dependent on God's direction; once the Temple was built, the Hebrews desired security more than

king of Egypt, who appointed him ruler over Egypt and over all his household. ¹¹Now there came a famine throughout Egypt and Canaan, and great suffering, and our ancestors could find no food. ¹²But when Jacob heard that there was grain in Egypt, he sent our ancestors there on their first visit. ¹³On the second visit Joseph made himself known to his brothers, and Joseph's family became known to Pharaoh. ¹⁴Then Joseph sent and invited his father Jacob and all his relatives to come to him, seventy-five in all; ¹⁵so Jacob went down to Egypt. He himself died there as well as our ancestors, ¹⁶and their bodies^x were brought back to Shechem and laid in the tomb that Abraham had bought for a sum of silver from the sons of Hamor in Shechem.

17 "But as the time drew near for the fulfillment of the promise that God had made to Abraham, our people in Egypt increased and multiplied ¹⁸until another king who had not known Joseph ruled over Egypt. ¹⁹He dealt craftily with our race and forced our ancestors to abandon their infants so that they would die. ²⁰At this time Moses was born, and he was beautiful before God. For three months he was brought up in his father's house; ²¹and when he was abandoned, Pharaoh's daughter adopted him and brought him up as her own son. ²²So Moses was instructed in all the wisdom of the Egyptians and was powerful in his words and deeds.

23 "When he was forty years old, it came into his heart to visit his relatives, the Israelites.^y ²⁴When he saw one of them being wronged, he defended the oppressed man and avenged him by striking down the Egyptian. ²⁵He supposed that his kinsfolk would understand that God through him was rescuing them, but they did not understand. ²⁶The next day he came to some of them as they were quarreling and tried to reconcile them, saying, 'Men, you are brothers; why do you wrong each other?' ²⁷But the man who was wronging his neighbor pushed Moses^z aside, saying, 'Who made you a ruler and a judge over us? ²⁸Do you want to kill me as you killed the Egyptian yesterday?' ²⁹When he heard this, Moses fled and became a resident alien in the land of Midian. There he became the father of two sons.

30 "Now when forty years had passed, an angel appeared to him in the wilderness of Mount Sinai, in the flame of a burning bush. ³¹When Moses saw it, he was amazed at the sight; and as he approached to look, there came the voice of the Lord: ³²'I am the God of your ancestors, the God of Abraham, Isaac, and Jacob.' Moses began to tremble and did not dare to look. ³³Then the Lord said to him, 'Take off the sandals from your feet, for the place where you are standing is holy ground. ³⁴I have surely seen the mistreatment of my people who are in Egypt and have heard their groaning, and I have come down to rescue them. Come now, I will send you to Egypt.'

35 "It was this Moses whom they rejected when they said, 'Who made you a ruler and a judge?' and whom God now sent as both ruler and liberator through the angel who appeared to him in the bush. ³⁶He led them out, having performed wonders and signs in Egypt, at the Red Sea, and in the wilderness for forty years. ³⁷This is the Moses who said to the Israelites, 'God will raise up a prophet for you from your own people^a as he raised me up.' ³⁸He is the one who was in the congregation in the wilderness with the angel who spoke to

^x Gk *they*   ^y Gk *his brothers, the sons of Israel*
^z Gk *him*   ^a Gk *your brothers*

God's direction by the Holy Spirit. Stephen finally accuses his judges of 'opposing the Holy Spirit': their ancestors killed the prophets, and they have murdered the 'Righteous One' (Jesus – but Stephen's speech never mentions Jesus' name) whose coming the prophets foretold. To the authorities, Stephen's words border on blasphemy because he equates Jesus with Messiah.

him at Mount Sinai, and with our ancestors; and he received living oracles to give to us. [39]Our ancestors were unwilling to obey him; instead, they pushed him aside, and in their hearts they turned back to Egypt, [40]saying to Aaron, 'Make gods for us who will lead the way for us; as for this Moses who led us out from the land of Egypt, we do not know what has happened to him.' [41]At that time they made a calf, offered a sacrifice to the idol, and reveled in the works of their hands. [42]But God turned away from them and handed them over to worship the host of heaven, as it is written in the book of the prophets:

'Did you offer to me slain victims and
     sacrifices
   forty years in the wilderness,
     O house of Israel?
[43] No; you took along the tent of
     Moloch,
   and the star of your god Rephan,
     the images that you made to
       worship;
so I will remove you beyond Babylon.'

44 "Our ancestors had the tent of testimony in the wilderness, as God[b] directed when he spoke to Moses, ordering him to make it according to the pattern he had seen. [45]Our ancestors in turn brought it in with Joshua when they dispossessed the nations that God drove out before our ancestors. And it was there until the time of David, [46]who found favor with God and asked that he might find a dwelling place for the house of Jacob.[c] [47]But it was Solomon who built a house for him. [48]Yet the Most High does not dwell in houses made with human hands;[d] as the prophet says,

[49] 'Heaven is my throne,
     and the earth is my footstool.
   What kind of house will you build for
     me, says the Lord,
     or what is the place of my rest?
[50] Did not my hand make all these
       things?'

51 "You stiff-necked people, uncircumcised in heart and ears, you are forever opposing the Holy Spirit, just as your ancestors used to do. [52]Which of the prophets did your ancestors not persecute? They killed those who foretold the coming of the Righteous One, and now you have become his betrayers and murderers. [53]You are the ones that received the law as ordained by angels, and yet you have not kept it."

The Stoning of Stephen

54 When they heard these things, they became enraged and ground their teeth at Stephen.[e] [55]But filled with the Holy Spirit, he gazed into heaven and saw the glory of God and Jesus standing at the right hand of God. [56]"Look," he said, "I see the heavens opened and the Son of Man standing at the right hand of God!" [57]But they covered their ears, and with a loud shout all rushed together against him. [58]Then they dragged him out of the city and began to stone him; and the witnesses laid their coats at the feet of a young man named Saul. [59]While they were stoning Stephen, he prayed, "Lord Jesus, receive my spirit." [60]Then he knelt down and cried out

[b] Gk *he*   [c] Other ancient authorities read *for the God of Jacob*   [d] Gk *with hands*   [e] Gk *him*

54–57. Stephen's speech has enraged his listeners who now hear him describe a vision of Jesus at God's right hand, further blasphemy to them.

58–60. A customary stoning entails not only taking the criminal from the city (v. 58) but also pushing him over a twelve-foot-high cliff and dropping stones on his chest until he is dead (cf. Luke 4:29). Stephen's stoning may be a lynching rather than formal justice. Stephen's dying words echo Luke's account of Jesus' words from the cross to God (Luke 23:34, 46), but here Stephen addresses the ascended Lord Jesus.

in a loud voice, "Lord, do not hold this sin against them." When he had said this, he died.[f] [8:1]And Saul approved of their killing him.

Saul Persecutes the Church

That day a severe persecution began against the church in Jerusalem, and all except the apostles were scattered throughout the countryside of Judea and Samaria. [2]Devout men buried Stephen and made loud lamentation over him. [3]But Saul was ravaging the church by entering house after house; dragging off both men and women, he committed them to prison.

Philip Preaches in Samaria

4 Now those who were scattered went from place to place, proclaiming the word. [5]Philip went down to the city[g] of Samaria and proclaimed the Messiah[h] to them. [6]The crowds with one accord listened eagerly to what was said by Philip, hearing and seeing the signs that he did, [7]for unclean spirits, crying with loud shrieks, came out of many who were possessed; and many others who were paralyzed or lame were cured. [8]So there was great joy in that city.

9 Now a certain man named Simon had previously practiced magic in the city and amazed the people of Samaria, saying that he was someone great. [10]All of them, from the least to the greatest, listened to him eagerly, saying, "This man is the power of God that is called Great." [11]And they listened eagerly to him because for a long time he had amazed them with his magic. [12]But when they believed Philip, who was proclaiming the good news about the kingdom of God and the name of Jesus Christ, they were baptized, both men and women. [13]Even Simon himself believed. After being baptized, he stayed constantly with Philip and was amazed when he saw the signs and great miracles that took place.

14 Now when the apostles at Jerusalem heard that Samaria had accepted the word of God, they sent Peter and John to them. [15]The two went down and prayed for them that they might receive the Holy Spirit [16](for as yet the Spirit had not come[i] upon any of them; they had only been baptized in the name of the Lord Jesus). [17]Then Peter and John[j] laid their hands on them, and they received the Holy Spirit. [18]Now when Simon saw that the Spirit was given through the laying on of the apostles' hands, he offered them money, [19]saying,

[f] Gk *fell asleep*   [g] Other ancient authorities read *a city*   [h] Or *the Christ*   [i] Gk *fallen*   [j] Gk *they*

ACTS 8

1–40. Luke introduces Saul/Paul at Stephen's execution and subsequent persecution of the believers before depicting his conversion and missionary work. Saul, like the council members, believes that the notion of the resurrection of the man Jesus is blasphemous. Hence, his virulent zeal takes him into believers' houses to drag men and women to prison. Persecution causes believers, particularly Hellenists, to flee Jerusalem. Luke now shows Philip, one of the seven (6:5), fulfilling the risen Lord's command to witness in Samaria and the ends of the earth (1:8). The apostles' approval, through Peter and John, is given to evangelism outside Jerusalem.
4–13. The Samaritans joyfully receive Philip's preaching and healing. Simon, a popular sorcerer, has previously amazed them with his abilities, but both men and women are amazed at Philip's preaching and healings. They believe and are baptized, as is Simon.
14–25. When this news comes to Jerusalem, Peter and John go to Samaria and lay hands on the baptized believers, who then receive the Holy Spirit. Simon, constantly amazed at the power of God, offers money for the power to bestow the Holy Spirit through laying on hands. Peter curses him and urges him to repent. Simon asks Peter's prayers to avert any evil. Luke never reports what ultimately happens to Simon.

"Give me also this power so that anyone on whom I lay my hands may receive the Holy Spirit." [20]But Peter said to him, "May your silver perish with you, because you thought you could obtain God's gift with money! [21]You have no part or share in this, for your heart is not right before God. [22]Repent therefore of this wickedness of yours, and pray to the Lord that, if possible, the intent of your heart may be forgiven you. [23]For I see that you are in the gall of bitterness and the chains of wickedness." [24]Simon answered, "Pray for me to the Lord, that nothing of what you[k] have said may happen to me."

25 Now after Peter and John[l] had testified and spoken the word of the Lord, they returned to Jerusalem, proclaiming the good news to many villages of the Samaritans.

Philip and the Ethiopian Eunuch

26 Then an angel of the Lord said to Philip, "Get up and go toward the south[m] to the road that goes down from Jerusalem to Gaza." (This is a wilderness road.) [27]So he got up and went. Now there was an Ethiopian eunuch, a court official of the Candace, queen of the Ethiopians, in charge of her entire treasury. He had come to Jerusalem to worship [28]and was returning

home; seated in his chariot, he was reading the prophet Isaiah. [29]Then the Spirit said to Philip, "Go over to this chariot and join it." [30]So Philip ran up to it and heard him reading the prophet Isaiah. He asked, "Do you understand what you are reading?" [31]He replied, "How can I, unless someone guides me?" And he invited Philip to get in and sit beside him. [32]Now the passage of the scripture that he was reading was this:

"Like a sheep he was led to the
        slaughter,
    and like a lamb silent before its
        shearer,
        so he does not open his mouth.
[33] In his humiliation justice was denied
        him.
    Who can describe his generation?
    For his life is taken away from the
        earth."

[34]The eunuch asked Philip, "About whom, may I ask you, does the prophet say this, about himself or about someone else?" [35]Then Philip began to speak, and starting with this scripture, he proclaimed to him the good news about Jesus. [36]As they were going along the

k The Greek word for you and the verb pray are plural   l Gk after they   m Or go at noon

---

26–40. God, through an angel (v. 26) and the Holy Spirit (vv. 29, 39), closely directs Philip as he travels southward toward Gaza with only enough information necessary for his next move. For Luke, specific direction by the Holy Spirit usually benefits the believers' community, is confirmed directly or indirectly by others' experiences, and is not merely a personal experience (see 9:1–19; 10:1–48; 16:9–10; 27:23–26). Philip meets an Ethiopian eunuch, a treasurer for the Candace, queen of the Ethiopians. The ancient Mediterranean world considered Ethiopia, territory south of Aswan, as the 'ends of the earth'. Eunuchs, castrated males, were often employed as officials in royal courts of Near Eastern countries. Some scholars think that the term 'eunuch' does not necessarily indicate castration but is simply another term for 'court official'. The Candace, the powerful queen mother of the Ethiopian king, ruled the country for her son, who was considered divine.

Luke relates little about the eunuch. He is African; he may be a 'God-fearer', a Gentile who believes in the God of Israel, but Luke does not say so. The eunuch has a scroll of Hebrew Scriptures with Is. 53. After Philip interprets the Scriptures by proclaiming the good news, the eunuch seeks baptism. Philip baptizes him, and the Spirit takes Philip – like Elijah and Ezekiel (1 Kings 18:12; 2 Kings 2:16; Ezek. 3:14) – to Azotus. Philip preaches along the way to Caesarea, where he next appears (Acts 21:8–9).

road, they came to some water; and the eunuch said, "Look, here is water! What is to prevent me from being baptized?"[n] [38]He commanded the chariot to stop, and both of them, Philip and the eunuch, went down into the water, and Philip[o] baptized him. [39]When they came up out of the water, the Spirit of the Lord snatched Philip away; the eunuch saw him no more, and went on his way rejoicing. [40]But Philip found himself at Azotus, and as he was passing through the region, he proclaimed the good news to all the towns until he came to Caesarea.

The Conversion of Saul

9 Meanwhile Saul, still breathing threats and murder against the disciples of the Lord, went to the high priest [2]and asked him for letters to the synagogues at Damascus, so that if he found any who belonged to the Way, men or women, he might bring them bound to Jerusalem. [3]Now as he was going along and approaching Damascus, suddenly a light from heaven flashed around him. [4]He fell to the ground and heard a voice saying to him, "Saul, Saul, why do you persecute me?" [5]He asked, "Who are you, Lord?" The reply came, "I am Jesus, whom you are persecuting. [6]But get up and enter the city, and you will be told what you are to do." [7]The men who were travel-

ing with him stood speechless because they heard the voice but saw no one. [8]Saul got up from the ground, and though his eyes were open, he could see nothing; so they led him by the hand and brought him into Damascus. [9]For three days he was without sight, and neither ate nor drank.

10 Now there was a disciple in Damascus named Ananias. The Lord said to him in a vision, "Ananias." He answered, "Here I am, Lord." [11]The Lord said to him, "Get up and go to the street called Straight, and at the house of Judas look for a man of Tarsus named Saul. At this moment he is praying, [12]and he has seen in a vision[p] a man named Ananias come in and lay his hands on him so that he might regain his sight." [13]But Ananias answered, "Lord, I have heard from many about this man, how much evil he has done to your saints in Jerusalem; [14]and here he has authority from the chief priests to bind all who invoke your name." [15]But the Lord said to him, "Go, for he is an instrument whom I have chosen to bring my name before Gentiles and kings and before the people of Israel; [16]I myself will show him

[n] Other ancient authorities add all or most of verse 37, *And Philip said, "If you believe with all your heart, you may." And he replied, "I believe that Jesus Christ is the Son of God."*   [o] Gk *he*   [p] Other ancient authorities lack *in a vision*

ACTS 9

1–31. Since Luke rarely repeats episodes, his three accounts of Saul's conversion (here; 22:6–16; 26:12–20) highlight its importance as an act of God. As with Philip (8:26:40), God's revelation to Saul is confirmed by Ananias' vision.

1–9. Saul, angry because he sees the believers' exaltation of Jesus as blasphemy, continues persecuting both men and women (v. 2), all the way to Damascus, nearly 150 miles from Jerusalem. In a moment of blinding light Saul hears the risen Jesus speaking to him, and he must reconsider what he believes about God. He spends three days, sightless and fasting. God reveals to Saul, like Philip, what to do, one step at a time.

10–22. The Lord appears in a vision to Ananias, a Damascus believer, and instructs him to approach Saul. Ananias protests, fearing Saul's reputation as persecutor, but is assured that God has chosen Saul to go to both Jew and Gentile. Ananias, as bidden, lays hands on Saul whose sight is restored. Saul is baptized and goes to synagogues to preach to an amazed audience that Jesus is the Son of God.

how much he must suffer for the sake of my name." [17]So Ananias went and entered the house. He laid his hands on Saul[q] and said, "Brother Saul, the Lord Jesus, who appeared to you on your way here, has sent me so that you may regain your sight and be filled with the Holy Spirit." [18]And immediately something like scales fell from his eyes, and his sight was restored. Then he got up and was baptized, [19]and after taking some food, he regained his strength.

Saul Preaches in Damascus

For several days he was with the disciples in Damascus, [20]and immediately he began to proclaim Jesus in the synagogues, saying, "He is the Son of God." [21]All who heard him were amazed and said, "Is not this the man who made havoc in Jerusalem among those who invoked this name? And has he not come here for the purpose of bringing them bound before the chief priests?" [22]Saul became increasingly more powerful and confounded the Jews who lived in Damascus by proving that Jesus[r] was the Messiah.[s]

Saul Escapes from the Jews

23 After some time had passed, the Jews plotted to kill him, [24]but their plot became known to Saul. They were watching the gates day and night so that they might kill him; [25]but his disciples took him by night and let him down through an opening in the wall,[t] lowering him in a basket.

Saul in Jerusalem

26 When he had come to Jerusalem, he attempted to join the disciples; and they were all afraid of him, for they did not believe that he was a disciple. [27]But Barnabas took him, brought him to the apostles, and described for them how on the road he had seen the Lord, who had spoken to him, and how in Damascus he had spoken boldly in the name of Jesus. [28]So he went in and out among them in Jerusalem, speaking boldly in the name of the Lord. [29]He spoke and argued with the Hellenists; but they were attempting to kill him. [30]When the believers[u] learned of it, they brought him down to Caesarea and sent him off to Tarsus.

31 Meanwhile the church throughout Judea, Galilee, and Samaria had peace and was built up. Living in the fear of the Lord and in the comfort of the Holy Spirit, it increased in numbers.

The Healing of Aeneas

32 Now as Peter went here and there among all the believers,[v] he came down also to the saints living in Lydda. [33]There he found a man named Aeneas, who had been bedridden for eight years, for he was paralyzed. [34]Peter said to him, "Aeneas, Jesus Christ heals you; get up and make your bed!" And immediately he got up. [35]And all the residents of Lydda and Sharon saw him and turned to the Lord.

[q] Gk him   [r] Gk that this   [s] Or the Christ   [t] Gk through the wall   [u] Gk brothers   [v] Gk all of them

---

23–31. Saul arouses Jewish opposition in Damascus by proclaiming that Jesus is the Messiah and flees for his life back to Jerusalem. Believers there, at first afraid of Saul because he previously persecuted them, accept him after Barnabas (see 4:36–37) vouches for his conversion. Saul then clashes with Jewish Hellenists who also try to kill him. The believers return him home to Tarsus, nearly 500 miles from Jerusalem. Luke does not indicate how much time has elapsed since Saul's conversion. The believers' community in Jerusalem is now at peace and well established outside the city.

32–43. Luke recounts healings in Lydda and Joppa, towns about ten miles apart.

32–35. Peter, visiting believers' communities, comes to Lydda and through the power of Jesus heals Aeneas, paralyzed for eight years.

Peter in Lydda and Joppa

36 Now in Joppa there was a disciple whose name was Tabitha, which in Greek is Dorcas.ʷ She was devoted to good works and acts of charity. ³⁷At that time she became ill and died. When they had washed her, they laid her in a room upstairs. ³⁸Since Lydda was near Joppa, the disciples, who heard that Peter was there, sent two men to him with the request, "Please come to us without delay." ³⁹So Peter got up and went with them; and when he arrived, they took him to the room upstairs. All the widows stood beside him, weeping and showing tunics and other clothing that Dorcas had made while she was with them. ⁴⁰Peter put all of them outside, and then he knelt down and prayed. He turned to the body and said, "Tabitha, get up." Then she opened her eyes, and seeing Peter, she sat up. ⁴¹He gave her his hand and helped her up. Then calling the saints and widows, he showed her to be alive. ⁴²This became known throughout Joppa, and many believed in the Lord. ⁴³Meanwhile he stayed in Joppa for some time with a certain Simon, a tanner.

Peter and Cornelius

10 In Caesarea there was a man named Cornelius, a centurion of the Italian Cohort, as it was called. ²He was a devout man who feared God with all his household; he gave alms generously to the people and prayed constantly to God. ³One afternoon at about three o'clock he had a vision in which he clearly saw an angel of God coming in and saying to him, "Cornelius." ⁴He stared at him in terror and said, "What is it, Lord?" He answered, "Your prayers and your alms have ascended as a memorial before God. ⁵Now send men to Joppa for a certain Simon who is called Peter; ⁶he is lodging with Simon, a tanner, whose house is by the seaside." ⁷When the angel who spoke to him had left, he called two of his slaves and a devout soldier from the ranks of those who served him, ⁸and

---

ʷ The name Tabitha in Aramaic and the name Dorcas in Greek mean *a gazelle*

36–39. In Joppa a devoted disciple named Tabitha has died. Peter is specifically summoned because Tabitha has meant so much to the believers. Tabitha is unique in the New Testament, singled out with *mathetria*, the feminine form of the word 'disciple' (*mathetes*). Elsewhere women are included as disciples by the inclusive masculine plural form of *mathetes*. Before her death Tabitha, like the Seven (6:1–6), cared for poor widows, some of the most vulnerable members of society. Luke underscores that community members know Tabitha is truly dead because they have prepared her body for burial. Women normally washed the body. Here, the Greek word for 'wash' is masculine plural, indicating that men and women take part. Perhaps the men bring water since they would not wash a woman's corpse.

40–43. Peter prays and bids Tabitha arise, similar to Jesus' healing of Jairus' daughter (Mark 5:22–24, 35–43). Tabitha is restored to the community, and news of her healing adds new believers.

ACTS 10 & 11

10:1–11:18. As news of Jesus' resurrection spreads outside Jerusalem, inevitably the believers' community, originally Jewish, must deal with Gentile believers. Luke has indicated in 1:8; 2:17; 9:15 that the gospel is not for Jews only. He now depicts the believers' community struggling with related practical problems: hospitality with Gentiles, and circumcision as part of initiation.

10:1–16. Cornelius, stationed at Caesarea, is a Roman professional soldier of modest family background (probably descended from a slave freed by the Roman Dictator L. Cornelius Sulla about 80 BC). As a centurion he leads about 100 soldiers. He is a 'God-fearer', an uncircumcised believer in the God of Israel – different from many Roman soldiers who worshiped numerous

after telling them everything, he sent them to Joppa.

9 About noon the next day, as they were on their journey and approaching the city, Peter went up on the roof to pray. ¹⁰He became hungry and wanted something to eat; and while it was being prepared, he fell into a trance. ¹¹He saw the heaven opened and something like a large sheet coming down, being lowered to the ground by its four corners. ¹²In it were all kinds of four-footed creatures and reptiles and birds of the air. ¹³Then he heard a voice saying, "Get up, Peter; kill and eat." ¹⁴But Peter said, "By no means, Lord; for I have never eaten anything that is profane or unclean." ¹⁵The voice said to him again, a second time, "What God has made clean, you must not call profane." ¹⁶This happened three times, and the thing was suddenly taken up to heaven.

17 Now while Peter was greatly puzzled about what to make of the vision that he had seen, suddenly the men sent by Cornelius appeared. They were asking for Simon's house and were standing by the gate. ¹⁸They called out to ask whether Simon, who was called Peter, was staying there. ¹⁹While Peter was still thinking about the vision, the Spirit said to him, "Look, three^x men are searching for you.

²⁰Now get up, go down, and go with them without hesitation; for I have sent them." ²¹So Peter went down to the men and said, "I am the one you are looking for; what is the reason for your coming?" ²²They answered, "Cornelius, a centurion, an upright and God-fearing man, who is well spoken of by the whole Jewish nation, was directed by a holy angel to send for you to come to his house and to hear what you have to say." ²³So Peter^y invited them in and gave them lodging.

The next day he got up and went with them, and some of the believers^z from Joppa accompanied him. ²⁴The following day they came to Caesarea. Cornelius was expecting them and had called together his relatives and close friends. ²⁵On Peter's arrival Cornelius met him, and falling at his feet, worshiped him. ²⁶But Peter made him get up, saying, "Stand up; I am only a mortal." ²⁷And as he talked with him, he went in and found that many had assembled; ²⁸and he said to them, "You yourselves know that it is unlawful for a Jew to associate with or to visit a Gentile; but God has shown me that I should not call

^x One ancient authority reads *two*; others lack the word   ^y Gk *he*   ^z Gk *brothers*

Greek, Roman, and Oriental divinities. In Jesus' ministry Luke records (Luke 7:2–10) that a centurion is the first Gentile Jesus approaches. Cornelius becomes God's agent. Through him Peter and the apostles learn that practical ethnic and religious barriers between Jew and Gentile must fall. Cornelius has a vision of an angel of God who assures him that God has heard his prayers and tells him, without giving reasons, to send for Peter in Joppa. Luke validates Cornelius' vision, pairing it with Peter's vision of the sheet containing clean and unclean animals (see Lev. 11). The voice urges him to eat them regardless of their ritual impurity because God has made them clean. Peter cannot yet understand the vision's significance.

10:17–33. Cornelius' messengers arrive at Simon the Tanner's house where Peter, still perplexed, is staying. The Spirit confirms their mission, and the next day Peter goes with them to Caesarea. Cornelius, knowing that God is acting, summons family and friends. When Peter arrives, Cornelius reverences him, but Peter insists (v. 28) that he is a mortal (*anthropos*: see on 5:29). Peter now understands the importance of his vision: fellowship with Gentiles who eat food dedicated to idols, who do not always remove all the blood from their meat, and who eat meat declared unclean by the Mosaic code, is acceptable to God. Understanding the vision further, Peter declares that no human being (*anthropos*, v. 28: NRSV translates it 'anyone') should be called 'profane or unclean'.

anyone profane or unclean. ²⁹So when I was sent for, I came without objection. Now may I ask why you sent for me?"

30 Cornelius replied, "Four days ago at this very hour, at three o'clock, I was praying in my house when suddenly a man in dazzling clothes stood before me. ³¹He said, 'Cornelius, your prayer has been heard and your alms have been remembered before God. ³²Send therefore to Joppa and ask for Simon, who is called Peter; he is staying in the home of Simon, a tanner, by the sea.' ³³Therefore I sent for you immediately, and you have been kind enough to come. So now all of us are here in the presence of God to listen to all that the Lord has commanded you to say."

Gentiles Hear the Good News

34 Then Peter began to speak to them: "I truly understand that God shows no partiality, ³⁵but in every nation anyone who fears him and does what is right is acceptable to him. ³⁶You know the message he sent to the people of Israel, preaching peace by Jesus Christ – he is Lord of all. ³⁷That message spread throughout Judea, beginning in Galilee after the baptism that John announced: ³⁸how God anointed Jesus of Nazareth with the Holy Spirit and with power; how he went about doing good and healing all who were oppressed by the devil, for God was with him. ³⁹We are witnesses to all that he did both in Judea and in Jerusalem. They put him to death by hanging him on a tree; ⁴⁰but God raised him on the third day and allowed him to appear, ⁴¹not to all the people but to us who were chosen by

God as witnesses, and who ate and drank with him after he rose from the dead. ⁴²He commanded us to preach to the people and to testify that he is the one ordained by God as judge of the living and the dead. ⁴³All the prophets testify about him that everyone who believes in him receives forgiveness of sins through his name."

Gentiles Receive the Holy Spirit

44 While Peter was still speaking, the Holy Spirit fell upon all who heard the word. ⁴⁵The circumcised believers who had come with Peter were astounded that the gift of the Holy Spirit had been poured out even on the Gentiles, ⁴⁶for they heard them speaking in tongues and extolling God. Then Peter said, ⁴⁷"Can anyone withhold the water for baptizing these people who have received the Holy Spirit just as we have?" ⁴⁸So he ordered them to be baptized in the name of Jesus Christ. Then they invited him to stay for several days.

Peter's Report to the Church at Jerusalem

11 Now the apostles and the believers[a] who were in Judea heard that the Gentiles had also accepted the word of God. ²So when Peter went up to Jerusalem, the circumcised believers[b] criticized him, ³saying, "Why did you go to uncircumcised men and eat with them?" ⁴Then Peter began to explain it to them, step by step, saying, ⁵"I was in the city of Joppa praying, and in a trance I saw a vision. There was something like a large sheet coming down

[a] Gk brothers   [b] Gk lacks believers

10:34–48. Peter, resolving his own issues of associating with Gentiles, now takes the opportunity to share the gospel with this Gentile group – the first direct example of this in Acts (the Ethiopian eunuch may be a Gentile, but Luke is unclear). Although they have already heard about Jesus (v. 36), they and Peter now experience that the good news is for Gentiles too. The Holy Spirit, to the amazement of the Jewish believers, falls on Gentiles as it has on Jews, and they are baptized in Jesus' name.

11:1–18. Facing opposition within the Jerusalem community, Peter reports his meeting with Cornelius. To emphasize these events, Luke repeats them. The Jerusalem believers praise God for the Gentiles' repentance and new life. The apostles' approval, particularly Peter's, now rests on the Gentile mission.

from heaven, being lowered by its four corners; and it came close to me. ⁶As I looked at it closely I saw four-footed animals, beasts of prey, reptiles, and birds of the air. ⁷I also heard a voice saying to me, 'Get up, Peter; kill and eat.' ⁸But I replied, 'By no means, Lord; for nothing profane or unclean has ever entered my mouth.' ⁹But a second time the voice answered from heaven, 'What God has made clean, you must not call profane.' ¹⁰This happened three times; then everything was pulled up again to heaven. ¹¹At that very moment three men, sent to me from Caesarea, arrived at the house where we were. ¹²The Spirit told me to go with them and not to make a distinction between them and us.ᶜ These six brothers also accompanied me, and we entered the man's house. ¹³He told us how he had seen the angel standing in his house and saying, 'Send to Joppa and bring Simon, who is called Peter; ¹⁴he will give you a message by which you and your entire household will be saved.' ¹⁵And as I began to speak, the Holy Spirit fell upon them just as it had upon us at the beginning. ¹⁶And I remembered the word of the Lord, how he had said, 'John baptized with water, but you will be baptized with the Holy Spirit.' ¹⁷If then God gave them the same gift that he gave us when we believed in the Lord Jesus Christ, who was I that I could hinder God?" ¹⁸When they heard this, they were silenced. And they praised God, saying, "Then God has given even to the Gentiles the repentance that leads to life."

◆ The Greek word used for the silence of the apostles in Acts 11:18 is *hesuchazo*. Interestingly enough, they are being 'silent' while praising God and making a theological statement! The term demonstrates that the apostles became acquiescent after having previously offered objections to Peter's evangelizing Gentiles. Now they see that it is God's purpose.

The same term, *hesuchazo*, is also used at Acts 21:14 and again involves speech on the part of the very people who are supposedly silent! Those who previously had resisted Paul's plan now desist and become supportive instead. The same word is used in Luke 14:4, where Jesus' opponents cease from further argumentation. The obstreperous crowd quietens and the people listen attentively when they realize that Paul is speaking to them in their own tongue (Acts 22:2).

Hesuchia, the noun form of *heschazo* is applied to women in 1 Tim. 2:11–12. Here too it may be understood as a call for women to concur with God's message rather than to adulterate it with false doctrine. The women of Luke 23:56 'rested' (*hesuchazo*) on the day before Christ commanded them to tell the apostles that he was risen from the dead.

The same root forms occur in 1 Thess. 4:11; 2 Thess. 3:12; 1 Pet. 3:4 where they appear to imply orderly deportment, tranquillity and minding one's own business. *Sige* and its derivatives, a second term used for the behavior of women, is used for keeping something secret (Luke 9:36; 18:39; Rom. 16:25) refraining from further comment or outcry (Luke 20:26; 1 Cor. 14:28, 30) and listening attentively (Acts 12:17; 15:12–13; 21:40). The rabbis expected students to learn in silence, and St Ignatius wrote that the more silent a bishop was, the more he should be respected.

In the Greek world, silence could mean reverence, acquiescence, receptivity, the keeping of a religious secret, an accompaniment of worship, or the perception of a profound spiritual revelation (cf. Rev. 8:1).

About AD 100, the Greek writer Plutarch observed that we learned speech from other human beings but silence from the gods. It was a prime requisite for an understanding of deity. We should bear in mind, he said, 'the solemn and holy, and mysterious nature of silence' (*Moralia*, 510 E).

In the first instance, silence was necessary for true learning to take place.

ᶜ Or *not to hesitate*

This did not necessarily mean absence of speech, for instruction usually requires that we listen to the words of a teacher. It has more to do with tranquillity of soul, with laying aside the hustle and bustle of the world. Plutarch wrote: 'How wise a thing, it would seem, is silence [hesuchia]. In particular it serves for studying to acquire knowledge and wisdom, by which I do not mean the wisdom of shop and market-place, but that mighty wisdom which makes the one who acquires it like to God' (On Quietude, Fragment no. 143, LCL). This kind of silence might open the door for unlearned women to apprehend the things of God ◆

The Church in Antioch

19 Now those who were scattered because of the persecution that took place over Stephen traveled as far as Phoenicia, Cyprus, and Antioch, and they spoke the word to no one except Jews. 20But among them were some men of Cyprus and Cyrene who, on coming to Antioch, spoke to the Hellenists[d] also, proclaiming the Lord Jesus. 21The hand of the Lord was with them, and a great number became believers and turned to the Lord. 22News of this came to the ears of the church in Jerusalem, and they sent Barnabas to Antioch. 23When he came and saw the grace of God, he rejoiced, and he exhorted them all to remain faithful to the Lord with steadfast devotion; 24for he was a good man, full of the Holy Spirit and of faith. And a great many people were brought to the Lord. 25Then Barnabas went to Tarsus to look for Saul, 26and when he had found him, he brought him to Antioch. So it was that for an entire year they met with[e] the church and taught a great many people, and it was in Antioch that the disciples were first called "Christians."

27 At that time prophets came down from Jerusalem to Antioch. 28One of them named Agabus stood up and predicted by the Spirit that there would be a severe famine over all the world; and this took place during the reign of Claudius. 29The disciples determined that according to their ability, each would send relief to the believers[f] living in Judea; 30this they did, sending it to the elders by Barnabas and Saul.

James Killed and Peter Imprisoned

12 About that time King Herod laid violent hands upon some who

---

d Other ancient authorities read Greeks   e Or were guests of   f Gk brothers

---

11:19–30. Luke introduces the Antioch 'Christians' who are to be prominent in the rest of Acts. Antioch, nearly 200 miles north of Damascus, was the third largest city in the Roman Empire. Nearby was a famous temple to the Greek divinities Artemis and Apollo. Like other large cities of the Empire, it was well known for its decadence. Some Hellenistic Jews, persecuted after Stephen's death, come to Antioch and evangelize fellow Jews. Also arriving are other believers from Cyprus and Cyrene who evangelize Greek Gentiles.

11:22–26. Barnabas (4:36–37), sent from Jerusalem, apparently unites Jewish and Gentile Christians. He also brings Saul from Tarsus, and the two teach in Antioch for a year. The believers are first called 'Christians' here.

11:27–29. Prophets from Jerusalem, specifically Agabus (21:10–11), come to Antioch. Agabus prophesies a wide-scale famine under the Roman Emperor Claudius, AD 41–54. No widespread famine at that time is recorded outside of Acts, but a series of local famines plagued Claudius' reign. Antioch believers send famine aid to Judea.

ACTS 12

1–20. Luke details Herod's hostility toward the church, Peter's deliverance from prison, and God's ultimate judgment on Herod.

1. King Herod Agrippa I, grandson of Herod the Great (Matt. 2) and his favorite wife Mariamme, grew up in Rome with the family of Augustus Caesar. As an adult, he was out of favor with the

belonged to the church. ²He had James, the brother of John, killed with the sword. ³After he saw that it pleased the Jews, he proceeded to arrest Peter also. (This was during the festival of Unleavened Bread.) ⁴When he had seized him, he put him in prison and handed him over to four squads of soldiers to guard him, intending to bring him out to the people after the Passover. ⁵While Peter was kept in prison, the church prayed fervently to God for him.

Peter Delivered from Prison

6 The very night before Herod was going to bring him out, Peter, bound with two chains, was sleeping between two soldiers, while guards in front of the door were keeping watch over the prison. ⁷Suddenly an angel of the Lord appeared and a light shone in the cell. He tapped Peter on the side and woke him, saying, "Get up quickly." And the chains fell off his wrists. ⁸The angel said to him, "Fasten your belt and put on your sandals." He did so. Then he said to him, "Wrap your cloak around you and follow me." ⁹Peter⁸ went out and followed him; he did not realize that what

was happening with the angel's help was real; he thought he was seeing a vision. ¹⁰After they had passed the first and the second guard, they came before the iron gate leading into the city. It opened for them of its own accord, and they went outside and walked along a lane, when suddenly the angel left him. ¹¹Then Peter came to himself and said, "Now I am sure that the Lord has sent his angel and rescued me from the hands of Herod and from all that the Jewish people were expecting."

12 As soon as he realized this, he went to the house of Mary, the mother of John whose other name was Mark, where many had gathered and were praying. ¹³When he knocked at the outer gate, a maid named Rhoda came to answer. ¹⁴On recognizing Peter's voice, she was so overjoyed that, instead of opening the gate, she ran in and announced that Peter was standing at the gate. ¹⁵They said to her, "You are out of your mind!" But she insisted that it was so. They said, "It is his angel." ¹⁶Meanwhile Peter continued knocking; and when they

⁸ Gk *He*

Emperor Tiberius (AD 14–37), but Emperors Gaius (Caligula) (37–41) and Claudius (41–54) made him king of several Palestinian regions. He worked hard to satisfy his Jewish subjects.

2–5. Luke acknowledges that Jewish attitudes toward the new faith have changed from goodwill to hostility after Stephen's death and believers' increasing association with Gentiles. Herod, for unstated reasons, has James, John's brother, beheaded. Since James' execution pleased the Jews, Herod now arrests Peter. The church prays for the apostle.

6–11. God's direct intervention brings about Peter's release from a closely guarded prison cell. God sends an angel to a sleeping, guarded, and shackled Peter. The angel awakes him, looses his chains, and leads him past sleeping guards through a miraculously opening gate.

12. An incredulous Peter finally realizes his rescue and goes to the house of Mary, John Mark's mother. For women's property rights, see Acts 5:1–10. Since Mary has her own property, she is probably widowed or divorced. She is wealthy and has a large house (many are gathered there, and it has an outer gate). Some scholars see her as a possible leader of this house church, but the passage leaves that unstated. For churches in women's houses see Acts 16:15, 40 (Lydia), Col. 4:15 (Nympha), Rom. 16:5 (Priscilla, with Aquila) and the 'elect lady' of 2 John.

13:17. The 'maid' Rhoda ('Rosie') is a slave with the responsible position of doorkeeper for the large home. Like the women bringing news of the resurrection (Luke 24:1–11), Rhoda endures the believers' disbelief. The scene alternates humor and fear: the church, praying fervently for Peter, cannot believe the miracle of his deliverance; he keeps knocking though he fears making noise that would attract the authorities. After he enters and tells what has happened, he leaves undetected by Herod's soldiers. An angry Herod executes the guards who allowed Peter's escape. Peter leaves the region for Caesarea.

opened the gate, they saw him and were amazed. [17]He motioned to them with his hand to be silent, and described for them how the Lord had brought him out of the prison. And he added, "Tell this to James and to the believers."[h] Then he left and went to another place.

◆ The slave woman Rhoda has been entrusted with the critical position of gate-keeper during a time of persecution. Issues of life and death hang upon her discernment in admitting believers and refusing entrance to interlopers and spies. She correctly identifies Peter's voice and refuses to be dissuaded from her insistence that he actually stands at the door. Another such door-keeper is mentioned in John 18:17.

Other slave women as well took a lively interest in the mission of early Christianity. Since they might move about more freely than citizen-class women, they were in a far better position to learn about the happenings of the outside world and to listen to the conversations of men. Two such women are well enough acquainted with Jesus' activities so that they recognize Peter and insist that he is one of the Galilean's followers (Matt. 26:69–72; Mark 14:66–70; Luke 22:54–57; John 18:16–18).

Mary the mother of Jesus identified herself as the 'slave' of God (Luke 1:48), and on the day of Pentecost, the Spirit was poured forth upon the women slaves of God (Acts 2:18). Paul incurred great wrath for having effected the healing of a slave woman whom he considered worthy of God's grace (Acts 16:16–21). Slaves were considered part of a Roman family and were surely included in those making up believing households. Pliny the younger in AD 112 wrote to the Emperor Trajan of two slave women called 'ministers' of the church in Bithynia. Early Christian writings indicate the strong allegiance to Christ demonstrated by many other slave women. Some, such as Blandina and Felicitas, died noble martyrs' deaths. In late antiquity the message of Christianity was ridiculed because it held such attraction for slaves, women and children. In the Christian community they found a transforming power and a caring fellowship that gave them inner freedom, equality, meaning and dignity ◆

18 When morning came, there was no small commotion among the soldiers over what had become of Peter. [19]When Herod had searched for him and could not find him, he examined the guards and ordered them to be put to death. Then Peter[i] went down from Judea to Caesarea and stayed there.

The Death of Herod

20 Now Herod was angry with the people of Tyre and Sidon. So they came to him in a body; and after winning over Blastus, the king's chamberlain, they asked for a reconciliation, because their country depended on the king's country for food. [21]On an appointed day Herod put on his royal robes, took his seat on the platform, and delivered a public address to them. [22]The people kept shouting, "The voice of a god, and not of a mortal!" [23]And immediately, because he had not given the glory to God, an angel of the Lord struck him down, and he was eaten by worms and died.

24 But the word of God continued to advance and gain adherents. [25]Then after completing their mission Barnabas and Saul returned to[j] Jerusalem and brought with them John, whose other name was Mark.

[h] Gk *brothers*   [i] Gk *he*   [j] Other ancient authorities read *from*

20–24. Luke indicates that Herod is struck down by God because Herod let himself be equated with God. For divine-human contrast, see 5:29. Herod died in AD 44.

Barnabas and Saul Commissioned

13 Now in the church at Antioch there were prophets and teachers: Barnabas, Simeon who was called Niger, Lucius of Cyrene, Manaen a member of the court of Herod the ruler,[k] and Saul. [2]While they were worshiping the Lord and fasting, the Holy Spirit said, "Set apart for me Barnabas and Saul for the work to which I have called them." [3]Then after fasting and praying they laid their hands on them and sent them off.

◆ The role of Africans in the New Testament is frequently overlooked. Persons from Cyrene took a lively interest in early Christianity and provided crucial leadership in the spreading of the gospel to the Gentile world. They are present at the day of Pentecost (Acts 2:10) and wish to debate the claims of Christianity critically with Stephen (6:9). If some were opposed, others were more positively disposed and were aggressive in their proclamation of the gospel (11:20–25). The Cyrenians appear to have played a major role in conceiving a missionary strategy that would reach out to Gentiles (13:1). Among the prime movers in the outreach are 'Simon the black' who may well be Simon of Cyrene, and Lucius, also a Cyrenian. It is these Africans who are instrumental in sending the gospel to Europe, and there is historical and archaeological evidence that the gospel reached Cyrene very rapidly ◆

The Apostles Preach in Cyprus

4 So, being sent out by the Holy Spirit, they went down to Seleucia; and from there they sailed to Cyprus. [5]When they arrived at Salamis, they proclaimed the word of God in the synagogues of the Jews. And they had John also to assist them. [6]When they had gone through the whole island as far as Paphos, they met a certain magician, a Jewish false prophet, named Bar-Jesus. [7]He was with the proconsul, Sergius Paulus, an intelligent man, who summoned Barnabas and Saul and wanted to hear the word of God. [8]But the magician

[k] Gk *tetrarch*

ACTS 13 & 14

13:1–14:29. Saul and Barnabas, commissioned by the Antioch church, make their first missionary journey to Cyprus, Pamphylia, and southern Galatia. Once they reach the mainland, each city's events normally follow a pattern: preaching in the synagogue, conversions, opposition, escape.

13:1–3. Prophets and teachers in the Antioch church are an internationally, socially, and ethnically diverse group. Barnabas is from Cyprus (4:36); Simeon is black ('Niger' is Latin for 'black'), presumably African; Lucius is from Cyrene, a city in northern Africa, west of Egypt; Manaen was brought up (Greek *syntrophos*) with Herod Antipas (another grandson of Herod the Great and his wife Malthake), tetrarch of Galilee (Mark 6:14; Luke 23:6–16); Saul is from Tarsus in Cilicia. They are worshipping and fasting when the Spirit commands them to set apart Barnabas and Paul for God's work.

13:4–12. The Holy Spirit leads them, along with John Mark (12:12), to Cyprus, Barnabas' native land, where they preach in synagogues from Salamis (east) to Paphos (west). Luke highlights one incident on Cyprus: conversion of the Roman proconsul Sergius Paulus from influence of a Jewish magician, Bar-Jesus. Luke emphasizes (8:27–39; 17:4, 12; 19:31; 26:30) that important officials are well disposed to the new faith. Proconsuls, from prominent Roman families, first advanced through a customary sequence of political offices and then became governors of provinces.

13:8–12. Like Luke's story of Simon (8:4–24), this incident depicts the triumph of the new faith over the power of magic. Luke does not describe the magician's practices which attract Paulus' allegiance but instead portrays the humiliation of Bar-Jesus with temporary blindness.

Elymas (for that is the translation of his name) opposed them and tried to turn the proconsul away from the faith. ⁹But Saul, also known as Paul, filled with the Holy Spirit, looked intently at him ¹⁰and said, "You son of the devil, you enemy of all righteousness, full of all deceit and villainy, will you not stop making crooked the straight paths of the Lord? ¹¹And now listen – the hand of the Lord is against you, and you will be blind for a while, unable to see the sun." Immediately mist and darkness came over him, and he went about groping for someone to lead him by the hand. ¹²When the proconsul saw what had happened, he believed, for he was astonished at the teaching about the Lord.

Paul and Barnabas in Antioch of Pisidia

13 Then Paul and his companions set sail from Paphos and came to Perga in Pamphylia. John, however, left them and returned to Jerusalem; ¹⁴but they went on from Perga and came to Antioch in Pisidia. And on the sabbath day they went into the synagogue and sat down. ¹⁵After the reading of the law and the prophets, the officials of the synagogue sent them a message, saying, "Brothers, if you have any word of exhortation for the people, give it." ¹⁶So Paul stood up and with a gesture began to speak:

"You Israelites,ˡ and others who fear God, listen. ¹⁷The God of this people Israel chose our ancestors and made the people great during their stay in the land of Egypt, and with uplifted arm he led them out of it. ¹⁸For about forty years he put up withᵐ them in the wilderness. ¹⁹After he had destroyed seven nations in the land of Canaan, he gave them their land as an inheritance ²⁰for about four hundred fifty years. After that he gave them judges until the time of the prophet Samuel. ²¹Then they asked for a king; and God gave them Saul son of Kish, a man of the tribe of Benjamin, who reigned for forty years. ²²When he had removed him, he made David their king. In his testimony about him he said, 'I have found David, son of Jesse, to be a man after my heart, who will carry out all my wishes.' ²³Of this man's posterity God has brought to Israel a Savior, Jesus, as he promised; ²⁴before his coming John had already proclaimed a baptism of repentance to all the people of Israel. ²⁵And as John was finishing his work, he said, 'What do you suppose that I am? I am not he. No, but one is coming after me; I am not worthy to untie the thong of the sandalsⁿ on his feet.'

26 "My brothers, you descendants of Abraham's family, and others who fear God, to usᵒ the message of this salvation has been sent. ²⁷Because the residents of Jerusalem and their leaders did not

ˡ Gk *Men, Israelites*   ᵐ Other ancient authorities read *cared for*   ⁿ Gk *untie the sandals*   ᵒ Other ancient authorities read *you*

13:13–52. Paul and Barnabas, now in Pisidian Antioch (west and north of Syrian Antioch, where the church commissioned them) again go to Jews in the synagogue to preach. No reasons are given for John Mark's departure. Luke terms his departure desertion (16:37–39).

13:16–20a. The first section of Paul's speech quickly passes over the period of the patriarchs and Moses (already treated in Stephen's speech, 7:1–43). NRSV footnote 1 (v. 18) gives the reading 'cared for' for 'put up with'. The difference in Greek is one letter: *etrophophoresen* vs. *etropophoresen*. The footnoted reading emphasizes God's nurturing love for the people of Israel whereas the primary reading emphasizes God's tolerance of their bad behavior: two different models of parenting.

13:20b–25. This speech highlights Hebrew history from Saul to David, emphasizing David as Christ's progenitor, as well as John the Baptist's witness to the need for repentance.

13:26–41. Paul now centers on fulfillment of prophecy in Jesus and his resurrection (Pss. 2:7; 16:10; Is. 55:3, Septuagint) and declares forgiveness of sins for them, too.

recognize him or understand the words of the prophets that are read every sabbath, they fulfilled those words by condemning him. ²⁸Even though they found no cause for a sentence of death, they asked Pilate to have him killed. ²⁹When they had carried out everything that was written about him, they took him down from the tree and laid him in a tomb. ³⁰But God raised him from the dead; ³¹and for many days he appeared to those who came up with him from Galilee to Jerusalem, and they are now his witnesses to the people. ³²And we bring you the good news that what God promised to our ancestors ³³he has fulfilled for us, their children, by raising Jesus; as also it is written in the second psalm,

'You are my Son;
today I have begotten you.'

³⁴As to his raising him from the dead, no more to return to corruption, he has spoken in this way,

'I will give you the holy promises made to David.'

³⁵Therefore he has also said in another psalm,

'You will not let your Holy One experience corruption.'

³⁶For David, after he had served the purpose of God in his own generation, died,ᵖ was laid beside his ancestors, and experienced corruption; ³⁷but he whom God raised up experienced no corruption. ³⁸Let it be known to you therefore, my brothers, that through this man forgiveness of sins is proclaimed to you; ³⁹by this Jesusᑫ everyone who believes is set free from all those sinsʳ from which you could not be freed by the law of Moses. ⁴⁰Beware, therefore, that what the prophets said does not happen to you:

⁴¹ 'Look, you scoffers!
Be amazed and perish,
for in your days I am doing a work,

a work that you will never believe,
even if someone tells you.' "

42 As Paul and Barnabasˢ were going out, the people urged them to speak about these things again the next sabbath. ⁴³When the meeting of the synagogue broke up, many Jews and devout converts to Judaism followed Paul and Barnabas, who spoke to them and urged them to continue in the grace of God.

44 The next sabbath almost the whole city gathered to hear the word of the Lord.ᵗ ⁴⁵But when the Jews saw the crowds, they were filled with jealousy; and blaspheming, they contradicted what was spoken by Paul. ⁴⁶Then both Paul and Barnabas spoke out boldly, saying, "It was necessary that the word of God should be spoken first to you. Since you reject it and judge yourselves to be unworthy of eternal life, we are now turning to the Gentiles. ⁴⁷For so the Lord has commanded us, saying,

'I have set you to be a light for the Gentiles,
so that you may bring salvation to the ends of the earth.' "

48 When the Gentiles heard this, they were glad and praised the word of the Lord; and as many as had been destined for eternal life became believers. ⁴⁹Thus the word of the Lord spread throughout the region. ⁵⁰But the Jews incited the devout women of high standing and the leading men of the city, and stirred up persecution against Paul and Barnabas, and drove them out of their region. ⁵¹So they shook the dust off their feet in protest against them, and went to Iconium. ⁵²And the disciples were filled with joy and with the Holy Spirit.

ᵖ Gk *fell asleep*   ᑫ Gk *this*   ʳ Gk *all*   ˢ Gk *they*
ᵗ Other ancient authorities read *God*

13:42–51. Here, Gentiles (v. 48) receive the preaching and believe, but city leaders and socially prominent women arouse persecution (v. 50).

◆ The opposition which Paul arouses in the women of Pisidian Antioch invites reflection as to the nature of his offense. The word *euschemonai* may convey the sense either of social prominence or of proper deportment. In any event, these women are incensed by the intrusion of a heathen into the synagogue (13:50). The congregation was composed of Jews, converts to Judaism and inquirers. Gentiles would not have been unwelcome in the synagogue unless they had been unfamiliar with Jewish patterns of worship. The text says that the congregation saw the *ochloi*, a word that could mean either 'crowds' or 'disturbance'. Pagan women were notorious in that area of Asia Minor for their wild, abandoned and indecorous forms of worship, and this would certainly have been unacceptable to socially prominent women who had espoused the orderly and reverent ways of the synagogue.

Shortly after Paul was driven out of Pisidian Antioch by the women, he was summoned to Jerusalem to discuss methods of integrating Jew and Gentile into the body of Christ (Acts 15; Gal. 2). The matter is carefully considered, and Paul returns to all of the churches to share with them the insights gathered from the Council (Acts 14:26–15:29, 36; 21:25). He realizes that he must use principles of adaptation in order to respect the sensibilities of others (Rom. 14:1–15:3; 1 Cor. 8:1–13; 9:1–10; 10:23–33). The restraints which Paul appears to put upon the religious expressions of women can be understood in light of the need for fusing Jew and Gentile into a cohesive fellowship in Christ.

Thereafter Paul becomes successful with the very type of woman who had previously rejected his ministry

(Acts 16:1, 13–15; 17:4, 12; 18:1; 24:24; 25:13, 23; 26:30). Though he had formerly persecuted them (Acts 8:3; 9:1-2; 22:4), Paul enjoyed a ministry to women (Acts 16:12-40; 17:1-4, 10, 34) and considered them significant in his ministry (Acts 18:1-4, 18-28; Rom. 16:1-16; 1 Cor. 16:19; Phil. 4:2-3; 2 Tim. 4:19) ◆

Paul and Barnabas in Iconium

14 The same thing occurred in Iconium, where Paul and Barnabas[u] went into the Jewish synagogue and spoke in such a way that a great number of both Jews and Greeks became believers. [2]But the unbelieving Jews stirred up the Gentiles and poisoned their minds against the brothers. [3]So they remained for a long time, speaking boldly for the Lord, who testified to the word of his grace by granting signs and wonders to be done through them. [4]But the residents of the city were divided; some sided with the Jews, and some with the apostles. [5]And when an attempt was made by both Gentiles and Jews, with their rulers, to mistreat them and to stone them, [6]the apostles[u] learned of it and fled to Lystra and Derbe, cities of Lycaonia, and to the surrounding country; [7]and there they continued proclaiming the good news.

Paul and Barnabas in Lystra and Derbe

[8] In Lystra there was a man sitting who could not use his feet and had never walked, for he had been crippled from birth. [9]He listened to Paul as he was speaking. And Paul, looking at him intently and seeing that he had faith to be

[u] Gk *they*

14:8–20. Events in Iconium follow the usual pattern: synagogue, conversion, opposition, departure. Lystra, about 20 miles from Iconium, provides a different challenge for Paul and Barnabas. Because they heal a man lame from his mother's womb (see 3:2), the Gentile crowds think that the Greek gods Zeus and Hermes are in the midst. For Jews, calling a human being a god is blasphemy (see 5:29). When Paul and Barnabas realize what is happening, they implore the crowd to desist from sacrificing oxen to them.

healed, [10]said in a loud voice, "Stand upright on your feet." And the man[v] sprang up and began to walk. [11]When the crowds saw what Paul had done, they shouted in the Lycaonian language, "The gods have come down to us in human form!" [12]Barnabas they called Zeus, and Paul they called Hermes, because he was the chief speaker. [13]The priest of Zeus, whose temple was just outside the city,[w] brought oxen and garlands to the gates; he and the crowds wanted to offer sacrifice. [14]When the apostles Barnabas and Paul heard of it, they tore their clothes and rushed out into the crowd, shouting, [15]"Friends,[x] why are you doing this? We are mortals just like you, and we bring you good news, that you should turn from these worthless things to the living God, who made the heaven and the earth and the sea and all that is in them. [16]In past generations he allowed all the nations to follow their own ways; [17]yet he has not left himself without a witness in doing good – giving you rains from heaven and fruitful seasons, and filling you with food and your hearts with joy." [18]Even with these words, they scarcely restrained the crowds from offering sacrifice to them.

19 But Jews came there from Antioch and Iconium and won over the crowds. Then they stoned Paul and dragged him out of the city, supposing that he was dead. [20]But when the disciples surrounded him, he got up and went into the city. The next day he went on with Barnabas to Derbe.

The Return to Antioch in Syria

21 After they had proclaimed the good news to that city and had made many disciples, they returned to Lystra, then on to Iconium and Antioch. [22]There they strengthened the souls of the disciples and encouraged them to continue in the faith, saying, "It is through many persecutions that we must enter the kingdom of God." [23]And after they had appointed elders for them in each church, with prayer and fasting they entrusted them to the Lord in whom they had come to believe.

24 Then they passed through Pisidia and came to Pamphylia. [25]When they had spoken the word in Perga, they went down to Attalia. [26]From there they sailed back to Antioch, where they had been commended to the grace of God for the work[y] that they had completed. [27]When they arrived, they called the church together and related all that God had done with them, and how he had opened a door of faith for the Gentiles. [28]And they stayed there with the disciples for some time.

The Council at Jerusalem

15 Then certain individuals came down from Judea and were teaching the brothers, "Unless you are

[v] Gk *he* [w] Or *The priest of Zeus-Outside-the-City*
[x] Gk *Men* [y] Or *committed in the grace of God to the work*

14:15–17. Paul's brief speech contains basic ingredients of his preaching to Gentiles (see 17:22–31): he urges them to turn from idols to the living Creator God who, while allowing Gentiles to 'follow their own ways' (v. 16), cares for them by providing food.

14:22–29. After a successful mission to Derbe, Paul and Barnabas, realizing that new believers need strengthening, encouraging, and structure for their church, revisit disciples in Lystra, Iconium, Pisidian Antioch, preach in Perga in Pamphylia, and return to Antioch.

ACTS 15

1–35. As further reports of Gentiles' conversions come to Jerusalem, debate continues among apostles and elders about Gentiles' responsibility to keep the Law of Moses. The immediate question concerns circumcision: should Gentile men who believe in Jesus be circumcised for admission to the church? Luke presents only one side of the debate, with Peter, Paul, Barnabas, and James as speakers.

circumcised according to the custom of Moses, you cannot be saved." [2]And after Paul and Barnabas had no small dissension and debate with them, Paul and Barnabas and some of the others were appointed to go up to Jerusalem to discuss this question with the apostles and the elders. [3]So they were sent on their way by the church, and as they passed through both Phoenicia and Samaria, they reported the conversion of the Gentiles, and brought great joy to all the believers.[z] [4]When they came to Jerusalem, they were welcomed by the church and the apostles and the elders, and they reported all that God had done with them. [5]But some believers who belonged to the sect of the Pharisees stood up and said, "It is necessary for them to be circumcised and ordered to keep the law of Moses."

6 The apostles and the elders met together to consider this matter. [7]After there had been much debate, Peter stood up and said to them, "My brothers,[a] you know that in the early days God made a choice among you, that I should be the one through whom the Gentiles would hear the message of the good news and become believers. [8]And God, who knows the human heart, testified to them by giving them the Holy Spirit, just as he did to us; [9]and in cleansing their hearts by faith he has made no distinction between them and us. [10]Now therefore why are you putting God to the test by placing on the neck of the disciples a yoke that neither our ancestors nor we have been able to bear? [11]On the

contrary, we believe that we will be saved through the grace of the Lord Jesus, just as they will."

12 The whole assembly kept silence, and listened to Barnabas and Paul as they told of all the signs and wonders that God had done through them among the Gentiles. [13]After they finished speaking, James replied, "My brothers,[a] listen to me. [14]Simeon has related how God first looked favorably on the Gentiles, to take from among them a people for his name. [15]This agrees with the words of the prophets, as it is written,

[16] 'After this I will return,
 and I will rebuild the dwelling of
  David, which has fallen;
   from its ruins I will rebuild it,
    and I will set it up,
[17] so that all other peoples may seek the
  Lord –
   even all the Gentiles over whom my
    name has been called.
     Thus says the Lord, who has been
      making these things [18]known
       from long ago.'[b]

[19]Therefore I have reached the decision that we should not trouble those Gentiles who are turning to God, [20]but we should write to them to abstain only from things polluted by idols and from fornication and from whatever has been strangled[c] and from

[z] Gk *brothers*   [a] Gk *Men, brothers*   [b] Other ancient authorities read *things.* [18]*Known to God from of old are all his works.'*   [c] Other ancient authorities lack *and from whatever has been strangled*

6–12. In his last appearance in Acts, Peter refers indirectly to his experiences with Cornelius (vv. 7–9) and asks why the church would burden Gentiles with a 'yoke' that even Jews cannot bear – the rigors of the Law. He emphasizes that all Christians, Jewish and Gentile, will be saved by God's grace. Since Luke has just reported Paul's and Barnabas' mission among Gentiles, he alludes only briefly to their speeches about God's powerful work there.

13–21. James, Jesus' brother, provides scriptural basis (Amos 9:11–12, Septuagint) to show that God 'looks favorably' on Gentiles. He also proposes a solution to the immediate issue: circumcision is not required, but Gentiles should not offend Jewish believers particularly in table fellowship and marriage: Gentiles must not eat food offered to idols or slaughtered improperly (Mosaic Law forbids eating blood; when animals are strangled, blood remains in their flesh, Gen. 9:4–5; Lev. 3:17; 17:10–14); nor should Gentiles marry people of those relationships forbidden in Lev. 18:6–18 (fornication).

blood. [21]For in every city, for generations past, Moses has had those who proclaim him, for he has been read aloud every sabbath in the synagogues."

The Council's Letter to Gentile Believers

22 Then the apostles and the elders, with the consent of the whole church, decided to choose men from among their members[d] and to send them to Antioch with Paul and Barnabas. They sent Judas called Barsabbas, and Silas, leaders among the brothers, [23]with the following letter: "The brothers, both the apostles and the elders, to the believers[e] of Gentile origin in Antioch and Syria and Cilicia, greetings. [24]Since we have heard that certain persons who have gone out from us, though with no instructions from us, have said things to disturb you and have unsettled your minds,[f] [25]we have decided unanimously to choose representatives[g] and send them to you, along with our beloved Barnabas and Paul, [26]who have risked their lives for the sake of our Lord Jesus Christ. [27]We have therefore sent Judas and Silas, who themselves will tell you the same things by word of mouth. [28]For it has seemed good to the Holy Spirit and to us to impose on you no further burden than these essentials: [29]that you abstain from what has been sacrificed to idols and from blood and from what is strangled[h] and from fornication. If you keep yourselves from these, you will do well. Farewell."

30 So they were sent off and went down to Antioch. When they gathered the congregation together, they delivered the letter. [31]When its members[i] read it, they rejoiced at the exhortation. [32]Judas and Silas, who were themselves prophets, said much to encourage and strengthen the believers.[e] [33]After they had been there for some time, they were sent off in peace by the believers[e] to those who had sent them.[j] [35]But Paul and Barnabas remained in Antioch, and there, with many others, they taught and proclaimed the word of the Lord.

Paul and Barnabas Separate

36 After some days Paul said to Barnabas, "Come, let us return and visit the believers[e] in every city where we proclaimed the word of the Lord and see how they are doing." [37]Barnabas wanted to take with them John called Mark. [38]But Paul decided not to take with them one who had deserted them in Pamphylia and had not accompanied them in the work. [39]The disagreement became so sharp that they parted company; Barnabas took Mark with him and sailed away to Cyprus. [40]But Paul chose Silas and set out, the believers[e] commending him to the grace of the Lord. [41]He went through Syria and Cilicia, strengthening the churches.

[d] Gk *from among them*   [e] Gk *brothers*   [f] Other ancient authorities add *saying, 'You must be circumcised and keep the law,'*   [g] Gk *men*   [h] Other ancient authorities lack *and from what is strangled*   [i] Gk *When they*   [j] Other ancient authorities add verse 34, *But it seemed good to Silas to remain there*

22–35. James' proposal is accepted, and the Jerusalem church sends Silas and Judas Barsabbas to churches in Antioch, Syria, and Cilicia, communicating their decision by letter. Again, Luke's repetition of material indicates its importance.

15:35–18:17. Luke relates events of Paul's second missionary journey. He revisits churches already established and then a vision of a Macedonian man leads him to Greece, which was divided into the Roman provinces of Macedonia (north) and Achaia (south).

15:35–41. Paul and Barnabas return to Antioch and teach and preach there. Paul wants to revisit the young churches created during their missionary journey. Disagreement arises over John Mark's participation (see 13:13). Conflict is resolved as Barnabas takes John Mark and returns to his native Cyprus while Paul chooses Silas (who is still communicating the Jerusalem letter to other churches) to accompany him through Syria and Cilicia.

Timothy Joins Paul and Silas

16 Paul[k] went on also to Derbe and to Lystra, where there was a disciple named Timothy, the son of a Jewish woman who was a believer; but his father was a Greek. [2]He was well spoken of by the believers[l] in Lystra and Iconium. [3]Paul wanted Timothy to accompany him; and he took him and had him circumcised because of the Jews who were in those places, for they all knew that his father was a Greek. [4]As they went from town to town, they delivered to them for observance the decisions that had been reached by the apostles and elders who were in Jerusalem. [5]So the churches were strengthened in the faith and increased in numbers daily.

Paul's Vision of the Man of Macedonia

6 They went through the region of Phrygia and Galatia, having been forbidden by the Holy Spirit to speak the word in Asia. [7]When they had come opposite Mysia, they attempted to go into Bithynia, but the Spirit of Jesus did not allow them; [8]so, passing by Mysia, they went down to Troas. [9]During the night Paul had a vision: there stood a man of Macedonia pleading with him and saying, "Come over to Macedonia and help us." [10]When he had seen the vision, we immediately tried to cross over to Macedonia, being convinced that God had called us to proclaim the good news to them.

The Conversion of Lydia

11 We set sail from Troas and took a straight course to Samothrace, the following day to Neapolis, [12]and from there to Philippi, which is a leading city of the district[m] of Macedonia and a Roman colony. We remained in this city for some

k Gk *He*   l Gk *brothers*   m Other authorities read *a city of the first district*

ACTS 16

1–5. In Lystra, Paul adds Timothy to his travelling group. Occasionally the New Testament offers glimpses of families, and Timothy's is one of them. Luke indicates that Timothy's mother was Jewish and a believer, probably converted during Paul's first visit to Lystra. 2 Tim. 1:5 mentions the 'sincere faith' of Timothy's grandmother Lois and his mother Eunice. His father, however, was Greek – apparently neither Jewish nor a believer. Jews considered that children of a Jewish mother were Jewish. Though his mother was Jewish, Timothy was not circumcised (thus not in good standing in most Jewish communities). Perhaps his Gentile father objected. Jewish-Gentile marriages, illegal by Jewish Law, would have been unacceptable in Jerusalem, but in Lystra separation between Jew and Gentile must have been less rigid. For another mixed marriage, see Acts 24:24. Since the Jerusalem church has just refused to burden Gentiles with circumcision, why would Timothy need circumcision? Perhaps because Paul goes first to synagogues in his work, he needs colleagues to be Jews in good standing in order to gain a hearing.

6–10. After travelling northward in Galatia and then westward to Troas on the Aegean Sea, Paul has a vision of a Macedonian man urging their help. This first 'we' section suggests that Luke sometimes accompanied Paul.

12. Sailing from Troas to Neapolis takes two days. Then the group goes by land to Philippi on one of the many roads built by the Romans as their empire expanded. Near Philippi was the site of a historically significant battle between the murderers of Julius Caesar, Brutus and Cassius and his avengers, Antony and Octavian (later Augustus Caesar), in 42 BC. Afterwards it became a Roman 'colony', settled by soldiers, with Roman laws and customs.

After Alexander the Great (356–323 BC), Macedonian princesses and queens were well known for their political, intellectual, and civic activity. By the first century, well-to-do Macedonian women had more opportunities for education and participation in government, civic, and business than women elsewhere in Greece. Opportunities, however, were not automatic: women had to seize them.

days. [13]On the sabbath day we went outside the gate by the river, where we supposed there was a place of prayer; and we sat down and spoke to the women who had gathered there. [14]A certain woman named Lydia, a worshiper of God, was listening to us; she was from the city of Thyatira and a dealer in purple cloth. The Lord opened her heart to listen eagerly to what was said by Paul.

◆ Women engaged in a variety of occupations both inside and outside the home (see the note on 'The occupations of women', p. 591). Two of Paul's most influential women associates were business women. Lydia was involved in the dyeing industry (Acts 16:14), and Priscilla was a tent-maker (Acts 18:2–3). She shared a business with her husband, and the couple may have owned or set up workshops in Corinth, Ephesus, and Rome. A number of instances are known in which an owner had branches of a business at several widely separated population centers. If the couple had sufficient capital, it would not have been difficult to set up a shop in a new location; for tent-making tools were portable and easily installed.

In all probability, Phoebe who delivered the epistle to the Romans was also a business woman used to travel and to conducting negotiations in her own right (Rom. 16:1–2).

These women used the opportunities afforded them by the circumstances of their businesses and by their efforts contributed substantively to the furtherance of the gospel ◆

[15]When she and her household were baptized, she urged us, saying, "If you have judged me to be faithful to the Lord, come and stay at my home." And she prevailed upon us.

◆ The ministry of hospitality was an important one in the early church as it had been in Israel (1 Kings 17:7–24; 2 Kings 4:8–37; 8:1–20; Job 31:32). Jesus sent his disciples out with a command to go into a house that would receive them and to remain there as long as their mission continued in that location (Matt. 10:11; Luke 9:4). Early missionaries found it necessary to stay with those who would receive them (Acts 16:15; 18:1–3; 21:8–9; Philem. 22). Almost always, when we read of instances of hospitality in the Bible, we read of women who were involved in this ministry.

Since the great need for homes which might become launching pads for the gospel in a community was fully acknowledged by the itinerant leaders (2 John 5–10), hospitality is mentioned as a particular grace that furthered the spread of the gospel (Matt. 10:41; Rom. 12:13; Gal. 4:14; 1 Tim. 3:2; 5:10; Titus 1:8; Heb. 13:2; 1 Pet. 4:9). Great help or hindrance could result from the giving or withholding of hospitality, and great care should be taken as to whom Christians should receive (2 John 10–11).

Beyond a desire for furthering the gospel, Christians are enjoined to take into their homes those in need, for thereby they are receiving Christ (Matt. 18:8; 10:40–41;

---

13. On the Sabbath, Paul seeks out a local Jewish service and finds several women. Since ten men are required for a synagogue service and none is mentioned, the women have a 'place of prayer' instead.

14–15. Lydia, the most enterprising woman in Acts, is converted through Paul's preaching. She and her household are baptized, and she offers hospitality to the travelling missionaries. The name 'Lydia' suggests that she may have been a slave and then freed (slave names sometimes reflect the slave's country of origin, here Lydia in the Roman province of Asia). She is from the city of Thyatira (see Rev. 2:18–29) where the madder plant, a key ingredient in a popular purple fabric dye, grew. She is now a competent business woman selling purple cloth in Philippi, knowledgeable about trade routes westward from Thyatira, with a large house and her own slaves.

25:35, 38, 40). Our outreach should not be directed merely at those who will repay the social obligation of an invitation but much more to those whose blessing to our house is simply that they represent Christ (Luke 14:12–14).

True hospitality is making another feel welcome. It has little to do with elegant appointments in our homes, picture-perfect spreads upon the table, or impeccable decor. It is quite possible to welcome folk in Christ's name with shabby furniture, mismatched dishes upon the table, ragged curtains at the window, and a warm heart. A caring and responsive attitude is so much better than a flustered hostess who must have everything perfect but has no time for the guest. Paul speaks with appreciation of those with whom he found rest for his spirit, and he remembers them and their hospitality fondly ◆

Paul and Silas in Prison

16 One day, as we were going to the place of prayer, we met a slave-girl who had a spirit of divination and brought her owners a great deal of money by fortune-telling. [17]While she followed Paul and us, she would cry out, "These men are slaves of the Most High God, who proclaim to you[n] a way of salvation." [18]She kept doing this for many days. But Paul, very much annoyed, turned and said to the spirit, "I order you in the name of Jesus Christ to come out of her." And it came out that very hour.

19 But when her owners saw that their hope of making money was gone, they seized Paul and Silas and dragged them into the marketplace before the authorities. [20]When they had brought them before the magistrates, they said, "These men are disturbing our city; they are Jews [21]and are advocating customs that are not lawful for us as Romans to adopt or observe." [22]The crowd joined in attacking them, and the magistrates had them stripped of their clothing and ordered them to be beaten with rods. [23]After they had given them a severe flogging, they threw them into prison and ordered the jailer to keep them securely. [24]Following these instructions, he put them in the innermost cell and fastened their feet in the stocks.

25 About midnight Paul and Silas were praying and singing hymns to God, and the prisoners were listening to them. [26]Suddenly there was an earthquake, so violent that the foundations of the prison were shaken; and immediately all the doors were opened and everyone's chains were unfastened. [27]When the jailer woke up and saw the prison doors wide open, he drew his sword and was about to kill himself, since he supposed that the prisoners had escaped. [28]But Paul shouted in a loud voice, "Do not harm yourself, for we are all here." [29]The jailer[o] called for lights, and rushing in, he fell down trembling

[n] Other ancient authorities read *to us*   [o] Gk *He*

16–19. Luke next depicts a third confrontation (see 13:8–12) between Paul and magical powers. A young female slave is possessed by an oracular spirit called a Python, which enables her to tell fortunes by speaking through her, sometimes uncontrollably. She follows Paul and his companions for several days, crying out that they are God's slaves and proclaim salvation. This dvertisement for their preaching, though accurate, is nagging and disruptive. Paul finally casts out the spirit and enrages her owners concerned with her money-making potential.

20–34. Her owners drag Paul and Silas before the authorities and accuse them of disturbing the peace and possible treason (see 17:7). Flogged and imprisoned, they make the best of an ugly situation by praying and singing. An earthquake shakes the prison, making possible their escape. The jailer, believing the worst, prepares to commit suicide; Paul prevents him, as all the prisoners are safe. The jailer believes in Jesus; he and his household are baptized and care for the wounded and hungry Paul and Silas. The jailer's conversion is paired with Lydia's (see Introduction p. 229).

before Paul and Silas. ³⁰Then he brought them outside and said, "Sirs, what must I do to be saved?" ³¹They answered, "Believe on the Lord Jesus, and you will be saved, you and your household." ³²They spoke the word of the Lord^p to him and to all who were in his house. ³³At the same hour of the night he took them and washed their wounds; then he and his entire family were baptized without delay. ³⁴He brought them up into the house and set food before them; and he and his entire household rejoiced that he had become a believer in God.

35 When morning came, the magistrates sent the police, saying, "Let those men go." ³⁶And the jailer reported the message to Paul, saying, "The magistrates sent word to let you go; therefore come out now and go in peace." ³⁷But Paul replied, "They have beaten us in public, uncondemned, men who are Roman citizens, and have thrown us into prison; and now are they going to discharge us in secret? Certainly not! Let them come and take us out themselves." ³⁸The police reported these words to the magistrates, and they were afraid when they heard that they were Roman citizens; ³⁹so they came and apologized to them. And they took them out and asked them to leave the city. ⁴⁰After leaving the prison they went to Lydia's home; and when they had seen and encouraged the brothers and sisters^q there, they departed.

The Uproar in Thessalonica

17 After Paul and Silas^r had passed through Amphipolis and Apollonia, they came to Thessalonica, where there was a synagogue of the Jews. ²And Paul went in, as was his custom, and on three sabbath days argued with them from the scriptures, ³explaining and proving that it was necessary for the Messiah^s to suffer and to rise from the dead, and saying, "This is the Messiah,^s Jesus whom I am proclaiming to you." ⁴Some of them were persuaded and joined Paul and Silas, as did a great many of the devout Greeks and not a few of the leading women. ⁵But the Jews became jealous, and with the help of some ruffians in the marketplaces they formed a mob and set the city in an uproar. While they were searching for Paul and Silas to bring them out to the assembly, they attacked Jason's house. ⁶When they could not find them, they dragged Jason and some believers^q before the city authorities,^t shouting, "These people who have been turning the world upside down have come here also, ⁷and Jason has entertained them as guests. They are all acting contrary to the decrees of the emperor, saying that there is another king named Jesus." ⁸The people and the city officials were disturbed when they heard this, ⁹and after they had taken bail from Jason and the others, they let them go.

Paul and Silas in Beroea

10 That very night the believers^q sent Paul and Silas off to Beroea; and when they arrived, they went to the Jewish synagogue.

^p Other ancient authorities read *word of God* ^q Gk *brothers* ^r Gk *they* ^s Or *the Christ* ^t Gk *politarchs*

35–39. Paul uses his legal trump card: he and Silas are Roman citizens and have been treated improperly. The magistrates release them, apologize, but ask them to leave.
40. What starts as Lydia's hospitality leads to a house-church in her home.

ACTS 17

1–9. In Thessalonica, a port city named after a daughter of Philip of Macedon, Paul follows the customary pattern of events. New believers include leading women (v. 4).
10–15. Similar events occur in Beroea. Luke emphasizes again that believers include Greek women of high standing (v. 12). Paul is sent away before Jews from Thessalonica cause trouble.

[11]These Jews were more receptive than those in Thessalonica, for they welcomed the message very eagerly and examined the scriptures every day to see whether these things were so. [12]Many of them therefore believed, including not a few Greek women and men of high standing. [13]But when the Jews of Thessalonica learned that the word of God had been proclaimed by Paul in Beroea as well, they came there too, to stir up and incite the crowds. [14]Then the believers[u] immediately sent Paul away to the coast, but Silas and Timothy remained behind. [15]Those who conducted Paul brought him as far as Athens; and after receiving instructions to have Silas and Timothy join him as soon as possible, they left him.

Paul in Athens

[16] While Paul was waiting for them in Athens, he was deeply distressed to see that the city was full of idols. [17]So he argued in the synagogue with the Jews and the devout persons, and also in the marketplace[v] every day with those who happened to be there. [18]Also some Epicurean and Stoic philosophers debated with him. Some said, "What does this babbler want to say?" Others said, "He seems to be a proclaimer of foreign divinities." (This was because he was telling the good news about Jesus and the resurrection.) [19]So they took

him and brought him to the Areopagus and asked him, "May we know what this new teaching is that you are presenting? [20]It sounds rather strange to us, so we would like to know what it means." [21]Now all the Athenians and the foreigners living there would spend their time in nothing but telling or hearing something new.

[22] Then Paul stood in front of the Areopagus and said, "Athenians, I see how extremely religious you are in every way. [23]For as I went through the city and looked carefully at the objects of your worship, I found among them an altar with the inscription, 'To an unknown god.' What therefore you worship as unknown, this I proclaim to you. [24]The God who made the world and everything in it, he who is Lord of heaven and earth, does not live in shrines made by human hands, [25]nor is he served by human hands, as though he needed anything, since he himself gives to all mortals life and breath and all things. [26]From one ancestor[w] he made all nations to inhabit the whole earth, and he allotted the times of their existence and the boundaries of the places where they would live, [27]so that they would search for God[x] and perhaps grope for him

---

[u] Gk brothers   [v] Or civic center; Gk agora
[w] Gk From one; other ancient authorities read From one blood   [x] Other ancient authorities read the Lord

---

16–34. Athens was in the Roman province of Achaia. Once a dominant force in Greek politics, it has become primarily a 'university town'. The numerous idols and altars dedicated to divinities distress Paul, who regards idol worship as blasphemy (Exod. 20:4–6).

18–21. Paul debates Jews and Gentiles in the synagogue and the agora, the city's civic and business center. Luke mentions two schools of Greek philosophy: the Epicureans, who saw the gods as far removed from human activity and the chief purpose of existence as a tranquil life; and the Stoics, who believed that divinity showed itself in reason and that humans should live a self-sufficient life governed by reason. The Epicureans (v. 18) scoff at 'this babbler' and the Stoics, thinking that 'Resurrection' is a foreign divinity, misunderstand him.

22–31. Luke portrays Paul addressing Gentiles at the Court of the Areopagus. He approaches them differently from Jewish audiences (see 14:15–18). First, he urges them to change from worshipping unknown gods to the Creator God who, unlike pagan idols made by humans, has made the earth and created the human race to search and find God. He quotes Greek poets who also suggest that humans are God's offspring. Paul then urges his hearers to repent because of coming judgment by Jesus (not named) who has been raised from the dead.

and find him – though indeed he is not far from each one of us. [28]For 'In him we live and move and have our being'; as even some of your own poets have said,

'For we too are his offspring.'

[29]Since we are God's offspring, we ought not to think that the deity is like gold, or silver, or stone, an image formed by the art and imagination of mortals. [30]While God has overlooked the times of human ignorance, now he commands all people everywhere to repent, [31]because he has fixed a day on which he will have the world judged in righteousness by a man whom he has appointed, and of this he has given assurance to all by raising him from the dead."

32 When they heard of the resurrection of the dead, some scoffed; but others said, "We will hear you again about this." [33]At that point Paul left them. [34]But some of them joined him and became believers, including Dionysius the Areopagite and a woman named Damaris, and others with them.

Paul in Corinth

18 After this Paul[y] left Athens and went to Corinth. [2]There he found a

◆ We first learn from Luke that Priscilla is married to a Jew named Aquila, and is perhaps herself a Roman Gentile (Acts 18:2). When the Jews were banished from Rome by decree of Claudius, Priscilla and Aquila leave Italy, reaching Corinth shortly before the Apostle Paul in AD 51. Scripture mentions not that Priscilla and Aquila were Christians and hence Paul's visit, but that he visits them because they are tent-makers. Priscilla and Aquila invite Paul to live with them, and because Paul does not mention leading them to faith, they were Christians at the time of Paul's visit, or become so before all three relocate to Ephesus, 18 months later.

While in Ephesus, Priscilla and Aquila gain prominence not only through the church they establish in their home (1 Cor. 16:19), but by risking their lives for Paul (perhaps during the riots mentioned in Acts 19:23-41), a deed for which the Gentile churches gave thanks (Rom. 16:4). Moreover, Luke recognizes Priscilla and Aquila as skilled teachers for having instructed the eloquent Apollos. Though

[y] Gk *he*

32–33. Paul's reception in Athens is lukewarm. Some (the Epicureans) scoff; others (the Stoics) want to hear more. Some believe. Among them is a woman, otherwise unknown, named Damaris. Scholars think that she must be prominent to be specifically identified.

ACTS 18

1–17. Paul leaves Athens for the port city of Corinth where Silas and Timothy arrive from Macedonia. Corinth, the capital of Achaia, is near the isthmus between mainland Greece and the Peloponnesus, the southern part of Greece. Two ports connected by a portage were associated with it: Lechaeum (west) and Cenchreae (east, v. 18). Luke describes the establishment of the believers' community and developing conflict. Paul stays there for 'a considerable time' and leaves under normal circumstances.

2–3. In Corinth Paul finds a couple, Priscilla and Aquila, who are already believers. They have travelled widely: Aquila is a Jew from Pontus, a Roman province on the Black Sea, and they have recently come from Rome after Claudius ordered them expelled, possibly because difficulties within the Jewish community have divided Jews and Jewish Christians. Possibly they were founding members of the church in Rome. They are tent-makers, as is Paul, who joins them as he works to support himself. When their names appear together, (Acts 18:18, 26; Rom. 16:13; 2 Tim. 4:19) Priscilla's name appears first – an unusual practice for Judaism or early Christianity. From this, scholars think that she was spiritually more gifted or socially more prominent than he (possibly a freedwoman or freeborn in a prominent Roman family), not Jewish but a 'God-fearer'.

Apollos was well versed in the Scriptures, his understanding of salvation was incomplete, and it was Priscilla and Aquila who furthered his knowledge. Apollos received Priscilla's instruction without reservation. Far from condemning Priscilla for having taught a man, both Luke and Paul promote Priscilla, who along with her husband explained the way of God more accurately (Acts 18:26).

Priscilla's authority in the early church is highlighted by Paul who calls her his 'co-worker' (Rom. 16:3), a term Paul uses to identify leaders such as Mark, Timothy, Titus, Philemon, Apollos, and Luke. Moreover, her name is mentioned first in four of the six references to Priscilla and Aquila, suggesting she is the more distinguished of the two, and both Luke and Paul honor her in this way.

Priscilla's position in the early church soon came under suppression. One scholar observed that several later manuscripts had been tampered with such that Aquila's name had been placed *before* Priscilla's (Acts 18:26), and in three different places Aquila's name was used *without* Priscilla's.

Because Priscilla's name has endured suppression, and due to her prominence with Paul, Luke, and the early church, scholars suggest Priscilla may have authored the Epistle to the Hebrews, an epistle lacking a prescript indicating both the author and persons to whom the letter was addressed. Some argue that Hebrews itself alludes to an author who is non-Jewish, an exile, and perhaps feminine, pointing again to Priscilla ◆

Jew named Aquila, a native of Pontus, who had recently come from Italy with his wife

Priscilla, because Claudius had ordered all Jews to leave Rome. Paul[z] went to see them, [3]and, because he was of the same trade, he stayed with them, and they worked together – by trade they were tentmakers. [4]Every sabbath he would argue in the synagogue and would try to convince Jews and Greeks.

5 When Silas and Timothy arrived from Macedonia, Paul was occupied with proclaiming the word,[a] testifying to the Jews that the Messiah[b] was Jesus. [6]When they opposed and reviled him, in protest he shook the dust from his clothes[c] and said to them, "Your blood be on your own heads! I am innocent. From now on I will go to the Gentiles." [7]Then he left the synagogue[d] and went to the house of a man named Titius[e] Justus, a worshiper of God; his house was next door to the synagogue. [8]Crispus, the official of the synagogue, became a believer in the Lord, together with all his household; and many of the Corinthians who heard Paul became believers and were baptized. [9]One night the Lord said to Paul in a vision, "Do not be afraid, but speak and do not be silent; [10]for I am with you, and no one will lay a hand on you to harm you, for there are many in this city who are my people." [11]He stayed there a year and six months, teaching the word of God among them.

12 But when Gallio was proconsul of Achaia, the Jews made a united attack on Paul and brought him before the tribunal.

[z] Gk *he*   [a] Gk *with the word*   [b] Or *the Christ*
[c] Gk *reviled him, he shook out his clothes*
[d] Gk *left there*   [e] Other ancient authorities read *Titus*

5–11. Faced with conflict within the synagogue, Paul leaves for the house of Titius Justus, a 'God-fearing' Gentile. In a vision, the Lord tells Paul to speak boldly.

12–17. Further conflict arises between Paul and the Jews. They bring him before Gallio, proconsul of Achaia (for Proconsul, see 13:7) in AD 51. He was a brother of Seneca, the Stoic philosopher and political advisor to Nero. Both brothers were forced to commit suicide by Nero. Uninterested in disputes within Judaism, Gallio refuses to hear the complaint. Roman officials still see the developing Christian faith as part of Judaism. Paul has spent at least 18 months in Corinth.

[13]They said, "This man is persuading people to worship God in ways that are contrary to the law." [14]Just as Paul was about to speak, Gallio said to the Jews, "If it were a matter of crime or serious villainy, I would be justified in accepting the complaint of you Jews; [15]but since it is a matter of questions about words and names and your own law, see to it yourselves; I do not wish to be a judge of these matters." [16]And he dismissed them from the tribunal. [17]Then all of them[f] seized Sosthenes, the official of the synagogue, and beat him in front of the tribunal. But Gallio paid no attention to any of these things.

Paul's Return to Antioch

18 After staying there for a considerable time, Paul said farewell to the believers[g] and sailed for Syria, accompanied by Priscilla and Aquila. At Cenchreae he had his hair cut, for he was under a vow. [19]When they reached Ephesus, he left them there, but first he himself went into the synagogue and had a discussion with the Jews. [20]When they asked him to stay longer, he declined; [21]but on taking leave of them, he said, "I[h] will return to you, if God wills." Then he set sail from Ephesus.

22 When he had landed at Caesarea, he went up to Jerusalem[i] and greeted the church, and then went down to Antioch.

[23]After spending some time there he departed and went from place to place through the region of Galatia[j] and Phrygia, strengthening all the disciples.

Ministry of Apollos

24 Now there came to Ephesus a Jew named Apollos, a native of Alexandria. He was an eloquent man, well-versed in the scriptures. [25]He had been instructed in the Way of the Lord; and he spoke with burning enthusiasm and taught accurately the things concerning Jesus, though he knew only the baptism of John. [26]He began to speak boldly in the synagogue; but when Priscilla and Aquila heard him, they took him aside and explained the Way of God to him more accurately. [27]And when he wished to cross over to Achaia, the believers[g] encouraged him and wrote to the disciples to welcome him. On his arrival he greatly helped those who through grace had become believers, [28]for he powerfully refuted the Jews in public, showing by the scriptures that the Messiah[k] is Jesus.

---

[f] Other ancient authorities read *all the Greeks*
[g] Gk *brothers*   [h] Other ancient authorities read *I must at all costs keep the approaching festival in Jerusalem, but I*   [i] Gk *went up*   [j] Gk *the Galatian region*   [k] Or *the Christ*

18–22. Paul leaves Corinth for Syria, first stopping at Cenchreae, Corinth's east port, to cut his hair because of a vow. The nature of this vow is unclear. Rom. 16:1 mentions the Cenchreae church with its deacon Phoebe. Paul also stops in Ephesus, visiting its synagogue briefly. Priscilla and Aquila remain in Ephesus while Paul returns to Caesarea, Jerusalem and Antioch.

18:24–21:16. In his third missionary journey, Paul revisits cities where he has left young churches. Luke highlights events in Ephesus and Troas since he has previously mentioned events there only briefly

18:24–28. Luke's first major episode in Ephesus describes Apollos, a Jew from Alexandria (in Egypt) and a learned and passionate preacher who knows only John's baptism. Priscilla and Aquila instruct him more accurately. Luke portrays Priscilla, here mentioned first (see 18:2–3), as part of a teaching team. Apollos respects her knowledge and experience as he accepts the couple's correction in doctrinal matters. Their previous connection with Corinth enables Apollos to work among the Corinthians (1 Cor. 3:1–9).

Paul in Ephesus

19 While Apollos was in Corinth, Paul passed through the interior regions and came to Ephesus, where he found some disciples. [2]He said to them, "Did you receive the Holy Spirit when you became believers?" They replied, "No, we have not even heard that there is a Holy Spirit." [3]Then he said, "Into what then were you baptized?" They answered, "Into John's baptism." [4]Paul said, "John baptized with the baptism of repentance, telling the people to believe in the one who was to come after him, that is, in Jesus." [5]On hearing this, they were baptized in the name of the Lord Jesus. [6]When Paul had laid his hands on them, the Holy Spirit came upon them, and they spoke in tongues and prophesied – [7]altogether there were about twelve of them.

8 He entered the synagogue and for three months spoke out boldly, and argued persuasively about the kingdom of God. [9]When some stubbornly refused to believe and spoke evil of the Way before the congregation, he left them, taking the disciples with him, and argued daily in the lecture hall of Tyrannus.[1] [10]This continued for two years, so that all the residents of Asia, both Jews and Greeks, heard the word of the Lord.

The Sons of Sceva

11 God did extraordinary miracles through Paul, [12]so that when the handkerchiefs or aprons that had touched his skin were brought to the sick, their diseases left

◆ Ephesus, as this incident shows, was famous in antiquity as a center for magical arts. Practices like magic, sorcery witchcraft, and the like which sought knowledge of the future and personal control of events by the supernatural aid of spirits were widespread throughout the ancient Mediterranean world.

Charms and amulets to wear for protection, love potions to drink, incantations to utter to bind spirits to certain actions, spells to cast, curse tablets to bring disaster to enemies, mediums to summon the spirits of the dead – all these and other means served to help people who felt powerless before an uncertain future. Details of such practices deemed successful were collected into books such as those the Ephesian practitioners burned.

Some of these practices were not malicious, intended simply to promote personal well-being and to ward off evil spirits from the lives of people who knew that sudden and inexplicable illness and disaster were always awaiting them. Other practices, however, were intended to invoke supernatural powers or spirits to gain personal ends at others' expense or to harm other people.

Biblical attitudes against magic, sorcery and witchcraft are particularly severe against practitioners, male and female, who use such practices to glorify themselves, to harm others, and to manipulate

[1] Other ancient authorities read *of a certain Tyrannus, from eleven o'clock in the morning to four in the afternoon*

ACTS 19

1–10. This second Ephesian episode depicts Paul's more than two years of work among believers who know only John's baptism (vv. 1–7). In the synagogue he meets with the usual opposition. When he leaves the synagogue, he uses a lecture hall daily. Since Ephesian women had considerable freedom, holding some political and religious offices, they possibly attended such lectures. Paul also teaches in homes (20:20) where women could hear him.

11–20. Luke's third Ephesian episode portrays another conflict between Christianity and magic (8:9; 13:8; 16:16–19). Through Paul God heals many sick and demon-possessed people. When 'itinerant Jewish exorcists', the seven sons of Scaeva, try imitating Paul by expelling evil spirits in Jesus' name, the evil spirit in a possessed man attacks them. When this becomes known, many believe in Jesus, stop practising magic, and burn their valuable books.

the spirit world against the Spirit of God. In the Old Testament there are strong prohibitions against this sort of activity. In Exod. 22:18 the penalty for a female (but not a male) sorcerer is death. Deut. 18:9–14 emphasizes that the Hebrew people are not to engage in divination, soothsaying, augury, sorcery, or consultation with the dead but instead are to be 'completely loyal to the LORD your God'. The terrifying effects of a consultation with the dead are described in 1 Sam. 28:3–25 as Saul consults a medium to bring up Samuel from the dead. The prophets, too, urge the Hebrew people (Is. 2:6) and others (Jer. 27:8–11) not to listen to soothsayers and other practitioners of occult arts.

The New Testament assumes the existence of an extensive spirit world but shows that Spirit of God, manifest in Jesus and his apostles, is triumphant over these spirits. The Gospels demonstrate that these spirits recognize and submit to Jesus (Matt. 8:28–34; Mark 1:21–28; 5:1–20; 9:14–29; Luke 4:31–37; 9:37–43; 11:14–26). Acts provides four accounts showing the gospel's triumph over people who use spirits or are possessed by them. Simon Magus, with a wide following in Samaria, is amazed by the power of the Holy Spirit and wants to buy the power of bestowing it (Acts 8:4–25). On Cyprus a Jewish false prophet named Bar Jesus realizes that he will lose his power over his client, the Roman proconsul Sergius Paulus, if Paulus believes in Jesus (13:8–12). In Philippi, Paul expels the spirit of divination that recognized that Paul and Silas are 'slaves of the Most High God' with the result that her owners lose the money that can be earned by her divination (16:16–24). And finally, here in Ephesus, the seven sons of the Jewish high priest Scaeva attempt to use the Name, and hence the power, of Jesus, to expel evil spirits without understanding the implications of it (19:11–20). These four passages indicate that attempts to use the Spirit of God for personal benefit are doomed to failure and that real dangers await those who try to manipulate the powers of the spirit world. Most import-

antly, Acts shows that the new community of believers in the risen Christ know that the Spirit of God is more powerful than the forces of evil and death itself. In the Epistles, Paul asks the Galatians who has bewitched them (Gal. 3:1). He may not be speaking figuratively but instead appealing literally to their culture's belief in the power of magic.

Today, whatever we believe about human ability to manipulate spirits, it is vital to evaluate our own lives in respect to the issues underlying the use of magic, witchcraft, sorcery, and similar practices. How anxious are we over our own future? our family's success? How much do we need to manipulate others to gain our own ends? How do we deal with angry and vengeful feelings against others? How deep is our loyalty to God, who has exposed Jesus to all the powers of evil and overcome them for our sake? ◆

them, and the evil spirits came out of them. [13]Then some itinerant Jewish exorcists tried to use the name of the Lord Jesus over those who had evil spirits, saying, "I adjure you by the Jesus whom Paul proclaims." [14]Seven sons of a Jewish high priest named Sceva were doing this. [15]But the evil spirit said to them in reply, "Jesus I know, and Paul I know; but who are you?" [16]Then the man with the evil spirit leaped on them, mastered them all, and so overpowered them that they fled out of the house naked and wounded. [17]When this became known to all residents of Ephesus, both Jews and Greeks, everyone was awestruck; and the name of the Lord Jesus was praised. [18]Also many of those who became believers confessed and disclosed their practices. [19]A number of those who practiced magic collected their books and burned them publicly; when the value of these books[m] was calculated, it was found to come to fifty thousand silver coins. [20]So the word of the Lord grew mightily and prevailed.

[m] Gk them

The Riot in Ephesus

21 Now after these things had been accomplished, Paul resolved in the Spirit to go through Macedonia and Achaia, and then to go on to Jerusalem. He said, "After I have gone there, I must also see Rome." [22]So he sent two of his helpers, Timothy and Erastus, to Macedonia, while he himself stayed for some time longer in Asia.

23 About that time no little disturbance broke out concerning the Way. [24]A man named Demetrius, a silversmith who made silver shrines of Artemis, brought no little business to the artisans. [25]These he gathered together, with the workers of the same trade, and said, "Men, you know that we get our wealth from this business. [26]You also see and hear that not only in Ephesus but in almost the whole of Asia this Paul has persuaded and drawn away a considerable number of people by saying that gods made with hands are not gods. [27]And there is danger not only that this trade of ours may come into disrepute but also that the temple of the great goddess Artemis will be scorned, and she will be deprived of her majesty that brought all Asia and the world to worship her."

28 When they heard this, they were enraged and shouted, "Great is Artemis of the Ephesians!" [29]The city was filled with the confusion; and people[n] rushed together to the theater, dragging with them Gaius and Aristarchus, Macedonians who were Paul's travel companions. [30]Paul wished to go into the crowd, but the disciples would not let him; [31]even some officials of the province of Asia,[o] who were friendly

◆ Artemis of Ephesus was the supreme manifestation of the mother goddesses whose worship began in Asia and spread to Greece and Rome. These powerful deities captivated the imaginations of women and the less-educated classes. Their appeal was to the individual rather than to a political entity, such as the city or the Roman Empire, and those in lives of wretchedness were promised a happier hereafter.

No other goddess so teemed with fertility. Though she bore the same name, Artemis the Ephesian goddess was far different from the virgin huntress goddess of Greece. Artemis of Ephesus, known as 'Diana' among the Romans, was represented as a long, attentuated statue covered by a pectoral displaying multiple breasts. Scholarly debate continues as to whether these might not also indicate the scrota of the bulls sacrificed in her cult. On her stiffly projected arms sat lions, and on her skirt's front were triplet goats, sheep, and bulls, while the sides were adorned with rosettes, priestesses, and bees. On her head rose a high crown depicting the city, of which she was the tutelary deity. The zodiac sometimes ornamented the neck-plate of this mistress of moon and stars. Deer stood beside her strange, stiff body, sometimes wrapped in mummy-like bindings. Artemidorus of Ephesus insisted that this image form had a special sanctity, so different from the graceful gods carved by sculptors further west. Concealed somewhere on her statue were said to be the six mystic words upon which all Ephesian

[n] Gk *they*   [o] Gk *some of the Asiarchs*

21–22. Paul resolves to go back to Jerusalem at the end of this second missionary journey and then to Rome. This itinerary dominates the rest of Acts.

23–40. Luke's culminating Ephesian episode involves conflict between Christians and the very ancient cult of the goddess Artemis whose temple in Ephesus was one of the Seven Wonders of the World. Conflict comes in terms of economics and theology. An artisan who makes silver shrines of Artemis realizes he is losing sales as more Gentiles become Christians. Puzzled by Christians' assertions that idols made by human hands are not divinities, he incites other silversmiths by appealing to fears of lost income and declining prestige for the temple of Artemis. They respond by chanting 'Great is Artemis of the Ephesians!' (a customary type of acclamation for a pagan divinity). A riot ensues, and the people rush to the theater, a

magic was based. The original wooden image was said to have been brought by the Amazons and set up in an oak tree at Ephesus.

Her sanctuary, larger than the size of a modern football field, was one of the Seven Wonders of the ancient world. The goddess was served by thousands of functionaries, among them temple prostitutes and castrated priests. There were also acrobats, toe dancers, and hermaphrodites. The grounds surrounding the temple were very extensive and contained many splendid buildings for the accommodation of the cult. The shrine was used as a banking center for all of Asia, and enormous sums were deposited within the sacred enclosure for safe keeping.

Other sanctuaries dedicated to the Ephesian Artemis were to be found in every Greek city throughout the Mediterranean world, and Strabo insisted that the goddess was the deity most widely worshipped in private devotion. Evidence of her cult has been found at Rome, southern France, and Spain. Her devotees frequently conflated her aspects with those of Isis, Cybele, and Hecate.

Artemis may be understood as epitomizing the maternal principle, that the feminine is ultimate source of all life and being. She was the goddess of childbirth but was also said to guard tombs as mistress of the dead. This embodiment and divinization of the feminine as supreme reality of the universe was countered by Paul's view of a God who stood above and beyond sexuality or representation as a sexual being. Neither masculinity nor femininity nor any image can convey the essence of our God ◆

to him, sent him a message urging him not to venture into the theater. [32]Meanwhile, some were shouting one thing, some another; for the assembly was in confusion, and most of them did not know why they had come together. [33]Some of the crowd gave instructions to Alexander, whom the Jews had pushed forward. And Alexander motioned for silence and tried to make a defense before the people. [34]But when they recognized that he was a Jew, for about two hours all of them shouted in unison, "Great is Artemis of the Ephesians!" [35]But when the town clerk had quieted the crowd, he said, "Citizens of Ephesus, who is there that does not know that the city of the Ephesians is the temple keeper of the great Artemis and of the statue that fell from heaven?[p] [36]Since these things cannot be denied, you ought to be quiet and do nothing rash. [37]You have brought these men here who are neither temple robbers nor blasphemers of our[q] goddess. [38]If therefore Demetrius and the artisans with him have a complaint against anyone, the courts are open, and there are proconsuls; let them bring charges there against one another. [39]If there is anything further[r] you want to know, it must be settled in the regular assembly. [40]For we are in danger of being charged with rioting today, since there is no cause that we can give to justify this commotion." [41]When he had said this, he dismissed the assembly.

[p] Meaning of Gk uncertain   [q] Other ancient authorities read *your*   [r] Other ancient authorities read *about other matters*

---

traditional place for regular civic meetings, where confusion reigns for two hours as the people continue chanting. The disciples and some officials of the province of Asia keep Paul from participating. Again, Luke portrays officials as favorably disposed to Christianity. The town clerk finally quiets the crowds by insisting that everyone knows that Ephesus is the seat of the cult of Artemis and that the Christians in the theater are not harming the temple or its reputation. He urges the silversmiths to complain to the proper authorities. This satisfies the crowds.

Paul Goes to Macedonia and Greece

20 After the uproar had ceased, Paul sent for the disciples; and after encouraging them and saying farewell, he left for Macedonia. ²When he had gone through those regions and had given the believers⁸ much encouragement, he came to Greece, ³where he stayed for three months. He was about to set sail for Syria when a plot was made against him by the Jews, and so he decided to return through Macedonia. ⁴He was accompanied by Sopater son of Pyrrhus from Beroea, by Aristarchus and Secundus from Thessalonica, by Gaius from Derbe, and by Timothy, as well as by Tychicus and Trophimus from Asia. ⁵They went ahead and were waiting for us in Troas; ⁶but we sailed from Philippi after the days of Unleavened Bread, and in five days we joined them in Troas, where we stayed for seven days.

Paul's Farewell Visit to Troas

7 On the first day of the week, when we met to break bread, Paul was holding a discussion with them; since he intended to leave the next day, he continued speaking until midnight. ⁸There were many lamps in the room upstairs where we were meeting. ⁹A young man named Eutychus, who was sitting in the window, began to sink off into a deep sleep while Paul talked still longer. Overcome by sleep, he fell to the ground three floors below and was picked up dead. ¹⁰But Paul went down, and bending over him took him in his arms, and said, "Do not be alarmed, for his life is in him." ¹¹Then Paul went upstairs, and after he had broken bread and eaten, he continued to converse with them until dawn; then he left. ¹²Meanwhile they had taken the boy away alive and were not a little comforted.

The Voyage from Troas to Miletus

13 We went ahead to the ship and set sail for Assos, intending to take Paul on board there; for he had made this arrangement, intending to go by land himself. ¹⁴When he met us in Assos, we took him on board and went to Mitylene. ¹⁵We sailed from there, and on the following day we arrived opposite Chios. The next day we touched at Samos, andᵗ the day after that we came to Miletus. ¹⁶For Paul had decided to sail past Ephesus, so that he might not have to spend time in Asia; he was eager to be in Jerusalem, if possible, on the day of Pentecost.

Paul Speaks to the Ephesian Elders

17 From Miletus he sent a message to Ephesus, asking the elders of the church to

⁸ Gk *given them*   ᵗ Other ancient authorities add *after remaining at Trogyllium*

ACTS 20

1–6. Luke briefly summarizes Paul's itinerary and travelling companions for Macedonia and Achaia and focuses on Paul's week's visit to Troas.

7–12. The second 'we' passage begins here (to 21:18). Luke reports a miracle. On the eve of his departure Paul preaches well past midnight, and a young man, Eutychus, sitting in a window, grows drowsy and falls into a deep sleep. He falls three floors to the ground and is thought dead. Paul, reminiscent of Elijah (1 Kings 17:17–24) and Elisha (2 Kings 4:8–37), lies upon (a better translation than NRSV 'bending over') Eutychus and revives him.

13–16. Paul, hastening to Jerusalem, bypasses Ephesus but summons the elders of the Ephesian church to meet him in Miletus.

20:17–21:16. Until now, Luke has not portrayed emotions involving grief, separation, and loss. Luke now anticipates somber events in Jerusalem and beyond and shows the deep feelings of the believers for each other.

20:17–35. Paul's speech, the only one in Acts addressed to believers, is a poignant, emotional farewell to these leaders. The Holy Spirit has foretold imprisonment and persecution, but Paul realizes that his goal is to complete the ministry given by the Lord Jesus. He advises the

meet him. ¹⁸When they came to him, he said to them:

"You yourselves know how I lived among you the entire time from the first day that I set foot in Asia, ¹⁹serving the Lord with all humility and with tears, enduring the trials that came to me through the plots of the Jews. ²⁰I did not shrink from doing anything helpful, proclaiming the message to you and teaching you publicly and from house to house, ²¹as I testified to both Jews and Greeks about repentance toward God and faith toward our Lord Jesus. ²²And now, as a captive to the Spirit,ᵘ I am on my way to Jerusalem, not knowing what will happen to me there, ²³except that the Holy Spirit testifies to me in every city that imprisonment and persecutions are waiting for me. ²⁴But I do not count my life of any value to myself, if only I may finish my course and the ministry that I received from the Lord Jesus, to testify to the good news of God's grace.

²⁵ "And now I know that none of you, among whom I have gone about proclaiming the kingdom, will ever see my face again. ²⁶Therefore I declare to you this day that I am not responsible for the blood of any of you, ²⁷for I did not shrink from declaring to you the whole purpose of God. ²⁸Keep watch over yourselves and over all the flock, of which the Holy Spirit has made you overseers, to shepherd the church of Godᵛ that he obtained with the blood of his own Son.ʷ ²⁹I know that after I have gone, savage wolves will come in among you, not sparing the flock. ³⁰Some

even from your own group will come distorting the truth in order to entice the disciples to follow them. ³¹Therefore be alert, remembering that for three years I did not cease night or day to warn everyone with tears. ³²And now I commend you to God and to the message of his grace, a message that is able to build you up and to give you the inheritance among all who are sanctified. ³³I coveted no one's silver or gold or clothing. ³⁴You know for yourselves that I worked with my own hands to support myself and my companions. ³⁵In all this I have given you an example that by such work we must support the weak, remembering the words of the Lord Jesus, for he himself said, 'It is more blessed to give than to receive.' "

36 When he had finished speaking, he knelt down with them all and prayed. ³⁷There was much weeping among them all; they embraced Paul and kissed him, ³⁸grieving especially because of what he had said, that they would not see him again. Then they brought him to the ship.

Paul's Journey to Jerusalem

21 When we had parted from them and set sail, we came by a straight course to Cos, and the next day to Rhodes, and from there to Patara.ˣ ²When we found a ship bound for Phoenicia, we went on

ᵘ Or *And now, bound in the spirit*   ᵛ Other ancient authorities read *of the Lord*   ʷ Or *with his own blood;* Gk *with the blood of his Own*   ˣ Other ancient authorities add *and Myra*

Ephesian elders to watch the flock and keep out those who distort truth. He commends them to God and God's grace, urging them to follow his example and support themselves by working. He concludes with some words of Jesus not found in the Gospels.

36–38. Luke depicts an emotional farewell between Paul and the elders: they kneel, pray, weep, embrace, kiss, and grieve that they will not see each other again.

ACTS 21–23

21:1–6. In Tyre (on the coast of Syria), Paul meets with believers who warn him through the Spirit of danger ahead. As he leaves, their whole families (v. 5) go to the seashore; there they kneel, pray, and say farewell.

board and set sail. ³We came in sight of Cyprus; and leaving it on our left, we sailed to Syria and landed at Tyre, because the ship was to unload its cargo there. ⁴We looked up the disciples and stayed there for seven days. Through the Spirit they told Paul not to go on to Jerusalem. ⁵When our days there were ended, we left and proceeded on our journey; and all of them, with wives and children, escorted us outside the city. There we knelt down on the beach and prayed ⁶and said farewell to one another. Then we went on board the ship, and they returned home.

7 When we had finished^y the voyage from Tyre, we arrived at Ptolemais; and we greeted the believers^z and stayed with them for one day. ⁸The next day we left and came to Caesarea; and we went into the house of Philip the evangelist, one of the seven, and stayed with him. ⁹He had four unmarried daughters^a who had the gift of prophecy. ¹⁰While we were staying there for several days, a prophet named Agabus came down from Judea. ¹¹He came to us and took Paul's belt, bound his own feet and hands with it, and said, "Thus says the Holy Spirit, 'This is the way the Jews in Jerusalem will bind the man who owns this belt and will hand him over to the Gentiles.'" ¹²When we

heard this, we and the people there urged him not to go up to Jerusalem. ¹³Then Paul answered, "What are you doing, weeping and breaking my heart? For I am ready not only to be bound but even to die in Jerusalem for the name of the Lord Jesus." ¹⁴Since he would not be persuaded, we remained silent except to say, "The Lord's will be done."

15 After these days we got ready and started to go up to Jerusalem. ¹⁶Some of the disciples from Caesarea also came along and brought us to the house of Mnason of Cyprus, an early disciple, with whom we were to stay.

Paul Visits James at Jerusalem

17 When we arrived in Jerusalem, the brothers welcomed us warmly. ¹⁸The next day Paul went with us to visit James; and all the elders were present. ¹⁹After greeting them, he related one by one the things that God had done among the Gentiles through his ministry. ²⁰When they heard it, they praised God. Then they said to him, "You see, brother, how many thousands of believers there are among the Jews, and

^y Or *continued*   ^z Gk *brothers*   ^a Gk *four daughters, virgins,*

21:7–16. In Caesarea, the travelling group stays at the house of Philip (see 6:5; 8:4–40) who has four virgin daughters with the gift of prophecy. Nothing is known of these young women, but women clearly were prophets in the early church. By linking these female prophets with Agabus (21:10–14), Luke suggests that God uses both women and men to reveal divine purpose to the believers' community and that the church attends carefully to their prophecies. Agabus (11:28) vividly dramatizes his prophecy of Paul's imprisonment in Jerusalem. Paul declares emotionally that he is ready to die in Jerusalem for Jesus.

21:17–end of Acts. The events in the rest of Acts cover about five years (AD 57–62) but center on several events which Luke has for the most part foreshadowed: Paul's arrest, defense, and imprisonment in Jerusalem, a hearing in Caesarea, and his trip to Rome. Women's roles in these events can only be surmised, since they are rarely mentioned.

21:17–23.35. Luke carefully structures and dramatizes his account of Paul's stay in Jerusalem: the conflict which leads to his arrest in the Temple (21:17–36), his defense before the people of Jerusalem (21:37–22:21), threats of scourging (22:22–29), his speech to the Council (22:30–23:11), the plot to kill him (23:12–22), and his removal to Caesarea (23:23–35).

21:17–36. Christian Jews, still part of Judaism, urge Paul to show other Jews that he keeps the Law of Moses. He agrees to go through a week of purification rites (since he has been among Gentiles, he cannot participate in Temple worship until purified). He also agrees to pay the

they are all zealous for the law. [21]They have been told about you that you teach all the Jews living among the Gentiles to forsake Moses, and that you tell them not to circumcise their children or observe the customs. [22]What then is to be done? They will certainly hear that you have come. [23]So do what we tell you. We have four men who are under a vow. [24]Join these men, go through the rite of purification with them, and pay for the shaving of their heads. Thus all will know that there is nothing in what they have been told about you, but that you yourself observe and guard the law. [25]But as for the Gentiles who have become believers, we have sent a letter with our judgment that they should abstain from what has been sacrificed to idols and from blood and from what is strangled[b] and from fornication." [26]Then Paul took the men, and the next day, having purified himself, he entered the temple with them, making public the completion of the days of purification when the sacrifice would be made for each of them.

Paul Arrested in the Temple

27 When the seven days were almost completed, the Jews from Asia, who had seen him in the temple, stirred up the whole crowd. They seized him, [28]shouting, "Fellow Israelites, help! This is the man who is teaching everyone everywhere against our people, our law, and this place; more than that, he has actually brought

Greeks into the temple and has defiled this holy place." [29]For they had previously seen Trophimus the Ephesian with him in the city, and they supposed that Paul had brought him into the temple. [30]Then all the city was aroused, and the people rushed together. They seized Paul and dragged him out of the temple, and immediately the doors were shut. [31]While they were trying to kill him, word came to the tribune of the cohort that all Jerusalem was in an uproar. [32]Immediately he took soldiers and centurions and ran down to them. When they saw the tribune and the soldiers, they stopped beating Paul. [33]Then the tribune came, arrested him, and ordered him to be bound with two chains; he inquired who he was and what he had done. [34]Some in the crowd shouted one thing, some another; and as he could not learn the facts because of the uproar, he ordered him to be brought into the barracks. [35]When Paul[c] came to the steps, the violence of the mob was so great that he had to be carried by the soldiers. [36]The crowd that followed kept shouting, "Away with him!"

Paul Defends Himself

37 Just as Paul was about to be brought into the barracks, he said to the tribune, "May I say something to you?" The tribune[c] replied, "Do you know Greek? [38]Then you

[b] Other ancient authorities lack *and from what is strangled*   [c] Gk *he*

---

considerable expenses of four men who have taken a vow. Other Jews would consider this the act of a devout man. Just before his purification is accomplished, Jews from Asia (Minor) incite others to seize him, claiming that Paul has defiled the Temple by bringing in Gentiles (an act punishable by death). The Roman tribune (a junior officer from a prominent Roman family) brings troops to quell the disturbance. The tribune binds Paul (fulfilling Agabus' prophecy, 21:11) and brings him from the Temple precinct toward the nearby Antonia fortress with its barracks.

21:37–22:21. Paul asks (in Greek) to address the people. The tribune, who thought Paul was an Egyptian revolutionary, allows him to speak. Paul summarizes, in Hebrew, his life as a 'persecutor of the Way', again emphasizing that he cast both men and women (22:4) into prison, and relates his conversion (a shorter version of 9:1–19). He explains that Jesus himself appeared to him in a vision in the Temple and bid him go to the Gentiles. Luke has saved this detail of Paul's Jerusalem visit (9:26–30) until now.

are not the Egyptian who recently stirred up a revolt and led the four thousand assassins out into the wilderness?" [39]Paul replied, "I am a Jew, from Tarsus in Cilicia, a citizen of an important city; I beg you, let me speak to the people." [40]When he had given him permission, Paul stood on the steps and motioned to the people for silence; and when there was a great hush, he addressed them in the Hebrew[d] language, saying:

22 "Brothers and fathers, listen to the defense that I now make before you."

2 When they heard him addressing them in Hebrew,[d] they became even more quiet. Then he said:

3 "I am a Jew, born in Tarsus in Cilicia, but brought up in this city at the feet of Gamaliel, educated strictly according to our ancestral law, being zealous for God, just as all of you are today. [4]I persecuted this Way up to the point of death by binding both men and women and putting them in prison, [5]as the high priest and the whole council of elders can testify about me. From them I also received letters to the brothers in Damascus, and I went there in order to bind those who were there and to bring them back to Jerusalem for punishment.

Paul Tells of His Conversion

6 "While I was on my way and approaching Damascus, about noon a great light from heaven suddenly shone about me. [7]I fell to the ground and heard a voice saying to me, 'Saul, Saul, why are you persecuting me?' [8]I answered, 'Who are you, Lord?' Then he said to me, 'I am Jesus of Nazareth[e] whom you are persecuting.' [9]Now those who were with me saw the light but did not hear the voice of the one who was speaking to me. [10]I asked, 'What am I to do, Lord?' The Lord said to me, 'Get

up and go to Damascus; there you will be told everything that has been assigned to you to do.' [11]Since I could not see because of the brightness of that light, those who were with me took my hand and led me to Damascus.

12 "A certain Ananias, who was a devout man according to the law and well spoken of by all the Jews living there, [13]came to me; and standing beside me, he said, 'Brother Saul, regain your sight!' In that very hour I regained my sight and saw him. [14]Then he said, 'The God of our ancestors has chosen you to know his will, to see the Righteous One and to hear his own voice; [15]for you will be his witness to all the world of what you have seen and heard. [16]And now why do you delay? Get up, be baptized, and have your sins washed away, calling on his name.'

Paul Sent to the Gentiles

17 "After I had returned to Jerusalem and while I was praying in the temple, I fell into a trance [18]and saw Jesus[f] saying to me, 'Hurry and get out of Jerusalem quickly, because they will not accept your testimony about me.' [19]And I said, 'Lord, they themselves know that in every synagogue I imprisoned and beat those who believed in you. [20]And while the blood of your witness Stephen was shed, I myself was standing by, approving and keeping the coats of those who killed him.' [21]Then he said to me, 'Go, for I will send you far away to the Gentiles.'"

Paul and the Roman Tribune

22 Up to this point they listened to him, but then they shouted, "Away with such a fellow from the earth! For he should not be allowed to live." [23]And while they were

[d] That is, *Aramaic*   [e] Gk *the Nazorean*   [f] Gk *him*

22:22–29. The crowd, to whom a vision of Jesus in the Temple is blasphemy, now call for Paul's death. The tribune brings Paul to the barracks and prepares to scourge him to gain information (more deadly punishment than the flogging in Philippi, 16:22–23). Thus Paul immediately invokes the protection of his Roman citizenship (as in Philippi, 9:37–39).

shouting, throwing off their cloaks, and tossing dust into the air, [24]the tribune directed that he was to be brought into the barracks, and ordered him to be examined by flogging, to find out the reason for this outcry against him. [25]But when they had tied him up with thongs,[g] Paul said to the centurion who was standing by, "Is it legal for you to flog a Roman citizen who is uncondemned?" [26]When the centurion heard that, he went to the tribune and said to him, "What are you about to do? This man is a Roman citizen." [27]The tribune came and asked Paul,[h] "Tell me, are you a Roman citizen?" And he said, "Yes." [28]The tribune answered, "It cost me a large sum of money to get my citizenship." Paul said, "But I was born a citizen." [29]Immediately those who were about to examine him drew back from him; and the tribune also was afraid, for he realized that Paul was a Roman citizen and that he had bound him.

Paul before the Council

[30] Since he wanted to find out what Paul[i] was being accused of by the Jews, the next day he released him and ordered the chief priests and the entire council to meet. He brought Paul down and had him stand before them.

23 While Paul was looking intently at the council he said, "Brothers,[j] up to this day I have lived my life with a clear conscience before God." [2]Then the high priest Ananias ordered those standing near him to strike him on the mouth. [3]At this Paul said to him, "God will strike you, you whitewashed wall! Are you sitting there to judge me according to the law, and yet in violation of the law you order me to be struck?" [4]Those standing nearby said, "Do you dare to insult God's high priest?" [5]And Paul said, "I did not realize, brothers, that he was high priest; for it is written, 'You shall not speak evil of a leader of your people.'"

[6] When Paul noticed that some were Sadducees and others were Pharisees, he called out in the council, "Brothers, I am a Pharisee, a son of Pharisees. I am on trial concerning the hope of the resurrection[k] of the dead." [7]When he said this, a dissension began between the Pharisees and the Sadducees, and the assembly was divided. [8](The Sadducees say that there is no resurrection, or angel, or spirit; but the Pharisees acknowledge all three.) [9]Then a great clamor arose, and certain scribes of the Pharisees' group stood up and contended, "We find nothing wrong with this man. What if a spirit or an angel has spoken to him?" [10]When the dissension became violent, the tribune, fearing that they would tear Paul to pieces, ordered the soldiers to go down, take him by force, and bring him into the barracks.

[11] That night the Lord stood near him and said, "Keep up your courage! For just as you have testified for me in Jerusalem, so you must bear witness also in Rome."

The Plot to Kill Paul

[12] In the morning the Jews joined in a conspiracy and bound themselves by an

[g] Or *up for the lashes* [h] Gk *him* [i] Gk *he* [j] Gk *Men, brothers* [k] Gk *concerning hope and resurrection*

22:30–23:11. Because the tribune wants to understand why the Jews accuse Paul, he lets the Council (see 4:1–21; 6:12–7:57) examine Paul. Paul unwittingly insults the high priest, the Sadducee Ananias (murdered in AD 66), but manages a dignified apology. Capitalizing on the Council's division between Sadducee and Pharisee, Paul claims Pharisee heritage and insists he is on trial concerning the theological issue of resurrection. This causes intense division within the Council, and the tribune removes Paul to the barracks. An angel encourages him that he will witness in Rome.

23:12–22. Luke relates a dramatic account of a plot by 40 men who forswear food until they have killed Paul (they could be released from the oath if it could not be kept). The son of Paul's sister (little is known of Paul's family) learns of the plot and informs the tribune.

oath neither to eat nor drink until they had killed Paul. [13]There were more than forty who joined in this conspiracy. [14]They went to the chief priests and elders and said, "We have strictly bound ourselves by an oath to taste no food until we have killed Paul. [15]Now then, you and the council must notify the tribune to bring him down to you, on the pretext that you want to make a more thorough examination of his case. And we are ready to do away with him before he arrives."

[16] Now the son of Paul's sister heard about the ambush; so he went and gained entrance to the barracks and told Paul. [17]Paul called one of the centurions and said, "Take this young man to the tribune, for he has something to report to him." [18]So he took him, brought him to the tribune, and said, "The prisoner Paul called me and asked me to bring this young man to you; he has something to tell you." [19]The tribune took him by the hand, drew him aside privately, and asked, "What is it that you have to report to me?" [20]He answered, "The Jews have agreed to ask you to bring Paul down to the council tomorrow, as though they were going to inquire more thoroughly into his case. [21]But do not be persuaded by them, for more than forty of their men are lying in ambush for him. They have bound themselves by an oath neither to eat nor drink until they kill him. They are ready now and are waiting for your consent." [22]So the tribune dismissed the young man, ordering him, "Tell no one that you have informed me of this."

Paul Sent to Felix the Governor

[23] Then he summoned two of the centurions and said, "Get ready to leave by nine o'clock tonight for Caesarea with two hundred soldiers, seventy horsemen, and two hundred spearmen. [24]Also provide mounts for Paul to ride, and take him safely to Felix the governor." [25]He wrote a letter to this effect:

[26] "Claudius Lysias to his Excellency the governor Felix, greetings. [27]This man was seized by the Jews and was about to be killed by them, but when I had learned that he was a Roman citizen, I came with the guard and rescued him. [28]Since I wanted to know the charge for which they accused him, I had him brought to their council. [29]I found that he was accused concerning questions of their law, but was charged with nothing deserving death or imprisonment. [30]When I was informed that there would be a plot against the man, I sent him to you at once, ordering his accusers also to state before you what they have against him.[l]"

[31] So the soldiers, according to their instructions, took Paul and brought him during the night to Antipatris. [32]The next day they let the horsemen go on with him, while they returned to the barracks. [33]When they came to Caesarea and delivered the letter to the governor, they presented Paul also before him. [34]On reading the letter, he asked what province he belonged to, and when he learned that he was from Cilicia, [35]he said, "I will give you a hearing when your accusers arrive." Then he ordered that he be kept under guard in Herod's headquarters.[m]

---

[l] Other ancient authorities add *Farewell*

[m] Gk *praetorium*

23:23–35. The tribune protects Paul by sending him to Caesarea to Felix, governor of Syria, who has jurisdiction in such cases. The tribune's letter, generally favorable to Paul, explains the situation. Felix will give Paul a hearing when his accusers arrive.

Felix with his brother Pallas were slaves of Antonia, the mother of the Emperor Claudius (AD 41–54) before they were freed by the imperial family. Pallas moved in the highest circles of Claudius' government; Felix gained this office of governor but had difficulties controlling Jewish-Gentile conflicts.

Paul before Felix at Caesarea

24 Five days later the high priest Ananias came down with some elders and an attorney, a certain Tertullus, and they reported their case against Paul to the governor. ²When Paul[n] had been summoned, Tertullus began to accuse him, saying:

"Your Excellency,[o] because of you we have long enjoyed peace, and reforms have been made for this people because of your foresight. ³We welcome this in every way and everywhere with utmost gratitude. ⁴But, to detain you no further, I beg you to hear us briefly with your customary graciousness. ⁵We have, in fact, found this man a pestilent fellow, an agitator among all the Jews throughout the world, and a ringleader of the sect of the Nazarenes.[p] ⁶He even tried to profane the temple, and so we seized him.[q] ⁸By examining him yourself you will be able to learn from him concerning everything of which we accuse him."

9 The Jews also joined in the charge by asserting that all this was true.

Paul's Defense before Felix

10 When the governor motioned to him to speak, Paul replied:

"I cheerfully make my defense, knowing that for many years you have been a judge over this nation. ¹¹As you can find out, it is not more than twelve days since I went up to worship in Jerusalem. ¹²They did not find me disputing with anyone in the temple or stirring up a crowd either in the synagogues or throughout the city. ¹³Neither can they prove to you the charge that they now bring against me. ¹⁴But this I admit to you, that according to the Way, which they call a sect, I worship the God of our ancestors, believing everything laid down according to the law or written in the prophets. ¹⁵I have a hope in God – a hope that they themselves also accept – that there will be a resurrection of both[r] the righteous and the unrighteous. ¹⁶Therefore I do my best always to have a clear conscience toward God and all people. ¹⁷Now after some years I came to bring alms to my nation and to offer sacrifices. ¹⁸While I was doing this, they found me in the temple, completing the rite of purification, without any crowd or disturbance. ¹⁹But there were some Jews from Asia – they ought to be here before you to make an accusation, if they have anything against me. ²⁰Or let these men here tell what crime they had found when I stood before the council, ²¹unless it was this one sentence that I called out while

[n] Gk *he*   [o] Gk lacks *Your Excellency*
[p] Gk *Nazoreans*   [q] Other ancient authorities add *and we would have judged him according to our law. ⁷But the chief captain Lysias came and with great violence took him out of our hands, ⁸commanding his accusers to come before you.*
[r] Other ancient authorities read *of the dead, both of*

ACTS 24–26

24:1–26:32. Paul defends himself before a succession of Roman authorities in Caesarea: Felix (24:1–27), his successor Porcius Festus (25:1–22), Herod Agrippa II, son of Agrippa (12:1; 25:23–26:32).

24:1–27. When Jewish leaders arrive in Caesarea, Felix hears both sides of the case. Tertullus for the Jewish authorities accuses Paul of being a no-good agitator and ringleader, and one who profaned the Temple. Paul's defense reiterates his recent participation in events in Jerusalem. He admits he is a member of the 'Way' which believes the Law and the prophets, with the hope of resurrection. He states his reasons for coming to Jerusalem: to offer sacrifices and bring alms. This reference to alms is Luke's only mention of the extensive collection Paul made for Jerusalem (2 Cor. 8:1–9:15). He insists he is really on trial for believing in the resurrection of the dead. Felix adjourns the hearing, deferring a decision until the tribune arrives. Paul is in relaxed custody.

standing before them, 'It is about the resurrection of the dead that I am on trial before you today.' "

22 But Felix, who was rather well informed about the Way, adjourned the hearing with the comment, "When Lysias the tribune comes down, I will decide your case." [23]Then he ordered the centurion to keep him in custody, but to let him have some liberty and not to prevent any of his friends from taking care of his needs.

Paul Held in Custody

24 Some days later when Felix came with his wife Drusilla, who was Jewish, he sent for Paul and heard him speak concerning faith in Christ Jesus. [25]And as he discussed justice, self-control, and the coming judgment, Felix became frightened and said, "Go away for the present; when I have an opportunity, I will send for you." [26]At the same time he hoped that money would be given him by Paul, and for that reason he used to send for him very often and converse with him.

27 After two years had passed, Felix was succeeded by Porcius Festus; and since he wanted to grant the Jews a favor, Felix left Paul in prison.

Paul Appeals to the Emperor

25 Three days after Festus had arrived in the province, he went up from Caesarea to Jerusalem [2]where the chief priests and the leaders of the Jews gave him a report against Paul. They appealed to him [3]and requested, as a favor to them against Paul,[s] to have him transferred to Jerusalem. They were, in fact, planning an ambush to kill him along the way. [4]Festus replied that Paul was being kept at Caesarea, and that he himself intended to go there shortly. [5]"So," he said, "let those of you who have the authority come down with me, and if there is anything wrong about the man, let them accuse him."

6 After he had stayed among them not more than eight or ten days, he went down to Caesarea; the next day he took his seat on the tribunal and ordered Paul to be brought. [7]When he arrived, the Jews who had gone down from Jerusalem surrounded him, bringing many serious charges against him, which they could not prove. [8]Paul said in his defense, "I have in no way committed an offense against the law of the Jews, or against the temple, or against the

[s] Gk *him*

24:24. To Paul's next hearing, the Gentile governor Felix brings his Jewish wife Drusilla (AD 38–79?). She was the daughter of Herod Agrippa I (12:1-23) and the sister of Agrippa II and Bernice (25:13–26:32). She was about 20 years old at this time (about AD 57) and was married for the second time. Her first husband, a Gentile who accepted circumcision before their marriage, was King of Emesa, north of Damascus. Felix employed a Jewish magician from Cyprus to win her away, and the couple were married. She and a son probably died in Italy in the eruption of Mt Vesuvius (AD 79). Luke portrays Paul as having a reputation which attracts Roman officials and their families (see Bernice and Agrippa, 25:13–26:32).

24:25–27. When Paul talks to Felix and Drusilla about 'justice, self-control, and the coming judgment', he frightens Felix, whose marriage with Drusilla is thereby questioned. Felix's interest in Paul's faith decreases, and his interest in a bribe increases. Paul has been imprisoned for two years when a new governor, Porcius Festus, succeeds Felix who keeps Paul imprisoned to avoid unnecessary conflict with Jewish authorities. Porcius Festus, from a prominent Roman family, came to Judaea about AD 58–59 as governor and was moderately successful in controlling local uprisings.

25:1–22. Immediately after Festus arrives, Jewish leaders request a Jerusalem trial, for Paul's case, planning another ambush. Festus holds a hearing in Caesarea and suggests moving the trial to Jerusalem. Paul, as a Roman citizen, appeals to Caesar's tribunal in Rome. Agrippa (AD 27–100), king of areas of Palestine, and his sister Bernice (born AD 28) pay their respects to the emperor." ⁹But Festus, wishing to do the Jews a favor, asked Paul, "Do you wish to go up to Jerusalem and be tried there before me on these charges?" ¹⁰Paul said, "I am appealing to the emperor's tribunal; this is where I should be tried. I have done no wrong to the Jews, as you very well know. ¹¹Now if I am in the wrong and have committed something for which I deserve to die, I am not trying to escape death; but if there is nothing to their charges against me, no one can turn me over to them. I appeal to the emperor." ¹²Then Festus, after he had conferred with his council, replied, "You have appealed to the emperor; to the emperor you will go."

Festus Consults King Agrippa

13 After several days had passed, King Agrippa and Bernice arrived at Caesarea to welcome Festus. ¹⁴Since they were staying there several days, Festus laid Paul's case before the king, saying, "There is a man here who was left in prison by Felix. ¹⁵When I was in Jerusalem, the chief priests and the elders of the Jews informed me about him and asked for a sentence against him. ¹⁶I told them that it was not the custom of the Romans to hand over anyone before the accused had met the accusers face to face and had been given an opportunity to make a defense against the charge. ¹⁷So when they met here, I lost no time, but on the next day took my seat on the tribunal and ordered the man to be brought. ¹⁸When the accusers stood up, they did not charge him with any of the crimes[t] that I was expecting. ¹⁹Instead they had certain points of disagreement with him about their own religion and about a certain Jesus, who had died, but whom Paul asserted to be alive. ²⁰Since I was at a loss how to investigate these questions, I asked whether he wished to go to Jerusalem and be tried there on these charges.[u] ²¹But when Paul had appealed to be kept in custody for the decision of his Imperial Majesty, I ordered him to be held until I could send him to the emperor." ²²Agrippa said to Festus, "I would like to hear the man myself." "Tomorrow," he said, "you will hear him."

Paul Brought before Agrippa

23 So on the next day Agrippa and Bernice came with great pomp, and they entered the audience hall with the military tribunes and the prominent men of the city. Then Festus gave the order and Paul was brought in. ²⁴And Festus said, "King Agrippa and all here present with us, you see this man about whom the whole Jewish community petitioned me, both in Jerusalem and here, shouting that he ought not to live any longer. ²⁵But I found that he had done nothing deserving death; and when he appealed to his Imperial Majesty, I decided to send him. ²⁶But I have nothing definite to

[t] Other ancient authorities read *with anything*
[u] Gk *on them*

---

new governor. Herod Agrippa II, son of Herod Agrippa I (12:1–23), had a relationship with his sister Bernice which some scholars think was incestuous. Her first husband, her uncle, died, and she lived with her brother from AD 48–63 when she married the King of Cilicia who died in 66. After 70, she lived with the soon-to-be Roman Emperor Titus; popular disapproval hindered their marriage. At this time Agrippa is about 31 years old and Bernice 30. Festus explains Paul's situation to Agrippa.

25:23–26:32. At the hearing before Agrippa and Bernice, Festus asks Agrippa's advice about how to handle Paul's appeal to Caesar. Agrippa bids Paul state his defense. Paul gives an account of himself similar to those in 22:3–21 and 24:10–21. Again, Luke's repetition of events indicates their importance. Festus exclaims that Paul's excessive theological study has driven him mad. Paul, always seeking new converts, insists that he is telling the truth and appeals to Agrippa's belief in the prophets. Luke again emphasizes that rulers and Roman officials think well of Paul by reporting that they all agree Paul could be freed had he not appealed to Caesar.

write to our sovereign about him. Therefore I have brought him before all of you, and especially before you, King Agrippa, so that, after we have examined him, I may have something to write – [27]for it seems to me unreasonable to send a prisoner without indicating the charges against him."

Paul Defends Himself before Agrippa

26 Agrippa said to Paul, "You have permission to speak for yourself." Then Paul stretched out his hand and began to defend himself:

2 "I consider myself fortunate that it is before you, King Agrippa, I am to make my defense today against all the accusations of the Jews, [3]because you are especially familiar with all the customs and controversies of the Jews; therefore I beg of you to listen to me patiently.

4 "All the Jews know my way of life from my youth, a life spent from the beginning among my own people and in Jerusalem. [5]They have known for a long time, if they are willing to testify, that I have belonged to the strictest sect of our religion and lived as a Pharisee. [6]And now I stand here on trial on account of my hope in the promise made by God to our ancestors, [7]a promise that our twelve tribes hope to attain, as they earnestly worship day and night. It is for this hope, your Excellency,[v] that I am accused by Jews! [8]Why is it thought incredible by any of you that God raises the dead?

9 "Indeed, I myself was convinced that I ought to do many things against the name of Jesus of Nazareth.[w] [10]And that is what I did in Jerusalem; with authority received from the chief priests, I not only locked up many of the saints in prison, but I also cast my vote against them when they were being condemned to death. [11]By punishing them often in all the synagogues I tried to force them to blaspheme; and since I was so furiously enraged at them, I pursued them even to foreign cities.

Paul Tells of His Conversion

12 "With this in mind, I was traveling to Damascus with the authority and commission of the chief priests, [13]when at midday along the road, your Excellency[v] I saw a light from heaven, brighter than the sun, shining around me and my companions. [14]When we had all fallen to the ground, I heard a voice saying to me in the Hebrew[x] language, 'Saul, Saul, why are you persecuting me? It hurts you to kick against the goads.' [15]I asked, 'Who are you, Lord?' The Lord answered, 'I am Jesus whom you are persecuting. [16]But get up and stand on your feet; for I have appeared to you for this purpose, to appoint you to serve and testify to the things in which you have seen me[y] and to those in which I will appear to you. [17]I will rescue you from your people and from the Gentiles – to whom I am sending you [18]to open their eyes so that they may turn from darkness to light and from the power of Satan to God, so that they may receive forgiveness of sins and a place among those who are sanctified by faith in me.'

Paul Tells of His Preaching

19 "After that, King Agrippa, I was not disobedient to the heavenly vision, [20]but declared first to those in Damascus, then in Jerusalem and throughout the countryside of Judea, and also to the Gentiles, that they should repent and turn to God and do deeds consistent with repentance. [21]For this reason the Jews seized me in the temple and tried to kill me. [22]To this day I have had help from God, and so I stand here, testifying to both small and great, saying nothing but what the prophets and Moses said would take place: [23]that the Messiah[z] must suffer, and that, by being the first to rise from the dead, he would proclaim light both to our people and to the Gentiles."

Paul Appeals to Agrippa to Believe

24 While he was making this defense, Festus exclaimed, "You are out of your

---

[v] Gk O king [w] Gk the Nazorean [x] That is, Aramaic [y] Other ancient authorities read the things that you have seen [z] Or the Christ

mind, Paul! Too much learning is driving you insane!" ²⁵But Paul said, "I am not out of my mind, most excellent Festus, but I am speaking the sober truth. ²⁶Indeed the king knows about these things, and to him I speak freely; for I am certain that none of these things has escaped his notice, for this was not done in a corner. ²⁷King Agrippa, do you believe the prophets? I know that you believe." ²⁸Agrippa said to Paul, "Are you so quickly persuading me to become a Christian?"ᵃ ²⁹Paul replied, "Whether quickly or not, I pray to God that not only you but also all who are listening to me today might become such as I am – except for these chains."

30 Then the king got up, and with him the governor and Bernice and those who had been seated with them; ³¹and as they were leaving, they said to one another, "This man is doing nothing to deserve death or imprisonment." ³²Agrippa said to Festus, "This man could have been set free if he had not appealed to the emperor."

Paul Sails for Rome

27 When it was decided that we were to sail for Italy, they transferred Paul and some other prisoners to a centurion of the Augustan Cohort, named Julius. ²Embarking on a ship of Adramyttium that was about to set sail to the ports along the coast of Asia, we put to sea, accompanied by Aristarchus, a Macedonian from Thessalonica. ³The next day we put in at Sidon; and Julius treated Paul kindly, and allowed him to go to his friends to be cared for. ⁴Putting out to sea from there, we sailed under the lee of Cyprus, because the winds were against us. ⁵After we had sailed across the sea that is off Cilicia and Pamphylia, we came to Myra in Lycia. ⁶There the centurion found an Alexandrian ship bound for Italy and put us on board. ⁷We sailed slowly for a number of days and arrived with difficulty off Cnidus, and as the wind was against us, we sailed under the lee of Crete off Salmone. ⁸Sailing past it with difficulty, we came to a place called Fair Havens, near the city of Lasea.

9 Since much time had been lost and sailing was now dangerous, because even the Fast had already gone by, Paul advised them, ¹⁰saying, "Sirs, I can see that the voyage will be with danger and much heavy loss, not only of the cargo and the ship, but also of our lives." ¹¹But the centurion paid more attention to the pilot and to the owner of the ship than to what Paul said. ¹²Since the harbor was not suitable for spending the winter, the majority was in favor of putting to sea from there, on the chance that somehow they could reach Phoenix, where they could spend the winter. It was a harbor of Crete, facing southwest and northwest.

ᵃ Or *Quickly you will persuade me to play the Christian*

ACTS 27–28

27:1–28:31. Paul's desire to go to Rome, first expressed in Ephesus (19:21), will be realized but not without many difficulties. The 'we' narrative, indicating Luke's participation, continues throughout the trip (27:2–28:16). Under favorable circumstances sailing from the eastern Mediterranean to Rome against prevailing winds would take more than five weeks.

27:9–12. In antiquity, navigation in the Mediterranean was treacherous after mid-September and virtually impossible after mid-November until February or March. Paul's journey starts in early fall since he is at Fair Havens on Crete after the Fast (vv. 8–9: the Day of Atonement, occurring in early October in AD 59). Paul foresees loss of life and cargo if the trip proceeds, but most want to winter at Phoenix, a suitable harbor also in southern Crete.

The Storm at Sea

13 When a moderate south wind began to blow, they thought they could achieve their purpose; so they weighed anchor and began to sail past Crete, close to the shore. [14]But soon a violent wind, called the northeaster, rushed down from Crete.[b] [15]Since the ship was caught and could not be turned head-on into the wind, we gave way to it and were driven. [16]By running under the lee of a small island called Cauda[c] we were scarcely able to get the ship's boat under control. [17]After hoisting it up they took measures[d] to undergird the ship; then, fearing that they would run on the Syrtis, they lowered the sea anchor and so were driven. [18]We were being pounded by the storm so violently that on the next day they began to throw the cargo overboard, [19]and on the third day with their own hands they threw the ship's tackle overboard. [20]When neither sun nor stars appeared for many days, and no small tempest raged, all hope of our being saved was at last abandoned.

21 Since they had been without food for a long time, Paul then stood up among them and said, "Men, you should have listened to me and not have set sail from Crete and thereby avoided this damage and loss. [22]I urge you now to keep up your courage, for there will be no loss of life among you, but only of the ship. [23]For last night there stood by me an angel of the God to whom I belong and whom I worship, [24]and he said, 'Do not be afraid, Paul; you must stand before the emperor; and indeed, God has granted safety to all those who are sailing with you.' [25]So keep up your courage, men, for I have faith in God that it will be exactly as I have been told. [26]But we will have to run aground on some island."

27 When the fourteenth night had come, as we were drifting across the sea of Adria, about midnight the sailors suspected that they were nearing land. [28]So they took soundings and found twenty fathoms; a little farther on they took soundings again and found fifteen fathoms. [29]Fearing that we might run on the rocks, they let down four anchors from the stern and prayed for day to come. [30]But when the sailors tried to escape from the ship and had lowered the boat into the sea, on the pretext of putting out anchors from the bow, [31]Paul said to the centurion and the soldiers, "Unless these men stay in the ship, you cannot be saved." [32]Then the soldiers cut away the ropes of the boat and set it adrift.

33 Just before daybreak, Paul urged all of them to take some food, saying, "Today is the fourteenth day that you have been in suspense and remaining without food, having eaten nothing. [34]Therefore I urge you to take some food, for it will help you survive; for none of you will lose a hair from your heads." [35]After he had said this, he took bread; and giving thanks to God in the presence of all, he broke it and began to eat. [36]Then all of them were encouraged and took food for themselves. [37](We were in all two hundred seventy-six[e] persons in the

[b] Gk *it*   [c] Other ancient authorities read *Clauda*
[d] Gk *helps*   [e] Other ancient authorities read *seventy-six*; others, *about seventy-six*

27:13–44. Luke's vivid account of a two-week storm at sea provides a fitting climax to the acts of God detailed throughout, here working in Paul. God does not quell the storm but consistently reassures Paul that he will stand before the Emperor and that there will be no loss of life (vv. 23–26). Paul, in turn, tries to encourage all in the ship and give occasional advice to crew and soldiers. When it is apparent that they are near land, Paul, in an act verbally reminiscent of the Lord's Supper (Luke 22:16; 1 Cor. 11:23–24: take bread, give thanks, break bread), urges them to eat for their own well-being (Greek *soteria* suggests both physical and spiritual well-being). This meal is offered to all but must have been the Lord's Supper to the believers on board. The ship finally breaks up while on a reef. After two weeks of tribulation, they reach shore safely.

ship.) ³⁸After they had satisfied their hunger, they lightened the ship by throwing the wheat into the sea.

The Shipwreck

39 In the morning they did not recognize the land, but they noticed a bay with a beach, on which they planned to run the ship ashore, if they could. ⁴⁰So they cast off the anchors and left them in the sea. At the same time they loosened the ropes that tied the steering-oars; then hoisting the foresail to the wind, they made for the beach. ⁴¹But striking a reef,ⁱ they ran the ship aground; the bow stuck and remained immovable, but the stern was being broken up by the force of the waves. ⁴²The soldiers' plan was to kill the prisoners, so that none might swim away and escape; ⁴³but the centurion, wishing to save Paul, kept them from carrying out their plan. He ordered those who could swim to jump overboard first and make for the land, ⁴⁴and the rest to follow, some on planks and others on pieces of the ship. And so it was that all were brought safely to land.

Paul on the Island of Malta

28 After we had reached safety, we then learned that the island was called Malta. ²The natives showed us unusual kindness. Since it had begun to rain and was cold, they kindled a fire and welcomed all of us around it. ³Paul had gathered a bundle of brushwood and was putting it on the fire, when a viper, driven out by the heat, fastened itself on his hand. ⁴When the natives saw the creature hanging from his hand, they said to one another, "This man must be a murderer; though he has escaped from the sea, justice has not allowed him to live." ⁵He, however, shook off the creature into the fire and suffered no harm. ⁶They were expecting him to swell up or drop dead, but after they had waited a long time and saw that nothing unusual had happened to him, they changed their minds and began to say that he was a god.

7 Now in the neighborhood of that place were lands belonging to the leading man of the island, named Publius, who received us and entertained us hospitably for three days. ⁸It so happened that the father of Publius lay sick in bed with fever and dysentery. Paul visited him and cured him by praying and putting his hands on him. ⁹After this happened, the rest of the people on the island who had diseases also came and were cured. ¹⁰They bestowed many honors on us, and when we were about to sail, they put on board all the provisions we needed.

Paul Arrives at Rome

11 Three months later we set sail on a ship that had wintered at the island, an Alexandrian ship with the Twin Brothers as its figurehead. ¹²We put in at Syracuse and stayed there for three days; ¹³then we weighed anchor and came to Rhegium. After one day there a south wind sprang up, and on the second day we came to Puteoli. ¹⁴There we found believersˢ and were invited to stay with them for seven days. And so we came to Rome. ¹⁵The believersˢ from there, when they heard of us, came as far as the Forum of Appius and Three Taverns to meet us. On seeing them, Paul thanked God and took courage.

16 When we came into Rome, Paul was allowed to live by himself, with the soldier who was guarding him.

ⁱ Gk *place of two seas*　　ˢ Gk *brothers*

28:13–15. Puteoli is about 100 miles south of Rome. Believers from Rome meet Paul 30–40 miles outside the city.
28:16. As a prisoner in Rome, Paul is allowed to live alone with one guard.

Paul and Jewish Leaders in Rome

17 Three days later he called together the local leaders of the Jews. When they had assembled, he said to them, "Brothers, though I had done nothing against our people or the customs of our ancestors, yet I was arrested in Jerusalem and handed over to the Romans. [18]When they had examined me, the Romans[h] wanted to release me, because there was no reason for the death penalty in my case. [19]But when the Jews objected, I was compelled to appeal to the emperor – even though I had no charge to bring against my nation. [20]For this reason therefore I have asked to see you and speak with you,[i] since it is for the sake of the hope of Israel that I am bound with this chain." [21]They replied, "We have received no letters from Judea about you, and none of the brothers coming here has reported or spoken anything evil about you. [22]But we would like to hear from you what you think, for with regard to this sect we know that everywhere it is spoken against."

Paul Preaches in Rome

23 After they had set a day to meet with him, they came to him at his lodgings in great numbers. From morning until evening he explained the matter to them, testifying to the kingdom of God and trying to convince them about Jesus both from the law of Moses and from the prophets. [24]Some were convinced by what he had said, while others refused to believe. [25]So they disagreed with each other; and as they were leaving, Paul made one further statement: "The Holy Spirit was right in saying to your ancestors through the prophet Isaiah,

[26] 'Go to this people and say,
  You will indeed listen, but never
    understand,
  and you will indeed look, but never
    perceive.
[27] For this people's heart has grown dull,
  and their ears are hard of hearing,
   and they have shut their eyes;
   so that they might not look with
    their eyes,
  and listen with their ears,
and understand with their heart and
    turn –
and I would heal them.'
[28]Let it be known to you then that this salvation of God has been sent to the Gentiles; they will listen."[j]

30 He lived there two whole years at his own expense[k] and welcomed all who came to him, [31]proclaiming the kingdom of God and teaching about the Lord Jesus Christ with all boldness and without hindrance.

[h] Gk *they* [i] Or *I have asked you to see me and speak with me* [j] Other ancient authorities add verse 29, *And when he had said these words, the Jews departed, arguing vigorously among themselves* [k] Or *in his own hired dwelling*

28:17–22. Paul explains to the Jewish leaders in Rome that he is a prisoner 'for the sake of the hope of Israel'. They have heard nothing from Jerusalem authorities and agree to hear him on 'this sect'.

28:23–31. When Paul talks with them, as is usual, some believe and others refuse. As they leave, Paul quotes from Is. 6:9–10 to show that the Holy Spirit has already rebuked the Jews' ancestors for not listening to God. God's salvation has been sent to the Gentiles who will listen.

Acts ends abruptly. Luke states that Paul lives in Rome for two years at his own expense and proclaims the gospel boldly. The last word, 'without hindrance', suggests that neither Paul nor the gospel is restricted by his imprisonment. Christian tradition relates that both Peter and Paul met their deaths in Rome during the persecutions of the Emperor Nero about AD 65. Luke does not follow Peter's story beyond Acts 15, and he ends Paul's story with his Roman imprisonment. Nero's savage persecutions are to Luke an aberration in the relationship between the emerging Christian community and the government and not the proper conclusion for a work dedicated to Theophilus, himself a Roman official. Furthermore, Luke does not see his writing as a biography of a few Christian disciples: it contains none other than the acts of God.

THE LETTER OF PAUL
TO THE ROMANS

INTRODUCTION

This first letter of the apostle Paul in the New Testament is unusual because it is addressed to a church which he had not founded or even visited. There is a well-established body of Christian believers from both Jewish and Gentile backgrounds in the capital of the Empire. Paul is on his way to Jerusalem with money collected from the prosperous churches in Achaia and Macedonia to meet the needs of poor believers in Jerusalem (Rom. 15:25–26).

These facts correlate with Paul's movements described in Acts 20:1–3, 16. He hopes to travel next to Rome (Rom. 1:10–11) which he probably saw as an important launching pad for a mission into Spain (Rom. 15:28). The earliest Christians in Rome may have been Jews returning home after the feast of Pentecost described in Acts 2. There was a large Jewish population in first-century Rome, but in AD 49 they were expelled by edict of the Emperor Claudius because of 'riots at the instigation of Chrestus'. The trouble may have been a reaction to many Jews becoming disciples of Christ ('Christus'). By the time of this letter, the middle to late AD 50s, Jews will have been filtering back into Rome, but meanwhile Gentiles may have become dominant in the Roman church.

In this letter Paul sets out the gospel he preaches, a message with double effect. It draws a person into a right relationship with God, rooted in faith in Jesus. It also makes individuals into members of a loving community with other believers whatever their background. The second task is by no means easy, given the strength of cultural and religious barriers between communities, in Paul's day and our own. When a Jewish mother took her eight-day-old son to be circumcised, when she made the family seek out the last hint of yeast from the house before Passover, when she planned menus and bought meat with care according to the Bible's food laws, she acted as guardian of a way of life she believed to be rooted in the Word of God. Many Gentile converts, on the other hand, had turned their backs on a lifestyle which had been degrading and destructive. The news of God's love had given them a new sense of freedom and dignity. How were they to work it out in practice? The apostles stressed that the Hebrew Bible contained the foundations for knowing God and understanding who Jesus is, but as Jewish and Gentile believers read the texts together, urgent questions kept arising. Did certain specific commandments still apply?

In Romans Paul lays out his approach to this issue with many Old Testament quotations and much close-packed argument. The prophets in Scripture speak of a moment at the end of history when God will hold a great trial and call the human race to account. It will finally become clear who are the people in right standing with God. Paul's message is that all those who have faith in Jesus and identify with his death for forgiveness of sin can know in advance that they will be acquitted. They are 'justified by faith' (Rom. 1–4). This future hope is linked with a strong sense of having access now to the presence of a God who gives us loving acceptance as a free and gracious gift (5:1–5, 17). Paul is not only talking about developing an inner spiritual life of prayer, though that is important (8:26). He contrasts life 'in the flesh' (his way of referring to every aspect of human life lived without God) with life 'in the Spirit'. In the latter the Holy Spirit is actively transforming everything: thought, behavior, social relationships (Rom. 8:12).

In places Paul appears to speak quite strongly against the Law. He is attacking a way of living under the Law which boosts ethnic pride and creates a burden of perfection. He takes his readers through the Scriptures to show that from Abraham onwards the people of God are those who respond in faith to God's saving activity. Then he looks in more detail at how the believer lives out God's love at home, at work, in public life and in church.

In our age of mobility and family fragmentation, this letter speaks of how the Christian gospel can put confidence into the hearts of those who discover that they can stand and be showered with the grace and love of God. But the message will be distorted and fail to do its healing work if local churches are places of discrimination or disapproval.

Salutation

1 Paul, a servant[a] of Jesus Christ, called to be an apostle, set apart for the gospel of God, [2]which he promised beforehand through his prophets in the holy scriptures, [3]the gospel concerning his Son, who was descended from David according to the flesh [4]and was declared to be Son of God with power according to the spirit[b] of holiness by resurrection from the dead, Jesus Christ our Lord, [5]through whom we have received grace and apostleship to bring about the obedience of faith among all the Gentiles for the sake of his name, [6]including yourselves who are called to belong to Jesus Christ,

7 To all God's beloved in Rome, who are called to be saints:

Grace to you and peace from God our Father and the Lord Jesus Christ.

Prayer of Thanksgiving

8 First, I thank my God through Jesus Christ for all of you, because your faith is proclaimed throughout the world. [9]For God, whom I serve with my spirit by announcing the gospel[c] of his Son, is my witness that without ceasing I remember you always in my prayers, [10]asking that by God's will I may somehow at last succeed in coming to you. [11]For I am longing to see you so that I may share with you some spiritual gift to strengthen you – [12]or rather so that we may be mutually encouraged by each other's faith, both yours and mine. [13]I want you to know, brothers and sisters,[d] that I have often intended to come to you (but thus far have been prevented), in order that I may reap some harvest among you as I have among the rest of the Gentiles. [14]I am a debtor both to Greeks and to barbarians, both to the wise and to the foolish [15] – hence my eagerness to proclaim the gospel to you also who are in Rome.

The Power of the Gospel

16 For I am not ashamed of the gospel; it is the power of God for salvation to everyone who has faith, to the Jew first and

[a] Gk *slave*   [b] Or *Spirit*   [c] Gk *my spirit in the gospel*   [d] Gk *brothers*

ROMANS 1

Paul introduces himself to the Romans and briefly mentions his hope to visit them soon. He announces his theme that God's rescue strategy for the human race is related to faith, and begins by interpreting the moral and religious life he sees round about him, relating it to the story of humanity since Adam.

1–7. When introducing himself, Paul puts the focus on Jesus. Prophets had promised that God would do something decisive to change history with a Messiah (Christ) in the family line of David. Though Jesus had not been the forceful political deliverer a Messiah was expected to be, his resurrection powerfully demonstrated his unique and intimate relationship as 'Son' of God. As 'Lord', a title frequently used for God by both Jews and pagans, Jesus calls people to belong to him (v. 6), to obey him (v. 5) and in some cases to be his apostle or messenger (v. 1). The dominance of Christ invites a submission which is about trusting and receiving grace and love (vv. 5, 7).

8–15. Paul has a rich prayer life which includes praying for this church he has not yet visited. He seems sensitive to the danger that a forceful personality like his own might try to take control. He spells out that his visit would be for sharing a gift and giving and receiving encouragement. But he is an irrepressible evangelist and longs to make some converts in Rome. He is not elitist. He preaches to a range of ethnic groups and educational backgrounds.

16–17. The prophet Habakkuk once looked out on a world where oppression was flourishing and heard God assuring him that in the end wrong would be put right. Meanwhile 'the righteous live by their faith' (Hab. 2:4). For Paul, as for the prophets, the righteousness of God is not just the goodness of God's character but also God's activity to restore justice and bring people back to himself. Paul is going to argue that it is through faith and faith alone that people experience the

also to the Greek. ¹⁷For in it the righteousness of God is revealed through faith for
faith; as it is written, "The one who is
righteous will live by faith."ᵉ

The Guilt of Humankind

18 For the wrath of God is revealed from
heaven against all ungodliness and wickedness of those who by their wickedness
suppress the truth. ¹⁹For what can be
known about God is plain to them, because
God has shown it to them. ²⁰Ever since the
creation of the world his eternal power and
divine nature, invisible though they are,
have been understood and seen through the
things he has made. So they are without
excuse; ²¹for though they knew God, they
did not honor him as God or give thanks
to him, but they became futile in their
thinking, and their senseless minds were
darkened. ²²Claiming to be wise, they
became fools; ²³and they exchanged the
glory of the immortal God for images
resembling a mortal human being or birds
or four-footed animals or reptiles.

24 Therefore God gave them up in the
lusts of their hearts to impurity, to the
degrading of their bodies among themselves, ²⁵because they exchanged the truth
about God for a lie and worshiped and
served the creature rather than the Creator,
who is blessed forever! Amen.

26 For this reason God gave them up
to degrading passions. Their women

exchanged natural intercourse for unnatural, ²⁷and in the same way also the men,
giving up natural intercourse with women,
were consumed with passion for one
another. Men committed shameless acts
with men and received in their own
persons the due penalty for their error.

◆ Jewish Law set clear boundaries for
sexual behavior and all homosexual
activity was excluded. Christians
followed the Jewish position and in many
Western countries, until recently, male
homosexual acts were criminal offences,
female ones unmentionable. With the
easing of the law in recent decades, the
issue has come under close scrutiny.

A proportion of adults is exclusively
attracted to people of the same sex (the
percentage is disputed). Experiences in
early family life often seem to play a part
in this, but there may also be genetic
factors. The full story is not known, but
medical staff and pastoral workers agree
that there are those for whom the direction of attraction is homosexual and
unlikely to change. Should we view this
as 'natural' and encourage these men and
women to form committed, loving, same-
sex relationships?

Pagan culture, in Paul's day, was highly

ᵉ Or *The one who is righteous through faith will
live*

---

power of God which brings them into the category 'righteous', meaning 'in a right relationship
with God', power which helps them live in ways that reflect the righteous character of God.
18–32. This section builds up to a description of the extremes of human wickedness (vv. 29–31).
If there is a powerful and loving God, why does he tolerate it? Paul indirectly affirms the love of
God by talking about his wrath: a capacity for great love includes the capacity for anger.
Although God cannot be known through the five senses, evidence about God is available to the
human mind (v. 20). We are created with a capacity to love and worship God, responses which
imply some space for choice. Rebellion has led to a downward spiral. To believe in a glorious
Creator and not worship him is too uncomfortable. A process of denial takes place. People
transfer their worship to images representing aspects of creation rather than the whole character
of the Creator. Values, such as sexual values, get distorted. Meanwhile God is not distant or
indifferent. The repeated phrase 'God gave them up' (vv. 24, 26, 28) indicates that God upholds
the moral nature of his world making sure that sin can be seen to be harmful. The most brazenly
destructive people may have a painful sense that they themselves deserve to be destroyed (v. 32).

permissive. Temples were often centres for homosexual as well as heterosexual prostitution. Paul's language in Rom. 1:24–27 is strong because he is responding to a situation in which sexual experience is being glorified, and promiscuity, including homosexual experimentation, is being encouraged. The church has tended to employ a similarly condemning tone towards all those with homosexual feelings, encouraging a climate in which they have been subjected to fear and abuse. This ignores the example of Jesus who flouted social taboos and befriended people who broke the sexual code.

Jesus, however, called his followers to a standard of sexual behavior which seemed to them impossible (Matt. 19:10). He emphasized from the creation story in Gen. 2 that the uniting of the bodies of a man and woman in sexual intercourse was not just a biological function. It was intended by God to be linked with uniting their lives in personal intimacy and in the public partnership of founding a new family. Jesus went on to speak in positive ways about the possibilities of a single life.

For Paul the intimacy and mystery of relating to the sexual other reflects the depth and mystery of our relationship with God who is Other than us. His concept of what is 'natural' for human beings looks beyond what we find in the world, towards the Creator's intention.

Same-sex intercourse is unnatural because it denies the significance of sexual complementarity. If Paul were here to engage in our modern debates on this issue, he would surely want to affirm the value of intimate same-sex friendships but conclude that, in such cases, sexual celibacy is still the Christian way ◆

28 And since they did not see fit to acknowledge God, God gave them up to a debased mind and to things that should not be done. [29]They were filled with every kind of wickedness, evil, covetousness, malice. Full of envy, murder, strife, deceit, craftiness, they are gossips, [30]slanderers, God-haters,[f] insolent, haughty, boastful, inventors of evil, rebellious toward parents, [31]foolish, faithless, heartless, ruthless. [32]They know God's decree, that those who practice such things deserve to die – yet they not only do them but even applaud others who practice them.

The Righteous Judgment of God

2 Therefore you have no excuse, whoever you are, when you judge others; for in passing judgment on another you condemn yourself, because you, the judge, are doing the very same things. [2]You say,[g] "We know that God's judgment on those

[f] Or *God-hated*   [g] Gk lacks *You say*

ROMANS 2

Paul has painted a black picture which seemed to be aimed at pagan worship. He imagines readers, especially from a Jewish background, agreeing that such groups deserve the full weight of God's judgment. Now he turns to them and argues that despite all the privileges of the Jews there is godless behavior, arrogance, theft, adultery to be found in their community too. When it comes to the final judgment there will be no favoritism (v. 11). God will weigh up good and evil in people's lives and the standards will be recognizable even to the consciences of those who know nothing of the written Law of God (v. 15). The important covenant sign of circumcision will no longer be relevant. The issue will be the goodness of life and heart (vv. 7, 29). Note how, in the day of judgment, Jesus occupies a central role (v. 16).

1–11. An Old Testament faith, with all its emphasis on the patient forgiveness and kindness of God, should lead to a humble repentant heart, slow to criticize others (v. 4). But a religious community can breed a hard self-satisfaction in its members with dangerous eternal consequences (vv. 5–8).

who do such things is in accordance with truth." ³Do you imagine, whoever you are, that when you judge those who do such things and yet do them yourself, you will escape the judgment of God? ⁴Or do you despise the riches of his kindness and forbearance and patience? Do you not realize that God's kindness is meant to lead you to repentance? ⁵But by your hard and impenitent heart you are storing up wrath for yourself on the day of wrath, when God's righteous judgment will be revealed. ⁶For he will repay according to each one's deeds: ⁷to those who by patiently doing good seek for glory and honor and immortality, he will give eternal life; ⁸while for those who are self-seeking and who obey not the truth but wickedness, there will be wrath and fury. ⁹There will be anguish and distress for everyone who does evil, the Jew first and also the Greek, ¹⁰but glory and honor and peace for everyone who does good, the Jew first and also the Greek. ¹¹For God shows no partiality.

12 All who have sinned apart from the law will also perish apart from the law, and all who have sinned under the law will be judged by the law. ¹³For it is not the hearers of the law who are righteous in God's sight, but the doers of the law who will be justified. ¹⁴When Gentiles, who do not possess the law, do instinctively what the law requires, these, though not having the law, are a law to themselves. ¹⁵They show that what the law requires is written on their hearts, to which their own conscience also bears witness; and their conflicting thoughts will accuse or perhaps excuse them ¹⁶on the day when, according to my gospel, God, through Jesus Christ, will judge the secret thoughts of all.

The Jews and the Law

17 But if you call yourself a Jew and rely on the law and boast of your relation to God ¹⁸and know his will and determine what is best because you are instructed in the law, ¹⁹and if you are sure that you are a guide to the blind, a light to those who are in darkness, ²⁰a corrector of the foolish, a teacher of children, having in the law the embodiment of knowledge and truth, ²¹you, then, that teach others, will you not teach yourself? While you preach against stealing, do you steal? ²²You that forbid adultery, do you commit adultery? You that abhor idols, do you rob temples? ²³You that boast in the law, do you dishonor God by breaking the law? ²⁴For, as it is written, "The name of God is blasphemed among the Gentiles because of you."

25 Circumcision indeed is of value if you obey the law; but if you break the law, your circumcision has become

---

12–13. We meet for the first time the verb 'justify', which is from the same root as 'righteousness' (see on 1:17). 'To be justified' means to be declared in the right by God the Judge, for an eternal life in relationship with him (vv. 7, 10). There is no mention yet of faith in Jesus Christ. Paul is establishing that it is possible to listen to God's Law without the response that leads to changed lives.

14:16. 'Conscience' means knowing or debating within yourself about right and wrong. It was a Greek concept roughly equivalent to the Hebrew idea of a heart responsive or hardened to God. These verses say people have moral knowledge whether they know the Scriptures or not. God can justly hold them accountable for the inconsistency of their lives.

17–24. The history of Christian prejudice against the Jews should alert us to the dangers of reading this section as a blanket attack on them. It is precisely because of their high standards of moral excellence that Paul points out that at the end of the day there is still crime, broken marriages, and some spiritual arrogance to be found in their community too. No group or individual can be complacent before God.

25–29. For a Jewish man circumcision was an essential sign of membership of the people of God. There was no equivalent physical mark for women. It is, however, significant that it touched a

uncircumcision. ²⁶So, if those who are uncircumcised keep the requirements of the law, will not their uncircumcision be regarded as circumcision? ²⁷Then those who are physically uncircumcised but keep the law will condemn you that have the written code and circumcision but break the law. ²⁸For a person is not a Jew who is one outwardly, nor is true circumcision something external and physical. ²⁹Rather, a person is a Jew who is one inwardly, and real circumcision is a matter of the heart – it is spiritual and not literal. Such a person receives praise not from others but from God.

3 Then what advantage has the Jew? Or what is the value of circumcision? ²Much, in every way. For in the first place the Jews[h] were entrusted with the oracles of God. ³What if some were unfaithful? Will their faithlessness nullify the faithfulness of God? ⁴By no means! Although everyone is a liar, let God be proved true, as it is written,

"So that you may be justified in your
        words,
    and prevail in your judging."[i]

⁵But if our injustice serves to confirm the justice of God, what should we say? That God is unjust to inflict wrath on us? (I speak in a human way.) ⁶By no means! For then how could God judge the world? ⁷But if through my falsehood God's truthfulness abounds to his glory, why am I still being condemned as a sinner? ⁸And why not say (as some people slander us by saying that we say), "Let us do evil so that good may come"? Their condemnation is deserved!

None Is Righteous

9 What then? Are we any better off?[j] No, not at all; for we have already charged that all, both Jews and Greeks, are under the power of sin, ¹⁰as it is written:

"There is no one who is righteous, not
        even one;
¹¹   there is no one who has
        understanding,
    there is no one who seeks God.
¹² All have turned aside, together they
        have become worthless;
    there is no one who shows kindness,
        there is not even one."

h Gk *they*   i Gk *when you are being judged*
j Or *at any disadvantage?*

---

man at the point of intimate sexual contact so within marriage and family life circumcision would have been part of women's experience too. (See also the note on Gal. 5:6.) The irrevocable commitment of cutting something off has meaning only if it corresponds to a commitment to the will of God.

ROMANS 3

Paul touches briefly on some issues he will return to later. Then he completes his presentation of the state of humanity before God, using texts that emphasize the universal scope of sin. Everyone is under its power. No one can reach God's standard. In vv. 24–26 he puts the spotlight on the death of Christ Jesus. It is linked with God's generous forgiveness in such a way that those who have faith can know that they will be put right with God.

1–8. Paul's lively mind anticipates a barrage of questions. What was the point of all those years of Jewish history? God trusted them with important promises (v. 2). Does the fact that so few recognize Jesus as the Messiah undermine the promises? No, human faithlessness simply highlights God's faithfulness (v. 4). So why does God condemn any sin if it highlights his goodness? This malicious question is hardly worth an answer (see 6:1).

9–20. Sin exerts power over us; we feel helpless to live up to our own standards. A string of quotations follows (Pss. 14:1–3; 53:1–3; 5:9; 140:3; Is. 59:7–8; Pss. 36:1; 143:2). At first sight they might seem to be saying we are all as bad as we possibly could be. But Paul has already made clear there is considerable moral variation among people. It is more likely that he intends the quotations to support a double message. Firstly, there is no community in which we cannot find very blatant

¹³ "Their throats are opened graves;
   they use their tongues to deceive."
"The venom of vipers is under their
   lips."
¹⁴ "Their mouths are full of cursing
   and bitterness."
¹⁵ "Their feet are swift to shed blood;
¹⁶ ruin and misery are in their paths,
¹⁷ and the way of peace they have not
   known."
¹⁸ "There is no fear of God before their
   eyes."

19 Now we know that whatever the law
says, it speaks to those who are under the
law, so that every mouth may be silenced,
and the whole world may be held accountable to God. ²⁰For "no human being will be
justified in his sight" by deeds prescribed
by the law, for through the law comes the
knowledge of sin.

Righteousness through Faith

21 But now, apart from law, the righteousness of God has been disclosed, and is
attested by the law and the prophets, ²²the
righteousness of God through faith in Jesus
Christᵏ for all who believe. For there is no
distinction, ²³since all have sinned and fall
short of the glory of God; ²⁴they are now
justified by his grace as a gift, through the
redemption that is in Christ Jesus, ²⁵whom
God put forward as a sacrifice of atone-
mentˡ by his blood, effective through faith.
He did this to show his righteousness,
because in his divine forbearance he had
passed over the sins previously committed;
²⁶it was to prove at the present time that he
himself is righteous and that he justifies
the one who has faith in Jesus.ᵐ

27 Then what becomes of boasting? It
is excluded. By what law? By that of works?
No, but by the law of faith. ²⁸For we hold
that a person is justified by faith apart
from works prescribed by the law. ²⁹Or is
God the God of Jews only? Is he not the
God of Gentiles also? Yes, of Gentiles also,
³⁰since God is one; and he will justify the

ᵏ Or *through the faith of Jesus Christ*   ˡ Or *a place
of atonement*   ᵐ Or *who has the faith of Jesus*

---

examples of evil. Secondly, even the very best people within any community do not measure up
to the standard 'righteous' when seen from God's perspective. These two pieces of bad news
knock away pride and level the ground for the good news which follows.
21–23. Something new happened. It bypasses the system of atonement in Israel's Law, but once
known about, it proves to be consistent with the Scriptures (v. 21). It is God's righteous way of
putting people right with him. It is available to everybody and needed by all (vv. 22–23).
24–26. Hebrew worshippers were encouraged to come to God and trust him to forgive the wrongs
they confessed. But there is a terrible complexity about God passing over (v. 25) what has often
caused irrevocable hurt and harm. This was brought home in the vividness of a ceremony of
sacrifice. Blood and life of an innocent and beautiful creature was poured out as God's provided
atonement for their own lives (Lev. 17:11). Those mysterious illustrations, sacrifices of one on
behalf of others, have pointed towards an event in history in which God takes the initiative.
Jesus Christ dies and people justify them as a free gift of his grace. All that is required is a
response of faith.
   Paul has not been very specific here about how Christ's death can be the effective basis for
God's forgiveness. This needs careful thought because there is a danger of presenting a God who
is distant and angry while his Son bears the brunt of evil and pain. People feeling knocked down
by life sometimes suspect that God is like that. We see in other texts that Paul does not make that
split between the Son of God and his Father. They are so united in love and purpose that the cross
is the supreme demonstration of God's love (5:8). The atonement was the self-sacrifice of God.
27–31. Anyone who has received the gift just described should not boast about or rely on any
other tradition. God is not the God of any specific race or group. There is only one God and it is
only by faith that anyone will finally be justified before God. This might appear to contradict the
idea that God has given us his Law to live by; Paul will argue there is no contradiction.

circumcised on the ground of faith and the uncircumcised through that same faith. [31]Do we then overthrow the law by this faith? By no means! On the contrary, we uphold the law.

The Example of Abraham

4 What then are we to say was gained by[n] Abraham, our ancestor according to the flesh? [2]For if Abraham was justified by works, he has something to boast about, but not before God. [3]For what does the scripture say? "Abraham believed God, and it was reckoned to him as righteousness." [4]Now to one who works, wages are not reckoned as a gift but as something due. [5]But to one who without works trusts him who justifies the ungodly, such faith is reckoned as righteousness. [6]So also David speaks of the blessedness of those to whom God reckons righteousness apart from works:

[7] "Blessed are those whose iniquities
    are forgiven,
  and whose sins are covered;
[8] blessed is the one against whom the
    Lord will not reckon sin."

9 Is this blessedness, then, pronounced only on the circumcised, or also on the uncircumcised? We say, "Faith was reckoned to Abraham as righteousness." [10]How then was it reckoned to him? Was it before or after he had been circumcised? It was not after, but before he was circumcised.

◆ The word faith carries with it a multitude of meanings and conjures up a myriad of ideas. For the majority of people, faith is the intellectual ascent to a particular belief system, accepting that certain things are true while others are not. It is viewed as the reliance or trust in a person or thing. We all experience this to varying degrees on an everyday basis – we all have 'faith' that the brakes on our motor car will work when we need them to, that the sun will rise and that our friends will not let us down.

Religious faith is often treated in a negative manner by those who do not hold any religious beliefs, viewing it as a type of lesser knowledge, something to be looked down upon, used by those who are weak and by those who cannot cope, as the opposite to intellect and science.

For the Christian, faith is more than intellectual assent to certain beliefs about God, although of course that is part of it. It is also placing complete trust in God, being totally dependent on him and receiving all he has to offer. Faith is the response of the whole person, intellect, emotions, imagination, to God. It is seeing him as the only way out of the situation mankind had created for itself – that

[n] Other ancient authorities read *say about*

ROMANS 4

Two key biblical figures demonstrate that justification by faith has always been God's way. When God promised Abraham and Sarah innumerable descendants despite their childlessness, Abraham's belief was 'reckoned to him as righteousness' (Gen. 15:6). Traditional interpretations of Abraham stressed that he was circumcised, obedient to God (Gen. 17; 22), righteous because he kept the Law although he lived before Moses. Paul claims it was faith which was the key to Abraham's right relationship with God. Abraham is the ancestor of God's people in a different sense from the physical; he is the father of all who have faith. David is mentioned as someone with faith that his sin, which was serious, could be forgiven.

1–5. Paul connects the phrase 'reckoned as righteousness' with 'being justified'. (Just and righteous are the same word in Greek.) He illustrates it with a metaphor of money reckoned to our account. God viewing us as one of his righteous people is a gift to be received in faith. It is not something to be earned.

6–8. If righteousness can be compared with credit on an account, sin is a debt. Ps. 32 speaks of God cancelling the debt of sin when David confesses and trusts he has been forgiven.

is, a state of alienation from God, sinful and condemned to death. It is accepting and entering into the reality of what Christ has done through his death and resurrection in securing our salvation. Realizing that, there is nothing anyone can do to better themselves, to make themselves right and pure before God. No amount of prayer, Bible study, worship, good deeds or other Christian activities can bring us closer to God. None of these things, however commendable, are able to give us access to God, however hard we work and strive to please him, to obey his commandments, it is not enough. With regard to salvation, in becoming righteous before God, works are of no avail. They do not, in fact they cannot help us. We cannot work our way to God to gain his approval and forgiveness. All we can do is to accept by faith what Christ has done for us, to accept his totally unconditional love, acknowledging that we even need his help in doing this ◆

¹¹He received the sign of circumcision as a seal of the righteousness that he had by faith while he was still uncircumcised. The purpose was to make him the ancestor of all who believe without being circumcised and who thus have righteousness reckoned to them, ¹²and likewise the ancestor of the circumcised who are not only circumcised but who also follow the example of the faith that our ancestor Abraham had before he was circumcised.

God's Promise Realized through Faith

13 For the promise that he would inherit the world did not come to Abraham or to his descendants through the law but through the righteousness of faith. ¹⁴If it is the adherents of the law who are to be the heirs, faith is null and the promise is void. ¹⁵For the law brings wrath; but where there is no law, neither is there violation.

16 For this reason it depends on faith, in order that the promise may rest on grace and be guaranteed to all his descendants, not only to the adherents of the law but also to those who share the faith of Abraham (for he is the father of all of us, ¹⁷as it is written, "I have made you the father of many nations") – in the presence of the God in whom he believed, who gives life to the dead and calls into existence the things that do not exist. ¹⁸Hoping against hope, he believed that he would become "the father of many nations," according to what was said, "So numerous shall your descendants be." ¹⁹He did not weaken in faith when he considered his own body, which was alreadyᵒ as good as dead (for he was about a hundred years old), or when he considered the barrenness of Sarah's womb. ²⁰No distrust made him waver concerning the promise of God, but he grew strong in his faith as he gave glory to God, ²¹being fully convinced that God was able to do what he had promised. ²²Therefore his faithᵖ "was

ᵒ Other ancient authorities lack *already*
ᵖ Gk *Therefore it*

9–12. With Abraham circumcision happens after righteousness is accounted to him (Gen. 15:6; 17:24). It is a visible sign or symbol (Rom. 4:11). Faith and not the outward rite makes Abraham an ancestor and role model.
13–15. Abraham was promised that God would bring blessing to all the world through his descendants (Gen. 12:2–3). If keeping the rites and duties of Moses' Law was a condition of that blessing, the promise was an empty one. No one can succeed in keeping the Law.
16–22. The promise was about God's initiative of grace (v. 16). Abraham and Sarah clung on to it despite the tremendous suffering it brought into their lives, rubbing on the raw nerve of her infertility (v. 19). Abraham believed something about what God was going to do in the future. Faith and praise of God shaped his character, making him strong (v. 20).

reckoned to him as righteousness." [23]Now the words, "it was reckoned to him," were written not for his sake alone, [24]but for ours also. It will be reckoned to us who believe in him who raised Jesus our Lord from the dead, [25]who was handed over to death for our trespasses and was raised for our justification.

Results of Justification

5 Therefore, since we are justified by faith, we[q] have peace with God through our Lord Jesus Christ, [2]through whom we have obtained access[r] to this grace in which we stand; and we[s] boast in our hope of sharing the glory of God. [3]And not only that, but we[s] also boast in our sufferings, knowing that suffering produces endurance, [4]and endurance produces character, and character produces hope, [5]and hope does not disappoint us, because God's love has been poured into our hearts through the Holy Spirit that has been given to us.

6 For while we were still weak, at the right time Christ died for the ungodly. [7]Indeed, rarely will anyone die for a righteous person – though perhaps for a good person someone might actually dare to die. [8]But God proves his love for us in that while we still were sinners Christ died for us. [9]Much more surely then, now that we have been justified by his blood, will we be saved through him from the wrath of God.[t] [10]For if while we were enemies, we were reconciled to God through the death of his Son, much more surely, having been reconciled, will we be saved by his life. [11]But more than that, we even boast in God through our Lord Jesus Christ, through whom we have now received reconciliation.

Adam and Christ

12 Therefore, just as sin came into the world through one man, and death came through sin, and so death spread to all

[q] Other ancient authorities read *let us* [r] Other ancient authorities add *by faith* [s] Or *let us* [t] Gk *the wrath*

23–24. Abraham had only a glimpse of what God's plan was all about. The death and resurrection of Jesus reveal much more of how faith and righteousness connect.

ROMANS 5

Following the look at Abraham and Sarah there is a description of how Christian character is shaped in hope and love, including through suffering. This leads back to more detail on the significance of Christ suffering on the cross. The contrast is explored between the human race, in solidarity with Adam, ruined by sin and Christ's new people, enjoying the gift he brings.

1–5. A child thrives in the presence of loving parents who provide for it unconditionally. It gains confidence to take risks and endure knocks as it grows up. Being justified by faith means trusting we can have the attention of God now and look forward to a future in his glorious presence. There is no opting out of the pressure and pain of human life, but a confident hope that through suffering, God will shape our lives. Hope risks disappointment as Sarah well knew (4:19), but the Holy Spirit pours the encouragement of God's love into believing hearts.

6–11. Our sense that God loves us grows as we dwell on the significance of Jesus' death. Someone might dare to die for her own community or a deserving friend, but no one willingly dies for the enemy. God's Son died for sinners who were hostile to him. With that as the measure of God's love, we can be sure that the risen Christ accompanies us through our struggles in life (v. 10) and will still be around when we die (v. 9).

12–21. In this comparison between Adam and Jesus Christ each 'one man' represents or includes 'many'. Each makes a choice and acts; many are affected. Adam's choice is for self. Jesus' choice is a gift to others (5:15). Adam deliberately disobeys God; sin enters the world, and also death, which is linked to God's disapproval of sin. All die, whether they are conscious of transgressing because all have sinned – [13]sin was indeed in the world before the law, but sin is not reckoned when there is no law. [14]Yet death exercised dominion from Adam to Moses, even over those whose sins were not like the transgression of Adam, who is a type of the one who was to come.

15 But the free gift is not like the trespass. For if the many died through the one man's trespass, much more surely have the grace of God and the free gift in the grace of the one man, Jesus Christ, abounded for the many. [16]And the free gift is not like the effect of the one man's sin. For the judgment following one trespass brought condemnation, but the free gift following many trespasses brings justification. [17]If, because of the one man's trespass, death exercised dominion through that one, much more surely will those who receive the abundance of grace and the free gift of righteousness exercise dominion in life through the one man, Jesus Christ.

18 Therefore just as one man's trespass led to condemnation for all, so one man's act of righteousness leads to justification and life for all. [19]For just as by the one man's disobedience the many were made sinners, so by the one man's obedience the many will be made righteous. [20]But law came in, with the result that the trespass multiplied; but where sin increased, grace abounded all the more, [21]so that, just as sin exercised dominion in death, so grace might also exercise dominion through justification[u] leading to eternal life through Jesus Christ our Lord.

Dying and Rising with Christ

6 What then are we to say? Should we continue in sin in order that grace may abound? [2]By no means! How can we who died to sin go on living in it? [3]Do you not know that all of us who have been baptized into Christ Jesus were baptized into his death? [4]Therefore we have been buried with him by baptism into death, so that, just as Christ was raised from the dead by the glory of the Father, so we too might walk in newness of life.

5 For if we have been united with him in a death like his, we will certainly be united with him in a resurrection like his. [6]We know that our old self was crucified with him so that the body of sin might be destroyed, and we might no longer be

[u] Or *righteousness*

---

a law of God or not. Some, such as those who lived before Moses, do not even know the laws of God (5:14). They are still shot through with sin (2:15) and death dominates them. Now Jesus chooses to obey and many receive the gift of eternal life, empowered to live through Jesus (5:17).

Paul does not mention Eve, who was first to break the command (Gen. 3:6). In 2 Cor. 11:3 he uses her as an example. Here he perhaps names only Adam because the solidarity of the human race is in view. In Genesis 'Adam' is both the name of the first man and the generic word for humankind, male and female together (see especially Gen. 5:2). When 'one man' occurs in this passage the Greek inclusive word *anthropos* is used rather than the gender specific word. Men and women sin; Christ in his humanity, not his maleness, is our representative who brings the free gift of grace into the world.

ROMANS 6

Saying that God accepts sinners by grace through faith has been criticized as encouraging irresponsibility (3:8). Will some continue to sin, thinking, 'God will forgive; grace is his business'? For a Christian united with Christ, Paul replies, such an attitude is unthinkable. Conversion is like a transfer of employment from slavery in sin to serving God from the heart.

1–11. Entry into the Christian community is publicly marked by baptism which women and men equally receive. We wash in water and drink it but it is also the medium of death and burial by drowning. Baptism vividly acts out the reality that Christians are united with Christ. They

enslaved to sin. ⁷For whoever has died is freed from sin. ⁸But if we have died with Christ, we believe that we will also live with him. ⁹We know that Christ, being raised from the dead, will never die again; death no longer has dominion over him. ¹⁰The death he died, he died to sin, once for all; but the life he lives, he lives to God. ¹¹So you also must consider yourselves dead to sin and alive to God in Christ Jesus.

12 Therefore, do not let sin exercise dominion in your mortal bodies, to make you obey their passions. ¹³No longer present your members to sin as instruments of wickedness, but present yourselves to God as those who have been brought from death to life, and present your members to God as instruments of righteousness. ¹⁴For sin will have no dominion over you, since you are not under law but under grace.

Slaves of Righteousness

15 What then? Should we sin because we are not under law but under grace? By no means! ¹⁶Do you not know that if you present yourselves to anyone as obedient slaves, you are slaves of the one whom you obey, either of sin, which leads to death, or of obedience, which leads to righteousness?

¹⁷But thanks be to God that you, having once been slaves of sin, have become obedient from the heart to the form of teaching to which you were entrusted, ¹⁸and that you, having been set free from sin, have become slaves of righteousness. ¹⁹I am speaking in human terms because of your natural limitations. For just as you once presented your members as slaves to impurity and to greater and greater iniquity, so now present your members as slaves to righteousness for sanctification.

20 When you were slaves of sin, you were free in regard to righteousness. ²¹So what advantage did you then get from the things of which you now are ashamed? The end of those things is death. ²²But now that you have been freed from sin and enslaved to God, the advantage you get is sanctification. The end is eternal life. ²³For the wages of sin is death, but the free gift of God is eternal life in Christ Jesus our Lord.

An Analogy from Marriage

7 Do you not know, brothers and sisters – for I am speaking to those who know

ᵛ Or *weapons*   ʷ Gk *the weakness of your flesh*
ˣ Gk *brothers*

---

have left the community of Adam and entered a new one where what is true of Christ is true of his people. When he died, they died. That is emphatic, but Paul is more cautious about the next step. Christ has been raised from the dead. His people come out of the water of baptism to a new life (v. 4), but the full benefits of resurrection lie ahead (v. 8).

12–13. Christians sometimes still feel as if sin is in control. The terms 'bodies', 'passions' and 'members' (parts of the body) might seem to emphasize sin as physical appetites and emotional reactions. An overview of Paul's letters reveals that he uses 'body' to refer to the whole of human life as an embodied person, including intellectual achievements and social relationships. Believers choose and act in all aspects of life on earth as Christ's people offering themselves to God's service.

14–15. Paul is still shocking his readers by linking the Law with sin and death rather than with grace. He reckons attempts to create a godly community by attention to the detail of the Law are futile. They merely increase the number of acts which are sins, without reducing the powerful grip of sin. Only the grace of God can do that.

16–23. Describing the life of grace as slavery seems equally shocking. It conveys the paradox that only God's power can enable human freedom. He breathes into believers a new attitude. They start to view themselves as free to become what they have been taught they should be.

ROMANS 7

An example from marriage law indicates that death brings certain duties to an end. Uniting with

the law – that the law is binding on a person only during that person's lifetime? ²Thus a married woman is bound by the law to her husband as long as he lives; but if her husband dies, she is discharged from the law concerning the husband. ³Accordingly, she will be called an adulteress if she lives with another man while her husband is alive. But if her husband dies, she is free from that law, and if she marries another man, she is not an adulteress.

4 In the same way, my friends,ʸ you have died to the law through the body of Christ, so that you may belong to another, to him who has been raised from the dead in order that we may bear fruit for God. ⁵While we were living in the flesh, our sinful passions, aroused by the law, were at work in our members to bear fruit for death. ⁶But now we are discharged from the law, dead to that which held us captive, so that we are slaves not under the old written code but in the new life of the Spirit.

The Law and Sin

7 What then should we say? That the law is sin? By no means! Yet, if it had not been for the law, I would not have known sin. I would not have known what it is to covet if the law had not said, "You shall not covet." ⁸But sin, seizing an opportunity in the commandment, produced in me all kinds of covetousness. Apart from the law sin lies dead. ⁹I was once alive apart from the law, but when the commandment came, sin revived ¹⁰and I died, and the very commandment that promised life proved to be death to me. ¹¹For sin, seizing an opportunity in the commandment, deceived me and through it killed me. ¹²So the law is holy, and the commandment is holy and just and good.

13 Did what is good, then, bring death to me? By no means! It was sin, working death in me through what is good, in order that sin might be shown to be sin, and through the commandment might become sinful beyond measure.

The Inner Conflict

14 For we know that the law is spiritual; but I am of the flesh, sold into slavery

ʸ Gk *brothers*

Christ and becoming identified with his death (6:3–8) ends the grip of the Law on those who had been trying to live under it. They are free to live in new ways under the Spirit of God. That said, Paul speaks more positively about the Law, especially the Ten Commandments. They are good even though they do not contain the power to prevent sin. The command, 'Do not covet' is used to illustrate the inner struggle that goes on in those who want to do good and find they are constantly doing the opposite.

1–3. Paul is illustrating a point, not laying down rules for marriage, though we may note he views it as a commitment for live. A specific sexual relationship might be sinful now and completely innocent later, a death having changed how the Law applies.

4–6. The death of Christ has changed how the biblical Law applies and our new relationship with him has power to bear fruit. As with 'body', Paul gives 'flesh' a wider meaning than the physical. It refers to the weakness and sinfulness of lives not filled with the Spirit of God (8:4–8).

7–13. Paul may be saying something about Law which rings bells in the experience of those who rear children. Rules parents make for good reasons, are challenged as the child tests out boundaries and moves towards independence. But Paul sees a deceitful twist of sin in the process of human maturing. We were not created just to be assertive but to be loving towards each other and dependent on God. If we push over God's boundaries, we edge towards spiritual disaster. He may also have in mind that greater moral knowledge brings more responsibility and complexity of conscience. It is less obvious that it is wrong to covet than to kill but once we see coveting as sin we may feel guilty in areas of life previously taken for granted.

14–25. It is not clear if this description of inner conflict is to be seen as pre-Christian experience or a struggle that goes on in us until the resurrection. The issue has been long debated. The

under sin.[z] [15]I do not understand my own actions. For I do not do what I want, but I do the very thing I hate. [16]Now if I do what I do not want, I agree that the law is good. [17]But in fact it is no longer I that do it, but sin that dwells within me. [18]For I know that nothing good dwells within me, that is, in my flesh. I can will what is right, but I cannot do it. [19]For I do not do the good I want, but the evil I do not want is what I do. [20]Now if I do what I do not want, it is no longer I that do it, but sin that dwells within me.

[21] So I find it to be a law that when I want to do what is good, evil lies close at hand. [22]For I delight in the law of God in my inmost self, [23]but I see in my members another law at war with the law of my mind, making me captive to the law of sin that dwells in my members. [24]Wretched man that I am! Who will rescue me from this body of death? [25]Thanks be to God through Jesus Christ our Lord!

So then, with my mind I am a slave to the law of God, but with my flesh I am a slave to the law of sin.

Life in the Spirit

8 There is therefore now no condemnation for those who are in Christ Jesus. [2]For the law of the Spirit[a] of life in Christ Jesus has set you[b] free from the law of sin and of death. [3]For God has done what the law, weakened by the flesh, could not do: by sending his own Son in the likeness of sinful flesh, and to deal with sin,[c] he condemned sin in the flesh, [4]so that the just requirement of the law might be fulfilled in us, who walk not according to the flesh but according to the Spirit.[a] [5]For those who live according to the flesh set their minds on the things of the flesh, but those who live according to the Spirit[a] set their minds on the things of the Spirit.[a] [6]To set the mind on the flesh is death, but to set the mind on the Spirit[a] is life and peace. [7]For this reason the mind that is set on the flesh is hostile to God; it does not submit

[z] Gk *sold under sin*   [a] Or *spirit*   [b] Here the Greek word *you* is singular number; other ancient authorities read *me* or *us*   [c] Or *and as a sin offering*

---

words 'sold into slavery under sin' (v. 14) sound too strong to describe those already in Christ. But later (v. 25) he sounds a victory note, thanking God for rescuing him through Jesus and then restates the conflict. Perhaps the clear distinction is not so important to Paul who is aware that the Christian lives in the overlap between the old life and the new, as Rom. 8 will show.

ROMANS 8

After a summary of previous themes the focus moves to the Holy Spirit. Life lived in the sphere of influence of the Spirit is contrasted with life without the Spirit (in the flesh). But life in the Spirit still involves suffering. Paul compares it with the pain of childbirth where those involved are looking forward with hope to a birth. Meanwhile we are assured that none of life's pressure points can separate us from the love of God.

1–4. After the reminder of inner struggles these verses are full of encouragement. We stand before God and he is not disapproving. We are free from the downward pull of sin towards death, made worse by trying to keep God's Law. The Law is too weak to make an impact on the power of sin in human lives. So God sent reinforcements, firstly his own Son. (There are echoes of Jesus' story about a vineyard owner sending his son to the tenants, Mark 12.) 'In the likeness of sinful flesh' means that Jesus is genuinely human but not sinful. Sin, the terminal disease in 'the flesh', is dealt a death blow on the cross. In the second stage of the rescue the Holy Spirit comes to give those in Christ the power to live as the Law intends. Under his influence the laws of God are no longer weak but take their rightful place.

5–11. Freedom begins in the mind. Even the most imprisoned or dominated person has some freedom if he or she can think. Freedom for a Christian starts to be a reality when the mind

to God's law – indeed it cannot, [8]and those who are in the flesh cannot please God.

9 But you are not in the flesh; you are in the Spirit,[d] since the Spirit of God dwells in you. Anyone who does not have the Spirit of Christ does not belong to him. [10]But if Christ is in you, though the body is dead because of sin, the Spirit[d] is life because of righteousness. [11]If the Spirit of him who raised Jesus from the dead dwells in you, he who raised Christ[e] from the dead will give life to your mortal bodies also through[f] his Spirit that dwells in you.

12 So then, brothers and sisters,[g] we are debtors, not to the flesh, to live according to the flesh – [13]for if you live according to the flesh, you will die; but if by the Spirit you put to death the deeds of the body, you will live. [14]For all who are led by the Spirit of God are children of God. [15]For you did not receive a spirit of slavery to fall back into fear, but you have received a spirit of adoption. When we cry, "Abba![h] Father!" [16]it is that very Spirit bearing witness[i] with our spirit that we are children of God, [17]and if children, then heirs, heirs of God and joint heirs with Christ – if, in fact, we suffer with him so that we may also be glorified with him.

Future Glory

18 I consider that the sufferings of this present time are not worth comparing with the glory about to be revealed to us. [19]For the creation waits with eager longing for the revealing of the children of God; [20]for the creation was subjected to futility, not of its own will but by the will of the one who subjected it, in hope [21]that the creation itself will be set free from its bondage to decay and will obtain the freedom of the glory of the children of God. [22]We know that the whole creation has been groaning in labor pains until now; [23]and not only the creation, but we ourselves, who have the first fruits of the Spirit, groan inwardly while we wait for adoption, the redemption of our bodies. [24]For in[j] hope we were saved. Now hope that is seen is not hope. For who hopes[k] for what is seen? [25]But if we hope for what we do not see, we wait for it with patience.

[d] Or *spirit*   [e] Other ancient authorities read *the Christ* or *Christ Jesus* or *Jesus Christ*   [f] Other ancient authorities read *on account of*
[g] Gk *brothers*   [h] Aramaic for *Father*   [i] Or [15]*a spirit of adoption, by which we cry, "Abba! Father!"* [16]*The Spirit itself bears witness*   [j] Or *by*   [k] Other ancient authorities read *awaits*

---

begins to give attention to the 'things of the Spirit'. This is not becoming abstract and distant from family and friends, work and possessions. It is looking at these from a new perspective in which love for God and Christ are central.

12–17. Sometimes in the New Testament a believer is described as being born again into God's family. Here the image is adoption. A convert may have memories of a former insecure life but there is no need to fear now. We may sometimes ask how can we be sure all this is true? Paul does not provide proof but he asserts an answer. God is not accessible to our five senses but God can communicate with us and does by the Spirit in our spirit. 'Mind' (vv. 5–8) and 'spirit' (v. 16) are not separate categories. They overlap as do the activities of thinking and praying. Every time we address God with the intimacy of 'Father' the Spirit of God is actively encouraging us that we have the right to pray.

18–25. The adopted children will eventually share with God's own Son a breath-taking inheritance, not only resurrected bodies but a renewed environment. Paul had nothing like our modern awareness of the earth as a fragile environment in danger of being destroyed by our greed, yet a connection between human sin and the environment, hinted at in Gen. 1–3, is picked up here. All creation is groaning in pain and Christ's people are groaning too. Our faith can be rocked by sudden suffering, agonizing and apparently meaningless, like the excruciating experience of child-birth, especially without modern pain-control. Paul does not try to explain or justify suffering in the world but he asks us to note how the hope for a child may sustain the mother through labor.

26 Likewise the Spirit helps us in our weakness; for we do not know how to pray as we ought, but that very Spirit intercedes[l] with sighs too deep for words. [27]And God,[m] who searches the heart, knows what is the mind of the Spirit, because the Spirit[n] intercedes for the saints according to the will of God.[o]

28 We know that all things work together for good[p] for those who love God, who are called according to his purpose. [29]For those whom he foreknew he also predestined to be conformed to the image of his Son, in order that he might be the firstborn within a large family.[q] [30]And those whom he predestined he also called; and those whom he called he also justified; and those whom he justified he also glorified.

God's Love in Christ Jesus

31 What then are we to say about these things? If God is for us, who is against us? [32]He who did not withhold his own Son, but gave him up for all of us, will he not with him also give us everything else? [33]Who will bring any charge against God's elect? It is God who justifies. [34]Who is to condemn? It is Christ Jesus, who died, yes, who was raised, who is at the right hand of God, who indeed intercedes for us.[r] [35]Who will separate us from the love of Christ? Will hardship, or distress, or persecution, or famine, or nakedness, or peril, or sword? [36]As it is written,

"For your sake we are being killed all
    day long;
we are accounted as sheep to be
    slaughtered."

[37]No, in all these things we are more than conquerors through him who loved us. [38]For I am convinced that neither death, nor life, nor angels, nor rulers, nor things present, nor things to come, nor powers, [39]nor height, nor depth, nor anything else in all creation, will be able to separate us from the love of God in Christ Jesus our Lord.

God's Election of Israel

9 I am speaking the truth in Christ – I am not lying; my conscience confirms it by the Holy Spirit – [2]I have great sorrow

---

[l] Other ancient authorities add *for us* [m] Gk *the one* [n] Gk *he* or *it* [o] Gk *according to God* [p] Other ancient authorities read *God makes all things work together for good*, or *in all things God works for good* [q] Gk *among many brothers* [r] Or *Is it Christ Jesus . . . for us?*

26–27. The birth imagery seems to continue here. The Spirit 'sighs' – this is the same word as 'groaning in labor' (v. 22). The Spirit like a mother, or perhaps a midwife, is alongside us sharing and comforting our pain, understanding how inarticulate we are when we attempt to pray about the things that really touch our lives.

28–39. The Spirit retreats from the limelight as Paul surveys the sweep of God's plan in history. In the midst of human sin and a groaning creation, from Abraham onwards, God had a covenant of grace with a community of people chosen for himself. Now his covenant is with the people who belong to Jesus. Their destiny is secure. Nothing need make them anxious about separation from his love.

ROMANS 9

Not separated from God's love, Paul nevertheless feels enormous anguish at being cut off from the family and ethnic community he grew up in. Israel as a whole does not accept Jesus as Messiah. Has God been unfaithful to his promise to them? Starting with Abraham Paul works through biblical examples to show how many of the physical descendants of Abraham have been excluded along the way.

1–5. Despite the negative tone of earlier chapters about the Law, Paul counted it a great privilege to live in the covenant community of Israel, into which Jesus was born. But he emphasizes that the Messiah is for all. Notice how once again Paul names Christ as God. (See on 1:4 and 10:12.)

and unceasing anguish in my heart. ³For I could wish that I myself were accursed and cut off from Christ for the sake of my own people,ˢ my kindred according to the flesh. ⁴They are Israelites, and to them belong the adoption, the glory, the covenants, the giving of the law, the worship, and the promises; ⁵to them belong the patriarchs, and from them, according to the flesh, comes the Messiah,ᵗ who is over all, God blessed forever.ᵘ Amen.

6 It is not as though the word of God had failed. For not all Israelites truly belong to Israel, ⁷and not all of Abraham's children are his true descendants; but "It is through Isaac that descendants shall be named for you." ⁸This means that it is not the children of the flesh who are the children of God, but the children of the promise are counted as descendants. ⁹For this is what the promise said, "About this time I will return and Sarah shall have a son." ¹⁰Nor is that all; something similar happened to Rebecca when she had conceived children by one husband, our ancestor Isaac. ¹¹Even before they had been born or had done anything good or bad (so that God's purpose of election might continue, ¹²not by works but by his call) she was told, "The elder shall serve the younger." ¹³As it is written,

"I have loved Jacob,
    but I have hated Esau."

14 What then are we to say? Is there injustice on God's part? By no means! ¹⁵For he says to Moses,

"I will have mercy on whom I have
    mercy,
and I will have compassion on
    whom I have compassion."

¹⁶So it depends not on human will or exertion, but on God who shows mercy. ¹⁷For the scripture says to Pharaoh, "I have raised you up for the very purpose of showing my power in you, so that my name may be proclaimed in all the earth." ¹⁸So then he has mercy on whomever he chooses, and he hardens the heart of whomever he chooses.

God's Wrath and Mercy

19 You will say to me then, "Why then does he still find fault? For who can resist his will?" ²⁰But who indeed are you, a human being, to argue with God? Will what is molded say to the one who molds it, "Why have you made me like this?" ²¹Has the potter no right over the clay, to make out of the same lump one object for special use and another for ordinary use? ²²What if God, desiring to show his wrath and to make known his power, has endured with

ˢ Gk *my brothers*   ᵗ Or *the Christ*   ᵘ Or *Messiah,*
who is God over all, blessed forever; or *Messiah.*
May he who is God over all be blessed forever

6–13. Already in the second and third generations God's selection process considerably reduced the number of Abraham's physical descendants who inherit the promise. The choice of Isaac not Ishmael, Jacob the younger son, not Esau the heir was planned by God in advance, not in reaction to their behavior.

14–18. While Moses was writing out the law on the mountain, Israel was indulging in idolatry with a golden calf. If God was merciful to them it was his choice, not anything they deserved. Another side of the Exodus story was Pharaoh, whose opposition was also in God's plan. Exodus says God hardened his heart.

19–24. There is a mystery about God carrying out his plan, yet calling to account those who oppose him. Many explanations have been attempted which never adequately solve it (9:19–20). Paul has already made it plain that God's final judgment will be seen to be utterly fair (2:6–11). But is it fair that particular groups of people are chosen to be part of God's covenant community at particular periods of history? Some of the prophets pictured God as a potter shaping nations and empires, being patient with them but eventually destroying them as a demonstration of his indignation over sin. Within this pattern Israel, the object for special use, is destroyed in Exile and reshaped in the return from Babylon (Jer. 18; Is. 45:9–13).

much patience the objects of wrath that are made for destruction; ²³and what if he has done so in order to make known the riches of his glory for the objects of mercy, which he has prepared beforehand for glory – ²⁴including us whom he has called, not from the Jews only but also from the Gentiles? ²⁵As indeed he says in Hosea,

"Those who were not my people I will
  call 'my people,'
and her who was not beloved I will
  call 'beloved.' "

²⁶ "And in the very place where it was
  said to them, 'You are not my
  people,'
there they shall be called children of
  the living God."

27 And Isaiah cries out concerning Israel, "Though the number of the children of Israel were like the sand of the sea, only a remnant of them will be saved; ²⁸for the Lord will execute his sentence on the earth quickly and decisively."ᵛ ²⁹And as Isaiah predicted,

"If the Lord of hosts had not left
  survivorsʷ to us,
we would have fared like Sodom
and been made like Gomorrah."

Israel's Unbelief

30 What then are we to say? Gentiles, who did not strive for righteousness, have attained it, that is, righteousness through faith; ³¹but Israel, who did strive for the righteousness that is based on the law, did not succeed in fulfilling that law. ³²Why not? Because they did not strive for it on the basis of faith, but as if it were based on works. They have stumbled over the stumbling stone, ³³as it is written,

"See, I am laying in Zion a stone that
  will make people stumble, a
  rock that will make them fall,
and whoever believes in himˣ will
  not be put to shame."

10 Brothers and sisters,ʸ my heart's desire and prayer to God for them is that they may be saved. ²I can testify that they have a zeal for God, but it is not enlightened. ³For, being ignorant of the righteousness that comes from God, and

ᵛ Other ancient authorities read *for he will finish his work and cut it short in righteousness, because the Lord will make the sentence shortened on the earth*   ʷ Or *descendants*; Gk *seed*   ˣ Or *trusts in it*   ʸ Gk *Brothers*

25–26. Hosea had two children resulting from his wife's unfaithfulness. He called them, 'Not beloved' and 'Not my kin'. Out of the depth of his experience he wrote of the mercy of God changing the status of 'Not my people' to make them his people again. Paul extends the application of this to Gentiles who were not God's people and are now being included in Christ.

27–29. Contrast that with Isaiah's description of the people who would be restored after the Exile as a remnant, a minority of the original Israel. Only a remnant of Jews are being included in Christ.

30–33. In the lifetime of Jesus the religious leaders were looking at boundary issues of the law, 'Did he keep the Sabbath, wash properly, teach in an orthodox way?' and they failed to recognize the One who embodied the righteousness of God. Two texts in Isaiah (8:14; 28:16) provide the idea of Jesus as a stone, a foundation for the people who have faith in him, something to stumble over for those who do not.

ROMANS 10

The journey through biblical history reaches a climax in 10:4. Christ is the end or the goal. The promise that Abraham should be father of many nations (4:17) has become true. The message, 'Jesus is Lord, raised from the dead', is spreading all over the world, and many people both Jewish and Gentile believe and confess him. Others are rejecting it. Sadly this includes a majority of Jews.

1–4. In 9:1 Paul anguished over separation from his people. He turns his longing into prayer. He is not content nor contemptuous about synagogues which reject Jesus. If only they could see that the Law has reached its goal and takes on new meaning in Christ.

seeking to establish their own, they have not submitted to God's righteousness. ⁴For Christ is the end of the law so that there may be righteousness for everyone who believes.

Salvation Is for All

5 Moses writes concerning the righteousness that comes from the law, that "the person who does these things will live by them." ⁶But the righteousness that comes from faith says, "Do not say in your heart, 'Who will ascend into heaven?'" (that is, to bring Christ down) ⁷"or 'Who will descend into the abyss?'" (that is, to bring Christ up from the dead). ⁸But what does it say?

"The word is near you,
    on your lips and in your heart"

(that is, the word of faith that we proclaim); ⁹because² if you confess with your lips that Jesus is Lord and believe in your heart that God raised him from the dead, you will be saved. ¹⁰For one believes with the heart and so is justified, and one confesses with the mouth and so is saved. ¹¹The scripture says, "No one who believes in him will be put to shame." ¹²For there is no distinction between Jew and Greek; the same Lord is Lord of all and is generous to all who call on him. ¹³For, "Everyone who calls on the name of the Lord shall be saved."

14 But how are they to call on one in whom they have not believed? And how are they to believe in one of whom they have never heard? And how are they to hear without someone to proclaim him? ¹⁵And how are they to proclaim him unless they are sent? As it is written, "How beautiful are the feet of those who bring good news!" ¹⁶But not all have obeyed the good news;ª for Isaiah says, "Lord, who has believed our message?" ¹⁷So faith comes from what is heard, and what is heard comes through the word of Christ.ᵇ

◆ When we think of women in mission we tend to think of those faithful and dedicated women who made many sacrifices to serve God in far-off countries – giving up all hope of marriage and a normal family life and home comforts, suffering attacks and disease, some even losing their lives. Many generations of these women had taken seriously the words of Paul in Romans (10:15) and seen themselves as part of the answer to the

² Or *namely, that*   ª Or *gospel*   ᵇ Or *about Christ*; other ancient authorities read *of God*

5–11. An example of that new meaning is given. 'Do these things and live by them', said Moses. 'The commands are not far away, up in the sky or hidden in the depths. They are within your reach.' Without faith they had always been out of reach. Now they are within reach in a new way. Christ has come down from heaven and risen from the dead. Christians believe it in their hearts and confess him without shame in their baptism. They 'do the law' by believing and living their lives by him.

12–13. Joel foretold a day when the Spirit will be poured out on men and women, young and old, employee and employer; everyone who calls on the name of the Lord will be saved (Joel 2:28–32). Paul includes another category where barriers are broken down. Gentiles received the Spirit without having to become circumcised Jews (Acts 10:45–47). Jesus is now universal Lord. Early Christians often applied Old Testament texts about God the Lord to Jesus the Lord, as Paul has done here. It expressed a growing understanding of Jesus as God without denying that God is one.

14–17. The Lord of all becomes Lord indeed by sending messengers who announce the news which people hear and believe. They respond to the summons to call on Jesus' name. Many have not heard the news. Many who have heard do not 'obey'. Believing is being equated with doing or obeying. Faith for Paul is trust put into action, not just intellectual assent (as in James 2:17–19).

question, 'How can the gospel be proclaimed if the messengers are not sent out?' It is their work that has done much to reach the 'unreached' peoples of the earth, taking the gospel of Christ to all areas of the world. The determination, courage and commitment of such women is to be admired.

One dictionary definition of missionary is 'a person who is sent to spread the Christian faith amongst a community'. We all belong to a community of some description, we all come into contact with a variety of people, whether it is at work, taking the children to school, going shopping or socializing. The majority of us will never go abroad as full-time missionaries, but that does not prevent us from serving Christ and sharing the good news of salvation. It is not just those people in far-off countries who need to hear the gospel; it is also our friends and neighbors, those we come into contact with everyday in very ordinary situations.

Christian service is not limited to a certain type of person who we may consider to be super-spiritual but it is part of every Christian's life. People in our local community need to hear the gospel. If they do not hear, then how can they believe; if they do not believe, then how can they be saved? ◆

18 But I ask, have they not heard? Indeed they have; for

"Their voice has gone out to all the earth,
and their words to the ends of the world."

[19]Again I ask, did Israel not understand? First Moses says,

"I will make you jealous of those who are not a nation;
with a foolish nation I will make you angry."

[20]Then Isaiah is so bold as to say,

"I have been found by those who did not seek me;
I have shown myself to those who did not ask for me."

[21]But of Israel he says, "All day long I have held out my hands to a disobedient and contrary people."

Israel's Rejection Is Not Final

11 I ask, then, has God rejected his people? By no means! I myself am an Israelite, a descendant of Abraham, a member of the tribe of Benjamin. [2]God has not rejected his people whom he foreknew. Do you not know what the scripture says of Elijah, how he pleads with God against Israel? [3]"Lord, they have killed your prophets, they have demolished your altars; I alone am left, and they are seeking my life." [4]But what is the divine reply to him? "I have kept for myself seven thousand who have not bowed the knee to Baal."

18–21. The previous verses could apply to Jew or Gentile but the focus returns to the Jews. V. 18 may refer to the speed with which the message has passed around the synagogue network. As in past history, Israel has 'disobeyed'. A suggestion that God intends to make them jealous of Gentiles (Deut. 32:21) will be developed in the next chapter.

ROMANS 11

God has not been unfaithful to his people. A substantial remnant have found grace. Through the hardness of the others riches have spread to Gentiles. The people of God are like an olive tree which has been cut back and had a wild shoot grafted into a cultivated stump. But cultivated branches can also be grafted back in. Paul is confident that in the end God will be seen to have been faithful to his call to Israel. He has discussed the place of Israel within God's plan in such detail because he is concerned about possible prejudice of Gentile Christians towards Jews.
1–6. Feeling deeply about Jewish unbelief Paul recalls that when Elijah was depressed he failed to notice how large the believing remnant was.

[5]So too at the present time there is a remnant, chosen by grace. [6]But if it is by grace, it is no longer on the basis of works, otherwise grace would no longer be grace.[c]

[7] What then? Israel failed to obtain what it was seeking. The elect obtained it, but the rest were hardened, [8]as it is written,

"God gave them a sluggish spirit,
  eyes that would not see
  and ears that would not hear,
down to this very day."

[9]And David says,

"Let their table become a snare and a
    trap,
  a stumbling block and a retribution
    for them;
[10] let their eyes be darkened so that they
    cannot see,
  and keep their backs forever bent."

The Salvation of the Gentiles

[11] So I ask, have they stumbled so as to fall? By no means! But through their stumbling[d] salvation has come to the Gentiles, so as to make Israel[e] jealous. [12]Now if their stumbling[d] means riches for the world, and if their defeat means riches for Gentiles, how much more will their full inclusion mean!

[13] Now I am speaking to you Gentiles. Inasmuch then as I am an apostle to the Gentiles, I glorify my ministry [14]in order to make my own people[f] jealous, and thus save some of them. [15]For if their rejection is the reconciliation of the world, what will their acceptance be but life from the dead! [16]If the part of the dough offered as first fruits is holy, then the whole batch is holy; and if the root is holy, then the branches also are holy.

[17] But if some of the branches were broken off, and you, a wild olive shoot, were grafted in their place to share the rich root[g] of the olive tree, [18]do not boast over the branches. If you do boast, remember that it is not you that support the root, but the root that supports you. [19]You will say, "Branches were broken off so that I might be grafted in." [20]That is true. They were broken off because of their unbelief, but you stand only through faith. So do not become proud, but stand in awe. [21]For if God did not spare the natural branches, perhaps he will not spare you[h] [22]Note then the kindness and the severity of God: severity toward those who have fallen, but God's kindness toward you, provided you continue in his kindness; otherwise you also will be cut off. [23]And even those of Israel,[i] if they do not persist in unbelief, will be grafted in, for God has the power to graft them in again. [24]For if you have been cut from what is by nature a wild olive tree and grafted, contrary to nature, into a cultivated olive tree, how much more will these natural branches be grafted back into their own olive tree.

All Israel Will Be Saved

[25] So that you may not claim to be wiser than you are, brothers and sisters,[j] I

---

[c] Other ancient authorities add *But if it is by works, it is no longer on the basis of grace, otherwise work would no longer be work*   [d] Gk *transgression*   [e] Gk *them*   [f] Gk *my flesh*   [g] Other ancient authorities read *the richness*   [h] Other ancient authorities read *neither will he spare you*   [i] Gk lacks *of Israel*   [j] Gk *brothers*

7–12. Hardening is what happens when people refuse the mercy and patience of God (2:3–5). In God's plan this is linked with salvation to Gentiles. Note how Pharaoh's hardening (9:17–18) was linked with salvation to Jews.

13–24. Paul's work is to bring Gentiles to faith but he hopes that the quality of life in the Christian community will make Jews jealous (v. 13) and assist in bringing them to Christ (vv. 23–24). Meanwhile he is concerned that Gentile believers are showing signs of arrogance towards Jews and warns them that is incompatible with faith in the grace of God (vv. 18–22).

25–31. Paul's mystery here remains mysterious, a matter of on-going debate. Some think Paul is introducing a revelation he has been given. Towards the end of history, when enough Gentiles are saved, Israel as an ethnic and religious community will be saved, perhaps by believing Jesus is

want you to understand this mystery: a hardening has come upon part of Israel, until the full number of the Gentiles has come in. [26]And so all Israel will be saved; as it is written,

> "Out of Zion will come the Deliverer;
>   he will banish ungodliness from
>   Jacob."
> [27] "And this is my covenant with them,
>   when I take away their sins."

◆ With great feeling, Paul has taken us through Israel's history in Rom. 9–11. Convinced of the privilege of the Jewish role, he is alarmed at signs that Christians are despising the people to whom God gave his unconditional love. We can imagine how horrified he would be at the subsequent history. Far from making Jews jealous by the quality of our common life of love and care, church-going communities have frequently been active in mistreating them. A Jew today hears the story of the crucifixion of Jesus through the emotional barrier of memories of the holocaust. We cannot reverse history, but we can make sure we learn the vital message Paul is teaching. We too have experienced God's unconditional love and our attitudes to the Jewish community are a good test of how much grace is shaping our lives.

There are other applications of this too. Churches sometimes allow traditions, developed as attempts to be faithful to the Word of God, to become boundary conditions dividing one group of Christians from another, as the Law was the dividing Jew from Gentile. Even this letter to the Romans has been used that way. Paul would have been indignant to see interpretations of the less clear aspects of his letter being used to create division among those who believe in Christ. Women excluded from official church leadership structures have often led the way in crossing such divides. But women are also prone to reinforce them out of anxiety to keep the family or community safe and pure ◆

[28]As regards the gospel they are enemies of God[k] for your sake; but as regards election they are beloved, for the sake of their ancestors; [29]for the gifts and the calling of God are irrevocable. [30]Just as you were once disobedient to God but have now received mercy because of their disobedience, [31]so they have now been disobedient in order that, by the mercy shown to you, they too may now[l] receive mercy. [32]For God has imprisoned all in disobedience so that he may be merciful to all.

33 O the depth of the riches and wisdom and knowledge of God! How unsearchable are his judgments and how inscrutable his ways!
[34] "For who has known the mind of the
            Lord?
        Or who has been his counselor?"
[35] "Or who has given a gift to him,
        to receive a gift in return?"
[36]For from him and through him and to him are all things. To him be the glory forever. Amen.

[k] Gk lacks *of God*   [l] Other ancient authorities lack *now*

the Messiah (11:26). Meanwhile they live out their irrevocable call under the old covenant (11:29). Others think Paul is summing up what he has been arguing throughout. All of the true Israel of faith (9:6) will be saved. The gifts and calling of God to the Jews are fulfilled through the remnant and through Jews in each generation who have come to Christ and brought with them the richness of being 'cultivated' stock.

32–36. Either way, his confidence in the wisdom and mercy of God fills him with wonder and praise.

The New Life in Christ

12 I appeal to you therefore, brothers and sisters,[m] by the mercies of God, to present your bodies as a living sacrifice, holy and acceptable to God, which is your spiritual[n] worship. [2]Do not be conformed to this world,[o] but be transformed by the renewing of your minds, so that you may discern what is the will of God – what is good and acceptable and perfect.[p]

◆ In Rom. 12, we are urged to present ourselves as a living sacrifice, holy and acceptable to God. This involves handing over every area of our lives – our everyday, even mundane, activities; our spiritual life and relationships; and our gifts and talents – both natural and spiritual. We all come into the body of Christ as individuals with something unique to offer, to add to the richness and variety of church life. This diversity of background, personality and experience brings a wholesome balance where individual gifts can be used to complement each other to form a fully functioning unit. Each person and each of the gifts they have been given is vitally important. If any are not used, for whatever reason, then the whole is impoverished and weakened. Just as in the human body, each part is dependent on the other for survival, good health and strength, so it is with the church, that each member is needed to play their part and exercise their gifts. It is not important who has which gifts or how many an individual may have but rather their willingness to use them to glorify God and build up the church.

Problems occur when Christians, for whatever reason, dismiss their gifts as irrelevant, as being of no importance, feel they are not up to standard or are reluctant to use them until they have been perfected and are ready for 'public performance'. It is at this point that we need to look at what the apostle Paul writes concerning the way we should see ourselves i.e. to view ourselves with 'sober judgment'. Those who do not appreciate themselves or their gifts as being of value will be less inclined to utilize them. They may not even be able to recognize or accept the fact that they are gifted and will, therefore, need the support and encouragement of others to see, use and develop their gifts.

On the other hand, problems arise when individuals think too highly of themselves and seek the more public prestigious gifts, putting others down in the process and trying to obtain a position which is not really theirs to have. In both these cases gifts can either be misused or not used at all. But a healthy perception of oneself will lead to a recognition of where an individual's strengths and weaknesses lay, enabling a genuine and cheerful acceptance of the gifts and talents God has given, even though they may not be those which we would have chosen for our self, nor which we consider to be of most importance. To see some gifts as more important or to long for and desire those

[m] Gk brothers   [n] Or reasonable   [o] Gk age   [p] Or what is the good and acceptable and perfect will of God

---

ROMANS 12

Paul now gives more practical detail about what righteous or holy lives are like. He reminds us that change in our lives begins in an attitude of mind (6:13; 8:5). There will be plenty of variety as God gives individuals different gifts, but there are qualities like love which are a common thread running through all Christian character.

1–2. A Christian does not offer any sacrifice in order to be acceptable to God. No death but Christ's death is required. In the light of that mercy we are encouraged to view every aspect of our embodied life as worship presented to God like a sacrifice. Paul has made the strongest possible connection between what happens when believers meet to 'worship' and what happens in the rest of the week. We are to develop minds that can make choices about everyday matters with a wisdom compatible with the will of God.

we do not have points to the fact that we are all in need of having our minds renewed – having our thoughts transformed and brought into line with God's point of view, perceiving ourselves, our gifts, others and their gifts, not from a worldly perspective, but from God's ◆

3 For by the grace given to me I say to everyone among you not to think of yourself more highly than you ought to think, but to think with sober judgment, each according to the measure of faith that God has assigned. [4]For as in one body we have many members, and not all the members have the same function, [5]so we, who are many, are one body in Christ, and individually we are members one of another. [6]We have gifts that differ according to the grace given to us: prophecy, in proportion to faith; [7]ministry, in ministering; the teacher, in teaching; [8]the exhorter, in exhortation; the giver, in generosity; the leader, in diligence; the compassionate, in cheerfulness.

Marks of the True Christian

9 Let love be genuine; hate what is evil, hold fast to what is good; [10]love one another with mutual affection; outdo one another in showing honor. [11]Do not lag in zeal, be ardent in spirit, serve the Lord.[q] [12]Rejoice in hope, be patient in suffering, persevere in prayer. [13]Contribute to the needs of the saints; extend hospitality to strangers.

14 Bless those who persecute you; bless and do not curse them. [15]Rejoice with those who rejoice, weep with those who weep. [16]Live in harmony with one another; do not be haughty, but associate with the

◆ Women's particular gift of empathy can become a real ministry. Actions of weeping and rejoicing are normally associated with the corresponding feelings of sadness and happiness. Can such feelings be made to order, in response to some injunction such as Rom. 12:15? Do they conveniently exist in some ready-made package? Can they be conjured up by an effort of will – ours, or someone else's? Or do they develop naturally, in appropriate response to some trigger such as the evident pain or pleasure of a person with whom we are in contact?

This injunction in Romans is not actually addressed to everyone in every situation. It is a directive to those who are members together of the body of Christ. It is designed to encourage, indeed demand, that God's people share in each other's feelings. When others are sad, we are to weep with them; when others are happy, we are to join in their rejoicing. Even though Jesus knew that he would soon raise Lazarus from the grave, he wept in sympathy with the bereaved sisters. By contrast the well-meaning but thoroughly unattuned friends of Job made matters far worse in his time of agony and despair.

2 Cor. 1:3–7 points out that we can share with other believers the insights and consolation which we have found in our own afflictions. The most meaningful comfort comes from those who have already walked through a similar experience and found God's grace within the crucible ◆

[q] Other ancient authorities read *serve the opportune time*

3–8. Having just used 'body' to mean a person, Paul now uses it to describe Christians collectively. He has firmly established our human equality so he can safely encourage us to be relaxed about our differences. Paul lists a range of capacities which can be used to benefit others in Christ and describes them as gifts from God. Those who tend to overestimate themselves should aim for sober judgment, but a lack of confidence can be overcome by faith.

9–16. This portrait of Christian character contains a range of qualities. Some are often seen as particularly male others as typically female. Jesus in the Gospels is clearly male, yet he displayed the qualities Paul mentions here and is the model for all believers.

lowly;' do not claim to be wiser than you are.
[17]Do not repay anyone evil for evil, but take
thought for what is noble in the sight of all.
[18]If it is possible, so far as it depends on
you, live peaceably with all. [19]Beloved, never
avenge yourselves, but leave room for the
wrath of God;' for it is written, "Vengeance
is mine, I will repay, says the Lord." [20]No, "if
your enemies are hungry, feed them; if they
are thirsty, give them something to drink;
for by doing this you will heap burning coals
on their heads." [21]Do not be overcome by
evil, but overcome evil with good.

Being Subject to Authorities

13 Let every person be subject to the
governing authorities; for there is
no authority except from God, and those
authorities that exist have been instituted
by God. [2]Therefore whoever resists authority resists what God has appointed, and
those who resist will incur judgment.
[3]For rulers are not a terror to good conduct,
but to bad. Do you wish to have no fear of
the authority? Then do what is good, and
you will receive its approval; [4]for it is God's
servant for your good. But if you do what is
wrong, you should be afraid, for the authority' does not bear the sword in vain! It is the
servant of God to execute wrath on the
wrongdoer. [5]Therefore one must be subject,
not only because of wrath but also because
of conscience. [6]For the same reason you
also pay taxes, for the authorities are God's
servants, busy with this very thing. [7]Pay to
all what is due them – taxes to whom taxes
are due, revenue to whom revenue is due,
respect to whom respect is due, honor to
whom honor is due.

Love for One Another

8 Owe no one anything, except to love
one another; for the one who loves another

' Or *give yourselves to humble tasks*   ' Gk *the
wrath*   ' Gk *it*

17–21. It is easy to feel that goodness and popularity should go together. In fact Christ's
followers will have enemies as he did and not every relationship that goes wrong will be put
right. The vivid quote from Prov. 25:21–22 stresses that we should continue to act with loving
respect and care towards those who are hostile to us.

ROMANS 13

Paul now addresses the question of how Christians relate to the state. Then he returns to love as
the central command. He also urges them to be alert that there may be a sudden end.
1–7. Under Roman law Jews were allowed to be virtually a state within a state but Christians as
a multi-racial grouping were no longer eligible for that. Paul is against withdrawing into a sacred
enclave where Christ is Lord and passively or forcefully resisting the secular power of Rome. In
fact he is not allowing sacred and secular to be divided. God is the author of all authority (13:1)
in two senses. Firstly, it is God's will there should be government with power to restrain bad
behavior (13:4). Secondly, all who govern are servants, accountable to God whether they know it
or not (13:1). So Christians should 'be subject'. This is a key verb in many of the New Testament
letters, meaning ordering oneself under someone in an ordered relationship. While most
Christians at this time had little political power, they could respect and co-operate with those
who had, not merely for fear of reprisal but as a conscientious choice (13:5). Christians have
sometimes read this passage as a divine command that the existing government must always be
obeyed. It then becomes a frightening charter for legitimizing tyranny. Rather Paul is giving a
Christian basis for being an involved citizen. With a transformed mind they will be able to
discern the will of God (12:2). God uses human instruments to overthrow unjust rule and
Christians at times have judged it right to be involved in that.
8–10. Jesus highlighted 'Love your neighbor as yourself' together with 'Love God' as summing up
the Law. But that does not mean the Ten Commandments are cancelled. They remain boundaries which give content to the command to love.

has fulfilled the law. [9]The commandments, "You shall not commit adultery; You shall not murder; You shall not steal; You shall not covet"; and any other commandment, are summed up in this word, "Love your neighbor as yourself." [10]Love does no wrong to a neighbor; therefore, love is the fulfilling of the law.

◆ Christians are called upon to be responsible for every area of activity in their lives, including financial matters. In Romans, Paul urges them not to incur any debts except the debt to love which will always remain outstanding and never paid in full. Whatever the size of income and whether it is obtained through employment, housekeeping, benefits or inheritance, it is the Christian's duty to use it wisely and responsibly, recognizing that all good gifts, including a means of financial support, ultimately come from God.

This responsibility covers a wide expanse of circumstances from the more obvious ones of the punctual payment of taxes and bills, not exceeding credit limits, supporting the local church through tithes, and budgeting for the weekly grocery bill, through to the responsibility to one's dependents to provide a home and, therefore, possibly a mortgage, and security for the future – life assurance, joining a pension scheme and maybe investments, making sure that the family is well catered for. Many of these need professional input to ensure that wise choices are made.

On a more everyday level, most of us need to budget carefully, making sure that the essentials are taken care of and paid for before more extravagant items are purchased; calculating first whether an item is affordable and repayments can be kept up to date. The responsible Christian attitude to money management should perhaps be that of the man in Jesus' parable who decided to build a tower but first sat down to consider whether he could afford to complete it (Luke 14:28) ◆

An Urgent Appeal

11 Besides this, you know what time it is, how it is now the moment for you to wake from sleep. For salvation is nearer to us now than when we became believers; [12]the night is far gone, the day is near. Let us then lay aside the works of darkness and put on the armor of light; [13]let us live honorably as in the day, not in reveling and drunkenness, not in debauchery and licentiousness, not in quarreling and jealousy. [14]Instead, put on the Lord Jesus Christ, and make no provision for the flesh, to gratify its desires.

Do Not Judge Another

14 Welcome those who are weak in faith,[u] but not for the purpose of quarreling over opinions. [2]Some believe in

[u] Or *conviction*

11–14. The end of the present order, the day of judgment and renewal (2:5; 8:21) could come any moment. Paul compresses two images. One is dawn, the expected light which comes at the end of night. The other reminds us of Jesus' story of the home-owner who returns unexpectedly in the middle of the night to find the staff misbehaving. This is not a call for extraordinary action but for a steady alertness and a strand of urgency to run through all our daily living.

ROMANS 14

It is hard to have a good relationship with someone who strongly disapproves and is openly critical of what you eat. If you are both Christians and the disapproval stems from a conviction that God is being dishonored the difficulty increases. Paul is not very explicit about whether the problem was the Jewish food and Sabbath laws or meat and wine which might have been sacrificed to pagan gods. What he says could cover a variety of situations. Some basic principles are very clear.

eating anything, while the weak eat only vegetables. ³Those who eat must not despise those who abstain, and those who abstain must not pass judgment on those who eat; for God has welcomed them. ⁴Who are you to pass judgment on servants of another? It is before their own lord that they stand or fall. And they will be upheld, for the Lord[v] is able to make them stand.

5 Some judge one day to be better than another, while others judge all days to be alike. Let all be fully convinced in their own minds. ⁶Those who observe the day, observe it in honor of the Lord. Also those who eat, eat in honor of the Lord, since they give thanks to God; while those who abstain, abstain in honor of the Lord and give thanks to God.

7 We do not live to ourselves, and we do not die to ourselves. ⁸If we live, we live to the Lord, and if we die, we die to the Lord; so then, whether we live or whether we die, we are the Lord's. ⁹For to this end Christ died and lived again, so that he might be Lord of both the dead and the living.

10 Why do you pass judgment on your brother or sister?[w] Or you, why do you despise your brother or sister?[w] For we will all stand before the judgment seat of God.[x] ¹¹For it is written,

"As I live, says the Lord, every knee
   shall bow to me,
and every tongue shall give praise
   to[y] God."
¹²So then, each of us will be accountable to God.[z]

Do Not Make Another Stumble

13 Let us therefore no longer pass judgment on one another, but resolve instead never to put a stumbling block or hindrance in the way of another.[a] ¹⁴I know and am persuaded in the Lord Jesus that nothing is unclean in itself; but it is unclean for anyone who thinks it unclean. ¹⁵If your brother or sister[w] is being injured by what you eat, you are no longer walking in love. Do not let what you eat cause the ruin of one for whom Christ died. ¹⁶So do not let your good be spoken of as evil. ¹⁷For the kingdom of God is not food and drink but righteousness and peace and joy in the Holy Spirit. ¹⁸The one who thus serves Christ is acceptable to God and has human approval. ¹⁹Let us then pursue what makes for peace and for mutual upbuilding. ²⁰Do

[v] Other ancient authorities read *for God*   [w] Gk *brother*   [x] Other ancient authorities read *of Christ*   [y] Or *confess*   [z] Other ancient authorities lack *to God*   [a] Gk *of a brother*

1–4. Those who eat and drink what they want and do not feel obliged to observe certain days, Paul calls strong; he himself is strong. The others might consider themselves strong in living out their principles, but Paul thinks those principles are unnecessary. The first essential, however, is that they must not despise and criticize each other. God's welcoming grace and God's right to judge make this inappropriate.

5–6. Individuals should make a decision of conscience and be convinced, even though others disagree. They should be able to act, thanking God and feeling they are honoring him.

7–12. The same points are reinforced by a reminder that Christ died and rose for each individual in his church.

13–23. So, since it is hard in practice to differ and accept each other, the strong should be willing to try and find a pattern of behavior that makes it possible for strong and weak to love and encourage each other. There is a danger that the weak will actually be harmed. They may copy the strong when they know in their hearts that this thing is wrong for them. Paul does not want principles such as 'Do not drink wine' or 'You must observe this day of worship in this way' to become enshrined as laws in the church. He does want the strong to work out loving compromises in specific situations. The letter sent out from Jerusalem in Acts 15 was perhaps an example of such a temporary compromise.

not, for the sake of food, destroy the work of God. Everything is indeed clean, but it is wrong for you to make others fall by what you eat; [21]it is good not to eat meat or drink wine or do anything that makes your brother or sister[b] stumble.[c] [22]The faith that you have, have as your own conviction before God. Blessed are those who have no reason to condemn themselves because of what they approve. [23]But those who have doubts are condemned if they eat, because they do not act from faith;[d] for whatever does not proceed from faith[d] is sin.[e]

Please Others, Not Yourselves

15 We who are strong ought to put up with the failings of the weak, and not to please ourselves. [2]Each of us must please our neighbor for the good purpose of building up the neighbor. [3]For Christ did not please himself; but, as it is written, "The insults of those who insult you have fallen on me." [4]For whatever was written in former days was written for our instruction, so that by steadfastness and by the encouragement of the scriptures we might have hope. [5]May the God of steadfastness and encouragement grant you to live in harmony with one another, in accordance with Christ Jesus, [6]so that together you may with one voice glorify the God and Father of our Lord Jesus Christ.

The Gospel for Jews and Gentiles Alike

[7] Welcome one another, therefore, just as Christ has welcomed you, for the glory of God. [8]For I tell you that Christ has become a servant of the circumcised on behalf of the truth of God in order that he might confirm the promises given to the patriarchs, [9]and in order that the Gentiles might glorify God for his mercy. As it is written,

"Therefore I will confess[f] you among
the Gentiles,
and sing praises to your name";
[10]and again he says,
"Rejoice, O Gentiles, with his people";
[11]and again,
"Praise the Lord, all you Gentiles,
and let all the peoples praise him";
[12]and again Isaiah says,
"The root of Jesse shall come,
the one who rises to rule the
Gentiles;
in him the Gentiles shall hope."
[13]May the God of hope fill you with all joy and peace in believing, so that you may abound in hope by the power of the Holy Spirit.

[b] Gk brother   [c] Other ancient authorities add or be upset or be weakened   [d] Or conviction   [e] Other authorities, some ancient, add here 16.25-27   [f] Or thank

---

ROMANS 15

Paul winds up the themes of Rom. 12–15 by urging pastoral care for each other based on the example of Christ and encouragement from the written Scriptures. He reminds them that this includes a welcoming attitude between Jew and Gentile. He outlines a plan to come to Rome on the way to Spain. Meanwhile he asks them to pray for him as he takes the collection to Jerusalem.

1–3. The quotation from Ps. 69 is frequently applied to Christ's death. The insult was, 'Let him come down from the cross.'

4. Paul has said strong things about the wrong way that some people live under God's Law. He has also been showing positively how to teach and encourage others from the written Scriptures.

7–8. Welcoming guests at the door and serving the family at table are two pictures of what Christ does for us and they are to be metaphors for our attitude to others in the church.

9–13. The quotations emphasize that it has always been God's will for people of all nations to enjoy praising him together.

Paul's Reason for Writing So Boldly

14 I myself feel confident about you, my brothers and sisters,[g] that you yourselves are full of goodness, filled with all knowledge, and able to instruct one another. [15]Nevertheless on some points I have written to you rather boldly by way of reminder, because of the grace given me by God [16]to be a minister of Christ Jesus to the Gentiles in the priestly service of the gospel of God, so that the offering of the Gentiles may be acceptable, sanctified by the Holy Spirit. [17]In Christ Jesus, then, I have reason to boast of my work for God. [18]For I will not venture to speak of anything except what Christ has accomplished[h] through me to win obedience from the Gentiles, by word and deed, [19]by the power of signs and wonders, by the power of the Spirit of God,[i] so that from Jerusalem and as far around as Illyricum I have fully proclaimed the good news[j] of Christ. [20]Thus I make it my ambition to proclaim the good news,[j] not where Christ has already been named, so that I do not build on someone else's foundation, [21]but as it is written,

"Those who have never been told of
          him shall see,
and those who have never heard of
          him shall understand."

Paul's Plan to Visit Rome

22 This is the reason that I have so often been hindered from coming to you. [23]But now, with no further place for me in these regions, I desire, as I have for many years, to come to you [24]when I go to Spain. For I do hope to see you on my journey and to be sent on by you, once I have enjoyed your company for a little while. [25]At present, however, I am going to Jerusalem in a ministry to the saints; [26]for Macedonia and Achaia have been pleased to share their resources with the poor among the saints at Jerusalem. [27]They were pleased to do this, and indeed they owe it to them; for if the Gentiles have come to share in their spiritual blessings, they ought also to be of service to them in material things. [28]So, when I have completed this, and have delivered to them what has been collected,[k] I will set out by way of you to Spain; [29]and I know that when I come to you, I will come in the fullness of the blessing[l] of Christ.

30 I appeal to you, brothers and sisters,[g] by our Lord Jesus Christ and by the love of the Spirit, to join me in earnest prayer to God on my behalf, [31]that I may be rescued from the unbelievers in Judea, and that my ministry[m] to Jerusalem may be acceptable to the saints, [32]so that by God's will I may come to you with joy and be refreshed in your company. [33]The God of peace be with all of you.[n] Amen.

[g] Gk *brothers*   [h] Gk *speak of those things that Christ has not accomplished*   [i] Other ancient authorities read *of the Spirit* or *of the Holy Spirit*   [j] Or *gospel*   [k] Gk *have sealed to them this fruit*   [l] Other ancient authorities add *of the gospel*   [m] Other ancient authorities read *my bringing of a gift*   [n] One ancient authority adds 16.25-27 here

---

14–19. Priests, in Paul's day, led worship by offering sacrifices. Paul sees his work of bringing Gentiles to Jesus as a great offering that gladdens the heart of God (v. 16). It is by the power of the Holy Spirit that converts have believed (v. 19) and their lives are being changed (v. 16). Yet Paul can speak of his role with confidence; he is sure it has been given to him by God (v. 15).

20–33. So he lays out his future plans and invites the Roman Christians to share in his work by prayer. Although keen to press on and preach in places where the message is unknown, he is also giving time and energy to organize financial help for the needy in Jerusalem. He sees giving as an important part of being members of Christ's worldwide church.

Personal Greetings

16 I commend to you our sister Phoebe, a deacon° of the church at Cenchreae, ²so that you may welcome her in the Lord as is fitting for the saints, and help her in whatever she may require from you, for she has been a benefactor of many and of myself as well.

◆ We know from Phil. 1 that by the early AD 60s some churches had at least one officer called a 'deacon', and from this text, that Phoebe was deacon of the assembly of Christians at Cenchreae. Since then various churches have entrusted various duties to deacons. We do not know precisely which duties were entrusted to Phoebe in addition to delivering the Epistle to the Romans to the church in Rome. At that time the word 'deacon' connoted an extremely high standard of service, skill at perceiving needs and resources, an ability to negotiate and enable things to happen with speed, and trustworthiness. At Cana, it was the 'deacons' who perceived that the good wine had come from Jesus.

The reference to the 'church' at Cenchreae is to the people, the assembly of Christians, rather than to the later building there which was dedicated to St Phoebe. Corinth had two harbors on either side of the isthmus. Cenchreae was the eastern one on the Saronic Gulf and received and sent shipping towards Athens, Asia, Egypt, and other eastern points. We do not know to what extent this was a 'daughter' church to the major assembly of Christians at Corinth. In the case of Rome, a Christian assembly met in the house of Prisca (Priscilla) and Aquila. At Cenchreae it probably met in the house of an unnamed person.

Phoebe also has been a patron to many and even Paul himself. Patronage in the first century implied moral and/or social and/or financial support. Being a patron, and being in a position to travel to Rome and conduct Paul's affairs there suggests several things about Phoebe which we cannot know for certain but which are extremely likely. The experience in travelling would suggest that Phoebe had been the wife of an official or a merchant. What we know about other deacons and her freedom at this time, suggests that by now she was a widow. Her husband may have had a long illness which necessitated her taking on more and more responsibility. At any rate, her being a patron suggests that by now she is the head of her own household.

Yet at Rome she is expected to require things about which Paul does not elaborate. This has led at least one scholar to hypothesize that Paul is sending her to Rome to make preparations for his mission to Spain ◆

3 Greet Prisca and Aquila, who work with me in Christ Jesus, ⁴and who risked their necks for my life, to whom not only I give thanks, but also all the churches of the Gentiles. ⁵Greet also the church in their house. Greet my beloved Epaenetus, who

◆ Rom. 16 affords us a remarkable glimpse into the involvement of women in the early church at Rome. In the first instance there is Phoebe (vv. 1–2). She is called a 'deacon' or 'minister' of the church at Cenchrae, a community adjacent to Corinth. As such, she is the only deacon named in the New Testament as serving in a specific local church.

° Or *minister*

ROMANS 16

Phoebe, a deacon and a person of influence has business in Rome. Paul asks the Christians to offer her help as needed. He knows and greets a large number of individuals by name. This may indicate that the church was subdivided into house churches (v. 5) and Paul is eager to underline their connections with each other as well as with himself

Her title as *prostatis* ('benefactor' in the NRSV translation) may be rendered 'champion', 'protector', 'leader' or 'presider'. Justin Martyr used the term to indicate the person presiding at Communion. The verbal equivalent occurs at Rom. 12:8; 1 Thess. 5:12; 1 Tim. 3:4–5, 12; 5:17; Titus 3:8, 14, in all of which it describes the action of governing. Some scholars have suggested that the last phrase of Rom. 16:2 should be translated 'She has been ordained, even by me, as an officer over many.'

There has been a scholarly suggestion that the errand on which she went to Rome was that of procuring support for Paul in his proposed visit to Spain. The political, economic and military exigencies of the Iberian peninsula were far different from those further east. A missionary journey would have required letters of introduction, governmental permission, funding and careful planning. Phoebe may have been a person capable of undertaking just such arrangements, with the right connections in imperial Rome. At any rate, Phoebe has been entrusted with an important mission for the church and travelled to Rome to fulfill the charge given her by Paul.

In Rom. 16:3–4, Paul commends Priscilla and Aquila (see note at Acts 18:1–2). We do not know what the occasion was nor the heroic action in which they risked their lives to save that of Paul. We know only that all the churches of the Gentiles gave thanks to God for their brave loyalty. Paul calls Priscilla and Aquila 'fellow-laborers' as they worked with him in the gospel ministry. (For others called fellow-laborers in Rom. 16, see vv. 9, 21.)

Priscilla and Aquila were perhaps a sort of advance team whom Paul brought to Ephesus to establish a band of believers who might serve as a beach-head for Paul's wider endeavors. One of this couple's first pupils was the learned Apollos whom they instructed more perfectly in the way of the Lord. Thereafter the student was able to reason with great power that Jesus was indeed

the Christ (Acts 18:24–28). As Priscilla's name comes first, she is thought to have been more active in ministry.

Other names appear in the greeting: Mary, Junia the apostle, Tryphaena and Tryphosa, Persis, the mother of Rufus, Julia, the sister of Nereus and Olympas. At least eleven women are mentioned as leaders in the Roman church, and there are eight whose work is particularly singled out for commendation (Rom. 16:2–3, 5–7, 12–13). In the early centuries of the church, women continued to play a major role in the leadership at Rome ◆

---

was the first convert[p] in Asia for Christ. [6]Greet Mary, who has worked very hard among you. [7]Greet Andronicus and Junia,[q] my relatives[r] who were in prison with me; they are prominent among the apostles, and they were in Christ before I was. [8]Greet Ampliatus, my beloved in the Lord. [9]Greet Urbanus, our co-worker in Christ, and my beloved Stachys. [10]Greet Apelles, who is

---

◆ Although the gender of Junia(s) is questioned, early commentators took the name to be feminine, which is consistent with Greek and Latin literature of the first century. The name was a very common one in Rome, though the masculine form 'Junias' is not attested. No question about her gender was raised until the thirteenth century. St John Chrysostom declared, 'O how great is the devotion of this woman.'

Paul's identification of Junia as an apostle, and a prominent one at that, is significant. Given his defense of his own apostleship in Gal. 1:1, it is unlikely Paul would have considered Junia an apostle unless he was certain she had been specifically called by God to serve as a missionary in the church. Such a recognition indicates that at least one woman held a position of leadership and authority early in the life of the Christian church community ◆

---

[p] Gk *first fruits*   [q] Or *Junias*; other ancient authorities read *Julia*   [r] Or *compatriots*

approved in Christ. Greet those who belong to the family of Aristobulus. [11]Greet my relative[s] Herodion. Greet those in the Lord who belong to the family of Narcissus. [12]Greet those workers in the Lord, Tryphaena and Tryphosa. Greet the beloved Persis, who has worked hard in the Lord. [13]Greet Rufus, chosen in the Lord; and greet his mother – a mother to me also. [14]Greet Asyncritus, Phlegon, Hermes, Patrobas, Hermas, and the brothers and sisters[t] who are with them. [15]Greet Philologus, Julia, Nereus and his sister, and Olympas, and all the saints who are with them. [16]Greet one another with a holy kiss. All the churches of Christ greet you.

Final Instructions

[17] I urge you, brothers and sisters,[t] to keep an eye on those who cause dissensions and offenses, in opposition to the teaching that you have learned; avoid them. [18]For such people do not serve our Lord Christ, but their own appetites,[u] and by smooth talk and flattery they deceive the hearts of the simple-minded. [19]For while your obedience is known to all, so that I rejoice over you, I want you to be wise in what is good and guileless in what is evil. [20]The God of peace will shortly crush Satan under your feet. The grace of our Lord Jesus Christ be with you.[v]

[21] Timothy, my co-worker, greets you;

so do Lucius and Jason and Sosipater, my relatives.[w]

[22] I Tertius, the writer of this letter, greet you in the Lord.[x]

[23] Gaius, who is host to me and to the whole church, greets you. Erastus, the city treasurer, and our brother Quartus, greet you.[y]

Final Doxology

[25] Now to God[z] who is able to strengthen you according to my gospel and the proclamation of Jesus Christ, according to the revelation of the mystery that was kept secret for long ages [26]but is now disclosed, and through the prophetic writings is made known to all the Gentiles, according to the command of the eternal God, to bring about the obedience of faith – [27]to the only wise God, through Jesus Christ, to whom[a] be the glory forever! Amen.[b]

---

[s] Or *compatriot*   [t] Gk *brothers*   [u] Gk *their own belly*   [v] Other ancient authorities lack this sentence   [w] Or *compatriots*   [x] Or *I Tertius, writing this letter in the Lord, greet you*   [y] Other ancient authorities add verse 24, *The grace of our Lord Jesus Christ be with all of you. Amen.*   [z] Gk *the one*   [a] Other ancient authorities lack *to whom.* The verse then reads, *to the only wise God be the glory through Jesus Christ forever. Amen.*   [b] Other ancient authorities lack 16.25-27 or include it after 14.23 or 15.33; others put verse 24 after verse 27

17–20. A final urgent footnote is not uncommon in Paul's letters. The major plea of the letter has been for loving inclusiveness, but there comes a point where the church has to have boundaries. Its members are to be firm against teachers who undermine their common faith in Christ (v. 17) and the commitment to live his way (v. 18).

25–27. This final song of praise attempts to sum up the themes of the letter. It puts our individual stories in perspective as it makes the point that the beginning and end of all our lives is God himself.

THE FIRST LETTER OF PAUL
TO THE CORINTHIANS

INTRODUCTION

1 Corinthians is one of the earliest parts of the New Testament to have been written. It was addressed to immature Christians struggling to live for Christ in one of the richest and most dissolute cities of the Mediterranean world. Corinth had been destroyed by the Romans in 144 BC and rebuilt a century later, primarily to provide land holdings for retired veterans from the Roman army. At first they found survival hard, but the city soon became the most prosperous in Greece at a time when the rest of the land lay desolate. One writer remarked that there were less than 500 men with any significant property holdings in the entire country. The wealth of Corinth as over against the destitution of the surrounding area caused resentment, and the new inhabitants became objects of derision.

The advent of Roman veterans had created little good will; but with the arrival of a mercantile class, the character of the population began to change, and the city became more Greek. Although Corinth could not boast the intellectual or artistic climate of Athens, it was a bustling city swollen every two years by the Isthmian Games. Here persons from every region, class and calling mingled, and here philosophers of various persuasions proffered their ideas alongside jugglers, mountebanks, and hawkers of every sort. The Games of AD 51–52 would have afforded Paul an opportunity both to sell tents and to preach the gospel.

1 Corinthians has been called an 'occasional letter' because it was written about AD 55 to address a particular set of difficulties. Paul, who was then residing in Ephesus (1 Cor. 16:5–9), has been notified of the troubles and perplexities of the Corinthian congregation and is seeking to give specific responses to specific needs. There is uncertainty as to whether the epistle was first composed as a single document or whether it may not in its present form be a compilation of several letters dealing with particular problems. In any event, the advice given by Paul has proved invaluable to Christians throughout the ages and contains much that is still applicable to our present-day lives.

The first section (1 Cor. 1–4) deals with the intellectual challenges of Christianity and the competing philosophies of the ancient world. In all likelihood, these issues would have concerned educated males of that time.

Next follows a lengthy discussion of sexual issues (1 Cor. 5–7), a most important topic for women who were often categorized according to their sexual functions. It was said that Greek males had *hetaerae* (high-class courtesans) for companionship, concubines to meet their daily sexual needs and legitimate wives to bear them children and keep the house. Corinth was a sexually preoccupied city, with a large and prosperous group of prostitutes famed throughout the entire world. Some travellers visited Corinth only to try out the charms of these women. Paul saw the need to address many aspects of human sexuality when he wrote to a city whose patron was Aphrodite, the goddess of love.

There is then a section concerning personal freedom and concern for others in the body of Christ (1 Cor. 8–10), with precedents drawn from the spiritual history of Israel.

The last section (1 Cor. 11–16) treats the integrity of the believing community and seeks to set right abuses and doctrines which threaten its unity. The behavior of women becomes one of the issues which must be specifically addressed as persons from many different traditions and cultures seek to grow together as the people of God.

Salutation

1 Paul, called to be an apostle of Christ Jesus by the will of God, and our brother Sosthenes,

2 To the church of God that is in Corinth, to those who are sanctified in Christ Jesus, called to be saints, together with all those who in every place call on the name of our Lord Jesus Christ, both their Lord[a] and ours:

3 Grace to you and peace from God our Father and the Lord Jesus Christ.

4 I give thanks to my[b] God always for you because of the grace of God that has been given you in Christ Jesus, [5]for in every way you have been enriched in him, in speech and knowledge of every kind – [6]just as the testimony of[c] Christ has been strengthened among you – [7]so that you are not lacking in any spiritual gift as you wait for the revealing of our Lord Jesus Christ. [8]He will also strengthen you to the end, so that you may be blameless on the day of our Lord Jesus Christ. [9]God is faithful; by him you were called into the fellowship of his Son, Jesus Christ our Lord.

Divisions in the Church

10 Now I appeal to you, brothers and sisters,[d] by the name of our Lord Jesus Christ, that all of you be in agreement and that there be no divisions among you, but that you be united in the same mind and the same purpose. [11]For it has been reported to me by Chloe's people that there are quarrels among you, my brothers and sisters.[e] [12]What I mean is that each of you says, "I belong to Paul," or "I belong to Apollos," or "I belong to Cephas," or "I belong to Christ." [13]Has Christ been divided? Was Paul crucified for you? Or were you baptized in the name of Paul? [14]I thank God[f] that I baptized none of you except Crispus and Gaius, [15]so that no one can say that you were baptized in my name. [16](I did baptize also the household of Stephanas; beyond that, I do not know whether I baptized anyone else.) [17]For Christ did not send me to baptize but to proclaim the gospel, and not with eloquent wisdom, so that the cross of Christ might not be emptied of its power.

Christ the Power and Wisdom of God

18 For the message about the cross is foolishness to those who are perishing, but

---

[a] Gk theirs [b] Other ancient authorities lack my [c] Or to [d] Gk brothers [e] Gk my brothers [f] Other ancient authorities read I am thankful

---

1 CORINTHIANS 1

2. Here Paul issues a great call of Christian unity. All those who trust in Jesus Christ are called 'saints', though their personal lives may fall far short of the model provided by their Savior. The apostle declares that he writes not only to the church in Corinth but to those in every place who call upon the name of our Lord Jesus Christ. This is a particular challenge to Christian women, who have often been the first to reach out hands of caring and fellowship to others around the world who serve the same Lord.

5–9. Because of our social conditioning, women are often shy to voice their concerns and convictions. We may take courage as we understand that God will enrich us in all knowledge and utterance – not only what to say but how to say it. We shall not be deficient in any grace or gifts (1 Cor. 1:7). The encouragement of both brothers and sisters is needed as women venture forth in the strength of this promise. For women leaders of house churches, see Acts 12:12; 16:13–15, 40; Col. 4:15; 1 Cor. 16:19; Rom. 16:3–5; 2 John. A city might have more than one small group meeting in a private house, and partitions in some of these houses were demolished to make room for more believers to assemble. This was the normal pattern for Christian worship until AD 311 when Christianity became a legally recognized religion.

18. Apparently some members of the congregation were attempting either to over-intellectualize the gospel or to use their superior education to insist that everyone adopt their

to us who are being saved it is the power of God. [19]For it is written,

> "I will destroy the wisdom of the wise,
>   and the discernment of the
>   discerning I will thwart."

[20]Where is the one who is wise? Where is the scribe? Where is the debater of this age? Has not God made foolish the wisdom of the world? [21]For since, in the wisdom of God, the world did not know God through wisdom, God decided, through the foolishness of our proclamation, to save those who believe. [22]For Jews demand signs and Greeks desire wisdom, [23]but we proclaim Christ crucified, a stumbling block to Jews and foolishness to Gentiles, [24]but to those who are the called, both Jews and Greeks, Christ the power of God and the wisdom of God. [25]For God's foolishness is wiser than human wisdom, and God's weakness is stronger than human strength.

◆ Some recent scholars have defined Christ as wisdom (*Sophia*) incarnate. Traditional biblical scholarship holds that Christ *does* embody wisdom as an attribute along with other qualities such as love, holiness and justice. Yet Christ is more than wisdom. Indeed, he is more than the sum of all his many attributes.

In the writings of Paul there are several explicit references to Christ as wisdom. Paul refers to 'Christ the power of God and the wisdom of God' (1 Cor. 1:24). Paul then states that Christ 'became for us wisdom from God' (v. 30). Paul is not inferring that either power or wisdom are in themselves divine. Christ is called God's wisdom (1 Cor. 1:24) because the hidden wisdom of God is fully revealed in Christ Jesus.

Christ is wisdom, but wisdom cannot fully define Christ. All that is true of wisdom is true of Christ, but not vice versa. Christ goes beyond wisdom, wisdom being only one of God's many attributes. Wisdom is not God. Christ is God ◆

[26] Consider your own call, brothers and sisters:[g] not many of you were wise by human standards,[h] not many were powerful, not many were of noble birth. [27]But God chose what is foolish in the world to shame the wise; God chose what is weak in the world to shame the strong; [28]God chose what is low and despised in the world, things that are not, to reduce to nothing things that are, [29]so that no one[i] might boast in the presence of God. [30]He is

[g] Gk *brothers*   [h] Gk *according to the flesh*   [i] Gk *no flesh*

interpretations of the Christian message. Paul maintained that those who appear to be wise must learn the ways of God, who subverts the paths of the supposedly wise.

At Athens the apostle had hoped to engage in a meaningful debate with members of the Academy on their own terms, but found the intellectuals of the day unwilling to entertain a serious consideration of his concepts. He had discovered the superficiality and emptiness of the bankrupt philosophical systems of his day, and instead he now offered a radically new perception of the wisdom of God.

24. Women sometimes have feelings of inferiority because they have been afforded limited educational opportunities. Here they are told that in Christ they have a power and wisdom which far exceeds that of the finest secular institutions.

26. The congregation was composed mostly of quite humble folk who had neither family nor fortune nor education nor even mental prowess to commend them. Like the simple fishermen of Galilee, they were called to a commitment against which the world was no match.

30. The concept of the wisdom (*Sophia*) of God is an important one to women seeking new avenues of spirituality. This wisdom is wiser than that of human beings (1 Cor. 1:25; 2:9) allows people freedom of will (1:21), is hidden from those who are supposedly wise but available to those who ask for it (Is. 29:14; Luke 10:21; 1 Cor. 1:27–29; 2:8–10; James 1:5), is distinguished by the source of your life in Christ Jesus, who became for us wisdom from God, and righteousness and sanctification and redemption, [31]in order that, as it is written, "Let the one who boasts, boast in[j] the Lord."

Proclaiming Christ Crucified

2 When I came to you, brothers and sisters,[k] I did not come proclaiming the mystery[l] of God to you in lofty words or wisdom. [2]For I decided to know nothing among you except Jesus Christ, and him crucified. [3]And I came to you in weakness and in fear and in much trembling. [4]My speech and my proclamation were not with plausible words of wisdom,[m] but with a demonstration of the Spirit and of power, [5]so that your faith might rest not on human wisdom but on the power of God.

The True Wisdom of God

6 Yet among the mature we do speak wisdom, though it is not a wisdom of this age or of the rulers of this age, who are doomed to perish. [7]But we speak God's wisdom, secret and hidden, which God decreed before the ages for our glory. [8]None of the rulers of this age understood this; for if they had, they would not have crucified the Lord of glory. [9]But, as it is written,

"What no eye has seen, nor ear heard,
    nor the human heart conceived,
what God has prepared for those who
        love him" –

[10]these things God has revealed to us through the Spirit; for the Spirit searches everything, even the depths of God. [11]For what human being knows what is truly human except the human spirit that is within? So also no one comprehends what is truly God's except the Spirit of God. [12]Now we have received not the spirit of the world, but the Spirit that is from God, so that we may understand the gifts bestowed on us by God. [13]And we speak of these things in words not taught by human

[j] Or of   [k] Gk brothers   [l] Other ancient authorities read *testimony*   [m] Other ancient authorities read *the persuasiveness of wisdom*

---

peace, purity, kindness and gentleness (James 3:17), imparts a knowledge of salvation (1 Cor. 1:21; 2:6–13) and is brought to us by a personal relationship with Jesus Christ (1 Cor. 1:30).

Scripture presents wisdom as an attribute of God rather than as a separate entity deserving of worship. In 1 Cor. 1:30 wisdom appears not only as that which lies within the mind of God but as that which is communicated through Jesus Christ, himself the incarnation of that divine wisdom (1 Cor. 1:24).

1 CORINTHIANS 2

1. The missionary-evangelist came to them with a straightforward and homely strategy – to preach Jesus Christ as crucified and risen again for the redemption of humanity. The simplicity of the message was to be its very power.

6. Already he has discussed those who try to intellectualize the gospel, and now he turns to those who attempt to pour Christianity into the mold of the mystery religions. These cults were enormously popular, especially among socially marginalized segments of the population, and women in particular. A secret knowledge of exotic 'mysteries' was supposed to guarantee a happy hereafter. For people who had known only misery and deprivation in this life, the prospect was enticing. Furthermore, the adherents of mystery religions felt that they gained new identity with the gods as they underwent mystic initiation.

Paul offered a knowledge of the mysteries which God had revealed. To gain this wisdom, one did not need to pay a heavy fee or go through the ordeals of the mystery ceremonies. Rather, one needed to discern the truth of the Holy Spirit, available to all who repented of their sins and entered into the new birth. Only the Spirit could reveal the hidden things of God. For this reason, a very simple-minded person might perceive what escaped a learned individual.

wisdom but taught by the Spirit, interpreting spiritual things to those who are spiritual.ⁿ

14 Those who are unspiritualº do not receive the gifts of God's Spirit, for they are foolishness to them, and they are unable to understand them because they are spiritually discerned. ¹⁵Those who are spiritual discern all things, and they are themselves subject to no one else's scrutiny.

¹⁶ "For who has known the mind of the
       Lord
    so as to instruct him?"
But we have the mind of Christ.

On Divisions in the Corinthian Church

3 And so, brothers and sisters,ᵖ I could not speak to you as spiritual people, but rather as people of the flesh, as infants in Christ. ²I fed you with milk, not solid food, for you were not ready for solid food. Even now you are still not ready, ³for you are still of the flesh. For as long as there is jealousy and quarreling among you, are you not of the flesh, and behaving according to human inclinations? ⁴For when one says, "I belong to Paul," and another, "I belong to Apollos," are you not merely human?

5 What then is Apollos? What is Paul?

Servants through whom you came to believe, as the Lord assigned to each. ⁶I planted, Apollos watered, but God gave the growth. ⁷So neither the one who plants nor the one who waters is anything, but only God who gives the growth. ⁸The one who plants and the one who waters have a common purpose, and each will receive wages according to the labor of each. ⁹For we are God's servants, working together; you are God's field, God's building.

10 According to the grace of God given to me, like a skilled master builder I laid a foundation, and someone else is building on it. Each builder must choose with care how to build on it. ¹¹For no one can lay any foundation other than the one that has been laid; that foundation is Jesus Christ. ¹²Now if anyone builds on the foundation with gold, silver, precious stones, wood, hay, straw – ¹³the work of each builder will become visible, for the Day will disclose it, because it will be revealed with fire, and the fire will test what sort of work each has done. ¹⁴If what has been built on the

ⁿ Or *interpreting spiritual things in spiritual language,* or *comparing spiritual things with spiritual*   º Or *natural*   ᵖ Gk *brothers*

---

14. The understanding of spiritual things is based not only upon the presentation of their knowledge but also upon their *reception* in the heart and mind of a believer. There is a two-fold action, for the Spirit works not only in giving the Word but also in interpreting it to the one who hears and makes the effort to comprehend it. For this reason a study Bible is designed to call for a response of faith and obedience in the reader. This work is further predicated upon the belief that the Spirit can shed special light upon the experiences and meditations of women and that they can make creative and meaningful responses.

1 CORINTHIANS 3

1. Images of birthing and family relationships occur frequently in this section of the epistle. Here Paul pictures himself as busy with child care, providing suitable nourishment for infants not able to tolerate an adult diet. It is usually the responsibility of mothers to undertake the arduous task of feeding the immature child, whether by suckling or spoon-feeding, while teaching an infant to feed her or himself can be truly daunting. Just so nurturing young believers requires patience, endurance, and gentle sympathy.

3. Like quarrelsome children whose disputes must be settled by their mother or nurse, the Corinthians take sides among their leaders and fail to see the team play which had been at work in building their congregation. The image shifts next to farming and then to that of a building, but the underlying call is for cohesion and deep-seated unity among mature believers.

foundation survives, the builder will receive a reward. [15]If the work is burned up, the builder will suffer loss; the builder will be saved, but only as through fire.

16 Do you not know that you are God's temple and that God's Spirit dwells in you?[q] [17]If anyone destroys God's temple, God will destroy that person. For God's temple is holy, and you are that temple.

18 Do not deceive yourselves. If you think that you are wise in this age, you should become fools so that you may become wise. [19]For the wisdom of this world is foolishness with God. For it is written,

"He catches the wise in their
    craftiness,"

[20]and again,

"The Lord knows the thoughts of the
    wise,
  that they are futile."

[21]So let no one boast about human leaders. For all things are yours, [22]whether Paul or Apollos or Cephas or the world or life or death or the present or the future – all belong to you, [23]and you belong to Christ, and Christ belongs to God.

The Ministry of the Apostles

4 Think of us in this way, as servants of Christ and stewards of God's mysteries. [2]Moreover, it is required of stewards that they be found trustworthy. [3]But with me it is a very small thing that I should be judged by you or by any human court. I do not even judge myself. [4]I am not aware of anything against myself, but I am not thereby acquitted. It is the Lord who judges me. [5]Therefore do not pronounce judgment before the time, before the Lord comes, who will bring to light the things now hidden in darkness and will disclose the purposes of the heart. Then each one will receive commendation from God.

6 I have applied all this to Apollos and myself for your benefit, brothers and sisters,[r] so that you may learn through us the meaning of the saying, "Nothing beyond what is written," so that none of you will be puffed up in favor of one against another. [7]For who sees anything different in

[q] In verses 16 and 17 the Greek word for *you* is plural   [r] Gk *brothers*

16–17. Ancient philosophers often viewed the body as the prison or tomb of the soul, while Paul considered the body of a believer to be the temple of the Holy Spirit. Our bodies, like a house of God, are to be respected, to be kept clean and well maintained.

V. 17 expresses God's concern for our bodies both individually and corporately as composing the body of Christ, the church. Frequently in this letter the concept of individual body is merged with that of the church.

'Body', as used by Paul in this epistle, means not only our physical being but also the totality of personality, intellect and consciousness. Even after death, he insists that believers will be clothed with spiritual bodies (1 Cor. 15:35–49; 2 Cor. 5:1–5).

1 CORINTHIANS 4

1. God asks that we be faithful stewards. How often women have 'put their light under a bushel' because their poor self-image does not allow them to respond to the divine challenge for their lives. How could God possibly be calling *them* for so significant a task? The deciding factor is God's call, rather than human assessments of our frailties or deficiencies.

6. If we tend to undervalue ourselves, we sometimes find our importance by glorifying our own particular leader and giving that human being an honor that is appropriate for God alone. To combat these attitudes, Paul figuratively places the theatrical masks of comic buffoons upon himself and Apollos. He declares that God has placed apostles upon a burlesque stage as fools and objects of derision. Sometimes persons condemned to death were made to play such roles in the arena before a jeering crowd.

you?[s] What do you have that you did not receive? And if you received it, why do you boast as if it were not a gift?

8 Already you have all you want! Already you have become rich! Quite apart from us you have become kings! Indeed, I wish that you had become kings, so that we might be kings with you! [9]For I think that God has exhibited us apostles as last of all, as though sentenced to death, because we have become a spectacle to the world, to angels and to mortals. [10]We are fools for the sake of Christ, but you are wise in Christ. We are weak, but you are strong. You are held in honor, but we in disrepute. [11]To the present hour we are hungry and thirsty, we are poorly clothed and beaten and homeless, [12]and we grow weary from the work of our own hands. When reviled, we bless; when persecuted, we endure; [13]when slandered, we speak kindly. We have become like the rubbish of the world, the dregs of all things, to this very day.

Fatherly Admonition

14 I am not writing this to make you ashamed, but to admonish you as my beloved children. [15]For though you might have ten thousand guardians in Christ, you do not have many fathers. Indeed, in Christ Jesus I became your father through the gospel. [16]I appeal to you, then, be imitators of me. [17]For this reason I sent[t] you Timothy, who is my beloved and faithful child in the Lord, to remind you of my ways in Christ Jesus, as I teach them everywhere in every church. [18]But some of you, thinking that I am not coming to you, have become

[s] Or Who makes you different from another?   [t] Or am sending

---

The words which Paul uses evoke degrading images of that which must be wiped off, whether scum or slime, and of that which is refuse. Far from being an exalted leader, he views himself as the lowest of the low, a spectacle for mockery. In v. 16, he invites his readers also to become impersonators of such a role.

14–15. Paul maintains that he is the father of the Corinthian believers and that he has also brought them to birth in the Lord. The verb which he employs here (gennao) is one used to denote the feminine activity of giving birth. At other points too Paul expresses the concern of a mother or wetnurse for his children in the faith (see Gal. 4:18; 1 Thess. 2:7). He is not concerned about rigidly defined sex roles but rather about bringing souls to Christ and nurturing them in the faith.

16. This instruction is repeated at 1 Cor. 11:1; 1 Thess. 1:6; and Phil. 3:17. Most of the Scriptures of the New Testament were not yet written, and Christians had to look at the lives of other believers to discover godly patterns of living. This epistle is one of the earliest parts of the New Testament to be set down in writing. Since there were as yet few written guidelines, it was necessary for believers to follow living examples in order to see the behavior patterns which were pleasing to Christ. Paul himself was very careful to transmit to others what had been given to him by those who had known the Lord personally (Gal. 2:1–2). For this reason Paul does not merely send a letter but, as so often, sends an actual live Christian along with the epistle (cf. 2 Cor. 3:2). In this case it is Timothy (1 Cor. 4:17) who will bring the ways of the Lord to the Corinthians' memory by his visible example.

Timothy, his beloved son in the Lord, is able to reproduce his father's behavior and doctrine (cf. Phil. 2:19–22). In an era when many supposed teachers were wandering from church to church, it was important to document those who could be trusted by the newborn believers. The power of Christian influence and example is so strong that it is often said personal faith is caught rather than taught.

18. Some believers have become 'puffed up', literally, blown full of wind, distorted or distended. The same Greek word recurs at 1 Cor. 4:18–19; 5:2; 8:1; 13:4. It is a good indicator that the Corinthians have too exalted a view of themselves and their particular favorites.

arrogant. [19]But I will come to you soon, if the Lord wills, and I will find out not the talk of these arrogant people but their power. [20]For the kingdom of God depends not on talk but on power. [21]What would you prefer? Am I to come to you with a stick, or with love in a spirit of gentleness?

Sexual Immorality Defiles the Church

5 It is actually reported that there is sexual immorality among you, and of a kind that is not found even among pagans; for a man is living with his father's wife. [2]And you are arrogant! Should you not rather have mourned, so that he who has done this would have been removed from among you?

◆ The majority of this passage focuses on the responsibility of the church at Corinth regarding the incestuous man's behavior. The incestuous relationship itself was clearly forbidden by both Jewish and Roman law. The church, however, had not only accepted it, but appeared to support this man's actions. This entire passage can be understood as addressing not only this particular sexual immorality, but the morality of the church in general. That the congregation would condone this immoral behavior indicates the church had embraced a gnostic teaching which downplayed bodily sins. This teaching asserted that once the spirit had been saved, sins of the body were no longer relevant. Such a belief had resulted in a loose morality in the Corinthian church.

Paul's response to the congregation is a clear call to a higher standard of moral conduct. Not only is the incestuous man's behavior unacceptable, the congregation's morally lax and arrogant attitude is equally unacceptable. To make his point, Paul introduced the image of the unleavened bread. Yeast, as the symbol of evil, represents both the man's actions as well as the church's attitude. Just as the yeast had to be removed from the Jewish household, all traces of moral evil needed to be removed from the church. The unleavened bread is the symbol of holiness. In the same way, the church is to be pure, for they are the unleavened bread, having already been redeemed by Christ. The congregation, in its arrogance, is not living out its status in Christ. Thus, this entire discourse dealing with the incestuous man is an instruction for the church members to begin demonstrating in their actions what is already true of them as a believing community. They are to be a holy people, to live morally pure lives. In essence, they are to become what they already are ◆

3 For though absent in body, I am present in spirit; and as if present I have already pronounced judgment [4]in the name of the Lord Jesus on the man who has done such a thing.[u] When you are assembled,

[u] Or *on the man who has done such a thing in the name of the Lord Jesus*

---

1 CORINTHIANS 5

1. In Paul's absence some believers are displaying a deplorable arrogance and complacency about sin, whether their own or that of another member of the congregation. In a sexually preoccupied city such as Corinth, it is not surprising that new believers might display attitudes and actions that needed correction. Sacred prostitution and ritual promiscuity were required in some of the pagan cults but had no part in the body of Christ. Some of the Corinthians appear to have been quite unprepared for the claims of chastity which Christ makes on a believer's life.

3. Here we see the firmness which Paul demonstrates toward incest. The situation has become known both inside and outside the church, and the congregation has an obligation to deal with the problem. Ostensibly, this was a sexual liaison between consenting adults, though the woman may have been a very young girl married to a man who already had a grown son. Since the son is the one to be disciplined, we may suppose that the woman was being victimized.

and my spirit is present with the power of our Lord Jesus, [5]you are to hand this man over to Satan for the destruction of the flesh, so that his spirit may be saved in the day of the Lord.[v]

6 Your boasting is not a good thing. Do you not know that a little yeast leavens the whole batch of dough? [7]Clean out the old yeast so that you may be a new batch, as you really are unleavened. For our paschal lamb, Christ, has been sacrificed. [8]Therefore, let us celebrate the festival, not with the old yeast, the yeast of malice and evil, but with the unleavened bread of sincerity and truth.

Sexual Immorality Must Be Judged

9 I wrote to you in my letter not to associate with sexually immoral persons – [10]not at all meaning the immoral of this world, or the greedy and robbers, or idolaters, since you would then need to go out of the world. [11]But now I am writing to you not to associate with anyone who bears the name of brother or sister[w] who is sexually

immoral or greedy, or is an idolater, reviler, drunkard, or robber. Do not even eat with such a one. [12]For what have I to do with judging those outside? Is it not those who are inside that you are to judge? [13]God will judge those outside. "Drive out the wicked person from among you."

Lawsuits among Believers

6 When any of you has a grievance against another, do you dare to take it to court before the unrighteous, instead of taking it before the saints? [2]Do you not know that the saints will judge the world? And if the world is to be judged by you, are you incompetent to try trivial cases? [3]Do you not know that we are to judge angels – to say nothing of ordinary matters? [4]If you have ordinary cases, then, do you appoint as judges those who have no standing in the church? [5]I say this to your shame. Can it be that there is no one among you wise enough to decide between one believer[w]

[v] Other ancient authorities add *Jesus*   [w] Gk *brother*

The removal of the offender is still a valid form of action on the part of a group of believers, along with a ministry to the survivor of an abusive situation. The Corinthians are specifically rebuked because they have failed to provide the necessary discipline and protection. Allowing such a situation to continue rapidly spreads the evil throughout the church (vv. 6–8), just as yeast permeates an entire mass of dough.

11. Paul offers different pieces of advice regarding the treatment of those involved in sexual misconduct. Little better can be expected from unbelievers, and it is the duty of Christians to maintain a witness to them. It is quite another matter if one who is called a brother or sister in Christ displays the same kind of behavior. We are becoming increasingly aware that inappropriate conduct on the part of a very few can endanger the mental, emotional, spiritual, and physical health of a whole community (cf. Num. 25:1–16).

Among the types of conduct which are specifically unacceptable in a fellow believer are sexual immorality, greed, idolatry, verbal abuse, drunkenness and rape (1 Cor. 5:11). Though many translations fail to make the identification, there are references to rape in 1 Cor. 5:10–11; 6:10. Paul identifies it as a heinous crime that has no place among Christians.

1 CORINTHIANS 6

1. Just as Moses needed to set up judges to arbitrate disagreements for the newborn nation Israel (Exod. 18:13–26), so Paul instructs the Corinthians to set up leaders to whom they may turn rather than taking church disputes to a pagan court of law.

He implies that there are people within the congregation wise enough to arbitrate and that they ought to be utilized. This sort of wisdom is indeed a gift of the Holy Spirit, one that Deborah exercised in Israel (Judg. 4–5).

◆ Sometimes Christians misunderstand this instruction as meaning that they are to allow themselves to be wronged and defrauded by other believers without any recourse. It is sad that unscrupulous persons with a knowledge of this passage take an unfair advantage of committed Christians in the expectation that they will not seek justice even when they are wronged. This is not what Paul asks. Rather he directs that church-related problems should be judged within the body of Christ by competent people. The Scriptures are very clear that misbehavior should be checked and that Christians are responsible for dealing appropriately with erring brothers and sisters (Matt. 18:15–17; Luke 17:3; 2 Cor. 2:5–7; Gal. 6:1; James 5:19–20).

Believers are entitled to justice and may appropriately use secular courts of law for secular matters. Indeed, Jesus made a spiritual example of a woman who persisted in her quest for justice (Luke 18:1–5) ◆

7 In fact, to have lawsuits at all with one another is already a defeat for you. Why not rather be wronged? Why not rather be defrauded? [8]But you yourselves wrong and defraud – and believers[y] at that.

9 Do you not know that wrongdoers will not inherit the kingdom of God? Do not be deceived! Fornicators, idolaters, adulterers, male prostitutes, sodomites, [10]thieves, the greedy, drunkards, revilers, robbers – none of these will inherit the kingdom of God. [11]And this is what some of you used to be. But you were washed, you were sanctified, you were justified in the name of the Lord Jesus Christ and in the Spirit of our God.

Glorify God in Body and Spirit

12 "All things are lawful for me," but not all things are beneficial. "All things are lawful for me," but I will not be dominated by anything. [13]"Food is meant for the stomach and the stomach for food,"[z] and God will destroy both one and the other. The body is meant not for fornication but

and another, [6]but a believer[x] goes to court against a believer[x] – and before unbelievers at that?

[x] Gk *brother*   [y] Gk *brothers*   [z] The quotation may extend to the word *other*

9–11. Here we are given a compendium of persons engaging in undesirable activities. The list of unacceptable behaviors includes both explicitly sexual conduct and practices which often contain a sexual element. Idolatry, for instance, frequently involved fertility rites of a gross nature. Women were often encouraged to participate in such practices in order to enhance their ability to bear children. The term *pornoi* (here translated 'fornicators') usually referred to immoral persons of either sex, although it could also mean a male prostitute. The terms *malakoi* and *arsenkoites* (here rendered 'male prostitutes' and 'sodomites') are used elsewhere in Greek literature to refer to persons engaged in penetrating or being penetrated in homosexual intercourse, not necessarily for pay.

The individuals are labelled by their behavior; but our God loves the sinner while hating the sin. The good news is that we are not defined by past sin. We may be washed, sanctified, and justified by the forgiving grace of Jesus. (See the note on 'Homosexuality', p. 293.)

13ff. One of the great forces which God has placed in human beings is that of sexuality. It has within it spiritual, social, emotional and bodily aspects and may be properly used for expression of love and delight, for communication with one's beloved, for bonding, for the experience of intense pleasure and for procreation of another human being made in God's image. This powerful gift may enrich and ennoble or degrade and devastate.

The inappropriate use of sexuality is called *porneia*, a term which covers any illicit sex, obscenity, exploitation, or indecency. Paul deals with spiritual aspects of *porneia* within a context which blends both the human body and the body of Christ, the church. Sex is represented as a strong bonding force by which even casual sex with a prostitute may bring about a

for the Lord, and the Lord for the body.
[14]And God raised the Lord and will also
raise us by his power. [15]Do you not know
that your bodies are members of Christ?
Should I therefore take the members of
Christ and make them members of a
prostitute? Never! [16]Do you not know that
whoever is united to a prostitute becomes
one body with her? For it is said, "The two
shall be one flesh." [17]But anyone united to
the Lord becomes one spirit with him.
[18]Shun fornication! Every sin that a person
commits is outside the body; but the fornicator sins against the body itself. [19]Or do
you not know that your body is a temple[a]
of the Holy Spirit within you, which you
have from God, and that you are not your
own? [20]For you were bought with a price;
therefore glorify God in your body.

◆ We are called into being, created in
God's image, as embodied persons. We
don't 'have' a body (as though an added part
to what is an essential spirit or mind);
rather, we are enfleshed human beings.
This is most profoundly revealed in Jesus –
God's Word – becoming flesh, born to
Mary, a woman, as a human baby, and
growing through all the stages of childhood
into a mature adult who ate, slept,
touched, healed, spoke, taught, lived and
died and was bodily resurrected to new life.

Thus, grounded in a deep understanding

of God's purpose in creation, the apostle
Paul was able to write to the community
of Christians in Rome, an appeal which
speaks to us today: 'present your bodies as
a living sacrifice, holy and acceptable to
God, which is your spiritual worship'
(Rom. 12:1). As with all of God's good
gifts, we are to take responsibility for our
bodies, and to be stewards of our bodily
selves, being 'transformed by the renewing
of your minds, so that you may discern
what is the will of God – what is good and
acceptable and perfect' (Rom. 12:2).

It is a byproduct of the competitive
'spirit of our age' that women in First
World countries report, with ever-
increasing anguish, that they 'hate' their
bodies. The modern beauty culture seeks
to portray the myth of the perfect female body which can be manufactured
by continual dieting, plastic surgery,
cosmetics, hair styles and fashion. This
image is being exported around the world
by mass media, thus creating a universal
culture of fashion and exploitation of
women's bodies. Such images not only
objectify women, but profoundly affect
women's self-esteem and health.

Thus, 'to present our bodies as a living
sacrifice' requires that we refuse to
conform to the present standards and lies
of our age, and to learn instead, in our own

[a] Or *sanctuary*

---

union between her and the body of Christ. The body of the believer is not his or her own but
belongs rather to Christ and to the church. A supposedly private act may have wide social and
spiritual implications both inside and outside the church.

15ff. Here Paul refers to sex as glue, bonding two persons into one flesh. In 1 Cor. 7 he will speak
of sex as representing power.

18. Sexuality constitutes a mystic link between body and soul so that the misdirection of sexual
expression may result in psychological and spiritual damage to the individual as well as to
others.

19. The concept of the body as temple of the Holy Spirit is also expressed in 1 Cor. 3:16 and in
2 Cor. 6:16.

20. Women's understanding of their own bodies should be first as vessels with which they may
honor God (see Rom. 6:12–13). Our bodies do not make us sex objects, status symbols, baby
machines, clothes horses, or beasts of burden. Our bodies exist first and foremost for God's
glory, indwelt by the Holy Spirit, to be used in the demonstration of Christ's love in every dimension of life.

cultural context, how to love and care for our bodies as 'temples of God's Holy Spirit' and to rejoice in the mutual sharing of sexuality in loving and trothful relationships. Such a vision will enable us as Christian women to resist the violence against women and children, of wife beating, sexual abuse, rape and enforced pregnancy and abortion (all world-wide symptoms of the Fall); and will empower us to work for justice and reconciliation between men and women, speaking the truth in love, so that we all may grow into full maturity – wholeness and holiness – in Christ (Eph. 4:13–16).

Such a transforming vision will enable us to speak out against other abuses of the bodies of women and girl children, perpetrated by cultural patterns; to face the oppression of such practices as eating disorders (anorexia and bulimia), genital mutilation, shunning due to menstrual flow, selling and trading of young girls for sexual slavery, bride-burning, undernourishment of female children, female infanticide, silencing of women in churches, and other behaviors which shame and immobilize the bodies of those born female, made in God's image. Just as

19th-century Christians in China helped eradicate the binding of women's feet, and Christians in Europe helped eradicate child labor, today Christians around the world are helping to confront the evils of prostitution and pornography, wife abuse and child sexual abuse. Gender justice and reconciliation are vital dimensions of the good news of the gospel.

Thus, we are called to honor and to take responsibility for our bodies as we seek to follow Christ's command to love God, and our neighbor as ourselves ◆

Directions concerning Marriage

7 Now concerning the matters about which you wrote: "It is well for a man not to touch a woman." [2]But because of cases of sexual immorality, each man should have his own wife and each woman her own husband. [3]The husband should give to his wife her conjugal rights, and likewise the wife to her husband. [4]For the wife does not have authority over her own body, but the husband does; likewise the husband does not have authority over his own body, but the wife does. [5]Do not deprive one

---

1 CORINTHIANS 7

1. The Corinthians' perplexity over sexual matters is indicated by Paul's acknowledgement that they have sent inquiries to him. Many early Christians totally repudiated sexual activity, and some men took into their homes 'virgins' in what they insisted was a completely celibate relationship.

2. God has placed within members of the human race a desire for sexual communion and for progeny. This legitimate longing must be respected and given adequate outlet for expression. Marriage is an honorable estate and one mightily used by God. There are those given the ability to remain single without bringing reproach upon the name of Christ, but many others are most effective within the privileges and limits of marriage (v. 9).

3. Paul sets forth a remarkable rubric of equality in marriage in vv. 3–6. In an era when Greek women were often deprived both emotionally and sexually, he begins by insisting that the husband recognize and fulfill the needs of the wife. The apostle demands a mutual reciprocity from each partner, nor may either spouse willfully deny the other his or her due. Temporary abstinence must be arranged by mutual consent (v. 5). Each wields a formidable power over the other's body, a power to be used constructively and chastely within the bonds of marriage.

The absolute equality in sexual matters extends as well to relationships within other aspects of marriage. The same enjoinders to mutuality may be detected in Eph. 5:21–22 (literally translated 'being subject one to another, wives to their own husbands') and in 1 Pet. 3:7, where husbands must live with their wives as joint heirs of 'the gracious gift of life – so that nothing may hinder [their] prayers'.

another except perhaps by agreement for a set time, to devote yourselves to prayer, and then come together again, so that Satan may not tempt you because of your lack of self-control. ⁶This I say by way of concession, not of command. ⁷I wish that all were as I myself am. But each has a particular gift from God, one having one kind and another a different kind.

8 To the unmarried and the widows I say that it is well for them to remain unmarried as I am. ⁹But if they are not practicing self-control, they should marry. For it is better to marry than to be aflame with passion.

10 To the married I give this command – not I but the Lord – that the wife should not separate from her husband ¹¹(but if she does separate, let her remain unmarried or else be reconciled to her husband), and that the husband should not divorce his wife.

12 To the rest I say – I and not the Lord – that if any believerᵇ has a wife who is an unbeliever, and she consents to live with him, he should not divorce her. ¹³And if any woman has a husband who is an unbeliever, and he consents to live with her, she should not divorce him. ¹⁴For the unbelieving husband is made holy through his wife, and the unbelieving wife is made holy through her husband. Otherwise, your children would be unclean, but as it is, they are holy. ¹⁵But if the unbelieving partner separates, let it be so; in such a case the brother or sister is not bound. It is to peace that God has called you.ᶜ ¹⁶Wife, for all you know, you might save your husband. Husband, for all you know, you might save your wife.

ᵇ Gk *brother*   ᶜ Other ancient authorities read *us*

The typical pagan husband, often much older and frequently preoccupied with other sexual liaisons, married to obtain legitimate children. The wife was compelled to enter an arranged marriage, often with a man whom she had never met, at the age of twelve or fourteen. Frequently she was sexually deprived, and there was little communication, cooperation or affection between the two. A new life in Christ called forth new patterns in marriage. The husband must love his wife tenderly and seek to implement her personal development (Eph. 5:25–29; Col. 3:19), while the wife should respond to that love whole-heartedly. Too often 'submission' is misunderstood as subordination rather than as the commitment, attachment and loyalty which the Greek term implies.

7. Both marriage and singleness are special gifts from God. Throughout this passage, singleness is affirmed as more desirable in Christ's Kingdom and the celibate person as worthy of special respect. On the other hand, Paul encourages believers to make an earnest effort to maintain their marriages unless the other partner is unwilling.

8ff. This passage is unusual in the ancient world because it gives both men and women the freedom to remain unmarried if they so chose. Social pressures as well as heavy imperial taxation usually forced even the unwilling into marriages that might raise the birth rate of the Roman Empire.

9. Sexual passion is a legitimate gift from God that may be channeled to cement the marriage bond. As both glue and power, it can weld two persons together into 'one flesh' (Eph. 5:31). One Church Father urged Christians to marry off their sons at a young age so that they might bring their ardor to their wives rather than to their mistresses.

14. Even if one member of a marriage does not know Christ, the union provides a sanctifying effect on spouse and children of a believer. This has proven a source of great comfort and encouragement to praying Christian mothers. Children of believers are promised the gift of the Holy Spirit (Acts 2:39; 16:31; Mal. 2:15). This passage does not give sanction to Christians wishing to contract a marriage to an unbeliever but offers constructive exhortation to those who find themselves in such a situation.

15. Here there is a recognition that an unfortunate marriage can constitute a very real bondage. The text literally reads 'A brother or sister is not enslaved in such circumstances.' One of these circumstances is desertion by an unbelieving spouse. Some have argued that abuse constitutes

The Life That the Lord Has Assigned

17 However that may be, let each of you lead the life that the Lord has assigned, to which God called you. This is my rule in all the churches. ¹⁸Was anyone at the time of his call already circumcised? Let him not seek to remove the marks of circumcision. Was anyone at the time of his call uncircumcised? Let him not seek circumcision. ¹⁹Circumcision is nothing, and uncircumcision is nothing; but obeying the commandments of God is everything. ²⁰Let each of you remain in the condition in which you were called.

21 Were you a slave when called? Do not be concerned about it. Even if you can gain your freedom, make use of your present condition now more than ever.ᵈ ²²For whoever was called in the Lord as a slave is a freed person belonging to the Lord, just as whoever was free when called is a slave of Christ. ²³You were bought with a price; do not become slaves of human masters. ²⁴In whatever condition you were called, brothers and sisters,ᵉ there remain with God.

◆ Slavery is viewed both positively and negatively within the New Testament. The seizing and selling of slaves is severely condemned (1 Tim. 1:10; Rev. 18:13; see also Ezek. 27:13). During the New Testament era many slaves were born within the household of their owners and were viewed as part of the Roman family.

Sometimes slavery becomes a metaphor for salvation and service to Christ, while at other times – even within the same passage (Rom. 6:6–22) – it stands for bondage and intolerable suffering (Rom. 8:12–17, 21–23; Gal. 4:1–9, 24–25;

5:1). The institution itself bore many aspects in the Roman world. Slaves in the mines or on the galleys usually died in a short time because of the inhumane and utterly callous treatment which they endured.

Slavery provided others with educational and employment opportunities, as well as social and political advancement. Some individuals even sold themselves into slavery in order to gain advantages which they might not otherwise have had. Slaves of Roman citizens gained citizenship themselves upon their liberation. Wealthy masters sent promising young people to excellent schools for training in medicine, philosophy and the arts. Slaves might earn their own money, establish their own businesses, and even own other slaves. They were usually set free after seven to 21 years of service. Many of the manumission agreements are still preserved at Delphi. Typically a percentage of the slave's income the first few years would be assigned to the former master or mistress, and in return the freed persons might count upon their previous owners for patronage and protection as they launched themselves into the mainstream of Roman society.

The early church encouraged slaves to earn enough money to buy their own freedom, in the expectation that they would then have the ability to support themselves. Unless they had a special skill, freed persons sometimes experienced substantial hardships as they competed against cheap slave labor.

Jewish slave-holders were bound to very high standards in their treatment of

---

ᵈ Or *avail yourself of the opportunity*   ᵉ Gk *brothers*

---

such a desertion and that refusal to change destructive behavior patterns renders a person's status equal to that of an infidel (Matt. 18:15–17). A separation, though sometimes needed, is not the most desirable path, but God has called us to peace.

17–24. Believers were not ordinarily to disrupt their established social patterns but rather to live out their Christian calling within these frameworks.

21. Paul does not condone the existence of slavery but rather acknowledges it as a social reality of his day.

slaves, so that it was considered desirable to sell oneself to a Jew. There was a saying that he who had a Jewish slave had actually procured for himself a master.

Emperors tended to appoint trusted freedmen to positions of political prominence. The governor Felix, before whom Paul was tried, is an example of the power and influence a former slave might wield. As a protegé of the Emperor Claudius, his former status did not prevent him from marrying three queens, the third of whom was Drusilla (Acts 23:26–25:14).

Some have speculated that the apostle Paul was himself the child of freedmen who had received their citizenship at the time of their emancipation in the city of Tarsus. He may have been associated with the Synagogue of Freedmen in Jerusalem (Acts 6:9–14). In any event, he was aware of the advantages which Roman citizenship conferred upon him (Acts 16:37–39; 22:25–29; 23:27–29).

While proclaiming that Christ has done away with distinctions between slave and free (Gal. 3:28), Paul designates himself a slave of Christ (Rom. 1:1; Gal. 1:10; Phil. 1:1) and maintains that as a steward he has no right to wages (1 Cor. 9:16–17). Furthermore, he has made himself slave of all (1 Cor. 9:19), and calls on all believers not to misuse their freedom but to be slaves of one another (Gal. 5:13). Both slaves and masters are exhorted to remember that they belong to God and must give an answer for their behavior (Eph. 6:5–9; Col. 3:22–23; Titus 2:9–10; cf. 1 Pet. 2:18). The apostle commends to Philemon's care the erring Onesimus, whom some have thought a truant brother rather than a slave (Philem. 16).

Some scholars have suggested that Paul's very slavery to Christ legitimates his message (1 Cor. 9). His meaning in 1 Cor. 7:21–24 is that either slavery or freedom might be used as a means of proclaiming God's grace ◆

The Unmarried and the Widows

25 Now concerning virgins, I have no command of the Lord, but I give my opinion as one who by the Lord's mercy is trustworthy. [26]I think that, in view of the impending[f] crisis, it is well for you to remain as you are. [27]Are you bound to a wife? Do not seek to be free. Are you free from a wife? Do not seek a wife. [28]But if you marry, you do not sin, and if a virgin marries, she does not sin. Yet those who marry will experience distress in this life,[g] and I would spare you that. [29]I mean, brothers and sisters,[h] the appointed time has grown short; from now on, let even those who have wives be as though they had none, [30]and those who mourn as though they were not mourning, and those who rejoice as though they were not rejoicing, and those who buy as though they had no possessions, [31]and those who deal with the world as though they had no dealings with it. For the present form of this world is passing away.

32 I want you to be free from anxieties. The unmarried man is anxious about the affairs of the Lord, how to please the Lord; [33]but the married man is anxious about the affairs of the world, how to please his wife, [34]and his interests are divided. And the unmarried woman and the virgin are anxious about the affairs of the Lord, so that they may be holy in body and spirit; but the married woman is anxious about the affairs of the world, how to please her husband. [35]I say this for your own benefit, not to put any restraint upon you, but to promote good order and unhindered devotion to the Lord.

36 If anyone thinks that he is not behaving properly toward his fiancée,[i] if his

[f] Or present   [g] Gk in the flesh   [h] Gk brothers
[i] Gk virgin

---

36. Some scholars understand this passage as a warning against fathers marrying off the daughters at too young an age. Greek girls might be married as young as ten years old, and grave inscriptions attest there were many deaths from childbirth. Roman girls were generally married

passions are strong, and so it has to be, let him marry as he wishes; it is no sin. Let them marry. [37]But if someone stands firm in his resolve, being under no necessity but having his own desire under control, and has determined in his own mind to keep her as his fiancée,[j] he will do well. [38]So then, he who marries his fiancée[j] does well; and he who refrains from marriage will do better.

39 A wife is bound as long as her husband lives. But if the husband dies,[k] she is free to marry anyone she wishes, only in the Lord. [40]But in my judgment she is more blessed if she remains as she is. And I think that I too have the Spirit of God.

Food Offered to Idols

8 Now concerning food sacrificed to idols: we know that "all of us possess knowledge." Knowledge puffs up, but love builds up. [2]Anyone who claims to know something does not yet have the necessary knowledge; [3]but anyone who loves God is known by him.

4 Hence, as to the eating of food offered to idols, we know that "no idol in the world really exists," and that "there is no God but one." [5]Indeed, even though there may be so-called gods in heaven or on earth – as in fact there are many gods and many lords – [6]yet for us there is one God, the Father, from whom are all things and for whom we exist, and one Lord, Jesus Christ, through whom are all things and through whom we exist.

7 It is not everyone, however, who has this knowledge. Since some have become so accustomed to idols until now, they still think of the food they eat as food offered to

[j] Gk *virgin*   [k] Gk *falls asleep*

---

between the ages of twelve and fourteen and often clung to their mothers as they were torn away and escorted to their new husband's home. Remaining unmarried was usually not an option for young women.

Paul's advice may be an instruction to fathers to give their daughters a choice in the matter once they had passed through puberty. It may be translated, 'If anyone thinks that he is not doing the right thing by his unmarried daughter and she is fully mature, and ought to be married, then let him do as she wishes, he does not sin, let him give her in marriage. The father does well who stands firm in his own heart, not having to yield to pressure, but choosing freely in his own heart to keep his daughter as a virgin. Therefore he who gives his virgin daughter in marriage does well, and he who does not give her in marriage does better.'

The translators of our text believe that Paul is speaking of engaged couples, but some scholars consider this passage to be directed toward men who have entered into a supposedly celibate relationship with a 'virgin' living under the same roof. In that case, Paul is arguing that marriage might be a better option.

39–40. Paul ends the long passage on sexual considerations by again affirming the validity of marriage but calling upon believers to marry only 'in the Lord'. Marriage at its highest is a spiritual covenant, to be entered by two persons committed to Christ and to one another. The many experiences and conditions which they share – spirituality, intellectual and social communion, sexuality, children, home, property, grief, disappointment, joy, fatigue, responsibilities and pleasures – are all sanctified by the love and grace of the Savior.

1 CORINTHIANS 8

1. The consumption of meat previously offered to an idol presented a very real difficulty to new believers who ordinarily obtained their meat supply either from the actual sacrifice of an animal or from the butchers who operated a commercial outlet for the offerings from the temple. Some Christians were uncomfortable in partaking of that which had first been offered to a heathen god while others considered it ridiculous to maintain such scruples. The real issue became how to respect those with different convictions on such a matter.

an idol; and their conscience, being weak, is defiled. [8]"Food will not bring us close to God."[l] We are no worse off if we do not eat, and no better off if we do. [9]But take care that this liberty of yours does not somehow become a stumbling block to the weak. [10]For if others see you, who possess knowledge, eating in the temple of an idol, might they not, since their conscience is weak, be encouraged to the point of eating food sacrificed to idols? [11]So by your knowledge those weak believers for whom Christ died are destroyed.[m] [12]But when you thus sin against members of your family,[n] and wound their conscience when it is weak, you sin against Christ. [13]Therefore, if food is a cause of their falling,[o] I will never eat meat, so that I may not cause one of them[p] to fall.

The Rights of an Apostle

9 Am I not free? Am I not an apostle? Have I not seen Jesus our Lord? Are you not my work in the Lord? [2]If I am not an apostle to others, at least I am to you; for you are the seal of my apostleship in the Lord.

[3] This is my defense to those who would examine me. [4]Do we not have the right to our food and drink? [5]Do we not have the right to be accompanied by a believing wife,[q] as do the other apostles and the brothers of the Lord and Cephas? [6]Or is it only Barnabas and I who have no right to refrain from working for a living? [7]Who at any time pays the expenses for doing military service? Who plants a vineyard and does not eat any of its fruit? Or who tends a flock and does not get any of its milk?

[8] Do I say this on human authority? Does not the law also say the same? [9]For it is written in the law of Moses, "You shall not muzzle an ox while it is treading out the grain." Is it for oxen that God is concerned? [10]Or does he not speak entirely for our sake? It was indeed written for our sake, for whoever plows should plow in hope and whoever threshes should thresh

[l] The quotation may extend to the end of the verse   [m] Gk *the weak brother . . . is destroyed*   [n] Gk *against the brothers*   [o] Gk *my brother's falling*   [p] Gk *cause my brother*   [q] Gk *a sister as wife*

---

9. The answer to the perplexity is that we should be careful not to make our sister or brother stumble. It is better to forego a legitimate pursuit than to create a compromising situation for one who is weaker in the faith.

Women in particular have been trained to observe many rigidly traditional types of behavior, whether in social situations, personal appearance, manner of speech, etc. Modesty in one culture may be quite different than in another. It behooves Christian women to be especially considerate of the feelings and traditions of others so as not to give offense. The claims of the gospel supercede our personal rights and preferences.

10. It is indeed a surprise to discover that converts were still returning to pagan temples to participate in their feasts. Ritual meals were a part of many cults, and dining rooms associated with a shrine of the wine-god Dionysos have been excavated at Corinth.

1 CORINTHIANS 9

1. Paul here tells us that he is willing to renounce his personal rights for the sake of making Christ known to others. Specifically, he has renounced his right to a wife who might comfort him in his times of loneliness when others had deserted him. As a young rabbi, Paul was probably married, perhaps into a family highly connected with the temple personnel in Jerusalem, those most bitterly opposed to Jesus and his followers. It has been surmised that his wife, at the vehement insistence of her family, refused to be part of the apostle's gospel ministry and chose to separate from him. In view of the dangers and ordeals which Paul underwent (2 Cor. 11:23–33; Acts 9:23–25; 14:19; 16:23), he cannot have failed to find that his ministry was enhanced by his freedom from the encumbrances of a family.

in hope of a share in the crop. [11]If we have sown spiritual good among you, is it too much if we reap your material benefits? [12]If others share this rightful claim on you, do not we still more?

Nevertheless, we have not made use of this right, but we endure anything rather than put an obstacle in the way of the gospel of Christ. [13]Do you not know that those who are employed in the temple service get their food from the temple, and those who serve at the altar share in what is sacrificed on the altar? [14]In the same way, the Lord commanded that those who proclaim the gospel should get their living by the gospel.

15 But I have made no use of any of these rights, nor am I writing this so that they may be applied in my case. Indeed, I would rather die than that – no one will deprive me of my ground for boasting! [16]If I proclaim the gospel, this gives me no ground for boasting, for an obligation is laid on me, and woe to me if I do not proclaim the gospel! [17]For if I do this of my own will, I have a reward; but if not of my own will, I am entrusted with a commission. [18]What then is my reward? Just this: that in my proclamation I may make the gospel free of charge, so as not to make full use of my rights in the gospel.

19 For though I am free with respect to all, I have made myself a slave to all, so that I might win more of them. [20]To the Jews I became as a Jew, in order to win Jews. To those under the law I became as one under the law (though I myself am not under the law) so that I might win those under the law. [21]To those outside the law I became as one outside the law (though I am not free from God's law but am under Christ's law) so that I might win those outside the law. [22]To the weak I became weak, so that I might win the weak. I have become all things to all people, that I might by all means save some. [23]I do it all for the sake of the gospel, so that I may share in its blessings.

24 Do you not know that in a race the runners all compete, but only one receives the prize? Run in such a way that you may win it. [25]Athletes exercise self-control in all things; they do it to receive a perishable wreath, but we an imperishable one. [26]So I

---

12. The lack of a family enabled him to support himself and thereby to maintain his ministry at no expense to the recipients. Later, when he would be imprisoned and no longer able to provide for his own needs, he would be grateful to receive the gifts of his converts.

16. The propagation of the gospel is the driving motivational force in Paul's life. He cannot accept remuneration for that from which he cannot be restrained. Jeremiah declared that God's message was a burning fire which he was unable to keep to himself (Jer. 20:9). Others found the same necessity laid upon them (Amos 3:8; Acts 4:20). Today's believing women and men also understand the urgency of the call which is laid upon them. If God's hand is upon them for gospel ministry, they must obey no matter what the opposition. Like the Ethiopians Jehudi and Ebed-Melek, who believed that Jeremiah's message was truly of God and gained him a hearing in the king's court (Jer. 36:14, 21–24; 38:7–14; 39: 15–18), let the saints of God offer encouragement and support to women seeking to respond to their divine calling.

19–23. Paul presents his principle of adaptation. He is willing to make the adjustments himself to each culture, each society, and each regional and ethnic group. All too often Christians have expected other people to conform to their particular notions of architecture, style of worship, music, dress, politics, language, church government, convention and so forth. Rather we should be challenged to bring the love of Christ and the power of the gospel into each new situation and condition. It is important to understand the difference between *adaptation*, accommodating one's ministry style so as to be most effective with each people group and *assimilation*, adopting non-Christian practices, ideas or attitudes and incorporating them into Christian faith and practice.

do not run aimlessly, nor do I box as though beating the air; [27]but I punish my body and enslave it, so that after proclaiming to others I myself should not be disqualified.

Warnings from Israel's History

10 I do not want you to be unaware, brothers and sisters,[r] that our ancestors were all under the cloud, and all passed through the sea, [2]and all were baptized into Moses in the cloud and in the sea, [3]and all ate the same spiritual food, [4]and all drank the same spiritual drink. For they drank from the spiritual rock that followed them, and the rock was Christ. [5]Nevertheless, God was not pleased with most of them, and they were struck down in the wilderness.

6 Now these things occurred as examples for us, so that we might not desire evil as they did. [7]Do not become idolaters as some of them did; as it is written, "The people sat down to eat and drink, and they rose up to play." [8]We must not indulge in sexual immorality as some of them did, and twenty-three thousand fell in a single day. [9]We must not put Christ[s] to the test, as some of them did, and were destroyed by serpents. [10]And do not complain as some of them did, and were destroyed by the destroyer. [11]These things happened to them to serve as an example, and they were written down to instruct us, on whom the ends of the ages have come. [12]So if you think you are standing, watch out that you do not fall. [13]No testing has overtaken you that is not common to everyone. God is faithful, and he will not let you be tested beyond your strength, but with the testing he will also provide the way out so that you may be able to endure it.

> ◆ The promise is that God will 'provide the way out'. This makes it incumbent on a believer in unbearable circumstances to look for God's avenue of escape. These might include prayer, pastoral or professional counselling, group intervention, appeal to the wider Christian community, support groups, social service agencies – even appropriate use of courts of law. All too often the Christian woman feels trapped with no place to turn. If the first source to which she turns will not believe her story or render assistance, she should be emboldened to seek another avenue that God might have for her (Matt. 18:15–17; Gal. 6:1; 1 Tim. 5:20; James 5:19–20). It is important for her to understand that God does not wish his children to stay in impossible or abusive situations for which there is a possible remedy. It is the responsibility of the Christian community to watch for opportunities to

[r] Gk brothers   [s] Other ancient authorities read the Lord

---

1 CORINTHIANS 10

1ff. Paul now draws on the experiences of Israel to warn of the dangers of assimilation. These situations are not reproduced exactly in our own lives, but they can provide us with important spiritual examples. Paul maintains that the all too human failings of the children of Israel may serve as a warning to us. There was still the danger that the new believers might slip back into idolatry as did the Israelites. Idolatry, let us remember can be of many different sorts – whether wealth, prestige, power, or comfort. When we become overly involved with work, hobbies, possessions or even a preoccupation with church work that leaves no time for communion with Christ, then we like the children of Israel may be drawn into the world around us and away from the God who redeemed us.

8. The warning continues with a warning against fornication, and then a very pertinent admonition against grumbling and complaining. How easy it is to forget God's goodness and provision for our needs – how easy to descend to petty carping – and to the demoralization of others!

13. There follows a reassurance that God understands our trials and difficulties, and that his faithfulness will prevail even while we are in the crucible.

implement such a way of escape for those who come to them in desperation. Simple measures such as taking the children for an afternoon or a week-end, providing short-term respite care for an invalid, lending a sympathetic ear or even bringing in a meal may bring significant relief. We should always be aware that we may be the ones whom God will use to bring that 'way of escape' to another believer ◆

14 Therefore, my dear friends,[t] flee from the worship of idols. [15]I speak as to sensible people; judge for yourselves what I say. [16]The cup of blessing that we bless, is it not a sharing in the blood of Christ? The bread that we break, is it not a sharing in the body of Christ? [17]Because there is one bread, we who are many are one body, for we all partake of the one bread. [18]Consider the people of Israel;[u] are not those who eat the sacrifices partners in the altar? [19]What do I imply then? That food sacrificed to idols is anything, or that an idol is anything? [20]No, I imply that what pagans sacrifice, they sacrifice to demons and not to God. I do not want you to be partners with demons. [21]You cannot drink the cup of the Lord and the cup of demons. You cannot partake of the table of the Lord and the table of demons. [22]Or are we provoking the Lord to jealousy? Are we stronger than he?

Do All to the Glory of God

23 "All things are lawful," but not all things are beneficial. "All things are lawful," but not all things build up. [24]Do not seek your own advantage, but that of the other. [25]Eat whatever is sold in the meat market without raising any question on the ground of conscience, [26]for "the earth and its fullness are the Lord's." [27]If an unbeliever invites you to a meal and you are disposed to go, eat whatever is set before you without raising any question on the ground of conscience. [28]But if someone says to you, "This has been offered in sacrifice," then do not eat it, out of consideration for the one who informed you, and for the sake of conscience – [29]I mean the other's conscience, not your own. For why should my liberty be subject to the judgment of someone else's conscience? [30]If I partake with thankfulness, why should I be denounced because of that for which I give thanks?

31 So, whether you eat or drink, or whatever you do, do everything for the glory of God. [32]Give no offense to Jews or to Greeks or to the church of God, [33]just as I try to please everyone in everything I do, not seeking my own advantage, but that of many, so that they may be saved.

[t] Gk *my beloved*   [u] Gk *Israel according to the flesh*

---

14. The Corinthians are plagued with many holdovers from their previous religious practice. Some were still returning to the pagan temples for feasts involving the consumption of meat offered to idols (1 Cor. 8:10). Paul now argues that there is more at stake than just the conscience of a weaker believer. The participants of a pagan ritual have allied themselves with spiritual forces which are wholly incompatible with the worship of Jesus Christ.

20. Although an idol has no spiritual power nor is there reality in other gods, forces of evil may well use misguided religion to draw away the people of God. The word for 'demon' is used in Greek literature for an actual spiritual being, a mood or attitude, human personality, or intellect. Paul is aware of a spiritual warfare that deflects the allegiance and devotion of believers away from Christ.

23. This is the principle of Christian liberty: that we have freedom to do many things but that we must take care not to give offense to others. We must be careful that a perfectly legitimate action on our part does not put a stumbling block in the way of another. Every believer is worthy of our respect and of our consideration.

11 ¹Be imitators of me, as I am of Christ.

Head Coverings

2 I commend you because you remember me in everything and maintain the traditions just as I handed them on to you. ³But I want you to understand that Christ is the head of every man, and the

---

◆ Usually 'head' in the New Testament refers to the physical head of a person. However, at least seven times head has a metaphorical meaning, including 1 Cor. 11:3; Eph. 1:22; 4:15; 5:23; Col. 1:18; 2:10, 19.

'Leader or chief or authority over' is the meaning traditionally assumed for the metaphorical meanings of head in these passages *even though such meaning does not appear in the most complete Greek-English lexicon.*

The most comprehensive Greek-English Lexicon covering New Testament times, compiled by Liddell, Scott, Jones, McKenzie, lists more than 25 possible metaphorical meanings of 'head' (Gk. *kephale*). These meanings include source,

---

origin, starting point, top or crown, capital (of a column), completion or consummation, noblest part, and several others, but *none that suggest chief, authority over* etc.

'Head' appears ten times in 1 Cor. 11:2–13. It obviously refers to the physical head in the first and last part of v. 5. But does 'disgraces her head' mean her own physical head or her metaphorical head—husband or man? The same problem appears in v. 4. The meaning of the text is not clear and can be read either as her own head or her metaphorical head.

What does 'head' mean in 1 Cor. 11:3 if it does not mean 'authority over'? The discussion in vv. 8–13 refers to the 'beginning' of man and woman in Gen. 1–2, which would seem to indicate the idea of beginning or source is the meaning of 'head' in v. 3. Probably that is the way the first readers would have understood it.

In Col. 1:18 where Christ is spoken of as the 'head', the text says 'he is the *beginning, the firstborn from the dead*'. Col. 2:10 says '*you have come to fullness in him*, who is the head of every ruler and authority'. Col. 2:19 calls Christ the head

---

1 CORINTHIANS 11

1. Although Paul addresses various disorders in worship in this chapter, he uses the occasion to discuss theological and sociological issues as well. Many in the congregation were recently idol-worshippers (1 Cor. 12:2). Yet their meetings took place next door to the Jewish synagogue whose members were likely to condemn the conduct of people newly converted from paganism (Acts 18:7). **3.** Three of the words in this verse have more than one meaning. Among the Greeks, communication between married partners was so minimal that there were no common words for 'husband' and 'wife'. Rather, the ordinary words for 'man' and 'woman' were used. It seems more logical here to understand Paul's intent as being a reference to 'man' and 'woman', since the passage twice refers to the Genesis account of woman being taken from man (vv. 8, 11). *Kephale*, the Greek word for 'head', was often used metaphorically to mean 'beginning' or 'source'.

The early Greek Fathers went to great lengths to insist that this is the sense in which 'head' should be understood here. Christ brought into being every man (John 1:3), and woman had her beginning in man, while Son is begotten from the Father and Spirit proceed forth from the Father. The church held that all three were equal in goodness, power and love but distinguished between the members of the Godhead in terms of *origin*. (See the essay on 'The doctrine of the Trinity', p. 570.)

Seldom did 'head' imply 'chief' or 'boss'. John Chrysostom, an ardent defender of the Trinity, maintained that only a heretic would gather from this passage that there was subordination within the Godhead, for the Scriptures speak of the equality of Father and Son (John 5:18; Phil. 2:6). Rather one should understand 'head' as 'perfect oneness and primal cause and beginning'.

'from whom the whole body . . . grows'. In all these instances the concept of source or beginning fits the meaning of 'head'.

In Eph. 1:22, the concept of 'top or crown' fits; in Eph. 4:15, source seems to be the meaning of head; in Eph. 5:23, the meaning of 'one who brings to completion or consummation' may be indicated. All of these fall within the range of Greek meanings ◆

husband[v] is the head of his wife,[w] and God is the head of Christ. [4]Any man who prays or prophesies with something on his head disgraces his head, [5]but any woman who prays or prophesies with her head unveiled

disgraces her head – it is one and the same thing as having her head shaved. [6]For if a woman will not veil herself, then she should cut off her hair; but if it is disgraceful for a woman to have her hair cut off or to be shaved, she should wear a veil. [7]For a man ought not to have his head veiled, since he is the image and reflection[x] of God; but woman is the reflection[x] of man. [8]Indeed, man was not made from woman, but woman from man. [9]Neither was man created for the sake of woman, but woman for the sake of man. [10]For this

[v] The same Greek word means *man* or *husband*
[w] Or *head of the woman*   [x] Or *glory*

---

4. This must of necessity refer to a particular practice of the local congregation as Israelite priests were required to have a covering on their heads (Exod. 28:4, 37–38, 40; 29:6, 9; 39:28, 31; Lev. 8:9). To this day orthodox Jewish males wear headshawls during prayer; and Greek and Roman males usually prayed with covered heads except before the Father of the Gods and before a deity known as 'Glory'. Probably Paul is seeking to restrict the custom of men and women cross-dressing as they had during certain pagan rites. Here he affirms the identity of both sexes and encourages identity with one's own gender.

5. (See the note on 'Women prophets', p. 124.) Veiling of women was practised extensively by both Jewish and Gentile women. Some rabbis even maintained that a man was obliged to divorce his wife if she was seen on the street with uncovered head (see the note on 'Jewish marriage law', p. 97). Paul's hometown of Tarsus seems to have been particularly strict in the observance of this custom, though its women were said to be no more chaste than elsewhere. During pagan ceremonies, women sometimes discarded their veils as a sign of liberation from their husbands.

6. Shaving the head of a woman was a sign of disgrace, sometimes used as a punishment for unchastity and sometimes as a punishment for refusing to serve as a sacred prostitute.

7. Here Paul picks up the language of Gen. 1:27 and 5:1–2 in which male and female are made in the image of God (Gen. 1:26–27; 5:2–3). The word here translated 'reflection' is actually the word for 'glory', a term used to imply the manifestation of God's power or attributes. In human terms, several Christians are described as a 'glory' or being transformed 'from glory to glory' (2 Cor. 3:13; 8:23; 1 Thess. 2:20). The concept would be an important one in a society which considered it an embarrassment for a woman to be seen in public. Here Paul encourages husbands to take pride in their wives as they participate in public services of worship.

8. Greek myth held that woman was taken from a substance inferior to that from which man had been formed. Philosophers insisted that a woman could never equal a man in moral or spiritual qualities and was therefore unworthy to be his true companion. By contrast, Paul maintains that woman is of the self-same substance, 'Bone of his bone and flesh of his flesh.' She is man's fit partner in the journey through life.

9. The Hebrew Bible declares that woman was called into being as a 'help of man's like', sharing his humanity but able to render him the strength and aid of which he had such need. The phrase 'for the sake of' is often used to describe the purpose of a person's ministry (1 Cor. 4:6, 10; 9:10, 23; 2 Cor. 4:5, 11, 15). Jesus, though rich, was made poor 'for our sakes' (2 Cor. 8:9). Thus woman was created for ministry.

10. The Greek reads simply, 'Therefore a woman should have power over her head, because of the

reason a woman ought to have a symbol of[y] authority on her head,[z] because of the angels. [11]Nevertheless, in the Lord woman is not independent of man or man independent of woman. [12]For just as woman came from man, so man comes through woman; but all things come from God. [13]Judge for yourselves: is it proper for a woman to pray to God with her head unveiled? [14]Does not nature itself teach you that if a man wears long hair, it is degrading to him, [15]but if a woman has long hair, it is her glory? For her hair is given to her for a covering. [16]But if anyone is disposed to be contentious – we have no

such custom, nor do the churches of God.

Abuses at the Lord's Supper

[17] Now in the following instructions I do not commend you, because when you come together it is not for the better but for the worse. [18]For, to begin with, when you come together as a church, I hear that there are divisions among you; and to some extent I believe it. [19]Indeed, there have to be factions among you, for only so will it become clear who among you are genuine.

[y] Gk lacks *a symbol of*   [z] Or *have freedom of choice regarding her head*

---

angels.' A great many alterations have been offered in order to deal with the meaning. The footnote rightly suggests that the word for 'power' used here, *exousia*, offers a woman freedom of choice, since the term implies just this at seven other points in the same epistle (1 Cor. 7:27; 8:9; 9:4–6, 12, 18). The term may also be translated 'a woman should have power over her head'.

The Greek word 'angel' also means 'messenger'. Paul may be concerned about the tale-bearers who might carry the news of unveiled women next door to the synagogue, or perhaps there were marriage brokers who might take advantage of the opportunity to evaluate the personal appearance of young women of marriageable age.

11. This is perhaps the strongest statement of mutuality in the Bible. Man and woman belong to one another, both to reflect the image of God, and to comprise the body of Christ. Neither is adequate without the other, and neither is to take advantage of the other.

12. Here the interdependence is carried one step further. Both sexes find their point of origin in one another. In antiquity both males and females claimed supremacy for their sex as the source of being, but Paul points beyond them to the God who made all and who gave man and woman to one another. Here the apostle abolishes the sex hostility which has characterized both the ancient and the modern world, and here he calls all believers to a new unity in Christ (see Gal. 3:28).

14. This is puzzling in light of the long hair of Samson and Absalom. Indeed Nazarites were not permitted to cut their hair, and ancient Greek warriors who participated in the Trojan War were called 'long-haired Achaeans'. (Probably the cross-dressing associated with pagan cults is being addressed here.) But long hair on boys or men was described by poets as exciting the admiration of homosexual lovers. If the entire passage constitutes a call for men and women to belong to one another, it is also a call to find one's identity within the gender assigned to the individual by God.

15. The Bible often commands that the manifestation of glory should be concealed or covered from eyes not ready to behold it (Exod. 13:21–22; 19:16–18; 24:16–17; 34:29–35; 40:34–35; 1 Kings 8:10–13; Ps. 18:11; Is. 4:5–6; Ezek. 10:4).

16. The entire foregoing passage is a very difficult one, but it is clear that Paul is calling for propriety, particularly on the part of women. To bring women out of the seclusion of their homes and to allow them to participate in worship was a daring step in a society that often prohibited such practices. Women are to have full freedom to pray and prophesy, but they should be careful not to offend the sensibilities of either the pagan or Jewish community.

17. Often we idealize the early church, but here we see the deplorable state of a Communion service at Corinth. Some of the former pagans had brought their old ways into the celebration of the Lord's death. Communion, like any other ministry of the church, can become perverted and destructive when individuals seek their own interests rather than those of Christ.

18. For Paul's earlier discussion of these quarreling factions, see 3:1–9.

²⁰When you come together, it is not really to eat the Lord's supper. ²¹For when the time comes to eat, each of you goes ahead with your own supper, and one goes hungry and another becomes drunk. ²²What! Do you not have homes to eat and drink in? Or do you show contempt for the church of God and humiliate those who have nothing? What should I say to you? Should I commend you? In this matter I do not commend you!

The Institution of the Lord's Supper

23 For I received from the Lord what I also handed on to you, that the Lord Jesus on the night when he was betrayed took a loaf of bread, ²⁴and when he had given thanks, he broke it and said, "This is my body that is for[a] you. Do this in remembrance of me." ²⁵In the same way he took the cup also, after supper, saying, "This cup is the new covenant in my blood. Do this, as often as you drink it, in remembrance of me." ²⁶For as often as you eat this bread and drink the cup, you proclaim the Lord's death until he comes.

Partaking of the Supper Unworthily

27 Whoever, therefore, eats the bread or drinks the cup of the Lord in an unworthy manner will be answerable for the body and blood of the Lord. ²⁸Examine yourselves, and only then eat of the bread and drink of the cup. ²⁹For all who eat and drink[b] without discerning the body,[c] eat and drink judgment against themselves. ³⁰For this reason many of you are weak and ill, and some have died.[d] ³¹But if we judged ourselves, we would not be judged. ³²But when we are judged by the Lord, we are disciplined[e] so that we may not be condemned along with the world.

33 So then, my brothers and sisters,[f] when you come together to eat, wait for one another. ³⁴If you are hungry, eat at home, so that when you come together, it will not be for your condemnation. About

[a] Other ancient authorities read *is broken for*
[b] Other ancient authorities add *in an unworthy manner,*   [c] Other ancient authorities read *the Lord's body*   [d] Gk *fallen asleep*   [e] Or *When we are judged, we are being disciplined by the Lord*
[f] Gk *brothers*

---

20. People accustomed to pagan festivals behaved very differently from normal standards of Christian worship. In wild binges celebrating Dionysus, the god of wine, it was an act of worship to become drunk. (See the note on 'Chemical dependency', p. 444.) Women in particular availed themselves of this avenue of escape from the virtual imprisonment in which many of them lived, and Dionysus was viewed as the 'liberator of women'.

21. This text insists on equal treatment for all believers and on the care we must have for one another's welfare. Significantly, he does not direct that the men should eat first and that the women take the leftovers as is frequently done in Mediterranean societies. All are to share in the common meal and to do so with propriety.

Since it was considered an embarrassment for Greek men to take their wives out to a dinner party, we may reasonably conclude that women as well as men probably needed some instruction in how to behave at a non-pagan gathering. In a society where women and slaves were not given the same opportunity to consume meat, there may have been a temptation to take more than one's share without regard for the next person.

22. Paul here shows a deep sensitivity for those who were disadvantaged, including the humiliation which they would feel at being slighted during the common meal. The Bible repeatedly calls upon the 'haves' to share with the 'have nots' as well as to preserve their dignity and self-worth in a respectful and considerate manner. Within the body of Christ, this is a very great obligation, especially as we approach the Communion table.

29. This indicates that people should honor not only the Communion elements but also the body of believers, the church. Even the most humble or dysfunctional member must be treated as a valued part of the body of Christ. To do otherwise is to harm both oneself and the church.

the other things I will give instructions when I come.

Spiritual Gifts

12 Now concerning spiritual gifts,[g] brothers and sisters,[h] I do not want you to be uninformed. [2]You know that when you were pagans, you were enticed and led astray to idols that could not speak. [3]Therefore I want you to understand that no one speaking by the Spirit of God ever says "Let Jesus be cursed!" and no one can say "Jesus is Lord" except by the Holy Spirit.

4 Now there are varieties of gifts, but the same Spirit; [5]and there are varieties of services, but the same Lord; [6]and there are varieties of activities, but it is the same God who activates all of them in everyone. [7]To each is given the manifestation of the Spirit for the common good. [8]To one is given through the Spirit the utterance of wisdom, and to another the utterance of knowledge according to the same Spirit, [9]to another faith by the same Spirit, to another gifts of healing by the one Spirit, [10]to another the working of miracles, to another prophecy, to another the discernment of spirits, to another various kinds of tongues, to another the interpretation of tongues. [11]All these are activated by one and the same Spirit, who allots to each one individually just as the Spirit chooses.

One Body with Many Members

12 For just as the body is one and has many members, and all the members of the body, though many, are one body, so it is with Christ. [13]For in the one Spirit we were all baptized into one body – Jews or Greeks, slaves or free – and we were all made to drink of one Spirit.

14 Indeed, the body does not consist of one member but of many. [15]If the foot would say, "Because I am not a hand, I do not belong to the body," that would not make it any less a part of the body. [16]And if the ear would say, "Because I am not an eye, I do not belong to the body," that would not make it any less a part of the body. [17]If the whole body were an eye, where would the hearing be? If the whole body were hearing, where would the sense of smell be? [18]But as it is, God arranged the members in the body, each one of them, as he chose. [19]If all were a single member, where would the

[g] Or *spiritual persons*   [h] Gk *brothers*

---

1 CORINTHIANS 12

2. Many of the Corinthian believers were former idol-worshippers, heathen who possessed no knowledge of the true and living God nor of the Hebrew Scriptures. They had been 'carried away' by frenzied pagan cults and had still to struggle with divesting themselves of the remnants of their former religion.

3. In certain cults, that of Hercules in particular, good luck could be secured by cursing a divine figure. This was most certainly not an appropriate response to the Savior who died for our redemption. Early Christians were asked to curse Jesus and to affirm the lordship of the Emperor rather than of Christ. It was the work of the Holy Spirit which kept them faithful in their profession.

4. Often we tend to view a very few types of ministry as the ones that are really important, or to value some gifts far more highly than others. This passage teaches clearly that God has given a diversity of gifts to meet the many demands of people all over the world. Just as no two blades of grass, or leaves or flowers are alike, so our differences and varieties of ability are both ordained and valued by God. No two of us possess exactly the same blend of aptitudes and potentials. Women often fail to acknowledge and evaluate the gifting which is theirs, nor do they always use this enablement as they should. When this happens, the whole body suffers from the loss. The body requires that all of us be involved, men and women alike, caring for one another, supporting one another and depending upon one another.

body be? ²⁰As it is, there are many members, yet one body. ²¹The eye cannot say to the hand, "I have no need of you," nor again the head to the feet, "I have no need of you." ²²On the contrary, the members of the body that seem to be weaker are indispensable, ²³and those members of the body that we think less honorable we clothe with greater honor, and our less respectable members are treated with greater respect; ²⁴whereas our more respectable members do not need this. But God has so arranged the body, giving the greater honor to the inferior member, ²⁵that there may be no dissension within the body, but the members may have the same care for one another. ²⁶If one member suffers, all suffer together with it; if one member is honored, all rejoice together with it.

27 Now you are the body of Christ and individually members of it. ²⁸And God has appointed in the church first apostles, second prophets, third teachers; then deeds of power, then gifts of healing, forms of assistance, forms of leadership, various kinds of tongues. ²⁹Are all apostles? Are all prophets? Are all teachers? Do all work miracles? ³⁰Do all possess gifts of healing? Do all speak in tongues? Do all interpret?

³¹But strive for the greater gifts. And I will show you a still more excellent way.

The Gift of Love

13 If I speak in the tongues of mortals and of angels, but do not have love, I am a noisy gong or a clanging cymbal. ²And if I have prophetic powers, and understand all mysteries and all knowledge, and if I have all faith, so as to remove mountains, but do not have love, I am nothing. ³If I give away all my possessions, and if I hand over my body so that I may boast,[i] but do not have love, I gain nothing.

4 Love is patient; love is kind; love is not envious or boastful or arrogant ⁵or rude. It does not insist on its own way; it is not irritable or resentful; ⁶it does not rejoice in wrongdoing, but rejoices in the truth. ⁷It bears all things, believes all things, hopes all things, endures all things.

8 Love never ends. But as for prophecies, they will come to an end; as for tongues, they will cease; as for knowledge, it will come to an end. ⁹For we know only in part, and we prophesy only in part; ¹⁰but when the complete comes, the partial will come

[i] Other ancient authorities read *body to be burned*

---

21. Here the head is seen as a part of the body which cannot deny the need of another bodily member. The concept of the head is not as supreme but as interdependent with the rest of the body. (See the note on 'The head', p. 343.)

27. Of the many gifts mentioned, perhaps the one least prized by modern Christians is that of administration. We are in particular need of women whom God has so graced. Those who are reticent should receive particular encouragement from fellow believers to exercise the ability which has been entrusted to them.

1 CORINTHIANS 13

1–4. The gifts which Paul has already discussed are admirable, but the 'more excellent way' is the path of love. Without love, our ministry is a sham with no reality or substance.

4. The description of love's behavior is certainly a golden rule of desirable deportment for women. It may be considered the exemplar of the true Christian gentlewoman.

5. With love there is a lack of conceit and irritability, a willingness to put the good of another first. Another remarkable characteristic is that of thinking no evil. The tombstone of one Christian woman reads, 'Ever she looked for the best in people, and ever she found it!'

6. The challenge to rejoice not in iniquity but in the truth is surely the best antidote to unkind gossip and verbal abuse.

8. Love lasts after all the gifts fail.

to an end. [11]When I was a child, I spoke like a child, I thought like a child, I reasoned like a child; when I became an adult, I put an end to childish ways. [12]For now we see in a mirror, dimly,[j] but then we will see face to face. Now I know only in part; then I will know fully, even as I have been fully known. [13]And now faith, hope, and love abide, these three; and the greatest of these is love.

Gifts of Prophecy and Tongues

14 Pursue love and strive for the spiritual gifts, and especially that you may prophesy. [2]For those who speak in a tongue do not speak to other people but to God; for nobody understands them, since they are speaking mysteries in the Spirit. [3]On the other hand, those who prophesy speak to other people for their upbuilding and encouragement and consolation. [4]Those who speak in a tongue build up themselves, but those who prophesy build up the church. [5]Now I would like all of you to speak in tongues, but even more to prophesy. One who prophesies is greater than one who speaks in tongues, unless someone interprets, so that the church may be built up.

6 Now, brothers and sisters,[k] if I come to you speaking in tongues, how will I benefit you unless I speak to you in some revelation or knowledge or prophecy or teaching? [7]It is the same way with lifeless instruments that produce sound, such as the flute or the harp. If they do not give distinct notes, how will anyone know what is being played? [8]And if the bugle gives an indistinct sound, who will get ready for battle? [9]So with yourselves; if in a tongue you utter speech that is not intelligible, how will anyone know what is being said? For you will be speaking into the air. [10]There are doubtless many different kinds of sounds in the world, and nothing is without sound. [11]If then I do not know the meaning of a sound, I will be a foreigner to the speaker and the speaker a foreigner to me. [12]So with yourselves; since you are eager for spiritual gifts, strive to excel in them for building up the church.

13 Therefore, one who speaks in a tongue should pray for the power to interpret. [14]For if I pray in a tongue, my spirit prays but my mind is unproductive. [15]What should I do then? I will pray with the spirit, but I will pray with the mind also; I will sing praise with the spirit, but I will sing praise with the mind also. [16]Otherwise, if you say a blessing with the spirit, how can anyone in the position of an outsider say

---

[j] Gk *in a riddle*   [k] Gk *brothers*

---

1 CORINTHIANS 14

1. After his parenthetical discourse on love, Paul continues on with a discussion of the appropriate use of gifts during a service of worship – in this case those of prophecy and tongues.

3. Tongues may be used when God alone is being addressed, but prophecy builds up, comforts and admonishes those who hear (see v. 24). This is essentially the purpose of modern-day preaching.

5. Each gift has a legitimate use, but in Corinth there are abuses. Tongues may be used in praise although they are not as useful to the church as prophecy; but both may be used in worship.

6. More essential is the need for proper order so that there may be a meaningful and reverent expression of adoration (v. 40). One might say that there is a problem of noise control. Paul will allow only one person to speak at a time. If someone else wishes to share a message from God, the first person must cease. Furthermore all expressions must be given a meaning. Believers are not to speak in tongues during the worship service unless provision is made for an interpretation which can edify the church.

7–8. Here Paul addresses the meaningless jangle of musical instruments which characterized several ancient religions. Our word 'clamor' comes from the Latin *clamor*, the production of unregulated noise as a cultic exercise. By contrast, any instrument used by the Christians should issue structured notes to produce a meaningful harmony or tune.

the "Amen" to your thanksgiving, since the outsider does not know what you are saying? [17]For you may give thanks well enough, but the other person is not built up. [18]I thank God that I speak in tongues more than all of you; [19]nevertheless, in church I would rather speak five words with my mind, in order to instruct others also, than ten thousand words in a tongue.

[20] Brothers and sisters,[1] do not be children in your thinking; rather, be infants in evil, but in thinking be adults. [21]In the law it is written,

"By people of strange tongues
and by the lips of foreigners
I will speak to this people;
yet even then they will not listen to
me,"

says the Lord. [22]Tongues, then, are a sign not for believers but for unbelievers, while prophecy is not for unbelievers but for believers. [23]If, therefore, the whole church comes together and all speak in tongues, and outsiders or unbelievers enter, will they not say that you are out of your mind? [24]But if all prophesy, an unbeliever or outsider who enters is reproved by all and called to account by all. [25]After the secrets of the unbeliever's heart are disclosed, that person will bow down before God and worship him, declaring, "God is really among you."

Orderly Worship

[26] What should be done then, my friends?[1] When you come together, each one has a hymn, a lesson, a revelation, a tongue, or an interpretation. Let all things be done for building up. [27]If anyone speaks in a tongue, let there be only two or at most three, and each in turn; and let one interpret. [28]But if there is no one to interpret, let them be silent in church and speak to themselves and to God. [29]Let two or three prophets speak, and let the others weigh what is said. [30]If a revelation is made to someone else sitting nearby, let the first person be silent. [31]For you can all prophesy one by one, so that all may learn and all be encouraged. [32]And the spirits of prophets

[1] Gk brothers

---

23. The Greek literally says, 'Will they not say that you are mad?' Religious frenzy, known in antiquity as 'madness', was considered by many pagans to be a great blessing. Indeed, Plato held that the greatest benefits had come to mankind from persons in a state of madness. The famed Delphic sybil was said to be in a state of madness when she made her inspired utterances.

Here is yet another indication of the heathen accretions which still clung to the lives of Corinthian believers. Their behavior could lead observers to the conclusion that they were in a state of pagan frenzy. In particular, women tended to be swept along by this state of madness and were known as 'maenads' or 'mad ones'. One of their distinctives was a wild cry of exultation.

26. Instead Paul asks for an orderly sharing of what each finds meaningful and appropriate.

28. This is the first appeal for silence in this chapter. Two more will follow, one addressed to women. Paul is not asking tongues speakers to be permanently silent but simply to desist until an interpreter may be found.

30. A person prophesying must also be silent in order to give someone else a chance to share. Again the injunction is not permanent but, like the first command, intended to make sure that there is good order and good sense in the service. The decree is quite specific that all may prophesy and all may learn and be encouraged. No one is to be silenced permanently.

32. Here the word for 'be subject' is the same which will be used two verses further down, where it applies to women and has been rendered 'subordinate'. In v. 32, being subject appears to mean responsible behavior toward the congregation: not to speak when another is talking and to behave considerately toward others. *Hupotasso*, the word for 'submission', has many meanings in Greek literature and in the New Testament. Beside the traditional value of 'submit', it can mean to behave accountably toward another person or institution, to identify or associate with someone or something else, to join or unite with another, to relate to another in a meaningful fashion.

are subject to the prophets, [33]for God is a God not of disorder but of peace.

(As in all the churches of the saints, [34]women should be silent in the churches. For they are not permitted to speak, but should be subordinate, as the law also says. [35]If there is anything they desire to know, let them ask their husbands at home. For it is shameful for a woman to speak in church.[m] [36]Or did the word of God originate with you? Or are you the only ones it has reached?)

[37] Anyone who claims to be a prophet, or to have spiritual powers, must acknowledge that what I am writing to you is a command of the Lord. [38]Anyone who does not recognize this is not to be recognized. [39]So, my friends,[n] be eager to prophesy, and do not forbid speaking in tongues; [40]but all things should be done decently and in order.

[m] Other ancient authorities put verses 34-35 after verse 40   [n] Gk *my brothers*

---

34. Vv. 34–35 are missing from one significant New Testament text, and they appear in a number of texts after v. 39. This has led some scholars to wonder if this instruction may not have been a note which was originally placed in the margin and later was incorporated into the text. *Lalein*, the word used in v. 34 for 'speak', is frequently used in this chapter to indicate vocalization rather than the conveying of meaningful language (vv. 2, 4, 6, 9, 11 etc.). Sometimes the term was used to indicate *sound* rather than the *sense* that it conveyed. A nearly contemporary writer, Plutarch remarked that dogs and apes could *lalein* but they could not speak rationally.

The prohibition is not against women's prophesying or praying (see Acts 2:17–18; 21:8–9; 1 Cor 11:2–3; 12:31) but rather must refer to disruptive sorts of utterance which did not edify the congregation by meaningful communication. Paul asks women not to disrupt the service with inappropriate noise. This may be the chattering and gossip of women which to this day characterize the worship of certain orthodox Jewish groups where only men are involved in reading aloud from the Torah and reciting the prayers.

Christian congregations have sometimes experienced a similar problem in societies where women seldom have social contact with other women. Earlier missionaries reported difficulties in controlling women's visiting back and forth when a service was in progress.

35. The invitation to silence may perhaps have grown from disruptions due to women's inquiries as to the meaning of what was going on. Too many questions could prove a very great distraction. Unlettered and untutored women could begin their emancipation by engaging their husbands in dialogue about the significance of the various elements of the service.

Alternatively, the problem may have been the ecstatic cries of women who were still convinced that such behavior was expected of them at religious occasions. A plaque dedicated to the sacred cries of women has been excavated from a ruined temple at Corinth. Ancient texts tell us that these shouts could drown out all meaningful communication, and they would have been unacceptable in an orderly experience of worship.

The reference to the law is probably to the efforts which government authorities made to restrain the religious excesses of women. Both Greek and Roman authors tell us of the debauchery and destructive nature of certain cults of women, and efforts at legislation are documented in both cultures. No Jewish law is known that commands women to be subject.

Sometimes, as in v. 21, 'the law' referred to the Jewish Scriptures in their entirety. Possibly the reference is to three passages from the Psalms that call upon believers to be still and wait upon God: Pss. 37:7; 62:1, 5. The Jewish scholars who translated these texts into Greek did not use a word meaning 'keep silence' but rather *hupotasso*, the word often translated 'submission'. It was this Greek version of the Old Testament, known as the Septuagint, from which Paul usually quoted in his epistles. His words here may be a reminder that true worship demands stillness before the Lord.

40. The purpose of this chapter is to insist on propriety and due reverence in services of worship.

The Resurrection of Christ

15 Now I would remind you, brothers and sisters,° of the good news° that I proclaimed to you, which you in turn received, in which also you stand, ²through which also you are being saved, if you hold firmly to the message that I proclaimed to you – unless you have come to believe in vain.

3 For I handed on to you as of first importance what I in turn had received: that Christ died for our sins in accordance with the scriptures, ⁴and that he was buried, and that he was raised on the third day in accordance with the scriptures, ⁵and that he appeared to Cephas, then to the twelve. ⁶Then he appeared to more than five hundred brothers and sisters° at one time, most of whom are still alive, though some have died.⁹ ⁷Then he appeared to James, then to all the apostles. ⁸Last of all, as to one untimely born, he appeared also to me. ⁹For I am the least of the apostles, unfit to be called an apostle, because I persecuted the church of God. ¹⁰But by the grace of God I am what I am, and his grace toward me has not been in vain. On the contrary, I worked harder than any of them – though it was not I, but the grace of God that is with me. ¹¹Whether then it was I or they, so we proclaim and so you have come to believe.

The Resurrection of the Dead

12 Now if Christ is proclaimed as raised from the dead, how can some of you say there is no resurrection of the dead? ¹³If there is no resurrection of the dead, then Christ has not been raised; ¹⁴and if Christ has not been raised, then our proclamation has been in vain and your faith has been in vain. ¹⁵We are even found to be misrepresenting God, because we testified of God that he raised Christ – whom he did not raise if it is true that the dead are not raised. ¹⁶For if the dead are not raised, then Christ has not been raised. ¹⁷If Christ has not been raised, your faith is futile and you are still in your sins. ¹⁸Then those also who have died⁹ in Christ have perished. ¹⁹If for this life only we have hoped in Christ, we are of all people most to be pitied.

20 But in fact Christ has been raised from the dead, the first fruits of those who have died.⁹ ²¹For since death came through a human being, the resurrection of the dead has also come through a human being; ²²for as all die in Adam, so all will be made alive in

° Gk *brothers*   ᵖ Or *gospel*   ⁹ Gk *fallen asleep*

---

1 CORINTHIANS 15

1. This chapter helps the Corinthians to face their own future in the after-life and guides them as well into an understanding of God's being and purpose after the end of this world as we know it. The dominant theme is that of resurrection.

3–4. Here Paul outlines the essentials of the gospel message: the death, burial and resurrection of Jesus Christ. Of these events women were the main witnesses.

5. Although the story of the risen Christ's encounters with the women are noted by all four Gospels, little is recorded of Christ's appearance to Peter (Luke 24:34). Paul may have felt it more conciliatory to use his testimony when addressing a church where Peter had a considerable following (1 Cor. 1:12).

12. Some in the congregation were maintaining that the dead did not rise. Those who viewed the body as the prison or tomb of the soul had no wish to be incorporated in any kind of body whatsoever.

13. Now begins Paul's defense of a bodily resurrection. Like the book of Galatians, Colossians and many other New Testament portions, it contains a refutation of false teaching and a formulation of truth which we might not otherwise have.

22. Here we see that the responsibility for the original sin is laid at Adam's door as in Rom. 5:12–18. Eve is implicated at 2 Cor. 11:3 and 1 Tim. 2:14.

Christ. ²³But each in his own order: Christ the first fruits, then at his coming those who belong to Christ. ²⁴Then comes the end,ʳ when he hands over the kingdom to God the Father, after he has destroyed every ruler and every authority and power. ²⁵For he must reign until he has put all his enemies under his feet. ²⁶The last enemy to be destroyed is death. ²⁷For "Godˢ has put all things in subjection under his feet." But when it says, "All things are put in subjection," it is plain that this does not include the one who put all things in subjection under him. ²⁸When all things are subjected to him, then the Son himself will also be subjected to the one who put all things in subjection under him, so that God may be all in all.

29 Otherwise, what will those people do who receive baptism on behalf of the dead? If the dead are not raised at all, why are people baptized on their behalf?

30 And why are we putting ourselves in danger every hour? ³¹I die every day! That is as certain, brothers and sisters,ᵗ as my boasting of you – a boast that I make in Christ Jesus our Lord. ³²If with merely human hopes I fought with wild animals at Ephesus, what would I have gained by it? If the dead are not raised,

"Let us eat and drink,
    for tomorrow we die."

³³Do not be deceived:

"Bad company ruins good morals."

³⁴Come to a sober and right mind, and sin no more; for some people have no knowledge of God. I say this to your shame.

The Resurrection Body

35 But someone will ask, "How are the dead raised? With what kind of body do

ʳ Or *Then come the rest*   ˢ Gk *he*   ᵗ Gk *brothers*

27–28. In vv. 27–28, we have a play on words that uses *hupotasso* five times. Its frequency in these two verses alerts us to the possibility that the term is being used in more than one sense. The term may refer to subordination or control but also to integration, alignment, association, accountable behavior, identification, or meaningful relationship.

The passage deals with the ultimate control of the universe, which will be ruled by Christ until every enemy has been placed under his feet, including death. Disintegration will be replaced by unity, and rebellion by resolution, as the Son delivers up to the Father every force and power in the world. All things will be brought in line with the Father's will and purposes.

V. 27 begins with a quotation from Ps. 8:6. Paul makes it clear that 'God has put all things in subjection under his feet' does not mean that God the Father is made subject to Christ. On the other hand, v. 28 suggests that the Son in a certain sense will be made subject (or associated, identified with or integrated) to God the Father. That this does not mean inferiority of person or nature is shown by the future tense of the verb: 'the Son himself will also be subjected to the one who put all things in subjection under him'. If there were inherent inferiority, the present tense would be expected, e.g. 'he is ever subjected to the Father'. The future aspect of Christ's subjection to the Father must rather be viewed in the light of an integrative process in which the world is brought from its sin and disorder into order and harmony. This is effected by the power and distinctive function of the Son, who died and was raised to restore a fallen humanity to God. His mission accomplished, he renders back all to the administrative function of God the Father so that Christ becomes unified with the Father and the triune God recognized by all.

This scenario for the consummation of human history stands in marked contrast to the stories told of father-son relationships among the Greek gods. Zeus was obliged to kill his father, Cronos, who in turn had supplanted and slain his father, Uranos, in order to become ruler of the universe. The last use of *hupotasso* in this text may be understood to indicate Christ does not supplant the Father nor arrogate power to himself. Rather he fully aligns, associates and integrates himself with relation to the other members of the Godhead.

33. The quotation comes from Menander's *Thais*, a comedy about a famous courtesan – an appropriate touch when Paul writes to a city in which prostitutes played so large a role.

they come?" ³⁶Fool! What you sow does not come to life unless it dies. ³⁷And as for what you sow, you do not sow the body that is to be, but a bare seed, perhaps of wheat or of some other grain. ³⁸But God gives it a body as he has chosen, and to each kind of seed its own body. ³⁹Not all flesh is alike, but there is one flesh for human beings, another for animals, another for birds, and another for fish. ⁴⁰There are both heavenly bodies and earthly bodies, but the glory of the heavenly is one thing, and that of the earthly is another. ⁴¹There is one glory of the sun, and another glory of the moon, and another glory of the stars; indeed, star differs from star in glory.

42 So it is with the resurrection of the dead. What is sown is perishable, what is raised is imperishable. ⁴³It is sown in dishonor, it is raised in glory. It is sown in weakness, it is raised in power. ⁴⁴It is sown a physical body, it is raised a spiritual body. If there is a physical body, there is also a spiritual body. ⁴⁵Thus it is written, "The first man, Adam, became a living being"; the last Adam became a life-giving spirit. ⁴⁶But it is not the spiritual that is first, but the physical, and then the spiritual. ⁴⁷The first man was from the earth, a man of dust; the second man isᵘ from heaven. ⁴⁸As was the man of dust, so are those who are of the dust; and as is the man of heaven, so are those who are of heaven. ⁴⁹Just as we have borne the image of the man of dust, we willᵛ also bear the image of the man of heaven.

50 What I am saying, brothers and sisters,ʷ is this: flesh and blood cannot inherit the kingdom of God, nor does the perishable inherit the imperishable. ⁵¹Listen, I will tell you a mystery! We will

not all die,ˣ but we will all be changed, ⁵²in a moment, in the twinkling of an eye, at the last trumpet. For the trumpet will sound, and the dead will be raised imperishable, and we will be changed. ⁵³For this perishable body must put on imperishability, and this mortal body must put on immortality. ⁵⁴When this perishable body puts on imperishability, and this mortal body puts on immortality, then the saying that is written will be fulfilled:

> "Death has been swallowed up in
> victory."
> ⁵⁵ "Where, O death, is your victory?
> Where, O death, is your sting?"

⁵⁶The sting of death is sin, and the power of sin is the law. ⁵⁷But thanks be to God, who gives us the victory through our Lord Jesus Christ.

58 Therefore, my beloved,ʸ be steadfast, immovable, always excelling in the work of the Lord, because you know that in the Lord your labor is not in vain.

The Collection for the Saints

16 Now concerning the collection for the saints: you should follow the directions I gave to the churches of Galatia. ²On the first day of every week, each of you is to put aside and save whatever extra you earn, so that collections need not be taken when I come. ³And when I arrive, I will send any whom you approve with letters to take your gift to Jerusalem. ⁴If it seems advisable that I should go also, they will accompany me.

ᵘ Other ancient authorities add *the Lord*   ᵛ Other ancient authorities read *let us*   ʷ Gk *brothers*   ˣ Gk *fall asleep*   ʸ Gk *beloved brothers*

---

42. Throughout their lives, women have been intimately bound to their bodies in vicissitudes such as menarche, menstruation, premenstrual stress, pregnancy, birthing, lactation, menopause, and osteoporosis. In the life everlasting, we shall not be divested of our bodies but given new ones of spiritual power, made in the likeness of Christ's resurrection body. For women this means eternal significance and heavenly transformation of all that they have known in their earthly bodies. It means too that distinctions between male and female shall be done away in the glory of the resurrection.

Plans for Travel

5 I will visit you after passing through Macedonia – for I intend to pass through Macedonia – [6]and perhaps I will stay with you or even spend the winter, so that you may send me on my way, wherever I go. [7]I do not want to see you now just in passing, for I hope to spend some time with you, if the Lord permits. [8]But I will stay in Ephesus until Pentecost, [9]for a wide door for effective work has opened to me, and there are many adversaries.

10 If Timothy comes, see that he has nothing to fear among you, for he is doing the work of the Lord just as I am; [11]therefore let no one despise him. Send him on his way in peace, so that he may come to me; for I am expecting him with the brothers.

12 Now concerning our brother Apollos, I strongly urged him to visit you with the other brothers, but he was not at all willing[z] to come now. He will come when he has the opportunity.

Final Messages and Greetings

13 Keep alert, stand firm in your faith, be courageous, be strong. [14]Let all that you do be done in love.

15 Now, brothers and sisters,[a] you know that members of the household of Stephanas were the first converts in Achaia, and they have devoted themselves to the service of the saints; [16]I urge you to put yourselves at the service of such people, and of everyone who works and toils with them. [17]I rejoice at the coming of Stephanas and Fortunatus and Achaicus, because they have made up for your absence; [18]for they refreshed my spirit as well as yours. So give recognition to such persons.

19 The churches of Asia send greetings. Aquila and Prisca, together with the church in their house, greet you warmly in the Lord. [20]All the brothers and sisters[a] send greetings. Greet one another with a holy kiss.

21 I, Paul, write this greeting with my own hand. [22]Let anyone be accursed who has no love for the Lord. Our Lord, come![b] [23]The grace of the Lord Jesus be with you. [24]My love be with all of you in Christ Jesus.[c]

[z] Or *it was not at all God's will for him*
[a] Gk *brothers*   [b] Gk *Marana tha*. These Aramaic words can also be read *Maran atha*, meaning *Our Lord has come*   [c] Other ancient authorities add *Amen*

---

1 CORINTHIANS 16

16. The Greek uses here the word *hupotasso*, often rendered 'be subject', but here translated 'put yourselves at the service of' all Paul's fellow-workers. Among these were Priscilla (Rom. 16:3), Euodias and Syntyche (Phil. 4:2–3) and many others mentioned in Rom. 16.

16–17. Here we discover that some of the news brought to Paul had not been only from Chloe's household but also from three other emissaries: Stephanas, Fortunatus and Achaicus. It may have been they who carried the request that Paul comment on various issues (1 Cor. 7:1; 8:1;12:1; 16:1).

19. This reference to Priscilla and Aquila is unusual because here the husband's name stands first. Ordinarily the name of Priscilla stands before that of her husband (Acts 18:18, 26; Rom. 16:3; 2 Tim. 3:19), indicating that she was perhaps more active in the ministry. The interchange-ability of the naming order suggests that they worked well together and that neither dominated the other.

Paul had brought this couple from Corinth to Ephesus to assist him in his missionary labors. Apparently they served as a sort of advance team (Acts 18:18–21; 20:1) in making preparations for his ministry at Ephesus. They have established a church in their home which now joins them in sending back its greetings.

THE SECOND LETTER OF PAUL TO THE CORINTHIANS

INTRODUCTION

When 1 Corinthians was not able to win over the Corinthians, now manipulated by false teachers, Paul followed it (AD 56) with this masterpiece of persuasive, artistic literature. Writing to this business center, refounded as a Roman colony in 44 BC, Paul is not manipulative or motivated by personal gain. He defends his team's style of leadership as an honorable one in order that the Corinthians may not be misled. He fleshes out a cooperative, egalitarian, loving structure for ministry, modeled after Jesus' life of suffering for others. Christ did not teach a hierarchical, worldly-successful, abusive religion.

The letter is a model for dealing with conflict, misunderstandings about money, and distrust. By treating it as a unity, the reader will appreciate the subtlety of Paul's communication. Although Paul often is envisioned as theoretical and abstract, this letter demonstrates that truth and passion and love should coexist. Believers should never give up on reaching others.

Paul defends his team's concepts of leadership by explaining that its members behave sincerely with pure motives in God's grace (1:3–2:17) and their competence comes from God (3:1–5:21) and by warning the Corinthians not to accept God's grace in vain (6:1–9:15) but rather to change or be disciplined (10:1–13:11).

Salutation

1 Paul, an apostle of Christ Jesus by the will of God, and Timothy our brother,

To the church of God that is in Corinth, including all the saints throughout Achaia:

2 Grace to you and peace from God our Father and the Lord Jesus Christ.

Paul's Thanksgiving after Affliction

3 Blessed be the God and Father of our Lord Jesus Christ, the Father of mercies and the God of all consolation, ⁴who consoles us in all our affliction, so that we may be able to console those who are in any affliction with the consolation with which we ourselves are consoled by God. ⁵For just as the sufferings of Christ are abundant for us, so also our consolation is abundant through Christ. ⁶If we are being afflicted, it is for your consolation and salvation; if we are being consoled, it is for your consolation, which you experience when you patiently endure the same sufferings that we are also suffering. ⁷Our hope for you is unshaken; for we know that as you share in our sufferings, so also you share in our consolation.

◆ God's 'Fatherhood' is often confused with maleness. Is God male? Certainly not. God is neither male nor female. God is beyond gender. God is formless Spirit (John 4:24; Col. 1:15; Deut. 4:12–20). This is why we are warned: 'take care and watch yourselves closely, so that you do not act corruptly by making an idol for yourselves, in the form of any figure – the likeness of male or female' (Deut. 4:15–16). The Fatherhood of God has no sexual implications anywhere in Scripture. If God's fatherhood does not mean maleness, then what does it mean? Fatherhood actually describes God's otherness and God's relatedness. 'Father' is shorthand

---

2 CORINTHIANS 1

1. 'Our' – Paul's style was to work along with male and female co-workers. Timothy is included as a representative of Paul's teachings. In 2 Corinthians, 'we' and 'our' often refer to the leadership style of the team (1:3-13; 3:1-18; 5:12; 7:2, 5-6; 10:3-7; 11:12; 13:6).

2. 'Lord' is the most frequent metaphor for Jesus (1:2-3, 14; 2:12; 3:16-18; 4:5, 14; 8:9; 11:31). Like an ancient master, Jesus deserves obedience and submission. Unlike ancient masters, Jesus does not force us to obey or submit, never abuses or mistreats but even serves us (Mark 10:45). In 2 Corinthians Jesus is also described as 'son' (1:19), 'face' (2:10; 4:6), 'image' (3:18; 4:4), 'rich' (8:9), 'poor' (8:9), 'husband' (11:2), and 'strong' (12:9; 13:4).

3. 'Father' is a metaphor for God, principally meaning 'source'. As a human father can be a source for a child, God is the source of mercies. God is 'father' of Jesus in so far as God was instrumental in the human birth of Jesus (Luke 1:35; John 8:42; 10:36) and guided Jesus while on earth (John 8:28; 14:31; 15:15). God is 'father' of Jesus not by physical intercourse nor creation. God has a unique relationship to Jesus (John 1:14; 5:18) and a special loving relationship to all Christians (1:2; 6:18). The Greeks did not have a singular inclusive term for 'parent'.

3–4. God is not impersonal. Humans should never feel alone in their troubles. God is the source of all 'mercies' (deeply felt pity) (Rom. 12:1; Phil. 2:1; James 5:11) and 'consolation'. 'Console' (encourage) means literally to testify on someone's behalf at a trial. God empathizes with humans and acts to vindicate them. God encourages Paul and Timothy in their troubles so that they can encourage the Corinthians in their troubles. 'Consolation' is both vertical (between God and humans) and horizontal (between one human and another).

4–6. The troubles Paul writes about are ones which arise from serving Christ. 'Affliction' (1:4) literally is 'pressure' (Mark 3:9). Christ suffered from unbelievers, so will Christians (Matt. 24:9; John 15:20).

7. If believers are partners in suffering, they will also be partners in consolation. This paragraph has the heart of all the themes Paul will develop in this letter. Ministry is 'sharing', a partnership. A *koinonia* was a financial partnership (Luke 5:10). Here it is also a joint venture in mutual suffering and encouragement (2 Tim. 1:8).

for 'Father of our Lord Jesus Christ'. Father and Son describes a family relationship, a personal relationship. God is the Father of Christ. God is our Father only insofar as we are in Christ.

Our Father-God is neither a wife-beater nor a child-abuser. God is not a tyrant or a dictator. He 'did not withhold his own Son, but gave him up for all of us' (Rom. 8:32). In reality, God became a man and took the role of a servant (Matt. 20:25-28). He humbled himself and poured himself out: 'God himself – the Mighty One of Israel, the heavenly King, the God of the Fathers – sends his Son and heir to be the scapegoat, the Victim. Far from justifying male dominance, this [father/son] symbolism calls it under judgment' (1 Cor. 1:28-29).

The Son did not claim power and lordship over his subjects but 'emptied himself, taking the form of a slave . . . he humbled himself and became obedient to the point of death – even death on a cross' (Phil. 2:7-8). In him 'there is no longer slave or free, there is no longer male and female' (Gal. 3:28). As king he wills to dwell with his people, to 'wipe every tear from their eyes' (Rev. 21:4). These masculine metaphors are liberating, not oppressive. They reveal to us God's true intention for his children – to love, not to wield power.

Masculine language for God and Christ points to a radical shift in the way power is to be understood. Susanne Heine writes, 'A woman could not represent the humiliated because she herself is already where these people are.' Christ, as a man in a patriarchal society, had power. Yet he voluntarily renounced this power. He quite literally turned the patriarchal hierarchy upside down – and put himself at the bottom rather than the top. 'An image of a suffering female would not challenge the powers of this world because she would merely be one more victim.' It was therefore a wonderful gift from God that Christ became a man. God in Christ emptied himself of power in order to overcome the powers of this world.

Human fatherhood is only a dim reflection of divine Fatherhood. Barth explained that 'true and proper fatherhood resides in God, and from this Fatherhood of God what we know as fatherhood among us men is derived'. The Fatherhood of God defines human fatherhood, and not the reverse. 'We do not call God Father because we know what that is; on the contrary, because we know God's Fatherhood we afterwards understand what human fatherhood truly is.' God's definition of Fatherhood is radically different from the human definition. We must be careful not to super-impose our notions of human fatherhood onto God.

There is a great irony in the Fatherhood of God and the Sonship of Christ. The God of the Bible is not a God of 'sexism and patriarchy but the God of the gospel who saves men and women from their sin and liberates them for love, discipleship, and joyous fellowship in the Father, Son and Holy Spirit'. We must attend carefully to the Scriptures in order to understand our God truly. We must allow God to define himself, rather than making God in our own image ◆

8 We do not want you to be unaware, brothers and sisters,[a] of the affliction we experienced in Asia; for we were so utterly, unbearably crushed that we despaired of life itself. [9]Indeed, we felt that we had

[a] Gk *brothers*

---

8. 'Brothers and sisters' – *adelphos* in the plural included men and women. Paul writes to the whole church including Chloe (1 Cor. 1:11). 'Brothers' clearly included women in Acts 16:40 and Phil. 4:1-3.

8-9. Paul describes events in Asia that occurred to him and his co-workers during the time between Acts 18:23-19:40, after 1 Corinthians was written (1 Cor. 16:9). His co-workers in Asia included both men and women: Timothy (2 Cor. 1:1), Silvanus (1:19), Titus (2:13), Priscilla and Aquila (Acts 18:18; 1 Cor. 16:19; Rom. 16:3-4), Erastus (Acts 19:22), Gaius and Aristarchus (Acts 19:29).

received the sentence of death so that we would rely not on ourselves but on God who raises the dead. [10]He who rescued us from so deadly a peril will continue to rescue us; on him we have set our hope that he will rescue us again, [11]as you also join in helping us by your prayers, so that many will give thanks on our[b] behalf for the blessing granted us through the prayers of many.

◆ Paul's second letter to the Corinthians includes his most sustained treatment of his suffering (2 Cor. 1:3–11; 2:14–17; 4:7–12, 16–17; 6:3–10; 11:23–33; 12:7–10). The hardships to which Paul refers in 2 Cor. 1:8–9 included the riot at Ephesus (Acts 19), and the subsequent plot against Paul's life (Acts 20:1–6), from which he safely escaped. Nevertheless, he had been deeply affected emotionally by the experience, as he reminded the Corinthians. He had felt, he told them, great pressure, more than he was able to endure, so that he had despaired of life itself, feeling in his heart 'the sentence of death'. The sense of overwhelming hopelessness and despair that Paul experienced is commonly termed depression.

Rather than seeking to discount the trouble he had endured and his subsequent depression, Paul wanted the Corinthians to have a full understanding of both. Such openness on Paul's part is particularly notable in light of Paul's critics in the Corinthian church who had contemptuously cited Paul's weakness as evidence against the legitimacy of his apostleship. Paul, in response, fully acknowledged his weakness and suffering as a characteristic mark of his apostolic calling (Gal. 6:17; 1 Cor. 2:1–5; 2 Cor. 11:23–29; Phil. 1:30; 2 Tim. 1:11–12; 2:9). He presented this, however, as something about which, unashamed, he could rightly 'boast' (2 Cor. 11:30; 12:10; Phil. 1:12–30).

Paul's boasting, however, was dramatically different than that found in the descriptions of the philosophical heroes of Paul's day. In these descriptions, suffering was viewed as a show-case in which an individual's *personal* virtue could be revealed. In contrast, Paul presented his suffering and weakness as a show-case in which *God* could display *his* sovereign power, and demonstrate the reality of the cross and resurrection of Christ through Paul's life (1 Cor. 2:1–5; 2 Cor. 2:14; 4:11). For Paul, *either* his ability to endure suffering and weakness, *or* God's action of deliverance from it, were an expression of the same divine power revealed in Christ's resurrection (1 Cor. 4:8–13; 2 Cor. 1:3–10; 4:7–12; 6:4–10; Phil. 3:10–11; 2 Tim. 3:10–11).

Paul's vulnerability regarding his emotional response is a practical encouragement to those who suffer from depression. Paul believed that God 'in Christ always leads us in triumphal procession' (2 Cor. 2:14), yet, while believing strongly in God's power and his ultimate triumph, Paul experienced deep depression in which he found himself despairing even of life. Paul's testimony clearly indicates that depression is not an evidence of lack of faith.

Scientific evidence indicates that women experience depression at a rate approximately twice that of men. The reason for this significant gender difference is not fully understood. Some aspects of stereotyped roles to which women have traditionally been assigned (powerlessness and dependency, for example) may

---

[b] Other ancient authorities read *your*

8–10. Paul does *not* say that these troubles come from God. The ministering team does not stoically accept them. They feel 'crushed', despair of life, and feel as though they have received the 'sentence of death'. They feel free to express their feelings, since God can rescue from persecution. **10–11.** God's sovereignty, human action and cooperation all work together. God answers prayer for needs when humans pray for each other and thank God for answering their prayers for others. Believers should be thankful for God's blessings to others, as well as to themselves (1 Cor. 12:26). The church should be a community of suffering, consolation (2 Cor. 1:6–7) and thanksgiving.

contribute to higher rates of depression for women. The high incidence of poverty and the emotional abuse and interpersonal violence frequently experienced by women are probable contributors as well.

'Depression' as a general term is used to describe feelings of grief and deep discouragement evoked by the ordinary but painful events of life such as loss of a job, death of a close friend or family member, or failure to achieve an important goal. This type of depression is temporary; as time passes and circumstances change, the painful feelings fade.

In contrast, clinical depression does not diminish with time or changed circumstances. In order to recover, clinically depressed individuals require the help of a professional counselor, and often require medication. Undiagnosed, untreated clinical depression can lead to dangerous self-medicating use of food, alcohol, or other drugs as the individual seeks to relieve the emotional pain. Clinical depression is often accompanied by suicidal thoughts. Untreated, such thinking can lead an individual to attempt suicide, sometimes with tragically successful results.

Seeking professional help for depression is *not* a spiritual failure. Release from emotional pain enables us to comfort others, Paul reminds us (2 Cor. 1:3-7), with 'the consolation with which we ourselves are consoled by God' ◆

The Postponement of Paul's Visit

12 Indeed, this is our boast, the testimony of our conscience: we have behaved in the world with frankness[c] and godly sincerity, not by earthly wisdom but by the grace of God – and all the more toward you. [13]For we write you nothing other than what you can read and also understand; I hope you will understand until the end – [14]as you have already understood us in part – that on the day of the Lord Jesus we are your boast even as you are our boast.

15 Since I was sure of this, I wanted to come to you first, so that you might have a double favor;[d] [16]I wanted to visit you on my way to Macedonia, and to come back to you from Macedonia and have you send me on to Judea. [17]Was I vacillating when I wanted to do this? Do I make my plans according to ordinary human standards,[e] ready to say "Yes, yes" and "No, no" at the same time? [18]As surely as God is faithful, our word to you has not been "Yes and No." [19]For the Son of God, Jesus Christ, whom we proclaimed among you, Silvanus and Timothy and I, was not "Yes and No"; but in him it is always "Yes." [20]For in him every one of God's promises is a "Yes." For this reason it is through him that we say the "Amen," to the

[c] Other ancient authorities read *holiness*   [d] Other ancient authorities read *pleasure*   [e] Gk *according to the flesh*

---

12. This is the thesis for the letter. The better ancient manuscripts support 'holiness', not 'frankness'. Paul here assumes a tension in his relationship with the Corinthians which becomes explicit later (2 Cor. 6:2; 7:2; 10:1; 11:1; 13:5, 10–11). 'Holiness' and 'sincerity' are a pleonasm, two words with similar meanings to intensify one idea. Paul and his co-workers have pure motives ('sincerity') in their actions. They act within the sphere of God's grace, not in 'earthly wisdom' (1:17; 2:17; 11:20).

13. Paul's sincerity (1:12) is demonstrated by understandable writing and trustable promises (1:15–16).

14. Paul uses variations of 'boast' 28 times in 2 Corinthians. Mutual boasting counterpoints mutual submission (Eph. 5:21). To boast that we have done alone what either another human or God has done with us is wrong (2 Cor. 3:5; 10:13, 15). But 'boasting', if it means truthful 'praising' of another is not a sin. (And self-effacement and false modesty are not the same as genuine humility.)

18, 23. Paul's 'Yes' was to love the Corinthians. He changed his plans so they could prepare for his visit by changing their wrong behavior.

glory of God. [21]But it is God who establishes us with you in Christ and has anointed us, [22]by putting his seal on us and giving us his Spirit in our hearts as a first installment.

23 But I call on God as witness against me: it was to spare you that I did not come again to Corinth. [24]I do not mean to imply that we lord it over your faith; rather, we are workers with you for your joy, because

2 you stand firm in the faith. [1]So I made up my mind not to make you another painful visit. [2]For if I cause you pain, who is there to make me glad but the one whom I have pained? [3]And I wrote as I did, so that when I came, I might not suffer pain from those who should have made me rejoice; for I am confident about all of you, that my joy would be the joy of all of you. [4]For I wrote you out of much distress and anguish of heart and with many tears, not to cause you pain, but to let you know the abundant love that I have for you.

Forgiveness for the Offender

5 But if anyone has caused pain, he has caused it not to me, but to some extent – not to exaggerate it – to all of you. [6]This punishment by the majority is enough for such a person; [7]so now instead you should forgive and console him, so that he may not be overwhelmed by excessive sorrow. [8]So I urge you to re-affirm your love for him. [9]I wrote for this reason: to test you and to know whether you are obedient in everything. [10]Anyone whom you forgive, I also forgive. What I have forgiven, if I have forgiven anything, has been for your sake in the presence of Christ. [11]And we do this so that we may not be outwitted by Satan; for we are not ignorant of his designs.

Paul's Anxiety in Troas

12 When I came to Troas to proclaim the good news of Christ, a door was opened for

---

24. Ministry is not subjugation. Paul, Silvanus and Timothy are 'co-workers' with the Corinthians.

2 CORINTHIANS 2

2–4. Paul demonstrates a balance of compassion (2 Cor. 1:3; 6:11–13; 13:6) and truth (2 Cor. 13:8; John 1:14). Often people today *contrast* love and truth, but genuine love rejoices in truth (1 Cor. 13:6). Genuine love persists and endures with people (1 Cor. 13:4, 7). Here Paul expresses his passions (one characteristic of endurance, 'patient', 1 Cor. 13:4), he is pained when their relationship is ruptured, he wants their love to increase. He cries (silently – *dakruo*) because he must ask the Corinthians to do something they do not want to do. (Christians should be cheering each other up, compassionately exhorting to truth, and gently restoring sinners, Gal. 6:1.)
3–4. The previous letter may be 1 Corinthians, 2 Cor. 10–13, or a lost letter. If 1 Corinthians is the letter 'of tears', then 1 Cor. 16:5–6 describes Paul's future plans and 1 Cor. 5 discusses the same person as does 2 Cor. 2:5–11. Paul refers to one lost letter in 1 Cor. 5:9. Paul probably refers here to another lost letter and a different person because 1 Corinthians does not seem to be a letter of '*much* distress and *anguish* of heart and with *many* tears', and the person in 1 Cor. 5:5 was rightly handed over to Satan but the person in 2 Cor. 2:6–7 was too heavily punished.
7. Christians who sin should be encouraged to be righteous, but also pardoned.
11. Excessive discipline without forgiveness, encouragement, and compassion can lead someone away from the truth.
12. A map is necessary to understand 2 Corinthians. Paul uses a chronological schema and inserts truths about God that these different events taught him. In 1:3–11 Paul speaks of troubles in Asia teaching about comfort and suffering. In 1:15–17 he speaks of his plans to go to Macedonia and the importance of trust and love. In 2:12–13 at Troas, a seaport town in Asia across from Macedonia, he discusses the paradoxes of his life. In 7:5–7 when he crossed the Aegean Sea into Macedonia and found Titus, he writes about joy. In 8:17 Paul begins to envision future travel south to Achaia, and discusses plans for the collection. In 10:2 he envisions his

me in the Lord; ¹³but my mind could not rest because I did not find my brother Titus there. So I said farewell to them and went on to Macedonia.

14 But thanks be to God, who in Christ always leads us in triumphal procession, and through us spreads in every place the fragrance that comes from knowing him. ¹⁵For we are the aroma of Christ to God among those who are being saved and among those who are perishing; ¹⁶to the one a fragrance from death to death, to the other a fragrance from life to life. Who is sufficient for these things? ¹⁷For we are not peddlers of God's word like so many;ᶠ but in Christ we speak as persons of sincerity, as persons sent from God and standing in his presence.

Ministers of the New Covenant

3 Are we beginning to commend ourselves again? Surely we do not

ᶠ Other ancient authorities read *like the others*

---

entrance into Corinth itself. The reasons for the disciplinary action he hesitates to take move to the forefront. Paul relives mentally what has happened or will happen at each locale.

12–13. An 'open door' is an opportunity to preach the good news of Christ. Having an 'open door' should not be the ultimate criteria for life's decisions. Loving our Christian family and encouraging people to mature are more important (3:2). Titus preceded Paul in Macedonia and Achaia to ascertain the Corinthians' spiritual condition (7:7) and to help them prepare their contribution for the Christians in Jerusalem (8:6). Titus was going to join Paul at Troas after visiting the Corinthians.

13. 'Brother' is a common metaphor in the New Testament for the close, loving bonds between Christians. Jesus officially began the Christian family at the cross (John 19:26–27).

14–16. Paul develops the metaphor of a triumphal political parade after a victorious battle. God is the general. Paul's team is the army. Incense-bearers precede the general. Tablets would be carried that listed the spoils and pictured the different battles (2 Cor. 3:1–3). When God is the general, the army always wins, no matter how despairing the way may seem, though in 1 Cor. 4:9–13 Paul and his co-workers feel like the captives.

14–17. Paul's benediction presages the good news about Titus and a good response to Paul's letter (7:6–16).

15. The church here is symbolized as a smell. 'Aroma' (*euodia*) is a sweet, pleasant bouquet. To God we are always an attractive aroma because we represent Christ.

Sanctification, becoming Christ-like, is a process of 'being saved'. Similarly, those who reject Christ are in a process toward total separation from God, 'perishing'. Of course, a decision to be justified or not justified by God precedes both stages (2 Cor. 5:11, 15; Rom. 10:9–10).

16. 'Fragrance' (*osme*), a synonym for 'aroma' (vv. 14, 16), can be either a foul or fragrant smell. In the same way as the incense reminded the captives that they might be killed or be granted life, Christians who live and preach the good news remind others that either they will receive eternal death or eternal life. If Christ's good news is received as good news, it will 'smell' good. If it is rejected, it will 'smell' foul.

17. Christians should measure their effectiveness by whether they have spoken out *God's* message, despite human response. 'Peddlers' were petty retail dealers who would sell by hawking something ('earthly' wisdom, 1:12). In contrast, *Christian* leaders should not manipulate human wills, use God's Word for their own excessive financial benefit, nor adulterate God's teachings to sell the product more. (Genuine teachers have a pure desire to please God by loving those they serve, 2:4, 15, 17.)

2 CORINTHIANS 3

1–3. Paul explains now the reasons for his actions at Troas (2:13). Paul's team wants the people they serve to be their 'letters of recommendation', unlike others who brought literal letters (10:12).

need, as some do, letters of recommendation to you or from you, do we? ²You yourselves are our letter, written on our^g hearts,
to be known and read by all; ³and you show
that you are a letter of Christ, prepared by
us, written not with ink but with the Spirit
of the living God, not on tablets of stone
but on tablets of human hearts.

4 Such is the confidence that we have
through Christ toward God. ⁵Not that we
are competent of ourselves to claim
anything as coming from us; our competence is from God, ⁶who has made
us competent to be ministers of a new
covenant, not of letter but of spirit; for the
letter kills, but the Spirit gives life.

7 Now if the ministry of death, chiseled
in letters on stone tablets,ʰ came in glory so
that the people of Israel could not gaze at
Moses' face because of the glory of his face, a
glory now set aside, ⁸how much more will
the ministry of the Spirit come in glory? ⁹For
if there was glory in the ministry of condemnation, much more does the ministry of
justification abound in glory! ¹⁰Indeed, what
once had glory has lost its glory because of
the greater glory; ¹¹for if what was set aside
came through glory, much more has the
permanent come in glory!

12 Since, then, we have such a hope, we
act with great boldness, ¹³not like Moses,
who put a veil over his face to keep the
people of Israel from gazing at the end of
the glory thatⁱ was being set aside. ¹⁴But
their minds were hardened. Indeed, to this
very day, when they hear the reading of the
old covenant, that same veil is still there,
since only in Christ is it set aside. ¹⁵Indeed,
to this very day whenever Moses is read, a
veil lies over their minds; ¹⁶but when one
turns to the Lord, the veil is removed.
¹⁷Now the Lord is the Spirit, and where the
Spirit of the Lord is, there is freedom. ¹⁸And
all of us, with unveiled faces, seeing the
glory of the Lord as though reflected in a
mirror, are being transformed into the
same image from one degree of glory to
another; for this comes from the Lord, the
Spirit.

ᵍ Other ancient authorities read *your*   ʰ Gk *on
stones*   ⁱ Gk *of what*

2–3. Paul uses an extended metaphor, alluding to triumphal parades (2:14–16) and probably also
to Moses' receiving the Ten Commandments (Exod. 32:15–19). The Corinthians are the tablet,
visible to all, engraved by Christ, carried by Paul and Timothy. Unlike Moses who broke God's
tablets out of exasperation with the sin of the people, God wrote this message on the 'hearts' or
inmost beings of Paul's team. Their affection for the Corinthians is visible to all, genuine, and
long-lasting.

5–6. God, not gender, enables competency for ministry (Matt. 28:1–10).

6. The new covenant brings life and therefore requires *living* letters of recommendation (3:2).

12. The hope is described in 3:8–11. The greater glory of the new covenant is yet to come (cf.
4:7–10). 'Boldness' is action which follows from the principle in 3:7–11. See also 4:1–2. Paul's
team can act with great 'boldness', open and visible to all, without deceit or shame, because the
new covenant is open and visible to all (3:7–11).

13. Moses placed a veil over his face after he finished speaking with the people so they would not
see God's shekinah glory was temporary because then they might have questioned Moses' God-
given authority. Moses' shining face created fear as a spur to worship the one living God rather
than a human-made god (Exod. 34:29–35; 32:1). Similarly, the women at Corinth wore a veil
temporarily so that they could continue in their God-given authority to pray and preach in
public (1 Cor. 11:5, 10).

17. This is the climax to this passage. Paul believes in *one* God, not three.

18. The Greek has unveiled 'face'. The church has one 'face', because Christ has only one 'body'
on earth (11:2; 1 Cor. 12:12; John 17:11).

Transformation into becoming Christ-like is a process. The growing Christian has a continually increasing glory from the Lord, in contrast to Moses' decreasing glory (3:13).

Treasure in Clay Jars

4 Therefore, since it is by God's mercy that we are engaged in this ministry, we do not lose heart. ²We have renounced the shameful things that one hides; we refuse to practice cunning or to falsify God's word; but by the open statement of the truth we commend ourselves to the conscience of everyone in the sight of God. ³And even if our gospel is veiled, it is veiled to those who are perishing. ⁴In their case the god of this world has blinded the minds of the unbelievers, to keep them from seeing the light of the gospel of the glory of Christ, who is the image of God. ⁵For we do not proclaim ourselves; we proclaim Jesus Christ as Lord and ourselves as your slaves for Jesus' sake. ⁶For it is the God who said, "Let light shine out of darkness," who has shone in our hearts to give the light of the knowledge of the glory of God in the face of Jesus Christ.

7 But we have this treasure in clay jars, so that it may be made clear that this extraordinary power belongs to God and does not come from us. ⁸We are afflicted in every way, but not crushed; perplexed, but not driven to despair; ⁹persecuted, but not forsaken; struck down, but not destroyed; ¹⁰always carrying in the body the death of

---

In 1 Cor. 11:5, 13 Paul exhorts women to wear a veil while ministering in order not to offend anyone at Corinth (10:32). The freedom of these women was temporarily curtailed for the sake of weaker believers (1 Cor. 8:11). The essence of the good news is freedom in Christ (2 Cor. 3:17) and removal of veils. In the Old Testament an 'uncovered' face often describes a dishonoring or shaming act (Is. 47:2–3). That is no longer true. As believers gaze into the Lord's face, as into a mirror, they are slowly transformed to look like the Person they behold.

2 CORINTHIANS 4

1–2. The new covenant causes co-workers, like the Lord of the covenant (3:18), not to 'lose heart' ('behave badly'), and no longer do 'shameful things' that must be hidden. No 'alloys' are added to their message. They never use deception even for a worthwhile cause. God is their ultimate audience.

4. The good news is delivered in an honest and clear fashion, but Satan blinds people from seeing Christ's life-giving shekinah glory.

4–5. Christ is the living 'image' or representation of God. Humans must look to Christ to get God's glory and therefore must preach 'Jesus Christ as Lord'. V. 5 is an excellent summary of the style of leadership Paul's team maintains: the Christian's *reflected* glory is neither a *self-generated* glory nor unique only to special people. Leaders are *not* 'people set aside' with a special 'mission'. They are 'slaves' of people. But they are not enslaved by people. They serve people voluntarily, but their ultimate master is Jesus. Jesus is the Lord who sends his servants to take care of a neighbor's problems.

6–7. 4:1–6 describes the great glory of the new covenant, but 4:7–12 brings out that the full glory has not yet come (3:8–11).

A synonym for 'light' recurs four times in v. 6 to accentuate the magnificence of God's presence. However, this treasure is stored in fragile, everyday clay containers. No one can confuse treasure and containers if containers are not themselves treasure (4:5).

7. Ancient Corinth had a potter's quarter one mile west of its center. Often precious treasures would be hidden in cheap containers, unlike during triumphal processions (2:14) where treasures were exhibited for show. The clay containers are defined in 4:8–9, as lives of difficulties arising from external and internal opposition to genuine Christian ministry.

8–10. A 'clear' message may also be a stylistically attractive message. Good oratory does not have to be deceptive. Paul writes here rhythmically and forcefully. Godly power prevents the natural result, but does not prevent the difficulties: trouble need not degenerate into destruction, uncertainty into despair, persecution into abandonment, being hurled down into death.

10. This is the climax of the list of difficulties. 'The death' of Jesus is a synonym for experiencing

Jesus, so that the life of Jesus may also be made visible in our bodies. ¹¹For while we live, we are always being given up to death for Jesus' sake, so that the life of Jesus may be made visible in our mortal flesh. ¹²So death is at work in us, but life in you.

13 But just as we have the same spirit of faith that is in accordance with scripture – "I believed, and so I spoke" – we also believe, and so we speak, ¹⁴because we know that the one who raised the Lord Jesus will raise us also with Jesus, and will bring us with you into his presence. ¹⁵Yes, everything is for your sake, so that grace, as it extends to more and more people, may increase thanksgiving, to the glory of God.

Living by Faith

16 So we do not lose heart. Even though our outer nature is wasting away, our inner nature is being renewed day by day. ¹⁷For this slight momentary affliction is preparing us for an eternal weight of glory beyond all measure, ¹⁸because we look not at what can be seen but at what cannot be seen; for what can be seen is temporary, but what cannot be seen is eternal.

5 For we know that if the earthly tent we live in is destroyed, we have a building from God, a house not made with hands, eternal in the heavens. ²For in this tent we groan, longing to be clothed with our heavenly dwelling – ³if indeed, when we have taken it off¹ we will not be found naked. ⁴For while we are still in this tent, we groan under our burden, because we wish not to be unclothed but to be further clothed, so that what is mortal may be swallowed up by life. ⁵He who has prepared us for this very thing is God, who has given us the Spirit as a guarantee.

◆ Paul and Peter both use the simile of bodily life as dwelling in a tent in contrast to the fixed abode of eternity (cf. 2 Cor. 5:1–4; and 'I know that the putting off of my tent will come soon', 2 Pet. 1, 13–14). The black tents, spun and woven of goat hair by women, were a typical feature of life in Palestine and Asia Minor of the Old and New Testament periods. Sedentary people lived in them in the summer to be

¹ Other ancient authorities read *put it on*

---

difficulties in ministry. When believers suffer, they model after a crucified Messiah (1 Cor. 2:2). Only this road leads to glory (2 Cor. 4:6–9). 'Death', a concept, is personified as a dead person one must carry. 'Always carrying' indicates the process is continual. Paul alludes to Jesus' teaching on taking up a cross daily (Luke 9:23), but here the 'cross' is the carpenter Jesus. The paradox comes when the dead body one carries becomes a living body within our own bodies, a microcosm of Jesus' death and resurrection (2 Cor. 4:14) mirrored in every genuine Christian, and done for others (4:12, 15).

16–18. Paul summarizes 2 Cor. 4 by repeating the same verb used in 4:1 'we do not lose heart'. The 'outer' physical body is another symbol for the difficulties from opposition to genuine Christian ministry (4:8–9). Christians who have to undergo difficulties may not look impressive. The 'inner nature', 'unseen' reward, becoming Christ-like (3:18), which happens 'day by day' lasts eternally.
17. The troubles of 4:8–9 become 'slight' and 'momentary' in light of the future 'eternal weight of glory beyond all measure'.

2 CORINTHIANS 5

1–4. 'Earthly tent' versus 'heavenly dwelling' are metaphors referring to mortality with its difficulties and eternal life and its glory. It may also refer to an individual physical body on earth and a spiritual resurrected body, or a corporate body of Christians on earth and a corporate body of Christians in the new earth. In light of the context on ministry (2 Cor. 4; 5:11) the permanent 'heavenly *dwelling*' most likely refers to eternal life (metaphorically a cloak to 'put on over') which protects Paul's team from all the difficulties they experience in ministry. The Spirit is a down payment guaranteeing their glorious future.

closer to their fields and flocks, and nomads all year round, as both groups still do today. A bedouin expression refers to future children as 'waiting outside the tent'. So the tent provides a well-known basis for metaphor.

The Tabernacle itself was a tent that could be transported about as the Israelites changed locations. In John 1:14, the evangelist builds on the deep-seated memory of God dwelling among the people in a tent just as they did (Exodus story and 2 Sam. 7:1ff.) to express the earliest Semitic (in contrast to the Hellenistic) understanding of the incarnation. Typically obscured in translation by 'dwell' or 'live', the original Greek of this verse says that the Word became flesh and 'lived in a tent' among us. This is an example of Semitic poetic parallelism (saying the same thing twice with different words) in which 'became flesh' is restated in other words, 'pitched his tent' ◆

6 So we are always confident; even though we know that while we are at home in the body we are away from the Lord – [7]for we walk by faith, not by sight. [8]Yes, we do have confidence, and we would rather be away from the body and at home with the Lord. [9]So whether we are at home or away, we make it our aim to please him. [10]For all of us must appear before the judgment seat of Christ, so that each may receive recompense for what has been done in the body, whether good or evil.

The Ministry of Reconciliation

11 Therefore, knowing the fear of the Lord, we try to persuade others; but we ourselves are well known to God, and I hope that we are also well known to your consciences. [12]We are not commending ourselves to you again, but giving you an opportunity to boast about us, so that you may be able to answer those who boast in outward appearance and not in the heart. [13]For if we are beside ourselves, it is for God; if we are in our right mind, it is for you. [14]For the love of Christ urges us on, because we are convinced that one has died for all;

2–4. Some commentators suggest 'being naked' refers to Paul's fear of becoming a spirit or soul apart from the body in an interim state between death and the resurrection. However, in the Bible 'soul' is a living being (Phil. 2:30; Rom. 2:9; 1 Cor. 15:45). Unlike some ancient Greeks who believed the body was evil, Paul looks forward to a heavenly *body* (1 Cor. 15:44). Rather, 'being naked' probably refers to Christians' present mortal state, susceptibility to physical and mental hardships.

9. If Christians are becoming more like Jesus (3:18), they would naturally want to please Jesus.

10. The 'judgment seat' was a raised platform in the agora that is, market place, of many ancient cities. Some judges would carry their own ivory seats to use when making a judicial decision while traveling. No one can avoid Christ's final judgment.

11. Because everyone must be judged by Christ, Paul's team tries to persuade people to please Christ.

12. Boasting in itself is not wrong. When the Corinthians profess publicly their pride in Paul's team, they profess their belief in all for which they stood.

What is 'in the heart' is a synonym for the 'inner nature', 'what cannot be seen', the 'eternal' (4:16, 18). 'Outward appearance' literally is 'face'. The 'face' stands for what can be easily seen but is temporary (e.g. letter of recommendation, 3:1; laws on tablets, 3:7). God, too, is not impressed merely by anyone's 'face' (Acts 10:34; Matt. 22:16).

14–15. Paul has a succinct summary of the good news. Paul's team concluded that Christ represents all people, those being saved and those perishing (2:15). When he died, therefore, every human 'died'. No humans need any longer to die to cleanse themselves from the evil they have done. However, making a decision to accept Christ's action is insufficient in itself. In addition, if humans have 'died' in God's sight, they cannot live to please themselves because then they would be striving to please a dead person. They must live for the living Christ.

therefore all have died. [15]And he died for all, so that those who live might live no longer for themselves, but for him who died and was raised for them.

16 From now on, therefore, we regard no one from a human point of view;[k] even though we once knew Christ from a human point of view,[k] we know him no longer in that way. [17]So if anyone is in Christ, there is a new creation: everything old has passed away; see, everything has become new! [18]All this is from God, who

> ◆ Paul here speaks of the transformation which occurs when individuals repent of their sins and enter into a personal relationship with Jesus Christ. The work of the Holy Spirit causes the believer to be born anew, and a radical transformation takes place. Old things are passed away and new ones take their place.
>
> This second birth is not wholly unlike the first. A midwife who worked for many years in Africa and America wrote, 'There is something very thrilling and exciting about delivering a baby. There was nothing like the feel of the baby's head in my hands during delivery. I could feel new life, and each time I would be deeply moved. As I watched the parents becoming acquainted with their infant, I sometimes felt I was intruding on a very intimate and personal experience and almost felt out of place until I remembered I was part of it. I remember one father, with tears running down his cheeks, saying, "She's just what I wanted." I had helped to make a successful delivery possible, and I revelled in it. I know no other way to describe the feelings I had at the birth of a baby except to say that it was something spiritual and sacred.'
>
> If this is true of the first birth, how much more is it true of the second birth, where God labors over our delivery as a midwife (Is. 66:9). As loving Father, he exclaims 'She's just what I wanted!' ◆

reconciled us to himself through Christ, and has given us the ministry of reconciliation; [19]that is, in Christ God was reconciling the world to himself,[l] not counting their trespasses against them, and entrusting the message of reconciliation to us. [20]So we are ambassadors for Christ, since God is making his appeal through us; we entreat you on behalf of Christ, be reconciled to God. [21]For our sake he made him to be sin who knew no sin, so that in him we might become the righteousness of God.

[k] Gk *according to the flesh*   [l] Or *God was in Christ reconciling the world to himself*

---

16. If the flesh is 'dead' (5:15), then it is no longer a means by which to know anyone. Knowing someone 'according to the flesh' ('a human point of view') means to miss the reflecting glory that is hidden behind a life of difficulties and mortality.

18–19. 'Reconcile' literally referred to changing money and to exchanging one thing for another, such as prisoners. Humans are enemies of God because they violate God's commands, which results in death (Num. 16). God took the initiative, through Christ, to take the place of all persons (also 2 Cor. 5:21). Their sins no longer will be 'counted' or 'credited to their account'. Reconciliation is an ongoing process because not all humans are God's 'friends'.

20. God's action of reconciliation is a model for all genuine Christians. Paul emphasizes *who* sends them out as ambassadors and *who* they ultimately must please: 'we are ambassadors for Christ'. 'We are ambassadors' literally is 'we are elders'. Ancient elders were both judges and representatives defending a community. Paul applies the theory directly to the Corinthians: 'Be reconciled to God by listening to God's ambassadors.'

21. Christ served as a human sin offering (Exod. 29:10–14; Lev. 16:20–22) so that people could become righteous (holy and just) and live for Christ (2 Cor. 5:15).

6 As we work together with him,[m] we urge you also not to accept the grace of God in vain. [2]For he says,

"At an acceptable time I have listened
    to you,
and on a day of salvation I have
    helped you."

See, now is the acceptable time; see, now is the day of salvation! [3]We are putting no obstacle in anyone's way, so that no fault may be found with our ministry, [4]but as servants of God we have commended ourselves in every way: through great endurance, in afflictions, hardships, calamities, [5]beatings, imprisonments, riots, labors, sleepless nights, hunger; [6]by purity, knowledge, patience, kindness, holiness of spirit, genuine love, [7]truthful speech, and the power of God; with the weapons of righteousness for the right hand and for the left; [8]in honor and dishonor, in ill repute and good repute. We are treated as impostors, and yet are true; [9]as unknown, and yet are well known; as dying, and see— we are alive; as punished, and yet not killed; [10]as sorrowful, yet always rejoicing; as poor, yet making many rich; as having nothing, and yet possessing everything.

[11] We have spoken frankly to you Corinthians; our heart is wide open to you. [12]There is no restriction in our affections, but only in yours. [13]In return – I speak as to children – open wide your hearts also.

The Temple of the Living God

[14] Do not be mismatched with unbelievers. For what partnership is there between righteousness and lawlessness? Or what fellowship is there between light and darkness? [15]What agreement does Christ have with Beliar? Or what does a believer share with an unbeliever? [16]What

[m] Gk *As we work together*

---

2 CORINTHIANS 6

2. Word for word quotation of Greek Old Testament (Is. 49:8, LXX). Context in Is. 49:7–11 is the hope and mercy God wants to offer.

3. Paul uses a pleonasm or repetition – literally, 'no obstacle in no-one's way' – to accentuate that his team is not offending anyone.

4. The best commendation is not what others write (3:1), but one's own actions in obedience to God. Paul's team commends itself as leaders who obey God by their morality and endurance of physical and emotional hardships (vv. 4–10).

4–7. Paul repeats 'in' 18 times, as the first word(s) in consecutive phrases (anaphora), to create a rhythm and expectancy. He omits 'and' between all these phrases (asyndeton). He has four groups of phrases, each group is increasingly stressed: general synonyms (v. 4), specific types of troubles (v. 5), positive personal virtues (v. 6). The last four nouns all have adjectives central to 2 Corinthians. The Corinthians thought they had the Holy Spirit (1 Cor. 1:5; 2 Cor. 8:7), but they did not have the genuine love which the Spirit brings. Leadership which is Spirit-based is done in love, truth, and with God's power.

7–10. Paul uses two anaphoras: 'with' three times, 'as' seven times to continue the expectancy.

7. The right hand was used to attack, while the left hand was used for defense. The weapons are described in 6:8–10.

8. 'Good repute' causes 'honor' ('glory'). 'Ill repute' ('slander') causes 'dishonor'.

11. The eloquent list of difficulties (6:4–10) builds up dramatically to this conclusion and exhortation (6:13), rephrasing 6:12.

14. Being mismatched with 'unbelievers' in its context (6:11–13) first has to do with allegiance to wrong leaders (2:17; 11:13–15, 20). But what is true of the church family would also apply to marriage.

15. 'Beliar', 'worthlessness', is a synonym for the Devil or the Antichrist.

16. 'Temple' is singular. It refers to the holy place and holy of holies (Exod. 26:33), not the entire

agreement has the temple of God with idols? For we[n] are the temple of the living God; as God said,

"I will live in them and walk among them,
and I will be their God,
and they shall be my people.
[17] Therefore come out from them,
and be separate from them, says the Lord,
and touch nothing unclean;
then I will welcome you,
[18] and I will be your father,
and you shall be my sons and daughters,
says the Lord Almighty."

7 Since we have these promises, beloved, let us cleanse ourselves from every defilement of body and of spirit, making holiness perfect in the fear of God.

Paul's Joy at the Church's Repentance

2 Make room in your hearts[o] for us; we have wronged no one, we have corrupted no one, we have taken advantage of no one. [3]I do not say this to condemn you, for I said before that you are in our hearts, to die together and to live together. [4]I often boast about you; I have great pride in you; I am filled with consolation; I am overjoyed in all our affliction.

5 For even when we came into Macedonia, our bodies had no rest, but we were afflicted in every way – disputes without and fears within. [6]But God, who consoles the downcast, consoled us by the arrival of Titus, [7]and not only by his coming, but also by the consolation with which he was consoled about you, as he told us of your longing, your mourning, your zeal for me, so that I rejoiced still more. [8]For even if I made you sorry with my letter, I do not regret it (though I did regret it, for I see that I grieved you with that letter, though only briefly). [9]Now I rejoice, not because you were grieved, but because your grief led to repentance; for you felt a godly grief, so that you were not harmed in any way by us. [10]For godly grief produces a repentance that leads to salvation and brings no regret, but worldly grief produces death.

[n] Other ancient authorities read *you*   [o] Gk lacks *in your hearts*

---

building and grounds (John 2:14). 'We' is plural because God's sanctuary, place of dwelling, now is two or three people (Matt. 18:20), not a building (Lev. 16:1–5), not an individual (Eph. 5:15–18).
16–18. Paul refers to at least four Old Testament passages (a practice known as 'pearl stringing'): Lev. 26:11; Ezek. 37:27; Is. 52:11; 2 Sam. 7:14. Most of Paul's Old Testament quotations are in Rom. 1; 2 Corinthians; Gal. 2. 2 Cor. 6:16 is the basis for 6:17.
18. Paul adds 'and daughters' to 2 Sam. 7:14 to highlight the new covenant's inclusion of women (Acts 2:17).

2 CORINTHIANS 7

1. Because Christians have the promise of a personal and special relationship to God (6:16, 18), they need to act to become purified inwardly and outwardly.
1–12. This chapter offers guidelines on conflict resolution: (a) 1–3. Paul loves the Corinthians in the midst of their conflict, even though they have rejected his leadership style. (b) 4. Paul expects the best of those who reject him. (c) 6. Paul works in community. (d) 7. The Corinthians have some positive feelings for Paul. (e) 7. Titus listened to their point of view. Listening, face-to-face, is the best communication when possible. (f) 8–9. Brief pain from direct communication may have to precede improved relationships. Quiet acceptance is not always the most loving act. (g) 9–10. Pain in itself is not the goal, rather a pain which leads to repentance which leads to salvation or deliverance. Inflicting pain for its own sake will be harmful. (h) 12. All restoration of relationships should be done conscious of God's presence.

11 For see what earnestness this godly
grief has produced in you, what eagerness to clear yourselves, what indignation,
what alarm, what longing, what zeal,
what punishment! At every point you
have proved yourselves guiltless in the
matter. 12 So although I wrote to you, it
was not on account of the one who did
the wrong, nor on account of the one
who was wronged, but in order that
your zeal for us might be made known
to you before God. 13 In this we find comfort.

In addition to our own consolation, we
rejoiced still more at the joy of Titus,
because his mind has been set at rest by
all of you. 14 For if I have been somewhat
boastful about you to him, I was not
disgraced; but just as everything we said to
you was true, so our boasting to Titus has
proved true as well. 15 And his heart goes out
all the more to you, as he remembers the
obedience of all of you, and how you
welcomed him with fear and trembling. 16 I
rejoice, because I have complete confidence in you.

Encouragement to Be Generous

8 We want you to know, brothers and
sisters,[p] about the grace of God that
has been granted to the churches of
Macedonia; 2 for during a severe ordeal of
affliction, their abundant joy and their
extreme poverty have overflowed in a
wealth of generosity on their part. 3 For, as I
can testify, they voluntarily gave according
to their means, and even beyond their
means, 4 begging us earnestly for the privilege[q] of sharing in this ministry to the
saints – 5 and this, not merely as we expected; they gave themselves first to the
Lord and, by the will of God, to us, 6 so that
we might urge Titus that, as he had already
made a beginning, so he should also
complete this generous undertaking[r]
among you. 7 Now as you excel in everything – in faith, in speech, in knowledge, in
utmost eagerness, and in our love for you[s] –
so we want you to excel also in this
generous undertaking.[r]

[p] Gk *brothers* [q] Gk *grace* [r] Gk *this grace*
[s] Other ancient authorities read *your love for us*

---

11. Because the Corinthians disciplined this unknown person (2:4), Paul is encouraged to ask directly for their financial contribution (2 Cor. 8–9) and their loyalty (2 Cor. 10–13).
13, 15. Titus' 'mind' literally is 'spirit', which 'has been set at rest'. Titus' 'heart' literally is 'intestines', or 'gut-level feelings'. Genuine leadership involves the whole person.

2 CORINTHIANS 8

1. The churches are collecting gifts for the poor Christians in Jerusalem who were in need (1 Cor. 16:1–3; 2 Cor. 8:14–15; 9:12; Rom. 15:25–28; Gal. 2:10; Acts 6:1–3; 24:17). It does *not* refer to Acts 11:28 because Nero was now reigning over the Roman Empire (AD 54–68). This generous Macedonian church had many able women leaders.
8:1–9:15. The Corinthians should give because of: (a) the example of the Macedonian Christians who gave although poor (8:1–6); (b) the demonstration of the Corinthians' love (8:7–8, 24); (c) the example of Jesus who gave up all riches (8:9); (d) the need to fulfill their promises (8:10–11; 9:1–5), since God wants equality of benefits (8:12–15); (e) the reliability of the people who will pick up and transport the gift (8:16–23); (f) the benefits to themselves, the whole church, and God (9:6–15).
8:2. Not everyone at Philippi was necessarily poor. Lydia of Thyatira, a dealer in purple cloth, was probably well-to-do (Acts 16:15, 40). The Romans did not allow trading between the regions of Macedonia and kept the profit from the gold and silver mines and the timber, thereby causing economic distress.
7. Paul compliments before he exhorts. The Corinthians should have a balance of word ('speech', 'knowledge') and deed ('generous' giving).

8 I do not say this as a command, but I am testing the genuineness of your love against the earnestness of others. ⁹For you know the generous act[t] of our Lord Jesus Christ, that though he was rich, yet for your sakes he became poor, so that by his poverty you might become rich. ¹⁰And in this matter I am giving my advice: it is appropriate for you who began last year not only to do something but even to desire to do something – ¹¹now finish doing it, so that your eagerness may be matched by completing it according to your means. ¹²For if the eagerness is there, the gift is acceptable according to what one has – not according to what one does not have. ¹³I do not mean that there should be relief for others and pressure on you, but it is a question of a fair balance between ¹⁴your present abundance and their need, so that their abundance may be for your need, in order that there may be a fair balance. ¹⁵As it is written,

"The one who had much did not have too much,
and the one who had little did not have too little."

Commendation of Titus

16 But thanks be to God who put in the heart of Titus the same eagerness for you that I myself have. ¹⁷For he not only accepted our appeal, but since he is more eager than ever, he is going to you of his own accord. ¹⁸With him we are sending the brother who is famous among all the churches for his proclaiming the good news;[u] ¹⁹and not only that, but he has also been appointed by the churches to travel with us while we are administering this generous undertaking[v] for the glory of the Lord himself[w] and to show our goodwill. ²⁰We intend that no one should blame us about this generous gift that we are administering, ²¹for we intend to do what is right not only in the Lord's sight but also in the sight of others. ²²And with them we are sending our brother whom we have often tested and found eager in many matters, but who is now more eager than ever because of his great confidence in you. ²³As for Titus, he is my partner and co-worker in

[t] Gk the grace   [u] Or the gospel   [v] Gk this grace
[w] Other ancient authorities lack himself

---

8. Genuine Christianity does not force people to give, but it does exhort people to be consistent.
9. This sentence contains a microcosm of the whole letter. The graciousness or generosity of Jesus is defined by the whole sentence. Jesus went beyond fulfillment of obligations.
10. Because of this data, we know 1 Corinthians was written about one year before 2 Corinthians.
10–11. Paul gives two guidelines on how to give: plan and organize giving and fulfill promises.
12–15. The proportion of giving depends on one's own resources. The goal is 'a fair balance' or 'equality' of benefits. The goal is not paternalistic, for one always to give, another to receive. The parallel sentence structure (v. 15) mirrors the concept of 'fair balance'. Even in the Old Testament, more than 10% of the harvest was given away: the first tithe was given to Levi's tribe (Deut. 18:4–5; 26:1–11; Num. 18:21–32; Mal. 3:8); the second tithe was eaten with Levites, strangers, orphans, and widows (Deut. 14:22–29; 26:12–15); produce not picked at the first harvest was left for foreigners, orphans, and widows (Deut. 24:19–22; Ruth 2:2–12), and offerings were made for other special events (e.g. Lev. 12:6–8).
18. Some early Christians thought this brother was 'Luke', and the 'good news' was the Gospel of Luke (Tertullian, Origen, Jerome).
23. A 'co-worker' is a 'colleague'. The term signifies the equality of Christian workers (2 Cor. 1:24; 1 Cor. 3:5–9). People are subject to them out of love (1 Cor. 16:15–18). Timothy is called a 'co-worker', as were several women, Euodia, Syntyche, and Prisca (Rom. 16:3, 21; Phil. 4:2–3). Stephana, another co-worker, could be female or male (1 Cor. 16:15). These co-workers had different spiritual gifts for equipping Christians for ministry (Eph. 4:11–12). Titus seems to be a gifted organizer. He was helping to set up this collection and he would make sure elders were appointed at Crete (Titus 1:5; 3:12–13). He was 'urged', not sent to go to Corinth (2 Cor. 8:17; 12:18).

your service; as for our brothers, they are messengers[x] of the churches, the glory of Christ. [24]Therefore openly before the churches, show them the proof of your love and of our reason for boasting about you.

The Collection for Christians at Jerusalem

9 Now it is not necessary for me to write you about the ministry to the saints, [2]for I know your eagerness, which is the subject of my boasting about you to the people of Macedonia, saying that Achaia has been ready since last year; and your zeal has stirred up most of them. [3]But I am sending the brothers in order that our boasting about you may not prove to have been empty in this case, so that you may be ready, as I said you would be; [4]otherwise, if some

Macedonians come with me and find that you are not ready, we would be humiliated – to say nothing of you – in this undertaking.[y] [5]So I thought it necessary to urge the brothers to go on ahead to you, and arrange in advance for this bountiful gift that you have promised, so that it may be ready as a voluntary gift and not as an extortion.

[6] The point is this: the one who sows sparingly will also reap sparingly, and the one who sows bountifully will also reap bountifully. [7]Each of you must give as you have made up your mind, not reluctantly or under compulsion, for God loves a cheerful giver. [8]And God is able to provide you with

[x] Gk *apostles*   [y] Other ancient authorities add *of boasting*

The Jews had 'apostles' who would be sent by the rulers of a city to collect tribute for the Temple at Jerusalem. These 'apostles' or 'messengers' ('angels') were sent by the churches to deliver gifts (Phil. 2:25; 1 Cor. 11:10; 16:3), whereas Jesus' 'apostles' were sent to report his life and resurrection (Acts 1:21–22; 9:15–16; Matt. 28:7; Rom. 16:7; 2 Cor. 1:1).

24. Refusal to give in this case would signify a rejection of Paul, Paul's gospel, partnership with the other churches for the body of Christ and an acceptance of rival apostate apostles.

2 CORINTHIANS 9

1. Giving is a 'ministry' (9:1, 12–13), 'blessing' ('bountiful gift', 9:5), 'grace' ('blessing', 9:8), and 'partnership' ('sharing', 9:13).

2. The Corinthians express eagerness and zealousness, but they do not always keep their promises (8:10–11).

2–4. The use of various tenses here suggests that Paul writes 2 Corinthians in Macedonia and sends it before he leaves for Achaia (Acts 20:1–2). (His boasting is in the present tense, the possibility of the Macedonian Christians coming with him in the subjunctive, the mood of possibility, the giving of the Macedonian Christians in the past tense, 2 Cor. 8:15.)

5. Paul's co-workers precede him to prepare the Corinthians.

6. This sentence is almost perfectly parallel. The style reflects the content. The way one acts towards others rebounds to oneself. The gift is 'bountiful' (9:5), the harvest is 'bountiful' (9:6).

7. These givers are 'cheerful' since they trust in God, expect good things, fulfill their promises, and are not forced to give (9:5–6, 8, 10).

8. Christians do need, however, to evaluate what is a '*good* work' or worthwhile cause to which to give.

8, 10–11. The benefits of giving are both material ('seed') and spiritual ('righteousness', 9:10). 'Enough' was a Stoic virtue of self-reliance, supporting oneself without help from others. Paul accentuates 'enough' by repeating 'always', 'everything', and 'in all' (9:8). However, God gives material benefits so that Christians can give *more* to others (9:8), become more righteous, and thank God, be they messengers (9:11), receivers (9:12), or givers (9:15). Nevertheless, lack of wealth is *not* a sign of less spirituality (8:1–2), nor is presence of wealth a sign of more spirituality (8:14).

'Enough' is a relative term. God promises the basic necessities to those who seek God's reign first (Luke 12:22–24, 27–28).

every blessing in abundance, so that by always having enough of everything, you may share abundantly in every good work. ⁹As it is written,

"He scatters abroad, he gives to the poor;

his righteousness^z endures forever."

¹⁰He who supplies seed to the sower and bread for food will supply and multiply your seed for sowing and increase the harvest of your righteousness.^z ¹¹You will be enriched in every way for your great generosity, which will produce thanksgiving to God through us; ¹²for the rendering of this ministry not only supplies the needs of the saints but also overflows with many thanksgivings to God. ¹³Through the testing of this ministry you glorify God by your obedience to the confession of the gospel of Christ and by the generosity of your sharing with them and with all others, ¹⁴while they long for you and pray for you because of the surpassing grace of God that he has given

◆ Here the Greek word *hupotage*, ordinarily translated 'submission' when applied to women, occurs in the phrase given in the NRSV as 'obedience to the confession'. The word is best understood as implying commitment or adherence to the confession which the Corinthians had already made. They were willing to follow through with their lives what they had already proclaimed with their mouths ◆

you. ¹⁵Thanks be to God for his indescribable gift!

Paul Defends His Ministry

10 I myself, Paul, appeal to you by the meekness and gentleness of Christ – I who am humble when face to face with you, but bold toward you when I am away! – ²I ask that when I am present I

^z Or *benevolence*

9. In Ps. 112:1, 9 'those who fear the Lord' distribute alms.
13. Giving is a 'confession' that one trusts God because God is 'able' (9:8) and ultimately the source for all material benefits (9:10).

2 CORINTHIANS 10

1. Paul directly refers to the Corinthians' accusations: his actions in person and his words by letter were inconsistent, his letters were impressive but not his speech (10:10–11), the team lived by 'human standards' (10:2), not according to Christ (10:7). These accusations have been more implicit in 1 Cor. 4:3; 9:1–3, 6; 2 Cor. 1:12–14, 17–18, 23–24; 2:5–9, 17; 3:1–2, 5–6; 4:2–7, 18; 5:11–12, 16; 6:1–3, 11–14; 7:2; 8:7–8, 10–14, 24; 9:3–5.

Paul's tone becomes abrupt at 10:1 because now he directly confronts his opponents. He is filled with righteous anger as he writes about so-called believers who have been undermining his entire ministry. That same tone change can be found in Rom. 16:17; 1 Cor. 16:22; Gal. 6:12; Phil. 3:2.

Paul highlights *who* makes this appeal: 'Myself, I, Paul, I appeal.' Paul is the Corinthians' spiritual parent: Acts 18:1–5; 1 Cor. 4:15; 2 Cor. 11:2; 12:14. Paul appeals, does not command, figuratively, standing between Christ's 'meekness' and 'gentleness', the overflow of a loving spirit. He does not appeal on the basis of God's justice because God's justice has been met by Christ (2 Cor. 5:21), and the Corinthians need to appreciate God's compassion (2 Cor. 1:3).

Throughout this letter, Paul reinterprets the slander of his critics as compliments. They accuse Paul of being 'humble' when face to face. Jesus too is gentle and 'humble' or 'lowly' (Matt. 11:29; Is. 53:8, LXX; Phil. 2:8). Christians also should be 'lowly' (Matt. 18:4; Luke 1:48).
2–3. Paul keeps the critics' noun 'flesh' ('human standards', 10:2) but develops a play on words: 'in flesh walking not according to flesh fighting' (10:3). Matter or flesh is not evil or unreal. However, he and his co-workers do not 'wage war' or organize their lives and ministry according to the rules of a sinful world.

need not show boldness by daring to oppose those who think we are acting according to human standards.[a] [3]Indeed, we live as human beings,[b] but we do not wage war according to human standards;[a] [4]for the weapons of our warfare are not merely human,[c] but they have divine power to destroy strongholds. We destroy arguments [5]and every proud obstacle raised up against the knowledge of God, and we take every thought captive to obey Christ. [6]We are ready to punish every disobedience when your obedience is complete.

[7] Look at what is before your eyes. If you are confident that you belong to Christ, remind yourself of this, that just as you belong to Christ, so also do we. [8]Now, even if I boast a little too much of our authority, which the Lord gave for building you up and not for tearing you down, I will not be ashamed of it. [9]I do not want to seem as though I am trying to frighten you with my letters. [10]For they say, "His letters are weighty and strong, but his bodily presence is weak, and his speech contemptible." [11]Let such people understand that what we say by letter when absent, we will also do when present.

[12] We do not dare to classify or compare ourselves with some of those who commend themselves. But when they measure themselves by one another, and compare themselves with one another, they do not show good sense. [13]We, however, will not boast beyond limits, but will keep within the field that God has assigned to us, to reach out even as far as you. [14]For we were not overstepping our limits when we reached you; we were the first to come all the way to you with the good news[d] of Christ. [15]We do not boast beyond limits, that is, in the labors of others; but our hope is that, as your faith increases, our sphere of action among you may be greatly enlarged, [16]so that we may proclaim the good news[d] in lands beyond you, without boasting of work already done in someone else's sphere of action. [17]"Let the one who boasts, boast in the

[a] Gk according to the flesh   [b] Gk in the flesh   [c] Gk fleshly   [d] Or the gospel

---

4–6. Corinth was a Roman colony and the residence of the proconsul (Acts 18:12). To a city overrun with military personnel, Paul develops a military image for his team's leadership style. Challenging the false arguments of his opponents and defeating those who reject God's dominion are two 'fortresses'. An 'obstacle' literally is a 'height' or 'stronghold'. Paul may have had in mind the Acrocorinth, the fortified mountain that loomed 1,886 feet over ancient Corinth. Their 'captives' or prisoners are thoughts. Christ is the rightful ruler.

8. The purpose of authority is to 'build' people up. This is a different word from 'have authority' in 1 Tim. 2:12. Women (and men) are not to have a destructive power.

10. The Corinthians liked Paul's letters. 'Weighty' might refer to Paul's commands stated authoritatively or to an impressive and effective writing style. Paul consciously chose to have an unrhetorical speaking style (1 Cor. 2:1–5). He may also have been unimpressive physically (short? 2 Cor. 10:1). Apollos may have unintentionally attracted some Corinthians by his oratorical style (Acts 18:24; 1 Cor. 1:12; 16:12).

12–16. Corinth was a business center. The ports at Lechaum and Cenchreae (Rom. 16:1) produced duties and commerce. Crafts such as pottery and bronze products were world famous. The biannual Isthmian games and surrounding immorality both resulted in much money (2 Cor. 8:14; 1 Cor. 5:1). Sophists, too, would be paid to dazzle people with their oratory. Paul uses business imagery and measurement. 'Field' (10:13) and 'sphere' (10:15–16) refer to the same Greek word, 'canon'. A canon was a straight rod or bar that kept something straight. For masons it was a line by which the tiles were placed. Christians will become 'crooked' if they seek to be approved by those people who commend themselves. Paul uses the metaphor of measuring space as a springboard to discuss people who were apportioning 'fields', work done by others, as their own.

Lord." ¹⁸For it is not those who commend themselves that are approved, but those whom the Lord commends.

Paul and the False Apostles

11 I wish you would bear with me in a little foolishness. Do bear with me! ²I feel a divine jealousy for you, for I promised you in marriage to one husband, to present you as a chaste virgin to Christ. ³But I am afraid that as the serpent deceived Eve by its cunning, your thoughts will be led astray from a sincere and pure^e devotion to Christ. ⁴For if someone comes and proclaims another Jesus than the one we proclaimed, or if you receive a different spirit from the one you received, or a different gospel from the one you accepted, you submit to it readily enough. ⁵I think that I am not in the least inferior to these super-apostles. ⁶I may be untrained in speech, but not in knowledge; certainly in every way and in all things we have made this evident to you.

7 Did I commit a sin by humbling myself so that you might be exalted,

^e Other ancient authorities lack *and pure*

---

18. Rather than follow people who commend themselves, people need to ask: 'who is commended by God?' and 'Will my actions please God?' Following human examples is good as long as they also follow God's standards (1 Cor. 4:16–17; Phil. 3:17).

2 CORINTHIANS 11

1, 4. The Corinthians would not 'bear' with Paul's defense (11:1), but they would 'bear' with ('submit to', 'put up with') false teachers (11:4, 19–20).

2. In ancient times, a father would arrange a marriage and give the daughter to the groom. After the engagement the bride and groom would save their funds for their marriage. Sexual purity was expected. All the Corinthian believers make up one entity, a virgin. The church as a bride is only one of many images Paul uses: 'aroma', 'fragrance' (2:14–16), 'letter' (3:2–3), 'sanctuary' (6:16), and 'face' (3:18; 8:24). Paul also uses masculine imagery for the church (Eph. 4:13).

3. Deception is a major way the Corinthians are being misled. The 'cunning' serpent's conversation with Eve is an archetypal example of deception as a means to mislead. The Corinthians have not yet been misled: they '*may be* led astray'. They stand like Eve, admiring the tree of the knowledge of good and evil (Gen. 2:9; 3:6). Desire for knowledge is a temptation to the Corinthians (1 Cor. 1:5; 8:1, 11; 2 Cor. 8:7).

Paul uses the same analogy for the church at Ephesus which also was being misled by false knowledge from false teachers (1 Tim. 1:7; 2:14). At Corinth the whole church was affected. At Ephesus ignorant women were especially susceptible.

4. Paul does not explicitly state the heretical teachings of the 'super-apostles'. They emphasized their Jewish background (11:18,22), but did *not* emphasize sharing Christ's sufferings (11:23–33; 13:4). They were deceitful (11:4, 13–15). Probably they were some kind of Jewish legalists similar to Paul's other opponents (2 Cor. 3:3, 7, 12, 17; 4:2; 10:5; Phil. 3:2–6, 9; Gal. 1:6–7; 2:4, 12–13; 5:1–6, 11–13; Rom. 16:17–18; Acts 11:1–3; 15:1–5; 21:20–21).

5. Paul first directly mentions his opponents. 'Super-apostles' is ironic. The real meaning is opposite the literal meaning, 'inferior-apostles'. 'Super' literally is 'beyond, exceedingly', 'beyond measure'. His view of them is directly expressed in 11:13.

6. 'Untrained' in speech refers to lay people without advanced rhetorical knowledge, probably in contrast to professional orators or sophists. Oratory was one of the most popular forms of entertainment, rivaling the theater. In contrast to philosophic rhetoric which sought to discover truth, sophists used artificial rhythms, exotic words, novel figures of speech, quotable sentences, accompanied by music, to attract wealthy students.

7. Jesus taught that the laborer is worthy of wages (Matt. 10:10). However, since the Corinthians thought that being paid was a necessary sign of apostleship and yet were suspicious of being robbed (1 Cor. 9:2–6; 2 Cor. 2:17; 11:12; 12:12–18), Paul chose to take his salary from the

because I proclaimed God's good news[f] to you free of charge? [8]I robbed other churches by accepting support from them in order to serve you. [9]And when I was with you and was in need, I did not burden anyone, for my needs were supplied by the friends[g] who came from Macedonia. So I refrained and will continue to refrain from burdening you in any way. [10]As the truth of Christ is in me, this boast of mine will not be silenced in the regions of Achaia. [11]And why? Because I do not love you? God knows I do!

[12] And what I do I will also continue to do, in order to deny an opportunity to those who want an opportunity to be recognized as our equals in what they boast about. [13]For such boasters are false apostles, deceitful workers, disguising themselves as apostles of Christ. [14]And no wonder! Even Satan disguises himself as an angel of light. [15]So it is not strange if his ministers also disguise themselves as ministers of righteousness. Their end will match their deeds.

Paul's Sufferings as an Apostle

[16] I repeat, let no one think that I am a fool; but if you do, then accept me as a fool, so that I too may boast a little. [17]What I am saying in regard to this boastful confidence, I am saying not with the Lord's authority, but as a fool; [18]since many boast according to human standards,[h] I will also boast. [19]For you gladly put up with fools, being wise yourselves! [20]For you put up with it when someone makes slaves of you, or preys upon you, or takes advantage of you, or puts on airs, or gives you a slap in

[f] Gk the gospel of God   [g] Gk brothers   [h] Gk according to the flesh

---

churches at Macedonia who had a healthy view of money (2 Cor. 11:8–9; Phil. 1:5; 4:10–18; Acts 18:5). The 'super-apostles' did receive money as proof of their apostleship (2 Cor. 11:12).

9. These 'friends' ('brothers') included women (Acts 16:13–15, 40; Phil. 4:2–3).

12, 18. Paul's opponents boast about their salary (11:7–11), comfort, style of leadership (11:20), pure Jewish background (11:22), and false accomplishments (10:13–15).

13. To 'disguise' is to change the outward form perceptible to the senses. The inward form though remains the same. People need to become discerning. Not everyone who claims to tell God's truth or who looks or sounds attractive is truthful.

14–15. Satan, not Jesus (1:3–5; 8:9; 13:4) is the super-apostles' model.

16–17. Paul's 'boasting' and 'foolish' words are irony (11:18; 12:6). The opponents falsely boast (11:12). What Paul really says is that only fools boast and the Corinthians only listen to fools who boast a lot (11:1, 19). Therefore, Paul claims he must pretend to be foolish and boastful to be heard by them. But he will not boast 'according to the flesh' (1:17; 10:2–3; 11:18). Paul uses indirect communication because the Corinthians are not open to listening to him. In contrast, with the ignorant he directly commands education (1 Tim. 1:7; 2:11). Paul 'boasts' about difficulties (2 Cor. 11:23–33; 12:9–10) which would *not* impress the super-apostles. Paul's real goal is not to impress but to teach them about authentic Christian leadership (Luke 9:23). 'Boasting' of one's own accomplishments is impossible if it is God who sustains one in difficulties (2 Cor. 4:7; 12:9–10).

19. The Corinthians define themselves as 'wise' (1 Cor. 4:10). Paul adopts that self-description but demonstrates what their 'wisdom' looks like (2 Cor. 11:20).

20. Paul describes difficulties they inflict on others, *not* that opponents endure. The 'super-apostles' were autocratic, impressive-looking, and skillful speakers (11:6): personality leaders who spiritually, economically, and physically abused their followers. Literally, 'prey' is 'eat up', 'take advantage' is to catch unawares as in fishing or hunting. These metaphors denote activities which destroy the recipient's life. Slapping probably is literal. The super-apostles, like the high priest, thought they had the right to slap people (Acts 23:1–5). The Greek has no conjunctions ('or') joining clauses (asyndeton), making Paul's list impassioned, hurried, and inexhaustible. The final clause is the longest and most concrete because it is most outrageous.

the face. [21]To my shame, I must say, we were too weak for that!

But whatever anyone dares to boast of – I am speaking as a fool – I also dare to boast of that. [22]Are they Hebrews? So am I. Are they Israelites? So am I. Are they descendants of Abraham? So am I. [23]Are they ministers of Christ? I am talking like a madman – I am a better one: with far greater labors, far more imprisonments, with countless floggings, and often near death. [24]Five times I have received from the Jews the forty lashes minus one. [25]Three times I was beaten with rods. Once I received a stoning. Three times I was shipwrecked; for a night and a day I was adrift at sea; [26]on frequent journeys, in danger from rivers, danger from bandits, danger from my own people, danger from Gentiles, danger in the city, danger in the wilderness, danger at sea, danger from false brothers and sisters;[i] [27]in toil and hardship, through many a sleepless night, hungry and thirsty, often without food, cold and naked. [28]And, besides other things, I am under daily pressure because of my anxiety for all the churches. [29]Who is weak, and I am not weak? Who is made to stumble, and I am not indignant?

30 If I must boast, I will boast of the things that show my weakness. [31]The God and Father of the Lord Jesus (blessed be he forever!) knows that I do not lie. [32]In Damascus, the governor[j] under King Aretas guarded the city of Damascus in order to[k] seize me, [33]but I was let down

[i] Gk brothers   [j] Gk ethnarch   [k] Other ancient authorities read and wanted to

---

21. 'Weak' here is ironic. Helping people mature looks like 'weakness' compared to the super-apostles' 'strength' (11:20). Paul has used the slander 'weak' (10:10) and begins to redefine it.
22. These synonyms may have subtle nuances: 'Hebrew' may refer to being fluent in Hebrew, 'Israelite' to religious training, and 'descendant of Abraham' to race. Paul, too, impressed the crowd by speaking Hebrew (Acts 22:2).
22–23. The sentences are parallel (11:22) until 'ministers of Christ' (11:23), because as ministers of Christ they are not parallel.
23. Paul appears to be 'mad' to the Corinthians' mental immaturity. 'Countless' and 'better' have the same prefix as 'super-apostles' (11:5). The super-apostles had 'super' comfort while Paul had 'super' difficulties.
23–28. In Greek it is one sentence illustrating what genuine 'ministers of Christ' act like. Paul uses asyndeton (no conjunctions) vividly to impress the details on the reader. He also uses anaphora, repeating 'with' (literally 'in') eight times (2 Cor. 11:23, 27), 'danger' eight times (11:26–27), creating a marked rhythm.
24. 40 lashes were considered tantamount to death. For this reason, Jewish Law prescribed that one less lash should be administered.
26. Ancients would often travel in large groups as protection against robbers (Acts 20:4; Luke 23:19).
27. 'Toil and hardship', a pleonasm, two synonyms joined by 'and', summarize Paul's whole list.
29. The first 'weak' probably refers to someone who is tempted to 'stumble' or sin. The second 'weak' probably refers to being 'indignant', having empathy with the person made to sin and outrage at the person who caused the temptation (Luke 17:2–3).
30. Paul here completely embraces being 'weak' (10:10) as a virtue. 'Weakness' does not refer to moral, physical, or mental deficiencies or sins (Exod. 4:10–12; Luke 18:9–14), but rather to physical and mental discomforts for Christ's sake from persecution, a strenuous life, and concern for people's spiritual and physical well-being (11:23–33; 12:9–10). In the gospels 'weakness' (literally 'not strong') often refers to 'sickness' (Luke 5:15). Of the 45 times Paul uses a derivative of 'weak', 30 times it occurs in the two letters to the Corinthians (15 times in 2 Corinthians).
32. Aretas IV was king of Nabataean Arabia 9 BC–AD 40.
    Paul did not suffer when he could avoid it (Acts 17:10; 22:25; 23:17; Phil. 4:11–13).

in a basket through a window in the wall,[1] and escaped from his hands.

Paul's Visions and Revelations

12 It is necessary to boast; nothing is to be gained by it, but I will go on to visions and revelations of the Lord. [2]I know a person in Christ who fourteen years ago was caught up to the third heaven – whether in the body or out of the body I do not know; God knows. [3]And I know that such a person – whether in the body or out of the body I do not know; God knows – [4]was caught up into Paradise and heard things that are not to be told, that no mortal is permitted to repeat. [5]On behalf of such a one I will boast, but on my own behalf I will not boast, except of my weaknesses. [6]But if I wish to boast, I will not be a fool, for I will be speaking the truth. But I refrain from it, so that no one may think better of me than what is seen in me or heard from me, [7]even considering the exceptional character of the revelations. Therefore, to keep[m] me from being too elated, a thorn was given me in the flesh, a messenger of Satan to torment me, to keep me from being too elated.[n] [8]Three times I appealed to the Lord about this, that it would leave me, [9]but he said to me, "My grace is sufficient for you, for power[o] is made perfect in weakness." So, I will boast all the more gladly of my weaknesses, so that the power of Christ may dwell in me.

[1] Gk *through the wall*   [m] Other ancient authorities read *To keep*   [n] Other ancient authorities lack *to keep me from being too elated*   [o] Other ancient authorities read *my power*

---

2 CORINTHIANS 12

1. Possibly the super-apostles boasted of special revelations. Paul uses the third person, 'such a one', to refer to himself, since he only 'boasts' of actions which show his 'weakness' (12:5). 'Weaknesses' do not include visions.

2. The three heavens probably were clouds, sun and stars, and God's presence. The 'dome' that separates the waters separates the first from the second heaven (Gen. 1:7–8, 14). In the *Book of the Secrets of Enoch*, composed by a contemporary of Paul, ten heavens are described (the third is Eden, the seventh and tenth are God's presence).

Paul does not care about specifics. However, what happened to him (around AD 42 if 2 Corinthians was written around AD 56, about seven years after his conversion, before any missionary journeys) was not self-induced. He 'was caught up' (seized and carried off, Matt. 12:29; John 6:15; 10:12; Acts 23:10). In the same way, Philip was 'snatched' away by the Spirit from the Ethiopian treasurer (Acts 8:39) and all Christians will be 'caught up' with the returning Jesus (1 Thess. 4:17).

7. Commentators differ over the meaning of the metaphor 'thorn'. The thorn is anything pointed, especially a pale or stake. To 'torment', literally is to 'strike with a fist', as had been done to Jesus and Paul (Matt. 26:67; 1 Cor. 4:11; 2 Cor. 11:23–25). These metaphors, a thorn piercing, a messenger hitting, suggest external, localized, periodic problems. Since other uses of 'torment' refer to physical persecution, Paul could have asked God that he no longer be physically persecuted (2 Cor. 12:10; 4:7–11). Or, these metaphors could refer to some intermittent eye problem such as ophthalmia (Gal. 4:13–15; 6:11).

8. 'Appeal' was often used for communication with the gods, but in the New Testament it refers to prayer only here.

9. God 'said' is in the perfect tense: past action that affects the present state. Therefore, Paul no longer needs to ask. The quality of God's strength is figuratively presented as a person coming to live with one ('may dwell'), alluding to Christ's incarnation (John 1:14) and the descent of God's shekinah glory (Exod. 25:8; 40:34–35). Moses could not enter the Tabernacle when God's glory was present, but Paul could be filled by God's glory while alive.

[10]Therefore I am content with weaknesses, insults, hardships, persecutions, and calamities for the sake of Christ; for whenever I am weak, then I am strong.

Paul's Concern for the Corinthian Church

11 I have been a fool! You forced me to it. Indeed you should have been the ones commending me, for I am not at all inferior to these super-apostles, even though I am nothing. [12]The signs of a true apostle were performed among you with utmost patience, signs and wonders and mighty works. [13]How have you been worse off than the other churches, except that I myself did not burden you? Forgive me this wrong!

14 Here I am, ready to come to you this third time. And I will not be a burden, because I do not want what is yours but you; for children ought not to lay up for their parents, but parents for their children. [15]I will most gladly spend and be spent for you. If I love you more, am I to be loved less? [16]Let it be assumed that I did not burden you. Nevertheless (you say) since I was crafty, I took you in by deceit. [17]Did I take advantage of you through any of those whom I sent to you? [18]I urged Titus to go, and sent the brother with him. Titus did not take advantage of you, did he? Did we not conduct ourselves with the same spirit? Did we not take the same steps?

19 Have you been thinking all along that we have been defending ourselves before you? We are speaking in Christ before God. Everything we do, beloved, is for the sake of building you up. [20]For I fear that when I come, I may find you not as I wish, and that you may find me not as you wish; I fear that there may perhaps be quarreling, jealousy, anger, selfishness, slander, gossip, conceit, and disorder. [21]I fear that when I come again, my God may humble me before you, and that I may have to mourn over many who previously sinned and have not repented of the impurity, sexual immorality, and licentiousness that they have practiced.

---

10. This sentence is the climax to 11:1ff. and the discussion of 'weaknesses'. 'Gladly' and 'I am content' (12:9–10) describe Paul's present attitude to difficulties. The Corinthians want 'strength' (a 'weighty and strong' bodily as well as literary presence, 10:10). However, they forget this paradox: difficulties encountered in advancing God's reign are opportunities for God to empower and for genuine leaders to demonstrate sincere intentions. Paul has restated and personally appropriated Jesus' teachings (Luke 6:22–23; 9:23). Accepting all difficulties, in itself, is *not* God's intention. Rather, they should be welcomed only 'for the sake of Christ'.

11. Paul states the main purpose of the letter.

12–15. Paul summarizes three reasons he is not inferior to the 'super-apostles': (1) Paul has exhibited the 'supernatural' types of gifts such as healing and exorcism that encourage people to repent (Matt. 11:20); (2) Paul's team refused to take money; (3) Paul loves them.

12. One 'wonder' was women and men of all economic classes prophesying at Pentecost (Acts 2:17–19). Paul could have highlighted all the powerful 'mighty works' he accomplished to dazzle the Corinthians. However, these 'mighty works' only reflect *God's* power, not human power (2 Cor. 4:7; 13:4).

13. 'Forgive' and 'wrong' ('injustice') are ironic.

14. Paul's first visit to Corinth is recorded in Acts 18:1 and his third visit in Acts 20:2 (2 Cor. 13:1). The second visit is mentioned only in the letters (1 Cor. 4:19; 2 Cor. 2:1).

17–18. Paul's defense had to include his co-workers since someone may have accused them of taking financial advantage of the Corinthians.

19. Paul repeats the wording of 2:17. He summarizes 2 Cor. 1–5, Paul's defense of their behavior (13:8–9). His 'defense' is not a public, oratorical debate to impress the Corinthians, but a conversation in God's presence and an attempt to help the Corinthians mature.

20–21. The false apostles flourished because of the sinful environment at Corinth.

12:20–13:7, 10–11. Paul directly urges the Corinthians to change, summarizing 2 Cor. 6–12.

Further Warning

13 This is the third time I am coming to you. "Any charge must be sustained by the evidence of two or three witnesses." [2]I warned those who sinned previously and all the others, and I warn them now while absent, as I did when present on my second visit, that if I come again, I will not be lenient – [3]since you desire proof that Christ is speaking in me. He is not weak in dealing with you, but is powerful in you. [4]For he was crucified in weakness, but lives by the power of God. For we are weak in him,[p] but in dealing with you we will live with him by the power of God.

5 Examine yourselves to see whether you are living in the faith. Test yourselves. Do you not realize that Jesus Christ is in you? – unless, indeed, you fail to meet the test! [6]I hope you will find out that we have not failed. [7]But we pray to God that you may not do anything wrong – not that we may appear to have met the test, but that you may do what is right, though we may seem to have failed. [8]For we cannot do anything against the truth, but only for the truth. [9]For we rejoice when we are weak and you are strong. This is what we pray for, that you may become perfect. [10]So I write these things while I am away from you, so that when I come, I may not have to be severe in using the authority that the Lord has given me for building up and not for tearing down.

Final Greetings and Benediction

11 Finally, brothers and sisters,[q] farewell.[r] Put things in order, listen to my appeal,[s] agree with one another, live in peace; and the God of love and peace will be with you. [12]Greet one another with a holy kiss. All the saints greet you.

[p] Other ancient authorities read *with him*
[q] Gk *brothers*   [r] Or *rejoice*   [s] Or *encourage one another*

---

2 CORINTHIANS 13

1. Paul cites a key Old Testament practice to prevent slander (2 Cor. 12:20) and ensure Christ's presence (Matt. 18:20).

2–3. Paul alludes to the Corinthian complaints (1:17; 10:1–2, 7).

3–4. In v. 3 'weak' is the Corinthians' use of weak: authoritative punishment (12:21). In relation to sin, Christ is 'strong'. In v. 4, Paul summarizes his reinterpretation of 'weak'. In suffering for others, Christ is 'weak'. Christ is the ultimate model for Paul's team. Christ's followers need to live through difficulties for Christ's sake, because God's strength will empower them.

5–6. The test is probably Christ's example (13:3–4). 'You' is plural. Christ's model is imitated where at least two or three are present (13:1).

7. Paul wants the Corinthians to do good. He does not want a competitive relationship. Like Christ, he would give his life for their sakes (8:9).

9. Paul hearkens back to 2 Cor. 1–5, his defense of his team's behavior. 'Perfect' has the sense of mature, put in order (13:11), adjusted, restored, as to 'mend' a net (Matt. 4:21). The Corinthians are now a 'ripped net' which needs to be 'mended'.

10. Paul expresses the purpose of his whole letter. Warning before punishment is a key biblical concept (Ezek. 33:11; 2 Pet. 3:9).

11. Paul hearkens back to 2 Cor. 6–12, his exhortation to change.

12. Paul ends the letter with three levels of relationships: local congregation, church as a whole, God (13:10). The 'holy' kiss, probably given to persons of the same sex, became a regular part of early church services before the Eucharist, symbolizing unity and reconciliation. Paul reminds the Corinthians of the Macedonians' care for them as well as for the Jerusalem church (8:1; 9:14).

13 The grace of the Lord Jesus Christ,
the love of God, and the communion of[t] the
Holy Spirit be with all of you.

[t] Or *and the sharing in*

---

13. The Bible does not always refer to God, the Trinity, as Father and Son and Holy Spirit (Matt. 28:19). Here the sequence is Jesus and God and Holy Spirit. In 1 Cor. 12:4–6 Paul follows the sequence Spirit, Lord, God. The qualities of 'grace', 'love' and 'communion' are true of all persons of the Trinity. As in Matt. 28:19, Paul treats the three Persons as equal by using the connective 'and' between each Person. By repeating 'the' in the same number, gender, and case, Paul highlights the distinctiveness of each person of the Trinity. Unity in diversity is the key idea expressed by the 'Trinity'.

Grace, love, and communion (partnership) are three key concepts he has highlighted in this letter as necessary especially for the Corinthians.

THE LETTER OF PAUL
TO THE GALATIANS

INTRODUCTION

Paul wrote this epistle in the middle of the first century AD to a community of believers which he had founded (Acts 16:6) in the Roman province of Galatia in central Asia Minor. Apparently Judaizers who contradicted Paul's gospel had infiltrated the community, confusing recent converts. It is evident that Gentile Christians were part of the community at Galatia (3:8–9), 14, 28, 4:8) and were particularly confused by the infiltrators' different gospel (1:7) that obedience to the Mosaic Law was still necessary for one to be identified as a member of the people of God (4:10; 5:2–4; 6:12–13).

Paul's response to the damage done by these agitators is among his most defensive which is made obvious when he omits his usual thanksgiving section (cf. Phil. 1:3–11), replacing it instead with several statements of rebuke (Gal. 1:6–10). In the body of the letter he argues not only for the validity of his apostleship (1:11–12, 15–19; 2:1–2, 7–9) and hence his gospel, but also now that Jews and Gentiles are justified by faith in Christ and are fully members of the people of God (2:15–16; 3:8–9), the Mosaic Law has been rendered obsolete (3:24–26).

Now the indication that they are the people of God is that they have received the Holy Spirit (3:2–5, 14; 4:6–7). Although they are no longer guided by Mosaic Law, their behavior should not be characterized by vice (5:19–21) but by the virtuous fruit of the Spirit (5:22–23). Paul provides them with particular examples of how they are to live according to the Spirit as a community (6:1–10) before he closes the letter with further warnings (6:12–13) and a blessing (6:18).

This letter is of utmost importance because it provides the theological basis upon which Christianity could flourish beyond the boundaries of what might have become another Jewish sect.

Salutation

1 Paul an apostle – sent neither by human commission nor from human authorities, but through Jesus Christ and God the Father, who raised him from the dead – ²and all the members of God's family[a] who are with me,

To the churches of Galatia:

3 Grace to you and peace from God our Father and the Lord Jesus Christ, ⁴who gave himself for our sins to set us free from the present evil age, according to the will of our God and Father, ⁵to whom be the glory forever and ever. Amen.

There Is No Other Gospel

6 I am astonished that you are so quickly deserting the one who called you in the grace of Christ and are turning to a different gospel – ⁷not that there is another gospel, but there are some who are confusing you and want to pervert the gospel of Christ. ⁸But even if we or an angel[b] from heaven should proclaim to you a gospel contrary to what we proclaimed to you, let that one be accursed! ⁹As we have said before, so now I repeat, if anyone proclaims to you a gospel contrary to what you received, let that one be accursed!

10 Am I now seeking human approval, or God's approval? Or am I trying to please people? If I were still pleasing people, I would not be a servant[c] of Christ.

Paul's Vindication of His Apostleship

11 For I want you to know, brothers and sisters,[d] that the gospel that was proclaimed by me is not of human origin; ¹²for I did not receive it from a human source, nor was I taught it, but I received it through a revelation of Jesus Christ.

13 You have heard, no doubt, of my earlier life in Judaism. I was violently persecuting the church of God and was trying to destroy it. ¹⁴I advanced in Judaism beyond many among my people of the same age, for I was far more zealous for the traditions of my ancestors. ¹⁵But when God, who had set me apart before I was born and called me through his grace, was pleased ¹⁶to reveal his Son to me,[e] so that I might proclaim him among the Gentiles, I did not confer with any human being, ¹⁷nor did I go up to Jerusalem to those who were already apostles before me, but I went away at once

[a] Gk all the brothers   [b] Or a messenger   [c] Gk slave
[d] Gk brothers   [e] Gk in me

INTRODUCTION (GAL. 1:1–10)

Paul begins all of his letters with an introductory section which usually includes a greeting and a prayer of thanksgiving.

1. The apostle interrupts the flow of his opening greeting to state that his appointment as apostle is a divine appointment and not a human one – a similar point is made later in connection with the gospel he preaches (v. 11).

6–10. It is at this point in his letter that Paul would usually include a prayer of thanksgiving. Here, however, it is replaced by a rebuke which describes the serious situation into which the Galatian church is sliding. They are in grave danger of abandoning the gospel based on grace, which Paul presented to them, in favor of false teachings.

PAUL DEFENDS HIS GOSPEL AND HIS AUTHORITY (GAL. 1:11–2:21)

Paul includes an autobiographical section in order to add strength to his claim to be an apostle and to preach the true gospel of Jesus Christ.

1:11–12. Here Paul claims to have received the gospel through a revelation of Christ and not through human teaching and thereby validates the divine nature of his message.

1:13–17. Gives an account of Paul's zealous activities as a devout Jew prior to conversion. In spite of his persecution of the church Paul, by the grace of God, has been chosen to preach the gospel to the Gentiles.

into Arabia, and afterwards I returned to Damascus.

18 Then after three years I did go up to Jerusalem to visit Cephas and stayed with him fifteen days; ¹⁹but I did not see any other apostle except James the Lord's brother. ²⁰In what I am writing to you, before God, I do not lie! ²¹Then I went into the regions of Syria and Cilicia, ²²and I was still unknown by sight to the churches of Judea that are in Christ; ²³they only heard it said, "The one who formerly was persecuting us is now proclaiming the faith he once tried to destroy." ²⁴And they glorified God because of me.

Paul and the Other Apostles

2 Then after fourteen years I went up again to Jerusalem with Barnabas, taking Titus along with me. ²I went up in response to a revelation. Then I laid before them (though only in a private meeting with the acknowledged leaders) the gospel that I proclaim among the Gentiles, in order to make sure that I was not running, or had not run, in vain. ³But even Titus, who was with me, was not compelled to be circumcised, though he was a Greek. ⁴But because of false believers^f secretly brought in, who slipped in to spy on the freedom we

have in Christ Jesus, so that they might enslave us – ⁵we did not submit to them even for a moment, so that the truth of the gospel might always remain with you. ⁶And from those who were supposed to be acknowledged leaders (what they actually were makes no difference to me; God shows no partiality) – those leaders contributed nothing to me. ⁷On the contrary, when they saw that I had been entrusted with the gospel for the uncircumcised, just as Peter had been entrusted with the gospel for the circumcised ⁸(for he who worked through Peter making him an apostle to the circumcised also worked through me in sending me to the Gentiles), ⁹and when James and Cephas and John, who were acknowledged pillars, recognized the grace that had been given to me, they gave to Barnabas and me the right hand of fellowship, agreeing that we should go to the Gentiles and they to the circumcised. ¹⁰They asked only one thing, that we remember the poor, which was actually what I was^g eager to do.

Paul Rebukes Peter at Antioch

11 But when Cephas came to Antioch, I opposed him to his face, because he stood

^f Gk *false brothers*   ^g Or *had been*

1:18–26. Three years after his conversion Paul goes to Jerusalem to meet with the apostles Peter and James. He then moves on to Syria and Cilicia where the churches glorify God when they hear of his conversion.
2:1–10. Fourteen years later Paul returns to Jerusalem, with Barnabas and Titus, to present the gospel he has been preaching to the apostles for their approval and validation.
2:3. 'Titus . . . was not compelled to be circumcised . . .' In the New Testament world, circumcision was a sign that a man was Jewish, which signified that he was one of God's covenant people. Titus, who was a Gentile, would not have been circumcised when he was a boy. It is significant to Paul that the leaders in Jerusalem did not compel Titus to be circumcised because as Jewish leaders of the new Christian movement they could have compelled other members to take on this mark of the covenant. Consequently, Paul's conviction of justification by faith alone without assuming any of the typical characteristics of Judaism such as circumcision, food laws, and Sabbath observance, won the day during this visit to Jerusalem.
2:7–9. The recognized 'pillars' of the church, James, Cephas (Peter), and John validate Paul's ministry to the Gentiles, or the 'uncircumcised' through giving Barnabas and Paul the 'right hand of fellowship'. This signified a formal agreement which was to be honored by both parties.
2:11f. On his visit to Antioch Peter draws back from dining with Gentiles even though he has done so previously without hesitation, thus bringing a sharp rebuke from Paul who views his actions as

self-condemned; [12]for until certain people came from James, he used to eat with the Gentiles. But after they came, he drew back and kept himself separate for fear of the circumcision faction. [13]And the other Jews joined him in this hypocrisy, so that even Barnabas was led astray by their hypocrisy. [14]But when I saw that they were not acting consistently with the truth of the gospel, I said to Cephas before them all, "If you, though a Jew, live like a Gentile and not like a Jew, how can you compel the Gentiles to live like Jews?"[h]

Jews and Gentiles Are Saved by Faith

15 We ourselves are Jews by birth and not Gentile sinners; [16]yet we know that a person is justified[i] not by the works of the law but through faith in Jesus Christ.[j] And we have come to believe in Christ Jesus, so that we might be justified by faith in Christ,[k] and not by doing the works of the law, because no one will be justified by the works of the law. [17]But if, in our effort to be justified in Christ, we ourselves have been found to be sinners, is Christ then a servant of sin? Certainly not! [18]But if I build up again the very things that I once tore down, then I demonstrate that I am a transgressor. [19]For through the law I died to the law, so that I might live to God. I have been crucified with Christ; [20]and it is no longer I who live, but it is Christ who lives in me. And the life I now live in the flesh I live by faith in the Son of God,[l] who loved me and gave himself for me. [21]I do not nullify the grace of God; for if justification[m] comes through the law, then Christ died for nothing.

Law or Faith

3 You foolish Galatians! Who has bewitched you? It was before your eyes that Jesus Christ was publicly exhibited as crucified! [2]The only thing I want to learn from you is this: Did you receive the Spirit by doing the works of the law or by believing what you heard? [3]Are you so foolish? Having started with the Spirit, are you now ending with the flesh? [4]Did you experience so much for nothing? – if it really was for nothing. [5]Well then, does God[n] supply you with the Spirit and work miracles among you by your doing the works of the law, or by your believing what you heard?

6 Just as Abraham "believed God, and it was reckoned to him as righteousness," [7]so, you see, those who believe are the

---

[h] Some interpreters hold that the quotation extends into the following paragraph   [i] Or *reckoned as righteous*; and so elsewhere   [j] Or *the faith of Jesus Christ*   [k] Or *the faith of Christ*   [l] Or *by the faith of the Son of God*   [m] Or *righteousness*   [n] Gk *he*

---

insincere. Peter's reason for doing this was, perhaps, due to fear at the appearance of the 'circumcision faction'. This seems to have been a body of Jews or Jewish Christians who held tenaciously to traditional Jewish practices and who directed their efforts against any Jew who appeared to deviate from them.

2–15f. Paul concludes that if the Judaizers are correct in holding to the Law and tradition, and trying to persuade others to do the same, then the death of Christ was in vain, it achieved nothing. The Law was still necessary and grace is invalid.

PAUL DEFENDS HIS GOSPEL (GAL. 3)

In the major section of his letter Paul defends the truth of the message he has been proclaiming.
1–14. His main argument is that faith has priority over the Law. It is faith in Christ not the works of the Law which is the essential element of the gospel on which the whole of the Christian faith relies.
3. Paul equates the Law with the flesh and faith with the spirit.
6ff. Paul takes his argument back to Abraham. He lived long before the Law was given to Moses yet he was considered as righteous because of his faith in God. Faith is superior to the Law.

descendants of Abraham. [8]And the scripture, foreseeing that God would justify the Gentiles by faith, declared the gospel beforehand to Abraham, saying, "All the Gentiles shall be blessed in you." [9]For this reason, those who believe are blessed with Abraham who believed.

10 For all who rely on the works of the law are under a curse; for it is written, "Cursed is everyone who does not observe and obey all the things written in the book of the law." [11]Now it is evident that no one is justified before God by the law; for "The one who is righteous will live by faith."[o] [12]But the law does not rest on faith; on the contrary, "Whoever does the works of the law[p] will live by them." [13]Christ redeemed us from the curse of the law by becoming a curse for us – for it is written, "Cursed is everyone who hangs on a tree" – [14]in order that in Christ Jesus the blessing of Abraham might come to the Gentiles, so that we might receive the promise of the Spirit through faith.

The Promise to Abraham

15 Brothers and sisters,[q] I give an example from daily life: once a person's will[r] has been ratified, no one adds to it or annuls it. [16]Now the promises were made to Abraham and to his offspring;[s] it does not say, "And to offsprings,"[t] as of many; but it says, "And to your offspring,"[s] that is, to one person, who is Christ. [17]My point is this: the law, which came four hundred thirty years later, does not annul a covenant previously ratified by God, so as to nullify the promise. [18]For if the inheritance comes from the law, it no longer comes from the promise; but God granted it to Abraham through the promise.

The Purpose of the Law

19 Why then the law? It was added because of transgressions, until the offspring[s] would come to whom the promise had been made; and it was ordained through angels by a mediator. [20]Now a mediator involves more than one party; but God is one.

21 Is the law then opposed to the promises of God? Certainly not! For if a law had been given that could make alive, then righteousness would indeed come through the law. [22]But the scripture has imprisoned all things under the power of sin, so that what was promised through faith in Jesus Christ[u] might be given to those who believe.

23 Now before faith came, we were imprisoned and guarded under the law until faith would be revealed. [24]Therefore the law was our disciplinarian until Christ came, so that we might be justified by faith. [25]But now that faith has come, we are no longer subject to a disciplinarian, [26]for in Christ Jesus you are all children of God

[o] Or *The one who is righteous through faith will live* [p] Gk *does them* [q] Gk *Brothers* [r] Or *covenant* (as in verse 17) [s] Gk *seed* [t] Gk *seeds* [u] Or *through the faith of Jesus Christ*

10f. Adherence to the Law also brings with it the curse of the Law. No one, Paul argues, can keep all the laws, however hard they try, however devoted they are; it just is not possible. As they then fail to keep the Law, then they cannot be considered as righteous.

13f. Christ, however, has taken that curse on himself through his death and made it possible to be made righteous through faith in him.

15ff. Paul gives an example to illustrate the relationship between the Law and the promise of God.

21ff. These verses look at the purpose of the Law. It kept mankind under restraint, it gave rules to live by, it showed sin up for what it is.

25–26. Now that Christ has come, the Law no longer functions as the *paidagogos* which literally referred to the slave who protected and disciplined a child. Those who are 'in Christ Jesus' are children of God by virtue of their faith alone, not by virtue of their adherence to the Law.

through faith. [27]As many of you as were baptized into Christ have clothed yourselves with Christ. [28]There is no longer Jew or Greek, there is no longer slave or free, there is no longer male and female; for all of you are one in Christ Jesus. [29]And if you belong to Christ, then you are Abraham's offspring,[v] heirs according to the promise.

4 My point is this: heirs, as long as they are minors, are no better than slaves, though they are the owners of all the property; [2]but they remain under guardians and trustees until the date set by the father. [3]So with us; while we were minors, we were enslaved to the elemental spirits[w] of the world. [4]But when the fullness of time had come, God sent his Son, born of a woman, born under the law, [5]in order to redeem those who were under the law, so that we might receive adoption as children. [6]And because you are children, God has sent the Spirit of his Son into our[x] hearts, crying, "Abba![y] Father!" [7]So you are no longer a slave but a child, and if a child then also an heir, through God.[z]

Paul Reproves the Galatians

8 Formerly, when you did not know God, you were enslaved to beings that by nature are not gods. [9]Now, however, that you have come to know God, or rather to be

[v] Gk *seed*   [w] Or *the rudiments*   [x] Other ancient authorities read *your*   [y] Aramaic for *Father*   [z] Other ancient authorities read *an heir of God through Christ*

---

27. It is now baptism which formally signifies the incorporation of believers into the covenant community. This rite of initiation is open to all regardless of gender in contrast with the initiation rite of circumcision which was gender specific as practised by the Jews.
28. In the epistle Paul is concerned to show how it is that Gentile believers need not take on the characteristics of Jewish Law and that the Judaizers are in no way superior to Gentile believers by virtue of their adherence to the law (cf. Gal. 4:21–5:1). In society at large slaves were at the lower end of the economic spectrum and were viewed with disdain because their lives were antithetical to the Greek ideal of freedom. Women were viewed as being inferior to men in the Mediterranean world as a whole. This view was perpetuated by their lack of education and curtailed exposure to the outside world. Essentially Paul is stating that race, status, and gender are not factors for consideration for membership in the people of God. In the context of the epistle this means that all members of God's people are equal in God's sight. Concurrently, a new era in God's eschatological purposes has begun. Because Christ has come, the era of confinement under the Law is over (Gal. 3:23–24). God's people are now guided by the Holy Spirit in regard to their character (Gal. 5:22–23) and in regard to their giftedness (Rom. 12:6–8; Eph. 4:11–12) irrespective of gender.

FROM SLAVERY TO SONSHIP (GAL. 4)

4–5. In Jewish and Christian literature roughly contemporary with Paul the phrase 'born of a woman' was another way of describing someone as a human person (cf. Matt. 11:11). Paul uses the phrase 'born of a woman' to describe Jesus' human condition. That he was 'born under the law' also points to his being born a Jew by a Jewish mother. In the context of Paul's struggle with the Judaizers (see Introduction, p. 382) Paul is showing his opponents that Jesus was born not only in accord with God's purposes, in 'the fullness of time', but that Jesus was born a Jew just like they were, under the confining character of the Law, described earlier as the enslaving 'elemental spirits' (Gal. 4:3). Jesus redeemed his own people from the Law which once alienated Jew and Gentile. This meant that all persons could then become God's children (Gal. 4:5). The contrast here is that God's Son, who was born and lived as an ordinary human being during his mission on earth, through God's purposes provided for ordinary human beings to inherit divine adoption as sons and daughters of God.
8ff. Paul is concerned for the spiritual welfare of the Galatians. They have been set free from being enslaved by sin and 'elemental spirits' but are now in danger of giving away their freedom and being enslaved once more.

known by God, how can you turn back again to the weak and beggarly elemental spirits?[a] How can you want to be enslaved to them again? [10]You are observing special days, and months, and seasons, and years. [11]I am afraid that my work for you may have been wasted.

[12] Friends,[b] I beg you, become as I am, for I also have become as you are. You have done me no wrong. [13]You know that it was because of a physical infirmity that I first announced the gospel to you; [14]though my condition put you to the test, you did not scorn or despise me, but welcomed me as an angel of God, as Christ Jesus. [15]What has become of the goodwill you felt? For I testify that, had it been possible, you would have torn out your eyes and given them to me. [16]Have I now become your enemy by telling you the truth? [17]They make much of you, but for no good purpose; they want to exclude you, so that you may make much of them. [18]It is good to be made much of for a good purpose at all times, and not only when I am present with you. [19]My little children, for whom I am again in the pain of childbirth until Christ is formed in you, [20]I wish I were present with you now and could change my tone, for I am perplexed about you.

◆ Paul is willing to liken himself to both a birthing (Gal. 4:19) and a breast-feeding mother (1 Thess. 2:7). He even pictures himself as a mother or wet-nurse engaged in the weaning process (1 Cor. 3:2). He emphasizes the tenderness of mothers, the faithful constancy of their care, and the good judgment which they must use in perceiving what is appropriate for the young infant.

A mother pours her life into the child not only in the birth process but also in the constant care and nourishment which must be given to the newborn. She must respond to the infant's needs 24 hours a day, often at great personal sacrifice. To establish a good nursing relationship with a baby sometimes requires considerable patience and persistence. Then the mother has the satisfaction of seeing the infant thrive, and she knows that this is the result of the nutrition which she has provided. Her work and wakefulness and exhaustion bear blessed fruit. Paul is

---

[a] Or beggarly rudiments   [b] Gk Brothers

19. While speaking of someone as born or begotten of a male was not uncommon in Paul's time, and a man might speak metaphorically of giving birth amidst pain, for example, to ideas or to a literary work, Paul's description of himself bearing the anguish of labor is surprising at first glance. His use of his paternal imagery (cf. 1 Cor. 4:14–15; Philem. 10; 1 Thess. 2:11) is usually more familiar to readers of his letters. However, Paul does describe himself with maternal imagery elsewhere, as a 'nurse tenderly caring for her own children' (1 Thess. 2:7) and as feeding the Corinthians 'with milk, not solid food' (1 Cor. 3:1–3). In Gal. 4:19 Paul describes himself as a pregnant mother again in the midst of 'the pain of childbirth' (cf. Gal. 4:27 and below, Is. 54:1; the word is to be distinguished from the word which actually means 'to give birth'). He sees himself as the founder who had given birth to the Galatian community previously but who again is in the pain of labor to re-establish them because of their confusion over the gospel. He further states that his present travail will last 'until Christ is formed' in them. The word 'formed' could be used symbolically to describe the formation of an embryo during the time period in which Paul was writing. So the imagery here is not only of Paul as a pregnant mother, but also of the Galatians bearing a fetus in their wombs which needs a further gestation period until it is fully formed. Paul's pain will last until the Galatians have established vital, lasting fellowship with Christ. Elsewhere Paul speaks of anguish like that of labor anticipated in the apocalyptic era which will bring about the rebirth of the whole created order (Rom. 8:22–23; 1 Thess. 5:3; cf. Mark 13:8; Matt. 24:8). Paul's theological emphasis in Gal. 4:19 may be that his apostolic vocation is part of that apocalyptic rebirth and that the formation of Christ in believers in Galatia will continue until the culmination of God's purposes when Christ returns.

proud of his children for whom he has sacrificed much just as a mother is proud of her lovely babes. Women might well take their cue from Paul and realize that their gifts and experiences fit them admirably to exercise a gospel ministry ◆

The Allegory of Hagar and Sarah

21 Tell me, you who desire to be subject to the law, will you not listen to the law? [22]For it is written that Abraham had two sons, one by a slave woman and the other by a free woman. [23]One, the child of the

◆ The Galatians would understand very well Paul's identification of two half-brothers through their respective mothers. Just as a Jew was considered to be one whose mother was Jewish, so too the people in the areas surrounding Galatia understood themselves in terms of their mothers. Men identified themselves by giving their mother's name rather than that of their father, and property was inherited through the mother. Descent was traced through the mother,

and social and political rank might be determined by the maternal family, even if the father was unknown. Magic charms and curses frequently involved the name of the person's mother rather than of the father as this was supposed to give greater power by providing the individual's secret identity.

We too may understand ourselves better as we recognize the heritage which we receive from our mothers and how it has shaped our lives and personalities. The mother preoccupied with the incessant care of a small child has influence far greater than she imagines, and the impression that she creates will carry through to many generations. Spiritual foundations are formed even before the child can talk, and godly attitudes are imbibed with mother's milk ◆

slave, was born according to the flesh; the other, the child of the free woman, was born through the promise. [24]Now this is an allegory: these women are two covenants. One woman, in fact, is Hagar, from Mount Sinai, bearing children for slavery. [25]Now Hagar is

---

4:21–5:1. Paul has just admitted his perplexity concerning the Galatians (4:20) and now provides them with a pointed example from their own Law (4:21) upon which they must act. His example is in the form of an allegory which is constructed around the birth of the sons of Abraham, Isaac and Ishmael, and their mothers Sarah and Hagar. Because his interpretation of the text seems rather arbitrary and because none of the principle participants are named at first, it seems likely that Paul has revised the story used by the opponents to his own advantage. The opponents probably argued that to be a true son of Abraham it was necessary to be circumcised like Isaac.

4:22. Ishmael is the child who was born of the slave Hagar (Gen. 16:15). In the Genesis account Sarah, Abraham's wife who has despaired of ever bearing a child, gives him her Egyptian maid, Hagar, as a concubine so that she might bear children by Abraham. On the other hand, Isaac is said to be the child of a free woman, Sarah (Gen. 21:2), who conceived and bore a son even though she was beyond her child-bearing years (cf. Rom. 4:19–21).

23. Paul states that Ishmael was 'born according to the flesh'. Paul seems to be referring to the natural process of procreation. Paul's use of the word 'flesh' is negative in Galatians where it often refers to obedience to the Law (Gal. 6:12–13), particularly over against life in the Spirit (Gal. 3:3; 6:8). In contrast to Ishmael, Paul notes that Isaac was born 'through the promise', referring, of course, to God's promise that Abraham and Sarah would bear a son (Gen. 15:4–6; 17:1–8) even though his wife was past her child-bearing years (Gen. 17:15–19; 18:10–11) in accord with God's own design (Gen. 17:16; 18:12–14).

24–26. Paul states that he is using an 'allegory'. An allegorical exposition of a text usually refers to the text having a deeper meaning than appears on the surface. In Paul's allegory, Hagar and Sarah represent two covenants. What is noteworthy is that in reality no covenant was ever made with Ishmael (Gen. 17:20–21). Thus only one covenant – the covenant with Abraham and his

Mount Sinai in Arabia[c] and corresponds to the present Jerusalem, for she is in slavery with her children. [26]But the other woman corresponds to the Jerusalem above; she is free, and she is our mother. [27]For it is written,

"Rejoice, you childless one, you who
        bear no children,
    burst into song and shout, you who
        endure no birth pangs;
for the children of the desolate woman
    are more numerous
than the children of the one who is
    married."

[28]Now you,[d] my friends,[e] are children of the promise, like Isaac. [29]But just as at that time the child who was born according to the flesh persecuted the child who was born according to the Spirit, so it is now also. [30]But what does the scripture say? "Drive out the slave and her child; for the child of the slave will not share the inheritance with the child of the free woman."

[c] Other ancient authorities read *For Sinai is a mountain in Arabia*   [d] Other ancient authorities read *we*   [e] Gk *brothers*

---

progeny – is of concern here. Paul's two covenants are actually two ways of understanding the same covenant with Abraham. The covenant of Hagar is the understanding of God's covenant with Abraham in terms of Law and flesh. But the covenant of Sarah is Abraham's covenant seen in the fuller terms of freedom and promise and is an understanding which includes all nations through God's grace in Christ irrespective of the Law. Hagar stands for Mount Sinai (Gal. 4:24), the location where God gave the Law to Moses (Lev. 7:38; 26:46). Paul further states that Hagar bore 'children for slavery'. Paul has already argued in Galatians that those who maintain obedience to the Law are enslaved (Gal. 4:1–10). His message here would be understood: those who are under the Law are really the offspring of the slave Hagar, not Sarah.

25. Paul links Hagar with Mt Sinai. He states that although Mt Sinai is in Arabia geographically, as some Jews may have believed at the time, allegorically it can be linked with the present Jerusalem. Jerusalem, of course, had the reputation of being linked with Judaism and its Law. Additionally, the leaders of the Jerusalem church had reached an agreement with Paul in which he was free to propagate his Law-free gospel in the Gentile world (Gal. 2:9–10) but may have reversed their decision in regard to the Law. One indication of this reversal may be the 'certain people [who] came from James' (Gal. 2:3–5, 12) who, when they visited Antioch, caused so much commotion over the Law that even Peter disassociated himself from the Gentiles. It may be that the Judaizers in Galatia originated in Jerusalem or that they had been influenced by others who were from Jerusalem. By linking Hagar and Mt Sinai with the present Jerusalem Paul makes the striking point that those in Jerusalem who maintain that the Law is necessary for the people of God in Christ are actually the ones who are in slavery.

26. The 'other woman', of course, is Sarah. In contrast to Hagar who represents the earthly Jerusalem, Sarah represents the Jerusalem of the heavens. For Jews of the time an ideal form of Jerusalem existed, waiting in heaven to be revealed at the end of time (Rev. 3:12; 21:1–3, 10–11, 22–27). Sarah represents the Jerusalem that is the culmination of God's plans in history over the earthly Jerusalem which it ultimately temporary. In contrast to the enslavement under Law which the earthly Jerusalem represented, the heavenly Jerusalem is 'free'. The reference to Jerusalem being 'our mother' draws on a Jewish heritage in which Jerusalem is praised as the mother of God's people (Ps. 87; Is. 66:7–11). Paul's use of the word 'our' would refer to all believers in Christ, in this case particularly those in Galatia.

27. Paul uses Is. 54:1 in order to represent Sarah as the once childless woman who would bear numerous children.

28–30. Whereas vv. 21–27 revolve around the mothers, in these verses Paul centers on the offspring, Isaac and Ishmael. Believers in Galatia are children of the promise born according to the Spirit, like Isaac. And like Isaac was understood as being persecuted by Ishmael in some Jewish tradition (based upon Gen. 21:9) so Paul understands the Galatians who were free and born according to the Spirit as being persecuted by those who are under the Law. The citation of

[31]So then, friends,[f] we are children, not of the slave but of the free woman. [1]For freedom Christ has set us free. Stand firm, therefore, and do not submit again to a yoke of slavery.

The Nature of Christian Freedom

2 Listen! I, Paul, am telling you that if you let yourselves be circumcised, Christ will be of no benefit to you. [3]Once again I testify to every man who lets himself be circumcised that he is obliged to obey the entire law. [4]You who want to be justified by the law have cut yourselves off from Christ; you have fallen away from grace. [5]For through the Spirit, by faith, we eagerly wait for the hope of righteousness. [6]For in Christ Jesus neither circumcision nor uncircumcision counts for anything; the only thing that counts is faith working[g] through love.

7 You were running well; who prevented you from obeying the truth? [8]Such persuasion does not come from the one who calls you. [9]A little yeast leavens the whole batch of dough. [10]I am confident about you in the Lord that you will not think otherwise. But whoever it is that is confusing you will pay the penalty. [11]But my friends,[f] why am I still being persecuted if I am still preaching circumcision? In that case the offense of the cross has been removed. [12]I wish those who unsettle you would castrate themselves!

13 For you were called to freedom, brothers and sisters;[f] only do not use your freedom as an opportunity for self-indulgence,[h] but through love become slaves to one another. [14]For the whole law is summed up in a single commandment, "You shall love your neighbor as yourself." [15]If, however, you bite and devour one another, take care that you are not consumed by one another.

The Works of the Flesh

16 Live by the Spirit, I say, and do not gratify the desires of the flesh. [17]For what the flesh desires is opposed to the Spirit, and what the Spirit desires is opposed to the flesh; for these are opposed to each other, to prevent you from doing what you want. [18]But if you are led by the Spirit, you are not subject to the law. [19]Now the works of the flesh are obvious: fornication, impurity, licentiousness, [20]idolatry, sorcery, enmities, strife, jealousy, anger, quarrels, dissensions, factions, [21]envy,[i] drunkenness, carousing, and things like these. I am warning you, as I warned you before: those who do such things will not inherit the kingdom of God.

The Fruit of the Spirit

22 By contrast, the fruit of the Spirit is love, joy, peace, patience, kindness, generosity, faithfulness, [23]gentleness, and self-control. There is no law against such things. [24]And those who belong to Christ Jesus have crucified the flesh with its passions and desires. [25]If we live by the Spirit, let us also be guided by the Spirit. [26]Let us not become conceited, competing against one another, envying one another.

[f] Gk *brothers*   [g] Or *made effective*   [h] Gk *the flesh*
[i] Other ancient authorities add *murder*

Gen. 21:10 which refers to Sarah's command that Hagar and Ishmael be sent away furnishes Paul's rebuke for the believing community in Galatia. Just as the slave and her child were cast out, so should the believing community cast out the Judaizers and their influence.

4:31–5:1. Paul and all those who were born of the Spirit are children of the free woman, Sarah. In Paul's discussion of Hagar and Sarah, the importance of the Old Testament matriarchs is underlined. Abraham's line was perpetuated through both of these women. Although the Jews were originally the sole descendants of Abraham and Sarah, through Paul's argument he shows that by virtue of the Holy Spirit alone one is now shown to be among the progeny of the free woman. Paul closes this section by commanding the Galatians to stand firm in their freedom without again taking on aspects of the Law – the yoke of slavery (cf. Gal. 4:1–10, 22–24).

Bear One Another's Burdens

6 My friends,[j] if anyone is detected in a transgression, you who have received the Spirit should restore such a one in a spirit of gentleness. Take care that you yourselves are not tempted. [2]Bear one another's burdens, and in this way you will fulfill[k] the law of Christ. [3]For if those who are nothing think they are something, they deceive themselves. [4]All must test their own work; then that work, rather than their neighbor's work, will become a cause for pride. [5]For all must carry their own loads.

6 Those who are taught the word must share in all good things with their teacher.

7 Do not be deceived; God is not mocked, for you reap whatever you sow. [8]If you sow to your own flesh, you will reap corruption from the flesh; but if you sow to the Spirit, you will reap eternal life from the Spirit. [9]So let us not grow weary in doing what is right, for we will reap at harvest time, if we do not give up. [10]So then, whenever we have an opportunity, let us work for the good of all, and especially for those of the family of faith.

Final Admonitions and Benediction

11 See what large letters I make when I am writing in my own hand! [12]It is those who want to make a good showing in the flesh that try to compel you to be circumcised – only that they may not be persecuted for the cross of Christ. [13]Even the circumcised do not themselves obey the law, but they want you to be circumcised so that they may boast about your flesh. [14]May I never boast of anything except the cross of our Lord Jesus Christ, by which[l] the world has been crucified to me, and I to the world. [15]For[m] neither circumcision nor uncircumcision is anything; but a new creation is everything! [16]As for those who will follow this rule – peace be upon them, and mercy, and upon the Israel of God.

17 From now on, let no one make trouble for me; for I carry the marks of Jesus branded on my body.

18 May the grace of our Lord Jesus Christ be with your spirit, brothers and sisters.[j] Amen.

[j] Gk *Brothers*   [k] Other ancient authorities read *in this way fulfill*   [l] Or *through whom*   [m] Other ancient authorities add *in Christ Jesus*

GALATIANS 6

1–5. Here Paul encourages the Galatians towards mature Christian community. First, believers are to deal with those who have fallen into transgression with gentleness and humility, the implication being that each member is as apt to fall prey to sin as any other (v. 1). The 'burdens' which are to be shared are probably those which have become too much for one person to handle. It is by sharing their burdens that believers 'fulfill the law of Christ', which refers to Jesus' central teachings that his disciples are to love God and their neighbor (Gal. 6:2; Lev. 19:18; cf. Gal. 5:14). While groundless boasting is to be avoided (Gal. 6:3), one may boast when it is based upon reflection on one's own work and not in comparison with another's (v. 4). Paul's statement that they 'Bear one another's burdens' in v. 2 is tempered by his statement in v. 5 that each is responsible for his or her own load, referring to the common struggles of everyday life. Thus it would seem that although there are excessive burdens with which believers must assist one another, that in terms of the issues of daily life, one is also to be responsible.

11ff. Paul concludes this letter with both a warning and a greeting. He warns against boasting about external matters, about things that ultimately are not important. Paul himself will only boast about the love of Christ. This last section is written by Paul himself – the rest of the letter would have been dictated to a secretary.

THE LETTER OF PAUL
TO THE EPHESIANS

INTRODUCTION

The letter begins by stating that Paul is the writer, and 3:1; 4:1 imply that he is in prison, probably in Rome, which would date the letter in the early years of AD 60. We know from Acts 18–20 that Paul planted and worked with a church in Ephesus. However, it is unusual for Paul's letters that he makes no mention of any individuals here, and gives no personal greetings. Some people therefore think that the letter was a circular to a number of different churches in the area, especially as the teaching is general and does not specify circumstances or problems. Some of the best manuscripts leave out the words 'in Ephesus' from 1:1, although traditionally it has been believed that Paul is writing to Gentile believers (3:1) in Ephesus and sending the letter with Tychicus (6:21) for their encouragement.

Ephesus was the major city in the province of Asia (now western Turkey), center of the Roman Emperor cult, many magic cults, and worship of the goddess Artemis/Diana (cf. Acts 19:34).

Paul reminds the readers of his authority to write to them because of his apostleship and commission (1:1; 3:2, 7; 6:20) and his suffering on behalf of the Gentiles (3:1). Paul is concerned that these Gentile readers should know that they also are accepted by God through faith, even though they are not Jews.

Among the important themes of the letter is that of the church, which Paul describes in lofty terms, concentrating not on the local church, but on the whole church universal. He uses different metaphors where the church is a body (1:23; 4:16), temple (2:21) and bride (5:32). Paul reminds the believers of the benefits of their salvation in terms of spiritual blessings (1:3), adoption (1:5), redemption and forgiveness (1:7), inheritance (1:11), and that these are by grace through faith, not their own achievements (2:8). He explains how believers are part of God's plan which has cosmic dimensions, and that there is no part of the universe over which Christ is not Lord. What is true of them in Christ in the heavenly places (1:3, 20; 2:6; 3:10) is an encouragement and spur to holy living (4:17–6:9) and the winning of spiritual battles here and now (6:10–18).

In his concern for their lives to be Christlike in every way, Paul gives instruction to households (probably after the known pattern of early 'household codes') addressing wives and husbands, children and parents, and slaves and masters, under the general concern for mutual submission in Christ (5:21).

Salutation

1 Paul, an apostle of Christ Jesus by the will of God,

To the saints who are in Ephesus and are faithful[a] in Christ Jesus:

2 Grace to you and peace from God our Father and the Lord Jesus Christ.

Spiritual Blessings in Christ

3 Blessed be the God and Father of our Lord Jesus Christ, who has blessed us in Christ with every spiritual blessing in the heavenly places, 4just as he chose us in Christ[b] before the foundation of the world to be holy and blameless before him in love. 5He destined us for adoption as his children through Jesus Christ, according to the good pleasure of his will, 6to the praise of his glorious grace that he freely bestowed on us in the Beloved. 7In him we have redemption through his blood, the forgiveness of our trespasses, according to the riches of his grace 8that he lavished on us. With all wisdom and insight 9he has made known to us the mystery of his will, according to his good pleasure that he set forth in Christ, 10as a plan for the fullness of time, to gather up all things in him, things in heaven and things on earth. 11In Christ we have also obtained an inheritance,[c] having been destined according to the purpose of him who accomplishes all things according to his counsel and will, 12so that we, who were the first to set our hope on Christ, might live for the praise of his glory. 13In him you also, when you had heard the word of truth, the gospel of your salvation, and had believed in him, were marked with the seal of the promised Holy Spirit; 14this[d] is the pledge of our inheritance toward redemption as God's own people, to the praise of his glory.

[a] Other ancient authorities lack *in Ephesus*, reading *saints who are also faithful* [b] Gk *in him* [c] Or *been made a heritage* [d] Other ancient authorities read *who*

EPHESIANS 1

1. The 'saints' were not a group of specially canonized people (i.e. made official saints by the church), but this was a New Testament way of speaking of Christians as a whole, those who are 'holy ones' before God; comprising men and women, young and old – every type of believer.

5. NIV has 'to be adopted as his sons', rendering literally the Greek word used for son. NRSV is right to use 'children'. 'Children of God' and 'sons of God' are used interchangeably in the New Testament, and 'children' removes any doubt that women may not be included, and corrects any idea that sons are more important to God than daughters. God's adoption is for both men and women, whom he regards as equally important.

Paul is unique in the New Testament in using the image of adoption with reference to God's relationship with believers, even though the theme of God as Father is widely used. Adoption emphasizes God's own initiative in making people his own, and shows that people are not naturally or biologically born Christians, but are made so through the work of Christ on their behalf, which is entirely a result of God's free grace and will.

Comparative Ancient Near Eastern peoples practised adoption as a legal act of giving full rights, responsibilities and inheritance to a person as if they had truly been a child by birth. Adoption was a fairly rare procedure in the Old Testament, but the New Testament usage probably relies on the Old Testament background (emphasizing the change of relationship and status for the child) rather than the Roman law (emphasizing the need of a son to carry on the family line).

11. In a sense Christ, as first-born (Col. 1:15), should be heir. It is still a custom in many countries that the first-born son inherits everything. However, as adopted brothers and sisters of Christ, we also share in the inheritance, of which the 'seal of the promised Holy Spirit' (the already full possession of God's blessing, Eph. 1:13) is but a preliminary pledge or first instalment of all that awaits us in the fullness of future redemption. Both male and female believers inherit equally.

Paul's Prayer

15 I have heard of your faith in the Lord Jesus and your love^e toward all the saints, and for this reason ¹⁶I do not cease to give thanks for you as I remember you in my prayers. ¹⁷I pray that the God of our Lord Jesus Christ, the Father of glory, may give you a spirit of wisdom and revelation as you come to know him, ¹⁸so that, with the eyes of your heart enlightened, you may know what is the hope to which he has called you, what are the riches of his glorious inheritance among the saints, ¹⁹and what is the immeasurable greatness of his power for us who believe, according to the working of his great power. ²⁰God^f put this power to work in Christ when he raised him from the dead and seated him at his right hand in the heavenly places, ²¹far above all rule and authority and power and dominion, and above every name that is named, not only in this age but also in the age to come. ²²And he has put all things under his feet and has made him the head over all things for the church, ²³which is his body, the fullness of him who fills all in all.

From Death to Life

2 You were dead through the trespasses and sins ²in which you once lived, following the course of this world, following the ruler of the power of the air, the spirit that is now at work among those who are disobedient. ³All of us once lived among them in the passions of our flesh, following the desires of flesh and senses, and we were by nature children of wrath, like everyone else. ⁴But God, who is rich in mercy, out of the great love with which he loved us ⁵even when we were dead through our trespasses, made us alive together with Christ^g – by grace you have been saved – ⁶and raised us up with him and seated us with him in the heavenly places in Christ Jesus, ⁷so that in the ages to come he might show the immeasurable riches of his grace in kindness toward us in Christ Jesus. ⁸For by grace you have been saved through faith, and this is not your own doing; it is the gift of God – ⁹not the result of works, so that no one may boast. ¹⁰For we are what he has made us, created in Christ Jesus for good works, which God prepared beforehand to be our way of life.

One in Christ

11 So then, remember that at one time

---

^e Other ancient authorities lack *and your love*
^f Gk *He*   ^g Other ancient authorities read *in Christ*

---

22. The word 'head' may be used in different ways, even within the same letter. Sometimes it may mean ruler and sometimes origin or source. Context must prove the deciding factor for meaning. Here Paul is saying that Christ is Lord and ruler *over* all things (the 'all things' being cosmic and all-embracing) for the church. A literal link is not to be made between Christ as head and the church as the body, but the presence of the two images does show the close and special union between Christ and his church. There is nothing in all of creation over which Christ does not have ultimate power and authority on behalf of his people.

EPHESIANS 2

2. Literally 'the sons of disobedience', a Semitic idiom which denotes not gender, but anybody who has the characteristics of disobedience. NRSV translation is correct and avoids ambiguity. The same phrase is used in 5:6.

11. Circumcision was a primary sign of belonging to God's covenant people, the Jews, and marked out Jews from Gentiles. It was restricted to males, and Jewish families would cut the foreskins of their sons at eight days old. No form of cutting was ever practised or advocated for women or daughters, but this did not mean that they were in any sense less a part of the covenant. In some parts of the world female circumcision is practised widely today, but this is not a biblical practice, and Christians should find ways to protect women from this. In the New Testament circumcision finds its parallels in baptism, which is inclusive for men and women (see 4:5–6). (See the note on 'Circumcision', p. 411.)

you Gentiles by birth,[h] called "the uncircumcision" by those who are called "the circumcision" – a physical circumcision made in the flesh by human hands – [12]remember that you were at that time without Christ, being aliens from the commonwealth of Israel, and strangers to the covenants of promise, having no hope and without God in the world. [13]But now in Christ Jesus you who once were far off have been brought near by the blood of Christ. [14]For he is our peace; in his flesh he has made both groups into one and has broken down the dividing wall, that is, the hostility between us. [15]He has abolished the law with its commandments and ordinances, that he might create in himself one new humanity in place of the two, thus making peace, [16]and might reconcile both groups to God in one body[i] through the cross, thus putting to death that hostility through it.[j] [17]So he came and proclaimed peace to you who were far off and peace to those who were near; [18]for through him both of us have access in one Spirit to the Father. [19]So then you are no longer strangers and aliens, but you are citizens with the saints and also members of the household of God, [20]built upon the foundation of the apostles and prophets, with Christ Jesus himself as the cornerstone.[k] [21]In him the whole structure is joined together and grows into a holy temple in the Lord; [22]in whom you also are built together spiritually[l] into a dwelling place for God.

Paul's Ministry to the Gentiles

3 This is the reason that I Paul am a prisoner for[m] Christ Jesus for the sake of you Gentiles – [2]for surely you have already heard of the commission of God's grace that was given me for you, [3]and how the mystery was made known to me by revelation, as I wrote above in a few words, [4]a reading of which will enable you to perceive my understanding of the mystery of Christ. [5]In former generations this mystery[n] was not made known to humankind, as it has now been revealed to his holy apostles and prophets by the Spirit: [6]that is, the Gentiles have become fellow heirs, members of the same body, and sharers in the promise in Christ Jesus through the gospel.

7 Of this gospel I have become a servant according to the gift of God's grace that was given me by the working of his power. [8]Although I am the very least of all the saints, this grace was given to me to bring to the Gentiles the news of the boundless riches of Christ, [9]and to make everyone see[o] what is the plan of the mystery hidden for ages in[p] God who created all things; [10]so that through the church the wisdom of God in its rich variety might now be made known to the rulers and authorities in the heavenly places. [11]This was in accordance with the eternal purpose that he has carried out in Christ Jesus our Lord, [12]in whom we have access to God in boldness and confidence through faith in him.[q] [13]I pray therefore that you[r] may not lose heart over my sufferings for you; they are your glory.

Prayer for the Readers

14 For this reason I bow my knees before the Father,[s] [15]from whom every family[t] in heaven and on earth takes its name.

[h] Gk *in the flesh*   [i] Or *reconcile both of us in one body for God*   [j] Or *in him*, or *in himself*   [k] Or *keystone*   [l] Gk *in the Spirit*   [m] Or *of*   [n] Gk *it*   [o] Other ancient authorities read *to bring to light*   [p] Or *by*   [q] Or *the faith of him*   [r] Or *I*   [s] Other ancient authorities add *of our Lord Jesus Christ*   [t] Gk *fatherhood*

EPHESIANS 3

14. In the Greek there is a word-play here between Father (*pater*) and family (*patria*, i.e. a group of people coming from one ancestor), which the English cannot reproduce. The word 'family' here is not therefore meaning 'fatherhood' or something patriarchal. The word is used simply to mean family group or household in the earthly sense; and perhaps groupings of angels or angelic powers (good or evil) where 'in heaven' is mentioned. God is both creator and author, and is being extolled here.

¹⁶I pray that, according to the riches of his glory, he may grant that you may be strengthened in your inner being with power through his Spirit, ¹⁷and that Christ may dwell in your hearts through faith, as you are being rooted and grounded in love. ¹⁸I pray that you may have the power to comprehend, with all the saints, what is the breadth and length and height and depth, ¹⁹and to know the love of Christ that surpasses knowledge, so that you may be filled with all the fullness of God.

20 Now to him who by the power at work within us is able to accomplish abundantly far more than all we can ask or imagine, ²¹to him be glory in the church and in Christ Jesus to all generations, forever and ever. Amen.

Unity in the Body of Christ

4 I therefore, the prisoner in the Lord, beg you to lead a life worthy of the calling to which you have been called, ²with all humility and gentleness, with patience, bearing with one another in love, ³making every effort to maintain the unity of the Spirit in the bond of peace. ⁴There is one body and one Spirit, just as you were called to the one hope of your calling, ⁵one Lord, one faith, one baptism, ⁶one God and Father of all, who is above all and through all and in all.

7 But each of us was given grace according to the measure of Christ's gift. ⁸Therefore it is said,

"When he ascended on high he made
          captivity itself a captive;
     he gave gifts to his people."

⁹(When it says, "He ascended," what does it mean but that he had also descended[u] into the lower parts of the earth? ¹⁰He who descended is the same one who ascended far above all the heavens, so that he might fill all things.) ¹¹The gifts he gave were that some would be apostles, some prophets, some evangelists, some pastors and teachers, ¹²to equip the saints for the work of ministry, for building up the body of Christ, ¹³until all of us come to the unity of the faith and of the knowledge of the Son of God, to maturity, to the measure of the full stature of Christ. ¹⁴We must no longer be children, tossed to and fro and blown about by every wind of doctrine, by people's trickery, by their craftiness in deceitful scheming. ¹⁵But speaking the truth in love, we must grow up in every way into him who is the head, into Christ, ¹⁶from whom the whole body, joined and knit together by every ligament with which it is equipped, as each part is working properly, promotes the body's growth in building itself up in love.

[u] Other ancient authorities add *first*

---

16. 'in your inner being' translates the Greek *anthropos* or 'person'. NRSV is a much better translation than the old AV or RSV which had 'inner man'!

EPHESIANS 4

2. Humility and gentleness are often seen as feminine characteristics in many modern societies. The New Testament teaches that men *and* women are to be humble and gentle, after the example of Christ.

8. Ps. 68 may well have had associations with the Jewish festival of Pentecost, and Paul uses this quotation from Ps. 68:18 to refer to Christ giving gifts to the church. The older translations often rendered this verse 'he gave gifts to men', which is ambiguous, especially in the light of the gifts specified in Eph. 4:11, which have been male dominated in most churches. The early part of Eph. 4 is emphasizing the unity of the church, and 4:7 gives the context that gifts are to *each of us*.

11. There is no gender distinction in the text here. Paul is not saying that these gifts are for men only. Rather, the 'some' implies that these gifts are given throughout the whole church for our upbuilding.

The Old Life and the New

17 Now this I affirm and insist on in the Lord: you must no longer live as the Gentiles live, in the futility of their minds. [18]They are darkened in their understanding, alienated from the life of God because of their ignorance and hardness of heart. [19]They have lost all sensitivity and have abandoned themselves to licentiousness, greedy to practice every kind of impurity. [20]That is not the way you learned Christ! [21]For surely you have heard about him and were taught in him, as truth is in Jesus. [22]You were taught to put away your former way of life, your old self, corrupt and deluded by its lusts, [23]and to be renewed in the spirit of your minds, [24]and to clothe yourselves with the new self, created according to the likeness of God in true righteousness and holiness.

Rules for the New Life

25 So then, putting away falsehood, let all of us speak the truth to our neighbors, for we are members of one another. [26]Be angry but do not sin; do not let the sun go down on your anger, [27]and do not make room for the devil. [28]Thieves must give up stealing; rather let them labor and work honestly with their own hands, so as to have something to share with the needy. [29]Let no evil talk come out of your mouths, but only what is useful for building up,[v] as there is need, so that your words may give grace to those who hear. [30]And do not grieve the Holy Spirit of God, with which you were marked with a seal for the day of redemption. [31]Put away from you all bitterness and wrath and anger and wrangling and slander, together with all malice, [32]and be kind to one another, tenderhearted, forgiving one another, as God in Christ has forgiven you.[w] **5** [1]Therefore be imitators of God, as beloved children, [2]and live in love, as Christ loved us[x] and gave himself up for us, a fragrant offering and sacrifice to God.

Renounce Pagan Ways

3 But fornication and impurity of any kind, or greed, must not even be mentioned among you, as is proper among saints. [4]Entirely out of place is obscene, silly, and vulgar talk; but instead, let there be

◆ Sexual harrassment, in whatever form it takes, whether it involves verbal obscene suggestions or any form of unwanted physical contact is degrading and humiliating. It violates the victim's privacy and her person, even if it is done lightheartedly or in so-called 'fun', causing deep distress. It treats its victims as less than a person, as an object or plaything not to be taken seriously, whose feelings do not count, rather than as a person of value who God created and loves. It appears to give the perpetrators some sense of power or control over their victims to 'keep them in their place', to put them down, almost as if they are

[v] Other ancient authorities read *building up faith*
[w] Other ancient authorities read *us*   [x] Other ancient authorities read *you*

---

25. Cf. Zech. 8:16.
26. Cf. Ps. 4:4.

EPHESIANS 5

3. Sexual sins may have been a specific problem for the readers, and Paul is realistic about the temptations and results of even talking about such things. Christians are to be radically different in their moral attitudes and behavior. 'Fornication' covers sexual immorality in general, but also specifically adultery. Some male commentators note that it covers intercourse with female prostitutes, but presumably it is a ban for women's behavior as well as men's. Three types of sexually immoral behavior are specified in v. 3, as well as three types of sinful speech in v. 4.

another species which is less than they are and, therefore, worthy of misuse when in fact it is they that prove themselves, by their offensive behavior, to be less than they should be and belittle themselves.

What of the victim? How can she be helped to overcome the trauma of sexual harassment? At its worse, she is left feeling hurt, dirty, used, humiliated, guilty, angry and unable to trust. She must be allowed to express all her feelings in a safe environment with an understanding and compassionate listener to support her. To demonstrate that, whereas the perpetrator treated her as an object without respect and with no regard for her feelings, she is in fact a person of worth, beauty and dignity; pure and lovely; a real person who is loved and respected for who she is ◆

thanksgiving. ⁵Be sure of this, that no fornicator or impure person, or one who is greedy (that is, an idolater), has any inheritance in the kingdom of Christ and of God.

6 Let no one deceive you with empty words, for because of these things the wrath of God comes on those who are disobedient. ⁷Therefore do not be associated with them. ⁸For once you were dark-

ness, but now in the Lord you are light. Live as children of light – ⁹for the fruit of the light is found in all that is good and right and true. ¹⁰Try to find out what is pleasing to the Lord. ¹¹Take no part in the unfruitful works of darkness, but instead expose them. ¹²For it is shameful even to mention what such people do secretly; ¹³but everything exposed by the light becomes visible, ¹⁴for everything that becomes visible is light. Therefore it says,
"Sleeper, awake!
   Rise from the dead,
   and Christ will shine on you."

15 Be careful then how you live, not as unwise people but as wise, ¹⁶making the most of the time, because the days are evil. ¹⁷So do not be foolish, but understand what the will of the Lord is. ¹⁸Do not get drunk with wine, for that is debauchery; but be filled with the Spirit, ¹⁹as you sing psalms and hymns and spiritual songs among yourselves, singing and making melody to the Lord in your hearts, ²⁰giving thanks to God the Father at all times and for everything in the name of our Lord Jesus Christ.

The Christian Household
21 Be subject to one another out of reverence for Christ.

---

5. This does not mean that sexual sins are outside the scope of God's redemption. There is always the possibility of repentance and forgiveness for any sin committed before or after conversion. However, it is true to say that those who practise such things and do not repent, prove themselves by their behavior not to belong to the Kingdom of God. A mark of being a Christian is purity. Some societies are harder on women than men regarding sexual sins, requiring women to be virgins before marriage, but not men. Scripture makes no such distinction – both are to be holy.
6. See the note on 2:2.
18. A prohibition of the folly of drunkenness is followed by a command to the wisdom of being filled with and by the Holy Spirit. This main verb, the command to be filled, issues in five dependent participles which link the sentences together (though the punctuation and separation of vv. 21 and 22 obscure this in the NRSV and most other translations). The dependent participles are *speaking* (not 'singing' here) psalms and hymns, *singing, making melody* (5:19), *giving thanks* (5:20) and *submitting* (5:21). All of these require, and are a result of, being filled with the Spirit.
21. 'Be subject to' would be better rendered 'Submit to', since the verb does not denote subjection or subjugation, but rather willing and voluntary submission. It is not a statement implying any inferior nature of women, but talking about the relationship between two equals, where submission is always required to make a relationship work. This submission is required of every believer to every other, regardless of class, race, status or gender.

◆ Mutuality infers two people thinking, feeling and acting for the good of each other. The intimacy required in marriage is the perfect relationship for practising such mutuality. The word translated 'to know' in the OT refers to the intimate sexual relationship enjoyed by marriage partners, but must include every kind of communication necessary for those partners to become truly 'one'. Whether we consider men and women to be very different, or not as different as might be imagined, there is the necessity of 'knowing' our partner before true mutuality can be practised. As we experience life together, there are opportunities to talk about what we think and feel, always aiming to have the 'mind of Christ', considering the other as better than ourselves (Phil. 2:3) and making possible the knowledge of the other person that allows us to help our partner to develop to be what they uniquely were meant to be 'in Christ'.

Although true Christian mutuality cannot be practised in a marriage of unequally yoked partners, where one is a Christian and the other is not (cf. 1 Pet. 3:1–2 for how to deal with this situation as women), the knowledge of the other and consequent loving responses may be the first step to a partner's conversion and the resulting deeper intimacy available in a shared Christian faith.

Eph. 5:21 carries an injunction for all Christians which is then narrowed down to marriage, to 'Be subject to one another out of reverence for Christ'. It is the prior

and more important relationship with Christ that provides the motivation for our relationships with others. There can never be another person who can be put first in our lives. Just as the Bible never instructs us to trust anyone but God, so, in Christ, we are never expected to treat others in a certain way because *they* deserve it.

Our Christian mutuality takes into account that we will fall short of what's expected of us, bringing mutual forgiveness, only possible with Christ, into the equation. He is the third person who makes continuing mutuality possible, and allows us to be accountable to each other because of the standards he sets. In him we become responsible for seeking our partner's best, not only in what *we* do and say, but in what we encourage our partner to be. In an atmosphere of true mutuality, this may sometimes include either partner calling the other to account for something which may not be in line with a life in Christ.

Where there has been the prior love and respect spoken of in Eph. 5:22–33, there should be no reason why an exhortation or admonition from our partner should not be accepted in all humility. The confession of our sins to one another is a further function in mutuality. Who would be better to confess to than someone who knows us best of all, and yet loves and respects us in Christ? ◆

22 Wives, be subject to your husbands as you are to the Lord. [23]For the husband is the

---

The wife is never commanded to 'obey' her husband, whereas children are commanded to obey their parents (6:1) and slaves their masters (6:5). Women should therefore not be required to pledge obedience to their husbands as part of the marriage service. The husband is never told on any occasion to make the wife submit; it is to be a voluntary personal act of free yielding. Submission is nothing feeble, and the wife is not being required to be a doormat. Submission may prove to be difficult, which is why it requires being filled with the Holy Spirit. But it is a mark of mature Christian love.

22. The NRSV has a new paragraph here, as the NIV, which also gives a new heading. More accurately, v. 21 belongs with the verses following, and would be more literally translated, 'Submit to one another out of reverence for Christ, wives to your husbands . . .' as the better Greek manuscripts have no separate verb after wives, but rely instead on the verb being understood from

◆ The worldly concept of authority, that someone must always be at the top telling others what to do, may lead us to assume that when the Bible talks about submission, it naturally goes hand in hand with the exercise of authority. However, when the Bible talks about submission, or directs someone to submit, it is instead an expansion on the particulars of the Servanthood principle (Matt. 7:12; 22:39; Gal. 5:13).

When we read the word 'submit' in the Bible it often registers as 'to be in a God-ordained subordinate position', or 'to be under the authority of'. But that is the definition of 'subordinate'.

The words 'submit' and 'subordinate' are not synonymous. Submit means a voluntary yielding of oneself to another. It may or may not be to someone in authority over you. The word 'subordinate' indicates a position under the authority of a superior. Subordinate does not mean one who is submissive. Submit defines an action. Subordinate defines a position. Submit comes from within. Subordinate is imposed from without.

One says, 'I will serve you.' The other says, 'You must do as I tell you.'

Submit and subordinate may occur together. The patriot soldier freely gives himself to fight for his country. At the same time he is subordinate to the authority structures of that country and its army.

But submit and subordinate do not necessarily go together. A student is subordinate to his teacher, but at the same time may be completely rebellious and unsubmissive.

Likewise, we can all think of a circumstance when someone has been submissive, but not subordinate. It happens all the time in everyday life. Equals submit to equals. Someone simply gives in, yields their will to someone else's. There can be many reasons for being submissive, and being subordinate is only one of them.

Jesus is the prime example of one who was submissive, even though not subordinate (John 10:17–18; Luke 2:51; Phil. 2:6–7). The biblical concept of submission is ultimately linked to the example of Jesus, and his divine character (1 Pet.

v. 21. Grammatically and logically then, the submission required of the wife is a further specification of the mutual submission required of all believers, and even of both wife *and* husband. Paul is not teaching that the wife alone has the responsibility to submit any more than the husband alone must love (5:25). Both obviously do both!

'Husband' translates the Greek word which can mean man or husband. Paul is not teaching that women should be subordinate to all men. If anything, Paul is giving a restriction of submission which would have been expected of women at that time. The Greek also has the word 'own' before husband, implying that it is the marital relationship to which Paul refers. Neither is the submission of the wife to be unconditional. Paul qualifies it with 'as to the Lord'. This does not mean that the husband is lord to the wife (or the Greek would require 'lord' to be plural). It is most likely that this meaning is similar to the 'as is fitting in the Lord' of Col. 3:18, or that Christ is the motivation for submission. It is like a training ground, that in submitting to the husband a wife is in fact submitting to Christ.

23. Strictly speaking, the analogy of the husband as head of (not 'over'!) the wife is not a responsibility, but a statement of fact. It appears in this verse as part of the injunction to wives, not to husbands. Nowhere is there a command for the husband to 'be head'! Neither is the word 'headship' ever used in the New Testament. The husband is stated to be head, but his duty is to love.

Some have drawn from this statement that Paul is teaching authority for husbands and subjugation of wives. This view is usually based on the fact that the word 'head' (see the note on 'The head', p. 343) can mean chief or ruler from its Old Testament background, doubtless having with it a sense of leadership or authority. But it may also mean source or origin, and many think that this is the force here, emphasizing the closeness of relationship and unity between the head and body, Christ and the church, the husband and the wife, not any authority structure.

2:20–21; 3:1, 7; 5:5). We are to submit 'in the same way' Jesus did.

Jesus is God. Jesus is of the same substance, and equal in power and glory with God the Father and the Holy Spirit. This has been the understanding of orthodox Christianity since the doctrine of the Trinity was fully enunciated with the formulation of the Athanasian Creed in about AD 450. Jesus has all authority (Phil. 2:6; Matt. 23:8–12; 28:16–20; John 13:3).

But even though not subordinate, Jesus submitted his life to God for us (Eph. 5:1–2). His submission was completely voluntary (John 10:17–18). Jesus demonstrated his love by choosing to be a servant rather than by exercising authority (Phil. 2:6–8; John 13:3, 5).

A similar false assumption is often made when we discuss equality for women. We may jump to the conclusion that if there is equality there can be no submission. But every believer must have a commitment to servanthood. We must serve because Christ came to serve. Equality does not exclude submission. Equality makes submission the responsibility of every believer (1 Cor. 16:15–16; Eph. 5:21; 1 Pet. 5:5).

One example of how we incorrectly assume that the word 'submit' goes with an authority structure is in the very familiar passage in Ephesians which talks about the relationship between husbands and wives (Eph. 5:22–33). This section is introduced by two restatements of the Servanthood principle which are directed to all believers (Eph. 5:1–2, 21).

Then comes the example that wives are to submit to their husbands in the same

way that the church submits to Christ. Jesus made plain his definition of submission. 'If any want to become my followers, let them deny themselves and take up their cross *and follow me*' (Mark 8:34). Our submission must be characterized by humility, just as Jesus' was (James 4:6–12; Phil. 2:8). The essence of our submission to Jesus is our own death to ourselves so that we can live to God (Rom. 6:11–13; 12:1–2; 1 Pet. 2:24).

At this point the false assumption is often made that if wives are to submit, then husbands must be in authority over them. Not so. Instead, Paul continues, 'Husbands, love your wives, just as Christ loved the church and *gave himself up* for her . . .' (Eph. 5:22–25).

The essence of loving your wife (Eph. 5:25), and of loving each other (Eph. 5:1–2) is servanthood, just as the essence of Jesus' love for the church was giving himself up (John 15:13).

Both love and submission mean a completely voluntary giving up of oneself for another, first to God and then to each other (Matt. 22:37–40), through the reconciling power of God's grace which brings new life in Christ (Eph. 2:13–22; 4:1–6). Jesus gave himself and we respond by denying ourselves. This is servanthood, the way of Christ and his Kingdom ◆

head of the wife just as Christ is the head of the church, the body of which he is the Savior. [24]Just as the church is subject to Christ, so also wives ought to be, in everything, to their husbands.

25 Husbands, love your wives, just as Christ loved the church and gave himself up

---

24. Throughout these verses there is a see-saw effect of comparison between the church's relationship with Christ and the wife with her husband, as well as Christ's love for the church and the husband's love for his wife. The point of comparison is the submission of both church and wife. The husband is not being compared with Christ; he is in no sense in the place of Christ for her, but their relationship may be understood by reference to the *example* of Christ and the church.

25. Those who see 'head' in 5:23 meaning an authoritative power to rule often see this as implying a husband's role as decision-maker or even boss. However, in a passage speaking so much of submission and love, ideas of power and ruling are out of place. The analogies drawn

for her, [26]in order to make her holy by cleansing her with the washing of water by the word, [27]so as to present the church to himself in splendor, without a spot or wrinkle or anything of the kind – yes, so that she may be holy and without blemish. [28]In the same way, husbands should love their wives as they do their own bodies. He who loves his wife loves himself. [29]For no one ever hates his own body, but he nourishes and tenderly cares for it, just as Christ does for the church, [30]because we are members of his body.[y] [31]"For this reason a man will leave his father and mother and be joined to his wife, and the two will become one flesh." [32]This is a great mystery, and I am applying it to Christ and the church. [33]Each of you, however, should love his wife as himself, and a wife should respect her husband.

Children and Parents

6 Children, obey your parents in the Lord,[z] for this is right. [2]"Honor your father and mother" – this is the first commandment with a promise: [3]"so that it may be well with you and you may live long on the earth."

4 And, fathers, do not provoke your children to anger, but bring them up in the discipline and instruction of the Lord.

◆ As with any relationship between Christians, it is Christ who has the last word. So when Paul admonishes fathers not to exasperate their children, he explains what to do instead: 'bring them up in the discipline and instruction of the Lord'. A home that acknowledges Christ as the final authority, gives a tenderness and humility to the demands placed on children. It is not simply the whim of the parent that certain expectations are set.

Training and instruction take time, a commodity lacking for many. The commitment to set time aside to get to know our child and to apply God's teaching to his/her specific situation will develop habits of thought which will be invaluable in later life.

Deut. 6:7 gives us a clue as to where

[y] Other ancient authorities add *of his flesh and of his bones* [z] Other ancient authorities lack *in the Lord*

---

from Christ are all in the area of giving up and sacrifice, not of power or rule. Christ did not rule or assert himself in order to be Savior to the church, but sacrificed himself. It is not Christ's Lordship which is analogous to the husband's headship, but Christ's self-giving, and it is to such a headship of sacrificial love that the wife is to submit herself. The pattern and mandate for the husband's love is to be nothing less than the very love of Christ himself.

26–27. This is an elaboration on Christ's work, not that of the husband. The husband is not expected to sanctify, cleanse or present his wife holy, as Christ does the church. These are illustrations and results of the sacrificial love of Christ. But it is the sacrificial aspect of Christ's love which is the point of comparison for the husband's love.

31. Most commentaries on this verse (a quotation from Gen. 2:24) rightly point out the deep union of the husband and wife in marriage, but few deal with the prelude of leaving parents in order to form the new union. Leaving *and* cleaving are vital to the marriage relationship. Neither Paul nor Genesis elaborates on what exactly constitutes leaving. It is obviously not an excuse for abandoning responsibility toward parents, or for ceasing to love, respect, honor and obey them as appropriate in the Lord (6:1). However, it should be a challenge to some societies where the wife is forced to turn her back on her own family and become a virtual slave in her husband's family.

EPHESIANS 6

2. Cf. Exod. 20:12; Deut. 5:16. Both parents share in honor and obedience from their children.
4. Fathers are to have no less responsibility than mothers in bringing up their children in the Lord.

and when we can teach: 'when you are at home and when you are away, when you lie down and when you rise'. In other words, be so aware of God's continual presence, that whenever you are with your child, the response to any situation is to apply God's teaching to it ◆

Slaves and Masters

5 Slaves, obey your earthly masters with fear and trembling, in singleness of heart, as you obey Christ; [6]not only while being watched, and in order to please them, but as slaves of Christ, doing the will of God from the heart. [7]Render service with enthusiasm, as to the Lord and not to men and women, [8]knowing that whatever good we do, we will receive the same again from the Lord, whether we are slaves or free.

9 And, masters, do the same to them. Stop threatening them, for you know that both of you have the same Master in heaven, and with him there is no partiality.

The Whole Armor of God

10 Finally, be strong in the Lord and in the strength of his power. [11]Put on the whole armor of God, so that you may be able to stand against the wiles of the devil. [12]For our[a] struggle is not against enemies of blood and flesh, but against the rulers, against the authorities, against the cosmic powers of this present darkness, against the spiritual forces of evil in the heavenly places. [13]Therefore take up the whole armor of God, so that you may be able to withstand on that evil day, and having done everything, to stand firm.

[14]Stand therefore, and fasten the belt of truth around your waist, and put on the breastplate of righteousness. [15]As shoes for your feet put on whatever will make you ready to proclaim the gospel of peace. [16]With all of these,[b] take the shield of faith, with which you will be able to quench all the flaming arrows of the evil one. [17]Take the helmet of salvation, and the sword of the Spirit, which is the word of God.

18 Pray in the Spirit at all times in every prayer and supplication. To that end keep alert and always persevere in supplication for all the saints. [19]Pray also for me, so that when I speak, a message may be given to me to make known with boldness the mystery of the gospel,[c] [20]for which I am an ambassador in chains. Pray that I may declare it boldly, as I must speak.

Personal Matters and Benediction

21 So that you also may know how I am and what I am doing, Tychicus will tell you everything. He is a dear brother and a faithful minister in the Lord. [22]I am sending him to you for this very purpose, to let you know how we are, and to encourage your hearts.

23 Peace be to the whole community,[d] and love with faith, from God the Father and the Lord Jesus Christ. [24]Grace be with all who have an undying love for our Lord Jesus Christ.[e]

---

[a] Other ancient authorities read *your*   [b] Or *In all circumstances*   [c] Other ancient authorities lack *of the gospel*   [d] Gk *to the brothers*   [e] Other ancient authorities add *Amen*

---

21. 'Minister' translates *diakonos*, the same word used in Eph. 3:7 of Paul, but better translated there as 'servant', since 'minister' in English is often unfortunately associated with the male idea of the office of Minister or Pastor, rather than the function of serving. *Diakonos* is a word used in the New Testament of either male or female (e.g. Phoebe, Rom. 16:1).(See note on 'Women Deacons', p. 407.)

23. Literally, 'peace to the brothers', but 'brothers' always include sisters in the Greek (unless deliberately speaking of men only), and the NRSV conveys the idea here.

THE LETTER OF PAUL TO THE PHILIPPIANS

INTRODUCTION

The church at Philippi was unique in its beginnings. Paul had had a vision in the night of a man from Macedonia pleading with him, 'Come over to Macedonia and help us' (Acts 16:9). Paul knew that he must go. Together with Timothy and Silas, Paul sailed to the province of Macedonia, in the northern part of Greece and established a church there.

In Acts 16, we read about two women who were involved with Paul leading to the establishment of the church in Philippi. These two women represent opposite extremes in terms of their social standing. The first was Lydia, a prosperous business-woman from an Asiatic background – a trader of textiles for which her city was famous. When Paul and the others arrived in Philippi, they found no synagogue, but on the day of worship, a small group of women had gathered for prayer on the bank of the river. Lydia came into contact with the gospel when Paul and the others came there and spoke to these women. It appears that Lydia was the first convert at Philippi. She and her family were baptized, and she opened her home to Paul (Acts 16:14). Lydia's home became the first church at Philippi (Acts 16:40). The second was a demon-possessed slave girl from a Greek background who was being used by her owners to make money through fortune telling (Acts 16:16–18). Through Paul's ministry, she was set free from demons and it is likely that she joined the church at Philippi also.

The remarkable conversion of the jailer also took place in Philippi (Acts 16:25–34). Paul and Silas baptized the jailer, his wife, his children and all the other members of his household. After that, the jailer's wife and her servants prepared a meal for Paul and Silas. They all ate together and their hearts were filled with joy. Thus, when Paul addresses the leaders and members of the church at Philippi, it is clear that this congregation included people from all levels of society, both men and women.

One of Paul's strategies for evangelism was to establish churches in major cities. The city of Philippi, located in the part of northern Greece, was one such influential city that set the pace for the surrounding territories at that time. It is said to have been founded by Philip II, the father of Alexander the Great, and later made a Roman colony by Octavian. It was strategic and important in Paul's mission because it was a great commercial center situated in a passage-way linking Europe and Asia. It was a gateway in a range of hills dividing Europe and Asia. Then, as a Roman colony, it had developed good roads, an asset to trade and to the spread of the gospel. It was a strategic place to establish a church because traders passing through would come in contact with the gospel and carry the gospel back to their destinations. Philippi became the first city in Europe to hear the gospel.

The key factor in the life of the church at Philippi was their union with Christ (1:1; 2:1). This caused them to have compassion and love for fellow-believers and led to the spirit of generosity that characterized this church (1:15). Having supported Paul's ministry, they have become partners with him in spreading the gospel (1:4–11, 24–30; 2:1–4, 17–30; 3:10–11, 17; 4:1–3, 10, 14–19). Not only did they give gifts of money, but as mentioned above, Lydia opened her home to Paul; and two other women, Euodia and Syntyche (4:2) worked side by side with him in preaching and teaching.

Despite the serious nature of some of the issues addressed, this letter comes out with a clear and strong expression of joy. The word *joy* is repeated over and over (1:4, 18–19, 25–26; 2:2, 17–18, 29–30; 3:1; 4:1, 4, 10). This is even more significant considering that Paul wrote this letter while he was in prison. It is believed that at the time of writing this letter, Paul was imprisoned in Rome, having been accused of treason. His life was in great danger because of preaching the gospel of Jesus Christ. While awaiting trial, he was confined in a rented house, and chained to a soldier who guarded him day and night. For two years, Paul remained under house arrest in Rome. Yet he even preached to the soldiers who guarded him and whilst a prisoner in Rome, Paul wrote many letters to encourage God's people (Acts 28:16, 20, 30–31).

At the time of writing this letter, it was about ten years after Paul's first visit to Philippi. It is evident that Paul loved the members of this church dearly. During the ten years, it is likely that letters from Paul went back and forth to maintain ties of friendship. The church at Philippi heard that Paul was in prison in Rome and in need of money. Although Paul was in prison, it appears that he was obliged to buy his food and other essentials. Having been accused of treason, it is possible that the believers in Rome would have disassociated themselves from him; it is unlikely that they would have helped him.

Thus, it was the church at Philippi who sent one of their members, Epaphroditus, to bring Paul a gift of money and to take care of him while he was in prison (2:25; 4:14–18). Epaphroditus, after reaching Paul, had fallen sick and almost died. Having now recovered (2:26–28), he was about to return to Philippi. With him, Paul intended to send this letter. It was more than an ordinary letter of thanks; it expresses Paul's deep, personal feelings for this church.

Questions on Philippians

There is a real danger that Christians become so preoccupied with their own personal needs and circumstances that they neglect the needs of others. What are our responsibilities toward fellow Christians, especially Christian missions?

In any church, personalities can sometimes come into conflict. Thus, disagreements will at times arise between influential members or leaders of the church. In such situations, how do we help bring about reconciliation?

Salutation

1 Paul and Timothy, servants[a] of Christ Jesus,

To all the saints in Christ Jesus who are in Philippi, with the bishops[b] and deacons:[c]

◆ We know from Phil. 1:1 that by the early AD 60s some churches had at least one officer called a 'deacon'. If it was an individual 'from the first day' (v. 5) at Philippi, then that person must have been a woman (see Acts 16:13). Phoebe was deacon of the assembly of Christians at Cenchreae (Rom. 16:1). Since then various churches have entrusted various duties to deacons.

'Deacon' connoted an extremely high standard of service, skill at perceiving needs and resources, an ability to negotiate and enable things to happen with speed, and trustworthiness (see Acts 6:1–7).

The early women deacons (Rom. 16:1–2; 1 Tim. 3:11) were probably recruited from the corps of enrolled widows (1 Tim. 5). In that society only a widow would have the freedom of movement and the experience of managing a household. Older widows were preferred, but Deacon Olympias in Constantinople was quite young. The Council of Chalcedon decided the minimum age of ordination was 40. At a time of financial stringency, their numbers were reduced to 40 at Hagia Sophia and to six at the larger parishes!

Except for Latin-speaking Rome (and places it influenced) where the diaconate was limited to seven men only, the diaconate of women developed in various churches. We know most about that of the Syrian Church from the *Didascalia*. Its women deacons had teaching, sacramental, and administrative roles. In a society segregated by gender and age, their ministry was mainly, but not exclusively, to women of all ages and young boys. Today we might advertise the post as 'Personal Assistant to the Bishop for Ministry to Women'. A woman deacon especially accompanied women through all the stages of preparation for baptism, baptism itself, and gave the post-baptismal ethical instruction. She visited and took Communion to sick and house-bound women.

When some women deacons became responsible for women's religious communities, the *deacon*-abbess evolved into the deacon-*abbess*; eventually her diaconate was forgotten. But in the 19th and 20th centuries the diaconate of women has been restored in many Lutheran, Reformed and Anglican churches, and its restoration now is being discussed in the Orthodox, Oriental, and Roman Catholic churches ◆

2 Grace to you and peace from God our Father and the Lord Jesus Christ.

Paul's Prayer for the Philippians

3 I thank my God every time I remember you, [4]constantly praying with joy in every one of my prayers for all of you, [5]because of your sharing in the gospel from the first day until now. [6]I am confident of this, that the one who began a good work among you will bring it to completion by the day of Jesus Christ. [7]It is right for me to think this way about all of you, because you hold me in your heart,[d] for all of you share in God's grace[e] with me, both in my imprisonment and in the defense and confirmation of the

[a] Gk *slaves*   [b] Or *overseers*   [c] Or *overseers and helpers*   [d] Or *because I hold you in my heart*   [e] Gk *in grace*

PHILIPPIANS 1

1–11. Paul begins with an affectionate greeting and a prayer for the spiritual development of the little group of believers. V. 6 is a special encouragement to all those who focus more on their own shortcomings than on God's transforming power. A contemporary slogan reads, 'Please be patient with me. God hasn't finished with me yet!'

gospel. [8]For God is my witness, how I long for all of you with the compassion of Christ Jesus. [9]And this is my prayer, that your love may overflow more and more with knowledge and full insight [10]to help you to determine what is best, so that in the day of Christ you may be pure and blameless, [11]having produced the harvest of righteousness that comes through Jesus Christ for the glory and praise of God.

Paul's Present Circumstances

12 I want you to know, beloved,[f] that what has happened to me has actually helped to spread the gospel, [13]so that it has become known throughout the whole imperial guard[g] and to everyone else that my imprisonment is for Christ; [14]and most of the brothers and sisters,[f] having been made confident in the Lord by my imprisonment, dare to speak the word[h] with greater boldness and without fear.

15 Some proclaim Christ from envy and rivalry, but others from goodwill. [16]These proclaim Christ out of love, knowing that I have been put here for the defense of the gospel; [17]the others proclaim Christ out of selfish ambition, not sincerely but intending to increase my suffering in my imprisonment. [18]What does it matter? Just this, that Christ is proclaimed in every way, whether out of false motives or true; and in that I rejoice.

Yes, and I will continue to rejoice, [19]for I know that through your prayers and the help of the Spirit of Jesus Christ this will turn out for my deliverance. [20]It is my eager expectation and hope that I will not be put to shame in any way, but that by my speaking with all boldness, Christ will be exalted now as always in my body, whether by life or by death. [21]For to me, living is Christ and dying is gain. [22]If I am to live in the flesh, that means fruitful labor for me; and I do not know which I prefer. [23]I am hard pressed between the two: my desire is to depart and be with Christ, for that is far better; [24]but to remain in the flesh is more necessary for you. [25]Since I am convinced of this, I know that I will remain and continue with all of you for your progress and joy in faith, [26]so that I may share abundantly in your boasting in Christ Jesus when I come to you again.

27 Only, live your life in a manner worthy of the gospel of Christ, so that, whether I come and see you or am absent and hear about you, I will know that you are standing firm in one spirit, striving side by side with one mind for the faith of the gospel, [28]and are in no way intimidated by your opponents. For them this is evidence of their destruction, but of your salvation. And this is God's doing. [29]For he has graciously granted you the privilege not only of believing in Christ, but of suffering for him as well – [30]since you are having the same struggle that you saw I had and now hear that I still have.

[f] Gk *brothers*   [g] Gk *whole praetorium*   [h] Other ancient authorities read *word of God*

9–11. Paul prays for his children in the faith that they may mature and that God's work may be perfect in them. Do we pray in this manner for other Christians?

12–19. Paul wanted to reassure them of his well-being and take away any anxiety that his imprisonment was a set-back for the gospel.

20–26. Here is our most intimate view of the apostle's philosophy of life and death. This passage can give meaning to our own existence, whatever the circumstances.

28–30. Paul appealed to the church at Philippi to persevere in the midst of hardship. He encourages them to endure without fear because they were simply undergoing what Paul himself had experienced. His departure from Philippi was prompted by hostilities and imprisonment. The church must have been experiencing the same persecution. Paul wanted them to know that their courageous endurance should spring from the knowledge of the fact that their victory comes from God (1:29).

Imitating Christ's Humility

2 If then there is any encouragement in Christ, any consolation from love, any sharing in the Spirit, any compassion and sympathy, ²make my joy complete: be of the same mind, having the same love, being in full accord and of one mind. ³Do nothing from selfish ambition or conceit, but in humility regard others as better than yourselves. ⁴Let each of you look not to your own interests, but to the interests of others. ⁵Let the same mind be in you that was[i] in Christ Jesus,

⁶ who, though he was in the form of God,
   did not regard equality with God
   as something to be exploited,
⁷ but emptied himself,
   taking the form of a slave,
   being born in human likeness.
And being found in human form,
⁸   he humbled himself
   and became obedient to the point of
      death –
   even death on a cross.
⁹ Therefore God also highly exalted him

and gave him the name
   that is above every name,
¹⁰ so that at the name of Jesus
   every knee should bend,
   in heaven and on earth and under
      the earth,
¹¹ and every tongue should confess
   that Jesus Christ is Lord,
   to the glory of God the Father.

Shining as Lights in the World

12 Therefore, my beloved, just as you have always obeyed me, not only in my presence, but much more now in my absence, work out your own salvation with fear and trembling; ¹³for it is God who is at work in you, enabling you both to will and to work for his good pleasure.

14 Do all things without murmuring and arguing, ¹⁵so that you may be blameless and innocent, children of God without blemish in the midst of a crooked and perverse generation, in which you shine

[i] Or *that you have*

PHILIPPIANS 2

Paul wanted to appeal for unity among members of the church at Philippi (1:27; 2:1-11; 4:2). Throughout this letter, there are hints of disunity (1:9, 27; 2:1-4, 5, 15). Apparently, the church was being threatened by divisive elements of disunity which made it difficult for them to attain unity. There is a need to stand firm together and be of one mind (1:27; 2:2). Here the word *mind* refers to an attitude or outlook. It is unlikely that Paul would expect the believers to have the same opinions on every matter, but he would expect them to have a common faith and a common desire to serve Jesus Christ together. To achieve this oneness of mind and purpose, Paul admonished them to avoid acting from selfish ambition and pride (2:3); they must seek and remain faithful to God (2:12-13); avoid complaining and arguing among themselves (2:14-16).

1-5. He begins this portion by discussing attitudes. He speaks of humility and of mutual concern for one another (vv. 3-4) and then moves into a most important discussion of the nature of Jesus Christ. In one of the most moving passages in the whole of the New Testament (2:1-18), Paul deals with the ultimate goal of the Christian life – obedience to God and humility among believers.

6-8. He offers the humility and obedience of Christ as the supreme example for Christians to emulate. Although he was equal with God (v. 6), he moved to a servant's place and endured execution as a criminal (v. 8).

9-11. In Christ's abasement he procured our salvation, but he was raised up in exaltation. Paul emphasizes the need for a humble, self-sacrificial attitude and life among believers (2:4-11) who will seek to put the interests of others above their own personal ambitions.

12-18. Reflecting his glory, Christians shine forth (v. 15) in a darkened world. Life, attitudes and speech all bear witness to the One who is the Word of God.

like stars in the world. [16]It is by your holding fast to the word of life that I can boast on the day of Christ that I did not run in vain or labor in vain. [17]But even if I am being poured out as a libation over the sacrifice and the offering of your faith, I am glad and rejoice with all of you – [18]and in the same way you also must be glad and rejoice with me.

Timothy and Epaphroditus

19 I hope in the Lord Jesus to send Timothy to you soon, so that I may be cheered by news of you. [20]I have no one like him who will be genuinely concerned for your welfare. [21]All of them are seeking their own interests, not those of Jesus Christ. [22]But Timothy's[j] worth you know, how like a son with a father he has served with me in the work of the gospel. [23]I hope therefore to send him as soon as I see how things go with me; [24]and I trust in the Lord that I will also come soon.

25 Still, I think it necessary to send to you Epaphroditus – my brother and co-worker and fellow soldier, your messenger[k] and minister to my need; [26]for he has been longing for[l] all of you, and has been distressed because you heard that he was ill. [27]He was indeed so ill that he nearly died. But God had mercy on him, and not only on him but on me also, so that I would not have one sorrow after another. [28]I am the more eager to send him, therefore, in order that you may rejoice at seeing him again, and that I may be less anxious. [29]Welcome him then in the Lord with all joy, and honor such people, [30]because he came close to death for the work of Christ,[m] risking his life to make up for those services that you could not give me.

3 Finally, my brothers and sisters,[n] rejoice[o] in the Lord.

Breaking with the Past

To write the same things to you is not troublesome to me, and for you it is a safeguard.

2 Beware of the dogs, beware of the evil workers, beware of those who mutilate the flesh![p] [3]For it is we who are the circumcision, who worship in the Spirit of

[j] Gk *his*   [k] Gk *apostle*   [l] Other ancient authorities read *longing to see*   [m] Other ancient authorities read *of the Lord*   [n] Gk *my brothers*   [o] Or *farewell*   [p] Gk *the mutilation*

19–30. Paul wanted to explain to the church at Philippi why he was sending Epaphroditus and Timothy to them. Apparently, they had sent Epaphroditus to remain with Paul and take care of him while he was in prison. Paul expresses gratitude for Epaphroditus' services. He had served Paul with dedication but fell ill and almost died. Paul is full of praise for Epaphroditus and encouraged the church to accept Epaphroditus back with joy. Paul also expressed hope that Timothy, his trusted young friend and co-worker would visit them soon (2:19–24). With his mother and grandmother, Timothy had earlier accepted Christ during Paul's visit to Lystra (2 Tim. 1:5). Timothy had joined Paul and Silas on their first journey to Philippi.

PHILIPPIANS 3

1–3. Paul was aware of the dangers to which the believers at Philippi were being exposed. There were false teachers going around preaching, attempting to lead them astray. They threatened to undermine the basic teachings of the church. The church at Philippi needed to be aware of this because such a situation would pose a threat to them.

3–11. Here Paul parades his pedigree but not for the sake of declaring himself better than anyone else. Rather it is but dung compared to the excellency which is to be found in Jesus Christ (v. 8). He warns them against those who wanted to give pre-eminence to religious laws concerning outward ceremonies and rituals (3:3–11). Some of them were genuine, but genuinely wrong. He also wanted to warn them about other false teachers who were claiming to have attained perfection (3:15–17) and urging people to put their confidence in things other than Christ. Paul had found that all the things he had relied on in his old life such as family background, wealth, education and personal achievements (3:4–7) were worthless garbage compared with living in the knowledge of Jesus Christ.

God[q] and boast in Christ Jesus and have no confidence in the flesh – [4]even though I, too, have reason for confidence in the flesh.

If anyone else has reason to be confident in the flesh, I have more: [5]circumcised on the eighth day, a member of the people of Israel, of the tribe of Benjamin, a Hebrew born of Hebrews; as to the law, a Pharisee; [6]as to zeal, a persecutor of the church; as to righteousness under the law, blameless.

◆ Gentiles and Jews were working to achieve a somewhat uneasy truce as they merged their traditions in a new commitment to Christ. It was easy for the Jews to assume a cultural and religious superiority because they had been the people chosen by God to bear witness to his being, to receive and preserve the Scriptures, and to bring forth from their ranks the prophets and the Messiah.

Circumcision was viewed as a sign of religious correctness (Phil. 3:5) but that was not its original intention. It was rather a sign of the covenant between Abraham and God, a token of the pledge that he would be their God and they would be his people (Gen. 17:10–14). It served as a perpetual reminder to males of Israel's covenantal relationship and of the conduct which God expected of his people. The bodily member sometimes employed in aggression and exploitation of others was marked for divinely designed, constructive uses.

Paul reminds his readers repeatedly that circumcision is not a spiritual imperative (Rom. 2:25–29) but rather a distinguishing mark. He insisted that it should not be mandatory for Gentile Christians (Gal. 5:2–6), being well aware that it had been an exclusive rite for Jewish males. By contrast, all believers are included in baptism, all divisions are done away, and all become one in Christ (Gal. 3:28) ◆

---

[7] Yet whatever gains I had, these I have come to regard as loss because of Christ. [8]More than that, I regard everything as loss because of the surpassing value of knowing Christ Jesus my Lord. For his sake I have suffered the loss of all things, and I regard them as rubbish, in order that I may gain Christ [9]and be found in him, not having a righteousness of my own that comes from the law, but one that comes through faith in Christ,[r] the righteousness from God based on faith. [10]I want to know Christ[s] and the power of his resurrection and the sharing of his sufferings by becoming like him in his death, [11]if somehow I may attain the resurrection from the dead.

Pressing toward the Goal

[12] Not that I have already obtained this or have already reached the goal;[t] but I press on to make it my own, because Christ Jesus has made me his own. [13]Beloved,[u] I do not consider that I have made it my own;[v] but this one thing I do: forgetting what lies behind and straining forward to what lies ahead, [14]I press on toward the goal for the prize of the heavenly[w] call of God in Christ Jesus. [15]Let those of us then who are mature be of the same mind; and if you think differently about anything, this too God will reveal to you. [16]Only let us hold fast to what we have attained.

[17] Brothers and sisters,[u] join in imitating me, and observe those who live according to the example you have in us. [18]For many live as enemies of the cross of Christ; I have often told you of them, and now I tell

---

[q] Other ancient authorities read *worship God in spirit*   [r] Or *through the faith of Christ*   [s] Gk *him*   [t] Or *have already been made perfect*   [u] Gk *Brothers*   [v] Other ancient authorities read *my own yet*   [w] Gk *upward*

9–14. He had learned not to put confidence in who he is or what he has done but to put confidence in who Christ is and what he has done. He urges them not to seek security in earthly things, but to maintain the right focus on things of God and to strive towards the prize, the life above (3:14).
17–21. Paul encourages his children to walk joyfully in the Lord but warns them of those who might subvert the simplicity of their faith and practice.

you even with tears. ¹⁹Their end is destruction; their god is the belly; and their glory is in their shame; their minds are set on earthly things. ²⁰But our citizenship˟ is in heaven, and it is from there that we are expecting a Savior, the Lord Jesus Christ. ²¹He will transform the body of our humiliationʸ that it may be conformed to the body of his glory,ᶻ by the power that also enables him to make all things subject to himself.

4 ¹Therefore, my brothers and sisters,ᵃ whom I love and long for, my joy and crown, stand firm in the Lord in this way, my beloved.

Exhortations

2 I urge Euodia and I urge Syntyche to be of the same mind in the Lord. ³Yes, and I ask you also, my loyal companion,ᵇ help these women, for they have struggled beside me

◆ Interpersonal conflict is a fact of life. It is fundamentally rooted in the sinful nature of human beings who ever since the Fall have put their own perceived needs over obedience to God or the welfare of others. Satan is constantly at

work to create brokenness, disorder, and chaos in human affairs. And although Christians partake of a new nature in Christ, the old nature, aided and abetted by Satan, too often asserts itself and conflict between brothers and sisters in the faith is the result.

So it was that two faithful women co-workers with the apostle Paul came into conflict. Euodia and Syntyche were Macedonian women in the church at Philippi. In contrast to other women in Greek culture, it is clear that Macedonian women took much stronger roles in commercial and social life.

These women were named by Paul as co-workers who had struggled with him in the work of the gospel. Here is a clear instance of women who had public ministry roles in the apostolic church. Quite possibly the dispute had to do with church leadership. But if this case provides biblical support for women in ministry, it also makes quite clear that women in ministry are just as vulnerable

˟ Or *commonwealth*   ʸ Or *our humble bodies*
ᶻ Or *his glorious body*   ᵃ Gk *my brothers*   ᵇ Or *loyal Syzygus*

PHILIPPIANS 4

1–3. It is evident that a dispute had arisen in the church at Philippi. Some scholars have suggested that the two women mentioned in this letter (4:2), Euodia and Syntyche may have been leaders of two separate house churches and although united, by working side by side with Paul, they were at odds over some doctrinal issue. Other scholars have suggested that the dispute in the church arose because of the failure to recognize the proper place of women, either by giving them more authority than in other churches or by failing to give them due recognition.

Although the cause of the dispute is not made clear, it is clear that these two women, Euodia and Syntyche, had worked side by side with Paul in spreading the gospel and were probably leaders within the congregation. Paul expressed concern that they be reconciled; he appeals to the church to help resolve the conflict between the two women so that the unity and well-being of the congregation would not be jeopardized. The strong warning in 3:2 indicates the seriousness of the dispute between these two prominent church members. Apparently, Paul sensed that there was a danger of the church taking sides over the issue and splitting. Thus, he urges reconciliation so that the church will not be adversely affected.

It is significant that Paul does not take sides, nor does he scorn these two women; he has words of encouragement for Euodia and Syntyche and supports their leadership in the church as women who have worked with him. In Bible times, names were often regarded as indicators of character, performance or expectation. It is significant to me that the name Euodia means fragrant or successful journey and the name Syntyche means blessed. It appears that these two women fit their names well.

as men to temptations from the evil one.

Paul prescribes strong medicine for the Philippian's affliction. He reminds them that the Christian life is one of humiliation and suffering. He emphasizes its corporate nature 'in Christ' as against a gnostic, individualistic piety. They were to be 'of one mind' – the mind of Christ Jesus and conform to the lowly Christ's selfless and sacrificial way of life. That would put an end to the petty squabbles and wrangling.

Paul had enlisted the help of a third party or mediator in the dispute. This suggests that in addition to theological principles, concrete ways of dealing with conflict are important.

Western jurisprudence operates by identifying the guilty party and meting out punishment. In some other cultures, mending the fabric of society is more important, so the goal is pacification of both parties in the dispute without regard to moral standards. This process can easily lead to tyranny of the group over the individual without justice.

The biblical way of transforming interpersonal conflict is to approach the parties in a spirit of humility and gentleness. It is noteworthy that Paul did not exhibit a superior attitude. He had learned from his own conflict with Barnabas and Peter that people can be sincerely wrong.

Paul did not ask the mediator to remove the women from their positions of responsibility or to be silent. He did not even ask that they confess their sin, although confession and forgiveness may be a vital part of the reconciliation process. It should never be coerced, but Christians in conflict need to be reminded that our own forgiveness by God is conditional on our willingness to forgive others.

The mediator should be a person of mature faith. Paul addresses the mediator by the term *syzyge*, a companion who is his 'true yokefellow'. This 'sharing the same yoke' suggests that the mediator may have been a partner in the apostolic mission, but not a new Christian.

It is important for a mediator to bring the parties in conflict into direct contact with each other and to listen to both sides of the story objectively. In order for the parties to achieve more objectivity themselves, it is often helpful to ask them to state the other's position and then ask the other if that was a correct evaluation. The goal is to help the persons in conflict to understand each other's thinking. Just here some new insights may begin to break down the wall between them. Contrary to some Christian opinion, disagreement is not wrong. We often need to see opposing viewpoints in order to come to the truth. But the kind of conflict that results in hatred and alienation is always wrong.

Although the goal of mediation is reconciliation, it is not enough only to bring people into a state of withdrawal from conflict. And although each party believes in his or her own rightness, issues must be judged according to God's standards as revealed in Scripture. Euodia and Syntyche's disappearance from the scene suggests that Paul's admonition to be of one mind was heeded ◆

Paul pleads with one of his closest co-workers to help the two women who have worked hard with him to spread the gospel (4:3). Apparently, there were other co-workers in the church at Philippi who deserved recognition. Paul's statement (4:3b) could be taken as an admonition to the church to give due recognition to those – both men and women – who worked with him to spread the gospel. Although he does not mention them by name, he asserts the most important thing, that their names are in the God's book of life. This probably comes from the ancient practice in cities of keeping a register in which the names of its citizens are recorded. In the Old Testament it is a common symbol for God's record of the covenant people. It is significant that the women who preached with Paul would have their names written in the book of life with the men who had preached with him.

in the work of the gospel, together with Clement and the rest of my co-workers, whose names are in the book of life.

4 Rejoice[c] in the Lord always; again I will say, Rejoice.[c] [5]Let your gentleness be known to everyone. The Lord is near. [6]Do not worry about anything, but in everything by prayer and supplication with thanksgiving let your requests be made known to God. [7]And the peace of God, which surpasses all understanding, will guard your hearts and your minds in Christ Jesus.

8 Finally, beloved,[d] whatever is true, whatever is honorable, whatever is just, whatever is pure, whatever is pleasing, whatever is commendable, if there is any excellence and if there is anything worthy of praise, think about[e] these things. [9]Keep on doing the things that you have learned and received and heard and seen in me, and the God of peace will be with you.

Acknowledgment of the Philippians' Gift

10 I rejoice[f] in the Lord greatly that now at last you have revived your concern for me; indeed, you were concerned for me, but had no opportunity to show it.[g] [11]Not that I am referring to being in need; for I have learned to be content with whatever I have. [12]I know what it is to have little, and I know what it is to have plenty. In any and all circumstances I have learned the secret of being well-fed and of going hungry, of having plenty and of being in need. [13]I can do all things through him who strengthens me. [14]In any case, it was kind of you to share my distress.

15 You Philippians indeed know that in the early days of the gospel, when I left Macedonia, no church shared with me in the matter of giving and receiving, except

[c] Or *Farewell*　[d] Gk *brothers*　[e] Gk *take account of*　[f] Gk *I rejoiced*　[g] Gk lacks *to show it*

2–9. In the final chapter Paul gives an action plan to believers to help them to foster peace and sound relationships in their life together. These are:

(1) Agree in the Lord (4:2). Believers may differ, but for the sake of the unity in the church, believers should seek to avoid disagreements.

(2) Rejoice in the Lord (4:4). Union with Christ is a source of great joy for the believer.

(3) Show a gentle attitude towards everyone (4:5). The Lord is coming soon and there is no need to be negative and judgmental toward others.

(4) Shun worry (4:6). Worry is always destructive and counter-productive. A child of God has confidence in the Lord.

(5) Pray with thanksgiving (4:6). Christians have the great privilege of making their requests known to God with the assurance that is theirs in Christ.

(6) Think of things that are good and praiseworthy (4:8). Believers need not pollute their minds with the filth of the corrupt life. In Christ there is excellence and things worthy of praise.

(7) Practise what you have learned (4:9). Paul urges the believers at Philippi to put into practice what they have learned and received from him. All these teachings are worthless and meaningless if they are not put into practice.

The end result of all these is the obtaining of God's peace which keeps the believers' hearts and minds safe in Christ (4:7, 9).

10–20. Paul wanted to thank the church at Philippi for their generosity towards him. When Paul expresses his gratitude to them for helping him with their gifts and prayers, it becomes clear that this was an unusually caring and supportive congregation where women were key and influential members and leaders. Their support for Paul came early, soon after he established the church at Philippi (2 Cor. 11:8–9). Other churches contributed while Paul was in their midst, but the church at Philippi sent gifts of money to him even when he was not present with them. They were faithful in praying for him and in sending him money while he was in Thessalonica establishing a church there (4:16). Apparently, they were the only ones who remembered Paul at that time. Later, when they heard that he was short of funds, they sent him money again (2 Cor. 11:19).

you alone. [16]For even when I was in Thessalonica, you sent me help for my needs more than once. [17]Not that I seek the gift, but I seek the profit that accumulates to your account. [18]I have been paid in full and have more than enough; I am fully satisfied, now that I have received from Epaphroditus the gifts you sent, a fragrant offering, a sacrifice acceptable and pleasing to God. [19]And my God will fully satisfy every need of yours according to his riches in glory in Christ Jesus. [20]To our God and Father be glory forever and ever. Amen.

Final Greetings and Benediction

21 Greet every saint in Christ Jesus. The friends[h] who are with me greet you. [22]All the saints greet you, especially those of the emperor's household.

23 The grace of the Lord Jesus Christ be with your spirit.[i]

[h] Gk *brothers*   [i] Other ancient authorities add *Amen*

Paul's joy is not so much the gift itself, but like a mother who receives a gift from her children, she rejoices more in the fact that the children have given it than in the gift itself. In 4:18, he compares the gifts from the church at Philippi to an offering laid on the altar. The words 'a fragrant offering, a sacrifice acceptable and pleasing to God' (4:18) are taken from the Old Testament and reveals the attributes of sacrificial giving that God welcomes. Paul acknowledges that although he cannot repay the debt, God will repay them on his behalf (4:19).

21–23. Paul's letter to the church at Philippi begins with the senders (1:1), next comes a greeting and a prayer for the receivers (1:2). The letter ends as it begins, with closing greetings and a prayer (4:21–23).

THE LETTER OF PAUL TO THE COLOSSIANS

INTRODUCTION

Background and authorship

Paul dictated this short letter from prison. Although it may have been composed and sent while he was being held in Caesarea or possibly Ephesus, the most probable explanation is that it was sent from Rome between AD 60–62. The letter centers on the hymn in praise of Christ (1:15–20) which is then applied and expounded into the specific situation of a congregation facing inroads of heresy. Though he reminds his readers of his suffering (1:24) and chains (4:18) Paul's concern is to speak of Christ in the most exalted terms of any of his letters: 'Christ is all and in all!' (3:11).

Some have commented on significant differences in words, style and theology from the 'authentic' Pauline letters, leading to the suggestion that Colossians (and the similar letter, Ephesians) are later compositions by followers of Paul, after the pattern of his genuine letters. Such differences, however, would be natural if Paul is responding to a specific situation in Colossae which necessitates a different approach including the use of the distinctive poetic language of the Christological Hymn. He needs to stress the overwhelming greatness of Christ and his sufficiency in person and work for all the needs of believers both now and in the 'not yet' of Christ's ultimate purpose for their lives.

Colossae

The Christian groups in the Lycus valley (modern Turkey), in Colossae, Laodicea and Hierapolis had been established through the preaching of Epaphras (Col. 1:7; 4:12–13; Philem. 23) and had probably resulted from Paul's work in Ephesus in AD 52–55. People converted in Ephesus spread the message to the surrounding regions of the Roman province of Asia. Though Paul himself had not visited the area his relationship with Epaphras, a 'fellow servant' and 'faithful minister of Christ' (Col. 1:7) indicates that his apostolic authority supports, augments and authenticates Epaphras' witness to the house-fellowships established (4:13).

Reasons for writing

This letter is not merely a courteous note of greeting from a well-known figure to be taken back to little Colossian community, but a serious and important apostolic communication to be read to them and shared with the Laodicean believers (Col. 4:16). Paul is pleased at their faith and progress so far (cf. Col. 1:3ff., Gal. 1:6–9) but he is concerned to warn against wrong teachings and beliefs to which they might be susceptible (Col. 2:6–23). There are indications that he is not just anticipating dangers but warning against a specific teaching, a possible 'Colossian heresy' which had already gained influence and adherents.

The indigenous Phrygian people had long been joined by people of Greek descent and a sizeable community of Jews who had been settled in Colossae for over a century. In this cosmopolitan mix of peoples, traditional religious beliefs, polytheism, incipient gnosticism and Judaism were all present. Paul's warnings (2:8–23) may be in response to the influence of an unorthodox Jewish group with specific ascetic and mystic teachings who were gaining ground among the Christians or to a syncretistic mix of philosophies.

Salutation

1 Paul, an apostle of Christ Jesus by the will of God, and Timothy our brother,

2 To the saints and faithful brothers and sisters[a] in Christ in Colossae:

Grace to you and peace from God our Father.

Paul Thanks God for the Colossians

3 In our prayers for you we always thank God, the Father of our Lord Jesus Christ, [4]for we have heard of your faith in Christ Jesus and of the love that you have for all the saints, [5]because of the hope laid up for you in heaven. You have heard of this hope before in the word of the truth, the gospel [6]that has come to you. Just as it is bearing fruit and growing in the whole world, so it has been bearing fruit among yourselves from the day you heard it and truly comprehended the grace of God. [7]This you learned from Epaphras, our beloved fellow servant.[b] He is a faithful minister of Christ on your[c] behalf, [8]and he has made known to us your love in the Spirit.

9 For this reason, since the day we heard it, we have not ceased praying for you and asking that you may be filled with the knowledge of God's[d] will in all spiritual wisdom and understanding, [10]so that you may lead lives worthy of the Lord, fully pleasing to him, as you bear fruit in every good work and as you grow in the knowledge of God. [11]May you be made strong with all the strength that comes from his glorious power, and may you be prepared to endure everything with patience, while joyfully [12]giving thanks to the Father, who has enabled[e] you[f] to share in the inheritance of the saints in the light. [13]He has rescued us from the power of darkness and transferred us into the kingdom of his beloved Son, [14]in whom we have redemption, the forgiveness of sins.[g]

The Supremacy of Christ

15 He is the image of the invisible God, the firstborn of all creation; [16]for in[h] him all things in heaven and on earth were created,

[a] Gk *brothers* [b] Gk *slave* [c] Other ancient authorities read *our* [d] Gk *his* [e] Other ancient authorities read *called* [f] Other ancient authorities read *us* [g] Other ancient authorities add *through his blood* [h] Or *by*

GREETING: COLOSSIANS 1

1–2. Paul's special authority as Christ's chosen apostle makes the letter an authoritative one. As usual the conventional term 'brothers' is not intended to exclude females, Paul means to address all as 1:28; 3:18.

9. 'Spiritual wisdom and understanding' does not mean some high-powered philosophy or spiritual mystery (cf. 2:8ff.) available only to some, but the knowledge of God's intents and purposes.

12–14. These sentences may derive from early baptismal or eucharistic liturgies where the imagery of the Exodus experience of the Israelites was applied to the present experience of believers as the accepted, forgiven people of God.

14. The sacrificial death of Christ is complete in its efficacy, needing no supplementation by his apostolic sufferings (Col. 2:9–10). Yet at his conversion Paul realized that Christ is identified with his people in their persecutions (Acts 9:4). A person 'in Christ' suffering persecution, as he was, participates in the sufferings predicted for the age of the Messiah (Zeph. 1:14ff.; Matt. 24:7ff.) which are not yet complete (Col. 1:26).

15–20. The exalted poetic language of this Hymn to Christ and its stylistic and linguistic difference from the surrounding text, seem to indicate that Paul is quoting from a hymn of early Christian or possibly pre-Christian origins adapted by himself or others to apply to Christ.

15. The use of the term 'the image of the invisible God' probably derives from Jewish Wisdom literature rather than speculation on humanity, male and female, as created in 'the image of God' (Gen. 1:27). God's wisdom, his wise creation and government of the world, reveals his nature as an 'image' would (Prov. 8:22–25). Paul applies to Jesus Christ (cf. Col. 2:3) language which Jewish thinkers had used of Wisdom in the intertestamental period and applied to God's

things visible and invisible, whether thrones or dominions or rulers or powers – all things have been created through him and for him. [17]He himself is before all things, and in[i] him all things hold together. [18]He is the head of the body, the church; he is the beginning, the firstborn from the dead, so that he might come to have first place in everything. [19]For in him all the fullness of God was pleased to dwell, [20]and through him God was pleased to reconcile to himself all things, whether on earth or in heaven, by making peace through the blood of his cross.

[21] And you who were once estranged and hostile in mind, doing evil deeds, [22]he has now reconciled[j] in his fleshly body[k] through death, so as to present you holy and blameless and irreproachable before him – [23]provided that you continue securely established and steadfast in the faith, without shifting from the hope promised by the gospel that you heard, which has been proclaimed to every creature under heaven. I, Paul, became a servant of this gospel.

Paul's Interest in the Colossians

[24] I am now rejoicing in my sufferings for your sake, and in my flesh I am completing what is lacking in Christ's afflictions for the sake of his body, that is, the church. [25]I became its servant according to God's commission that was given to me for you, to make the word of God fully known, [26]the mystery that has been hidden throughout the ages and generations but has now been revealed to his saints. [27]To them God chose to make known how great among the Gentiles are the riches of the glory of this mystery, which is Christ in you, the hope of glory. [28]It is he whom we proclaim, warning everyone and teaching everyone in all wisdom, so that we may present everyone mature in Christ. [29]For this I toil and struggle with all the energy that he powerfully inspires within me.

2 For I want you to know how much I am struggling for you, and for those in Laodicea, and for all who have not seen me face to face. [2]I want their hearts to be encouraged and united in love, so that they may have all the riches of assured understanding and have the knowledge of God's mystery, that is, Christ himself,[l] [3]in whom are hidden all the treasures of wisdom and knowledge. [4]I am saying this so that no one may deceive you with plausible arguments. [5]For though I am absent in body, yet I am with you in spirit, and I rejoice to see your morale and the firmness of your faith in Christ.

[i] Or *by* [j] Other ancient authorities read *you have now been reconciled* [k] Gk *in the body of his flesh* [l] Other ancient authorities read *of the mystery of God, both of the Father and of Christ*

---

self-expression in the Torah (Wisdom 7; Sirach 24). It is Jesus Christ, ascended and exalted, who is now revealed as pre-existent, God's agent both in the creation and the reconciliation of the world to himself: God revealed to humankind. The use of 'firstborn' here stresses both his prior existence and his superiority over the universe. There is no necessary implication that he is a created being.

19. Christ possesses all the attributes of deity, the 'fullness' (Gk. *pleroma*). This term was probably used in Colossae by groups offering 'fullness' through philosophy, asceticism or mystic experiences.

21–23. Cf. Col. 1:13–14.

26. The term 'mystery' was common in the Old Testament and Judaism, in gnostic and pagan cults. Here Paul means that a part of God's purpose, his intention to include the Gentiles in his people, was hitherto unknown. But now it is now revealed as an 'open secret' through Christ.

27. The experience of being united to Christ is not a mystic one limited to special initiates.

28. Paul's message is utterly Christ-centered and maturity in him is for everyone without discrimination (cf. Col. 3:11–4:1).

Fullness of Life in Christ

6 As you therefore have received Christ Jesus the Lord, continue to live your lives[m] in him, [7]rooted and built up in him and established in the faith, just as you were taught, abounding in thanksgiving.

8 See to it that no one takes you captive through philosophy and empty deceit, according to human tradition, according to the elemental spirits of the universe,[n] and not according to Christ. [9]For in him the whole fullness of deity dwells bodily, [10]and you have come to fullness in him, who is the head of every ruler and authority. [11]In him also you were circumcised with a spiritual circumcision,[o] by putting off the body of the flesh in the circumcision of Christ; [12]when you were buried with him in baptism, you were also raised with him through faith in the power of God, who raised him from the dead. [13]And when you were dead in trespasses and the uncircumcision of your flesh, God[p] made you[q] alive together with him, when he forgave us all our trespasses, [14]erasing the record that stood against us with its legal demands. He set this aside, nailing it to the cross. [15]He disarmed[r] the rulers and authorities and made a public example of them, triumphing over them in it.

16 Therefore do not let anyone condemn you in matters of food and drink or of observing festivals, new moons, or sabbaths. [17]These are only a shadow of what is to come, but the substance belongs to Christ. [18]Do not let anyone disqualify you, insisting on self-abasement and worship of angels, dwelling[s] on visions,[t] puffed up without cause by a human way of thinking,[u] [19]and not holding fast to the head, from whom the whole body, nourished and held together by its ligaments and sinews, grows with a growth that is from God.

Warnings against False Teachers

20 If with Christ you died to the elemental spirits of the universe,[v] why do you live as if you still belonged to the world? Why do you submit to regulations, [21]"Do not handle, Do not taste, Do not touch"? [22]All these regulations refer to things that perish with use; they are simply human commands and teachings. [23]These have indeed an appearance of wisdom in promoting self-imposed piety, humility, and severe treatment of the body, but they are of no value in checking self-indulgence.[w]

[m] Gk *to walk*   [n] Or *the rudiments of the world*
[o] Gk *a circumcision made without hands*   [p] Gk *he*
[q] Other ancient authorities read *made us*; others, *made*   [r] Or *divested himself of*   [s] Other ancient authorities read *not dwelling*   [t] Meaning of Gk uncertain   [u] Gk *by the mind of his flesh*   [v] Or *the rudiments of the world*   [w] Or *are of no value, serving only to indulge the flesh*

COLOSSIANS 2

8. 'Elemental spirits' in the Colossian context are understood to be personal and active spiritual beings; active in the universe, but disarmed and conquered by Christ's death (2:15).

9–10. Nothing needs to be added to Christ, he is fully divine and, in being united with him, all believers have all that is needed for present spiritual growth and future maturity.

11–12. The old rebellious nature is stripped off, not now by physical circumcision as a covenant sign, but by identification with Christ in his death. In the Hebrew culture circumcision was not applied to women even though they were included in the people of God. This passage may be seen as teaching that Christian baptism replaces circumcision as a new covenant symbol which is now available to all.

16–23. The mixture of beliefs and ascetic practices mentioned may derive from Jewish observances and the reverence some unorthodox Jewish groups gave to angels as mediators of the Law delivered to Moses.

19. The body is not a male figure but men and women together in the community of faith.

The New Life in Christ

3 So if you have been raised with Christ, seek the things that are above, where Christ is, seated at the right hand of God. [2]Set your minds on things that are above, not on things that are on earth, [3]for you have died, and your life is hidden with Christ in God. [4]When Christ who is your[x] life is revealed, then you also will be revealed with him in glory.

5 Put to death, therefore, whatever in you is earthly: fornication, impurity, passion, evil desire, and greed (which is idolatry). [6]On account of these the wrath of God is coming on those who are disobedient.[y] [7]These are the ways you also once followed, when you were living that life.[z] [8]But now you must get rid of all such things – anger, wrath, malice, slander, and abusive[a] language from your mouth. [9]Do not lie to one another, seeing that you have stripped off the old self with its practices [10]and have clothed yourselves with the new self, which is being renewed in knowledge according to the image of its creator. [11]In that renewal[b] there is no longer Greek and Jew, circumcised and uncircumcised, barbarian, Scythian, slave and free; but Christ is all and in all!

12 As God's chosen ones, holy and beloved, clothe yourselves with compassion, kindness, humility, meekness, and patience. [13]Bear with one another and, if anyone has a complaint against another, forgive each other; just as the Lord[c] has forgiven you, so you also must forgive. [14]Above all, clothe yourselves with love, which binds everything together in perfect harmony. [15]And let the peace of Christ rule in your hearts, to which indeed you were called in the one body. And be thankful. [16]Let the word of Christ[d] dwell in you richly; teach and admonish one another in all wisdom; and with gratitude in your hearts sing psalms, hymns, and spiritual songs to God.[e] [17]And whatever you do, in word or deed, do everything in the name of the Lord Jesus, giving thanks to God the Father through him.

Rules for Christian Households

18 Wives, be subject to your husbands, as is fitting in the Lord. [19]Husbands, love your wives and never treat them harshly.

[x] Other authorities read *our*　[y] Other ancient authorities lack *on those who are disobedient* (Gk *the children of disobedience*)　[z] Or *living among such people*　[a] Or *filthy*　[b] Gk *its creator,* [11]*where*　[c] Other ancient authorities read *just as Christ*　[d] Other ancient authorities read *of God,* or *of the Lord*　[e] Other ancient authorities read *to the Lord*

COLOSSIANS 3

11. Unlike Gal. 3:28 there is no male/female contrast here. However the removal of all human distinctions in spiritual renewal is sufficiently clear elsewhere. (1:28ff.)

17. The whole of life in every part is to be lived consciously in relationship to the Lordship of Jesus, and is applied in 3:18ff.

3:18–4:1. Wives, children and slaves were of low value in contemporary culture, but Paul's evaluation is very different. They are not only mentioned but addressed, and addressed first in each pair. They too are 'God's chosen ones' (3:12ff.) and are responsible for themselves and the conduct of their relationships even if society despises them, orders their existences, or disregards them.

3:18. Comparison with Eph. 5:21 and 1 Cor. 15:28 indicates that subjection does not imply inferior dignity or value. The wife is told to submit not to 'obey' as with the children or slaves. The Lord's approval is what motivates her, not just conformity to first-century cultural norms.

19. The husband's responsibility is to show love and not cause his wife to become bitter. He is to show *agape*-love, a divinely motivated self-giving, not merely affection or sexual attraction. In a society where arranged marriages were the norm this demand on the husband is extraordinarily high.

◆ The household instructions found in the Epistle to the Colossians are carefully balanced to show a concern for all the members of the family. Those with greater power (the father, husband, master) are expected to take special care not to alienate, frustrate, or radicalize those with less status (children, wives, slaves). Oppression begets resentment and bitterness. Harmony was to be achieved not by a heavy hand but by the respectful treatment of every person in the household.

Wives are asked to 'submit' rather than to 'obey' as are children and slaves. This may be understood as a responsible and mature relationship, characterized by honesty and integrity. A wife can do much to create a healthy and reciprocal relationship with her husband.

Men are bidden to love their wives, a duty not generally expected in pagan society. The next directive to the husbands may be translated 'Do not make yourself a bad taste in your wife's mouth.'

Quite clearly the unmarried Paul was well aware of the stresses which may be put upon family life. Legalism will not resolve them, but a considerate attitude will do much to dispel them ◆

◆ Slavery conjures up distressing pictures of men and women shackled together, crowded into cramped and squalid conditions on board sailing ships. Being brutally forced away from their homelands and families, thrown into an airless and putrid enclosed ship's hold, unable to clean themselves, exercise or relieve themselves in private – hundreds squashed together for a voyage into the unknown where they are shown no kindness, no mercy and where there is no escape, only a future of enforced labor. They are no longer people with feelings and personality, they are more like animals or worse – a commodity to be sold as used and if it becomes ill or dies then there is no pity – another one can easily be bought as a replacement. A cargo of human flesh bought and sold for profit. Of course, some slaves were treated well and certainly in New Testament times there were slaves who held quite high positions in households, businesses or even government. But even there the sense of being perceived as of lesser value or of being somehow dehumanized remains.

The evils of slavery are obvious to us now in the twentieth century and we should be grateful to those Christian men, like William Wilberforce, and women who courageously campaigned during the last century to have this repugnant trade abolished. It seems almost unbelievable to us now that mankind could have been so inhuman, placing so little value on

20 Children, obey your parents in everything, for this is your acceptable duty in the Lord. [21]Fathers, do not provoke your children, or they may lose heart. [22]Slaves, obey your earthly masters[f] in everything, not only while being watched and in order to please them, but wholeheartedly, fearing the Lord.[g] [23]Whatever your task, put

[f] In Greek the same word is used for *master* and *Lord*   [g] In Greek the same word is used for *master* and *Lord*

---

20. Children are addressed in their own right and their responsibility as believers is more than just respect or 'honor' of parents but obedience in all things to both father and mother.
21. Fathers in particular are reminded of their duties to their children rather than of their powers over them. They are not to irritate or provoke them and cause discouragement, perhaps inculcating a low self-image.
22. Christian slaves receive a longer exhortation perhaps reflecting the social structure of the congregation or the special need for encouragement in their difficult situation. They are free in Christ yet enslaved by society. Paul contrasts by his use of the word *kyrios* ('Lord') the dual relationship experienced; Christ is *the* Lord whom they are to fear above their owners, male or female.

another person's life, treating the slaves literally as objects. Today we see this as totally offensive but would we, if we had lived at the height of the slave trade, have joined in with the campaigners to do something to relieve the suffering of others? Do we today campaign against evil and offensive ideas that are anti-Christian, that devalue or seek to destroy human life that was created in the image of God or do we sit by and let it happen?

At one time we were all slaves, not to human captors, but slaves to sin. This master treated us harshly and there was absolutely no way of escape, only the promise of eventual death. This master kept us in a life in which we could never be free to truly be ourselves but chained us to habits, lies, deceit and sin which devalued us and made us less than the people God had intended us originally to be, and spoilt our relationship with him. But God in his great mercy set us free from the power of sin and death so, through Jesus Christ, we are no longer slaves to sin and fear but are now sons and daughters of God and joint heirs with Jesus. No longer subject to a yoke of slavery – but free! ◆

time pray for us as well that God will open to us a door for the word, that we may declare the mystery of Christ, for which I am in prison, ⁴so that I may reveal it clearly, as I should.

5 Conduct yourselves wisely toward outsiders, making the most of the time.ʲ ⁶Let your speech always be gracious, seasoned with salt, so that you may know how you ought to answer everyone.

Final Greetings and Benediction

7 Tychicus will tell you all the news about me; he is a beloved brother, a faithful minister, and a fellow servantᵏ in the Lord. ⁸I have sent him to you for this very purpose, so that you may know how we areˡ and that he may encourage your hearts; ⁹he is coming with Onesimus, the faithful and beloved brother, who is one of you. They will tell you about everything here.

10 Aristarchus my fellow prisoner greets you, as does Mark the cousin of Barnabas, concerning whom you have received instructions – if he comes to you, welcome him. ¹¹And Jesus who is called Justus greets you. These are the only ones of the circumcision among my co-workers for the kingdom of God, and they have been a comfort to me. ¹²Epaphras, who is one of you, a servantᵏ of Christ Jesus, greets you. He is always wrestling in his prayers on your behalf, so that you may stand mature and fully assured in everything that God wills. ¹³For I testify for him that he has worked hard for you and for those in Laodicea and in Hierapolis. ¹⁴Luke, the beloved physician, and Demas greet you. ¹⁵Give my greetings to the brothers and

yourselves into it, as done for the Lord and not for your masters,ʰ ²⁴since you know that from the Lord you will receive the inheritance as your reward; you serveⁱ the Lord Christ. ²⁵For the wrongdoer will be paid back for whatever wrong has been done, and there is no partiality. ¹Masters, treat your slaves justly and fairly, for you know that you also have a Master in heaven.

Further Instructions

2 Devote yourselves to prayer, keeping alert in it with thanksgiving. ³At the same

ʰ Gk *not for men*   ⁱ Or *you are slaves of*, or *be slaves of*   ʲ Or *opportunity*   ᵏ Gk *slave*   ˡ Other authorities read *that I may know how you are*

COLOSSIANS 4

15. Having referred to the 'brothers' Paul mentions Nympha, one of a number of women whose households became bases for Christian congregations in New Testament times (cf. Lydia, Acts 16:15; Chloe, 1 Cor. 1:11).

sisters[m] in Laodicea, and to Nympha and the church in her house. [16]And when this letter has been read among you, have it read also in the church of the Laodiceans; and see that you read also the letter from Laodicea. [17]And say to Archippus, "See that you complete the task that you have received in the Lord."

[18] I, Paul, write this greeting with my own hand. Remember my chains. Grace be with you.[n]

[m] Gk *brothers*   [n] Other ancient authorities add *Amen*

THE FIRST LETTER OF PAUL TO THE THESSALONIANS

INTRODUCTION

1 Thessalonians was probably the first book of the New Testament to be written (dated usually at AD 51); therefore, Paul's letter gives us great insight into the lives, faith and sufferings of the earliest Christians. Consequently, the book is especially helpful for new believers and those who disciple them.

With the main theme of the second coming of Christ, the letter gives us important instructions for living in the light of eternity. Paul comforts those Thessalonians who grieved that their brothers and sisters had died before Jesus came back (4:13–18). He reminds them that all believers, both dead and alive, will be reunited and brought together with Jesus at the end of time (see the note on 'Clouds', p. 430). Furthermore, he encourages them not to be bothered about the date of Christ's return, but instead to live faithfully and carefully, ready for his coming, and building each other up in the meanwhile (1:9–10; 3:13; 5:1–11).

Thessalonica, named for Alexander the Great's half-sister, was at that time the largest city in Macedonia, the capital of the province, a thriving seaport, and a communications/trade hub. Believers there suffered persecution from the very beginning, and according to Acts 17:5–10, the apostle Paul himself was chased away shortly after arriving. The contemporary challenges of holding to faith and a godly life in the midst of a busy society are much the same as the Thessalonians and Paul faced – the hardships of proclaiming and receiving the gospel (1 Thess. 2); the need to minister to others as a mother caring for her children (vv. 7–9); the importance of a godly life (1 Thess. 4); and especially the necessity of purity in sexual matters (vv. 3–8) and of life-sustaining labor (vv. 11–12). We can face the trials of life for the same reasons that the Thessalonians did – because of the power of the gospel, the indwelling of the Holy Spirit, the partnership of believers, and the hope of Christ's return (1:4–10).

Paul gives us a wonderful model for encouraging each other in the faith and for the intensity of love that can characterize the Christian community (1 Thess. 3; 4:9–10). His final instructions (5:12–28) present one of the finest summaries of Christian community life in the New Testament.

Salutation

1 Paul, Silvanus, and Timothy,
To the church of the Thessalonians in God the Father and the Lord Jesus Christ:

Grace to you and peace.

The Thessalonians' Faith and Example

2 We always give thanks to God for all of you and mention you in our prayers, constantly ³remembering before our God and Father your work of faith and labor of love and steadfastness of hope in our Lord Jesus Christ. ⁴For we know, brothers and sisters[a] beloved by God, that he has chosen you, ⁵because our message of the gospel came to you not in word only, but also in power and in the Holy Spirit and with full conviction; just as you know what kind of persons we proved to be among you for your sake. ⁶And you became imitators of us and of the Lord, for in spite of persecution you received the word with joy inspired by the Holy Spirit, ⁷so that you became an example to all the believers in Macedonia and in Achaia. ⁸For the word of the Lord has sounded forth from you not only in Macedonia and Achaia, but in every place your faith in God has become known, so that we have no need to speak about it. ⁹For the people of those regions[b] report about us what kind of welcome we had among you, and how you turned to God from idols, to serve a living and true God, ¹⁰and to wait for

his Son from heaven, whom he raised from the dead – Jesus, who rescues us from the wrath that is coming.

Paul's Ministry in Thessalonica

2 You yourselves know, brothers and sisters,[a] that our coming to you was not in vain, ²but though we had already suffered and been shamefully mistreated at Philippi, as you know, we had courage in

---

◆ 1 Thess. 2:1–12 is one of the most powerful descriptions of the apostles' ministry; these verses model for us all the care with which we undertake whatever services God gives us. Paul answers slanders against him by reminding the Thessalonians that he is doing his utmost for them. Vv. 7 and 11 especially demonstrate the equality of men and women in Paul's perspectives. Functions in the church aren't limited by gender. Even as we women want men to share in the gentle nursing of children, so women must participate also in the urging and encouraging of fathers. Wives can nurture their husbands in both roles. By 'each one of you' in v. 11 Paul emphasizes his care both for individual women and men and the corporate community. In whatever functions to which God calls us we image his maternal and paternal care. Cf. Is. 66:13; Ps. 103:13 ◆

---

[a] Gk brothers   [b] Gk For they

---

1 THESSALONIANS 1

1. 'Silvanus' is the 'Silas' of Acts, just as 'Saul' is 'Paul' (Acts 15:22, 27, 32, 40; 16:19, 22, 39; 17:4 etc.).

4. With profound affection, Paul wrote 'brothers' in 1:4; 2:1, 9, 14, 17; 3:7; 4:1, 6, 9–10, 13; 5:1, 12. We know that this includes the sisters, too, because of 2:11 and 5:4–5, 27.

6. The Thessalonians imitated Paul and his companions as models of Christ. Similarly, Christ's reflection in us today attracts others to become Christ-like. Often we fear that we cannot demonstrate Christ when we are in the midst of our own troubles, but that is sometimes when the witness is most powerful.

7. Bearing affliction with joy (not necessarily happiness) is a model to other Christians.

1 THESSALONIANS 2

2. See Acts 16:19–40.

our God to declare to you the gospel of God in spite of great opposition. ³For our appeal does not spring from deceit or impure motives or trickery, ⁴but just as we have been approved by God to be entrusted with the message of the gospel, even so we speak, not to please mortals, but to please God who tests our hearts. ⁵As you know and as God is our witness, we never came with words of flattery or with a pretext for greed; ⁶nor did we seek praise from mortals,

◆ How often we are disappointed in Christian leaders whose motives are indeed those which Paul describes: greed, perpetration of error, impurity, fame, power, financial gain and personal popularity (cf. 2 Cor. 2:17; 4:2; Titus 1:11)! Their external piety is simply a cover-up, a mask by which they deceive the gullible. While it is always distressing, such elements are not new in the church. Against such people and situations Jesus has warned us in advance (Matt. 7:15–16; 24:23–5). Those in positions of influence have more asked of them and bear a greater responsibility (Matt. 13:11–12; 1 Cor. 4:2). It is important to examine our motives carefully and to do everything possible to avoid even the appearance of dishonest, immoral or underhanded dealings (1 Thess. 5:22). The ministry of women as well as that of men needs to be conducted with integrity ◆

whether from you or from others, ⁷though we might have made demands as apostles of Christ. But we were gentle[c] among you, like a nurse tenderly caring for her own chil-

dren. ⁸So deeply do we care for you that we are determined to share with you not only the gospel of God but also our own selves,

◆ A mother's love for her small child can be expressed in many ways, but breast-feeding creates a deep bond between mother and baby. Despite aggressive promotion of infant formula, mother's milk remains the most perfect form of nutrition. It provides important antibodies to protect the newborn against infectious diseases. Furthermore it establishes a calm stability for the child as the mother must stop whatever else she is doing and attend to her baby's needs. No one else will do.

Through this unique relationship, a child receives more than just physical nourishment. It gains the first spiritual food of love, gentleness and caring. Ps. 22:9 beautifully illustrates the fact that God uses that first experience of trust gained at the breast to then develop our trust in him. The Scriptures liken God to a nursing mother. The image is used to express the comfort which God gives (Ps. 131:2–3; Is. 66:13) and the continual concern and compassion (Is. 49:15). Some scholars consider the name for God 'El Shaddai' to mean the Breasted One, referring to God's all-sufficiency in meeting our needs ◆

because you have become very dear to us.

9 You remember our labor and toil, brothers and sisters;[d] we worked night and

[c] Other ancient authorities read *infants*　　[d] Gk *brothers*

---

5. 'God is our witness' is not a curse, but the confident assurance of a Christian living constantly under God's eye. Our credibility is established by integrity and steadfastness in the cause of Christ.
7. 'Caring for her own children' indicates that 'nurse' signifies a nursing mother. Cf. Gal. 4:19 and the note on 'Mother imagery in ministry of Paul', p. 388.
8. 'So deeply do we care for you' utilizes a Greek verb not found elsewhere in the New Testament. This verb, also found in the Septuagint version of Job 3:21, shows an intense 'longing for'.
9. Paul's tent-making, involving hardship and fatigue, models for us the importance of serving God in every occupation. Rabban Gamaliel III emphasized the tradition that the study of Torah was excellent if combined with a secular occupation. 'Proclaimed' is the Greek verb 'to act as a herald, proclaiming publicly what an authority (in this case, God) commissioned'.

day, so that we might not burden any of you while we proclaimed to you the gospel of God. [10]You are witnesses, and God also, how pure, upright, and blameless our conduct was toward you believers. [11]As you know, we dealt with each one of you like a father with his children, [12]urging and encouraging you and pleading that you lead a life worthy of God, who calls you into his own kingdom and glory.

13 We also constantly give thanks to God for this, that when you received the word of God that you heard from us, you accepted it not as a human word but as what it really is, God's word, which is also at work in you believers. [14]For you, brothers and sisters,[e] became imitators of the churches of God in Christ Jesus that are in Judea, for you suffered the same things from your own compatriots as they did from the Jews, [15]who killed both the Lord Jesus and the prophets,[f] and drove us out; they displease God and oppose everyone [16]by hindering us from speaking to the Gentiles so that they may be saved. Thus they have constantly been filling up the measure of their sins; but God's wrath has overtaken them at last.[g]

Paul's Desire to Visit the Thessalonians Again

17 As for us, brothers and sisters,[e]

when, for a short time, we were made orphans by being separated from you – in person, not in heart – we longed with great eagerness to see you face to face. [18]For we wanted to come to you – certainly I, Paul, wanted to again and again – but Satan blocked our way. [19]For what is our hope or joy or crown of boasting before our Lord Jesus at his coming? Is it not you? [20]Yes, you are our glory and joy!

◆ The Greek word *parousia* (signifying Christ's 'coming') was used in the papyri to denote the arrival and visit of a Roman emperor to some city, by which the inhabitants dated a new era. Christ's parousia instead is the consummation of an old era, the supreme apocalyptic presence, the climax of all Christian faith and certainty. Cf. 1 Cor. 15:23; Matt. 24:3, 27, 37, 39; James 5:7–8; 1 John 2:28; 2 Pet. 1:16; 3:4, 12. Cf. also references to God coming down in the Old Testament: Pss. 50:3; 68:1–7; 80:1–2; 82:8; 107:20; Is. 26:19–21; 42:13; 63:9; 64:1; 66:13; Hab. 2:3; Zeph. 1:14–16; Mal. 4:1 ◆

---

[e] Gk *brothers*   [f] Other ancient authorities read *their own prophets*   [g] Or *completely* or *forever*

13ff. Many scholars suggest that the presence of this second thanksgiving indicates that 1 Thessalonians comprises pieces of several letters from Paul. Rather, this thanksgiving is necessary to introduce the difficult subjects which follow. Modern canonical criticism (studying biblical books as whole pieces passed on by the Jewish and Christian communities) looks instead for the message given to the church by the book's shape which has been valued through history.

14–16 is sometimes thought to be a later addition (after the destruction of Jerusalem) because of its seemingly harsh judgment of Jews. This section is definitely not anti-Semitic, but emphasizes that their own fellow-citizens' persecution of the Thessalonians parallels that of those Jews, who, though chosen as God's own nation, spurned his covenant and gospel, killed the prophets, and finally crucified God's own Son. Cf. Matt. 21:33–46; 23:34–39.

17. See Acts 17:5–10.

18. Satan constantly obstructs Christians' path to prevent God's will from being accomplished in and through them.

19. All our efforts at ministering to others give us joy in the light of Christ's coming. Paul emphasizes here not our reward for serving God, but the hope and delight of being in God's will caring for others.

3 Therefore when we could bear it no longer, we decided to be left alone in Athens; [2]and we sent Timothy, our brother and co-worker for God in proclaiming[h] the gospel of Christ, to strengthen and encourage you for the sake of your faith, [3]so that no one would be shaken by these persecutions. Indeed, you yourselves know that this is what we are destined for. [4]In fact, when we were with you, we told you beforehand that we were to suffer persecution; so it turned out, as you know. [5]For this reason, when I could bear it no longer, I sent to find out about your faith; I was afraid that somehow the tempter had tempted you and that our labor had been in vain.

Timothy's Encouraging Report

[6] But Timothy has just now come to us from you, and has brought us the good news of your faith and love. He has told us also that you always remember us kindly and long to see us – just as we long to see you. [7]For this reason, brothers and sisters,[i] during all our distress and persecution we have been encouraged about you through your faith. [8]For we now live, if you continue to stand firm in the Lord. [9]How can we thank God enough for you in return for all the joy that we feel before our God because of you? [10]Night and day we pray most earnestly that we may see you face to face and restore whatever is lacking in your faith.

[11] Now may our God and Father himself and our Lord Jesus direct our way to you. [12]And may the Lord make you increase and abound in love for one another and for all, just as we abound in love for you. [13]And may he so strengthen your hearts in holiness that you may be blameless before our God and Father at the coming of our Lord Jesus with all his saints.

A Life Pleasing to God

4 Finally, brothers and sisters,[i] we ask and urge you in the Lord Jesus that, as you learned from us how you ought to live and to please God (as, in fact, you are doing), you should do so more and more. [2]For you know what instructions we gave you through the Lord Jesus. [3]For this is the will of God, your sanctification: that you abstain from fornication; [4]that each one of

[h] Gk lacks *proclaiming*   [i] Gk *brothers*

---

1 THESSALONIANS 3

1–6. It entailed less danger to send Timothy, of Greek lineage on his father's side, since Paul and Silas were recognizably Jewish.

3–5. True Christianity necessarily entails suffering; our unwillingness to suffer weakens Christianity. Paul models the need to care for community members who suffer. We must help each other not to be wheedled away from faith or fooled by persuasive talk amid afflictions. Sometimes well-meaning friends can be the worst kind of temptation.

6–13 demonstrates the importance of following up with encouragement when others persevere. Cf. 1 Cor. 16:13; Gal. 5:1; Phil. 1:27; 4:1.

8. Timothy's news releases Paul from the leaden weight of fear (as when our child finally comes safely home).

13. Is a 'wish-prayer' (with optative verbs), perhaps echoing the language of synagogue liturgy. (See also 5:23.)

1 THESSALONIANS 4

1–12. Here we are offered a model of praising others, while yet calling them to greater discipline in areas of weakness.

3–8. Paul's call for sexual sanctification is especially important for our age of rife sexual immorality.

4. Older versions depreciated women by translating the Greek word for 'vessel' as 'wife'. The word means 'body' and underscores the mutual responsibility of sexual relationships.

◆ The call for sexual purity is made forcefully: God's will for us is holiness, including keeping ourselves from immorality. The Greek term *porneia* (here translated as 'fornication') could denote genital activity outside of marriage, but could also include other kinds of behavior and attitudes. The issue was important for Paul to address because ancient paganism encouraged many inappropriate types of sexuality within its practice. Religious art was frequently pornographic, and lewd gestures were part of the worship. Sacred prostitution was widespread in the temples of the ancient world, and many religious festivals entailed sexual couplings outside the confines of marriage. Ritual obscenity was used to promote fertility and blessing, and it is specifically condemned at Eph. 5:4 and Col. 3:8. Promiscuity, whether in religious or secular settings, has no place in the community of believers (1 Cor. 6:9–10; Gal. 5:19; Eph. 5:5; Col. 3:4; Rev. 22:15).

By contrast Christians were called to lives that shunned even the entertainment of lustful thoughts (Matt. 5:27) and sexual stimuli (1 Cor. 6:18; 2 Tim. 2:22). Purity was to replace the old patterns (2 Cor. 7:1; 1 Tim. 2:15; 5:22), and the chaste behavior of women was a means of winning unbelievers to Christ (Titus 2:5; 1 Pet. 3:2). Marriage is affirmed as honorable and holy, the appropriate vehicle for sexual communion (1 Cor. 7:2; 1 Thess. 4:3–4; Heb. 13:4). Chaste celibacy is equally to be prized and cultivated and may be used to further the purposes of the Kingdom of God (Matt. 19:12; 1 Cor. 7:7–8, 25–39) ◆

you know how to control your own body[j] in holiness and honor, [5]not with lustful passion, like the Gentiles who do not know God; [6]that no one wrong or exploit a brother or sister[k] in this matter, because the Lord is an avenger in all these things, just as we have already told you beforehand and solemnly warned you. [7]For God did not call us to impurity but in holiness. [8]Therefore whoever rejects this rejects not human authority but God, who also gives his Holy Spirit to you.

[9] Now concerning love of the brothers and sisters,[l] you do not need to have anyone write to you, for you yourselves have been taught by God to love one another; [10]and indeed you do love all the brothers and sisters[l] throughout Macedonia. But we urge you, beloved,[l] to do so more and more, [11]to aspire to live quietly, to mind your own affairs, and to work with your hands, as we directed you, [12]so that you may behave properly toward outsiders and be dependent on no one.

The Coming of the Lord

[13] But we do not want you to be uninformed, brothers and sisters,[l] about those who have died,[m] so that you may not grieve as others do who have no hope. [14]For since we believe that Jesus died and rose again, even so, through Jesus, God will bring with him those who have died.[m]

[j] Or *how to take a wife for himself*   [k] Gk *brother*
[l] Gk *brothers*   [m] Gk *fallen asleep*

6. Older versions understood this verse to concern business relationships, rather than the sexual 'covetousness' of fornication. See also 1 Cor. 5:9–11; Eph. 4:19; 5:3, 5.

7. Because of the sexual laxity of Greek society, the new life in Christ demanded a complete break from pagan mores (cf. 1 Cor. 6:12–20, esp. v. 18). God called the Thessalonians from their former pagan state into the new divine work.

9–10 parallels all Paul's calls for community love, but adds instructions in vv. 11–12 not to meddle in others' business and not to cease working, practices which gave Christianity a bad reputation.

13–18 fulfills a major purpose of the letter with its special emphasis on comforting those who worried because loved ones had died before Christ returned. There should be no chapter break before 5:1–11, which adds the necessity for Christians to build each other up so everyone can be awake and ready for Christ's coming – whenever that might happen. The almost parallel conclusions in 4:18 and 5:11 show the relationship of the two paragraphs.

¹⁵For this we declare to you by the word of the Lord, that we who are alive, who are left until the coming of the Lord, will by no means precede those who have died.ⁿ ¹⁶For the Lord himself, with a cry of command, with the archangel's call and with the sound of God's trumpet, will descend from heaven, and the dead in Christ will rise first. ¹⁷Then we who are alive, who are left, will be caught up in the clouds together with them to meet the Lord in the air; and so we will be with the Lord forever. ¹⁸Therefore encourage one another with these words.

> ◆ 'Clouds' are used throughout the Scriptures to signify the presence of God, beginning with the pillar of cloud in the escape of Israel from Egypt (Exod. 13:21–22). God appears in the clouds on Mt Sinai (Exod. 19:9; 34:5), at the Tabernacle (Exod. 40:34), and in the Temple (1 Kings 8:10; 2 Chron. 5:13–14; 6:1). The presence of the Father in the life of Jesus is noted by a cloud at his transfiguration (Matt. 17:5 and parallels). Certainly here in Thessalonians the cloud image is meant to assure grieving believers that at the end of time we will all together experience the presence of God ◆

5 Now concerning the times and the seasons, brothers and sisters,° you do not need to have anything written to you. ²For you yourselves know very well that the day of the Lord will come like a thief in the night. ³When they say, "There is peace and security," then sudden destruction will come upon them, as labor pains come upon a pregnant woman, and there will be no

> ◆ The onset of labor for a pregnant woman is inevitable. There is no doubt as to the certainty of the actual occurrence, but without medical intervention there can be no accurate prediction of the time. When that hour comes, the importance of all other priorities dwindles in comparison to the one compelling claim.
> It is a distressing circumstance for a woman to go into labor before adequate preparation has been made. Although the time is uncertain, it is essential to make suitable arrangements not only for the actual birth but also for the care of the infant and the mother. First-time parents must have considerable instruction, and they need the support of family, friends, the church and community.

ⁿ Gk *fallen asleep*   ° Gk *brothers*

These verses comfort those who are anxious about those who have died before the parousia while 5:1–11 warns against false security about its timing. The best explanation for the delay of the parousia comes from John Henry Newman: 'Up to Christ's coming in the flesh, the course of things ran straight towards that end, nearing it by every step, but now, under the Gospel, that course has . . . altered its direction . . . and runs, not towards the end, but along it, and on the brink of it; and is at all times equally near that great event, which, did it run towards it, it would at once run into. Christ, then, is ever at our doors.'

15. Both translations, 'fallen asleep' and 'died', are valuable here – the former because Paul emphasized throughout his ministry that death holds no sting for those saved from eternal death through the forgiveness of sins and the promise of resurrection in Christ; the latter, 'died', because we must also acknowledge the sorrow of those who are left behind.

1 THESSALONIANS 5

3. Mothers can best convey the urgency of watchfulness because they know personally the image of sudden pain and helplessness when labor takes one by surprise. Just as a woman wants to be packed and ready to go to the hospital, so Paul urges the Thessalonians always to prepare for Christ's return. Cf. Exod. 15:14; Is. 13:8; Jer. 13:21; Hos. 13:13.

> Just so we look forward to Christ's return as a network of believers, all working together in anticipation. Even though we do not know the hour, we must be prepared. The return of Jesus Christ is a dominant theme in the New Testament, and repeatedly we are told to be ready for his blessed appearing and to be faithful and holy in our calling.
>
> The onset of labor is the announcement of an impending arrival. The event is filled with expectation of fulfillment, though there may be emotions of joy, anticipation, relief at the end of a long wait, excitement – or even dread and fear. There will be a realization of long-cherished hopes to look upon the face of one who is already loved while yet unseen. The new arrival will drastically transform the world of the family or community awaiting the event, and nothing will be the same thereafter ◆

escape! ⁴But you, beloved,ᵖ are not in darkness, for that day to surprise you like a thief; ⁵for you are all children of light and children of the day; we are not of the night or of darkness. ⁶So then let us not fall asleep as others do, but let us keep awake and be sober; ⁷for those who sleep sleep at night, and those who are drunk get drunk at night. ⁸But since we belong to the day, let us be sober, and put

on the breastplate of faith and love, and for a helmet the hope of salvation. ⁹For God has destined us not for wrath but for obtaining salvation through our Lord Jesus Christ, ¹⁰who died for us, so that whether we are awake or asleep we may live with him. ¹¹Therefore encourage one another and build up each other, as indeed you are doing.

Final Exhortations, Greetings, and Benediction

12 But we appeal to you, brothers and sisters,ᵖ to respect those who labor among you, and have charge of you in the Lord and admonish you; ¹³esteem them very highly in love because of their work. Be at peace among yourselves. ¹⁴And we urge you, beloved,ᵖ to admonish the idlers, encourage the faint hearted, help the weak, be patient with all of them. ¹⁵See that none of you repays evil for evil, but always seek to do good to one another and to all. ¹⁶Rejoice always, ¹⁷pray without ceasing, ¹⁸give thanks in all circumstances; for this is the will of God in Christ Jesus for you. ¹⁹Do not quench the Spirit. ²⁰Do not despise the words of prophets,�q ²¹but test everything; hold fast to what is good; ²²abstain from every form of evil.

ᵖ Gk *brothers*   q Gk *despise prophecies*

12-13 reminds all Christians to respect and encourage all 'those [both women and men] who labor', 'have charge', and 'admonish' the church. These participles are not titles but functions. Paul did not write 'men', as in former translations, since he had many female colleagues in leadership positions in the early church.

13 bridges the phrases about those who serve among us and the next section about the Christian community's life together.

14-24 is one of the finest descriptions of the Christian life in the whole New Testament. All this section's verbs are plural; we don't have to try to crank up our own joy or thanksgiving, but together in the community we experience them. 5:18 does not say that we give thanks *for* everything – then we would never fight evil! – but that *in* every circumstance we can give thanks for God's presence and sovereignty that will turn everything (even evil) into good.

When set down in Greek lines, all the verbs of this section are last for emphasis. A preponderance of Greek words beginning with *pi* indicates that this section might be headings for a worship service – glad adoration, prayer and thanksgiving, liberty of Spirit and avoidance of anything unseemly – concluded appropriately with a comprehensive prayer for the entire fellowship (v. 23) and the confident expression that God will hear and bless (v. 24). Cf. 1 Cor. 14. As Thomas Erskine said, 'Religion is grace; ethics is gratitude.'

23 May the God of peace himself sanctify you entirely; and may your spirit and soul and body be kept sound[r] and blameless at the coming of our Lord Jesus Christ. [24]The one who calls you is faithful, and he will do this.

25 Beloved,[s] pray for us.

26 Greet all the brothers and sisters[s] with a holy kiss. [27]I solemnly command you by the Lord that this letter be read to all of them.[t]

28 The grace of our Lord Jesus Christ be with you.[u]

[r] Or *complete*   [s] Gk *Brothers*   [t] Gk *to all the brothers*   [u] Other ancient authorities add *Amen*

---

26. The 'holy kiss' urges godly affection in the Christian community that encourages the faithful to refrain from sexual immorality. Liturgically, the kiss was exchanged usually before the Sacrament; mentioning it here might indicate that this letter was to be read in worship before the Supper.

27. Every member of the church needs to hear the matters in this letter; especially, comfort in times of persecution, the death of beloved ones, and the strong words about sexual purity.

THE SECOND LETTER OF PAUL
TO THE THESSALONIANS

INTRODUCTION

The Thessalonian correspondence together with the book of Galatians constitutes the earliest epistles penned by Paul the apostle (early AD 50s). The book's relevance for the contemporary church remains. In the twentieth century alone, at least nine different groups or people boldly predicted various dates for Christ's return. Around the world men and women have been alarmed and deceived by believing these self-proclaimed prophets. Paul's words of comfort, assurance and correction find an audience in today's church. But if one looks only for a specific twentieth century eschatological timetable, the relevant application and the thrust of the book are lost.

In his closing words of 1 Thessalonians Paul exhorts the believers not to quench the Spirit, not to despise prophesying, but to test everything, and to hold fast to good things (1 Thess. 5:19). Afterward the congregation had received a misleading communication sent in Paul's name that wreaked devastation in their midst. Apparently in their zeal not to limit the Spirit and to give proper value to prophesying, the Thessalonians failed to test the nature of words recently conveyed to them by someone pretending to be Paul (2:2; 3:17).

Whether in the form of Spirit-inspired words of prophecy, orally transmitted words, or hand-written words, the forgery plunged the recipients into turmoil. They lost their mental composure (2:2). They wavered from their beliefs and Paul's teachings concerning Jesus' return (2:2, 15, 17; 3:3, 16). Deception led them to believe they had actually missed the Lord's return (2:1–3). They questioned God's justice in their persecution since they understood suffering for believers to end on the Day of the Lord (1:5–6, 11; 2:13–14, 16; 3:5, 16). As a result, some ceased working and chose to live in shameful idleness (3:6–15).

Paul wrote to the Thessalonians a second time with clearly defined purposes. He aimed to bring comfort, assurance and proof that this Day had not arrived. In so doing, he establishes a chronology of events preceding Jesus' return. At the same time he explains the vindication of divine justice in the face of evil and commands them to go back to work.

Salutation

1 Paul, Silvanus, and Timothy,
To the church of the Thessalonians in God our Father and the Lord Jesus Christ:

2 Grace to you and peace from God our[a] Father and the Lord Jesus Christ.

Thanksgiving

3 We must always give thanks to God for you, brothers and sisters,[b] as is right, because your faith is growing abundantly, and the love of everyone of you for one another is increasing. [4]Therefore we ourselves boast of you among the churches of God for your steadfastness and faith during all your persecutions and the afflictions that you are enduring.

The Judgment at Christ's Coming

5 This is evidence of the righteous judg-

ment of God, and is intended to make you worthy of the kingdom of God, for which you are also suffering. [6]For it is indeed just of God to repay with affliction those who afflict you, [7]and to give relief to the afflicted as well as to us, when the Lord Jesus is revealed from heaven with his mighty angels [8]in flaming fire, inflicting vengeance on those who do not know God and on those who do not obey the gospel of our Lord Jesus. [9]These will suffer the punishment of eternal destruction, separated from the presence of the Lord and from the glory of his might, [10]when he comes to be glorified by his saints and to be marveled at on that day among all who have believed, because our testimony to you was believed. [11]To this end we always pray for you, asking

[a] Other ancient authorities read *the*   [b] Gk *brothers*

---

2 THESSALONIANS 1

In 2 Thess. 1 we find the dominant themes of the book stated. Against the setting of severe persecution, Paul discusses Christ's return and details its meaning for both believers and those outside.

1–4. The church in Thessalonica, made up of Jews and devout Greeks, including 'leading women' (Acts 17:4), could boast of growth. This was not realized so much in terms of church membership but in more important areas: their faith and love. This should not surprise us since Paul's prayer in 1 Thess. 3:12 requests such an increase. But the surprising element is how Paul could boast of such character growth while persecutions and afflictions escalated. Both Luke and Paul alluded to the nature of the persecution in Acts 17:5–9 and 1 Thess. 3:14–15. Apparently the severity of the persecution allowed Paul to draw the parallel between the Thessalonian church's suffering under their own countrymen and the afflictions of the Judean church (1 Thess. 3:14–15). In spite of the violent nature of the persecutions, Paul encourages the Thessalonians to endure.

5–10. Paul lays out two reasons for their continued endurance. First, their persecutions actually signified that God considered them worthy of his Kingdom (1:5, 11). The Thessalonians were by no means the objects of God's wrath.

Secondly there awaited a reward for their sufferings (v. 7). Paul spoke of Jesus' return (*parousia*) as the day when God, the just judge, would execute his righteous judgment on evildoers (1 Thess. 2:19; 3:13; 4:15; 5:23; 2 Thess 2:1, 8–9). Paul turns the attention of his readers to this specific day not because he wanted to give them an end time calendar of events but because he wanted to give them hope and reason to endure present persecutions. This eschatological admonition is given to correct the unstable situation in Thessalonica. Correcting their inaccurate view of God's justice, he emphasizes his wrath not upon believers but upon the disobedient, the persecutors of God and his people. That day will bring punishment of an eternal nature: exclusion from the Divine Presence. For the Thessalonians it would mean experiencing the Divine Presence (1 Thess. 4:17), and relief from all persecution and suffering.

11–12. Paul's prayer emphasizes how God's power energizes the saints to right conduct (good intentions and works of faith) while they endure. The apostle envisions a goal of reciprocal glorification. The name of Jesus will be glorified in Thessalonica by the actions of these believers and

that our God will make you worthy of his call and will fulfill by his power every good resolve and work of faith, [12]so that the name of our Lord Jesus may be glorified in you, and you in him, according to the grace of our God and the Lord Jesus Christ.

The Man of Lawlessness

2 As to the coming of our Lord Jesus Christ and our being gathered together to him, we beg you, brothers and sisters,[c] [2]not to be quickly shaken in mind or alarmed, either by spirit or by word or by letter, as though from us, to the effect that the day of the Lord is already here. [3]Let no one deceive you in any way; for that day will not come unless the rebellion comes first and the lawless one[d] is revealed, the one destined for destruction.[e] [4]He opposes and exalts himself above every so-called god or object of worship, so that he takes his seat in the temple of God, declaring himself to be God. [5]Do you not remember that I told you these things when I was still with you? [6]And you know what is now restraining him, so that he may be revealed when his time comes. [7]For the mystery of lawlessness is already at work, but only until the one who now restrains it is removed. [8]And then the lawless one will be revealed, whom the Lord Jesus[f] will destroy[g] with the breath of his mouth, annihilating him by the manifestation of

◆ The 'mystery of lawlessness' constitutes a very great perplexity. Those who believe in the goodness and love of God are baffled at the existence of profound evil in the world. The saints in all generations have struggled to explain why God allows it. But that explanation lies beyond our understanding. Our faith is severely strained as we witness devastating wars, humanly engineered famines, holocausts, and genocides. The twentieth century has witnessed hundreds of thousands of martyrdoms for the sake of Jesus Christ, more than any other century. Such events can rob the moral universe of meaning unless we hold onto a conviction in the ultimate righteousness of God.

Our response must be either faith or frustration. Those who walk through the fiery furnace with God find the divine presence and purpose in ways that they had not imagined. In the midst of horrifying circumstances, women with steadfast faith have comforted children, tended the sick and wounded, proclaimed Christ and given hope to the hopeless. Corrie Ten Boom was a prime example of one who lighted a bright lamp of faith in an abysmally dark place.

[c] Gk brothers [d] Gk the man of lawlessness; other ancient authorities read the man of sin [e] Gk the son of destruction [f] Other ancient authorities lack Jesus [g] Other ancient authorities read consume

---

in turn their glorification takes place with Christ's assistance. The glorification, Paul concludes, takes place fundamentally because of the amazing grace of God.

2 THESSALONIANS 2

Against the setting of doctrinal and emotional upheaval and deception in the Thessalonian church, Paul discusses Christ's return once again and details its meaning for both non-believers and believers.

1–12. The purpose of this chapter was to remind the Thessalonians there was no cause for being dismayed nor swept into deception. Paul gives reasons why they need not be alarmed. Contrary to popular misunderstandings, they had not missed the eschatological return of Christ (2:3b–10)! Paul proves this by stating two events that must precede Christ's second coming: (1) Apostasy must come. This includes the public appearance of the man of lawlessness under Satanic direction (2:3, 8). (2) The removal of the 'restrainer' in preparation for the lawless one's appearance (2:7). Since these events had not taken place, Paul argues the Day of the Lord had not been ushered in. The Thessalonians had missed nothing.

2 Thessalonians, Daniel, and Revelation assure us that the final victory belongs to God and not to the wicked. Again and again these promises have sustained believers in the darkest periods of history. Although the unrighteous are for a time allowed to wreak harm on millions, there will come a day of accounting and vindication. God is still in control of the universe ◆

his coming. [9]The coming of the lawless one is apparent in the working of Satan, who uses all power, signs, lying wonders, [10]and every kind of wicked deception for those who are perishing, because they refused to love the truth and so be saved. [11]For this reason God sends them a powerful delusion, leading them to believe what is false, [12]so that all who have not believed the truth but took pleasure in unrighteousness will be condemned.

Chosen for Salvation

[13] But we must always give thanks to God for you, brothers and sisters[h] beloved by the Lord, because God chose you as the first fruits[i] for salvation through sanctification by the Spirit and through belief in the truth. [14]For this purpose he called you through our proclamation of the good news,[j] so that you may obtain the glory of our Lord Jesus Christ. [15]So then, brothers and sisters,[h] stand firm and hold fast to the traditions that you were taught by us, either by word of mouth or by our letter.

[h] Gk brothers   [i] Other ancient authorities read *from the beginning*   [j] Or *through our gospel*

10b–12. When that day finally comes, there will be deception of great magnitude for those who have resisted the truth. The person of lawlessness draws unbelievers into further deception. God will permit the situation to exist for a time. The apparent success of the perpetrator of evil will create greater confusion for those who have turned their backs upon God's grace and love. In the end, unbelievers will receive more of the evil they desired and chose to embrace. They will receive condemnation for their wickedness.

13–15. In contrast to their unbelieving persecutors, the Thessalonian Christians are not subject to God's final wrath. In fact they had been graciously chosen and called by God to obtain his glory, not his wrath. Thus Paul offers a second reason they should not be alarmed. Therefore Paul urges that they stand strong once again by holding to his teachings.

In order to understand the person of lawlessness, a few things must be kept in mind. Other biblical passages speak of such an apocalyptic figure. Both the eschatological king in Daniel and numerous passages in Revelation refer to what Paul describes as the person of lawlessness (Dan. 7:25; Rev. 11:7; 13:1–18; 17:10; 19:19; 20:7–9). However, 2 Thessalonians provides the clearest information of the three passages. Paul's image points to a literal person as a key player in the sudden surge of evil immediately preceding Christ's return. Paul's audience would have understood the characteristics of this figure since they were reminiscent of a well known figure from the Maccabean period in Jewish history.

In 167 BC Antiochus Epiphanes took his seat in the Temple of God in Jerusalem as a self-proclaimed god. He erected a statue of Zeus in the Holy of Holies and sacrificed a pig on the altar. Based on this historical figure, Paul alerted his audience for the coming (*parousia*) of a wicked figure surpassing Antiochus' example. Attempts to identify this person of lawlessness with more precision result in conjecture at best. Paul wanted the Thessalonian believers and believers today to anticipate and be warned of the final act of rebellion against God before Jesus returns.

The identification of 'the restrainer' in vv. 6–7 presents problems for two reasons. First, there are numerous exegetical difficulties. Secondly, they suggest that the Thessalonians possessed an interpretative key to the meaning that we no longer have. Paul's teachings had given them this key (2 Thess. 2:5–6; 1 Thess. 2:9; 3:3; 4:2). Whatever the conclusion, one must account for the shift from the neuter participle in v. 6 translated as 'what is restraining' to the masculine

16 Now may our Lord Jesus Christ himself and God our Father, who loved us and through grace gave us eternal comfort and good hope, [17]comfort your hearts and strengthen them in every good work and word.

Request for Prayer

3 Finally, brothers and sisters,[k] pray for us, so that the word of the Lord may spread rapidly and be glorified everywhere, just as it is among you, [2]and that we may be rescued from wicked and evil people; for not all have faith. [3]But the Lord is faithful; he will strengthen you and guard you from the evil one.[l] [4]And we have confidence in the Lord concerning you, that you are doing and will go on doing the things that we command. [5]May the Lord direct your hearts to the love of God and to the steadfastness of Christ.

Warning against Idleness

6 Now we command you, beloved,[k] in the name of our Lord Jesus Christ, to keep away from believers who are[m] living in idleness and not according to the tradition that they[n] received from us. [7]For you yourselves know how you ought to imitate us; we were not idle when we were with you, [8]and we did not eat anyone's bread without paying for it; but with toil and labor we worked night and day, so that we might not burden any of you. [9]This was not because we do not have that right, but in order to give you an example to imitate. [10]For even when we were with you, we gave you this command: Anyone unwilling to work should not eat. [11]For we hear that some of you are living in idleness, mere busybodies, not doing any work. [12]Now such persons we command and exhort in the Lord Jesus Christ to do their work quietly and to earn

k Gk *brothers*   l Or *from evil*   m Gk *from every brother who is*   n Other ancient authorities read *you*

---

participle in v. 7 translated as 'he who restrains or the one who restrains'. This grammatical gender shift has allowed numerous and widely variant interpretations to be put forward.

Some see vv. 6–7 as the Roman Empire and the Emperor respectively, some suggest the preaching of the gospel and Paul or the preaching of the gospel and an angel. Still others would argue for an evil power and some evil person or a principle of rebellion and Satan. Some even suggest the Holy Spirit as a viable possibility for both verses. The interpretation best suited to the grammar, syntax and immediate context of v. 7 would seem to identify the 'restrainer' as an evil power and some evil person hostile to God.

16–17. Paul's prayer summarizes what he attempts to accomplish in the letter. Realizing his limitations, Paul appeals to Christ and the Father, asking God to do for the Thessalonians what no human could do.

2 THESSALONIANS 3

1–5. After offering two chapters of assurance, hope and comfort for the Thessalonians in their difficult circumstances, Paul requests their prayers for the success of the gospel ministry in Corinth. His associates, like the Thessalonians, needed relief from persecution generated by hostile opponents. This passage reveals Paul's initial impressions of his year and a half stay in Corinth (Acts 18).

6–15. Now that he has corrected their beliefs concerning Jesus' return and tried to restore composure to the group, Paul moves on to rebuke their shameful behavior. Three times he commands them to get to work (vv. 6, 10, 12). No excuses remain for such unacceptable behavior. Christ had not returned. Paul neither had modeled nor taught such behavior or attitudes. He urges disciplinary measures upon the disobedient brother or sister who refuses to work. In order to promote right conduct, he discourages giving handouts or sustaining fellowship with such people. He admonishes the congregation not to treat the idlers as they would hostile outsiders, that is, as enemies, but as brothers and sisters in Christ needing correction.

their own living. [13]Brothers and sisters,° do not be weary in doing what is right.

14 Take note of those who do not obey what we say in this letter; have nothing to do with them, so that they may be ashamed. [15]Do not regard them as enemies, but warn them as believers.ᴾ

Final Greetings and Benediction

16 Now may the Lord of peace himself give you peace at all times in all ways. The Lord be with all of you.

17 I, Paul, write this greeting with my own hand. This is the mark in every letter of mine; it is the way I write. [18]The grace of our Lord Jesus Christ be with all of you.ᑫ

° Gk *Brothers*   ᴾ Gk *a brother*   ᑫ Other ancient authorities add *Amen*

16–17. The Thessalonians needed peace in their time of turmoil, to reflect upon the teachings in this letter. They needed to know that the words of this letter came from a trustworthy authoritative source. Believers today need the same peace, assurance and authoritative proof given in 2 Thessalonians to deal with rampant predictions of the Lord's return.

THE FIRST LETTER OF PAUL
TO TIMOTHY

INTRODUCTION

Some scholars have argued that all the 'Pastoral Epistles', including 1 Timothy, are *pseude-pigrapha* – that is, writings using a false name – appearing to be Paul's but actually the work of an unnamed writer early in the second century. However, according to the text, the author of 1 Timothy is the apostle Paul, and there are a number of personal references difficult to explain if the letter is not authentic.

One strong theme of this letter is that 'God our Savior' wants everyone to be saved. The salvation Christ offers is available to all people through all time with no exceptions.

Purity of Christian doctrine, which is a recurring theme in other letters ascribed to Paul (2 Cor. 11:4; Gal. 1:6–7; 2 Tim. 4:4; Titus 1:14), is also important here. One fifth of the content of this letter deals with false teachers and their erroneous views. To counter this, truth must be proclaimed.

One contemporary false teaching was Gnosticism: a religious system that distorted Jewish ideas and opposed Christianity too. It believed all material things to be evil; only spirit could be good. Some felt this meant that God was evil because he created the material world. Gnosticism turned upside-down the Genesis account of the Creation and Fall, making the snake a hero who leads Adam and Eve away from God's deception, and presenting Eve as the source of life and enlightenment. One of the hallmarks of Gnosticism was nonsense, ranging from meaningless syllables to futile arguments about words. The writer of the first epistle to Timothy is at pains to refute Gnostic ideas.

The letter also deals with prayer in Christian congregations, qualities of Christian leadership, and practical aspects of church life including the place of widows.

The reputation of the gospel and of the church is to be protected, and on several occasions (1 Tim. 3:7; 5:12, 14; 6:1) this priority is advanced as a justification for courses of action advocated by the writer.

Salutation

1 Paul, an apostle of Christ Jesus by the command of God our Savior and of Christ Jesus our hope,

2 To Timothy, my loyal child in the faith: Grace, mercy, and peace from God the Father and Christ Jesus our Lord.

Warning against False Teachers

3 I urge you, as I did when I was on my way to Macedonia, to remain in Ephesus so that you may instruct certain people not to teach any different doctrine, **4**and not to occupy themselves with myths and endless genealogies that promote speculations rather than the divine training[a] that is known by faith. **5**But the aim of such instruction is love that comes from a pure heart, a good conscience, and sincere faith. **6**Some people have deviated from these and turned to meaningless talk, **7**desiring to be teachers of the law, without understanding either what they are saying or the things about which they make assertions.

8 Now we know that the law is good, if one uses it legitimately. **9**This means understanding that the law is laid down not for the innocent but for the lawless and disobedient, for the godless and sinful, for the unholy and profane, for those who kill their father or mother, for murderers, **10**fornicators, sodomites, slave traders, liars, perjurers, and whatever else is contrary to the sound teaching **11**that conforms to the glorious gospel of the blessed God, which he entrusted to me.

Gratitude for Mercy

12 I am grateful to Christ Jesus our Lord, who has strengthened me, because he judged me faithful and appointed me to his service, **13**even though I was formerly a blasphemer, a persecutor, and a man of violence. But I received mercy because I had acted ignorantly in unbelief, **14**and the grace of our Lord overflowed for me with the faith and love that are in Christ Jesus. **15**The saying is sure and worthy of full acceptance, that Christ Jesus came into the world to save sinners – of whom I am the foremost. **16**But for that very reason I received mercy, so that in me, as the foremost, Jesus Christ might display the utmost patience, making me an example to those who would come to believe in him for eternal life. **17**To the King of the ages, immortal, invisible, the only God, be honor and glory forever and ever.[b] Amen.

[a] Or *plan*   [b] Gk *to the ages of the ages*

INTRODUCTION (1 TIM. 1:1–2)

Paul, who sees himself as commanded by God to be an apostle of Jesus Christ, is writing a letter of instruction to Timothy (see Acts 16:1–3), who will in turn teach the church.

TIMOTHY THE TEACHER (1 TIM. 1:3–11)

Timothy was now a leader of the Christians in the city of Ephesus, on the west coast of Asia Minor, the site of one of the seven wonders of the ancient world, the Temple of Artemis (Diana).

Instruction should be motivated by love, be relevant to everyday life and promote understanding. The Law is to be taught to show up sin for what it is. The examples of things which don't measure up to the gospel vary from sexual perversion to telling lies. Note the specific mention of father and mother, quoted from the Ten Commandments; a parent is a parent regardless of gender.

PAUL THE CONSULTANT (1 TIM. 1:12–20)

15. The gospel Timothy is to announce is: 'Christ Jesus came into the world to save sinners.' The writer counts himself 'foremost of sinners' – probably because of Paul's persecution of Christian 'men and women' (Acts 8:3) – and also a recipient of mercy (1 Tim. 1:16).

18 I am giving you these instructions, Timothy, my child, in accordance with the prophecies made earlier about you, so that by following them you may fight the good fight, [19]having faith and a good conscience. By rejecting conscience, certain persons have suffered shipwreck in the faith; [20]among them are Hymenaeus and Alexander, whom I have turned over to Satan, so that they may learn not to blaspheme.

Instructions concerning Prayer

2 First of all, then, I urge that supplications, prayers, intercessions, and thanksgivings be made for everyone, [2]for kings and all who are in high positions, so that we may lead a quiet and peaceable life in all godliness and dignity. [3]This is right and is acceptable in the sight of God our Savior, [4]who desires everyone to be saved and to come to the knowledge of the truth.

[5]For
> there is one God;
>> there is also one mediator between
>> God and humankind,
> Christ Jesus, himself human,

[6] who gave himself a ransom for all – this was attested at the right time. [7]For this I was appointed a herald and an apostle (I am telling the truth,[c] I am not lying), a teacher of the Gentiles in faith and truth.

8 I desire, then, that in every place the men should pray, lifting up holy hands without anger or argument; [9]also that the women should dress themselves modestly and decently in suitable clothing, not with their hair braided, or with gold, pearls, or expensive clothes, [10]but with good works, as is proper for women who profess reverence for God. [11]Let a woman[d] learn in

[c] Other ancient authorities add *in Christ*   [d] Or *wife*

---

20. Deliberately rejecting the gospel or ignoring the need to live in the light of the gospel leads to disaster. Hymenaeus (2 Tim. 2:17) and Alexander (Acts 19:33–34 and/or 2 Tim. 4:14–15) came into this category and therefore were understood as being outside the community of the church.

THE QUIET LIFE (1 TIM. 2:1–15)

Faithful prayer is to be offered for everyone, 'so that we may lead a quiet and peaceable life'. God wants all people 'to be saved and to come to the knowledge of the truth'; which they are unable to do if society is not stable or false teaching is not exposed.

5. It is as a human being, *anthropos*, and not as a male, *aner*, that Jesus is the one mediator between God and people. God in human form is a representative of all humanity, women as well as men. The writer could have emphasized Jesus' maleness, in a situation where people were practising goddess-worship, if it was important.

8. Gentile men and women often worshipped differently and separately, often in somewhat disorderly ways. Christian worship is to be corporate and reverent. When men pray, they should be doing so without the arguments that accompany false teachers.

9. Women too are to pray. They are to dress modestly (some pagan women undressed to worship) but they are not to concentrate on expensive externals, neither flaunting wealth nor drawing undue attention to their appearance. Christian women should be noted instead for their good works.

11. The phrase 'Let a woman learn' uses the imperative or command form of the verb. The readers are enjoined to let women 'learn through instruction' as Mary did from Jesus in Luke 10:39. This is the crucial focus of this command. The 'silence' is the same word as is used in 1 Tim. 2:2 - 'peaceable life'. It refers to the manner in which women are to learn; not to what they do with their learning. (See the note on 'Silence', p. 252.)

'Silence and submission' is a Near Eastern formula of that period that implies willingness to obey instruction. 'With full submission' – women who had not received any formal education would need to be told even now to sit and listen to instruction about God.

silence with full submission. ¹²I permit no woman[e] to teach or to have authority over a man;[f] she is to keep silent. ¹³For Adam was formed first, then Eve; ¹⁴and Adam was not deceived, but the woman was deceived and became a transgressor. ¹⁵Yet she will be saved through childbearing, provided they continue in faith and love and holiness, with modesty.

[e] Or *wife* [f] Or *her husband*

---

12. 'I permit no' or 'I am not permitting' – nowhere else in the New Testament does the use of this verb tense imply that what is being said is a rule that applies to every situation.

The word translated 'to teach' is used elsewhere in the Pastoral Epistles only to refer to countering false teaching, and that may be what is being referred to here. It would be strange if the writer's point here was to be that women cannot teach at all, since it was at Ephesus that Priscilla (and her husband, Aquila) taught Apollos the way of God more accurately (Acts 18:26).

The Greek word here translated 'have authority over' is extremely rare. It could mean 'usurp authority'; or 'dominate'; or it may relate to contexts involving sex and murder. It can also refer to origin and authenticity. The verse might then be understood: 'I am not permitting a woman to teach or proclaim herself originator of man'. This rebukes the Gnostic idea that woman was responsible for the creation of man, and creates a logical link with v. 13.

13. Both Adam and Eve (men and women) should study Scripture. Adam was not alone at creation. Traditionalists have seen in this verse an appeal to a so-called 'order of creation' – Adam first, then Eve – implying the superiority of Adam over Eve. Such a view fails to attribute both the subordination of women to men and women's inferiority in status to the Fall rather than to creation. It makes better sense of the context of this verse to realize that Gnostics believed Eve pre-existed Adam and was the source of all life. The writer is saying Eve did *not* give Adam life, and could not have done so, since she was formed after him.

14. Traditionally, the idea that Eve was deceived but Adam was not has been taken to imply that women are more open to deception than men, and are thus disqualified from teaching in a Christian congregation. But what, then, of Adam? It cannot be right to say that sinning deliberately is less serious than sinning through being deceived. The writer is not asserting here that Eve is responsible for the Fall. That would be inconsistent with identifying the Fall with Adam (1 Cor. 15:22) and with the account in Gen. 3. It makes better sense to realise that Gnostics believed Adam had been misled by the Creator God. The writer is simply saying Adam was not deceived. The reference to Eve's deception in 2 Cor. 11:3 is applied to all believers and makes nonsense of the assumption that 'being deceived' happens to women and not to men.

15. This verse cannot mean that Christian women will be saved by bearing children, because that would exclude from salvation those who have not given birth. Nor can it mean that Christian women will be kept safe through childbirth – too many have died for that to be the case. The word used is one associated with salvation (as in 1 Tim. 1:15–16; 2:4), not safekeeping. It has been suggested that the verse should read 'through the Childbirth' – meaning through Mary's giving birth to Jesus. But this would contradict the thrust of New Testament teaching that salvation is through faith in the atoning death of Christ – not through the Incarnation, or by Mary's deed. The noun concerns 'bearing' children, as opposed to 'birth' or 'a child'.

The enmity between the serpent and Eve, and the prediction of greater pain in giving birth of Gen. 3:15–16 are alluded to in the promise that 'she will be saved through childbearing'. Some Gnostic texts condemned childbearing, and others implied that it is impossible to gain eternal life as a woman. The writer concludes this section that refutes Gnostic teaching by affirming that any woman may be saved as she is, distinct from men, and retaining the capacity to bear children, only on condition that she lives as befits Christian people.

Qualifications of Bishops

3 The saying is sure:[g] whoever aspires to the office of bishop[h] desires a noble task. [2]Now a bishop[i] must be above reproach, married only once,[j] temperate, sensible, respectable, hospitable, an apt teacher, [3]not a drunkard, not violent but gentle, not quarrelsome, and not a lover of money. [4]He must manage his own household well, keeping his children submissive

◆ Although polygamy was not permitted by Greeks or Romans, it was still a practice in first-century Judaism. 'It is an ancestral custom of ours to have several wives at the same time,' wrote Josephus. This first-century Jewish author tells of his four wives and of at least one divorce; but it is possible that he was married to two or three of his wives at the same time. Several other aristocratic Jews are known to have contracted multiple marriages without the necessity of divorce. The most notorious example was that of Herod the Great, who had nine wives.

Scholars had ordinarily assumed that this practice existed only at the upper echelons of society, but the discovery of a series of documents from the Dead Sea area shows that there was polygamy in the middle classes. The legal brief of a twice-widowed woman named Babatha has been recovered. As second wife of a deceased husband, she brought to the courts a dispute with the first wife over the claim to a field which had been purchased with funds inherited from Babatha's first marriage. We do not know how the case was ever settled, but we do know that Jewish polygamy was finally outlawed by the Code of Justinian.

We may appropriately ask, therefore, whether the instruction as to an elder having but one wife is a reference to this custom. A church official with multiple wives would have been totally unacceptable to a congregation including both Jews and Gentiles. Sometimes this reference is used to prove that only men are in view, though qualifications for female deacons are listed in 3:11.

This instruction about having one wife would apply only to males as no woman was permitted to have more than one husband. Women were particularly admired by the Romans if they were *univira* – having had only one husband ◆

and respectful in every way – [5]for if someone does not know how to manage his

[g] Some interpreters place these words at the end of the previous paragraph. Other ancient authorities read *The saying is commonly accepted* [h] Or *overseer* [i] Or *an overseer* [j] Gk *the husband of one wife*

BISHOPS (1 TIM. 3:1-7)

Anyone may aspire to the noble office of 'bishop' (or 'overseer'). The Greek pronoun is not gender-specific. The writer assumes aspirants will be older married men with children, but if these were definite qualifications Paul himself would be ineligible, as he was unmarried (1 Cor. 7:8).

2. The phrase 'married only once' (also in 1 Tim. 3:12 and Titus 1:6) could be a prohibition: of a second marriage after divorce or widow(er)hood; or of polygamy; or of sexual immorality generally. It might imply that the bishop must be married, as false teachers were forbidding marriage and would not be married themselves.

3. Leadership is forbidden to anyone who physically abuses other people.

4. Those who wish to 'manage' the church must show management skills first of all in their home. 'Manage' is also used in 1 Tim. 3:12 of deacons; and in 1 Tim. 5:17 of elders, where it is translated 'rule'. The same word is used of Phoebe in Rom. 16:1, herself a deacon. In 1 Tim. 5:17, where remarried widows are to manage their households, a different word is used but one where ruling connotations are even stronger. The author is certainly not arguing here that men as opposed to women should be household leaders.

own household, how can he take care of God's church? ⁶He must not be a recent convert, or he may be puffed up with conceit and fall into the condemnation of the devil. ⁷Moreover, he must be well thought of by outsiders, so that he may not fall into disgrace and the snare of the devil.

Qualifications of Deacons

8 Deacons likewise must be serious, not double-tongued, not indulging in much wine, not greedy for money; ⁹they must hold fast to the mystery of the faith with a clear conscience. ¹⁰And let them first be tested; then, if they prove themselves blameless, let them serve as deacons. ¹¹Womenᵏ likewise must be serious, not slanderers, but temperate, faithful in all things. ¹²Let deacons be married only once,ˡ and let them manage their children and their households well; ¹³for those who serve well as deacons gain a good standing for themselves and great boldness in the faith that is in Christ Jesus.

◆ When Paul lists his qualifications for those in leadership in the Christian community, both women and men, prominent among them is the need to be sober and to avoid drunkenness. In contemporary terms, this can be broadened to include all forms of chemical dependency. While alcoholism and hard drugs are most visible, chemical dependency can be as simple as 'needing' to take a tablet each day to cope with the demands of everyday life. Thus this problem is widespread, and with the increasing complexity of our world and ready access to all forms of drugs, affects the Christian community no less than the rest of society.

There are three dimensions to this problem, the physical, behavioral and spiritual. The physical effects of chemical dependency are relatively easy to identify, and may include damage to the brain and other organs. Children born to people with chemical dependency may inherit the dependency, and their growth is frequently inhibited. Such physical effects are both short and long term, and may inhibit practical functioning. Our bodies are part of God's good creation, which we are to care for: to submit them to this form of chemical control is to deny that good gift and to deny their nature as temples of the Holy Spirit (1 Cor. 6:19–20).

There are also behavioral effects of chemical dependency. This is evident, for example, in alcohol abuse, which may result in an inability to control emotions and behavior, often issuing in violence. There may be an inability to care for one's own self or for other people, such as children. These are not only the outcomes of 'serious' drug abuse, but are behaviors which can be seen in those who misuse prescription and over-the-counter drugs such as tranquilizers. What begins as medicinal aids in a time of crisis become necessary agents in living daily life and coping with everyday stresses.

Chemical dependency can have a major and detrimental impact on relationships, both for the person who is dependent and for their family and friends. A frequently observed condition in those close to someone with a chemical dependency is that of codependency, a state of secondary dependency in which a person's whole life is oriented around reaching the person with the dependency and meeting their perceived needs. This secondary dependency can result in a life characterized by loss of freedom and loss of control. What begins as a desire to love one's neighbor, becomes a means of maintaining them in their destructive behavior and destroying one's own self.

ᵏ Or *Their wives,* or *Women deacons*   ˡ Gk *be husbands of one wife*

DEACONS (1 TIM. 3:8–13)

Deacons can be male or female. Explicit qualities to be shown by women deacons are set forth in v. 11.

However even more fundamental is the spiritual impact. To the extent that we are dependent on chemicals as a means of surviving the stresses of everyday life, our relationship with and dependence on God is impaired. Control becomes vested in the chemical, rather than in the Holy Spirit. The loss of freedom for people with both primary and secondary dependencies impairs their ability to live lives of obedience to God, and obscures the gracious work of God in them ◆

The Mystery of Our Religion

14 I hope to come to you soon, but I am writing these instructions to you so that, [15]if I am delayed, you may know how one ought to behave in the household of God, which is the church of the living God, the pillar and bulwark of the truth. [16]Without any doubt, the mystery of our religion is great:

He[m] was revealed in flesh,
vindicated[n] in spirit,[o]
seen by angels,
proclaimed among Gentiles,
believed in throughout the world,
taken up in glory.

False Asceticism

4 Now the Spirit expressly says that in later[p] times some will renounce the

faith by paying attention to deceitful spirits and teachings of demons, [2]through the hypocrisy of liars whose consciences are seared with a hot iron. [3]They forbid marriage and demand abstinence from foods, which God created to be received with thanksgiving by those who believe and know the truth. [4]For everything created by God is good, and nothing is to be rejected, provided it is received with thanksgiving; [5]for it is sanctified by God's word and by prayer.

A Good Minister of Jesus Christ

6 If you put these instructions before the brothers and sisters,[q] you will be a good servant[r] of Christ Jesus, nourished on the words of the faith and of the sound teaching that you have followed. [7]Have nothing to do with profane myths and old wives' tales. Train yourself in godliness, [8]for, while physical training is of some value, godliness is valuable in every way, holding promise for both the present life and the life to come. [9]The saying is sure and worthy of full acceptance. [10]For to this end we toil and struggle,[s] because we have our

[m] Gk *Who*; other ancient authorities read *God*; others, *Which*   [n] Or *justified*   [o] Or *by the Spirit*   [p] Or *the last*   [q] Gk *brothers*   [r] Or *deacon*   [s] Other ancient authorities read *suffer reproach*

PAUL'S CONTINGENCY PLAN (1 TIM. 3:14–16)

Metaphors from the Temple – 'pillar' and 'bulwark' – and the family – 'household of God' – are used of the church, which is entrusted with 'the truth'. The writer quotes from what was probably an early Christian hymn – the 'mystery' is Christ himself.

BAD INFLUENCES (1 TIM 4:1–6)

Those who 'renounce the faith' are attending to 'deceitful spirits' and 'demons'. The writer denounces those who forbid marriage and the eating of certain foods, referring again to the Gnostics.
6. The Greek word which is often translated as 'brethren' or 'brothers' is here translated in its actual inclusive sense as 'brothers and sisters'.

GOOD INFLUENCES (1 TIM. 4:6–16)

Timothy himself is a servant (deacon) of Christ Jesus. He is to keep clear of false teaching, and the serious threat of 'profane myths and old wives' tales' (v. 7). Timothy is given detailed instructions about his teaching ministry, which he is to practise for his own sake and for the sake of his hearers.

hope set on the living God, who is the Savior of all people, especially of those who believe.

11 These are the things you must insist on and teach. [12]Let no one despise your youth, but set the believers an example in speech and conduct, in love, in faith, in purity. [13]Until I arrive, give attention to the public reading of scripture,[t] to exhorting, to teaching. [14]Do not neglect the gift that is in you, which was given to you through prophecy with the laying on of hands by the council of elders.[u] [15]Put these things into practice, devote yourself to them, so that all may see your progress. [16]Pay close attention to yourself and to your teaching; continue in these things, for in doing this you will save both yourself and your hearers.

Duties toward Believers

5 Do not speak harshly to an older man,[v] but speak to him as to a father, to younger men as brothers, [2]to older women as mothers, to younger women as sisters – with absolute purity.

3 Honor widows who are really widows. [4]If a widow has children or grandchildren, they should first learn their religious duty to their own family and make some repayment to their parents; for this is pleasing in God's sight. [5]The real widow, left alone, has set her hope on God and continues in supplications and prayers night and day; [6]but the widow[w] who lives for pleasure is

◆ A recurring theme in both Old and New Testament is the care of widows (Deut. 10:18; Job 22:9; 24:3; 31:16; Ps. 94:6; Is. 1:23; 10:2; Mark 12:40; James 1:18). God pronounces a curse against those who withhold justice from widows (Deut. 27:19) while those who care for them are promised God's blessing (Jer. 7:5–7). 'You shall not abuse any widow,' warns Exod. 22:22, for God is the defender of widows (Deut. 10:17; Pss. 68:5; 146:9). Mal. 3:5 declares that those who defraud laborers of their wages and oppress widows do not fear the LORD Almighty. God repeatedly commanded that his people should relieve the affliction of widows.

There is also an emphasis on letting widows help themselves. The tithe of the produce every third year was designated for the widow, the fatherless, the stranger and the Levite (Deut. 26:12; 27:19). Widows and other economically disadvantaged persons were given special rights to glean at harvest time (Deut. 24:19–21). Ruth, a foreign widow who is further burdened by having taken on the care of the widowed Naomi, is given an opportunity by Boaz to provide for both her mother-in-law and herself. His generosity ensures that her many hours of hot, hard labor bring adequate compensation. Often we see Ruth as a love story. It is also the story of a man righteous enough to support the legitimate claims of a widow.

[t] Gk *to the reading*   [u] Gk *by the presbytery*   [v] Or *an elder*, or *a presbyter*   [w] Gk *she*

RELATIONSHIPS WITH THE CHURCH (1 TIM. 5:1–6:2A)

In Christian relationships, the emphasis is to be on 'absolute purity'.

Real widows (with no family left to support them) should be honored. Such women are to be 'put on the list' for church assistance, under certain conditions of age and lifestyle (vv. 9–10). Younger widows are to be encouraged to marry again to prevent the church from being reviled because of pledges to remain unmarried being violated. This list does not necessarily denote the existence of a female order of ministry called 'widows'.

Elders are to be paid, especially teachers (v. 17). Timothy is to look for witnesses when elders are accused of sin, and to rebuke them 'in the presence of all' – he is not to act alone (vv. 19–20). There is to be no partiality or prejudice. Those in leadership roles can be the focus of unjust criticism and they must be protected from this – but leaders are not sacrosanct and just criticism must be followed up.

(See Is. 1:17 for the command to defend the rights of widows.) Her rights are to glean and to contract a levirate marriage.

Behind the story of Ruth lies the ancient law whereby a widow was given in marriage to her dead husband's brother, so that she might have a son to provide for her old age (Deut. 25:5–10). A story of another widow's rights is told in Gen. 38, where the father-in-law declares that Tamar acted more righteously than he in her efforts to gain the protection afforded her by law.

The Bible mentions other ways in which widows were enabled to improve their own condition. Elijah asked an impoverished widow to supply what she had – enough flour and oil to make a little cake for him. As she ministered to his needs, her own were miraculously supplied during the three and a half years of the drought. She was helped to help herself (1 Kings 17:7–16). Elisha was once approached by a destitute widow who was threatened with the sale of her two sons into slavery. His first command was that she go out and borrow jars from the neighbors. Next she must utilize what she had: the little oil she still possessed. By God's grace it is multiplied until she has enough to provide for herself and for her sons (2 Kings 4:1–7).

Jesus expressed concern for the legal rights of widows and told a parable affirming a widow who persisted in her struggles to obtain justice (Luke 18:2–5). He restored to life a widow's only son, so that he might continue to support her in her old age (Luke 7:11–17). The early church appointed deacons to see that the needs of widows were being met equitably and adequately (Acts 6:1ff.). Peter's prayers returned to life a disciple named Dorcas because of her ministry to widows (Acts 9:36–41).

An individual who leaves a widow in destitution has denied the faith and is worse than an infidel (1 Tim. 5:4, 8). 1 Timothy arranged for widows in financial need to be compensated in return for their labors in the church (5:3–16); and Paul was of the opinion that a laborer was worthy of her hire (5:18).

Widows were regarded as persons having special opportunities for Christian service. They were widely used in the ministry of the early church and given special seats of honor in front of the congregation. A large church, such as Hagia Sophia in Constantinople, might have hundreds of widows on its staff. They visited homes, brought food for the hungry, cared for the sick, comforted the bereaved, prayed for all who made their requests known, assisted in Christian instruction and baptism, and counselled those in need. So powerful were they in prayer that early Christian literature sometimes calls widows 'the altar of God' ◆

---

dead even while she lives. [7]Give these commands as well, so that they may be above reproach. [8]And whoever does not provide for relatives, and especially for family members, has denied the faith and is worse than an unbeliever.

9 Let a widow be put on the list if she is not less than sixty years old and has been married only once;[x] [10]she must be well attested for her good works, as one who has brought up children, shown hospitality, washed the saints' feet, helped the afflicted, and devoted herself to doing good in every way. [11]But refuse to put younger widows on the list; for when their sensual desires alienate them from Christ, they want to marry, [12]and so they incur condemnation for having violated their first pledge. [13]Besides that, they learn to be idle, gadding about from house to house; and they are not merely idle, but also gossips and busybodies, saying what they should not say. [14]So I would have younger widows marry, bear children, and manage their households, so as to give the adversary no occasion to revile us. [15]For some have already turned away to follow Satan. [16]If any believing woman[y] has relatives who are

[x] Gk *the wife of one husband*   [y] Other ancient authorities read *believing man or woman*; others, *believing man*

really widows, let her assist them; let the church not be burdened, so that it can assist those who are real widows.

17 Let the elders who rule well be considered worthy of double honor,[z] especially those who labor in preaching and teaching; [18]for the scripture says, "You shall not muzzle an ox while it is treading out the grain," and, "The laborer deserves to be paid." [19]Never accept any accusation against an elder except on the evidence of two or three witnesses. [20]As for those who persist in sin, rebuke them in the presence of all, so that the rest also may stand in fear. [21]In the presence of God and of Christ Jesus and of the elect angels, I warn you to keep these instructions without prejudice, doing nothing on the basis of partiality. [22]Do not ordain[a] anyone hastily, and do not participate in the sins of others; keep yourself pure.

23 No longer drink only water, but take a little wine for the sake of your stomach and your frequent ailments.

24 The sins of some people are conspicuous and precede them to judgment, while the sins of others follow them there. [25]So also good works are conspicuous; and even when they are not, they cannot remain hidden.

6 Let all who are under the yoke of slavery regard their masters as worthy of all honor, so that the name of God and the teaching may not be blasphemed. [2]Those who have believing masters must not be disrespectful to them on the ground that they are members of the church;[b]

rather they must serve them all the more, since those who benefit by their service are believers and beloved.[c]

False Teaching and True Riches

Teach and urge these duties. [3]Whoever teaches otherwise and does not agree with the sound words of our Lord Jesus Christ and the teaching that is in accordance with godliness, [4]is conceited, understanding nothing, and has a morbid craving for controversy and for disputes about words. From these come envy, dissension, slander, base suspicions, [5]and wrangling among those who are depraved in mind and bereft of the truth, imagining that godliness is a means of gain.[d] [6]Of course, there is great gain in godliness combined with contentment; [7]for we brought nothing into the world, so that[e] we can take nothing out of it; [8]but if we have food and clothing, we will be content with these. [9]But those who want to be rich fall into temptation and are trapped by many senseless and harmful desires that plunge people into ruin and destruction. [10]For the love of money is a root of all kinds of evil, and in their eagerness to be rich some have wandered away from the faith and pierced themselves with many pains.

[z] Or *compensation*   [a] Gk *Do not lay hands on*
[b] Gk *are brothers*   [c] Or *since they are believers and beloved, who devote themselves to good deeds*
[d] Other ancient authorities add *Withdraw yourself from such people*   [e] Other ancient authorities read *world – it is certain that*

5:22. 'Ordain' means 'lay hands on' – it may refer here to the restoration of repentant sinners, which is in keeping with the context. It is unlikely to refer here to any modern understanding of ordination to ministry.

6:1–2a. The writer invites slaves to honor their masters because he wants to protect the name of God and the teaching from blasphemy. These verses cannot be taken to support the system of enslavement. They deal only with the behavior of believing slaves.

GOOD TEACHING, GOOD LIFE (1 TIM. 6:2B–10)

The 'sound words' of Christ and 'the teaching' are contrasted with the 'controversy and disputes about words' of false teachers. Abuse by richer people of poorer ones is highlighted in v. 9. Overdependence on financial security is a perennial problem in the church.

◆ How often we hear references to love of money as the root of all evil! Money in itself is not wrong or evil. It is a necessary part of life in the West without which we could not obtain the essentials of everyday living. It can, of course, be put to good, proper and generous use where those in desperate need find aid and relief. It is rather the craving for money and possessions and their misuse which can be said to be 'the root of all evil'.

Here in the West the pursuit of material things has become more important, and more acceptable, than the pursuit of God. The chief philosophy has become that of materialism which affects not only our thinking but also our behavior. Where the emphasis in life is placed on possessions, reality becomes distorted. Human life consists of the here and now, with nothing beyond. In a world of material objects, eternity pales into insignificance. As the eternal realities fade, so does the searching after God. God ceases to be God in our lives.

Not only does the quality of our relationship with God diminish but also the relationship to those around us. Possessions become of more value than people. Something which could be used for good becomes a means to create power over others and to gain prestige. Even within the church, how often do we see the place of prominence given to the wealthy, and on a world scale how often are the Western wealthy nations seen to hold power over the poorer struggling nations. Wealth, possessions, control, power and prestige all go hand in hand, creating jealousy and resentment in those who do not have and will, therefore, never succeed in life.

Arguably the greatest sin in the West is that of materialism, encouraging possession and wealth to be treated with more respect and of having more value than people. Accumulating wealth, expanding greater properties, owning all the 'mod cons' and designer labels are all worthless when viewed from the perspective of eternity. What about the casualties which are created on the way – those who have nothing, the increasing numbers of homeless on our streets, those dying of starvation in the Third World? How will our attitude to them and to our possessions be viewed from eternity? ◆

The Good Fight of Faith

11 But as for you, man of God, shun all this; pursue righteousness, godliness, faith, love, endurance, gentleness. [12]Fight the good fight of the faith; take hold of the eternal life, to which you were called and for which you made[f] the good confession in the presence of many witnesses. [13]In the presence of God, who gives life to all things, and of Christ Jesus, who in his testimony before Pontius Pilate made the good confession, I charge you [14]to keep the commandment without spot or blame until the manifestation of our Lord Jesus Christ, [15]which he will bring about at the right time – he who is the blessed and only Sovereign, the King of kings and Lord of lords. [16]It is he alone who has immortality and dwells in unapproachable light, whom no one has ever seen or can see; to him be honor and eternal dominion. Amen.

[f] Gk *confessed*

KEEP ON KEEPING ON (1 TIM. 6:11-19)

Timothy is to pursue virtues that contrast with those possessed by the rich or the false teachers. His motivation is different, his security is different. The metaphor in 6:12 is an athletic one, alluding to the Games (not warfare) – see 1 Tim. 1:8 and 2 Tim. 4:7. Timothy is to persevere in his ministry until the 'manifestation' of Jesus Christ: there is urgency, for the return of Christ, his second coming, may be soon. The writer heaps up phrases to convey the wonder of the paradox of the coming one 'who dwells in unapproachable light'.

17 As for those who in the present age are rich, command them not to be haughty, or to set their hopes on the uncertainty of riches, but rather on God who richly provides us with everything for our enjoyment. [18]They are to do good, to be rich in good works, generous, and ready to share, [19]thus storing up for themselves the treasure of a good foundation for the future, so that they may take hold of the life that really is life.

Personal Instructions and Benediction

20 Timothy, guard what has been entrusted to you. Avoid the profane chatter and contradictions of what is falsely called knowledge; [21]by professing it some have missed the mark as regards the faith.

Grace be with you.[g]

---

[g] The Greek word for *you* here is plural; in other ancient authorities it is singular. Other ancient authorities add *Amen*

---

17. Those who are already rich are not to be proud, and instead of trusting in their riches are to hope in God, sharing their possessions in this life to prepare for the next.

CONCLUSION (1 TIM. 6:20-21)

This is a final word to Timothy to guard what he knows and avoid false teaching.

THE SECOND LETTER OF PAUL
TO TIMOTHY

Salutation

1 Paul, an apostle of Christ Jesus by the will of God, for the sake of the promise of life that is in Christ Jesus,

2 To Timothy, my beloved child:

Grace, mercy, and peace from God the Father and Christ Jesus our Lord.

Thanksgiving and Encouragement

3 I am grateful to God – whom I worship with a clear conscience, as my ancestors did – when I remember you constantly in my prayers night and day. ⁴Recalling your tears, I long to see you so that I may be filled with joy. ⁵I am reminded of your sincere faith, a faith that lived first in your grandmother Lois and your mother Eunice

◆ This passage speaks of the 'unfeigned' faith of Timothy, meaning that sincere faith which is an unpretentious faith of the heart. A multi-generational transmission of a rich spiritual heritage was given to Timothy from his godly mother and grandmother. Prov. 31:28 says of the upright woman that 'Her children rise up and call her happy' 2 Tim. 3:14–15 indicates that very early in infancy Timothy was instructed in the Holy Scriptures. Some have suggested that Timothy had been taught the letters of the alphabet from the Old Testament and had first learned to read in the sacred writings. It is generally believed that Lois and Eunice became converts to Christianity during

---

2 TIMOTHY 1

Paul begins his final letter to Timothy with a customary pattern of greeting almost similar to 1 Timothy 1:1–2. The formality is followed by a personal charge to the disciple to suffer with him in preserving the truth of the gospel. Paul writes with a tone of urgency hinged to his forthcoming death sentence.

1. Paul begins with the salutation by establishing his identity. That he is an apostle not by chance nor by man's appointment, but by the 'will of God' (Gal. 1:1). And the apostleship commissions him the task to communicate the message of the gospel which promises eternal life to those in union with Christ. The divine appointment is crucial to establish the authority and authenticity of the gospel (Gal. 1:11–12).

2. Paul's regard for Timothy as his 'beloved son', is a term of endearment and does not signify a flesh-and-blood relationship (Acts 16:1–3). The salutation ends with a pronouncement of 'grace, mercy and peace' upon Timothy – a blessing that can only be bestowed by the Father and the Son.

3. Paul is always in a constant act of giving thanks to his God. He has worshiped his God with sincerity and purity as inherited from his Jewish religious background and upbringing. Paul is also thankful to God for his co-worker whom he prays for daily.

4. The longing to see Timothy wells up whenever the apostle recalls the last tearful farewell when he was forced to leave the co-worker in Ephesus after the second arrest and taken to Rome. So, to meet with Timothy again will be a real joy, enabling him to cope with his loneliness (2 Tim. 4:9, 21).

5. Paul reminds Timothy that he is a third generation Christian. He owes his Christian heritage to his mother, Eunice and his grandmother, Lois. The apostle commends these two godly women (Jewesses) for their faithfulness in bringing up their respective children in the knowledge of Old Testament and the God of Israel (2 Tim. 3:15).

Paul's first missionary journey. Acts 16:1 informs us that when Paul came to Lystra a second time his mother Eunice was a believer. It is likely that Timothy was a product of a 'mixed marriage' in that his father was a Greek and his mother was a Jewess. It appears that Timothy's father was not a believer since his faith is not mentioned. 1 Cor. 7:14 speaks of the unbelieving husband being sanctified through his believing wife so that the children can be partakers of this new life in Christ.

How fortunate and blessed are children born into families where God's Word is passed to succeeding generations (Ps. 78:1–7). Many early church fathers such as Augustine, John Chrysostom, Gregory Nanzianzen, Basil, and Gregory of Nyssa celebrated the godly influence of their mothers. For example, Brothers Basil and Gregory of Nyssa, Cappadochian fathers and theologians par excellence, had a Christian heritage similar to Timothy's. They were under the care of their grandmother Macrina, mother Emmelia, and older sister Macrina, as their father Basil died at a young age. These three women served as powerful instruments of God in their lives through religious instruction, a devout lifestyle, and exemplary character. Gregory's conversion and decision to go into the monastery was credited to sister Macrina's fervent faith and persuasion. Even on her deathbed, at the convent she founded, Macrina was convincing Gregory of the doctrine of the resurrection of the dead, exhorting him not to sorrow for her as those who have no hope. Because of her ascetic lifestyle, she had no burial clothes, so Gregory bought a beautiful bridal dress for her burial.

Recent research relative to child-rearing emphasizes the interactive, developmental nature of the mother-child relationship – i.e., the reciprocal effect of the mother on the child, as well as the child on the mother. Observers of mother-child interaction note that mutual gazing is an indicator of maternal emotional involvement, thereby allowing a close and personally satisfying relationship to develop. Other positive maternal attitudes are manifested by mother's sensitivity and attentiveness to the needs of the infant, which affects the child's social and cognitive growth. Maternal stimulation matched to the infant's needs was predictive of the child's cognitive development.

Other researchers have studied the effect of parenting styles on child development. Authoritative parents direct the child in a rational manner, giving reasons behind demands, but also using power when needed to enforce set standards. The combination of firmness and warmth led to independent, self-directive, socially responsible children. Some further implications for child-rearing include the need for consistency in enforcement of rules, clear communication patterns where children can voice disagreements with parents, parental demands that are appropriate to the child's age with specific skills-training, a suggestive rather than intrusive parental method of helping their children with problem-solving tasks, and family commitment to a set of mutually agreed upon values. Religion may play a vital part in the formation of these values ◆

and now, I am sure, lives in you. ⁶For this reason I remind you to rekindle the gift of God that is within you through the laying on of my hands; ⁷for God did not give us a spirit of cowardice, but rather a spirit of power and of love and of self-discipline.

6–7. The nature of the 'charisma' is unclear but the gift was bestowed upon Timothy at his ordination or commissioning service for ministry (1 Tim. 4:14). He is reminded to 'stir up', to continue exercising the gift with the boldness, love and self-control endowed by the Holy Spirit. These three qualities will strengthen the natural disposition of God's servant to accomplish his work in the church.

8 Do not be ashamed, then, of the testimony about our Lord or of me his prisoner, but join with me in suffering for the gospel, relying on the power of God, ⁹who saved us and called us with a holy calling, not according to our works but according to his own purpose and grace. This grace was given to us in Christ Jesus before the ages began, ¹⁰but it has now been revealed through the appearing of our Savior Christ Jesus, who abolished death and brought life and immortality to light through the gospel. ¹¹For this gospel I was appointed a herald and an apostle and a teacher,ᵃ ¹²and for this reason I suffer as I do. But I am not ashamed, for I know the one in whom I have put my trust, and I am sure that he is able to guard until that day what I have entrusted to him.ᵇ ¹³Hold to the standard of sound teaching that you have heard from me, in the faith and love that are in Christ Jesus.

¹⁴Guard the good treasure entrusted to you, with the help of the Holy Spirit living in us.

15 You are aware that all who are in Asia have turned away from me, including Phygelus and Hermogenes. ¹⁶May the Lord grant mercy to the household of Onesiphorus, because he often refreshed me and was not ashamed of my chain; ¹⁷when he arrived in Rome, he eagerlyᶜ searched for me and found me ¹⁸– may the Lord grant that he will find mercy from the Lord on that day! And you know very well how much service he rendered in Ephesus.

A Good Soldier of Christ Jesus

2 You then, my child, be strong in the grace that is in Christ Jesus; ²and what you have heard from me through many

---

ᵃ Other ancient authorities add *of the Gentiles*
ᵇ Or *what has been entrusted to me*   ᶜ Or *promptly*

---

8. Paul urges Timothy to suffer with him for the sake of the gospel, and to avoid the temptation to feel ashamed in associating with the prisoner because Paul does not regard himself as Nero's prisoner. He is a prisoner for Christ and that is an honor!

9–10. Paul expands the content of the gospel emphasizing God's grace and work of salvation through Jesus Christ. The apostle encourages Timothy to recognize the worthiness of suffering for the gospel because of Christ's sacrificial offering on the cross.

11–12. Paul is not ashamed to be imprisoned because he is faithful to his role as God's appointed herald, apostle and teacher. And the strength to endure is stamped from the trust and confidence in God to guard his calling until the Day when Christ returns to judge and reward.

13. The disciple is exhorted to follow the master's model of sound teaching, that is, the doctrinal truths must not be altered because the words are given by God (verbal inspiration). And Timothy must do it with 'faith and love', not as a blind obedience to Paul's instruction.

14. Paul has entrusted the gospel to Timothy and, after his death, the gospel is in danger of being changed, adulterated and destroyed. Therefore, the disciple must guard it like an invaluable treasure to pass it on to the next generation of God's ministers with the help of the Holy Spirit.

15. It is not clear what Paul meant by 'all' in Asia and the situation that led to their desertion. They could have left him because they have deviated from doctrinal truths preached by the apostle based on the mention of Phygelus and Hermogenes in 2 Tim. 2:17–18.

16–18. Onesiphorus was commended for his loyalty and faithfulness to Paul. He was willing to take the risk to visit Paul in the Roman prison and Timothy would know how much he has helped to build the Ephesian church because Timothy too had worked in that church. Onesiphorus is indeed an example to Timothy as one who is not ashamed of Paul's imprisonment for the sake of the gospel.

Reminiscence of Onesiphorus, 'a bringer of profit', causes the apostle to pray for his household. Reference to his household could mean either he is dead or he is not in Ephesus when Paul wrote the letter.

2 TIMOTHY 2

The call to be a servant of God is an honor but not without difficulties as Paul has experienced it. In this chapter, the apostle continues to exhort the disciple to persevere and to carry on the

witnesses entrust to faithful people who will be able to teach others as well. ³Share in suffering like a good soldier of Christ Jesus. ⁴No one serving in the army gets entangled in everyday affairs; the soldier's aim is to please the enlisting officer. ⁵And in the case of an athlete, no one is crowned without competing according to the rules. ⁶It is the farmer who does the work who ought to have the first share of the crops. ⁷Think over what I say, for the Lord will give you understanding in all things.

8 Remember Jesus Christ, raised from the dead, a descendant of David – that is my gospel, ⁹for which I suffer hardship, even to the point of being chained like a criminal. But the word of God is not chained. ¹⁰Therefore I endure everything for the sake of the elect, so that they may also

obtain the salvation that is in Christ Jesus, with eternal glory. ¹¹The saying is sure:

If we have died with him, we will also
    live with him;
¹² if we endure, we will also reign with
    him;
if we deny him, he will also deny us;
¹³ if we are faithless, he remains
    faithful –
for he cannot deny himself.

A Worker Approved by God

14 Remind them of this, and warn them before God[d] that they are to avoid wrangling over words, which does no good but only ruins those who are listening. ¹⁵Do your best to present yourself to God as one

---

[d] Other ancient authorities read *the Lord*

---

mission entrusted to him. Paul expounds and prescribes certain principles to strengthen Timothy's aspiration and conduct.

1–2. It is imperative that Timothy draws his strength from Christ to do his ministry. The second imperative requires him to teach what Paul has taught him to trustworthy men and women who will in turn teach others. The discipling of converts ensures continuity in the ministry of teaching the Word.

3–4. Serving Christ means having suffering and hardship as companions. Paul uses three analogies to illustrate the costs of serving Christ and to exhort timid Timothy to endure the difficulties with him. The Christian worker is compared to a disciplined and long-suffering soldier who gives total devotion to Christ, battling against the enemies who are destroying the truth.

5. The Christian service is compared to a competing athlete in Greek games who assigned himself/herself to strict regulations of painstaking training and disciplined lifestyle in order to win the crown or wreath.

6. Hard-working servants of God who have labored faithfully can expect to receive rewards from God like a farmer who will reap the fruits of his labor.

7. Timothy must discover the meanings and implications of Paul's three analogies for his life and ministry with the help of his intellect and divine guidance.

8. The apostle reaffirms to Timothy that the content of the gospel entrusted to him to preach is centered on Jesus Christ – his incarnation, suffering, death and resurrection.

9–10. Paul uses himself as an example of suffering for the advancement of the gospel. He endures the hardships for the salvation of the 'elect' which may apply to those predestined to be saved but not yet (Rom. 8:33; Col. 3:12). Though Paul suffers imprisonment, the gospel remains free and the disciple must continue to preach it (2 Tim. 4:2).

11–13. The saying is worthy and could be extracted from an early church hymn. The conversion experience is about dying to self and becoming alive in Christ. Those who persist in the faith will join God in heaven. But for those who deny him, judgment will follow. God is faithful to his promises. He is consistent and is unaffected by any person's unfaithfulness toward him.

14. Timothy must warn the Ephesian Christians to resist disputing trivial matters with false teachers whose strategy is to destroy the church.

15. Contrary to the behavior of false teachers, God's servant should strive to preach and teach the Word of the truth honestly, the mark of a minister approved by God.

approved by him, a worker who has no need to be ashamed, rightly explaining the word of truth. ¹⁶Avoid profane chatter, for it will lead people into more and more impiety, ¹⁷and their talk will spread like gangrene. Among them are Hymenaeus and Philetus, ¹⁸who have swerved from the truth by claiming that the resurrection has already taken place. They are upsetting the faith of some. ¹⁹But God's firm foundation stands, bearing this inscription: "The Lord knows those who are his," and, "Let everyone who calls on the name of the Lord turn away from wickedness."

20 In a large house there are utensils not only of gold and silver but also of wood and clay, some for special use, some for ordinary. ²¹All who cleanse themselves of the things I have mentionedᵉ will become special utensils, dedicated and useful to the owner of the house, ready for every good work. ²²Shun youthful passions and pursue righteousness, faith, love, and peace, along with those who call on the Lord from a pure heart. ²³Have nothing to do with stupid and senseless controversies; you know that they breed quarrels. ²⁴And the Lord's servantᶠ must not be quarrelsome but kindly to everyone, an apt teacher, patient, ²⁵correcting opponents with gentleness. God may perhaps grant that they will repent and come to know the truth, ²⁶and that they may escape from the snare of the devil, having been held captive by him to do his will.ᵍ

Godlessness in the Last Days

3 You must understand this, that in the last days distressing times will come.

ᵉ Gk *of these things*   ᶠ Gk *slave*   ᵍ Or *by him, to do his* (that is, God's) *will*

---

16. God's worker and church must avoid heretical chatter because it begets ungodliness.

17–18. Furthermore, ungodly chattering will spread and ruin other believers. Hymenaeus and Philetus were two false teachers who denied the resurrection of believers on the last day and the false proclamation has affected the faith of some.

19. But, God is immovable and he can distinguish the faithful from false teachers. The faithful, therefore, should flee from the unholy.

20–21. A church is made up of saved and unsaved, righteous and unrighteous individuals. And God's servants and people must separate themselves from those who dishonor God to become honorable vessels set aside for God's use.

22. Paul elaborates on the ways Timothy and God's servants ought to behave to counteract false teachings. First, Timothy is cautioned to develop strong moral and spiritual virtues and to be in the company of those with like qualities.

23. Secondly, Timothy must avoid speculative, purposeless and ungodly talk that invites unnecessary contentions.

24–26. Thirdly, God's servant is not quarrelsome but gentle in treating those who oppose him/her or the truth. Correct them with patience, for God might give them a chance to turn over a new leaf. In this passage, the minister is reminded again to develop the skills of teaching the truth and to correct false teaching.

2 TIMOTHY 3

The apostle is held in captivity but his desire is preoccupied with the preservation and furtherance of the gospel. In this chapter, he charges and urges Timothy to stay faithful to what he has learned from him and others and to preserve the divine inspiration of the sacred Scripture. The charge is necessary because Paul wants Timothy to overcome his weaknesses, to stand firm against those who oppose the truth and preach a false gospel.

1. The 'last days' may refer to the eschatological phenomenon preceding the rapture of the church and the second coming of Christ. Paul is describing the deplorable situation and distressing happenings in the present time as a partial fulfillment of the worst that is yet to come (2 Tim. 3:13).

²For people will be lovers of themselves, lovers of money, boasters, arrogant, abusive, disobedient to their parents, ungrateful, unholy, ³inhuman, implacable, slanderers, profligates, brutes, haters of good, ⁴treacherous, reckless, swollen with conceit, lovers of pleasure rather than lovers of God, ⁵holding to the outward form of godliness but denying its power. Avoid them! ⁶For among them are those who make their way into households and captivate silly women, overwhelmed by their sins and swayed by all kinds of desires, ⁷who are always being instructed and can never arrive at a knowledge of the truth. ⁸As Jannes and Jambres opposed Moses, so these people, of corrupt mind and counterfeit faith, also oppose the truth. ⁹But they will not make much progress, because, as in the case of those two men,ʰ their folly will become plain to everyone.

Paul's Charge to Timothy

10 Now you have observed my teaching, my conduct, my aim in life, my faith, my patience, my love, my steadfastness, ¹¹my persecutions and suffering the things that happened to me in Antioch, Iconium, and Lystra. What persecutions I endured! Yet the Lord rescued me from all of them. ¹²Indeed, all who want to live a godly life in Christ Jesus will be persecuted. ¹³But wicked people and impostors will go from bad to worse, deceiving others and being deceived. ¹⁴But as for you, continue in what you have learned and firmly believed, knowing from whom you learned it, ¹⁵and how from childhood you have known the sacred writings that are able to instruct you for salvation through faith in Christ Jesus. ¹⁶All scripture is inspired by God and

ʰ Gk lacks *two men*

2–5. Paul warns Christians and God's servants to avoid adopting the unholy characteristics of individuals which they will encounter before the end-times. They are self-centeredness, materialism, slandering, pride, lack of self-control, infidelity, unfilial conduct towards parents, false spirituality, proneness to evil-doing and other unethical conduct.

6–7. Comparable to our present day cults who deceive and lead many away from the Christian faith by preaching the 'truth and yet not the truth'. These false teachers prey on women and manipulate their 'trusting' nature by tempting them to embrace the false religion's way of salvation to experience the forgiveness of their sins.

8–9. Paul compares the false teachers to Jannes and Jambres (pharoah's magicians, Exod. 7:11, 22) who opposed Moses by using magic. Similarly, the false teachers use deception to oppose the gospel. But the apostle is confident; eventually 'truth' will triumph and their false teaching will be exposed.

10–11. Paul urges Timothy to emulate his teaching and lifestyle of total commitment to Christ, faith in God and love for others. He has endured suffering and persecution, but it was God who protected and rescued him many times from dangers (1 Tim. 4:17–18).

12–13. Christians, as God's servants who desire to live a life of piety toward God, will experience opposition from the world and persecution. One such experience is the increasing effort and activity of impostors and evil men who will lead men and women to stray from the truth of God.

14–15. But Timothy is not to be deceived. He is to remain faithful to the foundations of the Christian faith (Old Testament Scripture, which was familiar to Timothy) he has learned from Paul, his grandmother and mother (1 Tim. 1:5).

16–17. Timothy must hold fast to the sacred Word of God (i.e. the Old Testament; the New Testament had not been completed), because every passage of Scripture is God-breathed. The divine inspiration empowers the Word for ministry. Timothy and God's ministers can use the Word either as the content for teaching and instruction; or to rebuke so as to bring about conviction of sins and confession; or to correct and expose false teachings; or to train and discipline godly living. An ultimate purpose of teaching the Word is to encourage every believer to be equipped for service and living a lifestyle to glorify God.

is[1] useful for teaching, for reproof, for correction, and for training in righteousness, [17]so that everyone who belongs to God may be proficient, equipped for every good work.

4 In the presence of God and of Christ Jesus, who is to judge the living and the dead, and in view of his appearing and his kingdom, I solemnly urge you: [2]proclaim the message; be persistent whether the time is favorable or unfavorable; convince, rebuke, and encourage, with the utmost patience in teaching. [3]For the time is coming when people will not put up with sound doctrine, but having itching ears, they will accumulate for themselves teachers to suit their own desires, [4]and will turn away from listening to the truth and wander away to myths. [5]As for you, always be sober, endure suffering, do the work of an evangelist, carry out your ministry fully.

◆ Women have wonderful opportunities to 'do the work of an evangelist'. Some go door to door, sharing the good news of God's love with their neighbors, often bringing their children with them. Others invite their friends in for a cup of coffee and a chat about the grace of Jesus Christ and how he can become real in a person's life. We can show God's love wherever there is a need in a neighbor's life.

Evangelist Daisy Osborn tells of an 80-year-old woman in Uganda who has an old Bible and an old bicycle. She asked God to show her where she might bring the good news of Jesus, and God showed her an area of the countryside where there were no churches or Christian leaders. Soon she had started seven little churches, each in a separate village. Now, with her message of grace, she pedals the rickety old bicycle around to a different church each day of the week. Daisy says, 'I'm talking about

[1] Or *Every scripture inspired by God is also*

---

2 TIMOTHY 4

Paul pens his last words to Timothy and the church. On looking back, he concludes that he has been faithful, completed his ministry calling and is now waiting to receive his reward from the Master. Death cannot take away what he has done for Christ.

1. Timothy is solemnly charged to assume spiritual responsibility, probably for the Ephesian church. Paul calls upon God, the Father and Jesus Christ, the Son to be witnesses which adds to the seriousness of the charge. And Timothy's faithfulness to the given task will be judged and rewarded at Christ's second coming and the establishment of his Kingdom.

2. The content of the charge is to preach the whole Word as given by God with authority and readiness to seize every opportunity available. In his preaching, the Word must be used to convict of sin in a way that results in conversions; to cause recognition and acknowledgment of sins; and to exhort listeners to repent or persevere in the faith. These three applications of the Word must be exercised with enduring patience and sound instruction.

3–4. Timothy is warned that he will experience increasing difficulties in preaching the Word after Paul's death. People will not endure listening to the objective truth of the Word. Instead, they will seek false preachers who will feed them with popular doctrines to satisfy their wants and not their needs. Together, they have abandoned the realities of God's Word for myths.

Therefore, Paul's final charge is urgent to warn preachers not to fall into the same trap – i.e. preaching to gain popularity. They must preach the Word to win respect for the authoritative Word and for themselves.

5. Timothy is exhorted to exert four qualities in response to the adverse conditions to come. God's worker must be alert and fearless. Secondly, the worker must be able to endure hardships in fighting against the threats of false doctrines. Thirdly, the minister must be evangelistic in preaching the gospel to win souls. Fourthly, the minister must persevere until the entrusted task is accomplished.

an old woman, an old Bible, and an old bicycle. The roads she has to travel, most of them are just dirt roads full of holes. Think of being that old and that happy and that full of love. She has no teeth, but she smiles. People can tell that she really cares about them. When we show that we really care, we're reflecting God's love.' That's being an evangelist! ◆

6 As for me, I am already being poured out as a libation, and the time of my departure has come. 'I have fought the good fight, I have finished the race, I have kept the faith. ⁸From now on there is reserved for me the crown of righteousness, which the Lord, the righteous judge, will give me on that day, and not only to me but also to all who have longed for his appearing.

Personal Instructions

9 Do your best to come to me soon, ¹⁰for Demas, in love with this present world, has deserted me and gone to Thessalonica; Crescens has gone to Galatia,ʲ Titus to Dalmatia. ¹¹Only Luke is with me. Get Mark and bring him with you, for he is useful in my ministry. ¹²I have sent Tychicus to Ephesus. ¹³When you come, bring the cloak that I left with Carpus at Troas, also the books, and above all the parchments. ¹⁴Alexander the coppersmith did me great harm; the Lord will pay him back for his deeds. ¹⁵You also must beware of him, for he strongly opposed our message.

ʲ Other ancient authorities read *Gaul*

---

6. Paul is certain that he will receive the death penalty. As a Roman citizen, he will not be crucified but faces decapitation. Death is not a dread because the apostle views it as the last act of the sacrifice of his life offered to God (Num. 15:1–10).

7. Reflecting on his past experience, Paul uses metaphors to evaluate his ministry. He believes he has finished the task entrusted honorably to him, like a noble contestant in a fight. He varies the metaphor to reemphasize that his ministry has reached its end, like an athlete in a race who stopped running when he reached the finishing line. His final assessment is that the truth which God has entrusted upon him, he has guarded and preserved faithfully.

8. Continuing with the metaphor from Greek athletics, Paul describes himself as a winner awaiting to receive his crown of victory from the judge. The crown will not be made of leaves but a wreath of 'righteousness'. It will be presented by the Judge, the Lord Jesus himself to the apostle and those who are eagerly waiting for his second coming.

9. Paul urges Timothy to make every effort to leave Ephesus as soon as possible to visit him in Rome.

10–12. Paul, a forlorn man, feels rejected by Demas, who was his dependable companion (Col. 4:14; Philem. 24). The deserter has abandoned the apostle and the Lord's ministry for worldly gains. Any Christian worker can succumb to such a temptation.

The other helpers, Crescens and Titus are laboring in Galatia and Dalmatia respectively. Luke is the only fellow-worker who remains with Paul. So, Mark's presence would be valuable for companionship and ministry. Apparently, Paul has arranged for Tychicus to replace Timothy in Ephesus when the latter brings Mark on his journey to Rome.

13. Timothy is also asked to pick up Paul's cloak which will be needed for the winter (4:21a); his papyrus rolls (made from plants) and parchments (made from calves' skins) from Carpus' home in Troas. The parchments may refer to Old Testament writings. It is thought-provoking to witness Paul's insatiable appetite for studying and researching the Scriptures even though death is crouching near.

14–15. Timothy is warned to guard against a certain Alexander, a metal craftsman in Ephesus who creates and sells idols. He is vehemently against Christianity because the preaching of the gospel has affected his business. For vengeance, he has done much harm to Paul but the extent of it is not made known to the reader. However, Paul takes comfort that the day will come when the Lord will judge and repay his evil deeds accordingly.

16 At my first defense no one came to my support, but all deserted me. May it not be counted against them! [17]But the Lord stood by me and gave me strength, so that through me the message might be fully proclaimed and all the Gentiles might hear it. So I was rescued from the lion's mouth. [18]The Lord will rescue me from every evil attack and save me for his heavenly kingdom. To him be the glory forever and ever. Amen.

Final Greetings and Benediction

19 Greet Prisca and Aquila, and the household of Onesiphorus. [20]Erastus remained in Corinth; Trophimus I left ill in Miletus. [21]Do your best to come before winter. Eubulus sends greetings to you, as do Pudens and Linus and Claudia and all the brothers and sisters.[k]

22 The Lord be with your spirit. Grace be with you.[l]

[k] Gk *all the brothers*   [l] The Greek word for *you* here is plural. Other ancient authorities add *Amen*

---

16. The apostle relates the trial experience at his second imprisonment (Acts 28:30f.). During the preliminary hearing, he appeared in court alone to defend the charges against him. None of his friends were there to support whether as a legal adviser, witness or advocate. Despite their desertion, Paul forgives them and hopes that God will forgive their actions.

17. Continuing his testimony, Paul relates how the Lord stood alongside with him, though forsaken by men. The Lord enabled him to conduct his own defence. Secondly, he was enabled to seize the opportunity to preach the gospel to the Gentiles, probably the Roman officials present in court. Thirdly, he was delivered from the lion's mouth and the metaphor could refer to Emperor Nero or Satan. Very likely, it refers to Paul's escape from an immediate death because the same metaphor also appears in Ps. 22:21.

18. Following the miraculous deliverance, Paul is confident that God will preserve him from evil and will protect him for the final entry into God's Kingdom. The doxology aptly echoes Paul's eschatalogical hope of the Lord's return. He has been faithful to the gospel entrusted to him and is ready to face martyrdom in triumph.

19. Paul concludes the letter with personal greetings to Priscilla and Aquila who are now in Ephesus. He must have fond memories of their initial meeting (Acts 18:2) and partnership in ministry (Acts 18:18–26; 1 Cor. 16:19).

He also sends regards to the family of Onesiphorus. Depending on the interpretation of 2 Tim. 1:16–18, Onesiphorus could be dead or he has not returned to his family in Ephesus.

20. The personal greeting is followed by news about certain individuals. Timothy would be interested to receive information about Erastus who was likely his travelling companion in Acts 19:22. Paul, however, did not explain why Erastus remained in Corinth and not in Ephesus.

Trophimus was an Ephesian (Acts 21:29) who travelled with Timothy to accompany the apostle (Acts 20:4). The nature of his illness was not disclosed but it forced him to remain in Miletus.

21. Paul echoes 2 Tim. 4:9 beckoning Paul to visit him soon because shipping will be closed during the winter months. Travelling to Rome will undoubtedly be impossible for him. Hence, the letter could be written in the summer or fall.

Lastly, Paul sends greetings to Timothy from Eubulus, Pudens, Linus, Claudia and others. The last three names are Latin, which seem to suggest that they are Roman Christians. They are likely to be leaders known to Timothy and it is significant that the apostle names a woman amongst them. Paul has regard for women like Priscilla and Claudia who are his co-laborers in the gospel of Jesus Christ.

22. Paul signs off with a two-part benediction. He addresses the first to Timothy. The second part includes members of the Ephesian church because the 'you' is plural in the Greek language. The benediction closes the earthly ministry of the apostle but the work of God must continue and for this reason, the baton is now in the hands of Timothy.

THE LETTER OF PAUL TO TITUS

INTRODUCTION

Although the traditional view accepts the apostle Paul as the writer of Titus, many critical scholars reject Pauline authorship. The text itself (Titus 1:1) supports Paul as author. The epistle was evidently penned from Macedonia between Paul's first and second Roman imprisonments, AD 62–66.

Titus, Paul's missionary associate and friend, received this letter. He served as Paul's example of the conversion of Gentiles at the Jerusalem conference (Gal. 2:1-3). Titus ministered as ambassador to Corinth and as overseer of the churches on Crete.

This pastoral letter was written to remind Titus of his task in Crete: to 'put in order what remained to be done', 'appoint elders in every town', and silence false teachers (Titus 1:5, 11). The epistle was intended not only for Titus personally but also for the Cretan churches.

The book includes passages concerning the qualifications of church leaders (1:6–9) and contrasts these with the false teachers (1:10–16). The conduct and motive of the Christian life is described (2:1–15), as well as the obligations of Christian citizenship (3:1–2). The nature of salvation (3:3–8) and how to treat false teachers (3:9–11) are discussed. Titus concludes with final admonitions and greetings (3:12–15).

Salutation

1 Paul, a servant[a] of God and an apostle of Jesus Christ, for the sake of the faith of God's elect and the knowledge of the truth that is in accordance with godliness, [2]in the hope of eternal life that God, who never lies, promised before the ages began – [3]in due time he revealed his word through the proclamation with which I have been entrusted by the command of God our Savior,

4 To Titus, my loyal child in the faith we share:

Grace[b] and peace from God the Father and Christ Jesus our Savior.

Titus in Crete

5 I left you behind in Crete for this reason, so that you should put in order what remained to be done, and should appoint elders in every town, as I directed you: [6]someone who is blameless, married only once,[c] whose children are believers, not accused of debauchery and not rebellious. [7]For a bishop,[d] as God's steward, must be blameless; he must not be arrogant or quick-tempered or addicted to wine or violent or greedy for gain; [8]but he must be hospitable, a lover of goodness, prudent, upright, devout, and self-controlled. [9]He must have a firm grasp of the word that is trustworthy in accordance with the teaching, so that he may be able both to preach with sound doctrine and to refute those who contradict it.

◆ Although translators usually fail to give the full weight to the word, the Greek text states that one who is a batterer (*plektes*) should not be a church officer (1 Tim. 3:3; Titus 1:7; see also 2 Tim. 2:24). *Plektes* literally means 'one who strikes or rains blows'. An individual who has not learned other ways of dealing with conflict resolution should not be given leadership in the Christian community.

Violence obstructs the prayer life of the batterer (Is. 58:4–6; 1 Pet. 3:7) and harms not only victim but also perpetrator (Ps. 7:16; Prov. 21:7). The Old Testament, and especially the Psalms, is filled with condemnations of violence (see, e.g., Pss. 58:2; 27:12; 140:110; Prov. 3:31; 10:6, 11; Ezek. 28:16; Hos. 12:1; Mic. 6:12; Zeph. 1:9) and of stalking and verbal abuse (Pss. 10:2, 8–9; 17:11; 37:33; 56:5–6; 59:3; Jer. 5:26; Mic. 7:2).

Battering of a wife is specifically condemned in Mal. 2:16, since the Hebrew word used there for 'garment' also means 'wife'. Thus we may read as an alternate translation, '"I hate covering one's wife with violence," says the LORD of hosts.'

Jesus spoke in the sternest tones of the evils of child abuse (Matt. 18:1–6; Mark 9:42; Luke 17:1–2) and of verbal abuse (Matt. 5:21–22; 12:34–37; 15:18–20). Wounds inflicted by the tongue may be at

---

[a] Gk *slave*   [b] Other ancient authorities read *Grace, mercy*   [c] Gk *husband of one wife*   [d] Or *an overseer*

TITUS 1

1. 'God's elect' stresses God's choice of his church. The text defines truth as 'in accordance with godliness', indicating the moral character of the gospel of Christ.

6–9. The qualifications for elders closely resemble those for the bishop found in 1 Tim. 3:2–7. These two positions are synonymous in the New Testament. The list of qualities includes family matters (v. 6), vices to be avoided (v. 7), virtues to be sought (v. 8), and a statement of duty (v. 9).

6. 'Married only once' literally means 'husband of one wife'. This phrase has several interpretative options. (1) The elder or pastor is required to be married. (2) Polygamy is prohibited. (3) Second marriages are prohibited, either after the death of a spouse or due to divorce. (4) Marital fidelity to one wife is required.

least as deep as those inflicted with fist or weapon. Verbal abuse (James 2:2–10; Eph. 4:29) and harassment are addressed in the epistles (Eph. 5:4; Col. 3:8) and antidotes offered (Rom. 12:10, 18; 14:19; Eph. 4:26–27, 31–32; Phil. 4:5; Heb. 12:14; 1 Pet. 1:22; cf. 2 Sam. 22:36; Pss. 18:35; 34:14; 37:37; Prov. 12:20).

Sexual abuse and exploitation is specifically and repeatedly repudiated in the New Testament (see, e.g., 1 Cor. 5:9–11; 1 Thess. 4:3–8). The Greek adjective used here *pornos* and the related noun *porneia*, cover a wide range of sexually inappropriate and exploitive behaviors, such as obscenity, prostitution, indecent exposure, rape, fornication, incest, and pederasty. No one English word implies the whole cluster of activities. This means that we often fail to understand the strength of the biblical condemnation of abuse.

Though often obliterated by translation, perpetrators of rape are specifically discussed (Luke 18:11; 1 Cor. 5:10–11; 6:10). The word used here, *harpax*, can refer to anyone who seizes by force against the will of another. Translators usually render this 'robber' or 'rapacious' but the term is used specifically of rapists. In passages dealing with sexual immorality, this is the most appropriate meaning. Rape is a very serious crime and should not be treated lightly by believers.

God's purpose is to give deliverance from violence (2 Sam. 22:3, 49; Pss. 10:17–18; 11:5; 18:48; 140:1–11) for victim and perpetrator alike. Means of succour may include removing an individual from a dangerous environment, providing food and shelter, counselling, group therapy, support networks, prayer and straightforward teaching of biblical truth.

Believers are called to renounce violence (Ezek. 45:9) and to join in freeing the helpless from oppression (Ps. 72:1–4, 14; Eccl. 4:1; Jer. 21:12; 22:3, 15–16). The need is stressed for Christian communities to deal with the problems associated with abuse (Matt. 18:15–17; 1 Cor. 5:1–5; 1 Thess. 5:14; 2 Thess. 3:14–15; 1 Tim. 4:20; Titus 3:2–11; James 5:19–20). Abuse is not simply a private domestic matter. The Bible teaches that it is the concern of the entire body of Christ. Submission should not be given to individuals whose behavior or communication is wrong, even though they pretend to be very pious or prayerful (Gal. 2:5–6) ◆

10 There are also many rebellious people, idle talkers and deceivers, especially those of the circumcision; ¹¹they must be silenced, since they are upsetting whole families by teaching for sordid gain what it is not right to teach. ¹²It was one of them, their very own prophet, who said,

"Cretans are always liars, vicious
    brutes, lazy gluttons."
¹³That testimony is true. For this reason rebuke them sharply, so that they may become sound in the faith, ¹⁴not paying attention to Jewish myths or to commandments of those who reject the truth.

---

10. Titus gives very few details of the actual content of the false teachings of the 'rebellious people, idle talkers and deceivers'. 'Those of the circumcision' implies that these people were Jewish converts who still insisted on adherence to the ritual Law. Some false teachers did forbid marriage and encourage abstaining from certain foods in order to attain spiritual perfection (1 Tim. 4:3). Such advice would upset whole families (v. 11).

11. 'Silenced' pictures the image of a horse being bridled or muzzled.

12–13. This quotation from a sixth-century BC Cretan poet, Epimenides, establishes the situation in Crete without exposing the writer to the charge of being anti-Cretan. His use of the quote did not indict all Cretans.

14. 'Jewish myths' consisted of useless speculations based on the Old Testament (see 1 Tim. 1:4; 4:7). The 'commandments of those who reject the truth' involved Jewish ritual.

¹⁵To the pure all things are pure, but to the corrupt and unbelieving nothing is pure. Their very minds and consciences are corrupted. ¹⁶They profess to know God, but they deny him by their actions. They are detestable, disobedient, unfit for any good work.

Teach Sound Doctrine

2 But as for you, teach what is consistent with sound doctrine. ²Tell the older men to be temperate, serious, prudent, and sound in faith, in love, and in endurance.

3 Likewise, tell the older women to be reverent in behavior, not to be slanderers or slaves to drink; they are to teach what is good, ⁴so that they may encourage the young women to love their husbands, to love their children, ⁵to be self-controlled, chaste, good managers of the household, kind, being submissive to their husbands, so that the word of God may not be discredited.

◆ The ancient Hebrews respected and trusted their older women, though scant honor was given them in the pagan world. Greek and Roman authors sometimes satirized their frailties in cruel fashion.

In this passage, the writer, realizing the potential problems of aging, sets out his list of what a grandmother or an elderly aunt ought to be. In early Christian times, the older woman was surrounded by her extended family; but as is the case today, she faced growing old. She found that she had to hand over her duties to her younger daughters-in-law. She saw that she was no longer needed, and fearing she was losing her position of authority, with less and less to do in the home, she took up gossiping with friends and perhaps took too much wine. Her friends also were aging and some were already dying. She had more and more time to think back over her life, ponder past decisions and review her mistakes.

---

15. The problem with the false teachers had to do with prohibitions of some kind, probably concerning food laws. The Cretan teachers were perpetuating ceremonial distinctions between the clean and unclean. What people eat, however, cannot defile them (Mark 7:14–19). The real place of purity is the conscience.

TITUS 2

3. Older women should possess personal godliness, be worthy of respect, and play an essential role in the lives of the young women in the church. The word translated 'reverent in behavior' often meant simply 'holy', but it could also carry the more specialized sense of 'acting like a priestess'. The way of life for the older women should be appropriate to a priestess serving in God's Temple. They should see themselves as given to God and his service. The exhortation to self-mastery of the tongue is especially directed toward women (1 Tim. 3:11), although self-control in this area applies to all believers (James 3:1–12). The first-century culture often admired heavy drinkers. Consequently, the writer urges both the older men (Titus 2:2) and older women in the church to set a different example. The older women must also teach what is good. The content of their instruction (vv. 4–5) has to do with being a model, godly wife.
4. 'Young women' implies 'wives', since most younger women of that day would be married. They are to love their husbands and children. These words have special significance in view of the home-disturbing tendencies of the false teachers (1:11). Believers should place high value on a loving, united family.
5. 'Self-controlled' coupled with 'chaste' may express the author's concern for marital fidelity. Certainly the prominence of the sex-oriented mystery cult of the Mother Goddess in Crete, as in Ephesus (1 and 2 Timothy), would prompt a social, though non-Christian, acceptance of sexual immorality. The writer, therefore, encourages sexual purity and marital fidelity for believers. 'Good managers of the household' translates 'keepers of the home'. This term taken together with 'kind' simply means 'good workers at home'. Also, the younger women are to be

Loneliness was inevitable. It opened the door to fear. The ache in the shoulder that wouldn't go away, the sudden, stabbing pain in the elbow that made her hands drop things unexpectedly were reminders of her decaying body. The sleeplessness that attacked in the night gave her plenty of time to listen to the thump of her irregular heart beats or the slow surge of thickening blood in her narrow veins.

With these and other, more dire illnesses, the door to the Great Unknown loomed closer, and despite their faith, despite their efforts to live productive lives, despair and the fear of death could engulf elderly women from all sides. However, Paul gave the grandmothers and aunts of the biblical world an important role to play in the newly forming Christian families of the time. They were to remember that they were the models of dignity and propriety for all other family members, for if proper behavior was not maintained, the Christian family would fall apart. They were the custodians of the gospel, the Word of God, for if the Word of God was not respected, then Christianity itself, as well as the family, was not to be respected. They were the upholders of the new religion, the places where their family's roots dug deepest, the wellsprings of all holiness and love.

The word *presbutis*, here used for 'elderly woman', was also used in the early church to denote a woman elder. There have been scholarly suggestions that their behavior, 'worthy of the priesthood', indicated official status within the Christian congregation ◆

6 Likewise, urge the younger men to be self-controlled. ⁷Show yourself in all respects a model of good works, and in your teaching show integrity, gravity, ⁸and sound speech that cannot be censured; then any opponent will be put to shame, having nothing evil to say of us.

9 Tell slaves to be submissive to their masters and to give satisfaction in every respect; they are not to talk back, ¹⁰not to pilfer, but to show complete and perfect fidelity, so that in everything they may be an ornament to the doctrine of God our Savior.

11 For the grace of God has appeared, bringing salvation to all,ᵉ ¹²training us to renounce impiety and worldly passions, and in the present age to live lives that are self-controlled, upright, and godly, ¹³while we wait for the blessed hope and the manifestation of the glory of our great God and

ᵉ Or *has appeared to all, bringing salvation*

'submissive to their husbands' (1 Tim. 2:11; Col. 3:18; Eph. 5:21–23; 1 Pet. 3:1). The Greek text includes the word 'own'. This indicates that the subordination is one of function within the context of the home and not that women are inferior to men. The writer gives more attention to the young women and is more specific in his exhortations. Possibly the behavior of this group was creating more problems for the Cretan church than that of the other groups (Titus 2:2–10). One emphasis of the Pastoral Epistles shows the need for Christian women to devote themselves to the home as an antidote to false teachings (1 Tim. 5:9–15; 2 Tim. 3:6–7). The reason for Christian wives to live out their faith in terms of these domestic responsibilities is for the sake of the gospel and how it would be viewed by outsiders. The writer does not want the Word of God discredited.

11–13. These verses provide a theological basis for the practical instructions for the conduct of believers (vv. 1–10). Christian conduct should be grounded in and motivated by Christian truth.
11. 'Has appeared' emphasizes God's manifestation of grace as an historical reality – the life of Jesus Christ.
12. God's grace instructs believers how to live. His people must give up 'impiety' or ungodly living and worldly passions. 'Worldly passions' refers to those desires of life not dedicated to God.
13. At the second coming of Christ, God's full glory will be manifested. The phrase, 'great God and Savior, Jesus Christ', affirms the deity of Jesus. He is the final manifestation of God's glory.

Savior,[f] Jesus Christ. [14]He it is who gave himself for us that he might redeem us from all iniquity and purify for himself a people of his own who are zealous for good deeds.

15 Declare these things; exhort and reprove with all authority.[g] Let no one look down on you.

Maintain Good Deeds

3 Remind them to be subject to rulers and authorities, to be obedient, to be ready for every good work, [2]to speak evil of no one, to avoid quarreling, to be gentle, and to show every courtesy to everyone. [3]For we ourselves were once foolish, disobedient, led astray, slaves to various passions and pleasures, passing our days in malice and envy, despicable, hating one another. [4]But when the goodness and loving kindness of God our Savior appeared, [5]he saved us, not because of any works of righteousness that we had done, but according to his mercy, through the water[h] of rebirth and renewal by the Holy Spirit. [6]This Spirit he poured out on us richly through Jesus Christ our Savior, [7]so that, having been justified by his grace, we might become heirs according to the hope of eternal life. [8]The saying is sure.

I desire that you insist on these things, so that those who have come to believe in God may be careful to devote themselves to good works; these things are excellent and profitable to everyone. [9]But avoid stupid controversies, genealogies, dissensions, and quarrels about the law, for they are unprofitable and worthless. [10]After a first and second admonition, have nothing more to do with anyone who causes divisions, [11]since you know that such a person is perverted and sinful, being self-condemned.

[f] Or *of the great God and our Savior*   [g] Gk *commandment*   [h] Gk *washing*

---

14. This verse presents Christ's work as voluntary, exhaustive, and substitutionary. 'Redeem' literally means 'to release on receipt of a ransom'. 'Iniquity' refers to the assertion of self-will in defiance of God's standards – the essence of sin. 'Purify' points to the moral defilement produced by humanity's rebellion.

TITUS 3

1. 'Rulers and authorities' relate to various forms of human government and not necessarily to individual leaders.

2. Believers are to refrain from slander, engaging in quarrels, and conflicts. Instead they are to be peaceable. 'Gentle' implies being conciliatory. Showing 'every courtesy to everyone' is the opposite of self-assertiveness.

3. These sins characteristic of human fallenness in general depict the ugly condition of humanity separated from God. Remembering what believers once were should serve as a powerful motive for them to witness to the unsaved.

4. The 'goodness and living kindness of God' appeared historically in the person and work of Jesus Christ.

5. The verb tense of 'saved' indicates the once-for-allness of the act. The basis of salvation is God's mercy, not because of any 'works of righteousness' done by the believer. Salvation is not due to personal merit but magnifies God's sovereign mercy and grace.

'Rebirth' and 'renewal' refer to the same spiritual reality – the re-creating work of the Holy Spirit in the life of the believer. This causes a new or restored relationship with God. The Holy Spirit accomplishes this re-creation by 'water' or washing. This is a metaphor for spiritual cleansing, although it likely also alludes to water baptism.

7. 'Justified' means declared righteous and given a standing of acceptance before God. It is always the act of God motivated solely by his grace.

8. A life of 'good works' cannot bring salvation but should result from it.

Final Messages and Benediction

12 When I send Artemas to you, or Tychicus, do your best to come to me at Nicopolis, for I have decided to spend the winter there. [13]Make every effort to send Zenas the lawyer and Apollos on their way, and see that they lack nothing. [14]And let people learn to devote themselves to good works in order to meet urgent needs, so that they may not be unproductive.

15 All who are with me send greetings to you. Greet those who love us in the faith. Grace be with all of you.[i]

[i] Other ancient authorities add *Amen*

THE LETTER OF PAUL TO PHILEMON

This short letter is a cameo of the early struggle to begin the process in which Christianity gradually changes traditional social norms. Although slavery was not legally abolished in the Western world until last century, Paul, in the first century, urges Philemon, the wealthy slave owner at Colossae, to receive back his runaway converted slave, Onesimus, to release him from the punishment due to him (possible death), and relate to him as 'a beloved brother' like Paul.

Paul's request is a model of tact and empathy. Philemon is called Paul's 'dear friend and co-worker', being converted through Paul's ministry and using his house as a Christian meeting place (v. 2). His argument is based on the unstated revolutionary principle which is prominent throughout Paul's writings, that all Christians are equal in God's sight and therefore we should treat each other equally as men and women, brothers and sisters loved by God and in whom Christ lives. Although it was not until last century that slavery was abolished, the principle of equality is established in this short epistle. We are no longer to be bound by whether we were born slave or free. We are free and no longer slaves to our old selves. 'If the Son makes you free you are free indeed' and need to treat each other and be treated with respect for the gift of freedom God gives us.

Paul delights in calling himself a prisoner of Christ Jesus and 'slave' in that sense only. This letter was written from prison, so there is double meaning to 'prisoner of Christ Jesus' (v. 9). Paul asks Philemon to welcome his slave 'as you would welcome me' (v. 17). He offers to pay his debts but he reminds Philemon he is in debt to Paul for his very life (v. 19). He appeals for Philemon to 'refresh [his] heart in Christ' (v. 20) by doing what he asks 'in love' and not as obedience (v. 8). He concludes in confidence that Philemon will do 'even more than I say' (v. 21).

Philemon is an example of a person challenged to change his perspective, to extend the bounds of social awareness beyond what was accepted as normal. As the letter was found at its destination, it is thought that it was acted upon. The letter to Philemon gives us a precedent to see situations of power, such as oppression of women, children, aged and refugees from the perspective of the gospel and to see what claims the gospel makes upon the way we govern the lives of our communities.

The principle of equality upon which our relationships are to be based is stated strongly here by Paul as it is in other places such as Gal. 3:26–28. Philemon was asked to put the principle into practice in everyday life in his own household. This is a precedent which needs to be followed wherever patriarchy, sexism, classism, racism or any form of power and oppression over others still exists.

Salutation

1 Paul, a prisoner of Christ Jesus, and Timothy our brother,[a]

To Philemon our dear friend and co-worker, **2** to Apphia our sister,[b] to Archippus our fellow soldier, and to the church in your house:

3 Grace to you and peace from God our Father and the Lord Jesus Christ.

Philemon's Love and Faith

4 When I remember you[c] in my prayers, I always thank my God **5** because I hear of your love for all the saints and your faith toward the Lord Jesus. **6** I pray that the sharing of your faith may become effective when you perceive all the good that we[d] may do for Christ. **7** I have indeed received much joy and encouragement from your love, because the hearts of the saints have been refreshed through you, my brother.

Paul's Plea for Onesimus

8 For this reason, though I am bold enough in Christ to command you to do your duty, **9** yet I would rather appeal to you on the basis of love – and I, Paul, do this as an old man, and now also as a prisoner of Christ Jesus.[e] **10** I am appealing to you for my child, Onesimus, whose father I have become during my imprisonment. **11** Formerly he was useless to you, but now he is indeed useful[f] both to you and to me. **12** I am sending him, that is, my own heart, back to you. **13** I wanted to keep him with me, so that he might be of service to me in your place during my imprisonment for the gospel; **14** but I preferred to do nothing without your consent, in order that your good deed might be voluntary and not something forced. **15** Perhaps this is the reason he was separated from you for a while, so that you might have him back forever, **16** no longer as a slave but more than a slave, a beloved brother – especially to me but how much more to you, both in the flesh and in the Lord.

17 So if you consider me your partner, welcome him as you would welcome me. **18** If he has wronged you in any way, or owes you anything, charge that to my account. **19** I, Paul, am writing this with my own hand: I will repay it. I say nothing about your owing me even your own self. **20** Yes, brother, let me have this benefit from you in the Lord! Refresh my heart in Christ. **21** Confident of your obedience, I am writing to you, knowing that you will do even more than I say.

22 One thing more – prepare a guest room for me, for I am hoping through your prayers to be restored to you.

Final Greetings and Benediction

23 Epaphras, my fellow prisoner in Christ Jesus, sends greetings to you,[g] **24** and so do Mark, Aristarchus, Demas, and Luke, my fellow workers.

25 The grace of the Lord Jesus Christ be with your spirit.[h]

---

[a] Gk the brother [b] Gk *the sister* [c] From verse 4 through verse 21, *you* is singular [d] Other ancient authorities read *you* (plural) [e] Or *as an ambassador of Christ Jesus, and now also his prisoner* [f] The name Onesimus means *useful* or (compare verse 20) *beneficial* [g] Here *you* is singular [h] Other ancient authorities add *Amen*

THE LETTER TO THE HEBREWS

INTRODUCTION

Author

The book of Hebrews was produced by a gifted writer with a profound knowledge of the Old Testament and of Jewish ritual. But there is no real indication who this person was. Unlike Paul's epistles there is no 'signature'. Paul himself being the author is ruled out because of the different style of writing, a different way of presenting quotations, and different emphases. The pattern is not a theological exposition followed by practical outworking; and the theme of Christ as High Priest is not in general found in Paul. In any case, the claim that instruction was received from others in 2:3 differs from Paul's standard claim to have received direct revelation. Many authors have been suggested, including Barnabas, Luke, Apollos, and Priscilla who taught Apollos, the anonymity then being explained by her being a woman. But basically we just do not know!

Readers

The title 'to the Hebrews' is found in some early manuscripts but not necessarily in the original text. However we can be reasonably certain that the book was written to a group of Jewish believers known to the writer (5:12; 13:7, 22–23). Some have been persecuted (10:32–33). There appears to be a danger of falling away from the original gospel teaching (2:1 and the strong warnings of Heb. 6 and 10). The phrase 'you ought to be teachers' (5:12) could indicate that this is addressed to a group within a church rather than the whole church. This maybe a separatist group, perhaps of ex-priests, who had been neglecting to meet with the whole church. The book is quoted as authoritative by Clement of Rome in AD 95 and therefore must have been written several years before that. Probably the date is before AD 70, because the destruction of the Temple is not mentioned at all, and that was of great importance to Jewish Christians.

Purpose

In 13:22 the letter is described as a 'word of exhortation'. It is clearly written not as a theological treatise but as an answer to a very real situation where there were issues of burning importance. The very strong warnings against turning away from Christianity are perhaps the key to the whole epistle. It is not absolutely certain whether they were tempted to turn back to Judaism, thus excluding Gentiles, or to other religions but the writer makes it clear that the Christian revelation is supreme and that any kind of apostasy is fatal.

Factors to keep in mind as one reads the book of Hebrews are firstly the background situation, that it was written to Christians who were tempted to backslide or renounce their faith probably for Judaism. And secondly that it was written as a whole and although there are digressions there is also a developing argument written to meet that particular situation. Looking at individual chapters or sections must not take away from our picture of the whole book.

God Has Spoken by His Son

1 Long ago God spoke to our ancestors in many and various ways by the prophets, [2]but in these last days he has spoken to us by a Son,[a] whom he appointed heir of all things, through whom he also created the worlds. [3]He is the reflection of God's glory and the exact imprint of God's very being, and he sustains[b] all things by his powerful word. When he had made purification for sins, he sat down at the right hand of the Majesty on high, [4]having become as much superior to angels as the name he has inherited is more excellent than theirs.

◆ The term angel (Greek *angelos*, 'messenger'), is ambiguous in Scripture. Sometimes it refers to human messengers, but sometimes to spiritual beings, members of the heavenly court.

References to the appearance and function of these spirit angels are vague, but that such beings existed is taken for granted. They are clearly presented as part of God's creation, and in no sense can be seen as divine. They do not enter into sexual relationships and gender seems to be an irrelevance (Matt. 22:30). They worshiped God and served God, but apparently could not enter into the kind of family relationship with God that, through Christ, is possible for human beings. Apart from specific tasks of bringing information to human beings (Judg. 14; Luke 1), angels seem to have general responsibility for looking after human beings, perhaps children in particular (Matt. 18:10), for fighting evil and for assisting God in the ongoing work of maintaining the creation.

[a] Or *the Son*   [b] Or *bears along*

INTRODUCING THE SON (HEB. 1:1–3)

These opening verses are vital to our understanding of the whole book. They make three important assumptions: (1) God has revealed himself to human beings – in lots of ways but most clearly through the prophets. (2) What has happened in the past does have a bearing on the present. (3) The revelation in Jesus is not just one more in a long line. It is something fundamentally different. He is God's final word. There is no possibility of going on from what they have learned of Jesus to some kind of better or higher or more well-developed revelation. The writer knew that it was vital that those who follow Jesus have a real understanding of who he is and of where he stands in relation to God. That is perhaps why he goes on to explain so clearly that there can be no question of treating Jesus as one of the angels, or as a great prophet like Moses.

Within these three short verses, seven important facts about Jesus are presented: (1) Looking forward: he is the heir, and his inheritance is all that God has. (2) Looking back: he was the means by which God created the world. (3) God's glory shines out through him. (4) He has an exact correspondence with God's nature, as when a stamp produces an image. (5) He keeps the universe going: the Bible never presents a picture of the world created and then left to its own devices. (6) He 'made purification for' sin (in the sense of 'cleared it up completely'). (7) He sat down at God's right hand: i.e. his work was completely finished, and his rightful place is to be enthroned beside God. The whole of the rest of the book must be seen in the light of this initial focus on Jesus.

HIGHER THAN THE ANGELS (HEB. 1:4–2:8A)

1:4–14. *The Old Testament lesson.* A whole collection of quotes from different parts of the Old Testament to emphasize the point that though angels were great and special, their function could never be compared with that of Jesus. He was a Son, which they could never be, and their response to him was one of worship. Perhaps so many quotes are included because the recipients of the letter were exalting angels – we know that around this time there was a tendency among some Jews to do this. Note the importance given to the authority of Old Testament Scripture. Note also that words applied in the Psalms directly to God are here transferred to Christ, reinforcing the high view of Christ given in the first three verses.

Because of their closeness to God, their ability to live in God's presence, and the significance of the task they have been given in caring for God's creatures, and carrying out God's will, angels are seen as glorious. This sense of awe and glory relating to angels has sometimes led groups of Jews and at a later stage Christians to have an excessive interest in them and even to be tempted to worship them. This tendency is firmly rejected in Scripture (Rev. 19:10; 22:9). Angels are to be respected and heeded (Heb. 2:2) but not regarded as anything other than created servants of God. There is no question in the author's mind about the superiority of Jesus to angels ◆

The Son Is Superior to Angels

5 For to which of the angels did God ever say,

"You are my Son;
    today I have begotten you"?
Or again,
"I will be his Father,
    and he will be my Son"?
6And again, when he brings the firstborn into the world, he says,
"Let all God's angels worship him."
7Of the angels he says,
"He makes his angels winds,
    and his servants flames of fire."
8But of the Son he says,
"Your throne, O God, isᶜ forever and ever,
    and the righteous scepter is the
        scepter of yourᵈ kingdom.
9 You have loved righteousness and
        hated wickedness;
therefore God, your God, has anointed
        you
    with the oil of gladness beyond your
        companions."

10And,
"In the beginning, Lord, you founded
        the earth,
    and the heavens are the work of
        your hands;
11 they will perish, but you remain;
    they will all wear out like clothing;
12 like a cloak you will roll them up,
    and like clothingᵉ they will be
        changed.
But you are the same,
    and your years will never end."
13But to which of the angels has he ever said,

"Sit at my right hand
    until I make your enemies a
        footstool for your feet"?
14Are not all angelsᶠ spirits in the divine service, sent to serve for the sake of those who are to inherit salvation?

Warning to Pay Attention

2 Therefore we must pay greater attention to what we have heard, so that we do not drift away from it. 2For if the message declared through angels was valid, and every transgression or disobedience received a just penalty, 3how can we escape if we neglect so great a salvation? It was declared at first through the Lord, and it was attested to us by those who heard him, 4while God added his testimony by signs and wonders and various miracles, and by gifts of the Holy Spirit, distributed according to his will.

ᶜ Or *God is your throne*   ᵈ Other ancient authorities read *his*   ᵉ Other ancient authorities lack *like clothing*   ᶠ Gk *all of them*

2:1–4. *Our response.* The writer of Hebrews is not interested in theology for its own sake. It constantly asks what difference this makes to their lives and challenges the readers to respond to these great truths. Thus if, as they rightly say, the message brought by angels had to be obeyed, with disobedience bringing punishment; then how much more dangerous it was to reject the message of salvation brought by Jesus who is so much greater. They must realise that to 'drift away' from the message of Christ is an awesome thing.

Exaltation through Abasement

5 Now God[g] did not subject the coming world, about which we are speaking, to angels. [6]But someone has testified somewhere,

"What are human beings that you are
      mindful of them,[h]
   or mortals, that you care for them?[i]
[7] You have made them for a little while
      lower[j] than the angels;
   you have crowned them with glory
      and honor,[k]
[8]   subjecting all things under their
      feet."

Now in subjecting all things to them, God[g] left nothing outside their control. As it is, we do not yet see everything in subjection to them, [9]but we do see Jesus, who for a little while was made lower[l] than the angels, now crowned with glory and honor because of the suffering of death, so that by the grace of God[m] he might taste death for everyone.

10 It was fitting that God,[g] for whom and through whom all things exist, in bringing many children to glory, should make the pioneer of their salvation perfect through sufferings. [11]For the one who sanctifies and those who are sanctified all have one Father.[n] For this reason Jesus[g] is not ashamed to call them brothers and sisters,[o] [12]saying,

"I will proclaim your name to my
      brothers and sisters,[o]
   in the midst of the congregation I
      will praise you."

[g] Gk he   [h] Gk What is man that you are mindful of him?   [i] Gk or the son of man that you care for him? In the Hebrew of Psalm 8.4-6 both man and son of man refer to all humankind   [j] Or them only a little lower   [k] Other ancient authorities add and set them over the works of your hands   [l] Or who was made a little lower   [m] Other ancient authorities read apart from God   [n] Gk are all of one   [o] Gk brothers

2:5–8a. *The Lord of All*. The greatness of Jesus is restressed. The world was created by Jesus and the world to come will also be subject not to angels but to him. *Oikumene*, 'world', is used for inhabited areas and often relates to the Roman world. It may refer to the after-life here, but it more probably refers to the new order inaugurated by Jesus and beginning now.

'Someone has testified somewhere' – actually in Ps. 8. The fact that it is in Scripture matters more than the exact reference. Ps. 8 was not usually seen as referring to the Messiah; in the original context it refers to humanity as a whole rather than to an individual person. The NRSV hence uses 'human beings' in the plural. However the writer uses the singular all the way through and in this context is clearly referring to the sovereignty of Christ, not the special place in creation of humanity. A fulfillment is seen which goes beyond the original context of Ps. 8 – the whole world is in subjection to Christ, nothing is outside his control.

BROTHER TO HUMANITY (HEB. 2:8B–18)

8b–9. *We see Jesus*. We can't see the outworking of this subjection of all things to the Son, but what we can see is Jesus himself. The one who became man, suffered and died. Jesus death was a problem for some. How could one who was greater than angels die, when angels don't die? But the problem is transformed. For Jesus, the path of death was in fact the way which led to him being crowned with glory and honour. The glory, which in Heb. 1 was seen as relating to the greatness of the Son in creation, is also related to his humiliation in becoming incarnate – a human being. Note that there is no stress here on Christ's maleness – it is Christ as *anthropos* (human) rather than as *aner* (male) who acts on our behalf.

10–13. *Suffering for us*. The concept of the Messiah suffering would have been abhorrent to some Jews, but here we are told that 'It was fitting' that the great and glorious Son should be made 'perfect through sufferings'. The writer assumes that the sufferings of Christ were essential for other human beings to be saved. It is because of what Jesus did that we can be saved and sanctified. Those who are sanctified in this way become related to Jesus as family – whether brothers and sisters (v. 11), or children (v. 13) (cf. Rom. 8:29).

[13]And again,
"I will put my trust in him."
And again,
"Here am I and the children whom
God has given me."

14 Since, therefore, the children share flesh and blood, he himself likewise shared the same things, so that through death he might destroy the one who has the power of death, that is, the devil, [15]and free those who all their lives were held in slavery by the fear of death. [16]For it is clear that he did not come to help angels, but the descendants of Abraham. [17]Therefore he had to become like his brothers and sisters[p] in every respect, so that he might be a merciful and faithful high priest in the service of God, to make a sacrifice of atonement for the sins of the people. [18]Because he himself was tested by what he suffered, he is able to help those who are being tested.

Moses a Servant, Christ a Son

3 Therefore, brothers and sisters,[p] holy partners in a heavenly calling, consider that Jesus, the apostle and high priest of our confession, [2]was faithful to the one who appointed him, just as Moses also "was faithful in all[q] God's[r] house." [3]Yet Jesus[s] is worthy of more glory than Moses, just as the builder of a house has more honor than the house itself. [4](For every house is built by someone, but the builder of all things is God.) [5]Now Moses was faithful in all God's[r] house as a servant, to testify to the things that would be spoken later. [6]Christ, however, was faithful over God's[r] house as a son, and we are his house if we hold firm[t] the confidence and the pride that belong to hope.

◆ Moses was held in great honor by the Jews at the time Hebrews was written, as at other times. Abraham was the father of the nation, but Moses was the founder of the faith. He was the one who brought them the Law and introduced them to the covenant – he gave meaning to the concept of Israel as the people of God. The house of Israel can, in one way at least, be seen as the house of Moses. It is easy to understand how a Jewish believer might want to see Jesus as coming after Moses in the scheme of things. He came later in time, bringing new teaching but perhaps

[p] Gk brothers   [q] Other ancient authorities lack all
[r] Gk his   [s] Gk this one   [t] Other ancient
authorities add to the end

14–18. *Sharing our nature.* The writer continues to reflect on the meaning of incarnation. The children given to Christ by God (note God's involvement here), are flesh and blood. Therefore Jesus himself took the same nature. If the power of the devil over death was to be broken it was necessary that one who was at the same time human and sinless should die and by his own death and resurrection remove the power of death. Death in Scripture is always linked with sin.

Having explained the purpose of the incarnation, the writer goes on to explain the implications. Because Jesus was 'in every respect' perfectly and completely human, he can act on behalf of the people as their high priest, fully able to understand their needs (the high priest theme is taken up in Heb. 4–5). He is able to help us in our suffering and temptations because he has been through the same experiences himself.

MORE GLORIOUS THAN MOSES (HEB. 3:1–19)

1–6. *Consider Jesus.* So far we have seen Jesus as so much greater than the angels and as fully identified with us – but the author makes it clear that there is much more to say. We need to put our minds to it, give it careful and continuous consideration. Moses was the great law-giver, a tremendous servant of God, but even he cannot be compared with Jesus. All his great qualities are superseded by Christ who was a Son rather than a servant. It is this Christ to whom the readers can belong if only they 'hold firm'.

only developing what Moses had already given them. It was in this context that the writer of Hebrews takes so much time to show the difference between Moses as a servant and Christ as a Son. There is no question in the author's mind about the superiority of Jesus to Moses ◆

Warning against Unbelief

7 Therefore, as the Holy Spirit says,
"Today, if you hear his voice,
8 do not harden your hearts as in the
        rebellion,
    as on the day of testing in the
        wilderness,
9 where your ancestors put me to the
        test,
    though they had seen my works ¹⁰for
        forty years.
    Therefore I was angry with that
        generation,
    and I said, 'They always go astray in
        their hearts,
    and they have not known my ways.'
11 As in my anger I swore,
    'They will not enter my rest.'"

¹²Take care, brothers and sisters,ᵘ that none of you may have an evil, unbelieving heart that turns away from the living God. ¹³But exhort one another every day, as long as it is called "today," so that none of you may be hardened by the deceitfulness of sin. ¹⁴For we have become partners of Christ, if only we hold our first confidence firm to the end. ¹⁵As it is said,

"Today, if you hear his voice,
    do not harden your hearts as in the
        rebellion."

¹⁶Now who were they who heard and yet were rebellious? Was it not all those who left Egypt under the leadership of Moses? ¹⁷But with whom was he angry forty years? Was it not those who sinned, whose bodies fell in the wilderness? ¹⁸And to whom did he swear that they would not enter his rest, if not to those who were disobedient? ¹⁹So we see that they were unable to enter because of unbelief.

The Rest That God Promised

4 Therefore, while the promise of entering his rest is still open, let us take care that none of you should seem to have failed to reach it. ²For indeed the good news came to us just as to them; but the message they heard did not benefit them, because they were not united by faith with those who listened.ᵛ ³For we who have believed enter that rest, just as Godʷ has said,

"As in my anger I swore,
    'They shall not enter my rest,'"

though his works were finished at the foundation of the world. ⁴For in one place it speaks about the seventh day as follows, "And God rested on the seventh day from all his works." ⁵And again in this place it says, "They shall not enter my rest."

ᵘ Gk *brothers* ᵛ Other ancient authorities read *it did not meet with faith in those who listened* ʷ Gk *he*

7–19. *Lessons from the wilderness.* In spite of the fact that Moses was appointed by God as a law-giver, most Israelites did not listen to him. The great majority were unfaithful. In spite of every opportunity to repent they continued in disobedience and unbelief. Eventually, therefore, they were excluded from the 'rest' which God had prepared for them. The same situation was existing among the recipients of this letter. Thus they are given a strong warning to 'Take care' and to learn carefully the lesson from history, lest they themselves should fall away from God.

GOD'S REST (HEB. 4:1–13)

1–5. *The need for faith.* There is in fact a far better rest than that eventually found in Canaan by the believing Israelites. This rest is the inheritance of believing Christians. It is a rest that can be paralleled by God's resting after creation. But this rest can never be reached by those who reject the good news or do not have faith.

◆ Work and rest were very important concepts in Hebrew thinking. God by his example in creation had made both concepts holy. Work was not, as in some other religions, simply a necessary evil to be relegated if possible to the lowest members of society. It was an honorable God-given task. This was true whether we are considering church work, as that of Phoebe, professional work, as that of Priscilla the tent-maker, or home-making as Martha and the Ephesian re-married widows (1 Tim. 5:14). Work is to be undertaken with commitment, effort and a sense of both rightness and joy that there are tasks to be done.

But rest is also presented very positively. It is not to be despised or at best tolerated as a sad necessity arising only because of laziness or weakness. God himself provides the model as he is pictured resting after the work of creation. That rest is not simply inactivity, but rather a glad satisfaction, revelling in the completion of something which can be seen to be 'very good'. God's rest provides both a basis for the concept of regular rest periods built into the structure of society, notably in the Sabbath concept, and also a hope for the future. The impression is sometimes given that the really spiritual person is the one who is constantly active, constantly achieving, constantly working. This is totally alien to biblical thinking where the one who never stops, who never takes time to reflect and to 'rest' is presented as disobedient and unfaithful.

The picture of God at rest is also a tremendous stimulus to hope. It is possible for human beings to share in God's glad satisfaction, sitting back with joy, knowing that everything that was intended for them in creation has been completed. That rest is not open to those without faith or those who are disobedient, it was not achieved when the people of Israel entered the Promised Land even though that was an achievement and a fulfillment of God's Word. The author of Hebrews tells us that this rest can come and indeed can only come through the work of Jesus which really does enable his followers to enter into God's presence and share in God's rest ◆

⁶Since therefore it remains open for some to enter it, and those who formerly received the good news failed to enter because of disobedience, ⁷again he sets a certain day – "today" – saying through David much later, in the words already quoted,

"Today, if you hear his voice,
    do not harden your hearts."

⁸For if Joshua had given them rest, God^x would not speak later about another day. ⁹So then, a sabbath rest still remains for the people of God; ¹⁰for those who enter God's rest also cease from their labors as God did from his. ¹¹Let us therefore make every effort to enter that rest, so that no one may fall through such disobedience as theirs.

12 Indeed, the word of God is living and active, sharper than any two-edged sword,

^x Gk *he*

6–11. *The need for obedience.* It is no use them thinking that the rest was achieved when Joshua entered the Promised Land and that they do not have to do any more about it. David still speaks of further opportunities to act. The rest is still available for them but they do have to take action. It involves obedience (v. 6) and effort (v. 11).

12–13. *The influence of God's Word.* Word here in the sense of God's complete revelation, probably includes both the written Word in Scripture and the personal Word in the Son. It is clear that neither the original readers nor we today can pretend before God or hide from God. The image of a sword contains various ideas – cutting to the heart of the situation, cutting in judgment, getting as close as possible to the individual. There is an overwhelming sense of the power involved in God's Word. V. 13 concludes the first part of the argument and backs up what has already been said about the relationship between Creator and created. Every creature is fully known by God, and will be held responsible by God.

piercing until it divides soul from spirit, joints from marrow; it is able to judge the thoughts and intentions of the heart. [13]And before him no creature is hidden, but all are naked and laid bare to the eyes of the one to whom we must render an account.

Jesus the Great High Priest

14 Since, then, we have a great high priest who has passed through the heavens, Jesus, the Son of God, let us hold fast to our confession. [15]For we do not have a high priest who is unable to sympathize with our weaknesses, but we have one who in every respect has been tested[y] as we are, yet without sin. [16]Let us therefore approach the throne of grace with boldness, so that we may receive mercy and find grace to help in time of need.

5 Every high priest chosen from among mortals is put in charge of things pertaining to God on their behalf, to offer gifts and sacrifices for sins. [2]He is able to deal gently with the ignorant and wayward, since he himself is subject to weakness; [3]and because of this he must offer sacrifice for his own sins as well as for those of the people. [4]And one does not presume to take this honor, but takes it only when called by God, just as Aaron was.

5 So also Christ did not glorify himself in becoming a high priest, but was

◆ In the early stages of Israel's history there appear to have been no appointed priests, with everybody offering their own sacrifices to God wherever they happened to be. But if the covenant community was going to carry out all the requirements of the Law it really needed professional trained priests both to carry out the sacrifices and to teach the people. Exod. 32 tells the story of how the tribe of Levi were first appointed as special servants of God. The whole tribe was set apart to carry out religious duties, Temple singing, administration and manual work of various kinds. Because of the need for them to be spread throughout the country supporting the faith of others they were not given any tribal land. The other Israelites were supposed to supply their needs.

Not all the Levites were priests. Aaron was a Levite and because of his initial responsibilities it was perhaps natural that his family and later on his descendants would be given the priestly tasks. In fact the only people who worked as priests were

[y] Or tempted

THE GREAT HIGH PRIEST (HEB. 4:14–5:14)

4:14–16. *Prologue.* These verses form the prologue to a detailed discussion on priesthood that goes right through to 10:18 with the section following 10:19 forming a kind of epilogue. The point of the whole discussion is that readers might recognize the importance of maintaining their faith, so both 4:14 and 10:23 speak of 'holding fast to our confession'.

The first thing to realize is that Jesus as high priest is fully qualified to act. Because he is great and has 'passed through the heavens' (as opposed to Aaronic high priests who only pass through the Temple curtain) and because he remains sinless Jesus can stand before God. Because he has known our temptations he can stand alongside us. Temptation itself is not sinful. The idea is of exposure to testing. Jesus' experience was not confined to the three wilderness temptations. He passed through a range of stresses and strains as wide as anyone has ever known. This factor, that he has stood in our shoes, means that we can have every confidence in him as our representative.

5:1–10. *Appointed by God.* High priests all have certain standard characteristics. They are chosen (the implication here is appointed by God) from other human beings, they act on behalf of humans in relation to God, they offer gifts and sacrifices. All these things apply to Jesus too, but there are differences. Aaronic high priests had to offer sacrifices for their own sins which Jesus did not, and Jesus is a member of a new order of priesthood, named after Melchizedek. This order lasts for ever and can never be improved upon. Vv. 7–10 re-emphasize that Jesus really did live a human life; the name Jesus, as opposed to Christ, is used to stress this. They must never lose sight of the fact that he is *their* high priest.

male descendants of Aaron aged between 30 and 50. Many conclusions have been drawn about the exclusion of women from the priestly role but the text itself makes no comment. It should be noted that it was not in any case, that men could be priests and women not, most male Israelites were also excluded. It is possible that the heavy work involved in moving around dead animals was one factor in excluding female Levites, or that the physical demands of pregnancy and breast-feeding would keep them away from duties too often. Any opinions here can only be speculative as no comment at all is made on the issue.

There was always one high priest who was particularly responsible for overseeing the system and for carrying out special sacrifices representing the whole nation, as on the Day of Atonement. Jesus was not from the tribe of Levi and certainly not a descendant of Aaron so in the context of the Old Testament covenant there was no possibility of his becoming or acting as a priest – his priesthood was therefore quite different from and in the opinion of the writer of Hebrews very much superior to that of the Aaronic priests ◆

appointed by the one who said to him,
  "You are my Son,
    today I have begotten you";
[6]as he says also in another place,
  "You are a priest forever,

according to the order of
  Melchizedek."
7 In the days of his flesh, Jesus[z] offered up prayers and supplications, with loud cries and tears, to the one who was able to save him from death, and he was heard because of his reverent submission. [8]Although he was a Son, he learned obedience through what he suffered; [9]and having been made perfect, he became the source of eternal salvation for all who obey him, [10]having been designated by God a high priest according to the order of Melchizedek.

Warning against Falling Away

11 About this[a] we have much to say that is hard to explain, since you have become dull in understanding. [12]For though by this time you ought to be teachers, you need someone to teach you again the basic elements of the oracles of God. You need milk, not solid food; [13]for everyone who lives on milk, being still an infant, is unskilled in the word of righteousness. [14]But solid food is for the mature, for those whose faculties have been trained by practice to distinguish good from evil.

The Peril of Falling Away

6 Therefore let us go on toward perfection,[b] leaving behind the basic teaching

[z] Gk he   [a] Or him   [b] Or toward maturity

5:11–14. *A challenging aside.* The writer has much more to tell them but it is hard to explain, simply because they have not kept their hearing faculties sharp. They ought by this stage to have got enough understanding to pass it on but not only had they not moved forward, they had gone backwards. They are living on baby-food, 'unskilled in the word of righteousness', their lack of skill indicating a lack of practice. The things of God need much more than just a passing acquaintance. Their minds need thorough training if they are to be mature – the word used here indicates the opposite of childhood. As this section speaks of every reader being a teacher, this may be evidence that a specific group, rather than the whole church, is being addressed. However there is certainly no indication that anything, other than a lack of skill and application, stood in the way of their being teachers.

APOSTASY (HEB. 6:1–20)

1–3. *On to maturity.* If they are to be mature, they need God's help, but some of it is also their own responsibility. It takes effort and an attitude of moving on from the foundation. The foundation itself, repentance, faith, baptism, with the recognition that they have been saved from eternal judgment into eternal life, is vital, but it can only be laid once and must then be built on.

about Christ, and not laying again the foundation: repentance from dead works and faith toward God, ²instruction about baptisms, laying on of hands, resurrection of the dead, and eternal judgment. ³And we will do^c this, if God permits. ⁴For it is impossible to restore again to repentance those who have once been enlightened, and have tasted the heavenly gift, and have shared in the Holy Spirit, ⁵and have tasted the goodness of the word of God and the powers of the age to come, ⁶and then have fallen away, since on their own they are crucifying again the Son of God and are holding him up to contempt. ⁷Ground that drinks up the rain falling on it repeatedly, and that produces a crop useful to those for whom it is cultivated, receives a blessing from God. ⁸But if it produces thorns and thistles, it is worthless and on the verge of being cursed; its end is to be burned over.

9 Even though we speak in this way,

beloved, we are confident of better things in your case, things that belong to salvation. ¹⁰For God is not unjust; he will not overlook your work and the love that you showed for his sake^d in serving the saints, as you still do. ¹¹And we want each one of you to show the same diligence so as to realize the full assurance of hope to the very end, ¹²so that you may not become sluggish, but imitators of those who through faith and patience inherit the promises.

The Certainty of God's Promise

13 When God made a promise to Abraham, because he had no one greater by whom to swear, he swore by himself, ¹⁴saying, "I will surely bless you and multiply you." ¹⁵And thus Abraham,^e

^c Other ancient authorities read *let us do* ^d Gk *for his name* ^e Gk *he*

4–8. *An impossibility.* This is the first of four impossible things that Hebrews talks about (in 6:18 God cannot prove false; in 10:4 animal blood cannot take away sins; and in 11:6 no-one can please God without faith). Here the impossibility is of somebody who has once been 'enlightened' and then falls away, coming back to repentance. It is made quite clear that what we are talking about here is those who have been well immersed in Christian experience, who have received the Spirit in a genuine and meaningful way. If people like that then turn against Christ, they are re-enacting the crucifixion. The language here is very strong. This is a very serious offense indeed.

This passage seems to imply that it is possible for those who have once been saved then to be lost again. However, this would contrast with 10:22 which speaks of 'full assurance of faith'. We need to remember that this is a hypothetical case, the writer is not speaking of a particular person. Also the main theme of the epistle is to show that having become a Christian one cannot possibly return then to Judaism. Again it may be that he is saying that the initial act of commitment and repentance can never be repeated, but maybe it can be remembered and re-affirmed. However, although we must be careful not to read too much into this text we do have a warning in the strongest possible terms. If a person gets into a hardened position then they simply cannot repent. An impenetrable barrier is built up so they become totally insensitive to any promptings of the Spirit. There is a point of no return. Of course it is very unlikely that anybody in that kind of hardened state of mind would even wish to return – so that if somebody is concerned about their sin that is evidence that this verse does not refer to them.

9–20. *The sure and steadfast Anchor.* Recognizing the severity of his warning the author goes on to reassure the readers. There is complete conviction that these particular people are not in any danger of losing their salvation. That conviction is based on God's justice and on the fruits of the Spirit that they have shown – a clear indication in their lives that they do belong to God. It is not being suggested here that their salvation is earned by their good works, but that their service to others is evidence of God's work in them. The previous warning is not intended to discourage them, but rather to encourage them to go on to inherit the promises.

having patiently endured, obtained the promise. [16]Human beings, of course, swear by someone greater than themselves, and an oath given as confirmation puts an end to all dispute. [17]In the same way, when God desired to show even more clearly to the heirs of the promise the unchangeable character of his purpose, he guaranteed it by an oath, [18]so that through two unchangeable things, in which it is impossible that God would prove false, we who have taken refuge might be strongly encouraged to seize the hope set before us. [19]We have this hope, a sure and steadfast anchor of the soul, a hope that enters the inner shrine behind the curtain, [20]where Jesus, a forerunner on our behalf, has entered, having become a high priest forever according to the order of Melchizedek.

The Priestly Order of Melchizedek

7 This "King Melchizedek of Salem, priest of the Most High God, met Abraham as he was returning from defeating the kings and blessed him"; [2]and

to him Abraham apportioned "one-tenth of everything." His name, in the first place, means "king of righteousness"; next he is also king of Salem, that is, "king of peace." [3]Without father, without mother, without genealogy, having neither beginning of days nor end of life, but resembling the Son of God, he remains a priest forever.

4 See how great he is! Even[f] Abraham the patriarch gave him a tenth of the spoils. [5]And those descendants of Levi who receive the priestly office have a commandment in the law to collect tithes[g] from the people, that is, from their kindred,[h] though these also are descended from Abraham. [6]But this man, who does not belong to their ancestry, collected tithes[g] from Abraham and blessed him who had received the promises. [7]It is beyond dispute that the inferior is blessed by the superior. [8]In the one case, tithes are received by those who are mortal; in the other, by one of whom it is

[f] Other ancient authorities lack *Even*   [g] Or *a tenth*
[h] Gk *brothers*

Their hope for the future goes right back to the promises given by God to Abraham, which are completely trustworthy (vv. 13–15). It is, contrary to the belief of some who wished to go back into Judaism, those who have accepted salvation through Jesus who are the true heirs of the promises to Abraham. Thus their hope is a sure and certain anchor (v. 19) – using a symbol of complete security, cutting away any doubt which the previous warning might have brought in. This hope takes them right into God's presence. Jesus has gone behind the curtain as a forerunner. The picture here is of the curtain which divided the very holiest place where the ark of God was kept from the rest of the Temple. This curtain was a symbol of the barrier keeping sinful human beings away from the presence of God. Only the chief priest could ever pass that curtain and then only once a year on the Day of Atonement. But Jesus' death splits the curtain in two (cf. Matt. 27:51) and makes the way open for his followers to enter into God's presence.

THE NEW PRIESTLY ORDER (HEB. 7:1–28)

1–10. *Melchizedek.* A few more details are given about Melchizedek, whom the author has chosen as the symbol of this new priesthood. He is the rather shadowy figure described in Gen. 14:17–20 as the king of Salem and priest of the most high God who blessed Abraham and received tribute from him. Hebrews develops this incident in Genesis as part of the argument that the order of priesthood to which Christ belonged was much superior to the Old Testament priesthood. This type of argument giving a spiritual interpretation to an Old Testament historical event was common at that time. It would probably have made more sense as an argument to the original readers than it does to us and we are not given a free hand to use this kind of interpretation ourselves. However the point being made by it is abundantly clear. Christ's priesthood is superior to any other available at the time.

testified that he lives. ⁹One might even say that Levi himself, who receives tithes, paid tithes through Abraham, ¹⁰for he was still in the loins of his ancestor when Melchizedek met him.

Another Priest, Like Melchizedek

11 Now if perfection had been attainable through the levitical priesthood – for the people received the law under this priesthood – what further need would there have been to speak of another priest arising according to the order of Melchizedek, rather than one according to the order of Aaron? ¹²For when there is a change in the priesthood, there is necessarily a change in the law as well. ¹³Now the one of whom these things are spoken belonged to another tribe, from which no one has ever served at the altar. ¹⁴For it is evident that our Lord was descended from Judah, and in connection with that tribe Moses said nothing about priests.

15 It is even more obvious when another priest arises, resembling Melchizedek, ¹⁶one who has become a priest, not through a legal requirement concerning physical descent, but through the power of an indestructible life. ¹⁷For it is attested of him,
"You are a priest forever,
    according to the order of
        Melchizedek."

¹⁸There is, on the one hand, the abrogation of an earlier commandment because it was weak and ineffectual ¹⁹(for the law made nothing perfect); there is, on the other hand, the introduction of a better hope, through which we approach God.

20 This was confirmed with an oath; for others who became priests took their office without an oath, ²¹but this one became a priest with an oath, because of the one who said to him,
"The Lord has sworn
    and will not change his mind,
'You are a priest forever' " –
²²accordingly Jesus has also become the guarantee of a better covenant.

23 Furthermore, the former priests were many in number, because they were prevented by death from continuing in office; ²⁴but he holds his priesthood permanently, because he continues forever. ²⁵Consequently he is able for all time to save¹ those who approach God through him, since he always lives to make intercession for them.

26 For it was fitting that we should have such a high priest, holy, blameless, undefiled, separated from sinners, and exalted above the heavens. ²⁷Unlike the otherʲ high priests, he has no need to offer sacrifices

¹ Or *able to save completely*   ʲ Gk lacks *other*

11–22. *The new priesthood means a new law.* Again we have a rather complicated argument which would have meant more to first-century readers than it does to us, but again the point is clear. The author firstly argues the need for a new priesthood as it is demonstrably clear that perfection is not available through the present system. And secondly, if there is to be a new priesthood then this means a new law and a new covenant. The old law is now set aside and a better hope introduced (v. 19). We need to keep in mind here the background of Jewish Christians who were tempted to go back into Judaism, perhaps in their hearts believing that the Law and the covenant that they had known all their lives were really the best thing for them. Hebrews totally rejects this belief.

23–28. *The permanent perfect High Priest.* Jesus once again becomes the centre of attention. The continual focal point of the argument is that if they do not keep their eyes fixed on Jesus they are likely to fall away. Unlike the Aaronic priests, Christ's priesthood is eternal because he never dies and can therefore always be relied upon to act on behalf of those who turn to God. We have already seen that Christ is able to help (2:18), able to sympathize (4:15) and able to save (7:25). Vv. 26–28 sum up the characteristics of this ideal high priest, emphasizing here his purity and the eternal effectiveness of the once-for-all sacrifice of himself.

day after day, first for his own sins, and then for those of the people; this he did once for all when he offered himself. [28]For the law appoints as high priests those who are subject to weakness, but the word of the oath, which came later than the law, appoints a Son who has been made perfect forever.

Mediator of a Better Covenant

8 Now the main point in what we are saying is this: we have such a high priest, one who is seated at the right hand of the throne of the Majesty in the heavens, [2]a minister in the sanctuary and the true tent[k] that the Lord, and not any mortal, has set up. [3]For every high priest is appointed to offer gifts and sacrifices; hence it is necessary for this priest also to have something to offer. [4]Now if he were on earth, he would not be a priest at all, since there are priests who offer gifts according to the law. [5]They offer worship in a sanctuary that is a sketch and shadow of the heavenly one; for Moses, when he was about to erect the tent,[k] was warned, "See that you make everything according to the pattern that was shown you on the mountain." [6]But Jesus[l] has now obtained a more excellent ministry, and to that degree he is the mediator of a better covenant, which has been enacted through better promises. [7]For if that first covenant had been faultless, there would have been no need to look for a second one.

[8] God[l] finds fault with them when he says:

"The days are surely coming, says the
         Lord,

when I will establish a new
         covenant with the house of
         Israel
    and with the house of Judah;
[9]   not like the covenant that I made with
         their ancestors,
    on the day when I took them by the
         hand to lead them out of the
         land of Egypt;
for they did not continue in my
         covenant,
    and so I had no concern for them,
         says the Lord.
[10] This is the covenant that I will make
         with the house of Israel
    after those days, says the Lord:
I will put my laws in their minds,
    and write them on their hearts,
and I will be their God,
    and they shall be my people.
[11] And they shall not teach one another
    or say to each other, 'Know the
         Lord,'
for they shall all know me,
    from the least of them to the
         greatest.
[12] For I will be merciful toward their
         iniquities,
    and I will remember their sins no
         more."

[13]In speaking of "a new covenant," he has made the first one obsolete. And what is obsolete and growing old will soon disappear.

k Or *tabernacle*   l Gk *he*

THE OLD AND THE NEW (HEB. 8:1–10:18)

8:1–13. *The High Priest's work.* The discussion of the relationship between the Aaronic high priesthood and the work of Christ continues, with further development of the idea of the new covenant. Christ's priesthood is heavenly not earthly. In fact the main use of the earthly Aaronic priesthood is as a model, a 'sketch and shadow' pointing to Christ. Useful as long as they remember how much 'more excellent' is the new than the old. The extensive quote from Jer. 31 is used to show that although the old covenant was needed in its time and was certainly used by God, now its time has passed. The old system, far from being really rather more special, which is what the Judaizers were implying, in fact has no validity at all within the new order.

The Earthly and the Heavenly Sanctuaries

9 Now even the first covenant had regulations for worship and an earthly sanctuary. [2]For a tent[m] was constructed, the first one, in which were the lampstand, the table, and the bread of the Presence;[n] this is called the Holy Place. [3]Behind the second curtain was a tent[m] called the Holy of Holies. [4]In it stood the golden altar of incense and the ark of the covenant overlaid on all sides with gold, in which there were a golden urn holding the manna, and Aaron's rod that budded, and the tablets of the covenant; [5]above it were the cherubim of glory overshadowing the mercy seat.[o] Of these things we cannot speak now in detail.

♦ The system in ancient Israel for public worship and in particular for bringing sacrifices was quite complicated. Regulations for sacrifices are described fairly fully in the book of Leviticus but certain things are taken for granted. It is not always easy to work out exactly what happened, and descriptions of actual sacrifices at various stages of Israel's history indicate that the regulations were applied in different ways at different times. As Heb. 9:5 indicates, the details are sometimes unclear and probably not of vital relevance to Christian believers. Nevertheless in order to understand the background of the teaching about the sacrifice of Christ it is helpful for us to have at least a basic awareness of what went on.

There were three main types of sacrifices and a whole range of others which applied in special circumstances. The first main type is gift offerings, sacrifices brought as presents for God, praising him and recognizing his greatness. These were sometimes animals which were either burnt in their entirety (hence the terms burnt offerings or whole offerings) or a portion was burnt and the rest went to the priests and their families as part of their wages. Sometimes the gift offerings were of grain or bread or cakes, and again they were either burnt or given to the priests. Secondly there were offerings which symbolized the relationship between God and his people which existed in the covenant. These are called in the NRSV 'sacrifices of well-being' and elsewhere known as fellowship offerings or peace offerings. In this instance a portion was burnt, a portion went to the priests and the rest was eaten by the offerer and their family in what was in effect a big party, symbolically shared with God. Thirdly there were sin offerings, which are probably what most people think of when they hear about Old Testament sacrifices; offerings where an animal, symbolically taking the place of a person, or group, who had sinned, was killed in order that the sin may be seen as dealt with and the person forgiven. It is important to note that the whole sacrificial system was symbolic and only made sense or was effective in the context of relationship between the offerer and God. It is quite clear, for example that sin offerings were only effective if the person concerned was genuinely repentant and intended to put right what had gone wrong. The sacrifices were not to be seen as magic formulae

[m] Or tabernacle   [n] Gk the presentation of the loaves   [o] Or the place of atonement

9:1–14. *Regulations for worship.* Early Jewish Christians were obviously impressed by the order and regulation of the old system and by the ritual involved. The author is not unappreciative of the glories of the past, but wants to keep stressing the greater glories of the new order. The old forms of worship in the Tent (Tabernacle) used before the Temple was even built are described with tremendous understanding and feeling, but they are nevertheless presented as inadequate. The rituals of the Tent and the Temple – even those of the great Day of Atonement – can only deal with outward surface things. On the other hand, when Christ came and acted as both the high priest and the perfect sacrifice, he could also purify and make perfect the conscience of the believer.

which guaranteed religious acceptability.

There was a system of corporate sacrifice, where daily offerings were brought by the priests on behalf of the whole nation, but individuals and families also brought their own sacrifices on feast days or on occasions when there was special reason to be either thankful or repentant. Although there is little in the regulations about it, it seems that in the patriarchal society of ancient Israel, the father brought sacrifices on behalf of the whole family. But there are some sacrifices particularly relating to women (Lev. 12:6; 15:19) and certainly in these and probably on other occasions where a sacrifice was required of an individual, women were expected to take an independent role. The need to bring a sacrifice as purification after the birth of a child is often taken as a negative view of childbirth, but that view misunderstands the Old Testament understanding of ritual purity. There were many activities that made people ritually unclean but that did not mean that the activities themselves were in any sense viewed negatively. In fact, the specific command for women to bring certain sacrifices which could only apply to them ensured that they could not be excluded from the whole cultic system in a way that otherwise might have happened ◆

6 Such preparations having been made, the priests go continually into the first tent[p] to carry out their ritual duties; [7]but only the high priest goes into the second, and he but once a year, and not without taking the blood that he offers for himself and for the sins committed unintentionally by the people. [8]By this the Holy Spirit indicates that the way into the sanctuary has not yet been disclosed as long as the first tent[p] is still standing. [9]This is a symbol[q] of the present time, during which gifts and sacrifices are offered that cannot perfect the conscience of the worshiper, [10]but deal only with food and drink and various baptisms, regulations for the body imposed until the time comes to set things right.

11 But when Christ came as a high priest of the good things that have come,[r] then through the greater and perfect[s] tent[p] (not made with hands, that is, not of this creation), [12]he entered once for all into the Holy Place, not with the blood of goats and calves, but with his own blood, thus obtaining eternal redemption. [13]For if the blood of goats and bulls, with the sprinkling of the ashes of a heifer, sanctifies those who have been defiled so that their flesh is purified, [14]how much more will the blood of Christ, who through the eternal Spirit[t] offered himself without blemish to God, purify our[u] conscience from dead works to worship the living God!

15 For this reason he is the mediator of a new covenant, so that those who are called may receive the promised eternal inheritance, because a death has occurred that redeems them from the transgressions

[p] Or *tabernacle* [q] Gk *parable* [r] Other ancient authorities read *good things to come* [s] Gk *more perfect* [t] Other ancient authorities read *Holy Spirit* [u] Other ancient authorities read *your*

9:15–28. *The Mediator.* There is a slight change of emphasis here although the same theme is being carried through. Christ is the mediator of the new covenant. Again the style of argument is somewhat unfamiliar to us but the point is clear. If sin is to be dealt with, there has to be a sacrifice – 'without the shedding of blood there is no forgiveness of sins' (v. 22). The old system helps to make this clear. But unlike all previous sacrifices, which needed to be repeated day by day and year by year, Christ's sacrifice was 'once for all'. His work was completely sufficient, he died, he rose, he appeared before God on our behalf and all our sins are now dealt with. There is no need for any other sacrifice or any other intermediary. Any who wish to retain the old system of sacrifices have missed this point completely. The reference to the second coming in v. 28 moves away from the main argument but was brought to mind by the mention of judgment in v. 27.

◆ Jesus is described as the mediator of the new covenant, that is the one who stands between the two parties to the covenant agreement and makes the whole thing function effectively. In this instance Jesus is the one who enables believers to come into the relationship with God and to remain in that relationship. For the old covenant there were a whole range of different mediators. Moses, who helped it to get off the ground is portrayed as a mediator. The priests enabled the cultic system to continue, and that provided a means by which sinful Israelites could regain the purity that made it possible for them to remain in touch with a holy God. The prophets helped Israel to know what God wanted from them and intended for them and the kings too are seen as having a mediatorial role in bringing God's blessing to the people. However as far as the new covenant is concerned there is only one mediator, Jesus himself (1 Tim. 2:5). No individual believer needs any other human mediator, Jesus is the only one needed to bring them into direct contact with God.

Often leaders in the church are compared with the different forms of leaders in the Old Testament, but it is important that neither they nor the people they lead envisage them as taking over a mediatorial role. To do that would be to usurp the position that belongs to Jesus alone. Christian leaders do not stand between the believer and God, they stand alongside as fellow believers with particular gifts who can encourage and enable others to take responsibility for living out their lives in a way that reflects the fact that they are in relationship with God. Certain views of marriage too have portrayed the husband as having a mediatorial role, but this again negates the New Testament teaching on Jesus as the sole mediator. In fact, even the Old Testament, though the husband and father, in practice if not necessarily in theory, is sometimes presented as having a representative role, does not reinforce this picture of the husband as mediator. The Christian wife, like every other believer,

must, in the context of the mediation of Jesus, take full responsibility for working out her own relationship with God ◆

under the first covenant.[v] [16]Where a will[v] is involved, the death of the one who made it must be established. [17]For a will[v] takes effect only at death, since it is not in force as long as the one who made it is alive. [18]Hence not even the first covenant was inaugurated without blood. [19]For when every commandment had been told to all the people by Moses in accordance with the law, he took the blood of calves and goats,[w] with water and scarlet wool and hyssop, and sprinkled both the scroll itself and all the people, [20]saying, "This is the blood of the covenant that God has ordained for you." [21]And in the same way he sprinkled with the blood both the tent[x] and all the vessels used in worship. [22]Indeed, under the law almost everything is purified with blood, and without the shedding of blood there is no forgiveness of sins.

Christ's Sacrifice Takes Away Sin

23 Thus it was necessary for the sketches of the heavenly things to be purified with these rites, but the heavenly things themselves need better sacrifices than these. [24]For Christ did not enter a sanctuary made by human hands, a mere copy of the true one, but he entered into heaven itself, now to appear in the presence of God on our behalf. [25]Nor was it to offer himself again and again, as the high priest enters the Holy Place year after year with blood that is not his own; [26]for then he would have had to suffer again and again since the foundation of the world. But as it is, he has appeared once for all at the end of the age to remove sin by the sacrifice of himself. [27]And just as it is appointed for mortals to die once, and after that the

[v] The Greek word used here means both *covenant* and *will* [w] Other ancient authorities lack *and goats* [x] Or *tabernacle*

judgment, [28]so Christ, having been offered once to bear the sins of many, will appear a second time, not to deal with sin, but to save those who are eagerly waiting for him.

Christ's Sacrifice Once for All

10 Since the law has only a shadow of the good things to come and not the true form of these realities, it[y] can never, by the same sacrifices that are continually offered year after year, make perfect those who approach. [2]Otherwise, would they not have ceased being offered, since the worshipers, cleansed once for all, would no longer have any consciousness of sin? [3]But in these sacrifices there is a reminder of sin year after year. [4]For it is impossible for the blood of bulls and goats to take away sins. [5]Consequently, when Christ[z] came into the world, he said,

"Sacrifices and offerings you have not
        desired,
    but a body you have prepared for me;
[6] in burnt offerings and sin offerings
    you have taken no pleasure.
[7] Then I said, 'See, God, I have come to
        do your will, O God'
    (in the scroll of the book[a] it is
        written of me)."

[8]When he said above, "You have neither desired nor taken pleasure in sacrifices and offerings and burnt offerings and sin offerings" (these are offered according to the law), [9]then he added, "See, I have come to do your will." He abolishes the first in order to estab-

lish the second. [10]And it is by God's will[b] that we have been sanctified through the offering of the body of Jesus Christ once for all.

11 And every priest stands day after day at his service, offering again and again the same sacrifices that can never take away sins. [12]But when Christ[c] had offered for all time a single sacrifice for sins, "he sat down at the right hand of God," [13]and since then has been waiting "until his enemies would be made a footstool for his feet." [14]For by a single offering he has perfected for all time those who are sanctified. [15]And the Holy Spirit also testifies to us, for after saying,

[16] "This is the covenant that I will make
        with them
    after those days, says the Lord:
    I will put my laws in their hearts,
        and I will write them on their
            minds,"
[17]he also adds,
    "I will remember[d] their sins and their
            lawless deeds no more."

[18]Where there is forgiveness of these, there is no longer any offering for sin.

A Call to Persevere

19 Therefore, my friends,[e] since we have confidence to enter the sanctuary by the blood of Jesus, [20]by the new and living way

---

[y] Other ancient authorities read *they*   [z] Gk *he*
[a] Meaning of Gk uncertain   [b] Gk *by that will*
[c] Gk *this one*   [d] Gk *on their minds and I will
remember*   [e] Gk *Therefore, brothers*

10:1–18. *The old order is ended.* It very much mattered to the writer that every reader really grasped the points that were being made and Heb. 10 reiterates much of what has already been said. It was necessary to be absolutely certain that they understood the difference between the old covenant expressed in Judaism and the new covenant expressed in Christ. They must realize that with the coming and sacrifice of Jesus the old order really was ended and abolished. Once an offering had been made which brings forgiveness of sins and purification of the conscience, then an order which is entirely based on the continual bringing of sin offerings is redundant. Christ has done the job. He is perfect and his work is perfect.

THE IMPLICATIONS OF FAITH (HEB. 10:19–35)

19–25. *'Therefore, my friends . . .'* Everything that has been considered so far has been in preparation for the conclusions which will now be drawn. All the arguments about the high priesthood of Jesus lead directly on to this. Teaching about Jesus, who he is and what he has done

that he opened for us through the curtain (that is, through his flesh), [21]and since we have a great priest over the house of God, [22]let us approach with a true heart in full assurance of faith, with our hearts sprinkled clean from an evil conscience and our bodies washed with pure water. [23]Let us hold fast to the confession of our hope without wavering, for he who has promised is faithful. [24]And let us consider how to provoke one another to love and good deeds, [25]not neglecting to meet together, as is the habit of some, but encouraging one another, and all the more as you see the Day approaching.

26 For if we willfully persist in sin after having received the knowledge of the truth, there no longer remains a sacrifice for sins, [27]but a fearful prospect of judg-ment, and a fury of fire that will consume the adversaries. [28]Anyone who has violated the law of Moses dies without mercy "on the testimony of two or three witnesses." [29]How much worse punishment do you think will be deserved by those who have spurned the Son of God, profaned the blood of the covenant by which they were sancti-fied, and outraged the Spirit of grace? [30]For we know the one who said, "Vengeance is mine, I will repay." And again, "The Lord will judge his people." [31]It is a fearful thing to fall into the hands of the living God.

32 But recall those earlier days when, after you had been enlightened, you endured a hard struggle with sufferings, [33]sometimes being publicly exposed to abuse and persecution, and sometimes

---

is not simply abstract doctrine, something to which we give our assent and then walk away from, it has a direct effect on our lives. Vv. 19–21 summarize the significance of the previous section. Since Jesus is our great high priest and since he has opened up the way into God's pres-ence for us – then let us take full advantage of that. There is nothing now to stop us drawing near to God, so let us do it!

There are three challenges given: (1) 'Approach with a true heart.' Come to God recognizing that sin really has been dealt with. Because of this we can have confidence in our own right to be there with God. This is what salvation is all about – being able to be comfortable in God's presence. (2) 'Hold fast to the confession of our hope.' Hope rather than faith is used here probably because it is more comprehensive. Note the link between hope and faith in 11:1. The basis of our confidence is again the character of the one who promised. (3) 'Provoke one another to love and good deeds.' Our faith is not a private thing. It is important to ensure as individuals that we hold fast to our own confession, stand firm on our own beliefs, but we always do this in a corporate context. The need for mutual support and encouragement is made explicit throughout the New Testament.

26–31. A warning. The warning against turning away from the gospel found in Heb. 6 is repeated and developed here in very strong terms. Having spoken of their hope and the way in which Christ has opened up the path into God's presence, the author again reminds them of the alter-native. There is no doubt here about the uniqueness of Christ and of the work of Christ as the only means of salvation. For anyone who has once learned of Christ but has rejected him, looking for some other way of reaching God, there is no hope at all. The only alternative to sal-vation in Christ is judgment. The use of terms like 'willfully persist in sin' and 'spurned' makes it clear that the reference is not to someone who backslides a little or slips away or who does not really understand. It is the one who in deliberate and calculated fashion rejects the message of the gospel for whom there is no hope. This really emphasizes the awesome nature of God. The fact that we can come freely into his presence with confidence does not lessen God's greatness.

32–39. Keep on keeping on. The readers are encouraged to use their memories, to focus on what their faith has meant to them in the past, the way they were enabled to cope in very difficult situ-ations. They did have confidence and that must not be thrown away. Rather they must endure and use the experiences of the past to lead them on into the future. V. 39 provides the link with Heb. 11. The writer and readers belong not to those who reject the gospel but to those who stand firm, the company of faith. They stand alongside the great names in the list of Old Testament believers about to be introduced.

being partners with those so treated. [34]For you had compassion for those who were in prison, and you cheerfully accepted the plundering of your possessions, knowing that you yourselves possessed something better and more lasting. [35]Do not, therefore, abandon that confidence of yours; it brings a great reward. [36]For you need endurance, so that when you have done the will of God, you may receive what was promised.

[37] For yet "in a very little while,
> the one who is coming will come
> > and will not delay;

[38] but my righteous one will live by faith.
> My soul takes no pleasure in anyone
> > who shrinks back."

[39]But we are not among those who shrink back and so are lost, but among those who have faith and so are saved.

The Meaning of Faith

11 Now faith is the assurance of things hoped for, the conviction of things not seen. [2]Indeed, by faith[f] our ancestors received approval. [3]By faith we understand that the worlds were prepared by the word of God, so that what is seen was made from things that are not visible.[g]

◆ Most people have a particular heroine or hero that they identify with or particularly admire; for children it is often television characters or pop stars, for adults the options are more varied but there seems to be a widespread human tendency to have somebody that we put on a pedestal. The New Testament is aware of this tendency and of both the strengths and the dangers of such an approach.

Bible characters are, in sermons and children's Bible study material, often presented as heroic figures and Christians are encouraged to identify with them. This can be a tremendously helpful activity. As in Heb. 11 we can see these characters as an encouragement and sometimes a model, we can learn from the way that God worked in their lives and draw strength from that as we continue in our own pilgrimage. The same can be true of stories of Christians in more modern times. However, men and women in the Bible are never portrayed as super-people. We are always given a realistic picture which includes strengths and failings, joys and sorrows. It is important not to expect too much of any human hero or heroine, whether a biblical character or not. We must beware in particular of thinking of a particular person as an ideal Christian. To do that almost inevitably leads to the situation where, when any failings become apparent, as is bound eventually to happen, we feel that the whole Christian faith has somehow lost its credibility. To look to role models, respecting them, valuing their experience, learning from their example is good. But putting them on a pedestal in a way that denies them their humanity is not fair to them, to ourselves or to the gospel.

---

[f] Gk *by this*   [g] Or *was not made out of visible things*

EXAMPLES OF FAITH (HEB. 11:1–40)

1–3. *A definition.* What is faith? That is faith in general terms, not 'the Christian faith' which has been so clearly defined. In this context the use of Old Testament believers is perfectly appropriate. Faith gives meaning to things that have not yet happened or makes you sure that they will happen. Faith is the proof of the reality of 'things not seen'. The hoped for things are not just a vague abstraction. It is as if faith is the attitude and dedication of the believer and hope the state of mind of those who have believed, but the 'things hoped for' are the very specific results of promises. 'By faith we understand' (v. 3), faith comes first and then faith makes understanding possible. The definition of faith here is slightly different from that found elsewhere. James uses the word to refer simply to doctrinal belief, Paul uses it for full commitment to Christ, but here it seems to be used more for the whole quality of life.

> The only hero who can be seen in that way as a faultless ideal is of course Christ himself ◆

The Examples of Abel, Enoch, and Noah

4 By faith Abel offered to God a more acceptable[h] sacrifice than Cain's. Through this he received approval as righteous, God himself giving approval to his gifts; he died, but through his faith[i] he still speaks. [5]By faith Enoch was taken so that he did not experience death; and "he was not found, because God had taken him." For it was attested before he was taken away that "he had pleased God." [6]And without faith it is impossible to please God, for whoever would approach him must believe that he exists and that he rewards those who seek him. [7]By faith Noah, warned by God about events as yet unseen, respected the warning and built an ark to save his household; by this he condemned the world and became an heir to the righteousness that is in accordance with faith.

The Faith of Abraham

8 By faith Abraham obeyed when he was called to set out for a place that he was to receive as an inheritance; and he set out, not knowing where he was going. [9]By faith he stayed for a time in the land he had been promised, as in a foreign land, living in tents, as did Isaac and Jacob, who were heirs with him of the same promise. [10]For he looked forward to the city that has foundations, whose architect and builder is God. [11]By faith he received power of procreation, even though he was too old – and Sarah herself was barren – because he considered him faithful who had promised.[i] [12]Therefore from one person, and this one as good as dead, descendants were born, "as many as the stars of heaven and as the innumerable grains of sand by the seashore."

13 All of these died in faith without having received the promises, but from a distance they saw and greeted them. They confessed that they were strangers and foreigners on the earth, [14]for people who speak in this way make it clear that they are seeking a homeland. [15]If they had been thinking of the land that they had left behind, they would have had opportunity to return. [16]But as it is, they desire a better country, that is, a heavenly one. Therefore God is not ashamed to be called their God; indeed, he has prepared a city for them.

[h] Gk *greater* [i] Gk *through it* [j] Other ancient authorities read *By faith Sarah herself, though barren, received power to conceive, even when she was too old, because she considered him faithful who had promised.*

4–40. *Faithful men and women.* The list of people who have shown faith is given in order to illustrate what is meant by faith and to encourage them in their own faith. Faith is portrayed very much as active, described by action rather than by attitude. It is a kind of committed piety that worked, but there are many different ways in which it can be worked out. Abel, Enoch, Abraham, Sarah, Isaac, Jacob, Moses' parents and all the others each trusted in God in a slightly different way. Their faith had many different aspects and stresses, sometimes obedience was the key, sometimes giving, sometimes sharing, sometimes overcoming obstacles, always relationship with God. The majority of the heroic figures here (though many of them were by no means heroic in the usual sense) are men. The most commonly told stories of the author's time as those in Victorian and some modern Sunday Schools were about such men. However, any implication that faith itself is restricted to men is set aside by the reference to women in general in v. 35, to Sarah in v. 11, Moses' parents in v. 23 and Rahab in v. 31. It is significant that the one woman mentioned in her own right is this foreign prostitute, perhaps deliberately included as a warning against restricting faith to those of acceptable race, background or gender. But the gender of the faithful people listed should not prevent readers, whether men or women from noting and learning from their example.

17 By faith Abraham, when put to the test, offered up Isaac. He who had received the promises was ready to offer up his only son, [18]of whom he had been told, "It is through Isaac that descendants shall be named for you." [19]He considered the fact that God is able even to raise someone from the dead – and figuratively speaking, he did receive him back. [20]By faith Isaac invoked blessings for the future on Jacob and Esau. [21]By faith Jacob, when dying, blessed each of the sons of Joseph, "bowing in worship over the top of his staff." [22]By faith Joseph, at the end of his life, made mention of the exodus of the Israelites and gave instructions about his burial.[k]

The Faith of Moses

23 By faith Moses was hidden by his parents for three months after his birth, because they saw that the child was beautiful; and they were not afraid of the king's edict.[l] [24]By faith Moses, when he was grown up, refused to be called a son of Pharaoh's daughter, [25]choosing rather to share ill-treatment with the people of God than to enjoy the fleeting pleasures of sin. [26]He considered abuse suffered for the Christ[m] to be greater wealth than the treasures of Egypt, for he was looking ahead to the reward. [27]By faith he left Egypt, unafraid of the king's anger; for he persevered as though[n] he saw him who is invisible. [28]By faith he kept the Passover and the sprinkling of blood, so that the destroyer of the firstborn would not touch the firstborn of Israel.[o]

The Faith of Other Israelite Heroes

29 By faith the people passed through the Red Sea as if it were dry land, but when the Egyptians attempted to do so they were drowned. [30]By faith the walls of Jericho fell after they had been encircled for seven days. [31]By faith Rahab the prostitute did not perish with those who were disobedient,[p] because she had received the spies in peace.

32 And what more should I say? For time would fail me to tell of Gideon, Barak, Samson, Jephthah, of David and Samuel and the prophets – [33]who through faith conquered kingdoms, administered justice, obtained promises, shut the mouths of lions, [34]quenched raging fire, escaped the edge of the sword, won strength out of weakness, became mighty in war, put foreign armies to flight. [35]Women received their dead by resurrection. Others were tortured, refusing to accept release, in order to obtain a better resurrection. [36]Others suffered mocking and flogging, and even chains and imprisonment. [37]They were stoned to death, they were sawn in two,[q] they were killed by the sword; they went about in skins of sheep and goats, destitute, persecuted, tormented – [38]of whom the world was not worthy. They wandered in deserts and mountains, and in caves and holes in the ground.

39 Yet all these, though they were commended for their faith, did not receive what was promised, [40]since God had provided something better so that they would not, apart from us, be made perfect.

---

[k] Gk *his bones*   [l] Other ancient authorities add *By faith Moses, when he was grown up, killed the Egyptian, because he observed the humiliation of his people* (Gk *brothers*)   [m] Or *the Messiah*   [n] Or *because*   [o] Gk *would not touch them*   [p] Or *unbelieving*   [q] Other ancient authorities add *they were tempted*

The element of future hope in the faith demonstrated here is very strong (vv. 13, 39–40). They never saw the full working out of promises made, but were able to envisage and expect that working out from a long distance away.

The Example of Jesus

12 Therefore, since we are surrounded by so great a cloud of witnesses, let us also lay aside every weight and the sin that clings so closely,[1] and let us run with perseverance the race that is set before us, [2]looking to Jesus the pioneer and perfecter of our faith, who for the sake of[2] the joy that was set before him endured the cross, disregarding its shame, and has taken his seat at the right hand of the throne of God.

3 Consider him who endured such hostility against himself from sinners,[3] so that you may not grow weary or lose heart. [4]In your struggle against sin you have not yet resisted to the point of shedding your blood. [5]And you have forgotten the exhortation that addresses you as children –
"My child, do not regard lightly the
        discipline of the Lord,
    or lose heart when you are punished
        by him;
[6] for the Lord disciplines those whom
        he loves,
    and chastises every child whom he
        accepts."
[7]Endure trials for the sake of discipline. God is treating you as children; for what child is there whom a parent does not discipline? [8]If you do not have that discipline in which all children share, then you are illegitimate and not his children. [9]Moreover, we had human parents to discipline us, and we respected them. Should we not be even more willing to be subject to the Father of spirits and live? [10]For they disciplined us for a short time as seemed best to them, but he disciplines us for our good, in order that we may share his holiness. [11]Now, discipline always seems painful rather than pleasant at the time, but later it yields the peaceful fruit of righteousness to those who have been trained by it.

12 Therefore lift your drooping hands and strengthen your weak knees, [13]and make straight paths for your feet, so that what is lame may not be put out of joint, but rather be healed.

Warnings against Rejecting God's Grace

14 Pursue peace with everyone, and the holiness without which no one will see the

---

[1] Other ancient authorities read *sin that easily distracts*   [2] Or *who instead of*   [3] Other ancient authorities read *such hostility from sinners against themselves*

THE PIONEER OF FAITH (HEB. 12:1-29)

1–2. *The race to be run.* The argument completes a full circle and brings us back to the focal point, Jesus as 'the pioneer and perfecter of our faith'. The point of including this list of faithful people is that they too should encourage us as we follow the trail blazed out for us by Jesus. The 'cloud of witnesses' calls to mind both those who give testimony – that the effort of following Christ is worth it – and those who stand in the arena watching our efforts and urging us on in our own race.

3–17. *The discipline to be endured.* The fact that things can sometimes be very bad indeed is not a reason for throwing in the towel and giving it all up. The writer's certainty of that does not take away from the real pastoral concern for those who suffer such difficulties. Three suggestions are made as to ways of looking at their situation to help them more easily bear it: (1) Think about Jesus and the hostility he faced, and be encouraged at the thought of standing alongside him. (2) Consider that there are those who are in a worse situation; these particular readers have not yet suffered torture or death and others certainly have. (3) Look on it as discipline, something which is given by God because he loves us and which is for our ultimate blessing. Something which seems hard at the time but which will bring benefits unobtainable in any other way. Thus the challenge is given to use their difficulties as a booster rather than a barrier in their ongoing progress. The encouragement is to gather one's resources and keep heading for the blessing to come rather than dropping out of the race at this stage. The fact that the path for the believer will involve difficulty, effort and endurance is taken for granted.

Lord. [15]See to it that no one fails to obtain the grace of God; that no root of bitterness springs up and causes trouble, and through it many become defiled. [16]See to it that no one becomes like Esau, an immoral and godless person, who sold his birthright for a single meal. [17]You know that later, when he wanted to inherit the blessing, he was rejected, for he found no chance to repent,[u] even though he sought the blessing[v] with tears.

[18] You have not come to something[w] that can be touched, a blazing fire, and darkness, and gloom, and a tempest, [19]and the sound of a trumpet, and a voice whose words made the hearers beg that not another word be spoken to them. [20](For they could not endure the order that was given, "If even an animal touches the mountain, it shall be stoned to death." [21]Indeed, so terrifying was the sight that Moses said, "I tremble with fear.") [22]But you have come to Mount Zion and to the city of the living God, the heavenly Jerusalem, and to innumerable angels in festal gathering, [23]and to the assembly[x] of the firstborn who are enrolled in heaven, and to God the judge of all, and to the spirits of the righteous made perfect, [24]and to Jesus, the mediator of a new covenant, and to the sprinkled blood that speaks a better word than the blood of Abel.

[25] See that you do not refuse the one who is speaking; for if they did not escape when they refused the one who warned them on earth, how much less will we escape if we reject the one who warns from heaven! [26]At that time his voice shook the earth; but now he has promised, "Yet once more I will shake not only the earth but also the heaven." [27]This phrase, "Yet once more," indicates the removal of what is shaken – that is, created things – so that what cannot be shaken may remain. [28]Therefore, since we are receiving a kingdom that cannot be shaken, let us give thanks, by which we offer to God an acceptable worship with reverence and awe; [29]for indeed our God is a consuming fire.

Service Well-Pleasing to God

13 Let mutual love continue. [2]Do not neglect to show hospitality to strangers, for by doing that some have entertained angels without knowing it. [3]Remember those who are in prison, as though you were in prison with them; those who are being tortured, as though you yourselves were being tortured.[y] [4]Let

[u] Or no chance to change his father's mind   [v] Gk it
[w] Other ancient authorities read a mountain   [x] Or angels, and to the festal gathering [23]and assembly
[y] Gk were in the body

18–29. *The unshakeable Kingdom.* A final reminder that all the difficulty, endurance and effort is worth it. The author reminds them of the greatness of the hope towards which they are striving. The inauguration of the first covenant was awesome enough but the Kingdom to which through Christ they belong, the heavenly Kingdom is infinitely more glorious. The continuing themes of the book are brought together here, the supremacy of the new order over the old, the focus on Jesus, who he is and what he has achieved and the fact that belonging to God's people has practical implications. The wonder of belonging to the great heavenly Kingdom and the awesome terrible consequences of rejecting God's Word are also restressed. V. 29 brings us another 'therefore . . . let us' parallel to those seen in 10:19–25 and in 12:1. In this instance it is let us worship God as he ought to be worshiped.

FINAL COMMENTS (HEB. 13:1–25)

1–7. *Live like Christians.* It is as if the author has now got off his chest this tremendous burden for them caused by the fear that they might possibly be contemplating moving away from their faith and back into Judaism. They have been shown why and how this is so completely unthinkable. Now there is time and space to encourage them in their general Christian living. The

marriage be held in honor by all, and let the marriage bed be kept undefiled; for God will judge fornicators and adulterers. [5]Keep your lives free from the love of money, and be content with what you have; for he has said, "I will never leave you or forsake you." [6]So we can say with confidence,

"The Lord is my helper;
I will not be afraid.
What can anyone do to me?"

7 Remember your leaders, those who spoke the word of God to you; consider the outcome of their way of life, and imitate their faith. [8]Jesus Christ is the same yesterday and today and forever. [9]Do not be carried away by all kinds of strange teachings; for it is well for the heart to be strengthened by grace, not by regulations about food,[z] which have not benefited those who observe them. [10]We have an altar from which those who officiate in the tent[a] have no right to eat. [11]For the bodies of those animals whose blood is brought into the sanctuary by the high priest as a sacrifice for sin are burned outside the camp.

[12]Therefore Jesus also suffered outside the city gate in order to sanctify the people by his own blood. [13]Let us then go to him outside the camp and bear the abuse he endured. [14]For here we have no lasting city, but we are looking for the city that is to come. [15]Through him, then, let us continually offer a sacrifice of praise to God, that is, the fruit of lips that confess his name. [16]Do not neglect to do good and to share what you have, for such sacrifices are pleasing to God.

17 Obey your leaders and submit to them, for they are keeping watch over your souls and will give an account. Let them do this with joy and not with sighing – for that would be harmful to you.

18 Pray for us; we are sure that we have a clear conscience, desiring to act honorably in all things. [19]I urge you all the more to do this, so that I may be restored to you very soon.

---

[z] Gk *not by foods*   [a] Or *tabernacle*

---

necessity for showing concern for other believers and in particular for strangers and any who are imprisoned or ill-treated is brought up. V. 3 calls to mind the 'one body' imagery used by Paul. The fact that the marriage covenant is taken seriously by God and must therefore also be honored by them is stressed. The primary reference here is to avoiding sexual immorality and unfaithfulness but he may also be speaking out against sexual asceticism that saw marriage as a lesser state than celibacy. The dangers of materialism are introduced; it was as much a danger then as it is today. Dependence on money can take away dependence on God, but money will fail whereas we can have absolute confidence in God's help. They are to look back to the ones who brought them to Christ and take encouragement from their lives. Faith and lifestyle must not and cannot be separated.

8–16. *Hold fast to the truth.* Do not be carried away by anybody who tries to persuade you that some kind of new laws must be kept, or new experiences must be obtained before we can really be in relationship with God. No, Jesus never changes, his sacrifice on our behalf is as effective today as when we first believed and will be so for ever. The truth of the gospel remains the same. The sacrifice that is looked for is not the animal sacrifices that they wanted to return to but praising God, doing good and sharing what you have. The author seems to be thinking here of Mic. 6:8: 'what does the LORD require of you but to do justice, and to love kindness, and to walk humbly with your God?'

17–19. *Obey and pray.* They are called to have the right attitude to their leaders actually following their lead. Note the assumptions here about Christian leadership, which as always in the New Testament is about service and responsibility rather than about control or power – leaders could not force them to obey and are nowhere ever called upon to enforce obedience, that is the responsibility of the followers. The leaders here are those who brought them to Christ and continue to proclaim the true gospel. The author then asks his readers for their personal prayer. He has done his best to help them and now it is as if he is asking that they do not reject him for saying all this but rather pray for him. Concern and love for the readers comes across again, he longs to be reunited with them.

Benediction

20 Now may the God of peace, who brought back from the dead our Lord Jesus, the great shepherd of the sheep, by the blood of the eternal covenant, [21]make you complete in everything good so that you may do his will, working among us[b] that which is pleasing in his sight, through Jesus Christ, to whom be the glory forever and ever. Amen.

Final Exhortation and Greetings

22 I appeal to you, brothers and sisters,[c] bear with my word of exhortation, for I have written to you briefly. [23]I want you to know that our brother Timothy has been set free; and if he comes in time, he will be with me when I see you. [24]Greet all your leaders and all the saints. Those from Italy send you greetings. [25]Grace be with all of you.[d]

[b] Other ancient authorities read *you*   [c] Gk *brothers*
[d] Other ancient authorities add *Amen*

20–25. *A closing prayer and a PS*. He prays for them that God, who raised Jesus from the dead, may enable them to do his will in all things. The focus in this lovely benediction is again on Jesus which sums up the point of all that has been said. He longs for them to have the full benefits of living their lives in God's presence, walking in God's will, and prays earnestly that this might happen.

The PS gives information about Timothy and brings greetings to the rest of the church, confirming the view that this letter was not sent to a whole church but to a particular group within it.

THE LETTER OF
JAMES

INTRODUCTION

This letter, has been likened to a number of different ancient writings including the book of Proverbs, a diatribe (an abusive speech, popular among Greek moral teachers), a collection of sermon notes or an exhortation. It has a strong Jewish orientation with many Old Testament quotes or allusions. But its message is immersed in the teaching of Jesus, referring on numerous occasions to the Sermon on the Mount.

There have always been questions concerning its authorship and place among the New Testament writings because it does not have direct apostolic authority. It has frequently been attributed to James, the brother of Jesus (Mark 6:3), who became leader of the early Jerusalem church and is mentioned with the apostles several times in Acts 1:14; 15:13–21; Gal. 1:19; 2:12; 1 Cor. 15:9.

Its intended readers are most likely to have been Jewish Christians in the first decades of the Christian church. They needed encouragement to work out the faith in their daily lives. The social situation behind this writing is typical of Jerusalem before its fall in AD 70. Merchants travelled widely seeking profits and wealthy land owners were oppressing poor laboring classes. Extreme poverty resulted (James 2:15). Violence and immorality were common and may have been part of the Christian community (2:11; 4:2).

This writing contributes significantly to our understanding of the teaching of the early Christian community. The author uses vivid imagery and paints strongly contrasting pictures. He communicates to his readers with a gentle love and a forthright honesty, calling them brothers and sisters, beloved, senseless persons, murderers, adulterers. He calls them to faithfulness and perseverance in the face of suffering, persecution and trials.

Salutation

1 James, a servant[a] of God and of the Lord Jesus Christ,

To the twelve tribes in the Dispersion: Greetings.

Faith and Wisdom

2 My brothers and sisters,[b] whenever you face trials of any kind, consider it nothing but joy, [3]because you know that the testing of your faith produces endurance; [4]and let endurance have its full effect, so that you may be mature and complete, lacking in nothing.

5 If any of you is lacking in wisdom, ask God, who gives to all generously and

---

◆ Wisdom for the believer is in fundamental contrast with the world's wisdom. It is knowledge of, and obedience to, God's way and will. God alone gives it generously to those who ask expecting to receive. Those suffering trials and testings of the faith receive it, thus enabling their perseverance. Some may boast about their wisdom, but if their lives contain envy and selfish ambition then disorder and wickedness will result. Their wisdom is not of God but is a lie from the devil. Their teaching is to be rejected. Wisdom produces God-like living, similar to the fruit of the Spirit ◆

---

ungrudgingly, and it will be given you. [6]But ask in faith, never doubting, for the one who doubts is like a wave of the sea, driven

---

◆ James believes that the Christian should relate to God in all life's circumstances including joy, suffering and sickness. His words in 5:14–16 seem to promise complete healing if certain

---

circumstances are fulfilled. On occasions God does work through these means, however it is not always so. James is not giving a fail-proof pattern for having prayers answered. In both Old and New Testament times God answered many different believing prayers. Jesus adopted no set method of healing. Mark's pattern (6:13) is the only similar one in the Bible.

In following these words, James uses Elijah's prayer for rain to be withheld and later given, as an example of God's answering believing prayer. This was of great importance to Elijah because many people of his day were leaving the worship of the Lord and turning to Baal, the Canaanite god who had particular responsibility for the weather. Elijah prayed so that God's power over the rain (and Baal), would be evident to everyone. God's name was vindicated and his glory shown.

When prayers are not answered, some defend James' words by seeking somewhere to lay the blame – maybe a lack in the amount or quality of the faith being exercised (1:6–7), selfish motives (4:3), unconfessed sin or unrighteousness of life (5:16). These could be valid reasons. Sickness may be caused by sin (see the paralysed man, John 5:14). Confession of sin may be part of physical healing (James 5:16). But Jesus taught that sometimes suffering is God's purpose, to reveal his works (see the blind man, John 9:1–3) and display his compassionate and merciful nature (James 5:11).

The psalmist observes that evil comes on the godly as well as the ungodly, and sometimes more so! The death of Jesus on the cross, shows God working out his glorious purposes through suffering. Paul could testify to the same in his experience (2 Cor. 1:8–9; 4:7–11; 12:7–10).

---

[a] Gk *slave*   [b] Gk *brothers*

JAMES 1

1. Dispersion Jews were scattered among the nations including those in Acts 2:9–11 from the eighth century BC. The twelve tribes as such no longer existed. James uses the expression to describe Christians, the new people of God, scattered as a result of persecution.

James commands his readers to count trials nothing but joy because of the anticipated endurance, maturity and completeness which God will bring (1:2–4). He encourages his readers to wait patiently and persevere in a similar way to the prophets and Job, who though faithful to God knew suffering and hardship. The Lord will come. He will act with judgment and compassion (5:7–11).

Believing prayer rather than seeking to relieve difficult circumstances should be for perseverance in trials and that God's glory may be shown. On some occasions he will work miraculously. At other times he will give his grace and strength to endure ◆

and tossed by the wind; [7, 8]for the doubter, being double-minded and unstable in every way, must not expect to receive anything from the Lord.

Poverty and Riches

9 Let the believer[c] who is lowly boast in being raised up, [10]and the rich in being brought low, because the rich will disappear like a flower in the field. [11]For the sun rises with its scorching heat and withers the field; its flower falls, and its beauty perishes. It is the same way with the rich; in the midst of a busy life, they will wither away.

Trial and Temptation

12 Blessed is anyone who endures temptation. Such a one has stood the test and will receive the crown of life that the Lord[d] has promised to those who love him. [13]No one, when tempted, should say, "I am being tempted by God"; for God cannot be tempted by evil and he himself tempts no one. [14]But one is tempted by one's own desire, being lured and enticed by it; [15]then, when that desire has conceived, it gives birth to sin, and that sin, when it is fully grown, gives birth to death. [16]Do not be deceived, my beloved.[e]

17 Every generous act of giving, with every perfect gift, is from above, coming down from the Father of lights, with whom there is no variation or shadow due to change.[f] [18]In fulfillment of his own purpose

[c] Gk *brother*   [d] Gk *he*; other ancient authorities read *God*   [e] Gk *my beloved brothers*   [f] Other ancient authorities read *variation due to a shadow of turning*

---

8. A double-minded person has loyalties divided between God and the world.

9. Most Christians in the early church were poor, powerless and of low status. But they belonged to God's Kingdom and already enjoyed a spiritual status which would one day be apparent when they joined the ascended Christ in the heavenlies (Eph. 4:8).

10. Though the rich have status and power now it has no lasting value. Both poor and rich Christians alike find their only true and lasting boasting in identifying with Christ and the lowliness of his death on the cross.

12. The 'crown of life' refers to a head wreath given to the victor in the Greek games. Eternal life is the reward of those who faithfully persevere through suffering and temptation.

13. God does allow obedience to be tested, in order to strengthen faith, not to destroy it. God cannot be blamed for sin.

14–15. Here the female, 'desire', is seen as a seductress luring, conceiving and giving birth to sin, which grows and finally results in death.

17. The phrase 'Father of lights' acknowledges God's creative work in the sun, moon and stars. Though these bodies are in a continual cycle of change, there is no variation in the Father's constancy.

18. The imagery of God as mother giving us birth complements the 'father' imagery in v. 17. It is used to describe God's bringing his people to new birth through the gospel. In Lev. 23:9–10 first fruit belong to God and show that all is really his. Early believers are as first fruit indicating the full harvest of God's redemption is coming.

he gave us birth by the word of truth, so that we would become a kind of first fruits of his creatures.

Hearing and Doing the Word

19 You must understand this, my beloved:[g] let everyone be quick to listen, slow to speak, slow to anger; [20]for your anger does not produce God's righteousness. [21]Therefore rid yourselves of all sordidness and rank growth of wickedness, and welcome with meekness the implanted word that has the power to save your souls.

22 But be doers of the word, and not merely hearers who deceive themselves. [23]For if any are hearers of the word and not doers, they are like those who look at themselves[h] in a mirror; [24]for they look at themselves and, on going away, immediately forget what they were like. [25]But those who look into the perfect law, the law of liberty, and persevere, being not hearers who forget but doers who act – they will be blessed in their doing.

26 If any think they are religious, and do not bridle their tongues but deceive their hearts, their religion is worthless.

◆ James warns his readers, with a number of colorful metaphors, that their speech is causing quarrels and splits among their number. Their behavior includes arrogant boasting, speaking behind one another's backs, criticism, anger, lack of truthfulness and grumbling. This certainly bears no resemblance to God's righteousness. He expects obedience which includes control of one's tongue, otherwise a person's religion is worthless. As the body of a horse is controlled by a bit in its mouth, so self-control learned in guarding the mouth from sin will enable believers to conquer whatever other bodily temptations may arise.

Control of speech particularly applies to teachers within the church community. James includes himself as he warns teachers of a stricter measure of judgment, for they are responsible to God for those they teach as well as themselves. It is hard to avoid mistakes, and to be consistently helpful in speaking to and about others, but enormous evil, spreading quickly like a forest fire, can result from misuse of the tongue even though it seems only small ◆

[27]Religion that is pure and undefiled before God, the Father, is this: to care for orphans and widows in their distress, and to keep oneself unstained by the world.

[g] Gk *my beloved brothers*   [h] Gk *at the face of his birth*

---

19. Being quick to listen is wise advice to promote harmony in the community. It may also relate to being quick to hear God's Word.

21. 'Sordidness' is used of filthy clothes and dirty morals. The expression 'rank growth' bespeaks abundance of wickedness and emphasizes its variety and extent. The gospel is 'implanted' after birth, and changes a person's very being.

23–25. The person looking in a mirror, goes away and forgets with no lasting effects. The contrast is with one who pores over the law of liberty in the Scriptures, and then acts upon it. This has lasting results.

26. 'Religion' describes outward acts of worship of a god. For a Christian the real test of religion is obedience, without which all is empty.

27. Pure religion includes caring for widows and orphans. These are the most helpless and easily exploited in society. As the heavenly Father cares, so must his children. Old Testament obligations include seeking justice, correcting oppression and defending their cause, expecting no repayment (Is. 1:17). Pure religion also involves keeping oneself unpolluted by the value system of the surrounding society.

◆ In James' day most believers were poor. Those designated as rich are probably wealthy landowners, who scorn the faith, by intimidating and exploiting poor laborers, sometimes on their own confiscated lands. James encourages believers to patiently wait for God, who will hear and comfort them and bring judgment to those who defraud and selfishly live in luxury. Jesus and the Old Testament taught that God has a particular concern for the pious poor and oppressed. God expects his people to reflect his concerns, helping to meet the needs of the poor, including women and children. By favoring the rich, the church neglects the poor, and the system which produced their oppression and exploitation is perpetuated ◆

Warning against Partiality

2 My brothers and sisters,[i] do you with your acts of favoritism really believe in our glorious Lord Jesus Christ?[j] ²For if a person with gold rings and in fine clothes comes into your assembly, and if a poor person in dirty clothes also comes in, ³and if you take notice of the one wearing the fine clothes and say, "Have a seat here, please," while to the one who is poor you say, "Stand there," or, "Sit at my feet,"[k] ⁴have you not made distinctions among yourselves, and become judges with evil thoughts? ⁵Listen, my beloved brothers and sisters.[l] Has not God chosen the poor in the world to be rich in faith and to be heirs of the kingdom that he has promised to those who love him? ⁶But you have dishonored the poor. Is it not the rich who oppress you? Is it not they who drag you into court? ⁷Is it not they who blaspheme the excellent name that was invoked over you?

8 You do well if you really fulfill the royal law according to the scripture, "You shall love your neighbor as yourself." ⁹But if you show partiality, you commit sin and are convicted by the law as transgressors. ¹⁰For whoever keeps the whole law but fails in one point has become accountable for all of it. ¹¹For the one who said, "You shall not commit adultery," also said, "You shall not murder." Now if you do not commit adultery but if you murder, you have become a transgressor of the law. ¹²So speak and so act as those who are to be judged by the law of liberty. ¹³For judgment will be without mercy to anyone who has shown no mercy; mercy triumphs over judgment.

[i] Gk *My brothers*   [j] Or *hold the faith of our glorious Lord Jesus Christ without acts of favoritism*   [k] Gk *Sit under my footstool*
[l] Gk *brothers*

JAMES 2

2–3. James contrasts a rich man (the Greek includes 'man') with a poor person (the Greek can include both sexes). If poor women and children are to be cared for (1:27), they should be equally honored and graciously welcomed into the Christian community.

4. Judges were frequently motivated by bribes and evil thinking instead of righteousness. Christians acting unfairly to others behave similarly.

5. James does not include all poor or exclude all rich in the Kingdom. Future blessings are for the chosen, who are rich in faith and love God.

7. The term 'excellent name' probably refers to the practice of calling upon the name of Jesus in baptism. It is incredible that the rich, who blaspheme and do not confess his name, are given preferential treatment over those who honor his name.

8. 'The royal law' could be referring to (1) the Old Testament Law as a whole, given by God's royal authority, or (2) Christ's (the King's) summation of all the Law under the command to love, or (3) God's entire will for those in his Kingdom.

13. God will judge the merciless with severity. Only those who show mercy and love coming from Christ to the needy can expect God's forgiveness at the last judgment.

Faith without Works Is Dead

14 What good is it, my brothers and sisters,[m] if you say you have faith but do not have works? Can faith save you? [15]If a brother or sister is naked and lacks daily food, [16]and one of you says to them, "Go in peace; keep warm and eat your fill," and yet you do not supply their bodily needs, what is the good of that? [17]So faith by itself, if it has no works, is dead.

◆ James is combating an under-emphasis on works. He describes faith as not just intellectual assent (demons do that, 2:19) but as a firm, unwavering commitment to Christ as Lord (2:1), even when tested by trials (1:2–4). Good works are produced by true faith, proving conversion is real (2:24). He says little about the conversion experience except that it is God's gift and purpose (1:18). He uses 'righteousness' as did the Jews, to describe being declared innocent because the facts have been judged.

Some believe James is contradicting Paul. However, Paul deals with different aspects of justification and faith. He counters the Jewish idea of gaining salvation by works and Law-keeping (Rom. 3:28). To Paul, faith is the response to God's offer declaring sinners right in his sight. Righteousness is God's gift. He justifies them, transferring them from the realm of sin and death into holiness and life (Rom. 4:5).

Both writers use Abraham as the great example of faith. James shows Abraham's willingness to sacrifice Isaac as evidence of faith and works (Gen. 15:6). Paul (Rom. 4:1–12) shows his belief, which was reckoned as righteousness.

James then shocks his readers by using Rahab (also Jesus' ancestor: Matt. 1:1, 5) as an example (James 2:25). Jewish men would have been insulted to be given a woman, especially a prostitute, as an example. Rahab is praised, not for her lifestyle, but for her faith in action (Heb. 11:31). She heard of God's mighty acts for his covenant people, believed he had given her land to Israel and helped the spies escape (Josh. 2) ◆.

18 But someone will say, "You have faith and I have works." Show me your faith apart from your works, and I by my works will show you my faith. [19]You believe that God is one; you do well. Even the demons believe – and shudder. [20]Do you want to be shown, you senseless person, that faith apart from works is barren? [21]Was not our ancestor Abraham justified by works when he offered his son Isaac on the altar? [22]You see that faith was active along with his works, and faith was brought to completion by the works. [23]Thus the scripture was fulfilled that says, "Abraham believed God, and it was reckoned to him as righteousness," and he was called the friend of God. [24]You see that a person is justified by works and not by faith alone. [25]Likewise, was not Rahab the prostitute also justified by works when she welcomed the messengers and sent them out by another road? [26]For just as the body without the spirit is dead, so faith without works is also dead.

Taming the Tongue

3 Not many of you should become teachers, my brothers and sisters,[m] for you know that we who teach will be judged with greater strictness. [2]For all of us make many mistakes. Anyone who makes no mistakes in speaking is perfect, able to keep the whole body in check with a bridle. [3]If we put bits into the mouths of horses to make them obey us, we guide their whole bodies. [4]Or look at ships: though they are so large that it takes strong winds to drive them, yet they are guided by a very small rudder wherever the will of the pilot directs. [5]So also the tongue is a small member, yet it boasts of great exploits.

[m] Gk *brothers*

How great a forest is set ablaze by a small fire! [6]And the tongue is a fire. The tongue is placed among our members as a world of iniquity; it stains the whole body, sets on fire the cycle of nature,[n] and is itself set on fire by hell.[o] [7]For every species of beast and bird, of reptile and sea creature, can be tamed and has been tamed by the human species, [8]but no one can tame the tongue – a restless evil, full of deadly poison. [9]With it we bless the Lord and Father, and with it we curse those who are made in the likeness of God. [10]From the same mouth come blessing and cursing. My brothers and sisters,[p] this ought not to be so. [11]Does a spring pour forth from the same opening both fresh and brackish water? [12]Can a fig tree, my brothers and sisters,[p] yield olives, or a grapevine figs? No more can salt water yield fresh.

Two Kinds of Wisdom

13 Who is wise and understanding among you? Show by your good life that your works are done with gentleness born of wisdom. [14]But if you have bitter envy and selfish ambition in your hearts, do not be boastful and false to the truth. [15]Such wisdom does not come down from above, but is earthly, unspiritual, devilish. [16]For where there is envy and selfish ambition, there will also be disorder and wickedness of every kind. [17]But the wisdom from above is first pure, then peaceable, gentle, willing to yield, full of mercy and good fruits, without a trace of partiality or hypocrisy. [18]And a harvest of righteousness is sown in peace for[q] those who make peace.

Friendship with the World

4 Those conflicts and disputes among you, where do they come from? Do they not come from your cravings that are at war within you? [2]You want something and do not have it; so you commit murder. And you covet[r] something and cannot obtain it; so you engage in disputes and conflicts. You do not have, because you do not ask. [3]You ask and do not receive, because you ask wrongly, in order to spend what you get on your pleasures. [4]Adulterers! Do you not know that friendship with the

[n] Or *wheel of birth*   [o] Gk *Gehenna*   [p] Gk *My brothers*   [q] Or *by*   [r] Or *you murder and you covet*

JAMES 3

6. The general meaning of this text is clear, but its details are difficult to interpret. The tongue represents the evil world present in the body often giving the first indication of sin's presence. Its evil influence and destructive nature spreads, because its evil originates in hell.

17. The qualities of God's wisdom as outlined here, are sometimes seen as more appropriate for women than men. God's way is very different from the world's. Christ-like behavior is for all his people, regardless of gender, and shows what humanity was designed to be like.

18. A proverb. Wisdom results in right living which is shown by peace in the community of God (Jesus' words, Matt. 5:9).

JAMES 4

1. James is not so much concerned with the various viewpoints in the disputes (military imagery) in the church as with the reasons contributing to them. These reasons resulted from selfish, lustful desires pursuing pleasure.

2. Where covetousness and unrestrained desires exist, violence breeds, and murder may eventuate. Rather than manipulating, competing or fighting for one's desires, the believer should pray.

4–5. The Greek is feminine, i.e. 'adulteresses', reminding Jews of God's Old Testament accusations of unfaithfulness to their covenant relationship (marriage vows) with him as they worshiped idols (Hos. 1–3). Here James accuses Christ's bride, the church, of being unfaithful in following the world. As a spurned husband God jealously desires her full devotion. The exact passage James quotes is not known. Cf. Exod. 20:5.

world is enmity with God? Therefore whoever wishes to be a friend of the world becomes an enemy of God. [5]Or do you suppose that it is for nothing that the scripture says, "God[s] yearns jealously for the spirit that he has made to dwell in us"? [6]But he gives all the more grace; therefore it says,

"God opposes the proud,
     but gives grace to the humble."
[7]Submit yourselves therefore to God. Resist the devil, and he will flee from you. [8]Draw near to God, and he will draw near to you. Cleanse your hands, you sinners, and purify your hearts, you double-minded. [9]Lament and mourn and weep. Let your laughter be turned into mourning and your joy into dejection. [10]Humble yourselves before the Lord, and he will exalt you.

Warning against Judging Another

11 Do not speak evil against one another, brothers and sisters.[t] Whoever speaks evil against another or judges another, speaks evil against the law and judges the law; but if you judge the law, you are not a doer of the law but a judge. [12]There is one lawgiver and judge who is able to save and to destroy. So who, then, are you to judge your neighbor?

Boasting about Tomorrow

13 Come now, you who say, "Today or tomorrow we will go to such and such a town and spend a year there, doing business and making money." [14]Yet you do not even know what tomorrow will bring. What is your life? For you are a mist that appears for a little while and then vanishes. [15]Instead you ought to say, "If the Lord wishes, we will live and do this or that." [16]As it is, you boast in your arrogance; all such boasting is evil. [17]Anyone, then, who knows the right thing to do and fails to do it, commits sin.

Warning to Rich Oppressors

5 Come now, you rich people, weep and wail for the miseries that are coming to you. [2]Your riches have rotted, and your clothes are moth-eaten. [3]Your gold and silver have rusted, and their rust will be evidence against you, and it will eat your flesh like fire. You have laid up treasure[u] for the last days. [4]Listen! The wages of the laborers who mowed your fields, which you kept back by fraud, cry out, and the cries of the harvesters have reached the ears of the Lord of hosts. [5]You have lived on

[s] Gk *He*   [t] Gk *brothers*   [u] Or *will eat your flesh, since you have stored up fire*

---

8. These people are 'double-minded', half-hearted Christians. James commands them to be committed in their hearts to God alone.

9. In the prophetic language of mourning James calls God's people to repent. In the Old Testament, laughter is that of unbelief (Sarah, Gen. 18:12) or the fool (Eccl. 7:6). Neither take sin or God's judgment seriously. The Christian is to be serious about sin not superficial and frivolous.

11. James warns people who habitually speak unkindly behind others' backs, to stop. They do not carry out the law of love; and their actions proclaim to the world that they think it is they who have authority, not the law.

JAMES 5

1–3. James, in prophetic vein, calls for the rich to mourn, their riches being of no hope for the future. Money and clothing are traditional forms of wealth. Hoarding leads only to decay, moths and rust. Wealth would be better used for the poor. Unless they repent they will be damned.

5. The rich have lived in self-indulgence, ignoring the just needs of the poor. James, using Jewish imagery, describes God judging them as animals fattened up, ready to be sacrificed, slaughtered and eaten.

the earth in luxury and in pleasure; you have fattened your hearts in a day of slaughter. [6]You have condemned and murdered the righteous one, who does not resist you.

Patience in Suffering

[7] Be patient, therefore, beloved,[v] until the coming of the Lord. The farmer waits for the precious crop from the earth, being patient with it until it receives the early and the late rains. [8]You also must be patient. Strengthen your hearts, for the coming of the Lord is near.[w] [9]Beloved,[v] do not grumble against one another, so that you may not be judged. See, the Judge is standing at the doors! [10]As an example of suffering and patience, beloved,[v] take the prophets who spoke in the name of the Lord. [11]Indeed we call blessed those who showed endurance. You have heard of the endurance of Job, and you have seen the purpose of the Lord, how the Lord is compassionate and merciful.

[12] Above all, my beloved,[v] do not swear, either by heaven or by earth or by any other oath, but let your "Yes" be yes and your "No" be no, so that you may not fall under condemnation.

The Prayer of Faith

[13] Are any among you suffering? They should pray. Are any cheerful? They should sing songs of praise. [14]Are any among you sick? They should call for the elders of the church and have them pray over them, anointing them with oil in the name of the Lord. [15]The prayer of faith will save the sick, and the Lord will raise them up; and anyone who has committed sins will be forgiven. [16]Therefore confess your sins to one another, and pray for one another, so that you may be healed. The prayer of the righteous is powerful and effective. [17]Elijah was a human being like us, and he prayed fervently that it might not rain, and for three years and six months it did not rain on the earth. [18]Then he prayed again, and the heaven gave rain and the earth yielded its harvest.

[19] My brothers and sisters,[x] if anyone among you wanders from the truth and is brought back by another, [20]you should know that whoever brings back a sinner from wandering will save the sinner's[y] soul from death and will cover a multitude of sins.

[v] Gk brothers   [w] Or is at hand   [x] Gk My brothers
[y] Gk his

---

9. Grumbling against one another is a serious temptation for members of a community under pressure. It is a common sin condemned by God. Believers are urged to 'get their house in order' before he comes shortly to judge.

11. As with Job, those who endure will be blessed. The Christian can expect God to work for good. His nature is 'extremely compassionate' (a term apparently created by the church or James to describe this unique quality of God).

12. Jews swore using an oath to guarantee the truth of a statement and invoke God's condemnation if they lied. Truthfulness is a quality of great importance for followers of Jesus. A simple 'yes' or 'no' should be enough (Matt. 5:34–37).

14. Use of the anointing oil is unclear. It may be that (1) Oil was used for medicinal purposes. Thus elders who came were to use both physical and spiritual means of healing. (2) Oil was a sign to show God's grace to heal and stimulate faith.

15. As the elders pray, if sin is the cause of particular sickness, then healing will include both body and soul.

16. God hears the voice of all (men, women and children) who are single-minded in devotion to him and committed to his will. That is the great power and effectiveness of prayer.

19–20. Believers who see others among them, moving away from and rejecting the faith, should seek in love and humility to bring them back. If they succeed, then a sinner has been forgiven and saved from judgment. Those who do not persevere in the faith will be lost.

THE FIRST LETTER OF PETER

INTRODUCTION

This letter has remarkable contemporary relevance. It was written around AD 64 when Christians were suffering for their faith and the persecution of Nero had begun. It speaks across the centuries to the many believers in different countries today who are suffering persecution, harassment, or discrimination. It was written to encourage those who were bewildered by all they faced and gives practical advice and guidance. There are indications that it was originally intended for those preparing for baptism.

Peter's letter focuses on the mercy and grace of God and the implications for discipleship. He speaks of how Christians should behave in various social settings and concludes the letter by addressing directly the issues of opposition and suffering. The practical teaching on discipleship and social relations makes the letter relevant to all believers and while its purpose was to encourage those in a hostile environment, it applies to all Christians as they relate to others and cope with indifference or discord because of their faith.

The letter was written by Peter, the original leader of the apostles. He mentions he is writing from Babylon (5:13) which is a code name for Rome, to congregations in Turkey, which were in Peter's day the four Roman provinces of northern Asia Minor (1:1). From the letter it would appear that the readers are a mixed group of people including converts from pagan backgrounds, wives with unbelieving husbands and slaves with unbelieving masters.

Salutation

1 Peter, an apostle of Jesus Christ,
To the exiles of the Dispersion in
Pontus, Galatia, Cappadocia, Asia, and
Bithynia, ²who have been chosen and
destined by God the Father and sanctified
by the Spirit to be obedient to Jesus Christ
and to be sprinkled with his blood:

May grace and peace be yours in abundance.

A Living Hope

3 Blessed be the God and Father of our
Lord Jesus Christ! By his great mercy he
has given us a new birth into a living hope
through the resurrection of Jesus Christ
from the dead, ⁴and into an inheritance that
is imperishable, undefiled, and unfading,
kept in heaven for you, ⁵who are being
protected by the power of God through faith
for a salvation ready to be revealed in the
last time. ⁶In this you rejoice,ᵃ even if now
for a little while you have had to suffer
various trials, ⁷so that the genuineness of
your faith – being more precious than gold
that, though perishable, is tested by fire –
may be found to result in praise and glory
and honor when Jesus Christ is revealed.
⁸Although you have not seenᵇ him, you love

◆ In *The Abolition of Man* C. S. Lewis
argues that modern men see suffering as
a scandal which needs to be overcome
whereas premodern men understood suffering differently. The lessons we might
learn are not the purpose of suffering and
our attempts at finding a purpose behind
suffering are likely to make God a sadist.

Indeed, God created a perfect world
without suffering (Gen 1:31). It is only
after sin entered this world that pain,
conflict, and death started to trouble our
lives which were meant to be spent in
peace and harmony with God.

Because our situation was so hopeless
after the Fall, God brought about the
remedy himself when he became man in
Christ in order to deliver us from sin and
its effects. It is because of Christ's death
and resurrection that we Christians have
the hope for eternal life after death where
there will be no more suffering. This
is the reason why Peter can say that
suffering is only temporary and does not
govern the whole of our life even if our
pains should never end in this world.

Since suffering is the result of sin, our

ᵃ Or *Rejoice in this*   ᵇ Other ancient authorities
read *known*

INTRODUCTORY GREETING (1 PET. 1:1–2)

Peter gives his credentials as an apostle and addresses the readers as those who are elect and
chosen but also exiled and scattered, which gives the theme of the letter in embryo form, God's
people in a hostile world. The familiar words of grace and peace sum up the whole of Christian
teaching, God's reconciling and undeserved love to his people.

THE BASIS OF CHRISTIAN HOPE (1 PET. 1:3–12)

3–5. Whatever the apparent discouragement there are always grounds for hope for God's people.
Words which are familiar and are paralleled in 2 Cor. 1:3 and Eph. 1:3 provide a framework
reminding the readers of God's mercy, that is his love and compassion. Through spiritual birth
readers have a hope of eternal dimensions and the promise of an inheritance being kept safely by
God.
6–7. Christians can rejoice, while facing difficulties, because of their future hope. Suffering
happens only as God allows and for a little while. This is important for when in pain or facing
distress the suffering seems unending. Further, suffering can purify faith proving it authentic
and increasing Christ's glory.
8–9. Unlike the writer of this letter, those reading it had not seen Jesus in the flesh. Despite this
they are filled with a depth of elation through their relationship with him and have already
experienced their salvation which has a present and a future dimension.

own suffering can make us aware of the sinfulness of this world and of ourselves. It forces us to think about the causes of pain more deeply than we do when our life runs along smoothly. Sometimes suffering is the direct result of our own personal sin and it thus offers us an opportunity to come to our senses and to repent (Ps. 51; 2 Sam. 12). But very often suffering does not have any discernible cause and we will struggle to find an answer as Job did whose questions about reasons for suffering were only brought to silence when he encountered God (Job 38–42).

Suffering challenges our assumption that our life is ordered. This is a very important lesson to learn in an age where health and success are the cherished ideals of the majority. Many Psalms reflect the fact that life is chaotic and unpredictable and they do not offer any solution as to why this is so and why God allows evil things to happen to those who love him. Their openendedness allows us, too, to come with our questions to God (Ps. 88).

Suffering can also teach us to recognize and acknowledge our own weakness and frailty. When we fail in our attempts to end pain we realize that we need to trust in God and to develop our relationship to him. God can then use our weakness to display his strength in our lives. This is what Paul means when he claims that he delights in weakness and hardship (2 Cor. 7–10). This is also the basic teaching of many saints over the centuries: We need to learn to put God first and to consecrate everything to him.

A great comfort for Christians must be the fact that they are not alone in their suffering. Christ himself suffered and understands what we feel. We must realize that his suffering did not only consist of the last few days of his life. His

life was continuous suffering because to encounter misunderstanding, sin, illness, and death over 30 years brought unceasing sorrow to his sinless soul. His sigh in Matt. 17:17 allows us a glimpse at his daily suffering. He has promised to his followers that he will not leave them alone. Therefore they will never have to go through the experience of being abandoned by God which he himself went through for their sake.

Another source of comfort for the Christian must be the church as the community which represents Christ here on earth. But this will only become reality if Christians do not attempt to blame the sufferer for his or her own suffering in the way Job's friends did. The responsibility of Christians who are not at present suffering themselves is to be listening and caring friends to those in physical or mental pain and to build up friendships with fellow Christians that will sustain them when they need help ◆

him; and even though you do not see him now, you believe in him and rejoice with an indescribable and glorious joy, ⁹for you are receiving the outcome of your faith, the salvation of your souls.

10 Concerning this salvation, the prophets who prophesied of the grace that was to be yours made careful search and inquiry, ¹¹inquiring about the person or time that the Spirit of Christ within them indicated when it testified in advance to the sufferings destined for Christ and the subsequent glory. ¹²It was revealed to them that they were serving not themselves but you, in regard to the things that have now been announced to you through those who brought you good news by the Holy Spirit sent from heaven – things into which angels long to look!

10–12. What the prophets foretold has been fulfilled, which gives a strong foundation for future hope. The same Holy Spirit who inspired the prophets is the one who makes real the gospel message of salvation which even God's messengers, the angels, long to know about.

A Call to Holy Living

13 Therefore prepare your minds for action;[c] discipline yourselves; set all your hope on the grace that Jesus Christ will bring you when he is revealed. [14]Like obedient children, do not be conformed to the desires that you formerly had in ignorance. [15]Instead, as he who called you is holy, be holy yourselves in all your conduct; [16]for it is written, "You shall be holy, for I am holy."

17 If you invoke as Father the one who judges all people impartially according to their deeds, live in reverent fear during the time of your exile. [18]You know that you were ransomed from the futile ways inherited from your ancestors, not with perishable things like silver or gold, [19]but with the precious blood of Christ, like that of a lamb without defect or blemish. [20]He was destined before the foundation of the world, but was revealed at the end of the ages for your sake. [21]Through him you have come to trust in God, who raised him from the dead and gave him glory, so that your faith and hope are set on God.

22 Now that you have purified your souls by your obedience to the truth[d] so that you have genuine mutual love, love one another deeply[e] from the heart.[f] [23]You have been born anew, not of perishable but of imperishable seed, through the living and enduring word of God.[g] [24]For

"All flesh is like grass
    and all its glory like the flower of
        grass.
The grass withers,
    and the flower falls,
[25] but the word of the Lord endures
        forever."

That word is the good news that was announced to you.

The Living Stone and a Chosen People

2 Rid yourselves, therefore, of all malice, and all guile, insincerity, envy, and all slander. [2]Like newborn infants, long for the pure, spiritual milk, so that by it you may grow into salvation – [3]if indeed you have tasted that the Lord is good.

4 Come to him, a living stone, though rejected by mortals yet chosen and precious

[c] Gk *gird up the loins of your mind*   [d] Other ancient authorities add *through the Spirit*   [e] Or *constantly*   [f] Other ancient authorities read *a pure heart*   [g] Or *through the word of the living and enduring God*

HOLINESS AND OBEDIENCE (1 PET. 1:13–2:3)

1:13–16. The call to hope is not a wistful dream but a practical reality which requires a response. Peter demands positive action, obedience and holiness. At one time before faith, believers' lives were shaped by values and behavior which were sinful but now that they know God their lives should be shaped by his values and teaching.

1:17–21. The readers are reminded of the enormous price paid for their hope and faith and they are exhorted to live in the knowledge of God as father and judge.

1:22–25. Peter focuses on the Christian community and emphasizes that love in the church is a priority. Love is possible because of the new life in Christ and that love should be as enduring as God's word from which it originates.

2:1–3. Everything which is contrary to love is to be rejected. Peter is concerned about spiritual maturity and the development of the Christian community. The vices listed are to be rejected and God's people should increase their appetite for the spiritual nourishment of the teaching of the Word of God.

THE SPIRITUAL HOUSE AND A CHOSEN PEOPLE (1 PET. 2:4–10)

4–6. Becoming a Christian means becoming part of the Church, the two cannot be separated. Peter paraphrases Ps. 118:22 to emphasize Christ as the living stone and the foundation of the spiritual house of which believers become a part. When Christians meet together they become a

in God's sight, and ⁵like living stones, let yourselves be built[h] into a spiritual house, to be a holy priesthood, to offer spiritual sacrifices acceptable to God through Jesus Christ. ⁶For it stands in scripture:

"See, I am laying in Zion a stone,
    a cornerstone chosen and precious;
and whoever believes in him[i] will not
        be put to shame."

⁷To you then who believe, he is precious; but for those who do not believe,

"The stone that the builders rejected
    has become the very head of the
        corner,"

⁸and

"A stone that makes them stumble,
    and a rock that makes them fall."

They stumble because they disobey the word, as they were destined to do.

9 But you are a chosen race, a royal priesthood, a holy nation, God's own people,[j] in order that you may proclaim the mighty acts of him who called you out of darkness into his marvelous light. ¹⁰ Once you were not a people,
    but now you are God's people;

once you had not received mercy,
    but now you have received mercy.

Live as Servants of God

11 Beloved, I urge you as aliens and exiles to abstain from the desires of the flesh that wage war against the soul. ¹²Conduct yourselves honorably among the Gentiles, so that, though they malign you as evildoers, they may see your honorable deeds and glorify God when he comes to judge.[k]

13 For the Lord's sake accept the authority of every human institution,[l] whether of the emperor as supreme, ¹⁴or of governors, as sent by him to punish those who do wrong and to praise those who do right. ¹⁵For it is God's will that by doing right you should silence the ignorance of the foolish. ¹⁶As servants[m] of God, live as free people, yet do not use your freedom as

[h] Or *you yourselves are being built*   [i] Or *it*
[j] Gk *a people for his possession*   [k] Gk *God on the day of visitation*   [l] Or *every institution ordained for human beings*   [m] Gk *slaves*

---

temple based on Christ and they offer spiritual sacrifices. Therefore, the Jerusalem Temple is no longer needed.

7–8. In Peter's time as today, Christians were in a minority. Peter explains to first-century Christians as he does to us that widespread unbelief was anticipated in the Old Testament and should not surprise us. The living stone which is the focus of our faith is rejected by others and causes them to stumble.

9–10. Peter encourages Christians to realize they are special. They are chosen by God through Jesus and they are a royal priesthood having access to God because of the sacrifice of Christ. Further, Christians are a holy people with a responsibility to live differently from others because they belong to God. Using images from Hosea, Peter shows how God has reached out to them in his grace and kindness.

CHRISTIAN BEHAVIOR IN THE WORLD (1 PET. 2:11–3:12)

2:11–12. Every generation of Christians finds itself alienated from the world. The values and goals of the world are not the values and goals of Christians. These verses emphasize that God's people should be different and that the temptations of contemporary society are to be resisted. More than that, Christians should live such exemplary lives that God's work in their lives will be recognized even by those who oppose them.

2:13–17. Peter encourages Christians to make a positive impact in their community and to show themselves as model citizens. Obedience to and respect for authorities is important because the authorities are appointed by God for the benefit of all. (Anarchy only benefits the minority who are powerful.) Christians should be active so far as doing good is concerned and they should be careful not to do wrong or to use their freedom in Christ as a cover for unprincipled activities.

a pretext for evil. [17]Honor everyone. Love the family of believers.[n] Fear God. Honor the emperor.

The Example of Christ's Suffering

18 Slaves, accept the authority of your masters with all deference, not only those who are kind and gentle but also those who are harsh. [19]For it is a credit to you if, being aware of God, you endure pain while suffering unjustly. [20]If you endure when you are beaten for doing wrong, what credit is that? But if you endure when you do right and suffer for it, you have God's approval. [21]For to this you have been called, because Christ also suffered for you, leaving you an example, so that you should follow in his steps.

[22] "He committed no sin,
    and no deceit was found in his
        mouth."

[23]When he was abused, he did not return abuse; when he suffered, he did not threaten; but he entrusted himself to the one who judges justly. [24]He himself bore our sins in his body on the cross,[o] so that, free from sins, we might live for righteousness; by his wounds[p] you have been healed. [25]For you were going astray like sheep, but now you have returned to the shepherd and guardian of your souls.

Wives and Husbands

3 Wives, in the same way, accept the authority of your husbands, so that, even if some of them do not obey the word, they may be won over without a word by their wives' conduct, [2]when they see the purity and reverence of your lives. [3]Do not adorn yourselves outwardly by braiding your hair, and by wearing gold ornaments or fine clothing; [4]rather, let your adornment be the inner self with the lasting beauty of a gentle and quiet spirit, which is very precious in God's sight. [5]It was in this way long ago that

[n] Gk *Love the brotherhood*   [o] Or *carried up our sins in his body to the tree*   [p] Gk *bruise*

2:18–20. The social structure which accepted slavery was different from social structures today. Peter is not condoning the evil structure of slavery and the suffering and indignity which surrounds it. He is teaching against personal retaliation but does not preclude social action against such injustice. This teaching relates to contemporary Christians as it links to employee and employer relations. The heart of what Peter is saying is that all our social relationships should develop from our relationship with God and our desire to do his will. Within that framework Christians should be seen to be meeting their obligations within the social relationships in which they find themselves.

2:21–25. Peter moves into a description of the suffering Christ drawn from Is. 53 to encourage suffering slaves that they have an example. Peter stresses that Jesus suffered physically, unjustly and that he endured the suffering patiently without attacking or condemning those who abused him leaving judgment of his abusers to God. To know that Jesus suffered unjustly does not take away physical pain but gives strength to maintain faith and hope (see note on 'Lessons to be learned from unexplained suffering', p. 504).

3:1–2. The emphasis of this teaching is winning husbands for Christ. Converted wives were in a difficult position because the conventions of the time required them to be submissive, but by becoming a Christian they had shown some independence and assertiveness. Therefore, Peter argues the wives should seek to please their husbands in all other ways. They should be prepared to use their freedom in Christ to observe the restraints of their unbelieving husband and be an example of godliness in their own home. This, of course, does not mean submitting to abuse, which would *not* glorify God. For Christian couples there should be mutual respect and a joint seeking of God's will.

3:3–6. In most cultures the outward appearance of women is highly valued. Peter overturns these values and teaches that it is the inner character which is important, not outward decoration. Christian wives are to display a reverence for God, gentleness of spirit and purity. In these days of changed roles for men and women these verses are not easy to interpret but the emphasis on inner character and the respect and honoring of others should be recognized.

the holy women who hoped in God used to adorn themselves by accepting the authority of their husbands. 6Thus Sarah obeyed Abraham and called him lord. You have become her daughters as long as you do what is good and never let fears alarm you.

7 Husbands, in the same way, show consideration for your wives in your life together, paying honor to the woman as the weaker sex,[q] since they too are also heirs of the gracious gift of life – so that nothing may hinder your prayers.

◆ The phrase which is in older translations rendered as 'the weaker vessel' is often misunderstood and has been used to devalue women. A careful reading of the text reveals that that was not Peter's intention. What Peter says about the way husbands are to treat their wives at first sight seems to balance what he has said to wives about their relationship to their husbands. In vv. 1–6 Peter seems to confirm traditional values about women held at this time. But he is talking to women with husbands who are not Christians and who would therefore not have any reason to accept Christian values. In v. 7 Peter addresses husbands directly: As far as Christian husbands are concerned, there is no place for abuse of the power which society grants to them. Instead he demands respect from them for their wives as somebody weaker. This corresponds to the teaching in the Gospels that those who are regarded as unimportant in society and those who humble themselves are valued highly by God (Matt. 18:2–5; 19:30; 20:25–28) and must be valued by God's children.

The Greek term Peter uses for the word 'weak' describes a physical state. It is used to depict material things, often pottery, and also metaphorically of the human body expressing physical weakness. It does therefore not speak of moral or mental weakness as the phrase 'the weaker sex' does. In this point Peter clearly does not share the views of Greek and Roman culture which regarded women as inferior to men in all aspects.

If Peter had admonished the believing men to honor their wives despite the fact that they are weaker, the sense might have been denigrating. But Peter places the Christian wife on the same level as her husband, because they are both heirs of the same inheritance, eternal life, and that in a social context which did not have equal rights of inheritance for men and women.

Failure to show respect to one's wife has serious spiritual consequences: prayers will be hindered. This warning re-inforces Peter's message that mutual respect is an essential principle in Christian marriage which cannot be disregarded ◆

◆ Peter's second reason why husbands must respect their wives is that they need to do so in order that their prayers may not be hindered. This suggests that there is a correlation between abuse – the extreme form of disrespect – and lack of spiritual growth. This applies to both the abuser and the abused.

Victims of abuse are frequently the physically weaker members of a family: children, women, and also the elderly. Since they are not treated with respect they have a very negative view of themselves and are unable to see themselves as loved children of the heavenly Father. Because they are so helpless in the face of attacks against them they are also likely to develop strong feelings of hatred which can become a consuming passion in their lives that leaves no room for a loving relationship to God (see note on 'Avenues of recourse for a believer', p. 341).

[q] Gk *vessel*

3:7. A husband also has responsibilities within marriage. He is to show respect for his wife and to be considerate. While the wife may be physically weaker, they are equally God's chosen people and partners in his grace.

And what about the abuser? He or she was probably also abused as a child and is unable to see himself or herself with God's eyes and knows little of God's love. Abusers suffer from similar problems as their victims and they, too, need the help of the church community so that they can change their attitude and behavior to become more like Christ ◆

Suffering for Doing Right

8 Finally, all of you, have unity of spirit, sympathy, love for one another, a tender heart, and a humble mind. [9]Do not repay evil for evil or abuse for abuse; but, on the contrary, repay with a blessing. It is for this that you were called – that you might inherit a blessing. [10]For

"Those who desire life
     and desire to see good days,
let them keep their tongues from evil
     and their lips from speaking deceit;
[11] let them turn away from evil and do
          good;
     let them seek peace and pursue it.
[12] For the eyes of the Lord are on the
          righteous,
     and his ears are open to their prayer.

But the face of the Lord is against
     those who do evil."

13 Now who will harm you if you are eager to do what is good? [14]But even if you do suffer for doing what is right, you are blessed. Do not fear what they fear,[r] and do not be intimidated, [15]but in your hearts sanctify Christ as Lord. Always be ready to make your defense to anyone who demands from you an accounting for the hope that is in you; [16]yet do it with gentleness and reverence.[s] Keep your conscience clear, so that, when you are maligned, those who abuse you for your good conduct in Christ may be put to shame. [17]For it is better to suffer for doing good, if suffering should be God's will, than to suffer for doing evil. [18]For Christ also suffered[t] for sins once for all, the righteous for the unrighteous, in order to bring you[u] to God. He was put to death in the flesh, but made alive in the spirit, [19]in which also he went and made a proclamation to the spirits in prison, [20]who in former times did not obey, when God waited patiently in the days of Noah, during the building of the ark, in

[r] Gk *their fear*   [s] Or *respect*   [t] Other ancient authorities read *died*   [u] Other ancient authorities read *us*

3:8–12. Christians are urged to get on with others and to show love rather than be guided by self-interest. They are to adopt a non-retaliatory manner and not follow the natural human desire for vengeance when wronged. Peter supports his comments from Ps. 34.

COPING WITH SUFFERING AND OPPOSITION (1 PET. 3:13–22)

13–17. Peter was writing to people facing fierce hostility because of their Christian discipleship. For those today, whose faith is tolerated or ignored, the exhortation is the same: maintain the highest standards of behavior in all situations and if you suffer for being a Christian you will be compensated by God's blessing. The readers are encouraged not to fear those who abuse them but their thoughts should be dominated by God. In all situations they should be ready to explain their faith in a gracious manner and with patient endurance which are a powerful witness to those who persecute them.

18–22. The significance of Christ's sacrifice is set forth in these verses as a source of powerful encouragement to those facing persecution. Christ's death was a unique act bringing about forgiveness. Unlike Old Testament sacrifices, it needed no repetition. Peter emphasizes that those who are Christ's disciples have been saved whatever they might face.

Precisely what Jesus did between his death and resurrection is not clear. However, the main idea which Peter seeks to show in vv. 19–20a is that the power of God is greater than the power of evil and has a restraining effect on evil. Those confronted by evil and suffering have the comfort of knowing that God is stronger.

which a few, that is, eight persons, were saved through water. [21]And baptism, which this prefigured, now saves you – not as a removal of dirt from the body, but as an appeal to God for[v] a good conscience, through the resurrection of Jesus Christ, [22]who has gone into heaven and is at the right hand of God, with angels, authorities, and powers made subject to him.

Good Stewards of God's Grace

4 Since therefore Christ suffered in the flesh,[w] arm yourselves also with the same intention (for whoever has suffered in the flesh has finished with sin), [2]so as to live for the rest of your earthly life[x] no longer by human desires but by the will of God. [3]You have already spent enough time in doing what the Gentiles like to do, living in licentiousness, passions, drunkenness, revels, carousing, and lawless idolatry. [4]They are surprised that you no longer join them in the same excesses of dissipation, and so they blaspheme.[y] [5]But they will have to give an accounting to him who stands ready to judge the living and the dead. [6]For this is the reason the gospel was proclaimed even to

the dead, so that, though they had been judged in the flesh as everyone is judged, they might live in the spirit as God does.

[7] The end of all things is near;[z] therefore be serious and discipline yourselves for the sake of your prayers. [8]Above all, maintain constant love for one another, for love covers a multitude of sins. [9]Be hospitable to one another without complaining. [10]Like good stewards of the manifold grace of God, serve one another with whatever gift each of you has received. [11]Whoever speaks must do so as one speaking the very words of God; whoever serves must do so with the strength that God supplies, so that God may be glorified in all things through Jesus Christ. To him belong the glory and the power forever and ever. Amen.

Suffering as a Christian

[12] Beloved, do not be surprised at the fiery ordeal that is taking place among you to

---

[v] Or *a pledge to God from*   [w] Other ancient authorities add *for us*; others, *for you*   [x] Gk *rest of the time in the flesh*   [y] Or *they malign you*   [z] Or *is at hand*

Peter uses the example of the Flood and the Ark as a parallel for baptism and Christians. The Ark was a means of salvation for God's people, baptism is a means of salvation for those who have responded to the gospel message. Peter is using the term baptism to represent the whole process by which people come to faith and is not suggesting that baptism alone, without faith, brings salvation. Whatever the readers of this letter are experiencing, Peter drives home the fact that they are God's people who can have confidence in his power and salvation.

A CHRISTIAN LIFESTYLE (1 PET. 4:1–19)

1–6. Christ is the model to be copied; he suffered but was obedient to God. This is the pattern for Christians, they should live according to God's will, not according to sinful desires. When we live according to God's principles, we may suffer but that should set us more firmly against sin because sin causes additional suffering in people's lives.

The temptations which surrounded Christians of Peter's day are no different in many respects to the temptations of today. Self-indulgence, corruption and idolatry may have different expressions in each generation but they are essentially the same and those who are involved in such activities will have to answer to God. God will have the last word on those who have lived in disobedience and wickedness.

The meaning of v. 6 is not clear but the most helpful explanation is that 'the dead' are those who heard and responded to the gospel when they were alive and have since died. They will, of course, be judged as righteous in Christ. The Spirit is at work in the person's life. Peter warns that suffering should be for Christ and not because of criminal or unpleasant behavior.

test you, as though something strange were happening to you. [13]But rejoice insofar as you are sharing Christ's sufferings, so that you may also be glad and shout for joy when his glory is revealed. [14]If you are reviled for the name of Christ, you are blessed, because the spirit of glory,[a] which is the Spirit of God, is resting on you.[b] [15]But let none of you suffer as a murderer, a thief, a criminal, or even as a mischief maker. [16]Yet if any of you suffers as a Christian, do not consider it a disgrace, but glorify God because you bear this name. [17]For the time has come for judgment to begin with the household of God; if it begins with us, what will be the end for those who do not obey the gospel of God? [18]And

"If it is hard for the righteous to be saved,
what will become of the ungodly and the sinners?"

[19]Therefore, let those suffering in accordance with God's will entrust themselves to a faithful Creator, while continuing to do good.

Tending the Flock of God

5 Now as an elder myself and a witness of the sufferings of Christ, as well as one who shares in the glory to be revealed, I exhort the elders among you [2]to tend the flock of God that is in your charge, exercising the oversight,[c] not under compulsion but willingly, as God would have you do it[d] – not for sordid gain but eagerly. [3]Do not lord it over those in your charge, but be examples to the flock. [4]And when the chief shepherd appears, you will win the crown of glory that never fades away. [5]In the same way, you who are younger must accept the authority of the elders.[e] And all of you must clothe yourselves with humility in your dealings with one another, for

"God opposes the proud,
but gives grace to the humble."

6 Humble yourselves therefore under the mighty hand of God, so that he may exalt you in due time. [7]Cast all your anxiety on him, because he cares for you. [8]Discipline yourselves, keep alert.[f] Like a

[a] Other ancient authorities add *and of power*
[b] Other ancient authorities add *On their part he is blasphemed, but on your part he is glorified*
[c] Other ancient authorities lack *exercising the oversight*   [d] Other ancient authorities lack *as God would have you do it*   [e] Or *of those who are older*
[f] Or *be vigilant*

17–19. Peter means that the persecution of the church, the family of God, is an element of the greater judgment of God which will be passed on all people.

DIRECTIONS FOR CHURCH LEADERS (1 PET. 5:1–5)

1–4. Any organization depends on effective leadership to function and meet the needs of its members and good leadership in a Christian community facing persecution is essential. Peter takes the image of a shepherd as his framework for teaching about leadership. The leader's role is to protect, lead, guide and feed, and the motivation for leadership should be a desire to serve and not a desire for money. The leaders are to be an example, not seeking to control or gain power. Peter is not advocating a particular pattern of leadership. The New Testament shows a variety of styles of leadership, but Peter here is advocating certain qualities and characteristics of godly leadership.
5. There is an emphasis on young men being gracious and respectful of their elders. Possibly some tensions had arisen from young leaders becoming arrogant. The new life of Christian faith may have caused some to claim too much for themselves and to show too little respect for others.

CONCLUDING ADVICE (1 PET. 5:6–14)

6–9. Being a Christian is a balance between reliance on God and diligent activity. Believers are to rely on God's strength and give him their anxieties but they are also to be self-disciplined, alert and resist the devil. This active and passive blend is a difficult stance to maintain but it is important that Christians in all situations actively do what they can in reliance on God.

roaring lion your adversary the devil prowls around, looking for someone to devour. ⁹Resist him, steadfast in your faith, for you know that your brothers and sisters[g] in all the world are undergoing the same kinds of suffering. ¹⁰And after you have suffered for a little while, the God of all grace, who has called you to his eternal glory in Christ, will himself restore, support, strengthen, and establish you. ¹¹To him be the power forever and ever. Amen.

Final Greetings and Benediction

12 Through Silvanus, whom I consider a faithful brother, I have written this short letter to encourage you and to testify that this is the true grace of God. Stand fast in it. ¹³Your sister church[h] in Babylon, chosen together with you, sends you greetings; and so does my son Mark. ¹⁴Greet one another with a kiss of love.

Peace to all of you who are in Christ.[i]

[g] Gk *your brotherhood*   [h] Gk *She who is*   [i] Other ancient authorities add *Amen*

10–11. As Peter draws to the close of his letter he brings a promise of God's sheer love and care for his people in whatever situation they face. The final comment about God is that he loves and while his people may suffer for a while his purpose is for their future glory. In the meantime he will strengthen, sustain and restore them for he has the power to do this.

12–14. Peter restates his purpose of writing to encourage and to teach. He uses the customary format to close his letter referring to Babylon, a code name for Rome, as the place from which he writes. The traditional greeting of peace comes with fresh meaning as the rich understanding of all that God has done in Christ is remembered.

THE SECOND LETTER OF PETER

INTRODUCTION

This book is included among the catholic or general epistles because it is not directed to a specific congregation. Its author is identified as Simeon (or Simon) Peter who purports to have been an eyewitness of the 'majesty' of Jesus Christ and to have heard the voice from heaven that proclaimed on the mountain, 'This is my Son, my Beloved, with whom I am well pleased' (1:17, NRSV). The reference appears to be to the Transfiguration (cf. Matt. 17:5; Mark 9:7; Luke 9:35).

Authorship is traditionally assigned to Peter. However, many scholars believe that Simon Peter's name was used as a literary device (a practice not unknown in the early church) because it refers to concerns that are thought to have developed in the Christian community only at the end of the first and beginning of the second century after the death of Peter, the apostle. It also apparently uses material from the book of Jude, refers to Paul's letters in the past tense, and was not considered to be apostolic by early Christian leaders such as Eusebius (fourth century AD) who lists 2 Peter as a book that was known but not acknowledged. The theological teachings of the book were not disputed but its origins were unclear. It was one of the last books to enter the canon.

The book contains a testament, an exhortation and a warning. The first generations of Christians were passing away and as the church moved into the late first and early second century and away from predominantly Jewish to largely Gentile Christianity it had to find its way. There were concerns because of the delay in the expected imminent return of Jesus. False teachers were arising who were attempting to make Christianity more compatible with the baser aspects of the Roman world. From the diatribe delivered in 2 Peter, it appears that they taught that the threat of a judgment by God was a hoax, that Christians need not restrain themselves in matters of morality and that Jesus is not coming again. The book responds that confirmation of God's judgment is evident in that God has already judged the sinning angels, the generation of the Flood and Sodom and Gomorrah. Christians must be aware of the character and motivation of those who practise and teach licentiousness so as to avoid a slide into error. God is not delaying the return of Jesus. God functions according to a divine timetable that is not set to accord with limited human notions of time.

2 Peter is directed to both women and men (all who have received faith) in a Christian community that was under the political and cultural hegemony of the Roman Empire. Roman women enjoyed more general freedom than many others in the ancient world. They had some legal rights. They could inherit wealth in land and possessions. They could acquire an education, hold down a job, and enjoy the public amusements of the day. The 'mystery religions' that flourished at the time may have had a particular pull for women who could join them of their own free will. An important part of the Christian message was that women (and men) are free in Christ. This strong affirmation that women (and men) are capable of thinking and making decisions is evident in 2 Peter. The author presents a reasoned argument for his position that he expects his readers to understand. Freedom, however, is not to be expressed in licentiousness, but in a godliness that includes responsibility and accountability to Christ for one's actions. 2 Peter encourages women to remain faithful to God in the midst of the twisted teachings and the temptations of the society in which they lived.

Salutation

1 Simeon[a] Peter, a servant[b] and apostle of Jesus Christ,

To those who have received a faith as precious as ours through the righteousness of our God and Savior Jesus Christ:[c]

2 May grace and peace be yours in abundance in the knowledge of God and of Jesus our Lord.

The Christian's Call and Election

3 His divine power has given us everything needed for life and godliness, through the knowledge of him who called us by[d] his own glory and goodness. [4]Thus he has given us, through these things, his precious and very great promises, so that through them you may escape from the corruption that is in the world because of lust, and may become participants of the divine nature. [5]For this very reason, you must make every effort to support your faith with goodness, and goodness with knowledge, [6]and knowledge with self-control, and self-control with endurance, and endurance with godliness, [7]and godliness with mutual[e] affection, and mutual[e] affection with love. [8]For if these things are yours and are increasing among you, they keep you from being ineffective and unfruitful in the knowledge of our Lord Jesus Christ. [9]For anyone who lacks these things is nearsighted and blind, and is forgetful of the cleansing of past sins. [10]Therefore, brothers and sisters,[f] be all the more eager to confirm your call and election, for if you do this, you will never stumble. [11]For in this way, entry into the eternal kingdom of our Lord and Savior Jesus Christ will be richly provided for you.

12 Therefore I intend to keep on reminding you of these things, though you know them already and are established in the truth that has come to you. [13]I think it right, as long as I am in this body,[g] to refresh your memory, [14]since I know that my death[h] will come soon, as indeed our Lord Jesus Christ has made clear to me. [15]And I will make every effort so that after my departure you may be able at any time to recall these things.

[a] Other ancient authorities read *Simon*   [b] Gk *slave*   [c] Or *of our God and the Savior Jesus Christ*   [d] Other ancient authorities read *through*   [e] Gk *brotherly*   [f] Gk *brothers*   [g] Gk *tent*   [h] Gk *the putting off of my tent*

2 PETER 1

1–2. The style of the greeting is typical of the letter form found elsewhere in the New Testament. The author identifies himself and his readers. In this case, the reader is not a specific person or congregation but members of the community of faith. The word 'knowledge' mentioned in v. 2 and repeated four times in the first chapter should not be overlooked. 2 Peter is concerned about heresies that are entering the church. One of those heresies has come to be called 'Gnosticism' because it taught that secret knowledge was necessary for salvation. This is refuted by 2 Peter. It is only the knowledge of God and of Jesus that is needed.

3–11. In this section the notions of 'call' (vv. 3, 10) and 'election' (v. 10) are prominent. However, being called is not enough. Human beings must respond. They must build up themselves by shoring up faith with goodness, knowledge, self-control, endurance, godliness, mutual affection and love. These attributes will make them participants in the divine nature and fruitful, productive Christians who are able to escape the corruption that is in the world.

12–21. The author indicates that he is not introducing new ideas but the truth as the readers already know it. He knows that he will soon die. Eyewitnesses such as himself are dying out and he wants to make sure that the faith will continue untarnished. Vv. 20–21 allude to prophetic confirmation of the author's claim. Prophecies of Scripture, they affirm, have a divine origin. This is in sharp contrast to the 'cleverly devised myths' referred to in v. 16.

Eyewitnesses of Christ's Glory

16 For we did not follow cleverly devised myths when we made known to you the power and coming of our Lord Jesus Christ, but we had been eyewitnesses of his majesty. [17]For he received honor and glory from God the Father when that voice was conveyed to him by the Majestic Glory, saying, "This is my Son, my Beloved,[i] with whom I am well pleased." [18]We ourselves heard this voice come from heaven, while we were with him on the holy mountain.

19 So we have the prophetic message more fully confirmed. You will do well to be attentive to this as to a lamp shining in a dark place, until the day dawns and the morning star rises in your hearts. [20]First of all you must understand this, that no prophecy of scripture is a matter of one's own interpretation, [21]because no prophecy ever came by human will, but men and women moved by the Holy Spirit spoke from God.[j]

◆ In the Ancient Near East lamps were very important to everyday life. Some speculate that shells such as the conch or bivalve may have been the very first lamp vessels. This type of lamp was not very popular and was quickly replaced by clay lamps. The earliest lamps were merely bowls, filled with oil, with a wick extending from the oil, leaning against the limp of the rim. Eventually, the bowls were pinched on one side, retaining a well for the oil, while creating a spout for the wick.

Lamps continued to develop, so that by the late Hellenistic and early Roman periods they looked quite different from those of earlier periods. These lamps became much smaller, fitting into the palm of the hand and are referred to as 'Herodian' lamps, since Herod and his family ruled during the early first century. This is the type of lamp with which Jesus would have been familiar. Most lamps continued to be wheel made; however, molded lamps were gaining popularity. Bases of the Herodian lamps were wide

and flat, and the oil well was completely closed, save for a single hole through which oil could be poured. Lamps begin to show decoration around the spout and well opening.

Wicks were generally made from flax, either one strand or several strands twisted into one. This material was placed in the spout, with one end immersed into the oil and the other protruding slightly beyond the spout for the flame.

The most common form of fuel was olive oil. Since matches had yet to be invented, flint was used to ignite first. This was a very hard thing to do, thus it was crucial to keep existing fires burning. When properly attended, a lamp could burn for four or five hours. It was the responsibility of the women of the household to keep the lamps going. According to Prov. 31:15, a woman was considered to be a good wife when she could keep the lamps burning all night long. In order to assure perpetual burning, several tasks were performed. First, oil had to be provided. Flasks and oil vessels were always kept on hand, for constant replacement of fuel for the flame. Second, wicks had to be trimmed. The flame consumed portions of the wicks, and the carbonized portion of the wick had to be cut off in order to burn oil more efficiently. Wicks were trimmed with portions of old combs, small bone tools or twigs. The housewife would have to attend to the lamps several times each night, waking every second or third hour to trim the wick and replenish the fuel. This is apparently the task which challenged the wise and foolish virgins in Matthew (25:1–12).

Light in the ancient world was very important. Light and fire symbolized life and suggested the presence, or constituted a remembrance of God (John 1:3–4; Rev. 4:5; 8:10; 21:23). There are numerous references of the lamp of God not being extinguished (1 Sam. 3:4). When the lamp of

---

[i] Other ancient authorities read *my beloved Son*
[j] Other ancient authorities read *but moved by the Holy Spirit saints of God spoke*

God does go out, there is utter tragedy (2 Sam. 21:17; Job 18:5ff.; Prov. 20:20; 24:20). The conversion of Paul in Acts (9:3; 13:47; 26:17) is described with reference to lamps and light. In the New Testament, Christians are referred to as being the lamps of God in the world (Matt. 5:14–16; 6:22; Mark 4:21; Luke 11:33–36; Phil. 2:15; 2 Pet. 1:19). For other uses of lamps, see Luke 12:35; 15:8; Acts 16:29 ◆

False Prophets and Their Punishment

2 But false prophets also arose among the people, just as there will be false teachers among you, who will secretly bring in destructive opinions. They will even deny the Master who bought them – bringing swift destruction on themselves. [2]Even so, many will follow their licentious ways, and because of these teachers[k] the way of truth will be maligned. [3]And in their greed they will exploit you with deceptive words. Their condemnation, pronounced against them long ago, has not been idle, and their destruction is not asleep.

[4] For if God did not spare the angels when they sinned, but cast them into hell[l] and committed them to chains[m] of deepest darkness to be kept until the judgment; [5]and if he did not spare the ancient world,

even though he saved Noah, a herald of righteousness, with seven others, when he brought a flood on a world of the ungodly; [6]and if by turning the cities of Sodom and Gomorrah to ashes he condemned them to extinction[n] and made them an example of what is coming to the ungodly;[o] [7]and if he rescued Lot, a righteous man greatly distressed by the licentiousness of the lawless [8](for that righteous man, living among them day after day, was tormented in his righteous soul by their lawless deeds that he saw and heard), [9]then the Lord knows how to rescue the godly from trial, and to keep the unrighteous under punishment until the day of judgment [10] – especially those who indulge their flesh in depraved lust, and who despise authority.

Bold and willful, they are not afraid to slander the glorious ones,[p] [11]whereas angels, though greater in might and power, do not bring against them a slanderous judgment from the Lord.[q] [12]These people,

[k] Gk *because of them*   [l] Gk *Tartaros*   [m] Other ancient authorities read *pits*   [n] Other ancient authorities lack *to extinction*   [o] Other ancient authorities read *an example to those who were to be ungodly*   [p] Or *angels;* Gk *glories*   [q] Other ancient authorities read *before the Lord;* others lack the phrase

---

2 PETER 2

1–3. Much of what follows in this second chapter presents the same argument as is found in the book of Jude, though in softer tones. The author enters into the heart of the concern. False prophets and false teachers have arisen who model licentiousness and even deny the Lord.

4–10a. The reader can rest assured that God will bring judgment upon the false prophets and teachers just as punishment was brought upon the people of Sodom and Gomorrah (Gen. 19), the world at the time of Noah (Gen. 7–8) and the angels. (This idea of fallen and punished angels appears primarily in extra-canonical literature elaborating on Gen. 6:1–4, but, see also, Jude 6; Matt. 25:41; Rev. 12:7–9.) The godly, however, will be rescued, just as Noah and Lot were rescued because they were righteous. The readers are to follow their example.

10b–22. The description of the false teachers charges them with slander of angels (and anything else that they do not understand), greediness, being irrational, participating in revelry and adultery, enticing 'unsteady souls', and following the ways of Balaam (see Num. 22–25; 31:16; Josh. 13:22). The false teachers are without substance and entice people to follow their licentious ways. The worst part is that these false teachers once knew the 'way of righteousness' but turned back to their pre-Christian ways. They once had the knowledge of Jesus Christ but have now turned their back on it. It will be worse for them now than if they had never known the Lord's way.

however, are like irrational animals, mere creatures of instinct, born to be caught and killed. They slander what they do not understand, and when those creatures are destroyed,[r] they also will be destroyed, [13]suffering[s] the penalty for doing wrong. They count it a pleasure to revel in the daytime. They are blots and blemishes, reveling in their dissipation[t] while they feast with you. [14]They have eyes full of adultery, insatiable for sin. They entice unsteady souls. They have hearts trained in greed. Accursed children! [15]They have left the straight road and have gone astray, following the road of Balaam son of Bosor,[u] who loved the wages of doing wrong, [16]but was rebuked for his own transgression; a speechless donkey spoke with a human voice and restrained the prophet's madness.

[17] These are waterless springs and mists driven by a storm; for them the deepest darkness has been reserved. [18]For they speak bombastic nonsense, and with licentious desires of the flesh they entice people who have just[v] escaped from those who live in error. [19]They promise them freedom, but they themselves are slaves of corruption; for people are slaves to whatever masters them. [20]For if, after they have escaped the defilements of the world through the knowledge of our Lord and Savior Jesus Christ, they are again entangled in them and overpowered, the last state has become worse for them than the first. [21]For it would have been better for them never to have known the way of righteousness than, after knowing it, to turn back from the holy commandment that was passed on to them. [22]It has happened to them according to the true proverb,

"The dog turns back to its own
vomit,"

and,

"The sow is washed only to wallow in
the mud."

The Promise of the Lord's Coming

3 This is now, beloved, the second letter I am writing to you; in them I am trying to arouse your sincere intention by reminding you [2]that you should remember the words spoken in the past by the holy prophets, and the commandment of the Lord and Savior spoken through your apostles. [3]First of all you must understand this, that in the last days scoffers will come, scoffing and indulging their own lusts [4]and saying, "Where is the promise of his coming? For ever since our ancestors died,[w] all things continue as they were from the beginning of creation!" [5]They deliberately ignore this fact, that by the word of God heavens existed long ago and an earth was formed out of water and by means of water, [6]through which the world of that time was deluged with water and perished. [7]But by the same word the present heavens and earth have been reserved for fire, being kept until the day of judgment and destruction of the godless.

[r] Gk *in their destruction*   [s] Other ancient authorities read *receiving*   [t] Other ancient authorities read *love feasts*   [u] Other ancient authorities read *Beor*   [v] Other ancient authorities read *actually*   [w] Gk *our fathers fell asleep*

---

2 PETER 3

1–7. It is clear that some time has passed since the first proclamation of the Word. This book is not directed to first-generation Christians. There has been a delay in what was expected to be an imminent return of Christ. Scoffers are arising who do not believe that Christ will return at all. They say everything goes on just as it has since the beginning of creation. But, the author warns in an allusion to the Flood (Gen. 7–8), that things, in fact, have not continued without interruption since creation.

8 But do not ignore this one fact, beloved, that with the Lord one day is like a thousand years, and a thousand years are like one day. [9]The Lord is not slow about his promise, as some think of slowness, but is patient with you,[x] not wanting any to perish, but all to come to repentance. [10]But the day of the Lord will come like a thief, and then the heavens will pass away with a loud noise, and the elements will be dissolved with fire, and the earth and everything that is done on it will be disclosed.[y]

11 Since all these things are to be dissolved in this way, what sort of persons ought you to be in leading lives of holiness and godliness, [12]waiting for and hastening[z] the coming of the day of God, because of which the heavens will be set ablaze and dissolved, and the elements will melt with fire? [13]But, in accordance with his promise, we wait for new heavens and a new earth, where righteousness is at home.

Final Exhortation and Doxology

14 Therefore, beloved, while you are waiting for these things, strive to be found by him at peace, without spot or blemish; [15]and regard the patience of our Lord as salvation. So also our beloved brother Paul wrote to you according to the wisdom given him, [16]speaking of this as he does in all his letters. There are some things in them hard to understand, which the ignorant and unstable twist to their own destruction, as they do the other scriptures. [17]You therefore, beloved, since you are forewarned, beware that you are not carried away with the error of the lawless and lose your own stability. [18]But grow in the grace and knowledge of our Lord and Savior Jesus Christ. To him be the glory both now and to the day of eternity. Amen.[a]

---

[x] Other ancient authorities read *on your account*
[y] Other ancient authorities read *will be burned up*
[z] Or *earnestly desiring*   [a] Other ancient authorities lack *Amen*

8–10. There has been no delay in carrying out the judgment. God's time is not counted according to the rhythms of nature. God has provided time so that people have the opportunity to repent. It is not God's desire that people perish. But the community must be aware that the Day of the Lord, a Day of Judgment, will come and will come suddenly (for a description of an Israelite understanding of the 'Day of the Lord' see Amos 5:18–20; Zeph. 1:14–18). The Christian community must be ready for it.

11–13. The readers are encouraged to live lives now that are holy and godly as they wait for that day. The 'day of the Lord' is not the end for the community of faith. There will follow new heavens and a new earth when, at last, they will be comfortable because righteousness will be the order of the day.

14–18. The author writes that he is following in the footsteps of Paul in his instructions to them. He warns that there are some things in the letters of Paul that are difficult to understand and that have been twisted (as have other Scriptures) but the readers must not be led astray. The letter ends with a salutation and benediction.

THE FIRST LETTER OF JOHN

INTRODUCTION

Listed among the general epistles, 1 John exhorts Christians in the true faith, a faith leading to obedience demonstrated in works. An apparent crisis had developed within the church as a result of the outspoken teaching of those holding a view of Christ and the Christian life far different from that of the author. The ensuing controversy resulted in a schism that ended in the formal separation of the two groups.

Early church tradition identified the author as the apostle John, one of the Twelve, who resided in Ephesus, a cosmopolitan center in which Greek philosophy and religion flourished. The Greek philosophy Gnosticism, along with the mystery religion cults, proved to entice certain groups within the church, who sought to combine various of their elements with Christian doctrine. On the basis of the Gnostic belief that matter is evil, the teaching of John's opponents theologically denied the Incarnation which resulted in the ethical behavior of lawlessness or asceticism.

John wrote to refute the false teaching and to affirm the necessity of accepting the truth that Jesus Christ is God in the flesh. John also sought to warn his readers not to fall into sin (2:1), because the opponents' lawlessness on one hand and asceticism on the other had confused their thinking about how Christians should conduct themselves. John's letter provides assurance of salvation to his readers as they test their relationship to God and the community through a number of self-tests he provides: theological, social, and moral.

The Word of Life

1 We declare to you what was from the beginning, what we have heard, what we have seen with our eyes, what we have looked at and touched with our hands, concerning the word of life – ²this life was revealed, and we have seen it and testify to it, and declare to you the eternal life that was with the Father and was revealed to us – ³we declare to you what we have seen and heard so that you also may have fellowship with us; and truly our fellowship is with the Father and with his Son Jesus Christ. ⁴We are writing these things so that our[a] joy may be complete.

God Is Light

5 This is the message we have heard from him and proclaim to you, that God is light and in him there is no darkness at all. ⁶If we say that we have fellowship with him while we are walking in darkness, we lie and do not do what is true; ⁷but if we walk in the light as he himself is in the light, we have fellowship with one another, and the blood of Jesus his Son cleanses us from all sin. ⁸If we say that we have no sin, we deceive ourselves, and the truth is not in us. ⁹If we confess our sins, he who is faithful and just will forgive us our sins and cleanse us from all unrighteousness. ¹⁰If we say that we have not sinned, we make him a liar, and his word is not in us.

Christ Our Advocate

2 My little children, I am writing these things to you so that you may not sin. But if anyone does sin, we have an advocate with the Father, Jesus Christ the righteous; ²and he is the atoning sacrifice for our sins, and not for ours only but also for the sins of the whole world.

3 Now by this we may be sure that we know him, if we obey his commandments.

---

[a] Other ancient authorities read *your*

---

1 JOHN 1:1–5

1–4. John's eyewitness account verifies the truth of the Incarnation and supports his apostolic authority. The purpose of his witness is to lead his readers to unity with each other and with the Father and the Son. (Some women have difficulty relating to God as Father because of comparisons to their own fathers who may have been abusive, absent, or condescending. God as parent is defined and limited within the identifying nature of the character of God as righteous, pure and just.)

5. 'God is light' describes God in terms of function. The character of God, described as 'light' (cleansing, purifying, exposing darkness), determines the character of our fellowship with God. Within God there is no darkness (error or evil).

1 JOHN 1:6–2:28

Because God is light, living in fellowship with the Father and Son requires our reflecting God's character. Moral living is not optional for the woman of God. Behavior and religious experience cannot be separated, nor ethics from faith.

1:6. *Peripatomen* (literally, 'walking about') has to do with the whole manner of living and suggests an attitude of mind.

1:7. The term 'fellowship' (*koinonia*) includes the idea of association, but the primary, root meaning is participation with others in the community of faith.

1:9. The reality of sin in the life of a believer is not ignored by John, who insists that confession of sin is essential for fellowship with the Father and with fellow believers.

2:1. John calls upon his readers to renounce their sin, to oppose their sinful nature, to be careful in their walk with God. In case of sin, our advocate and intercessor with God is Jesus Christ, whose fitness is based on his unique relationship to the Father and to humanity, his personal sinlessness and his sacrificial death.

⁴Whoever says, "I have come to know him," but does not obey his commandments, is a liar, and in such a person the truth does not exist; ⁵but whoever obeys his word, truly in this person the love of God has reached perfection. By this we may be sure that we are in him: ⁶whoever says, "I abide in him," ought to walk just as he walked.

A New Commandment

7 Beloved, I am writing you no new commandment, but an old commandment that you have had from the beginning; the old commandment is the word that you have heard. ⁸Yet I am writing you a new commandment that is true in him and in you, because[b] the darkness is passing away and the true light is already shining. ⁹Whoever says, "I am in the light," while hating a brother or sister,[c] is still in the darkness. ¹⁰Whoever loves a brother or sister[d] lives in the light, and in such a person[e] there is no cause for stumbling. ¹¹But whoever hates another believer[f] is in the darkness, walks in the darkness, and does not know the way to go, because the darkness has brought on blindness.

¹² I am writing to you, little children,
　　because your sins are forgiven on
　　　　account of his name.
¹³ I am writing to you, fathers,
　　because you know him who is from
　　　　the beginning.

I am writing to you, young people,
　　because you have conquered the evil
　　　　one.
¹⁴ I write to you, children,
　　because you know the Father.
I write to you, fathers,
　　because you know him who is from
　　　　the beginning.
I write to you, young people,
　　because you are strong
　　and the word of God abides in you,
　　　　and you have overcome the evil
　　　　one.

15 Do not love the world or the things in the world. The love of the Father is not in those who love the world; ¹⁶for all that is in the world—the desire of the flesh, the desire of the eyes, the pride in riches – comes not from the Father but from the world. ¹⁷And the world and its desire[g] are passing away, but those who do the will of God live forever.

Warning against Antichrists

18 Children, it is the last hour! As you have heard that antichrist is coming, so now many antichrists have come. From this we know that it is the last hour. ¹⁹They went out from us, but they did not belong to us; for if they had belonged to us, they

[b] Or that　[c] Gk *hating a brother*　[d] Gk *loves a brother*　[e] Or *in it*　[f] Gk *hates a brother*　[g] Or *the desire for it*

2:7–11. John makes love a commandment inclusive of all others. Jesus is the source of the commandment (cf. John 15:12; Mark 12:28f.) and the prime example of loving behavior. His love is dynamic, tough, honest, and without barriers. Lack of love betrays our commitment and blinds our spiritual vision. (Many women have been taught a distorted view of love in which they have not learned to include themselves. Jesus commanded us to love our neighbors *as* we love ourselves.)

2:12–17. The three groupings could perhaps refer to various stages of spiritual development. (The masculine forms do not preclude a message to females.) The basic theme is overcoming, with Christ as the example.

2:15. Here, *kosmos* refers to the 'godless world' of things that draw us away from God. To love the world means to embrace its ideals, customs and methods or to seek its approval or embrace.

2:18. An antichrist is one who assumes the guise of Christ, and who is a counterfeit, an adversary (inside or outside the church).

would have remained with us. But by going out they made it plain that none of them belongs to us. [20]But you have been anointed by the Holy One, and all of you have knowledge.[h] [21]I write to you, not because you do not know the truth, but because you know it, and you know that no lie comes from the truth. [22]Who is the liar but the one who denies that Jesus is the Christ?[i] This is the antichrist, the one who denies the Father and the Son. [23]No one who denies the Son has the Father; everyone who confesses the Son has the Father also. [24]Let what you heard from the beginning abide in you. If what you heard from the beginning abides in you, then you will abide in the Son and in the Father. [25]And this is what he has promised us,[j] eternal life.

[26] I write these things to you concerning those who would deceive you. [27]As for you, the anointing that you received from him abides in you, and so you do not need anyone to teach you. But as his anointing teaches you about all things, and is true and is not a lie, and just as it has taught you, abide in him.[k]

[28] And now, little children, abide in him, so that when he is revealed we may have confidence and not be put to shame before him at his coming.

Children of God

[29] If you know that he is righteous, you may be sure that everyone who does right has been born of him. [3] [1]See what love the Father has given us, that we should be called children of God; and that is what we are. The reason the world does not know us is that it did not know him. [2]Beloved, we are God's children now; what we will be has not yet been revealed. What we do know is this: when he[k] is revealed, we will be like him, for we will see him as he is. [3]And all who have this hope in him purify themselves, just as he is pure.

[4] Everyone who commits sin is guilty of lawlessness; sin is lawlessness. [5]You know that he was revealed to take away sins, and in him there is no sin. [6]No one who abides in him sins; no one who sins has either seen him or known him. [7]Little children, let no one deceive you. Everyone who does what is right is righteous, just as he is righteous. [8]Everyone who commits sin is a child of the devil; for the devil has been sinning from the beginning. The Son of God was revealed for this purpose, to destroy the works of the devil. [9]Those who have been born of God do not sin, because God's seed abides in them;[l] they cannot sin, because they have been born of God. [10]The children of God and the children of the devil are revealed in this way: all who do not do what is right are not from God, nor are those who do not love their brothers and sisters.[m]

[h] Other ancient authorities read *you know all things*   [i] Or *the Messiah*   [j] Other ancient authorities read *you*   [k] Or *it*   [l] Or *because the children of God abide in him*   [m] Gk *his brother*

2:20. 'Anointing' (*chrisma*) symbolizes the receiving of the Holy Spirit as consecration for service (cf. Is. 61:1). Some Gnostic groups and mystery cults claimed for their initiates special 'anointings' (as an initiation rite, not that of consecration) that would imbue them with a superior status of enlightenment.

1 JOHN 2:28–5:21

2:28–3:24. Christians are truly members of the family of God that results in their partaking of the divine gory (3:2-3), not achieving deity as the Gnostics and many current religions believe.
3:9. 'God's seed' may be a reference to God's Word, the new nature of the Christian, the reality of being God's children, or to the Holy Spirit within us.

Love One Another

11 For this is the message you have heard from the beginning, that we should love one another. [12]We must not be like Cain who was from the evil one and murdered his brother. And why did he murder him? Because his own deeds were evil and his brother's righteous. [13]Do not be astonished, brothers and sisters,[n] that the world hates you. [14]We know that we have passed from death to life because we love one another. Whoever does not love abides in death. [15]All who hate a brother or sister[o] are murderers, and you know that murderers do not have eternal life abiding in them. [16]We know love by this, that he laid down his life for us – and we ought to lay down our lives for one another. [17]How does God's love abide in anyone who has the world's goods and sees a brother or sister[p] in need and yet refuses help?

♦ Christianity is a faith characterized by social concerns and relationships. The New Testament contains over 52 instructions to believers using the phrase 'one another' (see Mark 9:50; John 13:14, 34–35; 15:12, 17; Rom. 12:5, 10, 16; 13:8; 14:13, 19; 15:5, 7, 14; 16:20; 1 Cor. 11:33; 12:25; 16:20; 2 Cor. 13:12; Gal. 5:13–15, 26; 6:2; Eph. 4:2, 25, 32; 5:19–21; Phil. 2:3; Col. 3:9, 13, 16; 1 Thess. 3:12; 4:9, 18; 5:11, 15; 2 Thess. 1:3; Heb. 10:24; James 4:11; 5:9, 16; 1 Pet. 1:22; 4:9–10; 5:5, 14; 1 John 1:7; 3:11, 23; 4:7, 11–12; 2 John 5). Of all these directives, the most important is to love one another. Some people stress the structures of authority that they profess to find in the New Testament, but the Scriptures themselves lay far more stress on mutuality. Jesus commanded his followers not to lord it over others (Matt. 20:25–27; Luke 22:25–27) but to become one with them in a common fellowship of love, concern, and support ♦

18 Little children, let us love, not in word or speech, but in truth and action. [19]And by this we will know that we are from the truth and will reassure our hearts before him [20]whenever our hearts condemn us; for God is greater than our hearts, and he knows everything. [21]Beloved, if our hearts do not condemn us, we have boldness before God; [22]and we receive from him whatever we ask, because we obey his commandments and do what pleases him.

23 And this is his commandment, that we should believe in the name of his Son Jesus Christ and love one another, just as he has commanded us. [24]All who obey his commandments abide in him, and he abides in them. And by this we know that he abides in us, by the Spirit that he has given us.

Testing the Spirits

4 Beloved, do not believe every spirit, but test the spirits to see whether they are from God; for many false prophets have gone out into the world. [2]By this you know the Spirit of God: every spirit that confesses that Jesus Christ has come in the flesh is from God, [3]and every spirit that does not confess Jesus[q] is not from God. And this is the spirit of the antichrist, of which you have heard that it is coming; and now it is already in the world. [4]Little children, you are from God, and have conquered them; for the one who is in you is greater than the one who is in the world. [5]They are from the world; therefore what they say is from the world, and the world listens to them. [6]We are from God. Whoever knows God listens to us, and whoever is not from God does not listen to

[n] Gk *brothers*   [o] Gk *his brother*   [p] Gk *brother*
[q] Other ancient authorities read *does away with Jesus* (Gk *dissolves Jesus*)

3:17. How does this relate to the economic injustice of the 20th century? Is not my sister or brother any Christian anywhere in the world who has a need for the basics of food and shelter?

us. From this we know the spirit of truth and the spirit of error.

God Is Love

7 Beloved, let us love one another, because love is from God; everyone who loves is born of God and knows God. [8]Whoever does not love does not know God, for God is love. [9]God's love was revealed among us in this way: God sent his only Son into the world so that we might live through him. [10]In this is love, not that we loved God but that he loved us and sent his Son to be the atoning sacrifice for our sins. [11]Beloved, since God loved us so much, we also ought to love one another. [12]No one has ever seen God; if we love one another, God lives in us, and his love is perfected in us.

◆ New Testament writers speak frequently of a spiritual birth that brings newness of life. In 2 Cor. 5:17 Paul speaks of the transformation which occurs when individuals repent of their sins and enter into a personal relationship with Jesus Christ. The work of the Holy Spirit causes the believer to be born anew, and a radical transformation takes place. Old things are passed away and new ones take their place.

This second birth is not wholly unlike the first (John 3:5–12). A midwife with many years of experience in both Africa and America wrote:

There is something very thrilling and exciting about delivering a baby. There was nothing like the feel of the baby's head in my hands during delivery. I could feel new life, and each time I would be deeply moved. As I would watch the parents becoming acquainted with their infant, I sometimes felt I was intruding in on a very intimate and personal experience and almost felt out of place until I remembered I was part of it. I remember one father with tears running down his cheeks saying, 'She's just what I wanted.' I had helped to make a successful delivery possible, and I revelled in it. I know no other way to describe the feelings I had at the birth of a baby except it was something spiritual and sacred.

If this is true of the first birth, how much more is it true of the second birth, where God labors over our delivery as a midwife (Is. 66:9). As a loving Father, he exclaims, 'She's just what I wanted!' ◆

13 By this we know that we abide in him and he in us, because he has given us of his Spirit. [14]And we have seen and do testify that the Father has sent his Son as the Savior of the world. [15]God abides in those who confess that Jesus is the Son of God, and they abide in God. [16]So we have known and believe the love that God has for us.

God is love, and those who abide in love abide in God, and God abides in them. [17]Love has been perfected among us in this: that we may have boldness on the day of judgment, because as he is, so are we in this world. [18]There is no fear in love, but perfect love casts out fear; for fear has to do with punishment, and whoever fears has not reached perfection in love. [19]We love[r] because he first loved us. [20]Those who say, "I love God," and hate their brothers or sisters,[s] are liars; for those who do not love a brother or sister[t] whom they have seen, cannot love God whom they have not seen. [21]The commandment we have from him is this: those who love God must love their brothers and sisters[s] also.

[r] Other ancient authorities add *him*; others add *God*   [s] Gk *brothers*   [t] Gk *brother*

4:11–12. Loving one another produces visible evidence that God dwells in us. His love *perfected* in us means that it has been brought to its proper end or fulfillment.

Faith Conquers the World

5 Everyone who believes that Jesus is the Christ[u] has been born of God, and everyone who loves the parent loves the child. [2]By this we know that we love the children of God, when we love God and obey his commandments. [3]For the love of God is this, that we obey his commandments. And his commandments are not burdensome, [4]for whatever is born of God conquers the world. And this is the victory that conquers the world, our faith. [5]Who is it that conquers the world but the one who believes that Jesus is the Son of God?

Testimony concerning the Son of God

6 This is the one who came by water and blood, Jesus Christ, not with the water only but with the water and the blood. And the Spirit is the one that testifies, for the Spirit is the truth. [7]There are three that testify:[v] [8]the Spirit and the water and the blood, and these three agree. [9]If we receive human testimony, the testimony of God is greater; for this is the testimony of God that he has testified to his Son. [10]Those who believe in the Son of God have the testimony in their hearts. Those who do not believe in God[w] have made him a liar by not believing in the testimony that God has given concerning his Son. [11]And this is the testimony: God gave us eternal life, and this life is in his Son. [12]Whoever has the Son has life; whoever does not have the Son of God does not have life.

Epilogue

13 I write these things to you who believe in the name of the Son of God, so that you may know that you have eternal life.

14 And this is the boldness we have in him, that if we ask anything according to his will, he hears us. [15]And if we know that he hears us in whatever we ask, we know that we have obtained the requests made of him. [16]If you see your brother or sister[x] committing what is not a mortal sin, you will ask, and God[y] will give life to such a one – to those whose sin is not mortal. There is sin that is mortal; I do not say that you should pray about that. [17]All wrongdoing is sin, but there is sin that is not mortal.

18 We know that those who are born of God do not sin, but the one who was born of God protects them, and the evil one does not touch them. [19]We know that we are God's children, and that the whole world lies under the power of the evil one. [20]And we know that the Son of God has come and has given us understanding so that we may know him who is true;[z] and we are in him who is true, in his Son Jesus Christ. He is the true God and eternal life.

21 Little children, keep yourselves from idols.[a]

[u] Or *the Messiah*   [v] A few other authorities read (with variations) [7]*There are three that testify in heaven, the Father, the Word, and the Holy Spirit, and these three are one.* [8]*And there are three that testify on earth:*   [w] Other ancient authorities read *in the Son*   [x] Gk *your brother*   [y] Gk *he*   [z] Other ancient authorities read *know the true God*   [a] Other ancient authorities add *Amen*

5:6. The terms 'water' and 'blood' point to historical realities in Christ's purpose. Possible interpretations are: (1) the water of his baptism and the blood of his death; (2) baptism and the Lord's Supper; or (3) the cleansing and atonement effected by Christ.

5:16. The author does not clarify his definition of a 'sin that is mortal'. Within the present context, perhaps the sin is one of false profession that reveals itself in lack of love for one's sisters and brothers.

THE SECOND LETTER OF JOHN

Some scholars have concluded that 'the elect lady and her children' (v. 1) refers to a local church and its members. Although it is true that John addresses a group in this letter (note plural in vv. 6, 8, 10, 12), it is also true that he addresses an individual (vv. 1, 5, 13). Due to the persecution of the early Christians, house churches were common. Perhaps the 'elect lady' is a leader of a house church and her children are church members, so that John has both a leader and a local church in mind. (See Rom. 16:5; 1 Cor. 16:19; Col. 4:15; Philem. 2.) In the light of the conditions of the time, it has also been suggested that the expression 'to the elect lady' was intended as a subterfuge. If the letter fell into the hands of the enemies of the early Christians, then it would appear to be a harmless letter to a dear friend. Even if this is the case, it is significant, that a church is symbolized as an honored mother.

John expresses joy at having found some of the elect lady's children 'walking in the truth' (2 John 4). Presumably, there were false teachers who were going around spreading error. These false teachers at one time professed to believe, but they turned from that faith and abandoned the truth (1 John 2:19). John expresses concern that this godly woman not allow anything false to come into her family or into the house church. If by 'children' (2 John 4) John includes members of the house church, it is possible that some of them had already gone astray after the false teachers. Thus, as an 'elder' (i.e. a respected, older person within the Christian community), he makes two requests. First, he asks them to 'love one another' (v. 5). Here the term 'love' means to behave toward sisters and brothers in the Christian community with *agape* love after the pattern of Jesus. Secondly, he asks them to be on guard against false teachers ('deceivers') who deny that Jesus has come as a real *flesh and blood* person (vv. 7–8). The Greek word for 'deceivers' refers to people who habitually deceive others, leading them not only into wrong teaching, but into wrong practices. John instructs the family (and the local church) to make an unyielding commitment to the teachings of Christ (v. 9).

The early Christians were bound together as members of one family. The unity of that family required that, whenever Christians travelled from one place to another, they should be received as welcome guests by the Christians residing there (see Rom. 12:13 ; 1 Tim. 3:2; 5:3–10; Heb. 13:2; 1 Pet. 4:8–10). However, John warns the family (and the local church) not to receive false teachers into their homes (2 John 10). Hospitality to false teachers incurs responsibility for their evil deeds (v. 11). Presumably, John visited the house churches from time to time. At the end of his letter, he expresses the hope that he will visit and communicate with them more fully face to face (v. 12). 'Your elect sister' (v. 13) could possibly be a leader of another house church or to a sister church from which John writes.

This one-page treasure has all the features of a real letter of that time: an introduction of the writer and the addressee (v. 1); a greeting (v. 3); joy over a good report (v. 4); a request and a warning (vv. 5–11); a conclusion (v. 12) and some final greetings (v. 13).

Salutation

1 The elder to the elect lady and her children, whom I love in the truth, and not only I but also all who know the truth, [2]because of the truth that abides in us and will be with us forever:

3 Grace, mercy, and peace will be with us from God the Father and from[a] Jesus Christ, the Father's Son, in truth and love.

Truth and Love

4 I was overjoyed to find some of your children walking in the truth, just as we have been commanded by the Father. [5]But now, dear lady, I ask you, not as though I were writing you a new commandment, but one we have had from the beginning, let us love one another. [6]And this is love, that we walk according to his commandments; this is the commandment just as you have heard it from the beginning – you must walk in it.

7 Many deceivers have gone out into the world, those who do not confess that Jesus Christ has come in the flesh; any such person is the deceiver and the antichrist! [8]Be on your guard, so that you do not lose what we[b] have worked for, but may receive a full reward. [9]Everyone who does not abide in the teaching of Christ, but goes beyond it, does not have God; whoever abides in the teaching has both the Father and the Son. [10]Do not receive into the house or welcome anyone who comes to you and does not bring this teaching; [11]for to welcome is to participate in the evil deeds of such a person.

Final Greetings

12 Although I have much to write to you, I would rather not use paper and ink; instead I hope to come to you and talk with you face to face, so that our joy may be complete.

13 The children of your elect sister send you their greetings.[c]

---

[a] Other ancient authorities add *the Lord*   [b] Other ancient authorities read *you*   [c] Other ancient authorities add *Amen*

THE THIRD LETTER OF JOHN

3 John is the shortest book of the Bible, and it is the only New Testament writing that does not mention Jesus Christ. It comes closer to a note than to a classic letter. Traditionally, due to doctrinal and literary resemblance, the author of this epistle was identified as the same who wrote the Gospel of John and the other two letters (1 and 2 John). However, there is not enough ground in research to confirm this, especially because the author of 3 John identifies himself solely as a Presbyter, or elder, not giving a personal name.

The date of the letter is probably the end of the first century AD. It is addressed not to a particular house-church, but to an individual named Gaius, a leader in the church. This letter deals primarily with ethical and practical issues, as opposed to the theological controversies that characterize the other two letters. The purpose of the epistle is to solve a leadership conflict in one of the local churches under the Presbyter's authority. He invites his followers (called 'Beloved') to imitate good, not evil (v. 11).

The central issue of this letter is conduct, especially hospitality toward itinerant brothers and sisters. The letter does not deal with theological controversies but with the way Christians ought to live out their faith through love. The issue of hospitality – rendering service to strangers, welcoming them and sending them on their journeys – is also the criterion to evaluate the actions of Gaius (who is praised for accepting the envoys sent by John) and Diotrephes (who not only refuses to welcome strangers, but prevents those who want to welcome them and puts them out of the church). The purpose of the church is to welcome, to be hospitable toward the itinerant, to receive and accept the strangers that come in the name of Christ.

3 John reveals the intricacies of the early church in the way leadership was exercised. This writing shows how an authoritarian leader can prevent a church from exercising the ministry it was called to do, that is, to demonstrate Christian love by welcoming strangers without distinction, sharing the table and opening homes to other Christians. In particular, it reveals how one individual can put other Christians out of the church. On the other hand, it also shows a movement of resistance insofar as the attitudes of Gaius, Demetrius and others are seen as worthy of imitation, since they practice hospitality and live in truth.

Salutation

1 The elder to the beloved Gaius, whom I love in truth.

Gaius Commended for His Hospitality

2 Beloved, I pray that all may go well with you and that you may be in good health, just as it is well with your soul. [3]I was overjoyed when some of the friends[a] arrived and testified to your faithfulness to the truth, namely how you walk in the truth. [4]I have no greater joy than this, to hear that my children are walking in the truth.

5 Beloved, you do faithfully whatever you do for the friends,[a] even though they are strangers to you; [6]they have testified to your love before the church. You will do well to send them on in a manner worthy of God; [7]for they began their journey for the sake of Christ,[b] accepting no support from non-believers.[c] [8]Therefore we ought to support such people, so that we may become co-workers with the truth.

Diotrephes and Demetrius

9 I have written something to the church; but Diotrephes, who likes to put himself first, does not acknowledge our authority. [10]So if I come, I will call attention to what he is doing in spreading false charges against us. And not content with those charges, he refuses to welcome the friends,[a] and even prevents those who want to do so and expels them from the church.

11 Beloved, do not imitate what is evil but imitate what is good. Whoever does good is from God; whoever does evil has not seen God. [12]Everyone has testified favorably about Demetrius, and so has the truth itself. We also testify for him,[d] and you know that our testimony is true.

Final Greetings

13 I have much to write to you, but I would rather not write with pen and ink; [14]instead I hope to see you soon, and we will talk together face to face.

15 Peace to you. The friends send you their greetings. Greet the friends there, each by name.

---

[a] Gk *brothers* [b] Gk *for the sake of the name* [c] Gk *the Gentiles* [d] Gk lacks *for him*

THE LETTER OF
JUDE

INTRODUCTION

This letter, which professes to be written by Jude the brother of James, is not addressed to a specific community and is categorized as one of the 'general' or 'catholic' epistles. Its date is unknown. The book quotes or alludes to two apocryphal works, 1 Enoch and the Testament of Moses, and shares subject matter with 2 Pet. 2, which may suggest a dependence of one on the other or a common source.

The book offers both an exhortation to the early church to remain faithful to the teachings of the apostles and a warning against a nascent heresy, not explicitly named, that is infiltrating it. Richard Bauckham suggests 'antinomianism' defined as 'the claim that the gospel frees Christians from moral "obligation"' ('Jude Epistle of', Anchor Bible Dictionary, 3:1102). Those adhering to this belief 'indulged in sexual immorality and pursued unnatural lust . . . defile the flesh, reject authority, and slander the glorious ones' (vv. 7–8). The Christian message of freedom in Christ must have been particularly attractive to women, but that freedom is tempered by responsibility. The believers must strengthen their own faith and have mercy on others. Judgment is God's prerogative.

Since Jesus had brothers named James and Judas (Matt. 13:55; Mark 6:3) some scholars think that the author was indeed a brother of Jesus. Others propose either that the letter is pseudonymous or another Jude penned it.

Salutation

1 Jude,[a] a servant[b] of Jesus Christ and brother of James,

To those who are called, who are beloved[c] in[d] God the Father and kept safe for[d] Jesus Christ:

2 May mercy, peace, and love be yours in abundance.

Occasion of the Letter

3 Beloved, while eagerly preparing to write to you about the salvation we share, I find it necessary to write and appeal to you to contend for the faith that was once for all entrusted to the saints. **4**For certain intruders have stolen in among you, people who long ago were designated for this condemnation as ungodly, who pervert the grace of our God into licentiousness and deny our only Master and Lord, Jesus Christ.[e]

Judgment on False Teachers

5 Now I desire to remind you, though you are fully informed, that the Lord, who once for all saved[f] a people out of the land of Egypt, afterward destroyed those who did not believe. **6**And the angels who did not keep their own position, but left their proper dwelling, he has kept in eternal chains in deepest darkness for the judgment of the great Day. **7**Likewise, Sodom and Gomorrah and the surrounding cities, which, in the same manner as they, indulged in sexual immorality and pursued unnatural lust,[g] serve as an example by undergoing a punishment of eternal fire.

8 Yet in the same way these dreamers also defile the flesh, reject authority, and slander the glorious ones.[h] **9**But when the archangel Michael contended with the devil and disputed about the body of Moses, he did not dare to bring a condemnation of slander[i] against him, but said, "The Lord rebuke you!" **10**But these people slander whatever they do not understand, and they are destroyed by those things that, like irrational animals, they know by instinct. **11**Woe to them! For they go the way of Cain, and abandon themselves to Balaam's error for the sake of gain, and perish in Korah's rebellion. **12**These are blemishes[j] on your love-feasts, while they feast with you without fear, feeding themselves.[k] They are waterless clouds carried along by the winds; autumn trees without fruit, twice dead, uprooted; **13**wild waves of the sea, casting up the foam of their own shame; wandering stars, for whom the deepest darkness has been reserved forever.

[a] Gk *Judas*   [b] Gk *slave*   [c] Other ancient authorities read *sanctified*   [d] Or *by*   [e] Or *the only Master and our Lord Jesus Christ*   [f] Other ancient authorities read *though you were once for all fully informed, that Jesus* (or *Joshua*) *who saved*   [g] Gk *went after other flesh*   [h] Or *angels*; Gk *glories*   [i] Or *condemnation for blasphemy*   [j] Or *reefs*   [k] Or *without fear. They are shepherds who care only for themselves*

3–4. The stated problem is that intruders who 'pervert the grace' of God and deny Jesus Christ are within the beloved community (v. 4). The necessity to 'contend' or 'struggle' for the faith points to a specific set of accepted theological beliefs.

5–6. These verses contain a number of allusions to Old Testament and extra-canonical texts. Those saved from Egypt but destroyed afterward are mentioned in Exod. 32. The reference to angels is taken from 1 Enoch 6–7; 10, which appear to be an elaboration of Gen. 6:1–2, where divine beings take human women for themselves. Jude lists sexual immorality and unnatural lust as the sins of Sodom and Gomorrah (Gen. 19; cf. Ezek. 16:49).

7–13. The intruders lack substance and judge others rather than leaving judgment to God (cf. Zech. 3:2). The allusion to a scene where Michael and the devil contend for the body of Moses is not biblical but possibly appears in the lost ending of a non-canonical book titled the *Testament of Moses*.

11–13. The references to Cain, Balaam, and Korah's rebellion are found in Gen. 4; Num. 25:1–4; 31:15–16; 16:14–16.

14 It was also about these that Enoch, in the seventh generation from Adam, prophesied, saying, "See, the Lord is coming[l] with ten thousands of his holy ones, [15]to execute judgment on all, and to convict everyone of all the deeds of ungodliness that they have committed in such an ungodly way, and of all the harsh things that ungodly sinners have spoken against him." [16]These are grumblers and malcontents; they indulge their own lusts; they are bombastic in speech, flattering people to their own advantage.

Warnings and Exhortations

17 But you, beloved, must remember the predictions of the apostles of our Lord Jesus Christ; [18]for they said to you, "In the last time there will be scoffers, indulging their own ungodly lusts." [19]It is these worldly people, devoid of the Spirit, who are causing divisions. [20]But you, beloved, build yourselves up on your most holy faith; pray in the Holy Spirit; [21]keep yourselves in the love of God; look forward to the mercy of our Lord Jesus Christ that leads to[m] eternal life. [22]And have mercy on some who are wavering; [23]save others by snatching them out of the fire; and have mercy on still others with fear, hating even the tunic defiled by their bodies.[n]

Benediction

24 Now to him who is able to keep you from falling, and to make you stand without blemish in the presence of his glory with rejoicing, [25]to the only God our Savior, through Jesus Christ our Lord, be glory, majesty, power, and authority, before all time and now and forever. Amen.

[l] Gk *came*   [m] Gk *Christ to*   [n] Gk *by the flesh.* The Greek text of verses 22–23 is uncertain at several points

---

14–16. The quotation appearing in these verses is from a slightly modified form of 1 Enoch 1:9. Judgment will come and those who have sinned will be found guilty.
17–24. The apostles warned that these things would happen (cf. 2 Pet. 3:3). Christians must build themselves up on the faith, 'pray in the Holy Spirit', keep themselves in the love of God, and look forward to the mercy of Jesus (vv. 20–21). This section ends with a call to save some and to have mercy on those who are wavering.
24–25. The doxology is a hymn of praise to God who is able to keep the Christian community from falling and preserve it to stand without blemish before God.

THE REVELATION TO JOHN

INTRODUCTION

Purpose

The opening verses of Revelation underscore the tremendous truth that God wants his servants aware of his mighty acts, particularly in relation to the second coming of Christ. As Christ's first advent did not happen 'in a corner' (Acts 26:26), so also events leading up to Christ's second advent and to the fulfillment of God's promise of a new heaven and a new earth will be plain for all to see. Symbolic references may be difficult to interpret in advance, but nevertheless John is instructed to write down these many visions so that God's people be informed and can heed the underlying message.

Author

Although exactly who John is cannot be established with absolute certainty, the church has traditionally held that he is the apostle John.

◆ The author writes under his own name (1:1, 4, 9; 22:8), classifies himself as a prophet (22:9) and refers to his work as prophesy (1:3; 22:7, 10, 18–19). This suggests that the author was well known in the early church as being a recognized authority figure who could deliver such a prophetic message in his own name.

The major problems of authorship seem to be internal, particularly the linguistic difference between the Apocalypse and the Gospel of John. For instance, the Greek of the Apocalypse is rougher and more unpolished than that of the Gospel. There are irregular uses of participles, broken sentence constructions, addition of unnecessary pronouns, confusion of genders, numbers and cases.

Guthrie points out, however, that 'in spite of linguistic and grammatical differences the Apocalypse has a closer affinity to the Greek of the other Johannine books than to any other New Testament Book' (Guthrie, *New Testament Introduction*, revised edition, IVP, 1990, p. 942). This close affinity can be further seen in common terminology: Christ is called *Logos* (John 1:1; Rev. 19:13); he is also described as a Lamb (although in different Greek words). The figures of water and springs are used, Christ is shown as a shepherd (John 10:1; Rev. 7:17). The idea that the Temple is no longer needed for the worship of God occurs (John 4:21; Rev. 21:22) and there is a symbolic allusion to manna (John 6:13f.; Rev. 2:17). Also, the dualistic themes, so common to the Gospel of John can be seen in the Apocalypse: light and darkness, truth and falsehood, good and evil, God and Satan. Another significant feature seen in common is the pattern of the number 7.

There is no evidence of another John existing in Asia with the authority suggested by the Apocalypse's author ◆

Date

Some scholars believe John was writing during the reign of the Emperor Nero, when Christians experienced initial, but localized, persecution by the Roman authorities (c. AD 64). Other scholars favor a later date, after the destruction of Jerusalem (c. AD 70), when the Palestinian Christian community had been dispersed and the churches in Asia Minor had become more prominent, and when during the reign of Domitian (AD 81–96) there was empire-wide persecution of Christians.

Style

The most noticeable feature of Revelation is its literary style, known as apocalyptic, which is radically different from the narratives and letters that comprise the rest of the New Testament. People have speculated that John used this style (as well as a very peculiar form of Greek) as a sort of code to avoid further persecution by the authorities should Revelation have fallen into Roman hands. However, because apocalyptic literature was already prevalent in the ancient world many images in Revelation would have been familiar to persons who knew the writings of Isaiah, Jeremiah, Ezekiel and Daniel; other images would have been familiar from extra-biblical apocalyptic writings.

Thus John may well have chosen this style as the best means to describe visions that, humanly speaking, were indescribable. Great care must be used in seeking to interpret these many word pictures, which John himself frequently qualifies by saying they are only 'like' something or someone. For example, consider the difficulty of describing a vision of late twentieth-century instruments of war to a first-century audience: armored vehicles and their weapons might indeed be rendered as stinging scorpions, missiles could be shooting stars.

Furthermore, over the years sincere Christians have differed widely in their interpretations of the events portrayed in John's experience and visions. Older readers may recall the certainty with which Adolf Hitler was identified as the Anti-Christ, or remember the confident assertions as to the exact date of Christ's return, based on the exegete's view of world events. More broadly, sincere Christians have also differed as to whether the Rapture (1 Thess. 4:13–18) will precede the Great Tribulation (Rev. 7:14), or exactly where the Millennium (Christ's 1,000-year reign, Rev. 20:4) fits into the sequence of events. Some of John's visions appear to be parallel descriptions of the same event, while others appear to be in a chronological sequence. In addition, some events are recorded as literal happenings, while others are obviously figurative.

John also employs numbers to highlight his visions. For example, the number seven features prominently and may represent completeness or fulfillment of a message or a judgment. If so, the use of half of seven would designate incompleteness or partial fulfillment. However, the reader does not need to know the exact meaning of these numbers to understand that their repeated usage underscores the importance of the various symbols to which they correspond. Thus Christ's specific emphasis on the seven churches with their seven angel guardians cautions us to study and profit from all seven of Christ's messages (2:1–3:22).

Interpretations

There are four general views of this challenging book:

(1) The symbolic view holds that Revelation is a spiritual allegory portraying the ultimate triumph of good over evil. The elaborate poetic images are used as a device to 'flesh out' abstract ideas and universal truths in order to give force and immediacy to the unseen realities that are the only true realities (2 Cor. 4:18).

(2) The preterist view considers Revelation to be a first-century tract written to encourage Christians undergoing persecution, and all the messages and visions applied to that time only. When Rome, with its cult of emperor worship, demanded the oath of allegiance to be 'Caesar is Lord', Christians could not bow down before such a 'beast'. John

wrote to urge them to stand firm, knowing that Jesus would ultimately triumph over Rome. Persons holding the preterist view find Revelation of great historical interest but of little or no prophetic value.

(3) The historicist view believes that Revelation gives a broad picture of world events from the end of the first century up until the close of human history, with particular reference to the different eras in church history as represented by the seven churches in Rev. 2–3. A difficulty with this view is that it forces all present and future visible manifestations of the body of Christ to fall under the condemnation of Laodicea, which is patently unrealistic in today's world where there are churches in renewal and also standing firm against persecution, as well as in dead orthodoxy.

(4) The futurist view places the bulk of Revelation in the future because the wording of Rev. 4:1 seems to signify a clear break between past and future events. This view has traditionally been the most popular among evangelicals, especially since the twentieth century has seen a renewed interest in the second coming of Christ.

Many modern interpreters draw from all four views, reading Revelation with an eye to its historical context but also aware that both literally and symbolically its overall message is clear: God is Sovereign, and in Christ the victory over evil is already won.

Application

Regardless of the interpreter's view or theological orientation, there is agreement that Revelation sets forth the cosmic battle between good and evil. And it is just as true today as in the reigns of Nero or Domitian that God and Caesar (what is not of God) cannot both be Lord of our lives. So although most persons are not confronted in so many words with the need to choose whether 'Jesus is Lord' or 'Caesar is Lord', certainly that choice must always be made. The refusal of those early Christians to bow down to Rome contains a timeless truth: God alone is worthy of our worship.

To heighten the crucial nature of this choice about lordship and its eternal consequences, Revelation centers on the person and work of Jesus Christ. The heart of prophecy (19:10) is not foretelling the future but proclaiming Christ as Savior, Lord, and returning, conquering King.

The letters to the seven churches are filled with awareness that Christ is coming again, and in the light of this truth all readers of Revelation are urged to heed the Spirit's messages. Therefore a related theme is our moral and spiritual responsibility: Will we have ears to hear God calling us to repentance, believing faith, and ongoing discipleship?

Those who deliberately choose 'Jesus is Lord' despite suffering or martyrdom are promised God's special protection and blessing. The perseverance of the saints is not a negative theme, but positive evidence of God's triumph over evil as God preserves these 'overcomers'.

Appreciation of these and other themes does not depend on identifying every symbol or matching every vision with historical events, past or future. Nor should we be put off reading Revelation because it does not answer our age-old queries about the origin of evil. Rather, building on the teaching of Job and Habakkuk, we are assured that evil will finally be conquered and cast away forever. Therefore Revelation demands a decision from its readers: On whose side of the conflict will we choose to be? The answer will determine our eternal destiny.

Introduction and Salutation

1 The revelation of Jesus Christ, which God gave him to show his servants[a] what must soon take place; he made[b] it known by sending his angel to his servant[c] John, [2]who testified to the word of God and to the testimony of Jesus Christ, even to all that he saw.

3 Blessed is the one who reads aloud the words of the prophecy, and blessed are those who hear and who keep what is written in it; for the time is near.

4 John to the seven churches that are in Asia:

Grace to you and peace from him who is and who was and who is to come, and from the seven spirits who are before his throne, [5]and from Jesus Christ, the faithful witness, the firstborn of the dead, and the ruler of the kings of the earth.

To him who loves us and freed[d] us from our sins by his blood, [6]and made[e] us to be a kingdom, priests serving[f] his God and Father, to him be glory and dominion forever and ever. Amen.

[7] Look! He is coming with the clouds;
      every eye will see him,
even those who pierced him;
      and on his account all the tribes of
            the earth will wail.
So it is to be. Amen.

8 "I am the Alpha and the Omega," says the Lord God, who is and who was and who is to come, the Almighty.

◆ These verses form an introduction to the 'unveiling' or revealing of future events. The channel of revelation is described. The message originates with God who gave it to Jesus for the purpose of passing it on to the followers (bond-servants). The message was communicated by an angel to John who then wrote the book to the churches.

Since the contents of the book are very important, it is necessary to emphasize that they constitute a divine message sent

[a] Gk slaves   [b] Gk and he made   [c] Gk slave
[d] Other ancient authorities read washed   [e] Gk and he made   [f] Gk priests to

---

REVELATION 1

1–3. Today we can emulate John by being faithful witnesses to what God has revealed to us. We are not to keep God's message to ourselves, but to pass it on (Rev. 1:11; see also 1 John 1:1–4; Matt. 28:19–20). The language suggests a situation where there were only limited copies of Revelation, so that the material would be read aloud in a group. With the availability of Scripture today, almost every believer can study and share God's Word. The specific blessing promised those who read, hear and keep the words of this book is surely a great incentive to heed its messages. Although John emphasizes the imminence of the events he records, rather than becoming mired in attempts to set exact dates the reader should remember that for each person 'now is the day of salvation' (2 cor. 6:2). God's Word explicitly states that humans are not to know the precise date of future events (Matt. 24:36), but does state explicitly that we are responsible for what we do know about God's free gift of eternal life (Heb. 2:1–4; John 3:36).

5b–6. These words praising Christ for the two-fold work of redemption and restoration in the lives of all believers teach that the Christian gospel is not elitist, but offers equal status to all God's servants (2 Cor. 5:16–20). The Bible begins with an affirmation of the full humanity of both men and women (Gen. 1:26–28) and states that both are to engage in the tasks of ruling and populating the earth. The biblical record now closes with an affirmation of the equally-shared priestly privileges of those who are Kingdom people (see also 1 Pet. 2:9–10). Significantly, this affirmation of the royal, priestly functions of the redeemed is repeated in Rev. 5:9–10; 20:6; 22:5. This teaching is particularly comforting for any persons whose congregations or denominations exclude women from decision-making or leadership posts. We can rejoice in the fact that God's Word itself designates all believers, regardless of gender, as mutual rulers and priests before God.

7. John's anticipation of Christ's return indicates an event that will be unmistakable and universally seen (Rev. 19:11f.; see also Matt. 24:30).

from God rather than merely a warning from John. This literary device is unusual in Greek literature. It heightens the impact of the book on the readers by stressing that the contents of the message are not available otherwise and that they deal with important divine events. Rev. 1:3 also emphasizes that the events are about to happen and that the reader who reads and obeys will be blessed.

Some see a problem with the statement 'for the time is near' (v. 3). One solution is that 'near' or 'short' could mean 'without delay' or 'suddenly' once the actual end time begins unfolding. An alternative is to understand it in terms of the certainty of the events. Perhaps the simplest interpretation is to realize that for Apocalyptists, the end is always imminent.

In vv. 4–6 the origin of the message is said to be from the eternal God, the seven spirits and Jesus. Jesus is given several titles which are significant in terms of his role with the revelation (v. 5). He is the Faithful Witness, which is the Greek word for 'martyr'. This would recall his death by crucifixion and identify him with the persecuted readers. Secondly, he is the firstborn of the dead. This probably refers to his resurrection. He is noted as the first resurrected and would look ahead to the reader's own hoped for resurrection. Finally, he is called the ruler of the kings of the earth. This would anticipate the final Kingdom when he would be supreme ruler and would again give hope to those being persecuted by their present governments.

Finally, Jesus is praised for loving us, for his work in redemption, and because he made us to be a Kingdom of priests unto God. This final description alludes to the Mosaic Covenant (Exod. 19) where Israel is promised to become a Kingdom of priests and a holy nation if the people obey God's voice. In Judaism, the priest was the only one who was worthy, through sacrificial atonements, to approach God in the holy of holies. Through he sacrificial death of Jesus the members of the church now were considered to be inheritors of this blessing. They are described in v. 6 collectively (a Kingdom) as well as individually (priests). This passage may suggest their current status as a spiritual Kingdom and also look ahead to a literal Kingdom as described in Revelation ◆

A Vision of Christ

9 I, John, your brother who share with you in Jesus the persecution and the kingdom and the patient endurance, was on the island called Patmos because of the word of God and the testimony of Jesus.[g] [10]I was in the spirit[h] on the Lord's day, and I heard behind me a loud voice like a trumpet [11]saying, "Write in a book what you see and send it to the seven churches, to Ephesus, to Smyrna, to Pergamum, to Thyatira, to Sardis, to Philadelphia, and to Laodicea."

◆ Patmos is a small island located off the coast of Asia Minor in the Aegean Sea, about 28 miles south of Samos. Approximately 10 miles long and 6 miles wide, the rocky, treeless island is shaped like a horse's head. Tacitus says that in Emperor Domitian's time it was used as an isolated place for political prisoners. Eusebius says that John was banished to the island by Domitian (around AD 95) and released by Nerva 18 months later (*Ecc. Hist.* 3.20.8–9) ◆

12 Then I turned to see whose voice it was that spoke to me, and on turning I saw seven golden lampstands, [13]and in the midst of the lampstands I saw one like the Son of Man, clothed with a long robe and with a golden sash across his chest. [14]His head and his hair were white as white wool, white as snow; his eyes were like a flame of fire, [15]his feet were like burnished bronze, refined as in a furnace, and his voice was like the sound of many waters. [16]In his right hand he held seven stars, and

[g] Or *testimony to Jesus*   [h] Or *in the Spirit*

from his mouth came a sharp, two-edged sword, and his face was like the sun shining with full force.

♦ This vision depicts the one who gives the revelation. His spiritual characteristics are reflected in his personal appearance: he is dressed as a priest (Exod. 25:37; 37:23; Zech. 4:2), but while the priest's girdle is made of fine linen and embroidered with needlework, Christ's is of gold symbolic of divinity. The white hair symbolizes wisdom, the eyes of fire show penetrating insight, the bronze feet stability and strength, the voice, like a waterfall is awe-inspiring. Christ controls the destiny of the seven churches and is able to discern good and evil by the sword of Divine judgment. Finally, his face shines brilliantly, which is reminiscent of Moses at Mt Sinai and Jesus at the Transfiguration. The placement of this vision is significant in that it presents a powerful, authoritative figure as the author of this apocalyptic message ♦

17 When I saw him, I fell at his feet as though dead. But he placed his right hand on me, saying, "Do not be afraid; I am the first and the last, ¹⁸and the living one. I was dead, and see, I am alive forever and ever; and I have the keys of Death and of Hades. ¹⁹Now write what you have seen, what is, and what is to take place after this. ²⁰As for the mystery of the seven stars that you saw in my right hand, and the seven golden lampstands: the seven stars are the angels of the seven churches, and the seven lampstands are the seven churches.

The Message to Ephesus

2 "To the angel of the church in Ephesus write: These are the words of him who holds the seven stars in his right hand, who walks among the seven golden lampstands:

2 "I know your works, your toil and your patient endurance. I know that you cannot tolerate evildoers; you have tested those who claim to be apostles but are not, and have found them to be false. ³I also know that you are enduring patiently and bearing up for the sake of my name, and that you have not grown weary. ⁴But I have this against you, that you have abandoned the love you had at first. ⁵Remember then from

♦ The seven churches (1:20), to whom the letters were addressed, were probably chosen for their location on the postal route and for their influence in the Mediterranean world. All lie in western Asia Minor and boasted early Christian communities. The first was Ephesus where the apostle John had maintained a ministry for many years. In this first letter, the image of a lover's enthusiastic burning passion is contrasted with the older patient, responsible attitude which is often perfunctory. God wanted the zealous deeds sparked by love rather than those dutifully performed out of habit ♦

---

17. Although Christ may appear in a manner that awes us, he also reassures us so that we are not paralyzed with fear (John 6:20). The placing of Christ's right hand (symbol of authority) on John indicates Christ has the power to allay our fears, especially fear of the unknown.

REVELATION 2

1. The imagery of Christ among the churches (lamp-stands) in 1:13 and 2:1 comforts us by its reminder of Christ's promise in Matt. 28:20 to be with his people always. The imagery should also remind us that we are accountable to the One among us who knows our words and deeds.
2–6. Although the church at Ephesus was hard at work for God (exhibiting purity of doctrine, discernment, perseverance, spiritual maturity, and fortitude), this congregation had nevertheless abandoned its first love. That love can either be loving Christ or loving others as Christ loves, or a combination of the two, because loving Christ *must* mean loving others (John 13:33–34; 1 John 4:20–21). Sadly, even the most zealous orthodoxy will be barren without love.

what you have fallen; repent, and do the works you did at first. If not, I will come to you and remove your lampstand from its place, unless you repent. [6]Yet this is to your credit: you hate the works of the Nicolaitans, which I also hate. [7]Let anyone who has an ear listen to what the Spirit is saying to the churches. To everyone who conquers, I will give permission to eat from the tree of life that is in the paradise of God.

The Message to Smyrna

8 "And to the angel of the church in Smyrna write: These are the words of the first and the last, who was dead and came to life:

9 "I know your affliction and your poverty, even though you are rich. I know the slander on the part of those who say that they are Jews and are not, but are a synagogue of Satan. [10]Do not fear what you are about to suffer. Beware, the devil is about to throw some of you into prison so that you may be tested, and for ten days you will have affliction. Be faithful until death, and I will give you the crown of life. [11]Let anyone who has an ear listen to what the Spirit is saying to the churches. Whoever conquers will not be harmed by the second death.

The Message to Pergamum

12 "And to the angel of the church in Pergamum write: These are the words of him who has the sharp two-edged sword:

13 "I know where you are living, where

◆ There were three dominant pagan elements in the city of Pergamum: a huge throne – like the altar to Zeus which overlooked the city; the temple and healing center of Asclepius, god of healing, symbolized by a serpent and called 'Savior'; and the pressure from emperor worship prevalent in the late first century AD. Satan's throne may be a reference to one of these or to the environment caused by all three ◆

Satan's throne is. Yet you are holding fast to my name, and you did not deny your faith in me[i] even in the days of Antipas my witness, my faithful one, who was killed among you, where Satan lives. [14]But I have a few things against you: you have some there who hold to the teaching of Balaam, who taught Balak to put a stumbling block before the people of Israel, so that they would eat food sacrificed to idols and practice fornication. [15]So you also have some who hold to the teaching of the Nicolaitans. [16]Repent then. If not, I will come to you soon and make war against them with the sword of my mouth. [17]Let anyone who has an ear listen to what the Spirit is saying to the churches. To everyone who conquers I will give some of the hidden manna, and I will give a white stone, and on the white stone is written a new name that no one knows except the one who receives it.

[i] Or *deny my faith*

9–10. With Smyrna located in a center of emperor worship, professing Christians there would be unable to escape persecution. But even if materially poor, this church knew the source of true riches (2 Cor. 6:10; Phil. 4:19). Christ's specific words of encouragement for this suffering congregation also encourage any today who are being persecuted for their faith, regardless of the form that persecution may take ('slander', 'prison', 'affliction').

13–16. Situated in another center of pagan worship ('Satan's throne'), the church at Pergamum firmly upheld faith in Christ. However, it also allowed immorality among some of its members. Christ's call to repentance is a timely warning to anyone who might feel that a loving God is not concerned with biblical standards of morality (1 Cor. 3:11–17; 1 Thess. 4:3–8). Rather, our loving Creator desires actions that do not mar or debase those created in God's image. The challenge is actively to uphold purity (and not just co-exist with immorality, which will eventually corrupt – v. 14–15), and to do so in a manner that cannot be confused with emotional prejudice or blind bigotry.

◆ The White Stone is a reward to those who overcome. A white stone was used in several ways in the ancient world. In ancient judicial cases jurors cast votes of guilt by submitting a black stone and innocence by a white stone. In a Thracian custom, white stones were used to mark a good day, and in other cultures white stones were given as awards at games. In this passage any or all could apply, for God is rewarding and could be pronouncing these overcomers innocent of the deeds done by others in Pergamum ◆

◆ A symbolic name for a false teacher in the early church at Thyatira, Jezebel is equated with the Old Testament queen who supported idolatry (1 Kings 16:31) because she promoted the churches's compromise with pagan temple practices of fornication and eating meat sacrificed to idols. 'Her children' probably refers to her followers. The negative description of her as a self-proclaimed prophetess is because her teaching was not in accord with acceptable practices of the church rather than because she was a woman ◆

The Message to Thyatira

18 "And to the angel of the church in Thyatira write: These are the words of the Son of God, who has eyes like a flame of fire, and whose feet are like burnished bronze:

19 "I know your works – your love, faith, service, and patient endurance. I know that your last works are greater than the first. ²⁰But I have this against you: you tolerate that woman Jezebel, who calls herself a prophet and is teaching and beguiling my servants^j to practice fornication and to eat food sacrificed to idols. ²¹I gave her time to repent, but she refuses to repent of her fornication. ²²Beware, I am throwing her on a bed, and those who commit adultery with her I am throwing into great distress, unless they repent of her doings; ²³and I will strike her children dead. And all the churches will know that I am the one who searches minds and hearts, and I will give to each of you as your works deserve. ²⁴But to the rest of you in Thyatira, who do not hold this teaching, who have not learned what some call 'the deep things of Satan,' to you I say, I do not lay on you any other burden; ²⁵only hold fast to what you have until I come. ²⁶To everyone who conquers and continues to do my works to the end,

I will give authority over the nations;
²⁷ to rule^k them with an iron rod,
        as when clay pots are shattered—
²⁸even as I also received authority from my Father. To the one who conquers I will also give the morning star. ²⁹Let anyone who has an ear listen to what the Spirit is saying to the churches.

^j Gk *slaves*   ^k Or *to shepherd*

19–25. Thyatira was another church active in loving, faithful service, persevering and even advancing despite outer trials ('your last works are greater than the first'). Yet the Christ who 'searches minds and hearts' uncovered there the practice of tolerating either sexual or more probably spiritual unfaithfulness. The language is similar to that of Old Testament prophets who considered idolatry as departure from single-minded loyalty to God, and thus spiritual adultery. The word 'tolerate' in v. 20 sounds a note of caution to those living in a pluralistic society. Toleration is not a virtue if it condones compromise with practices God has commanded against. This letter to Thyatira speaks to persons who may be tempted to compromise their faith in the name of 'toleration'. The related challenge is to be very sure that we have studied God's Word so that we know what God does require in matters of faith and practice.

The Message to Sardis

3 "And to the angel of the church in Sardis write: These are the words of him who has the seven spirits of God and the seven stars:

"I know your works; you have a name of being alive, but you are dead. ²Wake up, and strengthen what remains and is on the

---

◆ The archaeological remains at Sardis reveal that a surprising number of public works were never fully completed. This may explain the statement about knowing the works of Sardis – they were well begun but left unfinished.

Twice in its history Sardis fell to the enemy due to lack of vigilance: In 549 BC it was taken by Cyrus (a climber managed to scale the nearly perpendicular wall of the mountain fortress undetected) and again in 216 BC by Antiochus the Great. The church is admonished to wake up spiritually lest Christ also come unexpectedly ◆

---

point of death, for I have not found your works perfect in the sight of my God. ³Remember then what you received and heard; obey it, and repent. If you do not wake up, I will come like a thief, and you will not know at what hour I will come

to you. ⁴Yet you have still a few persons in Sardis who have not soiled their clothes; they will walk with me, dressed in white, for they are worthy. ⁵If you conquer, you will be clothed like them in white robes, and I will not blot your name out of the book of life; I will confess your name before my Father and before his angels. ⁶Let anyone who has an ear listen to what the Spirit is saying to the churches.

The Message to Philadelphia

7 "And to the angel of the church in Philadelphia write:

These are the words of the holy one,
    the true one,
who has the key of David,
who opens and no one will shut,
    who shuts and no one opens:

8 "I know your works. Look, I have set before you an open door, which no one is able to shut. I know that you have but little power, and yet you have kept my word and have not denied my name. ⁹I will make those of the synagogue of Satan who say that they are Jews and are not, but are lying – I will make them come and bow down before your feet, and they will learn that I have loved you. ¹⁰Because you have kept my word of patient endurance, I will keep you from the hour of trial that is

---

REVELATION 3

1–6. At the time Revelation was written, the city of Sardis was experiencing commercial decline and moral apathy; its Christian community was similarly moribund. Christ urged this congregation to rekindle its dying embers of faith and obediently join with those who had remained steadfast ('have not soiled their clothes' – possibly a reference to those 'robes of righteousness' promised believers in Is. 61:10). Christ's emphasis on 'waking up' to the urgency of being prepared for his return shows us that perseverance is of prime importance, and that apathy can be just as much a denial of Christ as verbal denial. Clothes need not be dragged through mud to become dirty; they can be just as deeply soiled if they are not regularly cleaned. So also we each need the continual spiritual cleansing Christ offers (1 John 1:8–9).

7–13. Like Smyrna, the church at Philadelphia was not condemned but praised for its firm stance against temptation to deny Christ, and also given a special promise of protection from harm. This faithful congregation would rejoice at news of Christ's return; so too will today's believers rejoice if they are faithful disciples. Those who keep God's Word (v. 10) will themselves be kept safe by God (v. 12).

coming on the whole world to test the inhabitants of the earth. [11]I am coming soon; hold fast to what you have, so that no one may seize your crown. [12]If you conquer, I will make you a pillar in the temple of my God; you will never go out of it. I will write on you the name of my God, and the name of the city of my God, the new Jerusalem that comes down from my God out of heaven, and my own new name. [13]Let anyone who has an ear listen to what the Spirit is saying to the churches.

The Message to Laodicea

14 "And to the angel of the church in Laodicea write: The words of the Amen, the faithful and true witness, the origin[1] of God's creation:

15 "I know your works; you are neither cold nor hot. I wish that you were either cold or hot. [16]So, because you are lukewarm, and neither cold nor hot, I am about to spit you out of my mouth. [17]For you say, 'I am rich, I have prospered, and I need nothing.' You do not realize that you are wretched, pitiable, poor, blind, and naked. [18]Therefore I counsel you to buy from me gold refined by fire so that you may be rich; and white robes to clothe you and to keep the shame of your nakedness from being seen; and salve to anoint your eyes so that

◆ The problem may not be spiritual temperature, but unproductivity of works. The hot medicinal waters of Hierapolis used for healing and the cold water of Colossae met at Laodicea in a tepid, lukewarm state. As such the water was good neither for healing or refreshment but was distasteful and useless. Because of Laodicea's apathy God considered the church as only worthy to be spat out ◆

you may see. [19]I reprove and discipline those whom I love. Be earnest, therefore, and repent. [20]Listen! I am standing at the door, knocking; if you hear my voice and open the door, I will come in to you and eat with you, and you with me. [21]To the one who conquers I will give a place with me on my throne, just as I myself conquered and sat down with my Father on his throne. [22]Let anyone who has an ear listen to what the Spirit is saying to the churches."

The Heavenly Worship

4 After this I looked, and there in heaven a door stood open! And the first voice, which I had heard speaking to me like a

[1] Or *beginning*

14–19. Laodicea is the only church for whom the Lord had nothing good to say because it was 'lukewarm'. Situated in a rich commercial and medical center, the Laodiceans had become complacent and self-satisfied, unable to discern their true poverty of spirit. Christ's message is a sobering reminder not to be blinded by wealth or achievement, but to focus on where true riches and security are found (Matt. 6:19:21; 1 Pet. 1:3–9). Yet the condemnation of Laodicea also contains a positive message: God's necessary discipline of persons who are Christians in name only springs from God's great love of humanity, and God's desire that all should come to the place of repentance and restoration (vv. 19–20). Significantly, it is to people caught up in the awful tragedy of spiritual indifference that Christ offers the closest fellowship, typified by a shared meal. This gracious invitation respects individual moral responsibility; Christ does not force repentance or belief but places the choice with each individual.

REVELATION 4

1. The remainder of Revelation not only shifts the vision between the earthly and heavenly realms, but does so in a manner that defies any rigid outline or uniform interpretation. However, the underlying teaching is that there is a cosmic drama (see Job 1–2) and our responsibility is to be God's faithful servants, however limited our understanding of that drama.

trumpet, said, "Come up here, and I will show you what must take place after this." [2]At once I was in the spirit,[m] and there in heaven stood a throne, with one seated on the throne! [3]And the one seated there looks like jasper and carnelian, and around the throne is a rainbow that looks like an emerald. [4]Around the throne are twenty-four thrones, and seated on the thrones are twenty-four elders, dressed in white robes, with golden crowns on their heads. [5]Coming from the throne are flashes of lightning, and rumblings and peals of thunder, and in front of the throne burn seven flaming torches, which are the seven spirits of God; [6]and in front of the throne there is something like a sea of glass, like crystal.

Around the throne, and on each side of the throne, are four living creatures, full of eyes in front and behind: [7]the first living creature like a lion, the second living creature like an ox, the third living creature with a face like a human face, and the fourth living creature like a flying eagle. [8]And the four living creatures, each of them with six wings, are full of eyes all around and inside. Day and night without ceasing they sing,

"Holy, holy, holy,
the Lord God the Almighty,
who was and is and is to come."

[9]And whenever the living creatures give glory and honor and thanks to the one who is seated on the throne, who lives forever and ever, [10]the twenty-four elders fall before the one who is seated on the throne and worship the one who lives forever and ever; they cast their crowns before the throne, singing,

[11] "You are worthy, our Lord and God,
to receive glory and honor and
power,
for you created all things,
and by your will they existed and
were created."

The Scroll and the Lamb

5 Then I saw in the right hand of the one seated on the throne a scroll written on the inside and on the back, sealed[n] with seven seals; [2]and I saw a mighty angel proclaiming with a loud voice, "Who is worthy to open the scroll and break its seals?" [3]And no one in heaven or on earth or

[m] Or *in the Spirit*   [n] Or *written on the inside, and sealed on the back*

6–11. Note that John is careful only to say these creatures were 'like' something else. The form of these creatures is not as important as their function: giving ceaseless praise to the One and Only Creator and Sustainer of all existence (v. 11). As elsewhere in Scripture, Revelation makes it plain that the Living God must be worshiped by living creatures. The God of the Bible can never be reduced to merely an abstract idea but is the One 'who lives forever and ever'. Nor does the Bible teach that God is only the highest personage in some 'chain of being'. Revelation emphasizes the distinct divide between Creator and creation, including as creatures even some heavenly beings that might seem to mortals to be semi-divine (19:10; 22:8–9). In their ceaseless praise, the 'living creatures' are joined by 24 elders. Who this group represents is not clear, but again their activity informs us of the importance of worship and praise. Further, as the hymn of 4:11 is expanded in chapter 5, we see a richness of worship that should prompt us to use the most creative words and music to honor and glorify our great Savior God.

REVELATION 5

1. The opening of this scroll sets in motion the consummation of all things, including the final judgment. God's perfect fairness is symbolized by designating the Lion/Lamb of v. 5 and 6 as the only One worthy to open this sequence: The Christ who returns as conquering King is also Suffering Servant who provides to all who believe escape from God's wrath (John 1:29; 3:36; 6:37).

under the earth was able to open the scroll or to look into it. ⁴And I began to weep bitterly because no one was found worthy to open the scroll or to look into it. ⁵Then one of the elders said to me, "Do not weep. See, the Lion of the tribe of Judah, the Root of David, has conquered, so that he can open the scroll and its seven seals."

6 Then I saw between the throne and the four living creatures and among the elders a Lamb standing as if it had been slaughtered, having seven horns and seven eyes, which are the seven spirits of God sent out into all the earth. ⁷He went and took the scroll from the right hand of the one who was seated on the throne. ⁸When he had taken the scroll, the four living creatures and the twenty-four elders fell before the Lamb, each holding a harp and golden bowls full of incense, which are the prayers of the saints. ⁹They sing a new song:

◆ Prayer is a privileged conversation which we have with God. Prayer is where we can do our personal business with God.

The language of prayer is the language of meeting and of encounter. It is not just a matter of sending requests up to God, but the means by which our relationship with God is strengthened. Whether alone or in a group, our prayer is a meeting with God.

Prayer depends fundamentally on Christ. Because God was incarnate in Christ, we know that God can understand what it is to be human, to be one of us. It is Jesus who taught his disciples, and us, to pray, 'Our Father' (Matt. 6:9–13); Jesus promised to be with us when we meet together to pray (Matt. 18:19–20).

Most importantly, our praying is based on the access we have to God through Christ (Heb. 10:19–22). It is made possible by the work of the Spirit (Rom. 8:26–27). Thus God as Father, Son and Spirit enables and directs our prayer. When we pray, we share in the divine conversation: we can therefore be confident that God will hear us. Nothing in our lives is too big or small to bring to the God with whom we meet in prayer.

Yet lest we become complacent, or too familiar with God, the descriptions of God in Revelation (1:12–18; 4:1–11) remind us of the danger of creating God in our own image. Language fails John when he tries to describe his visions of God. God cannot be contained. God is more holy than we can imagine. Thus we approach with reverence and awe, yet confident in the access won for us in Christ's death. God, who is beyond limitation, knows us and our limitation, and meets us in prayer ◆

"You are worthy to take the scroll
    and to open its seals,
for you were slaughtered and by your
      blood you ransomed for God
saints from° every tribe and language
    and people and nation;
¹⁰ you have made them to be a kingdom
    and priests servingᵖ our God,
    and they will reign on earth."

11 Then I looked, and I heard the voice of many angels surrounding the throne and the living creatures and the elders; they numbered myriads of myriads and thousands of thousands, ¹²singing with full voice,

° Gk *ransomed for God from*   ᵖ Gk *priests to*

---

8. The word 'saints' is the usual New Testament designation for Christians (see 1 Cor. 1:2), and not a special group of believers.

9. The new song builds on prior imagery to reveal the collegiality and inter-relation of the persons of the Godhead. In 4:11 the 'One seated on the throne' is 'worthy'; now the 'Lamb' is also 'worthy' (5:6, reinforced in v. 11). God who in 4:11 is Creator and Sustainer (which might be a reference to the Holy Spirit) is revealed as Redeemer in 5:9. Thus the heavenly beings sing a 'new song' as the first song of Creation (Job 38:7) is augmented by the song of redemption (Rev. 5:9–11).

"Worthy is the Lamb that was
  slaughtered
to receive power and wealth and
  wisdom and might
and honor and glory and blessing!"

[13]Then I heard every creature in heaven and on earth and under the earth and in the sea, and all that is in them, singing,

"To the one seated on the throne and
  to the Lamb
be blessing and honor and glory and
  might
forever and ever!"

[14]And the four living creatures said, "Amen!" And the elders fell down and worshiped.

The Seven Seals

6 Then I saw the Lamb open one of the seven seals, and I heard one of the four living creatures call out, as with a voice of thunder, "Come!"[q] [2]I looked, and there was a white horse! Its rider had a bow; a crown was given to him, and he came out conquering and to conquer.

[3] When he opened the second seal, I heard the second living creature call out, "Come!"[q] [4]And out came[r] another horse, bright red; its rider was permitted to take peace from the earth, so that people would slaughter one another; and he was given a great sword.

[5] When he opened the third seal, I heard the third living creature call out,

"Come!"[q] I looked, and there was a black horse! Its rider held a pair of scales in his hand, [6]and I heard what seemed to be a voice in the midst of the four living creatures saying, "A quart of wheat for a day's pay,[s] and three quarts of barley for a day's pay,[s] but do not damage the olive oil and the wine!"

[7] When he opened the fourth seal, I heard the voice of the fourth living creature call out, "Come!"[q] [8]I looked and there was a pale green horse! Its rider's name was Death, and Hades followed with him; they were given authority over a fourth of the earth, to kill with sword, famine, and pestilence, and by the wild animals of the earth.

[9] When he opened the fifth seal, I saw under the altar the souls of those who had been slaughtered for the word of God and for the testimony they had given; [10]they cried out with a loud voice, "Sovereign Lord, holy and true, how long will it be before you judge and avenge our blood on the inhabitants of the earth?" [11]They were each given a white robe and told to rest a little longer, until the number would be complete both of their fellow servants[t] and of their brothers and sisters,[u] who were soon to be killed as they themselves had been killed.

[q] Or "Go!"   [r] Or went   [s] Gk a denarius
[t] Gk slaves   [u] Gk brothers

---

13. The placing of this verse demonstrates the difficulty of attempting to force John's visions into rigid chronological order. Here the all-inclusive language indicates a time when everyone everywhere will praise God. Yet subsequent chapters describe massive rebellion against God, which certainly would antedate the universal praise of v. 13. The basic truth, however, is that this event will one day occur, in fulfillment of the yearning expressed in Rom. 8:18–23 and the prophecy of Phil. 2:9–11.

REVELATION 6

1–8. These images, traditionally known as The Four Horsemen of the Apocalypse, possibly represent tyranny, war, famine and death, all of which are instruments of destruction.
9–11. Significantly, persons who have suffered the most painful martyrdom understand that only God can effect final judgment on their enemies (Deut. 32:35; Rom. 12:19) because only God is able to execute righteous vengeance instead of unrighteous revenge. Equally significant, these martyrs are forever secure ('under the altar').

12 When he opened the sixth seal, I looked, and there came a great earthquake; the sun became black as sackcloth, the full moon became like blood, ¹³and the stars of the sky fell to the earth as the fig tree drops its winter fruit when shaken by a gale. ¹⁴The sky vanished like a scroll rolling itself up, and every mountain and island was removed from its place. ¹⁵Then the kings of the earth and the magnates and the generals and the rich and the powerful, and everyone, slave and free, hid in the caves and among the rocks of the mountains, ¹⁶calling to the mountains and rocks, "Fall on us and hide us from the face of the one seated on the throne and from the wrath of the Lamb; ¹⁷for the great day of their wrath has come, and who is able to stand?"

The 144,000 of Israel Sealed

7 After this I saw four angels standing at the four corners of the earth, holding back the four winds of the earth so that no wind could blow on earth or sea or against any tree. ²I saw another angel ascending from the rising of the sun, having the seal of the living God, and he called with a loud voice to the four angels who had been given power to damage earth and sea, ³saying, "Do not damage the earth or the sea or the trees, until we have marked the servants^v of our God with a seal on their foreheads."

4 And I heard the number of those who were sealed, one hundred forty-four thousand, sealed out of every tribe of the people of Israel:

5 From the tribe of Judah twelve thousand sealed,

from the tribe of Reuben twelve thousand,

from the tribe of Gad twelve thousand,

6 from the tribe of Asher twelve thousand,

from the tribe of Naphtali twelve thousand,

from the tribe of Manasseh twelve thousand,

7 from the tribe of Simeon twelve thousand,

from the tribe of Levi twelve thousand,

from the tribe of Issachar twelve thousand,

---

^v Gk *slaves*

12–17. This series of disasters are of such immense proportions that humans instinctively realize these woes are evidence of divine wrath towards the persecutors of God's people (v. 9–11). Persons who have rejected the sacrifice of the Lamb (and thus have rejected God's redemptive love) are now without excuse and must face the 'wrath of the Lamb'. However, mere desire to hide from God's judgment (v. 15–17, see also Luke 23:30) shows no understanding that the only effective covering from God's wrath is the covering provided by the shed blood of Christ. By itself, fear of God is an inadequate spiritual response. Nebuchadnezzar feared God but still trusted in his own personal power and might until God humbled him. Only those who move from fear to believing faith in God's mercy will be spared God's judgment; those who reject God's free gift of new life in Christ must face God's wrath.

REVELATION 7–10

1–17. Although the scene shifts to a new vision, the answer to who will be spared from God's wrath (6:16–17) is that God's specially marked servants are exempt. Whether the 144,000 who receive God's seal represent Jewish believers in Christ or all Christian believers as 'the Israel of God' (Gal. 6:16) does not affect the basic truth that God preserves his own (John 10:27–30). This truth is further taught through the next vision of the great multinational and multiethnic gathering of worshipers (vv. 9–10) whom God has specifically preserved from 'the great ordeal' (v. 14, also called the Great Tribulation). It is on account of their trust 'in the blood of the Lamb' that God will 'shelter them' (v. 15). The pastoral imagery of vv. 16–17 reinforces their complete security.

8 from the tribe of Zebulun twelve thousand,

from the tribe of Joseph twelve thousand,

from the tribe of Benjamin twelve thousand sealed.

The Multitude from Every Nation

9 After this I looked, and there was a great multitude that no one could count, from every nation, from all tribes and peoples and languages, standing before the throne and before the Lamb, robed in white, with palm branches in their hands. [10]They cried out in a loud voice, saying,

"Salvation belongs to our God who is seated on the throne, and to the Lamb!"

[11]And all the angels stood around the throne and around the elders and the four living creatures, and they fell on their faces before the throne and worshiped God, [12]singing,

---

◆ To worship is to respond to God. In the New Testament, 'worship' encompasses ideas ranging from bowing down before God (1 Cor. 14:25; Rev. 4:10) to service (Rom. 12:1-2). While worship is what we do in church, it is also what we do in the whole of our lives as Christians, in response to God.

Worship is focused in the meeting together of Christians expressly to declare the glory of God. In the New Testament, this expression of worship is frequently associated with bowing down, as a sign of humility and acknowledgment of the honor and greatness of God. It may be expressed in many ways, including prayer and song (Eph. 5:20-21), and predominantly takes place in the context of a faith community, although it may be formal or spontaneous. Worship has both horizontal and vertical dimensions, involving relationships both with God and with other people. While glorifying God, it serves to encourage other believers.

However, worship extends beyond what believers do when they meet together. It is also used in the New Testament to describe the response of Christians to God in the whole of their lives. Worship is about offering ourselves to God as living sacrifices (Rom. 12:1-2), in the service of God. All we do in our everyday life, whether caring for a family, working at a job or serving the church, as long as it is mindful of the glory of God, is an act of worship. Thus worship is the integrating factor in the Christian life. It extends beyond church to the way we live our whole lives.

Women's response to God in worship is frequently described in the New Testament. Luke's account of the birth of Christ records Mary's song of praise to God; it also tells of the prophetess Anna who worships in the Temple night and day. In Matt. 28:9, Mary again responds in worship, now to the risen Lord. In Acts, women are clearly part of the Christian community as it meets together; indeed, in Philippi, it is a woman, Lydia, described as a worshiper of God, who provides the home base for Paul's ministry in that city (Acts 16:11-15). 1 Cor. 11 makes explicit provision for women to lead in prayer. Women continue to worship today both in explicit declaration of God's glory, and in lives of service ◆

"Amen! Blessing and glory and wisdom
and thanksgiving and honor
and power and might
be to our God forever and ever! Amen."

13 Then one of the elders addressed me, saying, "Who are these, robed in white, and where have they come from?" [14]I said to him, "Sir, you are the one that knows." Then he said to me, "These are they who have come out of the great ordeal; they have washed their robes and made them white in the blood of the Lamb.

[15] For this reason they are before the throne of God,
and worship him day and night within his temple,

and the one who is seated on the
    throne will shelter them.
[16] They will hunger no more, and thirst
    no more;
    the sun will not strike them,
    nor any scorching heat;
[17] for the Lamb at the center of the
    throne will be their shepherd,
    and he will guide them to springs of
    the water of life,
and God will wipe away every tear
    from their eyes."

The Seventh Seal and the Golden Censer

8 When the Lamb opened the seventh seal, there was silence in heaven for about half an hour. [2] And I saw the seven angels who stand before God, and seven trumpets were given to them.

3 Another angel with a golden censer came and stood at the altar; he was given a great quantity of incense to offer with the prayers of all the saints on the golden altar that is before the throne. [4] And the smoke of the incense, with the prayers of the saints, rose before God from the hand of the angel. [5] Then the angel took the censer and filled it with fire from the altar and threw it on the earth; and there were peals of thunder, rumblings, flashes of lightning, and an earthquake.

◆ Translated 'firepan', 'tray', or 'snuffer' and usually handled by priests, the censer was a hand-held ladle or shovel-like device. It was used to carry live coals mixed with incense which provided a pleasant odor. In the Temple or Tabernacle the vessels were either brass (Exod. 27:3) or gold (1 Kings 7:50).

In this passage the angel performs an intercessory and avenging function. He offers the prayers of the saints to God (v. 4). Then, mixed with fire of judgment (v. 5), the contents are thrown to earth. The catastrophes which follow in the next chapters result ◆

The Seven Trumpets

6 Now the seven angels who had the seven trumpets made ready to blow them.

◆ In the book of Revelation the trumpet (*Shôphār*) is an important instrument. It was usually constructed from a ram's horn, but horns of the ibex or antelope were also used. The purpose of the trumpet in Judaism was to signal events such as the new moon, the Sabbath, or the death of an important person. It also warned of danger, heralded excommunication, was used in exorcisms and magic healing, and was used 'to terrorize the enemy into panic' (cf. Gideon's use of trumpets in Judg. 7:19–20).

The *Shôphār* was never used with other instruments and was not considered to be a musical instrument. Its function was to make noise since it could produce only limited musical tones.

In Revelation seven trumpets are used by seven angels to signal destructive events (Rev. 8:3ff.). It is interesting to note that voices announce other events (i.e. Rev. 18:2; 19:17; 21:3). It is also used to describe the voice of the Lord as he commissioned John to write (Rev. 1:10) ◆

8:1–5. Silence here indicates a pause, as in music, preceding a notable activity. The songs of praise are now quieted, possibly for a time of reflection on the unfolding events, but also possibly so that the 'prayers of all the saints' (v. 3, see also 5:8) can be clearly heard as they rise before God. If these prayers echo the cries for judgment in 6:10, then the bowl of fire the angel spills on the earth could represent God's answer of sending divine retribution on those who persecute his people.

8:6–9:21. The sounding of the first four trumpets unleashes a series of climactic, geological, and ecological disasters. The fifth trumpet signals the appearance of a falling star representing the emergence of some sort of supernatural personage and his demonic minions, evil forces who are told to spare both God's people and the innocent environment (9:4). But while those who reject

7 The first angel blew his trumpet, and there came hail and fire, mixed with blood, and they were hurled to the earth; and a third of the earth was burned up, and a third of the trees were burned up, and all green grass was burned up.

8 The second angel blew his trumpet, and something like a great mountain, burning with fire, was thrown into the sea. ⁹A third of the sea became blood, a third of the living creatures in the sea died, and a third of the ships were destroyed.

10 The third angel blew his trumpet, and a great star fell from heaven, blazing like a torch, and it fell on a third of the rivers and on the springs of water. ¹¹The name of the star is Wormwood. A third of the waters became wormwood, and many died from the water, because it was made bitter.

12 The fourth angel blew his trumpet, and a third of the sun was struck, and a third of the moon, and a third of the stars, so that a third of their light was darkened; a third of the day was kept from shining, and likewise the night.

13 Then I looked, and I heard an eagle crying with a loud voice as it flew in midheaven, "Woe, woe, woe to the inhabitants of the earth, at the blasts of the other trumpets that the three angels are about to blow!"

9 And the fifth angel blew his trumpet, and I saw a star that had fallen from heaven to earth, and he was given the key to the shaft of the bottomless pit; ²he opened the shaft of the bottomless pit, and from the shaft rose smoke like the smoke of a great furnace, and the sun and the air were darkened with the smoke from the shaft. ³Then from the smoke came locusts on the earth, and they were given authority like the authority of scorpions of the earth.

⁴They were told not to damage the grass of the earth or any green growth or any tree, but only those people who do not have the seal of God on their foreheads. ⁵They were allowed to torture them for five months, but not to kill them, and their torture was like the torture of a scorpion when it stings someone. ⁶And in those days people will seek death but will not find it; they will long to die, but death will flee from them.

7 In appearance the locusts were like horses equipped for battle. On their heads were what looked like crowns of gold; their faces were like human faces, ⁸their hair like women's hair, and their teeth like lions' teeth; ⁹they had scales like iron breastplates, and the noise of their wings was like the noise of many chariots with horses rushing into battle. ¹⁰They have tails like scorpions, with stingers, and in their tails is their power to harm people for five months. ¹¹They have as king over them the angel of the bottomless pit; his name in Hebrew is Abaddon,ʷ and in Greek he is called Apollyon.ˣ

12 The first woe has passed. There are still two woes to come.

13 Then the sixth angel blew his trumpet, and I heard a voice from the fourʸ horns of the golden altar before God, ¹⁴saying to the sixth angel who had the trumpet, "Release the four angels who are bound at the great river Euphrates." ¹⁵So the four angels were released, who had been held ready for the hour, the day, the month, and the year, to kill a third of humankind. ¹⁶The number of the troops of cavalry was two hundred million; I heard their number. ¹⁷And this was how I saw the horses in my vision: the riders wore breastplates the

ʷ That is, *Destruction*   ˣ That is, *Destroyer*
ʸ Other ancient authorities lack *four*

God experience utter misery (9:6), even after the next plagues these persons still defy God's sovereignty (9:20–21). The double emphasis on lack of repentance indicates both the voluntary nature of the decision to follow evil and also the fact that these individuals could have escaped God's wrath if they had but turned to seek God's salvation (see 5:9 and 7:10).

color of fire and of sapphire[z] and of sulfur; the heads of the horses were like lions' heads, and fire and smoke and sulfur came out of their mouths. [18]By these three plagues a third of humankind was killed, by the fire and smoke and sulfur coming out of their mouths. [19]For the power of the horses is in their mouths and in their tails; their tails are like serpents, having heads; and with them they inflict harm.

20 The rest of humankind, who were not killed by these plagues, did not repent of the works of their hands or give up worshiping demons and idols of gold and silver and bronze and stone and wood, which cannot see or hear or walk. [21]And they did not repent of their murders or their sorceries or their fornication or their thefts.

The Angel with the Little Scroll

10 And I saw another mighty angel coming down from heaven, wrapped in a cloud, with a rainbow over his head; his face was like the sun, and his legs like pillars of fire. [2]He held a little scroll open in his hand. Setting his right foot on the sea and his left foot on the land, [3]he gave a great shout, like a lion roaring. And when he shouted, the seven thunders sounded. [4]And when the seven thunders had sounded, I was about to write, but I heard a voice from heaven saying, "Seal up what the seven thunders have said, and do not write it down." [5]Then the angel whom I saw standing on the sea and the land raised his right hand to heaven

[6]   and swore by him who lives forever
           and ever,

who created heaven and what is in it, the earth and what is in it, and the sea and what is in it: "There will be no more delay, [7]but in the days when the seventh angel is to blow his trumpet, the mystery of God will be fulfilled, as he announced to his servants[a] the prophets."

8 Then the voice that I had heard from heaven spoke to me again, saying, "Go, take the scroll that is open in the hand of the angel who is standing on the sea and on the land." [9]So I went to the angel and told him to give me the little scroll; and he said to me, "Take it, and eat; it will be bitter to your stomach, but sweet as honey in your mouth." [10]So I took the little scroll from the hand of the angel and ate it; it was sweet as honey in my mouth, but when I had eaten it, my stomach was made bitter.

11 Then they said to me, "You must prophesy again about many peoples and nations and languages and kings."

The Two Witnesses

11 Then I was given a measuring rod like a staff, and I was told, "Come and measure the temple of God and the altar and those who worship there, [2]but do not measure the court outside the temple; leave that out, for it is given over to the nations, and they will trample over the holy city for forty-two months. [3]And I will grant my two witnesses authority to prophesy for one thousand two hundred sixty days, wearing sackcloth."

[z] Gk *hyacinth*   [a] Gk *slaves*

10:8–10. John's experience reminds us that while God's Word is sweet to his own people, Christians can never rejoice in God's judgment on unbelievers.

REVELATION 11

1–2. In Scripture, measuring tools can symbolize the demarcation between good and evil (Amos 7:7–9). Here the division between the Temple itself and the outside court depicts the deepening divide between those who turn to God in believing faith and those who 'trample' the things of God. **3–14.** God's two special witnesses are granted unique powers which should elicit repentance and belief, but (as with Pharoah during the Exodus) entrenched evil continues its defiance. In v. 7 the creature or evil power denoted as 'the beast' comes on the scene with no introduction or

4 These are the two olive trees and the two lampstands that stand before the Lord of the earth. ⁵And if anyone wants to harm them, fire pours from their mouth and consumes their foes; anyone who wants to harm them must be killed in this manner. ⁶They have authority to shut the sky, so that no rain may fall during the days of their prophesying, and they have authority over the waters to turn them into blood, and to strike the earth with every kind of plague, as often as they desire.

7 When they have finished their testimony, the beast that comes up from the bottomless pit will make war on them and conquer them and kill them, ⁸and their dead bodies will lie in the street of the great city that is prophetically[b] called Sodom and Egypt, where also their Lord was crucified. ⁹For three and a half days members of the peoples and tribes and languages and nations will gaze at their dead bodies and refuse to let them be placed in a tomb; ¹⁰and the inhabitants of the earth will gloat over them and celebrate and exchange presents, because these two prophets had been a torment to the inhabitants of the earth.

11 But after the three and a half days, the breath[c] of life from God entered them, and they stood on their feet, and those who saw them were terrified. ¹²Then they[d] heard a loud voice from heaven saying to them, "Come up here!" And they went up to heaven in a cloud while their enemies watched them. ¹³At that moment there was a great earthquake, and a tenth of the city fell; seven thousand people were killed in the earthquake, and the rest were terrified and gave glory to the God of heaven.

14 The second woe has passed. The third woe is coming very soon.

The Seventh Trumpet

15 Then the seventh angel blew his trumpet, and there were loud voices in heaven, saying,

"The kingdom of the world has
    become the kingdom of our
    Lord
    and of his Messiah,[e]
and he will reign forever and ever."

16 Then the twenty-four elders who sit on their thrones before God fell on their faces and worshiped God, ¹⁷singing,

"We give you thanks, Lord God
    Almighty,
    who are and who were,
for you have taken your great power
    and begun to reign.
¹⁸ The nations raged,
    but your wrath has come,
    and the time for judging the dead,

---

[b] Or *allegorically*; Gk *spiritually*   [c] Or *the spirit*
[d] Other ancient authorities read *I*   [e] Gk *Christ*

---

explanation, implying that John's contemporaries might have been familiar with the image. Clearly this 'beast' is the implacable enemy of God, as is the 'great city' of v. 8. Evidence of the depths of depravity among God's enemies is that they find the righteous witnesses a 'torment' and celebrate their absence (v. 10). While such perverse rejoicing is not always so blatant today, nevertheless a people's true allegiance can often be determined by what makes them glad (Est. 5:9–14).

11–14. In response to the intervention of God's resurrection power, some onlookers are 'terrified' while others go beyond terror to give God glory. This is a graphic example of the complementary truths Jesus taught in Matt. 10:28 and John 11:25–26.

15–19. Opening with an affirmation of God's inevitable triumphant reign and closing with a reminder that God keeps his promises to his covenant people, John's next vision greatly comforts the believer. It assures us that God will indeed answer our anguished cries for judgment against evil and that Christ's return will make God's Kingdom rule a reality. V. 18 reminds us that 'the earth is the Lord's' and that Creator God will sternly punish those who wantonly destroy the goodness of his created world.

for rewarding your servants,[f] the
      prophets
   and saints and all who fear your
      name,
   both small and great,
and for destroying those who destroy
      the earth."
19 Then God's temple in heaven was
opened, and the ark of his covenant was
seen within his temple; and there were
flashes of lightning, rumblings, peals of
thunder, an earthquake, and heavy hail.

The Woman and the Dragon

12 A great portent appeared in
heaven: a woman clothed with
the sun, with the moon under her feet,
and on her head a crown of twelve stars.
[2]She was pregnant and was crying out
in birth pangs, in the agony of giving
birth. [3]Then another portent appeared
in heaven: a great red dragon, with seven
heads and ten horns, and seven diadems
on his heads. [4]His tail swept down a third
of the stars of heaven and threw them
to the earth. Then the dragon stood before
the woman who was about to bear a
child, so that he might devour her child
as soon as it was born. [5]And she gave birth
to a son, a male child, who is to rule[g] all
the nations with a rod of iron. But her child
was snatched away and taken to God and
to his throne; [6]and the woman fled into
the wilderness, where she has a place
prepared by God, so that there she can be
nourished for one thousand two hundred
sixty days.

◆ The twentieth century world is filled
with high-tech visual media. We are
constantly exposed to sophisticated
multi-media images that become firmly
implanted in our memories. The book of
Revelation was given to John in a vision.
He saw it, but it has been passed down to
us in words. However, the word pictures
in Revelation, especially the symbols, are
unforgettable in their impact. The first-
century Christians didn't have personal
copies of Revelation, but after hearing
it read they could remember its vivid
imagery and symbols. They may forget
the exact words of the text, but they
would not easily forget the symbols and
word pictures that parade through the
vision.

A symbol is something that stands for
another meaning in addition to its ordinary meaning. It is usually a visual image
that represents an invisible concept. The
ordinary meaning for a lampstand is a
pedestal supporting one or more lamps. In
Revelation, the lampstands symbolize the
seven churches in Asia. In Rev. 5:8, there
are golden bowls of incense, but we find
that these stand for the prayers of the
saints.

Symbols are used because the indescribable is being described. We don't have a
reference point. How does one describe
the wonder, beauty and joy of eternity with
God except to describe it in symbols. It's a
wedding (this is a love relationship), where
the whole church (males and females) is a

[f] Gk *slaves*   [g] Or *to shepherd*

REVELATION 12

1–6. The similar number of days ascribed to this event and to the witnessing mission of 11:3 may
indicate that these are parallel accounts of the same era. Just as the two witnesses were eventually caught up into heaven (11:12), so also at her most vulnerable time (symbolized by childbirth)
the woman and her child are preserved (vv. 5–6). Even in the wilderness (those darkest places of
life) the woman finds refuge in 'a place prepared by God' (v. 6). Notably, John uses the woman as a
positive symbol (possibly representing the Virgin Mary or the church). This passage is particularly comforting to women who seek to serve God wholeheartedly, assuring them that while
others may abandon them when they are helpless, God cares for them and provides a place of
refuge.

bride. The long awaited day has arrived; the bride is adorned for her husband. She looks beautiful (doesn't every bride?). He thinks she's beautiful (doesn't every groom?). There will never be a separation, for God dwells with his people.

Rev. 12:1–5 illustrates the power of symbols. In this vision John sees a pregnant woman, in pain, giving birth. Next he sees a great red dragon wearing royal crowns. He is so powerful that his tail alone can knock out one third of the stars of heaven. The dragon's grizzly mission is to devour the child that is being born. In Rev. 12:9 we find out that the dragon is a symbol for 'that ancient serpent, who is called the Devil and Satan, the deceiver of the whole world'. The child being born is Jesus, 'who is to rule all the nations with a rod of iron' (12:5).

The woman is pictured as helpless, defenseless, vulnerable, weak (is a woman ever more vulnerable than in the middle of childbirth?). In contrast, the dragon is powerful. There is no way that he can be stopped. He will devour this child. What baby can stand a chance against the dragon? But the dragon fails! The child is 'snatched away and taken to God and to his throne' (12:5). God in his weakness is mightier than Satan with all his power.

John's message is conveyed by symbols that could have been understood by his audience but would escape the understanding of those for whom the message was not intended. In this way he could send a message of encouragement and hope unperceived in the midst of Roman censorship and persecution ◆

Michael Defeats the Dragon

7 And war broke out in heaven; Michael and his angels fought against the dragon.

The dragon and his angels fought back, [8]but they were defeated, and there was no longer any place for them in heaven. [9]The great dragon was thrown down, that ancient serpent, who is called the Devil and Satan, the deceiver of the whole world – he was thrown down to the earth, and his angels were thrown down with him.

10 Then I heard a loud voice in heaven, proclaiming,

"Now have come the salvation and the
          power
    and the kingdom of our God
    and the authority of his Messiah,[h]
for the accuser of our comrades[i] has
          been thrown down,
    who accuses them day and night
          before our God.
[11] But they have conquered him by the
          blood of the Lamb
    and by the word of their testimony,
for they did not cling to life even in the
          face of death.
[12] Rejoice then, you heavens
    and those who dwell in them!
But woe to the earth and the sea,
    for the devil has come down to you
with great wrath,
    because he knows that his time is
          short!"

The Dragon Fights Again on Earth

13 So when the dragon saw that he had been thrown down to the earth, he pursued[j] the woman who had given birth to the male child. [14]But the woman was given the two wings of the great eagle, so

[h] Gk *Christ*   [i] Gk *brothers*   [j] Or *persecuted*

7–12. Having been dramatically cast out of the heavenlies, Satan and his minions now concentrate on final persecution of God's people. As in Rom. 10:9–10, John's vision emphasizes the necessity of articulating our faith through verbal witness (v. 11).

13–17. With imagery echoing Is. 40:31, the woman is again rescued and nourished despite evil's new onslaught. The fact that Satan turns full force upon 'her children' (all other faithful believers) should not surprise us. All who 'keep the commandments of God and hold the testimony of Jesus' may expect to face spiritual warfare (John 15:18–20; 16:33; 1 Pet. 4:12–16).

that she could fly from the serpent into the wilderness, to her place where she is nourished for a time, and times, and half a time. ¹⁵Then from his mouth the serpent poured water like a river after the woman, to sweep her away with the flood. ¹⁶But the earth came to the help of the woman; it opened its mouth and swallowed the river that the dragon had poured from his mouth. ¹⁷Then the dragon was angry with the woman, and went off to make war on the rest of her children, those who keep the commandments of God and hold the testimony of Jesus.

The First Beast

18 Then the dragon[k] took his stand on the sand of the seashore. ¹And I saw a beast rising out of the sea; and on its horns were ten diadems, and on its heads were blasphemous names. ²And the beast that I saw was like a leopard, its feet were like a bear's, and its mouth was like a lion's mouth. And the dragon gave it his power and his throne and great authority. ³One of its heads seemed to have received a death-blow, but its mortal wound[l] had been healed. In amazement the whole earth followed the beast. ⁴They worshiped the dragon, for he had given his authority to the beast, and they worshiped the beast, saying, "Who is like the beast, and who can fight against it?"

5 The beast was given a mouth uttering haughty and blasphemous words, and it was allowed to exercise authority for forty-two months. ⁶It opened its mouth to utter blasphemies against God, blaspheming his name and his dwelling, that is, those who dwell in heaven. ⁷Also it was allowed to make war on the saints and to conquer them.[m] It was given authority over every tribe and people and language and nation, ⁸and all the inhabitants of the earth will worship it, everyone whose name has not been written from the foundation of the world in the book of life of the Lamb that was slaughtered.[n]

9 Let anyone who has an ear listen:
¹⁰ If you are to be taken captive,
    into captivity you go;
if you kill with the sword,
    with the sword you must be killed.
Here is a call for the endurance and faith of the saints.

The Second Beast

11 Then I saw another beast that rose out of the earth; it had two horns like a lamb and it spoke like a dragon. ¹²It exercises all the authority of the first beast on

[k] Gk *Then he;* other ancient authorities read *Then I stood*   [l] Gk *the plague of its death*   [m] Other ancient authorities lack this sentence   [n] Or *written in the book of life of the Lamb that was slaughtered from the foundation of the world*

REVELATION 13

1–10. The drama in Job 1–2 shows Satan focusing on one individual. Now the satanic forces assault the entire believing community. Note that these forces are 'allowed' to operate (v. 7, 15) but do not do so by right (see John 19:11). The imagery of the first beast as injured and then recovered is descriptive of the persistence of evil.

11–18. More subtle than the first beast, with its displays of raw power, the new deceiver of v. 11 appears somehow Christlike ('like a lamb', see also 2 Cor. 11:14). But this second beast is also evil because it too promotes blasphemy (vv. 13–15). No matter how clever or seductive a spiritual leader or movement may be, a good question to ask is: What is its true object of worship? Historically, the Christian-related cults have been the most insidious, leading astray persons not firmly grounded in the faith and therefore unable to discern what is and is not of God (Matt. 24:23–27). As in vv. 13–14, evil forces may even perform miraculous signs, but again the question is: To whom or what do these signs point? Whether these beasts in John's visions are actual

its behalf, and it makes the earth and its
inhabitants worship the first beast, whose
mortal wound[o] had been healed. [13]It
performs great signs, even making fire
come down from heaven to earth in the
sight of all; [14]and by the signs that it is
allowed to perform on behalf of the beast, it
deceives the inhabitants of earth, telling
them to make an image for the beast that
had been wounded by the sword[p] and yet
lived; [15]and it was allowed to give breath[q] to
the image of the beast so that the image of
the beast could even speak and cause those
who would not worship the image of the
beast to be killed. [16]Also it causes all, both
small and great, both rich and poor, both
free and slave, to be marked on the right
hand or the forehead, [17]so that no one can
buy or sell who does not have the mark,
that is, the name of the beast or the
number of its name. [18]This calls for
wisdom: let anyone with understanding
calculate the number of the beast, for it is
the number of a person. Its number is six
hundred sixty-six.[r]

The Lamb and the 144,000

14 Then I looked, and there was the
Lamb, standing on Mount Zion! And
with him were one hundred forty-four thousand who had his name and his Father's
name written on their foreheads. [2]And I
heard a voice from heaven like the sound of
many waters and like the sound of loud
thunder; the voice I heard was like the sound
of harpists playing on their harps, [3]and they
sing a new song before the throne and before
the four living creatures and before the
elders. No one could learn that song except
the one hundred forty-four thousand who
have been redeemed from the earth. [4]It is
these who have not defiled themselves with
women, for they are virgins; these follow the
Lamb wherever he goes. They have been
redeemed from humankind as first fruits for
God and the Lamb, [5]and in their mouth no
lie was found; they are blameless.

◆ Celibacy was a very attractive option to many in the ancient world. The erotic excesses of Rome created a strong revulsion that first caused the adherents of pagan philosophers to espouse and endorse a lifestyle free from sexual involvement. Christians too become

[o] Gk *whose plague of its death* [p] Or *that had received the plague of the sword* [q] Or *spirit*
[r] Other ancient authorities read *six hundred sixteen*

personages, world powers, or heretical spiritual movements is not as important as the warning to stand firm (v. 10) and to have wisdom (v. 18 and 17:9; see also Prov. 1:9; John 16:13; James 1:5). And once again John highlights the contrast between those sealed by God and those marked by evil. Whether there will be literal 'seals' or 'marks' does not affect the teaching that there will be an inevitable and recognizable divide between these two groups. Who we serve does indeed mark us (3:12; 7:4; 13:16; 14:1; 22:4). Similarly, more important than intricate interpretations of the beast's identifying number is the implication that the identification will be plain to the discerning person. Thus this complex vision reinforces the necessity of knowing Scripture, for only those familiar with God's Word will be able to recognize and stand against what is not of God.

REVELATION 14

1–5. The sexual reference in v. 4 need not be thought of as denigrating women. Because Scripture specifically terms marital relations honorable (Heb. 13:4) and because the sense of the Greek is not necessarily celibacy but rather moral purity, many scholars feel v. 4 refers to those who refused to engage in either cult prostitution or general promiscuity. Since these 144,000 witnesses are also scrupulously truthful (v. 5), the overall impression is that they are single-minded in upholding purity of conduct and doctrine (they 'follow the Lamb wherever he goes').

aware of the freedom made possible by celibacy. The phrase 'not defiled themselves with women' may refer to the sexual activity frequently connected with pagan religions – even with some of the quasi-Christian groups (2 Pet. 2:14; Jude 7; Rev. 2:14, 20), or it may refer to those who renounce marriage. Among the many anti-Roman sentiments expressed in the book of Revelation, 14:4 constituted a revolt against Roman convention.

Despite considerable reluctance on the part of young people, families usually placed strong pressure upon their sons to wed; and daughters were married off at a very young age. Because of a need to raise the birth rate, the state placed repressive taxation upon widows and widowers who resisted second marriages. Early Christian literature relates the trials of young women who tried to escape the marriages planned by their parents, thereby incurring the wrath of government officials. Shelters were founded, perhaps as early as the first century, for celibate Christian women shunning unwanted marital unions. Married couples, enamored by the same asceticism, sometimes covenanted together to remain celibate within the marriage. In a practice known as suneichatism, other men and women lived together under the same roof without the formal bonds of wedlock and without sexual union.

The New Testament affirms those who choose celibacy for the sake of the gospel (Matt. 19:12) and declares that singleness is a special gift from God (1 Cor. 7:7). The apostle Paul considered the state a blessed one that freed an individual from the demands and entanglements of matrimony (1 Cor. 7:28–34). It opened many opportunities for gospel ministry, and throughout the centuries the church has reaped untold benefits from the labors of those who have renounced marriage. The modern missionary movement has been implemented in large part by single women who carried the news of Jesus Christ to every corner of the globe ◆

The Messages of the Three Angels

6 Then I saw another angel flying in midheaven, with an eternal gospel to proclaim to those who live[s] on the earth – to every nation and tribe and language and people. [7]He said in a loud voice, "Fear God and give him glory, for the hour of his judgment has come; and worship him who made heaven and earth, the sea and the springs of water."

8 Then another angel, a second, followed, saying, "Fallen, fallen is Babylon the great! She has made all nations drink of the wine of the wrath of her fornication."

9 Then another angel, a third, followed them, crying with a loud voice, "Those who worship the beast and its image, and receive a mark on their foreheads or on their hands, [10]they will also drink the wine of

[s] Gk *sit*

Furthermore, if this group is symbolic of all the redeemed, then the imagery of virginity would not only be very suitable for the church as the pure Bride of Christ (19:7–8) but would also include both women and men in the symbolic language. The application for today would be for believers to emulate such faithfulness to God's standards.

6–7. God's merciful forbearance (Hab. 3:2; 2 Pet. 3:9) is implicit in this angelic call to return to God. Even though God's 'hour of judgment' is at hand, God graciously delays the 'point of no return'.

8. As with the first appearance of the beast (11:7), the image of Babylon is used with no introductory explanation and thus indicates that the original readers of Revelation were probably familiar with the apocalyptic use of the term.

9–13. Again John describes evil as being tormented by the presence of righteousness (see on 11:10). The passage predicts eternal disharmony and disquiet for those who voluntarily choose to worship the beast, in contrast to the eternal rest and blessing of the persevering saints.

God's wrath, poured unmixed into the cup of his anger, and they will be tormented with fire and sulfur in the presence of the holy angels and in the presence of the Lamb. [11]And the smoke of their torment goes up forever and ever. There is no rest day or night for those who worship the beast and its image and for anyone who receives the mark of its name."

12 Here is a call for the endurance of the saints, those who keep the commandments of God and hold fast to the faith of[t] Jesus.

13 And I heard a voice from heaven saying, "Write this: Blessed are the dead who from now on die in the Lord." "Yes," says the Spirit, "they will rest from their labors, for their deeds follow them."

Reaping the Earth's Harvest

14 Then I looked, and there was a white cloud, and seated on the cloud was one like the Son of Man, with a golden crown on his head, and a sharp sickle in his hand! [15]Another angel came out of the temple, calling with a loud voice to the one who sat on the cloud, "Use your sickle and reap, for the hour to reap has come, because the harvest of the earth is fully ripe." [16]So the one who sat on the cloud swung his sickle over the earth, and the earth was reaped.

17 Then another angel came out of temple in heaven, and he too had a sharp sickle. [18]Then another angel came out from the altar, the angel who has authority over fire, and he called with a loud voice to him who had the sharp sickle, "Use your sharp sickle and gather the clusters of the vine of the earth, for its grapes are ripe." [19]So the angel swung his sickle over the earth and gathered the vintage of the earth, and he threw it into the great wine press of the wrath of God. [20]And the wine press was trodden outside the city, and blood flowed from the wine press, as high as a horse's bridle, for a distance of about two hundred miles.[u]

The Angels with the Seven Last Plagues

15 Then I saw another portent in heaven, great and amazing: seven angels with seven plagues, which are the last, for with them the wrath of God is ended.

2 And I saw what appeared to be a sea of glass mixed with fire, and those who had conquered the beast and its image and the number of its name, standing beside the sea of glass with harps of God in their hands. [3]And they sing the song of Moses, the servant[v] of God, and the song of the Lamb:

"Great and amazing are your deeds,
  Lord God the Almighty!
Just and true are your ways,
  King of the nations![w]

[t] Or *to their faith in* [u] Gk *one thousand six hundred stadia* [v] Gk *slave* [w] Other ancient authorities read *the ages*

14–20. In nature there is an inevitable harvest time; so also there will come the divine harvest season (Matt. 13:36–43). This terrible reaping activity is God's prerogative (Deut. 32:35; Rom. 12:19) and the extravagant imagery of v. 20 indicates the horrible judgment upon those who reject the covering of the blood of the Lamb.

REVELATION 15–17

15:1–8. As 'the last' events begin to unfold on earth, songs in the heavenly realm celebrate the perfection of the judgment of the one true and holy God. This song of the redeemed emphasizes the centrality of worship in the lives of those whom God has delivered from the bondage of evil and made conquerors over evil's power (Exod. 15:2, 13; Rom. 8:37). Those who are secure in the Lord engage in active praise, suggesting an appropriate sequence for believers during their earthly lives because in God's economy the promise is as good as the reality yet to be experienced (Rom. 4:20–21; 8:30; Col. 3:3–4).

⁴ Lord, who will not fear
     and glorify your name?
For you alone are holy.
     All nations will come
     and worship before you,
for your judgments have been
     revealed."

5 After this I looked, and the temple of the tent[x] of witness in heaven was opened, ⁶and out of the temple came the seven angels with the seven plagues, robed in pure bright linen,[y] with golden sashes across their chests. ⁷Then one of the four living creatures gave the seven angels seven golden bowls full of the wrath of God, who lives forever and ever; ⁸and the temple was filled with smoke from the glory of God and from his power, and no one could enter the temple until the seven plagues of the seven angels were ended.

The Bowls of God's Wrath

16 Then I heard a loud voice from the temple telling the seven angels, "Go and pour out on the earth the seven bowls of the wrath of God."

2 So the first angel went and poured his bowl on the earth, and a foul and painful sore came on those who had the mark of the beast and who worshiped its image.

3 The second angel poured his bowl into the sea, and it became like the blood of a corpse, and every living thing in the sea died.

4 The third angel poured his bowl into the rivers and the springs of water, and they became blood. ⁵And I heard the angel of the waters say,

"You are just, O Holy One, who are
     and were,
     for you have judged these things;
⁶ because they shed the blood of saints
     and prophets,
     you have given them blood to drink.
     It is what they deserve!"
⁷And I heard the altar respond,
"Yes, O Lord God, the Almighty,
     your judgments are true and just!"

8 The fourth angel poured his bowl on the sun, and it was allowed to scorch them with fire; ⁹they were scorched by the fierce heat, but they cursed the name of God, who had authority over these plagues, and they did not repent and give him glory.

10 The fifth angel poured his bowl on the throne of the beast, and its kingdom was plunged into darkness; people gnawed their tongues in agony, ¹¹and cursed the God of heaven because of their pains and sores, and they did not repent of their deeds.

12 The sixth angel poured his bowl on the great river Euphrates, and its water was dried up in order to prepare the way for the kings from the east. ¹³And I saw three foul spirits like frogs coming from the mouth of the dragon, from the mouth of the beast, and from the mouth of the false prophet. ¹⁴These are demonic spirits, performing signs, who go abroad to the kings of the whole world, to assemble them for battle on the great day of God the Almighty. ¹⁵("See, I am coming like a thief! Blessed is

---

[x] Or *tabernacle*   [y] Other ancient authorities read *stone*

16:1–21. The vision of the seven bowls symbolizes final fearful judgments on all human and demonic powers that persist in defying God, judgments that with terrible symmetry 'fit the crime' (see Obad. 15). The imagery of being suitably 'clothed' (Is. 61:10; 2 Cor. 5:1–4) joins with the previous imagery of being 'sealed' and gives the believer further assurance that God fully protects his own. While it may seem incredible that unbelief continues during such dreadful plagues, ingrained spiritual defiance is the end result of a lifelong habit of ignoring God's loving offer of reconciliation and is the epitome of spiritual pride. Peoples and powers may have the most cleverly devised scientific, technological, or even supernatural 'armor' and yet be totally vulnerable because they are not clothed in Christ's righteousness (Matt. 22:1–14). Thus the greatest force that evil can muster in one place, Armageddon, will be decisively destroyed.

the one who stays awake and is clothed,[z] not going about naked and exposed to shame.") [16]And they assembled them at the place that in Hebrew is called Harmagedon.

17 The seventh angel poured his bowl into the air, and a loud voice came out of the temple, from the throne, saying, "It is done!" [18]And there came flashes of lightning, rumblings, peals of thunder, and a violent earthquake, such as had not occurred since people were upon the earth, so violent was that earthquake. [19]The great city was split into three parts, and the cities of the nations fell. God remembered great Babylon and gave her the wine-cup of the fury of his wrath. [20]And every island fled away, and no mountains were to be found; [21]and huge hailstones, each weighing about a hundred pounds,[a] dropped from heaven on people, until they cursed God for the plague of the hail, so fearful was that plague.

The Great Whore and the Beast

17 Then one of the seven angels who had the seven bowls came and said to me, "Come, I will show you the judgment of the great whore who is seated on many waters, [2]with whom the kings of the earth have committed fornication, and with the wine of whose fornication the inhabitants of the earth have become drunk." [3]So he carried me away in the spirit[b] into a wilderness, and I saw a woman sitting on a scarlet beast that was full

◆ The harlot image signifies faithlessness to God as well as prostitution of what is right in order to gain power, wealth and luxury. Appearing like a whore – gaudy, drunken and immoral – 'Babylon' has great economic influence (v. 18) and persecutes the righteous ones (v. 6).

The harlot metaphor is used to denote the deceptive and powerful influence which she uses for economic gain. The imagery does not reflect the author's negative view of women but is consistent with Old Testament prophetic descriptions of Israel and heathen nations which followed idolatry and pagan practices (see Is. 1:21; Jer. 2:20; 3:1; Ezek. 16:15; Hos. 2:5; 3:3; 4:15; Is. 23:17; Nah. 3:9) ◆

of blasphemous names, and it had seven heads and ten horns. [4]The woman was clothed in purple and scarlet, and adorned with gold and jewels and pearls, holding in her hand a golden cup full of abominations and the impurities of her fornication; [5]and on her forehead was written a name, a mystery: "Babylon the great, mother of whores and of earth's abominations." [6]And I saw that the woman was drunk with the blood of the saints and the blood of the witnesses to Jesus.

When I saw her, I was greatly amazed. [7]But the angel said to me, "Why are you so amazed? I will tell you the mystery of the

[z] Gk *and keeps his robes* [a] Gk *weighing about a talent* [b] Or *in the Spirit*

17:1–18. This vision uses the dual images of a whore and Babylon the great city to describe the very essence of evil, its wanton promiscuity and self-indulgence, and its ultimate self-destruction. The activities of 'the great whore' and those who traffic with her echo the many Old Testament depictions of idolatry as the spiritual adultery of persons seduced by the seeming attractions of evil into becoming intimate with what is not of God. Rarely do people today think in such stark terms, but spiritually there is no middle ground between faith in God and trusting in not-God. Concentrated into the image of the 'mother of whores and of earth's abominations' is everything past, present, and future that craves self-gratification and power, and thus hates God and finds its greatest satisfaction in destroying God's people. Similarly, 'the great city' is representative of every individual and government throughout human history that has sought to dominate the earth in defiance of God's created purpose. The Lamb will conquer this massive coalition, using even those who hate him to carry out their own destruction (vv. 16–17).

woman, and of the beast with seven heads and ten horns that carries her. [8]The beast that you saw was, and is not, and is about to ascend from the bottomless pit and go to destruction. And the inhabitants of the earth, whose names have not been written in the book of life from the foundation of the world, will be amazed when they see the beast, because it was and is not and is to come.

9 "This calls for a mind that has wisdom: the seven heads are seven mountains on which the woman is seated; also, they are seven kings, [10]of whom five have fallen, one is living, and the other has not yet come; and when he comes, he must remain only a little while. [11]As for the beast that was and is not, it is an eighth but it belongs to the seven, and it goes to destruction. [12]And the ten horns that you saw are ten kings who have not yet received a kingdom, but they are to receive authority as kings for one hour, together with the beast. [13]These are united in yielding their power and authority to the beast; [14]they will make war on the Lamb, and the Lamb will conquer them, for he is Lord of lords and King of kings, and those with him are called and chosen and faithful."

15 And he said to me, "The waters that you saw, where the whore is seated, are peoples and multitudes and nations and languages. [16]And the ten horns that you saw, they and the beast will hate the whore; they will make her desolate and naked; they will devour her flesh and burn her up with fire. [17]For God has put it into their hearts to carry out his purpose by agreeing to give their kingdom to the beast, until the words of God will be fulfilled. [18]The woman you saw is the great city that rules over the kings of the earth."

The Fall of Babylon

18 After this I saw another angel coming down from heaven, having great authority; and the earth was made bright with his splendor. [2]He called out with a mighty voice,

"Fallen, fallen is Babylon the great!
It has become a dwelling place of
    demons,
a haunt of every foul and hateful bird,
    a haunt of every foul and hateful
    beast.[c]
[3] For all the nations have drunk[d]
    of the wine of the wrath of her
    fornication,
and the kings of the earth have
    committed fornication with
    her,
and the merchants of the earth have
    grown rich from the power[e] of
    her luxury."

[c] Other ancient authorities lack the words *a haunt of every foul beast*   [d] Other ancient authorities read *she has made all nations drink*   [e] Or *resources*

REVELATION 18–19

18:1–24. The alternating songs of triumph by God's angels and mourning by evil's followers highlight both the utter depravity of the profane world systems and the culpability of individuals who choose to give allegiance to those systems (vv. 3, 9). The prostitute and her customers are both guilty: 'The devil made me do it' is no excuse. We are each answerable to God as to where we give our ultimate allegiance (Luke 6:46; Rom. 14:10–12). Notably, those who mourn Babylon's fall do so because they have found their meaning in losing themselves in her excesses, and without her they now feel lost (Mark 8:34–38). The warning in vv. 4–8 for God's people to disassociate themselves from Babylon is a timely reminder of how easy it is for anyone to become seduced by wealth and to believe that money and power insulate a person or a nation from sorrow or harm (Luke 12:15–21). And because wealth has traditionally been used as a means to gain power over others, the list of objects in vv. 11–13 ends with trading in that most precious commodity of all – human life.

4 Then I heard another voice from heaven saying,
"Come out of her, my people,
so that you do not take part in her
sins,
and so that you do not share
in her plagues;
5 for her sins are heaped high as
heaven,
and God has remembered her
iniquities.
6 Render to her as she herself has
rendered,
and repay her double for her deeds;
mix a double draught for her in the
cup she mixed.
7 As she glorified herself and lived
luxuriously,
so give her a like measure of
torment and grief.
Since in her heart she says,
'I rule as a queen;
I am no widow,
and I will never see grief,'
8 therefore her plagues will come in a
single day –
pestilence and mourning and
famine –
and she will be burned with fire;
for mighty is the Lord God who
judges her."

9 And the kings of the earth, who committed fornication and lived in luxury with her, will weep and wail over her when they see the smoke of her burning; 10they will stand far off, in fear of her torment, and say,
"Alas, alas, the great city,
Babylon, the mighty city!
For in one hour your judgment has
come."

11 And the merchants of the earth weep and mourn for her, since no one buys their cargo anymore, 12cargo of gold, silver, jewels and pearls, fine linen, purple, silk and scarlet, all kinds of scented wood, all articles of ivory, all articles of costly wood, bronze, iron, and marble, 13cinnamon, spice, incense, myrrh, frankincense, wine, olive oil, choice flour and wheat, cattle and sheep, horses and chariots, slaves – and human lives.[f]
14 "The fruit for which your soul longed
has gone from you,
and all your dainties and your
splendor
are lost to you,
never to be found again!"
15The merchants of these wares, who gained wealth from her, will stand far off, in fear of her torment, weeping and mourning aloud,
16 "Alas, alas, the great city,
clothed in fine linen,
in purple and scarlet,
adorned with gold,
with jewels, and with pearls!
17 For in one hour all this wealth has
been laid waste!"
And all shipmasters and seafarers, sailors and all whose trade is on the sea, stood far off 18and cried out as they saw the smoke of her burning,
"What city was like the great city?"
19And they threw dust on their heads, as they wept and mourned, crying out,
"Alas, alas, the great city,
where all who had ships at sea
grew rich by her wealth!
For in one hour she has been laid
waste.
20 Rejoice over her, O heaven,
you saints and apostles and
prophets!
For God has given judgment for you
against her."

21 Then a mighty angel took up a stone like a great millstone and threw it into the sea, saying,
"With such violence Babylon the great
city
will be thrown down,
and will be found no more;
22 and the sound of harpists and
minstrels and of flutists and
trumpeters

f Or *chariots, and human bodies and souls*

will be heard in you no more;
and an artisan of any trade
    will be found in you no more;
and the sound of the millstone
    will be heard in you no more;
23 and the light of a lamp
    will shine in you no more;
and the voice of bridegroom and bride
    will be heard in you no more;
for your merchants were the magnates
    of the earth,
and all nations were deceived by
    your sorcery.
24 And in you[g] was found the blood of
    prophets and of saints,
and of all who have been
    slaughtered on earth."

The Rejoicing in Heaven

19 After this I heard what seemed to be the loud voice of a great multitude in heaven, saying,
"Hallelujah!
Salvation and glory and power to our
    God,
2   for his judgments are true and just;
he has judged the great whore
    who corrupted the earth with her
      fornication,
and he has avenged on her the blood of
    his servants."[h]
3Once more they said,
"Hallelujah!
The smoke goes up from her forever
    and ever."
4And the twenty-four elders and the four living creatures fell down and worshiped God who is seated on the throne, saying, "Amen. Hallelujah!"

5 And from the throne came a voice saying,
"Praise our God,
    all you his servants,[h]
and all who fear him,
    small and great."
6Then I heard what seemed to be the voice of a great multitude, like the sound of many waters and like the sound of mighty thunderpeals, crying out,
"Hallelujah!
For the Lord our God
    the Almighty reigns.
7 Let us rejoice and exult
    and give him the glory,
for the marriage of the Lamb has
      come,
and his bride has made herself ready;
8 to her it has been granted to be clothed
    with fine linen, bright and pure" –
for the fine linen is the righteous deeds of the saints.

9 And the angel said[i] to me, "Write this: Blessed are those who are invited to the marriage supper of the Lamb." And he said to me, "These are true words of God." 10Then I fell down at his feet to worship him, but he said to me, "You must not do that! I am a fellow servant[j] with you and your comrades[k] who hold the testimony of Jesus.[l] Worship God! For the testimony of Jesus[l] is the spirit of prophecy."

[g] Gk her   [h] Gk slaves   [i] Gk he said   [j] Gk slave
[k] Gk brothers   [l] Or to Jesus

19:1–9. In dramatic contrast to the prostitute imagery depicting the promiscuity and unfaithfulness of evil, John uses the feminine imagery of a bride who is pure and loyal to symbolize God's people at the marriage supper of the Lamb.

19:10. Because Creator God is utterly distinct from his creation, it is just as false to worship an angelic being as a demonic being (see also 22:8–9). Only God is worthy of our worship, which we offer up in gratitude for the finished work of Christ on our behalf. Both the forthtelling and foretelling aspects of prophecy witness to the centrality of Christ as the One who reveals God to mortals (John 1:18).

The Rider on the White Horse

11 Then I saw heaven opened, and there was a white horse! Its rider is called Faithful and True, and in righteousness he judges and makes war. [12]His eyes are like a flame of fire, and on his head are many diadems; and he has a name inscribed that no one knows but himself. [13]He is clothed in a robe dipped in[m] blood, and his name is called The Word of God. [14]And the armies of heaven, wearing fine linen, white and pure, were following him on white horses. [15]From his mouth comes a sharp sword with which to strike down the nations, and he will rule[n] them with a rod of iron; he will tread the wine press of the fury of the wrath of God the Almighty. [16]On his robe and on his thigh he has a name inscribed, "King of kings and Lord of lords."

The Beast and Its Armies Defeated

17 Then I saw an angel standing in the sun, and with a loud voice he called to all the birds that fly in midheaven, "Come, gather for the great supper of God, [18]to eat the flesh of kings, the flesh of captains, the flesh of the mighty, the flesh of horses and their riders – flesh of all, both free and slave, both small and great." [19]Then I saw the beast and the kings of the earth with their armies gathered to make war against the rider on the horse and against his army. [20]And the beast was captured, and with it the false prophet who had performed in its presence the signs by which he deceived those who had received the mark of the beast and those who worshiped its image. These two were thrown alive into the lake of fire that burns with sulfur. [21]And the rest were killed by the sword of the rider on the horse, the sword that came from his mouth; and all the birds were gorged with their flesh.

The Thousand Years

20 Then I saw an angel coming down from heaven, holding in his hand the key to the bottomless pit and a great chain. [2]He seized the dragon, that ancient serpent, who is the Devil and Satan, and bound him for a thousand years, [3]and threw him into the pit, and locked and sealed it over him, so that he would deceive the nations no more, until the thousand years were ended. After that he must be let out for a little while.

4 Then I saw thrones, and those seated on them were given authority to judge. I also saw the souls of those who had been beheaded for their testimony to Jesus[o] and for the word of God. They had not worshiped the beast or its image and had not received

---

[m] Other ancient authorities read *sprinkled with*
[n] Or *will shepherd*   [o] Or *for the testimony of Jesus*

19:11–21. In Rev. 4:1 John was invited to come through a door into the heavenlies. Now John has a vision of heaven itself opening wide so that the returning Christ is in full view (Matt. 24:23–27), an unmistakable event whose implications are fully understood by the combined forces of evil (v. 19). A significant parallel occurs between God's servants and Satan's servants: No distinction is made between 'small and great' (vv. 5, 18). In God's economy, all individuals have equal moral and spiritual responsibility for their decision whom to serve. The ultimate tragedy is that while all persons are invited to share the blessing of gathering around God's festive table, not all choose to accept that invitation. Those who reject forfeit divine nourishment and will themselves be consumed. The reader is confronted with the need to choose at which table to be present.

REVELATION 20–21

20:1–6. In 12:9 John reported Satan being cast down to earth where, in chapters 13–19, Satan concentrates on deceiving humanity and marshalling every force of evil against God. Now Satan is cast 'into the pit', unable to continue any deception during Christ's millennial reign. John's language indicates not only bodily resurrection but also active service (reigning with Christ).

its mark on their foreheads or their hands. They came to life and reigned with Christ a thousand years. ⁵(The rest of the dead did not come to life until the thousand years were ended.) This is the first resurrection. ⁶Blessed and holy are those who share in the first resurrection. Over these the second death has no power, but they will be priests of God and of Christ, and they will reign with him a thousand years.

Satan's Doom

7 When the thousand years are ended, Satan will be released from his prison ⁸and will come out to deceive the nations at the four corners of the earth, Gog and Magog, in order to gather them for battle; they are as numerous as the sands of the sea. ⁹They marched up over the breadth of the earth and surrounded the camp of the saints and the beloved city. And fire came down from heaven[p] and consumed them. ¹⁰And the devil who had deceived them was thrown into the lake of fire and sulfur, where the beast and the false prophet were, and they will be tormented day and night forever and ever.

The Dead Are Judged

11 Then I saw a great white throne and the one who sat on it; the earth and the heaven fled from his presence, and no place was found for them. ¹²And I saw the dead, great and small, standing before the throne, and books were opened. Also another book was opened, the book of life. And the dead were judged according to their works, as recorded in the books. ¹³And the sea gave up the dead that were in it, Death and Hades gave up the dead that were in them, and all were judged according to what they had done. ¹⁴Then Death and Hades were thrown into the lake of fire. This is the second death, the lake of fire; ¹⁵and anyone whose name was not found written in the book of life was thrown into the lake of fire.

The New Heaven and the New Earth

21 Then I saw a new heaven and a new earth; for the first heaven and the first earth had passed away, and the sea was no more. ²And I saw the holy city, the new Jerusalem, coming down out of heaven from God, prepared as a bride adorned for her husband. ³And I heard a loud voice from the throne saying,

[p] Other ancient authorities read *from God, out of heaven,* or *out of heaven from God*

Whether those martyrs of v. 4 will be joined at this time by others who have died in the Lord (v. 6) is not clear. These 'priests of God' are not subject to the 'second death', or final separation from God described in vv. 14–15.

20:7–10. Difficult as it is for the human mind to understand, there will still be some who (given the opportunity of vv. 7–8) will exhibit the entrenched nature of sin by choosing to serve Satan rather than God.

20:11–15. Earlier visions of God's throne contained rich imagery, but now the stark language indicates the pure holiness of God's final judgment: There will be no place to hide from the One from whom no secrets are hidden. Any persons who have refused to accept the saving work of Christ (John 6:29) must now be judged on their own merits alone. We could say that God now finally ratifies the decisions of those who willingly choose not to believe and serve God; they are consigned to join the masters they have chosen to serve. How large a group this will be is not stated, but that there will be such a group seems clear from v. 15 (see also John 5:25–29). Now that the 'last enemy' of 1 Cor. 15:26 is defeated, the stage is set for the time when all things will be made new.

21:1–7. The many Old Testament allusions in this passage attest to the organic unity of Scripture (e.g. Is. 25:8). What John 19:30 guaranteed positionally now becomes an experienced reality. John's vision describes absence of turmoil, restlessness, or divisions between people

◆ The promise of a new world order which would last forever is described in prophetic literature (Is. 65:17; 66:22; cf. 1 Enoch 45:4–5; 72:1; 91:16; 2 Esdras 7:75; 2 Bar. 32:6). In Rev. 20:2 it is initiated by the new Jerusalem descending from heaven and is depicted metaphorically as a bride, brilliant as precious jewels (v. 11), pure gold and clear glass (v. 18). There is no darkness and her light illuminates the other nations (v. 24). There is no immorality or unrighteousness (v. 27), the Lamb and God are its Temple, its center of worship.

This imagery of the new city as a bride can be contrasted with Babylon, the harlot of the old order (see the note on 'The image of a harlot', p. 560). The 'bride's' appearance and influence is of beauty, righteousness, light, life and centers around the Lamb. 1 Pet. 3:10 describes the destruction by fire of the old order which will then make possible a new, clean, righteous Kingdom populated by the righteous and ruled by the Lamb ◆

"See, the home^q of God is among
    mortals.
He will dwell^q with them as their
    God;^r
they will be his peoples,^s
and God himself will be with them;^t
4 he will wipe every tear from their
    eyes.
Death will be no more;
mourning and crying and pain will be
    no more,
for the first things have passed away."
5 And the one who was seated on the throne said, "See, I am making all things

new." Also he said, "Write this, for these words are trustworthy and true." ⁶Then he said to me, "It is done! I am the Alpha and the Omega, the beginning and the end. To the thirsty I will give water as a gift from the spring of the water of life. ⁷Those who conquer will inherit these things, and I will be their God and they will be my children. ⁸But as for the cowardly, the faithless,^u the polluted, the murderers, the fornicators, the sorcerers, the idolaters, and all liars, their place will be in the lake that burns with fire and sulfur, which is the second death."

Vision of the New Jerusalem

9 Then one of the seven angels who had the seven bowls full of the seven last plagues came and said to me, "Come, I will show you the bride, the wife of the Lamb." ¹⁰And in the spirit^v he carried me away to a great, high mountain and showed me the holy city Jerusalem coming down out of heaven from God. ¹¹It has the glory of God and a radiance like a very rare jewel, like jasper, clear as crystal. ¹²It has a great, high wall with twelve gates, and at the gates twelve angels, and on the gates are inscribed the names of the twelve tribes of the Israelites; ¹³on the east three gates, on the north three gates, on the south three gates, and on the west three gates. ¹⁴And the wall of the city has twelve foundations,

^q Gk *tabernacle* ^r Other ancient authorities lack *as their God* ^s Other ancient authorities read *people* ^t Other ancient authorities add *and be their God* ^u Or *the unbelieving* ^v Or *in the Spirit*

groups (symbolized by no more sea). The new city (further described in vv. 9–21) comes 'down' from God, rather than emerging 'out of' the old world systems. This new Jerusalem will not be an 'urban renewal project' in which humanity brings about its own perfection, but a completely new community whose beauty, joy and unity can only be of divine origin (Eph. 2:4–10; Titus 3:4–8). Here the perseverance of the saints ('those who conquer') finds its final reward, as God's people experience the fullness of Emmanuel (God with us). Because in God's presence there can be nothing that mars or distorts, no one who has not received new life from God can be part of this new community.

and on them are the twelve names of the twelve apostles of the Lamb.

15 The angel^w who talked to me had a measuring rod of gold to measure the city and its gates and walls. ¹⁶The city lies foursquare, its length the same as its width; and he measured the city with his rod, fifteen hundred miles;^x its length and width and height are equal. ¹⁷He also measured its wall, one hundred forty-four cubits^y by human measurement, which the angel was using. ¹⁸The wall is built of jasper, while the city is pure gold, clear as glass. ¹⁹The foundations of the wall of the city are adorned with every jewel; the first was jasper, the second sapphire, the third agate, the fourth emerald, ²⁰the fifth onyx, the sixth carnelian, the seventh chrysolite, the eighth beryl, the ninth topaz, the tenth chrysoprase, the eleventh jacinth, the twelfth amethyst. ²¹And the twelve gates are twelve pearls, each of the gates is a single pearl, and the street of the city is pure gold, transparent as glass.

22 I saw no temple in the city, for its temple is the Lord God the Almighty and the Lamb. ²³And the city has no need of sun or moon to shine on it, for the glory of God is its light, and its lamp is the Lamb. ²⁴The nations will walk by its light, and the kings of the earth will bring their glory into it.

²⁵Its gates will never be shut by day – and there will be no night there. ²⁶People will bring into it the glory and the honor of the nations. ²⁷But nothing unclean will enter it, nor anyone who practices abomination or falsehood, but only those who are written in the Lamb's book of life.

The River of Life

22 Then the angel^w showed me the river of the water of life, bright as crystal, flowing from the throne of God and of the Lamb ²through the middle of the street of the city. On either side of the river is the tree of life^z with its twelve kinds of fruit, producing its fruit each month; and the leaves of the tree are for the healing of the nations. ³Nothing accursed will be found there any more. But the throne of God and of the Lamb will be in it, and his servants^a will worship him; ⁴they will see his face, and his name will be on their foreheads. ⁵And there will be no more night; they need no light of lamp or sun, for the Lord God will be their light, and they will reign forever and ever.

---

^w Gk *He*   ^x Gk *twelve thousand stadia*   ^y That is, almost seventy-five yards   ^z Or *the Lamb* ²*In the middle of the street of the city, and on either side of the river, is the tree of life*   ^a Gk *slaves*

21:22. When believers are united with their Lord there need be no special place set apart for worship. Nor will there be need for artificial illumination in the presence of God who is light (Ps. 36:9; Is. 60:19–20; John 8:12; 1 John 1:5). All human glory is now offered up to and absorbed by the heavenly glory (vv. 24–25). Although God's people will go in and out freely (v. 25), persons who practice 'abomination or falsehood' can have no part in a Kingdom ruled by One who is 'Faithful and True' (19:11).

REVELATION 22

1–6. The rich images of water, fruit, and light add further meaning to life in the new community, because human life needs water, food and light to survive. John's language leaves no doubt that every need of God's people will be perfectly provided for, thus fulfilling our deepest yearnings (Matt. 5:6). In the ultimate reward for those who have longed for God's Kingdom (2 Tim. 4:7–8), the eye of faith will become the reality of direct sight (John 20:29; 1 John 3:2). Significantly, all God's servants are depicted as eternally reigning, with no gender distinctive whatever. Just as there was no gender distinctive among the martyrs, there is no gender distinctive in the new community of the redeemed, who by God's own authority now equally and mutually share the royal and priestly functions forever (Rev. 1:6; 20:6; 21:5–6).

6 And he said to me, "These words are trustworthy and true, for the Lord, the God of the spirits of the prophets, has sent his angel to show his servants[b] what must soon take place."

7 "See, I am coming soon! Blessed is the one who keeps the words of the prophecy of this book."

Epilogue and Benediction

8 I, John, am the one who heard and saw these things. And when I heard and saw them, I fell down to worship at the feet of the angel who showed them to me; [9]but he said to me, "You must not do that! I am a fellow servant[c] with you and your comrades[d] the prophets, and with those who keep the words of this book. Worship God!"

10 And he said to me, "Do not seal up the words of the prophecy of this book, for the time is near. [11]Let the evildoer still do evil, and the filthy still be filthy, and the righteous still do right, and the holy still be holy."

12 "See, I am coming soon; my reward is with me, to repay according to everyone's work. [13]I am the Alpha and the Omega, the first and the last, the beginning and the end."

14 Blessed are those who wash their robes,[e] so that they will have the right to the tree of life and may enter the city by the gates. [15]Outside are the dogs and sorcerers and fornicators and murderers and idolaters, and everyone who loves and practices falsehood.

16 "It is I, Jesus, who sent my angel to you with this testimony for the churches. I am the root and the descendant of David, the bright morning star."

[17] The Spirit and the bride say, "Come."
And let everyone who hears say,
    "Come."
And let everyone who is thirsty come.
Let anyone who wishes take the water
    of life as a gift.

18 I warn everyone who hears the words of the prophecy of this book: if anyone adds to them, God will add to that person the plagues described in this book; [19]if anyone takes away from the words of the book of this prophecy, God will take away that person's share in the tree of life and in the holy city, which are described in this book.

[b] Gk *slaves*   [c] Gk *slave*   [d] Gk *brothers*   [e] Other ancient authorities read *do his commandments*

---

7. Revelation begins and ends with assurance of blessing for the person who heeds the message of John's visions and determines to be God's faithful servant.

10–16. God has graciously disclosed what we need to know in order to decide to whom we will give our eternal allegiance. Christians do not proclaim a 'secret' gospel; in this complex book we have enough information to know that Christ's work on the cross triumphs forever over evil, and it is in God's finished work of redemption that we find our eternal salvation. The somber fact that there will come a 'point of no return' when human choice is ratified (v. 11) is also the assurance of the 'right' of those who have chosen to serve God to be in God's holy city (v. 14). Significantly, those excluded are described as loving and practising falsehood (v. 15), that is, those who have willingly and deliberately set their heart on what is not of God (21:27). When faced with the difficulty of reconciling Rev. 22:11 with 2 Pet. 3:9, the safest approach is to echo Abraham's words in Gen. 18:25.

17. Revelation closes with this gracious and inclusive series of invitations to 'come' to God, leaving the reader in no doubt that one of Scripture's great themes is that God wants all persons to 'choose life' (Josh. 24:14–15; Is. 55:1–3, 6–9; 2 Cor. 6:2; Heb. 2:3; John 4:13–14).

18–19. John's words reinforce the imperative to treat 'this book' with great care. Elaborate interpretations that may well go beyond what the symbols represent are just as much a misuse of Scripture as ignoring or rationalizing away the great themes presented here.

20 The one who testifies to these things says, "Surely I am coming soon."

Amen. Come, Lord Jesus!

21 The grace of the Lord Jesus be with all the saints. Amen.ᶠ

ᶠ Other ancient authorities lack *all*; others lack *the saints*; others lack *Amen*

---

20. The Bible comes full circle. In Gen. 3 fallen humanity was fearful and ashamed before God's coming because they had no covering for sin. Now in Rev. 22:20 we have the great affirmation, 'Amen. Come, Lord Jesus!' because God has provided perfect covering through the shed bood of Christ (Rev. 1:5). Thus Revelation closes with a feeling of keen anticipation shared by every reader who also longs for Christ's appearing (Heb. 9:27–28).

THE DOCTRINE OF THE TRINITY: THE PERSONAL AND RELATIONAL GOD

The idea of the Trinity remains the great mystery of the Christian faith. A three-in-one God sets Christianity apart from the other religions of the world. We find it difficult to grasp that God is one and yet there are three who are God. We tend to conclude that this is some abstract description of the nature of God with little relevancy for the Christian life. However, properly understood, the doctrine of the Trinity teaches us about the inner life of God, God's life with us, and our life with each other and with all of creation.

In particular, we want to address the question: What do women risk in affirming that God is triune? We have seen a lack of enthusiasm and, in some cases, a dismissal of the doctrine by some women theologians. Feminist trinitarian writings have led to two areas of consensus. First, the Trinity is patriarchal and hierarchical since it focuses on God as Father; and that metaphor functions to legitimize the institutionalized system of male dominance in the family and in society and to proclaim it as ordained by God. Second, the predominantly male imagery and language contributes to a sense of God as male. The masculine metaphor calls into question the reality of women's ability to be the image of God and seems to exclude women. Thus, women are seen in a secondary and subordinate status in their imaging of God and in their relating to God. John B. Cobb states: 'Historically, whatever God's true nature and identity may be, God has been experienced, conceived, and spoken of as masculine,' (John B. Cobb, 'God and Feminism' in *Talking about God* by John B. Cobb and David Tracy, Seabury, New York, 1983, p. 79)

Theologians have traditionally claimed that God transcends sexuality and that it is Jesus' humanity, not his maleness, that is central to the Christian faith. The problem arises when 'these theological distinctions have no impact on the ways symbols and images actually function to support religious and cultural ideologies that are crippling to women' (Anne E. Carr, *Transforming Grace*, Harper & Row, San Francisco, 1988, p. 98). Although God is not male, for many women God is experienced, conceived, and spoken of as masculine. We should not underestimate the implications of making the Deity masculine. This establishes one of the primary categories of one's world-view as a male category. Ana-Maria Rizzuto, in *The Birth of the Living God* (University of Chicago Press, Chicago, 1979), points out that our God-image is a major determinative factor in our view of self, others, and the world. Consequently, describing God as 'male' or 'masculine' has tended to restrict the religious experience of women as well as men. In many cases the male language has alienated women from their church and the God of whom the church speaks.

The problem seems to be that we have either forgotten or misunderstood what it means to confess that God is triune. When rightly understood, the doctrine of the Trinity may be women's strongest ally. We will first consider the history of the development of the doctrine of the Trinity. Second, we will examine approaches to God-language. Third, we will reflect on particular concerns of women which a trinitarian understanding of God addresses.

THE HISTORICAL FORMULATION OF THE DOCTRINE

During the second half of the fourth century, three Cappadocian theologians in the early church, Basil of Caesarea, Gregory of Nyssa and Gregory of Nazianzus, were influential in bringing about the final form of the doctrine of the Trinity. We find some parallels between the issues that were addressed in the fourth century and those that are being raised today. The church was dealing with hierarchy in the Trinity and the meaning of God's fatherhood.

The early church faced the task of refuting two errors. Opponents of the church believed first that God the Father was absolutely transcendent and incapable of relating to the world. Therefore, Jesus was created as an intermediary, which made him inferior and subordinate to the Father. Second, they believed that they could name the essence of God: unbegottenness. To be God the Father is to be unbegotten, the one coming from no-one. Jesus cannot be of the same essence as the Father since he is begotten.

The fundamental error that God's nature or essence is knowable and within our comprehension was exposed by the church. It argued that all of our descriptions of God merely point to the mystery of God, but they do not signify what God's essence is in itself. Our framework of existence in space and time limits our knowledge of God. Therefore, unbegottenness is not the property of the unknowable divine essence.

Unbegottenness, begottenness, and procession are what distinguish the Father, the Son and the Spirit, respectively. These properties refer to the point of origin of each Person of the Trinity. Unbegottenness is the property of the divine Person the Father. Begottenness is the property of the divine Person the Son. Procession is the property of the divine Person the Spirit. Gregory of Nazianzus wrote: 'The Father is Father, and is Unoriginate, for He is of no one; the Son is Son, and is not unoriginate, for He is of the Father . . . The Holy Ghost is truly Spirit, coming forth from the Father indeed, but not after the manner of the Son, for it is not by Generation but by Procession' (*The Nicene and Post-Nicene Fathers*, 2nd series, ed. Philip Schaff, Eerdmans, Grand Rapids, repr. 1979, 7: 356). These three characteristics of origin have nothing to do with the essence or nature of God, but only with the source of each of the Persons of the Trinity. Neither do these points of origin indicate a pattern of hierarchy within the Trinity, where the one coming forth is less than the source and a primacy exists of one Person over another. Rather, each Person's identity and uniqueness are defined by their relation of origin. Thus, the Father, Son, and Spirit share the same essence as One, while their points of origin distinguish them as three Persons.

The early church then established that the Son and the Spirit are not in any sense subordinate to the Father. There is one God existing in three Persons. The essence of God is not found in God the Father as unbegotten. Father, Son and Spirit are equally God.

The early church also ascribed two meanings to the Fatherhood of God. Father means unbegottenness, the one coming from no-one, and begetter, the one in relation to the Son. The Father is the originator of and related to another. 'Father' implies that there is another. The Father is the Father because of the relationship with the Son and the Son is the Son because of the relationship with the Father. Gregory of Nazianzen wrote that Father 'is the name of the *Relation* in which the Father stands to the Son, and the Son to the Father,' (*NPF* 7:307). God the Father in the sense of the Father of the Son is a personal and specific way to name the first Person of the Trinity.

These meanings brought to the forefront the relational and personal nature of God. This contradicted the heretical idea of God as absolutely transcendent and essentially unrelated. The church rejected this and argued instead that relatedness is the primary characteristic of God. God is a communion of equal though unique and diverse Persons in which there is absolutely no subordination of one Person to another.

Beyond gender

The early church argued that the trinitarian names did not indicate that God was male. God transcends human gender just as God is beyond all human categories and beyond all comprehension. Confessing that the Father is God or that the Son is God has nothing to do with the gender of God. Gregory of Nazianzen ridiculed his opponents who 'would consider our God to be male . . . because He is called God and Father, and that deity is feminine, from the gender of the word, and Spirit is neuter, because it has nothing to do with generation' (*NPF* 7:320).

Likewise, the manner of the begetting or generation of the Son from the Father cannot be explained in terms of gender. This is an eternal generation not on the same order as human generation. To say the Son is begotten from the Father is referring to an eternal beginning, not to a temporal beginning. Divine generation cannot be restricted to nor defined by categories of created existence.

The only reason the issue of gender is mentioned is to repudiate such a notion. The nature or essence of the Father and the Son and the manner of the Son's generation from the Father are beyond description.

The theological significance of the doctrine

(1) The essence or nature of God is unknowable and incomprehensible.

(2) Three Persons exist co-eternally and co-equally as one God. God lives as Father, Son, Spirit. The trinitarian terms define the relationships within the being of God and the unique characteristics of each Person. God is a communion of equal though unique and diverse Persons.

(3) God's own life reflects what God is in relation to the world. For God to be means to ʹ in-communion both within God's eternal being as Father, Son, Spirit and in Godʹ to the world.

(4) The doctrine of the Trinity is that understanding of God which reflects tَ message. We come to the Father through the Son in the power of the Spirit.

(5) Fatherhood and Sonship transcend the category of gender. In confessing (Father and God the Son, we recognize the identity of each Person and the unique rₑ ship between the Father and the Son.

APPROACHES TO GOD-LANGUAGE

The movement to reconsider and expand imagery and language for the Trinity has re in various emotional responses. Some Christians recognize the necessity for the inc of feminine imagery and language for God for the vitality of the church. Other believerₛ that introducing feminine imagery and language for God will result in the collapse of Christian faith. Their accusations of blasphemy and opposition to the use of femₐ feminine language and imagery for the Trinity could be a good indication that theᵢ Christianity is based on a male God. This has resulted in several responses to the trinitarian language of Father, Son and Spirit. Our response depends on the perception of the depth and pervasiveness of sexism within Christianity and whether or not we can claim that the language and imagery are intrinsically patriarchal. We will look at three approaches.

The substitution approach

Those who find the traditional trinitarian formula inherently sexist and patriarchal propose to substitute language with gender-neutral terms or the use of both feminine and masculine terms. 'Father' and 'Son' as metaphors are replaced by other metaphors which evoke human gender quality. A metaphor is a direct comparison between two things. One thing is described in terms of something else. For example, the psalmist writes: 'Your word is a *lamp* to my feet and a *light* to my path' [Ps. 119:105, my italics].

This approach assumes two premises. First, God is incomprehensible and unknowable. We cannot speak literally about who God is. God transcends the limits of human language. This then requires a variety of images, words, symbols, and concepts to help us partially understand this God who is beyond all direct similarities to creatures. Therefore, all our language about God is based upon analogies drawn from human experience. The analogy affirms both the similarity and the dissimilarity between God and humanity. For example, when we say that God is a Father, we must also acknowledge the numerous ways in which God is unlike a human father. However, the danger arises when the unlikeness is forgotten and there is a more literal interpretation of 'Father' which results in an absolutizing of one metaphor over others. The solution is to speak of God in one of two ways. One way is to substitute the trinitarian language with gender neutral language. Creator, Redeemer, Sanctifier or Creator, Liberator, Advocate would substitute for Father, Son, Spirit.

A second way is to utilize both feminine and masculine images. God as our Mother is one such image which is built on a solid scriptural foundation. In Matt. 23:37, Jesus uses the image of the mother hen and her chicks to express the kind of relationship he yearned for with Jerusalem. Jesus as the mother hen desires to gather us like little chicks to love, protect, nurture, and shelter us. Hosea pictures God as the mother bear crazed by the loss of her cubs. As the mother bear is provoked to rage at her loss, so is God enraged toward the people (Hos. 13:8). The goal here is to use all the biblical language about God that we might more fully grasp our God who is neither female nor male, but contains and transcends both.

The second premise in this approach is that trinitarian language legitimizes and ordains a patriarchal culture. Therefore, the use of gender-neutral terms or of feminine and masculine terms will contribute to the restoration of female and male equality within society. Language change is essential because it has socially transforming power. Due to the relationship among language, thought, and action, the elimination of exclusive language will aid in altering attitudes about human equality.

The nonsubstitution approach

The second area includes those who argue that Father, Son, Spirit is the self-revealed name of God and, therefore, cannot be substituted with any other terms.

This approach affirms that God has revealed Godself exclusively as the Father of Jesus Christ. 'No one has ever seen God. It is God the only Son, who is close to the Father's heart, who has made him known' (John 1:18). In the event of the person of Jesus, the question of how God is revealed is answered. The Father is the Father in relationship to the Son, and the Son is the Son in relationship to the Father, and the Spirit is the Spirit of the Father and the Spirit of the Son.

The essence of the gospel is in the revelation of the triune name. We come to the Father through the Son in the power of the Spirit. It is here that we are invited to call God 'our Father'.

The status of the trinitarian name is based on revelation and salvation. Consequently, it cannot be substituted with other terms. This leads to a second premise in this approach. The trinitarian name of Father, Son, Spirit is exempt from a sexist, patriarchal origin because of its divinely revealed status. It is not the product of the biases of a patriarchal culture or of male theology. Rather, the trinitarian name is the product of divine authorship and, therefore, cannot be altered.

Mediating approaches

The third option includes a variety of responses between the substitution approach and the non-substitution approach. One premise of agreement seems to surface among those who hold to a mediating position: We must preserve the trinitarian formula because of its emphasis on the personal and relational nature of God. The essence of God is relational both within the being of God as Father, Son, Spirit and without as God relates to humanity. Variations within this approach are based on one's perspective on the metaphorical nature of the trinitarian language.

Those who lean toward the substitution approach encourage the use of different relational trinitarian analogies. One example of this is Abba, Servant, Paraclete. These analogies are meant to complement, not to replace, the traditional trinitarian language of Father, Son, Spirit. The goal is to communicate the inherently relational character of God by drawing from a variety of analogies and metaphors.

The substitution of the traditional trinitarian terms with other terms is not done because the terms are inherently patriarchal or sexist. The doctrine of the Trinity does not naturally or inevitably lead to the oppression of women. However, it is susceptible to misunderstanding and abuse since it is used to support a patriarchal view of God and of culture. In the process of conveying the relational character of God, a variety of relational trinitarian analogies will aid in resisting these abuses.

Those who lean toward the non-substitution approach have the same emphasis on the relational nature of God. However, the very terms 'Father, Son, Spirit' give access to and definition of who God is, how God relates within God's being and how God relates to humanity. These are precise theological terms which provide clues to the inner life of God and, therefore, are not exchangeable with other metaphors.

Toward inclusive language

Our task as Christians from generation to generation is to seek an understanding of God which is faithful to the Scriptures and yet sensitive to the newness of every changing moment. As we seek to remain faithful to the biblical witness of God as Father, Son, and Spirit, we want to be sensitive to the full range of human experience. In the triune God, we encounter the One who encompasses all of humanity, affirms all of humanity, and offers healing to all of humanity. Melanie May believes, 'The Orthodox image of the Triune God as communion that nurtures the specificity and uniqueness of persons can become a gift offered to women and men in need of theological words and images able to affirm each one in the human community,' ('Conversations on Language and Imagery of God', *Union Seminary Quarterly Review* 40 [1985], p. 19).

The doctrine of the Trinity, properly understood, is not inherently patriarchal and sexist. However, the oppression of women (and other groups of people) has resulted from the distortion and abuse of the doctrine. It is difficult not to hear a patriarchal Father-God behind the masculine language. In view of this, the mediating approach to God-language is a more tenable response which takes into account the biblical witness, the theological basis, and the Christian experience of women and men.

The church as traditionally affirmed that God is neither female nor male alone, but contains and transcends both. Therefore, it is consistent to say that God is neither 'masculine' nor 'male' and, yet, must be exclusively described in terms which are based on the human experience of men? Neither our language nor our thoughts will ever fully express God's nature or essence. However, they can partially reflect God's reality and truth. Although God transcends the distinction between female and male, *both* feminine and masculine images for God have biblical warrant and provide instructive disclosures of truth about God and God's relationship to humanity.

The use of different analogies should be considered complements to rather than replacements for the traditional formula. In the worthwhile attempt to avoid sexism, we must be careful that what is essential to the Christian faith is not discarded. The classic trinitarian formula reveals to us the One who is infinitely transcendent and yet became finitely present in Jesus Christ.

We would be naive to think that by changing language or by giving a rational explanation of the traditional trinitarian formula that hearts will be changed. However, the intentional use of different analogies for the Trinity raises our consciousness, which will aid in resisting the ways the traditional formula has been used to construct oppressive social systems, denigrate women, and restrict the religious experience of women. This will also lead us to a fuller understanding of who God is as we seek to use all the biblical language about God. Anne Carr states: 'While women can make no claim to a unique knowledge of God, they can trust that their experience and understanding of God provide an important and necessary corrective to an imagery and understanding derived from an over-masculinized church and culture' (*Transforming Grace*, p. 146).

Ultimately, all of this should enhance our appreciation of the triune God's essential incomprehensibility, God is not depicted adequately by either male or female images – or by both together. We must admit our inability to encapsulate and limit God.

THE DOCTRINE OF THE TRINITY: AN ALLY FOR WOMEN

God exists in community

Along with a commitment to inclusive language we must also have a commitment to inclusive community. Inclusivity is a fundamental truth of the triune God. The divine life is being-in-relationship or communion. The early church said about the three-Persons-in-God what should be said about human persons in community. In the triune God there is no contradiction between the one and the many – diversity and uniqueness exist within the framework of complete unity and equality. Human society should be a reflection of the triune God – within the unity and equality of humankind should exist the diversity and uniqueness of the many. This should first and foremost be true of the church. On several occasions Paul uses the word *koinonia*, communion or community, when speaking of the church and its way of being in the world. The orthodox understanding of the triune God as communion is our foundation, source, and power for a community of women and men in society and in the church without privilege or subjection to one another based on race, class, gender, age, or ability.

A theology of relationship

Trinitarian theology grounds relationality in the one God existing co-eternally and co-equally as three Persons. Catherine LaCugna states: 'The doctrine of the Trinity reminds us that in God there is neither hierarchy nor inequality, neither division nor competition, but only unity in love amid diversity,' (*Journal of Ecumenical Studies*, 26/2, p. 249).

This God is no respecter of persons. Rather, through the Son we all become equal partners and heirs in one body where 'There is no longer Jew or Greek, there is no longer slave or free, there is no longer male and female; for all of you are one in Christ Jesus' (Gal. 3:28). In this one body no division or hierarchy or inequality should exist. There is no hierarchical chain of being or chain of command between one individual and another or between one individual and God. We all have direct access to God. As we are engrafted into the trinitarian life of God, we are to reflect the communion that God is – unity in love amid diversity.

Trinitarian theology presents a relational and communal view both of God and all of creation. In confessing this, it becomes a radical critique of patriarchy as well as all forms of human relationships determined by domination and oppression. Our commitment to an inclusive community and to inclusive language expresses what we say we believe theologically – female and male are equally created in the image of God, female and male are equally offered redemption in Christ, female and male are equally one in Christ.

JESUS CHRIST

The church has always raised many questions about the person and nature of Jesus Christ. He is a controversial figure within feminist theology. He clearly occupies a position right at the centre of the Christian faith but feminist theologians do not agree as to whether this is something positive or negative for women.

Jesus has been hailed as a feminist – as a 'man for women' who broke with the patriarchal conventions of his time and who set ground-rules and an example for a new way of living where women and men are equally liberated from sin and oppression and are equally able to and invited to participate.

On the other hand, it has been argued that Jesus' centrality confirms and establishes the male bias of the Christian faith. Jesus was, as a male, one of the more privileged within first-century patriarchal society. He – unsurprisingly, in this context – chose twelve male disciples; he did not, it is argued, speak out directly against the oppression of women or in favor of the leadership of women; as God's Son he established a specifically male relationship as central to the being of God, whom he most characteristically addressed as 'Father'. The person of Jesus is seen by some as an essential part of the normative male perspective of Christianity within which women will never find true freedom, equality and justice.

So while many women may refer to Jesus as the reason for remaining Christian and as making it possible to be both Christian and pro-woman, others have left Christianity at least in part because of their view of the place and significance of Jesus for women.

This Study Bible speaks from a specifically Christian perspective – and yet it is important that we take seriously the obstacle which the person of Jesus presents to some women. Apart from anything else, if we do not do so we may be open to the charge of perpetuating the centuries-old assumption that womens' ideas and womens' problems are not of very great significance.

It is also important not only because the problem of Jesus for some women is very painful and genuine but also because of the very centrality of Jesus to the Christian faith. Christianity has always been a faith about a person, about the nature and history of an individual. It is also, of course, a faith with a particular view of the universe – of reality – and a particular interpretation of the place and destiny of human beings within that reality; but the historical individual Jesus of Nazareth has always been seen as having fundamental significance for that nature and destiny.

This means that a question about the value and effect of Jesus for women is not a marginal question. It is a question about the value and universality of the Christian faith itself.

So what sorts of arguments are presented about Jesus – and what can we say about Jesus particularly for women?

JESUS AS A FIRST-CENTURY MAN

Some feminists argue that Jesus' teaching about women is not sufficiently direct and revolutionary to found a truly egalitarian view – and, to be sure, we find in the Gospels no sermons denouncing patriarchy or supporting the priesthood of women. However, we do find the picture of a man who flouted first-century conventions and taboos in his dealings with women and whose attitudes and presuppositions about women do present a challenge to those of patriarchy. Jesus' view, for example, that the status of women is based on obedience to the Kingdom not on biological roles and functions (Luke 11:27-8) – or family relationships (Mark 3:33f.) – are no less significant for being almost throw-away comments. Indeed we can argue that such remarks and responses 'in passing' are at least as significant as formal speech-giving as an index of how someone genuinely and normatively thinks and feels about an issue.

It is clear from Jesus' behavior that women are not unclean – even when haemorraging, from Samaria or dead (Mark 5:25ff; John 4; Mark 5:41) – and, indeed, there is no suggestion that women are not equal to men in their capacity for understanding and discipleship (John 11:25ff; Luke 10:38ff.). There is an assumption in all of this which, measured against the assumptions of the first century about the inferiority and the specifically domestic and biological roles of women, is revolutionary.

Looking at Jesus' 'normal', day-to-day behavior and practice is of enormous significance for Christians. This is so not only because of belief in the Incarnation, because Jesus is significant as God – but also because he is significant as a human being. As we shall see below, part of Jesus' work of salvation was to establish a new way of being human. He is described by Paul as the second Adam (Rom. 5:12ff; 1 Cor.15) and in his life we see the beginning of the new creation. Whereas the original equality of creation was lost with the Fall, which resulted – among other things – in patterns of dominance and subservience between man and woman, in Christ we have the re-establishment of God's creation purposes. Christ is now the pattern, the prototype for what human beings should be, he is the measure of what is truly human. Whereas the first Adam and Eve were made in the image of God and that image was damaged by the Fall, we are to strive to be like Christ – and that prototype is characterized, as we have seen, by the breaking down of typical human patterns of dominance and subservience, of power, status and hierarchy.

As Elizabeth Moltmann-Wendel says, 'The story of Jesus which tells of exemplary mutuality, surrender and selfhood is the criterion by which we become sensitive and perceptive to human experiences and parallels,' (*A Land Flowing with Milk and Honey*, SCM, 1986, p. 70).

JESUS AS A MALE

It is undeniable, however, that no matter how liberated and egalitarian he was, Jesus was a first-century male. How far can a male truly represent and identify with the experience of women? Does not the centrality to Christianity of a man inevitably confirm assumptions that male-ness is superior to female-ness? that is to say – if God chose to become incarnate in the male human form, must this not be the highest human form? And does it not crucially confirm arguments that certain types of roles and behavior, while appropriate for men, may not be appropriate for women?

Our response to this issue will be affected by our views on the difference between the sexes. If the difference is purely physical, then we might want to suggest that Jesus' gender has little or no significance. However even purely physical difference cannot be separated from gender roles or from social and philosophical assumptions about the difference – even if we wanted to take such roles and assumptions as needing correction purely accidental and external. Even if we think that Jesus' maleness should be of no significance, it is more difficult to deny that it does have significance – in practice – within the context of a culture/cultures which favor the male over the female.

That Jesus was male has, accordingly, been used down the centuries to support arguments about the inferiority and susceptibility of women. (e.g. in 1486 the maleness of Christ was seen by Kramer and Sprenger, two Dominican monks, to protect men from witchcraft, whereas women are far more susceptible; see their *Malleus Maleficarum*) and in our own century especially as a major argument against the ordination and leadership of women. It has been argued (by C. S. Lewis, for example) that initiative, leadership, action are specifically male characteristics – they are part of a cosmic dichotomy, and are associated with a God who is only appropriately represented as male. Therefore, it is argued, it was not only suitable that Jesus was male – he had to be male.

There are a number of responses we may make to these arguments. Firstly, there has been a lot written recently about female representations of God in Scripture. Phyllis Trible, among others, has highlighted the way language and images of motherhood – birth and womb-language – are used to describe God in the Old Testament. Such language firstly throws doubt on the assertion that God is more appropriately seen in male terms than female. Secondly, it also undermines attempts to align leadership, initiative, strength with male-ness as these female images of God are by no means weak, submissive or passive.

Secondly, Jesus does not fit unambiguously into the usual pattern of male/female distinctions. Clearly we do see in Jesus the qualities of leadership, initiative and authority which are so often characterized as specifically male. But Jesus is also the one who is sent – he is the servant, relationships and mutuality are clearly absolutely vital to him. He is the one who is humbled, who is acted on as a victim. There is, maybe, an element of subversion here not only of human hierarchical patterns, but also of what are considered masculine and feminine characteristics. Hannah Wolff, in the 1970s, used Jungian terminology to describe Jesus as a man who had fully integrated the feminine dimension of his personality, his anima, despite living in an environment dominated by the male animus. We might argue that Jesus' behavior was all the more subversive and liberating because it was the behavior of a man.

Thirdly, we may of course question these kinds of gender designations on the basis of simple observation of the evidence of life, as well as on the grounds of exceptions found in Scripture (e.g. the roles of women such as Deborah and Huldah, in the Old Testament and Mary Magdalene, Priscilla, Junia in the New Testament). It simply does not seem to be the case that women universally or normatively possess a different set of characteristics and abilities from those of men. If such gender designations lose their grounds in observation then we must ask critical questions about where they come from.

This debate also leads us to reflect further upon the significance of our sex/gender. Of course it is undeniable that in most cultures of the world, whether we are male or female is likely to make a decisive difference to our whole existence. However, the Christian faith is concerned not only with the descriptive – with what is – but also with the prescriptive – with the way things should be.

Questions about the maleness of Christ must prompt further discussion about how essential is our sex/gender. Is it really – or should it be – the most important, or even a most important element in defining our being and determining our existence? There is clearly room for a range of opinion about this within Christianity and it is unlikely that all readers of this Study Bible would agree. We can, however, state that there is a major emphasis in the New Testament, an emphasis rooted in the life and teaching of Jesus, which stresses that it is our relationship with God and with our fellow human beings which determines how far we are fulfilling our destiny as part of God's creation, rather than our female-ness or male-ness. Jesus' characteristic response to both men and women in the New Testament is that obedience to the Kingdom of God, love of God, and love of others are the criteria for our behavior, and for assessing our status and roles.

JESUS AS THE SON OF GOD

Whatever we say about Jesus as a human being and as a male takes on a new dimension of significance in the light of our assertion that he is also the second Person of the Trinity, the Son of God. In a sense this is the whole point of the discussion – it is his divine status and universal significance which may be argued to make Jesus' maleness, his humanness, his attitudes to women, his teaching decisive. Whatever we conclude about Jesus' behavior and teaching on female-male relationships (as on any other topic) this will have ultimate significance when seen as part of God's revelation. But beyond this, not only does Jesus tell us about what it means to be human, but he also tells us about God, not solely through his words but through his very presence as Emmanuel, God with us.

If, therefore, we see Jesus as the ultimate fulfillment not only of humanness but of maleness as the height of human potential, as the best example we have – indeed as the prototype – of human existence in the image of God then this may be taken as telling us that maleness is nearer to Godliness. Indeed early Christian writers spoke about becoming Christian as a process of becoming male. We should note the implications of this not only for our view of human being, but also of divinity.

If, however, we see Jesus as breaking through 'normal' human, cultural, hierarchical, sinful patterns of relating, as exemplifying both sides of usual divide between male and female characteristics – as I suggested above – then this equally can be taken to tell us something about the way human beings should be in the image of God and something about divine being.

Again the debate about the significance of gender underlies the discussion: does the Sonship of Jesus tell us something about the importance of maleness, for human beings and for God? Or does it tell us about ways of being human and ways of relating to God and to one another which have no essential reference to gender?

In a way what I am saying here is that whichever side of the argument we may take, we may want to claim divine sanction for our views, through Jesus' identity as the Son of God. However, I think we can go further than this in considering Jesus as the Son of God.

One of the primary factors which establishes the Father-Son relationship as so central is Jesus' use of 'Father' to address and refer to God. This is very much a New Testament way of talking about God, it scarcely occurs in the Old Testament. Jesus establishes a distinctive name for God which has become characteristic of Christian talk about God and Christian worship. It has also been used (alongside arguments referred to already) to argue that it is more appropriate to see God in male terms and imagery than in female; that God is on the 'male' (giving, leading, initiating) side of a basic male/female polarity in reality; that, as representatives of God, men and not women are the appropriate leaders and initiaters in the Christian life.

Seeing God as Father is problematic for many Christian women – and for many Christian men also. For many with a negative experience of human fathering the emphasis on this image and language (which is often a virtually exclusive emphasis) may be the source of painful obstacles and dilemmas. Far from engendering a sense of the nearness and trustworthiness of God, it may promote a sense of alienation or absence. For women it may be a further vital part of the package of male language and images, male leaders and officials, male-dominated structures, male bias and the history of sexism which is seen in church worship, language and liturgy, hymns and prayers, organization and bureaucracy and everyday life and which seems to many women to have little place or regard for their experience and needs.

There are a number of issues raised here. What kind of reference does talk of God as Father have? That is to say, what does it really tell us about what God is, what God is like? How does this relate to our human experience of/as fathers? Is it an essential or mandatory part of the Christian view of God? Are there other alternative or different ways of thinking about God? Is this image and language replaceable?

Not all of these issues can be addressed in this article – but to take this debate a step further, we should consider how Jesus used Father-language. This must be a first step in determining what Jesus meant when he called God Father and in relating that to our own experience and use of his language.

It seems to me that these problems connected with the Fatherhood of God arise almost entirely, if not entirely, from human understandings and experience of fatherhood and from human use and abuse of this imagery rather than from Jesus' own use and intentions. Of course this does not solve the problem because it is impossible for us to disassociate the meaning of words we use in worship or prayer or theological discussion from their meaning and associations in our own lives. If we were abandoned or abused by our own father this is very likely to make it difficult if not impossible for us to pray to God as Father. However, as we have already noted, Christianity is concerned not only with the descriptive but with the prescriptive as well; and examination of what Jesus meant in calling God Father should contribute to our understanding of the essential message of Christianity and its implications for our view of God and for our behavior towards one another.

A lot of work has been done which wrestles with this problem. Theologians such as Rosemary Ruether, Elizabeth Schussler Fiorenza and Elisabeth Moltmann-Wendel point out that when Jesus talks about and to God as Father, in fact he is doing the very opposite of reinforcing human fatherly authority. Firstly in using this imagery Jesus is stressing our relationship with God and the nature of God's concerns for us. He is not using the term as a gender-designation. It has nothing to do with male-ness in its reference to God. (This is reinforced by the female imagery used of God which I mentioned earlier.) Thinking of God as Father should involve images of closeness, dependency, reliability, openness, confidence – not images of maleness, of men or of a man.

Secondly, Jesus stresses that God's Fatherhood is unique – and not only that, but it is an undermining of, not a mandate for, authority. Fiorenza points out that in Matt. 23:8-11 Jesus specifically links the recognition of God's Fatherhood with the rejection of human claims to authority. We are to call no-one on earth Father, for we have one Father, our Father in heaven. Jesus is clearly talking here about power structures as he goes on to reverse or subvert the usual patterns of domination, saying that the greatest will be servants and the most humble will be exalted. So Fiorenza concludes that 'liberation from patriarchal structures is not only explicitly articulated by Jesus but is in fact at the heart of the proclamation of the *basileia* (kingdom) of God' (*In Memory of Her*, SCM, 1983, p. 151).

This gives us a basis from which we can develop our critique of the way Jesus' teaching about God has been used, and is used, as an argument both that God is in some sense essentially male and that the nature of God lends authority to human male authority. Using the father-name for God is something which should be comforting and liberating for all people, it is not something which should ever be used to support domination; this is not what Jesus intended.

However, this does not solve all of the problems outlined above. It is extremely difficult if not impossible to separate the liberating message and life of Jesus from the ways in which it has been interpreted and used down the centuries. It is also impossible and inappropriate, I believe, for me – speaking as someone with a positive personal experience of human fatherhood – to tell someone who was abused by their father that they can and should find this imagery and language positive and meaningful, that they should use this language because it is the Christian view of God. This language may be irretrievable for some – women and men. However seeing the language in the context of Jesus' life and teaching can help us to separate the essential message and significance of Jesus, as something which should be liberating for all, from the ways in which it has been used; further, it can help us to evaluate different forms of expression which may also be appropriate and which may be more helpful terms of address for some Christians.

JESUS AS SAVIOR

Jesus' significance for us is not based only on the impact of his life and teaching nor solely on his divine status. He is also absolutely central and determinative for Christianity because he is our Savior. These different elements of Jesus' life and being, different perspectives we may focus on, are interrelated: it is as God incarnate that Jesus saves us, but it is also as the one who saves that we recognize Jesus as divine.

Is Jesus Savior for women in the same way and to the same extent that he is Savior for men? Is Jesus' role and activity as Savior of any particular significance for women as women? Does Jesus' maleness make a difference to this role and activity?

We find in Scripture and in the Christian tradition a wide range of different models which are used to explain the work of Jesus Christ – models which include healing, rebirth, re-creation, making whole, ransom, liberation, victory. However one particular cluster of models has been dominant in the West. This cluster focuses on Christ's work as a sacrifice which atones for sin and it corresponds to a model of self-giving and service as the supreme fulfillment of the Christian life, as the imitation of Christ. As part of this focus, Western understandings of the meaning of salvation have also emphasized Jesus' death as the primary means of salvation – we see this in traditional preaching, hymns and choruses – and much less has been said about the significance of Jesus' life as something which offers salvation.

This particular emphasis has been the focus of much criticism and discussion in recent years. (The work of Mary Grey, e.g. *Feminism, Redemption and the Christian Tradition*, Twenty Third Publications, 1990, is one example.) It has been seen as one-sided, as representing only a part of the teaching of Scripture and as neglecting other aspects of salvation. It has also been seen as a tradition which has been particularly harmful for women.

Women have, down the centuries been told that their role of service within church, home and society is part of their Christian duty – not only because this has been taken to be the God-given order of things, but because such self-giving is the way to be conformed with the image of Christ who was also humbled and gave himself. I have been in Christian discussions where women have been specifically told that they should be thankful for the role of service which our society so often gives them, because of this opportunity for Christ-likeness and there is a range of Christian teaching and writing available which takes this line.

There are a number of comments we could make about this debate. This kind of argument can lead to extremes where women are told to submit to their abusive husbands, to endure extreme physical and psychological or emotional oppression because of their Christian duty to be self-denying: because self-sacrifice is good for the soul. I would hope that most Christians would be appalled as I am by this kind of argument – but this may be only the logical conclusion of arguments which, in the first instance, sound much more acceptable and moderate. It has also, in the past, fitted in with a cluster of extremely harmful assumptions about the weakness of women and their status as victims. Some of the most influential and mainstream Christian thinkers of the past have seen women as more responsible than men for sin, or as more susceptible to sin than men; and there has been a strand in the Christian tradition which sees self-sacrifice as more necessary for women because of this. Writers such as Simone de Beauvoir and more recently Karen Armstrong have written on the ways in which women have taken this upon themselves and have subjected themselves to shocking physical suffering as self-punishment, and as an extremely negative form of identification with Christ's suffering as victim.

We should note the kinds of assumptions which may figure in these arguments – assumptions about the innate differences between women and men, women being seen as more altruistic than men, as better suited 'by nature' to certain kinds of service (normally those with less status, recognition and reward). We have already raised questions about such assumptions. We should also note the way such assumptions are taken to overlap with social and cultural views of 'womens' roles': even if women were naturally more altruistic than men, would this really mean they were less well-suited to be leaders or to have authority? Why should an association of women with service be translated more easily into the role of home-maker or secretary than into the role of Director or Principal? This may say more about our view of the nature of leadership than it does about the roles of women and men. A good example of this is Horace Bushnell, who argued in 1869 (speaking against womens' suffrage) that women have more natural affinity than men with the spiritual qualities of grace and altruistic love (men having natural affinity with the Law) – and that therefore men, not women should lead in society because the gospel is impracticable and cannot provide adequate public leadership. It may be that the model of service derived from the person of Christ should lead us to re-think all our assumptions not only about who should have power and authority, but about the essential nature of power and authority.

Does – or should – the model of service which we derive from Christ apply equally to women and to men? It is often argued – alongside the 'serving roles for women' arguments – that 'male' roles of leadership and authority are also roles of service but 'in different ways'. We have noted that we may want to question the 'in different ways' assumption. We also, however, have to remark that the roles seen as more normally and appropriately associated with men are certainly not seen as the more lowly, humble and serving in human terms. They are more likely to be associated with choice, responsibility, prestige, value and reward. We must be very aware that Christian models of service have been seen as a legitimation of power structures and role models which disadvantage or oppress women. We must also surely be suspicious of arguments which seem to give particular roles or situations a quite different 'spiritual' value to that which they have in particular society and culture.

As I have said, Christ as Savior represents and fulfills the humanity of the new creation – he is the new, the true human being and as such we should imitate him. However, Christ also has a role as substitute for us. There are certain things which Jesus did for us because we could not – or so that we should not have to do – do them ourselves. This includes Jesus' taking on himself of human sin and God-forsakenness – this is clearly not part of the imitation of Christ. We must be extremely careful about the ways in which we seek to emulate Jesus Christ. Being a victim, suffering may not – in and of itself – be a good thing. This may, also, be the place to note that Christ's maleness is not something which is part of the role-model to be imitated by the Christian. This might seem a strange point to make – and clearly such a view would exclude women – but there were early Christian theologians who talked about the process of becoming Christian as a process of 'becoming male', and the emphasis on celibacy and denial of femininity which has run through Western Christianity can still be seen, I believe, in some of the ordination debates.

We must also take account – in theory and in practice – of the message of Christ as liberator of the poor and oppressed. This was part of the purpose of Christ's self-giving and suffering. Given increasing concern, world-wide, over the 'feminization' of poverty – the fact that the poorest of the poor are increasingly and overwhelmingly women and young children – this message must apply especially to women.

Above all, I would want to stress that the model of Christ is a model not only of giving but of self-giving. Christ is not only a victim, not only passive and acted upon, he is also active. He is described in the New Testament not only as sent, but as the one who came for us, who gave himself because of the extent of his love for us, who suffered as a voluntary choice, to achieve a particular purpose. It may only increase the oppression of women to tell them that altruistic love and service is not a positive option for women, and we must understand the difference between giving of self, and being given or taken by others. It is an essential part of the oppression of women that they are so often, in our societies, assumed to be available for others in ways and situations which may entirely by-pass their own individual wishes and freedom.

Self-giving implies self-possession, control and real choice between alternatives. It may be that for some women there may be more value in some of the other images of salvation which can be found within Scripture and the Christian tradition. Salvation as healing, as re-creation, freedom, fulfillment may be a necessary first step before it is helpful or appropriate to talk of self-giving to others.

Taking on the imitation of Christ as the historical human Jesus who was also God incarnate, as the second Adam, the perfect human being and our Savior – taking this on as a genuine and personal choice implies that there are real alternatives. There is a great onus and opportunity here for the church as the community of Jesus Christ, the people of the Way. In relation to women, and to the issues and questions raised above, this challenge is twofold. Firstly, there is the task of differentiating the essential message of Christianity – of the person and practice of Jesus Christ – from the ways in which it has been interpreted and practised down the centuries. Of course this can only be done to a certain extent, and this is not an easy task. However we must recognize that the church, as a community of still sinful human beings, has not always interpreted and practised its faith in a way which is true to Jesus Christ, and its view and treatment of women is a particular case in point.

Secondly, we have the task of praxis – of putting the theory into concrete practice. This task is all the more urgent because of the poor – or at least mixed – track-record of Christianity in relation to women. The church has the responsibility not only for preaching the liberation and truly self-giving love of Jesus Christ, but for making this a real, demonstrable option, for translating this into reality within the concrete structures of its culture and society. If Jesus is truly the man for women this must be seen to be the case within the church which is the body of Christ on earth.

MEN AND WOMEN IN RELATIONSHIP

Many themes are woven into a biblical account of the relationship of men and women. There is not one static fixed concept of what that relationship is or must be, but the account is multifaceted, diverse, enriching and complex. At one point the central focus is on their union and similarity; at another on their diversity and difference; at another their complementarity and reciprocity. What is more, the relationship changes as the biblical themes themselves change. The story of men and women in Creation is very different from that after the Fall. The union and harmony of God's plan for humankind is spoiled by human rejection of God's will. The next theme, that of Redemption, is therefore anticipated from early in the Old Testament, and takes its specific shape in the Incarnation and the cross of Christ. This has profound implications for the relationship of man and woman. The final theme, that of Future Consummation, closes the story of our relationship in a very liberating way.

It is important therefore to distinguish where we are in the story of human relationships before we can begin to understand what these Scriptures are saying to us. It is a grave mistake to read the story of the Fall, for example, as the normative account of how men are to relate to women, or to take the ideas central to the future Consummation as the paradigm of how we should conduct our relationships today. To do that would be to misuse the Bible and distort the gospel.

CREATION

In the beginning of Genesis men and women first enter the scene, but the Creation theme is not limited to this book. It recurs in the Psalms, the book of Job, the prophesies of Isaiah, as elsewhere. What is clear is that women and men are *part* of creation, sharing a common createdness with the animals, the rocks, stones, trees, oceans, fish. They are *utterly reliant* on the love and creativity of the Maker, who puts us all into co-dependence on one another. But men and women are also *different* from the rest of creation. They are human. They are made in the image of God (Gen. 1:26).

There have been significant debates as to what constitutes the Image of God in male and female. Some significant heresies have been developed. The suggestion that the Image of God in men lies in male authority, whilst the Image of God in women is derived through men is not a conclusion which the Bible itself allows us to draw. It is difficult too to make a case for identifying the Image solely with any specific aspect of our humanness, such as our rationality or our creativity, although these are certainly given us by God. Nor does the Image reside in any roles that we play. Most recent biblical theologians focus on the fact that God is Trinity, three Persons in relationship. So it is in our relationality, rather than in our separateness that the Image of God is evident. Added to this, our ability to love, to experience compassion, to give sacrificially all show us what God is like, and thus are part of what it means to be God's Image. Imaging God is in fact our identity as personal beings. We are to reflect and represent God to all the other things which God has made.

In the creation of men and women there are some curious differences. The man, Adam, is formed from the 'dust of the ground' (Gen. 2:7). The woman is formed from the man. Why are these differences there? They are not, certainly, to indicate any 'superiority' of the man, because he is prior to woman in the creation order. If this were a key point then surely the stones and the animals would have priority over human beings! The difference in the process of creation is rather related to the joint status of male and female. It expresses their *union* as together they are image of God. For God did not make a second, separate, independent human being, in the same fashion as the first. But took the first and made another – inextricably linked, part of the same humanity, members of each other, and *together* imaging God. So when Adam cries 'bone of my bones and flesh of my flesh', he is not claiming *ownership* of the woman but rather crying in exaltation of their sameness. Out of all the animals he has named (Gen. 2:20) there has been nothing like him, but here at last is someone who is his equal, another human. He is also rejoicing in the bonding which is expressed in the one-flesh nature of their union. Woman is not man's subordinate, but rather his *ezer* or 'helpmeet' (used almost always in the Old Testament of an equal relationship, or even of one where the 'helpmeet' is of a higher status than the other, e.g. when used of God).

Man and woman in creation is therefore a relationship of union, of mutuality, of togetherness in the image of God, the plan of God and the calling of God. They are together given the task to be 'fruitful and multiply', together given the cultural mandate – to steward and care for the earth, and together, as God's image they live before the face of their Creator.

THE FALL INTO SIN

The account in Gen. 3 signals not only a central change in the intimacy between God and humankind, it also marks a serious deterioration in the relationship between man and woman. Their choice to seek their own autonomy and independence from God, by deliberately involving themselves in what God has said they should not do, was to mar their openness and closeness with each other, with God and with the rest of creation.

Three points emerge from this account. Both woman and man were responsible for the sin. Even though each person refused to fully accept the blame and 'passed the buck' elsewhere, they nevertheless together made the decision to eat of the fruit of the one tree which was not given to them. The second point is that both man and woman suffer as a result of their sin, but in different ways. The woman will have increased pain in childbirth, the man will struggle with other areas of life and work. The third point is that their own union will be spoiled. Her 'desire' would be for her husband but he would 'rule over' her (v. 16b). It is evident, therefore, that the male rule and dominance is ushered in by the Fall, as a result of the harmony and unity of creation being spoiled by human sin. It is, as Thielicke puts it, 'the element of disorder that disturbs the original peace'. There is no evidence that it is part of God's initial creation model.

The effects of sin in the relationship of man and woman are evident in much of the Old Testament. The gang-rape of the concubine in Judg. 19, or the deceitfulness of Abraham over his wife Sarah (Gen. 12:11-13), are two sobering examples. There are also the accounts of the men whose vision is distorted by lust, as is David's over his determination to acquire Bathsheba, another man's wife (2 Sam. 11), or Solomon's in his persistent polygamy (1 Kings 11).

The vulnerabilities of women and their need for special protection from the Law (Deut. 21-22; 24) all spell out the results of the Fall in male-female relations. This is not confined to the Old Testament. There are many women in the New Testament who suffer also because of the taboos, attitudes and demeaning stereotypes of women which have affected society. The menstruating woman who comes to Christ is crippled under heavy taboos about woman's 'uncleanness' (Luke 8:43-48); it is the *woman* who would have been stoned after adultery and not her partner (Mark 16:11) if Jesus had not intervened. And even the disciples are patronizing towards the women who have been given the resurrection message, not believing them because it 'seemed to them an idle tale' (Luke 24:11).

REDEMPTION

Sin had spoiled the relationship of woman and man to each other but it did not end it. The image was marred but not destroyed. Humankind was alienated but not abandoned. God himself was to heal that alienation by the redemptive act of Christ. Jesus was to die for our sins, restore us to the Father and give us life in abundance (Rom. 10:9; 1 Pet. 2:24; John 10:10). In this new Kingdom, this age of redemption, those who are his people do not therefore need to live in the old order: there is healing and freedom in the Spirit which has implications for the whole of our lives. This inevitably must incorporate the man-woman relationship. As Donald Wilson writes: 'Since one of the consequences of Adam's sin was the development of a dominant-submissive relationship that was foreign to the character of male-female relationships in Creation, the redemptive work of Christ will affect the nature of those relationships. Christ's work will have a restorative or corrective influence in this area' (Donald R. Wilson and Peter Djong, *Husband and Wife: The Sexes in Scripture and Society*, Zondervan, Grand Rapids, 1979).

FUTURE CONSUMMATION

In the final part of the biblical drama the new era will be ushered in. The return of Christ will herald the end of the world as we now know it, and there will be resurrection from the dead. The picture is often that of a marriage feast, when the church throughout the ages, as the bride of Christ, will be presented to the Bridegroom. The Scripture tells also of the new heavens and the new earth, when all evil will be done away and all things will be made new. This has inevitable implications for the relationship of men and women. For there 'in the resurrection they neither marry nor are given in marriage, but are like angels in heaven' (Matt. 22:30). It seems then that in this new era human sexuality will be a thing of the past, and what will define us and identify us is not our maleness or femaleness but our relationship with Christ.

THE BIBLE AND OUR RELATIONSHIPS TODAY

Today we are affected by creation, sin and redemption in our everyday lives. We recognize the structure of God's creation of us as male and female, but we are also subject to sin. Sin affects not only us ourselves but it pervades our institutions and often our relationships. As such it debases the quality and the openness of our lives. We see evidence of such sin in many aspects of the broken bond between men and women. Rape, pornography, and sexual violation are amongst the most extreme and distressing examples. But less spectacular examples are evident in the inequality of women at work, in the professions or in poverty. Amongst the world's poor women are often the poorest of all. Mothers are the ones who often are left to bring up children, and women frequently work for lower wages than men in many different societies. Women's vulnerability, economic and physical, has often been used as a way of forcing them into submission. It is very much a violation of what Peter writes to husbands (1 Pet. 3:7). Peter writes to husbands that they should give honor and consideration to their wives as being heirs together of the grace of life. This is urged 'so that nothing may hinder your prayers' (1 Pet. 3:7). Yet sin affects not only women detrimentally. Many men are subject to manipulation, scorn, and exclusion by women who are caught up in power games themselves. There are multiple characteristics of sin evident in human societies.

The Christian community, however, is asked to live differently. We are in the 'in-between times', the 'now and not yet'. Although sin is ubiquitous, and is there in our own heart, those who are 'in Christ', are called to live as redeemed people. Christians are therefore also to live out the implications of Christ's redemption in the way in which they organize, structure and develop our man-woman relationships. Essentially this calls for a recognition that the old sinful barriers must be dismantled. Gal. 3:28 is the most frequently quoted passage in this context: 'There is no longer Jew or Greek, there is no longer slaves or free, there is no longer male and female; for all of you are one in Christ Jesus.' The distortions of the Fall may now be revoked through Christ, and the church can lead the way into a new redemptive understanding and experience of man-woman relationships.

Inevitably there is no one single expression of redeemed male-female relationships. But there will be different expressions which relate to the various relationships in which men and women find themselves. Friendship, marriage, fellowship, family life, and work are all called to new norms of mutuality and respect. The differences between men and women are not abolished: that will only come with the final Resurrection. But what are abolished are all the ways in which we rival, debase, dishonor, manipulate or exercise power over each other.

So, in marriage there is to be reciprocal love and self-giving. Husband and wife are to enjoy mutual sexuality, each offering himself and herself to the other in love and concern. Paul sees no hierarchy, only reciprocal sexual fulfillment in this husband wife union (1 Cor. 7:1-7). In spite of what many have argued were Paul's teachings on 'headship', the meaning of man as the *kephale* of woman is a long way from its popular misunderstanding. When it is mentioned (Eph. 5) it is in the context of service, Christ-likeness and deep concern, where men are to love their wives as they love their own bodies. Not surprisingly there are several married couples amongst the early disciples. In one such each partner is given apostolic status (Rom. 16). Another, Aquila and Priscilla, evidently did not exhibit a hierarchical marriage relationship, for they were both Paul's fellow workers and it is clear that he regarded the ministries of each on the same level (Acts 18:19; 1 Cor. 16:19; Tim. 4:19).

In fellowship, brother and sister are to be subject to one another out of reverence to Christ (Eph. 5:21). This is to be the attitude which should exist among the church as a whole (Phil. 2). In family life parents are both to love and nurture their children and children are to honor and respect their parents (Eph. 6). There is no dividing or parenting into the disciplining father and the nurturing mother. In fact the only time fathers are singled out is with the warning, 'do not provoke your children to anger but bring them up in the discipline and instruction of the Lord' (Eph. 6:4). Christ's own love and respect for children should act as a central role model (Matt. 19:13-16).

In the New Testament church the relationship between women and men is complex. Often there is no differentiation. For example, the same word *diakonos* is used for Phoebe (Rom. 16:1) as is used for Paul and Timothy. As leaders or ministers they are all servants of the people of God. Elsewhere in some of his letters to the young churches, Paul seems to acknowledge the propriety of recognizing traditional styles of relationship, but even if this interpretation is drawn, there is no suggestion that this is to be the pattern for all churches in all times. On those few occasions where the letter writer seems to rein in some would-be women leaders, there is certainly a reason for that (1 Tim. 2). Women are first to learn, and to be in a position where they understand the truth before they may teach others, especially when they themselves are converted from very different cultures. In Paul's own ministry he accepts and reinforces the new place women are to occupy in Kingdom work. Women were teachers, encouragers, administrators and prophets in the early Church (Acts 18:24-26). They were 'fellow laborers' with the men disciples (Phil. 4:2-3), and many of them played an important part in housing the local church in their homes.

Both women and men are therefore called to express their union as the image of God and to exercise their gifts in the Kingdom of God. There is a new dynamic that comes for women and men when we recognize that in Christ sin is conquered and a new freedom is possible.

SOME CONTEMPORARY PROBLEMS

Many contemporary problems occur because the church has not grasped a biblical view of man-woman relationship. Often some aspects of a biblical perspective have been stressed (for example, male-female differences) whilst others have been ignored (for example their sameness, or union). Or writers have engaged in a 'renaming' process, whereby words are used but not in a biblical way. One clear instance of this is the way that the word 'comp-lementarity' has often misused. Rather than meaning the mutual acceptance and endorsement of woman and man, it has been used to evoke the idea of male dominance and female submission. Similarly, the terms 'equal but different' have often been twisted to mean 'unequal and hierarchical'. The result is that important words convey unbiblical concepts whilst purporting to be scriptural in their origin. The impact of this on both the church and society has been very damaging. Many kinds of oppressive practices have been unchallenged or ignored because they seemed to 'fit in' with the view which was presented by some people within the church. Only in recent years have we been able to see the scale of the problems which have resulted.

Other problems have resulted because of confusions about sexuality and gender. Whereas our sexuality is linked with male-female biology and is breathed into creation by God, gender is a cultural concept and is related to all the ways in which we have learned how to be men and women. Therefore there are many different expressions of gender throughout the world and over history. As one example, we can see how ideas of being a man have changed in the West over the last 50 years, not least in relation to fathering. Two generations ago men would be unlikely to be involved at all in the early nurturing process of their children. One generation ago they might have been already taking a full part in many more aspects of parenting. In recent years, however, the image of a father with a small baby in an intimate caring relationship has become an acceptable cultural image, and has been used in everything from Hollywood films, to advertising and baby clothes catalogues. What is important from a biblical perspective is that women and men develop both their sexuality and their gender in a redeemed way which honors Christ. This might mean recovering those aspects of our humanness which are lost in cultural stereotypes. Men may have to work harder on experiences of 'bonding' and emotional expression; women may have to develop more their detachment from over-dependency on others.

Women and men are to be in relationship in many areas of life, exercising their gifts, developing their personhood and sharing their insights with each other. Those gifts are not to be limited and chained down by restrictions placed on gender roles, but are to be the ones which God has endowed us with, and which the Holy Spirit has affirmed in us. Above all there is to be respect and honor among us, not a bid for power or an imposition of control. Central to our lives as women and men is the injunction to live according to the fruits of the Spirit. When women and men experience together more of the love, joy, peace, patience, kindness, goodness, faithfulness, gentleness, and self-control of the Spirit of God, they will be leaving behind the destructiveness of the Fall. When men and women allow each other the freedom in their lives which Christ himself brings, then we shall be moving closer to living our redemptive relationships. Then our diversity and differences, our sameness and complementarity will no longer be a cause for division, but will simply echo our union as persons made together by God and for God.

THE OCCUPATIONS OF WOMEN

'A capable wife who can find . . . She is far more precious than jewels . . . She seeks wool and flax, and works with willing hands . . . She perceives that her merchandise is profitable. Her lamp does not go out at night. She puts her hands to the distaff, and her hands hold the spindle . . . She makes linen garments and sells them; she supplies the merchant with sashes. Strength and dignity are her clothing, and she laughs at the time to come' (Prov. 31:10-24).

In antiquity, in Greece and Rome, both before and during the early Christian era, there is ample evidence for women's economic contributions to society from their occupations both inside and outside of the home. Many occupations can be documented from these periods, but one of women's primary marketable skills was the manufacture and sale of textiles, the weaving of cloth and the sale of garments.

Perenially and universally, women have been associated with wool-working. The evidence from Greek black and red figure vases suggests that nearly 500 years before the birth of Christ, the workbasket, or *kalathos*, became an inconographical symbol for the industrious and virtuous housewife. We know that even long before this, Mycenean craftswomen were working with wool, and that Mycenean craftsworkers of both sexes received the same rewards.

The Greek vases of sixth century Athens depict women spinning, weaving and producing textiles at home. There are scenes of young women, older women, those who spin alone and those who work in groups, all busily engaged in the occupation of textile working. Indeed, the *kalathos* became associated with immortality, for many examples of it are found on white ground *leckythoi*, the Greek vases used for funerary purposes.

Not just the Greek vases, but also ancient literary testimonia, and archeological evidence from sites of the fifth and fourth century BC, point to the existence of a cottage industry – women manufacturing fabrics or goods at home for sale in the marketplace.

The archeological evidence from several of these sites in ancient Greece documents that in many cases, women's quarters were used to provide areas suitable for textile working. The sizes of the women's rooms, or *gynoconitis*, were often the largest areas in the house, affording ample room for setting up and storing looms and other weaving equipment. Many excavation reports indicate by the large number of loom weights and spindle whorls found within, that these rooms were not simply women's quarters, but also workrooms where women did their spinning and weaving for the market. In most cases, in pre-Hellenistic Greece (fifth century BC Athens), the entire process of textile-making was carried out at home, including the preparation of fleeces or flax, which was done in the courtyard.

We know that the processes of textile manufacture involved many steps in preparation, and that most of these procedures are documented pictorially on the Athenian vases. There were many spinning and wool-working implements as well: the *epinitron*, or leg shield for working the wool, the distaff, the spindle, the spindle whorls and, of course, the looms themselves. All the equipment appears on vases where we see women busily working together, creating textiles not only for home usage but also for trade. Occasionally we will even see a money pouch being offered to women who are involved with textile-working.

Literary evidence from many sources confirms that Greek women were involved in such a home textile industry. As early as Hesiod's *Works and Days*, we have references to *erithoi*, or salaried wool-workers (ll. 602-3), and in Xenophon's *Memorabilia*, written in the fourth century BC, Aristarchus speaks to Socrates about his straitened economic situation and the fact that he is left with a large number of womenfolk in the house. The two men converse and it is decided that capital would be provided and wool purchased. The women then worked together, manufacturing and selling garments to provide for their own keep and to benefit Aristarchus monetarily (ll.vii.2-14). In his *Thesmophoriazusae*, Aristophanes also mentions women who work for pay (ll.813-20; 455-8).

In *The Frogs*, a young woman discusses her weaving and the fact that she sells it for income (ll.1346-51). Apollonias of Rhodes (*Argon* III.291), Pausanias (*Patras*) and Lucian (*D. Metr.* 6.293), among others, document that women often augmented the family income or supported themselves and their children by working at a cottage textile industry.

By the time we reach Hellenistic Greece and well into the first part of the early Christian era, there were many changes in the social status and economic opportunities open to women. The Hellenistic period in Greece was characterized by profound changes in political, philosophical and scientific ideas, in forms of art, and in concepts of life in general. In this period, women saw growing respect, broader economic opportunities and an extension of their legal capacities. Greek women and certainly Egyptian women acquired many new economic opportunities. For example, they could now buy and sell goods and property, mortgage their own goods, obtain and give loans, accept obligations of work, make wills, inherit legacies, and sometimes conclude their own marriage contracts.

Along with these expanded capacities came new opportunities for other professions for women. Although the clothing industry and the manufacture of textiles remained the primary occupation of working women, many other trades began to open up and become acceptable to them. Many laws and inscriptions from as early as 350 BC attest to the fact that women held other employment as well. We know that Phanostrate was a physician and midwife, Melitta, a nurse, Mania a grocer. Grave stele inscriptions also record Onesime, sesame seed seller . . . Thraitta, grocer . . . Sanno, acrobat . . . Demetria, harpist . . . Philrya, wet-nurse . . . Habroshye, perfume seller . . . and Rhodia, wool-worker.

By the time we reach the period of the Roman Empire and the early church (first century BC – first century AD), it appears that economic opportunities for women were greatly expanded. Just as we have more documentation of evidence of all types of material from Rome, we have much more evidence of women's employment in general (see note on 'Business women in the New Testament', p. 264).

There are multiple literary sources, biblical references, legal sources, inscriptions, archeological evidence and artistic and sculptural documentation attesting to the expanding economic opportunities available to Roman women and early Christian women.

The skills acquired by these women, although sometimes domestic in nature, were broad and varied, and many women practised skills that called for formal training. We know that among these categories were female physicians (*iatromae*), midwives (*opstetrices*), readers (*lectrices*), and scribes (*librariae*). There were also beauticians (*tractatrices*), barbers (*tonstrices*), hairdressers (*ornatrices*) and secretaries (*notariae*) (*Corpus Inscriptionum Latinarum* II.497, 4380; III.8820; VI.3473, 4458, 8786.

During the late Republic and early Empire, and certainly in Christian times, there is evidence of many different kinds of craftswomen. This is quite obvious in the case of crafts associated with the luxury trade which called for not only aptitude, but a long period of training or apprenticeships. One child, Viccentia, was already spinning gold thread (*auri netrix*) when she died at the age of nine. One Selli Epyre, who had a shop in the Via Sacra, sold golden cloth, and Thymele Marcella dealt in silk garments. Fulvia Melma and Septicia Rufa were both highly specialized craftswomen, for inscriptions record that they both were involved with the production of gold leaf. Cloth-dying, dye selling, cleaning and fulling were also practised by Roman women, but sometimes it is difficult to say whether these women were producers or retailers.

Nevertheless, documents do show us that many women were involved with very specialized crafts indeed. There is another shop along the Via Sacra in which five women specialized in the delicate job of cutting gemstones. We find biblical references to women involved with one of the most expensive of the luxury goods – the purple cloth trade. Sometimes these women worked in tandem with their husbands in the *purparia*, and often we cannot say whether the women produced or only sold these goods. Nevertheless, it is very notable that their names are included in inscriptions alongside their husbands.' *Unquentariae* (perfume producers/sellers), *sutrix* (shoemakers) and *furnariae* are some of the other crafts in the early Christian period.

Another occupation recorded for Roman and early Christian women is that of saleswoman such as Lydia (Acts 10:14). Sometimes, as in the trades, these women worked with their husbands or other non-related male patrons. Often we note shops involving twelve to fifteen saleswomen at one time. One woman, Hilarea, sold incense; another was a seed dealer; another dealt with preserved foods. There are many women who sold oil, wine, seeds, beans, meats, fish and fruits and vegetables. And several inscriptions furnish information of tradeswomen who clearly worked on their own, i.e., their names are not linked with men in any way. These included the barley dealer Pollecla, the Spanish cloth-seller Fulvia and the Pompeian money lender Faustilla, among others, (*CIL* VI.4528, 5923, 8203-8304, 9684).

The service industries and health-care fields, then as now, employed many women. In the health-care sector as mentioned above, there are inscriptions documenting the existence of female physicians – not only nurses. We also have ample evidence for contracts involving the hiring of wet-nurses. This is not surprising considering the fact that childbirth often claimed the life of the mother, and there were many abandoned infants who were picked up and reared as slaves. Midwives, companions, nurses and healers comprised the other occupations in which they were employed as health-care workers.

The service industries, especially the tavernas and wine shops, needed people to serve their customers. It was here that many women also found employment. The Greek and Latin literary portrait of barmaids and waitresses as women of loose morals was probably an upper-class prejudice. Male scholars tend to over-emphasize the number of women involved in prostitution, perhaps not realizing that of all the occupations available to women, prostitution would be the least desirable – entered into only under slave status or under the direst of economic conditions.

'Prostitute' is also a label often given to young freeborn women who found employment as actresses in the theatrical companies or as other female stage entertainers. Many were singers, flute players, cithra players, musicians, lute players, mimes, drummers, choral musicians and dancers. Cicero mentions that one of these actresses, Dionysia, earned an impressive sum from her work on stage (*Pro Roscio Amerino* 23); and a number of contracts show that entertainers could earn a respectable income even if they were limited to performing at local festivals. The incomes of many entertainers were adequate if not large, suggesting that prostitution would not have been an issue. Indeed, in one inscription, the parents of Eucharis went to great lengths to emphasize that their daughter was an entertainer of the highest class who graced the games of the nobles with her dancing.

Among the more exotic professions were those of mourner and gladiator. There seems to have been a market for hired female mourners as early as second century BC. Rome, which is not unusual considering women's ancient associations not only with birth but also with death. Female gladiators were participating in the Roman games as early as the Republican period. There is an inscription from Ostia referring to a gladiatorial exhibit which included female sword-fighters. Like entertainers and waitresses, female gladiators were often accused of being prostitutes, although nothing in the inscriptions points to this. One can imagine that at least in the case of gladiators, ancient literary sources reflect an upper-class bias as well as, perhaps, a case of 'wishful thinking'.

As in ancient Greece, in Imperial and early Christian Rome, the textile industry provided the greatest source of income for women. The manufacture of textiles and garments was one of the most marketable skills that virtually every freeborn Roman girl could expect to master and put to use throughout her life. Some women clearly produced, created and repaired clothing in a commercial setting from the loom to the salesfloor. Sewers, weavers, spinners and pieceworkers abound in literary references and inscriptions. Pausanias once remarked that there were so many women in Patrae employed as weavers that they heavily outnumbered the men in town (7.21.14).

There are many inscriptions from tombstones which have survived to document this large body of garment workers. These epitaphs record many women who were employed in this trade. Often their status is uncertain; but many were freed-women, while others were slaves. It is entirely possible that slave owners hired out women who worked as textile workers and pieceworkers during peak times of the year. Other inscriptions and monuments record women who profited quite handsomely from the garment trade, such as Eumachia, who owned and operated a large textile establishment in Pompeii.

Plautus counted spinning and weaving among the finest skills of women (*Mercator*, 396, 416, 515-527); and it is well known that the Emperor Augustus encouraged his daughters and granddaughters to learn how to spin and weave. He often made it a point to wear home-spun garments himself and credited his wife Livia as their source. In an epitaph from the same period, *Lanificum* is one of the virtues attributed to a wealthy woman named Murdie, along with the other apellations: *modestia, pudicita, obsequium, diligentia* and *fides*. 'Murdia worked in wool, and was modest, chaste, respectful, diligent and faithful' (*CIL* VI.11602, 1158402).

From the early Greek period to Roman and early Christian times, one of the highest praises a woman could be given, and one that was often inscribed on her tombstone, was *Lanam fecit* – she made wool. And of the many occupations of women in antiquity, it was long held to be the noblest.

That women in biblical times were still so employed and highly praised for their industry and virtue is indicated by the passage from Prov. 31: 'She makes linen garments and sells them; she supplies the merchant with sashes. Strength and dignity are her clothing, and she laughs at the time to come.'

INDEX